Professional C#, 2nd Edition

Simon Robinsons
K. Scott Allen
Ollie Cornes
Jay Glynn
Zack Greenvoss
Burton Harvey
Christian Nagel
Morgan Skinner
Karli Watson

wrox

Programmer to Programmer™

Professional C#, 2nd Edition

Published by
Wiley Publishing, Inc.
10475 Crosspoint Boulevard
Indianapolis, IN 46256
www.wiley.com

Copyright © 2003 by Wiley Publishing, Inc., Indianapolis, Indiana

Published simultaneously in Canada

Library of Congress Card Number: 2003107056

ISBN: 0-7645-4398-9

Manufactured in the United States of America

10 9 8 7 6 5 4 3 2 1

1B/QW/QW/QT/IN

Trademark Acknowledgements

Wrox has endeavored to provide trademark information about all the companies and products mentioned in this book by the appropriate use of capitals. However, Wrox cannot guarantee the accuracy of this information.

Credits

Authors
Simon Robinson
K. Scott Allen
Ollie Cornes
Jay Glynn
Zach Greenvoss
Burton Harvey
Christian Nagel
Morgan Skinner
Karli Watson

Additional Material
Steve Danielson
Julian Skinner

Managing Editors
Viv Emery
Louay Fatoohi

Commisioning Editor
Julian Skinner

Technical Editors
Douglas Paterson
Christian Peak
Mankee Cheng
Matthew Cumberlidge
Nick Manning

Project Manager
Beth Sacks

Author Agent
Cilmara Lion

Production Coordinator
Abbie Forletta

Indexing
Martin Brooks
Andrew Criddle

Technical Reviewers
Martin Beaulieu
Bill Burris
Martin Brooks
Ramu Choppa
Andreas Christiansen
Aravind Corera
Cristian Darie
Mitch Denny
Mike Erickson
Slavo Furman
Jeff Gabriel
Sam Gentile
Jacob Hammer
Hope Hatfield
Brian Hickey
Ben Hickman
Mark Horner
Amit Kalani
David Marcus
Jason Montgomery
Johan Normen
Juan Ramon Ravirosa
Jon Reid
Tomas Restrepo
Scott Robertson
David Schultz
Ian Smith
Gavin Smyth
Helmut Watson
David West

Proof Reader
Chris Smith

Illustrations
Abbie Forletta

Cover
Chris Morris

About the Authors

Simon Robinson

Simon Robinson lives in Lancaster in the UK, where he shares a house with some
students. He first encountered serious programming when he was doing his PhD in
physics, modeling all sorts of weird things to do with superconductors and
quantum mechanics. The experience of programming was nearly enough to put
him off computers for life (though, oddly, he seems to have survived all the
quantum mechanics), and he tried for a while being a sports massage therapist
instead. He then realized how much money was in computers compared to sports
massage, and therefore, rapidly got a job as a C++ programmer/researcher instead.
Simon is clearly the charitable, deep, spiritual type, who understands the true
meaning of life.

His programming work eventually lead him into writing, and he now makes a living mostly from writing great
books for programmers. He is a great enthusiast for C#, which he firmly believes is set to revolutionize
programming. His spare time is spent either at dance classes (he loves performing arts) or on his pet project
writing a computer strategy game. With what little time is left, he is an honorary research associate at Lancaster
University, where he does research in computational fluid dynamics with the environmental science department.
You can visit Simon's web site at http://www.SimonRobinson.com.

*Apart from the editors who've been great to work with, and who've worked incredibly hard to help bring
this book out, I'd like to thank:*

❑ *Joe Crump at Microsoft, for some very useful technical input and getting a number of queries answered*

❑ *Morgan Skinner for some useful suggestions for Chapter 5*

❑ *Jason Sickler, a student at MIT, and alias Darrius, President of the Chinese, for agreeing to have details
of his negotiations with me used in one of the samples in Chapter 12*

K. Scott Allen

Over the last 10 years Scott Allen has designed software for Windows, embedded
hardware, web applications, and massive multiplayer online games.

Scott holds an MS degree in Computer Science and an MCSD certification. He
lives in Hagerstown, Maryland, with his wife Vicky, and sons Alex and
Christopher.

Ollie Cornes

Ollie has been working with the Internet and the Microsoft platform since the early 90's. In 1999 he co-founded a business-to-business Internet company and until recently, was their Chief Technical Officer.

Prior to that, his various roles involved programming, technical authoring, network management, writing, leading development projects, and consulting. He has worked with Demon Internet, Microsoft, Saab, Tesco, Travelstore, and Vodafone. Ollie has a degree in computer science and is Microsoft certified.

When he's not working he spends his time devouring books on human potential, practicing Chinese internal martial arts, meditating, and juggling fire.

I want to say thank you to my friends and family for the support and love you've given me. Life throws the good and the bad at us all, and you have made the bad stuff much easier to get past.

Jay Glynn

Jay started developing software in the late 1980's, writing applications for the Pick operating system in Pick BASIC. Since then he has created applications using Paradox PAL and Object PAL, Delphi, Pascal, C/C++, Java, VBA, and Visual Basic. Currently, Jay is a Project Coordinator and Architect for a large insurance company based in Nashville TN. For the past five years he has been developing software for pen-based computers and, more recently, for ASP and server-based systems. When not sitting in front of a keyboard, Jay is busy restoring a house in Franklin TN, playing a round of golf whenever possible, and watching Disney movies with his wife and three year old son. Jay can be reached at jlsglynn@hotmail.com.

I would like to thank my wife Lydia and my son Samuel for being patient and understanding of all the late nights. They are my motivation and inspiration.

Zach Greenvoss

Zach Greenvoss is a Senior Consultant with Magenic Technologies, a Microsoft Gold Certified Solution Provider and industry leader in providing custom business solutions utilizing the latest Microsoft technologies. He specializes in middle-tier architecture and implementation, utilizing various technologies including COM+, MSMQ, BizTalk, XML, and the .NET Framework. Zach's hobbies include traveling, caving, and playing his new XBox. He can be reached at zachg@magenic.com.

I would like to thank my wife Amanda for being patient and understanding of all the long hours.

Burton Harvey

Burton Harvey builds software that elegantly fulfils users' needs. An MCSD with fifteen years' experience using Microsoft development tools, Burt is adept at a multitude of technologies including VB, COM, ASP, SQL, C#, C++, x86 assembler, UML, WML, and the Palm OS.

In 1998, Burt served as the founding editor of an online journal of scientific research, *Scientia*. His Master's thesis, "*The Outlaw Method for Solving Multimodal Functions with Parallel Genetic Algorithms*", was presented at the International Conference on Evolutionary Computation, and Burt has spoken on C# at Wrox conferences in Las Vegas and Amsterdam.

As a consultant, Burt provides services to healthcare companies, music publishers, financial institutions, and sports organizations. As the CEO of Promethean Personal Software, he develops handheld applications that empower the individual (http://www.propersonal.com).

Burt currently resides in Nashville, Tennessee, and can be reached at kbharvey@mindspring.com. This is his third book.

Christian Nagel

Christian Nagel works as a trainer and consultant for Global Knowledge, the largest independent information technology training provider. Christian started his computing career with PDP 11 and VAX/VMS platforms. Since then he has used a variety of languages and platforms, including Pascal, C, X-Windows, Motif, C++, Java, COM/ATL, COM+, and currently C# and .NET. With his profound knowledge of Microsoft technologies – he's certified as Microsoft Certified Trainer (MCT), Solution Developer (MCSD), and Systems Engineer (MCSE) – he enjoys teaching others programming and architecting distributed solutions. As founder of the .NET User Group Austria and as MSDN Regional Director he is speaker at European conferences (TechEd, VCDC), and is contacted by many developers for coaching, consulting, and teaching customized courses and boot camps. You will find Christian's web site at http://christian.nagel.net/.

I would like to thank the people at Wrox who got me started writing books, and Christian Seidler who supports my activities at Global Knowledge. Special thanks are also sent to the people at Microsoft, primarily to Alex Holy in Vienna for his organization of Visual Studio events and for his support of the .NET user community. Finally, and most importantly, I would like to thank my wife Elisabeth for her love and support.

Morgan Skinner

I started my computing at a tender age on a ZX80 at school, where I was underwhelmed by some code my teacher had put together and decided I could do better in assembly language. After getting hooked on Z80 (much better than those paltry three registers in 6502 land!) I graduated through the school ZX81s to my own ZX Spectrum.

Since then I've used all sorts of languages and platforms, including VAX Macro Assembler (way cool!), Pascal, Modula2, Smalltalk, x86 assembly language, PowerBuilder, C/C++, Visual Basic, and currently C#. I've managed to stay in the same company for nearly 12 years, largely down to the diversity of the job and a good working environment.

In my spare time I'm a bit of a DIY nut, I spend lots of money on bicycles, and 'relax' by fighting weeds on my allotment.

I can be reached by e-mail at morgan.skinner@totalise.co.uk.

Karli Watson

Karli Watson is an in-house author for Wrox Press with a penchant for multicolored clothing. He started out with the intention of becoming a world famous nanotechnologist, so perhaps one day you might recognize his name as he receives a Nobel Prize. For now, though, Karli's computing interests include all things mobile, and upcoming technologies such as C#. He can often be found preaching about these technologies at conferences, as well as after hours in drinking establishments. Karli is also a snowboarding enthusiast, and wishes he had a cat.

Thanks go to the Wrox team, both for helping me get into writing, and then for dealing with the results when I started. Finally, and most importantly, thanks to my wife, Donna, for continuing to put up with me.

Steve Danielson

Steve has been involved with programming since being introduced to the TRS-80 Model I computer in 1980 during the 6th grade, and began programming for Microsoft Windows with the release of Visual Basic 3.0. He is currently the Director of Architecture and Technology for Zeris Interactive, where he develops distributed applications for Zeris' clients using the gamut of Microsoft DNA tools and technologies.

Steve is also a private pilot and flies his Zenair CH-701 kitplane whenever he gets a chance. He lives with his family in Wake Forest, NC, and can be reached at **steve_danielson@hotmail.com**.

Table of Contents

Table of Contents

Table of Contents

Table of Contents

Table of Contents

Table of Contents

Table of Contents

Table of Contents

Table of Contents

Introduction

If we were to describe the C# language and its associated environment, the .NET Framework, as the most important new technology for developers for many years, we would not be exaggerating. .NET is designed to provide a new environment within which you can develop almost any application to run on Windows, and possibly in the future on other platforms too, while C# is a new programming language that has been designed specifically to work with .NET. Using C# you can, for example, write a dynamic web page, a component of a distributed application, a database access component, or a classic Windows desktop application.

Don't be fooled by the .NET label. The NET bit in the name is there to emphasize that Microsoft believes that distributed applications, in which the processing is distributed between client and server, are the way forward, but C# is not just a language for writing Internet or network-aware applications. It provides a means for you to code up almost any type of software or component that you might need to write for the Windows platform. Between them, C# and .NET are set both to revolutionize the way that you write programs, and to make programming on Windows much easier than it has ever been.

That's quite a substantial claim, and needs to be justified. After all, we all know how quickly computer technology changes. Every year Microsoft brings out new software, programming tools, or versions of Windows, with the claim that these will be hugely beneficial to developers. So what's different about .NET and C#?

The Significance of .NET and C#

In order to understand the significance of .NET it is useful to remind ourselves of the nature of many of the Windows technologies that have appeared in the last ten years or so. Although they may look quite different on the surface, all of the Windows operating systems from Windows 3.1 (introduced in 1992) through to Windows XP have the same familiar Windows API at their core. As we've progressed through new versions of Windows, huge numbers of new functions have been added to the API, but this has been a process of evolving and extending the API rather than replacing it.

The same can be said for many of the technologies and frameworks that we've used to develop software for Windows too. For example, **COM (Component Object Model)** originated as **OLE (Object Linking and Embedding)**. At the time it was, to a large extent, simply a means by which different types of office documents could be linked together, so that for example you could place a small Excel spreadsheet in your Word document. From that it evolved into COM, **DCOM (Distributed COM)**, and eventually COM+ – a sophisticated technology that formed the basis of the way almost all components communicated, as well as implementing transactions, messaging services, and object pooling.

Microsoft chose this evolutionary approach to software for the obvious reason that it is concerned about backward compatibility. Over the years a huge base of third-party software has been written for Windows, and Windows wouldn't have enjoyed the success it has had if every time Microsoft introduced a new technology it broke the existing code base!

While this backward compatibility issue has been a crucial feature of Windows technologies and one of the strengths of Windows, it does have a big disadvantage. Every time some technology evolves and adds new features, it ends up a bit more complicated than it was before.

It is clear that something had to change. Microsoft couldn't go on forever extending the same development tools and languages, always making them more and more complex in order to satisfy the conflicting demands of keeping up with the newest hardware, and maintaining backward compatibility with what was around when Windows first became popular in the early 1990s. There comes a point where you have to start with a clean slate if you want a simple yet sophisticated set of languages, environments, and developer tools, which make it easy for developers to write state-of-the-art software.

This fresh start is what C# and .NET are all about. Roughly speaking, .NET is a new framework – a new API – for programming on Windows. And C# is a new language that has been designed from scratch to work with .NET, as well as to take advantage of all the progress in developer environments and in our understanding of object-oriented programming principles that has taken place over the last 20 years.

Before we continue, we should make it clear that backward compatibility has not been lost in the process. Existing programs will continue to work, and .NET was designed with the ability to work with existing software. Communication between software components on Windows now almost entirely takes place using COM. Taking account of this, .NET does have the ability to provide wrappers around existing COM components so that .NET components can talk to them.

It is true that you don't need to learn C# in order to write code for .NET. Microsoft has extended C++, and made substantial changes to VB to turn it into the more powerful language VB.NET, in order to allow code written in either of these languages to target the .NET environment. Both of these languages, however, are hampered by the legacy of having evolved over the years rather than being written from the start with today's technology in mind.

Visual J++, which has been beset by legal difficulties, and never really took off in the first place, is now regarded as a legacy language. Microsoft will be offering instead J#, which is basically J++, but compiled to target .NET instead of compiling to Java byte code. There will also be a tool to convert existing J++ code to C# code for J++ developers who prefer to migrate to C#.

> **If you learn the C# language, and familiarize yourself with the .NET Framework, you will find that in many cases coding in C# is a far more pleasant and efficient business than it ever was using the older languages of C++ and VB.**

This book will equip you to program in C#, while at the same time providing the necessary background in how the .NET architecture works. We will not only cover the fundamentals of the C# language, but also go on to give examples of applications that use a variety of related technologies, including database access, dynamic web pages, advanced graphics, and directory access. The only requirement is that you are familiar with at least one other high-level language used on Windows – either C++, VB, or J++.

So What is .NET?

We can best answer the question, "what is .NET?" by comparing it with Windows and asking what Windows is to developers. The answer to that is twofold. In the first instance, Windows is a library; it is the set of all function calls in the Windows API, which are available for you to use in your program. These functions provide common features such as displaying dialog boxes, multiple-document-interface and single-document-interface windows, accessing base functions such as security features or component services, and so on. In the second instance, Windows is the environment in which your application runs, as well as the operating system itself.

In a similar way, .NET is two things. First, it is a library, one that is just as extensive as the Windows API. You can use it to call up all the same sorts of features that have traditionally been the role of the Windows operating system: displaying windows and dialog boxes, verifying security credentials, calling on base operating system services, creating threads, and so on, as well as newer areas such as accessing databases or connecting to the Internet or providing web services.

Second, .NET provides the environment ("the .NET runtime") in which your program is run. When .NET-aware code is executed, it will be .NET that starts up your code, manages the running threads, provides various background services, and in a real sense is the immediate environment seen by the code. You can therefore view .NET as something that provides a level of abstraction from the operating system.

We should stress, however, that .NET is not itself an operating system. The operating system is still Windows at least until (and unless) .NET gets ported to other systems, and the Windows API is still there behind the scenes. The .NET environment sits as a layer between the Windows OS and other applications, providing a much more up-to-date, object-oriented, and easy to use framework for developing and running code. Of course, older applications which are not .NET-aware, will continue to work with Windows and the Windows API directly just as they always have done.

Advantages of .NET

We've talked in general terms about how great .NET is, but we haven't said much about how it helps to make your life as a developer easier. In this section, we'll discuss some of the improved features of .NET in brief.

- ❑ **Object-Oriented Programming** – both .NET and C# are entirely based on object-oriented principles right from the start.

- ❑ **Good Design** – a base class library, which is designed from the ground up in a highly intuitive way.

- ❑ **Language Independence** – with .NET, all of the languages VB.NET, C#, J#, and managed C++ compile to a common **Intermediate Language**. This means that languages are interoperable in a way that has not been seen before.

❑ **Better Support for Dynamic Web Pages** – while ASP offers a lot of flexibility, it is also inefficient due to its use of interpreted scripting languages, and the lack of object-oriented design often results in messy ASP code. .NET offers an integrated support for web pages, using a new technology – ASP.NET. With ASP.NET, code in your pages is compiled, and may be written in a .NET-aware high-level language such as C# or VB.NET.

❑ **Efficient Data Access** – a set of .NET components, collectively known as ADO.NET, provide efficient access to relational databases and a variety of data sources. Components are also available to allow access to the file system, and to directories. In particular, XML support is built into .NET, allowing you to manipulate data, which may be imported from or exported to non-Windows platforms.

❑ **Code Sharing** – .NET has completely revamped the way that code is shared between applications, introducing the concept of the **assembly,** which replaces the traditional DLL. Assemblies have formal facilities for versioning, and different versions of assemblies can exist side by side.

❑ **Improved Security** – each assembly can also contain built-in security information that can indicate precisely who or what category of user or process is allowed to call which methods on which classes. This gives you a very fine degree of control over how the assemblies that you deploy can be used.

❑ **Zero Impact Installation** – there are two types of assembly: shared and private. Shared assemblies are common libraries available to all software, while private assemblies are intended only for use with particular software. A private assembly is entirely self-contained, so the process of installing it is simple. There are no registry entries; the appropriate files are simply placed in the appropriate folder in the file system.

❑ **Support for Web Services** – .NET has fully integrated support for developing web services as easily as you'd develop any other type of application.

❑ **Visual Studio .NET** – .NET comes with a new developer environment, Visual Studio .NET, which can cope equally well with C++, C#, and VB.NET, as well as with ASP.NET code. Visual Studio.NET integrates all the best features of the respective language-specific environments of Visual Studio 6.

❑ **C#** – C# is a new object-oriented language intended for use with .NET.

We will be looking more closely at the benefits of the .NET architecture in Chapter 1.

Where C# Fits In

In one sense, C# can be seen as being the same thing to programming languages as .NET is to the Windows environment. Just as Microsoft has been adding more and more features to Windows and the Windows API over the last decade, VB and C++ have undergone expansion. Although VB and C++ have ended up as hugely powerful languages as a result of this, both languages also suffer from problems due to the legacies of how they have evolved.

In the case of Visual Basic, the main strength of the language is the fact that it is simple to understand, and does make many programming tasks easy, largely hiding the details of the Windows API and the COM component infrastructure from the developer. The downside to this is that Visual Basic has never truly been object-oriented, so that large applications quickly become disorganized and hard to maintain. As well as this, because VB's syntax was inherited from early versions of BASIC (which, in turn, was designed to be intuitively simple for beginning programmers to understand, rather than to write large commercial applications), it doesn't really lend itself to well-structured or object-oriented programs.

C++, on the other hand, has its roots in the ANSI C++ language definition. It isn't completely ANSI-compliant for the simple reason that Microsoft first wrote its C++ compiler before the ANSI definition had become official, but it comes close. Unfortunately, this has lead to two problems. First, ANSI C++ has its roots in the state of technology over a decade ago and this shows up in a lack of support for modern concepts (such as Unicode strings and generating XML documentation), and in some archaic syntax structures designed for the compilers of yesteryear (such as the separation of declaration from definition of member functions). Secondly, Microsoft has been simultaneously trying to evolve C++ into a language that is designed for high-performance tasks on Windows, and in order to achieve that they've been forced to add a huge number of Microsoft-specific keywords as well as various libraries to the language. The result is that on Windows, the language has become a complete mess. Just ask a C++ developer how many definitions for a string they can think of: char*, LPTSTR, string, CString (MFC version), CString (WTL version), wchar_t*, OLECHAR*, and so on.

Now enter .NET – a completely new environment, which is going to involve new extensions to both languages. Microsoft has got around this by adding yet more Microsoft-specific keywords to C++, and by completely revamping VB into VB.NET, a language which retains some of the basic VB syntax, but which is so different in design that we can consider it to be, for all practical purposes, a new language.

It's in this context that Microsoft has decided to give developers an alternative – a language designed specifically for .NET, and designed with a clean slate. C# is the result. Officially, Microsoft describe C# as a "simple, modern, object-oriented, and type-safe programming language derived from C and C++". Most independent observers would probably change that to "derived from C, C++, and Java". Such descriptions are technically accurate, but do little to convey the beauty or elegance of the language. Syntactically, C# is very similar to both C++ and Java, to such an extent that many keywords are the same, and C# also shares the same block structure with braces ({}) to mark blocks of code, and semicolons to separate statements. The first impression of a piece of C# code is that it looks visually quite like C++ or Java code. Behind that initial similarity, however, C# is a lot easier to learn than C++, and of comparable difficulty to Java. Its design is more in tune with modern developer tools than both of those other languages, and it has been designed to give us simultaneously, the ease of use of Visual Basic, and the high-performance, low-level memory access of C++ if required. Some of the features of C# include:

- ❑ Full support for classes and object-oriented programming, including both interface and implementation inheritance, virtual functions, and operator overloading.

- ❑ A consistent and well-defined set of basic types.

- ❑ Inbuilt support for automatic generation of XML documentation.

- ❑ Automatic cleanup of dynamically allocated memory.

- ❑ The facility to mark classes or methods with user-defined attributes. This can be useful for documentation and can have some effects on compilation (for example, marking methods to be compiled only in debug builds).

- Full access to the .NET base class library, as well as easy access to the Windows API (if you really need it, which won't be all that often).

- Pointers and direct memory access are available if required, but the language has been designed in such a way that you can work without them in almost all cases.

- Support for properties and events in the style of VB.

- Just by changing the compiler options, you can compile either to an executable or to a library of .NET components that can be called up by other code in the same way as ActiveX controls (COM components).

- C# can be used to write ASP.NET dynamic web pages.

Most of the above statements it should be pointed out do also apply to VB.NET and Managed C++. The fact that C# is designed from the start to work with .NET, however, means that its support for the features of .NET is both more complete, and offered within the context of a more suitable syntax than for those other languages. While the C# language itself is very similar to Java, there are some improvements: in particular, Java is not designed to work with the .NET environment.

Before we leave the subject, we should point out a couple of limitations of C#. The one area the language is not designed for is time-critical or extremely high performance code – the kind where you really are worried about whether a loop takes 1000 or 1050 machine cycles to run through, and you need to clean up your resources the millisecond they are no longer needed. C++ is likely to continue to reign supreme among low-level languages in this area. C# lacks certain key facilities needed for extremely high performance apps, including the ability to specify inline functions and destructors that are guaranteed to run at particular points in the code. However, the proportion of applications that fall into this category are very low.

What You Need to Write and Run C# Code

.NET will run on Windows 98, 2000, or XP. In order to write code using .NET, you will need to install the .NET SDK. Unless you are intending to write your C# code using a text editor or some other third party developer environment, you will almost certainly also want Visual Studio .NET. The full SDK isn't needed to run managed code, but the .NET runtime is needed. You may find you need to distribute the .NET runtime with your code for the benefit of those clients who do not have it already installed.

What This Book Covers

In this book, we start by reviewing the overall architecture of .NET in the next chapter in order to give us the background we need to be able to write managed code. After that the book is divided into a number of sections that cover both the C# language and its application in a variety of areas.

Section I – The C# Language

This section gives us a good grounding in the C# language itself. This section doesn't presume knowledge of any particular language, although it does assume you are an experienced programmer. We start by looking at C#'s basic syntax and datatypes, and then discuss the object-oriented features of C# before moving on to look at more advanced C# programming topics.

Section II – .NET Programming

In this section, we look at the principles of programming in the .NET environment. In particular, we look at Visual Studio .NET, Windows Forms (how to code up classic Windows applications that display windows, or in more modern .NET parlance, forms), and we cover how to generate your own libraries as assemblies.

Section III – Data Access

We look at accessing databases with ADO.NET, and at interacting with directories and Active Directory. We also extensively cover support in .NET for XML and on the Windows operating system side, file and registry access.

Section IV – Internet Programming

In this section, we cover writing components that will run on web sites, serving up web pages. This covers both ASP.NET and the writing of web services.

Section V – Components

Backward compatibility with COM is an important part of .NET. Not only that, but COM+ is not strictly legacy – it will still be responsible for transactions, object pooling, and message queuing. In this section we'll look at the support .NET offers for working with COM and COM+, as well as discussing how to write C# code that interacts with these technologies.

Section VI – Advanced .NET Programming

This section is the concluding part of the main body of the book and covers some miscellaneous advanced topics. These include advanced graphics with GDI+, Windows services (formerly known as NT services), remoting, and security.

Conventions

We have used a number of different styles of text and layout in the book to help differentiate between the different kinds of information. Here are examples of the styles we use and an explanation of what they mean:

Bullets appear indented, with each new bullet marked as follows:

- ❑ **Important Words** are in a bold type font

- ❑ Words that appear on the screen in menus like the File or Window are in a similar font to the one that you see on screen

- ❑ Keys that you press on the keyboard, like *Ctrl* and *Enter*, are in italics

Code has several fonts. If it's a word that we're talking about in the text, for example, when discussing the `if...else` loop, it's in `this font`. If it's a block of code that you can type in as a program and run, then it's also in a gray box:

```
public static void Main()
{
    AFunc(1,2,"abc");
}
```

Sometimes you'll see code in a mixture of styles, like this:

```
// If we haven't reached the end, return true, otherwise
// set the position to invalid, and return false.
pos++;
if (pos < 4)
    return true;
else {
    pos = -1;
    return false;
}
```

The code with a white background is code we've already looked at and that we don't wish to examine further.

Advice, hints, and background information come in an italicized, indented font like this.

> **Important pieces of information come in boxes like this.**

We demonstrate the syntactical usage of methods, properties (and so on) using the following format:

```
Regsvcs BookDistributor.dll [COM+AppName] [TypeLibrary.tbl]
```

Here, italicized parts indicate object references, variables, or parameter values to be inserted; the square braces indicate optional parameters.

Technical Support

If you wish to directly query a problem in the book with an expert who knows it in detail then e-mail support@wrox.com with the title of the book and the last four numbers of the ISBN in the subject field. A typical e-mail should include the following things:

- ❑ The **name**, **last four digits of the ISBN**, and **page number** of the problem in the Subject field.

- ❑ Your **name**, **contact information**, and the **problem** in the body of the message.

We *won't* send you junk mail. We need the details to save your time and ours. When you send an e-mail message, it will go through the following chain of support:

- ❑ **Customer Support** – Your message is delivered to one of our customer support staff, who are the first people to read it. They have files on most frequently asked questions and will answer anything general about the book or the web site immediately.

- ❑ **Editorial** – Deeper queries are forwarded to the technical editor responsible for that book. They have experience with the programming language or particular product, and are able to answer detailed technical questions on the subject. Once an issue has been resolved, the editor can post the errata to the web site.

- ❑ **The Authors** – Finally, in the unlikely event that the editor cannot answer your problem, they will forward the request to the author. We do try to protect the author from any distractions to their writing, however, we are quite happy to forward specific requests to them. All Wrox authors help with the support on their books. They will mail the customer and the editor with their response, and again all readers should benefit.

The Wrox support process can only offer support to issues that are directly pertinent to the content of our published title. Support for questions that fall outside the scope of normal book support is provided via the community lists of our http://p2p.wrox.com/ forum.

p2p.wrox.com

For author and peer discussion, join the **P2P mailing lists**. Our unique system provides **programmer to programmer**™ contact on mailing lists, forums, and newsgroups, all *in addition* to our one-to-one e-mail support system. Be confident that your query is being examined by the many Wrox authors, and other industry experts, who are present on our mailing lists. At p2p.wrox.com you will find a number of different lists that will help you, not only while you read this book, but also as you develop your own applications.

To subscribe to a mailing list just follow this these steps:

1. Go to http://p2p.wrox.com/

2. Choose the appropriate category from the left menu bar

3. Click on the mailing list you wish to join

4. Follow the instructions to subscribe and fill in your e-mail address and password

5. Reply to the confirmation e-mail you receive

6. Use the subscription manager to join more lists and set your mail preferences

C# and .NET Architecture

You'll find that we emphasize throughout this book that the C# language cannot be viewed in isolation, but must be considered in parallel with the .NET Framework. The C# compiler specifically targets .NET, which means that all code written in C# will always run within the .NET Framework. This has two important consequences for the C# language:

❑   The architecture and methodologies of C# reflect the underlying methodologies of .NET

❑   In many cases, specific language features of C# actually depend upon features of .NET, or of the .NET base classes

Because of this dependence, it is important to gain some understanding of the architecture and methodology of .NET before we begin C# programming. That is the purpose of this chapter.

We will begin by going over what happens when all code (including C#) that targets .NET is compiled and run. Once we have this broad overview, we will take a more detailed look at the **Microsoft Intermediate Language** (**MS-IL**), the language which all compiled code ends up in on .NET. In particular, we will see how MS-IL, in partnership with the **Common Type System** (**CTS**) and **Common Language Specification** (**CLS**) works to give us interoperability between languages that target .NET. We'll also discuss where common languages (including VB and C++) fit into .NET.

Once we've done that, we will move on to examine some of the other features of .NET, including assemblies, namespaces, and the .NET base classes. We'll finish the chapter with a brief look at the kinds of applications we can create as C# developers.

The Relationship of C# to .NET

C# is a new programming language, and is significant in two respects:

❑ It is specifically designed and targeted for use with Microsoft's .NET Framework (a feature-rich platform for the development, deployment, and execution of distributed applications)

❑ It is a language based upon the modern object-oriented design methodology, and when designing it Microsoft has been able to learn from the experience of all the other similar languages that have been around over the 20 years or so since object-oriented principles came to prominence

One important thing to make clear is that C# is a language in its own right. Although it is designed to generate code that targets the .NET environment, it is not itself part of .NET. There are some features that are supported by .NET but not by C#, and you might be surprised to learn that there are actually features of the C# language that are not supported by .NET (for example operator overloading)!

However, since the C# language is intended for use with .NET, it is important for us to have an understanding of this Framework if we wish to develop applications in C# effectively. So, in this chapter we're going to take some time to peek beneath the surface of .NET. Let's get started.

The Common Language Runtime

Central to the .NET framework is its run-time execution environment, known as the **Common Language Runtime** (**CLR**) or the **.NET runtime**. Code running under the control of the CLR is often termed **managed** code.

However, before it can be executed by the CLR, any sourcecode that we develop (in C# or some other language) needs to be compiled. Compilation occurs in two steps in .NET:

1. Compilation of source code to **Microsoft Intermediate Language** (**MS-IL**)

2. Compilation of IL to platform-specific code by the CLR

At first sight this might seem a rather long-winded compilation process. Actually, this two-stage compilation process is very important, because the existence of the Microsoft Intermediate Language (managed code) is the key to providing many of the benefits of .NET. Let's see why.

Advantages of Managed Code

Microsoft Intermediate Language (often shortened to "Intermediate Language", or "IL") shares with Java byte code the idea that it is a low-level language with a simple syntax (based on numeric codes rather than text), which can be very quickly translated into native machine code. Having this well-defined universal syntax for code has significant advantages.

Platform Independence

First, it means that the same file containing byte code instructions can be placed on any platform; at runtime the final stage of compilation can then be easily accomplished so that the code will run on that particular platform. In other words, by compiling to Intermediate Language we obtain platform independence for .NET, in much the same way as compiling to Java byte code gives Java platform independence.

You should note that the platform independence of .NET is only theoretical at present because, at the time of writing, .NET is only available for Windows. However, porting .NET to other platforms is being explored (see for example the Mono project, an effort to create an open source implementation of .NET, at http://www.go-mono.com/).

Performance Improvement

Although we previously made comparisons with Java, IL is actually a bit more ambitious than Java byte code. Significantly, IL is always **Just-In-Time** compiled, whereas Java byte code was often interpreted. One of the disadvantages of Java was that, on execution, the process of translating from Java byte code to native executable resulted in a loss of performance (apart from in more recent cases, where Java is JIT-compiled on certain platforms).

Instead of compiling the entire application in one go (which could lead to a slow start-up time), the JIT compiler simply compiles each portion of code as it is called (just-in-time). When code has been compiled once, the resultant native executable is stored until the application exits, so that it does not need to be recompiled the next time that portion of code is run. Microsoft argues that this process is more efficient than compiling the entire application code at the start, because of the likelihood that large portions of any application code will not actually be executed in any given run. Using the JIT compiler, such code will never get compiled.

This explains why we can expect that execution of managed IL code will be almost as fast as executing native machine code. What it doesn't explain is why Microsoft expects that we will get a performance *improvement*. The reason given for this is that, since the final stage of compilation takes place at run time, the JIT compiler will know exactly what processor type the program will run on. This means that it can optimize the final executable code to take advantage of any features or particular machine code instructions offered by that particular processor.

Traditional compilers will optimize the code, but they can only perform optimizations that will be independent of the particular processor that the code will run on. This is because traditional compilers compile to native executable before the software is shipped. This means that the compiler doesn't know what type of processor the code will run on beyond basic generalities, such as that it will be an x86-compatible processor or an Alpha processor. Visual Studio 6, for example, optimizes for a generic Pentium machine, so the code that it generates cannot take advantages of hardware features of Pentium III processors. On the other hand, the JIT compiler can do all the optimizations that Visual Studio 6 can, and in addition to that it will optimize for the particular processor the code is running on.

Language Interoperability

So we can see how the use of IL enables platform independence, and how JIT compilation should improve performance. However, IL also facilitates **language interoperability**. Simply put, you can compile to IL from one language, and this compiled code should then be interoperable with code that has been compiled to IL from another language.

You're probably now wondering which languages aside from C# are interoperable via .NET, so let's now briefly discuss how some of the other common languages fit into .NET.

VB.NET

Visual Basic is undergoing a complete revamp to bring it up to date with .NET. The way that Visual Basic has evolved over the last few years means that in its previous version, Visual Basic 6, it is not a suitable language for running .NET programs. For example, it is heavily integrated into COM, and works by exposing only event handlers as sourcecode to the developer – most of the background code is not available as sourcecode. Not only that, it does not support implementation inheritance, and the standard data types Visual Basic uses are not compatible with .NET.

Visual Basic is being upgraded to Visual Basic .NET, but in the light of the previous comments, you won't be surprised to learn that the changes being made to VB are extensive. Although we might talk about an upgrade, for all practical purposes you may as well regard Visual Basic .NET as a new language. Existing VB 6 code will not compile as VB.NET code. Converting a VB 6 program to VB.NET requires extensive changes to the code. However, most of the changes can be done automatically for you by Visual Studio .NET (the upgrade of VS for use with .NET). If you attempt to read a VB 6 project into Visual Studio .NET, it will upgrade the project for you, which means that it will rewrite the VB 6 source code into VB.NET sourcecode. Although this means that the work involved for you is heavily cut down, you will need to check through the new VB.NET code to make sure that the project still works correctly.

One side effect of this is that it is no longer possible to compile VB.NET to native executable. VB.NET compiles only to IL, just as C# does. If you need to continue coding in VB 6, you may do so, but the executable code produced will completely ignore the .NET Framework, and you'll need to keep Visual Studio 6 installed if you rely on Visual Studio as your developer environment.

Managed C++

At the time of Visual C++ 6, C++ already had a large number of Microsoft-specific extensions on Windows. With Visual C++ .NET, extensions have been added to support the .NET framework. This means that existing C++ sourcecode will continue to compile to native executable without modification. It also means, however, that it will run independently of the .NET runtime. If you want your C++ code to run within the .NET Framework, then you can simply add the following line to the beginning of your code:

```
#using <mscorlib.dll>
```

You will also pass the flag `/clr` to the compiler, which will then assume you wish to compile to managed code, and will hence emit Intermediate Language instead of native machine code. The interesting thing about C++ is that when you compile to managed code, the compiler can emit IL that contains an embedded native executable. This means that you can mix managed types and unmanaged types in your C++ code. Thus the managed C++ code:

```
class MyClass
{
```

defines a plain C++ class, whereas the code:

```
__gc class MyClass
{
```

will give you a managed class, just as if you'd written the class in C# or VB.NET. Actually, an advantage of managed C++ over C# is that we can call unmanaged C++ classes from managed C++ code without having to resort to COM interop.

The compiler will raise an error if you attempt to use features that are not supported by .NET on managed types (for example, templates or multiple inheritance of classes). You will also find that you will need to use nonstandard C++ features (such as the __gc keyword shown in the above code) when using managed classes.

Because of the freedom that C++ allows in terms of low-level pointer manipulation and so on, the C++ compiler is not able to generate code that will pass the CLR's memory type safety tests. If it's important that your code is recognized by the CLR as memory type safe, then you'll need to write your sourcecode in some other language (such as C# or VB.NET).

J++ and J#

J++ itself will continue to be supported for backwards compatibility purposes only. Microsoft is not intending to further develop any platforms that compile to a Java virtual machine. Instead, Microsoft is separately developing two technologies for Java/J++ developers under the banner **JUMP** (**Java User Migration Path**) and the slogan "JUMP to .NET".

The first of these technologies is Visual J#. This is essentially an add-in to Visual Studio.NET that allows you to write and compile J++ code. The difference is that instead of compiling to a Java Virtual Machine, J# will compile to IL, so it will work as a .NET language. J# users will be able to take advantage of all the usual features of VS.NET. Microsoft expect that most J++ users will find it easiest to use J# if they wish to work with .NET.

The second option is a migration tool that will automatically convert J++ code into C# code. The similarities in syntax between J++ and C# are so great that this doesn't actually involve making many major changes to code structure.

Neither J# nor the language conversion tool are available as part of .NET or Visual Studio .NET itself, but are instead being supplied separately. For more information, go to http://msdn.microsoft.com/visualj/.

Scripting Languages

Scripting languages are still around, although, in general, their importance is likely to decline with the advent of .NET. JScript, on the other hand, has been upgraded to JScript.NET. ASP.NET (the upgrade of ASP intended for use with .NET, discussed later) pages may be written in JScript.NET, and it is now possible to run JScript.NET as a compiled rather than an interpreted language, and it is also possible to write strongly typed JScript.NET code. With ASP.NET there is no reason to use scripting languages in server-side web pages. VBA is, however, still used as a language for Microsoft Office and Visual Studio macros.

COM and COM+

Technically speaking, COM and COM+ aren't technologies targeted at .NET, because components based on them cannot be compiled into IL (although it's possible to do so to some degree using Managed C++, if the original COM component was written in C++). However, COM+ remains an important tool, since its features are not duplicated in .NET. Also, COM components will still work – and .NET incorporates COM interoperability features that make it possible for managed code to call up COM components and vice versa (this is discussed in Chapter 17). In general, however, you will probably find it more convenient for most purposes to code new components as .NET components, so that you can take advantage of the .NET base classes as well as the other benefits of running as managed code.

A Closer Look at Intermediate Language

From what we learned in the previous section, Intermediate Language obviously plays a fundamental role in the .NET Framework. As C# developers, we now understand that our C# code will be compiled into Intermediate Language before it is executed (indeed, the C# compiler *only* compiles to managed code). It makes sense, then, that we should now take a closer look at the main characteristics of IL, since any language that targets .NET would logically need to support the main characteristics of IL too.

Here are the important features of the Intermediate Language:

❑   Object-orientation and use of interfaces

❑   Strong distinction between value and reference types

❑   Strong data typing

❑   Error handling through the use of exceptions

❑   Use of attributes

Let's now take a closer look at each of these characteristics.

Support for Object Orientation and Interfaces

The language independence of .NET does have some practical limits. In particular, IL, however it is designed, is inevitably going to implement some particular programming methodology, which means that languages targeting it are going to have to be compatible with that methodology. The particular route that Microsoft has chosen to follow for IL is that of classic object-oriented programming, with single implementation inheritance of classes.

> *Those readers unfamiliar with the concepts of Object Orientation should refer to Appendix A for more information.*

Besides classic object-oriented programming, Intermediate Language also brings in the idea of interfaces, which saw their first implementation under Windows with COM. .NET interfaces are not the same as COM interfaces; they do not need to support any of the COM infrastructure (for example, they are not derived from IUnknown, and they do not have associated GUIDs). However, they do share with COM interfaces the idea that they provide a contract, and classes that implement a given interface must provide implementations of the methods and properties specified by that interface.

Object Orientation and Language Interoperability

We have now seen that working with .NET means compiling to the Intermediate Language, and that in turn means that you will need to be programming using traditional object-oriented methodologies. That alone is not, however, sufficient to give us language interoperability. After all, C++ and Java both use the same object-oriented paradigms, but they are still not regarded as interoperable. We need to look a little more closely at the concept of language interoperability.

To start with, we need to consider exactly what we mean by language interoperability. After all, COM allowed components written in different languages to work together in the sense of calling each other's methods. What was inadequate about that? COM, by virtue of being a binary standard, did allow components to instantiate other components and call methods or properties against them, without worrying about the language the respective components were written in. In order to achieve this however, each object had to be instantiated through the COM runtime, and accessed through an interface. Depending on the threading models of the relative components, there may have been large performance losses associated with marshaling data between apartments and/or running components on different threads. In the extreme case of components that are hosted in executable rather than DLL files, separate processes would need to be created in order to run them. The emphasis was very much that components could talk to each other, but only via the COM runtime. In no sense with COM did components written in different languages directly communicate with each other, or instantiate instances of each other – it was always done with COM as an intermediary. Not only that, but the COM architecture did not permit implementation inheritance, which meant that it lost many of the advantages of object-oriented programming.

An associated problem was that, when debugging, you would still have to independently debug components written in different languages. It was not possible to step between languages in the debugger. So what we *really* mean by language interoperability is that classes written in one language should be able to talk directly to classes written in another language. In particular:

❑ A class written in one language can inherit from a class written in another language

❑ The class can contain an instance of another class, no matter what the languages of the two classes are

❑ An object can directly call methods against another object written in another language

❑ Objects (or references to objects) can be passed around between methods

❑ When calling methods between languages we can step between the method calls in the debugger, even where this means stepping between sourcecode written in different languages

This is all quite an ambitious aim, but amazingly, .NET and the Intermediate Language have achieved it. For the case of stepping between methods in the debugger, this facility is really offered by the Visual Studio .NET IDE rather than from the CLR itself.

Distinct Value and Reference Types

As with any programming language, IL provides a number of predefined primitive data types. One characteristic of Intermediate Language however, is that it makes a strong distinction between value and reference types. **Value types** are those for which a variable directly stores its data, while **reference types** are those for which a variable simply stores the address at which the corresponding data can be found.

In C++ terms, reference types can be considered to be similar to accessing a variable through a pointer, while for Visual Basic, the best analogy for reference types are Objects, which in VB 6 are always accessed through references. Intermediate Language also lays down specifications about data storage: instances of reference types are always stored in an area of memory known as the **managed heap**, while value types are normally stored on the **stack** (although if value types are declared as fields within reference types, then they will be stored inline on the heap). We will discuss the stack and the heap and how they work in Chapter 3.

Strong Data Typing

One very important aspect of IL is that it is based on exceptionally **strong data typing**. What we mean by that is that all variables are clearly marked as being of a particular, specific data type (there is no room in IL, for example, for the `Variant` data type recognized by Visual Basic and scripting languages). In particular, IL does not normally permit any operations that result in ambiguous data types.

For instance, VB developers will be used to being able to pass variables around without worrying too much about their types, because VB automatically performs type conversion. C++ developers will be used to routinely casting pointers between different types. Being able to perform this kind of operation can be great for performance, but it breaks type safety. Hence, it is permitted only in very specific circumstances in some of the languages that compile to managed code. Indeed, pointers (as opposed to references) are only permitted in marked blocks of code in C#, and not at all in VB (although they are allowed as normal in managed C++). Using pointers in your code will immediately cause it to fail the memory type safety checks performed by the CLR.

You should note that some languages compatible with .NET, such as VB.NET, still allow some laxity in typing, but that is only possible because the compilers behind the scenes ensure the type safety is enforced in the emitted IL.

Although enforcing type safety might initially appear to hurt performance, in many cases this is far outweighed by the benefits gained from the services provided by .NET that rely on type safety. Such services include:

- ❑   Language Interoperability
- ❑   Garbage Collection
- ❑   Security
- ❑   Application Domains

Let's take a closer look at why strong data typing is particularly important for these features of .NET.

Importance of Strong Data Typing for Language Interoperability

One important reason that strong data typing is important is that, if a class is to derive from or contains instances of other classes, it needs to know about all the data types used by the other classes. Indeed, it is the absence of any agreed system for specifying this information in the past that has always been the real barrier to inheritance and interoperability across languages. This kind of information is simply not present in a standard executable file or DLL.

Suppose that one of the methods of a VB.NET class is defined to return an `Integer` – one of the standard data types available in VB.NET. C# simply does not have any data type of that name. Clearly, we will only be able to derive from the class, use this method, and use the return type from C# code if the compiler knows how to map VB.NET's `Integer` type to some known type that is defined in C#. So how is this problem circumvented in .NET?

Common Type System (CTS)

This data type problem is solved in .NET through the use of the **Common Type System** (**CTS**). The CTS defines the predefined data types that are available in IL, so that all languages that target the .NET framework will produce compiled code that is ultimately based on these types.

For the example that we were considering before, VB.NET's `Integer` is actually a 32-bit signed integer, which maps exactly to the IL type known as `Int32`. This will therefore be the data type specified in the IL code. Because the C# compiler is aware of this type, there is no problem. At source code level, C# refers to `Int32` with the keyword `int`, so the compiler will simply treat the VB.NET method as if it returned an `int`.

The CTS doesn't merely specify primitive data types, but a rich hierarchy of types, which includes well-defined points in the hierarchy at which code is permitted to define its own types. The hierarchical structure of the Common Type System reflects the single-inheritance object-oriented methodology of IL, and looks like this:

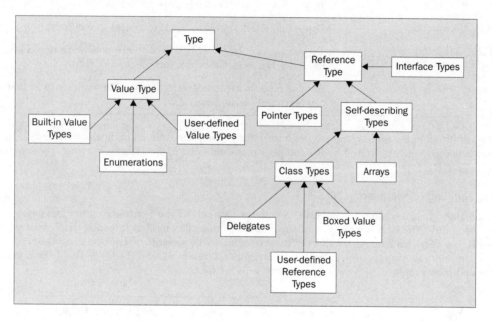

The types in this tree represent:

Type	Meaning
Type	Base class that represents any type.
Value Type	Base class that represents any value type.
Reference Types	Any data types that are accessed through a reference and stored on the heap.
Built-in Value Types	Includes most of the standard primitive types, which represent numbers, Boolean values, or characters.
Enumerations	Sets of enumerated values.
User-defined Value Types	Types that have been defined in sourcecode and are stored as value types. In C# terms, this means any struct.

Table continued on following page

Type	Meaning
Interface Types	Interfaces.
Pointer Types	Pointers.
Self-describing Types	Data types that provide information about themselves for the benefit of the garbage collector (see the next section).
Arrays	Any type that contains an array of objects.
Class Types	Types that are self-describing but are not arrays.
Delegates	Types that are designed to hold references to methods.
User-defined Reference Types	Types that have been defined in sourcecode and are stored as reference types. In C# terms, this means any class.
Boxed Value Types	A value type that is temporarily wrapped in a reference so that it can be stored on the heap.

We won't list all of the built-in value types here, because they are covered in detail in Chapter 2. In C#, each predefined type recognized by the compiler maps onto one of the IL built-in types. The same is true in VB.NET.

Common Language Specification (CLS)

The Common Language Specification works with the Common Type System to ensure language interoperability. The CLS is a set of minimum standards that all compilers targeting .NET must support. Since IL is a very rich language, writers of most compilers will prefer to restrict the capabilities of a given compiler to only support a subset of the facilities offered by IL and the CTS. That is fine, as long as the compiler supports everything that is defined in the CLS.

> It is perfectly acceptable to write non-CLS-compliant code. However, if you do, the compiled IL code isn't guaranteed to be fully language-interoperable.

An example is provided by case sensitivity. IL is case-sensitive. Developers who work with case-sensitive languages regularly take advantage of the flexibility this case sensitivity gives them when selecting variable names. VB.NET, however, is not case sensitive. The CLS works around this by indicating that CLS-compliant code should not expose any two names that differ only in their case. Therefore, VB.NET code can work with CLS-compliant code.

This example shows that the CLS works in two ways. First, it means that individual compilers do not have to be powerful enough to support the full features of .NET – this should encourage the development of compilers for other programming languages that target .NET. Second, it provides a guarantee that, if you restrict your classes to only exposing CLS-compliant features, then it is guaranteed that code written in any other compliant language can use your classes.

The beauty of this idea is that the restriction to using CLS-compliant features only applies to public and protected members of classes and public classes. Within the private implementations of your classes, you can write whatever non-CLS code you wish, because code in other assemblies (units of managed code, see later in the chapter) cannot access this part of your code anyway.

We won't go into the details of the CLS specifications here. In general, the CLS won't affect your C# code very much, because there are very few non-CLS-compliant features of C# anyway.

Garbage Collection

The **garbage collector** is .NET's answer to memory management, and in particular to the question of what to do about reclaiming memory that running applications ask for. Up until now there have been two techniques used on Windows platform for deallocating memory that processes have dynamically requested from the system:

- ❑ Make the application code do it all manually
- ❑ Make objects maintain reference counts

Having the application code responsible for de-allocating memory is the technique used by lower-level, high-performance languages such as C++. It is efficient, and it has the advantage that (in general) resources are never occupied for longer than unnecessary. The big disadvantage, however, is the frequency of bugs. Code that requests memory also should explicitly inform the system when it no longer requires that memory. However, it is easy to overlook this, resulting in memory leaks.

Although modern developer environments do provide tools to assist in detecting memory leaks, they remain difficult bugs to track down, because they have no effect until so much memory has been leaked that Windows refuses to grant any more to the process. By this point, the entire computer may have appreciably slowed down due to the memory demands being made on it.

Maintaining reference counts is favored in COM. The idea is that each COM component maintains a count of how many clients are currently maintaining references to it. When this count falls to zero, the component can destroy itself and free up associated memory and resources. The problem with this is that it still relies on the good behavior of clients to notify the component that they have finished with it. It only takes one client not to do so, and the object sits in memory. In some ways, this is a potentially more serious problem than a simple C++-style memory leak, because the COM object may exist in its own process, which means that it will never be removed by the system (at least with C++ memory leaks, the system can reclaim all memory when the process terminates).

The .NET runtime relies on the garbage collector instead. This is a program whose purpose is to clean up memory. The idea is that all dynamically requested memory is allocated on the heap (that is true for all languages, although in the case of .NET, the CLR maintains its own managed heap for .NET applications to use). Every so often, when .NET detects that the managed heap for a given process is becoming full and therefore needs tidying up, it calls the garbage collector. The garbage collector runs through variables currently in scope in your code, examining references to objects stored on the heap to identify which ones are accessible from your code – that is to say which objects have references that refer to them. Any objects that are not referred to are deemed to be no longer accessible from your code and can therefore be removed. Java uses a similar system of garbage collection to this.

Garbage collection works in .NET because Intermediate Language has been designed to facilitate the process. The principle requires, firstly, that you cannot get references to existing objects other than by copying existing references, and secondly, that Intermediate Language is type safe. In this context, what we mean is that if any reference to an object exists, then there is sufficient information in the reference to exactly determine the type of the object.

It would not be possible to use the garbage collection mechanism with a language such as unmanaged C++, for example, because C++ allows pointers to be freely cast between types.

One aspect of garbage collection that it is important to be aware of is that it is not deterministic. In other words, you cannot guarantee when the garbage collector will be called; it will be called when the CLR decides that it is needed (unless you explicitly call the collector).

Security

.NET can really excel in terms of complementing the security mechanisms provided by Windows because it can offer code-based security, whereas Windows only really offers role-based security.

Role-based security is based on the identity of the account under which the process is running, in other words, who owns and is running the process. Code-based security on the other hand is based on what the code actually does and on how much the code is trusted. Thanks to the strong type safety of IL, the CLR is able to inspect code before running it in order to determine required security permissions. .NET also offers a mechanism by which code can indicate in advance what security permissions it will require to run.

The importance of **code-based security** is that it reduces the risks associated with running code of dubious origin (such as code that you've downloaded from the Internet). For example, even if code is running under the administrator account, it is possible to use code-based security to indicate that that code should still not be permitted to perform certain types of operation that the administrator account would normally be allowed to do, such as read or write to environment variables, read or write to the registry, or to access the .NET reflection features.

Security issues are covered in more depth later in the book, in Chapter 23.

Application Domains

Application domains are an important innovation in .NET and are designed to ease the overhead involved when running applications that need to be isolated from each other, but which also need to be able to communicate with each other. The classic example of this is a web server application, which may be simultaneously responding to a number of browser requests. It will, therefore, probably have a number of instances of the component responsible for servicing those requests running simultaneously.

In pre-.NET days, the choice would be between allowing those instances to share a process, with the resultant risk of a problem in one running instance bringing the whole web site down, or isolating those instances in separate processes, with the associated performance overhead.

Up until now, the only means of isolating code has been through processes. When you start a new application running, it runs within the context of a process. Windows isolates processes from each other through address spaces. The idea is that each process has available 4 gigabytes of virtual memory in which to store its data and executable code (the figure of 4GB is for 32-bit systems; 64-bit systems will have more). Windows imposes an extra level of indirection by which this virtual memory maps into a particular area of actual physical memory or disk space. Each process will get a different mapping, with no overlap between the actual physical memories that the blocks of virtual address space map to. This situation is shown in the diagram:

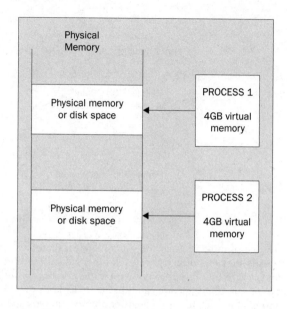

In general, any process is only able to access memory by specifying an address in virtual memory – processes do not have direct access to physical memory. Hence it is simply impossible for one process to access the memory allocated to another process. This provides an excellent guarantee that any badly behaved code will not be able to damage anything outside its own address space. (Note that on Windows 9x, these safeguards are not quite as thorough as they are on NT/2000/XP, so the theoretical possibility exists of applications crashing Windows by writing to inappropriate memory.)

Processes don't just serve as a way to isolate instances of running code from each other. On Windows NT/2000 systems, they also form the unit to which security privileges and permissions are assigned. Each process has its own security token, which indicates to Windows precisely what operations that process is permitted to do.

While processes are great for security in both of these senses, their big disadvantage is performance. Often a number of processes will actually be working together, and therefore need to communicate with each other. The obvious example of this is where a process calls up a COM component, which is an executable, and therefore is required to run in its own process. The same thing happens in COM when surrogates are used. Since processes cannot share any memory, a complex marshaling process has to be used to copy data between the processes. This gives a very significant hit for performance. If you need components to work together and don't want that performance hit, then the only way up till now has been to use DLL-based components and have everything running in the same address space – with the associated risk that a badly behaved component will bring everything else down.

Application domains are designed as a way of separating components without resulting in the performance problems associated with passing data between processes. The idea is that any one process is divided into a number of application domains. Each application domain roughly corresponds to a single application, and each thread of execution will be running in a particular application domain:

```
PROCESS - 4GB virtual memory


APPLICATION DOMAIN
- an application uses some
of this virtual memory


APPLICATION DOMAIN
- another application uses
some of this virtual memory
```

If different executables are running in the same process space, then they are clearly able to easily share data, because theoretically they can directly see each other's data. However, although this is possible in principle, the CLR makes sure that this does not happen in practice by inspecting the code for each running application, to ensure that the code cannot stray outside its own data areas. This sounds at first sight like an almost impossible trick to pull off – after all how can you tell what the program is going to do without actually running it?

In fact, it is usually possible to do this because of the strong type safety of the IL. In most cases, unless code is explicitly using unsafe features such as pointers, the data types it is using will ensure that memory is not accessed inappropriately. For example, .NET array types perform bounds checking to ensure that no out of bounds array operations are permitted. If a running application specifically does need to communicate or share data with other applications running in different application domains, then it must do so by calling on .NET's remoting services.

Code that has been verified to check that it cannot access data outside its application domain (other than through the explicit remoting mechanism) is said to be **memory type-safe**. Such code can safely be run alongside other type safe code in different application domains within the same process.

Error Handling Via Exceptions

.NET is designed to facilitate handling of error conditions using the same mechanism, based on exceptions, that is employed by Java and C++. C++ developers should note that, however, because of IL's stronger typing system, there is no performance penalty associated with the use of exceptions with IL in the way that there is in C++. Also, the `finally` block, which has long been on many C++ developers' wish list, is supported by .NET and by C#.

We will cover exceptions in detail in Chapter 4. Briefly, the idea is that certain areas of code are designated as exception handler routines, with each one able to deal with a particular error condition (for example, a file not being found, or being denied permission to perform some operation). These conditions can be defined as narrowly or as widely as you wish. The exception architecture ensures that when an error condition occurs, execution can immediately jump to the exception handler routine that is most specifically geared to handle the exception condition in question.

The architecture of exception handling also provides a convenient means to pass an object containing precise details of the exception condition to an exception handling routine. This object might include an appropriate message for the user and details of exactly where in the code the exception was detected.

Most exception handling architecture, including the control of program flow when an exception occurs, is handled by the high-level languages (C#, VB.NET, C++), and is not supported by any special IL commands. C#, for example, handles exceptions using `try{}`, `catch{}`, and `finally{}` blocks of code, as we'll see later in Chapter 4.

What .NET does do, however, is provide the infrastructure to allow compilers that target .NET to support exception handling. In particular, it provides a set of .NET classes that can represent the exceptions, and the language interoperability to allow the thrown exception objects to be interpreted by the exception handling code, irrespective of what language the exception handling code is written in. This language independence is absent from both the C++ and Java implementations of exception handling, although it is present to a limited extent in the COM mechanism for handling errors, which involves returning error codes from methods and passing error objects around. The fact that exceptions are handled consistently in different languages is a crucial aspect of facilitating multi-language development.

Use of Attributes

Attributes are a feature that will be familiar to developers who use C++ to write COM components (through their use in Microsoft's COM Interface Definition Language (IDL)) although they will not be familiar to Visual Basic or Java developers. The initial idea of an attribute was that it provided extra information concerning some item in the program that could be used by the compiler.

Attributes are supported in .NET – and hence now by C++, C#, and VB.NET. What is, however, particularly innovative about attributes in .NET is that a mechanism exists whereby you can define your own attributes in your sourcecode. These user-defined attributes will be placed with the metadata for the corresponding data types or methods. This can be useful for documentation purposes, where they can be used in conjunction with reflection technology (described) in order to perform programming tasks based on attributes. Also, in common with the .NET philosophy of language independence, attributes can be defined in sourcecode in one language, and read by code that is written in another language.

Attributes are covered in Chapters 4 and 5 of this book.

Assemblies

An **assembly** is the logical unit that contains compiled code targeted at .NET. We are not going to cover assemblies in great detail here, because they are covered in detail in Chapter 8, but we will summarize the main points here.

An assembly is completely self-describing, and is a logical rather than a physical unit, which means that it can be stored across more than one file (indeed dynamic assemblies are stored in memory, not on file at all). If an assembly is stored in more than one file, then there will be one main file that contains the entry point and describes the other files in the assembly.

Note that the same assembly structure is used for both executable code and library code. The only real difference is that an executable assembly contains a main program entry point, whereas a library assembly doesn't.

An important characteristic of assemblies is that they contain metadata that describes the types and methods defined in the corresponding code. An assembly, however, also contains assembly metadata that describes the assembly itself. This assembly metadata, contained in an area known as the **manifest**, allows checks to be made on the version of the assembly, and on its integrity.

> `ildasm`, *a Windows-based utility, can be used to inspect the contents of an assembly, including the manifest and metadata. We examine* `ildasm` *in Chapter 8.*

The fact that an assembly contains program metadata means that applications or other assemblies that call up code in a given assembly do not need to refer to the Registry, or to any other data source, in order to find out how to use that assembly. This is a significant break from the old COM way of doing things, in which the GUIDs of the components and interfaces had to be obtained from the Registry, and in some cases, the details of the methods and properties exposed would need to be read from a type library.

Having data spread out in up to three different locations meant there was the obvious risk of something getting out of synchronization, which would prevent other software from being able to use the component successfully. With assemblies, there is no risk of this happening, because all the metadata is stored with the program executable instructions. Note that even though assemblies are stored across several files, there are still no problems with data going out of synchronization. This is because the file that contains the assembly entry point also stores details of, and a hash of, the contents of the other files, which means that if one of the files gets replaced, or in any way tampered with, this will almost certainly be detected and the assembly will refuse to load.

Assemblies come in two types: **shared** and **private** assemblies.

Private Assemblies

Private assemblies are the simplest type. They normally ship with software, and are intended to be used only with that software. The usual scenario in which you will ship private assemblies is the case in which you are supplying an application in the form of an executable and a number of libraries, where the libraries contain code that should only be used with that application.

The system guarantees that private assemblies will not be used by other software, because an application may only load private assemblies that are located in the same folder that the main executable is loaded in, or in a subfolder of it.

Because we would normally expect that commercial software would always be installed in its own directory, this means that there is no risk of one software package overwriting, modifying, or accidentally loading private assemblies intended for another package. As private assemblies can only be used by the software package that they are intended for, this means that you have much more control over what software uses them. There is, therefore, less need to take security precautions, since there is no risk, for example, of some other commercial software overwriting one of your assemblies with some new version of it (apart from the case where software is designed specifically to perform malicious damage). There are also no problems with name collisions. If classes in your private assembly happen to have the same name as classes in someone else's private assembly that doesn't matter, because any given application will only be able to see the one set of private assemblies.

Because a private assembly is entirely self-contained, the process of deploying it is simple. You simply place the appropriate file(s) in the appropriate folder in the file system (there are no registry entries that need to be made). This process is known as **zero impact (xcopy) installation**.

Shared Assemblies

Shared assemblies are intended to be common libraries that any other application can use. Because any other software can access a shared assembly, more precautions need to be taken against the following risks:

- ❑ Name collisions, where another company's shared assembly implements types that have the same names as those in your shared assembly. Because client code can theoretically have access to both assemblies simultaneously, this could be a serious problem.

- ❑ The risk of an assembly being overwritten by a different version of the same assembly – the new version being incompatible with some existing client code.

The solution to these problems involves placing shared assemblies in a special directory subtree in the file system, known as the global **assembly cache**. Unlike with private assemblies, this cannot be done by simply copying the assembly into the appropriate folder – it needs to be specifically installed into the cache. This process can be performed by a number of .NET utilities, and involves carrying out certain checks on the assembly, as well as setting up a small folder hierarchy within the assembly cache that is used to ensure assembly integrity.

In order to avoid the risk of name collisions, shared assemblies are given a name that is based on private key cryptography (private assemblies are simply given the same name as their main file name). This name is known as a **strong name**, is guaranteed to be unique, and must be quoted by applications that wish to reference a shared assembly.

Problems associated with the risk of overwriting an assembly are addressed by specifying version information in the assembly manifest, and by allowing side-by-side installations.

Reflection

Since assemblies store metadata, including details of all the types and members of these types that are defined in the assembly, it is possible to access this metadata programmatically. Full details of this can be found in Chapter 5. This technique – known as **reflection** – raises interesting possibilities, since it means that managed code can actually examine other managed code, or can even examine itself, to determine information about that code. This will most commonly be used to obtain the details of attributes, although you can also use reflection, among other purposes, as an indirect way of instantiating classes or calling methods, given the names of those classes on methods as strings. In this way you could select classes to instantiate methods to call at run time, rather than compile time, based on user input (dynamic binding).

.NET Framework Classes

Perhaps one of the biggest benefits of writing managed code, at least from a developer's point of view, is that you get to use the .NET **base class library**.

The .NET base classes are a massive collection of managed code classes that have been written by Microsoft, and which allow you to do almost any of the tasks that were previously available through the Windows API. These classes follow the same object model as used by IL, based on single inheritance. This means that you can either instantiate objects of whichever .NET base class is appropriate, or you can derive your own classes from them.

The great thing about the .NET base classes is that they have been designed to be very intuitive and easy to use. For example, to start a thread, you call the `Start()` method of the `Thread` class. To disable a `TextBox`, you set the `Enabled` property of a `TextBox` object to `false`. This approach will be familiar to Visual Basic and Java developers, whose respective libraries are just as easy to use. It may however come as a great relief to C++ developers, who for years have had to cope with such API functions as `GetDIBits()`, `RegisterWndClassEx()`, and `IsEqualIID()`, as well as a whole plethora of functions that required Windows handles to be passed around.

On the other hand, C++ developers always had easy access to the entire Windows API, whereas Visual Basic and Java developers were more restricted in terms of the basic operating system functionality that they have access to from their respective languages. What is new about the .NET base classes is that they combine the ease of use that was typical of the Visual Basic and Java libraries with the relatively comprehensive coverage of the Windows API functions. There are still many features of Windows that are not available through the base classes, and for which you will need to call into the API functions, but in general, these are now confined to the more exotic features. For everyday use, you will probably find the base classes adequate. And if you do need to call into an API function, .NET offers a so-called "platform-invoke" which will ensure data types are correctly converted, so the task is no harder than calling the function directly from C++ code would have been, no matter whether you are coding in C#, C++, or VB.NET.

> *WinCV, a Windows-based utility, can be used to browse the classes, structs, interfaces, and enums in the base class library. We'll examine WinCV in Chapter 6.*

Although Chapter 5 is nominally dedicated to the subject of base classes, in reality, once we have completed our coverage of the syntax of the C# language, most of the rest of this book will essentially be showing you how to use various classes within the .NET base class library. That is how comprehensive base classes are. As a rough guide, the areas covered by the .NET base classes include:

❑ Core features provided by IL (including, say, the primitive data types in the CTS, Chapter 5)

❑ Windows GUI support and controls (Chapter 7)

❑ Web Forms (ASP.NET, Chapters 14-16)

❑ Data Access (ADO.NET, Chapters 9 and 10)

❑ Directory Access (Chapter 13)

❑ File system and registry access (Chapter 12)

❑ Networking and web browsing (Chapter 20)

❑ .NET attributes and reflection (Chapter 5)

❑ Access to aspects of the Windows OS (environment variables and so on, see Chapter 23)

❑ COM interoperability (Chapters 17 and 18)

Incidentally, according to Microsoft sources, a large proportion of the .NET base classes have actually been written in C#!

Namespaces

Namespaces are the way that .NET avoids name clashes between classes. They are designed, for example, to avoid the situation in which you define a class to represent a customer, name your class Customer, and then someone else does the same thing (quite a likely scenario – the proportion of businesses that have customers seems to be quite high).

A namespace is no more than a grouping of data types, but it has the effect that the names of all data types within a namespace automatically get prefixed with the name of the namespace. It is also possible to nest namespaces within each other. For example, most of the general-purpose .NET base classes are in a namespace called System. The base class Array is in this namespace, so its full name is System.Array.

.NET requires all types to be defined in a namespace, so for example you could place your Customer class in a namespace called YourCompanyName. This class would have the full name YourCompanyName.Customer.

If a namespace is not explicitly supplied, then the type will be added to a nameless global namespace.

Microsoft recommends that for most purposes you supply at least two nested namespace names, the first one being the name of your company, the second being the name of the technology or software package that the class is a member of, such as YourCompanyName.SalesServices.Customer. Doing this will, in most situations, protect the classes in your application from possible name clashes with classes written by other organizations.

We will look more closely at namespaces in Chapter 2.

Creating .NET Applications Using C#

C# can be used to create console applications: text-only applications that run in a DOS window. You'll probably use console applications when unit testing class libraries, and for creating Unix/Linux daemon processes. However, more often you'll use C# to create applications that use many of the technologies associated with .NET. In this section, we'll give you an overview of the different types of application that you can write in C#.

Creating ASP.NET Applications

ASP was a Microsoft technology for creating web pages with dynamic content. An ASP page is basically an HTML file with embedded chunks of server-side VBScript or JavaScript. When a client browser requested an ASP page, the web server would deliver the HTML portions of the page, processing the server-side scripts as it came to them. Often these scripts would query a database for data, and mark up that data in HTML. ASP was an easy way for clients to build browser-based applications.

ASP was not, however, without its shortcomings. First, ASP pages sometimes rendered slowly because the server-side code was interpreted instead of compiled. Second, ASP files could be difficult to maintain because they were unstructured; the server-side ASP code and plain HTML were all jumbled up together. Third, ASP sometimes made development difficult because there was little support for error handling and type-checking. Specifically, if you were using VBScript and wanted to implement error handling in your pages, you had to use the On Error Resume Next statement, and follow every component call with a check to Err.Number to make sure that the call had gone well.

ASP.NET is a revision of ASP that fixes many of its problems. It does not replace ASP; rather, ASP.NET pages can live side by side on the same server with legacy ASP applications. Of course, you can also program ASP.NET with C#!

Although subsequent chapters (14-16) discuss ASP.NET in greater detail, let's take a moment to explore some of its more significant features.

Features of ASP.NET

First, and perhaps most importantly, ASP.NET pages are **structured**. That is, each page is effectively a class that inherits from the .NET System.Web.UI.Page class, and can override a set of methods that are evoked during the Page object's lifetime. (You can think of these events as page-specific cousins of the OnApplication_Start and OnSession_Start events that went in the global.asa files of plain old ASP.) Because you can factor a page's functionality into event handlers with explicit meanings, ASP.NET pages are easier to understand.

Another nice thing about ASP.NET pages is that you can create them in VS.NET, the same environment in which you create the business logic and data access components that those ASP pages use. A VS.NET project group, or **solution**, contains all of the files associated with an application. Moreover, you can debug your ASP pages in the editor as well; in the old days of Visual InterDev, it was often a vexing challenge to configure InterDev and the project's web server to turn debugging on.

For maximum clarity, ASP.NET's code-behind feature lets you take the structured approach even further. ASP.NET allows you to isolate the server-side functionality of a page to a class, compile that class into a DLL, and place that DLL into a directory below the HTML portion. A code-behind directive at the top of the page associates the file with its DLL. When a browser requests the page, the web server fires the events in the class in the page's code-behind DLL.

Last but not least, ASP.NET is remarkable for its increased performance. Whereas ASP pages are interpreted with each page request, the web server caches ASP.NET pages after compilation. This means that subsequent requests of an ASP.NET page execute more quickly than the first.

ASP.NET also makes it easy to write pages that cause forms to be displayed by the browser, which you might use in an intranet environment. The traditional wisdom is that form-based applications offer a richer user interface, but are harder to maintain because they run on so many different machines. For this reason, people have relied on form-based applications when rich user interfaces were a necessity and extensive support could be provided to the users.

With the advent of Internet Explorer 5 and the lackluster performance of Navigator 6, however, the advantages of form-based applications are clouded. IE 5's consistent and robust support for DHTML allows the programmer to create web-based applications that are every bit as pretty as their fat client equivalents. Of course, such applications necessitate standardizing on IE and not supporting Navigator. In many industrial situations, this standardization is now common.

Web Forms

To make web page construction even easier, Visual Studio .NET supplies **Web Forms**. They allow you to build ASP.NET pages graphically in the same way that VB 6 or C++ Builder windows are created; in other words, by dragging controls from a toolbox onto a form, then flipping over to the code aspect of that form, and writing event handlers for the controls. When you use C# to create a Web Form, you are creating a C# class that inherits from the Page base class, and an ASP page that designates that class as its code-behind. Of course, you don't have to use C# to create a Web Form; you can use VB.NET or another .NET language just as well.

In the past, the difficulty of web development has discouraged some teams from attempting it. To succeed in web development, you had to know so many different technologies, such as VBScript, ASP, DHTML, JavaScript, and so on. By applying the Form concepts to web pages, Web Forms promise to make web development easier. Only time will tell, however, how successful Web Forms and Web Controls (which we'll look at next) will be at insulating the developer from the complexities of web design.

Web Controls

The controls used to populate a Web Form are not controls in the same sense as ActiveX controls. Rather, they are XML tags in the ASP namespace that the web browser dynamically transforms into HTML and client-side script when a page is requested. Amazingly, the web server is able to render the same server-side control in different ways, producing a transformation that is appropriate to the requestor's particular web browser. This means that it is now easy to write fairly sophisticated user interfaces for web pages, without having to worry about how to ensure that your page will run on any of the available browsers – because Web Forms will take care of that for you.

You can use C# or VB.NET to expand the Web Form toolbox. Creating a new server-side control is simply a matter of implementing .NET's System.Web.UI.WebControls.WebControl class.

Web Services

Today, HTML pages account for most of the traffic on the World Wide Web. With XML, however, computers have a device-independent format to use for communicating with each other on the Web. In the future, computers may use the Web and XML to communicate information rather than dedicated lines and proprietary formats such as **EDI** (**Electronic Data Interchange**). Web Services are designed for a service-oriented web, in which remote computers provide each other with dynamic information that can be analyzed and re-formatted, before final presentation to a user. A Web Service is an easy way for a computer to expose information to other computers on the Web in the form of XML.

In technical terms, a Web Service on .NET is an ASP.NET page that returns XML instead of HTML to requesting clients. Such pages have a code-behind DLL containing a class that derives from the WebService class. The VS.NET IDE provides an engine that facilitates Web Service development.

There are two main reasons that an organization might choose to use Web Services. The first reason is that because they rely on HTTP, Web Services can use existing networks (the Web) as a medium for conveying information. The other is that because Web Services use XML, the data format is self-describing, non-proprietary, and platform-independent.

Creating Windows Forms

Although C# and .NET are particularly suited to web development, they still offer splendid support for so-called "fat client" apps, applications that have to be installed on the end-user's machine where most of the processing takes place. This support is from **Windows Forms**.

A Windows Form is the .NET answer to a VB 6 Form. To design a graphical window interface, you just drag controls from a toolbox onto a Windows Form. To determine the window's behavior, you write event-handling routines for the form's controls. A Windows Form project compiles to an EXE that must be installed alongside the .NET runtime on the end user's computer. Like other .NET project types, Windows Form projects are supported by both VB.NET and C#. We will be examining Windows Forms more closely in Chapter 7.

Windows Controls

Although Web Forms and Windows Forms are developed in much the same way, you use different kinds of controls to populate them. Web Forms use Web Controls, and Windows Forms use **Windows Controls**.

A Windows Control is a lot like an ActiveX control. After a Window control is implemented, it compiles to a DLL that must be installed on the client's machine. In fact, the .NET SDK provides a utility that creates a wrapper for ActiveX controls, so that they can be placed on Windows Forms. As is the case with Web Controls, Windows Control creation involves deriving from a particular class, `System.Windows.Forms.Control`.

Windows Services

A Windows Service (originally called an NT Service) is a program that is designed to run in the background in Windows NT/2000/XP (but not Windows 9x). Services are useful where you want a program to be running continuously and ready to respond to events without having been explicitly started by the user. A good example would be the World Wide Web Service on web servers, which listens out for web requests from clients.

It is very easy to write services in C#. There are .NET Framework base classes available in the `System.ServiceProcess` namespace that handle many of the boilerplate tasks associated with services, and in addition, Visual Studio .NET allows you to create a C# Windows Service project, which starts you out with the Framework C# sourcecode for a basic Windows service. We'll explore how to write C# Windows Services in Chapter 22.

The Role of C# in .NET Enterprise Architecture

C# requires the presence of the .NET runtime, and it will probably be a few years before most clients – particularly most home machines – have .NET installed. In the meantime, installing a C# application is likely to mean also installing the .NET redistributable components. Because of that, it is likely that the first place we will see many C# applications is in the enterprise environment. Indeed, C# arguably presents an outstanding opportunity for organizations that are interested in building robust, n-tiered client-server applications.

When combined with **ADO.NET**, C# has the ability to quickly and generically access data stores like SQL Server and Oracle databases. The returned datasets can easily be manipulated via the ADO.NET object model, and automatically render as XML for transport across an office intranet.

Once a database schema has been established for a new project, C# presents an excellent medium for implementing a layer of data access objects, each of which could provide insertion, updates, and deletion access to a different database table.

Because it's the first component-based C language, C# is a great language for implementing a business object tier, too. It encapsulates the messy plumbing for inter-component communication, leaving the developer free to focus on gluing their data access objects together in methods that accurately enforce his organization's business rules. Moreover, with attributes, C# business objects can be outfitted for method-level security checks, object pooling, and JIT activation supplied by COM+ Services. Furthermore, .NET ships with utility programs that allow your new .NET business objects to interface with legacy COM components.

To create an enterprise application with C#, you'd probably create a Class Library project for the data access objects and another for the business objects. While developing, you could use Console projects to test the methods on your classes. Fans of extreme programming could build Console projects that could be automatically executed from batch files to unit test that working code has not been broken.

On a related note, C# and .NET will probably influence the way that you physically package your reusable classes. In the past, many developers crammed a multitude of classes into a single physical component because this arrangement made deployment a lot easier; if there was a versioning problem, you knew just where to look. Because deploying .NET enterprise components simply involves copying files into directories, developers can now package their classes into more logical, discrete components without encountering "DLL Hell".

Last but not least, ASP.NET pages coded in C# constitute an excellent medium for user interfaces. Because ASP.NET pages compile, they execute quickly. Because they can be debugged in the VS.NET IDE, they are robust. Because they support full-scale language features like early binding, inheritance, and modularization, ASP.NET pages coded in C# are tidy and easily maintained.

Seasoned developers acquire a healthy skepticism about strongly hyped new technologies and languages, and are reluctant to utilize new platforms simply because they are urged to. If you're an enterprise developer in an IT department, though, or if you provide application services across the World Wide Web, let me assure you that C# and .NET offer at least four solid benefits, even if some of the more exotic features like Web Services and server-side controls don't pan out:

❑ Component conflicts will become infrequent and deployment will be easier, because different versions of the same component can run side by side on the same machine without conflicting

❑ Your ASP code won't look like spaghetti anymore

❑ You can leverage a lot of the functionality in the .NET base classes

❑ For applications requiring a Windows Forms user interface, C# makes it very easy to write this kind of application

Windows Forms have to some extent been downplayed in the last year due to the advent of WebForms and Internet-based applications. However, if you or your colleagues lack expertise in JavaScript, ASP, or related technologies, then Windows Forms are still a viable option for creating a user interface with speed and ease. Just remember to factor your code so that the user interface logic is separate from the business logic and the data access code. Doing so will allow you to migrate your application to the browser at some point in the future if you need to do so. Also, it is likely that Windows Forms will remain the dominant user interface for applications for use in homes and small businesses for a long time to come.

Summary

We've covered a lot of ground in this chapter, briefly reviewing important aspects of the .NET Framework and C#'s relationship to it. We started by discussing how all languages that target .NET are compiled into Intermediate Language before this is compiled and executed by the Common Language Runtime. We also discussed the roles of the following features of .NET in the compilation and execution process:

- ❑ Assemblies and .NET base classes
- ❑ COM components
- ❑ JIT compilation
- ❑ Application domains
- ❑ Garbage Collection

The diagram opposite provides an overview of how these features come into play during compilation and execution:

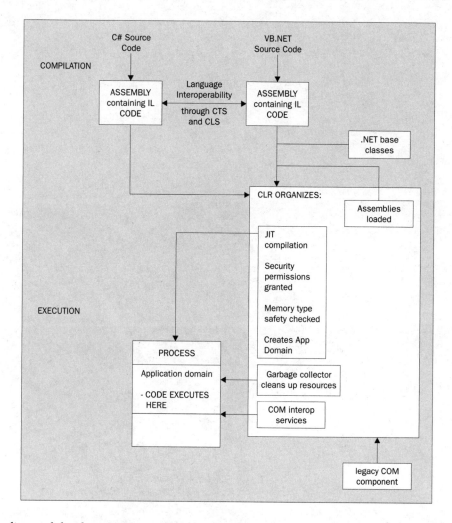

We also discussed the characteristics of the IL, particularly its strong data typing and object-orientation. We noted how these characteristics influence the languages that target .NET, including C#. We also noted how the strongly-typed nature of IL enables language interoperability, as well as CLR services such as garbage collection and security.

At the end of the chapter, we talked about how C# can be used as the basis for applications that are built upon several .NET technologies, including ASP.NET.

Now that we have this background, we will move on in the next chapter to see how to actually write code in C#.

2

C# Basics

Now that you understand a little more about *what* C# can do, you will want to learn *how* to use it. This chapter on the basics of C# will give you a good start in that direction by providing you with a basic knowledge of the fundamentals of C# programming, which we will build on in subsequent chapters. The main topics we will be covering are:

- ❑ Declaring variables
- ❑ Initialization and scope of variables
- ❑ C#'s predefined data types
- ❑ Dictating the flow of execution within a C# program using loops and statements
- ❑ Calling and declaring classes and methods
- ❑ Using arrays
- ❑ Operators
- ❑ Type safety and how to convert between data types
- ❑ Enumerations
- ❑ Namespaces
- ❑ The `Main()` method
- ❑ Basic command-line C# compiler options
- ❑ Using `System.Console` to perform console I/O
- ❑ Using commenting features in C# and Visual Studio .NET
- ❑ C# identifiers and keywords

By the end of this chapter you will know enough C# to write simple programs, though without using inheritance or other object-oriented features. We will be exposing these details in the next few chapters of the book.

Before We Start

As we have already mentioned, C# is an object-oriented language. As we get you up to speed in the fundamentals of the C# language, we will be assuming that you have a good grasp of the concepts behind object-oriented (OO) programming. In other words, we will expect you to understand what we mean by **classes**, **objects**, **interfaces**, and **inheritance**. If you have programmed in C++ or Java before, you should have a pretty good grounding in object oriented programming (OOP).

However, if you do not have a background in OOP, there are plenty of good sources of information on this subject. Indeed, Appendix A of this book provides an introduction to OOP. We also recommend the Wrox Press publication, *Beginning C#* (ISBN 1-861004-98-2) which teaches both object-orientation and C# from scratch.

If you are a very experienced developer in one of VB 6, C++, or Java, you should note that we make many comparisons between C#, C++, Java, and VB 6 as we walk though the basics of C#. However, you might prefer to learn C# initially by reading a comparison between C# and your selected language. If so, we have made available separate documents for download on the Wrox Press web site (http://www.wrox.com) that give introductions to C# from the point of view of each of those languages.

Our First C# Program

Let's start in the traditional way by compiling and running the simplest possible C# program – a simple class consisting of a console application that writes a message to the screen. Type the following into a text editor (such as Notepad), and save it with a .cs extension (for example, First.cs):

```
using System;

namespace Wrox.ProCSharp.Basics
{
    class MyFirstCSharpClass
    {
        static void Main()
        {
            Console.WriteLine("This isn't at all like Java!");
            Console.ReadLine();
            return;

        }
    }
}
```

Through the next chapters we will present a number of code samples. The most common technique for writing C# programs is to use Visual Studio .NET to generate a basic project and add your own code to this. However, since the aim of these early chapters is to teach the C# language, we are going to keep things simple and avoid relying on Visual Studio .NET until Chapter 6. Instead, we will present the code as simple files that you can type in using any text editor and compile from the command line.

You can compile this program simply running the C# command-line compiler (`csc.exe`) against the source file, like this:

```
csc First.cs
```

If you wish to compile code from the command line using the `csc` command, you should be aware that the .NET command-line tools, including `csc`, are only available if certain environment variables have been set up. Depending on how you installed .NET (and Visual Studio .NET), this may or may not be the case on your machine.

> *If you do not have them set up then there are two ways round this. The first is to run the batch file*
> `%Microsoft Visual Studio .NET%\Vc7\bin\vcvars32.bat` *from the command*
> *prompt before running* `csc`, *where* `%Microsoft Visual Studio .NET` *is the folder to which*
> *Visual Studio .NET has been installed. The second (easier) way is to use the Visual Studio .NET*
> *command prompt instead of the usual command-prompt window. You will find the Visual Studio*
> *.NET command prompt in the Start Menu, under the* **Programs** *then* **Microsoft Visual**
> **Studio.NET** *submenus. It is simply a command-prompt window that automatically runs*
> `vcvars32.bat` *when it opens.*

Compiling the code will produce an executable file named `First.exe`, which we can run from the command line or from Windows Explorer like any other executable. Give it a try:

```
csc First.cs
Microsoft (R) Visual C# .NET Compiler version 7.00.9466
for Microsoft (R) .NET Framework version 1.0.3705
Copyright (C) Microsoft Corporation 2001. All rights reserved.


First
This isn't at all like Java!
```

Well, maybe that message isn't quite true! There are some fairly fundamental similarities to Java in this program, although there are one or two points (such as the capitalized `Main()` function) to catch out the unwary Java or C++ developer. Let's look a little more closely at what's going on in the code.

A Closer Look

First, a few general comments about C# syntax. In C#, as in other C-style languages, every statement *must* end in a semi-colon, `;`, and can continue over multiple lines without needing a continuation character (such as the underscore in VB). Statements can be joined into blocks using curly braces, `{}`. Single-line comments begin with two forward slash characters, `//`, and multi-line comments begin with a slash and an asterisk, `/*`, and end with the same combination reversed, `*/`. In these aspects, C# is identical to C++ and Java, but different from VB. It is the semi-colons and curly braces that give C# code such a different visual appearance to VB code. If your background is predominantly VB, then take extra care to remember the semi-colon at the end of every statement. Omitting this is usually the biggest single cause of compilation errors among developers new to C-style languages.

The first couple of lines are to do with **namespaces** (mentioned in Chapter 1), which are a way to group associated classes together. This concept will be familiar to Java and C++ developers, but may be new to VB developers. C# namespaces are basically the same as C++ namespaces or, equivalently, Java packages, but there is no comparable concept in VB. The namespace keyword declares the namespace our class should be associated with. All code within the following braces is regarded as being within that namespace. The using statement specifies a namespace that the compiler should look at to find any classes that are referenced in your code but which aren't defined in the current namespace. This performs the same purpose as the import statement in Java and the using namespace statement in C++.

```
using System;

namespace Wrox.ProCSharp.Basics
{
```

The reason for the presence of the using statement in the First.cs file is that we are going to use a library class, System.Console. The using System statement allows us to refer to this class simply as Console (and similarly for any other classes in the System namespace). The standard System namespace is where the most commonly used .NET types reside. It is important to realize straight away that pretty well everything we do in C# depends on the .NET base classes; in this case, we are using the Console class within the System namespace in order to write to the console window.

> *Since almost every C# program uses classes in the* System *namespace, we will assume that a* using System; *statement is present in the file for all of the other code snippets in this chapter.*

C# has no built-in keywords of its own for input or output – it is completely reliant on the .NET classes.

Next, we declare a class ostensibly called MyFirstClass. However, because it has been placed in a namespace called Wrox.ProCSharp.Basics the fully qualified name of this class is Wrox.ProCSharp.Basics.MyFirstCSharpClass.

```
class MyFirstCSharpClass
{
```

As in Java, *all* C# code must be contained within a class. Classes in C# are similar to classes in Java and C++, and very roughly comparable to class modules in VB 6. The class declaration consists of the class keyword, followed by the class name and a pair of curly braces. All code associated with the class should be placed between these braces.

Next we declare a method called Main(). Every C# executable (such as console applications, Windows applications, and Windows services) must have an entry point – the Main() method (note the capital M):

```
static void Main()
{
```

The method is called when the program is started, like the `main()` function in C++ or Java, or `Sub Main()` in a VB 6 module. This method *must* return either nothing (`void`) or an integer (`int`). A C# method corresponds to a method in C++ and Java (sometimes referred to in C++ as a member function). It also corresponds to either a VB `Function` or a VB `Sub`, depending on whether the method returns anything (unlike VB, C# makes no conceptual distinction between functions and subroutines).

Note how method definitions in C# take the form:

```
[modifiers] return_type MethodName([parameters])
{
    // Method body
}
```

Here, the first square brackets represent certain optional keywords. Modifiers are used to specify certain features of the method we are defining, such as where the method can be called from. In our case, we have two modifiers: `public` and `static`. The `public` modifier means that the method can be accessed from anywhere, so it can be called from outside our class. This is the same meaning as `public` in C++ and Java, and `Public` in VB. The `static` modifier indicates that the method does not operate on a specific instance of our class, and therefore is called without first instantiating the class. This is important since we are creating an executable rather than a class library. Once again, this has the same meaning as the `static` keyword in C++ and Java, though in this case there is no VB equivalent (the `Static` keyword in VB has a different meaning). We set the `return_type` to `void`, and in our example, we don't include any parameters.

Finally we come the code statements themselves:

```
Console.WriteLine("This isn't at all like Java!");
Console.ReadLine();
return;
```

In this case, we simply call the `WriteLine()` method of the `System.Console` class to write a line of text to the console window. `WriteLine()` is a `static` method, so we don't need to instantiate a `Console` object before calling it.

`Console.ReadLine()` reads user input. Adding this line forces the application to wait for the carriage return key to be hit before the application exits, and, in the case of Visual Studio .NET, the console window disappears.

We then call `return` to exit from the method (and, since this is the `Main()` method, the program). We specified `void` in our method header, so we don't return any parameters. The `return` statement is equivalent to `return` in C++ and Java, and `Exit Sub` or `Exit Function` in VB.

Now that we have given you a taste of basic C# syntax, we are ready to go into more detail with the various aspects of C#. Since it is virtually impossible to write any non-trivial program without **variables**, we will start by looking variables in C#.

Variables

We declare variables in C# using the following syntax:

```
datatype identifier;
```

for example:

```
int i;
```

This statement declares an `int` named i. The compiler won't actually let us use this variable until we have initialized it with a value, but the declaration allocates four bytes on the stack to hold the value.

Once it has been declared, we can assign a value to the variable using the assignment operator, =:

```
i = 10;
```

We can also declare the variable and initialize its value at the same time:

```
int i = 10;
```

This syntax is identical to C++ and Java syntax, but very different from VB syntax for declaring variables. If you are coming from VB 6, you should also be aware that C# doesn't distinguish between objects and simple types, so there is no need for anything like the `Set` keyword, even if we want our variable to refer to an object. The C# syntax for declaring variables is the same no matter what the data type of the variable.

If we declare and initialize more than one variable in a single statement, all of the variables will be of the same data type:

```
int x = 10, y =20;    // x and y are both ints
```

To declare variables of different types, you need to use separate statements – don't assign different data types within a multiple variable declaration:

```
int x = 10;
bool y = true;            // Creates a variable that stores true or false
int x = 10, bool y = true;  // This won't compile!
```

Initialization of Variables

Variable initialization demonstrates another example of C#'s emphasis on safety. Briefly, the C# compiler requires that any variable be initialized with some starting value *before* we refer to that variable in an operation. Most modern compilers will flag violations of this as a warning, but the ever-vigilant C# compiler treats such violations as errors. This prevents us from unintentionally retrieving junk values from memory that is left over from other programs.

C# has two methods for ensuring that variables are initialized before use:

❑   Variables that are fields in a class or struct, if not initialized explicitly, are by default zeroed out when they are created.

❑   Variables that are local to a method must be explicitly initialized in your code prior to any statements in which their values are used. In this case, the initialization doesn't have to happen when the variable is declared, but the compiler will check all possible paths through the method and will flag an error if it detects any possibility of the value of a local variable being used before it is initialized.

C#'s approach contrasts with that of C++, in which the compiler leaves it up to the programmer to make sure that variables are initialized before use, and that of VB, in which all variables are zeroed out automatically.

For example, we can't do the following in C#:

```
public static int Main()
{
    int d;
    Console.WriteLine(d);   // Can't do this! Need to initialize d before use
    return 0;
}
```

Notice that for this code snippet we have demonstrated defining Main() so it returns an int instead of void.

When we attempt to compile these lines, we will receive this kind of error message:

```
Use of unassigned local variable 'd'
```

The same rules apply to reference types as well. Consider the statement:

```
Something objSomething;
```

In C++, the above line would create an instance of the Something class on the stack. In C#, this same line of code would only create a **reference** for a Something object, but this reference does not yet actually refer to any object. Any attempt to call a method or property against this variable would result in an error.

Instantiating a reference object in C# requires use of the new keyword. We create a reference as above, and then point the reference at an object allocated on the heap using the new keyword:

```
objSomething = new Something();   // This creates a Something on the heap
```

Variable Scope

The **scope** of a variable is the region of code from which the variable can be accessed. In general, the scope is determined by the following rules:

❑ A **field** (also known as a member variable) of a class is in scope for as long as its containing class is in scope (this is the same as for C++, Java, and VB).

❑ A **local variable** is in scope until a closing brace indicates the end of the block statement or method in which it was declared.

❑ A local variable that is declared in a `for`, `while`, or similar statement is in scope in the body of that loop. (C++ people will note that this is the same behavior as the ANSI standard for C++. Early versions of the MS C++ compiler did not comply with this standard, but scoped such variables to remain in scope after the loop terminated).

You should also note that variables with the same name can't be declared twice in the same scope, so we can't do this:

```
int x = 20;
// some more code
int x = 30;
```

Consider the following code sample:

```
using System;

namespace Wrox.ProCSharp.Basics
{
    public class ScopeTest
    {
        public static int Main()
        {
            for (int i = 0; i < 10; i++)
            {
                Console.WriteLine(i);
            }   // i goes out of scope here

            // We can declare a variable named i again, because
            // there's no other variable with that name in scope
            for (int i = 9; i >= 0; i--)
            {
                Console.WriteLine(i);
            }   // i goes out of scope here
            return 0;
        }
    }
}
```

This code simply prints out the numbers from 0 to 9, and then back again from 9 to 0, using a `for` loop. The important thing to note is that we declare the variable `i` twice in this code, within the same method. The reason that we can do this is that `i` is declared in two separate loops, so each `i` variable is local to its own loop.

Let's have a look at another example:

```
public static int Main()
{
    int j = 20;
    for (int i = 0; i < 10; i++)
    {
        int j = 30;    // Can't do this - j is still in scope
        Console.WriteLine(j + i);
    }
    return 0;
}
```

If we try to compile this, we'll get an error:

```
ScopeTest.cs(12,14): error CS0136: A local variable named 'j' cannot be declared
in this scope because it would give a different meaning to 'j', which is already
used in a 'parent or current' scope to denote something else
```

This is because the variable j, which we defined before the start of the for loop, is still in scope within the for loop, and won't go out of scope until the Main() method has finished executing. Although, the second j (the illegal one) is in the loop's scope, that scope is nested within the Main() method's scope. The compiler has no way to distinguish between these two variables, so it won't allow the second one to be declared. This is again different from C++ where variable hiding is permitted.

Fields and Local Variables

In certain circumstances, however, we *can* distinguish between two identifiers with the same name (although not the same fully qualified name) and the same scope, and in this case the compiler *will* allow us to declare the second variable. The reason is that C# makes a fundamental distinction between variables that are declared at the type level (fields), and variables declared within methods (local variables):

Consider this code:

```
using System;

namespace Wrox.ProCSharp.Basics
{
    class ScopeTest2
    {
        static int j = 20;

        public static void Main()
        {
            int j = 30;
            Console.WriteLine(j);
            return;
        }
    }
}
```

This code will compile, even though we have two variables named j in scope within the Main() method – the j that was defined at the class level, and doesn't go out of scope until the class is destroyed (in this case, when the Main() method terminates, and the program ends) and the j defined in Main(). In this case, the new variable named j which we declare in the Main() method **hides** the class-level variable with the same name, so when we run this code, the number **30** will be displayed.

However, what if we want to refer to the class-level variable? We can actually refer to fields of a class or struct from outside the object, using the syntax *object*.*fieldname*. In the example above, we are accessing a static field (we will look at what this means in the next section) from a static method, so we can't use an instance of the class; we just use the name of the class itself:

```
...
public static void Main()
{
    int j = 30;
    Console.WriteLine(ScopeTest2.j);
}
...
```

If we were accessing an instance field (a field that belongs to a specific instance of the class), we would need to use the this keyword instead. The this keyword is used within a class or struct to obtain a reference to the current instance; we will look at this in more detail later on in the chapter. this performs the same role as this in C++ and Java, and Me in VB.

Constants

Prefixing a variable with the const keyword when it is declared and initialized designates that variable as a constant. As the name implies, a constant is a variable whose value cannot be changed throughout its lifetime:

```
const int a = 100;   // This value cannot be changed
```

Constants will be familiar to developers in VB and C++. C++ developers should, however, note that C# doesn't permit all the subtleties of C++ constants. In C++, not only could variables be declared as constant, but depending on the declaration, you could have constant pointers, variable pointers to constants, constant methods (that don't change the contents of the containing object), constant parameters to methods, and so on. These subtleties have been discarded in C#, and all you can do is declare local variables and fields to be constant.

Constants have the following characteristics:

❑ They *must* be initialized when they are declared, and once a value has been assigned, it can never be overwritten.

❑ The value of a constant must be computable at compiletime. Therefore, we can't initialize a constant with a value taken from a variable. If you need to do this, you will need to use a read-only field.

❑ Constants are always implicitly static. However, notice that we don't have to (and, in fact, aren't permitted to) include the static modifier in the constant declaration.

There are at least three advantages to using constants in your programs:

❑ Constants make your programs easier to read by replacing 'magic numbers' and 'magic strings' with readable names whose values are easy to understand.

❑ Constants make your programs easier to modify. Say, for instance, that you have a `SalesTax` constant in one of your C# programs, and that constant is assigned a value of 6%. If the sales tax rate changes at a later point in time, you can modify the behavior of all tax calculations simply by assigning a new value to the constant; you don't have to hunt throughout your code for the value `.06` and change each one, hoping that you've found all of them.

❑ Constants make it easier to avoid mistakes in your programs. If you attempt to assign another value to a constant somewhere in your program after you've already assigned it a value, the compiler will flag the error.

Predefined Data Types

Now that we have seen how to declare variables and constants, we shall take a closer look at the data types available in C#. As we will see, C# is a lot fussier about the types available and their definitions than some other languages are.

Value Types and Reference Types

Before examining the data types in C#, it is important to understand that C# distinguishes between two categories of data type:

❑ Value types

❑ Reference types

We will look in detail at the syntax for value and reference types over the next few sections. Conceptually, the difference is that a **value type** stores its value directly, while a **reference type** stores a reference to the value. Comparing to other languages, value types in C# are basically the same thing as simple types (integer, float, but not pointers or references) in VB or C++. Reference types are the same as reference types in VB, or are similar to types accessed through pointers in C++.

These types are stored in different places in memory; value types in an area known as the **stack**, while reference types are stored in an area known as the **managed heap**. It is important to be aware of whether a type is a value type or a reference type because of the different effect that assignment has. For example, `int` is a value type, which means that the following statement will result in two locations in memory storing the value 20:

```
// i and j are both of type int
i = 20;
j = i;
```

However, consider the following code. This code uses a class, MathTest, which we will define in an example to be introduced later. For now, we need to know only that MathTest is a reference type:

```
// x and y are MathTest references
x = new MathTest();
x.value = 30;    // value is a field defined in MathTest sample
y = x;
Console.WriteLine(y.value);
y.value = 50;
Console.WriteLine(x.value);
```

The crucial point to understand is that after executing this code, there is only one MathTest object around. x and y both point to the memory location that contains this object. Since x and y are variables of a reference type, declaring each variable simply reserves a reference – it doesn't instantiate an object of the given type. This is the same as declaring a pointer in C++ or an object reference in VB – in neither case does an object actually get created. In order to create an object we have to use the new keyword, as shown. Since x and y refer to the same object, changes made to x will affect y and vice versa. Hence the above code will display 30 then 50.

> *C++ developers should note that this syntax is like a reference, not a pointer. We use the .*
> *notation, not ->, to access object members. Syntactically, C# references look more like C++*
> *reference variables. However, behind the superficial syntax, the real similarity is with*
> *C++ pointers.*

If a variable is a reference, it is possible to indicate that it does not refer to any object by setting its value to null:

```
y = null;
```

This is just the same as setting a reference to null in Java, a pointer to NULL in C++, or an object reference in VB to Nothing. If a reference is set to null, then clearly it is not possible to call any non-static member functions or fields against it – doing so will cause an exception to be thrown at run-time.

In languages like C++, the developer could choose whether a given value was to be accessed directly or via a pointer. VB was more restrictive, taking the view that COM objects were reference types and simple types were always value types. C# takes a similar view to VB: whether a variable is value or reference is determined solely by its data type, so int for example is always a value type. It is not possible to declare an int variable as a reference (although later on when we cover **boxing** we will see it is possible to wrap value types in references of type object).

In C#, basic data types like bool and long are value types. This means that if we declare a bool variable and assign it the value of another bool variable, we will have two separate bool values in memory. Later, if we change the value of the original bool variable, the value of the second bool variable does not change. These types are copied by value.

In contrast, most of the more complex C# data types, including all classes that we ourselves declare, are reference types. They are allocated upon the heap, have lifetimes that can span multiple function calls, and can be accessed via one or several aliases. The CLR implements an elaborate algorithm to track which reference variables are still reachable, and which have been orphaned. Periodically, the CLR will 'clean house', destroying orphaned objects and returning the memory that they once occupied back to the operating system. This is done by the garbage collector.

C# has been designed this way because high performance is best served by keeping primitive types (like int and bool) as value types, while having larger types that contain many fields (as is usually the case with classes) as reference types. If you wish to define your own type as a value type, you should declare it as a struct.

CTS Types

As we pointed out in Chapter 1, the basic predefined types recognized by C# are not intrinsic to the language but part of the .NET Framework. For example, when you declare an int in C#, what you are actually declaring is an instance of a .NET struct, System.Int32. This may sound like an esoteric point, but it has a profound significance: it means that you are able to treat all the primitive data types syntactically as if they were classes that supported certain methods. For example, to convert an int i to a string you can write:

```
string s = i.ToString();
```

It should be emphasized that, because of the way the .NET Framework implements these types, this syntactical convenience is achieved without any performance costs. In terms of performance, you really are dealing with primitive data types.

Let's now review the types defined in C#. We will list each type, along with its definition and the name of the corresponding .NET type (CTS type). C# has fifteen predefined types, thirteen value types, and two (string and object) reference types.

Predefined Value Types

The built-in value types represent primitives, such as integer and floating-point numbers, character, and Boolean types.

Integer Types

C# supports eight predefined integer types:

Name	CTS Type	Description	Range (min:max)
sbyte	System.SByte	8-bit signed integer	-128:127 (-2^7:2^7-1)
short	System.Int16	16-bit signed integer	-32,768:32,767 (-2^{15}:2^{15}-1)
int	System.Int32	32-bit signed integer	-2,147,483,648:2,147,483,647 (-2^{31}:2^{31}-1)
long	System.Int64	64-bit signed integer	-9,223,372,036,854,775,808: 9,223,372,036,854,775,807 (-2^{63}:2^{63}-1)
byte	System.Byte	8-bit unsigned integer	0:255 (0:2^8-1)

Table continued on following page

Name	CTS Type	Description	Range (min:max)
ushort	System.UInt16	16-bit unsigned integer	0:65,535 ($0:2^{16}-1$)
uint	System.UInt32	32-bit unsigned integer	0:4,294,967,295 ($0:2^{32}-1$)
ulong	System.UInt64	64-bit unsigned integer	0:18,446,744,073,709,551,615 ($0:2^{64}-1$)

Future versions of Windows will target 64-bit processors, which can move bits into and out of memory in larger chunks to achieve faster processing times. Consequently, C# supports provides a rich palette of signed and unsigned integer types ranging in size from 8 to 64 bits.

VB developers will of course find many of these type names to be new. C++ and Java developers should be careful; some of the names of C# types are the same as C++ and Java types, but the types nevertheless, have different definitions. For example, in C#, an int is always a 32-bit signed integer. In C++ an int is a signed integer, but the number of bits is platform-dependent (32 bits on Windows). In C#, all data types have been defined in a platform-independent manner in order to allow for the possible future porting of C# and .NET to other platforms.

A byte is the standard 8-bit type for values in the range 0 to 255 inclusive. Be aware that, in keeping with its emphasis on type safety, C# regards the byte type and the char type as completely distinct, and any programmatic conversions between the two must be explicitly requested. Also be aware that unlike the other types in the integer family, a byte type is by default unsigned. Its signed version bears the special name sbyte.

With .NET, a short is no longer quite so short; it is now 16 bits long. Even larger, the int type is 32 bits long. Now huge, the long type reserves 64 bits for values! All integer-type variables can be assigned values in decimal or in hex notation. The latter require the 0x prefix:

```
long x = 0x12ab;
```

If there is any ambiguity about whether an integer is int, uint, long, or ulong, it will default to an int. In order to specify which of the other integer types the value should take, you can append one of the following characters to the number:

```
uint ui = 1234U;
long l = 1234L;
ulong ul = 1234UL;
```

We can also use lower case u and l, although the latter could be confused with the integer 1.

Floating Point Types

Although C# provides a plethora of integer data types, it supports floating-point types as well. They will be familiar to C and C++ programmers:

Name	CTS Type	Description	Significant Figures	Range (approximate)
float	System. Single	32-bit single-precision floating-point	7	$\pm 1.5 \times 10^{-45}$ to $\pm 3.4 \times 10^{38}$
double	System. Double	64-bit double-precision floating-point	15/16	$\pm 5.0 \times 10^{-324}$ to $\pm 1.7 \times 10^{308}$

The float data type is for smaller floating-point values, for which less precision is required. The double data type is bulkier than the float data type, but offers twice the precision (15 digits).

If you hard-code in a non-integer number (such as 12.3) in your code, the compiler will normally assume you want the number interpreted as a double. If we want to specify that the value is a float, we append the character F (or f) to it:

```
float f = 12.3F;
```

Decimal Type

In addition, there is a decimal type representing higher precision floating-point numbers:

Name	CTS Type	Description	Significant Figures	Range (approximate)
decimal	System. Decimal	128-bit high precision decimal notation	28	$\pm 1.0 \times 10^{-28}$ to $\pm 7.9 \times 10^{28}$

One of the great things about the CTS and C# is the provision of a dedicated decimal type for financial calculations. How you use the 28 digits that the decimal type provides is up to you. In other words, you can track smaller dollar amounts with greater accuracy for cents, or larger dollar amounts with more rounding in the fractional area.

To specify that our number is of a decimal type rather than a double, float, or an integer, we can append the M (or m) character to the value, like so:

```
decimal d = 12.30M;
```

Boolean Type

The C# bool type is used to contain Boolean values of either true or false:

Name	CTS Type	Values
bool	System.Boolean	true or false

We cannot implicitly convert bool values to and from integer values. If a variable (or a function return type) is declared as a bool, then we can only use values of true and false. We will get an error if we try to use zero for false and a non-zero value for true.

Character Type

For storing the value of a single character, C# supports the char data type:

Name	CTS Type	Values
char	System.Char	Represents a single 16-bit (Unicode) character

Although this data type has a superficial resemblance to the char type provided by C and C++, there is a significant difference. C++ char represents an 8-bit character, whereas a C# char contains 16 bits. This is part of the reason that implicit conversions between the char type and the 8-bit byte type are not permitted.

Although 8 bits may be enough to encode every character in the English language and the digits 0-9, they aren't enough to encode every character in more expansive symbol systems (such as Chinese). In a gesture towards universality, the computer industry is moving away from the 8-bit character set and towards the 16-bit Unicode scheme, of which the ASCII encoding is a subset.

Literals of type char are signified by being enclosed in single quotes, for example 'A'. If we try to enclose a character in double quotes, the compiler will treat this as a string, and throw an error.

As well as representing chars as character literals, we can represent them with 4-digit hex Unicode values (for example '\u0041'), as integer values with a cast (for example, (char)65), or as hexadecimal values ('\x0041'). They can also be represented by an escape sequence:

Escape Sequence	Character
\'	Single quote
\"	Double quote
\\	Backslash
\0	Null
\a	Alert
\b	Backspace

Escape Sequence	Character
\f	Form feed
\n	Newline
\r	Carriage return
\t	Tab character
\v	Vertical tab

C++ developers should note that because C# has a native string type, we don't need to represent strings as arrays of chars.

Predefined Reference Types

C# supports two predefined reference types:

Name	CTS Type	Description
object	System.Object	The root type, from which all other types in the CTS derive (including value types)
string	System.String	Unicode character string

The object Type

Many programming languages and class hierarchies provide a root type, from which all other objects in the hierarchy derive. C# and .NET are no exception. In C#, the object type is the ultimate parent type from which all other intrinsic and user-defined types derive. This is a key feature of C#, which distinguishes it from both VB and C++, although its behavior here is very similar to Java. All types implicitly derive ultimately from the System.Object class. This means that we can use the object type for two purposes.

❑   We can use an object reference to bind to an object of any particular sub-type. For example, in the next chapter we'll see how we can use the object type to box a value object on the stack to move it to the heap. Object references are also useful in reflection, when code must manipulate objects whose specific types are unknown. This is similar to the role played by a void pointer in C++ or by a Variant data type in VB.

❑   The object type implements a number of basic, general-purpose methods, which include Equals(), GetHashCode(), GetType(), and ToString(). Responsible user-defined classes may need to provide replacement implementations of some of these methods using an object-oriented technique known as **overriding**, which we will discuss in Chapter 3. When we override ToString(), for example, we equip our class with a method for intelligently providing a string representation of itself. If we don't provide our own implementations for these methods in our classes, the compiler will pick up the implementations in object, which may or may not be correct or sensible in the context of our classes.

We'll examine the object type in more detail in subsequent chapters.

The string Type

Veterans of C and C++ probably have battle scars from wrestling with C-style strings. A C or C++ string was nothing more than an array of characters, so the client programmer had to do a lot of work just to copy one string to another or to concatenate two strings. In fact, for a generation of C++ programmers, implementing a string class that wrapped up the messy details of these operations was a rite of passage requiring many hours of teeth gnashing and head scratching, while chasing memory leaks and faulty overloaded operators. VB programmers had a somewhat easier life, with a string type, while Java people had it even better, with a String class that is in many ways very similar to C# string.

C# provides its own string type. With it, operations like string concatenation and string copying are a snap:

```
string str1 = "Hello ";
string str2 = "World";
string str3 = str1 + str2; // string concatenation
```

Despite this style of assignment, the CTS System.String class is a reference type. Behind the scenes, a string object is allocated on the heap, not the stack, and when we assign one string variable to another string, we get two references to the same string in memory. However, should we then make changes to one of these strings, note that this will create an entirely new string object, leaving the other string unchanged. Consider the code:

```
using System;

class StringExample
{
    public static int Main()
    {
        string s1 = "a string";
        string s2 = s1;
        Console.WriteLine("s1 is " + s1);
        Console.WriteLine("s2 is " + s2);
        s1 = "another string";
        Console.WriteLine("s1 is now " + s1);
        Console.WriteLine("s2 is now " + s2);
        return 0;
    }
}
```

The output from this is:

```
s1 is a string
s2 is a string
s1 is now another string
s2 is now a string
```

In other words, changing the value of s1 had no effect on s2, contrary to what we'd expect with a reference type! What's happening here is that when s1 is initialized with the value a string, a new string object is allocated on the heap. When s2 is initialized, the reference points to this same object, so s2 also has the value a string. However, when we now change the value of s1, instead of replacing the original value, a new object will be allocated on the heap for the new value. Our s2 variable will still point to the original object, so its value is unchanged.

String literals are enclosed in double quotes ("..."); if we attempt to enclose a string in single quotes, the compiler will take the value as a char, and throw an error. C# strings can contain the same Unicode and hexadecimal escape sequences as chars. Since these escape sequences start with a backslash, we can't use this character unescaped in a string. Instead, we need to escape it with two backslashes, \\:

```
string filepath = "C:\\ProCSharp\\First.cs";
```

Even if you are confident you can remember to do this all the time, it can prove annoying typing out all those double backslashes. Fortunately, C# gives us an alternative. We can prefix a string literal with the at character, @, and all the characters in it will be treated at face value – they won't be interpreted as escape sequences:

```
string filepath = @"C:\ProCSharp\First.cs";
```

This even allows us to include line breaks in our string literals:

```
string Jabberwocky = @"'Twas brillig and the slithy toves
Did gyre and gimble in the wabe.";
```

Then the value of Jabberwocky would be this:

```
'Twas brillig and the slithy toves
Did gyre and gimble in the wabe.
```

Flow Control

In this section, we will look at the real nuts and bolts of the language: the statements that allow us to control the **flow** of our program, rather than executing every line of code in the order it appears in the program.

Conditional Statements

Conditional statements allow us to branch our code depending on whether certain conditions are met or on the value of an expression. C# has two constructs for branching code – the if statement, which allows us to test whether a specific condition is met, and the switch statement, which allows us to compare an expression with a number of different values.

The if Statement

For conditional branching, C# inherits C and C++'s `if...else` construct. The syntax should be fairly intuitive for anyone who has done any programming with a procedural language:

```
if (condition)
    statement(s)
else
    statement(s)
```

If more than one statement is to be executed as part of either condition, these statements will need to be joined together into a block using curly braces ({ ... }) (this also applies to other C# constructs where statements can be joined into a block, such as the `for` and `while` loops we meet later):

```
bool isZero;
if (i == 0)
{
    isZero = true;
    Console.WriteLine("i is Zero");
}
else
{
    isZero = false;
    Console.WriteLine("i is Non-zero");
}
```

The syntax here is similar to C++ and Java but once again different from VB. VB developers should note that C# does not have any statement corresponding to VB's `EndIf`. Instead, the rule is that each clause of an `if` contains just one statement. If you need more than one statement, as in the above example, you should enclose the statements in braces, which will cause the whole group of statements to be treated as a single block statement.

If we want to, we can use an `if` statement without a final `else` statement. We can also combine `else if` clauses to test for multiple conditions. The following code example is called `WhatIsI`:

```
using System;

namespace Wrox.ProCSharp.Basics
{
    class MainEntryPoint
    {
        static void Main(string[] args)
        {
            Console.WriteLine("Type in a string");
            string input;
            input = Console.ReadLine();
            if (input == "")
            {
                Console.WriteLine("You typed in an empty string");
            }
            else if (input.Length < 5)
            {
```

```
        Console.WriteLine("The string had less than 5 characters");
    }
    else if (input.Length < 10)
    {
        Console.WriteLine("The string had at least 5 but less than 10
            characters");
    }
    Console.WriteLine("The string was " + input);
    }
  }
}
```

There is no limit to how many `else if`'s we can add to an `if` clause.

You'll notice that in the example above, we declare a string variable called `input`, get the user to enter text at the command line, feed this into `input`, and then test the length of this string variable. The code also shows us how easy string manipulation can be in C#. To find the length of `input`, for example, use `input.Length`.

One point to note about `if` is that we don't need to use the braces if there's only one statement in the conditional branch:

```
if (i == 0)
   Console.WriteLine("i is Zero");        // This will only execute if i == 0
Console.WriteLine("i can be anything");   // Will execute whatever the
                                          // value of i
```

However, for consistency, many programmers prefer to use curly braces whenever they use an `if` statement.

The `if` statements we have presented also illustrate some of the C# operators that compare values. Note in particular that, like C++ and Java, C# uses `==` to compare variables for equality. Do not use `=` for this purpose. A single `=` is used to assign values.

In C#, the expression in the `if` clause must evaluate to a Boolean. C++ programmers should be particularly aware of this; unlike C++, it is not possible to test an integer (returned from a function, say) directly. In C#, we have to explicitly convert the integer that is returned to a Boolean `true` or `false`, for example by comparing the value with zero or with `null`:

```
if (DoSomething() != 0)
{
   // Non-zero value returned
}
else
{
   // Returned zero
}
```

This restriction is there in order to prevent some common types of run-time bugs that occur in C++. In particular, in C++ it was common to mistype `=` when `==` was intended, resulting in unintentional assignments. In C# that will normally result in a compile-time error, since unless you are working with `bool` values, `=` will not return a `bool`.

The switch Statement

The `switch...case` statement is good for selecting one branch of execution from a set of mutually exclusive ones. It will be familiar to C++ and Java programmers, and is similar to the `Select Case` statement in VB.

It takes the form of a `switch` argument followed by a series of `case` clauses. When the expression in the switch argument evaluates to one of the values beside a `case` clause, the code immediately following that `case` clause executes. This is one case where we don't need to use curly braces to join statements into blocks; instead, we mark the end of the code for each case using the `break` statement. We can also include a `default` case in the `switch` statement, which will execute if the expression evaluates to none of the other cases. The following `switch` statement tests the value of the `integerA` variable:

```
switch (integerA)
{
    case 1:
        Console.WriteLine("integerA =1");
        break;
    case 2:
        Console.WriteLine("integerA =2");
        break;
    case 3:
        Console.WriteLine("integerA =3");
        break;
    default:
        Console.WriteLine("integerA is not 1,2, or 3");
        break;
}
```

Note that the case values *must* be constant expressions – variables are not permitted.

Though the `switch...case` statement should be familiar to C and C++ programmers, C#'s `switch...case` is a bit safer. Specifically, it prohibits fall-through conditions in almost all cases. This means that if a `case` clause is fired early on in the block, later clauses cannot be fired unless you use a `goto` statement to specifically mark that you want them fired too. The compiler enforces this restriction by flagging every `case` clause that is not equipped with a `break` statement as an error similar to this:

```
Control cannot fall through from one case label ('case 2:') to another
```

While it is true that fall-through behavior is desirable in a limited number of situations, in the vast majority of cases it is unintended and results in a logical error that's hard to spot. Isn't it better to code for the norm rather than for the exception?

By getting creative with `goto` statements (which C# does support) however, you can duplicate fall-through functionality in your `switch...cases`. However, if you find yourself really wanting to, you probably should re-consider your approach. The following code illustrates both how to use `goto` to simulate fall-through, and how messy the resultant code can get.

```
// assume country and language are of type string
switch(country)
{
   case "America":
      CallAmericanOnlyMethod();
      goto case "Britain";
   case "France":
      language = "French";
      break;
   case "Britain":
      language = "English";
      break;
}
```

There is one exception to the no-fall-through rule however, in that we can fall through from one case to the next if that case is empty. This allows us to treat two or more cases in an identical way (without the need for goto statements):

```
switch(country)
{
   case "au":
   case "uk":
   case "us":
      language = "English";
      break;
   case "at":
   case "de":
      language = "German";
      break;
}
```

One intriguing point about the switch statement in C# is that the order of the cases doesn't matter – we can even put the default case first! As a result, no two cases can be the same. This includes different constants that have the same value, so we can't, for example, do this:

```
// assume country is of type string
const string england = "uk";
const string britain = "uk";
switch(country)
{
   case england:
   case britain:
      language = "English";
      break;
}
```

The above code also shows another way in which the switch statement is different in C# from C++: In C#, you are allowed to use a string as the variable being tested.

Loops

C# provides four different loops (`for`, `while`, `do...while`, and `foreach`) that allow us to execute a block of code repeatedly until a certain condition is met. The `for`, `while`, and `do...while` loops are essentially identical to those encountered in C++. The `for` loop is the first that we shall examine.

The for Loop

C# `for` loops provide a mechanism for iterating through a loop where we test whether a particular condition holds before we perform another iteration. The syntax is:

```
for (initializer; condition; iterator)
    statement(s)
```

where:

❑ The *initializer* is the expression evaluated before the first loop is executed (usually initializing a local variable as a loop 'counter').

❑ The *condition* is the expression that is checked before each new iteration of the loop (this must evaluate to `true` for another iteration to be performed).

❑ The *iterator* is an expression that will be evaluated after each iteration (usually incrementing the loop counter). The iterations end when the *condition* evaluates to `false`.

The `for` loop is a so-called *pre-test loop*, because the loop condition is evaluated before the loop statements are executed, and so the contents of the loop won't be executed at all if the loop condition is `false`.

The `for` loop is excellent for repeating a statement or a block of statements for a pre-determined number of times. The following example is typical of the use of a `for` loop. This code will write out all the integers from 0 to 99:

```
for (int i = 0; i < 100; i = i+1)       // this is equivalent to
                                        // For i = 0 To 99 in VB.
{
    Console.WriteLine(i);
}
```

Here, we declare an `int` called `i` and initialize it to zero. This will be used as the loop counter. We then immediately test whether it is less than 100. Since this condition evaluates to `true`, we execute the code in the loop, displaying the value 0. We then increment the counter by one, and walk through the process again. Looping ends when `i` reaches 100.

This syntax is far more powerful than the VB `For...Next` loop, since the *iterator* can be any statement. In VB, all you can do is add or subtract some number from the loop control variable. In C# you can do anything – for example multiply the loop control variable by 2.

It's not unusual to nest `for` loops so that an inner loop executes once completely for each iteration of an outer loop. This scheme is typically employed to loop through every element in a rectangular multidimensional array. The outermost loop loops through every row, and the inner loop loops through every column in a particular row. The following code is available as the `NumberTable` sample, and displays rows of numbers. It also uses another `Console` method, `Console.Write()`, which does the same as `Console.WriteLine()` but doesn't send a carriage return to the output.

```
using System;

namespace Wrox.ProCSharp.Basics
{
    class MainEntryPoint
    {
        static void Main(string[] args)
        {
            // This loop iterates through rows...
            for (int i = 0; i < 100; i+=10)
            {
                // This loop iterates through columns...
                for (int j = i; j < i + 10; j++)
                {
                    Console.Write("  " + j);
                }
                Console.WriteLine();
            }
        }
    }
}
```

We also see from this sample that strings in C# can be concatenated by using the symbol +:

```
            Console.Write("  " + j);
```

Although `j` is an integer, it will be automatically converted to a string so that the concatenation can take place. C++ developers will note that this is far easier than string handling ever was in C++, though VB developers will be used to this.

C programmers should take note of one particular feature of the example above. The counter variable in the innermost loop is effectively re-declared with each successive iteration of the outer loop. This syntax is legal not only in C#, but in C++ as well.

The above sample results in this output:

```
csc NumberTable.cs
Microsoft (R) Visual C# .NET Compiler version 7.00.9466
for Microsoft (R) .NET Framework version 1.0.3705
Copyright (C) Microsoft Corporation 2001. All rights reserved.


NumberTable
  0  1  2  3  4  5  6  7  8  9
 10  11  12  13  14  15  16  17  18  19
```

```
20  21  22  23  24  25  26  27  28  29
30  31  32  33  34  35  36  37  38  39
40  41  42  43  44  45  46  47  48  49
50  51  52  53  54  55  56  57  58  59
60  61  62  63  64  65  66  67  68  69
70  71  72  73  74  75  76  77  78  79
80  81  82  83  84  85  86  87  88  89
90  91  92  93  94  95  96  97  98  99
```

Although it is technically possible to evaluate something other than a counter variable in a `for` loop's test condition, it is certainly not typical. It is also possible to omit one (or even all) of the expressions in the `for` loop. In such situations however, you should consider using the next type of loop that we will discuss.

The while Loop

The `while` loop is identical to the `while` loop in C++ and Java, and the `While...Wend` loop in VB. Like the `for` loop, `while` is a pre-test loop. The syntax is similar, but `while` loops take only one expression:

```
while(condition)
    statement(s);
```

Unlike the `for` loop, the `while` loop is most often used to repeat a statement or a block of a statements for a number of times that is not known before the loop begins. Usually, a statement inside the `while` loop's body will set a Boolean flag to `false` on a certain iteration, triggering the end of the loop, as in the following example:

```
bool condition = false;
while (!condition)
{
    // This loop spins until the condition is true
    DoSomeWork();
    condition = CheckCondition();   // assume CheckCondition() returns a bool
}
```

All of C#'s looping mechanisms, including the `while` loop, can forego the curly braces that follow them if they intend to repeat just a single statement and not a block of them. Again, many programmers consider it good practice to use braces all of the time.

The do...while Loop

The `do...while` loop is the post-test version of the `while` loop. It does the same thing with the same syntax as `do...while` in C++ and Java, and the same thing as `Loop...While` in VB. This means that the loop's test condition is evaluated after the body of the loop has been executed. Consequently, `do...while` loops are useful for situations in which a block of statements must be executed at least one time, as in this case:

```
bool condition;
do
{
```

```
    // this loop will at least execute once, even if Condition is false
    MustBeCalledAtLeastOnce();
    condition = CheckCondition();
} while (condition);
```

The foreach Loop

The `foreach` loop is the final C# looping mechanism that we will discuss. While the other looping mechanisms were present in the earliest versions of C and C++, the `foreach` statement is a new addition (borrowed from VB), and a very welcome one at that.

The `foreach` loop allows us to iterate through each item in a collection. For the time being we won't worry about exactly what a collection is – we'll explain fully in Chapter 5 on *C# and Base Classes*. For now, we will just say that it is a object that contains other objects. Technically, to count as a collection, it must support an interface called `IEnumerable`. Examples of collections include C# arrays, the collection classes in the `System.Collection` namespaces, and user-defined collection classes. We can get an idea of the syntax of `foreach` from the following code, if we assume that `arrayOfInts` is (unsurprisingly) an array if `ints`:

```
foreach (int temp in arrayOfInts)
{
    Console.WriteLine(temp);
}
```

Here, `foreach` steps through the array one element at a time. With each element, it places the value of the element in the `int` variable called `temp`, and then performs an iteration of the loop.

An important point to note with `foreach` is that we can't change the value of the item in the collection (`temp` above), so code such as the following will not compile:

```
foreach (int temp in arrayOfInts)
{
    temp++;
    Console.WriteLine(temp);
}
```

If you need to iterate through the items in a collection and change their values, you will need to use a `for` loop instead.

We will learn how to implement our own collection classes later in this book, in Chapter 5. Interestingly, such classes can be iterated through with Visual Basic .NET's `ForEach` statement, too.

Jump Statements

C# provides a number of statements that allow us to *jump* immediately to another line in the program. The first of these is, of course, the notorious `goto` statement.

The goto Statement

The goto statement allows us to jump directly to another specified line in the program, indicated by a **label** (this is just an identifier followed by a colon):

```
goto Label1;
    Console.WriteLine("This won't be executed");
Label1:
    Console.WriteLine("Continuing execution from here");
```

There are a couple of restrictions involved with goto. We can't jump into a block of code such as a for loop, we can't jump out of a class, and we can't exit a finally block after try...catch blocks (we will look at exception handling with try...catch...finally in Chapter 4).

The reputation of the goto statement probably precedes it, and in most circumstances, its use is sternly frowned upon. In general, it certainly doesn't conform to good object-oriented programming practice. However, there is one place where it is quite handy: jumping between cases in a switch statement, particularly since C#'s switch is so strict on fall-through. We saw the syntax for this earlier.

The break Statement

We have already met the break statement briefly – when we used it to exit from a case in a switch statement. In fact, break can also be used to exit from for, foreach, while, or do...while loops too. Control will switch to the statement immediately after the end of the loop.

If the statement occurs in a nested loop, control will switch to the end of the innermost loop. If the break occurs outside of a switch statement or a loop, a compile-time error will occur.

The continue Statement

The continue statement is similar to break, and must also be used within a for, foreach, while, or do...while loop. However, it exits only from the *current iteration* of the loop, meaning execution will restart at the beginning of the next iteration of the loop, rather than outside the loop altogether.

The return Statement

The return statement is used to exit a method of a class, returning control to the caller of the method. If the method has a return type, return must return a value of this type; otherwise if the method returns void, then you should use return without an expression. We will look at the syntax for writing and calling methods shortly.

Program Structure

So far, we've been introduced to some of the main 'building blocks' that make up the C# language – including declaring variables, data types, and program flow statements, and we have seen a very short complete program containing only the Main() method. What we haven't really seen is how we can put all these together to form a longer complete program. The key to this lies in working with classes.

Classes

As we've seen, **classes** play a huge role in C# programs, so much that we're going to dedicate Chapter 3 entirely to object-oriented programming in C#. However, since it really is pretty well impossible to write a C# program without using classes, we will need to say a little bit about them here. We will cover basic syntax for writing and calling into classes, but we will save inheritance and other OOP features for future chapters.

Classes are essentially templates from which we can create objects. Each object contains data and has methods to manipulate and access that data. The class defines what data and functionality each particular object (called an **instance**) of that class can contain, but doesn't usually contain any data itself. For example, if we have a class that represents a customer, it might define fields such as `CustomerID`, `FirstName`, `LastName`, and `Address`, which we will use to hold information about a particular customer. It might also define functionality that acts upon the data stored in these fields. We can then **instantiate** an object of this class to represent one specific customer, set the field values for that instance, and use its functionality.

Class Members

The data and functions within a class are known as the class's **members**. Microsoft's official terminology distinguishes between data members and function members. As well as these members, classes can also contain nested types (such as other classes). All members of a class can be declared as `public` (in which case they are directly accessible from outside the class) or as `private` (in which case they are only visible to other code within the class), just as in VB, C#, and Java. C# also has variants on this theme, such as `protected`, which we will explore in future chapters.

Microsoft has published detailed guidelines for the naming of variables, data types, and so on, which are available in the MSDN documentation and discussed in Chapter 6. We'll note for now that in this book, we are tending to name public fields and methods, as well as classes like this: PhoneNumber, CustomerAddress; while private fields and variables local to methods are named like this: phoneNumber, customerAddress. Note the capitalization in both cases. This broadly conforms to the guidelines and to standard practice among the C# community. These types of names are respectively referred to as *Pascal-cased* and *camel-cased* respectively.

Data Members

Data members are those members that contain the data for the class – fields, constants, and events.

Fields are any variables associated with the class. In fact, if we define any variable at the class level, that is in fact a field of the class. If fields are declared as `public`, they will be accessible from outside the class. For example, we can define a `PhoneCustomer` class with `CustomerID`, `FirstName` and `LastName` fields like this:

```
class PhoneCustomer
{
    public int CustomerID;
    public string FirstName;
    public string LastName;
}
```

Once we have instantiated a `PhoneCustomer` object, we can then access these fields using the `Object.FieldName` syntax, for example:

```
PhoneCustomer Customer1 = new PhoneCustomer();
Customer1.FirstName = "Burton";
```

Constants can be associated with classes in the same way as variables. We declare a constant using the `const` keyword. Once again, if it is declared as `public`, it will be accessible from outside the class.

```
class PhoneCustomer
{
    public const int DayOfSendingBill = 1;
    public int CustomerID;
    public string FirstName;
    public string LastName;
}
```

Events are class members that allow an object to notify a caller whenever something noteworthy happens, such as a field or property of the class changing, or some form of user interaction occurring. The client can have code known as an error handler that reacts to the event. We won't look at events in this chapter, but we'll look at them in detail in Chapter 4.

Function Members

Function members are those members that provide some functionality for manipulating the data in the class. They include methods, properties, constructors and destructors, operators, and indexers.

Methods are functions that are associated with a particular class. They can be either **instance methods**, which work on a particular instance of a class, or **static methods**, which provide more generic functionality that doesn't require us to instantiate a class (like the `Console.WriteLine()` method which we have already met). We will look at methods in the next section.

Properties are sets of functions that can be accessed from the client in a similar way to the public fields of the class. C# provides a specific syntax for implementing read and write properties on our classes, so we don't have to jury-rig methods whose names have the words `Get` or `Set` embedded in them. Since there's a dedicated syntax for properties that is distinct from that for normal functions, the illusion of objects as actual things is strengthened for client code. Even better, properties centralize the read/write aspects of a property, making property code easier to maintain for the developer of the class.

Constructors are functions called when an object is instantiated. They must have the same name as the class to which they belong, and cannot have a return type. Constructors are useful for setting the values of fields when an object is instantiated.

Destructors are similar to constructors, but are called when the object is destroyed. They have the name of the class, preceded by a tilde (~). Since the CLR handles garbage collection, it is impossible to predict when a destructor will be called, and destructors are used much less frequently in C# than in C++.

Classes may also contain definitions for **operators**, so that we can define our own operators, or specify how existing operators will work with our class. We'll look at defining operators in Chapter 3.

Indexers allow our objects to be indexed in the same way as an array or collection. We'll look at indexers in Chapter 3.

For reference, we will also list the modifiers that can be applied to a method, though we won't be covering most of these until the next two chapters:

Modifier	Description
new	The method hides an inherited method with the same signature.
public	The method can be accessed from anywhere, including outside the class.
protected	The method can be accessed from within the class to which it belongs, or a type derived from that class.
internal	The method can be accessed only from within the same assembly.
private	The method can only be accessed from inside the class to which it belongs.
static	The method does not operate on a specific instance of the class.
virtual	The method can be overridden by a derived class.
abstract	A virtual method that defines the signature of the method, but doesn't provide an implementation.
override	The method overrides an inherited virtual or abstract method.
sealed	The method overrides an inherited virtual method, but cannot be overridden by any classes that inherit from this class. Must be used in conjunction with override.
extern	The method is implemented externally, in a different language.

Structs

We will briefly mention that, besides classes, it is also possible to declare structs. The syntax is basically identical, except that we use the keyword struct instead of class. For example, if we wished to declare PhoneCustomer as a struct, we would write

```
struct PhoneCustomer
{
   public const int DayOfSendingBill = 1;
   public int CustomerID;
   public string FirstName;
   public string LastName;
}
```

We won't look at structs in detail until Chapter 3. They differ from classes in the way that they are stored in memory and accessed (classes are reference types stored in the heap, structs are value types stored on the stack), and in some of the features (structs don't support inheritance). You will tend to use structs for smaller data types for performance reasons.

C++ developers beware; structs in C# are very different from classes in their implementation. This is very different to the situation in C++, for which classes and structs are virtually the same thing.

Methods

Now that we have seen how to code up the flow of control within a method and how to define classes that can contain methods, we shall have a look at how to define methods in C#.

In VB and C, and even in C++, we could of course define global functions that were not associated with a particular class. This is not the case in C#. As noted earlier, in C# every function must be associated with a class or struct.

Note that official C# terminology does in fact make a distinction between functions and methods. In this terminology, the term 'function member' includes not only methods, but also other non-data members of a class or struct. This includes indexers, operators, constructors, destructors, and also – perhaps somewhat surprisingly – properties. These are contrasted with data members: fields, constants, and events. In this chapter, we will confine ourselves to looking at methods.

Declaring Methods

The syntax for defining a method in C# is just what you'd expect from a C-style language, and is virtually identical to the syntax in C++ and Java. The only difference is that, in C#, each method is separately declared as `public` or `private`. It is not possible to use `public:` blocks to group several method definitions. Also, all C# methods are declared and defined in the class definition. There is no facility in C# to separate the method implementation as in C++.

In C#, the definition of a method consists of any method modifiers (such as the method's accessibility), the type of the return value, followed by the name of the method, followed by a list of input arguments enclosed in parentheses, followed by the body of the method enclosed in curly braces:

```
[modifiers] return_type MethodName([parameters])
{
    // Method body
}
```

Each parameter consists of the name of the type of the parameter, and the name by which it can be referenced in the body of the method. Also, if the method returns a value, a `return` statement must be used with the return value to indicate the exit point. For example:

```
public bool IsSquare(Rectangle rect)
{
    return (rect.Height == rect.Width);
}
```

This code uses one of the .NET base classes, `System.Drawing.Rectangle`, which represents a rectangle.

If the method doesn't return anything, we specify a return type of void, as we can't omit the return type altogether, and if it takes no arguments, we still need to include an empty set of parentheses after the method name (as with the Main() method that we met early in the chapter). In this case, including a return statement is optional – the method returns automatically when the closing curly brace is reached. You should note that a method can contain as many return statements as required:

```csharp
public bool IsPositive(int value)
{
    if (value < 0)
        return false;
    return true;
}
```

Invoking Methods

The syntax for invoking a method is exactly the same in C# as it is in C++ and Java, and the only difference between C# and VB is that round brackets must always be used when invoking the method in C# – this is actually simpler than VB6 's set of rules whereby brackets were sometimes necessary and at other times not allowed.

The following sample, MathTest, illustrates the syntax for definition of and instantiation of classes, and definition of and invocation of methods. Besides the class that contains the Main() method, it defines a class named MathTest, which contains a couple of methods and a field. We briefly covered parts of this class earlier in the chapter:

```csharp
using System;

namespace Wrox.ProCSharp.Basics
{
    class MainEntryPoint
    {
        static void Main()
        {
            // Try calling some static functions
            Console.WriteLine("Pi is " + MathTest.GetPi());
            int x = MathTest.GetSquareOf(5);
            Console.WriteLine("Square of 5 is " + x);

            // Instantiate a MathTest object
            MathTest math = new MathTest();   // this is C#'s way of
                                              // instantiating a reference type

            // Call non-static methods
            math.value = 30;
            Console.WriteLine(
                "Value field of math variable contains " + math.value);
            Console.WriteLine("Square of 30 is " + math.GetSquare());
        }
    }

    // Define a class named MathTest on which we will call a method
    class MathTest
```

```
    {
        public int value;

        public int GetSquare()
        {
            return value*value;
        }

        public static int GetSquareOf(int x)
        {
            return x*x;
        }

        public static double GetPi()
        {
            return 3.14159;
        }
    }
}
```

Running the `MathTest` sample produces these results:

```
csc MathTest.cs
Microsoft (R) Visual C# .NET Compiler version 7.00.9466
for Microsoft (R) .NET Framework version 1.0.3705
Copyright (C) Microsoft Corporation 2001. All rights reserved.


MathTest
Pi is 3.14159
Square of 5 is 25
Value field of math variable contains 30
Square of 30 is 900
```

As you can see from the code, our `MathTest` class contains a field that contains a number, as well as a method to find the square of this number. It also contains two static methods, to return the value of pi, and to find the square of the number passed in as a parameter.

> *There are some features of this class that are not really good examples of C# program design. For example, `GetPi()` would usually be implemented as a `const` field, but good design would mean using concepts that we are not going to introduce until Chapter 3.*

Most of this syntax should be familiar to C++ and Java developers. If your background is in VB, then just think of the `MathTest` class as being like a VB class module that implements fields and methods. There are a couple of points to watch out for though, whatever your language.

For VB people, the idea of `static` methods will be new (and `static` in C# does not mean the same thing as `Static` in VB). As mentioned earlier, a `static` method (or field) is associated with the class definition as a whole, not with any particular instance of that class. This means they are called by specifying the class name, not the variable name. The difference between the `GetSquare()` and the `GetSquareOf()` methods in `MathSample` is that `GetSquare()` returns the square of the value field in the class, while `GetSquareOf()` returns the square of the value supplied as a parameter. Since `GetSquareOf()` does not use any data associated with any particular instance of the class, we can define it as `static`.

C++ programmers should note that C# class definitions should not be followed by semi-colons, and static members must always be called by specifying the class name. C++ allowed you alternatively to specify a variable name (in C++, the expression `math.GetPi()` would be allowed). This is not permitted in C#. Also, notice that the C# compiler is happy for the `MathTest` class to be referenced in the `Main()` function before the actual definition of the `MathTest` class. Unlike in C++, the C# compiler is not worried about the order in which classes are defined, as long as the class is defined somewhere in your sourcecode.

Finally, just as in C++, Java, and VB, you don't need to specify the object name if you are calling a method from within the same class. Specifying the name of the method or field is sufficient.

Passing Parameters to Methods

Arguments can in general be passed into methods by reference, or by value. A variable that is passed by reference to a method is affected by any changes that the called method makes to it, while a variable that is passed by value to a method is not changed by any changes made within the body of the method. This is because methods refer to the original variables when those variables are passed by reference, but only to copies of those variables when they are passed by value. For complex data types, passing by reference is more efficient because of the large amount of data that must be copied when passing by value.

In C#, all parameters are passed by value unless we specifically say otherwise. This is the same behavior as in C++, but the opposite to VB. However, the data type of the parameter also determines the effective behavior of any parameters passed to a method. Since reference types only hold a reference to an object, they will still only pass this reference into the method. Value types, in contrast, hold the actual data, so a copy of the data itself will be passed into the method. An `int`, for instance, is passed by value to a method, and any changes that the method makes to the value of that `int` do not change the value of the original `int` object. Conversely, if an array or any other reference type, such as a class, is passed into a method, and the method changes a value in that array, the new value is reflected in the original array object.

Here is an example, `ParameterTest.cs`, that demonstrates this:

```
using System;

namespace Wrox.ProCSharp.Basics
{
    class ParameterTest
    {
        static void SomeFunction(int[] ints, int i)
        {
            ints[0] = 100;
            i = 100;
        }

        public static int Main()
        {
            int i = 0;
            int[] ints = { 0, 1, 2, 4, 8 };
```

```
          // Display the original values
          Console.WriteLine("i = " + i);
          Console.WriteLine("ints[0] = " + ints[0]);
          Console.WriteLine("Calling SomeFunction...");

          // After this method returns, ints will be changed,
          // but i will not
          SomeFunction(ints, i);
          Console.WriteLine("i = " + i);
          Console.WriteLine("ints[0] = " + ints[0]);
          return 0;
       }
    }
}
```

The output of this is:

```
csc ParameterTest.cs
Microsoft (R) Visual C# .NET Compiler version 7.00.9466
for Microsoft (R) .NET Framework version 1.0.3705
Copyright (C) Microsoft Corporation 2001. All rights reserved.


ParameterTest
i = 0
ints[0] = 0
Calling SomeFunction...
i = 0
ints[0] = 100
```

Notice how the value of i remains unchanged, but the value we changed in ints is also changed in the original array.

One point to remember is that strings are **immutable** (if we alter a string's value, we create an entirely new string), so strings don't display the typical reference-type behavior. Any changes made to a string within a method call won't affect the original string.

The behavior described above is the default. We can, however, force value parameters to be passed by reference. To do so, we use the ref keyword. If a parameter is passed to a method, and if the input argument for that method is prefixed with the ref keyword, then any changes that the method makes to the variable will affect the value of the original object:

```
static void SomeFunction(int[] ints, ref int i)
{
   ints[0] = 100;
   i = 100;
}
```

We will also need to add the ref keyword when we invoke the method:

```
          SomeFunction(ints, ref i);
```

Adding the `ref` keyword in C# serves the same purpose as using the & syntax in C++ to specify passing by reference. However, C# makes the behavior more explicit (thus hopefully preventing bugs) by requiring the use of the `ref` keyword when invoking the method.

Finally, it is also important to understand that C# continues to apply initialization requirements to parameters passed to methods. Any variable must be initialized before it is passed into a method, whether it is passed in by value or reference.

The out Keyword

In C-style languages, it is common for functions to be able to output more than one value from a single routine. This is accomplished using **output parameters**, in other words, by assigning the output values to variables that have been passed to the method by reference. Often, the starting values of the variables that are passed by reference are unimportant. Those values will be overwritten by the function, which may never even look at them.

It would be convenient if we could use the same convention in C#, but if you remember, C# requires that variables be initialized with a starting value before they are referenced. Although we could initialize our input variables with meaningless values before passing them into a function that will fill them with real, meaningful ones, this practice seems at best needless, and at worst, confusing. However, there is a way to short-circuit the C# compiler's insistence on initial values for input arguments.

This is achieved with the `out` keyword. When a method's input argument is prefixed with the `out` keyword, that method can be passed a variable that has not been initialized with a starting value. The variable is passed by reference, so any changes that the method makes to the variable will persist when control returns from the called method. Again, we also need to use the `out` keyword when we call the method, as well as when we define it:

```
static void SomeFunction(out int i)
{
    i = 100;
}

public static int Main()
{
    int i; // note how i is declared but not initialized
    SomeFunction(out i);
    Console.WriteLine(i);
    return 0;
}
```

If the `out` parameter isn't assigned a value within the body of the function, the method won't compile.

The `out` keyword is an example of something new in C# that has no analogy in either VB or C++, and which has been introduced to make C# more secure against bugs.

Arrays

Arrays in C# differ substantially from arrays in both VB and C/C++, both in syntax and in the underlying implementation, although C# array syntax looks superficially similar to C++ syntax. As in C/C++ (and in Java), arrays in C# are indicated with square brackets.

In VB, arrays are actually SAFEARRAY variables. The use of a SAFEARRAY involves some overhead while making the arrays syntactically simpler to work with.

In C and C++, the name of an array is just a pointer to an address in memory, and the index to an array is simply an offset from that address. Although the C/C++ approach to arrays is flexible – you can do some fancy things with pointer arithmetic to move from element to element – it is also error-prone. Since C and C++ do not track the size of the arrays, there is nothing to stop a program from referencing an element outside the bounds of an array, possibly corrupting other data, and generating an error.

To overcome the shortcomings of C and C++, C# supports the array as a definite, distinct type. By treating arrays as objects with methods and properties (including ranges), the CLR is able to catch these kinds of out-of-bounds errors. Moreover, if an index-out-of-bounds error occurs during the course of a C# program, the CLR will throw a special type of error object that error handling routines can specifically respond to.

Array Syntax

C# takes such a different approach to arrays that it enforces a unique syntax for them. When you declare an array in C#, what is actually going on behind the scenes is that an instance of the .NET base class System.Array is being instantiated. C# array operations look to you like normal array code, but in fact the C# compiler translates your code into various method calls on System.Array. This gives the benefit of extra features compared to a plain C++-style array and even compared to a VB SAFEARRAY.

Arrays in C# are declared by fixing a set of square brackets to the end of the variable type of the individual elements (note that all the elements in an array must be of the same data type).

> **A note to VB users: arrays in C# use square brackets, not parentheses.**

For example, while int represents a single integer, int[] represents an array of integers:

```
int[] integers;
```

To initialize the array with specific dimensions, we can use the new keyword, giving the size in the square brackets after the type name:

```
// Create a new array of 32 ints
int[] integers = new int[32];
```

If you hadn't already guessed, `Array` is a reference type (as are all classes). The use of the new keyword strongly hints at this fact. However, each individual array element is an `int` and therefore a value type.

To access an individual element within the array, we use the usual syntax, placing the index of the element in square brackets after the name of the array. All C# arrays use zero-based indexing, so we can reference the first variable with the index zero:

```
integers[0] = 35;
```

Accordingly, we reference the thirty-second element value with an index value of 31:

```
integers[31] = 432;
```

C#'s array syntax is flexible, too. In fact, C# allows us to declare arrays without initializing them, so that the array can be dynamically sized later in the program. With this technique, we are basically creating a `null` reference, and later pointing that reference at a dynamically allocated stretch of memory locations requested with the new keyword:

```
int[] integers;
integers = new int[32];
```

This syntax is certainly a lot easier than using `malloc` and `sizeof`. It is a lot less prone to memory leaks, too. In C or C++, a segment of memory referenced by an array will remain allocated on the heap unless specifically deallocated. In contrast, C# arrays, like other C# objects, are managed by the CLR and marked for automatic deallocation once they are no longer referenced.

One of the nice features of C and C++ arrays was the way that you could declare and initialize an array with a hard-coded list of initial values in curly braces. Thankfully, C# preserves this handy capability:

```
string[] myArray = {"first element", "second element", "third element"};
```

Note that it is perfectly permissible to use a variable to set how many elements the array will contain, like this:

```
int len;
len = GetArraySize();    // assume this function works out how big we want
                         // the array to be
string[] myArray = new string[len];
```

However you cannot change the size of an array once it has been instantiated (other than by copying the contents to a new array). If you want to dynamically add elements to an array, you will have to create an instance of the `ArrayList` object, which is in the `System.Collections` namespace. This is covered in detail in Chapter 5.

Obviously, you cannot assign more values to an array than there are elements.

Working with Arrays

Since arrays are represented by a specific type in C#, they have their own methods, for example to get the length of the array. This means that working with arrays in C# is very easy indeed.

For example, to find out the size of a one-dimensional array called `integers`, we can use the `Length` property:

```
int arrayLength = integers.Length;
```

If the array elements are of one of the predefined types, we can also sort the array into ascending order using the static `Array.Sort()` method:

```
Array.Sort(myArray);
```

Notice that we call this as a static method of the `Array` class, and not as a method of our array instance. We specify the array we want to sort by passing it in as a parameter to the method.

> *Sorting can alternatively be achieved using the `System.Array.Sort()` method and the `IComparer` interface.*

Finally, we can reverse the existing order of the elements in an array using the static `Reverse()` method:

```
Array.Reverse(myArray);
```

The following short example stores a short list of famous artists' names in a string array, sorts the array into reverse alphabetical order, and then loops through the array to display each name in order in the console window:

```
string[] artists = {"Leonardo", "Monet", "Van Gogh", "Klee"};
Array.Sort(artists);
Array.Reverse(artists);

foreach (string name in artists)
{
    Console.WriteLine(name);
}
```

Multidimensional Arrays in C#

C# supports multidimensional arrays in two varieties. The first kind is the **rectangular** array. A two-dimensional rectangular array is one in which every row has the same number of columns. This is also known as a **matrix**. As demonstrated in the following example, rectangular arrays are relatively simple to declare and initialize. Here, we declare a two-dimensional rectangular array of four rows, each of which has exactly two columns:

```
string[,] beatleName = { {"Lennon","John"},
                         {"McCartney","Paul"},
                         {"Harrison","George"},
                         {"Starkey","Richard"} };
```

Note that we use a comma to separate the dimensions in the array declaration, even though we don't actual specify the size of the dimensions. In order to declare a three-dimensional string array, we would use:

```
string[,,] my3DArray;
```

An alternative way of initializing the array would be to use nested `for` loops, like this:

```
double [, ] matrix = new double[10, 10];
for (int i = 0; i < 10; i++)
{
    for (int j=0; j < 10; j++)
        matrix[i, j] = 4;
}
```

If the array has more than one dimension, we can get the length of any specific dimension using the `GetLength()` method:

```
// Get the length of the first dimension
int arrayLength = Integers.GetLength(0);
```

The second kind of multidimensional array that C# supports is the **orthogonal**, or so-called **jagged** array. A jagged two-dimensional array is one in which every row can have a different number of columns. Although obviously more flexible than rectangular arrays, jagged arrays are, as you might guess, more difficult to instantiate and initialize. In creating a jagged array, we're basically creating an array *of* arrays:

```
int[][] a = new int[3][];
a[0] = new int[4];
a[1] = new int[3];
a[2] = new int[1];
```

Here, instead of using commas to indicate the number of dimensions in the array, we use an extra set of square brackets for each dimension. Therefore, to declare a three-dimensional jagged array of `ints`, we would use:

```
int[][][] ints;
```

Iterating through the elements in a jagged array requires more work than iterating through the elements in a rectangular array, too. As you loop through each row, you have to use the array's `GetLength()` method to dynamically ascertain the number of columns that you should loop through. The following example, `AuthorNames`, illustrates this point.

```
using System;

namespace Wrox.ProCSharp.Basics
{
    class MainEntryPoint
    {
        static void Main()
```

```
    {
        // Declare a two-dimension jagged array of authors' names
        string[][] novelists = new string[3][];
        novelists[0] = new string[] {
            "Fyodor", "Mikhailovich", "Dostoyevsky"};
        novelists[1] = new string[] {
            "James", "Augustine", "Aloysius", "Joyce"};
        novelists[2] = new string[] {
            "Miguel", "de Cervantes", "Saavedra"};

        // Loop through each novelist in the array
        int i;
        for (i = 0; i < novelists.GetLength(0); i++)
        {
            // Loop through each name for the novelist
            int j;
            for (j = 0; j < novelists[i].GetLength(0); j++)
            {
                // Display current part of name
                Console.Write(novelists[i][j] + " ");
            }
            // Start a new line for the next novelist
            Console.Write("\n");
        }
    }
  }
}
```

Running this example gives the following result:

```
csc AuthorNames.cs
Microsoft (R) Visual C# .NET Compiler version 7.00.9466
for Microsoft (R) .NET Framework version 1.0.3705
Copyright (C) Microsoft Corporation 2001. All rights reserved.


AuthorNames
Fyodor Mikhailovich Dostoyevsky
James Augustine Aloysius Joyce
Miguel de Cervantes Saavedra
```

Operators

Although most of C#'s operators should be familiar to C and C++ developers, we will discuss the most important ones here for the benefit of new programmers and VB converts, and to shed some light on some of the changes introduced with C#.

C# supports the following operators, although four (`sizeof`, `*`, `->`, and `&`) are only available in unsafe code (code which bypasses C#'s type safety checking), which we will look at in Chapter 4:

Category	Operator
Arithmetic	+ - * / %
Logical	& | ^ ~ && || !
String concatenation	+
Increment and decrement	++ --
Bit shifting	<< >>
Comparison	== != < > <= >=
Assignment	= += -= *= /= %= &= |= ^= <<= >>=
Member access (for objects and structs)	.
Indexing (for arrays and indexers)	[]
Cast	()
Conditional (the Ternary Operator)	? :
Object Creation	new
Type information	`sizeof` (unsafe code only) is `typeof` as
Overflow exception control	checked unchecked
Indirection and Address	* -> & (unsafe code only) []

One of the biggest pitfalls to watch out for when using C# operators is that, like other C-style languages, it uses different operators for assignment =, and comparison ==. For instance, the following statement means 'let x equal three':

```
x = 3;
```

If we now want to compare x to a value, we need to use the double equals sign ==:

```
if (x == 3)
```

Fortunately, C#'s very strict type safety rules prevent the very common C error we mentioned earlier in the chapter, where using an assignment operator instead of the comparison operator caused unpredictable behavior. This means that in C# the following statement will generate an error, and won't compile:

```
if (x = 3)
```

VB programmers who are used to using the ampersand, &, to concatenate strings will have to make an adjustment. In C#, the plus sign + is used instead, while & denotes a bit-wise AND between two different integer values. | allows you to perform a bit-wise OR between two integers. VB programmers also might not recognize the % (modulus) arithmetic operator. This returns the remainder after division, so for example x % 5 will return 2 if x is equal to 7.

You will use few pointers in C#, and so, you will use few indirection operators ->. Specifically, the only place you will use them is within blocks of unsafe code, because that's the only place in C# where pointers are allowed.

Operator Shortcuts

The following table shows the full list of shortcut assignment operators available in C#:

Shortcut Operator	Equivalent To
x++, ++x	x = x + 1
x--, --x	x = x - 1
x += y	x = x + y
x -= y	x = x - y
x *= y	x = x * y
x /= y	x = x / y
x %= y	x = x % y
x >>= y	x = x >> y
x <<= y	x = x << y
x &= y	x = x & y
x |= y	x = x | y
x ^= y	x = x ^ y

You may be wondering why there are two examples each for the ++ increment and the -- decrement operators. Placing the operator *before* the expression is known as a **prefix**, and placing the operator *after* the expression is known as a **postfix**. The expressions x++ and ++x are both equivalent to x = x + 1, but there is a difference in the way they behave. The increment and decrement operators can act both as whole expressions and within expressions.

As lines on their own, they are identical and correspond to the statement x = x + 1. When they are used within expressions, however, there is a difference. The prefix example ++x will increment the value of x *before* the expression is evaluated; in other words, x is incremented and the new value is used in the expression. In contrast, the postfix operator increments the value of x *after* the expression is evaluated – the expression is evaluated using the original value. The following example shows the difference between the two operators:

```
int x = 5;
if (++x == 6)
{
    Console.WriteLine("This will execute");
}
if (x++ == 7)
{
    Console.WriteLine("This won't");
}
```

The first `if` condition evaluates to `true`, because x is incremented from 5 to 6 before the expression is evaluated. The condition in the second `if` statement is `false`, however, because x is only incremented to 7 after the entire expression has been evaluated.

The prefix and postfix operators `--x` and `x--` behave in the same way, but decrement rather than increment the operand.

The other shortcut operators, such as `+=` and `-=`, require two operands, and are used to modify the value of the first operand by performing an arithmetic, logical, or bit-wise operation on it. For example, the next two lines are equivalent:

```
x += 5;
x = x + 5;
```

The Ternary Operator

The ternary operator, `?:`, is a shorthand form of the `if...else` construction. It gets its name from the fact that it involves three operands. It allows us to evaluate a condition, returning one value if that condition is true, or another value if it is false. The syntax is:

```
condition ? true_value : false_value
```

Here, *condition* is the Boolean expression to be evaluated, *true_value* is the value that will be returned if *condition* is true, and *false_value* is the value that will be returned otherwise.

When used sparingly, the ternary operator can add a dash of terseness to your programs. It is especially handy for providing one of a couple of arguments to a function that is being invoked. You can use it to quickly convert a Boolean value to a string value of `true` or `false`. It is also quite handy for displaying a correct singular or plural form, for example:

```
int x = 1;
string s = x.ToString() + " ";
s += (x == 1 ? "man" : "men");
Console.WriteLine(s);
```

This code will display 1 man if x is equal to one, but will display the correct plural form for any other number. Note, however, that if your output needs to be localized to different languages then you will probably have to write more sophisticated routines to take account of the different grammatical rules of different languages.

checked and unchecked

Consider the following code:

```
byte b = 255;
b++;
Console.WriteLine(b.ToString());
```

The `byte` data type can only hold values in the range zero to 255, so incrementing the value of b causes an overflow. How the CLR handles this depends on a number of issues, including compiler options, so whenever there's a risk of an unintentional overflow, we really need some way of making sure that we get the result we want.

To do this, C# provides the `checked` and `unchecked` operators. If we mark a block of code as `checked`, the CLR will enforce overflow checking, and throw an exception if an overflow occurs. Let's change our code to include the `checked` operator:

```
byte b = 255;
checked
{
    b++;
}
Console.WriteLine(b.ToString());
```

When we try to run this, we will get an error message like this:

```
Unhandled Exception: System.OverflowException: Arithmetic operation resulted in an
overflow.
   at Wrox.ProCSharp.Basics.OverflowTest.Main(String[] args)
```

We can enforce overflow checking for all unmarked code in our program by compiling with the /checked option.

If we want to suppress overflow checking, we can mark the code as `unchecked`:

```
byte b = 255;
unchecked
{
    b++;
}
Console.WriteLine(b.ToString());
```

In this case, no exception will be raised, but we will lose data – since the `byte` type can't hold a value of 256, the overflowing bits will be discarded, and our b variable will hold a value of zero.

Note that unchecked is the default behavior. The only time where you are likely to need to explicitly use the unchecked keyword is if you need a few unchecked lines of code inside a larger block that you have explicitly marked as `checked`.

is

The is operator allows us to check whether an object is compatible with a specific type. For example, to check whether a variable is compatible with the object type:

By the phrase is 'compatible', we mean that an object is either of that type or is derived from that type.

```
int i = 10;
if (i is object)
{
    Console.WriteLine("i is an object");
}
```

int, like all other C# data types, inherits from object, therefore the expression i is object will evaluate to true, and the message will be displayed.

The as operator is used to perform certain explicit type conversions.

sizeof

We can determine the size (in bytes) required by a value type on the stack using the sizeof operator:

```
string s = "A string";
unsafe
{
    Console.WriteLine(sizeof(int));
}
```

This will display the number 4, as ints are four bytes long.

Notice that we can only use the sizeof operator in unsafe code. We will look at unsafe code in more detail in Chapter 4.

typeof

The typeof operator returns a Type object representing a specified type. For example, typeof(string) will return a Type object representing the System.String type. This is useful when we want to use reflection to find out information about an object dynamically. We will look at reflection in Chapter 5.

Operator Precedence

The following table shows the order of precedence of the C# operators. The operators at the top of the table are those with the highest precedence (that is, the ones which are evaluated first in an expression containing multiple operators):

Group	Operators
	() . [] x++ x-- new typeof sizeof checked unchecked
Unary	+ - ! ~ ++x --x and casts
Multiplication/Division	* / %
Addition/Subtraction	+ -
Bitwise shift operators	<< >>
Relational	< > <= >= is as
Comparison	== !=
Bitwise AND	&
Bitwise XOR	^
Bitwise OR	|
Boolean AND	&&
Boolean OR	||
Ternary operator	?:
Assignment	= += -= *= /= %= &= |= ^= <<= >>= >>>=

Type Safety

In Chapter 1 we noted that the Intermediate Language enforces strong type safety upon its code. We noted that strong typing enables many of the services provided by .NET, including security and language interoperability. As we would expect from a language that is compiled into IL, C# is also strongly typed.

Among other things, this means that the dedicated Boolean type mentioned earlier does not automatically convert to an integer type. If you want such conversions, you have to ask for them explicitly, with an explicit cast. In this section, we will look at casting between primitive types.

You should note that C# allows you to specify how data types that you yourself create behave in the context of implicit and explicit casts. The syntax for specifying such typecasting behavior is covered at length in Chapter 4 on *Advanced C# Topics*.

Type Conversions

We often need to convert data from one type to another. Consider the code:

```
byte value1 = 10;
byte value2 = 23;
byte total;
total = value1 + value2;
Console.WriteLine(total);
```

When we attempt to compile these lines, we get the error message:

```
Cannot implicitly convert type 'int' to 'byte'
```

The problem here is that when we add two bytes together, the result will be returned as an int, not as another byte. This is because a byte can only contain eight bits of data, so adding two bytes together could very easily result in a value that can't be stored in a single byte. If we do want to store this result in a byte variable, then we're going to have to convert it back to a byte. There are two ways this can happen, either **implicitly** or **explicitly**.

Implicit Conversions

Conversion between types can normally be achieved automatically (implicitly) only if by doing so, we can guarantee that the value is not changed in any way. This is why our previous code failed; by attempting a conversion from an int to a byte, we were potentially losing three bytes of data. The compiler isn't going to let us do that unless we explicitly tell it that that's what we want to do! If we store the result in a long instead of a byte however, we'll have no problems:

```
byte value1 = 10;
byte value2 = 23;
long total;              // this will compile fine
total = value1 + value2;
Console.WriteLine(total);
```

This is because a long holds more bytes of data than an int, so there is no risk of data being lost. In these circumstances, the compiler is happy to make the conversion for us, without us needing to ask for it explicitly.

The table below shows the implicit type conversions that are supported in C#:

From	To
sbyte	short, int, long, float, double, decimal
byte	short, ushort, int, uint, long, ulong, float, double, decimal
short	int, long, float, double, decimal
ushort	int, uint, long, ulong, float, double, decimal
int	long, float, double, decimal
uint	long, ulong, float, double, decimal
long, ulong	float, double, decimal
float	double
char	ushort, int, uint, long, ulong, float, double, decimal

As you would expect, we can only perform implicit conversions from a smaller integer type to a larger one, not from larger to smaller. We can also convert between integers and floating-point values. The rules are slightly different here. Though we can convert between types of the same size, such as int/uint to float and long/ulong to double, we can also convert from long/ulong back to float. We might lose four bytes of data doing this, but this only means that the value of the float we receive will be less precise than if we had used a double; this is regarded by the compiler as an acceptable possible error. The magnitude of the value would not be affected at all.

We can also assign an unsigned variable to a signed variable so long as the limits of value of the unsigned type fit between the limits of the signed variable.

Explicit Conversions

There are still many conversions that cannot be implicitly made between types and the compiler will give an error if any are attempted. These are some of the transformations that cannot be made implicitly:

- ❑   int to short – May lose data
- ❑   int to uint – May lose data
- ❑   uint to int – May lose data
- ❑   float to int – Will lose everything after the decimal point
- ❑   Any numeric type to char – Will lose data
- ❑   decimal to any numeric type – Since the decimal type is internally structured differently from both integers and floating-point numbers

However, we can explicitly carry out such transformations using **casts**. When we cast one type to another, we deliberately force the compiler to make the transformation. A cast looks like this:

```
long val = 30000;
int i = (int)val;    // A valid cast. The maximum int is 2147483647
```

We indicate the type we're casting to by placing the cast type in parentheses before the value to be modified. For programmers familiar with C, this is the typical syntax for casts. For those familiar with the C++ special cast keywords such as static_cast, these do not exist in C# and you have to use the older C-type syntax.

This can be a dangerous operation to undertake, so you need to know what you are doing. Even a simple cast from a long to an int can land you into trouble if the value of the original long is greater than the maximum value of an int:

```
long val = 3000000000;
int i = (int)val;         // An invalid cast. The maximum int is 2147483647
```

In this case, you will not get an error, but you also will not get the result you expect. If you run the code above and output the value stored in i, this is what you get:

```
-1294967296
```

In fact, you should never assume that the cast will give the results you expect. As we have seen earlier, C# provides a `checked` operator that we can use to test whether an operation causes an overflow. We can use this operator to check that a cast is safe and to cause the runtime to throw an overflow exception if it isn't:

```
long val = 3000000000;
int i = checked ((int)val);
```

Bearing in mind that all explicit casts are potentially unsafe, you should take care to include code in your application to deal with possible failures of the casts. We will introduce structured exception handling using `try` and `catch` in Chapter 4.

Using casts, we can convert most data types from one type to another, for example:

```
double price = 25.30;
int approximatePrice = (int)(price + 0.5);
```

This will give the price rounded to the nearest dollar. However, in this transformation, data is lost – namely everything after the decimal point. Therefore, such a transformation should never be used if you want to go on to do more calculations using this modified price value. However, it is useful if you want to output the approximate value of a completed or partially completed calculation – if you do not want to bother the user with lots of figures after the decimal point.

This example shows what happens if you convert an unsigned integer into a `char`:

```
ushort c = 43;
char symbol = (char)c;
Console.WriteLine(symbol);
```

The output is the character that has an ASCII number of 43, the + sign. You can try out any kind of transformation you want between the numeric types (including `char`), however ludicrous it appears, and it will work, such as converting a `decimal` into a `char`, or vice versa. However, if the value that results from the cast operation cannot be fitted into the new data type, the cast seems to work but the result is not as you would expect. Take this example:

```
int i = -1;
char symbol = (char)i;
```

This cast should not work, as the `char` type cannot take negative values. However, you do not get an error and instead the `symbol` variable is assigned the value of a question mark (?).

Converting between value types is not just restricted to isolated variables, as we have shown. We can convert an array element of type `double` to a struct member variable of type `int`:

```
struct ItemDetails
{
    public string Description;
    public int ApproxPrice;
}
```

```
//...

double[] Prices = { 25.30, 26.20, 27.40, 30.00 };

ItemDetails id;
id.Description = "Whatever";
id.ApproxPrice = (int)(Prices[0] + 0.5);
```

Using explicit casts and a bit of care and attention, you can just about transform any instance of a simple value type to any other. However there are limitations on what we can do with explicit type conversions – as far as value types are concerned, we can only convert to and from the numeric and char types and enum types. We can't directly cast Booleans to any other type or vice versa.

If we do need to convert between numeric and string, for example, there are methods provided in the .NET class library. The Object class implements a ToString() method, which has been overridden in all the .NET predefined types and which returns a string representation of the object:

```
int i = 10;
string s = i.ToString();
```

Similarly, if we need to parse a string to retrieve a numeric or Boolean value, we can use the Parse() method supported by all the predefined value types:

```
string s = "100";
int i = int.Parse(s);
Console.WriteLine(i + 50);    // Add 50 to prove it is really an int
```

Note that Parse() will register an error by throwing an exception if it is unable to convert the string (for example, if you try to convert the string Hello to an integer). We cover exceptions in Chapter 4.

We will see in Chapter 4 how we can define casts for our own classes and structs.

Boxing and Unboxing

Earlier in the chapter, we noted that all types, both the simple predefined types such as int and char, and the complex types such as classes and structs, derive from the object type. This means that we can treat even literal values as though they were objects:

```
string s = 10.ToString();
```

However, we also saw that C# data types are divided into value types, which are allocated on the stack, and reference types, which are allocated on the heap. How does this square with the ability to call methods on an int, if the int is nothing more than a four-byte value on the stack?

The way C# achieves this is through a bit of magic calling **boxing**. Boxing and unboxing allow us to convert value types to reference types and vice versa. This has been included in the section on casting as this is essentially what we are doing – we are casting our value to the object type. Boxing is the term used to describe the transformation of a value type to a reference type. Basically, the runtime creates a temporary reference-type 'box' for the object on the heap.

This conversion can occur implicitly, as in the example above, but we can also perform it manually:

```
int i = 20;
object o = i;
```

Unboxing is the term used to describe the reverse process, where the value of a reference type is cast to a value type. We use the term 'cast' here, as this has to be done explicitly. The syntax is similar to explicit type conversions already described:

```
int i = 20;
object o = i;      // Box the int
int j = (int)o;    // Unbox it back into an int
```

We can only unbox a variable that has previously been boxed. If we executed the last line when o is not a boxed int, we will get an exception thrown at runtime.

One word of warning. When unboxing, we have to be careful that the receiving value variable has enough room to store all the bytes in the value being unboxed. C#'s ints, for example, are only 32 bits long, so unboxing a long value (64 bits) into an int as shown below will result in an InvalidCastException:

```
long a = 333333423;
object b = (object)a;
int c = (int)b;
```

Enumerations

An **enumeration** is a user-defined integer type. When we declare an enumeration, we specify a set of acceptable values that instances of that enumeration can contain. Not only that, but we can give the values user-friendly names. If, somewhere in our code, we attempt to assign a value that is not in the acceptable set to an instance of that enumeration, the compiler will flag an error. This concept may be new to VB programmers. C++ does support enumerations (or enums), but C# enumerations are far more powerful than their C++ counterparts.

Creating an enumeration can end up saving you lots of time and headaches in the long run. There are at least three benefits to using enumerations instead of plain integers:

❑ As mentioned, enumerations make your code easier to maintain by helping to ensure that your variables are assigned only legitimate, anticipated values.

❑ Enumerations make your code clearer by allowing you to refer to integer values by descriptive names rather than by obscure 'magic' numbers.

❑ Enumerations make your code easier to type, too. When you go to assign a value to an instance of an enumerated type, the Visual Studio .NET IDE will, through IntelliSense, pop up a list box of acceptable values in order to save you some keystrokes and to remind you of what the possible options are.

We can define an enumeration as follows:

```
public enum TimeOfDay
{
   Morning = 0,
   Afternoon = 1,
   Evening = 2
}
```

In this case, we use an integer value to represent each period of the day in the enumeration. We can now access these values as members of the enumeration. For example, `TimeOfDay.Morning` will return the value 0. We will typically use this enumeration to pass an appropriate value into a method, and iterate through the possible values in a `switch` statement:

```
class EnumExample
{
   public static int Main()
   {
       WriteGreeting(TimeOfDay.Morning);
       return 0;
   }

   static void WriteGreeting(TimeOfDay timeOfDay)
   {
       switch(timeOfDay)
       {
       case TimeOfDay.Morning:
           Console.WriteLine("Good morning!");
           break;
       case TimeOfDay.Afternoon:
           Console.WriteLine("Good afternoon!");
           break;
       case TimeOfDay.Evening:
           Console.WriteLine("Good evening!");
           break;
       default:
           Console.WriteLine("Hello!");
           break;
       }
   }
}
```

The real power of enums in C# is that behind the scenes they are instantiated as structs derived from the base class, `System.Enum`. This means it is possible to call methods against them to perform some useful tasks. Note that because of the way the .NET Framework is implemented there is no performance loss associated with treating the enums syntactically as structs. In practice, once your code is compiled, enums will exist as primitive types, just like `int` and `float`.

You can retrieve the string representation of an enum. For example, using our earlier TimeOfDay enum:

```
TimeOfDay time = TimeOfDay.Afternoon;
Console.WriteLine(time.ToString());
```

This will write out the string Afternoon.

Alternatively you can obtain an enum value from a string.

```
TimeOfDay time2 = (TimeOfDay) Enum.Parse(typeof(TimeOfDay), "afternoon", true);
Console.WriteLine((int)time2);
```

This code snippet illustrates both obtaining an enum value from a string and converting to an integer. To convert from a string, we need to use the static Enum.Parse() method, which as shown here takes three parameters. The first is the type of enum we wish to consider. The syntax is the keyword typeof followed by the name of the enum class in brackets. We will explore the typeof operator briefly later this chapter and in more detail in Chapters 5. The second parameter is the string to be converted, and the third parameter is a bool indicating whether or not we should ignore case when doing the conversion. Finally, note that Enum.Parse() actually returns an object reference – we need to explicitly convert this to the required enum struct (this is an example of an unboxing operation). For the above code, this returns the value 1 as an object, corresponding to the enum value of TimeOfDay.Afternoon. On converting explicitly to an int, this produces the value 1 again.

There are other methods on System.Enum to do things like return the number of values in an enum definition or to list the names of the values. Full details are in the MSDN documentation.

Namespaces

As we have seen earlier, namespaces provide a way of organizing related classes and other types. Unlike a file or a component, a namespace is a logical, rather than a physical grouping. When we define a class in a C# file, we can include it within a namespace definition. Later, when we define another class that performs related work in another file, we can include it within the same namespace, creating a logical grouping that gives an indication to other developers using the classes how they are related and used:

```
namespace CustomerPhoneBookApp
{
    using System;

    public struct Subscriber
    {
        // Code for struct here...
    }
}
```

Placing a type in a namespace effectively gives that type a long name, consisting of the type's namespace as a series of names separated with periods (.), terminating with the name of the class. In the example above, the full name of the `Subscriber` struct is `CustomerPhoneBookApp.Subscriber`. This allows distinct classes with the same short name to be used within the same program without ambiguity.

We can also nest namespaces within other namespaces, creating a hierarchical structure for our types:

```
namespace Wrox
{
    namespace ProCSharp
    {
        namespace Basics
        {
            class NamespaceExample
            {
                // Code for the class here...
            }
        }
    }
}
```

Each namespace name is composed of the names of the namespaces it resides within, separated with periods, starting with the outermost namespace and ending with its own short name. So the full name for the `ProCSharp` namespace is `Wrox.ProCSharp`, and the full name of our `NamespaceExample` class is `Wrox.ProCSharp.Basics.NamespaceExample`.

We can use this syntax to organize the namespaces in our namespace definitions too, so the code above could also be written:

```
namespace Wrox.ProCSharp.Basics
{
    class NamespaceExample
    {
        // Code for the class here...
    }
}
```

Note that we are not permitted to declare a multi-part namespace nested within another namespace.

Namespaces are not related to assemblies. It is perfectly acceptable to have different namespaces in the same assembly, or define types in the same namespace in different assemblies.

The using Statement

Obviously, namespaces can grow rather long and tiresome to type, and the ability to indicate a particular class with such specificity may not always be necessary. Fortunately, as we noted at the beginning of the chapter, C# allows us to abbreviate a class's full name. To do this, we list the class's namespace at the top of the file, prefixed with the `using` keyword. Throughout the rest of the file, we can refer to the types in the namespace simply by their type names.

If two namespaces referenced by using statements contain a type of the same name, then we will have to use the full (or at least, a longer) form of the name to ensure that the compiler knows which type is to be accessed. For example, say classes called NamespaceExample exist both in the Wrox.ProCSharp.Basics and Wrox.ProCSharp.OOP namespaces. If we then create a class called Test in the Wrox.ProCSharp namespace, and instantiate one of the NamespaceExample classes in this class, we need to specify which of these two classes we're talking about:

```
using Wrox.ProCSharp;

class Test
{
   public static int Main()
   {
      Basics.NamespaceExample NSEx = new Basics.NamespaceExample();
      return 0;
   }
}
```

You will have noticed that we have been adding the using System; statement to the start of most of our examples. You will find that the vast majority of all C# code does the same, since the CTS types mentioned earlier are all contained within this namespace, as is much of .NET's core functionality, such as console I/O.

Since using statements occur at the top of C# files, in the same place that C and C++ list #include statements, namespaces are often confused with header files. Don't make this mistake. The using statement does no physical linking between files.

Your organization will probably want to spend some time developing a namespace schema so that its developers can quickly locate functionality that they need and so that the names of the organization's homegrown classes won't conflict with those in off-the-shelf class libraries. You can refer to Microsoft's .NET SDK documentation for guidelines on establishing your own namespace scheme.

Namespace Aliases

Another use of the using keyword is to assign aliases to classes and namespaces. If we have a very long namespace name that we want to refer to several times in our code, but don't want to include in a simple using statement (for example, to avoid type name conflicts), we can assign an alias to the namespace. The syntax for this is:

```
using alias = NamespaceName;
```

The following example (a modified version of the previous example) assigns the alias Introduction to the Wrox.ProCSharp.Basics namespace, and uses this to instantiate a NamespaceExample object, which is defined in this namespace. This object has one method, GetNamespace(), which uses the GetType() method exposed by every class to access a Type object representing the class's type. We use this object to return a name of the class's namespace:

```
using System;
using Introduction = Wrox.ProCSharp.Basics;
```

```
class Test
{
    public static int Main()
    {
        Introduction.NamespaceExample NSEx =
            new Introduction.NamespaceExample();
        Console.WriteLine(NSEx.GetNamespace());
        return 0;
    }
}

namespace Wrox.ProCSharp.Basics
{
    class NamespaceExample
    {
        public string GetNamespace()
        {
            return this.GetType().Namespace;
        }
    }
}
```

The Main() Method

We saw at the start of this chapter that C# programs start execution at a method named `Main()`. As we saw earlier, this must be a static method of a class (or struct), and must have a return type of either `int` or `void`.

Although it is common to specify the `public` modifier explicitly, since by definition the method must be called from outside the program, it doesn't actually matter what accessibility level we assign to the method – it will run even if we mark the method as `private`.

Multiple Main() Methods

When a C# console or Windows application is compiled, by default the compiler looks for exactly one `Main()` method in any class matching the signature listed above, and makes that class method the entry point for the program. If there is more than one `Main()` method, the compiler will return an error message. For example, consider the following code called `MainExample.cs`:

```
using System;

namespace Wrox.ProCSharp.Basics
{
    class Client
    {
        public static int Main()
        {
            MathExample.Main();
            return 0;
        }
```

```
    }

class MathExample
{
   static int Add(int x, int y)
   {
      return x + y;
   }

   public static int Main()
   {
      int i = Add(5,10);
      Console.WriteLine(i);
      return 0;
   }
}
}
```

This contains two classes, both of which have a `Main()` method. If we try to compile this in the usual way we will get the following errors:

```
csc MainExample.cs
Microsoft (R) Visual C# .NET Compiler version 7.00.9466
for Microsoft (R) .NET Framework version 1.0.3705
Copyright (C) Microsoft Corporation 2001. All rights reserved.

MainExample.cs(7,25): error CS0017: Program 'MainExample.exe' has more than one
entry point defined: 'Wrox.ProCSharp.Basics.Client.Main()'
MainExample.cs(21,25): error CS0017: Program 'MainExample.exe' has more than one
entry point defined: 'Wrox.ProCSharp.Basics.MathExample.Main()'
```

However, we can explicitly tell the compiler which of these methods to use as the entry point for the program using the `/main` switch, together with the full name (including namespace) of the class to which the `Main()` method belongs:

```
csc MainExample.cs /main:Wrox.ProCSharp.Basics.MathExample
```

Passing Arguments to Main()

In our examples so far, we have only shown the `Main()` method without any parameters. However, when the program is invoked, we can get the CLR to pass any command-line arguments to the program by including a parameter. This parameter is a string array, traditionally called `args` (although C# will accept any name). We can read this array to evaluate any options passed through the command line when the program is started.

The following sample, `ArgsExample.cs`, loops through the string array passed in to the `Main()` method, and writes the value of each option to the console window:

```csharp
using System;

namespace Wrox.ProCSharp.Basics
{
    class ArgsExample
    {
        public static int Main(string[] args)
        {
            for (int i = 0; i < args.Length; i++)
            {
                Console.WriteLine(args[i]);
            }
            return 0;
        }
    }
}
```

We can compile this as usual using command line. When we run the compiled executable, we can pass in arguments after the name of the program, for example:

```
ArgsExample /a /b /c
/a
/b
/c
```

More on Compiling C# Files

So far, we have seen how to compile console applications using `csc.exe`, but what about other types of application? What if we want to reference a class library? We will look at all the options for `csc.exe` in Appendix B on *C# Compilation Options*, but for now we will look at the most important options.

To answer the first question, we can specify what type of file we want to create using the `/target` switch, often abbreviated to `/t`. This can be one of the following:

Option	Output
`/t:exe`	A console application (the default)
`/t:library`	A class library with a manifest
`/t:module`	A component without a manifest
`/t:winexe`	A Windows application (without a console window)

If we want a non-executable file (such as a DLL) to be loadable by the .NET runtime, we must compile it as a library. If we compile a C# file as a module, no assembly will be created. Although modules cannot be loaded by the runtime, they can be compiled into another manifest using the `/addmodule` switch. As we will see later in the book (in Chapter 17), this is particularly useful for including metadata held in `AssemblyInfo.cs` files in an assembly.

Another option we need to mention is /out. This allows us to specify the name of the output file produced by the compiler. If the /out option isn't specified, the compiler will base the name of the output file on the name of the input C# file, adding an extension according to the target type (for example, .exe for a Windows or console application, or .dll for a class library). Note that the /out and /t, or /target, options must precede the name of the file we want to compile.

If we want to reference types in assemblies that aren't referenced by default, we can use the /reference or /r switch, together with the path and filename of the assembly. The following example demonstrates how we can compile a class library, and then reference that library in another assembly. It consists of two files:

❑   The class library

❑   A console application, which will call a class in the library.

The first file is called MathLibrary.cs and contains the code for our DLL. To keep things simple, it contains just one (public) class, MathLib, with a single method that adds two ints:

```
namespace Wrox.ProCSharp.Basics
{
    public class MathLib
    {
        public int Add(int x, int y)
        {
            return x + y;
        }
    }
}
```

We can compile this C# file into a .NET DLL using the following command:

csc /t:library MathLibrary.cs

The console application, MathClient.cs, will simply instantiate this object, and call its Add() method, displaying the result in the console window:

```
using System;

namespace Wrox.ProCSharp.Basics
{
    class Client
    {
        public static void Main()
        {
            MathLib mathObj = new MathLib();
            Console.WriteLine(mathObj.Add(7,8));
        }
    }
}
```

We can compile this using the /r switch to point at or reference our newly compiled DLL:

```
csc MathClient.cs /r:MathLibrary.dll
```

We can then run it as normal just by entering MathClient at the command prompt. This will display the number 15 – the result of our addition.

Console I/O

By this point, you should have a basic familiarity with C#'s data types, as well as some knowledge of how the thread-of-control moves through a program that manipulates those data types. During this chapter we have also used several of the Console class's static methods used for reading and writing data. Since these methods are so useful when writing basic C# programs, we will quickly go over them in a little more detail.

To read a character of text from the console window, we use the Console.Read() method. This will read an input stream from the console window and return the next character in the stream as an int. There are also two corresponding methods for writing to the console:

❑ Console.Write() – Writes the specified value to the console window

❑ Console.WriteLine() – Which does the same, but adds a new line character at the end of the output.

There are various forms (overloads) of these methods for all of the predefined types (including object), so in most cases we don't have to convert values to strings before we display them.

For example, the following code lets the user input a line of text, and displays the first character:

```
int x = Console.Read();
Console.WriteLine((char)x);
```

This is similar, but returns the entire line of text as a string:

```
string s = Console.ReadLine();
Console.WriteLine(s);
```

Console.WriteLine() also allows us to display formatted output in a way comparable to C's printf() function. To use WriteLine() in this way, we pass in a number of parameters. The first is a string containing markers in curly braces where the subsequent parameters will be inserted into the text. Each marker contains a zero-based index for the number of the parameter in the following list. For example, {0} represents the first parameter in the list. Consider the following code:

```
int i = 10;
int j = 20;
Console.WriteLine("{0} plus {1} equals {2}", i, j, i + j);
```

This will display:

```
10 plus 20 equals 30
```

We can also specify a width for the value, and justify the text within that width, using positive values for right justification, and negative values for left justification. To do this, we use the format {n, w}, where n is the parameter index, and w is the width value:

```
int i = 940;
int j = 73;
Console.WriteLine(" {0,4}\n+{1,4}\n ----\n {2,4}", i, j, i + j);
```

The result of this is:

```
   940
+   73
 ----
  1013
```

Finally, we can also add a format string, together with an optional precision value. It is not possible to give a complete list of possible format strings, since, as we will see in Chapter 5, it is possible to define your own format strings. However, the main ones in use for the predefined types are:

String	Description
C	Local currency format.
D	Decimal format. Converts an integer to base 10, and pads with leading zeros if a precision specifier is given.
E	Scientific (exponential) format. The precision specifier sets the number of decimal places (6 by default). The case of the format string (e or E) determines the case of the exponential symbol.
F	Fixed-point format; the precision specifier controls the number of decimal places. Zero is acceptable.
G	General format. Uses E or F formatting, depending on which is the most compact.
N	Number format. Formats the number with commas as thousands separators, for example 32,767.44.
P	Percent format.
X	Hexadecimal format. The precision specifier can be used to pad with leading zeros.

Note that the format strings are normally case-insensitive, except for e/E.

If you wish to use a format string, you should place it immediately after the marker that gives the parameter number and field width, and separated from it by a colon. For example, to format a `decimal` value as currency for the computer's locale, with precision to two decimal places, we would use `C2`:

```
decimal i = 940.23m;
decimal j = 73.7m;
Console.WriteLine(" {0,9:C2}\n+{1,9:C2}\n ---------\n {2,9:C2}", i, j, i + j);
```

The output of this in the United States is:

```
    $940.23
+    $73.70
  ---------
 $1,013.93
```

As a final trick, we can also use placeholder characters instead of these format strings to map out formatting. For example:

```
double d = 0.234;
Console.WriteLine("{0:#.00}", d);
```

This displays as `.23`, because the # symbol (#) is ignored if there is no character in that place, and zeros will either be replaced by the character in that position if there is one, or else printed as a zero.

Using Comments

The last topic we will look at in this chapter looks very simple on the surface – adding comments to our code. As we noted at the start of the previous chapter, C# uses the traditional C-type single-line (`//` ...) and multi-line (`/* ... */`) comments:

```
// This is a single-line comment
/* This comment
   spans multiple lines */
```

Everything in a single-line comment, from the `//` to the end of the line, will be ignored by the compiler, and everything from an opening `/*` to the next `*/` in a multi-line comment combination will be ignored. Obviously we can't include the combination `*/` in any multi-line comments, as this will be treated as the end of the comment.

It is actually possible (although definitely not recommended) to put multi-line comments *within* a line of code:

```
Console.WriteLine(/* Please don't do this! */ "This will compile");
```

Although having said that, inline comments like this can be useful when debugging if, say, you temporarily want to try running the code with a different value somewhere:

```
DoSomething(Width, /*Height*/ 100);
```

Comment characters included in string literals are of course treated like normal characters:

```
string s = "/* This is just a normal string */";
```

XML Documentation

In addition to the C-type comments, illustrated above, C# has a very neat feature that we can't leave this chapter without discussing: the ability to produce documentation in XML format automatically from special comments. These comments are single-line comments, but begin with three slashes (///), instead of the usual two. Within these comments, we can place XML tags containing documentation of the types and type members in our code.

The following tags are recognized by the compiler:

Tag	Description
`<c>`	Marks up text within a line as code, for example: `<c>int i = 10;</c>`
`<code>`	Marks multiple lines as code.
`<example>`	Marks up a code example.
`<exception>`	Documents an exception class. (Syntax verified by the compiler.)
`<include>`	Includes comments from another documentation file. (Syntax verified by the compiler.)
`<list>`	Inserts a list into the documentation.
`<param>`	Marks up a method parameter. (Syntax verified by the compiler.)
`<paramref>`	Indicates that a word is a method parameter. (Syntax verified by the compiler.)
`<permission>`	Documents access to a member. (Syntax verified by the compiler.)
`<remarks>`	Adds a description for a member.
`<returns>`	Documents the return value for a method.
`<see>`	Provides a cross-reference to another parameter. (Syntax verified by the compiler.)
`<seealso>`	Provides a 'see also' section in a description. (Syntax verified by the compiler.)
`<summary>`	Provides a short summary of a type or member.
`<value>`	Describes a property.

To see how this works, let's add some XML comments to the MathLibrary.cs file from an earlier section, and call it Math.cs. We will add a `<summary>` element for the class and for its Add() method, and also a `<returns>` element and two `<param>` elements for the Add() method:

```
// Math.cs
namespace Wrox.ProCSharp.Basics
{

    ///<summary>
    ///    Wrox.ProCSharp.Basics.Math class.
    ///    Provides a method to add two integers.
    ///</summary>
    public class Math
    {
        ///<summary>
        ///    The Add method allows us to add two integers
        ///</summary>
        ///<returns>Result of the addition (int)</returns>
        ///<param name="x">First number to add</param>
        ///<param name="y">Second number to add</param>
        public int Add(int x, int y)
        {
            return x + y;
        }
    }
}
```

The C# compiler can extract the XML elements from the special comments and use them to generate an XML file. To get the compiler to generate the XML documentation for an assembly, we specify the /doc option when we compile, together with the name of the file we want to be created:

csc /t:library /doc:Math.xml Math.cs

> **The compiler will throw an error if the XML comments do not result in a well-formed XML document.**

This will generate an XML file named Math.xml, which looks like this:

```
<?xml version="1.0"?>
<doc>
    <assembly>
        <name>Math</name>
    </assembly>
    <members>
        <member name="T:Wrox.ProCSharp.Basics.Math">
            <summary>
                Wrox.ProCSharp.Basics.Math class.
                Provides a method to add two integers.
            </summary>
        </member>
        <member name=
            "M:Wrox.ProCSharp.Basics.Math.Add(System.Int32,System.Int32)">
            <summary>
                The Add method allows us to add two integers
```

```
        </summary>
        <returns>Result of the addition (int)</returns>
        <param name="x">First number to add</param>
        <param name="y">Second number to add</param>
      </member>
    </members>
  </doc>
```

Notice how the compiler has actually done some work for us; it has created an <assembly> element, and also added a <member> element for each type or member of a type in the file. Each <member> element has a name attribute with the full name of the member as its value, prefixed by a letter that indicates whether this is a type (T:), field (F:), or member (M:).

XML Documentation in Visual Studio .NET

We don't want to concentrate too much on Visual Studio .NET this early in the book, as most of the functionality it provides is quite straightforward. However, it is worth mentioning in this context that if you're using Visual Studio .NET, it can save you quite a lot of typing when compiling XML documentation.

Open up the Math.cs file in Visual Studio .NET, and add a blank line before the definition of the Add() method. Now, type three forward slashes (///) at the start of the line. Visual Studio very kindly adds a whole lot of XML tags for us:

```
public class Math
{
    /// <summary>
    ///
    /// </summary>
    /// <param name="x"></param>
    /// <param name="y"></param>
    /// <returns></returns>
    public int Add(int x, int y)
    {
        return x + y;
    }
}
```

All we have to do is type in the actual descriptions. Notice how Visual Studio .NET has even managed to put in the correct values for the parameter names in the <param> tags.

In order to generate the XML documentation when the project is compiled, specify an XML Documentation File on the Build menu under Configuration Properties on the project's property pages.

Visual Studio .NET can also generate HTML-formatted documentation from these XML comments. To do this, select Tools | Build Comment Web Pages... from the menu. We are now asked whether we want to generate XML documentation for the entire solution, or just for selected projects. We are also asked where we want to save the generated HTML pages. When we select OK, Visual Studio .NET will generate a whole set of HTML pages documenting our project, which we can browse through Visual Studio .NET or any web browser:

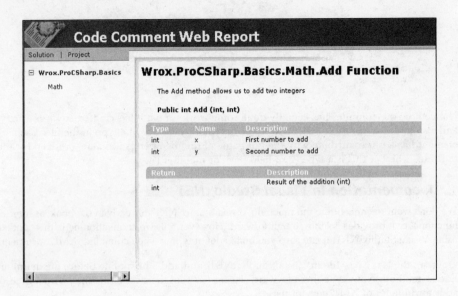

Identifiers and Keywords

In this final section of this basics of C# chapter, we examine the rules governing what names we can use for variables, classes, methods, and so on.

Identifiers are the names we give to variables, to user-defined types such as classes and structs, and to members of these types. Identifiers are case-sensitive, so `identifier` and `Identifier` would be different variables. There are a couple of rules determining what identifiers we can use in C#:

❑   They must begin with a letter or underscore, although they can contain numeric characters

❑   We can't use C# keywords as identifiers

C# has the following reserved keywords:

abstract	do	implicit	params	switch
as	double	in	private	this
base	else	int	protected	throw
bool	enum	interface	public	true
break	event	internal	readonly	try
byte	explicit	is	ref	typeof
case	extern	lock	return	uint
catch	false	long	sbyte	ulong

char	finally	namespace	sealed	unchecked
checked	fixed	new	short	unsafe
class	float	null	sizeof	ushort
const	for	object	stackalloc	using
continue	foreach	operator	static	virtual
decimal	goto	out	string	volatile
default	if	override	struct	void
delegate				while

If we do need to use one of these words as an identifier (for example, if we are accessing a class written in a different language), we can prefix the identifier with the @ symbol to indicate to the compiler that what follows is to be treated as an identifier, not as a C# keyword (so abstract is not a valid identifier, but @abstract is).

Finally, identifiers can also contain Unicode characters, specified using the syntax \uXXXX, where XXXX is the four-digit hex code for the Unicode character. The following are some examples of valid identifiers:

❑ Name

❑ überfluß

❑ _Identifier

❑ \u005fIdentifier

These last two are identical and interchangeable (005f is the Unicode code for the underscore character), so obviously couldn't both be declared in the same scope. Note that although syntactically you are allowed to use the underscore character in identifiers, usually this isn't recommended in most situations because it doesn't follow the guidelines for naming variables that Microsoft has written in order to ensure that developers use the same conventions, making it easier to read each other's code. We discuss these naming conventions in Chapter 6.

Summary

In this chapter, we have examined some of the basic syntax of C#, covering the areas needed to write simple C# programs. We have covered a lot of ground, but much of it will be instantly recognizable to developers who are familiar with any C-style language (or even JavaScript). Some of the topics we have covered include:

❑ Variable scope and access levels

❑ Declaring variables of various data types

❑ Controlling the flow of execution within a C# program

❑ Calling and declaring classes and methods

❑ Working with arrays

❑ C#'s operators

❑ Converting data between different types

❑ How the stack and heap are implemented by the CLR

❑ Commenting code, and XML auto-documentation

We have seen that the syntax is similar to C++/Java syntax, although there are many minor differences. We have also seen that in many areas this syntax is combined with facilities to write code very quickly, for example high quality string handling facilities. C# also has a strongly defined type system, based on a distinction between value and reference types. Now we have a grounding in the C# language, we will move on to an in-depth look at C#'s object-oriented programming features in the next chapter.

3

Object-Oriented C#

In this chapter, we will introduce the C# object-oriented features. In particular, we will cover:

- ❑ The C# syntax for **inheritance**, virtual functions and related features.

- ❑ **Method Overloading** – C# allows you to define different versions of a method in a class, and the compiler will automatically select the most appropriate one based on the parameters supplied.

- ❑ **Construction and Destruction** – it is possible to specify how objects should be initialized as well as any action that needs to be automatically taken when they are destroyed.

- ❑ **Structs** – on occasions you need something that has the many of the features of a class without all of the overhead involved in creating a class instance. Structs are value types that provide this facility.

- ❑ **Operator Overloading** – we will examine how to define operators for your classes.

- ❑ **Indexers** – indexers allow a class to be treated syntactically as if it is an array, and can simplify the use of classes that contain sets of objects.

- ❑ **Interfaces** – C# supports interface inheritance as well as implementation inheritance. We will examine this feature.

We will assume that you are already familiar with the principles of object-oriented programming, such as inheritance and polymorphism, so that we can focus largely on how C# implements OOP. If you are not familiar these with object-oriented principles then you should read Appendix A, which introduces object-oriented concepts, before attempting this chapter.

On the other hand, we will introduce and explain those concepts that are not necessarily supported by most object-oriented languages. For example, although object constructors are a widely used concept, **static constructors** are something new to C#, so we will explain in more detail how they work.

Classes and Inheritance

We have seen the use of classes in Chapter 2, but in order to get our bearings we'll briefly recap. Classes are defined in C# using the following syntax:

```csharp
class MyClass
{
    private int someField;

    public string SomeMethod(bool parameter)
    {
    }
}
```

Classes contain **members** – a member is the term used to refer to any data or function that is defined in the class. We use the term **function** to refer to any member that contains code – this includes methods, properties, constructors, and operator overloads.

All C# classes are reference types. This means that when you declare a variable of a class type, all you are getting is a variable (memory location) that can in principle store a reference to an instance of that class. You also need to instantiate an object myObject using the new operator:

```csharp
MyClass myObject;
myObject = new MyClass();
```

You can, in fact, declare and initialize an instance at the same time:

```csharp
MyClass myObject = new MyClass();
```

Consider the following line:

```csharp
MyClass myObjectRef = myObject;
```

Here myObjectRef will also refer to the same MyClass() instance as myObject. Methods against this instance may be called through either of these variables.

Single Implementation Inheritance

C# supports single inheritance of classes. In other words, a class may derive directly from one other class. The syntax for this is as follows.

```csharp
class MyDerivedClass : MyBaseClass
{
    // functions and data members here
}
```

This syntax differs from C++ only to the extent that there is no access modifier describing the inheritance. C# does not support the C++ concepts of public and private inheritance – doing so would complicate the language. In practice private inheritance is used extremely rarely in C++ anyway.

To be more exact, we should say that a class **must** derive from one other class. C# supports the concept of a universal base class, System.Object, from which all other classes are ultimately derived. If you do not specify a base class in your class definition, the C# compiler will assume that System.Object is the base class.

Method Overloading

C# supports method overloading – several versions of the method that have different signatures (name, number of parameters, and parameter types), but does not support default parameters in the way that, say, C++ or VB do. In order to overload methods, you simply declare the methods with the same name but different numbers or types of parameters:

```
class ResultDisplayer
{
    void DisplayResult(string result)
    {
        // implementation
    }

    void DisplayResult(int result)
    {
        // implementation
    }
}
```

Because C# does not directly support optional parameters, you will need to use method overloading to achieve the same effect:

```
class MyClass
{
    int DoSomething(int x)    // want 2nd parameter with default value 10
    {
        DoSomething(x, 10);
    }

    int DoSomething(int x, int y)
    {
        // implementation
    }
}
```

As in any language, method overloading carries with it the potential for subtle runtime bugs if the wrong overload is called. In the next chapter we will discuss how to code defensively against these problems. For now, we'll point out that C# does place some minimum differences on the parameters of overloaded methods.

- ❏ It is not sufficient for two methods to differ only in their return type
- ❏ It is not sufficient for two methods to differ only by virtue of a parameter having been declared as ref or out

Method Overriding and Hiding

By declaring a base class function as virtual, we allow the function to be overridden in any derived classes:

```
class MyBaseClass
{
    public virtual string VirtualMethod()
    {
        return "This method is virtual and defined in MyBaseClass";
    }
}
```

This means that we can create a different implementation of VirtualMethod() (with the same method signature) in a class derived from MyBaseClass, and when we call this method on an instance of the derived class, the derived class's method is called, not the base class's method. In C#, functions are not virtual by default, but (aside from constructors) may be explicitly declared as virtual. This follows the C++ methodology, in which for performance reasons, functions are not virtual unless explicitly indicated, and stands in contrast to Java, in which all functions are virtual. C# differs from C++ syntax, however, because it requires you to explicitly declare when a derived class's function overrides another function, using the override keyword:

```
class MyDerivedClass : MyBaseClass
{
    public override string VirtualMethod()
    {
        return "This method is an override defined in MyDerivedClass";
    }
}
```

Neither member fields nor static functions can be declared as virtual. It's easy to see why: a virtual member must have a signature and be associated with a particular object – and the only members that satisfy both requirements are instance functions.

This approach to method overriding removes potential run-time bugs where a method signature in a derived class unintentionally differs slightly from the base version, resulting in the method failing to override the base version. In C# this will be picked up as a compile-time warning.

If a method with the same signature is declared in both base and derived classes, but the methods are not declared as `virtual` and `override` respectively, then the derived class version is said to **hide** the base class version. The result is that which version of a method gets called depends on the type of the variable used to reference the instance, not the type of the instance itself.

In most cases you would want to override methods rather than hide them, because hiding them gives a strong risk of the "wrong" method being called for a given class instance. However, C# syntax is designed to ensure that the developer is warned at compile time about this potential problem. This also has versioning benefits for developers of class libraries.

Imagine that someone has written a class. Let's call it `HisBaseClass`:

```
class HisBaseClass
{
    // various members
}
```

At some point in the future you write a derived class of your own, which adds some functionality to `HisBaseClass`. In particular, you add a method called `MyGroovyMethod()`, which is not present in the base class:

```
class MyDerivedClass: HisBaseClass
{
    public int MyGroovyMethod()
    {
        // some groovy implementation
    }
}
```

Now one year later, the author of the base class decides to extend its functionality. By coincidence, he adds a method that is also called `MyGroovyMethod()`, which has the same name and signature as yours, but probably doesn't do the same thing. When you next compile your code using the new version of the base class, you have a potential clash about which method should be called. It's all perfectly legal C#, but since your `MyGroovyMethod()` is not intended to be related in any way to the base class `MyGroovyMethod()` the result of running this code probably won't be what you wanted. This sort of thing doesn't happen very often, but it does happen. Fortunately C# has been designed in such a way that it copes very well with the situation.

In the first place, you get warned about the problem. In C#, we should use the `new` keyword to declare that we intend to hide a method, like this:

```
class MyDerivedClass : HisBaseClass
{
    public new int MyGroovyMethod()
    {
        // some groovy implementation
    }
}
```

However, your version of `MyGroovyMethod()` wasn't declared as `new`, so the compiler will pick up on the fact that it's hiding a base class method, but not declared explicitly to do so and generate a warning (this applies whether or not you declared `MyGroovyMethod()` as `virtual`). If you wish, you can react to the warning by renaming your version of the method. If you can do so, that's probably the best course of action, since it'll save a lot of confusion. However, the great thing is that if you do decide that renaming your method isn't practical (for example, you've published your software as a library for other companies so you can't change any names of methods) and so you leave it, all your existing client code will still run correctly, picking up your version of `MyGroovyMethod()`. That's because any existing code that accesses this method must be doing so through a reference to `MyDerivedClass` (or a further derived class).

Any existing code cannot access this method through a reference to `HisBaseClass`, because that would have generated a compilation error when compiled against the earlier version of `HisBaseClass`. The problem can only happen in any future client code that is written. C# arranges things so that you get a warning that a potential problem might occur in future code – and you will need to pay attention to this warning, and take care not to attempt to call your version of `MyGroovyMethod()` through any reference to `HisBaseClass` in any future code you add, but all your existing code will still work fine. It may be a subtle point, but it's quite an impressive example of how C# is able to cope with different versions of classes.

Calling Base Versions of Functions

C# has a special syntax for calling base versions of a method from a derived class. To do this, you write `base.<MethodName>()`. For example, suppose a method in a derived class should return 90% of the value returned by the base class method:

```
class CustomerAccount
{
    public virtual decimal CalculatePrice()
    {
        // implementation
    }
}
```

```
class GoldAccount : CustomerAccount
{
    public override decimal CalculatePrice()
    {
        return base.CalculatePrice() * 0.9M;
    }
}
```

This syntax is similar to that in Java, although Java uses the keyword `super` rather than `base`. C++ has no similar keyword but instead requires explicit specification of the class name. Any equivalent to `base` in C++ would have been ambiguous since C++ allows multiple inheritance.

Note that you can use the `base.<MethodName>()` syntax to call any method in the base class – you don't have to be calling it from an override of the same method.

Abstract Classes and Functions

C# allows both classes and functions to be declared as abstract. An abstract class cannot be instantiated, while an abstract function does not have an implementation, and **must** be overridden in any non-abstract derived class. Obviously, an abstract function is automatically virtual (though you don't need to supply the virtual keyword as well – in fact it's regarded as a syntax error if you do). If any class contains any abstract functions, then that class is also abstract and must be declared as such.

```
abstract class Building
{
    public abstract decimal CalculateHeatingCost();    // abstract method
}
```

C++ developers will notice some syntactical differences in C# here. The =0 syntax has gone. In C#, this syntax would be misleading, since =<value> is allowed on member fields in class declarations to supply initial values:

```
abstract class Building
{
    private bool damaged = false;    // field
    public abstract decimal CalculateHeatingCost();    // abstract method
}
```

C++ developers should also note the slightly different terminology: In C++, abstract functions are often described as pure virtual; in the C# world, the only term to use is abstract.

Sealed Classes and Methods

C# allows classes and methods to be declared as sealed. For the case of a class, this means that you can't inherit from that class. For the case of a method, it means that you can't override that method further.

```
sealed class FinalClass
{
    // etc
}

class DerivedClass : FinalClass        // wrong. Will give compilation error
{
    // etc
}
```

Java developers will recognize sealed as the C# equivalent of Java's final.
The most likely situation when you'll mark a class or method as sealed will be if it is very much internal to the operation of the library, class or other classes that you are writing, so you are fairly sure that any attempt to override some of its functionality will cause problems. You might also mark a class or method as sealed for commercial reasons, in order to prevent a third party from extending your classes in a manner that is contrary to the licensing agreements. In general, however, you should be careful about marking a class or member as sealed, since by doing so you are severely restricting how it can be used. Even if you don't think it would be useful to inherit from a class or override a particular member of it, it's still possible that at some point in the future someone will encounter a situation you hadn't anticipated in which it is useful to do so. The .NET base class library makes quite a bit of use of sealed classes where Microsoft does not intend anyone to derive from the class. For example, string is a sealed class.

115

Declaring a method as sealed serves a similar purpose, although it's likely to be only rarely that you will want to declare a method as sealed.

```
class MyClass
{
   public sealed override void FinalMethod()
   {
      // etc.
   }
}

class DerivedClass : MyClass
{
   public override void FinalMethod()          // wrong. Will give compilation error
   {
   }
}
```

Note that it does not make sense to use the sealed keyword on a method unless that method is itself an override of another method in some base class. If you are defining a new method and you don't want anyone else to override it, then do not declare it as virtual in the first place. If, however, you have overridden a base class method then the sealed keyword provides a way of ensuring that the override you supply to a method is a "final" override in the sense that no-one else can override it again.

Access Modifiers

In common with other object-oriented languages, C# has a number of accessibility modifiers, which determine which other code is allowed to be aware of the existence of a given member of a class. We have already encountered public, private, and protected. C# actually has five such modifiers. The complete list is as follows.

Accessibility	Description
public	The variable or method can be accessed from anywhere as a field of the type to which it belongs
internal	The variable or method can only be accessed from the same assembly
protected	The variable or method can only be accessed from within the type to which it belongs, or from types derived from that type
protected internal	The variable or method can be accessed from the current assembly, or from types derived from the current type (that is, from anywhere that could access it if it were declared as protected or internal)
private	The variable or method can only be accessed from within the type to which it belongs

Of these, internal and protected internal are the ones that are new to C# and the .NET Framework. internal acts in much the same way as public, but access is confined to other code in the same assembly – in other words, code that is being compiled at the same time in the same program. You can use internal to ensure all the other classes that you are writing have access to a particular member, but at the same time hiding it from other code written by other organizations. protected internal combines protected and internal, but in an OR sense, not an AND sense. A protected internal member can be seen by any code in the same assembly. But it can also be seen by any derived classes, even those in other assemblies.

Properties

Properties are unusual in that they represent an idea that C# has taken from VB, not from C++/Java. The idea of a property is that it is a method or pair of methods that are dressed to look like a field as far as any client code is concerned. A good example of this is the `Height` property of a Windows Form. Suppose you have the following code.

```
// mainForm is of class System.Windows.Form
mainForm.Height = 400;
```

On executing this code, the height of the window will be set to 400 and you will see the window resize on the screen. Syntactically, the above code looks like we're setting a field, but in fact we are calling a property accessor that contains code to resize the form.

> *In this section we assume you are familiar with the concept and use of properties. If you are unsure about them, Appendix A of this book contains a section that explains the concept in detail.*

To define a property in C#, we use the following syntax.

```
public string SomeProperty
{
   get
   {
      return "This is the property value";
   }
   set
   {
      // do whatever needs to be done to set the property
   }
}
```

The usual restrictions apply. The `get` accessor takes no parameters and must return the same type as the property has been declared as. You should not specify any explicit parameters for the `set` accessor either, but the compiler assumes it takes one parameter, which is of the same type again, and which is referred to as `value`. As an example, the following code contains a property called `ForeName`, which sets a field called `foreName`, which has a length limit.

```
private string foreName;

public string ForeName
{
   get
   {
      return foreName;
   }
   set
   {
      if (value.Length > 20)
         // code here to take error recovery action
         // (eg. throw an exception)
      else
         foreName = value;
   }
}
```

Note the pattern of naming here. We take advantage of C#'s case sensitivity by using the same name, Pascal-cased for the public property and camel-cased for the equivalent private field if there is one. This is standard practice.

VB 6 programmers should note that the syntax for defining properties is very different in C#. Whereas in VB 6, `Get` and `Set` accessors are defined as separate functions, in C# they are placed together inside a single property declaration. In VB you also explicitly declare the parameter to the set accessor and can therefore choose its name, whereas in C# this parameter is implicitly assumed and always named `value`. Recall also that C# does not distinguish between VB `Set` and VB `Let`: in C#, the write accessor is always termed `set`, no matter what the property type.

Read-Only and Write-Only Properties

It is possible to create a **read-only property** by simply omitting the set accessor from the property definition. Thus, to make `ForeName` read-only in the above example:

```
private string foreName;

public string ForeName
{
   get
   {
      return foreName;
   }
}
```

It is similarly possible to create a **write-only property** by omitting the `get` accessor. However this is regarded as poor programming practice because it could be confusing to authors of client code. In general, it is recommended that if you are tempted to do this, you should use a method instead.

Access Modifiers

C# does not permit setting different access modifiers to the `get` and `set` accessor. This may affect you if you have a property that you need public access for reading, but where you want to restrict write access to derived classes. If you need this feature then you'll need to use some workaround, such as declaring a public read-only property and a protected `Set()` function.

```
public string ForeName
{
   get
   {
      return foreName;
   }
}

protected void SetForeName(string value)
{
   if (value.Length > 20)
      // code here to take error recovery action
      // (eg. throw an exception)
   else
      foreName = value;
}
```

Virtual and Abstract Properties

It is also permitted to declare a property as virtual or abstract. For a virtual or overridden property, the syntax is the same as for a non-virtual property except for the addition of `virtual` or `override` in the definition, as for methods. For an abstract property, the syntax looks like this:

```
public abstract string ForeName
{
   get;
   set;
}
```

Inlining

Some developers may worry that, in the above sections, we have presented a number of situations in which standard C# coding practices have led to very small functions – for example accessing a field via a property instead of directly, and having one overload of a method call another overload. In this kind of situation, C++ developers in particular will be accustomed to using the C++ `inline` keyword to request that small methods be **inlined** (replaced by inline code during compilation) in order to remove the excess method call (with all the associated overhead of adding and removing parameters and return address to/from the stack) – but C# does not have an inline or equivalent keyword. There is nevertheless no need to worry about performance loss from these kinds of programming methodologies in C#. Recall that C# code is compiled to IL then JIT-normally compiled at runtime to native executable code. Well the JIT compiler is designed to generate highly optimized code. Although it is not in general possible to predict what methods will be inlined in particular circumstances, experience has shown that the JIT compiler is ruthless when it comes to inlining any function calls that look suitable. A method or property whose implementation simply calls another method or returns a field will almost certainly be inlined.

The Object Class

We indicated earlier that all .NET classes are ultimately derived from `System.Object`, and that, in C#, if you don't specify that a class is derived from another class, the compiler will automatically assume that it derives from `Object`. The practical significance of this is that, besides the methods and properties and so on that you define, you also have access to a number of public and protected member methods that have been defined for the `Object` class. These methods are available in all other classes that you define.

The methods defined in `Object` are:

Method	Access Modifiers	Purpose
`string ToString()`	`public virtual`	Returns a string representation of the object
`int GetHashTable()`	`public virtual`	Used if implementing dictionaries (hash tables)
`bool Equals(object obj)`	`public virtual`	Compares instances of the object for equality
`bool Equals(object objA, object objB)`	`public static`	Compares instances of the object for equality
`bool ReferenceEquals(object objA, object objB)`	`public static`	Compares whether two references refer to the same object
`Type GetType()`	`public`	Returns details of the type of the object.
`object MemberwiseClone()`	`protected`	Makes a shallow copy of the object
`void Finalize()`	`protected virtual`	This is the .NET version of a destructor

Recall that C# uses the keyword `object` as a syntactical convenient shorthand for
`System.Object`. Writing `object` instead of `Object` might not seem that much more
convenient, but at least it means Visual Studio .NET will recognize it as a keyword and so display
it in a different color.

At this stage, you should consider this table as mostly for reference. We haven't yet covered enough of the C# language to be able to properly understand how to use all these methods. We're not going to examine most of them or how to use them in detail yet – for the most part, we'll do that in Chapter 5 when we look at the .NET base classes more thoroughly. We'll make a couple of observations however.

You'll gather from the three methods that are available to compare objects that .NET supports a fine degree of control in precisely how objects are compared. We'll go into this in detail in Chapter 5. If you are comparing two reference variables, then `ReferenceEquals()` will simply check whether the references point to the same object. The virtual and static `Equals()` methods, as well as the comparison operator, `==`, will usually do the same thing, but, as we will explain in Chapter 5, the behavior of these may be overridden in some classes.

`GetType()` returns an instance of the class `System.Type` – this is another of the many base classes that Microsoft has written for us, and which we'll examine in Chapter 5. `Object.GetType()` provides the usual means of access into the .NET reflection technology, allowing you to examine the definitions of types in assemblies.

We have already encountered `ToString()` in previous chapters. It forms the most convenient way to get a quick string representation of an object. We'll examine that method in detail now.

The ToString() method

ToString() is an incredibly convenient way of getting a string representation of an object. For example:

```
int i = -50;
string str = i.ToString();   // returns "-50"
```

Here's another example:

```
enum Colors {Red, Orange, Yellow};

// later on in code...

Colors favoriteColor = Colors.Orange;
string str = favoriteColor.ToString();           // returns "Orange"
```

Object.ToString() is actually declared as virtual, and in all these examples, we are taking advantage of the fact that its implementation in the C# predefined data types has been overridden for us in order to return correct string representations of those types. You might not think that our Colors enum counts as a predefined data type. It actually gets implemented as a struct derived from System.Enum, and System.Enum has a rather clever override of ToString() that deals with all the enums you define.

If you don't override ToString() in classes that you define, then your classes will simply inherit the System.Object implementation – which displays the name of the class. If you want ToString() to return a string that contains information about the value of objects of your class, then you will need to override it. We illustrate this with a sample, StringRepresentations, which defines two very simple classes that represent US$ money amounts. Money simply acts as a wrapper for the decimal class, while BetterMoney derives from Money and adds a ToString() override. The complete code for the sample is as follows. Note that it also illustrates use of properties to wrap fields, as well as inheritance:

```
using System;

namespace Wrox.ProCSharp.OOCSharp
{
    class MainEntryPoint
    {
        static void Main(string[] args)
        {
            Money cash1 = new Money();
            cash1.Amount = 40M;
            Console.WriteLine("cash1.ToString() returns: " + cash1.ToString());
            cash1 = new BetterMoney();
            cash1.Amount = 40M;
            Console.WriteLine("cash1.ToString() returns: " + cash1.ToString());
            Console.ReadLine();
        }
    }
```

```
class Money
{
    private decimal amount;

    public decimal Amount
    {
        get
        {
            return amount;
        }
        set
        {
            amount = value;
        }
    }
}

class BetterMoney : Money
{
    public override string ToString()
    {
        return "$" + Amount.ToString();
    }
}
```

You'll realize that this sample is there just to illustrate syntactical features of C#. C# already has a predefined type to represent currency amounts, decimal, so in real life, you wouldn't write such a class to do this unless you wanted to add various other methods to it. And you'd probably use the String.Format() method (details in the MSDN docs, and we cover this method in Chapter 5 too) to format a currency string.

In the Main() method we instantiate first a Money object, then a BetterMoney() object. In both cases we call ToString(). For the Money object, we'll pick up the Object version of this method that displays class information. For the BetterMoney object, we'll pick up our own override. Running this code gives the following results:

```
StringRepresentations
cash1.ToString() returns: Wrox.ProCSharp.OOCSharp.Money
cash1.ToString() returns: $40
```

Interfaces

C# supports **interfaces**, which act as contracts. By deriving from an interface, a class is declaring that it implements certain functions. Because not all object-oriented languages support interfaces, we will examine C#'s implementation of interfaces in some detail in this section.

Developers familiar with COM should be aware that, although conceptually C# interfaces are similar to COM interfaces, they are not the same thing. The underlying architecture is different – for example, C# interfaces do not derive from IUnknown. A C# interface provides a contract stated in terms of .NET functions. Unlike a COM interface, a C# interface does not represent any kind of binary standard.

We will illustrate interfaces by presenting the complete definition of one of the interfaces that has been predefined by Microsoft, `System.IDisposable`. `IDisposable` contains one method, `Dispose()`, which is intended to be implemented by classes to clean up code.

```
public interface IDisposable
{
    void Dispose();
}
```

The above code shows that declaring an interface works syntactically in pretty much the same way as declaring an abstract class, except that it is not permitted to supply implementations of any of the members of an interface. And the only things an interface can contain are declarations of methods, properties, indexers, and events.

You can't ever actually instantiate an interface; all it contains is the signatures for its members. An interface does not have constructors (how can you construct something that you can't instantiate?), or fields (because that would imply some internal implementation). An interface definition is also not allowed to contain operator overloads, though that's not because there is any problem in principle with declaring them – there isn't; it is because this would cause some incompatibility problems with other .NET languages, such as VB.NET, which do not support operator overloading.

It is also not permitted to declare modifiers on the members in an interface definition. Interface members are always public, and cannot be declared as `virtual` or `static`. That's up to implementing classes to do if required, and it is therefore fine for implementing classes to declare access modifiers, as we do in the above code.

If a class wishes to declare publicly that it implements the `Dispose()` method, then it must **implement** `IDisposable` – which in C# terms means that the class derives from `IDisposable`. `IDisposable` is a relatively simple interface, since it defines only one method. Most interfaces will contain more members.

```
class SomeClass : IDisposable
{
    // this class MUST contain an implementation of the
    // IDisposable.Dispose() method, otherwise
    // you get a compilation error

    public void Dispose()
    {
        // implementation of Dispose() method
    }
    // rest of class
}
```

Another good example of an interface is provided by the `foreach` loop in C#. In principle, the `foreach` loop works internally by querying the object to find out whether it implements the `System.Collections.IEnumerable` interface. If it does, then the runtime uses the methods on this interface to iterate through the members of the collection. If it doesn't, then `foreach` will raise an exception.

Defining and Implementing Interfaces

We're going to illustrate how to define and use interfaces by developing a short sample that follows the interface inheritance paradigm. The example is based on bank accounts. We assume we are writing code that will ultimately allow computerized transfers between bank accounts. There are many companies that may implement bank accounts, but they have all mutually agreed that any classes that represent bank accounts will implement an interface, IBankAccount, which exposes methods to pay in or withdraw money, and a property to return the balance. It is this interface that will allow outside code to recognize the various bank account classes implemented by different bank accounts. Although our aim is to allow the bank accounts to talk to each other to allow transfers of funds between accounts, we won't introduce that feature yet – that will come later, when we look at interface inheritance.

To keep things simple, we will keep all the code for our sample in the same source file, although in reality the different bank account classes would be compiling to different assemblies, and presumably hosted on different machines. We explore in Chapter 8 how .NET assemblies hosted on different machines can communicate. However, here, to maintain some attempt at realism, we will define different namespaces for the different companies.

To start with, we need bank account to define the IBank interface:

```
namespace Wrox.ProCSharp.OOCSharp.BankProtocols
{
    public interface IBankAccount
    {
        void PayIn(decimal amount);
        bool Withdraw(decimal amount);

        decimal Balance
        {
            get;
        }
    }
}
```

Notice the name of the interface, IBankAccount. It's a convention that an interface name traditionally starts with the letter I, so that we know that it's an interface.

In most cases, .NET usage guidelines discourage the so-called "Hungarian" notation in which names are preceded by a letter that indicates the type of object being defined. Interfaces are one of the few cases in which Hungarian notation is recommended. We'll discuss the usage guidelines at the end of Chapter 6.

The idea is that we can now write classes that represent bank accounts. These classes don't have to be related to each other in any way, they can be completely different classes. They will, however, all declare to the world that they represent bank accounts by the fact that they implement the IBankAccount interface.

Let's start off with the first class, a saver account run by the Royal Bank of Venus:

```
namespace Wrox.ProCSharp.OOCSharp.VenusBank
{
    public class SaverAccount : IBankAccount
    {
        private decimal balance;

        public void PayIn(decimal amount)
        {
            balance += amount;
        }

        public bool Withdraw(decimal amount)
        {
            if (balance >= amount)
            {
                balance -= amount;
                return true;
            }
            Console.WriteLine("Withdrawal attempt failed.");
            return false;
        }

        public decimal Balance
        {
            get
            {
                return balance;
            }
        }
        public override string ToString()
        {
            return String.Format("Venus Bank Saver: Balance = {0,6:C}", balance);
        }
    }
}
```

It should be pretty obvious what the implementation of this class does. We maintain a private field, balance, and adjust this amount when money is paid in or withdrawn. Note that we display an error message if an attempt to withdraw money fails because there is insufficient money in the account. Notice also that, because we want to keep the code as simple as possible, we are not implementing extra properties, such as the account holder's name! In real life that would be pretty essential information, but it's unnecessary complication for our sample.

The only really interesting line in this code is the class declaration:

```
public class SaverAccount : IBankAccount
```

We've declared that `SaverAccount` derives from one interface, `IBankAccount`, and we have not explicitly indicated any other base classes (which of course means that `SaverAccount` will derive directly from `System.Object`). Although we have chosen not to explicitly derive `SaverAccount` from any other class, we should note that derivation from interfaces acts completely independently from derivation from classes. A class will derive from one other class and can additionally inherit as many interfaces as required, like this:

```
public class MyDerivedClass : MyBaseClass, IInterface1, IInterface2
```

Being derived from `IBankAccount` means that `SaverAccount` gets all the members of `IBankAccount`. But since an interface doesn't actually implement any of its methods, `SaverAccount` *must* provide its own implementations of all of them. If any implementations are missing, you can rest assured that the compiler will complain. Recall also that the interface just indicates the presence of its members. It's up to the class to decide if it wants any of them to be virtual or abstract (though abstract is only allowed if the class itself is abstract and will be derived from). Here, we've decided that none of the interface methods should be public, though there wouldn't be any problems declaring any of them as virtual if we wished.

To illustrate how different classes can implement the same interface, we will assume the Planetary Bank of Jupiter also implements a class to represent one of its bank accounts – a Gold Account.

```
namespace Wrox.ProCSharp.OOCSharp.JupiterBank
{
    public class GoldAccount : IBankAccount
    {
        // etc
    }
}
```

We won't present details of the `GoldAccount` class because in our sample it's basically identical to the implementation of `SaverAccount`. We stress that `GoldAccount` has no connection with `VenusAccount`, other than that they happen to implement the same interface. Normally they would be implemented differently because they are independent classes. But for our sample, it keeps things simpler if we keep the same implementation.

Now we have our classes, we can test them out. We first need a couple of `using` statements:

```
using System;
using Wrox.ProCSharp.OOCSharp.BankProtocols;
using Wrox.ProCSharp.OOCSharp.VenusBank;
using Wrox.ProCSharp.OOCSharp.JupiterBank;
```

Then we need a `Main()` method:

```
namespace Wrox.ProCSharp.OOCSharp
{
    class MainEntryPoint
    {
        static void Main()
        {
```

```
        IBankAccount venusAccount = new SaverAccount();
        IBankAccount jupiterAccount = new GoldAccount();
        venusAccount.PayIn(200);
        venusAccount.Withdraw(100);
        Console.WriteLine(venusAccount.ToString());
        jupiterAccount.PayIn(500);
        jupiterAccount.Withdraw(600);
        jupiterAccount.Withdraw(100);
        Console.WriteLine(jupiterAccount.ToString());
      }
   }
}
```

This code (`BankAccounts.cs`) produces this output:

```
BankAccounts
Venus Bank Saver: Balance = £100.00
Withdrawal attempt failed.
Jupiter Bank Saver: Balance = £400.00
```

The main point to notice about this code is the way that we have declared both our reference variables as `IBankAccount` references. This means that they can point to any instance of any class that implements this interface. It does, however, mean that we can only call methods that are part of this interface through these references – if we want to call any methods implemented by a class that are not part of the interface, then we'd normally need to explicitly cast the reference to the appropriate type. In our code, we've got away with calling `ToString()` (not implemented by `IBankAccount`) without any explicit cast, purely because `ToString()` is a `System.Object` method, so the C# compiler knows that it will be supported by any class (or to put it another way, the cast from an interface to object is implicit).

Interface references can in all respects be treated like class references – but the power of them is that an interface reference can refer to *any* class that implements that interface. For example, this allows us to form arrays of interfaces, where each element of the array is a different class:

```
IBankAccount[] accounts = new IBankAccount[2];
accounts[0] = new SaverAccount();
accounts[1] = new GoldAccount();
```

Note, however, that we'd get a compiler error if we tried something like this

```
accounts[1] = new SomeOtherClass();    // SomeOtherClass does NOT implement
                                       // IBankAccount: WRONG!!
```

this will cause a compilation error similar to this:

```
Cannot implicitly convert type 'Wrox.ProCSharp.OOCSharp.SomeOtherClass' to
'Wrox.ProCSharp.OOCSharp.BankProtocols.IBankAccount'
```

You should note that it is also fine to implicitly convert references to any class that implements an interface to references to that interface. Conversions the other way round must be done explicitly.

Interface Inheritance

It's possible for interfaces to inherit from each other in the same way that classes do. We'll illustrate this concept by defining a new interface, ITransferBankAccount, which has the same features as IBankAccount, but also defines a method to transfer money directly to a different account:

```
namespace Wrox.ProCSharp.OOCSharp.BankProtocols
{
    public interface ITransferBankAccount : IBankAccount
    {
        bool TransferTo(IBankAccount destination, decimal amount);
    }
}
```

Because ITransferBankAccount derives from IBankAccount, it gets all the members of IBankAccount as well as its own. That means that any class that implements (derives from) ITransferBankAccount *must* implement all the methods of IBankAccount, as well as the new TransferTo() method defined in ITransferBankAccount. Failure to implement all of these methods will result in a compilation error.

One point to notice about the TransferTo() method is that it uses an IBankAccount interface reference for the destination account. This illustrates the usefulness of interfaces: when implementing and then invoking this method, we don't need to know anything about what type of object we are transferring money to – all we need to know is that this object implements IBankAccount.

We'll illustrate ITransferBankAccount by assuming that the Planetary Bank of Jupiter also offers a current account. Most of the implementation of the CurrentAccount class is identical to the implementations of SaverAccount and GoldAccount (again this is just in order to keep this sample simple – that won't normally be the case), so in the following code we've just highlighted the differences:

```
public class CurrentAccount : ITransferBankAccount
{
    private decimal balance;

    public void PayIn(decimal amount)
    {
        balance += amount;
    }

    public bool Withdraw(decimal amount)
    {
        if (balance >= amount)
        {
            balance -= amount;
            return true;
        }
        Console.WriteLine("Withdrawal attempt failed.");
        return false;
    }
```

```
     public decimal Balance
     {
       get
       {
         return balance;
       }
     }

     public bool TransferTo(IBankAccount destination, decimal amount)
     {
       bool result;
       if ((result = Withdraw(amount)) == true)
         destination.PayIn(amount);
       return result;
     }

     public override string ToString()
     {
       return String.Format("Jupiter Bank Current Account: Balance = {0,6:C}",
                                                            balance);
     }
}
```

We can demonstrate the class with this code:

```
static void Main()
{
    IBankAccount venusAccount = new SaverAccount();
    ITransferBankAccount jupiterAccount = new CurrentAccount();
    venusAccount.PayIn(200);
    jupiterAccount.PayIn(500);
    jupiterAccount.TransferTo(venusAccount, 100);
    Console.WriteLine(venusAccount.ToString());
    Console.WriteLine(jupiterAccount.ToString());
}
```

This code (`CurrentAccount.cs`) produces this output, which as you can verify shows the correct amounts have been transferred:

CurrentAccount
```
Venus Bank Saver: Balance = £300.00
Jupiter Bank Current Account: Balance = £400.00
```

Construction and Disposal

In this section we're going to look at how to define constructors and destructors for your classes in C#. Recall from Chapter 2 that constructors exist to provide automatic initialization routines for objects and classes, while destructors are in principle available to supply automatic cleanup code when an object is destroyed.

Constructors

The syntax for declaring basic constructors in C# is the same as in Java and C++. We declare a method that has the same name as the containing class, and which does not have any return type:

```
public class MyClass
{
   public MyClass()
   {
   }
   // rest of class definition
```

As in C++ and Java, it's not necessary to provide a constructor for your class. We haven't supplied one for any of our examples so far in the book. In general, if you don't explicitly supply any constructor, the compiler will just make a default one up for you behind the scenes. It'll be a very basic constructor that just initializes all the member fields to their normal default values (empty string for strings, zero for numeric data types, and `false` for `bools`, as we've already mentioned). Often, that will be adequate; otherwise, you'll need to write your own constructor.

> *For C++ programmers: because primitive fields in C# are by default initialized by being zeroed out, whereas primitive fields in C++ are by default uninitialized, you may find you don't need to write constructors in C# as often as you would in C++.*

Constructors follow the same rules for overloading as other methods. In other words, you can provide as many overloads to the constructor as you wish, providing they are clearly different in signature:

```
public MyClass()    // zero-parameter constructor
{
   // construction code
}
public MyClass(int number)   // another overload
{
   // construction code
}
```

Note however that if you supply any constructors that take parameters, then the compiler will not automatically supply a default one. This is only done if you have not explicitly defined any constructors at all. In the following example, because we have explicitly defined a one-parameter constructor, the compiler will assume that this is the only constructor we wish to be available, and so will not implicitly supply any others:

```
public class MyNumber
{
   private int number;
   public MyNumber(int number)
   {
      this.number = number;
   }
}
```

The above code also illustrates typical use of the `this` keyword to distinguish member fields from parameters of the same name. If we now try instantiating a `MyNumber` object using a no-parameter constructor, we will get a compilation error:

```
MyNumber numb = new MyNumber();    // causes compilation error
```

We should mention that it is possible to define constructors as private or protected, so that they are invisible to code in unrelated classes too:

```
public class MyNumber
{
    private int number;
    private MyNumber(int number)    // another overload
    {
        this.number = number;
    }
}
```

In this example we haven't actually defined any public or even any protected constructors for `MyNumber`. This would actually make it impossible for `MyNumber` to be instantiated by outside code using the new operator (though you might write a public static property or method in `MyNumber` that can instantiate the class). This is useful in two situations:

❑   If your class serves only as a container for some static members or properties, and therefore should never be instantiated

❑   If you want the class to only ever be instantiated by calling some static member function

Note, however, that if you declare only one or more private constructors, you will also make it impossible for any class derived from your class to ever be instantiated by any means whatsoever. This is because, as we will see soon when we examine derived class constructors, a derived class will always expect to call a base constructor – which means there must be an appropriate base class constructor to which the derived class has access.

Static Constructors

One novel feature of C# is that it is also possible to write a static no-parameter constructor for a class. Such a constructor will only ever be executed once, as opposed to the constructors we've written so far, which are instance constructors, and executed whenever an object of that class is created. One reason why you might want a static constructor is to initialize the values of any static variables. There is no equivalent to the static constructor in C++.

```
class MyClass
{
    static MyClass()
    {
        // initialization code
    }
    // rest of class definition
}
```

One reason for writing a static constructor would be if your class has some static fields or properties that need to be initialized from an external source before the class is first used.

The .NET runtime makes no guarantees about when a static constructor will be executed, so you should not place any code in it that relies on it being executed at a particular time (for example, when an assembly is loaded). Nor is it possible to predict what order static constructors of different classes will execute. However, what is guaranteed is that the static constructor will run at most once, and that it will be invoked before your code makes any reference to the class. In practice, in C#, the static constructor usually seems to be executed immediately before the first call to a member of the class.

Notice that the static constructor does not have any access modifiers. It's never called by any other C# code, but always by the .NET runtime when the class is loaded, so any access modifier like `public` or `private` would be meaningless. For this same reason, the static constructor cannot ever take any parameters, and there can only ever be one static constructor for a class. It should also be obvious that a static constructor can only access static members, not instance members, of the class.

Note that it is perfectly possible to have a static constructor and a zero-parameter instance constructor defined in the same class. Although the parameter lists are identical, there is no conflict here because the static constructor is executed when the class is loaded, but the instance constructor is executed whenever an instance is created – so there won't be any confusion about which constructor gets executed when!

One thing to watch is that if you have more than one class that has a static constructor, which static constructor will be executed first is undefined. This means that you should not put any code in a static constructor that depends on other static constructors having been or not having been executed. On the other hand, if any static fields have been given default values, these will be allocated before the static constructor is called.

We'll now present a sample that illustrates the use of a static constructor. The sample is imaginatively called `StaticConstructor`, and is based on the idea of a program that has user preferences (which are presumably stored in some configuration file). To keep things simple, we'll assume just one user preference – a quantity called `BackColor`, which might represent the background color to be used in an application. And since we don't want to get into coding up reading data from an external source here, we'll instead make the assumption that the preference is to have a background color of red on weekdays and green at weekends. All the program will do is display the preference in a console window – but this is enough to see a static constructor at work.

The preferences will be controlled by a class, `UserPreferences`. Since it doesn't make sense to have more than one set of preferences in a running application, everything in this class will be static. We'll even make the class sealed and define a private constructor to ensure it can't ever get instantiated. Here's the definition of `UserPreferences`.

```
namespace Wrox.ProCSharp.OOCSharp
{
    sealed class UserPreferences
    {
        public static readonly Color BackColor;

        static UserPreferences()
        {
            DateTime now = DateTime.Now;
```

```
            if (now.DayOfWeek == DayOfWeek.Saturday
                || now.DayOfWeek == DayOfWeek.Sunday)
                BackColor = Color.Green;
            else
                BackColor = Color.Red;
        }

        private UserPreferences()
        {
        }
    }
}
```

This code shows how the color preference is stored in a static variable, which is initialized in the static constructor. We have declared this field as `readonly`, which means that its value can only be set in a constructor. We'll look at `readonly` fields in more detail later. The code makes use of the (static) `Now` and (instance) `DayOfWeek` properties of the `System.DateTime` struct. It also uses the `System.Drawing.Color` struct that we will investigate more fully in Chapter 19. In order to use this struct, we need to reference the `System.Drawing.dll` assembly when compiling, and add a `using` statement for the `System.Drawing` namespace.

```
using System;
using System.Drawing;
```

We test the static constructor with this code:

```
    class MainEntryPoint
    {
        static void Main(string[] args)
        {
            Console.WriteLine("User-preferences: BackColor is: " +
                          UserPreferences.BackColor.ToString());
        }
    }
```

Compiling and running this code gives this:

StaticConstructor
```
User-preferences: BackColor is: Color [Red]
```

Calling Constructors from Other Constructors

You may sometimes find yourself in the situation where you have several constructors in a class, perhaps to accommodate some optional parameters, for which the constructors have some code in common. For example, consider this situation:

```
class Car
{
    private string description;
    private uint nWheels;
```

```
    public Car(string model, uint nWheels)
    {
        this.description = description;
        this.nWheels = nWheels;
    }

    public Car(string model)
    {
        this.description = description;
        this.nWheels = 4;
    }
// etc.
```

Both constructors initialize the same fields. It would clearly be neater to place all the code in one place, and C# has a special syntax, known as a **constructor initializer**, to allow this.

```
class Car
{
    private string description;
    private uint nWheels;

    public Car(string model, uint nWheels)
    {
        this.description = description;
        this.nWheels = nWheels;
    }

    public Car(string model) : this(model, 4)
    {
    }
    // etc
```

In this context, the `this` keyword simply causes the constructor with the nearest matching parameters to be called. Note that the constructor initializer is executed *before* the body of the constructor. Now say the following code is run:

```
Car myCar = new Car("Proton Persona");
```

In this case, the two-parameter constructor will execute before any code in the body of the one-parameter constructor (though in this particular case, since there is no code in the body of the one-parameter constructor, it makes no difference).

A C# constructor initializer may contain either one call to another constructor in the same class (using the syntax just presented) or one call to a constructor in the immediate base class (using the same syntax, but using the keyword `base` instead of `this`). It is not possible to put more than one call in the initializer.

The syntax for constructor initializers in C# is similar to that for constructor initialization lists in C++, but C++ developers should beware. Behind the similarity in syntax, C# initializers follow very different rules for what can be placed in them. Whereas you can use a C++ initialization list to indicate initial values of any member variables or to call a base constructor, the *only* thing you can put in a C# initializer is one call to one other constructor. This forces C# classes to follow a strict sequence for how they get constructed, where C++ allows some laxity. As we'll see soon, the sequence enforced by C# arguably amounts to no more than good programming practice anyway, and so is beneficial.

Constructors of Derived Classes

We've now seen how constructors work for simple classes, and we've also seen how classes can derive from other classes. An interesting question arises as to what happens when you start defining your own constructors for classes that are in a hierarchy, inherited from other classes that may also have custom constructors. This is quite a subtle issue so we'll investigate it in some detail.

When the compiler supplies default constructors everywhere, there is actually quite a lot going on, but the compiler is able to arrange it so that things work out nicely all throughout the class hierarchy and every field in every class gets initialized to whatever its default value is. From the moment that we add a constructor of our own, however, we are effectively taking control of construction right through the hierarchy, and we will therefore need to make sure that we don't inadvertently do anything to prevent construction through the hierarchy from taking place smoothly.

You might be wondering why there is any special problem with derived classes. The reason is that when you create an instance of a derived class, there is actually more than one constructor at work. The constructor of the class you instantiate isn't by itself sufficient to initialize the class – the constructors of the base classes must also be called. That's why I've been talking about construction through the hierarchy.

To see why base class constructors must be called, we're going to develop an example based on a cell phone company called `MortimerPhones`. If you've read Appendix A, you'll know that `MortimerPhones` is the example that we used through that appendix to illustrate the concepts of inheritance. If you haven't read the appendix, we'll just say that the example contains an abstract base class, `GenericCustomer`, which represents any customer. There is also a (non-abstract) class, `Nevermore60Customer`, which represents any customer on a particular tariff, called the Nevermore60 tariff. All customers have a name, represented by a private field. Under the Nevermore60 tariff, the first few minutes of the customer's call time are charged at a higher cost, necessitating the need for a field, `highCostMinutesUsed`, which details how far into these higher cost minutes each customer has reached. This means that the class definitions look like this:

```
abstract class GenericCustomer
{
    private string name;
    // lots of other methods etc.
}

class Nevermore60Customer : GenericCustomer
{
    private uint highCostMinutesUsed;
    // other methods etc.
}
```

We won't worry about what other methods might be implemented in these classes, as we are concentrating solely on the construction process here. And if you download the sample code for this chapter, you'll find the class definitions include only the constructors.

Let's look at what happens when you use the new operator to instantiate a `Nevermore60Customer` like this:

```
GenericCustomer arabel = new Nevermore60Customer();
```

Clearly both of the member fields `name` and `highCostMinutesUsed` must be initialized when `arabel` is instantiated. If we don't supply constructors of our own, but rely simply on the default constructors, then we'd expect `name` to be initialized to the `null` reference, and `highCostMinutesUsed` to zero. Let's look in a bit more detail at how this actually happens.

The `highCostMinutesUsed` field presents no problem: the default `Nevermore60Customer` constructor supplied by the compiler will initialize this to zero.

What about name? Looking at the class definitions, it's clear that the `Nevermore60Customer` constructor **can't** initialize these values. This field is declared as `private`, which means that derived classes don't have access to it. So the default `Nevermore60Customer` constructor simply won't even know that this field exists. The only things that have that knowledge are other members of `GenericCustomer`. This means that if `name` is going to be initialized, that'll have to be done by some constructor in `GenericCustomer`. No matter how big your class hierarchy is, this same reasoning applies right down to the ultimate base class, `System.Object`.

Now that we have an understanding of the issues involved, we can look at what actually happens whenever a derived class is instantiated. Assuming default constructors are used throughout, the compiler first grabs the constructor of the class it is trying to instantiate – in this case `Nevermore60Customer`. The first thing that the default `Nevermore60Customer` does is attempt to run the default constructor for the immediate base class, `GenericCustomer`. This is how default constructors *always* behave in C#. Then the `GenericCustomer` constructor attempts to run the constructor for its immediate base, `System.Object`. `System.Object` doesn't have any base classes, so its constructor just executes and returns control to the `GenericCustomer` constructor. That constructor now executes, initializing `name` to `null`, before returning control to the `Nevermore60Customer` constructor. That constructor in turn executes, initializing `highCostMinutesUsed` to zero, and exits. At this point, the `Nevermore60Customer` instance has been successfully constructed and initialized.

The net result of all this is that the constructors are called in order of `System.Object` first, then progressing down the hierarchy until we reach the class being instantiated. Notice also that in this process, each constructor handles initialization of the fields in its own class. That's how it should normally work, and when you start adding your own constructors you should try to stick to that principle where possible.

Incidentally, working up the hierarchy is a sensible order because it means that if required, a constructor for the derived class can, in its implementation, call up base class methods, properties and any other members it is allowed to be aware of, confident that the base class has already been constructed and its fields initialized. It also means that if the derived class doesn't like the way that the base class has been initialized, it can change the initial values of the data, provided it has access to do so. However, good programming practice means you'll try to avoid that situation occurring, if you can, but trust the base class constructor to deal with its fields.

Anyway, now we've understood how the process of construction works, we can start fiddling with it by adding our own constructors.

Adding a No-Parameter Constructor in a Hierarchy

We'll take the simplest case first and see what happens if we simply replace the default constructor somewhere in the hierarchy with another constructor that takes no parameters. Suppose that we decide that we want everyone's name to be initially set to <no name> instead of to the null reference. We'd modify the code in GenericCustomer like this:

```
public abstract class GenericCustomer
{
    private string name;

    public GenericCustomer()
        : base()  // we could omit this line without affecting the compiled code
    {
        name = "<no name>";
    }
}
```

Adding this code will work fine. Nevermore60Customer still has its default constructor, so the sequence of events described above will proceed as before, except that the compiler will use our custom GenericCustomer constructor instead of generating a default one, so the name field will be initialized to <no name> as required.

Notice that in our constructor, we've added an explicit call to the base class constructor before the GenericCustomer constructor is executed, using the same syntax as we were using earlier when we covered how to get different overloads of constructors to call each other. The only difference is that this time we use the base keyword instead of this, to indicate it's a constructor to the base class rather than a constructor to this class we want to call. There are no parameters in the brackets after the base keyword, so we are calling the no-parameter System.Object constructor, just as would happen by default.

In fact, we could have left that line out, and just written the following, as we've done for most of the constructors so far in the chapter:

```
public GenericCustomer()
{
    name = "<no name>";
}
```

If the compiler doesn't see any reference to another constructor before the opening curly brace, it assumes that we intended to call the base class constructor; this fits in with the way that we've just explained default constructors work.

> The **base** and **this** keywords are the only keywords allowed in the line which calls another constructor. Anything else will cause a compilation error. Also note that only one other constructor can be specified.

So far this code works fine. One good way to mess up the progression through the hierarchy of constructors, however, is to declare a constructor as `private`:

```
private GenericCustomer()
{
    name = "<no name>";
}
```

If you try this, you'll find you get an interesting compilation error, which could really throw you if you don't understand how construction down a hierarchy works:

```
'Wrox.ProCSharp.OOCSharp.GenericCustomer.GenericCustomer()' is inaccessible due to
its protection level
```

The interesting thing is that the error occurs not in the `GenericCustomer` class, but in the derived class, `Nevermore60Customer`. What's happened is that the compiler has tried to generate a default constructor for `Nevermore60Customer`, but not been able to because the default constructor is supposed to invoke the no-parameter `GenericCustomer` constructor. By declaring that constructor as `private`, we've made it inaccessible to the derived class. A similar error will occur if we supply a constructor to `GenericCustomer`, which takes parameters, but no no-parameter constructor. In this case the compiler will not generate a default constructor for `GenericCustomer`, so when it tries to generate the default constructors for any derived class, it'll again find that it can't because there is no no-parameter base class constructor available. The way round this problem would be to add your own constructors to the derived classes, even if you don't actually need to do anything in these constructors, so that the compiler doesn't try to generate any default constructor for them.

However, at this point I think we've had enough discussion of what can go wrong with constructors. We've got all the theoretical background we need and we're ready to move on to an example of how you should add constructors to a hierarchy of classes. In the next section we'll start adding constructors that take parameters to the `MortimerPhones` sample.

Adding Constructors with Parameters to a Hierarchy

We're going to start by arranging that customers can only be instantiated on supplying their name. This will mean writing a one-parameter constructor for `GenericCustomer`:

```
abstract class GenericCustomer
{
    private string name;

    public GenericCustomer(string name)
    {
        this.name = name;
    }
}
```

So far so good, but as we've just said, this will cause a compilation error when the compiler tries to create a default constructor for any derived classes, since the default compiler-generated constructors for `Nevermore60Customer` will both try to call a no-parameter `GenericCustomer` constructor, but `GenericCustomer` does not now possess such a constructor. Therefore, we'll need to supply our own constructors to the derived classes to avoid a compilation error.

```
class Nevermore60Customer : GenericCustomer
{
    private uint highCostMinutesUsed;
    public Nevermore60Customer(string name)
        : base(name)
    {
    }
}
```

Now instantiation of `Nevermore60Customer` objects can only take place when a string containing the customer's name is supplied, which is what we want anyway. The interesting thing is what our `Nevermore60Customer` constructor does with this string. Remember that it can't initialize the `name` field itself, because it has no access to a private field in a base class. Instead, it passes the name through to the base class for the `GenericCustomer` constructor to handle. It does this by specifying that the base class constructor to be executed first is the one that takes the name as a parameter. Other than that, it doesn't take any action of its own.

Now we're now going to make things a bit more complex. We're going to investigate what happens if you have different overloads of the constructor as well as a class hierarchy to deal with.

To this end we're going to assume that Nevermore60 customers may have been referred to `MortimerPhones` by a friend, you know, one of these sign up a friend and get a discount offers. This means that when we construct a `Nevermore60Customer`, we may need to pass in the referrer's name as well. In real life the constructor would have to do something complicated with the name, like process the discount, but here we'll just store the referrer's name in another field.

The `Nevermore60Customer` definition will look like this at this stage:

```
class Nevermore60Customer : GenericCustomer
{
    public Nevermore60Customer(string name, string referrerName)
        : base(name)
    {
        this.referrerName = referrerName;
    }

    private string referrerName;
    private uint highCostMinutesUsed;
```

The constructor takes the name and passes it to the `GenericCustomer` constructor for processing. `referrerName` is the variable that is our responsibility here, so the constructor deals with that parameter in its main body.

However, not all `Nevermore60Customers` will have a referrer, so we still need a constructor that doesn't require this parameter (or, equivalently, a constructor that gives us a default value for it). In fact we will specify that if there is no referrer, then the `referrerName` field should be set to <None>. Here's what the one-parameter constructor that does this looks like:

```
public Nevermore60Customer(string name)
    : this(name, "<None>")
{
}
```

We've now got all our constructors set up correctly. It's rather instructive to examine the chain of events that now occurs when we execute a line like this:

```
GenericCustomer arabel = new Nevermore60Customer("Arabel Jones");
```

The compiler sees that it needs a one-parameter constructor that takes one string, so the constructor it'll identify is the last one that we've defined:

```
public Nevermore60Customer(string Name)
    : this(Name, "<None>")
```

When we instantiate `arabel`, this constructor will be called. It will immediately transfer control to the corresponding `Nevermore60Customer` 2-parameter constructor, passing it the values `Arabel Jones`, and `<None>`. Looking at the code for this constructor, we see that it in turn immediately passes control to the one-parameter `GenericCustomer` constructor, giving it the string `Arabel Jones`, and in turn that constructor passes control to the `System.Object` default constructor. Now the constructors will actually execute. First, the `System.Object` constructor executes. Next comes the `GenericCustomer` constructor; this will initialize the `name` field. Then the `Nevermore60Customer` 2-parameter constructor gets control back, and sorts out initializing the `referrerName` to `<None>`. Finally, the `Nevermore60Customer` one-parameter constructor gets to execute; this constructor doesn't do anything else.

Although this is quite a complicated process as you can see, it's actually a very neat and well-designed one too. Each constructor has handled initialization of the variables that are obviously its responsibility, and in the process our class has been correctly instantiated and prepared for use. If you follow the same principles when you write your own constructors for your classes, you should find that even the most complex classes get initialized smoothly and without any problems.

Cleaning up: Destructors and Dispose()

We've seen that constructors allow you to specify certain actions that must take place whenever an instance of a class is created, so you might be wondering if it's possible to do the same thing whenever a class instance is destroyed. Indeed, if you're familiar with C++, you'll know that C++ allows you to do just that, by specifying a method known as a **destructor**. Destructors are called whenever a class instance goes out of scope or is otherwise removed from memory. Experienced C++ developers make extensive use of destructors, and sometimes not only to clean up resources, but also to provide debugging information or perform other tasks.

C# does support destructors, but they are used far less often than in C++, and the way they work is very different. Because reference objects in .NET and C# are removed by the garbage collector, there can be a delay between their the reference going out of scope and the object actually being deleted. This is perhaps the only disadvantage of a garbage-collection system of memory management. If your object is holding scarce and critical resources which need to be freed as soon as possible then you won't want to wait for garbage collection. Because of this, the destruction paradigm in C# works in two stages.

1. The class should implement the standard interface `System.IDisposable`. This means implementing the method, `IDisposable.Dispose()`. This method is explicitly called by client code when an object is no longer required.

2. A destructor may be defined, which will be automatically invoked when the object is garbage-collected. However, the aim should be that it's the client's responsibility to notify the object (by calling `Dispose()`) when it no longer needs it. The destructor is only there as a backup mechanism in case some badly-behaved client doesn't call `Dispose()`.

Although we talk about destructors in C#, in the underlying .NET architecture, these are known as `Finalize()` *methods. When you define a destructor in C#, what is emitted into the assembly by the compiler is actually a method called* `Finalize()`. *That's something that doesn't affect any of your sourcecode, but you'll need to be aware of the fact if for any reason you wish to examine the contents of the emitted assembly.*

In general, if objects of some class can contain references to other managed objects that are large and should be cleaned up as soon as we no longer need our object, then that class should implement `Dispose()`. If a class holds unmanaged resources, then it should implement both `Dispose()` and a destructor.

There are really two issues we need to consider here: what the syntax for destructors and `Dispose()` is, and how to write good implementations of these methods. We'll look at the syntax first. This class contains a `Dispose()` method and a destructor.

`Dispose()` is a normal method. So the syntax for defining it is no different from any other method.

```
class MyClass : IDisposable
{
   public void Dispose()
   {
      // implementation
   }


   ~MyClass()    // destructor. Only implement if MyClass directly holds
                 // unmanaged resources.
   {
      // implementation
   }
   // etc.
```

Notice that the class is derived from `IDisposable`. Notice also the signature of `Dispose()`: it returns a void and takes no parameters.

The syntax for the destructor will be familiar to C++ developers. It looks like a method, with the same name as the containing class, but prefixed with a tilde (~). It has no return type, takes no parameters and no access modifiers (it is always called by the .NET runtime, not by other C# code, so access modifiers would make no sense here).

Implementing Dispose() and a Destructor

Destructors are called when an object is destroyed. There are several things you should bear in mind when you implement a destructor:

- ❑ Destructors are not deterministic. This means that there's no way in general to predict when the instance will be destroyed, which means that you can't predict when a destructor will be called. In general, instances will be destroyed when the garbage collector detects that they are no longer referenced, but to a large extent the garbage collector comes into action when the .NET runtime decides it's needed – and that's up to the .NET runtime, not your program. Hence, you should not place any code in the destructor that relies on being run at a certain time, and you shouldn't even rely on the destructor being called for different class instances in any particular order.

- ❑ You can force the garbage collector to run at a certain point in your code, if you want, by calling System.GC.Collect(). System.GC is a .NET base class that represents the garbage collector, and the Collect() method actually calls the garbage collector. However, this is intended for rare situations in which you know that for example, it's a good time to call the garbage collector because a very large number of objects in your code have just stopped being referenced. You certainly wouldn't normally go to the trouble of calling up the entire garbage collection process just to get one destructor called!

- ❑ In general, you are advised not to implement a destructor unless your class really does need it. Due to the way the garbage collector has been implemented, if an object implements a destructor, that puts a significant performance hit on garbage-collecting that object. It also delays the final removal of that object from memory. Objects that do not have a destructor get removed from memory in one pass of the garbage collector, but objects that have destructors require two passes to be destroyed: the first one calls the destructor without removing the object, the second actually deletes the object. Do not implement a destructor unless your class directly holds some unmanaged resource (for example a database connection). If your class merely holds references to other objects that hold on to unmanaged resources, then do not implement a destructor – those other classes ought instead to have destructors of their own.

Now on to the typical usage pattern of destructors. We'll show you the general code structure you should implement, then discuss the reasons for this. The code you write ought to look like this.

```
public class ResourceHolder : IDisposable
{
    public void Dispose()
    {
        Dispose(true);
        GC.SuppressFinalize(this);
    }

    protected virtual void Dispose(bool disposing)
    {
        if (disposing)
        {
            // Cleanup managed objects
        }
```

```
        // Cleanup unmanaged objects
    }

    ~ResourceHolder()
    {
        Dispose (false);
    }
}
```

We see from this that there is a second overload of `Dispose()`, which takes one `bool` parameter – and this is the method that really does the cleaning up. `Dispose(bool)` is called by both the destructor, and by the no-parameter `Dispose()` method (which we'll refer to as `IDisposable.Dispose()`). The point of this approach is to ensure that all cleanup code is in one place.

The parameter passed to `Dispose(bool)` indicates whether `Dispose(bool)` has been invoked by the destructor or by `IDisposable.Dispose()` – `Dispose(bool)` should not be invoked from anywhere else in your code. The idea is this:

❑   If a client calls `IDisposable.Dispose()` then that client is indicating that all resources associated with that object – both managed and unmanaged – should be cleaned up.

❑   If a destructor has been invoked, then all resources still need in principle to be cleaned up. However, in this case, we know that the destructor must have been called by the garbage collector – and we can assume that the garbage collector will independently be ensuring that any other associated managed resources are being removed from the managed heap (and in the process will be invoking their destructors if they have any defined). Hence the only thing we need to explicitly do from the destructor is clean up any unmanaged resources. Not only that, but there is another very good reason for not referring to other managed objects from code that has been invoked from the destructor. Since it's not possible to predict what order objects will be destroyed in, any such managed objects may well have got destroyed first – in which case our references to them will be invalid anyway.

Looking again at the above code, we see that the final thing to happen in a call to `IDisposable.Dispose()` is a call to a method in the `System.GC` .NET Framework base class, `GC.SuppressFinalize()`. GC is the class that is responsible for managing the garbage collector, and the `SuppressFinalize()` method tells the garbage collector that a class no longer needs to have its destructor called – that makes the garbage collection process more efficient. Since `Dispose()` has already done all the cleanup required, there's nothing left for the destructor to do. Calling `SuppressFinalize()` means that the garbage collector will treat that object as if it doesn't have a destructor at all.

By doing it this way, you have a backup. If the client code remembers to call `Dispose()`, then the resources get cleaned up in good time. If the client forgets, then all is not lost because the destructor will be called eventually when the object is garbage-collected.

Note that there are never any parameters to a destructor, no return type, and no access modifier. Just as with constructors, each destructor should clean up only those resources that are defined within its own class. If any code in any of the base classes holds on to external resources, then those should be cleaned up in destructors in the relevant base classes. And there is no need to explicitly call the base class's destructor – the compiler will automatically arrange for all destructors that have been defined through the class hierarchy to be called.

Close() vs. Dispose()

The difference between the Close() and Dispose() methods is largely one of convention. Close() tends to suggest that it's a resource that might later be reopened, while Dispose() has more of an implication of finality – calling Dispose() means that the client has finished with this particular object for good. You can implement either one or both of these methods, but to avoid confusing other developers, you should implement them with those meanings in mind. You also might wish to implement Close() in situations in which a Close() method has been traditional programming practice or fits in with traditional terminology, such as closing a file or database connection. A case in which you might use Dispose() might be to release handles to various GDI or other Windows objects. You will also need to use Dispose() if you wish to take advantage of the IDisposable architecture, which we discuss next.

Using the IDisposable Interface

C# offers a syntax that you can use to guarantee that Dispose() (though not Close()) will automatically be called against an object when the reference goes out of scope. The syntax to do this involves the using keyword – though now in a very different context, which has nothing to do with namespaces. Suppose we have a class, let's call it ResourceGobbler, which relies on the use of some external resource, and we wish to instantiate an instance of this class. We could do it like this:

```
{
    ResourceGobbler theInstance = new ResourceGobbler();

    // do your processing

    theInstance.Dispose();
}
```

I've put braces around the above code. These aren't necessary, but I've put them there to emphasize that, after calling theInstance.Dispose(), we have presumably finished with theInstance, so there's presumably no more point the reference remaining in scope. A better approach is to transfer the processing above into a using block:

```
using (ResourceGobbler theInstance = new ResourceGobbler())
{
    // do your processing
}
```

The using block, followed in brackets by a reference variable definition, will cause that variable to be scoped to the accompanying compound statement. In addition, when that variable goes out of scope, its Dispose() method will automatically be called.

The using syntax does have the disadvantage that it forces extra indentation of the code, and it doesn't save you very much coding. We will also see in Chapter 4, when we examine exceptions, that a similar effect can alternatively be achieved anyway by placing the call to Dispose() in a finally block. If you are using exceptions anyway, this will likely be the preferred technique. For these reasons, you may prefer to avoid the using construct.

In order to use the alternative `using` syntax, we do have to define the `ResourceGobbler` class in a certain way. In order to see what this involves, we're going to have to jump ahead of ourselves a bit, since it relies on use of interfaces. The restriction is that we have to derive `ResourceGobbler` from an interface called `IDisposable`, which is defined in the `System` namespace:

```
class ResourceGobbler : IDisposable
{
    // etc.

    public void Dispose()
    {
        // etc.
    }
}
```

Deriving from an interface is a bit different from deriving from a class. We'll examine the details later in the chapter. We'll just say here that deriving from `IDisposable` has the effect of forcing the derived class to implement a method called `Dispose()`; you'll actually get a compilation error if you derive from `IDisposable` and don't implement this method. The reason that we have to derive from `IDisposable` in order to use the `using` syntax is that it gives the compiler a way of checking that the object defined in the `using` statement does have a `Dispose()` method that it can automatically call. As we'll see later in the chapter, deriving from an interface is the usual way that a class can declare that it implements certain features.

Implementing Destructors and Dispose()

Now we've had a look at the theory we'll expand out the above code to see how it works in practice. First, here's an example of a class that contains only a managed resource.

```
public class ManagedResourceGobbler : IDisposable
{
    private StreamReader sr;

    public void Dispose()
    {
        if (sr != null)
        {
            sr.Close();
            sr = null;
        }
    }
}
```

`ManagedResourceGobbler` doesn't contain any direct references to unmanaged resources, which means it doesn't need a destructor. However, it does contain a reference to a `StreamReader` object. We'll meet `StreamReader` in the chapter on file handling. It's a class defined in the `System.IO` namespace and is designed to read data from, for example, a file. Since `StreamReader` will internally hold an external resource, it's a fair guess that it will implement the destructor-dispose paradigm we've just seen. It certainly does have a `Dispose()` method, and if we are following good programming practices we will want to ensure that it gets called as soon as possible. Hence we implement a `Dispose()` method that calls the `StreamReader`'s `Close()`. That's what the above code illustrates. Notice that, because we don't have a destructor, we can keep all our cleanup code in our public `Dispose()` method.

Next let's look at the situation for a class that has references to managed and unmanaged resources.

```csharp
public class ResourceGobbler : IDisposable
{
    private StreamReader sr;
    private int connection;

    public void Dispose()
    {
        Dispose(true);
        GC.SuppressFinalize(this);
    }

    protected virtual void Dispose(bool disposing)
    {
        if (disposing)
        {
            if (sr != null)
            {
                sr.Close();
                sr = null;
            }
        }
        CloseConnection();
    }

    ~ResourceGobbler()
    {
        Dispose(false);
    }

    void CloseConnection()
    {
        // code here will close connection
    }
}
```

The `ResourceGobbler` class has a reference to a `StreamReader`. However, it also has an `int` called `connection`, which we will assume somehow represents some unmanaged object. This means we will need to implement a destructor. In the above code we assume that `CloseConnection()` is a method that closes the external resource.

readonly Fields

The concept of a constant, as a variable that contains a value that cannot be changed, is something that C# shares with most programming languages. However, constants don't necessarily meet all requirements. On occasions, you may have some variable whose value shouldn't be changed, but where the value is not known until runtime. C# provides another type of variable that is useful in this scenario: the `readonly` field.

The `readonly` keyword gives a bit more flexibility than `const`, allowing for the case in which you might want a field to be constant but also need to carry out some calculations to determine its initial value. The rule is that you can assign values to a `readonly` field inside a constructor, but not anywhere else. It's also possible for a `readonly` field to be an instance rather than a static field, having a different value for each instance of a class. This means that, unlike a `const` field, if you want a `readonly` field to be static, you have to explicitly declare it as such.

Suppose we have an MDI program that edits documents, and for licensing reasons we want to restrict the number of documents that can be opened simultaneously. But, because we are selling different versions of the software, and it's possible that customers can upgrade their licenses, we can't hard-code the maximum number in the sourcecode. We'd probably need a field to represent this maximum number. This field will have to be read in – perhaps from a registry key or some other file storage – each time the program is launched. So our code might look something like this:

```
public class DocumentEditor
{
    public static readonly uint MaxDocuments;

    static DocumentEditor()
    {
        // code here will read in the value of the max no. of documents.
        // for the sake of argument, let's assume the result is 20
        MaxDocuments = 20;
    }
```

In this case, the field is static, since the maximum number of documents only needs to be stored once per running instance of the program. This is why it is initialized in the static constructor. If we had an instance `readonly` field then we would initialize it in the instance constructor(s). For example, presumably each document we edit has a creation date, which you wouldn't want to allow the user to ever change (because that would be rewriting the past!). Note that the field is also public – we don't need to make `readonly` fields private, because by definition they cannot be modified externally (the same principle applies to constants too).

A date is represented by the base class, `System.DateTime`, which we've already encountered briefly. In this code we use a `System.DateTime` constructor that takes three parameters (the year, month, and day of the month):

```
public class Document
{
    public readonly DateTime CreationDate;

    public Document()
    {
        // read in creation date from file. Assume result is 1 Jan 2002
        // but in general this can be different for different instances
        // of the class
        CreationDate = new DateTime(2002, 1, 1);
    }
}
```

CreationDate and MaxDocuments in the above code snippets are treated like any other field, except that because they are readonly, it cannot be assigned to outside the constructors.

```
void SomeMethod()
{
    MaxDocuments = 10;  // compilation error here. MaxDocuments is readonly
}
```

It's also worth noting that you don't have to assign a value to a readonly field in a constructor. If you don't it will be left with the default value for its particular data type or whatever value you initialized it to at its declaration. That applies to both static and instance readonly fields.

Structs

So far, we have seen how classes can be great way of encapsulating objects in your program. We have also seen how they are stored on the heap in a way that gives you much more flexibility in data lifetime, but with a slight cost in performance. This performance cost is small thanks to the optimizations of managed heaps. However, there are some situations when all you really need is a small data structure. In this case, a class provides more functionality than you need, and for performance reasons you probably don't want the performance overhead of using the managed heap. Look at this example:

```
class Dimensions
{
    public double Length;
    public double Width;
}
```

We've defined a class called Dimensions, which simply stores the length and width of some item. Perhaps we're writing a furniture-arranging program to let people experiment with rearranging their furniture on the computer and we want to store the dimensions of each item of furniture. It looks like we're breaking the rules of good program design by making the fields public, but the point is that we don't really need all the facilities of a class for this at all. All we have is two numbers, which we find convenient to treat as a pair rather than individually. There is no need for lots of methods, or for us to be able to inherit from the class, and we certainly don't want to have the .NET runtime go to the trouble of bringing in the heap with all the performance implications, just to store two doubles.

Instead, we're better off defining Dimensions as something called a **struct**. To do this, the only thing we need to change in the code is to replace the keyword class with struct:

```
struct Dimensions
{
    public double Length;
    public double Width;
}
```

You can think of structs in C# as being like scaled down classes. They are basically the same as classes, but designed more for cases where you simply want to group some data together. They differ from classes in the following ways:

❑   Structs are value types, not reference types. This means they are stored either in the stack or inline (if they are part of another object that is stored on the heap), and have the same lifetime restrictions as the simple data types.

❑   Structs do not support inheritance.

❑   There are some differences in the way constructors work for structs. In particular, the compiler *always* supplies a default no-parameter constructor, which you are not permitted to replace.

❑   With a struct, you can (if you wish) specify how the fields are to be laid out in memory.

Also, because structs are really intended to group data items together, you'll sometimes find that most or all of their fields are declared as `public`. This is strictly speaking contrary to the guidelines for writing .NET code – according to Microsoft, fields (other than `const` fields) should always be private and wrapped by public properties. However, for simple structs, many developers would nevertheless consider public fields to be acceptable programming practice.

Over the following pages, we'll go through the differences between classes and structs in more detail. We won't, however, look at the facility to specify how the fields in a struct are laid out in memory. In C# this feature can be regarded as fairly esoteric; it is only rarely needed (usually for calling native API functions), so we are treating it as beyond the scope of this book. If you do need to do this, you should look up the `StructLayout` attribute in the MSDN documentation.

Structs Are Value Types

Although structs are value types, you can often treat them syntactically in the same way as classes. For example, with our definition of `Dimensions` above, we could write:

```
Dimensions point = new Dimensions();
point.Length = 3;
point.Width = 6;
```

Note that because structs are value types, the new operator does not work in the same way as it does for classes and other reference types. Instead of allocating memory on the heap, the new operator simply calls the appropriate constructor, according to the parameters passed to it, initializing all fields. Indeed, for structs it is perfectly legal to write:

```
Dimensions point;
point.Length = 3;
point.Width = 6;
```

If `Dimensions` was a class, this would produce a compilation error, because `point` would contain an uninitialized reference – an address that points nowhere, so we could not start setting values to its fields. For a struct however, the variable declaration actually allocates space on the stack for the entire struct, so it's ready to assign values to. Note, however, that the following code would cause a compilation error, with the compiler complaining that you are using an uninitialized variable:

```
Dimensions point;
Double D = point.Length;
```

Structs follow the same rules as any other data type: everything must be initialized before use. A struct is considered fully initialized either when the new operator has been called against it, or when values have been individually assigned to all its fields. And of course, a struct defined as a member field of a class is initialized by being zeroed-out automatically when the containing object is initialized.

The fact that structs are value types will affect performance, though depending on how you use your struct, this can be good or bad. On the positive side, allocating memory for structs is very fast because this takes place inline or on the stack. The same goes for removing structs when they go out of scope. On the other hand, whenever you pass a struct as a parameter or assign a struct to another struct (as in A=B, where A and B are structs), the full contents of the struct are copied, whereas for a class only the reference is copied. This will result in a performance loss that depends on the size of the struct – this should emphasize the fact that structs are really intended for *small* data structures. Note, however, that when passing a struct as a parameter to a method, you can avoid this performance loss by passing it as a ref parameter – in this case only the address in memory of the struct will be passed in, which is just as fast as passing in a class. On the other hand, if you do this, you'll have to be aware that it means the called method can in principle change the value of the struct.

Structs and Inheritance

Structs are not designed for inheritance. This means that it is not possible to inherit from a struct, and a struct cannot derive from any class. The only exception to this is that structs, in common with every other type in C#, derive ultimately from the class System.Object. Hence, structs also have access to the methods of System.Object, and it is even possible to override them in structs – an obvious example would be overriding the ToString() method.

> For structs, the derivation from System.Object is indirect: Structs derive from System.ValueType, which in turn derives from System.Object. ValueType adds no new methods of its own, but provides overridden implementations of some of the Object methods that are more appropriate to value types.

Defining methods for structs is exactly the same as defining them for classes:

```
struct Dimensions
{
    public double Length;
    public double Width;

    Dimensions(double length, double width)
    { Length=length; Width=width; }

    public override string ToString()
    {
        return "( " + Length.ToString() + " , " + Width.ToString() + " )";
    }
```

We declare the method exactly as we would for a class. Note, however, that it is not possible to declare any member of a struct as `virtual`, `abstract`, or `sealed`. To do so would imply that we were intending other classes to inherit from struct, but structs will not allow you to do that.

Constructors for Structs

You can define constructors for structs in exactly the same way that you can for classes, except that you are not permitted to define a constructor that takes no parameters. This may seem nonsensical, and the reason is buried in the implementation of the .NET runtime. There are some rare circumstances in which the .NET runtime would not be able to call a custom zero-parameter constructor that you have supplied. Microsoft has therefore taken the easy way out and banned zero-parameter constructors for structs in C#. This feature seems to be one of the few poor aspects of the design of .NET, and has caused some controversy in .NET– related newsgroups.

Having said that, the default constructor, which initializes all fields to zero values, is always present implicitly, even if you supply other constructors that take parameters. It's also not possible to sneakily work round the default constructor by explicitly supplying initial values for fields. The following code will cause a compile-time error:

```
struct Dimensions
{
    public double Length = 1;      // error. Initial values not allowed
    public double Width = 2;       // error. Initial values not allowed
```

Of course, if `Dimensions` had been declared as a class, this code would have compiled without any problems.

Incidentally, you can supply a `Close()` or `Dispose()` method for a struct in the same way you might choose to do so for a class, but it is not permitted to define a destructor.

Operator Overloading

In this and the next section, we're going to look at two of the other types of members that you can define for a class or a struct: **operator overloads** and **indexers**. We start by discussing operator overloading in this section.

Operator overloading is something that will be familiar to C++ developers. However, since the concept will be new to both Java and VB developers, we'll explain the concept of it here. C++ developers will probably prefer to skip straight to the main example.

The point of operator overloading is that you don't always just want to call methods or properties on class instances. Often you need to do things like adding quantities together, multiplying them, or performing logical operations such as comparing objects. Suppose for example you had defined a class that represents a mathematical matrix. Now in the world of math, matrices can be added together and multiplied, just like numbers. So it's quite plausible that you'd want to write code like this:

```
Matrix a, b, c;
// assume a, b and c have been initialized
Matrix d = c * (a + b);
```

By overloading the operators, you can effectively tell the compiler what + and * does to a `Matrix`, allowing you to write code like the above. If we were coding in a language that didn't have operator overloading, we'd have presumably have to define methods to perform those operations. The result would probably look a bit messy, like this:

```
Matrix d = c.Multiply(a.Add(b));
```

With what you've learned so far, operators like + and * have been strictly for the predefined data types, and for good reason: the compiler automatically knows what all the common operators mean for those data types. For example, it knows how to add two `longs` or how to divide one `double` by another `double`, and can generate the appropriate intermediate language code. When we define our own classes or structs, however, we have to tell the compiler everything: what methods are available to call, what fields to store with each instance, and so on. Similarly, if we want to use operators like + and * on our own classes, we'll have to tell the compiler what the relevant operators mean in the context of that class. The way we do that is by defining overloads for the operators.

We should also say that there are many classes you could write for which operator overloading would not be relevant. For example, multiplying together two `MortimerPhones` customers just doesn't make any sense conceptually. There are, however, a large number of cases where you might want to write overloads for operators, including:

❑ From the world of mathematics, almost any mathematical object: coordinates, vectors, matrices, tensors, functions, and so on. If you are writing a program that does some mathematical or physical modeling, you will almost certainly use classes representing these objects.

❑ Graphics programs will also use mathematical or coordinate-related objects when calculating positions on screen.

❑ A class that represents an amount of money (for example, in a financial program).

❑ A word processing or text analysis program might have classes representing sentences, clauses and so on, and you might wish to use operators to combine sentences together (a more sophisticated version of concatenation for strings).

The other thing we should stress is that overloading isn't just concerned with arithmetic operators. We also need to consider the comparison operators, ==, <, >, !=, >=, and <=. Take the statement `if (a==b)`. For classes, this statement will, by default, compare the references a and b – it tests to see if the references point to the same location in memory, rather than checking to see if the instances actually contain the same data. For the `string` class, this behavior is overridden so that comparing strings really does compare the contents of each string. You might wish to do the same for your own classes. For structs, the == operator doesn't do anything at all by default. Trying to compare two structs to see if they are equal will produce a compilation error unless you explicitly overload == to tell the compiler how to perform the comparison.

There are a large number of situations in which being able to overload operators will help greatly to allow us to generate more readable, intuitive code.

Over the next few sections we're going to illustrate operator overloading by developing a new example, a struct called Vector that represents a 3D mathematical vector. In the world of mathematics, vectors can be added together or multiplied by other vectors or by numbers. Incidentally, in this context we'll use the term **scalar,** which is math-speak for a simple number – in C# terms that's just a double. However, before we can understand how to overload operators, we need a bit of theoretical understanding about how operators work, which we cover next.

> *The fact that our example will be developed as a struct rather than a class is not significant. Operator overloading works in just the same way for both structs and classes.*

How Operators Work

In order to understand how to overload operators, it's quite useful to think about what happens when the compiler encounters an operator – and for this we'll take the addition operator, + , as an example. Suppose it meets the lines of code:

```
int a = 3;
uint b = 2;
double d = 4.0;
long l = a + b;
double x = d + a;
```

Consider the line:

```
long l = a + b;
```

Saying a+b is really just a very intuitive, convenient syntax for saying that we are calling a method to add the numbers together. The method takes two parameters, a and b, and returns their sum. For integers the compiler and the JIT compiler between them actually make sure this line is implemented internally as highly efficient inline code which does the addition using hardware, but the principle as far as the C# code is concerned is the same as if it was any ordinary method call.

The compiler will see it needs to add two integers and return a long, so it does the same thing as it does for any method call – it looks for the best matching overload of + given the parameter types. Adding two integers is fine – for modern processors there will be a specific machine code instruction to do this. The result will be an integer as well, so it will need to be cast to a long, which is allowed in C#, so there are no problems.

The next line demonstrates that there are actually quite a few overloads of "+" kicking around already, even before we start defining our own classes:

```
double x = d + a;
```

It appears that this overload takes a `double` and an `int`, adds them, and returns a `double`. Actually, on most machines, that's probably not directly possible – rather, we'll need to implicitly convert the `int` to a `double` and add the two `double`s together. In other words, we identify the best matching overload of "+" here as being a version of the operator that takes two `double`s as its parameters. Adding together two `double`s is a very different affair from adding two integers. Floating-point numbers are stored internally in modern processors as a mantissa and an exponent. Adding them involves bit-shifting the mantissa of one of the `double`s so that the two exponents have the same value, adding the mantissas, then shifting the mantissa of the result and adjusting its exponent to maintain the highest possible accuracy in the answer. There will be hardware support for this in a modern Pentium processor, but it's still a completely different operation from adding two integers. Finally, the compiler needs to make sure it can cast the result to the required return type if necessary. In this case there's no problem – adding two `double`s gives another `double`, which is what x is declared as.

Now, we're in a position to see what happens if the compiler finds something like this:

```
Vector vect1, vect2, vect3;
// initialise vect1 and vect2
vect3 = vect1 + vect2;
vect1 = vect1*2;
```

Here `Vector` is the struct that we shall define shortly. The compiler will see that it needs to add two `Vector`s, `vect1`, and `vect2` together. It'll look for an overload of the + operator which takes two `Vector`s as its parameters. This operator must also return either a `Vector` or something that can be implicitly converted to a `Vector`, so that we can set `vect3` equal to the return value. The compiler therefore needs to find a definition of an operator that has a signature something like this:

```
public static Vector operator + (Vector lhs, Vector rhs)
```

If it finds one, it'll call up the implementation of that operator. If it can't find one, it'll look to see if there is any other overload for + that it can use as a best match – perhaps something that has two parameters of other data types that can be implicitly converted to `Vector` instances. If it can't find anything suitable, it'll raise a compilation error, just as it would do if it couldn't find an appropriate overload for any other method call. Of course, a similar approach is used for the * and any other operator too:

```
vect1 = vect1*2;
```

Addition Operator Overloading Example: The Vector Struct

Now that we've delved into the theory of how operators work, it's time to introduce our example. We're going to write the struct `Vector`, which represents a 3-dimensional vector.

If you're worried that mathematics is not your strong point, don't worry. We'll keep things very simple. As far as we are concerned, a 3D-vector is just a set of three numbers (doubles) that tell you how far something is moving. The variables representing the numbers are called x, y, and z; x tells you how far something moves East, y tells you how far it moves North, and z tells you how far it moves upwards (in height). Combine the three numbers together and you get the total movement. For example, if x=3.0, y=3.0, and z=1.0, (which we'd normally write as (3.0, 3.0, 1.0) then you're moving 3 units East, 3 units North and rising upwards by 1 unit.

The significance of addition should be clear here. If you move first by the vector $(3.0, 3.0, 1.0)$ then you move by the vector $(2.0, -4.0, -4.0)$, the total amount you have moved can be worked out by adding the two vectors. Adding vectors means adding each component individually, so you get $(5.0, -1.0, -3.0)$. In this context, mathematicians will always write c=a+b, where a and b are the vectors and c is the result. We want to be able to use our Vector struct the same way.

The following is the definition for Vector – containing the member fields, constructors, and a ToString() override so we can easily view the contents of a Vector, and finally that operator overload:

```
namespace Wrox.ProCSharp.OOCSharp
{
    struct Vector
    {
        public double x, y, z;

        public Vector(double x, double y, double z)
        {
            this.x = x;
            this.y = y;
            this.z = z;
        }

        public Vector(Vector rhs)
        {
            x = rhs.x;
            y = rhs.y;
            z = rhs.z;
        }

        public override string ToString()
        {
            return "( " + x + " , " + y + " , " + z + " )";
        }
    }
```

Note that in order to keep things simple I've left the fields as public. I could have made them private and written corresponding properties to access them, but it wouldn't have made any difference to the example, other than to make the code a lot more complicated. Besides, for a simple struct like this, which to a large extent is just a grouping of the x, y, and z components, I think I can legitimately get away with keeping the fields public. Note that I have not supplied a default constructor, since it is not permitted for structs. Instead I've supplied two constructors that require the initial value of the vector to be specified, either by passing in the values of each component or by supplying another vector whose value can be copied.

Constructors like our second constructor, the one that takes just one argument, are often termed **copy constructors**, since they effectively allow you to initialize a class or struct instance by copying another instance.

Now let's have a closer look at the operator overload.

```
public static Vector operator + (Vector lhs, Vector rhs)
{
    Vector result = new Vector(lhs);
    result.x += rhs.x;
    result.y += rhs.y;
    result.z += rhs.z;
    return result;
}
    }
}
```

How does this work? The important syntax is in the declaration of the operator. It is declared in much the same way as a method, except the `operator` keyword tells the compiler it's actually an operator overload we're defining. `operator` is followed by the actual symbol for the relevant operator. The return type is whatever type you get when you use this operator. In our case, adding two `Vector`s gives us another `Vector`, so the return type is `Vector`. For this particular override of +, the return type is the same as the containing class, but that's not necessarily the case. Later on we'll define operators that return other types. The two parameters are the things you're operating on. For an operator that takes two parameters like "+", the first parameter is the object or value that goes on the left of the "+" sign, and the second parameter is the object or value that goes to the right of it.

Finally, note that the operator has been declared as `static`, which means that it is associated with the struct or class, not with any object, and so does not have access to a `this` pointer; C# requires that operator overloads are declared in this way. That's fine because the `lhs` and `rhs` parameters between them cover all the data the operator needs to know to perform its task.

Now we've dealt with the syntax for the operator + declaration, we can look at what happens inside the operator:

```
{
    Vector result = new Vector(lhs);
    result.x += rhs.x;
    result.y += rhs.y;
    result.z += rhs.z;
    return result;
}
```

This part of the code is exactly the same as if we were declaring a method, and you should easily be able to convince yourself that this really will return a vector containing the sum of `lhs` and `rhs` as defined above. We simply add the individual doubles `x`, `y`, and `z` individually.

Now all we need to do is write some simple test harness code to test our `Vector` struct. Here it is:

```
static void Main()
{
    Vector vect1, vect2, vect3;
    vect1 = new Vector(3.0, 3.0, 1.0);
    vect2 = new Vector(2.0, -4.0, -4.0);
```

```
        vect3 = vect1 + vect2;
        Console.WriteLine("vect1 = " + vect1.ToString());
        Console.WriteLine("vect2 = " + vect2.ToString());
        Console.WriteLine("vect3 = " + vect3.ToString());
    }
```

Saving this code as `Vectors.cs`, and compiling and running it gives this result:

```
Vectors
vect1 = ( 3 , 3 , 1 )
vect2 = ( 2 , -4 , -4 )
vect3 = ( 5 , -1 , -3 )
```

Adding More Overloads

Although the `Vectors` sample demonstrates in principle how you overload an operator, there's still not that much that we can do with the `Vector` struct. In real life, you can multiply vectors together, add and subtract them, and compare their values. In this section and the next we'll develop the sample by adding a few more operator overloads. Not the complete set that you'd probably need for a real and fully functional `Vector` type, but enough to demonstrate some other aspects of operator overloading. In the next section we'll see how to overload the process of comparing objects, but first, in this section we'll focus on more arithmetic operators. We'll overload multiplying vectors by a scalar and multiplying vectors together.

Multiplying a vector by a scalar simply means multiplying each component individually by the scalar: for example, 2 * (1.0, 2.5, 2.0) gives (2.0, 5.0, 4.0). The relevant operator overload looks like this:

```
    public static Vector operator * (double lhs, Vector rhs)
    {
        return new Vector(lhs * rhs.x, lhs * rhs.y, lhs * rhs.z);
    }
```

This by itself, however, is not sufficient. If a and b are declared as type `Vector`, it will allow us to write code like this:

```
b = 2 * a;
```

The compiler will implicitly convert the integer 2 to a `double` in order to match the operator overload signature. However, code like the following will not compile:

```
b = a * 2;
```

The thing is that the compiler treats operator overloads exactly like method overloads. It examines all the available overloads of a given operator to find the best match. The above statement requires the first parameter to be a `Vector` and the second parameter to be an integer, or something that an integer can be implicitly converted to. We have not provided such an overload. The compiler can't start swapping the order of parameters so the fact that we've provided an overload that takes a `double` followed by a `Vector` is not sufficient. We need to explicitly define an overload that takes a `Vector` followed by a `double` as well. There are two possible ways of implementing this. The first way involves explicitly breaking down the vector multiplication operation in the same way that we've done for all operators so far:

```
public static Vector operator * (Vector lhs, double rhs)
{
    return new Vector(rhs * lhs.x, rhs * lhs.y, rhs *1 hs.z);
}
```

Given that we've already written code to implement essentially the same operation, however, you might prefer to reuse that code by instead writing:

```
public static Vector operator * (Vector lhs, double rhs)
{
    return rhs * lhs;
}
```

This code works by effectively telling the compiler that if it sees a multiplication of a `Vector` by a `double`, it can simply reverse the parameters and call the other operator overload. Which you prefer is to some extent a matter of taste. In the actual sample code with this chapter we've gone for the second version, which looks neater and because we want to illustrate the idea in action. This version also makes for more maintainable code, since it saves duplicating the code to perform the multiplication in two separate overloads.

The next operator to be overloaded is `Vector` multiplication. In mathematics there are a couple of ways of multiplying vectors together, but the one we are interested in here is known as the **dot product** or **inner product**, and it actually gives a scalar as a result. That's the reason we're introducing that example, so that we can demonstrate that arithmetic operators don't have to return the same type as the class in which they are defined. In mathematical terms, if you have two vectors (x, y, z) and (X, Y, Z), then the inner product is defined to be the value of $x*X + y*Y + z*Z$. That might look like a strange way to multiply two things together, but it's actually very useful, since it can be used to calculate various other quantities. Certainly, if you ever end up writing any code that displays any complex 3D graphics, for example using Direct3D or DirectDraw, you'll almost certainly find your code needs to work out inner products of vectors quite often as an intermediate step in calculating where to place objects on the screen. At any rate, what concerns us here is that we want people to be able to write `double X = a*b` where `a` and `b` are vectors and what they intend is for the dot product to be calculated. The relevant overload looks like this:

```
public static double operator * (Vector lhs, Vector rhs)
{
    return lhs.x * rhs.x + lhs.y * rhs.y + lhs.z * rhs.z;
}
```

Now, we've defined the arithmetic operators, we can check that they work fine using a simple test harness routine:

```
static void Main()
{
    // stuff to demonstrate arithmetic operations
    Vector vect1, vect2, vect3;
    vect1 = new Vector(1.0, 1.5, 2.0);
    vect2 = new Vector(0.0, 0.0, -10.0);
    vect3 = vect1 + vect2;
    Console.WriteLine("vect1 = " + vect1);
```

```
Console.WriteLine("vect2 = " + vect2);
Console.WriteLine("vect3 = vect1 + vect2 = " + vect3);
Console.WriteLine("2*vect3 = " + 2*vect3);
vect3 += vect2;
Console.WriteLine("vect3+=vect2 gives " + vect3);
vect3 = vect1*2;
Console.WriteLine("Setting vect3=vect1*2 gives " + vect3);
double dot = vect1*vect3;
Console.WriteLine("vect1*vect3 = " + dot);
}
```

Running this code (`Vectors2.cs`) produces this result:

```
Vectors2
vect1 = ( 1 , 1.5 , 2 )
vect2 = ( 0 , 0 , -10 )
vect3 = vect1 + vect2 = ( 1 , 1.5 , -8 )
2*vect3 = ( 2 , 3 , -16 )
vect3+=vect2 gives ( 1 , 1.5 , -18 )
Setting vect3=vect1*2 gives ( 2 , 3 , 4 )
vect1*vect3 = 14.5
```

This shows that the operator overloads have given us the correct results, but if you look at the test harness code closely, you might be surprised to notice that we've actually sneakily used an operator that we hadn't overloaded – the addition assignment operator "+=":

```
vect3 += vect2;
Console.WriteLine("vect3 += vect2 gives " + vect3);
```

Amazingly, it gave us the correct result! So what's going on? Although += normally counts as a single operator, it really can be broken down into two steps – the addition and the assignment. Unlike C++, C# won't actually allow you to overload the = operator, but if you overload +, the compiler will automatically use your overload of + to work out how to carry out a += operation. The same principle works for the ++ operator, and for -=, --, *=, and /= (although in order for these operators to work, you'll need to have respectively overloaded the -, *, and / operators). For a struct, C# always interprets assignment as meaning just copy the contents of the memory where the struct is stored, while for a class C# always copies just the reference.

Overloading the Comparison Operators

There are six comparison operators in C#, and they come in three pairs:

- ❑ == and !=
- ❑ > and <
- ❑ >= and <=

The significance of the pairing is twofold. First, within each pair, the second operator should always give exactly the opposite (Boolean) result to the first (whenever the first returns true, the second returns false, and vice versa), and second, C# always requires you to overload the operators in pairs. If you overload "==", then you must overload "!=" too, otherwise you get a compiler error.

In the case of overriding $==$ and $!=$, you should strictly also override the Equals() method which all classes and structs inherit from System.Object; you'll get a compiler warning if you don't. However, we'll ignore that for now, since we're not covering System.Object in detail until Chapter 5.

One other restriction is that the comparison operators must return a bool. This is the fundamental difference between these operators and the arithmetic ones. The result of adding or subtracting two quantities, for example, might theoretically be any type depending on the quantities. We've already seen that multiplying two Vectors can be understood to give a scalar. Another example involves the .NET base class, System.DateTime, which we've briefly encountered. It's possible to subtract two DateTimes, but the result is not a DateTime, instead it is a System.TimeSpan instance. By contrast, it doesn't really make much sense for a comparison to return anything other than a bool.

Apart from these differences, overloading the comparison operators follows the same principles as overloading the arithmetic operators. Comparing quantities isn't always as simple as you'd think, however, as the example we use will illustrate. We're going to override the == and != operators for our Vector class. Let's start off with ==. Here's our implementation of ==:

```
public static bool operator == (Vector lhs, Vector rhs)
{
    if (lhs.x == rhs.x && lhs.y == rhs.y && lhs.z == rhs.z)
        return true;
    else
        return false;
}
```

This approach simply compared vectors for equality based on the values of their components. For most structs, that is probably what you will want to do, though in some cases you may need to think carefully about what you mean by equality. For example, if there are embedded classes, should you simply compare whether the references point to the same object (**shallow comparison**) or whether the values of the objects are the same (**deep comparison**)?

We also need to override the != operator. The simple way to do it is like this:

```
public static bool operator != (Vector lhs, Vector rhs)
{
    return ! (lhs == rhs);
}
```

As usual, we'll quickly check that our override works with a test harness. This time we'll define three Vectors, two of which are close enough that they should count as equal, and compare all the vectors:

```
static void Main()
{
    Vector vect1, vect2, vect3;
    vect1 = new Vector(3.0, 3.0, -10.0);
    vect2 = new Vector(3.0, 3.0, -10.0);
    vect3 = new Vector(2.0, 3.0, 6.0);
    Console.WriteLine("vect1==vect2 returns    " + (vect1==vect2));
    Console.WriteLine("vect1==vect3 returns    " + (vect1==vect3));
    Console.WriteLine("vect2==vect3 returns    " + (vect2==vect3));
```

```
            Console.WriteLine();
            Console.WriteLine("vect1!=vect2 returns  " + (vect1!=vect2));
            Console.WriteLine("vect1!=vect3 returns  " + (vect1!=vect3));
            Console.WriteLine("vect2!=vect3 returns  " + (vect2!=vect3));
      }
```

Compiling and running this code, (the `Vectors3.cs` sample in the code download) produces these results at the command line, which demonstrates the correct results. Notice also the compiler warning because we haven't overridden `Equals()` for our `Vector`. For our purposes here, that doesn't matter.

csc Vectors3.cs
```
Microsoft (R) Visual C# .NET Compiler version 7.00.9466
for Microsoft (R) .NET Framework version 1.0.3705
Copyright (C) Microsoft Corporation 2001. All rights reserved.

Vectors3.cs(5,11): warning CS0660: 'Wrox.ProCSharp.OOCSharp.Vector' defines
          operator == or operator != but does not override Object.Equals(object o)
Vectors3.cs(5,11): warning CS0661: 'Wrox.ProCSharp.OOCSharp.Vector' defines
          operator == or operator != but does not override Object.GetHashCode()
```

Vectors3
```
vect1==vect2 returns   True
vect1==vect3 returns   False
vect2==vect3 returns   False

vect1!=vect2 returns   False
vect1!=vect3 returns   True
vect2!=vect3 returns   True
```

Which Operators Can You Overload?

There are quite a number of operators in C#, some of which you can overload, and some of which you can't. Operators that you are allowed to overload include:

Category	Operators	Restrictions
Arithmetic binary	+, *, /, -, %	none
Arithmetic unary	+, -, ++, --	none
Bitwise binary	&, |, ^, <<, >>	none
Bitwise unary	!, ~, true, false	none
Comparison	==, !=, >=, <, <=, >	must be overloaded in pairs

This list leaves some gaps, but the gaps are there for logical reasons. A number of operators cannot be overloaded explicitly, but are evaluated in terms of other operators that can be overloaded. This includes the arithmetic and bitwise assignment operators +=, -=, *=, /=, >>=, <<=, %=, &=, |=, and ^=, as well as the conditional logical operators && and || (these last operators are evaluated using & and |). C++ developers will be surprised to learn that [] and () cannot be overloaded. The reason is that C# achieves the same functionality by other means: using indexers in place of [] overloading, and user-defined casts in place of () overloading; we cover user-defined casts in the next chapter.

Indexers

Indexers share with properties the fact that they are not really an essential part of object-oriented programming. Rather, they represent a syntactical convenience that allows certain classes to be used in a more intuitive manner. In the case of indexers, the convenience they allow is for you to access an object as if it was an array.

*C++ developers should note that indexers in C# serve the same purpose as overriding the []
operator in C++. The concept of an indexer may be new to Java and VB developers, however.*

Adding an Indexer to Vector

We're going to continue using our Vector struct as an example to demonstrate the use of indexers. As with operator overloads, indexers work in the same way for structs and classes, so the fact that we happen to be using a struct for our example is not significant.

Up to now we've referred to the components of our Vector struct with their names x, y, and z. The trouble is that mathematicians often prefer to treat vectors as if they are arrays, with x being the first element, y the second, and z the third. In other words, in order to set the x-component they will tend to write:

```
MyVector[0] = 3.6;
```

If we can treat Vectors as arrays then we should also be able to do things like iterate through the components:

```
for(int i = 0; i < 3; i++)
{
    vect2[i] = i;
}
```

With our current definition of Vector, these code snippets will produce a compile-time error, since the compiler won't understand what we mean by the first-element of a Vector. Indexers are a way of solving that. If you define an indexer for a class, you are telling the compiler what to do if it encounters code in which a class instance is being treated as if it were an array.

Indexers are defined in pretty much the same way as properties, with get and set accessors. The main difference is that the name of the indexer is the keyword this. To define an indexer for the Vector struct, we modify the strut definition as follows:

```
struct Vector
{
    public double x, y, z;

    public double this [int i]
    {
        get
        {
            switch (i)
```

```
        {
            case 0:
                return x;
            case 1:
                return y;
            case 2:
                return z;
            default:
                throw new IndexOutOfRangeException(
                        "Attempt to retrieve Vector element " + i) ;
        }
    }
    set
    {
        switch (i)
        {
            case 0:
                x = value;
                break;
            case 1:
                y = value;
                break;
            case 2:
                z = value;
                break;
            default:
                throw new IndexOutOfRangeException(
                        "Attempt to set Vector element " + i);
        }
    }
}
// etc.
```

There's a fair bit of new stuff in this code. To start with, let's look at the line that declares the indexer:

```
public double this [int i]
```

This line basically says that we want to be able to treat each Vector instance as a one-dimensional array with an int as the index (or, equivalently in this case, the parameter), and that when we do so the return type is a double. Indexers actually give us quite a lot of freedom – we can use any data type as the index, though the types you'll most often want to use are the integer types and string. Similarly, you can use whatever data type you think most appropriate for the return type.

Within the body of our indexer, we have the same get and set accessors that you see for properties. If we wanted to make our indexer read-only or write-only, we could do so by leaving out the appropriate accessor. The syntax for the accessors follows precisely that which is used when you define properties, except that we now have accessors to whatever variables we defined as the parameters to the indexer (recall that property get and set accessors never take any explicit parameters). The get accessor must return the type we have declared the indexer as returning, while the set accessor must not return anything, and has access to an additional implicit parameter, value, whose data type is the type we declared the indexer as (double in this case), and which is initialized as the value on the right-hand side of the assignment operator we use the indexer expression in.

Beyond that, the code should be self-explanatory to the extent that we simply use the parameter passed in to determine which of the components of the `Vector` should be accessed, and either return or set the appropriate field. Notice, however, that the `switch` statements also each have a `default` case to handle the situation in which the indexer is called with an inappropriate value for the parameter. The action taken in this case is to throw an exception:

```
throw new IndexOutOfRangeException(
                         "Attempt to retrieve Vector element " + i);
```

We haven't yet encountered exceptions – those will be covered in the next chapter. They are the way that you deal with unexpected error conditions in C#, and up to now in this chapter I've carefully avoided any error checking in any of the examples, precisely because we haven't yet covered exceptions. For an indexer, however, you can't really get away without checking that the index passed in is within the appropriate bounds – for our `Vector` class, 0 to 2. So for the time being I'll just ask you to accept that the line above is the way you'd handle an index out of bounds. What it actually should do is cause execution to jump to a special area of code that you'll ideally have written and marked as responsible for handling this particular error situation. Since we haven't written any such code yet, this statement will instead cause program execution to terminate.

Now we've added our indexer, let's try it out:

```
static void Main()
{
    Vector vect1 = new Vector(1.0, -5.0, 4.6);
    Vector vect2 = new Vector();
    Console.WriteLine("vect1 = " + vect1);
    Console.WriteLine("vect1[1] = " + vect1[1]);

    for(int i = 0; i < 3; i++)
    {
        vect2[i] = i;
    }
    Console.WriteLine("vect2 = " + vect2);
```

Note that in this example (`VectorWithIndexer`) we are demonstrating using a `for` loop to index the components of the `Vector`.

> *Although we are able to use* for, do, *and* while *loops with indexers, we cannot write a loop that uses* foreach. *The* foreach *statement works in a different way, treating the item as a collection rather than an array. It's possible to set up a class or struct so it acts as a collection, but that involves implementing certain interfaces rather than indexers. We'll show how to do this in Chapter 5.*

This is the result:

```
VectorWithIndexer
vect1 = ( 1 , -5 , 4.6 )
vect1[1] = -5
vect2 = ( 0 , 1 , 2 )
```

It is also possible to verify that our exception handling code does trap an out-of-bound index. If we try to access the `Vector` like this:

```
double tryThis = vect1[6];
```

Then our console application terminates and this dialog is displayed:

```
VectorWithIndexer
vect1 = ( 1 , -5 , 4.6 )
vect1[1] = -5


Unhandled Exception: System.IndexOutOfRangeException: Attempt
to retrieve Vector element 6
   at Wrox.ProCSharp.OOCSharp.Vector.get_Item(Int32 i)
   at Wrox.ProCSharp.OOCSharp.Vector.Main()
```

In the next chapter, we'll see how to handle exceptions so that you can determine what action your program takes, rather than simply terminating.

Other Indexer Examples

Indexers are extremely flexible. They are not, for example confined to one-dimensional arrays. We can treat classes and structs as multidimensional arrays as well, just by adding more than one parameter inside the square brackets. We can also overload indexers – a struct or class can have as many indexers as you want, provided they have different numbers or types of parameters.

One example to illustrate this would be that if we'd wanted to write that `Matrix` class, we'd probably want to be able to treat it as a 2D array of `doubles`. Not only that, but mathematicians would regard any individual row of the matrix as a vector. We won't actually work through the example, but in principle we could achieve this by defining two indexers like this:

```
// for struct Matrix
public double this [uint i, uint j]
public Vector this [uint i]
```

Another common use for indexers is to be able to access a part of a class or struct in a way that is described by a string. This means that you can have an array or some data structure that has named elements (although in this case, you might prefer to use a dictionary, as described in Chapter 5):

```
// for a class, ListOfCustomers
public Customer this[string Name]

// in client code
Customer nextCustomer = CustomerList["Simon Robinson"]
```

A useful variation of this is to access elements using an enumerated value.

Indeed, indexers are most commonly used for classes that represent some data structure, such as an array, a list, or a map, and are defined for the .NET base classes that represent these structures, which we'll examine in Chapter 5.

Summary

In this chapter we have examined some of the features that C# offers that make writing classes and objects easier and allow them to have a more intuitive syntax. We also looked at how C# handles its memory management internally. This information is useful if we are to write high–performance code. We have examined how constructors and destructors allow you to specify how your objects should be initialized and what action, if any, should be taken to clean up resources when they are destroyed. We've considered how performance can sometimes be improved by defining structs instead of classes, and we've examined the syntactical convenience that is provided by operator overloads, indexers, and method overloads.

In the next chapter we look at some advanced C# programming topics, including exception and event handling.

4

Advanced C# Topics

At this point, we have covered all the basics of C# syntax as well as object-oriented programming in C#. We have in effect, learned enough to be able to use C# to write well-designed object-oriented programs. However, we haven't yet completed our coverage of the C# language, because C# also offers a number of more advanced features that can be extremely useful in some circumstances. Those features are what we will be looking at over the next two chapters.

The C# language relies extensively on its interaction with the .NET Framework and the base classes. In this chapter we will focus more on those advanced features that are predominantly part of the language itself, and in the next chapter, we will examine the topics for which support is provided mainly through the base classes, with minimal help from the C# language syntax.

The topics that we cover in this chapter are:

❑ **Errors and exception handling** – C#'s mechanism for handling error conditions, which allows us to provide custom handling for each type of error condition, and also to cleanly separate the code that identifies errors from the code that handles them.

❑ **User-defined casts** – Defining casts between your own classes.

❑ **Delegates** – The way in which C# allows code to refer to a method, without specifying which method is being referred to until run-time.

❑ **Events** – Notifying code when a particular action takes place, for example when the user clicks a mouse button.

❑ **The C# preprocessor** – A look at the advantages of preprocessing just before compilation.

❑   **Attributes** – A technique for marking items in your code that are of interest in some way.

❑   **Memory management under the hood** – We look under the hood at the heap and the stack and how value and reference variables are stored and the performance implications.

❑   **Unsafe code** – Declaring blocks of code as 'unsafe' in order to obtain direct memory access.

Errors and Exception Handling

No matter how good your coding is, your programs will always have to be able to handle possible errors. For example, in the middle of some complex processing your code discovers that it doesn't have permission to read a file, or while it is sending network requests the network goes down. In such exceptional situations, it is not enough for a method to simply return an appropriate error code – there might be 15 or 20 nested method calls, so what you really need the program to do is jump back up through all those 15 or 20 calls in order to exit the task completely and sort out the mess. C# has very good facilities to handle this kind of situation, through the mechanism known as **exception handling**.

> *Error handling facilities in VB are very restricted, and is essentially limited to the* On Error GoTo *statement. If you are coming from a VB background, you will find C# exceptions open up a whole new world of error handling in your programs. On the other hand, Java and C++ developers will be familiar with the principle of exceptions since these languages also handle errors in a similar way to C#. Developers using C++ are sometimes wary of exceptions because of possible C++ performance implications, but this is not the case in C#. Using exceptions in C# code does not in general adversely affect performance in any way.*

Exception Classes

In C#, an exception is an object created (or **thrown**) when a particular exceptional error condition occurs. This object contains information that should help track down the problem. Although we can create our own exception classes (and we will be doing so later), .NET provides us with many predefined exception classes too.

Base Class Exception Classes

In this section, we will do a quick survey of some of the exceptions that are available in the base classes. There are a large number of exception classes that Microsoft has defined, and it is not possible to provide anything like an exhaustive list here. This class hierarchy diagram shows a few of them, however, in order to give a flavor of the general pattern:

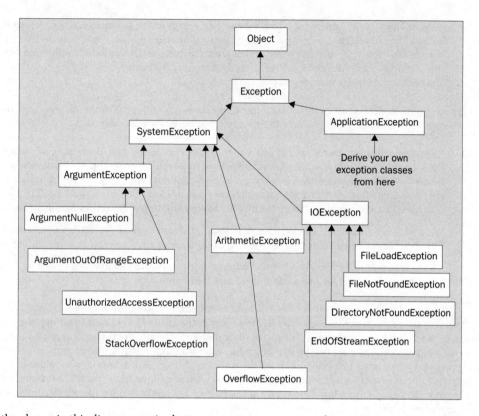

All the classes in this diagram are in the System namespace, apart from IOException and the classes derived from IOException. These are in the namespace System.IO, which deals with reading and writing data to files. In general, there is no specific namespace for exceptions; exception classes should be placed in whatever namespace is appropriate to the classes that they could be generated by – hence IO-related exceptions are in the System.IO namespace, and you will find exception classes in quite a few of the base class namespaces.

The generic exception class, System.Exception is derived from System.Object, as we would expect for a .NET class. In general, you should not throw generic System.Exception objects from your code, because they give no idea of the specifics of the error condition.

There are two important classes in the hierarchy that are derived from System.Exception.

❑ System.SystemException – This is for exceptions that are usually thrown by the .NET runtime, or which are considered of a very generic nature and may be thrown by almost any application. As examples, StackOverflowException will be thrown by the .NET runtime if it detects the stack is full. On the other hand, you might choose to throw ArgumentException, or its subclasses in your own code, if you detect that a method has been called with inappropriate arguments. Subclasses of System.SystemException include ones that represent both fatal and non-fatal errors.

❑ System.ApplicationException – This class is important, because it is the intended base for any class of exception defined by third parties (in other words, organizations other than Microsoft). Hence, if you define any exceptions covering error conditions unique to your application, you should derive these directly or indirectly from System.ApplicationException.

We are not going to discuss all of the other exception classes shown in the diagram, since, for the most part, their purposes should be clear from their names, but here is a small selection:

❑ As just mentioned, StackOverflowException occurs if the area of memory allocated to the stack becomes completely full. A stack overflow can occur if a method continuously calls itself recursively. This is generally a fatal error, since it prevents your application from doing anything apart from terminating (in which case it is unlikely that even the finally block will execute). There is usually little point in your attempting to handle errors like this yourself.

❑ We will cover streams in Chapter 12. A **stream** represents a flow of data between data sources. The usual cause of an EndOfStreamException is an attempt to read past the end of a file.

❑ An OverflowException is what will happen if for example you attempt to cast an int containing a value of –40 to a uint in a checked context.

The class hierarchy for exceptions is somewhat unusual in that most of these classes do not add any functionality to their respective base classes. However, in the case of exception handling, the usual reason for adding inherited classes is simply to indicate more specific error conditions, and there is often no need to override methods or add any new ones (although it is not uncommon to add extra properties that carry extra information about the error condition). For example, you might have a base ArgumentException class intended for method calls where inappropriate values are passed in, and an ArgumentNullException class derived from this, which is intended to be specifically for when a null argument is passed.

Catching Exceptions

Given that we have these predefined base class exception objects available to us, how do we make use of them in our code to trap error conditions? In order to deal with possible error conditions in C# code, you will normally divide the relevant part of your program into blocks of three different types:

❑ try blocks contain code that forms part of the normal operation of your program, but which might encounter some serious error conditions

❑ catch blocks contain the code that deals with the various error conditions

❑ finally blocks contain the code that cleans up any resources or takes any other action that you will normally want done at the end of a try or catch block. It is important to understand that the finally block is executed whether or not any exception is thrown. Since the aim is that the finally block contains cleanup code that should always be executed, the compiler will flag an error if you place a return statement inside a finally block.

So how do these blocks fit together to trap error conditions? Here's how:

1. The execution flow enters a `try` block.

2. If no errors occur, execution proceeds normally through the `try` block, and when the end of the `try` block is reached, the flow of execution jumps to the `finally` block (Step 5). However, if an error occurs within the `try` block, execution jumps to a `catch` block (next step).

3. The error condition is handled in the `catch` block.

4. At the end of the `catch` block, execution automatically transfers to the `finally` block.

5. The `finally` block is executed.

The C# syntax used to bring all this about looks roughly like this:

```
try
{
    // code for normal execution
}
catch
{
    // error handling
}
finally
{
    // clean up
}
```

Actually, there are a few variations on this theme:

❑   You can omit the `finally` block.

❑   You can also supply as many `catch` blocks as you want to handle different types of error.

❑   You can omit the `catch` blocks altogether, in which case the syntax serves not to identify exceptions, but as a way of guaranteeing that code in the `finally` block will be executed when execution leaves the `try` block. This is useful if there are several exit points in the `try` block.

So far so good, but this leaves the question: if the code is running in the `try` block, how does it know to switch to the `catch` block if an error has occurred? If an error is detected, the code does something that is known as **throwing an exception**. In other words, it instantiates an exception object class and throws it:

```
throw new OverflowException();
```

Here we have instantiated an exception object of the `OverflowException` class. As soon as the computer encounters a `throw` statement inside a `try` block, it immediately looks for the `catch` block associated with that `try` block. If there is more than one `catch` block associated with the `try` block, it identifies the correct `catch` block by checking which exception class the `catch` block is associated with. For example, when the `OverflowException` object is thrown, execution will jump to the following `catch` block:

```
catch (OverflowException e)
{
```

In other words, the computer looks for the `catch` block that indicates a matching exception class instance of the same class (or of a base class).

With this extra information, we can expand out the `try` block we have just demonstrated. Let's assume, for the sake of argument, that there are two possible serious errors that can occur in it: an overflow and an array out of bounds. We will assume that our code contains two Boolean variables, `Overflow` and `OutOfBounds`, which indicate whether these conditions exist. We have already seen that a predefined exception class exists to indicate overflow (`OverflowException`); similarly, an `IndexOutOfRangeException` class exists to handle an array out-of-bounds.

Now our `try` block looks like this:

```
try
{
    // code for normal execution

    if (Overflow == true)
        throw new OverflowException();

    // more processing

    if (OutOfBounds == true)
        throw new IndexOutOfRangeException();

    // otherwise continue normal execution
}
catch (OverflowException e)
{
    // error handling for the overflow error condition
}
catch (IndexOutOfRangeException e)
{
    // error handling for the index out of range error condition
}
finally
{
    // clean up
}
```

So far, this might not look like we have achieved much that you can't do with VB's `On Error GoTo`, beyond the fact that we have more cleanly separated the different parts of the code. In fact, we have here a far more powerful and flexible mechanism for error handling.

This is because we can have `throw` statements that are nested in several method calls inside the `try` block, but the same `try` block continues to apply even as execution flow enters these other methods. If the computer encounters a `throw` statement, it immediately goes back up through all the method calls on the stack, looking for the end of the containing `try` block and the start of the appropriate `catch` block. As it does so, all the local variables in the intermediate method calls will correctly go out of scope. This makes the `try...catch` architecture beautifully suited to the situation we described at the beginning of this section, where the error occurs inside a method call that is nested inside 15 or 20 method calls, and processing has to stop immediately.

As you can probably gather from the above discussion, `try` blocks can play a very significant part in controlling the flow of execution of your code. However, it is important to understand that exceptions are intended for exceptional conditions, hence their name. It would be considered very bad programming style to, for example, use exceptions as a way of controlling when to exit a `do...while` loop.

Implementing Multiple catch Blocks

The easiest way to see how `try...catch...finally` blocks work in practice is with a couple of examples. Our first example is called `SimpleExceptions`. It repeatedly asks the user to type in a number and displays it. However, for the sake of this example, we will imagine that the number needs to be between 0 and 5, or the program won't be able to process the number properly. Therefore we will throw an exception if the user types in something anything outside this range.

The program continues to ask for more numbers to be processed until the user simply hits the *Enter* key without entering anything.

> *You should note that this code does **not** provide a good example of when to use exception handling. As we have already indicated, the idea of exceptions is that they are provided for exceptional circumstances. Users are always typing in silly things, so this situation doesn't really count. Normally, your program will handle incorrect user input by performing an instant check and asking the user to retype the input if there is a problem. However, generating exceptional situations is difficult in a small sample that you can read through in a few minutes! So, we will tolerate this bad practice for now in order to demonstrate how exceptions would work. The examples that follow will present more realistic situations.*

The code for `SimpleExceptions` looks like this:

```
using System;

namespace Wrox.ProCSharp.AdvancedCSharp
{
    public class MainEntryPoint
    {
        public static void Main()
        {
            string userInput;
            while ( true )
            {
                try
                {
                    Console.Write("Input a number between 0 and 5 " +
```

```
                    "(or just hit return to exit)> ");
            userInput = Console.ReadLine();
            if (userInput == "")
                break;
            int index = Convert.ToInt32(userInput);
            if (index < 0 || index > 5)
                throw new IndexOutOfRangeException(
                    "You typed in " + userInput);
            Console.WriteLine("Your number was " + index);
        }
        catch (IndexOutOfRangeException e)
        {
            Console.WriteLine("Exception: " +
                "Number should be between 0 and 5. " + e.Message);
        }
        catch (Exception e)
        {
            Console.WriteLine(
                "An exception was thrown. Message was: " + e.Message);
        }
        catch
        {
            Console.WriteLine("Some other exception has occurred");
        }
        finally
        {
            Console.WriteLine("Thank you");
        }
    }
}
}
```

The core of this code is a `while` loop, which continually uses `Console.ReadLine()` to ask for user input. `ReadLine()` returns a string, so the first thing we do is convert it to an `int` using the `System.Convert.ToInt32()` method. The `System.Convert` class contains various useful methods to perform data conversions, and provides an alternative to the `int.Parse()` method. In general, `System.Convert` contains methods to perform various type conversions. Recall that the C# compiler resolves `int` to instances of the `System.Int32` base class.

> *It is also worth pointing out that the parameter passed to the `catch` block is scoped to that `catch` block – which is why we are able to use the same parameter name, e, in successive `catch` blocks in the above code.*

In the above code, we also check for an empty string, since this is our condition for exiting the `while` loop. Notice how the `break` statement actually breaks right out of the enclosing `try` block as well as the `while` loop – this is valid. Of course, as execution breaks out of the `try` block, the `Console.WriteLine()` statement in the `finally` block gets executed. Although we just display a greeting here, more commonly, you will be doing tasks like closing file handles and calling the `Dispose()` method of various objects in order to perform any cleaning up. Once the computer leaves the `finally` block, it simply carries on execution at the next statement that it would have executed, had the `finally` block not been present. In this case, we iterate back to the start of the `while` loop, and enter the `try` block again (unless the `finally` was entered as a result of executing the `break` statement in the `while` loop, in which case we simply exit the `while` loop).

Next, we check for our exception condition:

```
if (index < 0 || index > 5)
    throw new IndexOutOfRangeException("You typed in " + userInput);
```

When throwing an exception, we need to choose what type of exception to throw. Although the class `System.Exception` is available, it is really intended as a base class and it is considered bad programming practice actually to throw an instance of this class as an exception, because it conveys no information about the nature of the error condition. Instead, Microsoft has defined many other exception classes that are derived from `System.Exception`. Each of these matches a particular type of exception condition, and you are free to define your own ones too. The idea is that you give as much information as possible about the particular exception condition by throwing an instance of a class that matches the particular error condition. In this, case we have picked `System.IndexOutOfRangeException` as the best choice in the circumstances. `IndexOutOfRangeException` has several constructor overloads. The one we have chosen takes a string, which describes the error. Alternatively, we might choose to derive our own custom `Exception` object that describes the error condition in the context of our application.

Suppose the user then types in a number that is not between 0 and 5. This will be picked up by the `if` statement and an `IndexOutOfRangeException` object will be instantiated and thrown. At this point the computer will immediately exit the `try` block and hunt for a `catch` block that handles `IndexOutOfRangeException`. The first `catch` block it comes to is this:

```
catch (IndexOutOfRangeException e)
{
    Console.WriteLine(
        "Exception: Number should be between 0 and 5." + e.Message);
}
```

Since this `catch` block takes a parameter of the appropriate class, this will be passed the exception instance and executed. In this case, we display an error message and the `Exception.Message` property (which corresponds to the string we passed to `IndexOutOfRange's` constructor). After executing this `catch` block, control switches to the `finally` block, just as if no exception had occurred.

Notice that we have also provided another `catch` block:

```
catch (Exception e)
{
    Console.WriteLine("An exception was thrown. Message was: " + e.Message);
}
```

This `catch` block would also be capable of handling an `IndexOutOfRangeException` if it weren't for the fact that such exceptions will already have been caught by the previous `catch` block – a reference to a base class can also refer to any instances of classes derived from it, and all exceptions are derived from `System.Exception`. So why doesn't this `catch` block get executed? The answer is that the computer executes only the first suitable `catch` block it finds. So why is this second `catch` block here? Well, it is not only our code that is covered by the `try` block; inside the block, we actually make three separate calls to methods in the `System` namespace (`Console.ReadLine()`, `Console.Write()`, and `Convert.ToInt32()`), and any of these methods might throw an exception.

177

If we type in something that's not a number – say a or `hello`, then the `Convert.ToInt32()` method will throw an exception of the class `System.FormatException`, to indicate that the string passed into `ToInt32()` is not in a format that can be converted to an `int`. When this happens, the computer will trace back through the method calls, looking for a handler that can handle this exception. Our first `catch` block (the one that takes an `IndexOutOfRangeException`) won't do. The computer then looks at the second `catch` block. This one will do because `FormatException` is derived from `Exception`, so a `FormatException` instance can be passed in as a parameter here.

The structure of our example is actually fairly typical of a situation with multiple `catch` blocks. We start off with `catch` blocks that are designed to trap very specific error conditions. Then, we finish with more general blocks that will cover any errors for which we have not written specific error handlers. Indeed, the order of the `catch` blocks is important. If we had written the above two blocks in the opposite order, the code would not have compiled, because the second `catch` block is unreachable (the `Exception` catch block would catch all exceptions).

However, we have a third `catch` block in our code too:

```
catch
{
    Console.WriteLine("Some other exception has occurred");
}
```

This is the most general `catch` block of all – it doesn't take any parameter. The reason this `catch` block is here is to catch exceptions thrown by other code that isn't written in C#, or isn't even managed code at all. You see, it is a requirement of the C# language that only instances of classes that are derived from `System.Exception` can be thrown as exceptions, but other languages might not have this restriction – C++ for example allows any variable whatsoever to be thrown as an exception. If your code calls into libraries or assemblies that have been written in other languages, then it may find an exception has been thrown that is not derived from `System.Exception`, although in many cases, the .NET `PInvoke` mechanism will trap these exceptions and convert them into .NET `Exception` objects. However, there is not that much that this `catch` block can do, because we have no idea what class the exception might represent.

For our particular example, there is probably not much point adding this catch-all `catch` handler. Doing this is useful if you are directly calling into some other libraries that are not .NET-aware and which might throw exceptions. However, we have included it in our example to illustrate the principle.

Now that we have analyzed the code for the example, we can run it. The following screenshot illustrates what happens with different inputs, and demonstrates both the `IndexOutOfRangeException` and the `FormatException` being thrown:

```
SimpleExceptions
Input a number between 0 and 5 (or just hit return to exit)> 4
Your number was 4
Thank you
Input a number between 0 and 5 (or just hit return to exit)> 0
Your number was 0
Thank you
Input a number between 0 and 5 (or just hit return to exit)> 10
Exception: Number should be between 0 and 5. You typed in 10
```

```
Thank you
Input a number between 0 and 5 (or just hit return to exit)> hello
An exception was thrown. Message was: Input string was not in a correct format.
Thank you
Input a number between 0 and 5 (or just hit return to exit)>
Thank you
```

Catching Exceptions from Other Code

In our previous example, we have demonstrated the handling of two exceptions. One of them, `IndexOutOfRangeException`, was thrown by our own code. The other, `FormatException`, was thrown from inside one of the base classes. It is actually very common for code in a library to throw an exception if it detects that some problem has occurred, or if one of the methods has been called inappropriately by being passed the wrong parameters. However, library code rarely attempts to catch exceptions; this is regarded as the responsibility of the client code.

Often, you will find that exceptions get thrown from the base class libraries while you are debugging. The process of debugging to some extent involves determining why exceptions have been thrown and removing the causes. Your aim should be to ensure that by the time the code is actually shipped, exceptions really do only occur in very exceptional circumstances, and if possible, are handled in some appropriate way in your code.

System.Exception Properties

In our example, we have only illustrated the use of one property, `Message`, of the exception object. However, a number of other properties are available in `System.Exception`:

Property	Description
HelpLink	A link to a help file that provides more information about the exception.
Message	Text that describes the error condition.
Source	The name of the application or object that caused the exception.
StackTrace	Details of the method calls on the stack (to help track down the method that threw the exception).
TargetSite	A .NET reflection object that describes the method that threw the exception
InnerException	If this exception was thrown inside a `catch` block, it contains the exception object that sent the code into that `catch` block.

Of these properties, `StackTrace` and `TargetSite` are supplied automatically by the .NET runtime if a stack trace is available. `Source` will always be filled in by the .NET runtime as the name of the assembly in which the exception was raised (though you might wish to modify the property in your code to give more specific information), while `Message`, `HelpLink`, and `InnerException` must be filled in by the code that threw the exception, by setting these properties immediately before throwing the exception. So, for example, the code to throw an exception might look something like this:

```
if (ErrorCondition == true)
{
    Exception myException = new ClassmyException("Help!!!!");
    myException.Source = "My Application Name";
```

```
    myException.HelpLink = "MyHelpFile.txt";
    throw myException;
}
```

Here, `ClassMyException` is the name of the particular exception class you are throwing. Note that it is usual practice for the names of all exception classes to end with `Exception`.

What Happens if an Exception isn't Handled?

Sometimes an exception might be thrown, but there might not be a `catch` block in your code that is able to handle that kind of exception. Our `SimpleExceptions` example can serve to illustrate this. Suppose, for example, we omitted the `FormatException` and catch-all `catch` blocks, and only supplied the block that traps an `IndexOutOfRangeException`. In that event, what would happen if a `FormatException` got thrown?

The answer is that the .NET runtime would catch it. Later in this section we will see how it is possible to nest `try` blocks, and in fact, there is already a nested `try` block behind the scenes in the sample. The .NET runtime has effectively placed our entire program inside another huge `try` block – it does this for every .NET program. This `try` block has a `catch` handler that can catch any type of exception. If an exception occurs that your code doesn't handle, then the execution flow will simply pass right out of your program and get trapped by this `catch` block in the .NET runtime. However, the results probably won't be what you wanted. It means execution of your code will be promptly terminated and the user will get presented with a dialog box that complains that your code hasn't handled the exception, as well as any details about the exception the .NET runtime was able to retrieve. At least the exception will have been caught though! This is what actually happened in Chapter 3 in the `Vector` example when our program threw an exception.

In general, if you are writing an executable, you should try to catch as many exceptions as you reasonably can, and handle them in a sensible way. If you are writing a library, it is normally best not to handle exceptions (unless a particular exception represents something wrong in your code which you can handle), but to assume instead that the calling code will handle them. However, you may nevertheless want to catch any Microsoft-defined exceptions, so that you can throw your own exception objects that give more specific information to the client code.

Nested try Blocks

One nice feature of exceptions is that it is possible to nest `try` blocks inside each other, like this:

```
try
{
    // Point A
    try
    {
        // Point B
    }
    catch
    {
        // Point C
    }
    finally
    {
        // clean up
```

```
    }
    // Point D
}
catch
{
    // error handling
}
finally
{
    // clean up
}
```

Although each `try` block is only accompanied by one `catch` block in the example above, we could string several `catch` blocks together too. Let's now take a closer look at how nested `try` blocks work.

If an exception is thrown inside the outer `try` block but outside the inner `try` block (points A and D), then the situation is no different to any of the scenarios we have seen before: either the exception is caught by the outer `catch` block and the outer `finally` bock is executed, or the `finally` block is executed and the .NET runtime handles the exception.

If an exception is thrown in the inner `try` block (point B), and there is a suitable inner `catch` block to handle the exception, then again we are in familiar territory: the exception is handled there, and the inner `finally` block is executed before execution resumes inside the outer try block (at point D).

Now suppose an exception occurs in the inner `try` block but there *isn't* a suitable inner `catch` block to handle it. This time, the inner `finally` block is executed as usual, but then the .NET runtime will have no choice but to leave the entire inner `try` block in order to search for a suitable exception handler. The next obvious place to look is in the outer `catch` block. If the system finds one here, then that handler will be executed and then the outer `finally` block. If there is no suitable handler here, then the search for one will go on. In this case it means the outer `finally` block will be executed, and then, since there are no more `catch` blocks, control will transfer to the .NET runtime. Note that at no point is the code beyond point D in the outer `try` block executed.

An even more interesting thing happens if an exception is thrown at point C. If the program is at point C then it must be already processing an exception that was thrown at point B. It is in fact quite legitimate to throw another exception from inside a `catch` block. In this case, the exception is treated as if it had been thrown by the outer `try` block, so flow of execution will immediately leave the inner `catch` block, and execute the inner `finally` block, before the system searches the outer `catch` block for a handler. Similarly, if an exception is thrown in the inner `finally` block, control will immediately transfer to the best appropriate handler, with the search starting at the outer `catch` block.

> It is perfectly legitimate to throw exceptions from `catch` and `finally` blocks.

Although we have shown the situation with just two `try` blocks, the same principles hold no matter how many `try` blocks you nest inside each other. At each stage, the .NET runtime will smoothly transfer control up through the `try` blocks, looking for an appropriate handler. At each stage, as control leaves a `catch` block, any cleanup code in the corresponding `finally` block will be executed, but no code outside any `finally` block will be run until the correct `catch` handler has been found and run.

We have now shown how having nested `try` blocks can work. The obvious next question is why would you want to do that? There are two reasons:

❑   To modify the type of exception thrown

❑   To enable different types of exception to be handled in different places in your code

Modifying the Type of Exception

Modifying the type of the exception can be useful when the original exception thrown does not adequately describe the problem. What typically happens is that something – possibly the .NET runtime – throws a fairly low-level exception that says something like an overflow occurred (`OverflowException`) or an argument passed to a method was incorrect (a class derived from `ArgumentException`). However, because of the context in which the exception occurred, you will know that this reveals some other underlying problem (for example, an overflow can only have happened at that point in your code because a file you have just read contained incorrect data). In that case, the most appropriate thing that your handler for the first exception can do is throw another exception that more accurately describes the problem, so that another `catch` block further along can deal with it more appropriately. In this case, it can also forward the original exception through a property implemented by `System.Exception` called `InnerException`. `InnerException` simply contains a reference to any other related exception that was thrown – in case the ultimate handler routine will need this extra information.

Of course there is also the situation where an exception occurs inside a `catch` block. For example, you might normally read in some configuration file that contains detailed instructions for handling the error, and it might turn out that this file is not there.

Handling Different Exceptions in Different Places

The second reason for having nested `try` blocks is so that different types of exception can be handled at different locations in your code. A good example of this is if you have a loop where various exception conditions can occur. Some of these might be serious enough that you need to abandon the entire loop, while others might be less serious and simply require that you abandon that iteration and move on to the next iteration around the loop. You could achieve this by having one `try` block inside the loop, which handles the less serious error conditions, and an outer `try` block outside the loop, which handles the more serious error conditions. We will see how this works in the exceptions example that we are going to unveil next.

User-Defined Exception Classes

We are now ready to look at a second example that illustrates exceptions. This example, called `MortimerColdCall`, will contain two nested `try` blocks, and also illustrates the practice of defining our own custom exception classes, and throwing another exception from inside a `try` block.

For this example, we are going to return to the Mortimer Phones mobile phone company that we used in Chapter 3 (and Appendix A). We are going to assume that Mortimer Phones want some more customers. Its sales team is going to ring up a list of people to invite them to become customers, or to use sales jargon, they are going to 'cold-call' some people. To this end we have a text file available that contains the names of the people to be cold-called. The file should be in a well-defined format in which the first line contains the number of people in the file and each subsequent line contains the name of the next person. In other words a correctly formatted file of names might look like this:

```
4
Avon from 'Blake's 7'
Zbigniew Harlequin
Simon Robinson
Christian Peak
```

Since this is only an example, we are not really going to cold-call these people! Our version of cold-calling will be to display the name of the person on the screen (perhaps for the sales guy to read). That's why we have only put names, and not phone numbers in the file as well.

Our program will ask the user for the name of the file, and will then simply read it in and display the names of people.

That sounds like a simple task, but even here there are a couple of things that can go wrong and require us to abandon the entire procedure:

❑ The user might type in the name of a file that doesn't exist. This will be caught as a `FileNotFound` exception.

❑ The file might not be in the correct format. There are two possible problems here. Firstly, the first line of the file might not be an integer. Secondly, there might not be as many names in the file as the first line of the file indicates. In both cases, we want to trap this as a custom exception that we have written specially for this purpose, `ColdCallFileFormatException`.

There is also something else that could go wrong which won't cause us to abandon the entire process, but will mean we need to abandon that person and move on to the next person in the file (and hence this will need to be trapped by an inner `try` block). Some people are spies working for rival land-line telephone companies, and obviously, we wouldn't want to let these people know what we are up to by accidentally phoning one of them. Our research has indicated that we can identify who the land-line spies are because their names begin with Z. Such people should have been screened out when the data file was first prepared, but just in case any have slipped through, we will need to check each name in the file, and throw a `LandLineSpyFoundException` if we detect a land-line spy. This, of course, is another custom exception object.

Finally, we will implement this sample by coding up a class, `ColdCallFileReader`, which maintains the connection to the cold-call file and retrieves data from it. We will code up this class in a very safe way, which means its methods will all throw exceptions if they are called inappropriately, for example, if a method requiring a file read is called before the file has been opened. For this purpose, we will code up another exception class, `UnexpectedException`.

Catching the User-Defined Exceptions

Let's start with the `Main()` method of the `MortimerColdCall` sample, which catches our user-defined exceptions. Notice that we will need to call up file-handling classes in the `System.IO` namespace as well as the `System` namespace.

```
using System;
using System.IO;

namespace Wrox.ProCSharp.AdvancedCSharp
{
```

```
class MainEntryPoint
{
   static void Main()
   {
      string fileName;
      Console.Write("Please type in the name of the file " +
         "containing the names of the people to be cold-called > ");
      fileName = Console.ReadLine();
      ColdCallFileReader peopleToRing = new ColdCallFileReader();

      try
      {
         peopleToRing.Open(fileName);
         for (int i=0 ; i<peopleToRing.NPeopleToRing; i++)
         {
            peopleToRing.ProcessNextPerson();
         }
         Console.WriteLine("All callees processed correctly");
      }
      catch(FileNotFoundException e)
      {
         Console.WriteLine("The file {0} does not exist", fileName);
      }
      catch(ColdCallFileFormatException e)
      {
         Console.WriteLine(
       "The file {0} appears to have been corrupted", fileName);
         Console.WriteLine("Details of problem are: {0}", e.Message);
         if (e.InnerException != null)
            Console.WriteLine(
               "Inner exception was: {0}", e.InnerException.Message);
      }
      catch(Exception e)
      {
         Console.WriteLine("Exception occurred:\n" + e.Message);
      }
      finally
      {
         peopleToRing.Dispose();
      }
      Console.ReadLine();
   }
}
```

This code is basically little more than a loop to process people from the file. We start off by asking the user for the name of the file. Then we instantiate an object of a class called `ColdCallFileReader` that we will define later. This is the class that handles the file reading. Notice that we do this outside the initial `try` block – that's because the variables that we instantiate here need to be available in the subsequent `catch` and `finally` blocks, and if we declared them inside the `try` block they'd go out of scope at the closing curly brace of the `try` block.

In the `try` block we open the file (`ColdCallFileReader.Open()` method), and loop over all the people in it. The `ColdCallFileReader.ProcessNextPerson()` method reads in and displays the name of the next person in the file, while the `ColdCallFileReader.NPeopleToRing` property tells us how many people should be in the file (obtained by reading the first line of the file).

There are three `catch` blocks, one for each of `FileNotFoundException` and `ColdCallFileFormatException`, and a third `catch` block to trap any other .NET exceptions.

In the case of a `FileNotFoundException`, we display a message to that effect. Notice that in this `catch` block, we don't actually use the exception instance at all. The reason is that I decided to use this `catch` block to illustrate the user-friendliness of our application. Exception objects generally contain technical information that is useful for developers, but not the sort of stuff you want to show to your end users. So in this case, we create a simpler message of our own.

For the `ColdCallFileFormatException` handler, we have done the opposite, and illustrated how to give fuller technical information, including details of the inner exception, if one is present.

Finally, if we catch any other generic exceptions, we display a user-friendly message, instead of letting any such exceptions fall through to the .NET runtime. Note that we have chosen not to handle any other exceptions not derived from `System.Exception`, since we are not calling directly into non-.NET code.

The `finally` block is there to clean up resources. In this case, this means closing any open file – performed by the `ColdCallFileReader.Dispose()` method.

Throwing the User-Defined Exceptions

Now let's have a look at the definition of the class that handles the file reading, and (potentially) throws our user-defined exceptions: `ColdCallFileReader`. Since this class maintains an external file connection, we will need to make sure it gets disposed of correctly in accordance with the principles we laid down for the disposing of objects in Chapter 3. Hence we derive this class from `IDisposable`.

First, we declare some variables:

```
class ColdCallFileReader :IDisposable
{
    FileStream fs;
    StreamReader sr;
    uint nPeopleToRing;
    bool isDisposed = false;
    bool isOpen = false;
```

`FileStream` and `StreamReader`, both in the `System.IO` namespace, are the base classes that we will use to read the file. `FileStream` allows us to connect to the file in the first place, while `StreamReader` is specially geared up to reading text files, and implements a method, `StreamReader()`, which reads a line of text from a file. We will look at `StreamReader` more closely in Chapter 12 when we discuss file handling in depth.

The `isDisposed` field indicates whether the `Dispose()` method has been called. We have chosen to implement `ColdCallFileReader` so that once `Dispose()` has been called, it is not permitted to reopen connections and reuse the object. `isOpen` is also used for error checking – in this case, checking whether the `StreamReader` actually connects to an open file.

The process of opening the file and reading in that first line – the one that tells us how many people are in the file – is handled by the `Open()` method:

```
public void Open(string fileName)
{
    if (isDisposed)
        throw new ObjectDisposedException("peopleToRing");
    fs = new FileStream(fileName, FileMode.Open);
    sr = new StreamReader(fs);
    try
    {
        string firstLine = sr.ReadLine();
        nPeopleToRing = uint.Parse(firstLine);
        isOpen = true;
    }
    catch (FormatException e)
    {
        throw new ColdCallFileFormatException(
            "First line isn\'t an integer", e);
    }
}
```

The first thing we do in this method (as with all other `ColdCallFileReader` methods) is check whether the client code has inappropriately called it after the object has been disposed of, and throw a predefined `ObjectDisposedException` object if that has occurred. The `Open()` method checks the `isDisposed` field to see whether `Dispose()` has already been called. Since calling `Dispose()` implies the caller has now finished with this object, we regard it as an error to attempt to open a new file connection if `Dispose()` has been called.

Next, the method contains the first of two inner `try` blocks. The purpose of this one is to catch any errors resulting from the first line of the file not containing an integer. If that problem arises, the .NET runtime will throw a `FormatException`, which we trap and convert to a more meaningful exception that indicates there is actually a problem with the format of the cold-call file. Note that `System.FormatException` is there to indicate format problems with basic data types, not with files, and so is not a particularly useful exception to pass back to the calling routine in this case. The new exception thrown will be trapped by the outermost `try` block. Since there is no cleanup needed here, there is no need for a `finally` block.

If everything is fine, we set the `isOpen` field to `true` to indicate that there is now a valid file connection from which data can be read.

The `ProcessNextPerson()` method also contains an inner `try` block:

```
public void ProcessNextPerson()
{
    if (isDisposed)
```

```
            throw new ObjectDisposedException("peopleToRing");
        if (!isOpen)
            throw new UnexpectedException(
                "Attempt to access cold call file that is not open");
        try
        {
            string name;
            name = sr.ReadLine();
            if (name == null)
                throw new ColdCallFileFormatException("Not enough names");
            if (name[0] == 'Z')
            {
                throw new LandLineSpyFoundException(name);
            }
            Console.WriteLine(name);
        }
        catch(LandLineSpyFoundException e)
        {
            Console.WriteLine(e.Message);
        }

        finally
        {
        }
    }
```

There are two possible problems with the file here (assuming there actually is an open file connection – the `ProcessNextPerson()` method checks this first). First, we might read in the next name and discover that it is a land-line spy. If that condition occurs, the exception is trapped by the first of the `catch` blocks in this method. Since that exception has been caught here, inside the loop, it means that execution can subsequently continue in the `Main()` method of the program, and the subsequent names in the file will continue to be processed.

A problem may also occur if we try to read the next name and discover that we have already reached the end of the file. The way that the `StreamReader`'s `ReadLine()` method works, is if it has got past the end of the file, it doesn't throw an exception, but simply returns `null`. So if we find a null string, we know that the format of the file was incorrect because the number in the first line of the file indicated a larger number of names than were actually present in the file. If that happens, we throw a `ColdCallFileFormatException`, which will be caught by the outer exception handler (which will cause execution to terminate).

Once again, we don't need a `finally` block here since there is no cleanup to do, but this time we have put an empty one in, just to show that you can do so, if you want.

We have nearly finished the example. We have just two more members of `ColdCallFileReader` to look at: the `NPeopleToRing` property, which returns the number of people supposed to be in the file, and the `Dispose()` method, which closes an open file. Notice that the `Dispose()` method just returns if it has already been called – this is the recommended way of implementing it. It also checks that there actually is a file stream to close before closing it. This example is here to illustrate defensive coding techniques, so that's what we are doing!

```
        public uint NPeopleToRing
        {
            get
            {
                if (isDisposed)
                    throw new ObjectDisposedException("peopleToRing");
                if (!isOpen)
                    throw new UnexpectedException(
                        "Attempt to access cold call file that is not open");
                return nPeopleToRing;
            }
        }

        public void Dispose()
        {
            if (isDisposed)
                return;

            isDisposed = true;
            isOpen = false;
            if (fs != null)
            {
                fs.Close();
                fs = null;
            }
        }
```

Defining the Exception Classes

Finally, we need to define the three exceptions of our own. Defining our own exception is quite easy, since there are rarely any extra methods to add. It is just a case of implementing a constructor to ensure that the base class constructor is called correctly. Here is the full implementation of `LandLineSpyFoundException`:

```
class LandLineSpyFoundException : ApplicationException
{
    public LandLineSpyFoundException(string spyName)
        :   base("LandLine spy found, with name " + spyName)
    {
    }

    public LandLineSpyFoundException(
        string spyName, Exception innerException)
        :   base(
            "LandLine spy found with name " + spyName, innerException)
    {
    }
}
```

Notice we've derived it from `ApplicationException`, as you would expect for a custom exception. In fact, if we'd been going about this even more formally, we would probably have put in an intermediate class, something like `ColdCallFileException`, derived from `ApplicationException`, and derived both of our exception classes from this class, just to make sure that the handling code has that extra fine degree of control over which exception handlers handle which exception, but to keep the example simple, we won't do that.

We have done one bit of processing in `LandLineSpyFoundException`. We have assumed the 'message' passed into its constructor is just the name of the spy found, and so we turn this string into a more meaningful error message. We have also provided two constructors, one that simply takes a message, and one that also takes an inner exception as a parameter. When defining your own exception classes, it is best to include as a minimum, at least these two constructors (although we won't actually be using the second `LandLineSpyFoundException` constructor in this example).

Now for the `ColdCallFileFormatException`. This follows the same principles as the previous exception, except that we don't do any processing on the message:

```
class ColdCallFileFormatException : ApplicationException
{
    public ColdCallFileFormatException(string message)
        :   base(message)
    {
    }

    public ColdCallFileFormatException(
        string message, Exception innerException)
        :   base(message, innerException)
    {
    }
}
```

And finally, `UnexpectedException`, which looks much the same as `ColdCallFileFormatException`:

```
class UnexpectedException : ApplicationException
{
    public UnexpectedException(string message)
        :   base(message)
    {
    }

    public UnexpectedException(string message, Exception innerException)
        :   base(message, innerException)
    {
    }
}
```

Now we are ready to test the program. First, we try the `people.txt` file whose contents we displayed earlier. This has four names (which matches the number given in the first line of the file) including one spy. Then, we will try the following `people2.txt` file, which has an obvious formatting error:

```
49
Avon from 'Blake's 7'
Zbigniew Harlequin
Simon Robinson
Christian Peak
```

Finally, we will try the example but specify the name of a file that does not exist, `people3.txt`, say. Running the program three times for the three filenames gives these results:

```
MortimerColdCall
Please type in the name of the file containing the names of the people to be cold-
called > people.txt
Avon from 'Blake's 7'
LandLine spy found, with name Zbigniew Harlequin
Simon Robinson
Christian Peak
All callees processed correctly


MortimerColdCall
Please type in the name of the file containing the names of the people to be cold-
called > people2.txt
Avon from 'Blake's 7'
LandLine spy found, with name Zbigniew Harlequin
Simon Robinson
Christian Peak
The file people2.txt appears to have been corrupted
Details of the problem are: Not enough names


MortimerColdCall
Please type in the name of the file containing the names of the people to be cold-
called > people3.txt
The file people3.txt does not exist
```

User-Defined Casts

In Chapter 2, we examined how you can convert values between predefined data types. We saw that this is done through a process of **casting**. We also saw that C# allows two different types of casts:

- ❑ **Implicit**
- ❑ **Explicit**

For an explicit cast, you *explicitly* mark the cast in your code by writing the destination data type inside parentheses:

```
int I = 3;
long l = I;              // implicit
short s = (short)I;      // explicit
```

For the predefined data types, explicit casts are required where there is a risk that the cast might fail or some data might be lost – for example if converting from an int to a short, as the short might not be large enough to hold the value. Other examples are that converting from signed to unsigned data types will return incorrect results if the signed variable holds a negative value, and when converting from floating-point to integer data types, the fractional part of the number will be lost. The idea is that by making the cast explicit in your code, you are affirming to the compiler that you understand that there is a risk of data loss, and therefore presumably you have written your code to take this possibility into account.

Since C# allows you to define your own structs and classes, which in effect means that you are defining your own data types, you would expect that there would be some facility to allow casts between your data types too. C# does indeed allow this. The mechanism is that you can define a cast as a member operator of one of the relevant classes. Your cast must be marked as either implicit or explicit to indicate how you are intending it to be used. The expectation is that you follow the same guidelines as for the predefined casts: if you know the cast is always safe, whatever the value held by the source variable, then you define it as implicit. If on the other hand, you know there is a risk of something going wrong for certain values – perhaps some loss of data or an exception being thrown – then you should define the cast as explicit.

> **You should define any custom casts you write as explicit if there are any source data values for which the cast will fail, or if there is any risk of an exception being thrown.**

The syntax for defining a cast is a similar to that for overloading operators. This is not a coincidence, since in a way a cast can be regarded as an operator whose effect is to convert from the source type to the destination type. To illustrate the syntax, the following is taken from the example that we will introduce later in this section:

```
public static implicit operator float (Currency value)
{
   // processing
}
```

This code is part of a struct, Currency, which is used to store an amount of money. The cast defined here allows us to implicitly convert the value of a Currency into a float. Note that if a conversion has been declared as implicit, then the compiler will permit its use either implicitly or explicitly. If it has been declared as explicit, the compiler will only permit it to be used explicitly.

In this declaration, the cast has been declared as static. In common with operator overloads, C# requires casts to be static. This means that each cast also takes one parameter, which is of the data type of the source.

C++ developers will notice that this is the opposite of the situation in C++, in which casts are instance members of classes.

Implementing User-Defined Casts

In this section, we will illustrate the use of implicit and explicit user-defined casts in an example called SimpleCurrency (which, as usual, is found in the code download). In this example, we will define a struct, Currency, that holds a positive USD ($) monetary value. Normally, C# provides the decimal type for this purpose, but it is possible you might still want to write your own struct or class to represent monetary values if you want to perform sophisticated financial processing, and therefore, want to implement specific methods on such a class.

> *The syntax for casting is the same for structs and classes. Our example happens to be for a struct, but would work just as well if we declared Currency as a class. Other than that difference, C# syntax is similar to C++ syntax for defining casts.*

Initially, the definition of the Currency struct is as follows:

```
struct Currency
{
    public uint Dollars;
    public ushort Cents;

    public Currency(uint dollars, ushort cents)
    {
        this.Dollars = dollars;
        this.Cents = cents;
    }
```

The use of unsigned data types for the Dollar and Cents fields ensures that a Currency instance can only hold positive values. We are restricting it this way so that we can illustrate some points about explicit casts later on. The sort of situation in which you might wish to use a class like this might be, for example, to hold salary information for employees of a company (people's salaries tend not to be negative!). In order to keep the class simple, we are making our fields public, but usually, you would make them private and define corresponding properties for the dollars and cents.

Let's start off by assuming that we want to be able to convert Currency instances to float values, where the integer part of the float represents the dollars. In other words we would like to be able to write code like this:

```
Currency balance = new Currency(10,50);
float f = balance; // We want f to be set to 10.5
```

To be able to do this, we need to define a cast. Hence we add the following to our Currency definition:

```
public static implicit operator float (Currency value)
{
    return value.Dollars + (value.Cents/100.0f);
}
```

This cast is implicit. This is a sensible choice in this case, because, as should be clear from the definition of Currency, any value that can be stored in the currency can also be stored in a float. There's no way that anything should ever go wrong in this cast.

There is a slight cheat here – in fact, when converting a uint to a float, there can be a loss in precision, but Microsoft has deemed this error sufficiently marginal to count the uint-to-float cast as implicit anyway.

What about converting back? In other words, what if we have a float that we would like to be converted to a Currency? In this case the conversion is not guaranteed to work; floats can store negative values, which Currency instances can't, and they can store numbers of a far higher magnitude than can be stored in the (uint) Dollar field of Currency. So if a float contains an inappropriate value, converting it to a Currency could give unpredictable results. As a result of this risk, the conversion from float to Currency should be defined as explicit. Here is our first attempt, which we will say now won't give quite the correct results, but it is instructive to examine the try it out first:

```csharp
public static explicit operator Currency (float value)
{
   uint dollars = (uint)value;
   ushort cents = (ushort)((value-dollars)*100);
   return new Currency(dollars, cents);
}
```

The following code will now successfully compile:

```csharp
float amount = 45.63f;
Currency amount2 = (Currency)amount;
```

However, the following code, if we tried it, would generate a compilation error, because it attempts to use an explicit cast implicitly:

```csharp
float amount = 45.63f;
Currency amount2 = amount;   // wrong
```

Is this good enough? By making the cast explicit, you certainly warn the developer to be careful because data corruption might take place. As we will see soon though, for the above example though, this probably isn't what we really want. We will try writing a test harness and running the sample. Here is the Main() method, which instantiates a Currency struct, and attempts a few conversions. At the start of this code, we write out the value of balance in two different ways (because I will want to use this to illustrate something else later on):

```csharp
static void Main()
{
   try
   {
      Currency balance = new Currency(50,35);
      Console.WriteLine(balance);
      Console.WriteLine("balance is " + balance);
      Console.WriteLine("balance is (using ToString()) " +
         balance.ToString());
```

```
        float balance2= balance;
        Console.WriteLine("After converting to float, = " + balance2);
        balance = (Currency) balance2;
        Console.WriteLine("After converting back to Currency, = " + balance);

        Console.WriteLine("Now attempt to convert out of range value of " +
                          "-$100.00 to a Currency:");
        checked
        {
            balance = (Currency) (-50.5);
            Console.WriteLine("Result is " + balance.ToString());
        }
    }
    catch(Exception e)
    {
        Console.WriteLine("Exception occurred: " + e.Message);
    }
}
```

Notice that we have placed the entire code in a `try` block to catch any exceptions that occur during our casts. Also, we have placed the lines that test converting an out-of-range value to `Currency` in a `checked` block as well, so this looks like the negative value will be trapped. Or will it? Running this code gives this output:

```
SimpleCurrency
50.35
Balance is $50.35
Balance is (using ToString()) $50.35
After converting to float, = 50.35
After converting back to Currency, = $50.34
Now attempt to convert out of range value of -$100.00 to a Currency:
Result is $4294967246.60486
```

This output shows that the code didn't quite work as we expected. In the first place, converting back from `float` to `Currency` gave a wrong result of $50.34 instead of $50.35. In the second place, no exception was generated when we tried to convert an obviously out-of-range value.

The first problem is caused by rounding errors. If a cast is used to convert from a `float` to a `uint`, the computer will *truncate* the number rather than *rounding* it. The computer stores numbers in binary rather than decimal, and the fraction 0.35 cannot be exactly represented as a binary fraction (a bit like 1/3 cannot be represented exactly as a decimal fraction – it comes out as 0.3333 recurring). So, the computer ends up storing a value very slightly lower than 0.35, and which can be represented exactly in binary format. Multiply by 100 and you get a number fractionally less than 35, which gets truncated to 34 cents. Clearly in our situation, such errors caused by truncation are serious, and the way to avoid them is ensure that some intelligent rounding is performed in numerical conversions instead. Luckily, Microsoft has written a class that will do this, `System.Convert`. `System.Convert` contains a large number of static methods to perform various numerical conversions, and the one that we want is `Convert.UInt16()`. Note that the extra care taken by the `System.Convert` methods does come at a performance cost, so you should only use them when you need them.

Now let's examine why the expected overflow exception didn't get thrown. The problem here is this: the place where the overflow really occurs isn't actually in the `Main()` routine at all – it is inside the code for the cast operator, which is called from the `Main()` method. And we didn't mark that code as `checked`.

The solution here is to ensure that the cast itself is computed in a `checked` context too. With both of these changes, the revised code for the conversion looks like this:

```
public static explicit operator Currency (float value)
{
    checked
    {
        uint dollars = (uint)value;
        ushort cents = Convert.ToUInt16((value-dollars)*100);
        return new Currency(dollars, cents);
    }
}
```

Note that we use `Convert.UInt16()` to calculate the cents, as described above, but we do not use it for calculating the dollar part of the amount. `System.Convert` is not needed when working out the dollar amount because truncating the `float` value is what we want there.

> It is worth noting that the `System.Convert` methods also carry out their own overflow checking. Hence, for the particular case we are considering, there is no need to place the call to `Convert.UInt16()` inside the checked context. The checked context is still required, however, for the explicit casting of `value` to `dollars`.

We won't show a new screenshot with this new `checked` cast just yet, because we have some more modifications to make to the `SimpleCurrency` example later in this section.

> Of course, if you are defining a cast that will be used very often, and for which performance is at an absolute premium, you may prefer not to do any error checking. That's also a legitimate solution, provided the behavior of your cast and the lack of error checking are very clearly documented.

Casts Between Classes

Our `Currency` example involved only classes that converted to or from `float` – one of the predefined data types. However, it is not necessary to involve any of the simple data types. It is perfectly legitimate to define casts to convert between instances of different structs or classes that you have defined. There are a couple of restrictions to be aware of, however. These are:

❑ You cannot define a cast if one of the classes is derived from the other (these types of cast already exist, as we will see)

❑ The cast must be defined inside the definition of either the source or destination data type

To illustrate these requirements, suppose you have the following class hierarchy:

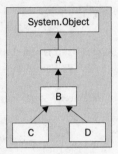

In other words, classes C and D are indirectly derived from A. In this case, the only legitimate user-defined cast between A, B, C, or D would be to convert between classes C and D, because these classes are not derived from each other. The code to do so might look like this (assuming you want the casts to be explicit, which is usually the case when defining casts between user-defined casts):

```
public static explicit operator D(C value)
{
    // and so on
}
public static explicit operator C(D value)
{
    // and so on
}
```

For each of these casts, you have a choice of where you place the definitions – inside the class definition of C, or inside the class definition of D, but not anywhere else. C# requires you to put the definition of a cast inside either the source class (or struct) or the destination class (or struct). A side effect of this is that you can't define a cast between two classes unless you have access to edit the source code for at least one of them. This is sensible because it prevents third parties from introducing casts into your classes.

Once you have defined a cast inside one of the classes, you also can't define the same cast inside the other class. Obviously, there should only be one cast for each conversion – otherwise the compiler wouldn't know which one to pick.

Casts Between Base and Derived Classes

To see how these casts work, let's start by considering the case where the source and destination are both reference types, and consider two classes, MyBase and MyDerived, where MyDerived is derived directly or indirectly from MyBase.

Firstly from MyDerived to MyBase; it is always possible (assuming the constructors are available) to write:

```
MyDerived derivedObject = new MyDerived();
MyBase baseCopy = derivedObject;
```

In this case, we are casting implicitly from `MyDerived` to `MyBase`. This works because of the rule that any reference to a type `MyBase` is allowed to refer to objects of class `MyBase` or to objects of anything derived from `MyBase`. In OO programming, instances of a derived class are, in a real sense, instances of the base class, plus something extra. All the functions and fields defined on the base class are defined in the derived class too.

Now the other way round, we can write:

```
MyBase derivedObject = new MyDerived();
MyBase baseObject = new MyBase();
MyDerived derivedCopy1 = (MyDerived) derivedObject;    // OK
MyDerived derivedCopy2 = (MyDerived) baseObject;        // Throws exception
```

All the above code is perfectly legal C# (in a syntactic sense, that is), and illustrates casting from a base class to a derived class. However, the final statement will throw an exception when executed. What happens when we perform the cast is that the object being referred to is examined. Since a base class reference can in principle refer to a derived class instance, it is possible that this object is actually an instance of the derived class that we are attempting to cast to. If that's the case, then the cast succeeds, and the derived reference is set to refer to the object. If, however, the object in question is not an instance of the derived class (or of any class derived from it) then the cast fails and an exception is thrown.

Notice the casts that the compiler has supplied, which convert between base and derived class do not actually do any data conversion on the object in question. All they do is set the new reference to refer to the object if it is legal for that conversion to occur. To that extent, these casts are very different in nature from the ones that you will normally define yourself. For example, in our `SimpleCurrency` sample earlier, we defined casts that convert between a `Currency` struct and a `float`. In the `float`-to-`Currency` cast, we actually instantiated a new `Currency` struct and initialized it with the required values. The predefined casts between base and derived classes do not do this. If you actually want to convert a `MyBase` instance into a real `MyDerived` object with values based on the contents of the `MyBase` instance, you would not be able to use the cast syntax to do this. The most sensible option is usually to define a derived class constructor that takes a base class instance as a parameter, and have this constructor perform the relevant initializations:

```
class DerivedClass : BaseClass
{
   public DerivedClass(BaseClass rhs)
   {
      // initialize object from the Base instance
   }
   // etc.
```

Boxing and Unboxing Casts

The above discussion focused on casting between base and derived classes where both were reference types. Similar principles apply when casting value types, although in this case it is not possible to simply copy references – some copying of data must take place.

It is not, of course, possible to derive from structs or primitive value types. So, casting between base and derived structs invariably means casting between a primitive type or a struct and `System.Object` (theoretically, it is possible to cast between a struct and `System.ValueType`, though it is hard to see why you would want to do this).

The cast from any struct (or primitive type) to `object` is always available as an implicit cast – since it is a cast from derived to base type – and is just the familiar process of boxing that we have encountered briefly in Chapter 2. For example, with our `Currency` struct:

```
Currency balance = new Currency(40,0);
object baseCopy = balance;
```

When the above implicit cast is executed, the contents of `balance` are copied onto the heap into a boxed object, and the `baseCopy` object reference set to this object. What actually happens behind the scenes is this: when we originally defined the `Currency` struct, the .NET Framework implicitly supplied another (hidden) class, a boxed `Currency` class, which contains all the same fields as the `Currency` struct, but is a reference type, stored on the heap. This happens whenever we define a value type – whether it is a `struct` or enum, and similar boxed reference types exist corresponding to all the primitive value types of `int`, `double`, `uint`, and so on. It is not normally possible to gain any direct programmatic access to any of these boxed classes in source code, but they are the objects that are working behind the scenes whenever a value type is cast to `object`. When we implicitly cast `Currency` to `object`, a boxed `Currency` instance gets instantiated, and initialized with all the data from the `Currency` struct. In the above code, it is this boxed `Currency` instance that `BaseCopy` will refer to. By these means, it is possible for casting from derived to base type to work in syntactically the same way for value types as for reference types.

Casting the other way is known as **unboxing**. Just as for casting between a base reference type and a derived reference type, it is an explicit cast, since an exception will be thrown if the object being cast is not of the correct type:

```
object derivedObject = new Currency(40,0);
object baseObject = new object();
Currency derivedCopy1 = (Currency)derivedObject;   // OK
Currency derivedCopy2 = (Currency)baseObject;       // Exception thrown
```

The above code works analogously to the similar code presented earlier for reference types. Casting `derivedObject` to `Currency` works fine because `derivedObject` actually refers to a boxed `Currency` instance – the cast will be performed by copying the fields out of the boxed `Currency` object into a new `Currency` struct. The second cast fails because `baseObject` does not refer to a boxed `Currency` object.

When using boxing and unboxing, it is important to understand both processes actually copy the data into the new boxed or unboxed object. Hence, manipulations on the boxed object for example will not affect the contents of the original value type.

Multiple Casting

One thing you will have to watch for when you are defining casts is if the C# compiler is presented with a situation in which no direct cast is available to perform a requested conversion, it will attempt to find a way of combining casts to do the conversion. For example, with our `Currency` struct, suppose the compiler encounters a couple of lines of code like this:

```
Currency balance = new Currency(10,50);
long amount = (long)balance;
double amountD = balance;
```

We first initialize a `Currency` instance, and then we attempt to convert it to a `long`. The trouble is that we haven't defined the cast to do that. However, this code will still compile successfully. What will happen is that the compiler will realize that you have defined an implicit cast to get from `Currency` to `float`, and it knows how to explicitly cast a `float` to a `long`. Hence, it will compile that line of code into IL code that converts balance first to a `float`, and then converts that result to a `long`. The same thing happens in the final line of the above code, when we convert `balance` to a `double`. However, since the cast from `Currency` to `float` and the predefined cast from `float` to `double` are both implicit, we can write this conversion in our code as an implicit cast. If we'd preferred, we could have specified the casting route explicitly:

```
Currency balance = new Currency(10,50);
long amount = (long)(float)balance;
double amountD = (double)(float)balance;
```

However, in most cases, this would be seen as needlessly complicating your code. The following code by contrast would produce a compilation error:

```
Currency balance = new Currency(10,50);
long amount = balance;
```

The reason is the best match for the conversion that the compiler can find is still to convert first to `float` then to `long`. The conversion from `float` to `long` needs to be specified explicitly, though.

All this by itself shouldn't give you too much trouble. The rules are, after all, fairly intuitive and designed to prevent any data loss from occurring without the developer knowing about it. However, the problem is that if you are not careful when you define your casts, it is possible for the compiler to figure out a path that leads to unexpected results. For example, suppose it occurs to someone else in the group writing the `Currency` struct, that it would be useful to be able to convert a `uint` containing the total number of cents in an amount into a `Currency` (cents not dollars because the idea is not to lose the fractions of a dollar). So, this cast might be written to try to achieve this:

```
public static implicit operator Currency (uint value)
{
    return new Currency(value/100u, (ushort)(value%100));
} // Don't do this!
```

Note the u after the first 100 in this code to ensure that value/100u is interpreted as a uint. If we'd written value/100 then the compiler would have interpreted this as an int, not a uint.

We have clearly commented Don't do this in this code, and here's why. Look at the following code snippet; all we do in it is convert a uint containing 350 into a Currency and back again. What do you think bal2 will contain after executing this?

```
uint bal = 350;
Currency balance = bal;
uint bal2 = (uint)balance;
```

The answer is not 350, but 3! And it all follows logically. We covert 350 implicitly to a Currency, giving the result Balance.Dollars=3, Balance.Cents=50. Then the compiler does its usual figuring out of best path for the conversion back. Balance ends up getting implicitly converted to a float (value 3.5), and this gets converted explicitly to a uint with value 3.

Of course, other instances exist in which converting to another data type and back again causes data loss. For example, converting a float containing 5.8 to an int and back to a float again will lose the fractional part, giving a result of 5, but there is a slight difference in principle between losing the fractional part of a number and 'accidentally' dividing an integer by more than 100! Currency has suddenly become a rather dangerous class that does strange things to integers!

The problem is that there is a conflict between how our casts interpret integers. Our casts between Currency and float interpret an integer value of 1 as corresponding to one dollar, but our latest uint-to-Currency cast interprets this value as one cent. This is an example of very poor design. If you want your classes to be easy to use, then you should make sure all your casts behave in a way that is mutually compatible, in the sense that they intuitively give the same results. In this case, the solution is obviously to rewrite our uint-to-Balance cast so that it interprets an integer value of 1 as one dollar:

```
public static implicit operator Currency (uint value)
{
    return new Currency(value, 0);
}
```

Incidentally, you might wonder whether this new cast is necessary at all. The answer is that it could be useful. Without this cast, the only way for the compiler to carry out a uint-to-Currency conversion would be via a float. Converting directly is a lot more efficient in this case, so having this extra cast gives performance benefits, but we need to make sure it gives the same result as we would get going via a float, which we have now done. In other situations, you may also find that separately defining casts for different predefined data types allows more conversions to be implicit rather than explicit, though that's not the case here.

A good test of whether your casts are compatible is to ask whether a conversion will give the same results (other than perhaps a loss of accuracy as in float-to-int conversions), irrespective of which path it takes. Our Currency class provides a good example of this. Look at this code:

```
Currency balance = new Currency(50, 35);
ulong bal = (ulong) balance;
```

At present, there is only one way that the compiler can achieve this conversion: by converting the Currency to a `float` implicitly, then to a `ulong` explicitly. The `float-to-ulong` conversion requires an explicit conversion, but that's fine because we have provided one here.

Suppose, however, that we then added another cast, to convert implicitly from a Currency to a `uint`. We will actually do this by modifying the Currency struct by adding the casts both to and from `uint`. This code is available as the `SimpleCurrency2` example:

```
public static implicit operator Currency (uint value)
{
    return new Currency(value, 0);
}

public static implicit operator uint (Currency value)
{
    return value.Dollars;
}
```

Now the compiler has another possible route to convert from Currency to `ulong`: to convert from Currency to `uint` implicitly then to `ulong` implicitly. Which of these two routes will it take? C# does have some precise rules (which we won't detail in this book; if you are interested, details are in the MSDN documentation) to say how the compiler decides which is the best route if there are several possibilities. The best answer is that you should design your casts so that all routes give the same answer (other than possible loss of precision), in which case it doesn't really matter which one the compiler picks. (As it happens in this case, the compiler picks the Currency-to-uint-to-ulong route in preference to Currency-to-float-to-ulong.)

To test the `SimpleCurrency2` sample, we will add this code to the test harness for `SimpleCurrency`:

```
try
{
    Currency balance = new Currency(50,35);
    Console.WriteLine(balance);
    Console.WriteLine("balance is " + balance);
    Console.WriteLine("balance is (using ToString()) " + balance.ToString());

    uint balance3 = (uint) balance;
    Console.WriteLine("Converting to uint gives " + balance3);
```

Running the sample now gives these results:

```
SimpleCurrency2
50
balance is $50.35
balance is (using ToString()) $50.35
Converting to uint gives 50
After converting to float, = 50.35
After converting back to Currency, = $50.34
Now attempt to convert out of range value of -$100.00 to a Currency:
Exception occurred: Arithmetic operation resulted in an overflow.
```

The output shows that the conversion to uint has been successful, though as expected, we have lost the cents part of the Currency in making this conversion. Casting a negative float to Currency has also produced the expected overflow exception now that the float-to-Currency cast itself defines a checked context.

However, the output also demonstrates one last potential problem that you need to be aware of when working with casts. The very first line of output has not displayed the balance correctly, displaying 50 instead of $50.35. Consider these lines:

```
Console.WriteLine(balance);
Console.WriteLine("balance is " + balance);
Console.WriteLine("balance is (using ToString()) " + balance.ToString());
```

Only the last two lines correctly displayed the Currency as a string. So what's going on? The problem here is that when you combine casts with method overloads, you get another source of unpredictability. We will look at these lines in reverse order.

The third Console.WriteLine() statement explicitly calls the Currency.ToString() method ensuring the Currency is displayed as a string. The second does not do so. However, the string literal "balance is " passed to Console.WriteLine() makes it clear to the compiler that the parameter is to be interpreted as a string. Hence the Currency.ToString() method will be called implicitly.

The very first Console.WriteLine() method, however, simply passes a raw Currency struct to Console.WriteLine(). Now, Console.WriteLine() has many overloads, but none of them takes a Currency struct. So the compiler will start fishing around to see what it can cast the Currency to in order to make it match up with one of the overloads of Console.WriteLine(). As it happens, one of the Console.WriteLine() overloads is designed to display uints quickly and efficiently, and it takes a uint as a parameter, and we have now supplied a cast that converts Currency implicitly to uint. I'm sure you can guess the rest.

In fact, Console.WriteLine() has another overload that takes a double as a parameter and displays the value of that double. If you look closely at the output from the first SimpleCurrency example, you will find the very first line of output displayed Currency as a double, using this overload. In that example, there wasn't a direct cast from Currency to uint, so the compiler picked Currency-to-float-to-double as its preferred way of matching up the available casts to the available Console.WriteLine() overloads. However, now that there is a direct cast to uint available in SimpleCurrency2, the compiler has opted for this route.

The upshot of this is that if you have a method call that takes several overloads, and you attempt to pass it a parameter whose data type doesn't match any of the overloads exactly, then you are forcing the compiler to decide not only what casts to use to perform the data conversion, but which overload, and hence which data conversion, to pick. The compiler always works logically and according to strict rules, but the results may not be what you expected. If there is any doubt, you are probably better off specifying casts explicitly.

Delegates

Delegates can best be seen as a new type of object in C#, which has some similarities to classes. They exist for situations in which you want to pass methods around to other methods. To see what we mean by that, consider this line of code:

```
int i = int.Parse("99");
```

We are so used to passing data to methods as parameters, as above, that we don't consciously think about it, and for this reason the idea of passing methods around instead of data might sound a little strange. However, there are cases in which you have a method that does something, and rather than operating on data, the method might need to do something that involves invoking another method. To complicate things further, you do not know at compile-time what this second method is. That information is only available at run-time, and hence will need to be passed in as a parameter to the first method. That might sound confusing, but should be clearer with a couple of examples:

❑ **Starting Threads** – It is possible in C# to tell the computer to start some new sequence of execution in parallel with what it is currently doing. Such a sequence is known as a thread, and starting one up is done using a method, `Start()` on an instance of one of the base classes, `System.Threading.Thread`. (We will look at threads more closely in Chapter 5.) Now, when your application first starts running, it has to start somewhere, and as we have just commented, the place it starts is `Main()`. Similarly, if you are going to tell the computer to start a new sequence of execution, you have got to tell it where to start that sequence. You have to supply it with the details of a method in which execution can start – in other words, the `Thread.Start()` method has to take a parameter that defines the method to be invoked by the thread.

❑ **Generic Library Classes** – There are of course many libraries around that contain code to perform various standard tasks. It is usually possible for these libraries to be self-contained, in the sense that you know when you write to the library exactly how the task must be performed. However, sometimes the task contains some sub-task, which only the individual client code that uses the library knows how to perform. For example, say we want to write a class that takes an array of objects and sorts them into ascending order. Part of the sorting process involves repeatedly taking two of the objects in the array, and comparing them in order to see which one should come first. If we want to make the class capable of sorting arrays of *any* object, there is no way that it can tell in advance how to do this comparison. The client code that hands our class the array of objects will also have to tell our class how to do this comparison for the particular objects it wants sorted. In other words, the client code will have to pass our class details of an appropriate method that can be called, which does the comparison.

❑ **Events** – The general idea here is that often, you have code that needs to be informed when some event takes place. GUI programming is full of situations like this. For example, at the moment I'm typing lots of characters into Word for Windows. Each time I hit a key on the keyboard, Windows calls up a particular method inside Word that takes the appropriate action – or, in the jargon, that **handles** the event. In order for Windows to be able to do this, Word must have informed Windows which method should be called in response to a key press. So, Word must have called a Windows API function, giving it the details of this method. Once again, we see that details of a method must have been passed as a parameter. Obviously, in C# programming, we will be interacting with the .NET runtime rather than directly with Windows, but when we come to do GUI programming with Windows Forms in Chapter 7, the same principles will hold: our code will need to inform the .NET runtime of what methods handle what events.

So, we have established the principle that sometimes, methods need to take details of other methods as parameters. Next, we need to figure out how we can do that. The simplest way would appear to be to just pass in the name of a method as a parameter. To take our example from threading, suppose we are going to start a new thread, and we have a method called `EntryPoint()`, which is where we want our thread to start running:

```
void EntryPoint()
{
    // do whatever the new thread needs to do
}
```

Could we perhaps start the new thread off with some code like this:

```
Thread NewThread = new Thread();
Thread.Start(EntryPoint);                    // WRONG
```

In fact, this is a simple way of doing it, and it is what some languages, such as C and C++, do in this kind of situation (in C and C++, the parameter `EntryPoint` is a function pointer). Incidentally, something like this is also going on behind the scenes in pre-.NET Visual Basic when you add event handlers, but the Visual Basic runtime is so good at shielding you from the details of what is happening, you would never realize that.

Unfortunately, this direct approach causes some problems with type safety, and it also neglects the fact that when we are doing object-oriented programming, methods rarely exist in isolation, but usually need to be associated with a class instance before they can be called. As a result of these problems, the .NET Framework does not syntactically permit this direct approach. Instead, if you want to pass methods around, you have to wrap up the details of the method in a new kind of object, a delegate. Delegates quite simply are a special type of object – special in the sense that, whereas all the objects we have defined up to now contain data, a delegate just contains the details of a method.

Using Delegates in C#

When we want to use a class in C#, there are two stages. First, we need to define the class – that is, we need to tell the compiler what fields and methods make up the class. Then (unless we are using only static methods), we instantiate an object of that class. With delegates it is the same thing. We have to start off by defining the delegates we want to use. In the case of a delegates, defining it means telling the compiler what kind of method a delegate of that type will represent. Then, we have to create one or more instances of that delegate.

The syntax for defining delegates looks like this:

```
delegate void VoidOperation(uint x);
```

In this case, we have defined a delegate called `VoidOperation`, and we have indicated that each instance of this delegate can hold a reference to a method that takes one `uint` parameter and returns `void`. The crucial point to understand about delegates is that they are very type-safe. When you define the delegate, you have to give full details of the signature of the method that it is going to represent.

> One good way of understanding delegates is by thinking of a delegate as something that gives a name to a method signature.

Suppose we wanted to define a delegate called `TwoLongsOp` that will represent a function that takes two `long`s as its parameters and returns a `double`. We could do it like this:

```
delegate double TwoLongsOp(long first, long second);
```

Or, to define a delegate that will represent a method that takes no parameters and returns a `string`, we might write this:

```
delegate string GetAString();
```

The syntax is similar to that for a method definition, except that there is no method body, and the definition is prefixed with the keyword `delegate`. Since what we are doing here is basically defining a new class, we can define a delegate in any of the same places that we would define a class – that is to say either inside another class, or outside of any class and in a namespace as a top-level object. Depending on how visible we want our definition to be, we can apply any of the normal access modifiers to delegate definitions – `public`, `private`, `protected`, and so on:

```
public delegate string GetAString();
```

> *We do literally mean what we say when we describe 'defining a delegate' as 'defining a new class'. Delegates are implemented as classes derived from the base class, `System.Delegate`. The C# compiler is aware of this class, and uses its delegate syntax to shield us from the details of the operation of this class. This is another good example of how C# works in conjunction with the base classes to make programming as easy as practicable.*

Once we have defined a delegate, we can create an instance of it so that we can use it to store details of a particular method.

> *There is an unfortunate problem with terminology here. With classes there are two distinct terms – 'class', which indicates the broader definition, and 'object', which means an instance of the class. Unfortunately, with delegates there is only the one term. When you create an instance of a delegate, what you have created is also referred to as 'a delegate'. You need to be aware of the context to know which meaning we are using when we talk about delegates.*

The following code snippet demonstrates the use of a delegate. It is a rather long-winded way of calling the `ToString()` method on an `int`:

```
private delegate string GetAString();

static void Main(string[] args)
{
    int x = 40;
    GetAString firstStringMethod = new GetAString(x.ToString);
    Console.WriteLine("String is" + firstStringMethod());
```

```
   // With firstStringMethod initialized to x.ToString(),
   // the above statement is equivalent to saying
   // Console.WriteLine("String is" + x.ToString());
```

In this code, we instantiate a delegate of type `GetAString`, and we initialize it so that it refers to the `ToString()` method of the integer variable x. Delegates in C# always syntactically take a one-parameter constructor, the parameter being the method to which the delegate will refer. This method must match the signature with which we originally defined the delegate. So in this case, we would get a compilation error if we tried to initialize `FirstStringMethod` with any method that did not take no parameters and return a string. Notice that since `int.ToString()` is an instance method (as opposed to a static one) we need to specify the instance (x) as well as the name of the method to initialize the delegate properly.

The next line actually uses the delegate to display the string. In any code, supplying the name of a delegate instance, followed by brackets containing any parameters, has exactly the same effect as calling the method wrapped by the delegate. Hence, in the above code snippet, the `Console.WriteLine()` statement is completely equivalent to the commented-out line.

One feature of delegates is that they are type-safe to the extent that they ensure the signature of the method being called is correct. However, interestingly, they do not care what type of object the method is being called against, or even whether the method is a static method or an instance method.

> **An instance of a given delegate can refer to any instance or static method on any object of any type, provided that the signature of the method matches the signature of the delegate.**

To see this, we will expand the above code snippet so that it uses the `FirstStringMethod` delegate to call a couple of other methods on another object – an instance method and a static method. For this, we will reuse the `Currency` struct that we defined earlier in the chapter. Recall that the `Currency` struct already has its own overload of `ToString()`. In order to demonstrate using delegates with static methods, we will also add a static method with the same signature to `Currency`:

```
struct Currency
{
   public static string GetCurrencyUnit()
   {
      return "Dollar";
   }
}
```

Now we can use our `GetAString` instance as follows.

```
private delegate string GetAString();

static void Main(string[] args)
{
   int x = 40;
   GetAString firstStringMethod = new GetAString(x.ToString);
   Console.WriteLine("String is " + firstStringMethod());
```

```
Currency balance = new Currency(34, 50);
firstStringMethod = new GetAString(balance.ToString);
Console.WriteLine("String is " + firstStringMethod());
firstStringMethod = new GetAString(Currency.GetCurrencyUnit);
Console.WriteLine("String is " + firstStringMethod());
```

This code shows how you can call a method via a delegate, and subsequently reassign the delegate to refer to different methods on different instances of classes, even static methods or methods against instances of different types of class, provided that the signature of each method matches the delegate definition.

However, we still haven't demonstrated the process of actually passing a delegate to another method. Nor have we actually achieved anything particularly useful yet. It is possible to call the ToString() method of int and Currency objects in a much more straightforward way than using delegates! Unfortunately, it is in the nature of delegates that we need a fairly complex example before we can really appreciate their usefulness. We are now going to present two delegate examples. The first one simply uses delegates to call a couple of different operations. It illustrates how to pass delegates to methods, and how you can use arrays of delegates – although arguably it still doesn't do much that you couldn't do a lot more simply without delegates. Then, we will present a second, much more complex example of a BubbleSorter class, which implements a method to sort out arrays of objects into increasing order. This class would be difficult to write without delegates.

SimpleDelegate Example

For this example, we will define a MathOperations class that has a couple of static methods to perform two operations on doubles. Then, we will use delegates to call up these methods. The math class looks like this:

```
class MathsOperations
{
    public static double MultiplyByTwo(double value)
    {
        return value*2;
    }

    public static double Square(double value)
    {
        return value*value;
    }
}
```

and we call up these methods like this:

```
using System;

namespace Wrox.ProCSharp.AdvancedCSharp
{
    delegate double DoubleOp(double x);

    class MainEntryPoint
    {
        static void Main()
```

```
    {
        DoubleOp [] operations =
            {
                new DoubleOp(MathsOperations.MultiplyByTwo),
                new DoubleOp(MathsOperations.Square)
            };

        for (int i=0 ; i<operations.Length ; i++)
        {
            Console.WriteLine("Using operations[{0}]:", i);
            ProcessAndDisplayNumber(operations[i], 2.0);
            ProcessAndDisplayNumber(operations[i], 7.94);
            ProcessAndDisplayNumber(operations[i], 1.414);
            Console.WriteLine();
        }
    }

    static void ProcessAndDisplayNumber(DoubleOp action, double value)
    {
        double result = action(value);
        Console.WriteLine(
            "Value is {0}, result of operation is {1}", value, result);
    }
```

In this code, we instantiate an array of `DoubleOp` delegates (remember that once we have defined a delegate class, we can basically instantiate instances just like we can with normal classes, so putting some into an array is no problem). Each element of the array gets initialized to refer to a different operation implemented by the `MathOperations` class. Then, we loop through the array, applying each operation to three different values. This illustrates one way of using delegates – that you can group methods together into an array using them, so that you can call several methods in a loop.

The key lines in this code are the ones in which we actually pass each delegate to the `ProcessAndDisplayNumber()` method, for example:

```
        ProcessAndDisplayNumber(operations[i], 2.0);
```

Here, we are passing in the name of a delegate, but without any parameters. Given that `operations[i]` is a delegate, syntactically:

❑ `operations[i]` means 'the delegate', in other words the method represented by the delegate

❑ `operations[i](2.0)` means 'actually call this method, passing in the value in parentheses'

The `ProcessAndDisplayNumber()` method is defined to take a delegate as its first parameter:

```
        static void ProcessAndDisplayNumber(DoubleOp action, double value)
```

Then, when in this method, we call:

```
        double result = action(value);
```

This actually causes the method that is wrapped up by the `action` delegate instance to be called, and its return result stored in `Result`.

Running this sample gives the following:

```
SimpleDelegate
Using operations[0]:
Value is 2, result of operation is 4
Value is 7.94, result of operation is 15.88
Value is 1.414, result of operation is 2.828

Using operations[1]:
Value is 2, result of operation is 4
Value is 7.94, result of operation is 63.0436
Value is 1.414, result of operation is 1.999396
```

BubbleSorter Example

We are now ready for an example that will show delegates working in a situation in which they are very useful. We are going to write a class called `BubbleSorter`. This class implements a static method, `Sort()`, which takes as its first parameter an array of objects, and rearranges this array into ascending order. In other words, suppose we were to pass it this array of ints: {0, 5, 6, 2, 1}. It would rearrange this array into {0, 1, 2, 5, 6}.

The bubble-sorting algorithm is a well-known and very simple way of sorting numbers. It is best suited to small sets of numbers, since for larger sets of numbers (more than about 10) there are far more efficient algorithms available). It works by repeatedly looping through the array, comparing each pair of numbers and, if necessary, swapping them, so that the largest numbers progressively move to the end of the array. For sorting ints, a method to do a bubble sort might look like this:

```
// Note that this isn't part of the sample
for (int i = 0; i < sortArray.Length; i++)
{
   for (int j = i + 1; j < sortArray.Length; j++)
   {
      if (sortArray[j] < sortArray[i])    // problem with this test
      {
         int temp = sortArray[i];   // swap ith and jth entries
         sortArray[i] = sortArray[j];
         sortArray[j] = temp;
      }
   }
}
```

This is all very well for ints, but we want our `Sort()` method to be able to sort any object. In other words, if some client code hands us an array of `Currency` structs or any other class or struct that it may have defined, we need to be able to sort the array. This gives us a problem with the line `if(sortArray[j] < sortArray[i])` in the above code, since that requires us to compare two objects on the array to see which one is greater. We can do that for ints, but how are we to do it for some new class that is unknown or undecided until run-time? The answer is the client code that knows about the class will have to pass in a delegate wrapping a method that will do the comparison.

We define the delegate like this:

```
delegate bool CompareOp(object lhs, object rhs);
```

and give our Sort method this signature:

```
static public void Sort(object [] sortArray, CompareOp gtMethod)
```

The documentation for this method will state that gtMethod must refer to a static method that takes two arguments, and returns true if the value of the second argument is 'greater than' (in other words should come later in the array than) the first one.

Although we are using delegates here, it is possible to solve this problem alternatively, by using interfaces. .NET in fact makes the IComparer interface available for that purpose. However, we will use delegates here since this is still the kind of problem that lends itself to delegates.

Now we are all set. Here is the definition for the BubbleSorter class:

```
class BubbleSorter
{
   static public void Sort(object [] sortArray, CompareOp gtMethod)
   {
      for (int i=0 ; i<sortArray.Length ; i++)
      {
         for (int j=i+1 ; j<sortArray.Length ; j++)
         {
            if (gtMethod(sortArray[j], sortArray[i]))
            {
               object temp = sortArray[i];
               sortArray[i] = sortArray[j];
               sortArray[j] = temp;
            }
         }
      }
   }
}
```

In order to use this class, we need to define some other class, which we can use to set up an array that needs sorting. For this example, we will assume that our Mortimer Phones mobile phone company has a list of employees, and wants them sorted according to salary. The employees are each represented by an instance of a class, Employee, which looks like this:

```
class Employee
{
   private string name;
   private decimal salary;

   public Employee(string name, decimal salary)
   {
      this.name = name;
      this.salary = salary;
```

```
        }

        public override string ToString()
        {
            return string.Format(name + ", {0:C}", salary);
        }

        public static bool RhsIsGreater(object lhs, object rhs)
        {
            Employee empLhs = (Employee) lhs;
            Employee empRhs = (Employee) rhs;
            return (empRhs.salary > empLhs.salary) ? true : false;
        }
    }
```

Notice that in order to match the signature of the CompareOp delegate, we have had to define RhsIsGreater in this class as taking two object references, rather than Employee references as parameters. This means that we have had to cast the parameters into Employee references in order to perform the comparison.

Now we are ready to write some client code to request a sort:

```
using System;

namespace Wrox.ProCSharp.AdvancedCSharp
{
    delegate bool CompareOp(object lhs, object rhs);

    class MainEntryPoint
    {
        static void Main()
        {
            Employee [] employees =
                {
                    new Employee("Karli Watson", 20000),
                    new Employee("Bill Gates", 10000),
                    new Employee("Simon Robinson", 25000),
                    new Employee("Mortimer", (decimal)1000000.38),
                    new Employee("Arabel Jones", 23000),
                    new Employee("Avon from 'Blake's 7'", 50000)};
            CompareOp employeeCompareOp = new CompareOp(Employee.RhsIsGreater);
            BubbleSorter.Sort(employees, employeeCompareOp);

            for (int i=0 ; i<employees.Length ; i++)
                Console.WriteLine(employees[i].ToString());
        }
    }
```

Running this code shows that the `Employees` are correctly sorted according to salary:

```
BubbleSorter
Bill Gates, £10,000.00
Karli Watson, £20,000.00
Arabel Jones, £23,000.00
Simon Robinson, £25,000.00
Avon from 'Blake's 7', £50,000.00
Mortimer, £1,000,000.38
```

Note that the above output shows salaries in £, because I'm in the UK, so my locale is set to UK, and this is picked up by the `decimal` struct when it formats each salary as a string. If you download and run this sample, £ will be replaced by the currency unit in your local currency. This might also make the salaries look a bit lower (10000 Yen, for example, aren't worth quite as much as GB£10000!). A number like a 1000 is a pure `int`, not a currency amount. Unfortunately there is no formal way in C# to specify the locale value (to be associated with the `int`) in a constructor and have the constructor invoke the proper converter delegate. If you were writing a `Currency` class in real life, and needed to be able to work with currencies other than the one associated with the computer's current culture setting, you would need to find some way round this. One possibility is for the `Currency` constructor to take strings allowing specification of the currency.

```
new Currency ("£1000");
```

Multicast Delegates

So far, each of the delegates we have used wraps just one single method call. Calling the delegate amounts to calling that method. If we want to call more than one method, we need to make an explicit call through a delegate more than once. However, it is possible for a delegate to wrap more than one method. Such a delegate is known as a **multicast delegate**. If a multicast delegate is called, it will successively call each method in order. For this to make sense, the delegate signature must return a `void` (otherwise, where would all the return values go?), and in fact, if the compiler sees a delegate that returns a `void`, it automatically assumes you mean a multicast delegate. Consider this code, which is adapted from the `SimpleDelegate` example. Although the syntax is the same as before, it is actually a multicast delegate, `Operations`, that gets instantiated:

```
    delegate void DoubleOp(double value);
//   delegate double DoubleOp(double value);    // can't do this now

    class MainEntryPoint
    {
        static void Main()
        {
            DoubleOp operations = new DoubleOp(MathOperations.MultiplyByTwo);
            operations += new DoubleOp(MathOperations.Square);
```

In our earlier example, we wanted to store references to two methods so we instantiated an array of delegates. Here, we simply add both operations into the same multicast delegate. Multicast delegates recognize the operators + and +=. If we'd preferred, we could have expanded out the last two lines of the above code to this, which has the same effect:

```
DoubleOp operation1 = new DoubleOp(MathOperations.MultiplyByTwo);
DoubleOp operation2 = new DoubleOp(MathOperations.Square);
DoubleOp operations = operation1 + operation2;
```

Multicast delegates also recognize the operators – and -= to remove method calls from the delegate.

In terms of what's going on under the hood, a multicast delegate is a class derived from System.MulticastDelegate, which in turn is derived from System.Delegate. System.MulticastDelegate has additional members to allow chaining of method calls together into a list.

To illustrate the use of multicast delegates, we have recast the SimpleDelegate sample into a new sample, MulticastDelegate. Since we now need the delegate to refer to methods that return void, we have had to rewrite the methods in the MathOperations class, so they display their results instead of returning them:

```
class MathOperations
{
    public static void MultiplyByTwo(double value)
    {
        double result = value*2;
        Console.WriteLine(
            "Multiplying by 2: {0} gives {1}", value, result);
    }

    public static void Square(double value)
    {
        double result = value*value;
        Console.WriteLine("Squaring: {0} gives {1}", value, result);
    }
}
```

To accommodate this change, we have rewritten ProcessAndDisplayNumber:

```
static void ProcessAndDisplayNumber(DoubleOp action, double value)
{
    Console.WriteLine("\nProcessAndDisplayNumber called with value = " +
                        value);
    action(value);
}
```

Now we can try out our multicast delegate like this:

```
static void Main()
{
    DoubleOp operations = new DoubleOp(MathOperations.MultiplyByTwo);
    operations += new DoubleOp(MathOperations.Square);

    ProcessAndDisplayNumber(operations, 2.0);
    ProcessAndDisplayNumber(operations, 7.94);
```

```
            ProcessAndDisplayNumber(operations, 1.414);
            Console.WriteLine();
    }
```

Now, each time that `ProcessAndDisplayNumber` is called, it will display a message to say that it has been called. Then the following statement:

```
    action(value);
```

will cause each of the method calls in the `action` delegate instance to be called in succession.

Running this code gives this result:

```
MulticastDelegate

ProcessAndDisplayNumber called with value = 2
Multiplying by 2: 2 gives 4
Squaring: 2 gives 4

ProcessAndDisplayNumber called with value = 7.94
Multiplying by 2: 7.94 gives 15.88
Squaring: 7.94 gives 63.0436

ProcessAndDisplayNumber called with value = 1.414
Multiplying by 2: 1.414 gives 2.828
Squaring: 1.414 gives 1.999396
```

If you are using multicast delegates, you should be aware that the order in which methods chained to the same delegate will be called is formally undefined. You should, therefore, avoid writing code that relies on such methods being called in any particular order.

Events

As we have indicated, **events** are the usual means by which an application running on the Windows platform can receive notifications when something interesting happens. Whenever Windows is running, you can be pretty sure a lot of events are firing. For example, when you click the mouse button, the application in whose window you clicked will almost certainly have been notified of this event. The same thing happens when you do almost anything with the mouse or keyboard. Similarly, when windows are minimized, restored, or maximized, the corresponding applications will be notified in case they wish to take any action in response.

> *Actually, we should point out that the above paragraph isn't completely accurate. Strictly, events aren't a part of the Windows operating system at all. Windows uses things called Windows messages in order to notify applications of interesting things that have happened. However, Windows messages are low-level C structures that are quite hard to work with, so high-level languages such as VB have traditionally wrapped up the messages in a high-level framework in which events are the main objects, to make things easier for the programmer. C# and the .NET runtime do this as well, which means we can work entirely in terms of events, even though it is the Windows messages that are actually doing the work behind the scenes.*

> **In C# terms, events are actually a special form of delegates.**

Believe it or not, in the preceding section on *Delegates*, we learned just about everything we needed to know to understand how events work. However, one of the great things about how Microsoft has designed C# events is that you don't actually need to understand anything about the underlying delegates in order to use them. So, we are going to start off with a short discussion of events from the point of view of the client software. We will focus on what code you need to write in order to receive notifications of events, without worrying too much about what is happening behind the scenes – just so we can show how easy handling events really is. After we have done that, we will write a sample that generates events, and as we do so, we will see how the underlying delegates framework is working with us.

The discussion in this section will be of most use to C++ developers since C++ does not have any concept similar to events. C# events on the other hand are quite similar in concept to VB events, although the syntax and the underlying implementation are different in C#.

In this context, we are using the term 'event' in two different senses. Firstly as something interesting that happens, and secondly as a precisely defined object in the C# language – the object that handles the notification process. When we mean the latter, we will usually refer to it either as a C# event, or, when the meaning is obvious from the context, simply as an event.

The Consumer's View of Events

The consumer here is any application that wants to be notified when something happens. For the sake of argument, we will assume that the thing that happens is the mouse being clicked, but the event can be anything you like. There will also be some other software (often the Windows operating system or the .NET Framework itself) that represents whatever it is that normally becomes aware that an event has occurred. This software is responsible for notifying our application (for things like mouse and keyboard events, this will be Windows itself). We will refer to this other software as the **event generator**.

The pattern looks like this:

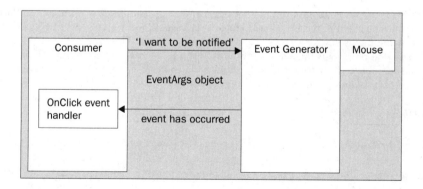

Now, somewhere inside the consumer, there will be a method, which is the one the consumer wants called when a `MouseClick` happens. This method is known as the **event handler** for the event, and a good name for it in this case is `OnClick` (this name isn't entirely random; in Chapter 19, we will see that the relevant Windows Forms base classes really do have a handler called `OnClick` for this purpose). At some point in the past, most likely when the consumer application started up, it will have informed the event generator of its interest in mouse clicks – and of the fact that it wants `OnClick()` to be called whenever a mouse click happens. You can see the delegates coming in here. In C# terms, in order to give the event generator this information, the consumer is going to have to somehow place a reference to `OnClick()` inside a delegate. Once the event generator has this information, whenever it detects that a mouse click happens, it can use this delegate to call the consumer's `OnClick()` method.

Let's look at the coding details now. The .NET Framework requires a very precise signature for any event handler. `OnClick()` and all other event handlers must look like this:

```
void OnClick(object sender, EventArgs e)    // e can also be derived
                                            // from EventArgs
{
    // code to handle event
}
```

Event handlers can't return anything other than `void`. There's no point in them returning any value – all the event generator wants to do is call the method. It doesn't usually want to know anything about what the consumer does in response – that's the consumer's business (There are occasions when an event handler will wish to cancel an event, but this is handled by the handler modifying a property of the `EventArgs` parameter, not through any return value). Handlers must also take two parameters. The first parameter is a reference to the object that generated the event. In other words, the event generator passes in a reference to itself. The second parameter must be a reference to either a .NET base class, `System.EventArgs`, or to a class derived from that. You can think of `EventArgs` as the generic base class for any notifications that events have occurred. In some cases, the event generator will document that it will actually send in a reference to a derived class in response to certain specific events. A derived class might contain extra information pertaining to that event, such as the location of the mouse, or which key on the keyboard was pressed.

That's the event handler sorted out. All we need to do now is notify the event generator that we are interested in the event in the first place. For this to happen, we need the event generator to make some item available that is able to receive requests for notifications. This item will be a public member of the .NET class that represents the event generator, and is a member of type `event`. This member is the C# event itself, and is a specialized form of multicast delegate. Let's suppose here that the consumer has a reference to the event generator, via a reference variable called `Generator`, and that the member that represents the event is called `MouseClick`. In the code for the consumer class, we would presumably see something like this:

```
EventGenerator Generator = GetAReferenceToTheEventGeneratorSomehow();
```

where we assume that `EventGenerator` represents the event generator class.

The consumer can notify the event generator that it wants to receive notifications of mouse clicks with this line of code:

```
// Generator is a reference to the event generator
Generator.MouseClick += OnClick();
```

That is literally all the consumer needs to do.

Since we have already given away the fact that the event, MouseClick, is a kind of multicast delegate, you can probably guess what is really going on here. The event will contain references to all the event handlers that various consumers have registered to receive notifications, and this line of code simply adds our own event handler to the list. Another point of this is if the consumer subsequently decides it is not interested in this particular event any more, it can inform the event generator like this:

```
Generator.MouseClick -= OnClick();
```

We might have had to learn a lot of concepts to get this far, but the amount of coding you need to do in the consumer is fairly trivial. Also bear in mind that you will find yourself writing event consumers a lot more often than you write event generators. At least in the field of the Windows user interface, Microsoft has already written all the event generators you are likely to need (these are in the .NET base classes, in the Windows.Forms namespace, and we'll look at them in Chapter 7).

There is just one point you might notice in the above discussion. We were a bit vague about just how the consumer obtains a reference to the events generator in the first place. That is not part of the general events framework. You should find that the documentation for the particular event generator will tell you how to get this reference. In the case of Windows Forms, you can often just derive your consumer from a generator class. Very often, you will simply instantiate the event generator as one of the .NET base classes.

This architecture is actually extremely flexible. It means that your consumer can request notifications of as many events as it pleases. It can even request notifications from different sources. This is the reason for the first parameter passed to the event handler, the sender reference. Since the consumer has a reference to the object that generated the event, this means that if there is more than one possible source for the event, the event handler can easily work out which source is responsible. An example of this is that your application might be a Windows form that has several buttons on it. Any one of these buttons might have notified you that it has been clicked, and by examining the sender reference you can figure out which button is the correct one. Not only that, but also, many different consumers can request to be notified of the same events. Each one simply adds its event handler to the events, and because of the way that multicast delegates work, when the event fires, all the event handlers will be triggered in turn.

Events Example: Console Notifications

We are now going to write an example that generates events. The example is called UserInputNotify. For this example, we are going back to the Mortimer Phones mobile phone company. The Mortimer Phones company is a fictional company that we have used for our examples to illustrate the principles of inheritance in Appendix A, and briefly in Chapter 3.

We are going to write a little console application for Mortimer Phones staff members, which displays a message to the user. The user gets a choice between seeing a personal message from Mortimer (the company president), or a general advertisement. The program keeps asking the user what message they want to see until the user hits *X* followed by *Enter* to exit the program. However, we are going to structure the program so that it uses events. It will follow a classic event-notification architecture that has a general applicability and is also very similar to the architecture that Windows Forms uses.

There are two objects of interest in our code:

❑ The `UserInputMonitor` – This is the object that deals with user input. It is responsible for asking users which messages they want to see.

❑ The `MessageDisplayer` – This is the object that is responsible for displaying the appropriate message.

Since the message displayer is not concerned with user input, it has no direct means of knowing when to display a message or which message to display – it has to rely on the `UserInputMonitor` to tell it. The `UserInputMonitor` will do so by raising events. The `MessageDisplayer` will notify the `UserInputMonitor` that it wishes to be told whenever the user has asked to display a message. After that, whenever the user makes such a request, the `UserInputMonitor` will fire an appropriate event, resulting in the event handler in the `MessageDisplayer` getting called.

At this point, we have just designed a program that illustrates events nicely, but which doesn't actually do anything that we couldn't have done with a simple loop inside one method in one single class, with the knowledge of C# that we picked up in Chapter 2! We are also now going to add something else that will demonstrate how flexible the events architecture is. You see, Mortimer quite likes to know when members of his staff have asked to see his personal message. It makes him feel popular and gives him a nice warm feeling inside. So he would like to be notified too whenever users request to see his personal messages.

To this end, we will code up another class, the `ManagersStaffMonitor`, which tells Mortimer when someone has asked to see his personal message. For the purposes of our sample, the `ManagersStaffMonitor` will simply display a dialog box that says **Kaark!** (Mortimer likes saying Kaark! when he's happy!). Doing this, we can see the beauty of the events architecture, because all we have to do to let Mortimer know about the events is plug the `ManagersStaffMonitor`'s own event handler into the event as well. Then, when a customer asks to see a message, the resulting event will call both event handlers in succession. If some other software wanted to be notified of this event, it would do the same thing: write an event handler and add it to the event in the `UserInputMonitor`. In this way, the event handlers can get effectively chained together.

The structure of our application looks like this:

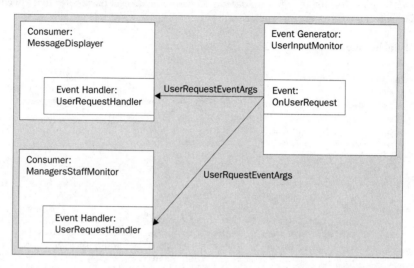

In this diagram, we have marked in the event handlers for our two consumer classes, the `MessageDisplayer` and the `ManagersStaffMonitor`, as well as the event in our event generator class, the `UserInputMonitor`. In order to pass details of the event, we are going to use a new class, `UserRequestEventArgs`, which we will derive from `System.EventArgs`, and which will implement one property, `Request`. This indicates which of the two possible requests the user has made.

To start off with, we need to write the `UserRequestEventArgs` class that will convey details of an event. For this, we will use an enumeration to list the possible events:

```csharp
enum RequestType {AdRequest, PersonalMessageRequest};

class UserRequestEventArgs : EventArgs
{
    private RequestType request;

    public UserRequestEventArgs(RequestType request)
        :   base()
    {
        this.request = request;
    }

    public RequestType Request
    {
        get
        {
            return request;
        }
    }
}
```

This code should be fairly self-explanatory. We simply add a field and corresponding property that specifies which request the user has made. Our constructor takes a parameter that specifies this value, and then calls the base class constructor.

Now for the event generator, the `UserInputMonitor`:

```
class UserInputMonitor
{
    public delegate void UserRequest(object sender, UserRequestEventArgs e);

    public event UserRequest OnUserRequest;

    public void Run()
    {
        bool finished = false;
        do
        {
            Console.WriteLine("Select preferred option:");
            Console.WriteLine("  Request advertisement - hit A then Return");
            Console.WriteLine("  Request personal message from Mortimer " +
                              "- hit P then Return");
            Console.WriteLine("  Exit - hit X then Return");
            string response = Console.ReadLine();

        char responseChar = (response == "") ? ' ' : char.ToUpper(response[0]);
            switch(responseChar)
            {
                case 'X':
                    finished = true;
                    break;
                case 'A':
                    OnUserRequest(this, new
                        UserRequestEventArgs(RequestType.AdRequest));
                    break;
                case 'P':
                    OnUserRequest(this, new
                        UserRequestEventArgs(RequestType.PersonalMessageRequest));
                    break;
            }
        }
        while (!finished);
    }
}
```

This class contains the only line of code in which we actually use the `event` keyword to declare an event. The two lines of code of interest are these:

```
public delegate void UserRequest(object sender, UserRequestEventArgs e);

public event UserRequest OnUserRequest;
```

The pattern is much the same as when we were declaring delegates in the previous section of this chapter. We first define a delegate, and then declare an instance of one. Note that the definition of the delegate signature matches the signature that .NET requires all event handlers to have: it returns a void, and takes an object and something derived from EventArgs as parameters.

The second line is more interesting – here we tell the compiler that this class contains a member event, of a type given by the delegate. You can think of this line as meaning something like:

```
// not actual code - just presented for comparison
public UserRequest OnUserRequest = new UserRequest(// method);
```

except that the event syntax allows the compiler to make sure the delegate has the correct signature. It also implies we are instantiating the object, but not yet supplying any methods for it to refer to, something that we could not do with the alternative delegate syntax.

The rest of the UserInputMonitor class is given over to a method, Run(), which repeatedly loops, asking the user for input. Notice how the event actually gets fired:

```
switch(responseChar)
{
    case 'X':
        finished = true;
        break;
    case 'A':
        OnUserRequest(this, new UserRequestEventArgs(RequestType.AdRequest));
        break;
    case 'P':
        OnUserRequest(this, new
            UserRequestEventArgs(RequestType.PersonalMessageRequest));
        break;
}
```

We simply call the event, which automatically invokes any methods that it currently references (these will be the event handlers that the consumers have notified it about). In each case, we instantiate a new EventArgs-derived class to pass to the event handler.

Now we can look at the consumer classes. First, the MessageDisplayer:

```
class MessageDisplayer
{
    public MessageDisplayer(UserInputMonitor monitor)
    {
        monitor.OnUserRequest +=
            new UserInputMonitor.UserRequest(UserRequestHandler);
    }

    protected void UserRequestHandler(object sender, UserRequestEventArgs e)
    {
        switch (e.Request)
        {
            case RequestType.AdRequest:
```

```
                  Console.WriteLine("Mortimer Phones is better than anyone " +
                     "else because all our software is written in C#!\n");
                  break;
               case RequestType.PersonalMessageRequest:
                  Console.WriteLine("Today Mortimer issued the following " +
                     "statement:\n  Nevermore!\n");
                  break;
            }
         }
      }
```

The constructor to the `MessageDisplayer` is where we actually tell the `UserInputMonitor` class that we want to receive event notifications. We do this by adding a reference to our event handler to the `UserRequest` event. The event handler is our `UserRequestHandler()` method, and it simply checks the `EventArgs` parameter to see what type of message the user has requested, and displays the appropriate event. Note that, in line with common practice, we make the event handler `protected`. Generally, event handlers are intended to be called through events, in other words, through delegates. There's usually no reason for them to be called directly, so there's no reason for outside classes to be able to see them. (Notice that the fact a method is invisible to outside classes does not prevent those classes from calling it through a delegate if that delegate has been supplied with a reference to that method.)

Mortimer's personal `ManagersStaffMonitor` class does basically the same thing, except it displays a dialog box instead of writing to the console:

```
class ManagersStaffMonitor
{
   public ManagersStaffMonitor(UserInputMonitor monitor)
   {
      monitor.OnUserRequest +=
         new UserInputMonitor.UserRequest(UserRequestHandler);
   }

   protected void UserRequestHandler(object sender, UserRequestEventArgs e)
   {
      if (e.Request == RequestType.PersonalMessageRequest)
      {
         MessageBox.Show("Kaark!", "Mortimer says ...");
      }
   }
}
```

Finally, we can see how the whole set of classes fit together. This is the code for the `Main` routine:

```
using System;
using System.Windows.Forms;

namespace Wrox.ProCSharp.AdvancedCSharp
{
   class MainEntryPoint
   {
      static void Main()
```

```
    {
        UserInputMonitor inputMonitor = new UserInputMonitor();
        MessageDisplayer inputProcessor =
            new MessageDisplayer(inputMonitor);
        ManagersStaffMonitor mortimer =
            new ManagersStaffMonitor(inputMonitor);
        inputMonitor.Run();
    }
}
```

Quite apart from the event architecture, this is actually a classic example of object-oriented programming. The main entry point does almost nothing itself. It simply instantiates the various objects that make up the application, and sets them off interacting with each other. In this sample, we create an instance of each of the three main classes, and initialize them appropriately. We then call the `inputMonitor`'s `Run()` method, which enters the main program loop, asking the user for input. When we cover Windows Forms in Chapter 7, we will find that a Windows Forms application has a very similar structure to this. For this type of application, we instantiate our objects, then call a static method, `Run()` on a .NET base class, `Windows.Forms.Application`, which sets the whole events process going.

If we run our sample, we get this result:

```
UserInputNotify
Select preferred option:
   Request advertisement - hit A then Return
   Request personal message from Mortimer - hit P then Return
   Exit - hit X then Return
A
Mortimer Phones is better than anyone else because all our software is written in
C#!

Select preferred option:
   Request advertisement - hit A then Return
   Request personal message from Mortimer - hit P then Return
   Exit - hit X then Return
P
Today Mortimer issued the following statement:
   Nevermore!
```

with the Windows Form when the user hits *P* looking like this:

The C# Preprocessor Directives

Besides the usual keywords, most of which we have now encountered, C# also includes a number of commands that are known as **preprocessor directives**. These commands never actually get translated to any commands in your executable code, but instead they affect aspects of the compilation process. For example, you can use preprocessor directives to prevent the compiler from compiling certain portions of your code. You might do this if you are planning to release two versions of the code, a basic version, and an enterprise version that will have more features. You could use preprocessor directives to prevent the compiler from compiling code related to the additional features when you are compiling the basic version of the software. Another scenario is that you might have written bits of code that are intended to provide you with debugging information. You probably don't want those portions of code compiled when you actually ship the software.

The preprocessor directives are all distinguished by beginning with the # symbol.

C++ developers will recognize the preprocessor directives as something that plays an important part in C and C++. However, there aren't as many preprocessor directives in C#, and they are not used as often. C# provides other mechanisms that achieve the same effect as many of the C++ directives. Also, note that C# doesn't actually have a separate preprocessor in the way that C++ does. The so-called preprocessor directives are actually handled by the compiler. Nevertheless, C# retains the name 'preprocessor directive' because these commands give the impression of a preprocessor.

We will briefly cover the purposes of the preprocessor directives here.

#define and #undef

#define is used like this:

```
#define DEBUG
```

What this does is tell the compiler that a symbol with the given name (in this case DEBUG) exists. It is a little bit like declaring a variable, except that this variable doesn't really have a value – it just exists. And this symbol isn't part of your actual code; it just exists while the compiler is compiling the code.

#undef does the opposite, and removes the definition of a symbol:

```
#undef DEBUG
```

If the symbol doesn't exist in the first place, then #undef has no effect. Similarly, #define has no effect if a symbol already exists.

You need to place any #define and #undef directives at the beginning of the C# source file, before any code that declares any objects to be compiled.

#define isn't much use on its own, but when combined with other preprocessor directives, especially #if, it becomes very powerful.

Incidentally, you might notice some changes from the usual C# syntax. Preprocessor directives are not terminated by semi-colons, and are normally the only command on a line. That's because for the preprocessor directives, C# abandons its usual practice of requiring commands to be separated by semicolons. If it sees a preprocessor directive, it assumes the next command is on the next line.

#if, #elif, #else, and #endif

These directives inform the compiler whether or not to compile a block of code. Consider this method:

```
int DoSomeWork(double x)
{
   // do something
#if DEBUG
      Console.WriteLine("x is " + x);
#endif
}
```

This code will compile as normal, except for the `Console.WriteLine()` method call that is contained inside the `#if` clause. This line will only be executed if the symbol `DEBUG` has been defined by a previous `#define` directive. When the compiler finds the `#if` directive, it checks to see if the symbol concerned exists, and only compiles the code inside the `#if` clause if the symbol does exist. Otherwise, the compiler simply ignores all the code until it reaches the matching `#endif` directive. Typical practice is to define the symbol `DEBUG` while you are debugging, and have various bits of debugging-related code inside `#if` clauses. Then, when you are close to shipping, you simply comment out the `#define` directive, and all the debugging code miraculously disappears, the size of the executable file gets smaller, and your end users don't get confused by being shown debugging information! (Obviously, you would do more testing to make sure your code still works without `DEBUG` defined). This technique is very common in C and C++ programming and is known as **conditional compilation**.

The `#elif` (=else if) and `#else` directives can be used in `#if` blocks and have the intuitively obvious meanings, and it is also possible to nest `#if` blocks:

```
#define ENTERPRISE
#define W2K

// further on in the file

#if ENTERPRISE
   // do something
   #if W2K
      // some code that is only relevant to enterprise
      // edition running on W2K
   #endif
#elif PROFESSIONAL
   // do something else
#else
   // code for the leaner version
#endif
```

Note that, unlike the situation in C++, using #if is not the only way to conditionally compile code. C# provides an alternative mechanism via the Conditional attribute, which we will explore in the next section.

#if and #elif support a limited range of logical operators too, using the operators !, ==, !=, and ||. A symbol is considered to be true if it exists and false if it doesn't. For example:

```
#if W2K && (ENTERPRISE==false)    // if W2K is defined but ENTERPRISE isn't
```

#warning and #error

Two other very useful preprocessor directives are #warning and #error. These will respectively cause a warning or an error to be raised when the compiler encounters them. If the compiler sees a #warning directive, then it will display whatever text appears after the #warning to the user, after which compilation continues. If it encounters a #error directive, it will display the subsequent text to the user as if it were a compilation error message, and then immediately abandon the compilation, so no IL code will be generated.

You can use these directives as checks that you haven't done anything silly with your #define statements, and you can also use the #warning statements to remind yourself to do something:

```
#if DEBUG && RELEASE
    #error "You've defined DEBUG and RELEASE simultaneously! "
#endif

#warning "Don't forget to remove this line before the boss tests the code! "
    Console.WriteLine("*I hate this job*");
```

#region and #endregion

The #region and #endregion directives are used to mark that a certain block of code is to be treated as a single block with a given name, like this:

```
#region Member Field Declarations
    int x;
    double d;
    Currency balance;
#endregion
```

This doesn't look that useful by itself; it doesn't affect the compilation process in any way. However, the real advantage is that these directives are recognized by some editors, including the Visual Studio. NET editor. These editors can use these directives to lay out your code better on the screen. We will see how this works in Chapter 6, when we look at Visual Studio. NET.

#line

The #line directive can be used to alter the file name and line number information that is output by the compiler in warnings and error messages. You probably won't want to use this directive that often. Its main use occurs if you are coding in conjunction with some other package that alters the code you are typing in before sending it to the compiler, since this will mean line numbers, or perhaps the file names reported by the compiler, won't match up to the line numbers in the files or the file names you are editing. The #line directive can be used to restore the match. You can also use the syntax #line default to restore the line to the default line numbering:

```
#line 164 "Core.cs"     // we happen to know this is line 164 in the file
                        // Core.cs, before the intermediate
                        // package mangles it.

// later on

#line default           // restores default line numbering
```

Attributes

Microsoft has defined a number of **attributes** in the .NET Framework base classes. For the most part, these are in some ways similar to preprocessor directives, to the extent that for the most part they don't actually translate into statements in your compiled code, but rather serve as directives to the compiler. There are also attributes that cause no compilation action, but cause extra data to be emitted to the compiled assembly – we will wait till the next chapter before we explore those ones however. Whereas preprocessor directives are specific to the C# compiler, attributes form part of the .NET Framework, and are even represented by .NET classes. And whereas there are a fixed number of preprocessor directives (we have just presented the full list in the last section), the number of attributes is theoretically unlimited, since the .NET Framework incorporates a mechanism for you to define your own custom attributes.

Essentially, an attribute is a marker that can be applied to an item in your code such as a method or class, or even an individual argument to a method, and which supplies extra information about that item. For example, the Conditional attribute can be used to mark a method as a debugging method like this:

```
[Conditional("DEBUG")]
public void DoSomeDebugStuff()
{
    // do something
}
```

From this example, we can see that in order to apply an attribute to an item, you supply the name of the attribute in square brackets immediately before the definition of the item. Certain attributes take parameters – these are supplied inside round brackets immediately following the name of the attribute.

At its most basic level, applying an attribute to an item might simply mean that the extra information about that item is left in the compiled assembly where it can be used for additional documentation purposes (using the technique of reflection, which we will discuss in the next chapter, you can also access this information programmatically from C# code). This will be the case for any custom attributes that you define. However, a number of attributes that are defined in the base classes are explicitly recognized by the C# compiler. For these particular attributes, the compiler will take certain actions, which may affect the generated code. This is the case for the `Conditional` attribute illustrated above, which will cause the compiler to compile the code for the `Conditional` item only if the named symbol has been defined using an earlier `#define` statement.

With such a wide variety of attributes, it is not really possible to give a systematic statement of what they do. However, we will give a flavor of what can be achieved using attributes in this section by introducing three commonly-used general-purpose attributes that are defined in the base classes, and which are recognized by the compiler. In Chapter 5, we will show you how to define your own custom attributes, and also provide examples of why you would want to do that. Also, in later chapters in the book, we will intermittently meet additional attributes from the .NET base classes.

Here we will consider the following three attributes:

❑   `Conditional` – It is possible to mark any method with the `Conditional` attribute. This will prevent the compiler from compiling that method or any statements that refer to it unless a named symbol has been defined. This can be used to give conditional compilation (for example, for debug builds).

❑   `DllImport` – Despite the extensive features of the .NET bass class library, there are occasions when you need to get access to the basic Windows API, or to other old-style functions that are implemented in classic Windows DLLs. The `DllImport` attribute exists for this purpose. It is used to mark a method as being defined in an external DLL rather than in any assembly.

❑   `Obsolete` – This attribute is used to mark a method that is now regarded as obsolete. Depending on the settings you apply to this attribute, it will cause the compiler to generate either a warning or an error if it encounters any code that attempts to use this method.

Although the details are beyond the scope of this book, we will also mention that it is possible to specify the exact layout of the fields in a struct in memory, using an attribute, `StructLayout`.

We will demonstrate the use of these attributes with a small example program, the `Attributes` sample. This sample displays a message box using the Windows API function, `MessageBox`, and also displays two debug messages if we are doing a debug build. One of these debug messages is called via an obsolete method.

> *In normal programming, you wouldn't use `DllImport` to display a message box, since the .NET base class method, `System.Windows.Forms.MessageBox.Show()` can do the job just as well. We have picked on this API function to use in our example because it is relatively well known. Usually, you would use `DllImport` for situations where there is no .NET class that will do the task at hand.*

This is what the code for the `Attributes` example looks like:

```
#define DEBUG    // comment out this line if doing a release build

using System;
using System.Runtime.InteropServices;
using System.Diagnostics;

namespace Wrox.ProCSharp.AdvancedCSharp
{

    class MainEntryPoint
    {
        [DllImport("User32.dll")]
        public static extern int MessageBox(int hParent, string Message,
                                            string Caption, int Type);

        static void Main()
        {
            DisplayRunningMessage();
            DisplayDebugMessage();
            MessageBox(0, "Hello", "Message", 0);
        }

        [Conditional("DEBUG")]
        private static void DisplayRunningMessage()
        {
            Console.WriteLine("Starting Main routine. Current time is " +
                            DateTime.Now);
        }

        [Conditional("DEBUG")]
        [Obsolete()]
        private static void DisplayDebugMessage()
        {
            Console.WriteLine("Starting Main routine");
        }
    }
}
```

We start off by indicating a number of additional namespaces to be used. This is because the `DllImport` attribute is defined in the `System.Runtime.InteropServices` namespace, while the `Conditional` attribute is defined in the `System.Diagnostics` namespace.

Inside the main entry class of the program, we define the method that we are going to call up from an external DLL. The `MessageBox()` API function is defined in the file `User32.dll`, so we pass the name of this file as a parameter to the `DllImport` attribute. Note that we also need to declare this method as `extern`. `MessageBox()` has been written in C, so the four parameters that it takes are strictly speaking defined in terms of data types available in C, but in C# terms these data types map to an `int` (used to store a Windows handle, which we can set to zero), two strings containing respectively the message to be displayed and the caption to be displayed in the title bar, and an integer that indicates what buttons should be displayed in the message box. Setting this final parameter to zero ensures there will be one button, entitled OK.

Usually, it would be better programming practice to use a class, `System.IntPtr` to store a handle, but we have stuck with `int` here to keep things simple.

Looking further down at the debugging functions we have defined, `DisplayDebugMessage()` simply writes a line to the console saying we are starting to run the program. We only want this method run if we are doing a debug build, so we mark it as conditional upon the DEBUG symbol being present. We also regard this method as being obsolete, since we have written a better version, `DisplayRunningMessage()`, which additionally displays the current date and time. We are trying to discourage people from using `DisplayDebugMessage()` any more, so we mark it with the `Obsolete` attribute to make sure a compiler warning gets displayed if this method gets used. There are a couple of other overloads to this attribute we could use:

```
[Obsolete("The DisplayDebugMessage is obsolete. Use " +
          "DisplayRunningMessage instead.")]
```

This will generate a compiler warning if this method is used, but it will be the specified custom error message instead of a default one, while:

```
[Obsolete("The DisplayDebugMessage is obsolete. Use " +
          "DisplayRunningMessage instead.", true)]
```

This will actually cause a compilation error instead of a warning if this method is used. The second, optional parameter is a `bool` that indicates whether the compiler should treat it as an error instead of a warning if this `Obsolete` item is used in your code.

Before we run the code, a quick word about the `Conditional` attribute. This attribute is actually quite sophisticated, since if the condition is not met, the compiler will not only not compile the code for the method, but will also automatically ignore any lines of code anywhere else in the source file that call up this method. In order for the compiler to be able to do this, the method must return a `void`. This makes the `Conditional` attribute a much neater way of arranging for a conditional compilation than the preprocessor `#if...#endif` directives that we saw in the last section, since these directives must be applied separately to each section of code that needs to be conditionally compiled. On the other hand, the preprocessor directives are a little more flexible because of their capacity to evaluate some logical expressions, and because they can be applied to any arbitrary section of code. The `Conditional` attribute can only be applied to a complete method as a unit.

Compiling and running the `Attributes` sample with the DEBUG symbol defined gives these results. Notice the warning given on compilation:

```
csc Attributes.cs
Microsoft (R) Visual C# .NET Compiler version 7.00.9466
for Microsoft (R) .NET Framework version 1.0.3705
Copyright (C) Microsoft Corporation 2001. All rights reserved.

Attributes.cs(19,10): warning CS0612:
        'Wrox.ProCSharp.AdvancedCSharp.MainEntryPoint.DisplayDebugMessage()'
        is obsolete

Attributes
Starting Main routine. Current time is 12/02/2002 18:47:32
Starting Main routine
```

Memory Management Under the Hood

One of the declared advantages of C# programming is that the programmer doesn't need to worry about detailed memory management; in particular the garbage collector deals with all memory cleanup on your behalf. The result is that you can get something close to the efficiency of languages like C++ without the complexity of having to handle memory management yourself in the way that you need to do in C++. However, although you don't have to manage the memory manually, if you are to write efficient code, it still pays to understand what is going on behind the scenes. In this section we will take a look at what happens in the computer's memory when you allocate variables. I should stress that the precise details of much of the content of this section are undocumented. You should interpret this section as a rather simplified guide to the general principles that are going on, rather than as a statement of exact implementation.

Value Data Types

We will start off by looking at what happens when you create a variable of a value type. We will examine what happens in memory when you execute these lines of code:

```
{
    int nRacingCars = 10;
    double engineSize = 3000.0;
    // do calculations;
}
```

In this code we have indicated to the compiler that we need space in memory to store an integer and a double, and that these memory locations are to be referred to respectively as nRacingCars and engineSize. The line that declares each variable indicates the point at which we will start requiring access to this variable, and the closing curly brace indicates the point at which the variables go out of scope.

Windows uses a system known as **virtual addressing**, in which the mapping from the memory address seen by your program to the actual location in hardware memory or on disk is entirely managed behind the scenes by Windows. The result of this is that each application on a 32-bit processor sees 4GB of available memory, irrespective of how much hardware memory you actually have in your computer (on 64-bit processors this number will be greater). This 4GB of memory is known as the **virtual address space** or **virtual memory**. For convenience we will continue referring to it simply as 'memory'.

Each memory location from this 4GB is numbered starting from zero. If you want to indicate a value stored at a particular location in memory, you need to supply the number that represents that memory location. In any high-level language, be it C#, VB, C++, Java or any other similar language, one of the things that the compiler does is convert the human-readable names that you have given your variables into the memory addresses that the processor understands. This 4GB of memory actually contains everything that is a part of the program, including the executable code and the contents of all variables used when the program runs. Any DLLs called up will all be loaded into this same address space; each item of code or data will have its own definite location.

Somewhere inside this memory is an area that is known as the **stack**. The stack is where value data types are usually stored. When you call a method, the stack is also used to copy any parameters passed in. In order to understand how the stack works, we need to notice the following important fact about the scope of variables in C#. It is *always* the case that if a variable a goes into scope before variable b, then b will go out of scope first. Look at this code:

```
{
    int a;
    // do something
    {
        int b;
        // do something else
    }
}
```

First, a gets declared. Then, inside the inner code block, b gets declared. Then the inner code block terminates and b goes out of scope, then a goes out of scope. So, the lifetime of b is entirely contained within the lifetime of a.

> Note that if the compiler hits a line like int i, j, the order of coming into scope looks indeterminate. Both variables are declared at the same time and go out of scope at the same time. In this situation, it doesn't matter to us in what order the two variables are removed from memory. The compiler will internally always ensure that the one that was put in memory first is removed last, thus preserving our rule about no crossover of variable lifetimes.

This idea that you always deallocate variables in the reverse order to how you allocate them might look a bit abstract, but it is crucial to the way that the stack works. Let's see what actually happens when we declare the variables nRacingCars and engineSize from our earlier example.

Somewhere in the program is something called the **stack pointer**. This is simply a variable (or an address in memory) that tells us the address of the next free location in the stack. When the program first starts running, the stack pointer will point to just past the end of the block of memory that is reserved for the stack. The stack actually fills downwards, from high memory addresses to low addresses. As data is put on the stack, the stack pointer will be adjusted accordingly, so it always points to just past the next free location. Now, we don't know exactly where in the address space the stack is – we don't need to know for C# development – but let's say for the sake of argument, that immediately before the above code that allocates the variables is executed, the stack pointer contains the value 800000 or, in hexadecimal, 0xC3500). We are taking this memory location just for the sake of argument, to keep the numbers simple. In fact, later on when we start running code that uses pointers, we will see that the stack actually starts round about memory location 1243328 (0x12F8C8). However, we can explain the principles of how the stack works just as well using any address, so we may as well pick a simple one. We will also mostly use decimal for addresses, again for simplicity, although it is more common to write memory addresses in hexadecimal format.

The situation is illustrated in the diagram. In the diagram, bold text indicates the contents of memory locations; plain text indicates the address or a description of the location:

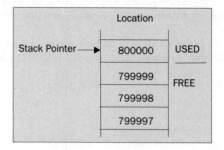

At this point, the variable nRacingCars comes into scope, and the value 10 is placed in it. What happens is that the value 10 will be placed in locations 799996-799999, the four bytes just below the location pointed to by the stack pointer – which are the first four free bytes on the stack. Four bytes because that's how much memory is needed to store an int. To accommodate this, 4 will be subtracted from to the stack pointer, so it now points to the location 799996, just after the new first free location.

The next line declares the variable engineSize, a double and initializes it to the value 3000.0. A double occupies 8 bytes, so the value 3000.0 will be placed in locations 799988-799995 in the stack, in whatever format the processor uses for 8-byte floating-point numbers, and the stack pointer will be decremented by 8, so that once again, it points just past the next free location on the stack.

When engineSize goes out of scope, the computer knows that it is no longer needed. Due to the way variable lifetimes are always nested, we can guarantee that, whatever else has happened while engineSize was in scope, the stack pointer will at this time happen to be pointing to the location just at where engineSize was stored. The process of removing this variable from scope is simple. The stack pointer is incremented by 8, so that it now points to where engineSize used to be. At this point in our code, we are at the closing curly brace, at which nRacingCars goes out of scope too, so the stack pointer gets incremented again, by 4 this time. If another variable were to come into scope at this point, it would just overwrite memory descending from location 799999, where nRacingCars used to be stored.

I've gone into a lot of detail about how variables are allocated, although even this discussion hasn't been exhaustive. For example, I've not touched on how the compiler is able to figure out the address of each variable. The thing I really want you to notice is just how fast and efficient the process of allocating variables on the stack is. There is little to be done other than increment the stack pointer – a simple arithmetic operation that will take just a few clock cycles.

Reference Data Types

While the stack gives very high performance, it is not really flexible enough to be used for all variables. The requirement that the lifetimes of variables must be nested is too restrictive for many purposes. Often, you may want to use some method to allocate some memory to store some data, and be able to keep that data available long after that method exited. This possibility exists whenever storage space is requested with the new operator – as is the case for all reference types. That's where the **managed heap** comes in.

If you have done any coding that requires low-level memory management in the past, you will be familiar with the stack and the heap as used in pre-.NET programs. The managed heap is not however quite the same as the heap that pre-.NET code such as classic C++ uses. It works under the control of the garbage collector and carries significant performance benefits compared to traditional heaps.

The managed heap (or just heap for short) is just another area of memory from that available 4GB. To see how the heap works and how memory is allocated for reference data types, examine this bit of code:

```
void DoWork()
{
    Customer arabel;
    arabel = new Customer();
    Customer mrJones = new Nevermore60Customer();
}
```

In this code, we have assumed the existence of two classes, Customer and Nevermore60Customer. These classes are in fact taken from Mortimer phones examples developed in Appendix A.

We declare a Customer reference called arabel. The space for this will be allocated on the stack, but remember that this is only a reference, not an actual Customer instance. The amount of space taken by the arabel reference will be 4 bytes for the address at which an instance of a Customer is actually stored. We need 4 bytes to be able to store an integer value between 0 and 4GB.

Then we get to the next line:

```
arabel = new Customer();
```

This line of code does several things. First, it allocates memory in the heap to store a Customer instance (a real instance, not just an address). Then, it sets the variable arabel to store the address of the memory it is allocated. It will also call the appropriate Customer() constructor to initialize the fields in the class instance, but we won't worry about that part here.

The customer instance will not be placed in the stack – it will be placed in the heap. Now, we don't know precisely how many bytes a Customer instance occupies, but let's say for the sake of argument it is 32. These 32 bytes contain the instance fields of Customer as well as some information that .NET uses to identify and manage its class instances, including the vtable.

The .NET runtime will look through the heap and grab the first contiguous block of 32 bytes that is unused. For the sake of argument, we will say that this happens to be at address 200000, and that the arabel reference occupied locations 799996-799999 on the stack. (Actually, from experiment, 20000 is nowhere near where the heap actually is – it is nearer locations 12000000, but we want to keep the numbers simple). This means that before instantiating the arabel object, the contents of memory will look like this.

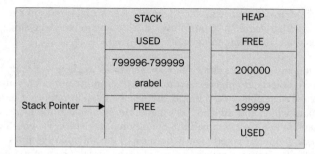

Note that, unlike the stack, memory in the heap is allocated upwards, so the free space can be found above the used space.

After allocating the object, memory looks like this.

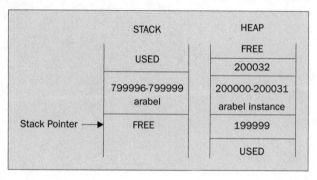

The next line of code that we execute does the same thing again, except that space on the stack for the mrJones reference needs to be allocated at the same time as the space for mrJones is allocated on the heap:

```
Customer mrJones = new Nevermore60Customer();
```

This line will result in 4 bytes being allocated on the stack to hold the mrJones reference. This will be stored at locations 799992-799995, while the mrJones instance itself will be allocated from locations 200032 upwards on the heap.

You can already see from this that the process of setting up a reference variable is more complex than it is for setting up a value variable, and inevitably there will be a performance hit. In fact we have somewhat oversimplified the process too, since the .NET runtime will need to maintain information about the state of the heap, and this information will also need to be updated whenever new data is added to the heap. However, we do now have a more flexible scheme for variable lifetime. To illustrate this, let's look at what happens when our method exits and the arabel and mrJones references go out of scope. In accordance with the normal working of the stack, the stack pointer will be incremented so these variables no longer exist. However, these variables only store addresses, not the actual class instances. The data for those class instances is still sitting there on the heap, where it will remain until either the program terminates, or the garbage collector is called. More importantly from our point of view, it is perfectly possible for us to set other reference variables to point to the same objects – this means that those objects will be available after the arabel and mrJones references have gone out of scope. And this is an important difference between the stack and the heap: objects allocated successively on the heap do not have nested lifetimes.

That's the power of reference data types, and you will see this feature used extensively in C# code. It means that we have a high degree of control over the lifetime of our data, since it is guaranteed to exist in the heap as long as we are maintaining some reference to it.

The above discussion and diagrams show the managed heap working very much like the stack, to the extent that successive objects are placed next to each other in memory. This means that we can work out where to place the next object very simply, by using a heap pointer that indicates the next free memory location, and which gets adjusted as we add more objects to the heap. However, there appears to be a problem here. When we explained the operation of the stack, we emphasized that it was only possible for the stack to operate so efficiently because of the way that lifetimes of stack variables are nested. The lifetimes of references have gone out of scope, yet the heap apparently works as if they also follow this rule. How is that possible? The answer is that it works thanks to the garbage collector. When the garbage collector runs, it will remove all those objects from the heap that are no longer referenced. Immediately after it has done this, the heap will have objects scattered on it, mixed up with memory that has just been freed, a bit like this:

If the managed heap stayed looking like that, allocating further objects on it would be an awkward process, with the computer having to search through it looking for a block of memory big enough to store each object. However, the garbage collector doesn't leave the heap in this state. As soon as it has freed up all the objects it can, it compacts all the others by moving them all back to the end of the heap to form one contiguous block again. This means that the heap can continue working just like the stack as far as locating where to store new objects is concerned. Of course, when the objects are moved about, all the references to those objects need to be updated with the correct new addresses, but the garbage collector handles that too.

This action of compacting by the garbage collector is where the managed heap really works differently from old unmanaged heaps. With the managed heap, it is just a question of reading the value of the heap pointer, rather than, say, trawling through a linked list of addresses to find somewhere to put the new data. For this reason, instantiating reference types under .NET is much faster. Interestingly, accessing them tends to be faster too, since the objects are compacted towards the same area of memory on the heap that will mean less page swapping may be required. Microsoft believes that these performance gains will compensate, and possibly more than compensate, for the performance penalty that we get whenever the garbage collector needs to do some work and has to change all those references to objects it has moved.

Unsafe Code

As we have just seen, C# is very good at hiding much of the basic memory management from the developer, thanks to the garbage collector and the use of references. However, there are cases in which you will want direct access to memory. This is most commonly for performance reasons, or because you wish to access a function in an external (non-.NET) DLL that requires a pointer to be passed as a parameter (as some Windows API functions do). Also, in some cases, you may wish to inspect memory contents for debugging purposes, or you may be writing an application such as a debugger that analyses other processes, and where the user needs direct access to memory. In this section, we will examine C#'s facilities that allow you to do this.

> *We should emphasize that although there are situations where you might need pointers, and we detail some of them below, they are really not that common. We would also strongly advise against using pointers unnecessarily, because if you do, your code will not only be harder to debug, but will fail the memory type-safety checks imposed by the CLR, which we discussed in Chapter 1. If you believe you have a good reason in the particular application you are developing for using pointers (the most likely reason is for backwards compatibility with some legacy code your application has to work with), then fine. Otherwise, you will usually find that using pointers is unnecessary. This advice particularly applies to ex-C++ developers who will be used to using pointers in C++ in a wide variety of situations. Pointers in C# are available in case you need them, but they are not needed nearly as often as they are in C++.*

Pointers

Although we are introducing **pointers** as if they are a new topic, in reality pointers are not new to us at all, because we have been using references freely in our code, and a reference is simply a dressed-up pointer. We have already seen how variables that represent classes and arrays actually store the address in memory of where the corresponding data (the **referent**) is actually stored. A pointer is simply a variable that stores the address of something else in the same way as a reference. The difference is that the C# syntax for reference does not allow you to access that address programmatically. With a reference, the variable is treated syntactically as if it stores the actual contents of the referent. If, say, the class instance referred to happened to be stored at memory location 0x334b38, then there is no way that you could gain access to that number 0x334b38 using a reference.

C# references are designed that way to make the language simpler to use, and to prevent you from inadvertently doing something that corrupts the contents of memory, and possibly prevents the garbage collector from being able to do its job properly. With a pointer, on the other hand, the actual memory address is available to you. This gives you a lot of power to perform new kinds of operations. For example, you can add 4 bytes onto the address, so that you can examine or even modify whatever data happens to be stored 4 bytes further on.

There are three advantages to using pointers:

❑ **Performance** – Provided you know what you are doing, you can ensure that the data is accessed or manipulated in the most efficient way possible – that is the reason why languages such as C and C++ have always allowed pointers.

❑ **Backwards compatibility** – Remember that, despite all of the facilities provided by the .NET runtime, it is still possible to call the old Windows API functions if you wish to, and for some operations, this may be the only way to accomplish your task. These API functions are all written in C, a language that uses pointers extensively, which means that many of these functions take pointers as parameters. Third parties may also in the past have supplied DLLs containing functions that take pointer parameters. Having said all that, in many cases it is possible to write the `DllImport` declaration in a way that avoids use of pointers, for example, by using the `System.IntPtr` class.

❑ You may need to **make memory addresses available to the user** – For example, if you are developing an application that provides some direct user interface to memory, such as a debugger).

However, this low-level memory access comes at various costs, in particular:

❑ The syntax required to get this functionality is more complex.

❑ Pointers are harder to use. You need very good programming skills and an excellent ability to think carefully and logically about what your code is doing in order to use them successfully. It is very easy to introduce subtle bugs to your program with pointers.

❑ In particular, if you are not careful, it is easy to overwrite other variables, cause stack overflows, access some area of memory that doesn't store any variables as if it did, or even overwrite information about your code that is needed by the .NET runtime, thereby crashing your program.

❑ For the case of .NET code, any use of pointers will cause the code to fail the .NET type-safety checks, which, depending on your security policies, may cause the .NET Framework to refuse to execute the code.

Incidentally, not so many decades ago it was possible for careless use of pointers to crash not just your program, but also other programs running on the system – or in extreme cases, the entire operating system itself. These days, operating systems have much more security built in to prevent you from overwriting memory that belongs to other processes or to the operating system, and generally, it is now only your own process that is at risk from careless use of pointers.

Despite these risks, pointers remain a very powerful and flexible tool in the writing of efficient code, and are worth learning about.

Due to the risks associated with pointer use, C# only allows the use of pointers in blocks of code that you have specifically marked for this purpose. The keyword to do this is `unsafe` (if the previous discussion wasn't enough to warn you of the potential dangers of pointers, Microsoft has even chosen a keyword that reinforces the point!). You can mark an individual method as being `unsafe` like this:

```
unsafe int GetSomeNumber()
{
    // code that can use pointers
}
```

Any method can be marked as `unsafe`, irrespective of what other modifiers may have been applied to it (for example, static methods, or virtual methods).

Or you can mark an entire class or struct as `unsafe`:

```
unsafe class MyClass
{
    // any method in this class can now use pointers
}
```

If you mark a class or struct as `unsafe`, all of its members are assumed to be unsafe.

Similarly, you can mark a field as `unsafe`:

```
class MyClass
{
    unsafe int *pX;    // declaration of a pointer field in a class
}
```

Or you can mark a block of code within a method as `unsafe`:

```
void MyMethod()
{
    // code that doesn't use pointers
    unsafe
    {
        // unsafe code that uses pointers here
    }
    // more 'safe' code that doesn't use pointers
}
```

Note, however, that you cannot mark a local variable by itself as `unsafe`:

```
int MyMethod()
{
    unsafe int *pX;    // WRONG
}
```

If you want to use an unsafe local variable, you will need to declare and use it inside a method or block statement that is unsafe. There is one more step before you can use pointers. The C# compiler will reject unsafe code unless you tell it that your code includes unsafe blocks. The flag to do this is `unsafe`. Hence, to compile a file named `MySource.cs` that contains unsafe blocks (assuming no other compiler options), the command is:

csc /unsafe MySource.cs

or:

csc -unsafe MySource.cs

If you are using Visual Studio .NET, you will find the option to compile unsafe code in the project properties. For the Visual Studio .NET versions of the downloadable samples in this section, you will find that we have already set the unsafe compilation option.

Pointer Syntax

Once you have marked a block of code as `unsafe`, you can declare a pointer using this syntax:

```
int * pWidth, pHeight;
double *pResult;
```

This code declares three variables. `pWidth` and `pHeight` are pointers to integers, and `pResult` is a pointer to a `double`. It is common practice to use the prefix `p` in front of names of pointer variables to indicate that they are pointers. When used in a variable declaration, the symbol `*` indicates that you are declaring a pointer, in other words, something that stores the address of a variable of the specified type.

> C++ developers should beware that syntax is different in C#. The C# statement *int *pX, pY;* corresponds to the C++ statement *int *pX, *pY;*. In C#, the * symbol is associated with the type rather than the variable name.

Once you have declared variables of pointer types, you can use them in the same way as normal variables, but first you need to learn two more operators:

❑ `&` means 'take the address of', and converts a value data type to a pointer, for example `int` to `*int`. This operator is known as the **address operator**.

❑ `*` means 'get the contents of this address', and converts a pointer to a value data type (for example, `*float` to `float`). This operator is known as the **indirection operator** (or sometimes as the **dereference operator**).

You will see from these definitions that `&` and `*` have the opposite effect to one another.

*You might be wondering how it is possible to use the symbols & and * in this manner, since these symbols also refer to the operators of bitwise AND (&) and multiplication (*). Actually, it is always possible for both you and the compiler to know what is meant in each case, because with the new pointer meanings, these symbols always appear as unary operators – they only act on one variable and appear in front of that variable in your code. On the other hand, bitwise AND and multiplication are binary operators – they require two variables.*

As examples of how to use these operators, consider this code:

```
int x = 10;
int *pX, pY;
pX = &x;
pY = pX;
*pY = 20;
```

We start off by declaring an integer, x, followed by two pointers to integers, pX and pY. We then set pX to point to x (in other words, we set the contents of pX to be the address of x). Then we assign the value of pX to pY, so that pY also points to x. Finally, we change the contents of x to 20 – since pY happens to point to x, *pY will evaluate to x. So the statement *pY = 20; will result in the value of x being changed to 20. Note that in all this code, there is no particular connection between the variables pY and x. It's just that at the present time, pY happens to point to the memory location at which x is held.

To understand what is going on further, let's suppose for the sake of argument that x is stored at memory locations 0x12F8C4 to 0x12F8C7 (1243332 to 1243335 in decimal) in the stack (there are 4 locations because an int occupies 4 bytes, and now we are choosing more realistic memory locations for our examples too). Since the stack allocates memory downwards, this means that the variables pX will be stored at locations 0x12F8C0 to 0x12F8C3, and pY will end up at locations 0x12F8BC to 0x12F8BF. Note that pX and pY also occupy 4 bytes each. That is not because an int occupies 4 bytes. It's because on a 32-bit processor you need 4 bytes to store an address. With these addresses, after executing the above code, the stack would look like this:

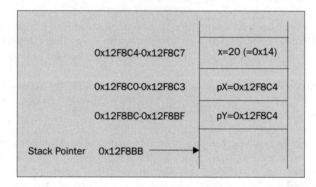

Although we have illustrated this process with ints, which will be stored consecutively on the stack on a 32-bit processor, this doesn't happen for all data types. The reason is that 32-bit processors work best retrieving data from memory in 4-byte chunks. Memory on such machines tends to be divided into 4-byte blocks, and each block is sometimes known under Windows as a DWORD because this was the name of a 32-bit unsigned int in pre-.NET days. It is most efficient to grab DWORDs from memory – storing data across DWORD boundaries normally gives a hardware performance hit. For this reason, the .NET runtime normally pads out data types so that the memory they occupy is a multiple of 4. For example, a short occupies 2 bytes, but if a short is placed on the stack, the stack pointer will still be decremented by 4, not 2, so that the next variable to go on the stack will still start at a DWORD boundary.

You can declare a pointer to any value type, in other words, any of the predefined types uint, int, byte, and so on, or to a struct. However, it is not possible to declare a pointer to a class or array; this is because doing so could cause problems for the garbage collector. In order to work properly, the garbage collector needs to know exactly what class instances have been created on the heap, and where they are, but if your code started manipulating classes using pointers, you could very easily corrupt the information on the heap concerning classes that the .NET runtime maintains for the garbage collector. In this context, any data type that the garbage collector can access is known as a **managed type**. Pointers can only be declared as **unmanaged types** since the garbage collector cannot deal with them.

Casting Pointers to Integer Types

Since a pointer really stores an integer that represents an address, you won't be surprised to know that the address in any pointer can be explicitly converted to or from any integer type. For example, it is perfectly legitimate to write the following:

```
int x = 10;
int *pX, pY;
pX = &x;
pY = pX;
*pY = 20;
uint y = (uint)pX;
int *pD = (int*)y;
```

y will now be a uint. We have then converted this quantity back to an int*, stored in the new variable pD. Hence, pD also points to the original value of x.

One reason for casting a pointer value to an integer type is in order to display it. The Console.Write() and Console.WriteLine() methods do not have any overloads that can take pointers, but will accept and display pointer values that have been cast to integer types:

```
Console.WriteLine("Address is" + pX);     // wrong - will give a
                                           // compilation error
Console.WriteLine("Address is" + (uint) pX);    // OK
```

Note that you can legally cast a pointer to any of the integer types. However, since an address occupies 4 bytes on 32-bit systems, casting a pointer to anything other than a uint, long, or ulong is almost certain to lead to overflow errors, and is therefore probably not a good idea. (An int can also cause problems, because its range is from roughly -2 billion to 2 billion, whereas an address runs from zero to about 4 billion). When C# is released for 64-bit processors, an address will occupy 8 bytes. Hence, on such systems, casting a pointer to anything other than ulong is likely to lead to overflow errors. It is also important to be aware that the checked keyword does not apply to conversions involving pointers. For such conversions, exceptions will not be raised when overflows occur, even in a checked context. The .NET runtime assumes that if you are using pointers you probably know what you are doing and are happy about the overflows!

Pointer-to-integer-type conversions must be explicit. Implicit conversions are not available for such conversions.

Casting Between Pointer Types

You can also explicitly convert between pointers pointing to different types. For example:

```
byte aByte = 8;
byte *pByte= &aByte;
double *pDouble = (double*)pByte;
```

This is perfectly legal code, though again, if you try something like this, be careful. With the above example, if we look up the double pointed to by pDouble, we will actually be looking up some memory that contains a byte, combined with some other memory, and treating it as if this area of memory contained a double, which won't give a meaningful value. However, you might want to convert between types in order to implement a union, or you might want to cast pointers to other types into pointers to sbyte in order to examine individual bytes of memory.

void Pointers

If you wish to maintain a pointer, but do not wish to specify what type of data it points to, you can declare it as a pointer to a void:

```
void *pointerToVoid;
pointerToVoid = (void*)pointerToInt;   // pointerToInt declared as int*
```

The main use of this is if you need to call any API functions that require void* parameters. Within the C# language, there isn't a great deal that you can do using void pointers. In particular, the compiler will flag an error if you attempt to dereference a void pointer using the * operator.

The sizeof Operator

Throughout this section, we have been referring to the sizes of various data types. If you need to explicitly use the size of a type in your code, you can use the sizeof operator, which takes the name of a data type as a parameter, and returns the number of bytes occupied by that type. For example:

```
int x = sizeof(double);
```

This will set x to the value 8.

The advantage of using sizeof is that you don't have to remember the sizes of particular types, and you can be certain the value you are using in your program is correct. For the predefined data types, sizeof returns the following values:

sizeof(sbyte) = 1;	sizeof(byte) = 1;
sizeof(short) = 2;	sizeof(ushort) = 2;
sizeof(int) = 4;	sizeof(uint) = 4;
sizeof(long) = 8;	sizeof(ulong) = 8;
sizeof(char) = 2;	sizeof(float) = 4;
sizeof(double) = 8;	sizeof(bool) = 1;

You can also use sizeof for structs that you define yourself, though in that case, the result will depend on what fields are in the struct. You cannot use sizeof for classes.

PointerPlayaround Example

We are now ready to present an example that uses pointers. The following code is a sample that I have named `PointerPlayaround`. It does some simple pointer manipulation and displays the results, allowing us to see for ourselves what is happening in memory and where variables are stored:

```
using System;

namespace Wrox.ProCSharp.AdvancedCSharp
{
    class MainEntryPoint
    {
        static unsafe void Main()
        {
            int x=10;
            short y = -1;
            byte y2 = 4;
            double z = 1.5;
            int *pX = &x;
            short *pY = &y;
            double *pZ = &z;

            Console.WriteLine(
                "Address of x is 0x{0:X}, size is {1}, value is {2}",
                (uint)&x, sizeof(int), x);
            Console.WriteLine(
                "Address of y is 0x{0:X}, size is {1}, value is {2}",
                (uint)&y, sizeof(short), y);
            Console.WriteLine(
                "Address of y2 is 0x{0:X}, size is {1}, value is {2}",
                (uint)&y2, sizeof(byte), y2);
            Console.WriteLine(
                "Address of z is 0x{0:X}, size is {1}, value is {2}",
                (uint)&z, sizeof(double), z);
            Console.WriteLine(
                "Address of pX=&x is 0x{0:X}, size is {1}, value is 0x{2:X}",
                (uint)&pX, sizeof(int*), (uint)pX);
            Console.WriteLine(
                "Address of pY=&y is 0x{0:X}, size is {1}, value is 0x{2:X}",
                (uint)&pY, sizeof(short*), (uint)pY);
            Console.WriteLine(
                "Address of pZ=&z is 0x{0:X}, size is {1}, value is 0x{2:X}",
                (uint)&pZ, sizeof(double*), (uint)pZ);

            *pX = 20;
            Console.WriteLine("After setting *pX, x = {0}", x);
            Console.WriteLine("*pX = {0}", *pX);

            pZ = (double*)pX;
            Console.WriteLine("x treated as a double = {0}", *pZ);

            Console.ReadLine();
        }
    }
}
```

This code declares three value variables:

- ❑ An int x

- ❑ A short y

- ❑ A double z

as well as pointers to these values. Then, we display the values of all these variables as well as their sizes and addresses. Note that in taking the address of pX, pY, and pZ, we are effectively looking at a pointer *to* a pointer – an address of an address of a value! Notice that, in accordance with usual practice when displaying addresses, we have used {0:X} format specifier in the Console.WriteLine() commands to ensure that memory addresses are displayed in hexadecimal format.

Finally, we use the pointer pX to change the value of x to 20, and do some pointer casting to see what rubbish results if we try to treat the content of x as if it was a double!

Compiling and running this code results in this output. In this screen output we have demonstrated the effects of attempting to compile both with and without the /unsafe flag:

```
csc PointerPlayaround.cs
Microsoft (R) Visual C# .NET Compiler version 7.00.9466
for Microsoft (R) .NET Framework version 1.0.3705
Copyright (C) Microsoft Corporation 2001. All rights reserved.

PointerPlayaround.cs(7,26): error CS0227: Unsafe code may only appear if
          compiling with /unsafe

csc /unsafe PointerPlayaround.cs
Microsoft (R) Visual C# .NET Compiler version 7.00.9466
for Microsoft (R) .NET Framework version 1.0.3705
Copyright (C) Microsoft Corporation 2001. All rights reserved.


PointerPlayaround
Address of x is 0x12F8C4, size is 4, value is 10
Address of y is 0x12F8C0, size is 2, value is -1
Address of y2 is 0x12F8BC, size is 1, value is 4
Address of z is 0x12F8B4, size is 8, value is 1.5
Address of pX=&x is 0x12F8B0, size is 4, value is 0x12F8C4
Address of pY=&y is 0x12F8AC, size is 4, value is 0x12F8C0
Address of pZ=&z is 0x12F8A8, size is 4, value is 0x12F8B4
After setting *pX, x = 20
*pX = 20
x treated as a double = 2.63837073472194E-308
```

Checking through these results confirms our description of how the stack operates, which we gave in the *Memory Management Under the Hood* section, earlier in the chapter. It allocates successive variables moving downwards in memory. Notice how it also confirms that blocks of memory on the stack are always allocated in multiples of 4 bytes. For example, y is a short (of size 2), and has the address 1243328, indicating that the memory locations reserved for it are locations 1243328-1243331. If the .NET runtime had been strictly packing variables up next to each other, then Y would have occupied just the two locations 1243328-1243329.

Pointer Arithmetic

It is possible to add or subtract integers to and from pointers. However, the compiler is quite clever about how it arranges for this to be done. For example, suppose you have a pointer to an int, and you try to add 1 on to its value. The compiler will assume you actually mean you want to look at the memory location following the int, and so will actually increase the value by 4 bytes – the size of an int. If it is a pointer to a double, adding 1 will actually increase the value of the pointer by 8 bytes, the size of a double. Only if the pointer points to a byte or sbyte (1 byte each) will adding 1 to the value of the pointer actually change its value by 1.

You can use the operators +, -, +=, -=, ++, and -- with pointers, with the variable on the right-hand side of these operators being a long or ulong.

Note that it is not permitted to carry out arithmetic operations on void pointers.

For example, let's assume these definitions:

```
uint u = 3;
byte b = 8;
double d = 10.0;
uint *pUint= &u;       // size of a uint is 4
byte *pByte = &b;      // size of a byte is 1
double *pDouble = &d;  // size of a double is 8
```

and let's assume the addresses to which these pointers point are:

❑   pUint: 1243332

❑   pByte: 1243328

❑   pDouble: 1243320

After executing this code:

```
++pUint;                // adds 1= 4 bytes to pUint
pByte -= 3;             // subtracts 3=3bytes from pByte
double *pDouble2 = pDouble - 4; // pDouble2 = pDouble - 32 bytes (4*8 bytes)
```

the pointers will contain:

❑   pUint: 1243336

❑   pByte: 1243321

❑   pDouble2: 1243328

> The general rule is that adding a number **X** to a pointer to type **T** with value **P** gives the result **P + X*(sizeof(T))**.

You need to be careful of this rule. If successive values of a given type are stored in successive memory locations, then pointer addition works very well to allow you to move pointers between memory locations. If you are dealing with types such as byte or char though, whose sizes are not multiples of 4, successive values will not by default be stored in successive memory locations.

You can also subtract one pointer from another pointer, provided both pointers point to the same data type. In this case, the result is a `long` whose value is given by the difference between the pointer values divided by the size of the type that they represent:

```
double *pD1 = (double*)1243324;    // note that it is perfectly valid to
                                   // initialize a pointer like this.
double *pD2 = (double*)1243300;
long L = pD1-pD2;                  // gives the result 3 (=24/sizeof(double))
```

Pointers to Structs – The Pointer Member Access Operator

We have not yet seen any examples of pointers that point to structs. In fact, pointers to structs work in exactly the same way as pointers to the predefined value types. There is, however, one condition – the struct must not contain any reference types. This is due to the restriction we mentioned earlier that pointers cannot point to any reference types. To avoid this, the compiler will flag an error if you create a pointer to any struct that contains any reference types.

Suppose we had a struct defined like this:

```
struct MyGroovyStruct
{
    public long X;
    public float F;
}
```

then we could define a pointer to it like this:

```
MyGroovyStruct *pStruct;
```

and initialize it like this:

```
MyGroovyStruct Struct = new MyGroovyStruct();
pStruct = &Struct;
```

It is also possible to access member values of a struct through the pointer:

```
(*pStruct).X = 4;
(*pStruct).F = 3.4f;
```

However, this syntax looks a bit complex. For this reason, C# defines another operator that allows you to access members of structs through pointers with a simpler syntax. It is known as the **pointer member access operator**, and the symbol is a dash followed by a greater than sign, so it looks like an arrow: ->.

C++ developers will recognize the pointer member access operator, since C++ uses the same symbol for the same purpose.

Using the pointer member access operator, the above code can be rewritten:

```
pStruct->X = 4;
pStruct->F = 3.4f;
```

You can also directly set up pointers of the appropriate type to point to fields within a struct:

```
long *pL = &(Struct.X);
float *pF = &(Struct.F);
```

or, equivalently:

```
long *pL = &(pStruct->X);
float *pF = &(pStruct->F);
```

Although these expressions also look syntactically rather complex, there is no equivalent of the `->` operator to help us out here.

Pointers to Class Members

We have indicated that it is not possible to create pointers to classes. That's because the garbage collector does not maintain any information about pointers, only about references, so creating pointers to classes could cause garbage collection to not work properly.

However, most classes do contain members that are themselves of value types, and you might wish to create pointers to them. This is possible, but requires a special syntax. For example, suppose we rewrite our struct from our previous example as a class:

```
class MyGroovyClass
{
    public long X;
    public float F;
}
```

Then you might wish to create pointers to its fields, X and F, in the same way as before. Unfortunately, doing so will produce a compilation error:

```
MyGroovyClass myGroovyObject = new MyGroovyClass();
long *pL = &( myGroovyObject.X);   // wrong
float *pF = &( myGroovyObject.F);  // wrong
```

So what's the problem? We are, after all, declaring pointers of perfectly legitimate types here – `long*` and `float*`. What is wrong is that although X and F are themselves unmanaged types, they are embedded in a class, which sits on the heap. This means that they are still indirectly under the control of the garbage collector. In particular, the garbage collector may at any time kick in and decide to move `MyGroovyClass` to a new location in memory in order to tidy up the heap. If it does that, then the garbage collector will of course update all references to the object, so that for example, the variable `myGroovyObject` will still point to the correct location. However, the garbage collector doesn't know about what pointers might be around, so if it moves the object referred to by `myGroovyObject`, `pL` and `pF` will still be unchanged and will end up pointing to the wrong memory locations. As a result of the risk of this problem, the compiler will not let you assign addresses of members of managed types to pointers in this manner.

The way round this problem is to use a new `fixed` keyword, which tells the garbage collector that there may be pointers pointing to members of certain class instances, and so those instances must not be moved. The syntax for using `fixed` looks like this if we just want to declare one pointer:

```
MyGroovyClass myGroovyObject = new MyGroovyClass();
// do whatever
fixed (long *pObject = &( myGroovyObject.X))
{
    // do something
}
```

In other words, we mark out a block of code as `fixed`. The block of code is bounded by braces, while in round brackets we define and initialize the pointer that we want to point to a class member. This pointer variable (`pObject` in the example) will now be scoped to the `fixed` block, and the garbage collector will then know not to move the instance `myGroovyObject` of `MyGroovyClass` while the code inside the `fixed` block is executing.

If you want to declare more than one such pointer, you can place multiple `fixed` statements before the same code block:

```
MyGroovyClass myGroovyObject = new MyGroovyClass();
fixed (long *pX = &( myGroovyObject.X))
fixed (float *pF = &( myGroovyObject.F))
{
    // do something
}
```

You can nest entire `fixed` blocks if you wish to fix several pointers for different periods:

```
MyGroovyClass myGroovyObject = new MyGroovyClass();
fixed (long *pX = &( myGroovyObject.X))
{
    // do something with pX
    fixed (float *pF = &( myGroovyObject.F))
    {
        // do something else with pF
    }
}
```

You can also initialize several variables within the same `fixed` block, provided they are of the same type:

```
MyGroovyClass myGroovyObject = new MyGroovyClass();
MyGroovyClass myGroovyObject2 = new MyGroovyClass();
fixed (long *pX = &( myGroovyObject.X), pX2 = &( myGroovyObject2.X))
{
    // etc.
```

In all these cases, it is immaterial whether the various pointers you are declaring point to fields in the same or different instances of classes, or to static fields not associated with any class instance.

Adding Classes and Structs to our Example

In this section, we will illustrate pointer arithmetic, as well as pointers to structs and classes, using a second example, which we will imaginatively title `PointerPlayaround2`. To start off, we will return to our earlier `Currency` struct we introduced in the section titled *User-Defined Casts*, and define a class and a struct that each represent a `Currency`. These types are similar to the `Currency` struct that we defined earlier, but simpler and with slightly different fields:

```
struct CurrencyStruct
{
    public long Dollars;
    public byte Cents;

    public override string ToString()
    {
        return "$" + Dollars + "." + Cents;
    }
}

class CurrencyClass
{
    public long Dollars;
    public byte Cents;

    public override string ToString()
    {
        return "$" + Dollars + "." + Cents;
    }
}
```

There is nothing significant about our choice of `Currency` for the struct and class, except to make our example look a bit less abstract and more realistic. Note also that `CurrencyStruct` and `CurrencyClass` are identical, aside from `CurrencyStruct` being a struct, and `CurrencyClass` being a class. This is just so we can demonstrate using pointers with both types of object.

Now we have our struct and class defined, we can apply some pointers to them. Here is the code for the new example. Since the code is fairly long, we will go through it in detail. We start off by displaying the size of the `Currency` struct, creating a couple of instances of it along with some pointers, and we use these pointers to initialize one of the `Currency` structs, `amount1`. Along the way we display the addresses of our variables:

```
public static unsafe void Main()
{
    Console.WriteLine(
        "Size of Currency struct is " + sizeof(CurrencyStruct));
    CurrencyStruct amount1, amount2;
    CurrencyStruct *pAmount = &amount1;
    long *pDollars = &(pAmount->Dollars);
    byte *pCents = &(pAmount->Cents);

    Console.WriteLine("Address of amount1 is 0x{0:X}", (uint)&amount1);
    Console.WriteLine("Address of amount2 is 0x{0:X}", (uint)&amount2);
    Console.WriteLine("Address of pAmt is 0x{0:X}", (uint)&pAmount);
    Console.WriteLine("Address of pDollars is 0x{0:X}", (uint)&pDollars);
    Console.WriteLine("Address of pCents is 0x{0:X}", (uint)&pCents);
    pAmount->Dollars = 20;
    *pCents = 50;
    Console.WriteLine("amount1 contains " + amount1);
```

Now we do some pointer manipulation that relies on our knowledge of how the stack works. Due to the order in which the variables were declared, we know that `amount2` will be stored at an address immediately below `amount1`. `sizeof(CurrencyStruc)` returns 16 (as demonstrated in the screen output coming up), so `CurrencyStruct` occupies a multiple of 4 bytes. Therefore, after we decrement our currency pointer, it will point to `amount2`:

```
--pAmount;    // this should get it to point to amount2
Console.WriteLine("amount2 has address 0x{0:X} and contains {1}",
    (uint)pAmount, *pAmount);
```

This `Console.WriteLine()` statement is interesting. We have displayed the contents of `amount2`, but we haven't yet initialized it to anything! What gets displayed will be random garbage – whatever happened to be stored at that location in memory before execution of the sample. There is an important point here, though. Normally, the C# compiler would prevent us from using an uninitialized value, but when you start using pointers, it is very easy to circumvent all the usual compilation checks. In this case we have done so because the compiler has no way of knowing that we are actually displaying the contents of `amount2`. Only we know that, because our knowledge of the stack means we can tell what the effect of decrementing `pAmount` will be. Once you start doing pointer arithmetic, you find you can access all sorts of variables and memory locations that the compiler would usually stop you from accessing, hence the description of pointer arithmetic as unsafe.

Next in our sample, we do something else that is equally cheeky. We do some pointer arithmetic on our `pCents` pointer. `pCents` currently points to `amount1.Cents`, but our aim here is to get it to point to `amount2.Cents`, again using pointer operations instead of directly telling the compiler that's what we want to do. Since to do this we need to decrement the address it contains by `sizeof(Currency)`, we need to do some casting to get the arithmetic to work out:

```
// do some clever casting to get pCents to point to cents
// inside amount2
CurrencyStruct *pTempCurrency = (CurrencyStruct*)pCents;
pCents = (byte*) ( --pTempCurrency );
Console.WriteLine("Address of pCents is now 0x{0:X}", (uint)&pCents);
```

Finally, we use the `fixed` keyword to create some pointers that point to the fields in a class instance, and use these pointers to set the value of this instance. Notice that this is also the first time that we have been able to look at the address of an item that is stored on the heap rather than the stack:

```
Console.WriteLine("\nNow with classes");
// now try it out with classes
CurrencyClass amount3 = new CurrencyClass();

fixed(long *pDollars2 = &(amount3.Dollars))
fixed(byte *pCents2 = &(amount3.Cents))
{
    Console.WriteLine(
        "amount3.Dollars has address 0x{0:X}", (uint)pDollars2);
    Console.WriteLine(
        "amount3.Cents has address 0x{0:X}", (uint) pCents2);
    *pDollars2 = -100;
    Console.WriteLine("amount3 contains " + amount3);
}
```

Running this code gives this output:

```
csc /unsafe PointerPlayaround2.cs
Microsoft (R) Visual C# .NET Compiler version 7.00.9466
for Microsoft (R) .NET Framework version 1.0.3705
Copyright (C) Microsoft Corporation 2001. All rights reserved.


PointerPlayaround2
Size of Currency struct is 16
Address of amount1 is 0x12F8A8
Address of amount2 is 0x12F898
Address of pAmt is 0x12F894
Address of pDollars is 0x12F890
Address of pCents is 0x12F88C
amount1 contains $20.50
amount2 has address 0x12F898 and contains $5340121818976080.102
Address of pCents is now 0x12F88C

Now with classes
amount3.Dollars has address 0xBA4960
amount3.Cents has address 0xBA4968
amount3 contains $-100.0
```

These results were obtained using the first release version of the .NET Framework. You may find that the actual addresses displayed are different if you run the sample on a different version of .NET.

Notice in this output the uninitialized value of `amount2` that we display, and that the size of the `Currency` struct is `16` – somewhat larger than we would expect given the sizes of its fields (1 long = 8 + 1 byte = 1). Evidently, some more word alignment is going on here. We can also see from this code the typical value of addresses on the heap: `12272624 = 0xBB43F0`. The heap clearly exists in a very different area of the virtual address space from the stack.

Using Pointers to Optimize Performance

Up to now, we have spent a lot of time looking at the various things that you can do with pointers, but in all our examples so far, we haven't really seen anything that would be very useful in many real applications. All we have done up to now essentially is to play around with memory in a way that is probably interesting to people who like to know what's happening under the hood, but doesn't really help us to write very good code. That's going to change in this section. Here we're going to apply our understanding of pointers and demonstrate an example in which judicious use of pointers will have a significant performance benefit.

Creating Stack-Based Arrays

In this section, we are going to look at the other main area in which pointers can be very useful; creating high-performance, low overhead arrays on the stack. We showed in Chapter 2 how C# includes rich support for handling arrays. While C# makes it very easy to use both one-dimensional and rectangular or jagged multidimensional arrays, it suffers from the disadvantage that these arrays are actually objects; they are instances of `System.Array`. This means that the arrays are stored on the heap with all of the overhead that it involves. There may be occasions when you just want to create an array for a short period of time and don't want the overhead of reference objects. It is possible to do this using pointers, although only for one-dimensional arrays.

In order to create a high-performance array we need another keyword, `stackalloc`. The `stackalloc` command instructs the .NET runtime to allocate a certain amount of memory on the stack. When you call it, you need to supply it with two pieces of information:

- ❑ The type of variable you want to store
- ❑ How many of these variables you need to store

As an example, to allocate enough memory to store 10 `decimal`s, you would write this:

```
decimal *pDecimals = stackalloc decimal [10];
```

Note that this command simply allocates the memory. It doesn't attempt to initialize it to any value – it is up to you to do that. The idea is that this is an ultra-high performance array, and initializing values unnecessarily would hurt performance.

Similarly, to store 20 `double`s you would write this:

```
double *pDoubles = stackalloc double [20];
```

Although this line of code specifies the number of variables to store as a constant, this can equally be a quantity evaluated at run-time. So you could equally write the second example above like this:

```
int size;
size = 20;   // or some other value calculated at run-time
double *pDoubles = stackalloc double [size];
```

You will see from these code snippets that the syntax of `stackalloc` is slightly unusual. It is followed immediately by the name of the data type you want to store (and this must be a value type), and then by the number of variables you need space for in square brackets. The number of bytes allocated will be this number multiplied by `sizeof(data type)`. The use of square brackets here suggests an array, which isn't too surprising, because if you have allocated space for, say, 20 `double`s, then effectively what you have is an array of 20 `double`s. The simplest, most basic type of array that it is possible to have is a block of memory that stores one element after another, like this:

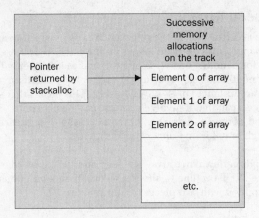

In this diagram, we have also shown the pointer returned by stackalloc, which always returns a pointer to the allocated data type, and sets this return value so that the pointer points to the start of the memory allocated.

The next question is how you use the memory you have just obtained. Carrying on our example, we have just said that the return value from stackalloc points to the start of the memory. It therefore follows that you can get to the first location of allocated memory by dereferencing that pointer. So, for example, to allocate our doubles and then set the first element (that is, element 0 of the array) to the value 3.0, you could write this:

```
double *pDoubles = stackalloc double [20];
*pDoubles = 3.0;
```

What about the next element? This is where the pointer arithmetic that we learned earlier comes in. Recall that if you syntactically add 1 to a pointer, its value will actually be increased by the size of whatever data type it points to. In this case, this will be just enough to take us to the next free memory location in the block that we have allocated. So, we can set the second element of a block (that is to say, element number 1 of the array, since we always count arrays from zero) like this:

```
double *pDoubles = stackalloc double [20];
*pDoubles = 3.0;
*(pDoubles+1) = 8.4;
```

And by the same reasoning in general, we can obtain the element with index X of the array with the expression *(pDoubles+X).

That's good as far as it goes – we effectively have a means by which we can access elements of our array, but for general purpose use, having to use that kind of syntax to get to array elements isn't going to win many friends. Fortunately, C# defines an alternative syntax. The way it works is that C# gives a very precise meaning to square brackets when they are applied to pointers. In general, if the variable p is any pointer type and X is any numeric type, then in C#, the expression p[X] is always interpreted by the compiler as meaning *(p+X). This is actually true in general – the pointer p doesn't need to have been initialized using stackalloc. And with this shorthand notation, we now have a very convenient syntax for accessing our array. In fact, it means that we have exactly the same syntax for accessing stack-based arrays as we do for accessing heap-based arrays that are represented by the System.Array class:

```
double *pDoubles = stackalloc double [20];
pDoubles[0] = 3.0;     // pDoubles[0] is the same as *pDoubles
pDoubles[1] = 8.4;     // pDoubles[1] is the same as *(pDoubles+1)
```

This idea of applying array syntax to pointers isn't new. It has been a fundamental part of both the C and the C++ languages ever since those languages were invented. Indeed, C++ developers will recognize the stack-based arrays we can obtain using stackalloc *as being essentially identical to classic stack-based C and C++ arrays. It is this syntax and the way it links pointers and arrays which was one of the reasons why the C language became popular back in the '70s, and the main reason why the use of pointers became such a popular programming technique in C and C++.*

Although our high-performance array can be accessed in the same way as a normal C# array, we do need to point out one word of warning. The following code in C# will raise an exception:

```
double [] myDoubleArray = new double [20];
myDoubleArray[50] = 3.0;
```

The exception occurs for the obvious reason that we are trying to access an array using an index that is out of bounds (the index is 50, maximum allowed value is 19). However, if you declare the equivalent array using stackalloc, there is now no object wrapped around the array that can do any bounds checking. Hence, the following code will *not* raise an exception:

```
double *pDoubles = stackalloc double [20];
pDoubles[50] = 3.0;
```

In this code, we allocate enough memory to hold 20 doubles. Then we set sizeof(double) memory locations starting at the location given by the start of this memory + 50*sizeof(double) to hold the double value 3.0. Unfortunately, that memory location is way outside the area of memory that we have allocated for the doubles. And who knows what data might be stored at that address? At best, we may have 'merely' corrupted the value of another variable, but it is equally possible for example that we may have just overwritten some locations in the stack that were being used to store the return address from the method currently being executed – the address that tells the computer where to carry on from when the method returns. In this case, the future execution path of our program is going to be, shall we say, novel! Once again, we see that the high performance to be gained from pointers comes at a cost; you need to be certain you know what you are doing, or you will get some very strange run-time bugs.

QuickArray Example

We will round off our discussion about pointers with a stackalloc example called QuickArray. In this example, the program simply asks the user how many elements they want to be allocated for an array. The code then uses stackalloc to allocate an array of longs that size. The elements of this array are populated with the squares of the integers starting from 0 and the results displayed on the console:

```
using System;

namespace Wrox.ProCSharp.AdvancedCSharp
{
    class MainEntryPoint
    {
```

```
    static unsafe void Main()
    {
        Console.Write("How big an array do you want? \n> ");
        string userInput = Console.ReadLine();
        uint size = uint.Parse(userInput);

        long *pArray = stackalloc long [(int)size];
        for (int i=0 ; i<size ; i++)
            pArray[i] = i*i;

        for (int i=0 ; i<size ; i++)
            Console.WriteLine("Element {0} = {1}", i, *(pArray+i));
    }
  }
}
```

QuickArray
```
How big an array do you want?
> 15
Element 0 = 0
Element 1 = 1
Element 2 = 4
Element 3 = 9
Element 4 = 16
Element 5 = 25
Element 6 = 36
Element 7 = 49
Element 8 = 64
Element 9 = 81
Element 10 = 100
Element 11 = 121
Element 12 = 144
Element 13 = 169
Element 14 = 196
```

Summary

This chapter has surveyed a number of separate topics in the C# language. We have covered the rich mechanism C# has for dealing with error conditions through exceptions, the ability of casting between different classes and structs, passing methods as parameters via delegates, and the related area of notifying applications of interesting things that have happened, via events. We have looked at the two main ways that C# gives us to control how code is compiled, through preprocessor directives and attributes, before finishing up with a discussion on what happens in-memory in the background and the use of pointers to gain that extra level of performance when you really need it.

We have already seen from previous chapters that C# is a powerful, object-oriented language that allows you to write well-structured code that follows the latest object-oriented methodologies. In this chapter, we have seen how C# actually goes beyond that to also provide facilities for handling a number of important programming paradigms that apply in specific circumstances on modern operating systems.

Although there are a couple of minor points of syntax that we are leaving until the next chapter, we have at this point covered pretty much the entire C# language, as far as keywords and language syntax are concerned. In the next chapter we will move on to investigate how C# interacts with the base classes to give you access to powerful programming techniques in a number of other areas, including string handling, custom attributes and threading. We will see how, through the technique of reflection, it is even possible for a C# program to access the assembly that describes its own objects, and those of other applications.

5

C# and the Base Classes

In this chapter, we are going to take a closer look at the **base classes** and how they interact with the C# language to give you support for writing code in a number of areas. In particular, we are going to examine the following topics:

❑ Strings and regular expressions

❑ Groups of objects, including array lists, collections, and dictionaries

❑ Custom attributes and how to use them

❑ Reflection

❑ Threading

We will also examine `System.Object`, the class from which everything else is derived, in more detail.

These look like a somewhat miscellaneous range of subjects to tackle in one chapter, but there is a good reason for it. You see, we have made it clear right from the start that it is not possible to view the C# language in isolation. The language interacts with both the .NET Framework and the associated class library, the .NET base classes, in a very fundamental way. We have seen numerous examples of this as we have explored C# in the last few chapters. For example, all of the C# keywords that represent data types, such as `int`, `long`, and `string`, are mapped by the compiler directly onto corresponding base classes (in these cases, `System.Int32`, `System.Int64`, and `System.String`). Another example is that in the case of exceptions, the `throw` and `catch` statements require that the exception object is inherited from `System.Exception`.

The interaction between C# and the base classes has made it impossible for us to introduce you to the C# language without covering a fair number of classes in the .NET base class library in the process. However, up to now the emphasis has largely been on features of C#, in which the language syntax is the predominant issue, and base classes have been seen as helpers. In this chapter, we will reverse that, and look at a number of features that are available in C# that are sufficiently fundamental to be considered as a part of the language, but which are explicitly implemented mainly through the use of certain base classes rather than through the C# language syntax. At the end of this chapter, we will have a sufficient grounding in C# so that we will be ready to look in detail at applications, and how the language is applied in a number of specific areas – the subject of the rest of the book.

System.Object

In Chapter 3, we have touched on `System.Object`. We indicated that it is the universal base class from which everything else is inherited, and listed its main member methods. However, in that chapter we hadn't yet learned sufficient C# to be able to understand the significance of all of the methods, and as a result, the only `System.Object` methods that we were able to look at in any detail were `ToString()` and `Finalize()` (implemented as a destructor in C#). As we work through this chapter, we will need to work with many of the remaining `System.Object` methods. In this section, we will provide a brief summary of them, and look in detail at the various ways of testing for equality.

To recap, below we reproduce the table from Chapter 3 that lists the methods available in `System.Object`:

Method	Access	Purpose
`string ToString()`	`public virtual`	Returns a string representation of the object
`int GetHashCode()`	`public virtual`	Returns a hash of the object designed to allow you to efficiently look up instances of the object in dictionaries
`bool Equals(object obj)`	`public virtual`	Compares this object with another instance of the class for equality
`bool Equals(object objA, object objB)`	`public static`	Compares instances of the class for equality
`bool ReferenceEquals(object objA, object objB)`	`public static`	Compares object references to see if they refer to the same object
`Type GetType()`	`public`	Returns an object derived from `System.Type` that can give details of a data type

Method	Access	Purpose
object MemberwiseClone()	protected	Makes a shallow copy of the object (in other words, copies data in the object but not other objects any fields refer to)
void Finalize()	protected virtual	Destructor

Four of these methods are declared as `virtual` and are therefore available for you to override. In all cases, however, good programming practice places restrictions on how you should implement your overrides.

We will note the following about the `System.Object` members:

❑ `ToString()` – This is intended as a fairly basic, quick and easy string representation, and is used for those situations when you just want a quick idea of the contents of an object, perhaps for debugging. If you need a more sophisticated string representation that, for example, takes account of the culture (the locale) and any requests that client code makes to have the object represented in a particular format, then you should implement the `IFormattable` interface, which we'll cover later in this chapter. For example, dates can be expressed in a huge variety of different formats, but `DateTime.ToString()` does not offer you any choice about format.

❑ `GetHashCode()` – This is used if objects are placed in a data structure known as a **map** (also known as a **hash table** or **dictionary**). It is used by classes that manipulate these structures in order to determine where to place an object in the structure. If you intend your class to be used as key for a dictionary, then you will need to override `GetHashCode()`. There are some fairly strong requirements for how you implement your overload, and we deal with these later in this chapter in the *Dictionaries* section.

❑ `Equals()` (both versions) and `ReferenceEquals()` – There are subtle differences between how these three methods, along with the comparison operator, `==`, are intended to be used. There are also restrictions on how you should override the virtual, one-parameter version of `Equals()` if you choose to do so, because certain base classes in the `System.Collections` namespace call the method and expect it to behave in certain ways. We will explore these issues in this chapter.

❑ `Finalize()` – We covered this method in Chapter 3. It is intended as the destructor, and is called when a reference object is garbage collected to clean up resources. The `Object` implementation of `Finalize()` actually does nothing, and is ignored by the garbage collector, but this is not true of any overrides. You should override it only when necessary, for example if your object uses external resources such as file or database connections. If you do need to override it, then you should provide a `Close()` or `Dispose()` method for clients to use too. Note that value types are not garbage-collected, so for these types there is no point overriding `Finalize()`. Overriding `Finalize()` in C# is not done explicitly (as this causes a compilation error), but implicitly, by supplying a destructor. The destructor is converted by the compiler into a `Finalize()` method.

❑ `GetType()` – This method returns an instance of a class derived from `System.Type`. This object can provide an extensive range of information about the class of which your object is a member, including base type, methods, properties, and so on. `System.Type` also provides the entry point into .NET's **reflection technology**. We will examine this area in detail later in the chapter in the *Reflection* section.

❑ MemberwiseClone() – This is the only member of System.Object that we don't examine in detail anywhere in the book. There is no need to, since it is fairly simple in concept. It simply makes a copy of the object and returns a reference (or in the case of a value type, a boxed reference) to the copy. Note that the copy made is a **shallow copy** – this means that it copies all the value types in the class. If the class contains any embedded references, then only the references will be copied, not the objects referred to.

Comparing Reference Objects for Equality

One aspect of System.Object that can look surprising at first sight is the fact that it defines three different ways of comparing objects for equality. Add to this the comparison operator, and we actually have four ways of comparing for equality. Why so many? There are in fact some subtle differences between the different methods, which we will now examine. We will look first at the case where we are comparing reference types.

ReferenceEquals()

ReferenceEquals() is exactly what it says. It is there to test whether two references refer to the same instance of a class: whether the two references contain the same address in memory. As a static method, it is not possible to override it, so the System.Object implementation is what you always have. ReferenceEquals() will always return true if supplied with two references refer to the same object instance, and false otherwise. It does, however, consider null to be equal to null:

```
SomeClass x, y;
x = new SomeClass();
y = new SomeClass();
bool B1 = ReferenceEquals(null, null);    // returns true
bool B2 = ReferenceEquals(null,x);        // returns false
bool B3 = ReferenceEquals(x, y);          // returns false because x and y
                                          // point to different objects
```

Virtual Equals() Method

The virtual, instance version of Equals() can be seen pretty much as the opposite of ReferenceEquals(). While it is true that the System.Object implementation of Equals() works by comparing references, this method is provided in case you wish to override it to compare the values of object instances. In particular, if you intend your instances of your class to be used as keys in a dictionary, then you will need to override this method to compare values. Otherwise, depending on how you override GetHashCode(), the dictionary class that contains your objects will either not work at all, or will work very inefficiently. One point you should note when overriding Equals() is that your override should never throw exceptions. Once again, this is because doing so could cause problems for dictionary classes and possibly certain other .NET base classes that internally call this method.

We will show an example of how to override this method in the MortimerPhonesEmployees example later in this chapter, in the section on dictionaries (hash tables).

Static Equals() Method

The static version of Equals() actually does the same thing as the virtual, instance version. The difference is that the static version of this method is able to cope when either of the objects is null, and therefore, provides an extra safety guard against throwing exceptions if there is a risk that an object might be null. The static overload first checks whether the references it has been passed are null. If they are both null, then it returns true (since null is considered to be equal to null). If just one of them is null, then it returns false. If both references actually refer to something, then it calls the virtual, instance version of Equals(). This means that when you override the instance version of Equals(), the effect is as if you were overriding the static version as well.

Comparison Operator (==)

The comparison operator can be best seen as an intermediate version between strict value comparison and strict reference comparison. In most cases, writing:

```
bool b = (x == y);    // x, y object references
```

should mean that you are comparing references. However, it is accepted that there are some classes whose meanings make more intuitive sense if they are treated as values. In those cases, it is better to override the comparison operator to perform a value comparison. The obvious example of this is for strings for which Microsoft has overridden this operator, because when developers think of performing string comparisons, they are almost invariably thinking of comparing the contents of the strings rather than the references.

One point to watch for if you are overriding comparison functions and Object.GetHashCode() is that there are certain guidelines about good coding practice, and the compiler will actually flag a warning if you don't adhere to the following guidelines:

1. You shouldn't override just one of Object.Equals() or Object.GetHashCode(). If you need to override one of these methods, then consider overriding the other one as well. This is because dictionary implementations require both methods to act in a consistent way (if Object.Equals() does value comparisons, then GetHashCode() should construct a code based on the value too). Having said this though, you might ignore this guideline if you *know* your class will never be used as a dictionary key (more on that later in the chapter).

   At the time of writing, overriding GetHashCode() without overriding Equals() doesn't generate a compiler warning, but you should still be careful about doing that – doing so will most likely prevent dictionaries based on your class from working.

2. If you override the == operator, then you ought to override Object.Equals() (and hence, from the first rule, Object.GetHashCode()). This is because the expectation of client code will be that, if == does a value comparison, then Object.Equals() will do a value comparison too.

If you get a compiler warning because you are not following these guidelines, then you need to make sure you know what you are doing and you have a good reason for not following them.

By the way, don't be tempted to overload the comparison operator by calling the one-parameter version of Equals(). If you do that, and somewhere in your code an attempt is made to evaluate (objA == objB) when objA happens to be null, you will get an instant exception as the .NET runtime tries to evaluate null.Equals(objB)! Working the other way round (overriding Equals() to call the comparison operator) should be safe.

Comparing Value Types for Equality

When comparing value types for equality, the same principles hold as for reference types: ReferenceEquals() is used to compare references, Equals() is intended for value comparisons, and the comparison operator is viewed as an intermediate case. However the big difference here is that value types need to be boxed in order to convert them to references, and that Microsoft has in fact already overloaded the instance Equals() method in the System.ValueType class in order to provide meanings more appropriate to value types. If you call sA.Equals(sB) where sA and sB are instances of some struct, then the return value will be true or false according to whether sA and sB contain the same values in all their fields. On the other hand, no overload of == is available by default for your own structs. Writing (sA == sB) in any expression will result in a compilation error unless you have provided an overload of == in your code for the struct in question.

Another point is that ReferenceEquals() will always return false when applied to value types, because in order to call this method, the value types will need to be boxed into objects. Even if you write:

```
bool b = ReferenceEquals(v,v);   // v is a variable of some value type
```

you will still get the answer of false because v will be boxed separately when converting each parameter, which will mean you get different references! Calling ReferenceEquals() to compare value types doesn't really make much sense.

Although the default override of Equals() supplied by System.ValueType will almost certainly be adequate for the vast majority of structs that you define, you may wish to override it again for your own structs in order to improve performance. Also, if a value type contains reference types as fields, you may wish to override Equals() to provide appropriate semantics for these fields, as the default override of Equals() will simply compare their addresses.

String Handling

Since Chapter 2, we have been almost constantly using strings, and have taken for granted the stated mapping that the string keyword in C# actually refers to the .NET base class System.String. System.String is a very powerful and versatile class, but it is not by any means the only string-related class in the .NET armory. In this section, we start off by reviewing the features of System.String, and then we will go on to have a look at some quite nifty things you can do with strings using some of the other .NET classes – in particular those in the System.Text and System.Text.RegularExpressions namespaces. We will cover the following areas:

❑ **Building Strings** – If you're performing repeated modifications on a string, for example in order to build up a lengthy string prior to displaying it or passing it to some other method or software, the String class can be very inefficient. For this kind of situation, another class, System.Text.StringBuilder is more suitable, since it has been designed exactly for this situation.

❑ **Formatting Expressions** – We will also take a closer look at those formatting expressions that we have been using in the `Console.WriteLine()` method throughout these last few chapters. These formatting expressions are processed using a couple of useful interfaces, `IFormatProvider` and `IFormattable`, and by implementing these interfaces on your own classes, you can actually define your own formatting sequences so that `Console.WriteLine()` and similar classes will display the values of your classes in whatever way you specify.

❑ **Regular Expressions** – .NET also offers some very sophisticated classes that deal with the situation in which you need to identify or extract substrings that satisfy certain fairly sophisticated criteria from a long string. By sophisticated, I mean situations such as needing to find all occurrences within a string where a character or set of characters is repeated, or needing to find all words that begin with 's' and contain at least one 'n'. Although you can write methods to perform this kind of processing using the string class, such methods are cumbersome to write. Instead, you can use some classes from `System.Text.RegularExpressions`, which are designed specifically to perform this kind of processing.

System.String

Before we examine the other string classes, we will quickly review some of the available methods on the `String` class.

`System.String` is a class that is specifically designed to store a string, and allow a large number of operations on the string. Not only that, but because of the importance of this data type, C# has its own keyword and associated syntax to make it particularly easy to manipulate strings using this class.

You can concatenate strings using operator overloads:

```
string message1 = "Hello";
message1 += ", There";
string message2 = message1 + "!";
```

C# also allows extraction of a particular character using an indexer-like syntax:

```
char char4 = message[4];    // returns 'a'. Note the char is zero-indexed
```

There are also a large number of methods to perform such common tasks as replacing characters, removing whitespace, and capitalization. The available methods include:

Method	Purpose
Compare	Compares the contents of strings, taking into account the culture (locale) in assessing equivalence between certain characters
CompareOrdinal	As Compare, but doesn't take culture into account
Format	Formats a string containing various values and specifiers for how each value should be formatted

Table continued on following page

Method	Purpose
IndexOf	Locates the first occurrence of a given substring or character in the string
IndexOfAny	Locates the first occurrence of any one of a set of characters in the string
LastIndexOf	As for IndexOf, but finds the last occurrence
LastIndexOfAny	As for IndexOfAny, but finds the last occurrence
PadLeft	Pads out the string by adding a specified repeated character to the beginning of it
PadRight	Pads out the string by adding a specified repeated character to the end of it
Replace	Replaces occurrences of a given character or substring in the string with another character or substring
Split	Splits the string into an array of substrings, the breaks occurring wherever a given character occurs
Substring	Retrieves the substring starting at a specified position in the string
ToLower	Converts string to lowercase
ToUpper	Converts string to uppercase
Trim	Removes leading and trailing whitespace

Note that this table is not comprehensive, but is intended to give you an idea of the features offered by strings.

Building Strings

As we have seen, String is an extremely powerful class that implements a large number of very useful methods. However, String has a problem that makes it very inefficient for making repeated modifications to a given string – it is actually an **immutable** data type, which is to say that once you initialize a string object, that string object can never change. The methods and operators that appear to modify the contents of a string actually create new strings, copying the contents of the old string over if necessary. For example, look at the following code:

```
string greetingText = "Hello from all the guys at Wrox Press. ";
greetingText += "We do hope you enjoy this book as much as we enjoyed
                 writing it.";
```

What happens when this code executes is this: first, an object of type System.String is created and initialized to hold the text "Hello from all the people at Wrox Press. " Note the space *after* the full stop. When this happens, the .NET runtime will allocate just enough memory in the string to hold this text (39 chars), and we set the variable greetingText to refer to this string instance.

In the next line, syntactically it looks like we're adding some more text onto the string – we are not. Instead, we create a new string instance, with just enough memory allocated to store the combined text – that's 103 characters in total. The original text, `"Hello from all the people at Wrox Press. "`, is copied into this new string along with the extra text, `"We do hope you enjoy this book as much as we enjoyed writing it. "`Then, the address stored in the variable `greetingText` is updated, so the variable correctly points to the new `String` object. The old `String` object is now unreferenced – there are no variables that refer to it – and so will be removed the next time the garbage collector comes along.

By itself, that doesn't look too bad, but suppose we wanted to encode that string by replacing each letter (not the punctuation) with the character which has an ASCII code one further on in the alphabet, as part of some extremely simple encryption scheme. This would turn the string to `"Ifmmp gspn bmm uif hvst bu Xspy Qsftt. Xf ep ipqf zpv fokpz uijt cppl bt nvdi bt xf fokpzfe xsjujoh ju."` There are several ways of doing this, but the simplest and (if you are restricting yourself to using the `String` class) almost certainly the most efficient way is to use the `String.Replace()` method, which replaces all occurrences of a given substring in a string with another substring. Using `Replace()`, the code to encode the text would look like this:

```
string greetingText = "Hello from all the guys at Wrox Press. ";
greetingText += "We do hope you enjoy this book as much as we enjoyed writing
it.";
```

```
for(int i = (int)'z'; i>=(int)'a' ; i--)
{
    char old = (char)i;
    char new = (char)(i+1);
    greetingText = greetingText.Replace(old, new);
}

for(int i = (int)'Z'; i>=(int)'A' ; i--)
{
    char old = (char)i;
    char new = (char)(i+1);
    greetingText = greetingText.Replace(old, new);
}
Console.WriteLine("Encoded:\n" + greetingText);
```

For simplicity, this code doesn't wrap Z to A or z to a. These letters get respectively encoded to [and {.

How much memory do you think we needed to allocate in total to perform this encoding? `Replace()` works in a fairly intelligent way, to the extent that it won't actually create a new string unless it does actually make some changes to the old string. Our original string contained 23 different lowercase characters and 3 different uppercase ones. `Replace()` will therefore have allocated a new string 26 times in total, each new string storing 103 characters. That means that as a result of our encryption process there will be string objects capable of storing a combined total of 2,678 characters now sitting on the heap waiting to be garbage-collected! Clearly, if you use strings to do text processing extensively, your applications will run into severe performance problems.

It is in order to address this kind of issue that Microsoft has supplied the `System.Text.StringBuilder` class. `StringBuilder` isn't as powerful as `String` in terms of the number of methods it supports. The processing you can do on a `StringBuilder` is limited to substitutions and appending or removing text from strings. However, it works in a much more efficient way.

Whereas when you construct a string, just enough memory gets allocated to hold the string, the `StringBuilder` will normally allocate more memory than needed. You have the option to explicitly indicate how much memory to allocate, but if you don't, then the amount will default to some value that depends on the size of the string that `StringBuilder` is initialized with. It has two main properties:

❑   `Length` – The length of the string that it actually contains

❑   `Capacity` – How long a string it has allocated enough memory to store

Any modifications to the string take place within this block of memory, which makes appending substrings and replacing individual characters within strings very efficient. Removing or inserting substrings is inevitably still inefficient, because it means that the following part of the string has to be moved. Only if you perform some operation that exceeds the capacity of the string will new memory need to be allocated and the entire contained string possibly moved. At the time of writing, Microsoft has not documented how much extra capacity will be added, but from experiments the `StringBuilder` appears to approximately double its capacity if it detects the capacity has been exceeded and no new value for the capacity has been explicitly set.

As an example, if we use a `StringBuilder` object to construct our original greeting string, we might write this code:

```
StringBuilder greetingBuilder =
    new StringBuilder("Hello from all the guys at Wrox Press. ", 150);
greetingBuilder.Append("We do hope you enjoy this book as much as we enjoyed
                       writing it");
```

In order to use the `StringBuilder` class, you will need a `System.Text` reference in your code.

In this code, we have set an initial capacity of 150 for the `StringBuilder`. It is always a good idea to set some capacity that covers the likely maximum length of string, to ensure the `StringBuilder` doesn't need to relocate because its capacity was exceeded. Theoretically, you can set as large a number as it is possible to pass in an `int` for the capacity, though the system will probably complain that it doesn't have enough memory if you try to actually allocate the maximum of 2 billion characters (this is the theoretical maximum that a `StringBuilder` instance is in principle allowed to contain).

When the above code is executed, we first create a `StringBuilder` object that initially looks like this:

Then, on calling the `Append()` method, the remaining text is placed in the empty space, without needing to allocate any more memory. However, the real efficiency gain from using a `StringBuilder` comes when we are making repeated text substitutions. For example, if we try to encrypt the text in the same way as before, then we can perform the entire encryption without allocating any more memory whatsoever:

```
StringBuilder greetingBuilder =
    new StringBuilder("Hello from all the guys at Wrox Press. ", 150);
greetingBuilder.Append("We do hope you enjoy this book as much as we enjoyed
                        writing it");
```

```
for(int i = (int)'z'; i>=(int)'a' ; i--)
{
    char old = (char)i;
    char new = (char)(i+1);
    greetingBuilder = greetingBuilder.Replace(old, new);
}

for(int i = (int)'Z'; i>=(int)'A' ; i--)
{
    char old = (char)i;
    char new = (char)(i+1);
    greetingBuilder = greetingBuilder.Replace(old, new);
}
Console.WriteLine("Encoded:\n" + greetingBuilder.ToString());
```

This code uses the `StringBuilder.Replace()` method, which does the same thing as `String.Replace()`, but without copying the string in the process. The total memory allocated to hold strings in the above code is 150 for the builder, as well as the memory allocated during the string operations performed internally in the final `Console.WriteLine()` statement.

Normally, you will use `StringBuilder` to perform any manipulation of strings, and `String` to store or display the final result.

StringBuilder Members

We have demonstrated one constructor of `StringBuilder`, which takes an initial string and capacity as its parameters. There are also several others. Among them, you can supply only a string:

```
StringBuilder sb = new StringBuilder("Hello");
```

or create an empty `StringBuilder` with a given capacity:

```
StringBuilder sb = new StringBuilder(20);
```

Apart from the `Length` and `Capacity` properties we have mentioned, there is a read-only `MaxCapacity` property, which indicates the limit to which a given `StringBuilder` instance is allowed to grow. By default, this is given by `int.MaxValue` (roughly 2 billion, as noted earlier), but you can set this value to something lower when you construct the `StringBuilder` object if you wish:

```
// These will both set initial capacity to 100, but the max will be 500.
// Hence, these StringBuilders can never grow to more than 500 characters,
// they will raise exception if you try to do that.

StringBuilder sb = new StringBuilder("Hello", 100, 500);
StringBuilder sb = new StringBuilder(100, 500);
```

You can also freely explicitly set the capacity at any time, though an exception will be raised if you set it to a value less than the current length of the string, or which exceeds the maximum capacity:

```
StringBuilder sb = new StringBuilder("Hello");
sb.Capacity = 100;
```

The main `StringBuilder` methods available include:

Method	Purpose
`Append()`	Appends a string to the current string
`AppendFormat()`	Appends a string that has been worked out from a format specifier
`Insert()`	Inserts a substring into the current string
`Remove()`	Removes characters from the current string
`Replace()`	Replaces all occurrences of a character by another character or a substring with another substring in the current string
`ToString()`	Returns the current string cast to a `System.String` object (overridden from `System.Object`)

There are several overloads of many of these methods available.

> `AppendFormat()` *is actually the method that is ultimately called when you call* `Console.WriteLine()`, *which has responsibility for working out what all the format expressions like* `{0:D}` *should be replaced with. We will examine this method in the next section.*

At the time of writing, there is no cast (either implicit or explicit) from `StringBuilder` to `String`. If you want to output the contents of a `StringBuilder` as a `String`, the only way to do so is through the `ToString()` method.

Format Strings

So far, we have written a large number of classes and structs for the code samples presented in this book, and we have normally implemented a `ToString()` method for each of these in order to be able to quickly display the contents of a given variable. However, quite often there are a number of possible ways that users might want the contents of a variable to be displayed, and often these are culture- or locale-specific. The .NET base class, `System.DateTime` provides the most obvious example of this. Ways that you might want to display the same date include 14 February 2002, 14 Feb 2002, 2/14/02 (in the USA, at least – in the UK, this would be written 14/2/02), or of course in Germany you'd write 14. Februar 2002, and so on.

Similarly, for our `Vector` struct that we wrote in Chapter 3, we implemented the `Vector.ToString()` method to display the vector in the format (4, 56, 8). There is, however, another very common way of writing vectors, in which this vector would appear as 4i + 56j + 8k. If we want the classes that we write to be user-friendly, then they need to support the facility to display their string representations in any of the formats that users are likely to want to use. The .NET runtime defines a standard way that this should be done: using an interface, `IFormattable`. Showing how to add this important feature to your classes and structs is the subject of this section.

The most obvious time that you need to specify the format in which you want a variable displayed is when you call `Console.WriteLine()`. Therefore, we are going to use this method as an example, although most of our discussion applies for any situation in which you wish to format a string. If for example, you wish to display the value of a variable in a listbox or textbox, you will normally use the `String.Format()` method to obtain the appropriate string representation of the variable, but the actual format specifiers you use to request a particular format are identical to those passed to `Console.WriteLine()`, and as we will see in this section, the same underlying mechanism is used. Hence, we will focus on `Console.WriteLine()` as an example. We start by examining what actually happens when you supply a format string to a primitive type, and from this we will see how we can plug in format specifiers for our own classes and structs into the process.

Recall from Chapter 2 that we use format strings in `Console.Write()` and `Console.WriteLine()` like this:

```
double d = 13.45;
int i = 45;
Console.WriteLine("The double is {0,10:E} and the int contains {1}", d, i);
```

The format string itself consists mostly of the text to be displayed, but wherever there is a variable to be formatted, its index in the parameter list appears in braces. The may be other information inside the brackets concerning the format of that item:

❑   The number of characters to be occupied by the representation of the item can appear; this information will be prefixed by a comma. A negative number indicates that the item should be left justified, while a positive number indicates that it should be right justified. If the item actually occupies more characters than have been requested, it will still appear in full.

❑   A format specifier can also appear. This will be preceded by a colon, and indicates how we wish the item to be formatted. For example, do we want a number to be formatted as a currency, or displayed in scientific notation?

We covered the common format specifiers for the numeric types in brief in Chapter 2. Here is the table again for reference:

Specifier	Applies to	Meaning	Example
C	numeric types	locale-specific monetary value	$4834.50 (USA) £4834.50 (UK)
D	integer types only	general integer	4834
E	numeric types	scientific notation	4.834E+003
F	numeric types	fixed point decimal	4384.50
G	numeric types	general number	4384.5
N	numeric types	usual locale-specific format for numbers	4,384.50 (UK/USA) 4 384,50 (continental Europe)
P	numeric types	Percentage notation	432,000.00%
X	integer types only	hexadecimal format	1120 (NB. If you want to display 0x1120, you'd need to write out the 0x separately)

If you want an integer to be padded with zeros, you can use the format specifier 0 (zero) repeated the required number of times. For example, the format specifier 0000 will cause 3 to be displayed as 0003, and 99 to be displayed as 0099, and so on.

It is not possible to give a complete list, because other data types can add their own specifiers. Showing how to define our own specifiers for our own classes is the aim of this section.

How the String is Formatted

As an example of how formatting of strings works, we will see what happens when the following statement is executed:

```
Console.WriteLine("The double is {0,10:E} and the int contains {1}", d, i);
```

In fact, Console.WriteLine() just hands the entire set of parameters straight over to the static method, String.Format() – the same method that you'd call if you wanted to format these values for use in a string to be used in some other way, such being displayed in a textbox. With the usual provisos about it being impossible to verify what the actual sourcecode for this method really is, the implementation of the 3-parameter overload of WriteLine() basically does this:

```
// Likely implementation of Console.WriteLine()

public void WriteLine(string format, object arg0, object arg1)
{
    Console.WriteLine(string.Format(format, arg0, arg1));
}
```

The one-parameter overload of this method, which is in turn getting called above, simply writes out the contents of the string it has been passed, without doing any further formatting on it.

String.Format() now needs to construct the final string by replacing each format specifier by a suitable string representation of the corresponding object. However, as we saw earlier, this kind of process of building up a string is exactly the situation in which we really need a StringBuilder instance rather than a string instance, and that's exactly what happens. For the particular example we are using here, a StringBuilder instance will be created and initialized with the first known portion of the string, the text "The double is ". The StringBuilder.AppendFormat() method will then be called, passing in the first format specifier, {0,10:E}, and the associated object, the double, in order to add the string representation of this object to the string being constructed, and this process will continue with StringBuilder.Append() and StringBuilder.AppendFormat() being called repeatedly until the entire formatted string has been obtained.

Now comes the interesting part, because StringBuilder.AppendFormat() will need to figure out how to actually format the object. The first thing it will do is probe the object to find out whether it implements an interface in the System namespace called IFormattable. You can find this out quite simply by trying to cast an object to this interface and seeing whether the cast succeeds, or by using the C# is keyword. If this test fails, then AppendFormat() will simply call the object's ToString() method, which all objects either inherit from System.Object or override. In the cases of all the classes and structs we have written so far, this is what will happen, since so far, none of the classes we have written have implemented this interface. That is why our overrides of Object.ToString() have been sufficient to allow our structs and classes from earlier chapters such as Vector to get displayed in Console.WriteLine() statements.

However, all of the predefined primitive numeric types do implement this interface, which means that for those types, and in particular for the `double` and the `int` in our example, the basic `ToString()` method inherited from `System.Object` will not be called. To understand what happens instead, we need to examine the `IFormattable` interface.

`IFormattable` defines just one method, which is also called `ToString()`. However, this method takes two parameters as opposed to the `System.Object` version, which doesn't takes any. This is the definition of `IFormattable`:

```
interface IFormattable
{
    string ToString(string format, IFormatProvider formatProvider);
}
```

The first parameter that this overload of `ToString()` expects is a string that specifies the requested format. In other words, it is the specifier portion of the string that appears in the `{}` in the string originally passed to `Console.WriteLine()` or `String.Format()`. For example, in our example the original statement was:

```
Console.WriteLine("The double is {0,10:E} and the int contains {1}", d, i);
```

Hence, when evaluating the first specifier, `{0,10:E}`, this overload will be called against the double variable, d, and the first parameter passed to it will be E. What `StringBuilder.AppendFormat()` will pass in here is always whatever text appears after the colon in the appropriate format specifier from the original string.

We won't worry about the second parameter to `ToString()` in this book. It is a reference to an object that implements the interface `IFormatProvider`. This interface gives further information that `ToString()` may need to consider when formatting the object, most notably including details of a culture to be assumed (recall that a .NET culture is similar to a Windows locale; if you are formatting currencies or dates then you need this information). If you are calling this `ToString()` overload directly from your sourcecode, you may wish to supply such an object. However, `StringBuilder.AppendFormat()` passes in null for this parameter. If `formatProvider` is null, then `ToString()` is expected to use the culture specified in the system settings.

Moving back to our example, the first item we wish to format is a double, for which we are requesting exponential notation, with the format specifier E. As just mentioned, the `StringBuilder.AppendFormat()` method will establish that the double does implement `IFormattable`, and will therefore call the two-parameter `ToString()` overload, passing it the string E for the first parameter and null for the second parameter. It is now up to the double's implementation of this method to return the string representation of the double in the appropriate format, taking into account the requested format and the current culture. `StringBuilder.AppendFormat()` will then sort out padding the returned string with spaces, if necessary, in order to fill the 10 characters the format string specified in this case.

The next object to be formatted is an `int`, for which we are not requesting any particular format (the format specifier was simply `{1}`). With no format requested, `StringBuilder.AppendFormat()` will pass in a null reference for the format string. Again the two-parameter overload of `int.ToString()` will be expected to respond appropriately. No format has been specifically requested, therefore it will most likely simply call the no-parameter `ToString()` method.

The whole process can be summarized in this diagram:

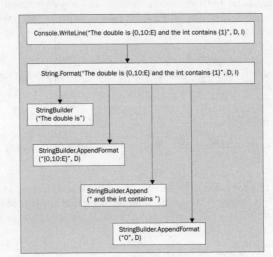

The FormattableVector Example

Now that we have established how format strings are constructed, we are going to extend the `Vector` example from Chapter 3, so that we can format vectors in a variety of ways. The sample code for this is downloadable as the `FormattableVector` sample. We will find that, now that we have understood the principles involved, the actual coding is quite simple. All we need to do is implement `IFormattable`, and supply an implementation of the `ToString()` overload defined by that interface.

The format specifiers we are going to support are:

❑　`N` – Should be interpreted as a request to supply a quantity known as the `Norm` of the `Vector`. This is just the sum of squares of its components, which for mathematics buffs happens to be equal to the square of the length of the `Vector`, and is usually displayed between double vertical bars, like this `||34.5||`.

❑　`VE` – Should be interpreted as a request to display each component in scientific format, just as the specifier `E` applied to a double indicates (`2.3E+01, 4.5E+02, 1.0E+00`).

❑　`IJK` – Should be interpreted as a request to display the vector in the form `23i + 450j + 1k`.

❑　Anything else should simply return the default representation of the `Vector` (`23, 450, 1.0`).

To keep things simple, we are not going to implement any option to display the vector in combined `IJK` and scientific format. We will, however, allow make sure we test the specifier in a case-insensitive way, so that we allow `ijk` instead of `IJK`. Note that it is entirely up to us which strings we use to indicate the format specifiers.

To achieve this, we first modify the declaration of `Vector` so it implements `IFormattable`:

```
struct Vector : IFormattable
{
    public double x, y, z;
```

Now we add our implementation of the 2-parameter `ToString()` overload:

```
public string ToString(string format, IFormatProvider formatProvider)
{
    if (format == null)
        return ToString();
    string formatUpper = format.ToUpper();
    switch (formatUpper)
    {
        case "N":
            return "|| " + Norm().ToString() + " ||";
        case "VE":
            return String.Format("( {0:E}, {1:E}, {2:E} )", x, y, z);
        case "IJK":
            StringBuilder sb = new StringBuilder(x.ToString(), 30);
            sb.Append(" i + ");
            sb.Append(y.ToString());
            sb.Append(" j + ");
            sb.Append(z.ToString());
            sb.Append(" k");
            return sb.ToString();
        default:
            return ToString();
    }
}
```

That is all we have to do! Notice how we take the precaution of checking whether format is `null` before we call any methods against this parameter – we want this method to be as robust as reasonably possible. The format specifiers for all the primitive types are case-insensitive, so that's the behavior that other developers are going to expect from our class too. For the format specifier VE, we need each component to be formatted in scientific notation, so we just use `String.Format()` again to achieve this. The fields x, y, and z are all doubles. For the case of the IJK format specifier, there are quite a few substrings to be added to the string, so we use a `StringBuilder` object to improve performance.

For completeness, we will also reproduce the no-parameter `ToString()` overload that we developed in Chapter 3:

```
public override string ToString()
{
    return "( " + x + " , " + y + " , " + z + " )";
}
```

Finally, we need to add a `Norm()` method that computes the square (norm) of the vector, since we didn't actually supply this method when we first developed the `Vector` struct in Chapter 3:

```
public double Norm()
{
    return x*x + y*y + z*z;
}
```

Now we can try out our formattable vector with some suitable test code:

```
static void Main()
{
    Vector v1 = new Vector(1,32,5);
    Vector v2 = new Vector(845.4, 54.3, -7.8);
    Console.WriteLine("\nIn IJK format,\nv1 is {0,30:IJK}\nv2 is {1,30:IJK}",
                      v1, v2);
    Console.WriteLine("\nIn default format,\nv1 is {0,30}\nv2 is {1,30}", v1,
                      v2);
    Console.WriteLine("\nIn VE format\nv1 is {0,30:VE}\nv2 is {1,30:VE}", v1,
                      v2);
    Console.WriteLine("\nNorms are:\nv1 is {0,20:N}\nv2 is {1,20:N}", v1,
                      v2);
}
```

The result of running this sample is this:

```
FormattableVector
In IJK format,
v1 is                  1 i + 32 j + 5 k
v2 is          845.4 i + 54.3 j + -7.8 k

In default format,
v1 is                    ( 1 , 32 , 5 )
v2 is              ( 845.4 , 54.3 , -7.8 )

In VE format
v1 is ( 1.000000E+000, 3.200000E+001, 5.000000E+000 )
v2 is ( 8.454000E+002, 5.430000E+001, -7.800000E+000 )

Norms are:
v1 is              || 1050 ||
v2 is          || 717710.49 ||
```

This shows that our custom specifiers are being picked up correctly.

Regular Expressions

Regular expressions form one of those little technology areas that is incredibly useful in a wide range of programs, but despite that isn't really that widely known among developers. It could almost be thought of as a mini programming language with one specific purpose: to locate substrings within a large string expression. It is not a new technology; it originated in the UNIX environment, and is commonly used with Perl. Microsoft ported it onto Windows, where it has up until now mostly been used with scripting languages. Regular expressions are, however, supported by a number of .NET classes in the namespace System.Text.RegularExpressions.

Many readers will not be familiar with the regular expressions language, so we will use this section as a very basic introduction to both regular expressions and to the related .NET classes. If you are already familiar with regular expressions then you'll probably want to just skim through this section to pick out the references to the .NET base classes. You might like to note that the .NET regular expression engine is designed to be mostly compatible with Perl 5 regular expressions, though it has a few extra features.

Introduction to Regular Expressions

The regular expressions language is a language designed specifically for string processing. It broadly contains two features:

- ❑ A set of **escape codes** for identifying types of characters. You will be familiar with the use of the * character to represent any substring in DOS expressions. (For example, the DOS command Dir Re* lists the names of files with names beginning Re.) Regular expressions use many sequences like this to represent items such as 'any one character', 'a word break', 'one optional character', and so on.

- ❑ A system for grouping parts of substrings and intermediate results during a search operation.

Using regular expressions, it is possible to perform quite sophisticated and high-level operations on strings. For example, you could:

- ❑ Identify (and perhaps either flag or remove) all repeated words in a string, for example, converting "The computer books books" to "The computer books"

- ❑ Convert all words to title case, such as convert "this is a Title" to "This Is A Title".

- ❑ Convert all words longer than three characters long to title case, for example convert "this is a Title" to "This is a Title"

- ❑ Ensure that sentences are properly capitalized

- ❑ Separate out the various elements of a URI (for example, given http://www.wrox.com, extract the protocol, computer name, file name, and so on)

These are all of course, tasks that can be performed in C# using the various methods on System.String and System.Text.StringBuilder. However, in some cases, this would involve writing a fair amount of C# code. If you use regular expressions, this code can normally be compressed down to just a couple of lines. Essentially, you instantiate a System.Text.RegularExpressions.RegEx object (or – even simpler – invoke a static RegEx() method), pass it the string to be processed, and a **regular expression** (a string containing the instructions in the regular expressions language), and you're done.

A regular expression string looks at first sight rather like a normal string, but interspersed with escape sequences and other characters that have a special meaning. For example, the sequence \b indicates the beginning or end of a word (a word boundary), so if we wanted to indicate we were looking for the characters th at the beginning of a word, we would search for the regular expression, \bth (that is, the sequence word boundary – t – h). If we wanted to search for all occurrences of th at the end of a word, we would write th\b (the sequence t – h – word boundary). However, as we have hinted, regular expressions are much more sophisticated than that, and include, for example, facilities to store portions of text that are found in a search operation. In this section, we will merely scratch the surface of the power of regular expressions.

As another example, suppose your application needed to convert UK phone numbers from national to international format. In the UK, national format would be something like 01233 345532, which would sometimes be written (01233) 345532. International format would mean this number should always be written +44 1233 345532, in other words the leading zero must be replaced by +44, and any brackets removed. As find-and-replace operations go, that's not too complicated, but would still require some coding effort if you were going to use the String class for this purpose (which would mean that you would have to write your code using the methods available on System.String); you would need to locate any zeros that occur at the beginning of a number or immediately following a left bracket. Again, the regular expressions language allows us to construct a short string that will be interpreted to have this meaning.

This section is intended only as a very simple example, so we will simply concentrate on searching strings to identify certain substrings, not on modifying them.

The RegularExpressionsPlayaround Example

For the rest of this section, we will develop a short sample that illustrates some of the features of regular expressions and how to use the .NET regular expressions engine in C# by performing and displaying the results of some searches. The text we are going to use as our sample 'document' to search through is the introduction to another Wrox Press book on XML (Professional XML 2nd Edition, ISBN 1-861005-05-9):

```
string Text =
@"XML has made a major impact in almost every aspect of software development
Designed as an open, extensible, self-describing language,
it has become the standard for data and document delivery on the web.
The panoply of XML-related technologies continues to develop at breakneck
speed, to enable validation, navigation, transformation, linking, querying,
description, and messaging of data.";
```

The above is valid C# code, despite all the line breaks. It nicely illustrates the utility of verbatim strings that are prefixed by the @ symbol.

We will refer to this text as the **input string**. To get our bearings and get used to the regular expressions .NET classes, we will start with a basic plain text search that doesn't feature any escape sequences or regular expression commands. Suppose that we want to find all occurrences of the string ion. We will refer to this search string as the **pattern**. Using regular expressions and the Text variable declared above, you could do it like this:

```
string Pattern = "ion";
MatchCollection Matches = Regex.Matches(Text, Pattern,
                                        RegexOptions.IgnoreCase |
                                        RegexOptions.ExplicitCapture);
foreach (Match NextMatch in Matches)
{
    Console.WriteLine(NextMatch.Index);
}
```

In this code, we have used the static method `Matches()` of the `Regex` class in the `System.Text.RegularExpressions` namespace. This method takes as parameters some input text, a pattern, and a set of optional flags taken from the `RegexOptions` enumeration. In this case, we have specified that all searching should be case-insensitive. The other flag, `ExplicitCapture`, modifies the way that the match is collected in a way that, for our purposes, makes the search a bit more efficient – we will see why this is later (although it does have other uses that we won't explore here). `Matches()` returns a reference to a `MatchCollection` object. A **match** is the technical term for the results of finding an instance of the pattern in the expression. It is represented by the class `System.Text.RegularExpressions.Match`. Therefore, we return a `MatchCollection` that contains all the matches, each represented by a `Match` object. In the above code, we simply iterate over the collection, and use the `Index` property of the `Match` class, which returns the index in the input text of where the match was found. When I ran this code, it found four matches.

So far, there is not really anything new here apart from some new .NET base classes. However, the power of regular collections really comes from that pattern string. The reason is that the pattern string doesn't only have to contain plain text. As hinted at earlier, it can also contain what are known as **metacharacters**, which are special characters that give commands, as well as escape sequences, which work in much the same way as C# escape sequences. They are characters preceded by a backslash, \, and also have special meanings.

For example, suppose we wanted to find words beginning with n. We could use the escape sequence \b, which indicates a word boundary (a word boundary is just a point where a an alphanumeric character precedes or follows a whitespace character or punctuation symbol). We would simply write this:

```
string Pattern = @"\bn";
MatchCollection Matches = Regex.Matches(Text, Pattern,
                                    RegexOptions.IgnoreCase |
                                    RegexOptions.ExplicitCapture);
```

Notice the @ character in front of the string. We want the \b to be passed to the .NET regular expressions engine at runtime – we don't want the backslash intercepted by a well-meaning C# compiler that thinks it's an escape sequence intended for itself! If we want to find words ending with the sequence ion, then we could do this:

```
string Pattern = @"ion\b";
```

What if we want to find all words beginning with the letter n and ending with the sequence ion? This would pick out the one word 'navigation' from the above text. That's a little more complicated. We clearly need a pattern that begins with \bn and ends with ion\b, but what goes in the middle? We need to somehow tell the application that between that the n and the ion there can be any number of characters as long as none of them are whitespace. In fact, the correct pattern looks like this:

```
string Pattern = @"\bn\S*ion\b";
```

One thing you will get used to with regular expressions is seeing weird sequences of characters like this, but it actually works quite logically. The escape sequence \S indicates any character that is not a whitespace character. The * is called a **quantifier**. It means that the preceding character can be repeated any number of time, including zero times. The sequence \S* means "any number of characters as long as they are not whitespace characters". The above pattern will, therefore, match any single word that begins with n and ends with ion.

The table shows some of the main special characters or escape sequences that you can use. It is not comprehensive, but a fuller list is available in the MSDN documentation:

	Meaning	Example	Examples that this will match
^	Beginning of input text	^B	B, but only if first character in text
$	End of the input text	X$	X, but only if last character in text
.	Any single character except the newline character (\n)	i.ation	isation, ization
*	Preceding character may be repeated 0 or more times	ra*t	rt, rat, raat, raaat, and so on
+	Preceding character may be repeated 1 or more times	ra+t	rat, raat, raaat and so on, (but not rt)
?	Preceding character may be repeated 0 or 1 times	ra?t	rt and rat only
\s	Any whitespace character	\sa	[space]a, \ta, \na (\t and \n have the same meanings as in C#)
\S	Any character that isn't a whitespace	\SF	aF, rF, cF, but not \tf
\b	Word boundary	ion\b	any word ending in ion
\B	Any position that isn't a word boundary	\BX\B	any X in the middle of a word

If you want to actually search for one of the metacharacters, you can do so by escaping the corresponding character with a backslash. For example, . (a single period) means any single character other than the newline character, while \. means a dot.

You can request a match that contains alternative characters by enclosing them in square brackets. For example [1|c] means one character that can be either 1 or c. If you wanted to search for any occurrence of the words map or man, you would use the sequence ma[n|p]. Within the square brackets, you can also indicate a range, for example [a-z] to indicate any single lower case letter, [A-E] to indicate any uppercase letter between A and E, or [0-9] to represent a single digit. If you want to search for an integer (that is, a sequence that contains only the characters 0 through 9), you could write [0-9]+ (note the use of the + character to indicate there must be at least one such digit, but there may be more than one – so this would match 9, 83, 854, and so on).

Displaying Results

Now we have the flavor what regular expressions are about, we will actually code up our RegularExpressionsPlayaround example. This is not really intended as a serious example of a real situation; it lets you set up a few regular expressions and displays the results so you can get a feel for how the regular expressions work.

The core of the example is a method called `WriteMatches()`, which writes out all the matches from a `MatchCollection` in a more detailed format. For each match, it displays the index of where the match was found in the input string, the string of the match, and a slightly longer string, which consists of the match plus up to ten surrounding characters from the input text – up to 5 characters before the match and up to 5 afterwards (it is less than 5 characters if the match occurred within 5 characters of the beginning or end of the input text). In other words, a match on the word messaging that occurs near the end of the input text quoted earlier would display `"'and messaging of d"` (five characters before and after the match), but a match on the final word data would display `"g of data."` (only one character after the match), because after that we hit the end of the string. This longer string lets you see more clearly where the regular expression located the match:

```
static void WriteMatches(string text, MatchCollection matches)
{
   Console.WriteLine("Original text was: \n\n" + text + "\n");
   Console.WriteLine("No. of matches: " + matches.Count);
   foreach (Match nextMatch in matches)
   {
      int Index = nextMatch.Index;
      string result = nextMatch.ToString();
      int charsBefore = (Index < 5) ? Index : 5;
      int fromEnd = text.Length - Index - result.Length;
      int charsAfter = (fromEnd < 5) ? fromEnd : 5;
      int charsToDisplay = charsBefore + charsAfter + result.Length;

      Console.WriteLine("Index: {0}, \tString: {1}, \t{2}",
         Index, result,
         text.Substring(Index - charsBefore, charsToDisplay));

   }
}
```

The bulk of the processing in this method is devoted to the logic of figuring out how many characters in the longer substring it can display without overrunning the beginning or end of the input text. Note that we use another property on the `Match` object, `Value`, which contains the string identified for the match. Other than that, `RegularExpressionsPlayaround` simply contains a number of methods with names like `Find1`, `Find2`, and so on, which perform some of the searches based on the examples in this section. For example, `Find2` looks for any string that contains n at the beginning of a word:

```
static void Find2()
{
   string text = @"XML has made a major impact in almost every aspect of
      software development. Designed as an open, extensible, self-describing
      language, it has become the standard for data and document delivery on
      the web. The panoply of XML-related technologies continues to develop
      at breakneck speed, to enable validation, navigation, transformation,
      linking, querying, description, and messaging of data.";
   string pattern = @"\bn";
   MatchCollection matches = Regex.Matches(text, pattern,
      RegexOptions.IgnoreCase);
   WriteMatches(text, matches);
}
```

Along with this is a simple `Main()` method that you can edit to select one of the Find<*n*>() methods:

```
static void Main()
{
   Find1();
   Console.ReadLine();
}
```

The code also makes use of the `RegularExpressions` namespace:

```
using System;
using System.Text.RegularExpressions;
```

Running the example with the `Find1()` method as above gives these results:

```
RegularExpressionsPlayaround
Original text was:

XML has made a major impact in almost every aspect of software development.
Designed as an open, extensible, self-describing language, it has become the
standard for data and document delivery on the web. The panoply of XML-related
technologies continues to develop at breakneck speed, to enable validation,
navigation, transformation, linking, querying, description, and messaging of data.

No. of matches: 1
Index: 364,     String: navigation,     ion, navigation, tra
```

Matches, Groups, and Captures

One nice feature of regular expressions is that you can group characters together. It works the same way as compound statements in C#. Recall that in C# you can group any number of statements together by putting them in braces, and the result is treated as one compound statement. In regular expression patterns, you can group any characters (including metacharacters and escape sequences) together, and the result is treated as a single character. The only difference is you use parentheses instead of braces. The resultant sequence is known as a **group**.

For example, the pattern `(an)+` will locate any recurrences of the sequence an. The + quantifier applies only to the previous character, but because we have grouped the characters together, it now applies to repeats of an treated as a unit. This means that `(an)+` applied to the input text, "bananas came to Europe late in the annals of history" will pick out the anan from bananas. On the other hand, if we'd written an+, that would pick out the ann from annals, as well as two separate sequences of an from bananas. The expression `(an)+` will pick out occurrences of an, anan, ananan, and so on, while the expression an+ will pick out occurrences of an, ann, annn, and so on.

> *You might wonder why with the above example, `(an)+` picks out anan from the word banana, but doesn't identify either of the two occurrences of an from the same word. The rule is that matches must not overlap. If there are a couple of possibilities that would overlap, then by default the longest possible sequence will be matched.*

However, groups are actually more powerful than that. By default, when you form part of the pattern into a group, you are also asking the regular expression engine to remember any matches against just that group, as well as any matches against the entire pattern. In other words you are treating that group as a pattern to be matched and returned in its own right. This can actually be extremely useful if you want to break up strings into component parts.

For example, URIs have the format: `<protocol>://<address>:<port>`, where the port is optional. An example of this is `http://www.wrox.com:4355`. Suppose you want to extract the protocol, the address, and the port from a URI, where you know that there may or may not be whitespace, (but no punctuation) immediately following the URI. You could do so using this expression:

```
\b(\S+)://(\S+)(?::(\S+))?\b
```

This is the way the expression works. First, the leading and trailing `\b` sequences ensure that we only consider portions of text that are entire words. Within that, the first group, `(\S+)://` will pick out one or more characters that don't count as whitespace, and which are followed by `://`. This will pick out the `http://` at the start of an HTTP URI. The brackets will cause the `http` to be stored as a group. The subsequent `(\S+)` will pick out expressions such as `www.wrox.com` in the above URI. This group will end either when it hits the end of the word (the closing `\b`) or when it hits a colon (`:`) as marked by the next group.

The next group is intended to pick out the port (`:4355` in our case). The following `?` indicates that this group is optional in the match – if there is no `:xxxx` then this won't prevent a match from being marked.

That's very important as the port number isn't always specified in a URI – in fact it is absent most of the time. However, things are a bit more complicated than that. We want to indicate that the colon might or might not appear too, but we don't want to store this colon in the group. We've achieved this by having two nested groups. The inner `(\S+)` will pick out anything that follows the colon (for example the `4355` in our example). The outer group contains the inner group preceded by the colon, and that in turn is preceded by the sequence `?:`. This sequence indicates that the group in question should not be saved (we only want to save the `4355`; we don't need the `:4355` as well!). Don't get confused by the two colons following each other – the first is part of the `?:` sequence that says 'don't save this group', and the second is text to be searched for.

If you run this pattern on this string:

```
Hey I've just found this amazing URI at http:// what was it - oh yes
http://www.wrox.com
```

you'll get one match: `http://www.wrox.com`. Within this match, there are the three groups just mentioned as well as a fourth group which represents the match itself. Theoretically, it is possible that each group itself might pick nothing, one or more than one match. Each of these individual matches is known as a **capture**. So, the first group, `(\S+)`, has one capture, `http`. The second group has one capture too, `www.wrox.com`, but the third group has no captures, since there is no port number on this URI.

Notice that the string contained a second `http://` on its own. Although this does match up to our first group, it will not be picked out by the search because the entire search expression will not match this part of the text.

We don't have space to show any examples of C# code that uses groups and captures, but we will mention that the .NET `RegularExpressions` classes support groups and captures, through classes known as `Group` and `Capture`. There are also the `GroupCollection` and `CaptureCollection` classes, which respectively represent collections of groups and captures. The `Match` class exposes a method, `Groups()`, which returns the corresponding `GroupCollection` object. The `Group` class correspondingly implements a method, `Captures()`, which returns a `CaptureCollection`. The relationship between the objects is as shown in the diagram:

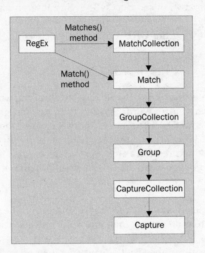

Returning a `Group` object every time you just want to group some characters together may not be what you want to do. There's a fair amount of overhead involved in instantiating the object, which is wasted if all you wanted was to group some characters together as part of your search pattern. You can disable this by starting the group with the character sequence `?:` for an individual group, as we did for our URI example, or for all groups by specifying the `RegExOptions.ExplicitCaptures` flag on the `RegEx.Matches()` method, as we did in the earlier examples.

Groups of Objects

We are now going to examine the support that the .NET base classes have for data structures in which a number of similar objects are grouped together. The simplest such data structure is the ordinary array, which we saw how to use in Chapter 2. The ordinary array is actually an instance of the class `System.Array`, but C# wraps its own syntax around this class. `System.Array` has the advantages of being relatively efficient for accessing an individual element given its index, and of having its own C# syntax, which obviously makes using it more intuitive. However, `Array` has the big disadvantage that you need to specify its size when you instantiate it. There is no facility for adding, inserting, or removing elements later on. You also have to have a numeric index in order to be able to access an element. This is not particularly useful if, for example, you are dealing with a set of employee records and need to look up a given record from the name of the employee.

.NET has quite extensive support for a number of other data structures that are useful in different circumstances. Not only that, but there are also a number of interfaces, which classes can implement in order to declare that they support all the functionality of a particular type of data structure. Here, we are going to survey three of these structures:

- ❏ Array lists
- ❏ Collections
- ❏ Dictionaries (also sometimes known as maps)

Other than the basic `System.Array`, all the data structure classes are in the `System.Collections` namespace.

> *The name* `System.Collections` *reflects another of those terminology ambiguities that plague computing.* **Collection** *is often used informally to denote any data structure. However, it also has the more specific meaning of a class that implements* `IEnumerable` *or* `ICollection` – *a particular type of data structure that we will investigate later in the chapter. In this chapter, we will always use the term 'collection' to refer to the more specific meaning, except where .NET base class names force us to use it in the general sense.*

Array Lists

An **array list** is very similar to an array, except that it has the ability to grow. It is represented by the class `System.Collections.ArrayList`.

The `ArrayList` class also has some similarities with the `StringBuilder` class that we looked at earlier. Just as a `StringBuilder` allocated enough space in memory to store a certain number of characters, and allowed you to manipulate characters within the space, the `ArrayList` allocates enough memory to store a certain number of object references. You can then efficiently manipulate these object references however you wish, within that limit. If you try to add more objects to the `ArrayList` than the capacity allows, then it will automatically increase its capacity by allocating a new area of memory big enough to hold twice as many elements as the current capacity, and relocating to there.

You can instantiate an array list by indicating the initial capacity you want. For this example, we will assume we are creating a list of `Vectors`:

```
ArrayList vectors = new ArrayList(20);
```

If you don't specify the initial size, it defaults to 16:

```
ArrayList vectors = new ArrayList();    // capacity of 16
```

You can then add elements using the `Add()` method:

```
vectors.Add(new Vector(2,2,2));
vectors.Add(new Vector(3,5,6));
```

The `ArrayList` treats all its elements as object references. That means you can store whatever objects you like in an `ArrayList`, but when accessing the objects, you will need to cast them back to the appropriate data type:

```
Vector element1 = (Vector)vectors[1];
```

This example also shows that `ArrayList` defines an indexer, so that you can access its elements with an array-like syntax. You can also insert elements into the `ArrayList`:

```
vectors.Insert(1, new Vector(3,2,2));    // inserts at position 1
```

There is also a useful override of `Insert` that allows you to insert all the elements of a collection into an `ArrayList`, given an `ICollection` interface reference.

You may remove elements:

```
vectors.RemoveAt(1);    // removes object at position 1
```

You can also supply an object reference to another method, `Remove()`. Doing this will take longer as it will cause the `ArrayList` to make a linear search through the array to find the object.

Note that adding or removing an element will cause all subsequent elements to have to be correspondingly shifted in memory, even if no reallocation of the entire `ArrayList` is needed,

You can modify or read the capacity via the `Capacity` property:

```
vectors.Capacity = 30;
```

Note, however, that changing the capacity will cause the entire `ArrayList` to be reallocated to a new block of memory with the required capacity.

The number of elements actually in the `ArrayList` can be obtained via the `Count` property:

```
int nVectors = vectors.Count;
```

An array list can be really useful if you need to build up an array of objects but you do not know in advance how big the array is going to end up. In that case, you can construct the 'array' in an `ArrayList`, and then copy the `ArrayList` back to a plain old array when you have finished if you actually need the data as an array (this would be the case, for example, if the array is to be passed to a method that expects an array as a parameter). The relationship between `ArrayList` and `Array` is in many ways similar to that between `StringBuilder` and `String`.

Unfortunately, unlike the `StringBuilder` class, there is no single method to do this conversion from an array list to an array. You have to use a loop to manually copy references back. Note, however, that you are only copying the references not the objects, so this shouldn't give too much of a performance hit:

```
// vectors is an ArrayList instance being used to store Vector instances
Vector [] vectorsArray = new Vector[vectors.Count];
for (int i=0 ; i< vectors.Count ; i++)
    vectorsArray[i] = (Vector)vectors [i];
```

Collections

The idea of a **collection** is that it represents a set of objects that you can access by stepping through each element in turn. In particular, it is the set of objects that you access using a `foreach` loop. In other words, when you write something like this:

```
foreach (string nextMessage in messageSet)
{
    DoSomething(nextMessage);
}
```

you are assuming that the variable `messageSet` is a collection. The ability to use a `foreach` loop is the main purpose of collections. They offer little in the way of additional features.

Over the next couple of pages, we are going to look in more detail at what a collection is and implement our own collection by converting the `Vector` sample that we have been developing. The broad concepts behind collections are actually not new to .NET. Collections have been a part of COM for years, and have also been used in Visual Basic with the convenient `For...Each` syntax. Java also has a `foreach` loop, and in both cases the underlying architecture is very similar to that for .NET collections.

What is a Collection?

Internally, an object is a collection if it is able to supply a reference to a related object, known as an **enumerator**, which is able to step through the items in the collection. More specifically, a collection must implement the interface `System.Collections.IEnumerable`. `IEnumerable` defines just one method, and looks like this:

```
interface IEnumerable
{
    IEnumerator GetEnumerator();
}
```

The purpose of `GetEnumerator()` is to return the enumerator object. As you will gather from the above code, the enumerator object is expected to implement an interface, `System.Collections.IEnumerator`.

> There is an additional collections interface, `ICollection`, which is derived from `IEnumerable`. More sophisticated collections will implement this interface as well. Besides `GetEnumerator()`, it implements a property that directly returns the number of elements in the collection. It also features support for copying the collection to an array and can supply information indicating if it is thread-safe. However, here we will only consider the simpler collection interface, `IEnumerable`.

`IEnumerator` looks like this:

```
interface IEnumerator
{
    object Current { get; }
    bool MoveNext();
    void Reset();
}
```

IEnumerator is intended to work like this: the object that implements it should be associated with one particular collection. When this object is first initialized, it does not yet refer to any elements in the collection, and you must call MoveNext(), which moves the enumerator so that it refers to the first element in the collection. You can then retrieve this element with the Current property. Current returns an object reference, so you will have to cast it to the type of object you are expecting to find in the collection. You can do whatever you want with that object then move to the next item in the collection by calling MoveNext() again. You repeat this process until there are no more items in the collection – you will know this has happened when the Current property returns null. If you wish, you can at any time return to the start of the collection by calling the Reset() method. Note that Reset() actually returns to just before the start of the collection so if you call this method, you will need to subsequently call MoveNext() again to get to the first element.

You can see from this that the point of the collection is simply to provide a way of stepping through all the elements when you don't want to supply an index, and you are happy to rely on the collection itself to choose the order in which the elements will be returned to you. This will usually mean that you are not bothered about the order in which the elements are retrieved, as long as you get to see all of them, although in some cases it may be that a particular collection is documented as returning the elements in a certain order. In one sense, a collection is a very basic type of group of objects, because it does not allow you to add or remove items from the group. All you can do is retrieve the items in an order determined by the collection, and examine them. It is not even possible to replace or modify items in the collection, because the Current property is read-only. The most frequent use of the collection is to give you the syntactical convenience of the foreach loop.

Arrays are also collections, as should be obvious because the foreach command works successfully with arrays. For the particular case of arrays, the enumerator supplied by the System.Array class steps through the elements in increasing order of index from zero upwards.

From the above discussion, we can see the above foreach loop in C# is just a syntactical shortcut for writing:

```
{
    IEnumerator enumerator = MessageSet.GetEnumerator();
    string nextMessage;
    enumerator.MoveNext();
    while ( (nextMessage = enumerator.Current) != null)
    {
        DoSomething(nextMessage);    // NB. We only have read access
                                     // toNextMessage
        enumerator.MoveNext();
    }
}
```

Note the enclosing curly braces around the above code snippet. We have supplied them in order to ensure that this code has exactly the same effect as the earlier foreach loop. If we hadn't included them, then this code would have differed to the extent that the nextMessage and enumerator variables would have remained in scope beyond the end of the loop.

One important aspect of collections is that the enumerator is returned as a separate object. It should not be the same object as the collection itself. The reason is to allow for the possibility that more than one enumerator might be applied simultaneously to the same collection.

Adding Collection Support to the Vector Struct

Our Vector struct that we started in Chapter 3, and to which we have already added formatting support earlier in this chapter, is about to get another extension with collection support.

When we last left the Vector struct, a Vector instance contained three components, x, y, and z, and because we had defined an indexer in Chapter 3, it was possible to treat a Vector instance as an array, so that we could access the x-component by writing SomeVector[0], the y-component by writing SomeVector[1], and the z-component by writing SomeVector[2].

We will now extend the Vector struct into a new code sample, the VectorAsCollection project, in which it is also possible to iterate through the components of a Vector by writing code like this:

```
foreach (double component in someVector)
   Console.WriteLine("Component is " + component);
```

Our first task is to mark Vector as a collection by having it implement the IEnumerable interface. We start by modifying the declaration of the Vector struct:

```
struct Vector : IFormattable, IEnumerable
{
    public double x, y, z;
```

Note that the IFormattable interface is present because we added support for string format specifiers earlier in this chapter. Now we need to implement the IEnumerable interface:

```
        public IEnumerator GetEnumerator()
        {
            return new VectorEnumerator(this);
        }
```

The implementation of GetEnumerator() could hardly be simpler, but it depends on the existence of a new class, VectorEnumerator, which we need to define. Since VectorEnumerator is not a class that any outside code needs to be able to see directly, we declare it as a private class inside the Vector struct. Its definition looks like this:

```
    private class VectorEnumerator : IEnumerator
    {
        Vector theVector;      // Vector object that this enumerato refers to
        int location;   // which element of theVector the enumerator is
                        // currently referring to

        public VectorEnumerator(Vector theVector)
        {
            this.theVector = theVector;
            location = -1;
        }

        public bool MoveNext()
        {
            ++location;
```

```
        return (location > 2) ? false : true;
    }

    public object Current
    {
        get
        {
            if (location < 0 || location > 2)
                throw new InvalidOperationException(
                    "The enumerator is either before the first element or " +
                    "after the last element of the Vector");
            return theVector[(uint)location];
        }
    }

    public void Reset()
    {
        location = -1;
    }
}
```

As required for an enumerator, `VectorEnumerator` implements the `IEnumerator` interface. It also contains two member fields, `theVector`, which is a reference to the `Vector` (the collection) that this enumerator is to be associated with, and `location`, an `int` that indicates where in the collection the enumerator should reference – in other words whether the `Current` property should retrieve the x, y, or z component of the vector.

The way we will work in this case is by treating `location` as an index and internally implementing the enumerator to access the `Vector` as an array. When accessing the `Vector` as an array, the valid indices are 0, 1, and 2 – we will extend this by using –1 as the value that indicates the enumerator is before the start of the collection, and 3 to indicate that it is beyond the end of the collection. Hence, the initialization of this field to –1 in the `VectorEnumerator` constructor:

```
public VectorEnumerator(Vector theVector)
{
    this.theVector = theVector;
    location = -1;
}
```

Notice the constructor also takes a reference to the `Vector` instance that we are to enumerate – this was supplied in the `Vector.GetEnumerator()` method:

```
public IEnumerator GetEnumerator()
{
    return new VectorEnumerator(this);
}
```

Dictionaries

Dictionaries represent a very sophisticated data structure that allows you to access an element based on some key, which can be of any data type you want. They are also known as **maps** or **hash tables**. Dictionaries are great for situations where you wish to store objects as if they were an array, but where you want to use some other data type rather than a numeric type to index into the structure. They also allow you to freely add and remove items, a bit like an `ArrayList`, but without the performance overhead of having to shift subsequent items in memory.

We will illustrate the kinds of situations in which dictionaries can be useful using the example that we will develop later in this section, the `MortimerPhonesEmployees` example. This example assumes that Mortimer Phones (the mobile phone company that we first introduced in Chapter 3) has some software that processes details of its employees. To that end, we need a data structure – something like an array – that contains data for employees. We assume that each Mortimer Phones employee is identified by an employee ID, which is a set of characters such as B342 or W435, and is stored as an `EmployeeID` object. The employee's details are stored as an `EmployeeData` object; for our example, this just contains the employee's ID, name, and salary.

Suppose we have this `EmployeeID`:

```
EmployeeID id = new EmployeeID("W435");
```

and we have a variable called `employees`, which we can treat syntactically as an array of `EmployeeData` objects. In actuality, it is not an array – it is a dictionary, and because it is a dictionary, we can get the details of an employee with the ID declared above like this:

```
EmployeeData theEmployee = employees[id];
   // Note that id is NOT a numeric type - it is an EmployeeID instance
```

That's the power of dictionaries. They look like arrays (but are more powerful than that; they are more like `ArrayLists` since you can dynamically set their capacity, and add and remove elements), but you don't have to use an integer to index into them; you can use any data type you want. For a dictionary, this is called a **key** rather than an index. Roughly speaking, what happens is that the dictionary takes the key supplied when you access an element (in the above example this is the ID object) and it does some processing on the value of this key. This processing returns an integer that depends on the value of the key, and is used to work out where in the 'array' the entry should be stored or retrieved from. Other examples where you would use a dictionary to store objects include:

❑ If you wish to store details of employees or other people, indexed by their social security numbers Although the social security number is basically an integer, you still couldn't use an array with social security numbers as the index since a US social security number can theoretically go up to the value 999999999. On a 32-bit system you'd never fit an array that big in a program's address space! Most of the array would be empty anyway. Using a dictionary, we can have a social security number to index an employee, but still keep the dictionary size small.

❑ If you want to store addresses, indexed by zip code. In the USA, zip codes are just numbers, but in Canada they have letters in too. In the UK, the equivalent (postal codes) are strings that contain both letters and numbers.

❑ Any data for objects or people that you wish to store, indexed by the name of the object or person.

Although the effect of a dictionary is that it looks to client code much like a dynamic array with a very flexible means of indexing into it, there is a lot of work that goes on behind the scenes to bring this about. Though in principle an object of any class can be used as the key to index into a dictionary, you do need to implement certain features on a class before it can be usefully used as a key. This also crucially involves the GetHashCode() method that all classes and structs inherit from System.Object. In this section, we will take a closer look under the hood at what a dictionary is, how it works, and how GetHashCode() is involved. Then, we will move on to our MortimerPhonesEmployees example, which demonstrates both how to use a dictionary, and how to set up a class so that it can be used as a key.

Dictionaries in Real Life

The name 'dictionary' is used because the structure is very similar to a real-life dictionary. In a real dictionary you will normally want to look up the meaning of a word (or in the case of a foreign dictionary, the details of how to translate a word). The couple of lines of text that give the meaning (or the translation) is the data that you are really interested in. The fact that a large dictionary will have tens of thousands of data items in it is no problem when you want to look up a meaning, because you just look for the word in alphabetical order. In a sense, the word you are looking up is equivalent to the key that you use to get at the data you are really interested in. It is not really the word itself you are interested in so much as the data associated with it. The word just provides the means to locate the entry in the dictionary. This means that there are really three things here that you need to make a dictionary:

❑ The data you want to look up

❑ The key

❑ The algorithm that allows you to find where the data is in the dictionary

The algorithm is a crucial part of the dictionary. Just knowing what the key is isn't sufficient – you also need a way that you can use the key to find out the location of the item in the data structure. In real-life dictionaries, this algorithm is provided by arranging words in alphabetical order.

Dictionaries in .NET

In .NET, the basic dictionary is represented by the class Hashtable, which works on the same principles as a real-life dictionary, except that it assumes that the key and item are both of type Object. This means that a Hashtable can store whatever data structure you want – whereas a real-life dictionary uses strings as the keys.

Although Hashtable represents the generic will-store-anything dictionary, it is permissible to define your own more specialized dictionary classes. Microsoft has provided an abstract base class, DictionaryBase, which provides basic dictionary functionality, and from which you can derive your classes. There is also a ready-made .NET base class, System.Collections.Specialized.StringDictionary, which you should use in place of Hashtable if your keys are strings.

When you create a Hashtable object, you can indicate its initial capacity, just as you would do for StringBuilder and ArrayList:

```
Hashtable employees = new Hashtable(53);
```

As usual there are many other constructors, but this is the one you will probably most commonly be using. Notice the unusual size of the initial capacity that I've chosen: 53. There is a good reason for this. Due to the internal algorithms used in dictionaries, they work most efficiently if their capacity is a prime number.

Adding an object to the `Hashtable` is done with the `Add()` method, but `Hashtable.Add()` takes two parameters, both of them object references. The first is a reference to the key; the second is a reference to the data. Carrying on with the `EmployeeID` and `EmployeeData` classes from the example that we will develop soon:

```
EmployeeID id;
EmployeeData data;

// initialize id and data to refer to some employee
// assume employees is a Hashtable instance
//that contains EmployeeData references

employees.Add(id, data);
```

In order to retrieve the data for an item, you need to supply the key. `Hashtable` implements an indexer so that you can retrieve data – this is how we get the array syntax we saw earlier:

```
EmployeeData data = employees[id];
```

You can also remove items from the dictionary, by supplying the key of the object to be removed:

```
employees.Remove(id);
```

You can also find out how many items are in the hash table using the `Count` property:

```
int nEmployees = employees.Count;
```

Notice, however, that there is no `Insert()` method. We have not yet looked at how a dictionary works internally, but there is no difference between adding and inserting data. Unlike an array or an `ArrayList`, you don't find one big block of data at the beginning of the structure and an empty block at the end. Instead, the situation looks more like the following diagram, in which any unmarked parts of the dictionary are empty:

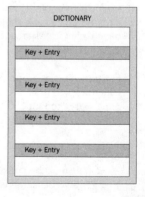

When you add an entry, it will actually be placed at some location that could be anywhere in the dictionary. How the location is worked out from the key is something that you don't need to know about when you are using the dictionary. The important point is that the algorithm used to work out the location of an item is reliable. As long as you remember what the key is, you can just hand it to the `Hashtable` object, and it will be able to use the key to quickly work out where the item is and retrieve it for you. We will examine how the algorithm works later in this section. We will just say here that it relies on the key's `GetHashCode()` method.

Note that the above diagram is simplified. Each key/entry pair is not actually stored inside the dictionary structure – as usual for reference types, what is stored are the object references that indicate where on the heap the objects themselves are located.

How the Dictionary Works

So far, we've seen that dictionaries (hash tables) are extremely convenient to use, but there is a snag: `Hashtable` (and indeed any other dictionary class) uses some sort of algorithm to work out where to place each object based on the key, and that algorithm isn't entirely provided by the `Hashtable` class. It has two stages, and the code for one of these stages must be provided by the key class. If you are using a class that Microsoft has written, and which may possibly be used as a key (such as `String`), then that's no problem (Microsoft will have written all the code already), but if the key class is one that you have written yourself, then you will have to write this part of the algorithm yourself.

In computer parlance, the part of the algorithm implemented by the key class is known as a **hash** (hence the term *hash table*), and the `Hashtable` class looks in a very particular place for the hash algorithm. It looks in your object's `GetHashCode()` method, which it inherits from `System.Object`. Whenever a dictionary class needs to work out where an item should be located, it simply calls the key object's `GetHashCode()` method. This is why we emphasized when we were discussing `System.Object()` that if you override `GetHashCode()`, there are fairly stringent requirements on how you do it, because your implementation needs to behave in certain ways for dictionary classes to work correctly (though if you don't intend your class to ever be used as a key in a dictionary, there's no need to override `GetHashCode()`).

The way it works is that `GetHashCode()` returns an `int`, and it somehow uses the value of the key to generate this `int`. `Hashtable` will take this `int` and do some other processing on it that involves some sophisticated mathematical calculations, and which returns the index of where in the dictionary an item with the given hash should be stored. We won't go into this part of the algorithm – that part has already been coded by Microsoft, so we don't need to know about it, but we will say that it involves prime numbers and is the reason why the hash table capacity should be a prime number.

For this to work properly, there are some fairly strict requirements for the `GetHashCode()` override, which we will look at here. These requirements are going to sound quite abstract and daunting, but don't worry too much. As our `MortimerPhonesEmployees` sample will demonstrate, it is not at all difficult to code up a key class that satisfies these requirements:

- ❑ It should be fast (because placing or retrieving entries in a dictionary is supposed to be fast)

- ❑ It must be consistent – if you regard two keys as representing the same value, then they must give the same value for the hash

- ❑ It should ideally give values that are likely to be evenly distributed across the entire range of numbers that an `int` can store

The reason for this last condition is because of a potential problem; what happens if you get two entries in the dictionary whose hashes both give the same index?

If this happens, the dictionary class will have to start fiddling about looking for the nearest available free location to store the second item – and will have to do some searching in order to retrieve this item later on. This is obviously going to hurt performance, and clearly, if lots of your keys are tending to give the same indexes for where they should be stored, this kind of clash becomes more likely. Due to the way Microsoft's part of the algorithm works, this risk is minimized when the calculated hash values are evenly distributed between `int.MinValue` and `int.MaxValue`.

The risk of clashes between keys also increases as the dictionary gets more full, so it's normally a good idea to make sure the capacity of the dictionary is substantially greater than the number of elements actually in it. For this reason, the `Hashtable` will automatically relocate in order to increase its capacity well before it actually becomes full. The proportion of the table that is full is termed the **load**, and you can set the maximum value that you want the load to reach before the `Hashtable` relocates in another of the `Hashtable` constructors:

```
// capacity =50, Max Load = 0.5

Hashtable employees = new Hashtable(50, 0.5);
```

The smaller you make the maximum load, the more efficiently your hash table will work, but the more memory it will occupy. Incidentally, when a hash table relocates in order to increase its capacity, it always chooses a prime number as its new capacity.

Another important point we listed above is that the hashing algorithm must be consistent. If two objects contain what you regard as the same data, then they must give the same hash value, and this is where we come to the important restrictions on how you override the `Equals()` and `GetHashCode()` methods of `System.Object`. You see, the way that the `Hashtable` determines whether two keys A and B are equal is that it calls `A.Equals(B)`. This means you must ensure that the following is always true:

> If **A.Equals(B)** is **true**, then **A.GetHashCode()** and **B.GetHashCode()** must always return the same hash code.

This probably seems a fairly subtle point, but it is crucial. If you contrived some way of overriding these methods so that the above statement is not always true, then a hash table that uses instances of this class as its keys will simply not work properly. You will find funny things happening. For example, you might place an object in the hash table and then find you can never retrieve it, or you might try to retrieve an entry and get the wrong entry returned.

For this reason, the C# compiler will display a compilation warning if you supply an override for `Equals()`, *but don't supply an override for* `GetHashCode()`.

For `System.Object` this condition is true, because `Equals()` simply compares references, and `GetHashCode()` actually returns a hash that is based solely on the address of the object. This means that hash tables based on a key that doesn't override these methods will work correctly. However, the problem with this way of doing things is that keys are regarded as equal only if they are the same object. That means that when you place an object in the dictionary, you then have to hang on to the reference to the key. You can't simply instantiate another key object later that has the same value, because the same value is defined as meaning the very same instance. This means that if you don't override the `Object` versions of `Equals()` and `GetHashCode()`, your class won't be very convenient to use in a hash table. It makes more sense to implement `GetHashCode()` to generate a hash based on the value of the key rather than its address in memory. This is why you will invariably need to override `GetHashCode()` and `Equals()` for any class that you want to be used as a key.

Incidentally, `System.String` has had these methods overloaded appropriately. `Equals()` has been overloaded to provide value comparison, and `GetHashCode()` has also been correspondingly overloaded to return a hash based on the value of the string. For this reason it is convenient to use strings as keys in a dictionary.

The MortimerPhonesEmployees Example

The `MortimerPhonesEmployees` example is a program that sets up a dictionary of employees. As mentioned earlier, the dictionary is indexed using `EmployeeID` objects, and each item stored in the dictionary is an `EmployeeData` object that stores details of an employee. The program simply instantiates a dictionary, adds a couple of employees to it, and then invites the user to type in employee IDs. For each ID the user types in, the program attempts to use the ID to index into the dictionary and retrieve the employee's details. The process iterates until the user types in X. The example, when run, looks like this:

```
MortimerPhonesEmployees
Enter employee ID (format:A999, X to exit)> B001
Employee: B001: Mortimer              £100,000.00

Enter employee ID (format:A999, X to exit)> W234
Employee: W234: Arabel Jones         £10,000.00

Enter employee ID (format:A999, X to exit)> X
```

This example contains a number of classes. In particular, we need the `EmployeeID` class, which is the key used to identify employees, and the `EmployeeData` class that stores employee data. We will examine the `EmployeeID` class first, since this is the one where all the action happens in terms of preparing it to be used as a dictionary key. The definition of this class is as follows:

```
class EmployeeID
{
    private readonly char prefix;
    private readonly int number;


    public EmployeeID(string id)
    {
        prefix = (id.ToUpper())[0];
        number = int.Parse(id.Substring(1,3));
```

```
    }

    public override string ToString()
    {
        return prefix.ToString() + string.Format("{0,3:000}", number);
    }

    public override int GetHashCode()
    {
        return ToString().GetHashCode();
    }

    public override bool Equals(object obj)
    {
        EmployeeID rhs = obj as EmployeeID;
        if (rhs == null)
            return false;
        if (prefix == rhs.prefix && number == rhs.number)
            return true;
        return false;
    }
}
```

The first part of the class definition simply stores the actual ID. Recall that we said the ID takes a format such as B001 or W234. In other words, it consists of a single letter prefix, followed by three numeric characters. We store this as a char for the prefix and an int for the remainder of the code.

The constructor simply takes a string and breaks it up to form these fields. Note that to keep the example simple, no error checking is performed. We will just assume the string passed into the constructor is in the correct format. The ToString() method simply returns the ID as a string:

```
        return prefix.ToString() + string.Format("{0,3:000}", number);
```

Note the format specifier (3:000) that ensures the int containing the number is padded with zeros, so we get for example B001, and not B1.

Now we come to the two method overrides that we need for the dictionary. First, we have overridden Equals() so that it compares the values of EmployeeID instances:

```
        public override bool Equals(object obj)
        {
            EmployeeID rhs = obj as EmployeeID;
            if (rhs == null)
                return false;
            if (prefix == rhs.prefix && number == rhs.number)
                return true;
            return false;
        }
    }
```

This is the first time we have seen an example of an override of Equals(). Notice that our first task is to check whether the object passed as a parameter is actually an EmployeeID instance. If it isn't, then it obviously isn't going to equal this object, so we return false. We test the type by attempting to cast it to EmployeeID using C#'s as keyword. Once we have established that we have an EmployeeID object, we just compare the values of the fields to see if they contain the same values as this object.

Next, we look at GetHashCode(). The implementation of this is shorter, though at first sight it is perhaps harder to understand what's going on:

```csharp
public override int GetHashCode()
{
   string str = this.ToString();
   return str.GetHashCode();
}
```

Earlier, we listed some strict requirements that the calculated hash code had to satisfy. Of course, there are all sorts of ways to devise simple and efficient hashing algorithms. Generally, taking the fields, multiplying them by large prime numbers, and adding the results together is a good way, but personally I'm not one for doing any more work than I have to, and Microsoft has already implemented a sophisticated, yet efficient hashing algorithm for the String class, so we may as well take advantage of that. String.GetHashCode() produces well-distributed numbers based on the contents of the string. It satisfies all the requirements of a hash code.

The only disadvantage of leveraging this method is that there is some performance loss associated with converting our EmployeeID class to a string in the first place. If you are concerned about that and need the last ounce of performance in your hashing algorithms, you will need to design your own hash. Designing hashing algorithms is a complex topic that we cannot go to in depth in this book. However, we will suggest one simple approach to the problem, which is to simply multiply numbers based on the component fields of the class by different prime numbers (for mathematical reasons, multiplying by different prime numbers helps to prevent different combinations of values of the fields from giving the same hash code). A suitable implementation of GetHashCode() would be:

```csharp
public override int GetHashCode()    // alternative implementation
{
   return (int)prefix*13 + (int)number*53;
}
```

This particular example, will work more quickly than the ToString()-based algorithm that we use in the example, but has the disadvantage that the hash codes generated by different EmployeeIDs are less likely to be evenly spread across the range of int. Incidentally, the primitive numeric types do have GetHashCode() methods defined, but these methods simply return the value of the variable, and are hence not particularly useful. The primitive types aren't really intended to be used as keys.

Notice that our GetHashCode() and Equals() implementations do between them satisfy the requirements for equality that we mentioned earlier. With our override of Equals(), two EmployeeID objects will be considered equal if, and only if they have the same values of prefix and number, but if that's the case, ToString() will give the same value for both of them, and so they will give the same hash code. That's the crucial test that we must make sure we satisfy.

Next, we can look at the class that contains the employee data. The definition of this class is fairly basic and intuitive:

```
class EmployeeData
{
   private string name;
   private decimal salary;
   private EmployeeID id;

   public EmployeeData(EmployeeID id, string name, decimal salary)
   {
      this.id = id;
      this.name = name;
      this.salary = salary;
   }

   public override string ToString()
   {
      StringBuilder sb = new StringBuilder(id.ToString(), 100);
      sb.Append(": ");
      sb.Append(string.Format("{0,-20}", name));
      sb.Append(" ");
      sb.Append(string.Format("{0:C}", salary));
      return sb.ToString();
   }
}
```

Notice how once again for performance reasons, we use a StringBuilder object to generate the string representation of an EmployeeData object. Finally, we create the test harness. This is defined in a class, TestHarness:

```
class TestHarness
{

   Hashtable employees = new Hashtable(31);

   public void Run()
   {
      EmployeeID idMortimer = new EmployeeID("B001");
      EmployeeData mortimer = new EmployeeData(idMortimer, "Mortimer",
                                     100000.00M);
      EmployeeID idArabel = new EmployeeID("W234");
      EmployeeData arabel= new EmployeeData(idArabel, "Arabel Jones",
                                     10000.00M);

      employees.Add(idMortimer, mortimer);
      employees.Add(idArabel, arabel);

      while (true)
      {
         try
         {
            Console.Write("Enter employee ID (format:A999, X to exit)> ");
```

```
            string userInput = Console.ReadLine();
            userInput = userInput.ToUpper();
            if (userInput == "X")
                return;
            EmployeeID id = new EmployeeID(userInput);
            DisplayData(id);
        }
        catch (Exception e)
        {
            Console.WriteLine("Exception occurred. Did you use the correct
                             format for the employee ID?");
            Console.WriteLine(e.Message);
            Console.WriteLine();
        }

        Console.WriteLine();
    }
}

private void DisplayData(EmployeeID id)
{
    object empobj = employees[id];
    if (empobj != null)
    {
        EmployeeData employee = (EmployeeData)empobj;
        Console.WriteLine("Employee: " + employee.ToString());
    }
    else
        Console.WriteLine("Employee not found: ID = " + id);
}
}
```

`TestHarness` contains the member field, which actually is the dictionary.

As usual for a dictionary, we have set the initial capacity to a prime number; in this case, 31. The guts of the test harness are in the `Run()` method. This method first sets up details for a couple of employees – `mortimer` and `arabel` – and adds their details to the dictionary:

```
        employees.Add(idMortimer, mortimer);
        employees.Add(idArabel, arabel);
```

Next, we enter the `while` loop that repeatedly asks the user to input an `employeeID`. There is a `try` block inside the `while` loop, which is just there to trap any problems caused by the user typing in something that's not the correct format for an `EmployeeID`, which would cause the `EmployeeID` constructor to throw an exception when it tries to construct an ID from the string:

```
        string userInput = Console.ReadLine();
        userInput = userInput.ToUpper();
        if (userInput == "X")
            return;
        EmployeeID id = new EmployeeID(userInput);
```

If the `EmployeeID` was constructed correctly, we display the associated employee by calling a method, `DisplayData()`. This is the method in which we finally get to access the dictionary with array syntax. Indeed, retrieving the employee data for the employee with this ID is the first thing we do in this method:

```
private void DisplayData(EmployeeID id)
{
    object empobj = employees[id];
```

If there is no employee with that ID in the dictionary, then `employees[id]` will return `null`, which is why we check for a `null` reference and display an appropriate error message if we find one. Otherwise, we simply cast our returned `empobj` reference to an `EmployeeData` (remember that `Hashtable` is a very generic dictionary class; as far as it is concerned, it is storing objects, so retrieving an element from it will return an object reference, which we need to explicitly cast back to the type that we originally placed in the dictionary.) Once we have our `EmployeeID` reference, we can simply display the employee data using the `EmployeeData.ToString()` method:

```
EmployeeData employee = (EmployeeData)empobj;
Console.WriteLine("Employee: " + employee.ToString());
```

We have one final part of the code – the `Main()` method that kicks the whole sample off. This simply instantiates a `TestHarness` object and runs it:

```
static void Main()
{
    TestHarness harness = new TestHarness();
    harness.Run();
}
```

Custom Attributes

We saw in Chapter 4 how it is possible to define attributes on various items within your program. The attributes that we encountered in that chapter were all ones that Microsoft has defined, however, and which the C# compiler has specific knowledge of. This means that for those particular attributes, the compiler could customize the compilation process in specific ways (for example laying out a struct in memory according to the details in the `StructLayout` and related attributes).

The architecture of attributes also allows you to define your own attributes in your sourcecode. Clearly, if you do this, these attributes will not have any effect on the compilation process itself, because the compiler has no intrinsic awareness of them, but these attributes will be emitted as metadata in the compiled assembly. By itself, this metadata may be useful for documentation purposes. However, what makes this idea really powerful is that using the classes in the `System.Reflection` namespace, your code can read this metadata at runtime. This means that the custom attributes that you define can have a direct effect on how your code runs.

We are going to examine the process of defining and using the custom attributes here, and then we will see how to use these in conjunction with reflection in the next section of the chapter. Over these two sections of the chapter, we will develop an example based on a company that regularly ships upgrades to its software, and wishes to have details of these upgrades documented automatically. In the example, we will define custom attributes that indicate the date that classes or methods in code were last modified or created, and what changes were made. We will then use reflection to develop an application that looks for these attributes in an assembly, and hence can automatically display all the details about what upgrades have been made to the software since a given date. This kind of application can be very useful in saving you work on documentation writing and ensuring your customers get all the up-to-date information whenever you ship a new version of the software package.

Another example of how you might use attributes and reflection would be if your application reads from or writes to a database; then you could use custom attributes as a way of marking which classes and properties correspond to which database tables and columns. Then, by reading these attributes in from the assembly at runtime, your program would be able to automatically retrieve or write data to the appropriate location in the database, without having to code up any specific logic for each table or column.

Writing Custom Attributes

In order to understand how to write custom attributes, it is useful to see what the compiler actually does when it encounters an item in your code that has been marked with an attribute, for which implicit support is not built into the compiler. To take our database example, suppose you have a C# property declaration that looks like this:

```
[FieldName("SocialSecurityNumber")]
public string SocialSecurityNumber
{
    get {
        // etc.
```

On seeing that this property has an attribute, `FieldName`, the C# compiler will start off by appending the string `Attribute` to this name, forming the combined name `FieldNameAttribute`, and will then search all the namespaces in its search path (that is, those namespaces that have been mentioned in a `using` statement) for a class that has the same name. Note, however, that if you mark an item with an attribute whose name already ends in the string `Attribute`, then the compiler won't bother adding that string to the name, but will leave the string that indicates the attribute name unchanged. The above code is exactly equivalent to this:

```
[FieldNameAttribute("SocialSecurityNumber")]
public string SocialSecurityNumber
{

    // etc.
```

The compiler will expect to find a class with this name and it will expect this class to be derived from `System.Attribute`. The compiler is also expecting that this class will contain information that governs the usage of this attribute in certain well-defined ways. In particular, the attribute class needs to specify which items in a program it can be applied to (classes, structs, properties, methods, and so on), and whether it is legal for it to be applied more than once to the same item, as well as what compulsory and optional parameters this attribute takes.

If the compiler cannot find a corresponding attribute class, or it finds one, but the way that you have used that attribute doesn't match the information in the attribute class (for example, if the attribute class indicates that the attribute could only be applied to fields, but you have applied it in your sourcecode to a struct definition), then the compiler will raise a compilation error. Therefore, the next step is to make sure we have defined an appropriate custom attribute class.

Custom Attribute Classes

Continuing the above example, let's assume we have defined a `FieldName` attribute like this:

```
[AttributeUsage(AttributeTargets.Property,
    AllowMultiple=false,
    Inherited=false)]
public class FieldNameAttribute : Attribute
{
    private string name;
    public FieldNameAttribute(string name)
    {
        this.name = name;
    }
}
```

What we have here is just enough information to let the compiler know how to use the attribute.

AttributeUsage Attribute

The first thing to note is that our attribute class itself is marked with an attribute – the `AttributeUsage` attribute. This is another one of those attributes that the C# compiler intrinsically knows what to do with (you could argue that `AttributeUsage` isn't an attribute at all; it is more like a meta-attribute, because it applies to other attributes, not simply to any class). `AttributeUsage` is there primarily to indicate to which items in your code your custom attribute can be applied. This information is given by its first parameter, which must be present. This parameter is of an enumerated type, `AttributeTargets`. In the above example, we have indicated that the `FieldName` attribute may be applied only to properties, which is fine, because that is exactly what we have applied it to in our earlier code fragment. The definition of the `AttributeTargets` enumeration is:

```
public enum AttributeTargets
{
    All = 0x00003FFF,
    Assembly = 0x00000001,
    Class = 0x00000004,
    Constructor = 0x00000020,
    Delegate = 0x00001000,
    Enum = 0x00000010,
    Event = 0x00000200,
    Field = 0x00000100,
    Interface = 0x00000400,
    Method = 0x00000040,
    Module = 0x00000002,
    Parameter = 0x00000800,
    Property = 0x00000080,
    ReturnValue = 0x00002000,
    Struct = 0x00000008
}
```

This list tells us all of the elements that attributes may be applied to. Note that when applying the attribute to a program element, we place the attribute in square brackets immediately before the element. However, there is one value in the above list that does not correspond to any program element: `Assembly`. An attribute can be applied to an assembly as a whole instead of to an element in your code; in this case the attribute can be placed anywhere in your sourcecode, but needs to be marked with the `assembly` keyword:

```
[assembly: SomeAssemblyAttribute(Parameters)]
```

When indicating the elements, it is quite possible to combine these values together using the bitwise `OR` operator. For example, if we wanted to indicate that our `FieldName` attribute could be applied to either a property or a field, we could have written:

```
[AttributeUsage(AttributeTargets.Property | AttributeTargets.Field,
    AllowMultiple=false,
    Inherited=false)]
public class FieldNameAttribute : Attribute
```

You can also use `AttributeTargets.All` to indicate that your attribute is allowed effectively anywhere. The `AttributeUsage` attribute as illustrated above also contains two other parameters, `AllowMultiple` and `Inherited`. These are indicated with a different syntax of `<AttributeName>=<AttributeValue>`, instead of simply giving the values for these attributes in order. These parameters are optional parameters – you can omit them if you wish.

The `AllowMultiple` parameter indicates whether an attribute may be applied more than once to the same item. The fact that it is set to `false` here indicates that the compiler should raise an error if it sees something like this:

```
[FieldName("SocialSecurityNumber")]
[FieldName("NationalInsuranceNumber")]
public string SocialSecurityNumber
{

    // etc.
```

If the `Inherited` parameter is set to `true`, then this indicates that an attribute that is applied to a class or interface will also automatically be applied to all inherited classes or interfaces. If the attribute is applied to a method or property, and so on, then it will automatically apply to any overrides of that method or property, and so on.

Specifying Attribute Parameters

Now let's examine how we can specify any parameters that our custom attribute takes. The way it works is that when the compiler encounters a statement such as:

```
[FieldName("SocialSecurityNumber")]
public string SocialSecurityNumber
{

    // etc.
```

it examines the parameters passed into the attribute – in this case, a string, and looks for a constructor to the attribute that will take exactly those parameters. If it finds one, that's OK. If it doesn't it will raise a compilation error. It's as if the compiler wants to instantiate an attribute object, although that's not actually what happens. The compiler simply emits metadata into the assembly. However, as we will see soon, an attribute object may later be instantiated if a later program uses reflection to examine the attributes in the assembly, so the compiler needs to make sure that the emitted metadata is of the appropriate types to allow this to happen.

In our case, we have supplied just one constructor for `FieldNameAttribute`, and this constructor takes one string parameter. Therefore, when applying the `FieldName` attribute to a property, we must supply one string as a parameter, as we have done in the code just presented.

If we want to allow a choice of what types of parameters should be supplied with an attribute, we can of course provide different overloads of the constructor, although normal practice is to supply just one constructor, and use properties to define any other optional parameters, as we explain next.

Optional Parameters

We have seen in the `AttributeUsage` attribute that there is an alternative syntax by which optional parameters can be added to an attribute. This syntax involves specifying the names of the optional parameters. It works through properties or fields in the attribute class. For example, suppose we modified our definition of the `SocialSecurityNumber` property as follows:

```
[FieldName("SocialSecurityNumber", Comment="This is the primary key field")]
public string SocialSecurityNumber
{

    // etc.
```

In this case, the compiler will recognize the `<ParameterName>=` syntax of the second parameter, and so not attempt to match this parameter to a `FieldNameAttribute` constructor. Instead, it will look for a public property (or field, but as indicated in previous chapters, public fields are not considered good programming practice, so normally you will work with properties) of that name that it can use to set the value of this parameter. If we want the above code to work, we had better add some code to `FieldNameAttribute`:

```
[AttributeUsage(AttributeTargets.Property,
    AllowMultiple=false,
    Inherited=false)]
public class FieldNameAttribute : Attribute
{
    private string comment;
    public string Comment
    {

        // etc.
```

With this code added and the implementation of the `Comment` property filled in, we can now supply optional attributes.

The WhatsNewAttributes Example

In this section, we will start developing the `WhatsNewAttributes` example described earlier, which provides for an attribute that indicates when an item was last modified. This is a rather more ambitious code sample than the others we have seen, in that it consists of three separate assemblies:

❑   The `WhatsNewAttributes` assembly itself, which contains the definitions of the attributes.

❑   The `VectorStruct` assembly, which contains the code to which the attributes have been applied. For this one, we have just taken the `Vector` sample that we have developed through the last few chapters.

❑   The `LookUpWhatsNew` assembly, which contains the project that displays details of items that have changed.

Of these, only `LookUpWhatsNew` is a console application of the type that we have used up until now. The remaining two assemblies are simply libraries – they each contain class definitions, but no program entry point. For the `VectorStruct` assembly, this means that we have taken the `VectorAsCollection` sample and removed the entry point and test harness class, leaving only the `Vector` class itself.

Managing three related projects by compiling at the command line is fiddly, so although we will present the commands for separately compiling all these source files, if you download this code sample from the Wrox Press web site, you may prefer to edit it as a combined Visual Studio .NET solution, in the way that we will demonstrate in Chapter 6. The files are alternatively available as Visual Studio .NET solutions to allow you to do this.

The WhatsNewAttributes Library Assembly

We will start off with the core `WhatsNewAttributes` project itself. The sourcecode is contained in the file `WhatsNewAttributes.cs`. We have not compiled to libraries before, but the syntax for doing this is quite simple. At the command line we supply the flag `target:library` to the compiler. To compile `WhatsNewAttributes`, type in:

```
csc /target:library WhatsNewAttributes.cs
```

The sourcecode for this assembly contains two attribute classes, `LastModifiedAttribute` and `SupportsWhatsNewAttribute`. `LastModifiedAttribute` is the attribute that we can use to mark when an item was last modified. It takes two compulsory parameters (the parameters that are passed to the constructor); the date of the modifications, and a string containing a description of the changes. There is also one optional parameter (the parameter for which a writeable property exists), `issues`, which can be used to describe any outstanding issues for the item.

> *There is no difference in the sourcecode between code intended as a library and code intended as an application, except there is no `Main()` method in a library.*

In real life you would probably want this attribute to apply to anything. In order to keep our code simple, we are going to limit its usage here to classes and methods. We will allow it to be applied more than once to the same item however, (`AllowMultiple=true`) since an item may get modified more than once, and each modification will need to be marked with a separate attribute instance.

SupportsWhatsNew is a smaller class representing an attribute that doesn't take any parameters. The idea of this attribute is that it's an assembly attribute that is used to mark an assembly for which we are maintaining documentation via the LastModifiedAttribute. This is so that the program that will examine this assembly later on knows that the assembly it is reading is one that we are actually using our automated documentation process on! Here is the complete sourcecode for this part of the example:

```
namespace Wrox.ProCSharp.WhatsNewAttributes
{
    [AttributeUsage(
      AttributeTargets.Class | AttributeTargets.Method,
      AllowMultiple=true, Inherited=false)]
    public class LastModifiedAttribute : Attribute
    {
        private DateTime dateModified;
        private string changes;
        private string issues;

        public LastModifiedAttribute(string dateModified, string changes)
        {
            this.dateModified = DateTime.Parse(dateModified);
            this.changes = changes;
        }

        public DateTime DateModified
        {
            get
            {
                return dateModified;
            }
        }

        public string Changes
        {
            get
            {
                return changes;
            }
        }

        public string Issues
        {
            get
            {
                return issues;
            }
            set
            {
                issues = value;
            }
        }
    }

    [AttributeUsage(AttributeTargets.Assembly)]
    public class SupportsWhatsNewAttribute : Attribute
    {
    }
}
```

From the previous descriptions, the above code should all be clear. Notice, however, that we have not bothered to supply set accessors to the Changes and DateModified properties. There is no need, since we are requiring these parameters to be set in the constructor as compulsory parameters (you may wonder what we need the get accessors for; that's so that when we need to read the values of these attributes later on, we will be able to do so).

Using these Attributes – The VectorClass Assembly

Next, we need to use these attributes. For this, as mentioned before, we are using a modified version of the earlier VectorAsCollection sample. Note that we need to explicitly reference the WhatsNewAttributes library that we have just created. We also need to indicate the corresponding namespace with a using statement if the compiler is to be able to recognize the attributes:

```
using System;
using Wrox.ProCSharp.WhatsNewAttributes;
using System.Collections;
using System.Text;

[assembly: SupportsWhatsNew]
```

In this code, we have also added the line that will mark the assembly itself with the SupportsWhatsNew attribute.

Now for the code for the Vector class. We are not really changing anything in this class, just adding a couple of LastModified attributes to mark out the work that we have done on this class in this chapter. We have made one change, however: we have defined Vector as a class instead of a struct. The only reason for this is to simplify the code that we will later write that displays the attributes. In the VectorAsCollection sample, Vector was a struct, but its enumerator was a class. This would have meant that our later sample that looks at this assembly would have had to pick out both classes and structs. Having both types as classes means we don't have to worry about the existence of any structs, thus making our example a bit shorter:

```
namespace Wrox.ProCSharp.VectorClass
{
    [LastModified("14 Feb 2002", "IEnumerable interface implemented\n" +
        "So Vector can now be treated as a collection")]
    [LastModified("10 Feb 2002", "IFormattable interface implemented\n" +
        "So Vector now responds to format specifiers N and VE")]
    class Vector : IFormattable, IEnumerable
    {
        public double x, y, z;

        public Vector(double x, double y, double z)
        {
            this.x = x;
            this.y = y;
            this.z = z;
        }

        [LastModified("10 Feb 2002",
                    "Method added in order to provide formatting support")]
        public string ToString(string format, IFormatProvider formatProvider)
```

```
    {
        if (format == null)
            return ToString();
```

We will also mark the contained `VectorEnumerator` class as new:

```
[LastModified("14 Feb 2002",
            "Class created as part of collection support for Vector")]
private class VectorEnumerator : IEnumerator
{
```

That's as far as we can get with this sample for now. We can't run anything yet, because all we have are two libraries. We will develop the final part of the example, in which we look up and display these attributes, as soon as we've had a look at how reflection works.

In order to compile this code from the command line you should type the following:

```
csc /target:library /reference:WhatsNewAttributes.dll VectorClass.cs
```

Reflection

Reflection is a generic term that covers the various .NET base classes that allow you to find out information about the types in your programs or in other assemblies, and also to read other metadata from assembly manifests. Most of these classes are in the namespace `System.Reflection`, and there are a huge number of classes in this namespace. We don't have space here to touch on more than a fraction of what you can do with the reflection classes, but we will give you enough to start you off.

In this section, we will start by having a closer look at the `System.Type` class, which lets you access information concerning the definition of any given data type. We will next have a brief look at the `System.Reflection.Assembly` class, which you can use to access information about a given assembly, or to load that assembly into your program. Finally, we will put everything in this section and the previous section about custom attributes together, by completing the `WhatsNewAttributes` sample.

The System.Type Class

We have already used the `Type` class on a number of occasions through this book, but so far only to retrieve the name of a type:

```
Type t = typeof(double)
```

In fact, although we loosely refer to `Type` as a class, it is in reality an abstract base class. Whenever you instantiate a `Type` object, you are actually instantiating a derived class of `Type`. `Type` has one derived class corresponding to each actual data type, though in general the derived classes simply provide different overloads of the various `Type` methods and properties that return the correct data for the corresponding data type. They do not generally add new methods or properties. In general, there are three common ways of obtaining a `Type` reference that refers to any given type:

❑ Use the C# typeof operator as illustrated above. This operator takes the name of the type (not in quote marks however) as a parameter.

❑ Use the GetType() method, which all classes inherit from System.Object:

```
double d = 10;
Type t = d.GetType();
```

GetType() is called against a variable, rather than taking the name of a type. Note, however, that the Type object returned is still associated with only that data type. It does not contain any information that relates to that instance of the type. However, this method can be useful if you have a reference to an object, but are not sure what class that object is actually an instance of.

❑ You can also call the static method of the Type class, GetType():

```
Type t = Type.GetType("System.Double");
```

Type is really the gateway to much of the reflection technology. It implements a huge number of methods and properties – again, far too many to give a comprehensive list here, but the following sub-sections should give you some idea of the kind of things you can do with this class.

Note that the available properties are all read-only; you use Type to find out about the data type – you can't use it to make any modifications to the type!

Type Properties

The properties implemented by Type can be split into three categories:

1. There are a number of properties that retrieve the strings containing various names associated with the class:

Property	Returns
Name	The name of the data type
FullName	The fully qualified name of the data type (including the namespace name)
Namespace	The name of the namespace in which the data type is defined

2. It is also possible to retrieve references to further type objects that represent related classes:

Property	Returns Type Reference Corresponding To
BaseType	Immediate base type of this type
UnderlyingSystemType	The type that this type maps to in the .NET runtime (recall that certain .NET base types actually map to specific predefined types recognized by IL)

3. There are a number of Boolean properties that indicate whether or not this type is, for example, a class, an enum, and so on. These properties include: `IsAbstract`, `IsArray`, `IsClass`, `IsEnum`, `IsInterface`, `IsPointer`, `IsPrimitive` (one of the predefined primitive data types), `IsPublic`, `IsSealed`, and `IsValueType`.

For example, using a primitive data type:

```
Type intType = typeof(int);
Console.WriteLine(intType.IsAbstract);      // writes false
Console.WriteLine(intType.IsClass);         // writes false
Console.WriteLine(intType.IsEnum);          // writes false
Console.WriteLine(intType.IsPrimitive);     // writes true
Console.WriteLine(intType.IsValueType);     // writes true
```

Or using our `Vector` class:

```
Type intType = typeof(Vector);
Console.WriteLine(intType.IsAbstract);      // writes false
Console.WriteLine(intType.IsClass);         // writes true
Console.WriteLine(intType.IsEnum);          // writes false
Console.WriteLine(intType.IsPrimitive);     // writes false
Console.WriteLine(intType.IsValueType);     // writes false
```

You can also retrieve a reference to the assembly that the type is defined in. This is returned as a reference to an instance of the `System.Reflection.Assembly` class, which we will examine soon:

```
Type t = typeof (Vector);
Assembly containingAssembly = new Assembly(t);
```

Methods

Most of the methods of `System.Type` are used to obtain details of the members of the corresponding data type – the constructors, properties, methods, events, and so on. There are quite a large number of methods, but they all follow the same pattern. For example, there are two methods that retrieve details of the methods of the data type: `GetMethod()` and `GetMethods()`. `GetMethod()` returns a reference to a `System.Reflection.MethodInfo` object, which contains details of a method. `GetMethods()` returns an array of such references. The difference is that `GetMethods()` returns details of all the methods, while `GetMethod()` returns details of just one method with a specified parameter list. Both methods have overloads that take an extra parameter, a `BindingFlags` enumerated value that indicates which members should be returned – for example, whether to return public members, instance members, static members and so on.

So for example, the simplest overload of `GetMethods()` takes no parameters and returns details of all the public methods of the data type:

```
Type t = typeof(double);
MethodInfo [] methods = t.GetMethods();
foreach (MethodInfo nextMethod in methods)
{

   // etc.
```

Following the same pattern are the following member methods of `Type`:

Type of object returned	Methods (the method with the plural name returns an array)
`ConstructorInfo`	`GetConstructor()`, `GetConstructors()`
`EventInfo`	`GetEvent()`, `GetEvents()`
`FieldInfo`	`GetField()`, `GetFields()`
`InterfaceInfo`	`GetInterface()`, `GetInterfaces()`
`MemberInfo`	`GetMember()`, `GetMembers()`
`MethodInfo`	`GetMethod()`, `GetMethods()`
`PropertyInfo`	`GetProperty()`, `GetProperties()`

The `GetMember()` and `GetMembers()` methods return details of any or all members of the data type, irrespective of whether these members are constructors, properties, methods, and so on. Finally, note that it is possible to invoke members either by calling the `InvokeMember()` method of `Type`, or by calling the `Invoke()` method of the `MethodInfo`, `PropertyInfo`, and the other classes.

The TypeView Example

We will now demonstrate some of the features of the `Type` class by writing a short example, `TypeView`, which we can use to list the members of a data type. We will demonstrate use of `TypeView` for a double, but we can swap to any other data type just by changing one line of the code for the sample. `TypeView` displays far more information than can be displayed in a console window, so we're going to take a break from our normal practice and display the output in a message box. Running `TypeView` for a double produces these results:

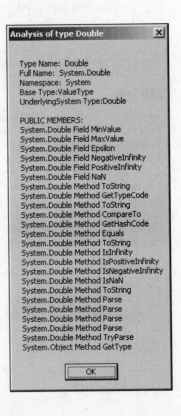

Analysis of type Double

Type Name: Double
Full Name: System.Double
Namespace: System
Base Type:ValueType
UnderlyingSystem Type:Double

PUBLIC MEMBERS:
System.Double Field MinValue
System.Double Field MaxValue
System.Double Field Epsilon
System.Double Field NegativeInfinity
System.Double Field PositiveInfinity
System.Double Field NaN
System.Double Method ToString
System.Double Method GetTypeCode
System.Double Method ToString
System.Double Method CompareTo
System.Double Method GetHashCode
System.Double Method Equals
System.Double Method ToString
System.Double Method IsInfinity
System.Double Method IsPositiveInfinity
System.Double Method IsNegativeInfinity
System.Double Method IsNaN
System.Double Method ToString
System.Double Method Parse
System.Double Method Parse
System.Double Method Parse
System.Double Method Parse
System.Double Method TryParse
System.Object Method GetType

OK

The message box displays the name, full name, and namespace of the data type as well as the name of the underlying type and the base type. Then, it simply iterates through all the public instance members of the data type, displaying for each member the declaring type, the type of member (method, field, and so on) and the name of the member. The **declaring type** is the name of the class that actually declares the type member (in other words, System.Double if it is defined or overridden in System.Double, or the name of the relevant base type if the member is simply inherited from some base class).

TypeView does not display signatures of methods because we are retrieving details of all public instance members through MemberInfo objects, and information about parameters is not available through a MemberInfo object. In order to retrieve that information, we would need references to MethodInfo and other more specific objects, which means we would need to separately obtain details of each type of member.

TypeView does display details of all public instance members, but it happens that for doubles, the only ones defined are fields and methods. We will compile TypeView as a console application – there is no problem with displaying a message box from a console application. However, the fact that we are using a message box means that we need to reference the base class assembly System.Windows.Forms.dll, which contains the classes in the System.Windows.Forms namespace in which the MessageBox class that we will need is defined. The code for TypeView is as follows. To start with, we need to add a couple of using statements:

```
using System;
using System.Text;
using System.Windows.Forms;
using System.Reflection;
```

We need System.Text because we will be using a StringBuilder object to build up the text to be displayed in the message box, and System.Windows.Forms for the message box itself. The entire code is in one class, MainClass, which has a couple of static methods, and one static field, a StringBuilder instance called OutputText, which will be used to build up the text to be displayed in the message box. The main method and class declaration look like this:

```
class MainClass
{
    static void Main()
    {
        // modify this line to retrieve details of any
        // other data type
        Type t = typeof(double);

        AnalyzeType(t);
        MessageBox.Show(OutputText.ToString(), "Analysis of type "
                                            + t.Name);
        Console.ReadLine();
    }
```

The Main() method implementation starts by declaring a Type object to represent our chosen data type. We then call a method, AnalyzeType(), which extracts the information from the Type object and uses it to build up the output text. Finally, we show the output in a message box. We have not encountered the MessageBox class before, but using it is fairly intuitive. We just call its static Show() method, passing it two strings, which will respectively be the text in the box and the caption. AnalyzeType() is where the bulk of the work is done:

```
static void AnalyzeType(Type t)
{
    AddToOutput("Type Name:   " + t.Name);
    AddToOutput("Full Name:   " + t.FullName);
    AddToOutput("Namespace:   " + t.Namespace);
    Type tBase = t.BaseType;
    if (tBase != null)
        AddToOutput("Base Type:" + tBase.Name);
    Type tUnderlyingSystem = t.UnderlyingSystemType;
    if (tUnderlyingSystem != null)
        AddToOutput("UnderlyingSystem Type:" + tUnderlyingSystem.Name);

    AddToOutput("\nPUBLIC MEMBERS:");
    MemberInfo [] Members = t.GetMembers();
    foreach (MemberInfo NextMember in Members)
    {
        AddToOutput(NextMember.DeclaringType + " " +
        NextMember.MemberType + " " + NextMember.Name);
    }
}
```

We implement this method by simply calling various properties of the `Type` object to get the information we need concerning the names, then call the `GetMembers()` method to get an array of `MemberInfo` objects that we can use to display the details of each method. Note that we use a helper method, `AddToOutput()`, to build up the text to be displayed in the message box:

```
static void AddToOutput(string Text)
{
    OutputText.Append("\n" + Text);
}
```

The Assembly Class

The `Assembly` class is defined in the `System.Reflection` namespace, and allows you access to the metadata for a given assembly. It also contains methods to allow you to execute an assembly, assuming the assembly is an executable. Like the `Type` class, it contains a very large number of methods and properties – too many for us to cover here. Instead, we will confine ourselves to covering those methods and properties that you need to get started, and which we will use to complete the `WhatsNewAttributes` sample.

Before you can do anything with an `Assembly` instance, you need to load the corresponding assembly into the running process. You can do this with either of the static members `Assembly.Load()` and `Assembly.LoadFrom()`. The difference between these methods is that `Load()` takes the name of the assembly, which must be an assembly that is already referenced from the currently executing assembly (in other words, it must be an assembly that you referenced when you were first compiling the project), while `LoadFrom()` takes the path name of an assembly, which can be any assembly that is present on your file system:

```
Assembly assembly1 = Assembly.Load("SomeAssembly");
Assembly assembly2 = Assembly.LoadFrom
    (@"C:\My Projects\GroovySoftware\SomeOtherAssembly");
```

There are a number of other overloads of both methods, which supply additional security information. Once you have loaded an assembly, you can use various properties on it to find out, for example, its full name:

```
string name = assembly1.FullName;
```

Finding Out About Types Defined in an Assembly

One nice feature of the `Assembly` class is it allows you to very conveniently obtain details of all the types that have been defined in the corresponding assembly. You simply call the `Assembly.GetTypes()` method, which returns an array of `System.Type` references containing details of all the types. You can then manipulate these `Type` references just as you would with a `Type` object obtained from the C# `typeof` operator, or from `Object.GetType()`:

```
Type[] types = theAssembly.GetTypes();
foreach(Type definedType in types)
   DoSomethingWith(definedType);
```

Finding Out About Custom Attributes

The methods you use to find out about what custom attributes are defined on an assembly or type depend on what type of object the type is attached to. If you want to find out what custom attributes are attached to an assembly as a whole, you need to call a static method of the `Attribute` class, `GetCustomAttributes()`, passing in a reference to the assembly:

```
Attribute [] definedAttributes =
         Attribute.GetCustomAttributes(assembly1);
         // assembly1 is an Assembly object
```

This is actually quite significant. You may have wondered why, when we defined custom attributes, we had to go to all the trouble of actually writing classes for them, and why Microsoft hadn't come up with some simpler syntax. Well, the answer is here. The custom attributes do genuinely exist as objects, and once an assembly is loaded you can read these attribute objects in, examine their properties, and call their methods.

`GetCustomAttributes()`, as used to get assembly attributes, has a couple of overloads: if you call it without specifying any parameters other than a reference to the assembly then it will simply return all the custom attributes defined for that assembly. You can also call it by specifying a second parameter, which is a `Type` object that indicates the attribute class. In this case `GetCustomAttributes()` returns an array consisting of all the attributes present that are of that class. We will use this overload in the `WhatsNewAttributes` example in order to find out whether the `SupportsWhatsNew` attribute is present in the assembly. To do this, we called `GetCustomAttributes()`, passing in a reference to the assembly, and the type of the `SupportWhatsNewAttribute` attribute. If this attribute is present, we get an array containing all instances of it. If there are no instances of it defined in the assembly, then we return `null`:

```
Attribute supportsAttribute =
         Attribute.GetCustomAttributes(assembly1,
         typeof(SupportsWhatsNewAttribute));
```

Note that all attributes are retrieved as plain `Attribute` references. If you want to call any of the methods or properties you defined for your custom attributes, then you will need to cast these references explicitly to the relevant custom attribute classes. You can obtain details of custom attributes that are attached to a given data type by calling another overload of `Assembly.GetCustomAttributes()`, this time passing a `Type` reference that describes the type for which you want to retrieve any attached attributes. On the other hand, if you want to obtain attributes that are attached to methods, constructors, fields, and so on, then you will need to call a `GetCustomAttributes()` method that is a member of one of the classes `MethodInfo`, `ConstructorInfo`, `FieldInfo`, and so on. That is outside the scope of this chapter.

Completing the WhatsNewAttributes Sample

We now have enough information to complete the `WhatsNewAttributes` sample by writing the sourcecode for the final assembly in the sample, the `LookUpWhatsNew` assembly. This part of the application is a console application. However, it needs to reference both of the other assemblies. Although this is going to be a command-line application, we will follow the previous `TypeView` sample in actually displaying our results in a message box, since there is again going to be rather a lot of text output – far too much to show in a console window screenshot.

The file is called `LookUpWhatsNew.cs`, and the command to compile it is

```
csc /reference:WhatsNewAttributes.dll /reference:VectorClass.dll LookUpWhatsNew.cs
```

In the sourcecode for this file, we first indicate the namespaces we wish to infer. `System.Text` is there because we need to use a `StringBuilder` object again:

```csharp
using System;
using System.Reflection;
using System.Windows.Forms;
using System.Text;
using Wrox.ProCSharp.VectorClass;
using Wrox.ProCSharp.WhatsNewAttributes;

namespace Wrox.ProCSharp.LookUpWhatsNew
{
```

Next, the class that will contain the main program entry point as well as the other methods, `WhatsNewChecker`. All the methods we define will be in this class, which will also have two static fields. `outputText` contains the text as we build it up in preparation for writing it to the message box. `backDateTo` stores the date we have selected – all modifications made since this date will be displayed. Normally, we would display a dialog box inviting the user to pick this date, but I don't want to get sidetracked into that kind of code (besides, we haven't reached the Windows Forms chapter yet, so we don't yet know how to display a dialog box other than a simple message box!). For this reason, I have initialized `backDateTo` to a hard-coded date of 1 Feb 2002. You can easily change this date if you want when you download the code:

```
class WhatsNewChecker
{
    static StringBuilder outputText = new StringBuilder(1000);
    static DateTime backDateTo = new DateTime(2002, 2, 1);

    static void Main()
    {
        Assembly theAssembly = Assembly.Load("VectorClass");
        Attribute supportsAttribute =
            Attribute.GetCustomAttribute(
                theAssembly, typeof(SupportsWhatsNewAttribute));
        string Name = theAssembly.FullName;

        AddToMessage("Assembly: " + Name);
        if (supportsAttribute == null)
        {
            AddToMessage(
                "This assembly does not support WhatsNew attributes");
            return;
        }
        else
            AddToMessage("Defined Types:");

        Type[] types = theAssembly.GetTypes();
        foreach(Type definedType in types)
            DisplayTypeInfo(theAssembly, definedType);

        MessageBox.Show(outputText.ToString(),
            "What\'s New since " + backDateTo.ToLongDateString());
        Console.ReadLine();
    }
```

The `Main()` method first loads the `VectorClass` assembly, and verifies that it is indeed marked with the `SupportsWhatsNew` attribute. It will do so, as we have only recently compiled that assembly with that attribute in, but this is a check that would be worth making if, more realistically, the user was given a choice of what assembly to check.

Assuming all is well, we use the `Assembly.GetTypes()` method to get an array of all the types defined in this assembly, and then loop through them. For each one, we call a method that we have written, `DisplayTypeInfo()`, which will add the relevant text, including details of any instances of `LastModifiedAttribute`, to the `outputText` field. Finally, we show the message box with the complete text. The `DisplayTypeInfo()` method looks like this:

```
static void DisplayTypeInfo(Assembly theAssembly, Type type)
{
    // make sure we only pick out classes
    if (!(type.IsClass))
        return;
    AddToMessage("\nclass " + type.Name);

    Attribute [] attribs = Attribute.GetCustomAttributes(type);
    if (attribs.Length == 0)
```

```
                AddToMessage("No changes to this class\n");
        else
            foreach (Attribute attrib in attribs)
                WriteAttributeInfo(attrib);

        MethodInfo [] methods = type.GetMethods();
        AddToMessage("CHANGES TO METHODS OF THIS CLASS:");
        foreach (MethodInfo nextMethod in methods)
        {
            object [] attribs2 =
                nextMethod.GetCustomAttributes(
                    typeof(LastModifiedAttribute), false);
            if (attribs2 != null)
            {
                AddToMessage(
                    nextMethod.ReturnType + " " + nextMethod.Name + "()");
                foreach (Attribute nextAttrib in attribs2)
                    WriteAttributeInfo(nextAttrib);
            }
        }
    }
}
```

Notice that the first thing we do in this method is check whether the `Type` reference we have been passed actually represents a class. Since, in order to keep things simple, we have specified that the `LastModified` attribute can only be applied to classes or member methods, we will be wasting our time doing any processing if the item is not a class (it might in principle be a class, delegate, or enum).

Next, we use the `Attribute.GetCustomAttributes()` method to find out if this class does have any `LastModifiedAttribute` instances attached to it. If it does, we add their details to the output text, using a helper method, `WriteAttributeInfo()`, which we will consider next.

Finally, we use the `Type.GetMethods()` method to iterate through all the member methods of this data type, and then basically do the same thing with each method; check if it has any `LastModifiedAttribute` instances attached to it, and display them using `WriteAttributeInfo()` if it has.

The next bit of code shows the `WriteAttributeInfo()` method, which is responsible for working out what text to display for a given `LastModifiedAttribute` instance. Note that this method is passed an `Attribute` reference, so it needs to cast this to a `LastModifiedAttribute` reference first. Once it has done that, it uses the properties that we originally defined for this attribute to retrieve its parameters. It checks that the date of the attribute is sufficiently recent before actually adding it to the text to be displayed:

```
static void WriteAttributeInfo(Attribute attrib)
{

    LastModifiedAttribute lastModifiedAttrib =
        attrib as LastModifiedAttribute;
    if (lastModifiedAttrib == null)
        return;

    // check that date is in range
    DateTime modifiedDate = lastModifiedAttrib.DateModified;
    if (modifiedDate < backDateTo)
        return;
```

```
        AddToMessage("  MODIFIED: " +
          modifiedDate.ToLongDateString() + ":");
      AddToMessage("     " + lastModifiedAttrib.Changes);
      if (lastModifiedAttrib.Issues != null)
        AddToMessage("     Outstanding issues:" +
          lastModifiedAttrib.Issues);
      AddToMessage("");
    }
```

Finally, here is the helper `AddToMessage()` method:

```
    static void AddToMessage(string message)
    {
      outputText.Append("\n" + message);
    }
```

Running this code produces these results:

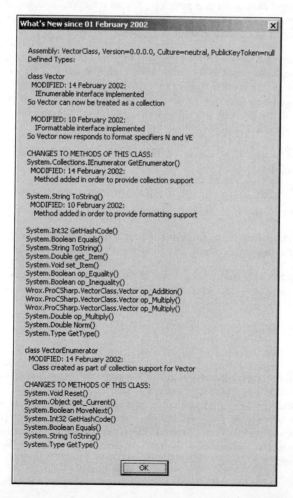

Notice that when we listed the types defined in the VectorClass assembly, we actually picked up two classes: Vector, and the embedded VectorEnumerator class that we added when we turned Vector into a collection earlier in the chapter. Also notice that since we hard-coded a backDateTo date of 1 Feb in this code, we have actually picked up the attributes that were dated 14 Feb (when we added the collection stuff), but not those dated 14 Jan (when we added the IFormattable interface).

Threading

In this section, we will look at the support that C# and the .NET base classes offer for developing applications that employ multiple threads. We will briefly examine the Thread class, through which much of the threading support takes place, and develop a couple of examples that illustrate threading principles. From there, we will examine some of the issues that arise when we consider thread synchronization. Due to the complexity of the subject, the emphasis will be on understanding some of the basic principles involved – we won't really go on to develop any real applications.

A **thread** is a sequence of execution in a program. For all programs that we have written so far in C#, there has been one entry point – the Main() method. Execution has started with the first statement in the Main() method and has continued until that method returns.

This program structure is all very well for programs in which there is one identifiable sequence of tasks, but often a program actually needs to be doing more than one thing at the same time. One familiar situation in which this occurs is when you have started up Internet Explorer and are getting increasingly frustrated as some page takes ages to load. Eventually, you get so fed up (if you're like me, after about 2 seconds!) that you click the Back button or type in some other URL to look at instead. For this to work, Internet Explorer must be doing at least three things:

❑ Grabbing the data for the page as it gets returned from the Internet, along with any accompanying files

❑ Rendering the page

❑ Watching for any user input that might indicate the user wants IE to do something else instead

More generally, the same situation applies to any case where a program is performing some task while at the same time displaying a dialog box that gives you the chance to cancel the task at any time.

Let's look at the example with Internet Explorer in more detail. We will simplify the problem a bit by ignoring the task of storing the data as it arrives from the Internet, and assume that Internet Explorer is simply faced with two tasks:

❑ Displaying the page

❑ Watching for user input

We will assume for the sake of argument that this is a page that takes a long time to display; it might have some processor-intensive JavaScript in it, or it might contain a marquee element in it that needs to be continually updated. One way that you could approach the situation is to write a method that does a little bit of work in rendering the page. After a short time, let us say a twentieth of a second, the method checks to see if there has been any user input. If there has been, this is processed (which may mean canceling the rendering task). Otherwise, the method carries on rendering the page for another twentieth of the second.

This approach would work, but it is going to be a very complicated method to implement. More seriously, it totally ignores the event-based architecture of Windows. Recall from our coverage of events in the last chapter that if any user input arrives, the system will want to notify the application by raising an event. Let's modify our method to allow Windows to use events:

❑   We will write an event handler that responds to user input. The response may include setting some flag to indicate that rendering should stop.

❑   We will write a method that handles the rendering. This method is designed to be executed whenever we are not doing anything else.

This solution is better, because it works with the Windows event architecture, but personally I wouldn't like to be the one who has to write this rendering method. Look at what it has to do. For a start, it will have to time itself carefully. While this method is running, the computer cannot respond to any user input. That means this method will have to make a note of the time that it gets called, continue monitoring the time as it works, and as soon as a fairly suitable period of time has elapsed (the absolute maximum to retain user responsiveness would be a bit less than a tenth of a second), should return. Not only that, but before this method returns, it will need to store the exact state of where it had got up to, so that the next time it is called it can carry on from there. It is certainly possible to write a method that would do that, and in the days of Windows 3.1, that's exactly what you would have to do to handle this sort of situation. Luckily, NT3.1 and then Windows 95 brought multi-threaded processes, which are a far more convenient way of solving problems like this.

Applications with Multiple Threads

The above example illustrates the situation in which an application needs to do more than one thing, so the obvious solution is to give the application more than one thread of execution. As we said, a thread represents the sequence of instructions that the computer executes. There is no reason why an application should only have one such sequence. In fact, it can have as many as you want. All that is required is that each time you create a new thread of execution, you indicate a method at which execution should start. The first thread in an application always starts at the Main() method because the first thread is started by the .NET runtime, and Main() is the method that the .NET runtime picks. Subsequent threads will be started internally by your application, which means that your application gets to choose where those threads start

How Does This Work?

So far, we have spoken rather loosely about threads happening at the same time. In fact, one processor can only be doing one thing at a time. If you have a multi-processor system, then it is theoretically possible for more than one instruction to be executed simultaneously, one on each processor, but for the majority of us who work on single-processor computers, things just don't happen simultaneously. What actually happens is that the Windows operating system gives the appearance of many things taking place at the same time by a procedure known as **pre-emptive multitasking**.

What pre-emptive multitasking means is that Windows picks a thread in some process and allows that thread to run for a short period of time. Microsoft hasn't documented how long this period is, because it is one of those internal operating system parameters that it wants to be free to tweak as Windows evolves in order to maintain optimum performance. In any case, it is not the kind of information you need to know to run the Windows applications. In human terms, this time is very short – certainly no more than milliseconds. It is known as the thread's **time slice**. When the time slice is finished, Windows takes control back and picks another thread, which will then be allocated a time slice. These time slices are so short that we get the illusion of lots of things happening simultaneously.

Even when your application only has one thread, this process of pre-emptive multitasking is going on because there are many other processes running on the system, and each process needs to be given time slices for each of its threads. That's how, when you have lots of windows on your screen, each one representing a different process, you can still click on any of them and have it appear to respond straight away. The response isn't instantaneous – it happens the next time that the thread in the relevant process that is responsible for handling user input from that window gets a time slice. However, unless the system is very busy, the wait before that happens is so short that you don't notice it.

Manipulating Threads

Threads are manipulated using the class Thread, which can be found in the System.Threading namespace. A thread instance represents one thread – one sequence of execution. You can create another thread by simply instantiating a thread object.

Starting a Thread

To make the following code snippets more concrete, let's suppose you are writing a graphics image editor, and the user requests to change the color depth of the image. I've picked this example because for a large image this can take a while to perform. It's the sort of situation where you'd probably create a separate thread to do the processing so that you don't tie up the user interface while the color depth change is happening. You'd start by instantiating a thread object like this:

```
// entryPoint has been declared previously as a delegate
// of type ThreadStart
Thread depthChangeThread = new Thread(entryPoint);
```

Here we have given the variable the name depthChangeThread.

Additional threads that are created within an application in order to perform some task are often known as worker threads.

The above code shows that the Thread constructor requires one parameter, which is used to indicate the entry point of the thread – that is, the method at which the thread starts executing. Since we are passing in the details of a method, this is a situation that calls for the use of delegates. In fact, a delegate has already been defined in the System.Threading class. It is called ThreadStart, and its signature looks like this:

```
public delegate void ThreadStart();
```

The parameter we pass to the constructor must be a delegate of this type.

After doing this, however, the new thread isn't actually doing anything so far. It is simply sitting there waiting to be started. We start a thread by calling the Thread.Start() method.

Suppose we have a method, ChangeColorDepth(), which does this processing:

```
void ChangeColorDepth()
{
    // processing to change color depth of image
}
```

You would arrange for this processing to be performed with this code:

```
ThreadStart entryPoint = new ThreadStart(ChangeColorDepth);
Thread depthChangeThread = new Thread(entryPoint);
depthChangeThread.Name = "Depth Change Thread";
depthChangeThread.Start();
```

After this point, both threads will be running simultaneously.

In this code, we have also assigned a user-friendly name to the thread using the `Thread.Name` property. It's not necessary to do this, but it can be useful.

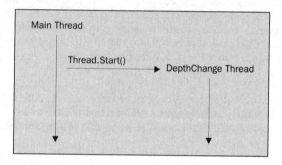

Note that because the thread entry point (`ChangeColorDepth()` in this example) cannot take any parameters, you will have to find some other means of passing in any information that the method needs. The most obvious way would be to use member fields of whatever class this method is a member. Also, the method cannot return anything. (Where would any return value be returned to? As soon as this method returns, the thread that is running it will terminate, so there is nothing around to receive any return value and we can hardly return it to the thread that invoked this thread, since that thread will presumably be busy doing something else.)

Once you have started another thread, you can also suspend, resume, or abort it. Suspending a thread means putting it to sleep – the thread will simply not run for a period, which means it will not take up any processor time. It can later be resumed, which means it will simply carry on from the point at which it was suspended. If a thread is aborted, then it will stop running for good. Windows will permanently destroy all data that it maintains relating to that thread, so the thread cannot subsequently be restarted.

Continuing the image editor example, we will assume that for some reason the user interface thread displays a dialog giving the user a chance to temporarily suspend the conversion process (it is not usual for a user to want to do this, but it is only an example; a more realistic example might be the user pausing the playing of a sound or video file). We would code the response like this in the main thread:

```
depthChangeThread.Suspend();
```

And if the user subsequently asked for the processing to resume:

```
depthChangeThread.Resume();
```

Finally, if the user (more realistically) decided that they didn't want to do the conversion after all, and chose to cancel it:

```
depthChangeThread.Abort();
```

Note that the `Suspend()` and `Abort()` methods do not necessarily work instantly. In the case of `Suspend()`, .NET may allow the thread being suspended to execute a few more instructions in order to reach a point at which .NET regards the thread as safely suspendable. This is for technical reasons to do with ensuring the correct operation of the garbage collector, and full details are in the MSDN documentation. In the case of aborting a thread, the `Abort()` method actually works by throwing a `ThreadAbortException` in the affected thread. `ThreadAbortException` is a special exception class that is never handled. The point of doing it this way is that it means that if that thread is currently executing code inside `try` blocks, any associated `finally` blocks will be executed before the thread is actually killed. This ensures that any appropriate cleaning up of resources can be done, and also gives the thread a chance to make sure that any data it was manipulating (for example, fields of a class instance that will remain around after the thread dies) is left in a valid state.

Prior to .NET, aborting a thread in this way was not recommended except in extreme cases because the affected thread simply got killed immediately, which meant that any data it was manipulating could be left in an invalid state, and any resources the thread was using would be left open. The exception mechanism used by .NET in this situation means that aborting threads is safer and so is acceptable programming practice.

Although this exception mechanism makes aborting a thread safe, it does mean that aborting a thread might actually take some time, since theoretically there is no limit on how long code in a finally block could take to execute. Due to this, after aborting a thread, you might want to wait until the thread has actually been killed before continuing any processing, if any of your subsequent processing relies on the other thread having been killed. You can wait for a thread to terminate by calling the `Join()` method:

```
depthChangeThread.Abort();
depthChangeThread.Join();
```

`Join()` also has other overloads that allow you to specify a time limit on how long you are prepared to wait. If the time limit is reached, then execution will simply continue anyway. If no time limit is specified, then the thread that is waiting will wait for as long as it needs to.

The above coded snippets will show one thread performing actions on another thread (or at least in the case of `Join()`, waiting for another thread). However, what happens if the main thread wants to perform some actions on itself? In order to do this it needs a reference to a thread object that represents its own thread. It can get such a reference using a static property, `CurrentThread`, of the `Thread` class:

```
Thread myOwnThread = Thread.CurrentThread;
```

`Thread` is actually a slightly unusual class to manipulate because there is always one thread present even before you instantiate any others – the thread that you are currently executing. This means that there are two different ways that you can manipulate the class:

❑   You can instantiate a thread object, which will then represent a running thread, and whose instance members apply to that running thread.

❑ You can call any of a number of static methods. These generally apply to the thread you are actually calling the method from.

One static method you may wish to call is `Sleep()`. This simply puts the running thread to sleep for a set period of time, after which it will continue.

The ThreadPlayaround Sample

We are going to start by illustrating how to use threads with a small example, called `ThreadPlayaround`. The aim of this example is to give us a feel for how manipulating threads works, so it is not intended to illustrate any realistic programming situations. We are simply going to kick off a couple of threads and see what happens.

The core of the `ThreadPlayaround` sample is a short method, `DisplayNumbers()`, that counts up to a large number, displaying how far it has counted up to every so often. `DisplayNumbers()` also starts by displaying the name and culture of the thread that it is being run on:

```
static void DisplayNumbers()
{
    Thread thisThread = Thread.CurrentThread;
    string name = thisThread.Name;
    Console.WriteLine("Starting thread: " + name);
    Console.WriteLine(name + ": Current Culture = " +
                    thisThread.CurrentCulture);
    for (int i=1 ; i<= 8*interval ; i++)
    {
        if (i%interval == 0)
            Console.WriteLine(name + ": count has reached " + i);
    }
}
```

How far the count runs up to depends on `interval`, which is a field whose value is typed in by the user. If the user types in `100`, then we will count up to 800, displaying the values `100`, `200`, `300`, `400`, `500`, `600`, `700`, and `800`. If the user types in `1000` then we will count up to 8000, displaying the values `1000`, `2000`, `3000`, `4000`, `5000`, `6000`, `7000`, and `8000` along the way, and so on. This might all seem like a pointless exercise, but the purpose of it is to tie up the processor for a period while allowing us to see how far the processor is progressing with its task.

What `ThreadPlayaround` does is to start a second worker thread, which will run `DisplayNumbers()`, but immediately after starting the worker thread, the main thread begins executing the same method. This means that we should see both counts happening at the same time.

The `Main()` method for `ThreadPlayaround` and its containing class looks like this:

```
class EntryPoint
{
    static int interval;

    static void Main()
    {
```

```
        Console.Write("Interval to display results at?> ");
        interval = int.Parse(Console.ReadLine());

        Thread thisThread = Thread.CurrentThread;
        thisThread.Name = "Main Thread";

        ThreadStart workerStart = new ThreadStart(StartMethod);
        Thread workerThread = new Thread(workerStart);
        workerThread.Name = "Worker";
        workerThread.Start();

        DisplayNumbers();
        Console.WriteLine("Main Thread Finished");

        Console.ReadLine();

    }
```

We have shown the start of the class declaration here so that we can see that `interval` is a static field of this class. In the `Main()` method, we first ask the user for the interval. Then, we retrieve a reference to the thread object that represents the main thread – this is done so that we can give this thread a name so that we can see what's going on in the output.

Next, we create the worker thread, set its name, and start it off, passing it a delegate that indicates that the method it must start in is a method called `workerStart`. Finally, we call the `DisplayNumbers()` method to start counting. The entry point for the worker thread is this:

```
    static void StartMethod()
    {
        DisplayNumbers();
        Console.WriteLine("Worker Thread Finished");
    }
```

Note that all these methods are static methods in the same class, `EntryPoint`. Note also that the two counts will take place entirely separately, since the variable i in the `DisplayNumbers()` method used to do the counting is a local variable. Local variables are not only scoped to the method they are defined in, but are also visible only to the thread that is executing that method. If another thread starts executing the same method, than that thread will get its own copy of the local variables. We will start by running the code, and selecting a relatively small value of 100 for the interval:

```
ThreadPlayaround
Interval to display results at?> 100
Starting thread: Main Thread
Main Thread: Current Culture = en-GB
Main Thread: count has reached 100
Main Thread: count has reached 200
Main Thread: count has reached 300
Main Thread: count has reached 400
Main Thread: count has reached 500
Main Thread: count has reached 600
```

```
Main Thread: count has reached 700
Main Thread: count has reached 800
Main Thread Finished
Starting thread: Worker
Worker: Current Culture = en-GB
Worker: count has reached 100
Worker: count has reached 200
Worker: count has reached 300
Worker: count has reached 400
Worker: count has reached 500
Worker: count has reached 600
Worker: count has reached 700
Worker: count has reached 800
Worker Thread Finished
```

As far as threads working in parallel are concerned, this doesn't immediately look like it's working too well! We see that the main thread starts, counts up to 800 and then claims to finish. The worker thread then starts and runs through separately.

The problem here is actually that starting a thread is quite a major process. After instantiating the new thread, the main thread hits this line of code:

```
workerThread.Start();
```

This call to `Thread.Start()` basically informs Windows that the new thread is to be started, then immediately returns. While we are counting up to 800, Windows is busily making the arrangements for the thread to be started. This internally means, among other things, allocating various resources for the thread, and performing various security checks. By the time the new thread is actually starting up, the main thread has finished its work!

We can solve this problem by simply choosing a larger interval, so that both threads spend longer in the `DisplayNumbers()` method. We'll try `1000000` this time:

ThreadPlayaround
```
Interval to display results at?> 1000000
Starting thread: Main Thread
Main Thread: Current Culture = en-GB
Main Thread: count has reached 1000000
Starting thread: Worker
Worker: Current Culture = en-GB
Main Thread: count has reached 2000000
Worker: count has reached 1000000
Main Thread: count has reached 3000000
Worker: count has reached 2000000
Main Thread: count has reached 4000000
Worker: count has reached 3000000
Main Thread: count has reached 5000000
Main Thread: count has reached 6000000
Worker: count has reached 4000000
Main Thread: count has reached 7000000
Worker: count has reached 5000000
```

```
Main Thread: count has reached 8000000
Main Thread Finished
Worker: count has reached 6000000
Worker: count has reached 7000000
Worker: count has reached 8000000
Worker Thread Finished
```

Now we can see the threads really working in parallel. The main thread starts and counts up to one million. At some point, while the main thread is counting the next million numbers, the worker thread starts off, and from then on, the two threads progress at the same rate until they both finish.

It is important to understand that unless you are running a multi-processor computer, using two threads in a CPU-intensive task will not have saved any time. On my single-processor machine, having both threads count up to 8 million will have taken just as long as having one thread count up to 16 million. Arguably, it will take slightly longer, since with the extra thread around, the operating system has to do a little bit more thread switching, but this difference will be negligible. The advantage of using more than one thread is two-fold. First, you gain responsiveness, in that one of the threads could be dealing with user input while the other thread does some work behind the scenes. Second, you will save time if one or more threads is doing something that doesn't involve CPU time, such as waiting for data to be retrieved from the Internet, because the other threads can carry out their processing while the inactive thread(s) are waiting.

Thread Priorities

It is possible to assign different priorities to different threads within a process. In general, a thread will not be allocated any time slices if there are any higher priority threads working. The advantage of this is that you can guarantee user responsiveness by assigning a slightly higher priority to a thread that handles receiving user input. For most of the time, such a thread will have nothing to do, and the other threads can carry on their work. However, if the user does anything, this thread will immediately take priority over other threads in your application for the short time that it spends handling the event.

High priority threads can completely block threads of lower priority, so you should be careful about changing thread priorities. The thread priorities are defined as values of the `ThreadPriority` enumeration. The possible values are `Highest`, `AboveNormal`, `Normal`, `BelowNormal`, `Lowest`.

You should note that each process has a base priority, and that these values are relative to the priority of your process. Giving a thread a higher priority may ensure that it gets priority over other threads in that process, but there may still be other processes running on the system whose threads get an even higher priority. Windows tends to give a higher priority to its own operating system threads.

We can see the effect of changing a thread priority by making the following change to the `Main()` method in the `ThreadPlayaround` sample:

```
ThreadStart workerStart = new ThreadStart(StartMethod);
Thread workerThread = new Thread(workerStart);
workerThread.Name = "Worker";
workerThread.Priority = ThreadPriority.AboveNormal;
workerThread.Start();
```

What we have done is indicate that the worker thread should have a slightly higher priority than the main thread. The result is dramatic:

```
ThreadPlayaroundWithPriorities
Interval to display results at?> 1000000
Starting thread: Main Thread
Main Thread: Current Culture = en-GB
Starting thread: Worker
Worker: Current Culture = en-GB
Main Thread: count has reached 1000000
Worker: count has reached 1000000
Worker: count has reached 2000000
Worker: count has reached 3000000
Worker: count has reached 4000000
Worker: count has reached 5000000
Worker: count has reached 6000000
Worker: count has reached 7000000
Worker: count has reached 8000000
Worker Thread Finished
Main Thread: count has reached 2000000
Main Thread: count has reached 3000000
Main Thread: count has reached 4000000
Main Thread: count has reached 5000000
Main Thread: count has reached 6000000
Main Thread: count has reached 7000000
Main Thread: count has reached 8000000
Main Thread Finished
```

This shows that when the worker thread has an AboveNormal priority, the main thread scarcely gets a look-in once the worker thread has started.

Synchronization

One crucial aspect of working with threads is the **synchronization** of access to any variables which more than one thread has access to. What we mean by synchronization is that only one thread should be able to access the variable at any one time. If we do not ensure that access to variables is synchronized, then subtle bugs can result. In this section, we will briefly review some of the main issues involved.

What is Synchronization?

The issue of synchronization arises because what looks like a single statement in your C# sourcecode in most cases will translate into many statements in the final compiled assembly language machine code. Take for example the statement:

```
message += ", there";   // message is a string that contains "Hello"
```

This statement looks syntactically in C# like one statement, but it actually involves a large number of operations when the code is being executed. Memory will need to be allocated to store the new longer string, the variable message will need to be set to refer to the new memory, the actual text will need to be copied, and so on.

Obviously, we've exaggerated the case here by picking a string – one of the more complex data types – as our example, but even when performing arithmetic operations on primitive numeric types, there is quite often more going on behind the scenes than you would imagine from looking at the C# code. In particular, many operations cannot be carried out directly on variables stored in memory locations, and their values have to be separately copied into special locations in the processor known as **registers**.

In any situation where a single C# statement translates into more than one native machine code command, it is quite possible that the thread's time slice might end in the middle of executing that 'statement' process. If this happens, then another thread in the same process may be given a time slice, and, if access to variables involved with that statement (message in the above example) is not synchronized, this other thread may attempt to read or write to the same variables. With our example, was the other thread intended to see the new value of message or the old value?

The problems can get worse than this, too. The statement we used in our example was relatively simple, but in a more complicated statement, some variable might have an undefined value for a brief period, while the statement is being executed. If another thread attempts to read that value in that instant, then it may simply read garbage. More seriously, if two threads simultaneously try to write data to the same variable, then it is almost certain that that variable will contain an incorrect value afterwards.

Synchronization was not an issue that affects the ThreadPlayAround sample, because both threads used mostly local variables. The only variable that both threads had access to was the Interval field, but this field was initialized by the main thread before any other thread started, and subsequently only ever read from either thread, so there was still not a problem. Synchronization issues only arise if at least one thread may be writing to a variable while other threads may be either reading or writing to it.

Fortunately, C# provides an extremely easy way of synchronizing access to variables, and unusually for this chapter, there's a C# language keyword that does it – lock. You use lock like this:

```
lock (x)
{
    DoSomething();
}
```

What the lock statement does is wrap an object known as a **mutual exclusion lock**, or **mutex**, around the variable in the round brackets. The mutex will remain in place while the compound statement attached to the lock keyword is executed. While the mutex is wrapped around a variable, no other thread is permitted access to that variable. We can see this with the above code; the compound statement will execute, and eventually this thread will lose its time slice. If the next thread to gain the time slice attempts to access the variable x, access to the variable will be denied. Instead, Windows will simply put the thread to sleep until the mutex has been released.

The mutex is the simplest of a number of mechanisms that can be used to control access to variables. We don't have the space to go into the others here, but we will mention that they are all controlled through the .NET bass class System.Threading.Monitor. In fact, the C# lock statement is simply a C# syntax wrapper around a couple of method calls to this class.

In general, you should synchronize variables wherever there is a risk that any thread might try writing to a variable at the same time as other threads are trying to read from or write to the same variable. We don't have space here to cover the details of thread synchronization, but we will point out that it is a fairly big topic in its own right. Here, we will simply confine ourselves to pointing out a couple of the potential pitfalls.

Synchronization Issues

Synchronizing threads is vitally important in multi-threaded applications. However, it's an area in which it is important to work carefully because a number of subtle and hard-to-detect bugs can easily arise, in particular **deadlocks** and **race conditions**.

Don't Overuse Synchronization

While thread synchronization is important, it is important to use it only where it is necessary, because it can hurt performance. This is for two reasons. First, there is some overhead associated with actually putting a lock on an object and taking it off, though this is admittedly minimal. Second, and more importantly, the more thread synchronization you have, the more threads can get held up waiting for objects to be released. Remember that if one thread holds a lock on any object, any other thread that needs to access that object will simply halt execution until the lock is released. It is important, therefore, that you place as little code inside `lock` blocks as you can without causing thread synchronization bugs. In one sense, you can think of `lock` statements as temporarily disabling the multi-threading ability of an application, and therefore temporarily removing all the benefits of multi-threading.

On the other hand, it has to be said that the dangers of using synchronization too much (performance and responsiveness go down) are not as great as the dangers associated with not using synchronization when you need it (subtle run-time bugs that are very hard to track down).

Deadlocks

A **deadlock** (or a deadly embrace) is a bug that can occur when two threads both need to access resources that are locked by each other. Suppose one thread is running the following code, where a and b are two object references that both threads have access to:

```
lock (a)
{

    // do something

    lock (b)
    {

        // do something

    }
}
```

At the same time another thread is running this code:

```
lock (b)
{

    // do something

    lock (a)
    {

        // do something

    }
}
```

Depending on the times that the threads hit the various statements, the following scenario is quite possible: the first thread acquires a lock on a, while at about the same time the second thread acquires a lock on b. A short time later, thread A hits the lock(b) statement, and immediately goes to sleep, waiting for the lock on b to be released. Soon afterwards, the second thread hits its lock(a) statement and also puts itself to sleep, ready for Windows to wake it up the instant the lock on a gets released. Unfortunately, the lock on a is never going to be released because the first thread, which owns this lock, is sleeping and won't wake up until the lock on b gets released, which won't happen until the second thread wakes up. The result is deadlock. Both threads just permanently sit there doing nothing, each waiting for the other thread to release its lock. This kind of problem can cause an entire application to just hang, so that you can't do anything with it apart from use the Task Manager to just terminate the entire process.

> *In this situation, it is not possible for another thread to release the locks; a mutual exclusion lock can only be released by the thread that claimed the lock in the first place.*

Deadlocks can usually be avoided by having both threads claim locks on objects in the same order. In the above example, if the second thread claimed the locks in the same order as the first thread, a first, then b, then whichever thread got the lock on a first would completely finish its task, then the other thread would start. This way, no deadlock can occur.

You might think that it is easy to avoid coding up deadlocks – after all, in the code shown above, it looks fairly obvious that a deadlock could occur so you probably wouldn't write that code in the first place, but remember that different locks can occur in different method calls. With this example, the first thread might actually be executing this code:

```
lock (a)
{

    // do bits of processing

    CallSomeMethod()
}
```

Here, CallSomeMethod() might call other methods, and so on, and buried in there somewhere is a lock(b) statement. In this situation, it might not be nearly so obvious when you write your code that you are allowing a possible deadlock.

Race Conditions

A **race condition** is somewhat subtler than a deadlock. It rarely halts execution of a process, but it can lead to data corruption. It is hard to give a precise definition of a race, but it generally occurs when several threads attempt to access the same data, and do not adequately take account of what the other threads are doing. Race conditions are best understood using an example.

Suppose we have an array of objects, where each element in the array needs to be processed somehow, and we have a number of threads that are between them doing this processing. We might have an object, let's call it ArrayController, which contains the array of objects as well as an int that indicates how many of them have been processed, and therefore, which one should be processed next. ArrayController might implement this method:

```
int GetObject(int index)
{

    // returns the object at the given index.

}
```

and this read/write property:

```
int ObjectsProcessed
{

    // indicates how many of the objects have been processed.

}
```

Now, each thread that is helping to process the objects might execute some code that looks like this:

```
lock(ArrayController)
{
    int nextIndex = ArrayController.ObjectsProcessed;
    Console.WriteLine("object to be processed next is " + nextIndex);
    ++ArrayController.ObjectsProcessed;
    object next = ArrayController.GetObject();
}
ProcessObject(next);
```

This by itself should work, but suppose that in an attempt to avoid tying up resources for longer than necessary, we decided not to hold the lock on `ArrayController` while we're displaying the user message. Therefore, we rewrite the above code like this:

```
lock(ArrayController)
{
    int nextIndex = ArrayController.ObjectsProcessed;
}
Console.WriteLine("object to be processed next is " + nextIndex);
lock(ArrayController)
{
    ++ArrayController.ObjectsProcessed;
    object next = ArrayController.GetObject();
}
ProcessObject(next);
```

Here, we have a possible problem. What could happen is that one thread gets an object (say the 11th object in the array), and goes to display the message saying that it is about to process this object. Meanwhile, a second thread also starts executing the same code, calls `ObjectsProcessed`, and determines that the next object to be processed is the 11th object, because the first thread hasn't yet updated `ArrayController.ObjectsProcessed`. While the second thread is happily writing to the console that it will now process the 11th object, the first thread acquires another lock on the `ArrayController` and inside this lock increments `ObjectsProcessed`. Unfortunately, it is too late. Both threads are now committed to processing the same object, and that's the kind of situation that we refer to as a race condition.

For both deadlocks and race conditions, it is not often obvious when the condition can occur, and when it does, it is hard to identify the bug. In general, this is an area where you largely learn from experience. It is, however, important to consider very carefully all the parts of the code where you need synchronization when you are writing multithreaded applications to check whether there is any possibility of deadlocks or a race conditions arising, bearing in mind that it is not possible to predict the exact times that different threads will hit different instructions.

Summary

In this chapter, we have examined some of the facilities provided by the .NET base classes. We have seen how to efficiently construct and process strings using the `StringBuilder` class, and also how to use the regular expressions engine to perform very sophisticated searches against strings. We then moved on and looked at the different collection objects available. The `System.Collections` and `System.Collections.Specialized` namespaces contain a huge number of classes that allow you to store different types of collections of objects. In particular, the `Hashtable` class enables code to store data in the dictionary with very efficient lookup based on any data type.

Custom attributes, used in conjunction with reflection, provide the very powerful ability for code to examine other code, or even to examine itself. This means that execution can depend on which user - defined attributes have been applied to objects in your code. We saw one example of this with the `WhatsNewAttributes` code sample, which was able to provide automatic reports on the new features that had been added to software. Finally, we examined some of the issues involved when we code up an application that uses multiple threads.

6

Programming in the .NET Environment

At this point we've familiarized ourselves with the C# language itself, and are almost ready to the move on to the applied sections of the book, in which we will look at how to use C# to program applications covering a variety of areas. Before we do that, however, we need to examine how we can use the tools and features provided by the .NET environment to get the best from our programs.

In this chapter we will look at what programming in the .NET environment means in practice, covering some of the tools that are available to help you write and debug programs as well as the guidelines for writing good applications. In particular we will examine:

❑   Visual Studio .NET – the main developer environment in which you will usually write, compile, debug, and optimize your C# programs

❑   WinCV – a useful utility that allows you to examine the base classes.

❑   Usage guidelines and naming conventions – the guidelines that you should adhere to when writing C# code, so that your code follows normal .NET practice, and can be easily understood by others.

❑ This will be followed in the next two chapters by a look at Windows Forms and how to write user interface code in Chapter 7, and in Chapter 8, we'll look at assemblies and resource files.

Visual Studio .NET

Visual Studio .NET is a fully integrated development environment. It is designed to make the process of writing your code, debugging it, and compiling it to an assembly to be shipped, as easy as possible. What this means in practice is that Visual Studio .NET gives you a very sophisticated multiple-document-interface application in which you can do just about everything related to developing your code. It offers:

❑ A **text editor** in which you can write your C# code (as well as VB.NET and C++ code). This text editor is quite sophisticated, and it is also aware of the syntax of C#. This means that as you type, it can automatically lay out your code, for example by indenting lines, matching start and end brackets of code blocks, and color coding keywords. It will also perform some syntax checks as you type, and will underline code that will cause compilation errors. Also, it features IntelliSense, which automatically displays the names of classes, fields or methods as you begin to type them. As you start typing parameters to methods, it will also show you the parameter lists for the available overloads. The screenshot below shows this feature at work with one of the .NET base classes, `ListBox`.

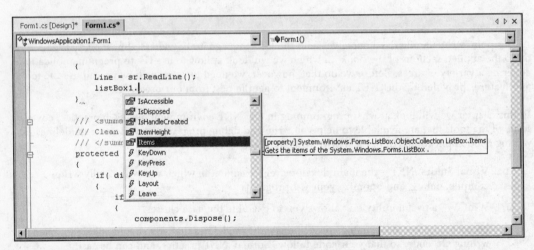

A useful shortcut to remember is that by pressing *CTRL+SPACE*, you can bring back the IntelliSense list box if you need it and for any reason it's not visible.

❑ A **design view editor** of your code, that allows you to visually place user-interface and data-access controls in your project. When you do this, Visual Studio .NET will automatically add the necessary C# code to your source files to instantiate these controls in your project. (This is possible as, under .NET, all the controls are actually just instances of particular base classes.)

❑ **Supporting windows** that allow you to view and modify aspects of your project. For example, there are windows available that show you the classes in your sourcecode as well as the available properties (and their startup values) for Windows Forms and Web Forms classes. You can also use these windows to specify compilation options, such as which assemblies your code needs to reference.

❑ **Compilation from within the environment**. Instead of having to run the C# compiler from the command line, you can simply select a menu option to compile the project and Visual Studio .NET will call the compiler for you. It will pass all the relevant command-line parameters to the compiler detailing such things as which assemblies to reference and what type of assembly you want to be emitted (executable or library .dll, for example). If you so wish, it will even run the compiled executable for you straight away so you can see whether it runs satisfactorily, and you can choose between different build configurations – for example, a release or debug build.

❑ An **integrated debugger**. It's in the nature of programming that you can virtually guarantee that your code won't run correctly the first time you try it. Or the second time. Or the third, etc. Visual Studio .NET will seamlessly link up to a debugger for you, allowing you to set breakpoints and watches on variables all from within the environment.

❑ **Integrated MSDN help**. Visual Studio .NET can call up the MSDN documentation for you. For example, this means that in the text editor if you're not sure of the meaning of a keyword, you can select it, hit the *F1* key, and Visual Studio .NET will then bring up MSDN to show you related topics. Similarly, if you're not sure what a certain compilation error means, you can bring up the documentation for that error by selecting the error message and hitting *F1*.

❑ **Access to other programs**. And if all that wasn't enough, Visual Studio .NET is also able to call on a number of other utilities that allow you to examine and modify aspects of your computer or network, without you having to leave the developer environment. Among the tools available, you can check running services, and database connections, and there's even an Internet Explorer window that lets you browse the Web.

Of course, assuming you are experienced in C++ or VB, you will already be familiar with the relevant Visual Studio 6 version of the developer environment for your particular language – so you will know that many of the features listed above are not new – you're probably already used to doing much the same things in Visual Studio 6. However, what's new in Visual Studio .NET is that it combines all the features that were previously available across all VS 6 developer environments. This means that, whatever language you used in VS 6, you'll find some new features in Visual Studio .NET. For example, in Visual Basic, you could not compile separate debug and release builds. On the other hand, if you are coming to C# from a background of C++, much of the support for data access and the ability to drop controls into your application with a click of the mouse, which has long been part of the Visual Basic developers experience, will be new to you. The C++ developer environment did include some support for this, but it was very limited, and was restricted to the most common user-interface controls.

We should point out to people coming from a C++ background that you will find two things from VS 6 missing in VS .NET: edit-and-continue debugging, and an integrated profiler. Microsoft was apparently unable to get edit-and-continue debugging for .NET working in time and has hinted that that facility will appear with a future service pack. MS is also not shipping any full profiler application with .NET. Instead, there are a number of .NET classes to assist with profiling in the System.Diagnostics *namespace. The* perfmon *profiling tool is available from the command line (just type* perfmon*) and has a number of new .NET-related performance monitors. At the time of writing, Microsoft is also working with a number of partner companies who are developing performance profilers.*

Whatever your background, you will find the overall look of the developer environment has changed to accommodate the new features, the single cross-language IDE, and the integration with .NET. There are new menu options and toolbar options, and many of the existing ones from VS 6 have been renamed. So you'll need to spend some time familiarizing yourself with the layout and commands available in Visual Studio .NET.

Since this is a professional-level book, we are not going to look in detail at every feature or menu option in Visual Studio .NET. We are assuming that you are a sufficiently competent programmer that you are capable of exploring the environment and seeing what's available for yourself. The real aim of our Visual Studio .NET coverage is to ensure that you are sufficiently familiar with all the concepts involved with building and debugging a C# application to be able to get the best out of Visual Studio .NET – and in particular to make sure that you are able to use particular features that might not have been available in the developer environment for whatever language you previously used.

To give you an idea of some of the features, the following screenshot shows what Visual Studio .NET might typically look like when you are coding (note that since the appearance of Visual Studio .NET is highly customizable, the windows might not be in the same locations or different windows might be visible when you launch the environment).

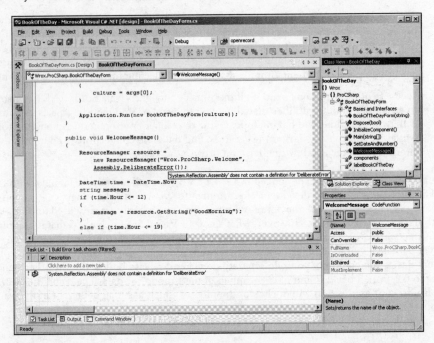

The way this part of the chapter is organized is that we are going to go through the process of creating, coding, and debugging a project, seeing what Visual Studio .NET can do to help you at each stage.

Creating a Project

Once you have installed Visual Studio .NET, you will want to start your first project. With Visual Studio .NET, you rarely start with a blank file that you type C# code into from scratch, in the way that we've been doing in the previous chapters in this book. Instead, the idea is that you tell Visual Studio .NET roughly what type of project you are going to create, and then Visual Studio .NET starts you off by automatically generating the C# code that gives you an outline framework for that type of project. You then work by adding your code to this outline. For example, if you are writing a Windows GUI-interface based application (or with .NET terminology, a Windows Form), Visual Studio .NET will start you off with a file containing C# sourcecode that creates a basic form. This form is capable of talking to Windows, and receiving events. It can let itself get maximized or minimized or resized – but it doesn't have any controls on it or any other functionality – that will be for you to add. If your application is intended to be a command-line utility (a console application) then Visual Studio .NET will give you a basic namespace, class, and `Main()` method to start you off. Of course, the option is there to ask for an empty application if you really do want to start writing your code from scratch.

However, Visual Studio .NET doesn't stop here in giving you your start-up project. Recall that we said earlier that Visual Studio .NET would call up the compiler for you when you need to compile your code? Well, when you create your project, it also sets up the compilation options that you are likely to need to supply to the C# compiler – whether or not it is to compile to a command-line application, a library, or a Windows application. It will also tell the compiler which base class libraries you will need to reference (a Windows GUI application will need to reference many of the `Windows.Forms`-related libraries; a console application probably won't). You can of course modify all these settings as you are editing, if you need to.

The first time you start Visual Studio .NET, you will be presented with what is known as the Start Page. The Start Page is an HTML page that contains various links to take you to useful web sites, let you set the appearance and configuration of Visual Studio .NET (the **My Profile** link), open existing projects, or start a new project.

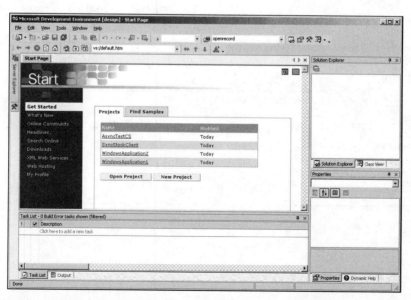

This screenshot shows the situation after I've used Visual Studio .NET a couple of times, and so features a list of the most recently edited projects. You can just click on one of these projects to open it again. Obviously the first time you start up Visual Studio, this list will be empty.

Under the My Profile option, you can even change the appearance of Visual Studio .NET to match what you will have been used to in the previous developer environment for whatever your preferred language was. For example you can set up Visual Studio .NET so its user interface looks a bit like the old VB or C++ IDEs. Note, however, that this option only really changes where the various windows are positioned on the screen. You'll still find that most of the menu and toolbar options, as well as the detailed features of each window, are new.

Selecting a Project Type

You can create a new project either by clicking on the appropriate link on the start page or by clicking on the File menu then choosing New, then Project. Either way, you will get presented with the New Project dialog that gives you the first inkling of the variety of different projects you can create.

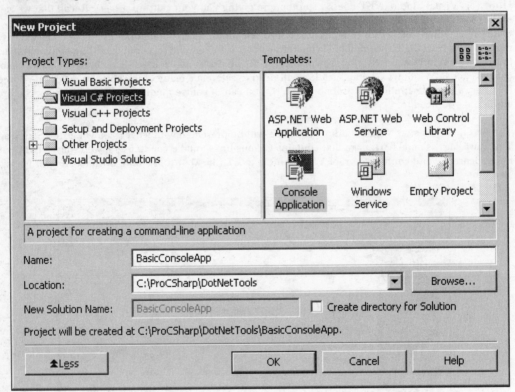

Effectively, what this dialog box is asking you is what kind of initial framework code you want Visual Studio .NET to generate for you, and what compilation options you want. And – for that matter – what compiler you want to compile your code with – the C#, VB.NET, or C++ compiler. We can immediately see the language integration that Microsoft has promised for .NET at work here! For this particular example, we've opted for a C# console application, the same type that we've been using up until now in the book.

We don't have space to cover all the various options for different types of project here. On the C++ side, all the old C++ project types are there – MFC application, ATL project, etc. On the VB.NET side, the options have changed somewhat – for example, you can create a VB.NET command-line application (Console Application), something that was impossible in VB 6. You can also create a .NET component (Class Library) or .NET control (Windows Control Library), but you can't create an old-style COM-based control (the .NET control is intended to replace such ActiveX controls).

However, since this is a C# book, we will list all the options that are available to you under Visual C# Projects. You should note that there are some other more specialized C# template projects available under the Other Projects option.

If You Choose...	You get the C# code and compilation options to generate...	Chapter
Windows Application	A basic empty form that responds to events.	7
Class Library	A .NET class that can be called up by other code.	8
Windows Control Library	A .NET class that can be called up by other code and which has a user interface. (Like an old-style ActiveX control.)	7
ASP.NET Web Application	An ASP.NET-based web site: ASP.NET pages and C# classes that generate the HTML response sent to browsers from those pages.	14
ASP.NET Web Service	A C# class that acts as a fully operational Web Service.	15
Web Control Library	A control that can be called up by ASP.NET pages, to generate the HTML code that gives the appearance of a control when displayed on a browser.	16
Console Application	An application that runs at the command-line prompt, or in a console window.	6
Windows Service	A service that runs in the background on Windows NT and Windows 2000.	22
Empty Project	Nothing. You have to write all your code from scratch – but you still get the benefit of all the Visual Studio .NET facilities when you are writing.	

Table continued on following page

If You Choose…	You get the C# code and compilation options to generate…	Chapter
Empty Web Project	As for Empty Project, but the compilation settings are set to instruct the compiler to generate code for ASP.NET pages.	
New Project In Existing Folder	New project files for an empty project. Use this option if you have some straight C# sourcecode (for example typed in a text editor) and want to turn it into a Visual Studio .NET project.	

The final column of this table gives the number of the chapter(s) in this book in which we cover that type of application (there are some types of project without chapter numbers. These project types aren't really complex enough to warrant their own chapters.)

The Newly Created Console Project

Let's see what happens when we OK the above dialog to generate a C# console application. Visual Studio .NET gives us a number of files, including a sourcecode file, Class1.cs, which contains the initial framework code. We'll discuss the case for a console application here, but the same principles hold for all the other types of project.

This screenshot shows exactly what code Visual Studio .NET has written for us.

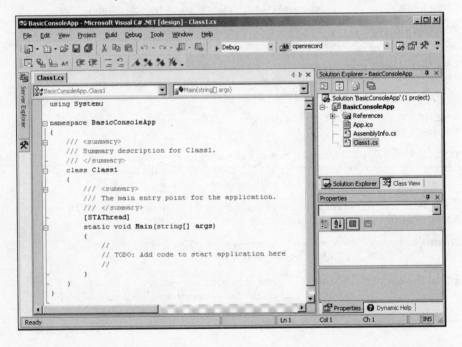

As you can see, we have here a C# program that doesn't yet actually do anything, but which contains the basic items required in any C# executable program: a namespace and a class that contains the `Main()` method, which is the program's entry point. (Strictly speaking, the namespace isn't necessary, but it would be very bad programming practice not to declare one.) This code is all ready to compile and run, which you can do immediately by hitting the *F5* key, or equivalently, by selecting the **Debug** menu and choosing **Start**. However, before we do that we'll just add one line of code – to make our application actually do something!

```
static void Main(string[] args)
{
    //
    // TODO: Add code to start application here
    //
    Console.WriteLine("Hello from all the editors at Wrox Press");
}
```

If you compile and run the project, you'll find a console window appears and disappears almost straight away, only just about giving you time to see the message. The reason this happens is that Visual Studio .NET, remembering the settings you specified when you created the project, arranged for it to be compiled as a console application and then immediately run. Windows then realized that it needed to run a console application but didn't have a console window to run it from. So Windows helpfully created a console window and ran the program. As soon as the program exited, Windows saw that it didn't need the console window any more and promptly destroyed it. That's all very logical but doesn't help you very much if you actually want to look at the output from your project!

A good way to avoid this problem is to insert the following line just before the `Main()` method returns in your code.

```
static void Main(string[] args)
{
    //
    // TODO: Add code to start application here
    //
    Console.WriteLine("Hello from all the editors at Wrox Press");
    Console.ReadLine();
}
```

That way, your code will run, display its output, and then it will hit the `Console.ReadLine()` statement, at which point it will wait for you to hit the *Return* key before the program exits. This means that the console window will hang around until you hit *Return*.

Note that all this is only a problem for console applications that you test-run from Visual Studio .NET – if you are writing a Windows application then the window displayed by the application will automatically stay on the screen until you explicitly exit it. Similarly, if you run a console application from the command-line prompt, as we've been doing up until now, you won't have any problems about the window disappearing.

Other Files Created

The `Class1.cs` sourcecode file isn't the only file that Visual Studio .NET has created for you. If you have a look in the folder in which you asked Visual Studio .NET to create your project, you will see not just the C# file, but a complete directory structure that looks like this:

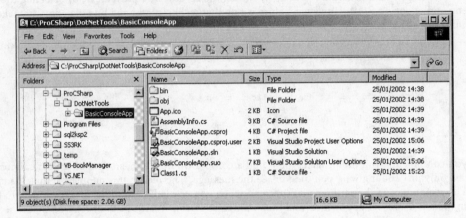

The two folders, `bin` and `obj`, are there for compiled and intermediate files. Subfolders of `obj` hold various temporary or intermediate files that may be generated, while subfolders of `bin` will hold the compiled assemblies.

> *This is something that may be unfamiliar to legacy VB developers. When running old VB 6 and earlier versions, you would traditionally simply write the code then run it. In VB, as with all languages, the code would need to be compiled into something containing executable instructions before being shipped – but VB tended to hide the process when debugging. In C#, it's more explicit: to run the code, you have to compile (or build) it first, which means an assembly must be created somewhere.*

The remaining files in the project's main folder, `BasicConsoleApp`, are there for Visual Studio .NET's benefit. They contain information about the project – what files are in it etc., so that Visual Studio .NET knows how to have the project compiled, and also how to read it in the next time you open the project.

Solutions and Projects

One important distinction we need to understand is that between a project and a solution.

❑ A **project** is a set of all the sourcecode files and resources that will compile into a single assembly (or in some cases, a single module). For example, a project might be a class library, or a windows GUI application.

❑ A **solution** is the set of all the projects that make up a particular software package (application).

To see the difference, we need to recall that when you ship an application it will probably consist of more than one assembly. For example, there might be a user interface; there may be certain custom controls and other components that ship as libraries of the parts of the application. There may even be a different user interface for administrators. Each of these parts of the application might be contained in a separate assembly, and hence, they are regarded by Visual Studio .NET as a separate project. However, it is quite likely that you will be coding these projects in parallel and in conjunction with each other. Thus it is quite useful to be able to edit them all as one single unit in Visual Studio .NET. Visual Studio .NET allows this by regarding all the projects as forming one solution, and treats the solution as the unit that it reads in and allows you to work on.

Up until now we have been loosely talking about creating a console project. In fact, in the example we are working on, Visual Studio .NET has actually created a solution for us – this particular solution contains just one project. We can see the situation in a window in Visual Studio .NET known as the **Solution Explorer**, which contains a tree structure that defines your solution.

This screenshot shows that the project contains our source file, `Class1.cs`, as well as another C# source file, `AssemblyInfo.cs`, which contains information describing the assembly and to specify versioning information. (We'll examine this file in Chapter 8). The Solution Explorer also indicates the assemblies that our project references, according to namespace.

If you haven't changed any of the default settings in Visual Studio .NET you will probably find the Solution Explorer in the top right corner of your screen. If you can't see it, just go to the **View** menu and click on **Solution Explorer**.

The solution is described by a file with the extension `.sln` – so in the case of our example it's `BasicConsoleApp.sln`. The project is described by various other files in the project's main folder. If you attempt to edit these files using Notepad, you'll find that they are mostly plain text files – and, in accordance with the principle that .NET and .NET tools rely on open standards wherever possible, they are mostly in XML format.

> *C++ developers will recognize that a Visual Studio .NET solution corresponds to an old Visual C++ project workspace (stored in a `.dsw` file) and a Visual Studio .NET project corresponds to an old C++ project (`.dsp` file). On the other hand, VB developers will recognize that a solution corresponds to an old Visual Basic project group (`.vbg` file) and the .NET project to an old Visual Basic project (`.vbp` file). Visual Studio .NET differs from the old VB IDE in that it always creates a solution for you automatically. In Visual Studio 6, Visual Basic developers would get a project initially, and a project group only if they explicitly asked the IDE for one.*

Adding Another Project to the Solution

As we work through this chapter we will want to demonstrate how Visual Studio .NET works with Windows applications as well as console ones. So at this point we are going to kill two birds with one stone, and simultaneously get ourselves a windows project while at the same time showing how to get a solution that contains more than one project. We are going to create a windows project called BasicForm, but instead of creating it as a new solution we will ask Visual Studio .NET to add it to our current solution, BasicConsoleApp.

> *This means we'll end up with a solution containing a Windows application and a console application. That's not a very common scenario – you're more likely to have one application and a number of libraries – but it allows us to demonstrate more code! You might, however, create a solution like our one if for example you are writing a utility that you want to be able to run either as a Windows application or as a command-line utility.*

There are a couple of ways of creating the new project. One way is to right-click on the name of the solution in the **Solution Explorer**. This will bring up a context menu in which one of the options is to add items to the solution. The other way is simply to go to the **File** menu and click on the **New | Project** option as we did before. Either way will bring up the **New Project** dialog box that we saw earlier, but this time, if we go through the file menu, we will notice it has two radio buttons near the bottom of the dialog which allow us to specify whether we want to create a new solution for this project or add it to the existing solution.

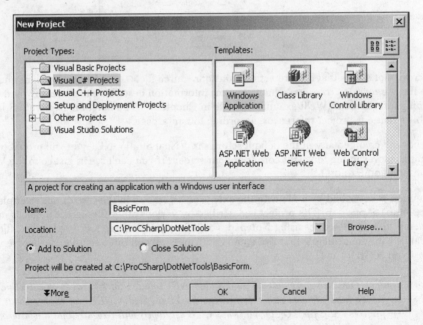

If we do this and specify **Add to Solution**, we will get a new project so that the BasicConsoleApp solution now contains a console application and a windows application.

In accordance with the language-independence of Visual Studio .NET, the new project doesn't have to be a C# project. It's perfectly acceptable to put a C# project, a VB.NET project and a C++ project in the same solution. But we'll stick with C# here since this is a C# book!

Of course, this means that BasicConsoleApp isn't really an appropriate name for the solution any more! We can change this by right-clicking on the name of the solution and choosing **Rename** from the context menu. If we rename the solution **DemoSolution**, the **Solution Explorer** window will now look like this.

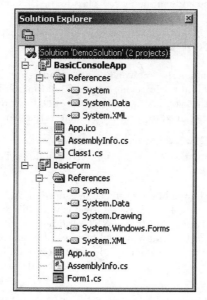

We can see from this that Visual Studio .NET has automatically made the windows project reference some of the extra base classes that are important for Windows Forms functionality.

You'll notice if you look in Windows Explorer that the name of the solution file has changed to `DemoSolution.sln`. In general, if you want to rename any files, the **Solution Explorer** window is the best place to do so, because Visual Studio .NET will then automatically be able to update any references to that file in the other project files. If you just rename files using Windows Explorer, you'll probably find you break the solution because Visual Studio .NET won't be able to locate all the files it needs to read in. You will then have to manually edit the project and solution files to update the file references.

Setting the Startup Project

One thing you'll need to bear in mind if you have multiple projects in a solution is that only one of them can be run at a time! When you compile the solution, all the projects in it will be compiled. However, you have to specify which one is the one you want Visual Studio .NET to start running when you press *F5* or select **Start**. If you have one executable and several libraries that it calls, then this will clearly be the executable. In our case, where we have two independent executables in the project, we'd simply have to debug each in turn.

You can tell Visual Studio .NET which project to run by right-clicking on that project in the Solution Explorer window and selecting Set as Startup Project from the context menu. You can tell which is the current startup project because it is the one that appears in bold in the Solution Explorer window – in the above screenshot it's BasicConsoleApp.

Windows Application Code

A Windows application contains a lot more code right from the off than a console application when VS .NET first creates it, because creating a window is an intrinsically more complex process. We're not going to discuss the code for a Windows application in detail here – that's the subject of the next chapter, but take a look at the code in the Form1 class in the BasicForm project to see for yourself how much is autogenerated.

Reading in Visual Studio 6 Projects

If you are coding in C#, then clearly you won't need to read in any old Visual Studio 6 projects, since C# doesn't exist in Visual Studio 6. However, language interoperability is a key part of the .NET framework, so it is possible that you may want your C# code to work alongside code written in VB or in C++. In that situation you may need to edit projects that were created with Visual Studio 6.

In fact, Visual Studio .NET is quite happy to read in Visual Studio 6 projects and workspaces, although as it does so it will upgrade them to Visual Studio .NET solutions. The situation is different for C++, VB, and J++ projects.

❑　In Visual C++, no change to the sourcecode is needed. All your old Visual C++ code will still work fine with the new C++ compiler. Obviously it will not be managed code, but it will still compile to code that runs outside the .NET runtime – if you want your code to integrate with the .NET Framework then you will need to edit it. If you get Visual Studio .NET to read in an old Visual C++ project, it will simply add a new solution file and updated project files. It will leave the old .dsw and .dsp files unchanged so that the project can still be edited by Visual Studio 6, if necessary.

❑　For Visual Basic we have more of a problem, since Visual Basic has been replaced by VB.NET. As we remarked in Chapter 1, although VB.NET has been designed very much around VB, and shares much of the same syntax, it is in many ways a new language. In Visual Basic, the sourcecode largely consisted of the event handlers for the controls. The code that actually instantiated the main window and many of the controls on it was not part of Visual Basic, but was instead hidden behind the scenes as part of the configuration of your project. By contrast, VB.NET works in the same way as C#, by putting the entire program out in the open as sourcecode, so all the code that displays the main window and all the controls on it needs to be in the source file. Also, like C#, VB.NET requires everything to be object-oriented and part of a class, whereas VB didn't even recognize the concept of classes in the .NET sense. If you try to read a Visual Basic project with Visual Studio .NET, it will have to upgrade the entire sourcecode to Visual Basic .NET before it can handle it – and this involves making a lot of changes to the VB code. Visual Studio .NET can, to a large extent, make these changes automatically and will then create a new VB.NET solution for you. You will find that the sourcecode it gives you looks very different from the corresponding VB code that it was converted from, and you will still need to carefully check through the generated code to make sure the project still works correctly. You may even find areas of code where Visual Studio .NET has left comments to the effect that it can't figure out exactly what you wanted the code to do, and you may have to edit the code manually.

❑ As far as Microsoft is concerned, J++ is now an obsolete language and is not directly supported in .NET. However, in order that existing J++ code can continue to operate, separate tools are available to allow J++ code to work with .NET. These include a developer environment known as Visual J# .NET, and a utility that can convert legacy J++ code to C# code – similar to the VB 6 to VB.NET upgrade facility. These tools are grouped under the name JUMP (Java User Migration Path), and at the time of writing are not bundled with .NET or VS .NET, but instead are available separately. Details are available at http://msdn.microsoft.com/visualj/jump/default.asp.

Exploring and Coding a Project

In this section we will look at the features that Visual Studio .NET gives us to help as we add code to our project.

The Folding Editor

One really exciting innovation with Visual Studio .NET is its use of a folding editor as its default code editor. Have a look at this screenshot:

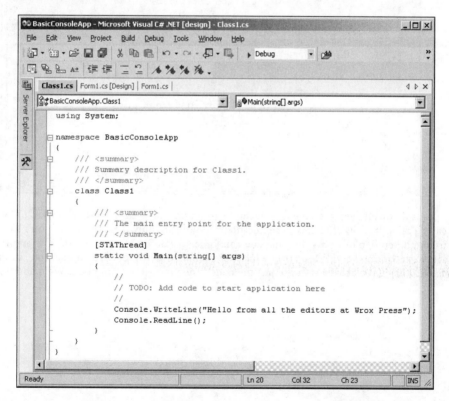

This shows the code for the console application that we generated earlier. Notice those little minus signs down the left-hand side of the window. These mark the points where the editor thinks a new block of code (or documentation comment) starts. You can click on these icons to close up the view of the corresponding block of code just as you would close a node in a tree control.

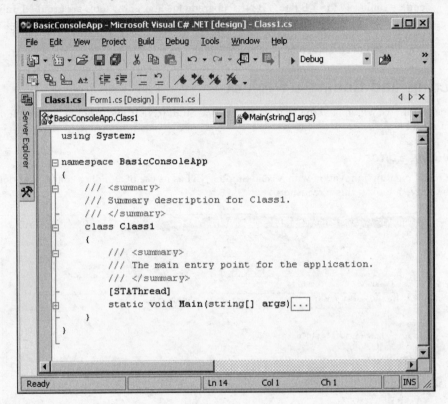

This means that while you are editing you can focus on just the areas of code you want to look at, and you can close up the bits of code you're not interested in. Not only that, but if you don't like the way the editor has chosen to block off your code you can indicate a different way with the C# preprocessor directives, #region and #endregion, which we examined in Chapter 4. For example, suppose we decide we'd like to be able to collapse just the code inside the Main() method. We'd add this code:

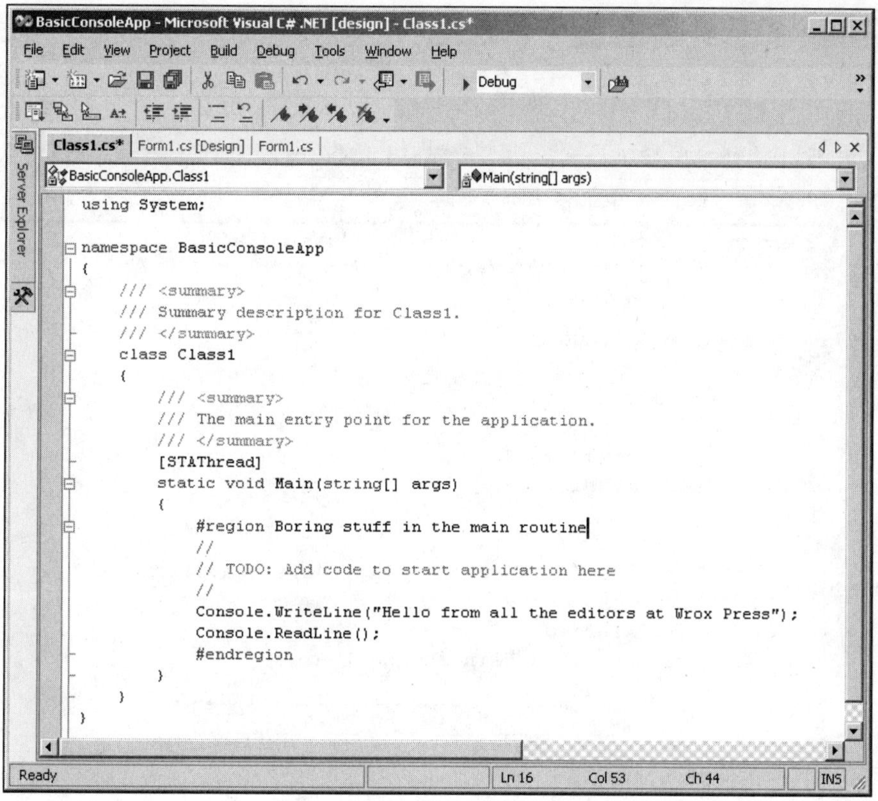

The code editor will automatically detect the #region block and place a new minus sign by the #region directive as shown above, allowing you to close the region. Enclosing this code in a region means that we can get the editor to close up the block of code, marking the area with the comment we specified in the #region directive. The compiler, however, will ignore the directives and compile the Main() method as normal.

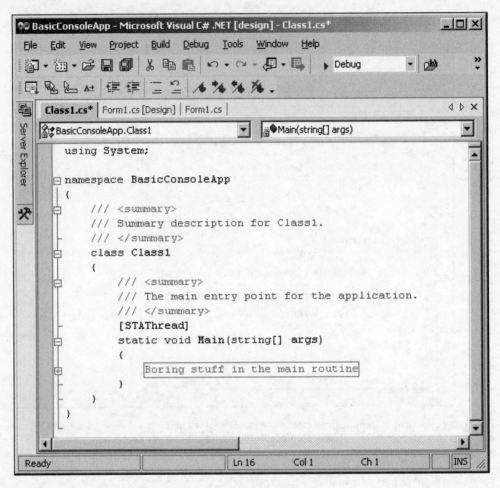

Besides the folding editor feature, Visual Studio .NET's code editor brings across all the familiar abilities from Visual Studio 6. In particular it features IntelliSense as we saw earlier. This not only saves you typing, but also helps make sure that you get the parameters correct. C++ developers will notice that the Visual Studio .NET IntelliSense feature is a bit more robust than the Visual Studio 6 version (which often missed items out of the listbox), and also works more quickly.

The code editor will also perform some syntax checking on your code and will underline most syntax errors with a short wavy line, even before you compile the code. Hovering the mouse pointer over the underlined text will bring up a small box telling you what the error is. This feature is something that VB developers have been used to for years, but will be new to developers coming to C# from C++.

Other Windows

Besides the code editor, Visual Studio .NET provides a number of other windows that allow you to view your project from different points of view.

For the rest of this section we'll be describing a number of other windows. If you find that one of these windows doesn't seem to be visible in your Visual Studio .NET setup, then you should just go to the View menu and click on the name of the appropriate window. The only exception to this is the Design View and Code Editor, since these are regarded as two tabs of the same window. You display these by either right clicking on the file name in the Solution Explorer and selecting View Designer or View Code from the context menu, or from the toolbar at the top of the Solution Explorer.

The Design View Window

If you are designing a user interface application, such as a Windows application, Windows control library, or ASP.NET application, then one window that you will use frequently is the Design View, which presents a visual overview of what your form will look like. You normally use the Design View in conjunction with a window known as the Toolbox (and the Layout toolbar). The Toolbox contains a large number of .NET components that you can drag onto your program:

The principle of the toolbox was applied in all developer environments in Visual Studio 6, but with .NET the number of components available from the toolbox has vastly increased. The categories of component available through the toolbox depend, to some extent, on the type of project you are editing – you'll find, for example, that you get a far wider range when you are editing the BasicForm project in the DemoSolution solution than you do when you are editing the BasicConsoleApp project. The most important ranges of items available include:

❑ **Data Access Components**. Classes that allow you to connect to data sources.

❑ **Windows Forms Components**. Classes that represent visual controls such as textboxes, listboxes, tree views etc.

❑ **Web Forms Components**. Classes that basically do the same thing as Windows controls, but which work in the context of web browsers, and which work by sending HTML output to simulate the controls to the browser.

❑ **Components**. Miscellaneous .NET classes that perform various useful tasks on your machine, such as connecting to directory services or to the event log.

You can also add your own custom categories of item to the toolbox if you wish, by right-clicking on any category and selecting Add Tab from the context menu. You can place other tools in the toolbox by selecting Customize Toolbox from the same context menu – this is particularly useful for adding your favorite COM components and ActiveX controls, which are not present in the toolbox by default. If you add a COM control, you can still click to place it in your project just as you would with a .NET control. Visual Studio .NET will automatically add all the required COM interoperability code to allow your project to call up the control. In this case, what will actually be added to your project is a .NET control that VS .NET creates behind the scenes, and which acts as a wrapper for your chosen COM control.

> *C++ developers will recognize the toolbox as Visual Studio .NET's (much enhanced) version of the resource editor. VB developers will probably think at first sight that there is not much new about the toolbox, since they have one in Visual Studio 6, but should beware because this toolbox has a dramatically different effect on your sourcecode from that which the one in the VB 6 IDE did.*

We'll see how the toolbox works by using it to place a textbox in our basic form project. We simply click on the TextBox in the toolbox then click again to place it in the form in the design view (or if you prefer, you can click and drag). Now the design view looks like this, showing roughly what BasicForm will look like if we compile and run it:

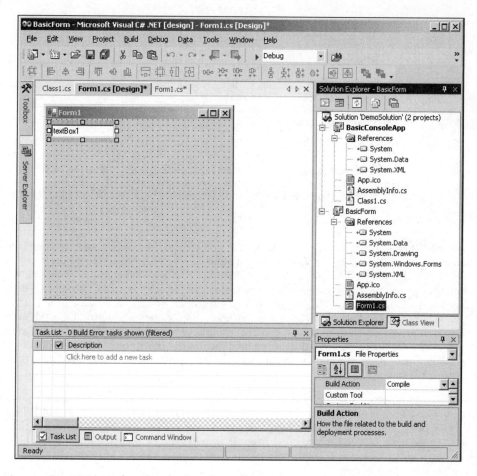

What is more interesting is that if we look at the code view, we see the developer environment has added the code that instantiates a `TextBox` object to go on the form. There's a new member variable in the `Form1` class:

```
public class Form1 : System.Windows.Forms.Form
{
    private System.Windows.Forms.TextBox textBox1;
```

There is also some code to initialize it in the method, `InitializeComponent()`, which is called from the `Form1` constructor:

```
/// <summary>
/// Required method for Designer support - do not modify
/// the contents of this method with the code editor.
/// </summary>
private void InitializeComponent()
{
```

357

```
            this.textBox1 = new System.Windows.Forms.TextBox();
this.SuspendLayout();
            //
            // textBox1
            //
            this.textBox1.Location = new System.Drawing.Point(8, 8);
            this.textBox1.Name = "textBox1";
            this.textBox1.TabIndex = 0;
            this.textBox1.Text = "textBox1";
            //
            // Form1
            //
            this.AutoScaleBaseSize = new System.Drawing.Size(5, 13);
            this.ClientSize = new System.Drawing.Size(292, 268);
            this.Controls.AddRange(new System.Windows.Forms.Control[] {

    this.textBox1});
```

In one sense there is no difference between the code editor and the design view: they simply present different views of the same code. What actually happened when we clicked to add the TextBox into the design view is that the toolbox (or strictly, Visual Studio .NET responding to our mouse clicks in the toolbox) has placed the above extra code in our C# source file. The design view simply reflects this change because Visual Studio .NET is able to read our sourcecode and determine from it what controls should be around when the application starts up. This is a fundamental shift from the old VB way of looking at things, in which everything was based around the visual design. Now, your C# sourcecode is what fundamentally controls your application, and the design view is just a different way of viewing the sourcecode. Incidentally, if you do write any VB.NET code with Visual Studio .NET, you'll find the same principles apply.

If we'd wanted to, we could have worked the other way round: if we manually added the same code as above to our C# source files, then Visual Studio .NET would have automatically detected from the code that our application contained a TextBox, and would have shown this textbox in the design view at the designated position. It is best to add these controls visually, and let Visual Studio handle the initial code generation – it's a lot quicker and less error-prone to click the mouse button a couple of times than to type quite a few lines of code!

Another reason for adding these controls visually is that, in order to recognize that they are there, Visual Studio .NET does need the relevant code to conform to certain criteria – and code that you write by hand might not do so. In particular, you'll notice that the InitializeComponent() method that contains the code to initialize the TextBox is commented to warn you against modifying it. That's because this is the method that Visual Studio .NET looks at in order to determine what controls are around when your application starts up, which it should be aware of. If you create and define a control somewhere else in your code, Visual Studio .NET won't be aware of it and you won't be able to edit it in the design view or certain other useful windows.

In fact, despite the warnings, you can modify the code in InitializeComponent(), provided you are careful. There's generally no harm in changing the values of some of the properties, for example, so that a control displays different text or so that it is a different size. In practice, the developer studio is pretty robust when it comes to working around any other code you place in this method. Just be aware, however, that if you make too many changes to InitializeComponent(), you do run the risk that Visual Studio .NET won't recognize some of your controls. We should stress that this won't affect your application whatsoever when it is compiled, but it may disable some of the editing features of Visual Studio .NET for those controls. Hence, if you want to add any other substantial initialization, it's probably better to do so in the Form1 constructor or in some other method.

The Properties Window

This is another window that has its origins in the old VB IDE. We know from Chapter 3 that .NET classes can implement properties. In fact, as we'll discover in the next chapter, the .NET base classes that represent forms and controls have a lot of properties that define their action or appearance – properties such as `Width`, `Height`, `Enabled` (whether the user can type input to the control), and `Text` (the text displayed by the control) – and Visual Studio .NET knows about many of these properties. The Properties window displays and allows you to edit the initial values of most of these properties for the controls that Visual Studio .NET has been able to detect by reading your sourcecode.

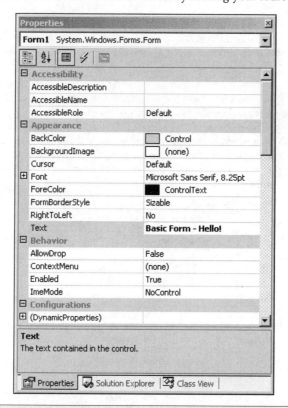

> The **Properties** window can also show events. You can view events by clicking on the icon that looks like a flash of lightning at the top of the window.

At the top of the Properties window is a listbox that allows you to select which control you want to view. We've selected `Form1`, the main form class for our **BasicForm** project, and have edited the text to 'Basic Form – Hello!' If we now check the sourcecode we can see that what we have actually done is edit the sourcecode – via a more friendly user interface.

```
this.AutoScaleBaseSize = new System.Drawing.Size(5, 13);
this.ClientSize = new System.Drawing.Size(292, 268);
this.Controls.AddRange(new System.Windows.Forms.Control[] {this.textBox1});
this.Name = "Form1";
this.Text = "Basic Form - Hello!";
```

Not all the properties shown in the Properties window are explicitly mentioned in our source code. For those that aren't, Visual Studio .NET will display the default values that were set when the form was created and which are set when the form is actually initialized. Obviously, if you change a value for one of these properties in the Properties window, a statement explicitly setting that property will magically appear in your sourcecode – and vice versa.

The Properties window provides a convenient way to get a broad overview of the appearance and properties of a particular control or window.

> *It is interesting to note that the Properties window is implemented as a*
> `System.Windows.Forms.PropertyGrid` *instance, which will internally use the reflection technology we described in the previous chapter to identify the properties and property values to display.*

The Class View

Unlike the Properties window, the Class View window owes its origins to the C++ (and J++) developer environments. It will, rather obviously, be new to VB developers since VB 6 did not even support the concept of the class, other than in the sense of a COM component. The class view is not actually treated by Visual Studio .NET as a window in its own right – rather it is an additional tab to the Solution Explorer window. The class view shows the hierarchy of the namespaces and classes in your code. It gives you a tree view that you can expand out to see what namespaces contain what classes and what classes contain what members.

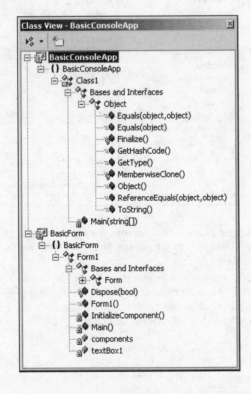

A nice feature of the **Class View** is that if you right-click on the name of any item for which you have access to the sourcecode, the context menu features an option, **Go To Definition**, which immediately takes you to the definition of the item in the code editor. You can alternatively do this by double-clicking on the item in **Class View** (or, indeed, by right-clicking on the item you want in the sourcecode editor and choosing the same option from the resulting context menu). The context menu also gives you the option to add a field, method, property, or indexer to a class. This means that you specify the details of the relevant member in a dialog box, and the code gets added for you. This is possibly not so useful for fields or methods, for which the effort to type in the definition manually into your code is small, but you may find it helpful for properties and indexers, where it can save you quite a bit of typing.

The Object Browser Window

One important aspect of programming in the .NET environment is being able to find out what methods etc. are available in the base classes and any other libraries that you are referencing from your assembly. This feature is available through a window called the **Object Browser**.

The **Object Browser** window is quite similar to the **Class View** window in that it displays a tree view that gives the class structure of your application, allowing you to inspect the members of each class. The user interface is slightly different in that it displays class members in a separate pane rather than in the tree view itself. The real difference is that it lets you look at not just the namespaces and classes in your project, but also the ones in all the assemblies that are referenced by the project. The screenshot below shows the object browser viewing the `SystemException` class from the .NET base classes.

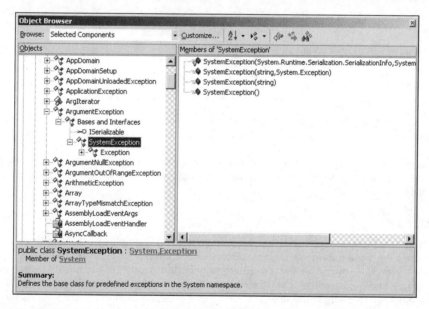

The only point you have to watch with the **Object Browser** is that it groups classes by the assembly in which they are located first, and by namespace second. Unfortunately, since namespaces for the base classes are often spread across several assemblies, this means you might have trouble locating a particular class unless you know what assembly it is in.

The object browser is there to view .NET objects. If for any reason you want to investigate installed COM objects, you'll find that the **OLEView** tool previously used in the C++ IDE is still available – it's under the **Tools** menu (the **OLE/COM Object Viewer** menu item), along with several other similar utilities.

> *VB developers should not confuse the .NET Object Browser with the Object Browser of the VB 6 IDE – they are different. The .NET Object Viewer is there to view .NET classes, whereas the tool of that name in VB 6 was there to view COM components. If you want the functionality of the old object browser, you should now use the OLEView tool.*

The Server Explorer Window

You can use the **Server Explorer** window to find out about aspects of the computer while coding.

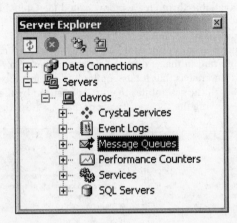

As you can see from the screenshot, among the things you can access through the Server Explorer are database connections, information about services, Web Services, and running processes.

The **Server Explorer** is linked to the **Properties** window so that, for example, if you open the **Services** node and click on a particular service, the properties of that service will be displayed in the **Properties** window.

Pin Buttons

While exploring Visual Studio .NET you may have noticed that many of the 'windows' we are describing have some interesting functionality more reminiscent of toolbars. In particular, apart from the code editor, they can all be docked. Another, very new, feature of them is that when they are docked, they have an extra icon that looks like a pin next to the minimize button in the top right corner of each window. This icon really does act like a pin – it can be used to pin the windows open. When they are pinned (the pin is displayed vertically), they behave just like all the 'normal' windows that you are used to. When they are unpinned, however, (the pin is displayed horizontally), they only remain open as long as they have the focus. As soon as they lose the focus (because you clicked somewhere else) they smoothly retreat into the main border around the entire Visual Studio .NET application.

Pinning and unpinning windows provides another way of making the best use of the limited space on your screen. It's not really been seen a great deal in Windows before, though a few third-party applications such as PaintShop Pro have used similar concepts. Pinned windows have, however, been around on many Unix-based systems for quite a while.

Building a Project

In this section we'll examine the options that Visual Studio .NET gives you for building your project.

Building, Compiling, and Making

Before we examine the various build options, we will just clarify one point of terminology. You'll often see three different terms used in connection with the process of getting from your sourcecode to some sort of executable code: compiling, building, and making. The origin of these various terms comes from the fact that until recently, the process of getting from sourcecode to executable code involved more than one step (and this is still the case in C++). This was largely because, typically, a program would contain many source files. In C++, for example, each source file needs to be compiled individually. This leads to what are known as object files, each containing something like executable code, but where each object file relates to only one source file. In order to generate an executable, these object files need to be linked together, a process that is officially known as **linking**. The combined process was usually referred to – at least on the Windows platform – as **building** your code. However, in C# terms the compiler is more sophisticated and is able to read in and treat all your source files as one block. Hence there isn't really a separate linking stage, so in the context of C# the terms "compile" and "build" are used interchangeably.

The term "make" basically means the same as "build", though it's not really used in the context of C#. The term originated on old mainframe systems on which, when a project was composed of many source files, a separate file would be written that contained instructions to the compiler on how to build a project – which files to include and what libraries to link in etc. This file was generally known as a **make file** and is still quite standard on Unix and Linux etc. Make files are not normally needed on Windows though you can still write them (or get Visual Studio .NET to generate them) if you need to.

Debug and Release Builds

The idea of having separate builds is something that will be well known to developers with C++ background, and less so to those with VB background. The point here is that when you are debugging you tend to want a rather different behavior from your executable from that which you do when you actually ship the software. When you ship, what you are mostly concerned with, besides the fact that your code works, is that the size of the executable should be as small as possible and that it should run as fast as possible. Unfortunately, these requirements aren't really compatible with your needs when you are debugging code, for the following reasons.

Optimization

High performance is achieved partly by the compiler doing a lot of optimizations on the code. This means that the compiler actively looks at your sourcecode as it's compiling in order to identify places where it can mangle the precise details of what you're doing in a way that doesn't change the overall effect, but which makes things more efficient. As one example of the principle, if the compiler encountered the following sourcecode:

```
double InchesToCm(double Ins)
{
    return Ins*2.54;
}

// later on in the code

Y = InchesToCm(X);
```

it might replace it with this:

```
Y = X * 2.54;
```

Or it might replace this code:

```
{
    string Message = "Hi";
    Console.WriteLine(Message);
}
```

with this:

```
Console.WriteLine("Hi");
```

Thereby saving having to declare an unnecessary object reference in the process.

It's not possible to exactly pin down what optimizations the C# compiler does – or whether the two above examples actually would occur with any particular example, because those kinds of details are not documented (it is most likely that for managed languages such as C#, the above optimizations would occur at JIT compilation time, not when the C# compiler compiles sourcecode to assembly). For obvious commercial reasons, companies that write compilers are usually quite reluctant to give too many details about the tricks that their compilers use. We should stress that optimizations do not affect your sourcecode – they affect only the contents of the executable code. However, the above examples should give you a good idea of what to expect from optimizations.

The problem is that while optimizations like the ones above help a great deal in making your code run faster, they aren't so good for debugging. Suppose with the first example, that you want to set a breakpoint inside the InchesToCm() method to see what's going on in there. How can you possibly do that if the executable code doesn't actually have an InchesToCm() method because the compiler has removed it? And how can you set a watch on the Message variable when that doesn't now exist in the compiled code either?

Debugger Symbols

When you're debugging, you often need to look at values of variables, and you will specify them by their sourcecode names. The trouble is that executable code generally doesn't contain those names – the compiler replaces the names with memory addresses. .NET has modified this situation somewhat, to the extent that certain items in assemblies are stored with their names, but this is only true of a small minority of items – such as public classes and methods – and those names will still be removed when the assembly is JIT-compiled. Asking the debugger to tell you what the value is in the variable called HeightInInches isn't going to get you very far if, when the debugger examines the executable code, it sees only addresses and no reference to the name HeightInInches anywhere. So, in order to debug properly, you need to have extra debugging information made available in the executable. This information will include, among other things, names of variables and line information that allows the debugger to match up which executable machine assembly language instructions correspond to those of your original sourcecode instructions. You won't, however, want that information in a release build, both for commercial reasons (debugging information makes it a lot easier for other people to disassemble your code) and because it increases the size of the executable.

Extra Source code Debugging Commands

A related issue is that quite often while you are debugging there will be extra lines in your code to display crucial debugging-related information. Obviously you want the relevant commands removed entirely from the executable before you ship the software. You could do this manually but wouldn't it be so much easier if you could simply mark those statements in some way so that the compiler ignores them when it is compiling your code to be shipped. We've already seen in Chapter 4 how this can be done in C# by defining a suitable processor symbol, and possibly using this in conjunction with the Conditional attribute – giving you what is known as conditional compilation.

What all these factors add up to is that you need to compile almost all commercial software in a slightly different way when debugging, compared to the final product that is shipped. Visual Studio .NET is able to take this into account because, as we have already seen, it stores details of all the options that it is supposed to pass to the compiler when it has your code compiled. All that Visual Studio needs to do in order to support different types of build is to store more than one set of such details. The different sets of build information are referred to as **configurations**. When you create a project Visual Studio .NET will automatically give you two configurations, called Debug and Release.

- ❑ The **Debug configuration** will usually specify that no optimizations are to take place, extra debugging information is to be present in the executable, and the compiler is to assume that the debug preprocessor symbol Debug is present unless it is explicitly #undefined in the sourcecode

- ❑ The **Release configuration** will usually specify that the compiler should optimize, that there should be no extra debugging information in the executable, and that the compiler should not assume that any particular preprocessor symbol is present

You can define your own configurations as well. You might do this, for example if you wish to set up professional-level builds and enterprise-level builds so you can ship two versions of the software. In the past, for C++ projects, because of issues concerning the Unicode character encodings being supported on Windows NT but not on Windows 95, it was common for C++ projects to feature a Unicode configuration and an MBCS (multibyte character set) configuration.

Selecting a Configuration

One obvious question is that, since Visual Studio .NET is storing details of more than one configuration, how does it determine which one to use when arranging for a project to be built? The answer is that there is always an active configuration, which is the configuration that will be used when you ask Visual Studio .NET to build a project. (Note that configurations are set for each project rather than for each solution.)

By default, when you create a project, the debug configuration will be the active configuration. You can change which configuration is the active one by clicking on the **Debug** menu option and selecting the item **Set Active Configuration**. It also available through a dropdown in the main VS .NET toolbar.

Editing Configurations

Besides choosing the active configuration you can also examine and edit the configurations. To do this, you need to click on the **Project** menu while the relevant project is selected in the Solution Explorer, and then select the **Properties** menu item. This brings up a very sophisticated dialog box. (You can alternatively reach the same dialog box by right-clicking on the name of the project in the Solution Explorer, and then selecting **Properties** from the context menu.)

This dialog contains a tree view, which allows you to select quite a lot of different general areas to examine or edit. We don't have space to show all of these areas but we will show a couple of the most important ones.

The screenshot below shows that the tree view has two top-level nodes, **Common Properties** and **Configuration Properties**. Common properties are those properties that are common across all the configurations while configuration properties are specific to a particular configuration:

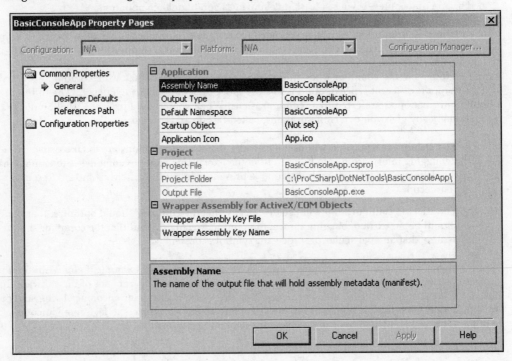

For this screenshot we are showing the general cross-configuration compiler options for the BasicConsoleApp project that we created earlier in the chapter. Among the points to note are that we can select the name of the assembly, as well as the type of assembly to be generated. The options here are console application, Windows application, and class library. You can, of course, change the assembly type if you want. (Though arguably, if you do want to, you might wonder why you didn't pick the correct project type at the time that you asked Visual Studio .NET to generate the project for you in the first place!)

The next screenshot shows the build configuration properties. You'll notice that a listbox near the top of the dialog allows you to specify which configuration you wish to look at. In this case we can see – for the Debug configuration – that the compiler will assume that the DEBUG and TRACE preprocessor symbols have been defined. Also, as we mentioned above is typical for Debug configurations, the code is not optimized and extra debugging information is generated.

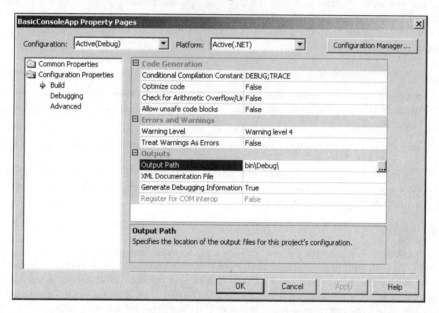

In general, although we've gone into some detail about configurations, it's not that often that you'll need to adjust them. However, you will need to be able to select the appropriate configuration depending on why you are building your project, and it is useful to know what the effect of the different configurations is.

Debugging

After the long discussion about building and build configurations, you might be surprised to learn that we're not going to spend a great deal of time discussing debugging itself. The reason for that is that the principles and the process of debugging – setting breakpoints and examining the values of variables – isn't really significantly different in Visual Studio .NET from in any of the various Visual Studio 6 IDE's. Instead we will briefly review the features offered by Visual Studio .NET, focusing on those areas that may be new to some developers. We will also discuss in more detail how to deal with exceptions, since these can cause problems for debugging.

In C#, as in pre-.NET languages, the main technique involved in debugging is simply setting breakpoints and using them to examine what is going on in your code at a certain point in its execution.

Breakpoints

You can set breakpoints from Visual Studio .NET on any line of your code that is actually executed. The simplest way is simply to click on the line in the code editor, in the shaded area towards the far left of the window (or hit the *F9* key when the appropriate line is selected). This will set up a breakpoint on that line, which will cause execution to break and control to be transferred to the debugger as soon as that line is reached. As in previous versions of Visual Studio, a breakpoint is indicated by a large circle to the left of the line in the code editor. Visual Studio .NET also highlights the line by displaying the text and background in a different color. Clicking on the circle again removes the breakpoint.

If breaking every time a particular line is hit isn't adequate for your particular problem, you can also set conditional breakpoints. To do this, click on the **Debug** menu, select the **Windows** then the **Breakpoints** menu options. This brings up the dialog box asking you for details of the breakpoint you wish to set. Among the options available you can:

❑ Specify that execution should break only after the breakpoint has been hit a certain number of times.

❑ Specify that the breakpoint should come into effect only every so-many times that the line is reached, for example every twentieth time that a line is executed (useful when debugging large loops).

❑ Set the breakpoints relative to a variable rather than to an instruction. In this case, the value of the variable will be monitored and the breakpoints will be triggered whenever the value of this variable changes. You may find, however, that using this option slows your code down very considerably. Checking whether the value of a variable has changed after every instruction adds a lot of processor time.

Watches

Once a breakpoint has been hit you will usually want to investigate the values of variables. The simplest way to do this is to simply hover the mouse cursor over the name of the variable in the code editor. This will cause a little box to appear that gives the value of that variable. However, you may also prefer to use the **Watch** window to examine the contents of variables. The watch window is a tabbed window that appears only when the program is running under the debugger. It looks like this:

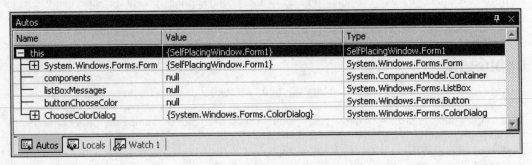

Variables that are classes or structs are shown with a + icon next to them, which you can click on to expand the variable and see the values of its fields.

The three tabs to this window are each designed to monitor different variables:

- ❑   **Autos** monitors the last few variables that have been accessed as the program was executing
- ❑   **Locals** monitors variables that are accessible in the method currently being executed
- ❑   **Watch** monitors any variables that you have explicitly specified by typing their names into the Watch window

Exceptions

Exceptions are great when you ship your application for making sure that error conditions are handled in an appropriate way within your application. Used well, they can ensure that your application copes well and the user never gets presented with some technical dialog box. Unfortunately, exceptions are not so great when you're trying to debug. The problem is twofold.

- ❑   If an exception occurs when you're debugging, then you quite often don't want it to be handled automatically – especially if automatically handling it means retiring gracefully and terminating execution! Rather, you want the debugger to help you find out why the exception has occurred. Of course the trouble is that if you have written good, robust, defensive code, then your program will automatically handle almost anything – including your bugs that you want to detect!

- ❑   If an exception occurs that you haven't written a handler for, the .NET runtime will still go off looking for a handler. But by the time it discovers that there isn't one, it will have terminated your program. There won't be a call stack left and you won't be able to look at the values of any of your variables because they will all have gone out of scope.

Of course, you can set breakpoints in your catch blocks, but that often doesn't help very much because when the `catch` block is reached, flow of execution will, by definition, have exited the corresponding `try` block. That means that the variables you probably wanted to examine the values of in order to find out what's gone wrong will have gone out of scope. You won't even be able to look at the stack trace to find out what method was being executed when the throw statement occurred – because control will have left that method. Setting the breakpoints at the `throw` statement will of course solve this, except that if you are coding defensively there will be a **lot** of `throw` statements in your code. How can you tell which one is the one that threw the exception?

In fact, Visual Studio has a very neat answer to all this. If you look at the main **Debug** menu, you'll find a menu item in it called **Exceptions**. This brings up the Exceptions dialog box that allows you to specify what happens when an exception is thrown. You can choose to continue execution or to automatically stop and start debugging – in which case execution stops and the debugger steps in at the `throw` statement itself.

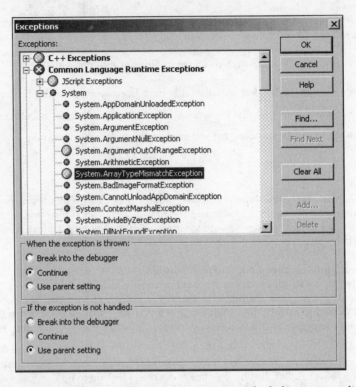

What makes this a really powerful tool is that you can customize the behavior according to which class of exception is thrown. For example, in the above screenshot, we've told Visual Studio .NET to break into the debugger whenever it encounters any exception thrown by a .NET base class (shown by the red cross next to the category of exception), but not to break into the debugger if the exception is an `ArgumentOutOfRangeException` or an `ArrayTypeMismatchException`.

Visual Studio .NET knows about all the exception classes available in the .NET base classes, and also about quite a few exceptions that can be thrown outside the .NET environment. Visual Studio .NET isn't automatically aware of your own custom exception classes that you write, but you can manually add your exception classes to the list and thereby specify which of your exceptions should cause execution to stop immediately. To do this you just click on the Add button above (which is enabled when you have selected a top-level node from the tree) and type in the name of your exception class.

Other .NET Tools

We've spent a lot of time exploring Visual Studio .NET, because that is the tool that you will almost certainly be spending most of your development time using. However, there are a number of other tools available to assist with your programming, which we will cover as we go through the book. Here we will mention one general-purpose utility, WinCV, which you can use to browse the base classes.

WinCV

You can use the WinCV utility, which Microsoft has provided, to explore the base classes and see what methods are available. It is very similar to the Visual Studio .NET object browser, except that it is an independent application, and it will show you *all* the base classes, whereas the object browser shows only those in the assemblies that are referenced by your project.

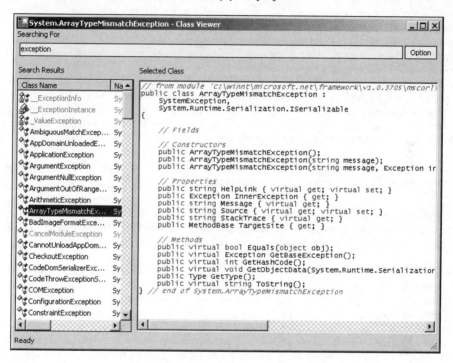

WinCV is quite simple to use. You run it from the Visual Studio .NET command-line prompt by typing in wincv. Then when it is running, you simply type in some text in the listbox near the top of the wincv window. As you type, wincv will search through the base classes and pick out all the classes whose name includes the word you have typed in. These classes are displayed in the left-hand listbox. If you click on a particular class, its members are displayed, roughly in a format that corresponds to C# syntax, on the right.

> *You'll find the Visual Studio .NET command prompt under Microsoft Visual Studio .NET in the Start menu. It is an ordinary command prompt, but with a couple of extra environment variables defined to allow you to use various .NET tools. You won't be able to run wincv (or other .NET tools) from the usual command prompt.*

.NET Usage Guidelines

In this final section of this .NET Programming chapter we're going to look at the guidelines Microsoft has written for .NET programming.

In any development language there usually arise certain traditional programming styles. The styles are not part of the language itself but are conventions concerning, for example, how variables are named or how certain classes, methods, or functions are used. If most developers using that language follow the same conventions, it makes it easier for different developers to understand each other's code – which in turn generally helps program maintainability. For example, a common (though not universal) convention in Visual Basic 6 was that variables that represents strings have names beginning with lowercase s or lowercase `str`, as in `sResult As String` or `strMessage As String`. Conventions do, however, depend on the language and the environment. For example, C++ developers programming on the Windows platform have traditionally used the prefixes `psz` or `lpsz` to indicate strings: `char *pszResult; char *lpszMessage;`, but on Unix machines it's more common not to use any such prefixes: `char *Result; char *Message;`.

You'll have gathered from the sample code in this book that the convention in C# is to name variables without prefixes: `string Result; string Message;`.

> *Incidentally, the convention by which variable names are prefixed with letters that represent the data type is known as* **Hungarian notation**. *It means that other developers reading the code can immediately tell from the variable name what data type the variable represents.*

Whereas, with many languages, usage conventions simply evolved as the language was used, with C# and the whole of the .NET Framework Microsoft has written very comprehensive usage guidelines, which are detailed in the .NET/C# MSDN documentation. This should mean that, right from the start, .NET programs will have a high degree of interoperability in terms of developers being able to understand code. The guidelines have also been developed with the benefit of some twenty years hindsight in object-oriented programming, and as a result, have been carefully thought out and appear to have been well received in the developer community to judge by the relevant newsgroups. Hence the guidelines are well worth following.

It should be noted, however, that the guidelines are not the same as language specifications. You should try to follow the guidelines when you can. Nevertheless, if you do have a good reason for not doing so then that's no problem. The general rule is that if you don't follow the usage guidelines you must have a convincing reason. Departing from the guidelines should be a positive decision rather than simply not bothering. Also, as you read the guidelines, you'll notice that in numerous examples in this book, we have chosen not to follow the conventions, usually because the conventions are designed for much larger programs than our samples, and while they are great if you are writing a complete software package, they are not really so suitable for small 20-line standalone programs. In many cases following the conventions would have made our samples harder rather than easier to follow.

The full guidelines for good programming style are quite extensive. Here we will confine ourselves to describing some of the more important guidelines, as well as the ones most likely to catch you out. If you want to make absolutely certain your code follows the usage guidelines completely, then you will need to refer to the MSDN documentation.

Naming Conventions

One important aspect to making your programs understandable is how you choose to name your items – and that includes naming variables, methods, classes, enumerations, and namespaces.

It is intuitively obvious that your names should reflect the purpose of the item, and should be designed not to clash with other names. The general philosophy in the .NET Framework is also that the name of a variable should reflect the purpose of that variable instance and not the data type. For example, `Height` is a good name for a variable, while `IntegerValue` isn't. However, you will probably feel that that principle is an ideal that is hard to achieve. Particularly when you are dealing with controls, in most cases, you'll probably feel happier sticking with variable names like `ConfirmationDialog` and `ChooseEmployeeListBox`.

Let's look at some of the things you need to think about when choosing names.

Casing of Names

In almost all cases you should use **Pascal casing** for names. Pascal casing means that the first letter of each word in a name is capitalized: `EmployeeSalary`, `ConfirmationDialog`, `PlainTextEncoding`. You will notice that essentially all of the names of namespaces, classes, and members in the base classes follow Pascal casing. In particular, the convention of joining words using the underscore character is discouraged. So you should try not to write names like `employee_salary`. It has also been common in other languages to use all-capitals for names of constants. This is not advised in C#, since such names are harder to read – the convention is to use Pascal casing throughout:

```
const int MaximumLength;
```

The only other casing scheme that you are advised to use is **camel casing**. Camel casing is similar to Pascal casing, except that the first letter of the first word in the name is not capitalized: `employeeSalary`, `confirmationDialog`, `plainTextEncoding`. There are two situations in which you are advised to use camel casing:

❑ Names of all parameters passed to methods should be camel-cased:

```
public void RecordSale(string salesmanName, int quantity);
```

❑ You should also use camel casing in order to distinguish between two items that would otherwise have the same name – a common case is when a property wraps around a field:

```
private string employeeName;

public string EmployeeName
{
   get
   {
      return employeeName;
   }
}
```

The above code is regarded by the guidelines as perfectly acceptable. Note, however, that if you are doing this, you should always use camel casing for the private member and Pascal casing for the public or protected member, so that other classes that use your code see only Pascal-cased names (except for parameter names).

You should also be wary about case-sensitivity. C# is case sensitive, so it is quite legal syntactically for names in C# to differ only by the case, as in the above examples. However, you should bear in mind that your assemblies might at some point be called from VB.NET applications – and **VB.NET is not case sensitive**. Hence, if you do use names that differ only by a case, it is important to do so only in situations in which both names will never be seen outside your assembly. (The above example qualifies as OK because the camel-cased name is attached to a `private` variable.) Otherwise you may prevent other code written in VB.NET from being able to use your assembly correctly.

Name Styles

You should try to be consistent about your style of names. For example, if one of the methods in a class is called `ShowConfirmationDialog()`, then you should not give another method a name like `ShowDialogWarning()`, or `WarningDialogShow()`. The other method should be called `ShowWarningDialog()`. Get the idea?

Namespace Names

Namespace names are particularly important to design carefully in order to the avoid risk of ending up with the same name for one of your namespaces as someone else uses. Remember, namespace names are the **only** way that .NET distinguishes names of objects in shared assemblies. So if you use the same namespace name for your software package as another package, and both packages get installed on the same computer, there are going to be problems. Because of this, it's almost always a good idea to create a top-level namespace with the name of your company, and then nest successive namespaces that narrow down the technology, group, or department you are working in or the name of the package your classes are intended for. Microsoft recommends namespace names that begin `<CompanyName>.<TechnologyName>`, for example `WeaponsOfDestructionCorp.RayGunControllers`, or `WeaponsOfDestructionCorp.Viruses`.

Names and Keywords

It is important the names should not clash with any keywords. In fact, if you attempt to name an item in your code with a word that happens to be a C# keyword, you'll almost certainly get a syntax error because the compiler will assume the name refers to a statement. However, because of the possibility that your classes will be accessed by code written in other languages, it is important that you don't use names that are keywords in other .NET languages. Generally speaking, C++ keywords are similar to C# keywords, so confusion with C++ is unlikely, and those commonly encountered keywords that are unique to Visual C++ tend to start with two underscore characters. Like C#, C++ keywords are spelled in lowercase, so if you hold to the convention of naming your public classes and members with Pascal-style names, then they will always have at least one uppercase letter in their names, and there will be no risk of clashes with C++ keywords. On the other hand, you are more likely to have problems with VB.NET, which has many more keywords than C# does, and being non-case sensitive means you cannot rely on Pascal-style names for your classes and methods.

The following table lists the keywords and standard function calls in VB.NET, which should not be used, in whatever case combination, for your public C# classes.

Abs	Do	Loc	RGB
Add	Double	Local	Right
AddHandler	Each	Lock	RmDir

AddressOf	Else	LOF	Rnd
Alias	ElseIf	Log	RTrim
And	Empty	Long	SaveSettings
Ansi	End	Loop	Second
AppActivate	Enum	LTrim	Seek
Append	EOF	Me	Select
As	Erase	Mid	SetAttr
Asc	Err	Minute	SetException
Assembly	Error	MIRR	Shared
Atan	Event	MkDir	Shell
Auto	Exit	Module	Short
Beep	Exp	Month	Sign
Binary	Explicit	MustInherit	Sin
BitAnd	ExternalSource	MustOverride	Single
BitNot	False	MyBase	SLN
BitOr	FileAttr	MyClass	Space
BitXor	FileCopy	Namespace	Spc
Boolean	FileDateTime	New	Split
ByRef	FileLen	Next	Sqrt
Byte	Filter	Not	Static
ByVal	Finally	Nothing	Step
Call	Fix	NotInheritable	Stop
Case	For	NotOverridable	Str
Catch	Format	Now	StrComp
CBool	FreeFile	NPer	StrConv
CByte	Friend	NPV	Strict
CDate	Function	Null	String
CDbl	FV	Object	Structure
CDec	Get	Oct	Sub
ChDir	GetAllSettings	Off	Switch
ChDrive	GetAttr	On	SYD
Choose	GetException	Open	SyncLock

Table continued on following page

Chr	GetObject	Option	Tab
CInt	GetSetting	Optional	Tan
Class	GetType	Or	Text
Clear	GoTo	Overloads	Then
CLng	Handles	Overridable	Throw
Close	Hex	Overrides	TimeOfDay
Collection	Hour	ParamArray	Timer
Command	If	Pmt	TimeSerial
Compare	IIf	PPmt	TimeValue
Const	Implements	Preserve	To
Cos	Imports	Print	Today
CreateObject	In	Private	Trim
CShort	Inherits	Property	Try
CSng	Input	Public	TypeName
CStr	InStr	Put	TypeOf
CurDir	Int	PV	UBound
Date	Integer	QBColor	UCase
DateAdd	Interface	Raise	Unicode
DateDiff	IPmt	RaiseEvent	Unlock
DatePart	IRR	Randomize	Until
DateSerial	Is	Rate	Val
DateValue	IsArray	Read	Weekday
Day	IsDate	ReadOnly	While
DDB	IsDbNull	ReDim	Width
Decimal	IsNumeric	Remove	With
Declare	Item	RemoveHandler	WithEvents
Default	Kill	Rename	Write
Delegate	LCase	Replace	WriteOnly
DeleteSetting	Left	Reset	Xor
Dim	Lib	Resume	Year
Dir	Line	Return	

Use of Properties and Methods

One area that can cause confusion in a class is whether a particular quantity should be represented by a property or a method. The rules here are not hard and fast, but in general, you ought to use a property if something really should look and feel like a variable. This means, among other things, that:

❑ Client code should be able to read its value. Write-only properties are not recommended, so for example use a `SetPassword()` method not a write-only `Password` property.

❑ Reading the value should not take too long. The fact that something is a property usually suggests that reading it will be relatively quick.

❑ Reading the value should not have any observable and unexpected side effect; for example, setting the value of a property will not have any side effect that is not directly related to the property. Setting the width of a dialog box has the obvious effect of changing the appearance of the dialog box on the screen. That's fine, as that's obviously related to the property in question.

❑ It should be possible to set properties in any order. In particular, it is not good practice when setting a property to throw an exception because another related property has not yet been set. For example, if in order to use a class that accesses a database you need to set `ConnectionString`, `UserName`, and `Password`, make sure the class is implemented so the user really can set them in any order.

❑ Successive reads of a property should give the same result. If the value of a property is likely to change unpredictably, then you should code it up as a method instead. `Speed`, in a class that monitors the motion of an automobile, is not a good candidate for a property. Use a `GetSpeed()` method here; on the other hand, `Weight` and `EngineSize` are good candidates for properties as they will not change for a given object.

If the item you are coding up satisfies all of the above criteria, then it is probably a good candidate for a property. Otherwise you should use a method.

Use of Fields

The guidelines are pretty simple here. Fields should almost always be private, except that in some cases it may be acceptable for constant or read-only fields to be public. The reason is that if you make a field public, you may hinder your ability to extend or modify the class in the future.

The above guidelines should give you a rough idea of good practices, and you should also use them in conjunction with good object-oriented programming style.

It's also worth bearing in mind that Microsoft has been fairly careful about being consistent, and has followed its own guidelines when writing the .NET base classes. So a very good way to get an intuitive feel for the conventions to follow when writing .NET code is to simply look at the base classes – see how classes, members, and namespaces are named, and how the class hierarchy works. If you try to write your code in the same style as the base classes, then you shouldn't go far wrong.

Summary

In this chapter we've looked at two sides of programming in the .NET environment. We spent the bulk of the chapter examining the tools that Microsoft has supplied to make your work writing C# (and C++ and VB.NET) code as easy as possible – particularly Visual Studio .NET. Then we finished off by examining some of the conventions you should try to follow when writing C# code. I quite like to think of the situation in terms of rights and responsibilities (by analogy with certain political debates): with .NET, you get the benefit of some really great tools that will have a huge impact on the speed with which you can get software written and debugged, but on the other hand you have the responsibility to use these tools carefully – by writing code that will be easy for others to use or maintain, and you can best show that responsibility by following the guidelines for writing good code.

In short, we have covered the following areas in this chapter:

❑ The look of Visual Studio .NET and some of the more common windows and tools that you will use when coding in the IDE

❑ WinCV – a useful utility that allows you to examine the base classes

❑ Usage guidelines and naming conventions – the guidelines that you should adhere to when writing C# code, so that your code follows normal .NET practice, and can be easily understood by others.

Windows Applications

While many business applications developed today are designed for the World Wide Web, the classic rich client still exists and will always be required. Whether it is an intranet application used within the organization, or a piece of shrink-wrapped software installed on enduser's desktops, the rich functionality and user experience such an environment provides will always be required for certain types of applications. Web applications are wonderful for ease of deployment and maintenance, but they cannot compare to the user experience possible through a good rich client.

Fortunately, .NET provides the ability to create rich clients that execute within the Common Language Runtime. These applications utilize a new Windows forms processing engine, called Windows Forms. Any .NET language can use Windows Forms to build Windows applications. These applications have access to the complete .NET Framework of namespaces and objects, and have all of the advantages we have discussed so far.

In this chapter we will discuss how to build Windows applications in .NET. We will cover the following topics:

❑   How to build Windows Forms applications using the .NET Framework

❑   How to use Visual Studio .NET to build Windows Forms applications quickly

❑   Adding menu support to an application, including dynamic and context-sensitive menus

❑   Utilizing custom and common dialog resources in a project

❑   How to use visual inheritance to build powerful and dynamic Windows Forms applications

❑   How to use Windows Forms controls in an application

❑   How to create and extend existing controls for specialized functionality

❑   Exposing and consuming custom events from a custom control

Windows Applications in .NET

It is important to understand the differences between rich and thin clients, as this is crucial to understanding why Windows applications are considered rich clients. A thin client does not require much installation or configuration before using the application itself. The classic example of this is a web application – all that is required to utilize the functionality is a Web browser and an Internet connection. Rich clients, sometimes called fat clients, require some form of installation or configuration on the client machine. Businesses have moved away from rich clients precisely for this reason – installing and upgrading an application installed on thousands of separate desktops can be a daunting challenge! However, because rich clients run on the client they can take full advantage of the environment and processing power of the client machine. This allows developers to create a much more interactive and user-friendly experience for the user.

Before .NET, developers had several choices in building a Windows application. They could go all the way down to the API layer and build a C or C++ application using the Win32 API. This is a very difficult and time consuming task, and not many businesses can afford to spend the time required to develop applications at this layer. Because of this, several environments have evolved to provide an easier interface into the Win32 API and allow developers to be more productive. Microsoft Foundation Classes (MFC) is a productivity class library using C++ that encapsulates the Win32 API. Visual Basic is a rapid application development tool utilizing a derivation of the Basic programming language that allows developers to create Windows applications relatively quickly. However, neither of these solutions utilizes the .NET Framework or the CLR.

The .NET Framework contains a new productivity layer that encapsulates the Win32 API, and much like MFC and Visual Basic, it allows for easier and more efficient development of Windows applications. This environment is called Windows Forms; it allows developers to create highly interactive and rich Windows applications using any .NET language. We will be examining the Windows Forms environment extensively in this chapter.

By using .NET itself to create Windows applications, developers gain access to the many new and exciting features exposed by .NET. All of the namespaces and classes available in the .NET Framework can be utilized within a .NET rich client. In addition, the application can be developed in any of the many .NET languages; different components of the application can even utilize different languages.

Almost all of the functionality we will be examining in this chapter is exposed through classes contained within the `System.Windows.Forms` namespace. This is an extremely large namespace containing many classes and additional namespaces, all of which facilitate creating Windows applications. The following diagram displays just some of the many classes that derive from `System.Windows.Forms.Control`. This object acts as a base class for the majority of classes within this namespace, and contains much of the basic functionality for interface display and interaction with the user:

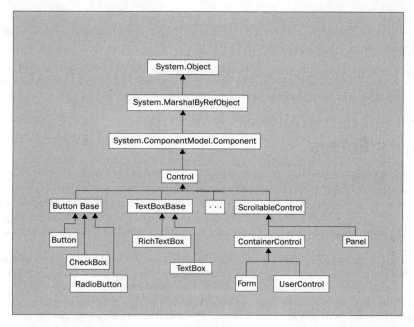

In this diagram, if a class is not prefixed with a namespace it is contained within the
System.Windows.Forms namespace. Not displayed are the incredibly large number of classes that
derive from Control, all of which provide specialized functionality. These provide access to the
extensive library of Windows Forms controls. This diagram provides an overview of how the hierarchy
is laid out and how the Form and Control classes fit into the big picture.

- ❑ System.Windows.Forms.Control – this acts as the base class for the majority of classes in
  the namespace. It contains very basic functionality for processing keyboard and mouse input
  and processing Windows messages.

- ❑ System.Windows.Forms.ButtonBase – this class supports the basic functionality of a
  button, which each of the three derived classes utilizes in different ways.

- ❑ System.Windows.Forms.TextBoxBase – again, this is a generic base class that is used to
  provide common functionality and properties to the derived classes. Both the TextBox and
  RichTextBox classes utilize the functionality provided by TextBoxBase.

- ❑ System.Windows.Forms.ScrollableControl – this is another base class that provides
  support for derived classes. This class manages the generation and display of scroll bars to
  enable the user to have access to the whole of a display.

- ❑ System.Windows.Forms.ContainerControl – this class manages the functionality
  required for a control to act as a container for other controls.

- ❑ System.Windows.Forms.Panel – this is another control that can contain additional
  controls, but unlike the ContainerControl class it simply groups controls. A perfect
  example is a set of mutually exclusive RadioButtons: the Panel groups the RadioButtons
  into sets.

❑ System.Windows.Forms.Form – this is the class that deals with creating and displaying windows. This class can be used to create any kind of window: standard, toolbox, borderless, even modal dialog boxes and multi-document interfaces.

❑ System.Windows.Forms.UserControl – this is the class that can be used to derive from when creating a custom control to be used in multiple places in an application or organization. This class will be covered extensively later in the chapter.

Windows Forms

Almost every Windows Forms application extends the functionality of System.Windows.Forms. The basic functionality of the Form class doesn't accomplish much more than to create a window that can live and interact in the Windows environment correctly. This is useful as a starting point, and by extending the Form class and adding custom controls and custom event handlers, a very useful application can be created that can interact with the user and present data through a sophisticated user-interface.

We are going to examine how this process works in two ways. To better understand how Windows Forms operates and how it interacts with the .NET Framework, we will first build a complete Windows application without the use of Visual Studio .NET. This should provide you with a healthy appreciation of Visual Studio .NET when we then move to building Windows Forms applications using it. VS .NET allows developers to create Windows Forms application faster and more efficiently than they can by hand.

Windows Forms Without Visual Studio .NET

Again, almost every Windows Forms application will extend the System.Windows.Forms class to customize and add business logic. Therefore, the simplest Windows Forms application would be the following:

```
using System;
using System.Windows.Forms;

namespace WindowsFormsApp
{
    class MyForm : Form
    {
        static void Main(string[] args)
        {
            MyForm aForm = new MyForm();
            Application.Run(aForm);
        }
    }
}
```

To see this in action, save the above code as BasicForm.cs, then compile and run it. Alternatively, this file can be found in the code download for this book in the BasicForm folder, under the WindowsApplications directory. You should see the following output:

```
Command Prompt                                          _ □ X
Microsoft Windows 2000 [Version 5.00.2195]
(C) Copyright 1985-2000 Microsoft Corp.

C:\>cd proc*

C:\ProCSharp>cd windo*

C:\ProCSharp\WindowsApplications>cd bas*

C:\ProCSharp\WindowsApplications\BasicForm>csc BasicForm.cs
Microsoft (R) Visual C# .NET Compiler version 7.00.9466
for Microsoft (R) .NET Framework version 1.0.3705
Copyright (C) Microsoft Corporation 2001. All rights reserved.


C:\ProCSharp\WindowsApplications\BasicForm>_
```

When the application is run (by double-clicking on the executable that has been output by the compiler) a very basic window will be opened. Note that the window acts like a standard window and can be minimized, maximized, dragged, and closed. Not the next killer app, but it is a fully functional Windows application in 13 lines of code. Let's take a look at the code itself to understand what is happening before we move on to more exciting things.

```
class MyForm : Form
```

This line shows that our class is deriving from the System.Windows.Forms.Form class, meaning we gain access to all the functionality of the basic Form class. Next, note that in the Main() method (which is the standard Main() method we have used for all .NET applications so far) we create an instance of the custom MyForm object and pass it to the Application.Run() method:

```
static void Main(string[] args)
{
    MyForm aForm = new MyForm();
    Application.Run(aForm);
}
```

Application is a static class available in the System.Windows.Forms namespace that contains methods to start and stop applications and threads. The Run() method can accept several parameters; by passing in a Form object we are signaling to the .NET Framework to begin processing Windows messages for this form, and to exit the application when this form closes.

Controls

Let's add a simple Button control to the form. We will cover events much more extensively later in the chapter; for now we will only examine what it takes to add a control to a .NET Windows Forms application without Visual Studio .NET.

Basically every control on a form is a data member of the custom Form class. Therefore, to add a button to our form we must add a new Button data member to the MyForm class. Add the following line to the BasicForm.cs file:

```
class MyForm : Form
{
    //Data member to hold Button control
    private Button BigButton;
```

Before this data member will do anything or display a button on the form it must be initialized and the `Button`'s various properties must be configured. This should be done in the constructor for the `MyForm` object. At this time we will also set the properties for the `Form` object itself, such as the size and name. Note that there are many properties that can be set, and doing so in the constructor is the best time to do so for initial values. Add the following block of code to the constructor of `MyForm`:

```
public MyForm()
{
    //Set the properties for the Button
    BigButton = new Button();
    BigButton.Location = new System.Drawing.Point(50, 50);
    BigButton.Name = "BigButton";
    BigButton.Size = new System.Drawing.Size(100, 100);
    BigButton.Text = "Click Me!";

    //Set properties of the Form itself
    ClientSize = new System.Drawing.Size(200, 200);
    Controls.Add(BigButton);
    Text = "My Windows Form!";
}
```

This code first instantiates a new `Button` object and assigns it to the private data member `BigButton`. It then sets the `Location`, `Name`, `Size`, and `Text` properties to appropriate values. Any properties not set here will retain their default settings, which vary depending on the property. For example, the `BackColor` property will remain the standard Windows button color.

The next lines set the size of the form itself, and then the `this.Controls.Add()` method is called to actually add the `Button` control to the `Controls` collection of the form. This is required before the button will actually be displayed on the form. The `Controls` collection contains all of the controls on a form, and can be dynamically updated and edited at runtime in order to add and remove controls as needed. We will be examining how this can be accomplished later in the chapter.

If you run the application at this point, you will see a slightly more exciting window:

However, nothing happens when the button is clicked. To change this we will need to add an event handler to the code.

Events

Recall our discussion of delegates and events from Chapter 4. Windows Forms uses these concepts to allow the developer to write code that responds to user interface and system events. Every object in a Windows Forms application has a set of events that can be responded to. These are all optional – the .NET Framework will take care of all of the basic plumbing required to make windows open and close, buttons press and depress, menus to draw themselves, and so on. However, if you want to have some code that actually does something useful when these events occur, you need to add an event handler to the class and associate it with the object.

For Windows Forms to utilize your custom code, you must give it the location of the event handler method in your code. You do this by creating an appropriate delegate instance associated with a method in the custom Form class. Later in the chapter we will explore how to throw our own events when we expose events from a custom control.

To add some functionality behind that pesky button we need to add some code to our class. Add the following method to our Form class. This will act as the event handler for the button's Click event. Note that the event handler can be called anything. The control's event itself defines the parameters expected by the handler.

```
static void Main(string[] args)
{
    MyForm aForm = new MyForm();
    Application.Run(aForm);
}

private void ClickHandler(object sender, System.EventArgs e)
{
    MessageBox.Show("Clicked!","My Windows Form",MessageBoxButtons.OK);
}
```

Most Windows Forms event handlers have exactly this method signature. The first parameter contains the object that raised the event. In this case it will be the `Button` object from the `MyForm` class. The next parameter contains data about the event in a `System.EventArgs` parameter or derived class. The `System.EventArgs` class actually contains no data – it only acts as a base class. If an event must pass data to the client it must utilize a derived class. The `Button.Click` event does not need to pass any additional information, so it utilizes the base `System.EventArgs` class. There are a huge number of derived classes that each contain information specific to the event they are tied to. We will cover some of these classes, but it is not possible to cover all of them in this chapter.

Finally, add the following code to the `MyForm` constructor to attach our event handler to the event in the `MyForm` class.

```
public MyForm()
{
    //Set the properties for the Button
    BigButton = new Button();
    BigButton.Location = new System.Drawing.Point(50, 50);
    BigButton.Name = "BigButton";
    BigButton.Size = new System.Drawing.Size(100, 100);
    BigButton.Text = "Click Me!";
    BigButton.Click += new EventHandler(ClickHandler);

    //Set properties for the Form itself
    ClientSize = new System.Drawing.Size(200, 200);
    Controls.Add(BigButton);
    Text = "My Windows Form!";
}
```

This example shows how Windows Forms uses delegates to wrap an object's method before assigning it to the event we want to handle. The `System.EventHandler` delegate is used to reference the `ClickHandler()` method and it is associated with the button's `Click` event by simply adding it to the `Click` event handler chain. Note the syntax used – this means additional event handlers can be associated with a single event. They will be processed in the order they were added to the event handler.

Compile this application again, just like we did before, and run it. This time when the button is clicked you should see a small `MessageBox` giving you some feedback:

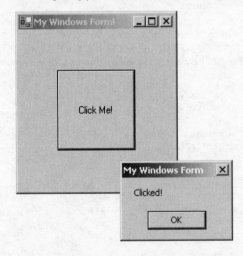

Now that we have seen how simple Windows Forms applications are structured in .NET, let's take a look at how Visual Studio .NET makes creating them even easier.

Windows Forms Using Visual Studio .NET

Like many things in .NET, using Visual Studio .NET makes writing Windows Forms applications much simpler. Visual Studio .NET reduces the amount of plumbing code developers must write themselves, allowing developers to concentrate on solving the business problem.

Let's jump right into this and see how to create a simple Windows Forms application using Visual Studio .NET. We are going to create a simple data entry screen for a fictitious personnel information management system. This type of screen would most likely be attached to some form of database used to store personnel data. We will wait to discuss data access issues until later in the book, but we will examine how to create the user-interface layer in this chapter. This project can be found in the online code in the `SimpleDataEntry` directory if you don't want to build the example yourself. Create a new C# Windows Application project in Visual Studio .NET titled `SimpleDataEntry`.

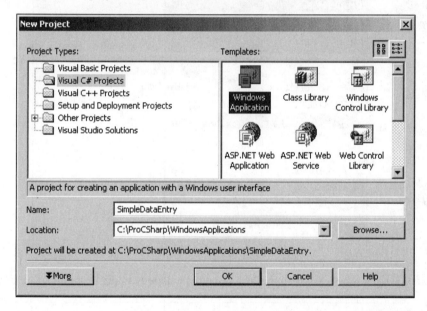

After the project is created, you will see a simple form in Visual Studio .NET in the design view. The design view is used to visually add controls to the form, much like the Visual Basic 6 IDE. Right-click on the `Form1.cs` file in the Solution Explorer and select **View Code**. This will display the code that generates the form displayed in the design view. Take a look through this code – it should look very familiar from our previous example. With the addition of some standards Visual Studio .NET complies with, such as the `InitializeComponent()` method, the code looks very much like our initial Windows Forms application. Note the use of `Application.Run` in the `Main` method, and the fact that this `Form` class derives from `System.Windows.Forms.Form`.

The `InitializeComponent()` method is used by Visual Studio .NET to build the designed Form at runtime. All of the controls and properties a developer sets during design time are set at run time in this method. As changes are made to the Form in design time Visual Studio .NET will update this method.

Switch back to design view in order to add some controls to this form to make it more useful and interesting. Note that when you select the form, the Properties window displays all of the available properties. We will use the Properties window extensively in setting the various properties of controls in our Windows Forms applications. It is a very important component of the Visual Studio .NET IDE, as using it is much easier than looking up the names of each property of every control in the .NET documentation. There are several buttons located at the top of this window. The first two change the way the properties are displayed. The first groups the displayed items into logical categories, such as all properties dealing with appearance, behavior, design, and so on. The second button sorts all of the properties in alphabetical order. The next two buttons toggle between displaying the properties or events. We will discuss events and how to add them to controls next. The last button opens this project's property pages:

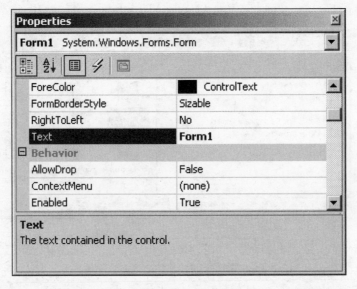

Set the following properties of the form by editing them directly in the Properties window.

Property	Value
Text	Data Entry Form
Size	300, 220
(Name)	frmMain
StartPosition	CenterScreen

These settings will create a 300 by 220 pixel window centered in the screen. The `Name` property is a very important property available on all controls. This value is used as the object name of the class's member variable, and is used to reference the control in code.

Now add two `Button` controls to the form. Set the properties of the two `Button` controls to the following:

Property	button1 Value	button2 Value
(Name)	btnSave	btnCancel
Location	125, 157	210, 157
Size	78, 25	78, 25
Text	Save	Cancel

Here we are changing the default names of the Buttons to a more standardized naming scheme, and positioning them to the location we want them on `Form1`, as well as sizing them to the correct size.

Return to the code view to examine what Visual Studio .NET has done during this time. You should see the addition of two new member variables in the `Form` class, much like we did previously when creating the class by hand. If you expand the region titled "Windows Form Designer generated code" you will see the `InitializeComponent()` method where all of the controls on the form are properly initialized and configured. This method is invoked in the form's constructor.

Next add three `TextBox` controls and three `Label` controls to the `Form`. Assign the following properties to each:

Property	TextBox1	TextBox2	TextBox3	Label1	Label2	Label3
(Name)	txt FName	txt LName	txtSSN	label1	label2	label3
Location	97, 25	97, 61	97, 99	20, 25	20, 62	20, 99
Size	115, 20	115, 20	115, 20	70, 18	70, 18	70, 18
Text	*(Blank)*	*(Blank)*	*(Blank)*	First Name:	Last Name:	SSN:

You should now have a Form that looks like a standard data entry screen for user information. An end-user could use this screen to enter their first and last name as well as their Social Security Number. At this point `Form1` should look like this:

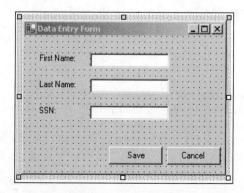

Events

Windows applications are event-driven, and without adding code that responds to events a Windows application cannot be very interactive for a user. Visual Studio .NET makes it very simple to add code to respond to the events generated by the user and the system.

The Properties window we examined earlier is the key to how Visual Studio .NET makes working with events simple. By selecting any Object, Control, MenuItem, Form, and so on, the Properties window is updated to reflect the complete list of events that can be handled from this object. To see this list, simply select the fourth button from the left (with a Potter-esque lightening bolt on it). This will display a list of the events for the currently selected object, and show any events that have code associated with them. The screenshot below shows the event list when a Form object is selected:

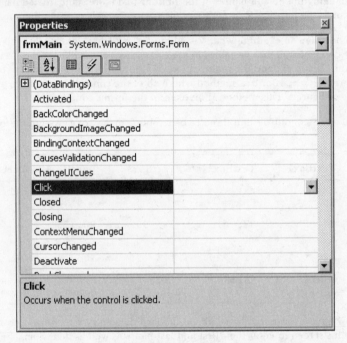

Adding an event can be accomplished in one of two ways. To add the default event for a control simply double-click on it in design view. For example, double-click on the btnSave button in the Designer; the appropriate event code will be included in the Form class, and you will be taken to the event handler for that button's Click event. This is because the Click event is the default event of the Button class. Note that if you look back through the code you will see similar code to what we did by hand previously, but VS .NET does all this work for you.

The other way to add event handlers to your code, and the only option if you are not adding the default event, is to utilize the Properties window. Select the object you wish to manipulate and then simply double-click on the desired event in the Properties window. Again, the correct plumbing code will be inserted into the Form class, and you will be taken to the event handler for the selected event.

Note that the **Properties** window displays the method that acts as the event handler for each event. If you select this field you will note that it acts as a combo box, and you can select from a list of available methods. This facility allows you to write a common event handler for multiple controls. Simply write an event handler and then associate it to each event in the **Properties** window. You might do this if you have many buttons that all do similar things and require similar processing, or textboxes that all require the same validation logic.

Let's add some code in the event handlers of our two Button controls. Add the `Click` event handler to the two existing `Buttons` (you can do this by double-clicking on a `Button` control or utilizing the **Properties** window). Add the following code to the file:

```csharp
private void btnSave_Click(object sender, System.EventArgs e)
{
    SaveFile();
}

private void btnCancel_Click(object sender, System.EventArgs e)
{
    Clear();
}


private void SaveFile()
{
    //Save the values to an XML file
    //Could save to data source, Message Queue, etc.
    System.Xml.XmlDocument aDOM = new System.Xml.XmlDocument();
    System.Xml.XmlAttribute aAttribute;

    aDOM.LoadXml("<UserData/>");

    //Add the First Name attribute to XML
    aAttribute = aDOM.CreateAttribute("FirstName");
    aAttribute.Value = txtFName.Text;
    aDOM.DocumentElement.Attributes.Append(aAttribute);

    //Add the Last Name attribute to XML
    aAttribute = aDOM.CreateAttribute("LastName");
    aAttribute.Value = txtLName.Text;
    aDOM.DocumentElement.Attributes.Append(aAttribute);

    //Add the SSN attribute to XML
    aAttribute = aDOM.CreateAttribute("SSN");
    aAttribute.Value = txtSSN.Text;
    aDOM.DocumentElement.Attributes.Append(aAttribute);

    //Save file to the file system
    aDOM.Save("UserData.xml");
}

private void Clear()
{
```

```
        //Erase all the text
        txtFName.Text = "";
        txtLName.Text = "";
        txtSSN.Text = "";
    }
```

This simple example saves the data entered by the user to an XML file on the file system. Most applications will utilize ADO.NET to save the information to a back-end data source, however, for this example we are simply going to export a small XML file.

We use private methods to perform the actual functionality so we can utilize the same functionality from menu options later on. Most of the code in the SaveFile() method involves writing out the XML file containing the user-supplied data. The Cancel button's Click event calls the Clear() method, which merely clears all the textbox controls to empty. Note that in a complete application this would probably also close this window and return the user to a main screen.

Note that as this book is going to press there is a bug in Visual Studio .NET that occasionally requires a developer to manually change the name of the Form class used in the Main() method. If you have an error when compiling navigate to the Main method and ensure it looks like the following code. Make sure the object creation code uses the frmMain class name. When a Form class' name is changed this line is not always updated.

```
static void Main()
{
    Application.Run(new frmMain());
}
```

If you run this application at this point you will have a small data entry window that is fully functional. You can enter data, save it to an XML file, and clear all the values. This is simple, but it demonstrates how to create applications using Visual Studio .NET.

Resizing Windows

One problem with our simple data entry window is that when it is resized the controls stay locked in place. This looks funny and unprofessional, and a high quality application should support the ability to resize and position a window in any fashion the user desires. Any developer who has written code to handle resizing and replacement of controls will appreciate how easy the .NET Framework and Windows Forms make this task. With a single property almost all of this work can be handled by the .NET Framework.

The Anchor property performs this magic, and it is a member of almost all classes in the System.Windows.Forms namespace because it is a property of the System.Windows.Forms.Control class. Recall that most controls derive from this class.

The Anchor property is set to a combination of one or more of the parent's edges. Setting one of these edges in the Anchor property will cause the control to maintain the relative position between its edge and its parent's as the form is resized and moved. For example, if a Button is placed on a form and the Anchor property is set to Left, Right then the Button will always maintain the same relative distance between the right edge of the form and the left edge of the form, without any custom code required. This property is very important to designing friendly user-interfaces, and should be experimented with extensively to understand how it works.

Visual Studio .NET includes a handy pop-up window to set this property to the correct combination. This pop-up window allows a developer to graphically select the sides to anchor the control to. This pop-up window can be found as part of the Properties window.

We are going to use the Anchor property to create a more effective and visually appealing user interface for our data entry screen.

Select the three TextBox controls in the Visual Studio .NET design environment. Change the Anchor property to Top, Left, Right using the pop-up window. This will maintain the distance between the top, left, and right of the parent's edges, thereby resizing the control correctly.

Select the two Button controls and change their Anchor property to Bottom, Right. This will maintain their position close to the bottom-right of the form. Run the application and resize the window to see how the controls now dynamically adjust themselves. Note that the window can be resized and the controls will resize and reposition themselves dynamically.

Again, this property is absolutely crucial in designing professional-level user-interfaces in .NET, and using it reduces the amount of work required by developers. This frees developers to concentrate on solving real business problems instead of low-level resizing issues.

Menus

Menus are used in almost every Windows application, and they provide an excellent way to present users with the options available to them in a non-invasive manner. There are two different types of menus. The most common is a main menu, which is located at the top of a window, and often includes items like File, Edit, and Help. Some applications also contain context-sensitive menus to allow users access to specialized information about specific topics or items. Context-sensitive menus are hidden until the user presses the right mouse button – then the menu is displayed at the cursor location.

Windows Forms provides full support for adding both types of menus to an application. The System.Windows.Forms.Menu class provides the base class for all menu classes in the system. The MainMenu class represents a main menu, and can be associated with a form, which causes it to display at the top of the form. This menu contains a collection of MenuItem objects, which each represent a separate menu option.

The ContextMenu class is available for adding context-sensitive menus to an application. This class also contains a collection of MenuItem objects, but the ContextMenu can appear in any location in a form, not just at the top of a window like the MainMenu class.

We are going to add a menu to our data entry application. Adding a menu to a Windows Forms application is as easy as adding any standard control like a Button or TextBox. Select the MainMenu control from the Toolbox and draw a box on the design surface. This will add the menu to the top of the form. Simply select the menu and type File to add the first menu item. Now when you click on File a new menu will display underneath, which can be added to just as we added the File menu item. You can continue to type in MenuItems, thereby creating the actual structure of the menu system graphically in the IDE:

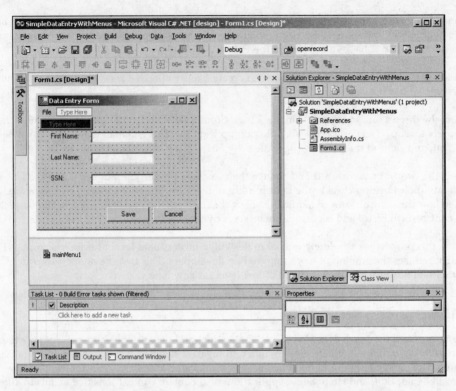

Use the menu system to create the following menu. Note that by entering a single dash character a separator line is created. This is very useful for partitioning off groups of choices in a menu. Another important thing to remember is that by prefacing a character with the ampersand (&) character that character becomes the accelerator key for this menu item. Therefore a user can select the menu choice by using only the keyboard, which is important for users who may not be able to or who prefer not to use a mouse.

Top Level Menu Item	Contained Menu Items
Text – &File Name – mnuFile	Text – &Save Name – mnuSave
	Text – &Cancel Name – mnuCancel
	Text – "-" (Single Dash)

Top Level Menu Item	Contained Menu Items
	Text – E&xit
	Name – mnuExit
Text – &Color Name – mnuColor	Text – &Gray Name – mnuGray RadioCheck – true Checked – true
	Text – G&reen Name – mnuGreen RadioCheck – true
	Text – &Blue Name – mnuBlue RadioCheck – true
	Text – &Red Name – mnuRed RadioCheck – true
	Text – &Purple Name – mnuPurple RadioCheck – true

Run the application and see that you now have a window with a working menu in place. However, nothing actually happens when a menu item is selected. To change this event handlers must be added behind the individual menu items. We will continue with this same example and add event handling so that users can actually use the menu.

The individual MenuItems are each controls like any other, and they can be selected in the design surface. Doing this exposes their available properties and events in the **Properties** window. Use the event list to add Click event handlers for the Save, Cancel, and Exit menu choices. Add the following code in the new event handlers.

```
private void mnuSave_Click(object sender, System.EventArgs e)
{
    SaveFile();
}

private void mnuCancel_Click(object sender, System.EventArgs e)
{
    Clear();
}
```

```
private void mnuExit_Click(object sender, System.EventArgs e)
{
    Close();
}
```

Note that the Save and Cancel menu options call the same methods that the Save and Cancel buttons call. This is a good design practice, because when code is updated and changed as project requirements change it is always a good idea to have to change things in one place only. Having duplicate code in the button event handlers and the menu event handlers is asking for trouble.

Dynamic Menus

Menus are often used to reflect the state of the application. As the user makes choices and changes in the application the menu must also reflect these changes. Menu items can be added, removed and modified to reflect the current application state. Again, MenuItems act like any other component and can be manipulated as such.

MenuItems can have a check placed next to them to illustrate the currently selected option. This is very useful to users as they can instantly appraise themselves of the state of the application. The Checked property is a Boolean flag that can be set to show or hide a check mark next to the menu item. Additionally, if the RadioCheck property is set to True the check will appear as a simple dot – this usually means the choices are mutually exclusive of each other. Therefore only a single menu item can be selected at a time with the RadioCheck property. It is important to remember that this is only a guideline; the .NET Framework does not enforce this rule.

We are going to add some code behind the color menu items to change the background color of the form. We will do this using a common event handler for all of the MenuItem objects.

In our application add the following method to the frmMain class.

```
private void mnuItems_Click(object sender, System.EventArgs e)
{

}
```

We are adding an event handler manually here instead of allowing the Visual Studio .NET IDE to do it for us. We need to do this so that we can associate this single method with each of the menu items' Click event handlers. This will enable us to control the state of the menu and the application from this single method.

Back in the design view of the IDE, click on the Gray menu item. In the Properties window switch to the event view and select the Click event. Click on the drop-down arrow to display a list of method names that can be associated to this event. This is how to attach custom methods to events. Select the mnuItems_Click() method from the list. Repeat this procedure with each of the color menu items. Each item's Click event should be associated with the same method.

Now that each object is associated with the same event handler method, add the following code to update the form's BackColor and the menu state as well.

```
private void mnuItems_Click(object sender, System.EventArgs e)
{
    MenuItem aObj;

    //Set the BackColor of the form based on the selected object
    if(sender == mnuGray)
        this.BackColor = System.Drawing.SystemColors.Control;
    else if(sender == mnuGreen)
        this.BackColor = Color.Green;
    else if(sender == mnuBlue)
        this.BackColor = Color.Blue;
    else if(sender == mnuRed)
        this.BackColor = Color.Red;
    else if(sender == mnuPurple)
        this.BackColor = Color.Purple;

    //Set all checkboxes to false
    mnuGray.Checked = false;
    mnuGreen.Checked = false;
    mnuBlue.Checked = false;
    mnuRed.Checked = false;
    mnuPurple.Checked = false;

    //Change the selected item to checked
    aObj = (MenuItem)sender;
    aObj.Checked = true;
}
```

This code uses the fact that the sender parameter to an event handler is the object that raised the event. This is required because this event handler is used by all of the MenuItem objects. Therefore, the first step is to determine the menu item selected by the user, and then change the form's BackColor to the respective color.

The next step is to set a check next to the appropriate menu item. We can do this by simply setting the sender's Checked property to true after casting it to a MenuItem object. However, before we do this we need to set all of the MenuItem objects to unchecked since we don't have anything telling us what menu item was checked previously. Remember that just by checking a menu item the previously checked item will not become unchecked – we must provide this custom logic ourselves, unfortunately.

Run the application and select different color options. You should see the background of the window change color, and the checkbox in the menu update to reflect the current color.

Context Menus

Most Windows applications allow the user to right-click and bring up a context-sensitive menu. This means the menu choices are based on the object, or context, the user has selected. Context menus allow the application to present additional information or choices to the user as they request additional information.

Context-sensitive menus can be added to Windows Forms applications very easily. We are going to add a context-sensitive menu to our data entry window that has the Save and Cancel choices available when the user right-clicks anywhere on the Form.

To add a context menu to a form simply add the ContextMenu control from the Toolbox to Form1. Once the ContextMenu object has been added to the form it will appear in the footer area below the form design surface. When this icon is selected, the main menu, if it exists, will disappear from the form and be replaced with the context menu itself. This can now be edited in the design surface by simply typing in the different menu items, just like editing the main menu. Although it appears that the menu will be displayed at the top of the form like the main menu, it will actually be invisible and not displayed until we assign it to the form.

After adding the ContextMenu to Form1, add the following menu items by typing in the following values:

Menu Item Name	Text Property Value
mnuSaveContext	Save
mnuCancelContext	Cancel

Again, each menu item is a separate MenuItem object and has properties that can be set in the **Properties** window. Instead of duplicating the existing methods, switch to the event view in the **Properties** window and select the Click event. In the drop-down list select mnuSave_Click for the mnuSaveContext MenuItem and mnuCancel_Click for the mnuCancelContext MenuItem. This will wire up these events to the same event handlers that are invoked when the main menu items are clicked.

Now we have a context menu, but we have yet to actually have it appear when we right click on the Form. To add a context menu to a Form the ContextMenu property of the Form object must be set to our ContextMenu object. Once this has been set the form will automatically display the ContextMenu when it receives a right-click from the user. It will display the ContextMenu at the location the user right-clicked without any additional code being required. Note that this property is dynamic and can be updated at run-time. It is also important to note that this property is actually a member of the Control class, meaning that almost all Windows Forms controls have this property, which can be set to a ContextMenu object. This allows you to hook a right-click context-sensitive menu into almost any control.

Set the ContextMenu property of Form1 to contextMenu1 using the **Properties** window. A combo box will display the current ContextMenu objects available to choose from on the form. Multiple ContextMenus can be added to a form, although only one can be assigned to a form at a time.

Run the application and right-click anywhere on the form to see the context menu displaying two options, Save and Cancel:

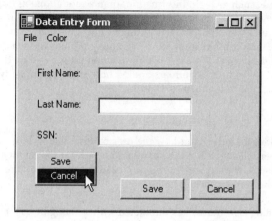

Note that when you right-click on one of the textboxes you will receive a very different context menu. This is because the `TextBox` control has a predefined context-sensitive menu, and when a custom context menu isn't set this default menu will be used. If you set the `contextMenu1` object to the `ContextMenu` of the `TextBox` controls you will see our custom context menu replace the standard `TextBox` menu.

Dialogs

Dialogs are a special type of Form used to capture user information or interact with the user in Windows applications. There exists a set of predefined dialog boxes for capturing common information such as file locations, colors, and printer settings. A custom application will often use custom dialog boxes to facilitate the collection of data from endusers.

Creating a dialog box is very similar to creating a standard Form. In fact, exactly the same process is used to add one to a Visual Studio .NET project. The key difference is the `FormBorderStyle` enumeration, which must be set to `FixedDialog`. This makes the window non-sizeable and causes it to look like a Windows dialog box. It is also the standard Windows practice to remove the `ControlBox`, `MinimizeBox`, and `MaximizeBox` from a dialog box, so these properties should be set to `false` in the Properties window.

Any of the standard Windows Forms controls can exist on a dialog box. The design surface in Visual Studio .NET is the same used to design standard `Forms`, and the same options are available to developers. Again, standard Windows practice is not to include a menu on a dialog box, but this is optional.

Modal vs. Modeless

When we want to display the dialog box itself, there are two choices: modal or modeless. These terms relate to how the dialog interacts with the rest of the application. A modal dialog blocks the current thread and requires the user to respond to the dialog box before continuing with the application. A modeless dialog box is more like a standard window that allows the user to switch the focus back and forth between it and other windows.

Deciding when to use the two types of activation depends entirely on the type of application being designed. If the application must get and process a key piece of data from the user before any other processing can continue, such as login information, then a modal dialog box is the only choice. Also, many users have come to expect dialog boxes to be modal and require processing before continuing with the application, much like the standard Windows **File Open** and **Save** dialogs. Therefore providing a modeless dialog box may confuse some users who don't understand why they can switch away from it. However, as every application and project is different you must evaluate the needs of your users before deciding the best course of action. By understanding how each type of activation is used in .NET hopefully you can make the best choice.

Dialog Box Results

It is often very important to understand how the user closes a dialog box. A perfect example is a **File Open** dialog. If the user selected a file the next obvious task for the application is to load that file, however if the user clicked the **Cancel** button or closed the dialog box the application should not load any file as this would be very confusing to the user!

The key to understanding how a user has interacted with a dialog box is the `DialogResult` enumeration. The calling code can interpret how the user closed the dialog box by reading this value. The possible values for this enumeration are below:

Value	Description
Abort	This value is usually returned when a user selects a button labeled **Abort**. In this case the user would like to cancel the current operation and not save the changes made.
Cancel	This value is usually returned when a user selects a button labeled **Cancel**, closes the dialog box by hitting the "x" button, or presses the *Esc* key. The user would like to cancel the changes made and return to the state before opening the dialog box.
Ignore	This value is usually returned when a user selects a button labeled **Ignore**. This could be used when the application warns the user of certain error conditions, but the user selected the **Ignore** command.
No	This value is usually returned when a user selects a button labeled **No**. This is common when the dialog box is used to ask the user a yes/no question, such as "Do you want to save the file?"
Yes	This value is usually returned when a user selects a button labeled **Yes**. This is the counterpoint to the No return result, and used in the same situations.
None	Nothing is returned from the dialog box. This means that the dialog box is still running.
OK	This value is usually returned when a user selects a button labeled **OK**. This is common for informational dialog boxes or warning messages where it is simply important for the user to acknowledge the receipt of the information.
Retry	This value is usually returned when a user selects a button labeled **Retry**. This is useful when an operation failed that might succeed if retried, such as a database connection or removable disk detection.

To gain access to this value you must use the Form's `DialogResult` property. This property is public, and can be accessed even after the user has closed a dialog box. When a user closes a dialog box the form is hidden from the user, not unloaded. This allows code to continue access any member variables and data the user may have set on the dialog box, and allows the developer to access the returned `DialogResult` value. In addition, if the application needs to display the dialog box again it is very quick to simply unhide the dialog instead of reloading it. As a result of this behavior, however, to actually destroy the dialog the `Form.Dispose()` method must be called when your code no longer requires the dialog resource.

Opening a Dialog

There are two ways to open a dialog box, one for modal display and one for modeless display. To show a dialog as a modal dialog, the following method is used:

```
DialogResult Form.ShowDialog()
```

This method is part of the `Form` class. The method itself accepts either no parameters or a single `Form` object as a parameter. This `Form` object represents the dialog box's owner, which is useful because all `Form` objects have a pointer back to their parent, allowing a dialog box to get or set data in its parent if passed the correct object in this parameter. If no parameter is passed the current window defaults to the parent.

Note that this method returns a `DialogResult` enumeration value. This method blocks execution, and no code after it will execute until the user closes the dialog box. When this occurs the `DialogResult` return code is returned and the application can continue processing. Code such as the following is very common when using modal dialog boxes:

```
if (aDialogObject.ShowDialog() == DialogResult.Yes)
{
    //User selected Yes
    //Use the properties of the aDialogObject to perform actions
}
else
{
    //User selected No - do not perform action
}
```

This displays the dialog box, which might ask the user if they want to save the current file. If the user selects Yes the code drops into the `if` block, and if they select No the `else` block is executed.

Displaying a modeless dialog box is much like displaying any `Form`, and the standard `Show()` method is used for this purpose. This method does not return a `DialogResult` value, nor does it block. The new dialog is simply displayed and the code continues to execute. Both the original window and the new dialog box are open and can be interacted with by the user. The `Form.DialogResult` property is the only way to retrieve the user's response. Often this form of dialog box will perform whatever action is required itself before closing.

Common Dialogs

Since Windows 95, developers have been able to utilize a set of dialogs for common functions, such as opening files, selecting fonts, and print previewing. Prior to Windows 95 each of these tasks was defined in custom dialog boxes for every application, thus creating a fragmented experience for the enduser. By standardizing these dialog resources and subsuming them into the operating system, any Windows application can take advantage of the functionality provided. These are the same dialogs all Windows users have used when opening a file or selecting a color, so people are automatically familiar with their use. This allows them to easily engage with the application and more quickly learn how to operate it.

The .NET Framework provides access to these underlying common dialogs through the following classes. Each of these classes represents a common dialog, and can be displayed as a dialog box. All of these classes exist in the `System.Windows.Forms` namespace:

Class	Description
ColorDialog	This allows a user to select a color from the available color palette as well as define and utilize custom defined colors
FontDialog	This dialog box displays all currently available fonts installed on the system and allows the user to choose one to use in the application
OpenFileDialog	Allows a user to open a file using the standard open file dialog box
SaveFileDialog	This allows a user to select a file, directory or network location to save the application's data to
PageSetupDialog	This dialog box allows the user to set page size, margins, and other printing features
PrintDialog	This dialog box allows the user to set common page formatting and printing features via the standard print properties dialog box
PrintPreviewDialog	This displays a document as it will appear on the currently-selected printer with the current page settings

All of these classes inherit from the `System.Windows.Forms.CommonDialog` class, except for the `PrintPreviewDialog` class. The `System.Windows.Forms.CommonDialog` class provides the basic functionality required to show a common dialog box. Each of the common dialog classes is displayed using the `ShowDialog()` method, but they each contain custom properties used to configure and query their custom functionality. We will examine each common dialog's main feature set and try to understand how each can be used in a business application.

ColorDialog

This dialog displays the common color picker dialog box. This is useful when a user is allowed to customize the background of a Form or control, and you want to provide them with an intuitive way to select their preferred color.

The main property that will be used with this class is the `Color` property. This contains the selected color when the dialog box returns control to the application. This property is a `Color` structure, which is useful because the .NET Framework expects this structure in other methods and properties that work with colors.

Another key feature of this dialog box is the ability for users to define and use a set of custom-defined colors. This feature is enabled by default, but can be disabled by setting the `AllowFullOpen` property to `false`.

Like all dialog boxes, the return value from `ShowDialog()` must be examined to understand how the user exited the dialog. Here is a snippet of code using this class:

```
ColorDialog aClrDialog = new ColorDialog();
aClrDialog.AllowFullOpen = false;
aClrDialog.Color = this.BackColor;
if (aClrDialog.ShowDialog() == DialogResult.OK)
{
    this.BackColor = aClrDialog.Color;
}

aClrDialog.Dispose();
```

This example creates a new `ColorDialog` object and sets the `AllowFullOpen` property to `false`. This disables the button that allows users to select custom colors. Note that then the `Color` property of the `ColorDialog` object is set to the current color of the `frmMain` Form object. This initializes the current color in the dialog and allows the user to see the existing color. The object that will be updated by the color selected in the dialog should initialize the dialog before displaying it to the user. Finally, the `ShowDialog()` method is called and the return value of that is checked. If the user selects **OK** then the code can now use the `Color` property of the `ColorDialog` class to access the color the user selected and update the `frmMain BackColor` property.

Note that you can use any common dialog box like this example, or you can add the component to a Form in Visual Studio .NET. The code will be very similar, but the dialog class will be available to all methods in the Form, and all of these properties can be set at design time in the **Properties** window. If you want to respond to an event raised by a common dialog box you must add the class to the Form in design view, as this allows you to write event handlers within the Form.

FontDialog

This class allows a user to select a font style, size, and color. This is very useful in applications that perform text processing, but again it could also be used to allow the user to customize their user experience by selecting the font type to display in the data input and reporting screens.

This class contains a large number of properties that can be set to configure the dialog box's functionality in exactly the right manner:

Property	Description
Color	This property gets or sets the currently selected font color. Note that the `ShowColor` property must be `true` for this to be a valid.
Font	This is the most important property of this dialog. It returns the `Font` structure representing the font selected by the user. This can then be applied to a `Control` or `Form` object to change the font.

Table continued on following page

Property	Description
MaxSize	Gets or sets the maximum point size a user can select in the dialog.
MinSize	Gets or sets the minimum point size a user can select in the dialog.
ShowApply	Boolean property that can be set to true to display an Apply button. If this is used, an event handler must be written to capture the Apply event when it occurs. This is because when the user selects Apply, the control still does not return to the application, but the event handler can then process the changed font in the application.
ShowColor	Boolean property that can be set to true to display a list of colors. This allows the user to select the color for the font as well as the style and size.
ShowEffects	Boolean property that can be set to true to allow the user to specify strikethrough, underline, and text color options.

An event handler can be written to respond to the Apply event when it is raised by the user pressing the Apply button. This event can be subscribed to and implemented exactly like the events we have seen before.

```
FontDialog aFontDialog = new FontDialog();
aFontDialog.ShowColor = true;
aFontDialog.ShowEffects = true;
aFontDialog.MinSize = 1;
aFontDialog.MaxSize = 35;
aFontDialog.Font = SomeControl.Font;
if (aFontDialog.ShowDialog() == DialogResult.OK)
{
    SomeControl.Font = aFontDialog.Font;
}

aFontDialog.Dispose ();
```

Note that we first initialize the FontDialog object with several settings, including the Font property of SomeControl, which represents the control object we are updating. It is good practice to initialize the Font property to the font of the control you will be replacing so the user sees the currently selected font in the dialog box, and is not confused. If the user selects OK in the FontDialog, then the Font property of SomeControl is updated to reflect the user-selected font.

OpenFileDialog

This class is very useful, as many applications require the user to navigate the file system in order to open and make use of data files. This dialog is the standard Windows dialog for opening files, and users should be very familiar with it.

This class contains a number of properties used to set the appearance and behavior of the dialog box itself. Both this class and the SaveFileDialog class inherit from the base class FileDialog that provides much of the basic functionality of working with files. For this reason many of the properties are shared. The key properties are in the following table.

Property	Description
CheckFileExists	Set this to `true` to cause the dialog box to display a warning if the user specifies a file name that does not exist. This way your code does not have to check for a valid path name. The default is `true`.
FileName	This important property is used to set and retrieve the file name selected in the file dialog box.
FileNames	If `Multiselect` is enabled, this property will return an array of file names the user selected.
Filter	This sets the file name filter string, which determines the choices that appear in the "Files of type" box in the dialog box.
FilterIndex	The index of the filter currently selected in the file dialog box.
InitialDirectory	The initial directory displayed by the file dialog box.
Multiselect	Boolean property that is set to indicate whether the dialog box allows multiple files to be selected. The default is `false`.
ReadOnlyChecked	Boolean property indicating if the read-only checkbox is selected. Default is `false`. This is used to indicate that the user wants to open the file as read-only.
RestoreDirectory	Boolean property indicating whether the dialog box restores the current directory before closing. The default is `false`.
ShowHelp	Boolean property indicating whether the **Help** button is displayed in the file dialog.
ShowReadOnly	Boolean property indicating whether the dialog contains a read-only check box. The default is `false`.
Title	The file dialog box title to display.

This class is used to get a file name or multiple file names from the user. Once this has been done the application can process the file or files indicated by the user. The `Filter` property is key to providing a useful interface to the user. By narrowing the displayed files to only those relevant to the current application the user is more likely to find the correct file.

The `Filter` property is a string that can contain multiple filtering options. Each filter contains a brief description, followed by a vertical bar (|) and the filter pattern as a DOS search string. The strings for different filtering options are also separated by a vertical bar. Therefore, a dialog that has two options: text files (`*.txt`) and all files (`*.*`) would utilize a filter string like this: `"Text files (*.txt)|*.txt|All files (*.*)|*.*"`

You can add multiple filter patterns to a single filter by separating the file types with semicolons. For example: `"Image Files(*.BMP;*.JPG;*.GIF)|*.BMP;*.JPG;*.GIF|All files (*.*)|*.*"`

The following code creates an `OpenFileDialog` object, configures some properties on it, and displays it to the user to allow them to select a file. The application can then use the `FileName` or `FileNames` property to process the referenced file or files. Note that these are mutually exclusive; if `Multiselect` has been set to `true` the code will use the `FileNames` property, otherwise it will use the `FileName` property.

```
OpenFileDialog aOpenFileDialog = new OpenFileDialog();
aOpenFileDialog.Filter = "Text Files (*.txt)|*.txt|Word Documents" +
                         "(*.doc)|*.doc|All Files (*.*)|*.*";
aOpenFileDialog.ShowReadOnly = true;
aOpenFileDialog.Multiselect = true;
aOpenFileDialog.Title = "Open files for custom application";
if (aOpenFileDialog.ShowDialog() == DialogResult.OK)
{
    //Do something useful with aOpenFileDialog.FileName
    //or aOpenFileDialog.FileNames
}

aOpenFileDialog.Dispose();
```

This dialog box has three options in the "Files of Type" combo box because of the `Filter` string. One option is **Text Files**, another **Word Documents**, and a third is **All Files**. It is a good practice to allow users to select an **All Files** option, as most Windows applications have this convention.

SaveFileDialog

This dialog box is very similar to the `OpenFileDialog`, and in fact they both derive from a common base class. The basic function of this dialog box is to allow a user to select a location to save data. Unlike the previous dialog box, this can be an entirely new file.

Many of the properties are the same as the `OpenFileDialog` class; however, the following properties are explicitly members of `OpenFileDialog` and do not exist in the `SaveFileDialog` class:

- ❑ `CheckFileExists`
- ❑ `Multiselect`
- ❑ `ReadOnlyChecked`
- ❑ `ShowReadOnly`

However, the following two properties are only valid as members of the `SaveFileDialog` class:

- ❑ `CreatePrompt` – boolean property that can be set to `true` to provide a prompt for the user if they specify a file name that does not exist. This reminds the user that a new file will be created, and can be a good check to ensure they did not simply misspell a file name. The default value is `false`.

- ❑ `OverwritePrompt` – boolean property than can be set to `true` to provide a warning prompt if the user selects a file name that already exists. This is a common warning to prevent a user from overwriting an important file accidentally. The default is `true`.

Note that the other properties operate in exactly the same manner, including the `Filter`, `Title`, and `FileName` properties. The following code shows how to use this class:

```
SaveFileDialog aSaveFileDialog = new SaveFileDialog();
aSaveFileDialog.Filter = "Text Files (*.txt)|*.txt|Word Documents" +
                         "(*.doc)|*.doc|All Files (*.*)|*.*";
aSaveFileDialog.CreatePrompt = true;
aSaveFileDialog.OverwritePrompt = true;
aSaveFileDialog.Title = "Save file for custom application";
if (aSaveFileDialog.ShowDialog() == DialogResult.OK)
{
    //Do something useful with aSaveFileDialog.FileName;
}

aSaveFileDialog.Dispose();
```

PageSetupDialog

This dialog box is used to set page orientation and margins.

The key property in this class is `Document`. This is required before the `ShowDialog()` method can be invoked, and an exception is raised if it has not been assigned a value. The `Document` property accepts a `PrintDocument` object, which is a member of the `System.Drawing.Printing` namespace. This object is crucial to the printing process in .NET, and represents the pages that an application will print out to. By setting the properties of this object and using GDI+ calls to draw to its surface, the application can print to the printer.

We are not going to cover printing in this chapter (for more on this you should refer to Chapter 19), although several of the common dialogs deal with configuring the printer and page settings. The examples in the following sections are not fully fleshed out, but demonstrate how the dialog boxes are invoked and utilized:

```
PageSetupDialog aPageSetup = new PageSetupDialog();
System.Drawing.Printing.PrintDocument aDoc = new
                                    System.Drawing.Printing.PrintDocument();
aPageSetup.Document = aDoc;
if (aPageSetup.ShowDialog() == DialogResult.OK)
{
    //Do something useful with aPageSetup.Document;
}

aPageSetup.Dispose();
```

This code creates a new `PageSetupDialog` object, associates a new `PrintDocument` object with it and displays the dialog.

PrintDialog

This dialog is used to select the printer, number of copies, and pages to print in a document. Like the previous dialog this object requires a valid `PrintDocument` object to be associated with the `Document` property before it can be displayed.

409

The object also contains the following key properties:

Property	Description
AllowPrintToFile	Boolean property that can be set to true to display the "Print to file" checkbox in the dialog. This is true by default.
AllowSelection	Boolean property that can be set to true to allow for printing only the current selection. This is false by default.
AllowSomePages	Boolean property that can be set to true to indicate the From Page and To Page option is enabled. This is false by default.
Document	The PrintDocument property representing the current printing surface.
PrintToFile	Boolean property that can be set to true to indicate the "Print to file" check box is checked. When the dialog returns this can be checked to see if the user wishes the application to print the document to a file. The default is false.
ShowHelp	Boolean property that can be set to true to indicate the Help button should be displayed. The default is false.

Like the other common dialog classes, these properties are configured before calling ShowDialog() in order to display the correct dialog box for the user. Once the ShowDialog() call has returned these can be queried to understand what the user wants. The code for using this class is very similar to the previous code:

```
PrintDialog aPrintDialog = new PrintDialog();
System.Drawing.Printing.PrintDocument aDoc = new
                                  System.Drawing.Printing.PrintDocument();
aPrintDialog.Document = aDoc;
aPrintDialog.AllowSomePages = true;
aPrintDialog.AllowSelection = true;
if (aPrintDialog.ShowDialog() == DialogResult.OK)
{
    //Do something useful with aPrintDialog.Document;
}

aPrintDialog.Dispose();
```

PrintPreviewDialog

This class provides a very quick way to introduce print previewing capabilities into an application without much custom code. This class accepts a PrintDocument object in its Document property, and the same code that handles printing to a printer will render the document to this dialog box.

This dialog box supports scaling, zooming, pagination, and a host of other options. The many properties are too numerous to list here, but the basic principle is much like the other classes we have examined.

Visual Inheritance

In previous chapters (and Appendix A) we have seen that the object-oriented nature of C# facilitates inheritance, which encourages code reuse, and thus allows for less code to be written. Recall that inheritance allows a class to utilize all of the properties and methods of its parent class (or interfaces) and gives it the ability to extend these methods and properties as desired.

The .NET Framework takes the concept of inheritance and allows a developer to use it to develop Windows Forms applications. A `Form` object can inherit from another `Form` object, thus gaining access to all the contained `Buttons`, `TextBoxes`, and `Menus`, as well as non-display-related methods and properties. This is a very powerful feature in .NET that when used properly dramatically reduces the amount of code required for creating similar screens and windows. This concept is called **visual inheritance**.

Recall that a `Form` always inherits from `System.Windows.Forms`. This means it gains access to all of the data members and methods of the base `Form` class. Implementing visual inheritance simply requires a developer to instead derive the `Form` object from a custom `Form` class instead of `System.Windows.Forms`. This causes all of the controls and properties in the custom Form class to pass over into the newly created `Form` class.

However, there are some important things to bear in mind. The access level of the various controls must be understood, just like the access level of standard inheritance. Recall that a private data member is inaccessible to any object outside of the original object, including derived objects. Therefore, unless a control is marked as protected or public the derived class cannot reference the control in any code, nor can it override any of the control's behavior. An important consideration is that private controls are still displayed in derived classes.

Using visual inheritance can be very useful when one must create a large number of screens that must have a similar design and/or do very similar functions. One common example is a data entry screen, much like the one we created earlier. If our application did not just need to input personnel records, but also automobile information, using visual inheritance to define a common style might be a good choice. Obviously we would want a similar looking screen, but some of the controls would change. Let's modify our previous example to utilize this technique.

Create a new C# Windows Application in Visual Studio .NET and name it **VisualInheritance**. This project can be found in the code download in the `VisualInheritance` folder.

Change the following properties of the default `Form1` object. We are going to create a simple menu window that will provide the user with the ability to enter either personnel records or automobile records.

- ❑ `FormBorderStyle` – `FixedDialog`
- ❑ `MaximizeBox` – `False`
- ❑ `MinimizeBox` – `False`
- ❑ `Size` – `200, 200`
- ❑ `StartPosition` – `CenterScreen`
- ❑ `Text` – `Main Menu`

Place two Button controls on the Form. Position them in the center of the window, label them **Person** and **Automobile**, and name them `btnPerson` and `btnAuto` respectively. We will add event handlers to these later to open up each derived Form.

We are now going to add our base `Form` class. This `Form` will never be displayed directly, but we will use its visual style in all of the derived forms.

Add a new Form to the application by selecting **Project | Add Windows Form**. Leave the default name and select **OK** in the Visual Studio .NET dialog box. Modify the following properties of the Form to generate a unique visual style.

- ❑   Name – `frmBase`
- ❑   BackColor – `White`
- ❑   FormBorderStyle – `FixedDialog`
- ❑   MaximizeBox – `False`
- ❑   MinimizeBox – `False`
- ❑   Size – `250, 250`
- ❑   StartPosition – `CenterScreen`
- ❑   Text – `Base Form`

This creates a white dialog box. Now add two `Buttons` to the lower right corner of the form. These will act as our **Save** and **Cancel** buttons. By adding them to the base class they will be visible on all derived forms, thus ensuring a common user-interface. Position the two `Buttons` in the lower right corner and set the following properties:

Button	Name	Anchor	Location	Modifiers	Size	Text
Button1	btnSave	Bottom, Right	159, 151	Protected	75, 23	Save
Button2	btnCancel	Bottom, Right	159, 185	Protected	75, 23	Cancel

The most important property to note is the `Modifiers` property. This sets the isolation level of the `Button` class within the form. This can be set to any valid C# isolation level: `public`, `protected`, `private`, or `internal`. After modifying the property in the **Properties** window examine the code to see that the declarations for the two `Button` objects have been modified to the protected isolation level. This will be very important in allowing derived `Form` objects access to the `Buttons`.

Recall that protected members can only be accessed by derived classes; they are inaccessible to any external code. Derived Forms cannot access controls declared with the default `private` isolation level. Interestingly the buttons will still be displayed on derived Forms, but no event handlers can be added, as the objects cannot be accessed from the derived class. Any event handlers placed within the parent Form would fire, so one could write code that remains in the parent Form but executes when a derived Form's buttons are clicked. This can be a very powerful design technique, but for our example we will write event handlers in each of the derived Forms. We are using visual inheritance to enforce a standard user-interface look and feel.

Finally we are ready to add a derived Form. However, Visual Studio .NET requires that base Form classes are compiled first, so we must first build the project at least once. Once this has completed, select **Project | Add Inherited Form**. Leave the default name of the class file by clicking **Open** in the resulting dialog box. Next select the correct base Form class to use. A dialog box displays the currently available Forms in the project, and allows you to derive the new Form class from any of them. Select the frmBase class and click **OK**.

A new Form will be generated, but it will look exactly like the original frmBase class. It has the same white BackColor and the two buttons: **Save** and **Cancel**. Change the Text property of the Form to Personnel Information, and add four Label controls and four TextBox controls. Change the Text property of the Labels to "First Name:," "Last Name:", "DOB:" and "SSN:" Change the Name property of the TextBox controls to txtFName, txtLName, txtDOB, and txtSSN, and blank out their Text properties. The new Form should look something like the following screen:

Repeat the process of adding a new **Inherited Form** to the project. Again derive it from the frmBase class. This time change the Text property of the Form to Automobile Information and the Name property to frmAuto and add four Labels to the Form titled: "Manufacturer:", "Model:", "Year:", and "Color:" Again add four TextBox controls positioned next to the Labels, and change the Name property to txtManufact, txtModel, txtYear, txtColor for each respective TextBox.

We are now ready to add event handlers to our derived Forms. Remember that in a functional application the **Save** button would likely utilize ADO.NET or a back-end business object to save the data to a data store. In this sample the data is simply persisted to a small XML file.

Add the following Click event handlers for the Personnel Information Form for both the **Save** and **Cancel** buttons. Even though these buttons have been inherited from a base class, they can still be manipulated and events added like any other controls. This is because the base class defines these objects' isolation level as protected – if they were private the derived classes would not be able to access the Button objects at all.

```csharp
private void btnSave_Click(object sender, System.EventArgs e)
{
    //Save the values to an XML file
    //Could save to data source, Message Queue, etc.
    System.Xml.XmlDocument aDOM = new System.Xml.XmlDocument();
    System.Xml.XmlAttribute aAttribute;

    aDOM.LoadXml("<PersonnelData/>");

    //Add the First Name attribute to XML
    aAttribute = aDOM.CreateAttribute("FirstName");
    aAttribute.Value = txtFName.Text;
    aDOM.DocumentElement.Attributes.Append(aAttribute);
    //Add the Last Name attribute to XML
    aAttribute = aDOM.CreateAttribute("LastName");
    aAttribute.Value = txtLName.Text;
    aDOM.DocumentElement.Attributes.Append(aAttribute);
    //Add the DOB attribute to XML
    aAttribute = aDOM.CreateAttribute("DOB");
    aAttribute.Value = txtDOB.Text;
    aDOM.DocumentElement.Attributes.Append(aAttribute);
    //Add the SSN attribute to XML
    aAttribute = aDOM.CreateAttribute("SSN");
    aAttribute.Value = txtSSN.Text;
    aDOM.DocumentElement.Attributes.Append(aAttribute);

    //Save file to the file system
    aDOM.Save("PersonnelData.xml");
}

private void btnCancel_Click(object sender, System.EventArgs e)
{
    txtLName.Text = "";
    txtFName.Text = "";
    txtDOB.Text = "";
    txtSSN.Text = "";
}
```

This code should look familiar to you, because it is very similar to the XML persistence code from the previous example. The basic idea is to serialize the contents of the TextBoxes into an XML file and save it to the file system. The Cancel button clears the TextBox controls.

The code for the Automobile Information Form is extremely similar except for the different TextBox names being used and a different XML file being generated. As it does not demonstrate anything new we will not show it, although the complete code for this project can be found in the code download in the VisualInheritance directory.

Finally, add the following event handlers for the `Form1` `Button`'s `Click` events. These open the appropriate derived `Form`.

```
private void btnPerson_Click (object sender, System.EventArgs e)
{
    Form3 aForm = new Form3();
    aForm.ShowDialog();
}

private void btnAuto_Click(object sender, System.EventArgs e)
{
    Form4 aForm = new Form4();
    aForm.ShowDialog();
}
```

The application is again fairly simple, with a small dialog box providing a basic menu for the user to enter either personnel records or automobile information. The user can select either choice and a window will be displayed that displays a common visual theme and interface. Obviously a more complex standardized userinterface can be developed than white backgrounds and two buttons, but this is a start.

Imagine an entire `Form` class library, with a base `Form` object providing the overall look and feel of the derived windows, with successive layers of classes defining specialized versions of Forms. Base classes could exist for data entry screens, About boxes, or any other required window in an application. This could be extended to the entire enterprise, enabling a common look and feel for the entire range of applications built by your organization. Ultimately this will lead to more positive user acceptance and greater user productivity, as users become accustomed to the organization's common application user interface.

Windows Controls

Windows Forms applications are largely composed of the many different available controls. These controls can be as simple as the `Button` and `TextBox` controls we have used so far, or they can be elaborate and complex like `Charting` and `TreeView` controls. The .NET Framework ships with many controls ready to incorporate into Windows Forms applications today, and there are already hundreds of third-party controls ready to be used in custom .NET application development. With so many, it is impossible to cover how to use each in the space of this chapter. Therefore, we will examine how all controls operate and interact at a higher level.

Controls in Windows Forms include those a developer would expect to find in a class library designed for graphical user interfaces including:

❑ Labels

❑ Buttons

❑ Checkboxes

❑ Menus

❑ Radio buttons

- ❑ Combo boxes
- ❑ Listboxes
- ❑ Textboxes
- ❑ Tabcontrols
- ❑ Toolbars
- ❑ Tree views

As we have seen, Visual Studio .NET can add these controls to a Form for you. We have already done this several times in the examples in this chapter. The steps that occur when a control is added to a Form are the following:

1. A variable of the type of control required is declared as a private object in the `Form` class

2. In the `InitializeComponent()` method the control object is created and assigned to the private variable

3. The properties of the control, such as the `Location`, `Size`, and the `Color` are all set within `InitializeComponent()` as well

4. The control is added to the collection of controls on the form

5. Finally, event handlers are implemented as the developer adds them through the IDE

Note that this is exactly the same process we went through when we manually added a button to our first Windows Forms application without Visual Studio .NET. The IDE simply makes this process easier – it does not perform any magic.

Most controls inherit from `System.Windows.Forms.Control`. This base class contains the basic methods and properties used by any control that provides a user interface to the user. This control manages the basic functionality required to capture keyboard and mouse input, as well defining its size and location on its parent.

Dynamic Controls

Since all displayable controls inherit from the `Control` class, we can take advantage of polymorphism when working with collections of controls. All controls contain a `Controls` property that acts as a collection of the contained controls. This allows you to write code that loops through the `Controls` collection and manipulates or queries each individual control using the base `Control` class's properties and methods.

This `Controls` property is also dynamic, and can be used to customize the appearance of a user-interface at run time by adding and removing controls to or from a `Form` or `Control`. Like all collections, the `Controls` collection exposes methods that allow for the addition and removal of objects, which cause visible controls to be added to and removed from the user-interface. This can be a very powerful technique for designing customizable user interfaces and elegant designs that display only the required information. In fact, if you examine the `InitializeComponent()` method created by Visual Studio .NET you will see this is exactly how the code itself adds controls to Forms initially, and it is also how we added our `Button` control to our first Windows Forms application at the beginning of the chapter. Let's create an application that takes advantage of this ability to customize the user interface at run time.

A common application requires different screens for each of the various objects that can be manipulated. One example is an inventory management system that must manage computers, software, and furniture. Each of these objects has unique properties; however each may also share some common characteristics. Depending on the interface design, it might be very useful to customize the user interface based on the type of object currently being manipulated in the system and display only those fields that are relevant to the current item being worked with. This dynamic customization of the user interface can be accomplished by manipulating the `Controls` property at runtime.

Open Visual Studio .NET and create a new C# Windows Application titled **DynamicUI**. This project can be found in the online code download in the `DynamicUI` directory.

Add three `Button` controls somewhere on the left of the Form. The exact placement is not important. Give the buttons the `Text` properties of `Computer`, `Software`, and `Furniture`. The Form should look approximately like the following screenshot:

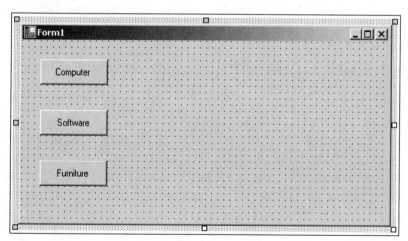

When a user selects the appropriate button the user interface will dynamically customize itself for the input of that type of object. An enterprise application would likely consume these settings from a back-end data source or configuration file; however, for brevity we will simply embed the logic of the display directly within the application. This is not a best practice, and if this example were expanded the first step should be to create an external method of representing the user interface.

There are a number of properties we will be setting for every control we add to the Form. These include the `Size` and `Location` properties, as all visible controls must be located somewhere. We will often also set the `Text` and `Name` properties as well. When adding a large number of controls to a Form this process can quickly lead to redundant and repetitive code, so to avoid this we will create a utility method to set these properties at once. We can then call this method for every control we add to the Form. Add the following private method to the `Form1` class.

```csharp
private void AddControl(Control aControl, Point Location, Size Size,
                        String strText, int TabIndex, string strName)
{
    aControl.Location = Location;
    aControl.Size = Size;
    aControl.Text = strText;
    aControl.TabIndex = TabIndex;
    aControl.Name = strName;
    this.Controls.Add(aControl);
}
```

This method accepts a `Control` object and sets various common properties on it. Note that when we invoke this method we will pass in a derived class, like a `Label` or `TextBox`. This is possible through polymorphism, because the base `Control` class defines the properties accessed by this method.

We are now ready to add event handlers for our `Button`s. Add a `Click` event handler for each of the three buttons and add the following code. The names of the event handlers may be different depending on the names used for the `Button`s themselves:

```csharp
private void btnComp_Click(object sender, System.EventArgs e)
{
    Controls.Clear();
    InitializeComponent();

    AddControl(new Label(),new Point(125,24),new Size(45,20),"ID:",0,"");
    AddControl(new TextBox(),new Point(174,21),new Size(125, 20),
            "",0,"txtID");
    AddControl(new Label(),new Point(125,54),new Size(45,20),"OS:",0,"");
    AddControl(new TextBox(),new Point(174,50),new Size(125,20),
            "",1,"txtOS");
    AddControl(new Label(),new Point(125,84),new Size(45,20),
            "Speed:",0,"");
    AddControl(new TextBox(),new Point(174,78),new Size(125,20),
            "",2,"txtSpeed");
}

private void btnSoft_Click(object sender, System.EventArgs e)
{
    Controls.Clear();
    InitializeComponent();

    AddControl(new Label(),new Point(125,24),new Size(45,20),
            "ID:",0,"");
    AddControl(new TextBox(),new Point(174,21),new Size(125, 20),
            "",0,"txtID");
```

```
        AddControl(new Label(),new Point(125,54),new Size(45,20),
                "Vendor:",0,"");
        AddControl(new TextBox(),new Point(174,50),new Size(125, 20),
                "",1,"txtVendor");
        AddControl(new Label(),new Point(125,84),new Size(45,20),
                "Name:",0,"");
        AddControl(new TextBox(),new Point(174,78),new Size(125, 20),
                "",2,"txtName");
    }

    private void btnFurn_Click(object sender, System.EventArgs e)
    {
        Controls.Clear();
        InitializeComponent();

        AddControl(new Label(),new Point(125,24),new Size(45,20),"ID:",0,"");
        AddControl(new TextBox(),new Point(174,21),new Size(125, 20),
                "",0,"txtID");
        AddControl(new Label(),new Point(125,54),new Size(45,20),
                "Color:",0,"");
        AddControl(new TextBox(),new Point(174,50),new Size(125, 20),
                "",1,"txtColor");
        AddControl(new Label(),new Point(125,84),new Size(45,20),
                "Type:",0,"");
        ComboBox aCombo = new ComboBox();
        aCombo.Items.AddRange(new Object[] {"Desk","Chair","Whiteboard"});
        AddControl(aCombo,new Point(174,78),new Size(125, 20),"",2,"");
    }
```

Run the application and select the different options available through the buttons. You will see the user interface customize itself based on the type of input expected from the user. The different data points possible for each type of object are displayed dynamically.

The code is relatively straightforward. Each method first clears the `Controls` collection before calling `InitializeComponent()`. Recall that Visual Studio .NET always generates this method; it is responsible for creating the user interface as designed at design time. Therefore it can be used as a quick and easy way to get back to the initial design state of the Form. In a more fully-featured application separate menu and input Forms would be used to customize the user interface, so clearing all of the controls on the input Form would be an acceptable option, since all of the controls would be generated dynamically every time anyway.

Once the code has cleared the Form and added the three buttons back, it adds the dynamic controls to the Form using the custom `AddControl()` method extensively. Note that for the majority of calls we simply create a new `TextBox` or `Label` object when calling the `AddControl()` method, as there is no need to retain a reference to the control object itself unless we need to set additional properties. However, in the `btnFurn_Click()` event handler we create a `ComboBox` control and add some string values to it before adding it to the Form. Therefore the control must be created externally to the method call and the reference used to add the values to the list. We will also use this technique next when we add event handlers to the dynamic controls.

Dynamic Event Handlers

The rich event model exposed by Windows Forms can still be utilized when implementing a dynamic user interface generated at runtime. All of the many events are still available to be hooked into, although these obviously cannot be set at design time in the Properties window. However, recall that our first example attached an event handler to a Button control using only code, proving it is possible to hook into events of dynamically generated controls.

To demonstrate how to add some event-processing code to our simple data entry application, let's add some validation logic to some of the TextBoxes. Specifically we are going to allow only numerical characters to be entered into the ID fields on the Form, which all of the object types contain.

First we need to add the event handler method itself. This is a very simply KeyPress event handler. Add the following method to the Form1 class.

```
private void ID_Validate(object sender,
                         System.Windows.Forms.KeyPressEventArgs e)
{
    //Check to make sure input is Numeric or Backspace Key
    if (!Char.IsNumber(e.KeyChar) && e.KeyChar != (char)8)
        e.Handled = true;
}
```

This event handler simply checks to see if the key that has been pressed is numeric or is the *BackSpace* key. If it is not then the event tells Windows that the application has processed the event, and Windows does not need to continue processing. This has the result of stopping the character from ever being entered on the TextBox control, thus filtering out any non-numeric data. Allowing users to use the *BackSpace* key is always a good idea, even if you are filtering out data or performing validation at the keystroke level – after all, any user can make a mistake.

Now we need to modify the three button Click event handlers to set this event handler. In order to do this the ID TextBox control must be created separately from the AddControl() method invocation, because the event handler must be attached to the KeyPress event. Therefore we will create a new TextBox object, set the event handler to the ID_Validate() method, and finally pass this object into the AddControl() method. The first Click event method is below with the changes highlighted.

```
private void btnComp_Click(object sender, System.EventArgs e)
{
    TextBox aTextBox;
    Controls.Clear();
    InitializeComponent();

    AddControl(new Label(),new Point(125,24),new Size(45,20),"ID:",0,"");
    aTextBox = new TextBox();
    aTextBox.KeyPress += new KeyPressEventHandler(ID_Validate);
    AddControl(aTextBox,new Point(174,21),new Size(125, 20),"",0,"txtID");
    AddControl(new Label(),new Point(125,54),new Size(45,20),"OS:",0,"");
    AddControl(new TextBox(),new Point(174,50),new Size(125, 20),"",1,"txtOS");
    AddControl(new Label(),new Point(125,84),new Size(45,20),"Speed:",0,"");
    AddControl(new TextBox(),new Point(174,78),new Size(125, 20),"",2,"txtSpeed");
}
```

The changes are identical in the other two event handlers, so you should be able to modify these methods on your own to reproduce the numeric validation logic in the other two methods. Again, the complete code is available in the online code download.

Run the application again, and now you should be unable to enter non-numerical characters into the ID TextBox control. This demonstrates how to dynamically generate and modify controls on a Form, as well as attach and respond to events within these dynamic controls.

Custom Controls

Custom controls are a very important aspect of Windows Forms development. These types of controls were called ActiveX controls or UserControls in Visual Basic. The basic concept is to allow a developer to generate new functionality and/or aggregate existing controls into a single common control that can be easily reused across the application or in multiple applications throughout an organization.

Custom controls allow developers to wrap functionality and presentation into a single class package that can be reused easily throughout an application. The user interface, events, properties, and methods can all be set and configured by the developer. This group of functionality can then be easily inserted into the project where it is needed. It is also possible to reuse custom controls across the enterprise as well, and entire control libraries can be developed for use by all developers within an organization.

In addition, if a custom control is very useful and exposes functionality that other developers external to a single organization will likely want, it is possible to sell the control commercially. An entire industry exists that provides custom controls for application developers. These companies have concentrated their time and resources into developing their controls' functionality extensively; therefore it is almost always cheaper to purchase one of these controls than attempt to duplicate the behavior manually. This is the classic build versus buy argument, and most businesses today agree that purchasing functionality off-the-shelf saves a significant amount of time and money.

To summarize, a custom control is a custom class that combines business logic functionality and/or multiple controls and custom display logic in a single package. This package can then be reused multiple times in a Form, just like a standard Button or Label control. An example of this in a business application might be a TextBox that contains special e-mail validation logic. E-mails are entered in many places throughout the application, so encapsulating the code into a single entity would cut down on the amount of code to write, debug, and maintain. A custom e-mail TextBox control could be created and used in place of the standard TextBox in all locations that require e-mail text entry.

The UserControl Class

Most custom controls should inherit from the System.Windows.Forms.UserControl class. This puts the appropriate plumbing in place that is required to host Controls, manage scrolling, and provide a design surface for the developer. This class acts much like the base Form class in that it provides a basic implementation and custom derived classes provide the business functionality. A control that does not need this plumbing code because the developer is going to write all of it themselves or it is not going to display a user-interface can simply inherit from System.Windows.Control directly.

In fact, building a custom control is very similar to building a Form. A User Control contains a client area in which Windows Forms controls can be situated and manipulated. Event handlers can be attached to these controls to respond to user interaction, and the overall look of the control is completely customizable. The difference is that one must always think about how another developer will utilize this custom control in a hosting application. The custom control acts as a simplification layer for the third-party developer who does not need to understand how the control works. The control will never exist independently; it will always execute within a hosting application.

Constituent Controls

The controls that make up the user interface of the custom control are called constituent controls. These are controls that are owned by the `UserControl` object. These are very useful for building reusable user interface components that can be manipulated and positioned as a group. For example, suppose every window in an application contains the same group of `RadioButton` controls. Instead of copying and pasting these controls into every Form, an alternative would be to create a custom control that contained this common `RadioButton` control group. A developer could then add this custom control to any Form, position it to the correct location, and the constituent `RadioButton` controls in the User Control would display and update properly without any interaction by the hosting application.

However, constituent controls are not accessible from outside the `UserControl` object, as they are declared as private variables by default. Although a developer can manually change this to expose certain constituent controls as public, this is generally regarded as violating encapsulation. The correct method of exposing required information is to define public properties, methods, and/or events in the custom `UserControl` class and map these requests to the constituent controls' various properties, methods and events. This allows the User Control to be editable within the Visual Studio .NET IDE, and provides a consistent design environment for the client developer.

Custom controls can be added to a Windows Forms project like any other class or component object. However, one can also create a standalone Windows Control Library application. This outputs an assembly DLL containing the custom control classes defined in the project. This assembly can then be included in other projects across the organization and enterprise. As custom controls are developed and refined this library can be expanded and shared across all applications, providing easy access to common functionality and user interface elements for developers.

Creating Constituent Controls

Let's create a custom control to demonstrate some of these concepts. We are going to create a custom control to encapsulate a common menu of `RadioButtons` featured across many Forms in an application. The menu exists on every window to allow the user to provide feedback to the application as to their likes and dislikes. In our fictional application, this data could be aggregated over time to develop user profiles and prediction data.

Create a new C# Windows Control Library application titled ControlLib. We will be creating several custom controls in this section, and we will package them all together in this single control library. The code for this project can be found in the code download in the `ControlLib` folder.

When the project is created, a default empty User Control is displayed in the design view. Much like a standard Form object, we can drag controls from the Toolbox onto this design surface and set their properties using the Properties window.

Add five `RadioButton` controls to the User Control design surface. You will have to resize the User Control to accommodate the `RadioButton` controls. Change the `Name` property of the User Control itself to `UserMenu`, and set the following properties of the `RadioButtons`.

Property	radioButton1	radioButton2	radioButton3	radioButton4	radioButton5
Name	rbtnAmazing	rbtnGood	rbtnOK	rbtnBad	rbtnTerrible
Text	Amazing	Good	OK	Bad	Terrible

At this point you should have a User Control that looks close to the following picture:

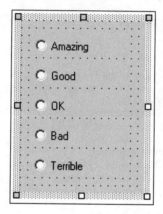

Recall that the radio buttons themselves cannot be accessed from the hosting application, as they are private members of the `UserMenu` class. To allow a hosting application to use this control we need to provide an easy way to query and update the selected option. Remember, part of the advantage of custom controls is the abstraction away from client developers; a developer using this control does not need to worry about looping through the radio buttons to get the selected one. Instead they should just be able to access a property and have the details abstracted away.

We are going to create a public property to represent the currently selected option. This property will be a custom enumeration, which will provide a friendly interface for the client developer that is more intuitive than an alternative like integer codes. Using an enumeration will also allow the Visual Studio .NET IDE to display the available options in the Properties window as a drop-down list. Add the following code to the `UserControl1.cs` file.

```
namespace ControlLib
{
    public enum SelectedOptionEnum
    {
        Amazing,
        Good,
        OK,
        Bad,
        Terrible,
        None
    }
```

We will now declare a public property with both set and get commands. When this property is set it will update the correct RadioButton to Checked. When the value is queried, the enumeration value representing the selected RadioButton will be returned. Add the following code to the UserMenu class:

```
public class UserMenu : System.Windows.Forms.UserControl
{
    private System.Windows.Forms.RadioButton rbtnAmazing;
    private System.Windows.Forms.RadioButton rbtnGood;
    private System.Windows.Forms.RadioButton rbtnOK;
    private System.Windows.Forms.RadioButton rbtnBad;
    private System.Windows.Forms.RadioButton rbtnTerrible;

    public SelectedOptionEnum SelectedOption
    {
        get
        {
            if(rbtnAmazing.Checked)
                return SelectedOptionEnum.Amazing;
            else if(rbtnGood.Checked)
                return SelectedOptionEnum.Good;
            else if(rbtnOK.Checked)
                return SelectedOptionEnum.OK;
            else if(rbtnBad.Checked)
                return SelectedOptionEnum.Bad;
            else if(rbtnTerrible.Checked)
                return SelectedOptionEnum.Terrible;
            else
                return SelectedOptionEnum.None;
        }
        set
        {
            if (value == SelectedOptionEnum.Amazing)
                rbtnAmazing.Checked = true;
            else if (value == SelectedOptionEnum.Good)
                rbtnGood.Checked = true;
            else if (value == SelectedOptionEnum.OK)
                rbtnOK.Checked = true;
            else if (value == SelectedOptionEnum.Bad)
                rbtnBad.Checked = true;
            else if (value == SelectedOptionEnum.Terrible)
                rbtnTerrible.Checked = true;
            else
            {
                rbtnAmazing.Checked = false;
                rbtnGood.Checked = false;
                rbtnOK.Checked = false;
                rbtnBad.Checked = false;
                rbtnTerrible.Checked = false;
            }
        }
    }
}
```

This code is long, but it is very simple to understand. On a get request it returns the correct enumeration value based on the currently selected RadioButton. On a set command it updates the correct RadioButton control. A client utilizing this control can simply use this property and never worry about the process required to actually get this value. Let's add a hosting application to understand how this control can be consumed.

Add a new project to the solution by selecting File | New | Project. An entirely new project must be added because a Windows Control Library project cannot execute; the controls are meant to be included within a hosting application. Select a new C# Windows Application, and ensure the Add to Solution option is checked on the bottom of the dialog box. Title the project HostApp.

Once this is completed we have our familiar looking Form ready for controls. Open the Toolbox and scroll to the very bottom to see the custom UserMenu control we created. Note that this is available in the Toolbox because Visual Studio .NET automatically adds a reference to existing projects when a new project is added. Incorporating a separate control library into the Toolbox would require the developer to add a reference to the location of the assembly file, just like the process for importing standard class libraries or components. Note that the ControlLib project must be compiled before a UserMenu control can be added to the Form.

Add a UserMenu control to the Form in the same way standard controls are added – drag and drop it onto the Form surface. Note that you can resize and position the UserMenu object, and the Properties window will display the many properties available to UserControl objects. Of special interest is our custom SelectedOption property. Notice that this property is displayed in the Properties window and a drop-down list is displayed containing the values from the SelectedOptionEnum enumeration. Even more exciting is the fact that as different options are selected in the Properties window the control itself updates the radio buttons to reflect the changes. Design-time support for developers is a very important aspect of control development.

Add a Button control to the Form, the position and size being irrelevant. Add a Click event handler with the following code.

```
private void button1_Click(object sender, System.EventArgs e)
{
    MessageBox.Show(userMenu1.SelectedOption.ToString());
}
```

This is a very simple way to test the control, but it is effective. The SelectedOption property is queried and displayed in a MessageBox. In a real application the value could be queried and persisted to a back-end database when the user clicked a Submit or Save button. As this code shows, using our custom UserMenu allows a developer to do this in a single line of code.

To actually run the application one last thing must be done. By default Visual Studio .NET has enabled the Windows Control Library project as the default project because it was the first project loaded, but it cannot run without a Form. Therefore, right-click on the HostApp project in the Solution Explorer and select the Set as StartUp project option. Compile and run the solution to see the custom control in action. The different menu options can be selected, and when the button is clicked the currently selected option is displayed in a MessageBox.

Extending Controls

Custom controls do not always need to be created by combining multiple constituent controls. Extending and customizing the functionality of a single Windows Forms control can be very useful because it can hide the customization behind a standard control for the user. The e-mail validation TextBox is a good example. Instead of rewriting a TextBox control, it makes much more sense to use the existing TextBox and simply add the additional functionality required. The e-mail validation TextBox can then be used in applications as a replacement for a standard TextBox and the user will never know the difference. This can be done in .NET using inheritance, and can be a very effective way of creating a custom control.

To extend an existing control the declaration for a User Control must be changed to inherit from the existing control instead of System.Windows.Forms.UserControl. Because of the power of inheritance, you now have access to all of the base class's properties, methods, and events.

Let's create a simple example to illustrate this properly. We are going to create an ActiveButton control that will provide visual feedback to the user when they position the mouse pointer over the button. The BackColor of the button will change gradually to reflect the user's position, and when the user's mouse pointer leaves the button its BackColor will gradually fade back to normal. This provides a very professional-looking user interface that gives users good subtle feedback as to their current selection.

Add a new User Control to our existing Windows Control Library project. Title the new file ActiveButton.cs. Note that even though we will be changing what class the control is derived from we still want to add a UserControl object in the project because then we get the correct Toolbox support in Visual Studio .NET. It is also important to name the file correctly, because this is used as the name of the control in the Toolbox, and cannot be updated once the base class is changed from UserControl.

Switch to the code view and change the declaration of the class to no longer derive from UserControl but instead from Button.

```
public class ActiveButton : System.Windows.Forms.Button
```

Switch back to design view and note the User Control design surface has changed. The same options are not available when a control does not inherit from UserControl. A derived control will assume the same look as the base class, and Visual Studio .NET does not allow for the option of building a custom user interface for the control.

The design surface can still accept non-visual controls from the Toolbox (in fact it can accept visual controls as well, but these will simply become private data members). One such non-visible control that is very useful is the Timer control. This can be found under the **Components** tab in the Toolbox. We will be using a Timer control to control the gradual changing of the background color. Add a Timer control to the design surface, and ensure that its **Enabled** property is set to true.

Add two private variables to record the state of the transformation in the control:

```
public class ActiveButton : System.Windows.Forms.Button
{
    private System.Timers.Timer timer1;
    private bool m_bActive;
    private int m_nSteps;
```

The Boolean variable m_bActive indicates the current state of the control. If this is true the user's mouse pointer is currently over the control and the background color should be increasing. If this is false it should be gradually decrementing the background to the original color. The m_nSteps variable represents the current step in the "animation" loop. This variable is used to stop the animation when it has reached the upper and lower limits.

These values need to be set in the constructor.

```
public ActiveButton ()
{
    // This call is required by the Windows.Forms Form Designer.
    InitializeComponent();

    m_nSteps = 0;
    m_bActive = false;
}
```

Finally we are ready to add some more interesting code. Back in the design view, select the background, causing the User Control itself to be active in the **Properties** window. Switch to the event view to see the list of possible events. Note that this is the list of exposed Button events, since this User Control now inherits from a Button control. We are going to hook into the MouseEnter and MouseLeave events to trigger the animation loops. Add an event handler for each of these events and add the following code:

```
private void ActiveButton_MouseEnter(object sender, System.EventArgs e)
{
    m_bActive = true;
    timer1.Interval = 50;
}

private void ActiveButton_MouseLeave(object sender, System.EventArgs e)
{
    m_bActive = false;
    timer1.Interval = 150;
}
```

This code merely sets the m_bActive flag, as well as telling the Timer control how often to fire off its Elapsed event. This event is fired every Interval milliseconds. When the user enters the area of the button the Timer's Interval property is set to a small value, causing the button to change color relatively quickly. When the user leaves the control this value is reduced, so the button will slowly lose its color. This is just a style issue, and can be easily played with to get your preferred look and feel.

Lastly we are going to add the Elapsed event of the Timer control, where the magic happens. Using the **Properties** window, add an event handler for the timer1's Elapsed event. Add the following code to the event; this is where the actual updates to the BackColor occur.

```
private void timer1_Elapsed(object sender, System.Timers.ElapsedEventArgs e)
{
    if(m_bActive && m_nSteps != 10)
    {
        try
        {
```

```
                BackColor = Color.FromArgb(BackColor.R - 10,
                                           BackColor.G - 10,
                                           BackColor.B - 10);
    }
    catch(Exception)
    {
    }
    finally
    {
        m_nSteps++;
    }
}
else if (!m_bActive && m_nSteps > 0)
{
    try
    {
        BackColor = Color.FromArgb(BackColor.R + 10,
                                   BackColor.G + 10,
                                   BackColor.B + 10);
    }
    catch(Exception)
    {
    }
    finally
    {
        m_nSteps--;
    }
}
}
}
```

This method checks to see if the control is currently under the user's mouse pointer and if it has not already executed the correct number of steps. The m_bActive flag indicates if the control is currently under the user's mouse pointer, and the m_nSteps variable represents the current state of the 'animation'. Based on these two factors the BackColor property is either incremented or decremented. The code to manipulate the BackColor property modifies the color by incrementing each constituent component of the color a set amount. This could raise an exception if one of the RGB values is modified above 255 or below 0. This exception is caught and ignored, and to ensure the m_nSteps variable is always incremented or decremented it is modified within a finally block.

This ActiveButton control is now done, and can be incorporated into other Windows applications just like any standard Windows Forms Button. The exact same properties, methods and events are exposed for this control as a Button control. The only difference is the visual interface exposed to the user, but a developer working on a hosting application that utilizes this custom control never need worry about this animation code. It is encapsulated away behind the implementation of the ActiveButton.

To see this button in action, add several ActiveButton controls to the Form in the HostApp project. It helps to add a number of them, as it is easier to see the effect of the gradual selection and de-selection. Run the application and move the mouse pointer over the ActiveButton controls. By providing good visual clues to the user an application interface is easier to use and more friendly to the end user. By extending existing Windows Forms controls a component designer can work to create custom business functionality while relying on the existing infrastructure for much of the plumbing code required. It is also convenient for client developers to be able to utilize the custom control exactly like the original control type in their applications.

Exposing Events

Events are another very important aspect of control development, and providing useful events to developers allows them to react to actions occurring within the custom control and respond in their own applications.

When designing custom controls several options are available for exposing events. One or more events of the constituent controls located within the User Control itself can be exposed. Recall that the constituent controls are declared private by default, and as such are not accessible by the client developer. For example, suppose a developer creates a custom control containing a ListBox control and a Button control, and the ListBox control is pre-populated with States and State codes. This custom control can be used to allow a user to choose a State from the list and click the button when they have made the correct selection. The client developer needs to be able to write code that is processed when the Button within the User Control is clicked, just like a developer would write code behind a standard Button's click event.

To perform this magic the User Control must raise the event to the hosting application. This is done by first adding an event handler behind the constituent control event that will be monitored. This is done in the User Control. For example, using the States User Control example, adding a Click event handler to the Button would be the first step.

From within this event handler an event must be raised to the hosting application. All Windows Forms controls contain a method for every exposed event that can be called to raise the event. This method is called "On" plus the name of the event. For example, to raise the Click event from the User Control the following code could be used.

```
private void button1_Click(object sender, System.EventArgs e)
{
    OnClick(e);
}
```

Note that the event handler required a System.EventArgs object. This can be created new and filled with custom information, which we will see next, or it can simply use the EventArgs object supplied by the Button's Click event.

Custom Events

Note that this process only works for events that are available to the UserControl class. We are not creating any new events; we are merely specifying when these events should be raised to a client application. Something that is often required in a User Control is to expose a custom event that can be processed by the hosting application.

The process for creating a custom event in a User Control uses the same technique that is used across the entire .NET Framework for exposing and consuming events – delegates.

A User Control must contain or utilize the following things in order to expose a custom event:

❑ A class to hold event state data. This must derive from System.EventArgs. This is how data is passed from an event to the client. This must be defined outside the UserControl class.

❑ A delegate for the event, again defined outside of the UserControl class.

❑ The User Control itself must contain the event declaration using the delegate type and a method that raises the event.

Exposing Custom Events

We will be creating a login User Control that contains UserID and Password `TextBox` controls and a Submit `Button` control. Instead of forcing client developers to manage the security of the application, this control will encapsulate the functionality of the entire user authentication process, and merely expose events the hosting application can respond to. The following events will be exposed:

❑ `GoodLogin` – the user has successfully entered their UserID and Password and it has been accepted.

❑ `FailedThreeTimes` – the user has failed to login three times. This event allows the hosting application to take some form of administrative action if required.

❑ `Cancel` – the user selected the Cancel button, indicating they do not want to log in to the application.

Add a new User Control to our existing Windows Control Library project. Add two `Label` controls, two `TextBox` controls, and two `Button` controls to the User Control design surface. The exact positioning is not important, but the following properties should be set.

Property	Label1	Label2	TextBox1	TextBox2
(Name)	n/a	n/a	txtUserID	txtPass
Text	UserID:	Password:	(Blank)	(Blank)
PasswordChar	n/a	n/a	n/a	*
TabIndex	n/a	n/a	0	1

Property	Button1	Button2	UserControl
(Name)	btnLogin	btnCancel	ActiveLogin
Text	Login	Cancel	n/a
PasswordChar	n/a	n/a	n/a
TabIndex	2	3	n/a

Note that when you change the name of a User Control you must close the design surface and reopen before the name is reflected in the Toolbox.

When you are finished you should have a User Control that looks something like the following screen. Again the exact positioning is not important, only that all of the individual controls exist and are named correctly.

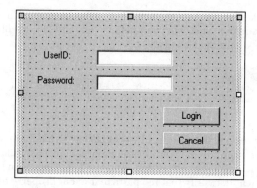

We are now ready to add the custom events to the class. Switch to the code view and add the class declaration below to the top of the file. This needs to be outside the User Control class definition, but within the namespace declaration. This is the event state data class and it represents the event data that will be passed to hosting applications when an event is raised. It contains the information a client application may require, such as the UserID and Password. Note that this class must derive from the System.EventArgs class.

```
namespace ControlLib
{
    public class LoginEventArgs : System.EventArgs
    {
        public LoginEventArgs(string sUserID, string sPassword, bool bValid)
        {
            UserID = sUserID;
            Password = sPassword;
            Valid = bValid;
        }

        public string UserID;
        public string Password;
        public bool Valid;
    }
}
```

The delegate objects must be added as well. Hosting applications will use these to hook into the custom events of this User Control. Add the following three declarations directly below the LoginEventArgs definition but still outside the class definition for the User Control. The LoginEventArgs class will be used for the GoodLogin and FailedThreeTimes event handlers; but the base EventArgs class will be used for the Cancel event. This is because the Cancel event does not need to pass any data back to the hosting application. Events not required to pass any additional information should use the base EventArgs class.

```
    //Delegate declarations
    public delegate void GoodLoginEventHandler(object sender, LoginEventArgs e);
    public delegate void FailedThreeTimesEventHandler(object sender,
                                                       LoginEventArgs e);
    public delegate void CancelEventHandler(object sender, EventArgs e);
```

Now add the event declarations within the `ActiveLogin` class itself. These will act as the bridge between the user code and our class. They are defined as public events of each of the delegate types. Add the following code within the class itself.

```
//Event declarations
public event GoodLoginEventHandler GoodLogin;
public event FailedThreeTimesEventHandler FailedThreeTimes;
public event CancelEventHandler Cancel;
```

The code that will raise the events must be added next. The .NET Framework coding convention advises us to name these methods "On" plus the name of the event. While it is possible to name them anything, it is wise to stick with the convention. Add the following three methods to the `ActiveLogin` class. These methods each first verify that the particular event property has at least one client attached before raising the event.

```
protected virtual void OnGoodLogin(LoginEventArgs e)
{
    if (GoodLogin != null)
    {
        //Invokes the delegates.
        GoodLogin(this, e);
    }
}

protected virtual void OnFailedThreeTimes(LoginEventArgs e)
{
    if (FailedThreeTimes != null)
    {
        //Invokes the delegates.
        FailedThreeTimes(this, e);
    }
}

protected virtual void OnCancel(EventArgs e)
{
    if (Cancel != null)
    {
        //Invokes the delegates.
        Cancel(this, e);
    }
}
```

We have now successfully exposed three events from this `UserControl` class, and a hosting application could utilize them. However these events will never be raised because the `ActiveLogin` control never actually raises them – it only contains code that allows them to be raised. The actual business functionality needs to be added so the control can react and raise the events at the appropriate times.

First add a private state variable that will hold the number of times a user has attempted to login:

```
//Event declarations
public event GoodLoginEventHandler GoodLogin;
public event FailedThreeTimesEventHandler FailedThreeTimes;
public event CancelEventHandler Cancel;

private int m_nLoginTimes;
```

Finally, to actually raise the different events add event handlers for each of the constituent Button controls. These will call the methods we just created that actually raise the event. In the Click event handlers for each Button add the following code.

```
private void btnLogin_Click(object sender, System.EventArgs e)
{
    //Increment this attempt
    m_nLoginTimes++;

    //Check userid and password
    if(txtUserID.Text == "Wrox" && txtPass.Text == "Wrox")
    {
        //Successful Login
        OnGoodLogin(new LoginEventArgs(txtUserID.Text,txtPass.Text,true));
        m_nLoginTimes = 0;
    }
    else if(m_nLoginTimes >= 3)
    {
        //Failed Three Times
        OnFailedThreeTimes(new
                    LoginEventArgs(txtUserID.Text,txtPass.Text,false));
        m_nLoginTimes = 0;
    }
    else
        MessageBox.Show("Invalid Login","Login",MessageBoxButtons.OK);

}

private void btnCancel_Click(object sender, System.EventArgs e)
{
    //Raise the cancel event
    OnCancel(new EventArgs());
}
```

This code causes the events to be raised and called in the hosting application. In a real application the login process would query a database, Active Directory, or LDAP data store, but for this example we simply compare the login values with simple static values. If the user successfully logs into the application the GoodLogin event is raised by calling the OnGoodLogin() method. Note that an object of type LoginEventArgs is created and passed into this method.

Note that the control does not do any branching after the user logs in successfully. It is up to the hosting application to respond to this event and navigate the user to the main screen of the application, open the requested resource, or perform whatever action the user required authentication for. This control simply encapsulates the login logic, and once that process is completed the control is passed back to the hosting application.

If the login failed, a MessageBox is displayed to the user for the first three times. On the third failure the FailedThreeTimes event is raised with an instantiated LoginEventArgs object. This allows the hosting application to perform any logging or lockout procedures when a user fails to login three times.

In the Cancel button's Click event the Cancel event is raised. This event uses only the basic EventArgs object to pass data since there is no state information passed to the hosting application on this event.

Consuming Custom Events

We are now ready to use this control from a hosting application. Navigate back to the Form in the HostApp project and scroll to the bottom of the Toolbox. If the ActiveLogin control is not displayed correctly you need to rebuild the Control Library project, as well as close the design surfaces of the open User Controls. This forces the changes to commit to the Toolbox.

Add an ActiveLogin control to the Form. Position it in a convenient location and switch to the Event view in the Properties window. Note that our three custom events, Cancel, FailedThreeTimes, and GoodLogin are all listed as events. Add event handlers to these three events in the same manner we have added events to any other control. Add the following code to handle the events raised by our custom control.

```
private void activeLogin1_GoodLogin(object sender, ControlLib.LoginEventArgs e)
{
    MessageBox.Show("Welcome " + e.UserID);
}

private void activeLogin1_FailedThreeTimes(object sender,
                                ControlLib.LoginEventArgs e)
{
    MessageBox.Show("Failed to login three times.");
}

private void activeLogin1_Cancel(object sender, System.EventArgs e)
{
    MessageBox.Show("Cancel");
}
```

The event handlers are very simple, but they illustrate how to consume custom events. Note that there is basically no difference between consuming custom events and standard Windows Forms events. In the GoodLogin event and the FailedThreeTimes event we have the custom LoginEventArgs object passed in as a parameter to the handler method. This can be queried for the various properties set by the User Control, such as UserID and Password.

Run the application and note that the client code is now responding to the business logic events exposed by the custom User Control. The hosting application can now delegate the responsibility of login processing to this control and receive notifications (through events) when significant state changes occur, such as a successful login. This is the essence of utilizing custom controls – allow the client application to concentrate on business functionality and hide the functional minutiae of tasks behind the interface to the custom control.

Summary

We have covered a lot of content in this chapter. Building Windows applications is a huge subject, and an entire book could easily be written on this subject alone. Hopefully this chapter has provided an understanding of the basic tenets used in building Windows Forms applications so you understand how and where to dive into more detail in any specific topic.

Although .NET makes building ASP.NET applications very simple, and provides a strong foundation for exposing and consuming Web Services, thick client applications will always be required. Understanding the power and versatility available with Windows Forms applications will be essential in creating enterprise .NET solutions. Rich clients can provide a dynamic, flexible, and interactive experience for the user that a web solution never can. With the incredibly rich functionality exposed by Windows Forms and the many Windows Forms controls, Windows application development may experience a renaissance as application developers return to the rich client.

In this chapter we have covered the following topics:

❑ How to build Windows Forms applications using the .NET Framework

❑ Using Visual Studio .NET to quickly build Windows Forms applications

❑ Adding menu support to an application, including dynamic and context-sensitive menus

❑ Utilizing custom and common dialog resources in a project

❑ How to use visual inheritance to build powerful and dynamic Windows Forms applications

❑ How to use Windows Forms controls in an application

❑ How to create and extend existing controls for specialized functionality

❑ Exposing and consuming custom events from a custom control

8

Assemblies

In this chapter we'll be discussing **assemblies**. An assembly is the .NET term for a deployment and configuration unit. We'll discuss exactly what they are, how they can be used, and why they're such a useful feature. In particular, we'll cover:

❑ The innovations offered by assemblies over previous technologies

❑ How to create and view assemblies

❑ What the Common Language Specification means, and how cross-language support is made possible

❑ How to create resource-only assemblies and use them for localization

❑ How to share assemblies – for this we have to create unique names and look at versioning

Let's begin this chapter with an overview of assemblies:

What are Assemblies?

Before the .NET Platform was introduced we had to deal with the predecessors of assemblies: normal DLLs exporting global functions, and COM DLLs exporting COM classes. Microsoft itself introduced the phrase "DLL-Hell" to describe traditional problems with DLLs – problems that we know all too well.

Often applications break because a newly installed application overwrites a DLL that was also used by another application. Sometimes it happens that the installation replaces a new DLL with an old one, because the installation program doesn't correctly check the versions, or the versions are not correctly set. More often, an old DLL is replaced by a new version. Normally, this shouldn't be a problem, but the reality is different. Although the new DLL should be backwardly compatible with the old version, sometimes it isn't. This situation arises far too often.

Windows 2000 introduced the **side-by-side** feature that allows the installation of DLLs in the application's directory. With side-by-side, a different version of an already-installed, shared DLL may be installed to the directory of the application. The LoadLibrary() Win32 API call was rewritten so that it first checks for a .local file in the application directory. If it's found, the API first checks if a DLL was in the same directory of the application, before the other mechanisms are used to find a shared DLL. This also modifies the fixed path that is in the Registry for COM DLLs. Side-by-side is an afterthought, and doesn't solve all of the issues, and also introduces some new problems with COM DLLs. Another feature of Windows 2000 that deals with DLL-Hell is file protection: system-DLLs are protected from being overwritten by unauthorized parties. All of these Windows 2000 features treat the symptoms and not the causes.

The versioning problems of DLLs exist because it's not clear which version of a specific DLL each application needs. Dependencies are not tracked or enforced with the traditional DLL architecture. **COM DLLs** seem to solve a lot of the DLL problems because of a better separation of the implementation and the interface. The interface is a contract between the client and the component, which, according to COM rules, may never be changed, and thus can't break. However, even with COM, changes of implementations can break existing applications.

Side-by-side also supports COM DLLs. If you're ever tried side-by-side with COM DLLs, you have seen it's just a hack. New problems arise when using side-by-side COM DLLs. Also, if we're not uninstalling, rather we're installing the new DLL over the old one, what happens when two versions of the same component use different threading configurations? The configuration information is taken from the last installed version. This problem exists because the configuration of a COM component is not stored in the component DLL itself, but in the Registry instead.

The Answer to DLL Hell

The .NET platform's answer to DLL Hell and all of its problems is **assemblies**. Assemblies are self-describing installation units, consisting of one or more files. One assembly could be a single DLL or EXE that includes metadata, or it can be made of different files, for example, resource files, metadata, DLLs, and an EXE. Installation of an assembly can be as simple as copying all of its files. An xcopy installation can be done. Another big feature of assemblies is that they can be **private** or **shared**. With COM this differentiation doesn't exist, since practically all COM components are shared. If you search for a COM component in the Registry or using OleView, you have to walk through hundreds and hundreds of components. Only a small number of these components were ever meant to be used from more than one application, but every component must have a global unique identifier (GUID).

There's a big difference between private and shared assemblies. Many developers will be happy with just private assemblies. No special management, registration, versioning, and so on need to be done with private assemblies. The only application that could have version problems with private assemblies is your own application. The private components you use within your application are installed at the same time as the application itself. Local application directories are used for the assemblies of the components, so you shouldn't have any versioning problem. No other application will ever overwrite your private assemblies. Of course it is still a good idea to use version numbers for private assemblies, too. This helps a lot with code changes, but this is not a requirement of .NET.

With private assemblies you can still have versioning problems during development time. Let's see an example: if a component you use in your application references version 1 of assembly X, and you use version 2 of assembly X in your application, which version of the assembly is copied to your application directory?

The answer to this depends on what assembly you referenced first – this versioning problem must be solved during development time. On the installed system, a hot fix can be easily applied to an application by simply replacing a private assembly with a new version. The only application that could have problems with the new version is the one where this fix is applied, as no other applications can be influenced.

When using shared assemblies, several applications can use this assembly and have a dependency on it. With shared assemblies, many rules must be fulfilled. A shared assembly must have a special version number, a unique name, and usually it's installed in the **global assembly cache**.

Features of Assemblies

The features of assemblies can be summarized as follows:

❑ Assemblies are **self-describing.** It's no longer necessary to pay attention to Registry keys for apartments, to get the type library from some other place, and so on. Assemblies include metadata that describes the assembly. The metadata includes the types exported from the assembly and a manifest; we'll look at exactly what a manifest is in the next section.

❑ **Version dependencies** are recorded inside an assembly manifest. By storing the version of any referenced assemblies in the manifest of the assembly, we are able to know exactly the version number of the referenced assembly that was used during development. The version of the referenced assembly that will be used can be configured by the developer and the system administrator. In a later section of this chapter, we will look at which version policies are available, and how they work.

❑ Assemblies can be loaded **side-by-side**. Using Windows 2000 we already have a side-by-side feature where different versions of the same DLL can be used on a system. .NET extends this functionality of Windows 2000, allowing different versions of the same assembly to be used inside a single process! Maybe you're asking where this could be useful? If assembly A references version 1 of the shared assembly Shared, and assembly B uses version 2 of the shared assembly Shared, and you are using both assembly A and B, guess which versions of the shared assembly Shared are needed in your application – you need both, and with .NET both versions are loaded and used.

❑ Application isolation is assured using **application domains**. With application domains a number of applications can run independently inside a single process. Faults in one application cannot directly affect other applications inside the same process.

❑ Installation can be as easy as copying the files that belong to an assembly. An xcopy can be enough. This feature is named **zero-impact installation**.

Why the Microsoft Windows Installer (MSI) is Still Important

I'm often asked why the Microsoft Windows Installer is still needed when xcopy is enough to install .NET applications. The simple answer is that we often want more than the simple copying of files when installing Windows applications.

Usually, you want to access the application from the **Start** menu, install it in a subdirectory of `Program Files`, let the user choose some options, show copyright screens, and so on. The Windows Installer supports a lot of additional features that can't be solved using assemblies. Applications can use their own Registry settings, **group policies** for easier management where specific users can access specific features, **advertisement** for installing parts of the application later, when requested by the user, and the repair feature to easily do repairs when files have become corrupted.

Application Domains and Assemblies

Before .NET, processes were used as isolation boundaries, with every process having its private virtual memory; an application running in one process cannot write to the memory of another application and thereby crash the other application. The process is used as an isolation and security boundary between applications. With the .NET architecture we have a new boundary for applications: **application domains**. With managed IL code the runtime can ensure that access to the memory of another application inside a single process can't happen. Multiple applications can run in a single process within multiple application domains:

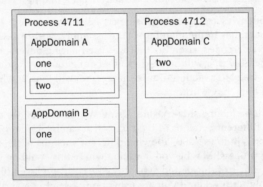

An assembly is loaded into an application domain. In the above figure you see process `4711` with two application domains. In application domain `A`, the objects `one` and `two` are instantiated, `one` probably in assembly `One`, and `two` in assembly `Two`. The second application domain in process `4711` has an instance `one`. To minimize memory consumption, the code of assemblies is only loaded once into an application domain. Instance and static members are not shared between application domains. It's not possible to directly access objects within another application domain; a proxy is needed instead. So in the figure above, the object `one` in application domain `B` cannot directly access the objects `one` or `two` in application domain `A` without a proxy. You can read more about proxies and communication across application domains in Chapter 21.

The `AppDomain` class is used to create and terminate application domains, load and unload assemblies and types, and to enumerate assemblies, and threads in a domain. Let's code a small example to see application domains in action.

Firstly, I'm creating a C# Console Application `AssemblyA`. I'm just doing a `Console.WriteLine()` in the `Main()` method so that we can see when this method gets called. In addition, I've added a constructor with two `int` values as arguments, so that we can also see how to create instances with the `AppDomain` class. The `AssemblyA.exe` assembly will be loaded from the second application that we're creating:

```
namespace Wrox.ProCSharp.Assemblies.AppDomains
{
    class Class1
    {
        public Class1(int val1, int val2)
        {
            Console.WriteLine("Constructor with the values {0}, {1}" +
                          " in domain {2} called", val1, val2,
                          AppDomain.CurrentDomain.FriendlyName);
        }
        [STAThread]
        static void Main(string[] args)
        {
            Console.WriteLine("Main in domain {0} called",
                          AppDomain.CurrentDomain.FriendlyName);
        }
    }
}
```

The second project created is again a C# Console Application: DomainTest. First, I'm displaying the name of the current domain. With the CreateDomain() method, a new application domain with the friendly name New AppDomain is created. Then we load the assembly AssemblyA into the new domain and call the Main() method by calling ExecuteAssembly():

```
using System;

namespace Wrox.ProCSharp.Assemblies.AppDomains
{
    class Test
    {
        [STAThread]
        static void Main(string[] args)
        {
            AppDomain currentDomain = AppDomain.CurrentDomain;
            Console.WriteLine(currentDomain.FriendlyName);
            AppDomain secondDomain = AppDomain.CreateDomain("New AppDomain");
            secondDomain.ExecuteAssembly("AssemblyA.exe");
        }
    }
}
```

Before starting the program DomainTest.exe, we have to copy the assembly AssemblyA.exe to the directory of DomainTest.exe so that the assembly can be found. It's not possible to add a reference to AssemblyA.exe, because Visual Studio .NET only supports adding references to assemblies stored in DLL formats, and not EXE formats. However, this is possible from the command line. If the assembly cannot be found, we get a System.IO.FileNotFoundException exception.

When `DomainTest.exe` is run, we see this console output:

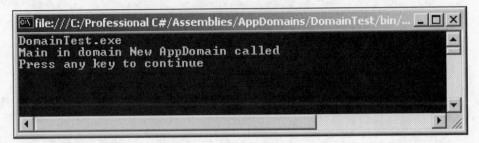

`DomainTest.exe` is the friendly name of the first application domain. The second line is the output of the newly loaded assembly in the `New AppDomain`. With a process viewer you will not see the process `AssemblyA.exe` executing because there's no new process created. `AssemblyA` is loaded into the process `DomainTest.exe`.

Instead of calling the `Main()` method in the newly loaded assembly, you can also create a new instance. In the following example I'm replacing the `ExecuteAssembly()` method with a `CreateInstance()`. The first argument is the name of the assembly, `AssemblyA`. The second argument defines the type that should be instantiated: `Wrox.ProCSharp.Assemblies.AppDomains.Class1`. The third argument, `true`, means that case is ignored. `System.Reflection.BindingFlags.CreateInstance` is a binding flag enumeration value to specify that the constructor should be called:

```
AppDomain secondDomain = AppDomain.CreateDomain("New AppDomain");
// secondDomain.ExecuteAssembly("AssemblyA.exe");

secondDomain.CreateInstance("AssemblyA",
                "Wrox.ProCSharp.Assemblies.AppDomains.Class1", true,
                System.Reflection.BindingFlags.CreateInstance,
                null, new object[] {7, 3}, null, null, null);
```

With a successful run we get this console output:

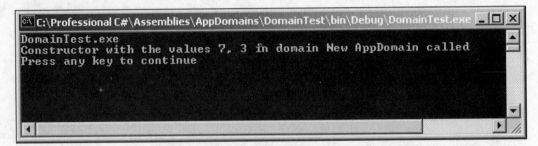

We have seen how to create and call application domains. In runtime hosts, application domains are created automatically. ASP.NET creates an application domain for each web application that runs on a web server. Internet Explorer creates application domains in which managed controls will run. For applications, it can be useful to create application domains if you want to unload an assembly. Unloading assemblies can only be done by terminating an application domain.

Assembly Structure

An assembly consists of assembly metadata describing the complete assembly, type metadata describing the exported types and methods, MSIL code, and resources. All these parts can be inside one file or spread across several files.

In this example represented in the figure on the right, the assembly metadata, type metadata, MSIL Code, and resources are all in one file – Component.dll. The assembly consists of a single file.

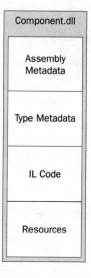

The second example below shows a single assembly spread across three files. Component.dll has assembly metadata, type metadata, and MSIL code, but no resources. The assembly uses a picture from picture.jpeg that is not embedded inside Component.dll, but is referenced from within the assembly metadata. The assembly metadata also references a module called Util.netmodule, which itself includes only type metadata and MSIL code for a class. A module has no assembly metadata. Thus the module itself has no version information; it also cannot be installed separately. All three files in this example make up a single assembly. The assembly is the installation unit. It would also be possible to put the manifest in a different file:

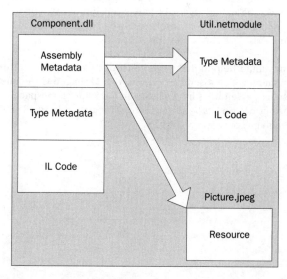

Assembly Manifests

An important part of an assembly is a **manifest**, which is part of the metadata. It describes the assembly with all the information that's needed to reference it, and lists all its dependencies. The parts of the manifest are:

- ❏ **Identity** (name, version, culture, and public key.)

- ❏ A **list of files** belonging to this assembly. A single assembly must have at least one file, but may contain a number of files.

- ❏ A list of **referenced assemblies**. Documented inside the manifest are all assemblies that are used from the assembly, including the version number, and the public key. The public key is used to uniquely identify assemblies. We will disuss the public key later.

- ❏ A set of **permission requests**. These are the permissions needed to run this assembly. We will not talk about permissions in this chapter. More information can be found in Chapter 23.

- ❏ **Exported types** are not part of the manifest, unless the types are included from a module. A module is a unit of reuse. The type description is stored as metadata inside the assembly. We can get the structures and classes with the properties and methods from the metadata. This replaces the type library that was used with COM to describe the types. For the use of COM clients it's easy to generate a type-library out of the manifest. The reflection mechanism uses the information about the exported types for late binding to classes. See Chapter 5 for more about reflection.

Namespaces, Assemblies, and Components

Maybe you're now confused by the meanings of namespaces, types, assemblies, and components. How does a namespace fit into the assembly concept? The namespace is completely independent of an assembly. You can have different namespaces in a single assembly, but the same namespace can be spread across assemblies. The namespace is just an extension of the type name – it belongs to the name of the type. Thus, the real name of the class `Class1` we used before is `Wrox.ProCSharp.Assemblies.AppDomains.Class1`.

The following diagram should help to make this concept clearer. It shows three assemblies, which we will build later in this chapter – an assembly written with Managed C++, one with Visual Basic .NET, and one with C#. All these assemblies have classes in the same namespace: `Wrox.ProCSharp.Assemblies.CrossLanguage`. The assembly `HelloCSharp` in addition, has a class `Math` that's in the namespace `Wrox.Utils`.

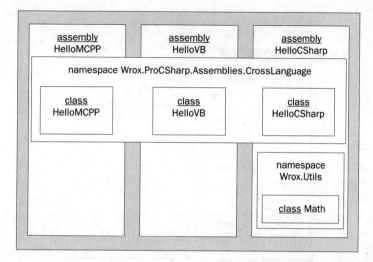

Now another question often arises: what is a component in the .NET language – is an assembly a component? The answer is "no". A component is the binary form of a class. A single assembly can have a lot of components.

Private and Shared Assemblies

Assemblies can be shared or private. A **private assembly** is found either in the same directory as the application, or within one of its subdirectories. With a private assembly, it's not necessary to think about naming conflicts with other classes or versioning problems. The assemblies that are referenced during the build process are copied to the application directory. Private assemblies are the normal way to build assemblies, especially when applications and components are built within the same company.

When using **shared assemblies**, we have to be aware of some rules. The assembly must be unique, and therefore have a unique name called a **strong name**. Part of the strong name is a mandatory version number. Shared assemblies will mostly be used when a vendor, different from that of the application, builds the component, or where a large application is split into sub-projects.

Viewing Assemblies

Assemblies can be viewed using the command-line utility **ildasm**, the MSIL disassembler. An assembly can be opened by starting ildasm from the command line, with the assembly as argument or by selecting the File | Open menu.

The screenshot overleaf shows ildasm opening the example that we are about to build, HelloCSharp.exe. ildasm shows the manifest, and the HelloCSharp type in the Wrox.ProCSharp.Assemblies.CrossLanguage namespace. Opening the manifest, we can see the version number, and the assembly attributes as well as the referenced assemblies and their versions. Opening the methods of the class, we can see the MSIL code:

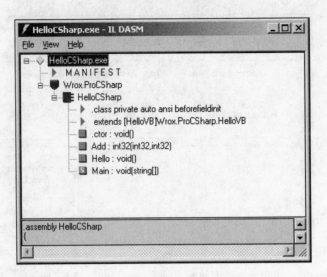

ildasm Symbols

The symbols that are used with `ildasm` are listed here:

Symbol	Description
	Represents a namespace.
	Represents a reference type, a class. Similar symbols are used by value types (structs) that have a light color, delegates that are real classes with the MSIL code, interfaces that have an "I" in the graphic, and enumerations with an "E".
	Represents a method and get and set accessors of a property; an "S" in the graphic means that this method is static.
	Represents a field
	Represents an event.
	Represents a property.
	This means that more information is available, for example. manifest information, or information about a class declaration.

Building Assemblies

Now we have learned what assemblies are, we are going to build some. Of course, we have already built assemblies as we have progressed through the book, because a .NET executable is an assembly anyway, but now we will have a look at special options for assemblies.

Creating Modules and Assemblies

All C# project types in Visual Studio .NET create an assembly. Whether you choose a DLL or EXE project type, an assembly is always created. With the command-line C# compiler csc, it's also possible to create modules. A module is a DLL without assembly attributes (so it's not an assembly, but it can be added to assemblies at a later time). The command

```
csc /target:module hello.cs
```

creates a module hello.netmodule. It's possible to view this module using ildasm.

A module also has a manifest, but there is no .assembly entry inside the manifest (except for the external assemblies that are referenced), since a module has no assembly attributes. It's not possible to configure versions or permissions with modules; that's only possible at the assembly scope. In the manifest of the module, references to assemblies can be found. With the /addmodule option of csc, it's possible to add modules to existing assemblies.

To compare modules to assemblies, I'm generating a simple class A and compiling it using:

```
csc /target:module A.cs
```

The compiler generates the file A.netmodule, which doesn't include assembly information (as we can see using ildasm looking at the manifest information). The manifest of the module shows the referenced assembly mscorlib and the .module entry:

```
MANIFEST                                                          _ □ ×
.assembly extern mscorlib
{
  .publickeytoken = (B7 7A 5C 56 19 34 E0 89 )                    // .z'
  .hash = (E6 5E CC 14 E3 F1 E6 AC 42 C3 F3 E9 B1 43 8C A9        // .^......B...
           AC 35 F0 BF )                                          // .5..
  .ver 1:0:3300:0
}
.module A.netmodule
// MVID: {CFA987F5-067E-4E97-9A52-731EB02A0FF9}
.imagebase 0x00400000
.subsystem 0x00000003
.file alignment 512
.corflags 0x00000001
// Image base: 0x030a0000
```

Next, I'm generating an assembly B that includes the module A.netmodule. It's not necessary to have a source file to generate this assembly. The command to build the assembly is:

```
csc /target:library /addmodule:A.netmodule /out:B.dll
```

When looking at the assembly using ildasm, only a manifest can be found. In the manifest, the assembly mscorlib is referenced. Next we see the assembly section with a hash algorithm and the version. The number of the algorithm defines the type of the algorithm that was used to create the hash code of the assembly. When creating an assembly programmatically it is possible to select the algorithm. Part of the manifest is a list of all modules belonging to the assembly. Here we see .module A.netmodule that belongs to the assembly. Classes exported from modules are part of the assembly manifest; classes exported from the assembly itself are not:

```
MANIFEST                                                            _ □ X
.assembly extern mscorlib
{
  .publickeytoken = (B7 7A 5C 56 19 34 E0 89 )                          //
  .hash = (E6 5E CC 14 E3 F1 E6 AC 42 C3 F3 E9 B1 43 8C A9   // .^......B.
           AC 35 F0 BF )                                      // .5..
  .ver 1:0:3300:0
}
.assembly B
{
  // --- The following custom attribute is added automatically, do not unc
  //   .custom instance void [mscorlib]System.Diagnostics.DebuggableAttribu
  //
  .hash algorithm 0x00008004
  .ver 0:0:0:0
}
.file A.netmodule
      .hash = (74 67 7D FC CC C0 D2 5F CB AB E4 9E 25 7F BC DF   // tg}...._
               21 B3 0D D2 )                                     // !...
.module B.dll
// MVID: {93652CF8-240C-4860-B8B9-178D2B2F5CA5}
.imagebase 0x00400000
.subsystem 0x00000003
.file alignment 512
.corflags 0x00000001
// Image base: 0x030a0000
```

What's the purpose of modules? Modules can be used for faster startup of assemblies because not all types are inside a single file. The modules are only loaded when needed. Another reason to use modules is if you want to create an assembly with more than one programming language; one module could be written using VB.NET, another module using C#, and these two modules can be included in a single assembly.

Creating Assemblies Using Visual Studio .NET

As already mentioned, all project types in Visual Studio .NET create assemblies. With Visual Studio .NET 7.0 there's no support for creating modules directly.

When creating a Visual Studio .NET project, the source file `AssemblyInfo.cs` is generated automatically. We can use using the normal sourcecode editor to configure the assembly attributes in this file. This is the file generated from the wizard:

```csharp
using System.Reflection;
using System.Runtime.CompilerServices;

//
// General Information about an assembly is controlled through the following
// set of attributes. Change these attribute values to modify the
// information associated with an assembly.
//

[assembly: AssemblyTitle("")]
[assembly: AssemblyDescription("")]
[assembly: AssemblyConfiguration("")]
[assembly: AssemblyCompany("")]
[assembly: AssemblyProduct("")]
[assembly: AssemblyCopyright("")]
[assembly: AssemblyTrademark("")]
[assembly: AssemblyCulture("")]


//
// Version information for an assembly consists of the following four
// values:
//
//      Major Version
//      Minor Version
//      Build Number
//      Revision
//
// You can specify all the values or you can default the Revision and Build
// Numbers by using the '*' as shown below:

[assembly: AssemblyVersion("1.0.*")]


//
// In order to sign your assembly you must specify a key to use. Refer to
// the Microsoft .NET Framework documentation for more information on
// assembly signing.
//
// Use the attributes below to control which key is used for signing.
//
// Notes:
//   (*) If no key is specified - the assembly cannot be signed.
//   (*) KeyName refers to a key that has been installed in the Crypto
//       Service Provider (CSP) on your machine.
//   (*) If the key file and a key name attributes are both specified, the
//       following processing occurs:
//       (1) If the KeyName can be found in the CSP - that key is used.
//       (2) If the KeyName does not exist and the KeyFile does exist, the
//           key in the file is installed into the CSP and used.
//   (*) Delay Signing is an advanced option - see the Microsoft .NET
//       Framework documentation for more information on this.
//

[assembly: AssemblyDelaySign(false)]
[assembly: AssemblyKeyFile("")]
[assembly: AssemblyKeyName("")]
```

This file is used for configuration of the assembly manifest. The compiler reads the assembly attributes to inject the specific information into the manifest.

[assembly], and [module] are global attributes. Global attributes are, in contrast to the other attributes, not attached to a specific language element. The arguments that can be used for the assembly attribute are classes of the namespaces System.Reflection, System.Runtime.CompilerServices, and System.Runtime.InteropServices.

You can read more about attributes and how to create custom attributes in Chapter 4.

Here's a list of all assembly attributes corresponding to classes in the System.Reflection namespace.

Assembly Attribute	Description
AssemblyCompany	Specifies the company name.
AssemblyConfiguration	Specifies build information such as retail or debugging information.
AssemblyCopyright and AssemblyTrademark	Hold the copyright and trademark information.
AssemblyDefaultAlias	Can be used if the assembly name is not easily readable (such as a GUID when the assembly name is created dynamically). With this attribute an alias name can be specified.
AssemblyDescription	Describes the assembly or the product. Looking at the properties of the executable file this value shows up as Comments.
AssemblyProduct	Specifies the name of the product where the assembly belongs.
AssemblyInformationalVersion	This attribute isn't used for version checking when assemblies are referenced, it is for information only. It is very useful to specify the version of an application that uses multiple assemblies. Opening the properties of the executable we can see this value as the Product Version.
AssemblyTitle	Used to give the assembly a friendly name. The friendly name can include spaces. With the file properties we can see this value as Description.

Here's an example of how these attributes might be configured:

```
[assembly: AssemblyTitle("Professional C#")]
[assembly: AssemblyDescription("")]
[assembly: AssemblyConfiguration("Retail version")]
[assembly: AssemblyCompany("Wrox Press")]
```

```
[assembly: AssemblyProduct("Wrox Professional Series")]
[assembly: AssemblyCopyright("Copyright (C) Wrox Press 2002")]
[assembly: AssemblyTrademark("Wrox is a registered trademark of Wrox Press Ltd")]
[assembly: AssemblyCulture("en-US")]
```

The following attributes correspond to classes in the `System.Runtime.CompilerServices` namespace:

- ❏ `AssemblyCulture` tells about the culture of the assembly. We will talk about the culture when covering localization.

- ❏ `AssemblyDelaySign`, `AssemblyKeyFile`, and `AssemblyKeyName` are used to create strong names for shared assemblies.

- ❏ `AssemblyVersion` specifies the version number of the assembly. Versioning plays an important part for shared assemblies.

Additional COM interoperability attributes within the `System.Runtime.InteropServices` *namespace can be used to make .NET types visible to COM, to specify application-ID's for example. COM interoperability is the subject of Chapter 17.*

Cross-Language Support

One of the best features of COM was its support for multiple languages. It's possible to create a COM component with Visual Basic and make use of it from within a scripting client such as JScript. On the other hand, it's also possible to create a COM component using C++ that a Visual Basic program can't make use of. A scripting client has different requirements from a VB client, and a C++ client is able to use many more COM features than any other client language.

When writing COM components it's always necessary to have the client in mind. The server must be developed for a specific client language, or for a group of client languages. If designing a COM component for a scripting client, this component can also be used from within C++, but the C++ client then has some disadvantages. Many rules must be followed when different clients should be supported, and the compiler can't help with COM; the COM developer has to know the requirements of the client language, and has to create the interfaces accordingly.

How does this compare with the .NET platform? With the **Common Type System (CTS)**, .NET defines how value types and reference types can be defined from a .NET language, the memory layout of such types. But the CTS does not guarantee that a type that is defined from any language can be used from any other language. This is the role of the **Common Language Specification (CLS)**. The CLS defines the minimum requirement of types that must be supported by a .NET language.

We briefly mentioned the CTS and CLS in the first chapter of this book. In this section, we shall go deeper, and explore:

- ❏ The Common Type System and the Common Language Specification.

- ❏ Language independence in action by creating a C++, Visual Basic .NET and a C# class that derive from each other. We look at the MSIL code that's generated from these compilers.

- ❏ The requirements of the Common Language Specification.

The CTS and the CLS

All types are declared with the guidance of the Common Type System (CTS). The CTS defines a set of rules that language compilers must follow to define, reference, use, and store both reference and value types. Therefore, by following the CTS, objects written in different languages can interact with each other.

However, not all types are available to all programming languages. To build components that are accessible from all .NET languages the Common Language Specification (CLS) should be used. With the CLS, the compiler can check for valid code according to the CLS specification.

Any language that supports .NET isn't just restricted to the common subset of features that is defined with the CLS; even with .NET it's still possible to create components that can't be used from different languages. Having said that, supporting all languages is much easier with .NET than it was with COM. If you do restrict yourself to the CLS, it's *guaranteed* that this component can be used from all languages. It is most likely that libraries written by thirdparties will restrict to the CLS to make the library available to all languages.

The .NET Framework was designed from the ground up to support multiple languages. During the design phase of .NET, Microsoft invited many compiler vendors to build their own .NET languages. Microsoft itself delivers Visual Basic .NET, Managed C++, C#, J#, and JScript.NET. In addition, more than twenty languages from different vendors, such as COBOL, Smalltalk, Perl, and Eiffel are available. Each of these languages has its specific advantages, and many different features. The compilers of all these languages have been extended to support .NET.

> **The CLS is the minimum specification of requirements that a language must support. This means that if we restrict our public methods to the CLS, all languages supporting .NET can use our classes!**

Most, but not all, of the classes in the .NET Framework are CLS-compliant. The non-compliant classes and methods are specially marked as not compliant in the MSDN documentation. One example is the `UInt32` structure in the `System` namespace. `UInt32` represents a 32-bit unsigned integer. Not all languages (for example Visual Basic .NET or J#) support unsigned data types; such data types are not CLS-compliant.

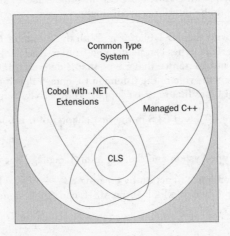

Language Independence in Action

Let's see CLS in action. The first assembly we create will include a base class with Visual C++. The second assembly has a VB.NET class that inherits from the C++ class. The third assembly is a C# console application with a class deriving from the VB.NET code, and a `Main` function that's using the C# class. The implementation should just show how the languages make use of .NET classes, and how they handle numbers, so all these classes have a simple `Hello()` method where the `System.Console` class is used, and an `Add()` method where two numbers are added:

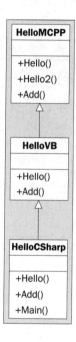

Writing the Managed C++ Class

The first project type to create is a Managed C++ Class Library, which is created from the Visual C++ Projects project type of Visual Studio .NET, and given the name `HelloMCPP`:

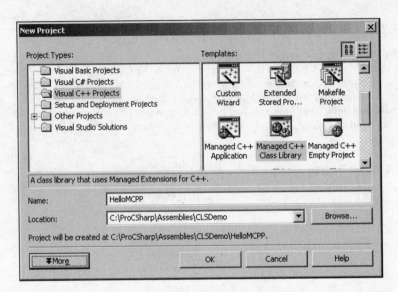

The application wizard generates a class `HelloMCPP` that is marked with `__gc` to make the class a managed type. Without a special attribute, the class would be a normal unmanaged C++ class generating native code.

In the generated header file `stdafx.h`, you'll see a `#using <mscorlib.dll>` directive. In C++, other assemblies can be referenced with the `#using` preprocessor directive. The code for the .NET class can be found in the file `HelloMCPP.h`:

```
// HelloMCPP.h

#pragma once

using namespace System;

namespace HelloMCPP
{
    public __gc class Class1
    {
        // TODO: Add your methods for this class here.
    };
}
```

For demonstration purposes, I'm changing the namespace and class name, and I'm adding three methods to the class. The virtual method `Hello2()` is using a C runtime function `printf()` that demonstrates the use of native code within a managed class. To make this method available the header file `stdio.h` must be included. Within the `Hello()` method we are using the `Console` managed class from the `System` namespace. The C++ `using namespace` statement is similar to the C# `using` statement. `using namespace System` opens the `System` namespace, so we needn't write `System::Console::WriteLine()`. The `Hello()` method is also marked `virtual`, so that it can be overridden. We will override `Hello()` in the VB and C# classes. C++ member functions are not `virtual` by default. A third method, which returns the sum of two `int` arguments, is added to the class so that we can compare the generated MSIL to the different languages to see how they handle numbers. All three examples use the same namespace `Wrox.ProCSharp.Assemblies.CrossLanguage`.

```
// HelloMCPP.h

#pragma once
#include <stdio.h>
using namespace System;
namespace Wrox
{
    namespace ProCSharp
    {
        namespace Assemblies
        {
            namespace CrossLanguage
            {
                public __gc class HelloMCPP
                {
                public:
                    virtual void Hello()
                    {
                        Console::WriteLine(S"Hello, Managed C++");
                    }
                    virtual void Hello2()
                    {
                        printf("Hello, calling native code\n");
                    }
                    int Add(int val1, int val2)
                    {
                        return val1 + val2;
                    }
                };
            }
        }
    }
}
```

To compare the programs with running code we are using the release build instead of the debug configuration. Looking at the generated DLL using ildasm, we see two static methods used, `printf()` and `DllMainCrtStartup()`. Both of these methods are native unmanaged functions using `pinvoke`. `DllMainCrtStartup()` is used within every Managed C++ program. It is the entry point in the DLL, and is called when the DLL is loaded. `printf()` is used within our `Hello()` method. The private field `$ArrayType$0xec5a014e` holds our native string "`Hello, calling native code\n`":

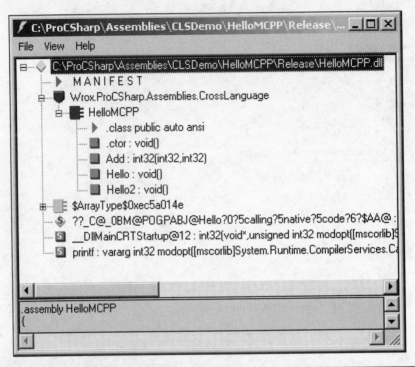

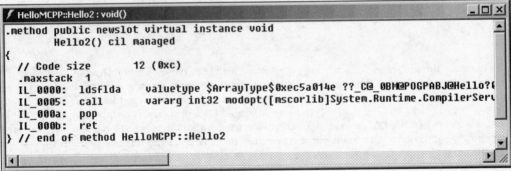

The Hello2() method pushes the address of the field $ArrayType$0xec5a014e, that keeps the string on the stack. In line IL_0005 a call to the static printf() method can be seen where a pointer to the string "Hello, calling native code" is passed.

printf() itself is called via the **platform invoke** mechanism (as shown below). With the platform invoke, we can call all native functions like the C runtime and Win32 API calls. There is more discussion of platform invoke in Chapter 17.

```
Global Functions::printf : vararg int32 modopt([mscorlib]System.Runtime.CompilerServices.Cal...  _ □ ×
.method public static pinvokeimpl(/* No map */)
        vararg int32 modopt([mscorlib]System.Runtime.CompilerServices.CallC
        printf(int8 modopt([Microsoft.VisualC]Microsoft.VisualC.NoSignSpeci
{
  .custom instance void [mscorlib]System.Security.SuppressUnmanagedCodeSecu
  // Embedded native code
  //  Disassembly of native methods is not supported.
  //  Managed TargetRVA = 0xa308
} // end of method 'Global Functions'::printf
```

The `Hello()` method is completely made up of MSIL code; there's no native code. Because the string was prefixed with an "S", a managed string is written into the assembly and it is put onto the stack with `ldstr`. In line `IL_0005` we are calling the `WriteLine()` method of the `System.Console` class using the string from the stack:

```
.method public newslot virtual instance void
        Hello() cil managed
{
  // Code size       11 (0xb)
  .maxstack  1
  IL_0000:  ldstr      "Hello, Managed C++"
  IL_0005:  call       void [mscorlib]System.Console::WriteLine(string)
  IL_000a:  ret
} // end of method HelloMCPP::Hello
```

```
HelloMCPP::Add : int32(int32,int32)                                        _ □ ×
.method public instance int32   Add(int32 val1,
                                    int32 val2) cil managed
{
  // Code size       4 (0x4)
  .maxstack  2
  IL_0000:  ldarg.1
  IL_0001:  ldarg.2
  IL_0002:  add
  IL_0003:  ret
} // end of method HelloMCPP::Add
```

To demonstrate how numbers are used within Managed C++, we're now going to take a look at the MSIL code of the `Add()` method. With `ldarg.1`, and `ldarg.2`, the passed arguments are put on the stack, `add` adds the stack values, and puts the result on the stack, and in line `IL_0003` the result is returned.

What's the advantage of using Managed C++ compared to C# and other languages of the .NET framework? Managed C++ makes it easier to make traditional C++ code available to .NET. MSIL code and native code can be mixed easily.

Be aware that it's not possible to create a Managed C++ application without native code. With the current implementation, there's always native start-up code.

Writing the VB.NET Class

Now we're going to use VB.NET to create a class. Again, we are using the Class Library wizard; the project will be called `HelloVB`:

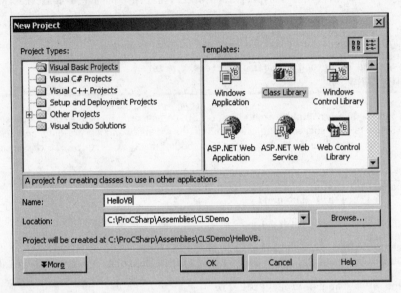

The namespace of the class should be changed to `Wrox.ProCSharp.Assemblies.CrossLanguage`. In a VB.NET project this can be done by changing the root namespace of the project in the project properties:

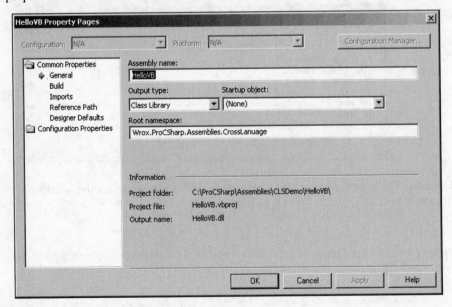

To make it possible to derive the class from `HelloMCPP` a reference to `HelloMCPP.dll` is needed. The reference is added using **Project | Add Reference**, or can also be added from inside the **Solution Explorer**. When building the assembly the reference can be seen inside the manifest: `.assembly extern HelloMCPP`. The referenced assembly is also copied to the output directory of the VB.NET project, so that we are independent of later changes made to the original referenced assembly:

```
MANIFEST
.assembly extern HelloMCPP
{
  .ver 1:0:759:30419
}
.assembly HelloVB
{
  // --- The following custom attribute is added automatically, do
  //   .custom instance void [mscorlib]System.Diagnostics.Debuggable
  //
  .custom instance void [mscorlib]System.Runtime.InteropServices.Gu

  .custom instance void [mscorlib]System.CLSCompliantAttribute::.ct
  .custom instance void [mscorlib]System.Reflection.AssemblyTradema
  .custom instance void [mscorlib]System.Reflection.AssemblyCopyrig
  .custom instance void [mscorlib]System.Reflection.AssemblyProduct
  .custom instance void [mscorlib]System.Reflection.AssemblyCompany
  .custom instance void [mscorlib]System.Reflection.AssemblyDescrip
  .custom instance void [mscorlib]System.Reflection.AssemblyTitleAt
  .hash algorithm 0x00008004
  .ver 1:0:759:30759
}
.module HelloVB.dll
// MVID: {FCBC582D-F654-447E-8A38-B11D467D3FD2}
.imagebase 0x11000000
.subsystem 0x00000002
.file alignment 512
.corflags 0x00000001
// Image base: 0x033F0000
```

The class `HelloVB` inherits from `HelloMCPP`. VB.NET has the keyword `Inherits` to derive from a base class. `Inherits` must be in the same line as, and follow the `Class` statement. The `Hello()` method in the base class is overridden. The VB.NET `Overrides` keyword does the same thing as the C# `override` keyword. In the implementation of the `Hello()` method, the `Hello()` method of the base class is called using the VB.NET keyword `MyBase`. The `MyBase` keyword is the same as `base` in C#. The method `Add()` is implemented so that we can examine the generated MSIL code to see how VB.NET works with numbers. The `Add()` method from the base class is not virtual, so it can't be overridden. VB.NET has the keyword `Shadows` to hide a method of a base class. `Shadows` is similar to C#'s `new`:

```vbnet
Public Class HelloVB
    Inherits HelloMCPP

    Public Overrides Sub Hello()
        MyBase.Hello()
        System.Console.WriteLine("Hello, VB.NET")
    End Sub
```

```
    Public Shadows Function Add(ByVal val1 As Integer, _
                               ByVal val2 As Integer) As Integer
        Return val1 + val2
    End Function

End Class
```

Let's look at the MSIL code that is generated from the VB.NET compiler.

The HelloVB.Hello() method first calls the Hello() method of the base class HelloMCPP. In line IL_0006, a string stored in the metadata is pushed on the stack using ldstr.

```
HelloVB::Hello : void()                                              _ □ x
.method public virtual instance void  Hello() cil managed
{
  // Code size       17 (0x11)
  .maxstack  8
  IL_0000:  ldarg.0
  IL_0001:  call         instance void [HelloMCPP]Wrox.ProCSharp.Assemblies.Cro:
  IL_0006:  ldstr        "Hello, VB.NET"
  IL_000b:  call         void [mscorlib]System.Console::WriteLine(string)
  IL_0010:  ret
} // end of method HelloVB::Hello
```

The other method we are looking at is Add(). VB.NET uses add.ovf instead of the add method that was used in the MC++ generated MSIL code. This is just a single MSIL statement that's different between MC++ and VB.NET, but the statement add.ovf generates more lines of native code, as add.ovf performs overflow checking. If the result of the addition of the two arguments is too large to be represented in the target type, add.ovf generates an exception of type OverflowException. In contrast, add just performs an addition of the two values, whether or not the target fits. In the case where the target is not big enough, the true value of the summation is lost, and the result is a wrong number. So, add is faster, but add.ovf is safer:

```
HelloVB::Add : int32(int32,int32)                                    _ □ x
.method public instance int32   Add(int32 val1,
                                    int32 val2) cil managed
{
  // Code size        4 (0x4)
  .maxstack  2
  .locals init (int32 V_0)
  IL_0000:  ldarg.1
  IL_0001:  ldarg.2
  IL_0002:  add.ovf
  IL_0003:  ret
} // end of method HelloVB::Add
```

Writing the C# Class

The third class is created using the language we know best: C#. For this project, we will create a C# Console Application. The HelloVB assembly is referenced to make a derivation of the class HelloVB, and a reference to HelloMCPP is also added.

The methods implemented in the C# class are similar to the MC++ and the VB.NET classes. Hello() is an overridden method of the base class; Add() is a new method:

```csharp
namespace Wrox.ProCSharp.Assemblies.CrossLanguage
{
    using System;

    /// <summary>
    ///     Summary description for HelloCSharp.
    /// </summary>

    public class HelloCSharp : HelloVB
    {
        public HelloCSharp()
        {
        }

        public override void Hello()
        {
            base.Hello();
            Console.WriteLine("Hello, C#");
        }

        public new int Add(int val1, int val2)
        {
            return val1 + val2;
        }

        [STAThread]
        public static void Main()
        {
            HelloCSharp hello = new HelloCSharp();
            hello.Hello();
        }
    }
}
```

As you can see, the generated MSIL code for the Hello() method is the same as the MSIL code from the VB.NET compiler:

```
HelloCSharp::Hello : void()                                    _ |O| x|
.method public hidebysig virtual instance void
        Hello() cil managed
{
  // Code size        17 (0x11)
  .maxstack  1
  IL_0000:  ldarg.0
  IL_0001:  call       instance void [HelloVB]Wrox.ProCSharp.Assemblies.Cros
  IL_0006:  ldstr      "Hello, C#"
  IL_000b:  call       void [mscorlib]System.Console::WriteLine(string)
  IL_0010:  ret
} // end of method HelloCSharp::Hello
```

The Add() method differs, and yet is similar to the MC++ code. When doing calculations, the C# compiler doesn't use the methods with overflow; checking with the default compiler settings in a Visual Studio .NET project. The faster MSIL method add is used instead of add.ovf; but it's possible to change this option using the configuration properties of the project both with C# and VB.NET. By setting **Check for overflow underflow** to true in a C# project, the MSIL code that the C# compiler generates for our example will be the same as that generated by the VB.NET compiler. Unlike VB.NET, with C# it's also possible to choose this option on an expression-by-expression basis with the checked and unchecked operators:

```
HelloCSharp::Add : int32(int32,int32)                             _|□|X|

.method public hidebysig instance int32    Add(int32 val1,
                                                int32 val2) cil managed
{
  // Code size        4 (0x4)
  .maxstack  2
  IL_0000:  ldarg.1
  IL_0001:  ldarg.2
  IL_0002:  add
  IL_0003:  ret
} // end of method HelloCSharp::Add
```

Finally, we can see the console application in action:

```
C:\ProCSharp\Assemblies\CLSDemo\HelloCSharp\bin\Debug\HelloCSharp.exe    _|□|X|
Hello, Managed C++
Hello, VB.NET
Hello, C#
```

Because all the .NET languages generate MSIL code and all the languages make use of the classes in the .NET framework, it's often said that there is no difference regarding performance. As you can see, however, small differences are still there. Firstly, depending on the language, some languages support different data types from others. Secondly, the generated MSIL code can still be different. One example that we've seen is that the number calculations are implemented differently: while the default configuration of VB.NET is for safety, the default for C# is for speed. C# is also more flexible.

CLS Requirements

We've just seen the CLS in action when we looked at cross-language inheritance between MC++, VB.NET, and C#. Until now we didn't pay any attention to the CLS requirements when building our project. We were lucky – the methods we defined in the base classes were callable from the derived classes. If a method had the System.UInt32 data type as one of its arguments, we wouldn't be able to use it from VB.NET. Unsigned data types are not CLS-compliant; for a .NET language, it's not necessary to support this data type.

The Common Language Specification exactly defines the requirements to make a component CLS-compliant, which enables it to be used with different .NET languages. With COM we had to pay attention to language-specific requirements when designing a component. JScript had different requirements from VB6, and the requirements of VJ++ were different again. That's no longer the case with .NET. When designing a component that should be used from other languages, we just have to make it CLS, compliant; it's guaranteed that this component can be used from all .NET languages. If we mark a class as CLS, compliant, the compiler can warn us about non-compliant methods.

All .NET languages must support the CLS. When talking about .NET languages we have to differentiate between **.NET consumer** and **.NET extender** tools.

A .NET consumer tool just uses classes from the .NET Framework – it can't create .NET classes that can be used from other languages. A consumer tool can use any CLS-compliant class. A .NET extender tool has the requirements of a consumer, and can in addition inherit any CLS-compliant .NET class, and define new CLS compliant classes that can be used by consumers. C++, VB.NET, and C# all are extender tools. With these languages, it's possible to create CLS compliant classes. The COBOL that's available for .NET currently is just a consumer tool. With COBOL.NET, we can use all CLS compliant classes, but not extend them.

CLSCompliant Attribute

With the `CLSCompliant` attribute, we can mark our assembly to be CLS compliant. Doing this guarantees that the classes in this assembly can be used from all .NET consumer tools. The compiler issues warnings when we are using non-CLS compliant data types in public and protected methods. The data types we use in the private implementation don't matter – when using other languages outside of the class, we don't have direct access to private methods anyway.

To get compiler warnings when a data type is not compliant in public and protected methods, we set the attribute `CLSCompliant` in the assembly by adding this attribute to the file `AssemblyInfo.cs`:

```
[assembly: System.CLSCompliant(true)]
```

This way, all the defined types and public methods inside the assembly must be compliant. Using a non-compliant `uint` type as argument type, we get this error from the compiler:

```
error CS3001: Argument type uint is not CLS-compliant
```

When we mark an assembly as compliant, it's still possible to define methods that are not compliant. This can be useful if you want to override some method to make it available with both compliant and non-compliant argument data types. The methods that are not compliant must be marked, within the class, by the `CLSCompliant` attribute with a value of `false`. The `CLSCompliant` attribute can be applied to types, methods, properties, fields, and events:

```
[CLSCompliant(false)]
void Method(uint i)
{
    //...
```

CLS Rules

The requirements for an assembly to be CLS-compliant are the following:

❑ All types appearing in a method prototype must be CLS-compliant.

❑ Array elements must have a CLS-compliant element type. Arrays must also be 0-indexed.

❑ A CLS compliant class must inherit from a CLS-compliant class. `System.Object` is CLS compliant.

❑ Although method names in CLS-compliant classes are not case-sensitive, no two method names can be different only in the case of the letters in their name.

❑ Enumerations must be of type `Int16`, `Int32`, or `Int64`. Enumerations of other types are not compliant.

All the listed requirements only apply to public and protected members. The private implementation itself doesn't matter – non-compliant types can be used there, and the assembly is still compliant.

Besides these requirements, there are the more general naming guidelines that we read about in Chapter 6. These guidelines are not a strict requirement of being CLS compliant, but do make life much easier.

In addition to these naming guidelines to support multiple languages, it's necessary to pay attention to method names where the type is part of the name. Data type names are language-specific, for example, the C# `int`, `long`, and `float` types are equivalent to the VB.NET `Integer`, `Long`, and `Single` types. When a data type name is used in a name of a method, the universal type names, and not the language-specific type names should be used, in other words `Int32`, `Int64`, and `Single`:

```
int ReadInt32();
long ReadInt64();
float ReadSingle();
```

As you can see when complying with the CLS specs and guidelines, it's easy to create components that can be used from multiple languages. It's not necessary to test the component using all .NET consumer languages.

Adding Resources to Assemblies

In this section, we will look at the .NET architecture's support for resource files, their use to facilitate internationalization, and the creation of satellite assemblies.

The advantage of using resource files instead of storing strings or pictures directly in program code is that non-programmers can easily change these resource files; although it may take a programmer, or at least the use of a few batch files to recompile them into new resource files. It's not necessary to search through the sourcecode for strings when using resource files, as the strings are all in one place. It is also advantageous to have strings or images in resource files when programs are localized to different languages, as translators simply need to edit the resource files. To this end, we can make use of satellite assemblies for **localization**; they hold resources, but no program code.

In this section, we shall explore:

- ❑ Creating resource files, using the `resgen` utility and the `ResourceWriter` object
- ❑ Using resource files, and accessing embedded resources with the `ResourceManager` class
- ❑ Localization by using satellite assemblies
- ❑ Visual Studio .NET localization support for Windows applications

Creating Resource Files

Resource files contain such things as pictures and string tables. A resource file is created using either a normal text file, or a `.resX` file that utilizes XML. We will start with a simple text file.

A resource that embeds a string table can be created using a normal text file. The text file just assigns strings to keys. The key is a name that can be used from a program to get the value. Spaces are allowed in both keys and values.

This example shows a simple string table in the file `strings.txt`:

```
Title = Professional C#
Chapter = Assemblies
Author = Christian Nagel
Publisher = WROX Press
```

ResGen

The `resgen.exe` utility can be used to create a resource file out of `strings.txt`. Typing:

```
resgen strings.txt
```

will create the file `strings.resources`. This resulting resource file can be added to an assembly either as an external file or embedded into the DLL or EXE. ResGen also supports the creation of resource files with XML-based `.resX` files. One easy way to build an XML file is by using ResGen itself: `resgen strings.resources strings.resX` creates the XML resource file `strings.resX`. We will look at how to work with XML resource files when we look at Localization, later in this chapter.

The `resgen` utility doesn't support adding pictures. With the .NET Framework SDK Samples, you'll get a ResXGen sample. With ResXGen it's possible to add pictures to a `.resX` file. Adding pictures to resources can also be easily done using the `ResourceWriter` class.

ResourceWriter

Instead of using the `resgen` utility to build resource files, a simple program can be written. `ResourceWriter` is a class in the `System.Resources` namespace that also supports pictures, and other resource types.

Here we're creating a `ResourceWriter` object `rw` using a constructor with the filename `Demo.resources`. After creating an instance, a number of resources of up to 2GB in total size can be added using the `AddResource()` method of the `ResourceWriter` class. The first argument of `AddResource()` specifies the key, and the second argument specifies the value. A picture resource can be added using an instance of the `Image` class. To use the `Image` class, the `System.Drawing` assembly must be referenced. We are also opening the namespace `System.Drawing` with the `using` directive.

Here I'm creating an `Image` object by opening the file `logo.gif`. You'll have to copy the picture to the directory of the executable, or specify the full path to the picture in the method argument of `Image.FromFile()`. The `using` statement specifies that the image resource should automatically be disposed of at the end of the using block. Additional simple string resources are added to the `ResourceWriter` object. The `Close()` method of the `ResourceWriter` class automatically calls `ResourceWriter.Generate()` to finally write the resources to the file `Demo.resources`:

```csharp
using System;
using System.Resources;
using System.Drawing;
class Class1
{
    [STAThread]
    public static void Main()
    {
        ResourceWriter rw = new ResourceWriter("Demo.resources");
        using (Image image = Image.FromFile("logo.gif"))
        {
            rw.AddResource("WroxLogo", image);
            rw.AddResource("Title", "Professional C#");
            rw.AddResource("Chapter", "Assemblies");
            rw.AddResource("Author", "Christian Nagel");
            rw.AddResource("Publisher", "Wrox Press");
            rw.Close();
        }
    }
}
```

Starting this small program creates the resource file `Demo.resources`. The resources will be used in a Windows application.

Using Resource Files

Resource files can be added to assemblies using the Assembly Generation Tool `Al.exe` using the `/embed` option, or directly with Visual Studio .NET. For a demonstration on how to use resource files with Visual Studio .NET, I'm creating a C# Windows Application and calling it `ResourceDemo`:

In the context menu of the Solution Explorer (Add | Add Existing Item), the previously created resource file Demo.resources can be added to this project. By default the BuildAction of this resource is set to Embedded Resource, so that this resource gets embedded into the output assembly:

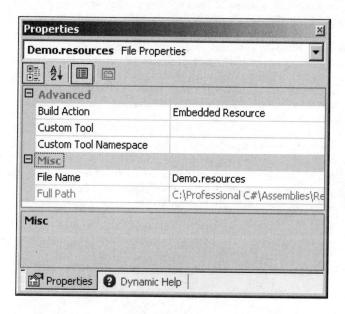

After building the project, viewing the assembly using ildasm shows .mresource in the manifest. .mresource declares the name for the resources in the assembly. If .mresource is declared public (as in our example), the resource is exported from the assembly and can be used from classes in other assemblies. .mresource private means the resource is not exported and only available within the assembly.

```
    .custom instance void [mscorlib]System.Reflection.AssemblyTitleAttribute::
    .hash algorithm 0x00008004
    .ver 1:0:714:30681
}
.mresource public ResourceDemo.Form1.resources
{
}
.mresource public ResourceDemo.Demo.resources
{
}
.module ResourceDemo.exe
// MVID: {732867A6-36FA-4593-8B82-496581883606}
.imagebase 0x00400000
.subsystem 0x00000002
.file alignment 512
.corflags 0x00000001
// Image base: 0x030a0000
```

When adding the resource to the assembly using Visual Studio .NET, the resource is always public as can be seen in the screenshot above. If the assembly generation tool is used to create assemblies, we can use command-line options to differentiate between adding public and private resources. The option /embed:demo.resources,Y adds the resource as public, while /embed:demo.resources,N adds the resource as private.

If the assembly was created using Visual Studio .NET it's possible to change the visibility of the resources later. Opening the assembly using ildasm with **File | Dump** generates an MSIL source file. The MSIL code can then be changed using a text editor such as Notepad. Using the text editor, we can change .mresource public to .mresource private. Using the tool ilasm, it's then possible to regenerate the assembly with the MSIL source code: ilasm /exe ResourceDemo.il /out:ResourceDemo.exe.

In our Windows application, we'll add some textboxes and a picture by dropping **Windows Forms** elements from the **Toolbox** to the designer where we will display the values from the resources. I'm changing the Text and Name properties of the textboxes and the labels to the values that you see below. The Name property of the PictureBox control is changed to **logo**. In the screenshot below, the PictureBox can be seen as a rectangle without grid in the upper left hand corner. The final form opened in the **Forms Designer** looks like this:

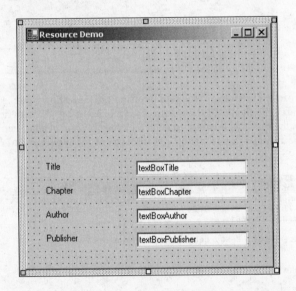

To use that embedded resource, the ResourceManager class from the System.Resources namespace can be used. We can pass the assembly where the resources are embedded in the constructor. In our case we have the resources embedded in the executing assembly, so we pass the result of Assembly.GetExecutingAssembly() as the second argument. The first argument is the root name of the resources. The root name is made of the namespace, with the name of the resource file, without the resources extension. As you've seen earlier, ildasm shows the name. It's just necessary to remove the file extension resources. We can also get the name programmatically using the GetManifestResourceNames() method of the System.Reflection.Assembly class.

Using the `ResourceManager` instance `rm` we can get all the resources by specifying the key:

```
using System.Reflection;
using System.Resources;
   // ...
   private System.Resources.ResourceManager rm;

      public Form1()
      {
         //
         // Required for Windows Form Designer support
         //
         InitializeComponent();
         Assembly assembly = Assembly.GetExecutingAssembly();

         rm = new ResourceManager("ResourceDemo.Demo", assembly);
         logo.Image = (Image)rm.GetObject("WroxLogo");
         textBoxTitle.Text = rm.GetString("Title");
         textBoxChapter.Text = rm.GetString("Chapter");
         textBoxAuthor.Text = rm.GetString("Author");
         textBoxPublisher.Text = rm.GetString("Publisher");
      }
```

When we run the code, we can see the string and picture resources, as the screenshot below shows:

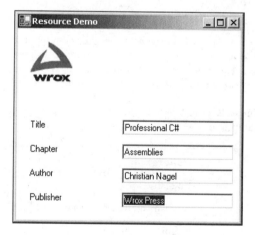

Now we will move on to look at internationalization and the use of resource files.

Internationalization and Resources

NASA's Mars Climate Orbiter was lost on September 23rd 1999 at a cost of $125 million because one engineering team used metric units, while another used different units for a key spacecraft operation.

When writing applications for international distribution, different cultures and regions must be kept in mind. A **culture** defines *who* you are, whereas a **region** defines *where* you are. Together, the culture and the region are called the **locale**. One example of the challenges with internationalization is the decimal divider: for the US, the decimal divider is ".", but for Germany it's a ",".

Here are some examples of different number formats:

US English	123,456,789.23
German	123.456.789,23
Swiss German	123'456'789.23
French	123 456 789,23

And some examples of different date formats:

US English	2/13/2002	Wednesday, February 13, 2002
UK English	13/02/2002	Wednesday 13 February 2002
German	13.02.2002	Mittwoch, 13. Februar 2002
French	13/02/2002	Mercredi 13 fevrier 2002

Cultures

A **culture** is a set of preferences based on a user's language and cultural conventions. The class `CultureInfo` is used to format dates, times, and numbers, to sort strings, and to determine the language choice for text. The user selects the culture during system installation and can configure it using the Regional Options in the Windows Control Panel.

The culture name defines a 2-letter language and a 2-letter country/region code that follow RFC1766 conventions. Some examples of the culture names are listed here:

Culture name	Culture
en	English
en-GB	English (United Kingdom)
en-US	English (United States)
fr	French
fr-FR	French (France)
de	German

Using the `System.Globalization.CultureInfo` class it's possible to get the name of the culture and supported cultures, create a new culture using a culture name string, and so on. Particular things to note are some of the static properties of `CultureInfo`. We have to differentiate between these culture types:

- ❑ `CurrentCulture` is the culture of the current thread. The default is set to the user settings, but the culture of the thread can be changed. This culture is used for locale-dependent formatting like numbers and dates.

- ❑ `CurrentUICulture` is the culture that is used for resource lookups. It is also dependent on the current thread. This culture can be used to get strings or pictures from resources. Contrary to the `CurrentCulture` this culture can only be configured by the user with a multi-language operating system. With a single-language operating system this culture is the same as the language of the operating system. There is a good reason it is done that way: if an English version of the operating system is installed that displays English dialogs, the same language should be used from applications, but the number and date formatting (`CurrentCulture`) should be configurable by the user. However, we also can change the `CurrentUICulture` programmatically.

- ❑ `InstalledUICulture` is the system default culture for resource lookups.

- ❑ `InvariantCulture` is a "neutral" culture. If you build a Windows service where the output and sorting should be independent of the logged on user, this culture should be used; it does not map to any real culture, and so it is not linguistically correct. If you want to store data, this culture is the preferred one as it does not change, and can easily be parsed and displayed in a culture-dependent manner.

Region

The **region** is different from the culture. The region does not represent the user's preferences, but defines the location. Switzerland is a multi-language country where the cultures `de-ch`, `fr-ch`, and `it-ch` are specified for Swiss people using their own versions of the German, French, and Italian languages. Be assured that the Swiss German language is different from German in Germany. In contrast to three cultures for Swiss people, only a single region, CH, is defined for Switzerland. When the language is defined by the culture, the region defines the currency and the unit of measurement. The currency used in a region is independent of the language. There's even one bigger aspect of culture vs. region: a Swiss person can go to a different country where they can still use their "home-culture", but of course they have to change the region.

The location can also be set using the **Regional Options** in Control Panel. The `System.Globalization.RegionInfo` class has methods to get to these values. `RegionInfo` has a static property `CurrentRegion` to get the configured region. It's also possible to create a `RegionInfo` object by passing a 2- or 3-letter ISO3166 name as a string to the constructor. Examples of this string are AT or AUT for Austria, DE or DEU for Germany, FR or FRA for France, GB or GBR for the United Kingdom, and US or USA for the United States of America.

System.Globalization Namespace

The `System.Globalization` namespace holds all the culture and region classes to support different date formats, different number formats, and even different calendars like `GregorianCalendar`, `HebrewCalendar`, `JapaneseCalendar`, and so on. By using these classes, it's possible to use different representations depending on the locale.

Numbers

The number structures Int16, Int32, Int64, and so on, in the System namespace all have an overloaded ToString() method. This method can be used to create a different representation of the number depending on the locale. For the Int32 structure, ToString() is overloaded with these four versions:

```
public string ToString();
public string ToString(IFormatProvider);
public string ToString(string);
public string ToString(string, IFormatProvider);
```

ToString() without arguments returns a string without formatting options. We can also pass a string and a class that implements IFormatProvider. The string specifies the format of the representation. The format can be a standard numeric formatting string, or a picture numeric formatting string. For standard numeric formatting, strings are predefined where C specifies a currency notation, D creates a decimal output, E scientific output, F fixed-point output, G general output, N number output, and X hexadecimal output. With a picture numeric format string, it's possible to specify the number of digits, section and group separators, percent notations, and so on. The picture numeric format string ###,### means two 3-digit blocks separated by a group separator.

With the default constructor of NumberFormatInfo in the System.Globalization namespace, a culture-independent or invariant object is created. Using the properties of this class it's possible to change all the formatting options like a positive sign, percent symbol, number group separator, currency symbol, and a lot more. A read-only culture-independent NumberFormatInfo object is returned from the static property InvariantInfo. A NumberFormatInfo object, where the format values are based on the CultureInfo of the current thread, is returned from the static property CurrentInfo.

The IFormatProvider interface is implemented by the NumberFormatInfo, DateTimeFormatInfo, and CultureInfo classes. This interface defines a single method GetFormat() that returns a format object.

In the next examples I'm using a simple **Console Project**. In this code, the first example shows a number displayed in the format of the culture of the current thread. On my operating system, the setting is en-us. That's the default for the thread. The second example uses the ToString() method with the IFormatProvider argument. CultureInfo implements IFormatProvider, so I'm creating a CultureInfo object with the French culture. The third example changes the culture of the current thread. Using the property CurrentCulture of the Thread instance the culture is changed to German:

```
using System;
using System.Globalization;
using System.Threading;

namespace Wrox.ProCSharp.Assemblies.Localization
{
    class Class1
    {
        [STAThread]
        static void Main(string[] args)
        {
            int val = 1234567890;
```

```
                // culture of the current thread
                Console.WriteLine(val.ToString("N"));
                // use IFormatProvider
                Console.WriteLine(val.ToString("N", new CultureInfo("fr-fr")));
                // change the culture of the thread
                Thread.CurrentThread.CurrentCulture = new CultureInfo("de-de");
                Console.WriteLine(val.ToString("N"));
            }
        }
    }
```

The output is shown in the screenshot here. You can compare the outputs with the previously listed differences for US English, French, and German:

```
Command Prompt                                          _ □ X
C:\ProCSharp\Assemblies\Localization>Localization
1,234,567,890.00
1 234 567 890,00
1.234.567.890,00
```

Dates

The same support for numbers is here for dates. The DateTime structure has some methods for date-to-string conversions. The public instance methods ToLongDateString(), ToLongTimeString(), ToShortDateString(), ToShortTimeString() all create string representations using the current culture. Using the ToString() method a different culture can be assigned:

```
public string ToString();
public string ToString(IFormatProvider);
public string ToString(string);
public string ToString(string, IFormatProvider);
```

With the string argument of the ToString() method, a predefined format character or a custom format string can be specified for converting the date to a string. The DateTimeFormatInfo class specifies the possible values. With the IFormatProvider argument the culture can be specified. Using an overloaded method without the IFormatProvider argument means that the culture of the current thread is used:

```
            DateTime d = new DateTime(2001, 6, 15);
            // current culture
            System.Console.WriteLine(d.ToLongDateString());
            // use IFormatProvider
            System.Console.WriteLine(d.ToString("D", new CultureInfo("fr-fr")));
            // use culture of thread
            CultureInfo ci = Thread.CurrentThread.CurrentCulture;
            Console.WriteLine(ci.ToString() + ": " + d.ToString("D"));
            ci = new CultureInfo("de-de");
            Thread.CurrentThread.CurrentCulture = ci;
            Console.WriteLine(ci.ToString() + ": " + d.ToString("D"));
```

The output of our example program shows `ToLongDateString()` with the current culture of the thread, a French version where a `CultureInfo` instance is passed to the `ToString()` method, and a German version where the `CurrentCulture` of the thread is changed to `de-de`:

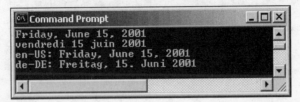

Besides having a different formatting and measurement system depending on the locale, strings should have different texts; perhaps some pictures should also be replaced depending on the locale. This is where satellite assemblies are used.

Satellite Assemblies

Satellite assemblies are used in applications to support language-dependent strings. Satellite assemblies are assemblies that hold only resources and no code. A string table, pictures, videos, and so on can be included. Of course, the `AssemblyCulture` attribute must be set. A satellite assembly for the `de` culture must be placed into the `de` subdirectory of the program. The satellite assembly supporting Austria's version of German is placed into the `de-at` subdirectory.

`de` and `de-at` have many translations in common. There are only a few differences. With the .NET architecture of satellite assemblies, it's not necessary to store all resources in the `de-at` assembly, just the differences. We just have to create a resource file with the different strings. If the user has a system where the region `de-at` is configured, and resources cannot be found there, the parent assembly is used; `de` is the parent assembly for `de-at`. If a resource can't be found there, then the resources of the neutral assembly are used. The neutral assembly is the assembly where no assembly culture is set. That's the reason why you shouldn't set a culture for the main assembly.

System.Resources Namespace

Before we move onto our example, we shall conclude this section with a review of the classes contained in the `System.Resources` namespace that deal with resources, some of which we've already met:

❑　The `ResourceManager` can be used to get resources for the current culture from satellite assemblies. Using the `ResourceManager` it's also possible to get a `ResourceSet` for a particular culture.

❑　A `ResourceSet` represents the resources for a particular culture. When a `ResourceSet` instance is created it enumerates over a class implementing the interface `IResourceReader`, and stores all resources in a `Hashtable`.

❑　The interface `IResourceReader` is used from the `ResourceSet` to enumerate resources. The class `ResourceReader` implements this interface.

❑　We already used the `ResourceWriter` class to create a resource file. `ResourceWriter` implements the interface `IResourceWriter`.

❑　Additionally there are some classes: `ResXResourceSet`, `ResXResourceReader`, and `ResXResourceWriter`. These classes are similar to `ResourceSet`, `ResourceReader`, and `ResourceWriter`, but create a XML-based resource file `.resX` instead of a binary file. `ResXFileRef` can be used to make a link to a resource instead of embedding it inside an XML file.

Localization Example Using Visual Studio .NET

We are going to create a simple Windows application to demonstrate localization using Visual Studio .NET. This application doesn't use complex Windows Forms, and doesn't have any real inner functionality because the main feature that is being demonstrated here is localization. In the sourcecode I'm changing the namespace to `Wrox.ProCSharp.Assemblies.Localization`, and the class name to `BookOfTheDayForm`. The namespace is not only changed in the source file `BookOfTheDayForm.cs`, but also in the project settings, so that all generated resource files will get this namespace, too. This is done within the **Common Properties** of **Project | Properties**.

To show some issues with localization, this program has a picture, some text, a date, and a number. The picture will also be localized so that the French version is different.

This form is created using the **Windows Forms Designer**:

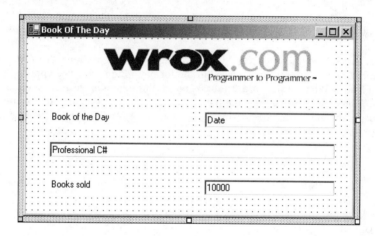

The values for the `Name` and `Text` properties for the Windows Forms elements are listed in this table:

Name	Text
labelBookOfTheDay	Book of the day
labelItemsSold	Books sold
textBoxDate	Date
textBoxTitle	Professional C#
textBoxItemsSold	10000

In addition to this form, we want to display a message box with a greeting, where the greeting message is different depending on the current time. This should demonstrate that the localization for dynamically created dialogs must be done differently. In the method `WelcomeMessage()`, we display a message box using `MessageBox.Show()`. We call the method `WelcomeMessage()` in the constructor of the form class `BookOfTheDayForm`, before the call to `InitializeComponent()`. Here's the code for the `WelcomeMessage` method:

```
public void WelcomeMessage()
{
    DateTime time = DateTime.Now;
    string message;
    if (time.Hour <= 12)
    {
        message = "Good Morning";
    }
    else if (time.Hour <= 19)
    {
        message = "Good Afternoon";
    }
    else
    {
        message = "Good Evening";
    }
    MessageBox.Show(message + " \nThis is a localization sample.");
}
```

The number and date in the form should be set using formatting options. We add a new method `SetDateAndNumber()` to set the values with the format option. In a real application these values could be received from a Web Service or a database, but in this example we are just concentrating on localization. The date is formatted using the D option (to display the long date name). The number is displayed using the picture number format string `###,###,###` where "#" represents a digit and "," is the group separator:

```
public void SetDateAndNumber()
{
    DateTime date = DateTime.Today;
    textBoxDate.Text = date.ToString("D");
    Int32 itemsSold = 327444;
    textBoxItemsSold.Text = itemsSold.ToString("###,###,###");
}
```

In the constructor of the `BookOfTheDayForm` class both the `WelcomeMessage` and `SetDateAndNumber()` methods are called.

```
public BookOfTheDayForm()
{
    WelcomeMessage();
    //
    // Required for Windows Form Designer support
    //
    InitializeComponent();
    SetDateAndNumber();
}
```

A magic feature of the Windows Forms designer is started when we set the `Localizable` property of the form from `false` to `true`: this results in the creation of an XML-based resource file for the dialog box that stores all resource strings, properties (including the location of Windows Forms elements), embedded pictures, and so on. In addition, the implementation of the `InitializeComponent()` method is changed; an instance of the class `System.Resources.ResourceManager` is created, and to get to the values and positions of the text fields and pictures, the `GetObject()` method is used instead of writing the values directly in the code. `GetObject()` uses the `CurrentUICulture` property of the current thread for finding the correct resources.

Here is part of `InitalizeComponent()` before the `Localizable` property is set to `true`, where all properties of `textBoxTitle` are set:

```
private void InitializeComponent()
{
    //...
    this.textBoxTitle = new System.Windows.Forms.TextBox();
    //...
    //
    // textBoxTitle
    //
    this.textBoxTitle.Cursor = System.Windows.Forms.Cursors.Default;
    this.textBoxTitle.Location = new System.Drawing.Point(32, 136);
    this.textBoxTitle.Name = "textBoxTitle";
    this.textBoxTitle.Size = new System.Drawing.Size(432, 20);
    this.textBoxTitle.TabIndex = 2;
    this.textBoxTitle.Text = "Professional C#";
```

This is the automatically changed code for `InitalizeComponent()` with the `Localizable` property set to `true`:

```
private void InitializeComponent()
{
    System.Resources.ResourceManager resources =
                new System.Resources.ResourceManager(typeof(BookOfTheDayForm));
    //...
    this.textBoxTitle = new System.Windows.Forms.TextBox();
    //...
    //
    // textBoxTitle
    //
    this.textBoxTitle.AccessibleDescription = ((string)
                (resources.GetObject("textBoxTitle.AccessibleDescription")));
    this.textBoxTitle.AccessibleName = ((string)
                    (resources.GetObject("textBoxTitle.AccessibleName")));
    this.textBoxTitle.Anchor = ((System.Windows.Forms.AnchorStyles)
                        (resources.GetObject("textBoxTitle.Anchor")));
    this.textBoxTitle.AutoSize = ((bool)
                    (resources.GetObject("textBoxTitle.AutoSize")));
    this.textBoxTitle.BackgroundImage = ((System.Drawing.Image)
                (resources.GetObject("textBoxTitle.BackgroundImage")));
    this.textBoxTitle.Cursor = ((System.Windows.Forms.Cursor)
                    (resources.GetObject("textBoxTitle.Cursor")));
    this.textBoxTitle.Dock = ((System.Windows.Forms.DockStyle)
                    (resources.GetObject("textBoxTitle.Dock")));
    this.textBoxTitle.Enabled = ((bool)
```

```
                          (resources.GetObject("textBoxTitle.Enabled")));
      this.textBoxTitle.Font = ((System.Drawing.Font)
                          (resources.GetObject("textBoxTitle.Font")));
      this.textBoxTitle.ImeMode = ((System.Windows.Forms.ImeMode)
                          (resources.GetObject("textBoxTitle.ImeMode")));
      this.textBoxTitle.Location = ((System.Drawing.Point)
                          (resources.GetObject("textBoxTitle.Location")));
      this.textBoxTitle.MaxLength = ((int)
                          (resources.GetObject("textBoxTitle.MaxLength")));
      this.textBoxTitle.Multiline = ((bool)
                          (resources.GetObject("textBoxTitle.Multiline")));
      this.textBoxTitle.Name = "textBoxTitle";
      this.textBoxTitle.PasswordChar = ((char)
                          (resources.GetObject("textBoxTitle.PasswordChar")));
      this.textBoxTitle.RightToLeft = ((System.Windows.Forms.RightToLeft)
                          (resources.GetObject("textBoxTitle.RightToLeft")));
      this.textBoxTitle.ScrollBars = ((System.Windows.Forms.ScrollBars)
                          (resources.GetObject("textBoxTitle.ScrollBars")));
      this.textBoxTitle.Size = ((System.Drawing.Size)
                          (resources.GetObject("textBoxTitle.Size")));
      this.textBoxTitle.TabIndex = ((int)
                          (resources.GetObject("textBoxTitle.TabIndex")));
      this.textBoxTitle.Text = resources.GetString("textBoxTitle.Text");
      this.textBoxTitle.TextAlign =
                          ((System.Windows.Forms.HorizontalAlignment)
                          (resources.GetObject("textBoxTitle.TextAlign")));
      this.textBoxTitle.Visible = ((bool)
                          (resources.GetObject("textBoxTitle.Visible")));
      this.textBoxTitle.WordWrap = ((bool)
                          (resources.GetObject("textBoxTitle.WordWrap")));
```

How does it work – where does the resource manager get the data? When we set the `Localizable` property to `true`, a resource file, `BookOfTheDay.resX`, was generated. In this file, the scheme of the XML resource can be found first, followed by all elements in the form: `Type`, `Text`, `Location`, `TabIndex`, and so on.

The following example shows a few of the properties of `textBoxTitle`: the `Location` property has a value of `36,136`, the `TabIndex` property has a value of `2`, the `Text` property is set to `Professional C#`, etc. For every value the type of the value is stored, as well. For example, the `Location` property is of type `System.Drawing.Point`, and this class can be found in the assembly `System.Drawing`.

Why are the locations and sizes also stored in this XML file? With translations, many strings will have completely different sizes and don't any longer fit in to the original positions. When the locations and sizes all are stored inside the resource file, everything that's needed for localizations is in these files, and is separate from the C# code:

```
<data name="textBoxTitle.Location" type="System.Drawing.Point, System.Drawing,
      Version=1.0.3300.0, Culture=neutral, PublicKeyToken=b03f5f7f11d50a3a">
   <value>36, 136</value>
</data>
<data name="textBoxTitle.TabIndex" type="System.Int32, mscorlib,
      Version=1.0.3300.0, Culture=neutral, PublicKeyToken=b77a5c561934e089">
   <value>2</value>
</data>
<data name="textBoxTitle.Text">
```

```
            <value>Professional C#</value>
    </data>
    <data name="textBoxTitle.TextAlign"
          type="System.Windows.Forms.HorizontalAlignment, System.Windows.Forms,
          Version=1.0.3300.0, Culture=neutral, PublicKeyToken=b77a5c561934e089">
        <value>Left</value>
    </data>
    <data name="textBoxTitle.Visible" type="System.Boolean, mscorlib,
          Version=1.0.3300.0, Culture=neutral, PublicKeyToken=b77a5c561934e089">
        <value>True</value>
    </data>
```

When changing some of these resource values, it's not necessary to work directly with the XML code. We can change these resources directly in the Visual Studio Designer. Whenever we change the Language property of the form and the properties of some form elements, a new resource file is generated for the specified language. We create a German version of the form by setting the Language property to German, and a French version by setting the Language property to French. For every language we get a resource file with the changed properties: BookOfTheDayForm.de.resx and BookOfTheDayForm.fr.resx. Here are the changes needed for the German version of the form:

German – Name	Value
$this.Text (title of the form)	Buch des Tages
labelItemsSold.Text	Bücher verkauft:
labelBookOfTheDay.Text	Buch des Tages

These are the changes for the French version. For the French version of the form we also change the picture, because Wrox Press has a French web site with a localized logo:

French – Name	Value
$this.Text (title of the form)	Le livre du jour
labelItemsSold.Text	Des livres vendus
labelBookOfTheDay.Text	Le livre du jour

Compiling the project now creates a **satellite assembly** for each language. Inside the debug directory (or release, depending on your active configuration), language subdirectories like de and fr are created. In such a subdirectory you'll find the file BookOfTheDay.resources.dll. These files are satellite assemblies that only include our localized resources. Opening this assembly using ildasm, we see this manifest with the embedded resources, and a defined locale. This assembly has the locale de in the assembly attributes, and so it can be found in the de subdirectory. You can also see the name of the resource with .mresource; it's prefixed with the namespace name Wrox.ProCSharp.Assemblies.Localization, followed by the class name BookOfTheDayForm and the language code de:

```
/ MANIFEST                                                          _ □ x

.assembly BookOfTheDay.resources
{
  .hash algorithm 0x00008004
  .ver 1:0:760:21574
  .locale = (64 00 65 00 00 00 )                          // d.e...
}
.mresource public Wrox.ProCSharp.Assemblies.Localization.BookOfTheDayForm.de
{
}
.module BookOfTheDay.resources.dll
// MVID: {42EB9B13-C17D-466F-B600-FC45CB9FB756}
.imagebase 0x00400000
.subsystem 0x00000003
.file alignment 512
.corflags 0x00000001
// Image base: 0x03670000
```

Outsourcing Translations

It is an easy task to outsource translations using resource files. When translating resource files, it is not necessary to install Visual Studio .NET, a simple XML editor would fulfill many requirements. The disadvantage of using an XML editor is that there is no real chance to rearrange Windows Forms elements and change the sizes if the translated text doesn't fit into the original borders of a label or button. Using a Windows Forms designer to do translations is a natural choice.

There is a tool delivered with the Microsoft .NET Framework SDK that fulfills all these requirements: the **Windows Resource Localization Editor** winres.exe. Users working with this tool don't need access to the C# source files, only binary or XML-based resource files are needed for translations. After these translations are completed, we can import the resource files to the Visual Studio .NET project to build satellite assemblies.

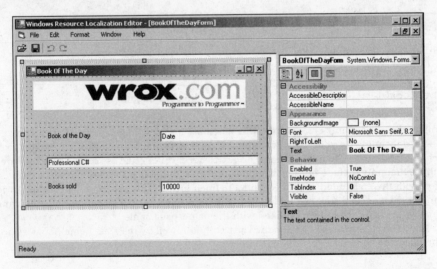

Changing the Culture Programmatically

After translating the resources and building the satellite assemblies we will get the correct translations depending on the configured culture for the user. The welcome message isn't translated at this time. This has been done in a different way, as we'll see shortly.

In addition to the system configuration, it should be possible to send the language code as command-line arguments to our application for testing purposes. The `Main()` method and the `BookOfTheDayForm` constructor are changed to support command-line arguments. In the `Main()` method we pass the culture string to the `BookOfTheDayForm` constructor. In the constructor we have to change something more: a `CultureInfo` instance is created to pass it to the `CurrentCulture` and `CurrentUICulture` properties of the current thread. Remember that the `CurrentCulture` is used for formatting, while the `CurrentUICulture` is used for loading of resources.

```
[STAThread]
static void Main(string[] args)
{
    string culture = "";
    if (args.Length == 1)
    {
        culture = args[0];
    }
    Application.Run(new BookOfTheDayForm(culture));
}
public BookOfTheDayForm(string culture)
{
    if (culture != "")
    {
        CultureInfo cultureInfo = new CultureInfo(culture);
        // set culture for formatting
        Thread.CurrentThread.CurrentCulture = cultureInfo;
        // set culture for resources
        Thread.CurrentThread.CurrentUICulture = cultureInfo;
    }
    WelcomeMessage();
    //
    // Required for Windows Form Designer support
    //

    InitializeComponent();
    SetDateAndNumber();
}
```

Now it's possible to start the application using command-line options. The formatting options and the resources that were generated from the Windows Forms Designer are used. Here are two screenshots where the application is started using the `fr-fr` and the `de-de` cultures:

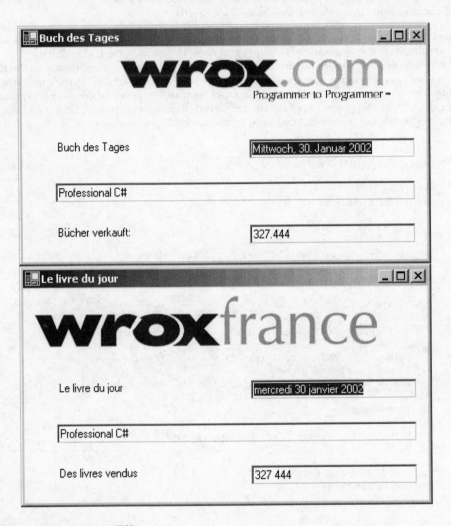

Using Binary Resource Files

There's still a problem with our welcome message box: the strings are hard-coded inside the program. Since these strings are not properties of elements inside the form, the Forms Designer doesn't extract XML resources like it does from the properties inside the `InitializeComponent()` method when we change the `Localizable` property of the form. We have to create resources ourselves.

The English text with a translation into German and French is listed in this table:

English	German	French
Good Morning	Guten Morgen	Bonjour
Good Afternoon	Guten Tag	Bonjour
Good Evening	Guten Abend	Bonsoir
This is a localization sample.	Das ist ein Beispiel mit Lokalisation.	C'est un exemple avec la localisation.

To support this I'm creating a simple text file (`Welcome.txt`), representing the default as well as German and French versions:

Default version, `Welcome.txt`:

```
GoodMorning=Good Morning
GoodAfternoon=Good Afternoon
GoodEvening=Good Evening
Description=This is a localization sample.
```

German version, `Welcome.de.txt`:

```
GoodMorning=Guten Morgen
GoodAfternoon=Guten Tag
GoodEvening=Guten Abend
Descpription=Das ist ein Beispiel mit Lokalisierung.
```

French version, `Welcome.fr.txt`:

```
GoodMorning=Bonjour
GoodAfternoon=Bonjour
GoodEvening=Bonsoir
Description=C'est un exemple avec la localisation.
```

We can use `resgen` to create the binary resource files `Welcome.resources`, `Welcome.de.resources`, and `Welcome.fr.resources`; for example, resgen `Welcome.de.txt` creates `Welcome.de.resources`. These files can be added to the solution using **Add | Add Existing Item in Solution Explorer**. In all these resource files the property `BuildAction` is automatically set to **Embedded Resource**, otherwise the satellite assembly won't be created. The name of the resources can be found using `ildasm`, as usual. The resources from the file `Welcome.de.resources` are named `Wrox.ProCSharp.Assemblies.Localization.Welcome.de` (the name of the namespace followed by the filename). Instead of using binary resource files, we can also add XML-based resource files to Visual Studio .NET projects, as we see next.

Using XML Resource Files

With the `resgen` command, we create XML resources out of the text based resource files:

❏   `resgen welcome.txt welcome.resx`

❏   `resgen welcome.de.txt welcome.de.resx`

❏   `resgen welcome.fr.txt welcome.fr.resx`

The generated XML-based resource files are then added to the project using **Add | Add Existing Item** in the **Solution Explorer**. Similar to binary resource files, the `BuildAction` for `.resx` files is set to **Embedded Resource**. When building the project, the resources are added to the satellite assemblies.

Now there are two `.mresource` entries in the satellite assembly – the resource `Wrox.ProCSharp.Assemblies.Localization.BookOfTheDayForm.de` was originally created from the Windows Forms Designer, and `Wrox.ProCSharp.Assemblies.Localization.Welcome.de` is the resource from the new `Welcome.de.resx` resource file:

```
/ MANIFEST                                                          _ |□| x|
.assembly BookOfTheDay.resources
{
    .hash algorithm 0x00008004
    .ver 1:0:760:22374
    .locale = (64 00 65 00 00 00 )                    // d.e...
}
.mresource public Wrox.ProCSharp.Assemblies.Localization.Welcome.de.resources
{
}
.mresource public Wrox.ProCSharp.Assemblies.Localization.BookOfTheDayForm.de.resour
{
}
.module BookOfTheDay.resources.dll
// MVID: {7F28F09A-1F2E-4988-BBBA-BE66D7B72254}
.imagebase 0x00400000
.subsystem 0x00000003
.file alignment 512
.corflags 0x00000001
// Image base: 0x03260000
```

Of course, the sourcecode of the `WelcomeMessage()` must also be changed to use the resources. A `ResourceManager` instance is created to get the resource named `Wrox.ProCSharp.Assemblies.Localization.Welcome` from the current assembly. With this resource manager we get the resources we created previously in the resource files using `GetString()` methods.

For the `ResourceManager` class, we have to declare the use of the `System.Resources` namespace; the `Assembly` class is in the `System.Reflection` namespace:

```
public void WelcomeMessage()
{
    ResourceManager resource = new
            ResourceManager("Wrox.ProCSharp.Assemblies.Localization.Welcome",
                                Assembly.GetExecutingAssembly());
    DateTime time = DateTime.Now;
    string message;
    if (time.Hour <= 12)
    {
```

```
            message = resource.GetString("GoodMorning");
    }
    else
        if (time.Hour <= 19)
        {
            message = resource.GetString("GoodAfternoon");
        }
        else
        {
            message = resource.GetString("GoodEvening");
        }
    MessageBox.Show(message + "\n\n" + resource.GetString("Description"));
}
```

When the program is started using English, German, or French we get these message boxes:

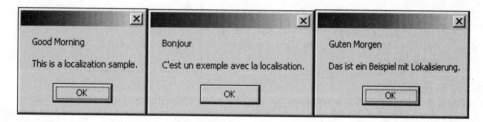

Changing Resources for Dialects

For the French and German versions, we've included all the resources inside the satellite assemblies. If not all the values are to change, that's not necessary. It's possible just to have the values that will change in the satellite assembly, with the other values are in the parent assembly. For example, for de-at (Austria) we could change the value for the GoodAfternoon resource to Grüß Gott, but no other values should be different. During runtime, when looking for the value of the resource GoodMorning that isn't in the de-at satellite assembly, the parent assembly would be searched. The parent for de-at is de. In cases where the de assembly doesn't have this resource either, the value would be searched for in the parent assembly of de; the neutral assembly. The neutral assembly doesn't have a culture code.

> **Remember: the culture code of the main assembly should be blank!**

Global Assembly Cache

The **global assembly cache** is, as the name implies, a cache for globally available assemblies. Most shared assemblies are installed inside this cache, but some private assemblies can also be found here. If a private assembly is compiled to native code using the native image generator, the compiled native code goes into this cache, too!

In this section, we shall explore:

❑ Creating native images at installation time

❑ Viewing shared assemblies with the Global Assembly Cache Viewer and the Global Assembly Cache Utility

Native Image Generator

With the native image generator Ngen.exe we can compile the IL code to native code at installation time. This way the program can start faster because the compilation during run time is no longer necessary. The ngen utility installs the native image in the **native image cache,** which is part of the global assembly cache.

> **Creating native images with ngen only makes sense if native images are created for all assemblies used by the application. Otherwise the JIT compiler would have to be started anyway.**

With ngen myassembly, we can compile the MSIL code to native code, and install it into the native image cache. This should be done from an installation program if we would like to put the assembly in the native image cache.

> **After compiling the assembly to native code you cannot delete the original assembly with the MSIL code because the metadata is still needed, and, if the security changes on the system, the native code will be rebuilt.**

With ngen we can also display all assemblies from the native image cache with the option /show. If we add an assembly name to the /show option we get the information about all installed versions of this assembly:

```
C:\ProCSharp>ngen /show System.Windows.Forms
Microsoft (R) CLR Native Image Generator - Version 1.0.3512.0
Copyright (C) Microsoft Corporation 1998-2001. All rights reserved.
System.Windows.Forms, Version=1.0.3300.0, Culture=neutral, PublicKeyToken=b77a5
561934e089
```

Global Assembly Cache Viewer

The global assembly cache can be displayed using shfusion.dll, which is a Windows shell extension to view and manipulate the contents of the cache. A Windows shell extension is a COM DLL that integrates with the Windows explorer. You just have to start the explorer and go to the <windir>/assembly directory.

The picture below shows the assembly cache viewer:

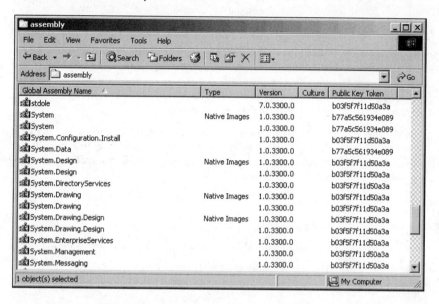

With the Assembly Viewer, the Global Assembly Name, Type, Version, Culture, and the Public Key Token can be seen. With the Type we can see if the assembly was installed using the native image generator. Using the context menu when selecting an assembly, it's possible to delete an assembly, and to view the properties:

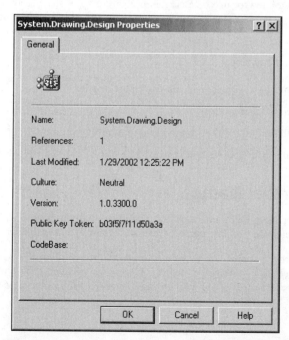

The real files and directories behind the assembly cache can be seen by viewing the directory from the command line. Inside the `<windir>\assembly` directory there's a GAC and `NativeImages_<runtime version>` directory. GAC is the directory for shared assemblies, and in `NativeImages_<runtime_version>` we can find the assemblies compiled to native code. If you go deeper in the directory structure you find directories names that are similar to the assembly names, and below that a version directory and the assemblies themselves. This makes it possible that different versions of the same assembly can be installed.

Global Assembly Cache Utility (gacutil.exe)

The assembly viewer can be used to view and delete assemblies using the Windows explorer, but it's not possible to use it from scripting code, such as to create installation programs. `gacutil.exe` is a utility to install, uninstall, and list assemblies using the command line. Naturally, it can be used within scripting code for administration purposes.

Some of the `gacutil` options are:

❑ `gacutil /l` lists all assemblies from the assembly cache

❑ `gacutil /i mydll` installs the shared assembly `mydll` into the assembly cache

❑ `gacutil /u mydll` uninstalls the assembly `mydll`

❑ `gacutil /ungen mydll` uninstalls the assembly from the native image cache

Creating Shared Assemblies

Assemblies can be isolated for use by a single application – not sharing an assembly is the default. When using private assemblies it's not necessary to pay attention to any requirements that are necessary for sharing.

In this section, we shall explore:

❑ Strong names as a requirement for shared assemblies

❑ Creating shared assemblies

❑ Installing shared assemblies in the global assembly cache

❑ Delayed signing of shared assemblies

Shared Assembly Names

The goal of a shared assembly name is that it must be globally unique, and it must be possible to protect the name. At no time may another person create an assembly using the same name.

COM solved only the first problem by using a globally unique identifier (GUID). The second problem, however, still existed as anyone could steal the GUID and create a different object with the same identifier. Both problems are solved with **strong names** of .NET assemblies.

A strong name is made of these items:

- ❏ The **name** of the assembly itself.

- ❏ A **version number**. This makes it possible to use different versions of the same assembly at the same time. Different versions can also work side-by-side, and can be loaded concurrently inside the same process.

- ❏ A **public key** guarantees that the strong name is unique. It also guarantees that a referenced assembly can't be replaced from a different source.

- ❏ A **culture**. We already talked about cultures when doing localization. Cultures are useful for private assemblies too.

> **A shared assembly must have a strong name to uniquely identify the assembly.**

A strong (shared) name is a simple text name accompanied by a version number, a public key, and a culture. You wouldn't create a new public key with every assembly, but you'd have one in the company, so the key uniquely identifies your company's assemblies.

However, this key this cannot be used as a trust key. Assemblies can carry Authenticode signatures to build up a trust. The key for the Authenticode signature can be a different one from the key used for the strong name.

> *For development purposes a different public key can be used, and later exchanged easily with the real key. We will look at this feature in the* Delayed Signing of Assemblies *section.*

To uniquely identify the assemblies in your companies, a useful namespace hierarchy should be used to name your classes. Here is a simple example showing how to organize namespaces: Wrox Press can use the major namespace `Wrox` for its classes and namespaces. In the hierarchy below the namespace, the namespaces must be organized so that all classes are unique. Every chapter of this book uses a different namespace of the form `Wrox.ProCSharp.<Description>`; this chapter uses `Wrox.ProCSharp.Assemblies`. So if there is a class `Hello` in two different chapters there's no conflict because of different namespaces. Utility classes that are used across different books can go into the namespace `Wrox.Utilities`.

A company name that usually is used as the first part of the namespace is not necessarily unique, so something more must be used to build a strong name. For this the public key is used. Because of the public/private key principle in strong names, no one without access to your private key can destructively create an assembly that could be unintentionally called by the client.

Public Key Cryptography

If you already know about public key cryptography, you can skip this section. For the rest of you, this is a simple introduction to keys. For encryption, we have to differentiate between **symmetric** encryption and **public/private key** encryption.

With a symmetric key, the same key can be used for encryption and decryption, but this is not the case with a public/private key pair. If something is encrypted using a public key, it can be decrypted using the corresponding private key, but not with the public key. This also works the other way around: if something is encrypted using a private key, it can be decrypted using the corresponding public key, but not the private key.

Public and private keys are always created as a pair. The public key can be made available to everybody, and it can even be put on a web site, but the private key must be safely locked away. Let's look at some examples where these public and private keys are used.

If Sarah sends a mail to Julian, and Sarah wants to make sure that no one else but Julian can read the mail, she uses Julian's public key. The message is encrypted using Julian's public key. Julian opens the mail and can decrypt it using his secretly stored private key. This way guarantees that no one else other than Julian can read Sarah's mail.

There's one problem left: Julian can't be sure that the mail is from Sarah. Anyone could use Julian's public key to encrypt mails sent to Julian. We can extend this principle. Let's start again with Sarah sending a mail to Julian. Before Sarah encrypts the mail using Julian's public key, she adds her signature and encrypts the signature using her own private key. Then she encrypts the mail using Julian's public key. Therefore, it is guaranteed that no one else but Julian can read the mail. When Julian decrypts the mail, he detects an encrypted signature. The signature can be decrypted using Sarah's public key. For Julian it's no problem to access Sarah's public key, because this key is public. After decrypting the signature, Julian can be sure that Sarah sent the mail.

Next we will look at how this public/private key principle is used with assemblies.

Integrity Using Strong Names

When creating a shared component, a public/private key pair must be used. The compiler writes the public key to the manifest, creates a hash of all files belonging to the assembly, and signs the hash with the private key. The private key is not stored within the assembly. This way it is guaranteed that no one can change your assembly. The signature can be verified with the public key.

During development, the client assembly must reference the shared assembly. The compiler writes the public key of the referenced assembly to the manifest of the client assembly. To reduce storage, it is not the public key that is written to the manifest of the client assembly, but a public key token. The public key token is the last eight bytes of a hash of the public key, and that is unique.

At run time, during loading of the shared assembly (or at install-time if the client is installed using the native image generator), the hash of the shared component assembly can be verified using the public key stored inside the client assembly. Only the owner of the private key can change the shared component assembly. There is no way a component Math that was created by vendor A, and referenced from a client can be replaced by a component from a hacker. Only the owner of the private key can replace the shared component with a new version. Integrity is guaranteed in so far that the shared assembly is from the expected publisher:

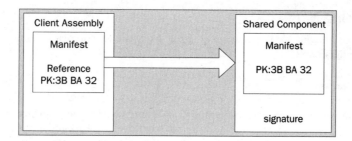

Creating a Shared Assembly

In our example, we will create a shared assembly and a client that uses it.

Before we create the shared assembly we start with a simple Visual C# Class Library project. I'm changing the namespace to `Wrox.ProCSharp.Assemblies.Sharing`, and the class name to `SimpleShared`. This class just reads all the lines of a file that's passed inside the constructor in a `StringCollection` at creation time, and returns a random string of this collection in the `GetQuoteOfTheDay()` method:

```csharp
using System;
using System.Collections.Specialized;
using System.IO;
namespace Wrox.ProCSharp.Assemblies.Sharing
{
    public class SimpleShared
    {
        private StringCollection quotes;
        private Random random;
        public SimpleShared(string filename)
        {
            quotes = new StringCollection();
            Stream stream = File.OpenRead(filename);
            StreamReader streamReader = new StreamReader(stream);
            string quote;
            while ((quote = streamReader.ReadLine()) != null)
            {
                quotes.Add(quote);
            }
            streamReader.Close();
            stream.Close();
            random = new Random();
        }
        public string GetQuoteOfTheDay()
        {
            int index = random.Next(1, quotes.Count);
            return quotes[index];
        }
    }
}
```

Create a Strong Name

To share this component we first need to create a strong name. To create such a name we can use the **strong name utility** (sn):

```
sn -k mykey.snk
```

The strong name utility generates and writes a public/private key pair, and writes this pair to a file; here the file is mykey.snk. Now we can set the AssemblyKeyFile attribute in the wizard-generated file Assemblyinfo.cs. The attribute must be either set to an absolute path to the key file, or the key file must be addressed relatively from the %ProjectDirectory%\obj\<configuration> directory, so ../../mykey.snk references a key in the project directory. When starting a build of the project, the key is installed in the **Crypto Service Provider** (**CSP**). If the key is already installed in the CSP, it's possible to use the AssemblyKeyName attribute instead.

Here are our changes to AssemblyInfo.cs. The attribute AssemblyKeyFile is set to the file mykey.snk:

```
[assembly: AssemblyDelaySign(false)]
[assembly: AssemblyKeyFile("../../mykey.snk")]
[assembly: AssemblyKeyName("")]
```

After rebuilding, the public key can be found inside the manifest when looking at the assembly using ildasm:

```
 MANIFEST                                                                    _|□|x|
    //   .custom instance void [mscorlib]System.Diagnostics.DebuggableAttribute ▲
    //
    .publickey = (00 24 00 00 04 80 00 00 94 00 00 00 06 02 00 00    // .$.....
                  00 24 00 00 52 53 41 31 00 04 00 00 01 00 01 00    // .$..RSA
                  DB 66 48 C3 A0 B8 E1 08 4E C4 2F F8 46 9C 4E 47    // .fH....
                  9C AA B7 F3 4B 0F C1 9B 72 72 28 FF 9D 56 29 94    // ....K..
                  E7 9E 11 2F 39 24 AD 53 B6 23 E3 24 50 FD 0B 6E    // .../9$.
                  EC C8 63 13 49 F2 D0 91 EC 50 3C A4 47 3E E3 90    // ..c.I..
                  AC 4E 7E 94 20 35 B9 D6 40 78 EA 07 FB 20 E8 19    // .N~. 5.
                  05 32 D1 B6 96 94 B5 97 0D E1 E3 E5 21 5D 5C 29    // .2.....
                  CE 52 70 F1 9C 19 68 45 88 9C F2 D3 D2 45 D3 1B    // .Rp...
                  9A AE 6D 78 34 02 D3 52 9B 7A 7F 6D 92 DD 31 C4 )  // ..mx4..
    .hash algorithm 0x00008004
    .ver 1:0:760:23717
}
.module SimpleShared.dll
// MVID: {337AFC96-ADAF-467F-BED1-E033FBA94C4E}
.imagebase 0x11000000
.subsystem 0x00000003
.file alignment 512
.corflags 0x00000009
// Image base: 0x03820000
◄|                                                                            ►|
```

Install the Shared Assembly

With a public key in the assembly, it's now possible to install it in the global assembly store using the global assembly cache tool gacutil with the /i option:

```
gacutil /i SimpleShared.dll
```

We can use the Global Assembly Cache Viewer to check the version of the shared assembly, and check if it is successfully installed.

Using the Shared Assembly

To use the shared assembly we will now create a C# Console Application called `Client`. Instead of adding the new project to the previous solution, you should create a new solution so that the shared assembly doesn't get rebuilt when rebuilding the client. I'm changing the name of the namespace to `Wrox.ProCSharp.Assemblies.Sharing`, and the name of the class to `Client`.

We reference the assembly `SimpleShared` in the same way as we are referencing private assemblies: use the menu **Project I Add Reference**, or use the context menu in **Solution Explorer**. Then select the **Browse** button to find the assembly `SimpleShared`. Because the `SimpleShared` assembly is shared, the `CopyLocal` property of the reference is automatically set to `false`, so that the shared assembly is not copied to the client directory; the assembly installed into the global assembly store will be used.

Here's the code for the client application:

```
using System;

namespace Wrox.ProCSharp.Assemblies.Sharing
{
   class Client
   {
      [STAThread]
      static void Main(string[] args)
      {
         SimpleShared quotes = new SimpleShared(
                             @"C:\ProCSharp\Assemblies\Quotes.txt");
         for (int i=0; i < 3; i++)
         {
            Console.WriteLine(quotes.GetQuoteOfTheDay());
            Console.WriteLine();
         }
      }
   }
}
```

When viewing the manifest in the client assembly using `ildasm` we can see the reference to the shared assembly `SimpleShared`: `.assembly extern SimpleShared`. Part of this referenced information is the version number we will talk about next, and the token of the public key.

```
┌─ MANIFEST ──────────────────────────────────────────────── _□×┐
│.assembly extern mscorlib                                        ▲│
│{                                                                 │
│  .publickeytoken = (B7 7A 5C 56 19 34 E0 89 )          // ·     │
│  .ver 1:0:3300:0                                                 │
│}                                                                 │
│.assembly extern SimpleShared                                    │
│{                                                                 │
│  .publickeytoken = (C1 4E 33 EF 37 2A E3 FC )          // ·     │
│  .ver 1:0:760:23717                                             │
│}                                                                 │
│.assembly Client                                                 │
│{                                                                 │
│  .custom instance void [mscorlib]System.Reflection.AssemblyCopyrightAttrib│
│  .custom instance void [mscorlib]System.Reflection.AssemblyKeyFileAttribut│
│  .custom instance void [mscorlib]System.Reflection.AssemblyDelaySignAttrib▼│
│◄ │                                                          ► │  │
└─────────────────────────────────────────────────────────────────┘
```

The token of the public key can also be seen within the shared assembly using the strong name utility: sn -T shows the token of the public key in the assembly, sn -Tp shows the token, and the public key. Pay attention to the use of the uppercase T!

The result of our program with a sample quotes file could now look like this:

```
┌─ Command Prompt ──────────────────────────────────────── _□×┐
│"I think there is a world market for maybe five computers", T. Watson, Chairman ▲│
│of IBM, 1943                                                     │
│                                                                 │
│"We will think about software more as a service than we have in the past.", Bill │
│ Gates, Microsoft Chief Software Architect, 2000                │
│                                                                 │
│"I think there is a world market for maybe five computers", T. Watson, Chairman │
│of IBM, 1943                                                    ▼│
└─────────────────────────────────────────────────────────────────┘
```

Delayed Signing of Assemblies

The private key of a company should be safely stored. Most companies don't give all the developers access to the private key; just a few security people have access to it. That's why the signature of an assembly can be added at a later time, such as before distribution. When the global assembly attribute AssemblyDelaySign is set to true, no signature is stored in the assembly, but enough free space is reserved so that it can be added later. However, without using a key, we can't test the assembly and install it in the global assembly cache. However, we can use a temporary key for testing purposes, and replace this key with the real company key later.

The following steps are required to delay signing of assemblies:

❑ Firstly we have to create a public / private key pair with the strong name utility sn. The generated file mykey.snk includes both the public and private key.

```
sn -k mykey.snk
```

❑ Next we can extract the public key to make it available to developers. The option -p extracts the public key of the keyfile. The file mypublickey.snk only holds the public key.

```
sn -p mykey.snk mypublickey.snk
```

❑ All developers in the company can use this keyfile `mypublickey.snk` and set the `AssemblyDelaySign` and `AssemblyKeyFile` attributes in the file `AssemblyInfo.cs`:

```
[assembly: AssemblyDelaySign(true)]
[assembly: AssemblyKeyFile("../../mypublickey.snk")]
```

❑ Before distribution the assembly can be resigned with the `sn` utility. The `-R` option is used to resign previously signed or delayed signed assemblies.

```
sn -R MyAssembly.dll mykey.snk
```

Configuration

COM components used the registry to configure components. Configuration of .NET applications is done using configuration files. With registry configurations, an `xcopy-deployment` is not possible. The configuration files use XML syntax to specify startup and runtime settings for applications.

In this section, we shall explore:

❑ What can be configured using the XML base configuration files

❑ How a strong named referenced assembly can be redirected to a different version

❑ How to specify the directory of assemblies to find private assemblies in subdirectories and shared assemblies in common directories or on a server

Configuration Categories

We can group the configuration into these categories:

❑ With **startup settings,** the version of the required runtime can be specified. It's possible that different versions of the runtime could be installed on the same system. With the `<startup>` element, the version of the runtime can be specified.

❑ With the **runtime settings** we can specify how garbage collection is performed by the runtime, and how the binding to assemblies works. We can also specify the version policy and the code base with these settings. We will take a more detailed look into the runtime settings later in this chapter.

❑ **Remoting settings** are used to configure applications using .NET Remoting. We will look into these configurations in Chapter 21.

❑ **Security settings** will be introduced in Chapter 23, and configuration for cryptography and permissions is done there.

These settings can be given in three types of configuration files:

❑ **Application configuration files** include specific settings for an application, such as binding information to assemblies, configuration for remote objects, and so on. Such a configuration file is placed into the same directory as the executable; it has the same name as the executable with a `.config` appended. ASP.NET configuration files are named `web.config`.

❏ **Machine configuration files** are used for system-wide configurations. We can also specify assembly binding and remoting configurations here. During a binding process, the machine configuration file is consulted before the application configuration file. The application configuration can override settings from the machine configuration. The application configuration file should be the preferred place for application-specific settings so that the machine configuration file stays smaller and manageable. A machine configuration file is located in `%runtime_install_path%\config\Machine.config`.

❏ **Publisher policy files** can be used by a component creator to specify that a shared assembly is compatible with older versions. If a new assembly version just fixes a bug of a shared component it is not necessary to put application configuration files in every application directory that uses this component; instead, the publisher can mark it as "compatible" by adding a publisher policy file. In the case that the component doesn't work with all applications it is possible to override the publisher policy setting in an application configuration file. In contrast to the other configuration files, publisher policy files are stored in the global assembly cache.

How are these configuration files used? How a client finds an assembly (also called **binding**) depends upon whether the assembly is private or shared. Private assemblies must be in the directory of the application or a subdirectory thereof. A process called **probing** is used to find such an assembly. For probing, the version number is not used, but the culture is an important aspect as we've seen in our localization example.

Shared assemblies can be installed in the global assembly cache, placed in a directory, a network share, or on a web site. We specify such a directory with the configuration of the **codeBase,** as we will see soon. The public key, version, and culture are all important aspects when binding to a shared assembly. The reference of the required assembly is recorded in the manifest of the client assembly, including the name, the version, and the public key token. All configuration files are checked to apply the correct version policy. The global assembly cache and code bases specified in the configuration files are checked, followed by the application directories, and probing rules are then applied.

Versioning

For private assemblies, versioning is not important because the referenced assemblies are copied with the client. The client uses the assembly it has in its private directories.

This is, however, different for shared assemblies. Let's look at the traditional problems that can occur with sharing. Using shared components, more than one client application can use the same component. The new version can break existing clients when updating a shared component with a newer version. We can't stop shipping new versions because new features are requested and introduced with new versions of existing components. We can try to program carefully to be backwards-compatible, but that's not always going to be possible.

A solution to this dilemma could be an architecture that allows installation of different versions of shared components, with clients using the version that they referenced during the build process. This solves a lot of problems, but not all of them. What happens if we detect a bug in a component that's referenced from the client? We would like to update this component and make sure that the client uses the new version instead of the version that was referenced during the build process.

Therefore, depending on the type in the fix of the new version, sometimes we want to use a newer version, and sometimes we want to use the older referenced version. All this is possible with the .NET architecture.

In .NET, the original referenced assembly is used by default. We can redirect the reference to a different version using configuration files. Versioning plays a key role in the binding architecture – how the client gets the right assembly where the components live.

Version Numbers

Assemblies have a four-part version number, for example. `1.0.479.36320`. The parts are:

```
<Major>.<Minor>.<Build>.<Revision>
```

How these numbers are used depends on your application configuration.

> **A good policy would be that you change the major or minor number on changes incompatible with the previous version, but just the build or revision number with compatible changes. This way we can assume that redirecting an assembly to a new version where just the build and revision changed is safe.**

We specify the version number in the assembly with the assembly attribute `AssemblyVersion`. In Visual Studio .NET projects we find this attribute in `AssemblyInfo.cs`:

```
[assembly: AssemblyVersion("1.0.*")]
```

The first two numbers specify the major and minor version, and the "*" means that the build and revision numbers are auto-generated. The build number is the number of days since January 1st, 2000, and the revision is the number of seconds since midnight local time. Of course, you can also specify four values, but be sure to change the numbers when rebuilding the assembly.

This version is stored in the `.assembly` section of the manifest.

Referencing the assembly in the client application stores the version of the referenced assembly in the manifest of the client application.

Getting the Version Programmatically

To make it possible to check the version of the assembly that is used from our client application, we are adding the method `GetAssemblyFullName()` to the `SimpleShared` class to return the strong name of the assembly. For easy use of the `Assembly` class, we have to add the `System.Reflection` namespace:

```
public string GetAssemblyFullName()
{
    Assembly assembly = Assembly.GetExecutingAssembly();
    return assembly.FullName;
}
```

The `FullName` property of the `Assembly` class holds the name of the class, the version, the locality, and the public key token as you see in our output below, when calling `GetAssemblyFullName()` in our client application.

In the client application, we just add a call to `GetAssemblyFullName()` in the `Main()` method after creating the shared component:

```
static void Main(string[] args)
{
    SimpleShared quotes = new SimpleShared(@"C:\ProCSharp\Assemblies\Quotes.txt");
    Console.WriteLine(quotes.GetAssemblyFullName());
```

Be sure to register the new version of the shared assembly `SimpleShared` again in the global assembly cache using `gacutil`. If the referenced version cannot be found, you will get a `System.IO.FileLoadException`, because the binding to the correct assembly failed.

With a successful run, we can see the full name of the referenced assembly:

Using this client program, we can now try different configurations of this shared component.

Application Configuration Files

With a configuration file we can specify that the binding should happen to a different version of a shared assembly. Let's say we create a new version of the shared assembly `SimpleShared` with major and minor versions 1.1. We don't want to rebuild the client – we just want to use the new version of the assembly with the existing client. This is useful in cases where either a bug is fixed with the shared assembly, or we just want to get rid of the old version because the new version is compatible.

With the global assembly cache viewer, we can see that the versions `1.0.735.36320`, `1.0.741.29127`, and `1.1.741.31355` are installed for the `SimpleShared` assembly:

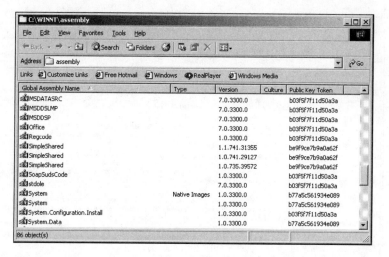

The manifest of the client application says that the client references version 1.0.741.29127 of the assembly SimpleShared:

Now we need an application configuration file. It's not necessary to work directly with XML; the .NET Framework Configuration tool can create application and machine configuration files. The .NET Framework Configuration tool is a MMC Snap-in that can be started from the Administrative Tools in the Control Panel:

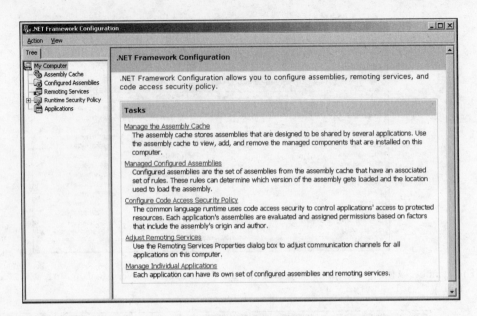

Selecting **Applications** on the left side, and the menu **Action | Add...** a list shows all .NET applications that have been previously started on this computer. We can select the `Client.exe` application to create an application configuration file for this application. After adding our client application to the .NET Admin Tool, we can view the assembly dependencies:

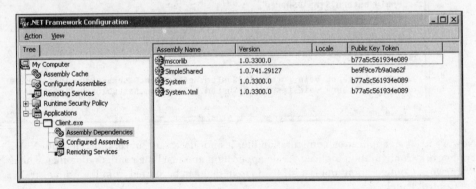

Selecting **Configured Assemblies** and the menu **Action | Add...** we can configure the dependency of the assembly `SimpleShared` from the dependency list:

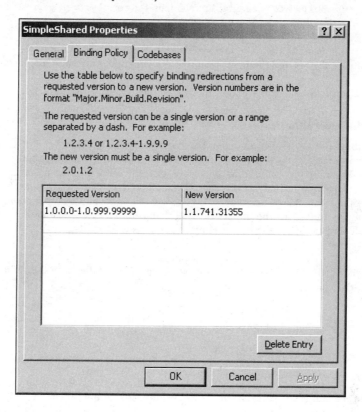

For the **Requested Version**, we specify the version that's referenced in the manifest of the client assembly. **New Version** specifies the new version of the shared assembly. In the above picture we specify that the version 1.1.741.31355 should be used instead of any version in the range of 1.0.0.0 to 1.0.999.99999.

Now we can find an application configuration file `Client.exe.config` in the directory of the `Client.exe` application that includes this XML code:

```xml
<?xml version="1.0"?>
<configuration>
    <runtime>
        <assemblyBinding xmlns="urn:schemas-microsoft-com:asm.v1">
            <dependentAssembly>
                <assemblyIdentity name="SimpleShared"
                                  publicKeyToken="be9f9ce7b9a0a62f" />
                <bindingRedirect oldVersion="1.0.0.0-1.0.999.99999"
                                 newVersion="1.1.741.31355" />
            </dependentAssembly>
        </assemblyBinding>
    </runtime>
</configuration>
```

With the `<runtime>` element, runtime settings can be configured. The sub-element of `<runtime>` is `<assemblyBinding>`, which in turn has a sub-element `<dependentAssembly>`. `<dependentAssembly>` has a required sub-element `<assemblyIdentity>`. We specify the name of the referenced assembly with `<assemblyIdentity>`. name is the only mandatory attribute for `<assemblyIdentity>`. The optional attributes are `publicKeyToken` and `culture`. The other sub-element of `<dependentAssembly>` that's needed for version redirection is `<bindingRedirect>`. With this element the old and the new version of the dependent assembly is specified.

Starting the client with this configuration file, we get the redirected version 1.1.741.31355.

Publisher Policy Files

Using assemblies that are shared in the global assembly cache it is also possible to use publisher policies to override versioning issues. Let's assume that we have a shared assembly that is used by some applications. What if a bug is found in the shared assembly? We have seen that it is not necessary to rebuild all the applications that use this shared assembly as we can use configuration files to redirect to the new version of this shared assembly. Maybe we don't know all the applications that use this shared assembly, but we want to get the bug fix to all of them. In that case we can create publisher policy files to redirect all applications to the new version of the shared assembly.

> Publisher policy files only apply to shared assemblies installed into the global assembly cache.

To set up publisher policies we have to:

- ❑ Create a publisher policy file
- ❑ Create a publisher policy assembly
- ❑ Add the publisher policy assembly to the global assembly cache

Create a Publisher Policy File

A publisher policy file is an XML file that redirects an existing version or version range to a new version. The syntax used is the same as for application configuration files, so we can use the same file we created earlier to redirect the old versions 1.0.0.0-1.0.999.99999 to the new version 1.1.741.31355.

I renamed the previously created file to `mypolicy.config` to use it as a publisher policy file.

```xml
<?xml version="1.0"?>
<configuration>
    <runtime>
        <assemblyBinding xmlns="urn:schemas-microsoft-com:asm.v1">
            <dependentAssembly>
                <assemblyIdentity name="SimpleShared"
                                  publicKeyToken="be9f9ce7b9a0a62f" />
                <bindingRedirect oldVersion="1.0.0.0-1.0.999.99999"
                                 newVersion="1.1.741.31355" />
            </dependentAssembly>
        </assemblyBinding>
    </runtime>
</configuration>
```

Create a Publisher Policy Assembly

To associate the publisher policy file with the shared assembly we have to create a publisher policy assembly that can be put into the global assembly cache. The tool that can be used to create such files is the assembly linker al. The option /linkresource adds the publisher policy file to the generated assembly. The name of the generated assembly must start with policy, followed by the major and minor version number of the assembly that should be redirected, and the filename of the shared assembly. In our case the publisher policy assembly must be named policy.1.0.SimpleShared.dll to redirect the assemblies SimpleShared with the major version 1, and minor version 0. The key that must be added to this publisher key with the option /keyfile is the same key that was used to sign the shared assembly SimpleShared to guarantee that the version redirection is from the same publisher.

```
al /linkresource:mypolicy.config /out:policy.1.0.SimpleShared.dll
   /keyfile:..\..\mykey.snk
```

Add the Publisher Policy Assembly to the Global Assembly Cache

The publisher policy assembly can now be added to the global assembly cache with the utility gacutil.

```
gacutil -i policy.1.0.SimpleShared.dll
```

Now we can remove the application configuration file that was placed in the directory of the client application, and start the client application. Although the client assembly references 1.0.741.29127 we use the new version 1.1.741.31355 of the shared assembly because of the publisher policy.

Overriding Publisher Policies

With a publisher policy, the publisher of the shared assembly guarantees that a new version of the assembly is compatible with the old version. As we know from changes of traditional DLLs, such guarantees don't always hold. Maybe all but one application is working with the new shared assembly. To fix the one application that has a problem with the new release, we can override the publisher policy by using an application configuration file.

With the .NET Framework configuration tool we can override the publisher policy by setting a checkbox:

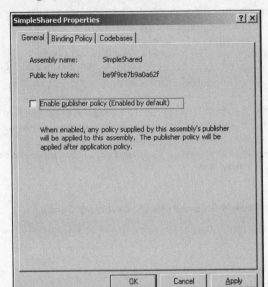

Disabling the publisher policy with the .NET Framework Configuration results in a configuration file with the XML element <publisherPolicy> and the attribute apply="no".

```
<?xml version="1.0"?>
<configuration>
  <runtime>
    <assemblyBinding xmlns="urn:schemas-microsoft-com:asm.v1">
      <dependentAssembly>
        <assemblyIdentity name="SimpleShared" publicKeyToken="be9f9ce7b9a0a62f" />
        <publisherPolicy apply="no" />
      </dependentAssembly>
    </assemblyBinding>
  </runtime>
</configuration>
```

Disabling the publisher policy we can configure different version redirection in the application configuration file.

Fixing an Application

If it happens that an application doesn't run because a configuration is wrong or because newly installed assemblies let it fail, the .NET Framework Configuration has an option to fix .NET applications. Clicking the Fix an Application hyperlink lists all .NET applications that were running previously and allows us to restore the last version of the application configuration file. With the Advanced option, it is also possible to reapply a specific configuration that probably was working, as can be seen in the screenshot opposite. Selecting the Application SafeMode disables publisher policies.

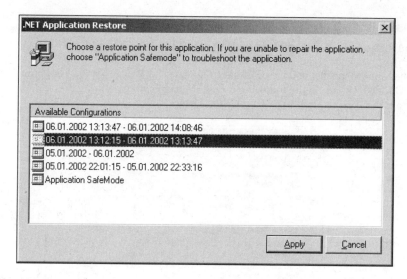

Runtime Version

In an application configuration file, it's not only possible to redirect versions of referenced assemblies; we can also define the required version of the runtime. Different .NET runtime versions can be installed on a single machine. We can specify the version that's required for the application in an application configuration file:

```
<?xml version="1.0"?>
<configuration>
   <startup>
      <requiredRuntime version="v1.0.3512" safeMode="true" />
   </startup>
</configuration>
```

The `version` attribute of the `<requiredRuntime>` element specifies the version number of the runtime. The version number must be the same name as the directory of the runtime. The runtime I'm using is in the directory `c:\winnt\Microsoft.NET\Framework\v1.0.3512`, so the version I have to specify is `v1.0.3512`.

Configuring Directories

We've already seen how to redirect referenced assemblies to a different version so that we can locate our assemblies, but there are more options to configure! For example, it's not necessary to install a shared assembly in the global assembly cache. It's also possible that shared assemblies can be found with the help of specific directory settings in configuration files. This feature can be used if you want to make the shared components available on a server. Another possible scenario is if you want to share an assembly between your applications, but you don't want to make it publicly available in the global assembly cache, so you put it into a shared directory instead.

There are two ways to find the correct directory for an assembly: the `codeBase` element in an XML configuration file, or through probing. The `codeBase` configuration is only available for shared assemblies, and probing is done for private assemblies.

<codeBase>

The <codeBase> can also be configured using the .NET Admin Tool. Codebases can be configured by selecting the properties of the configured application, SimpleShared, inside the Configured Assemblies in the Applications tree. Similar to the Binding Policy, we can configure lists of versions with the Codebases tab. In the following screen we have configured that the version 1.0 should be loaded from the Web server http://CNagel/WroxUtils:

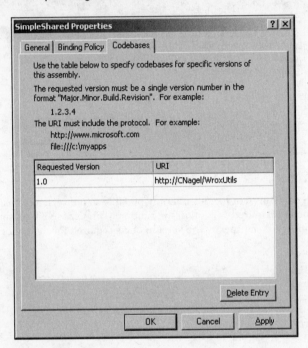

The .NET Admin tool creates this application configuration file:

```xml
<?xml version="1.0"?>
<configuration>
    <runtime>
        <assemblyBinding xmlns="urn:schemas-microsoft-com:asm.v1">
            <dependentAssembly xmlns="">
                <assemblyIdentity name="SimpleShared"
                                  publicKeyToken="6ca9587197f6f8c2" />
                <codeBase version="1.0" href="http://CNagel/WroxUtils" />
            </dependentAssembly>
        </assemblyBinding>
    </runtime>
</configuration>
```

The <dependentAssembly> element is the same used previously for the version redirection. The <codeBase> element has the attributes version and href. With version, the original referenced version of the assembly must be specified. With href, we can define the directory from where the assembly should be loaded. In our example, a path using the HTTP protocol is used. A directory on a local system or a share is specified using href="file:C:/WroxUtils".

When using that assembly loaded from the network a `System.Security.Permissions` *exception occurs. You must configure the required permissions for assemblies loaded from the network. In Chapter 23 we show how to configure security for assemblies.*

<probing>

When the `<codeBase>` is not configured and the assembly is not stored in the global assembly cache, the runtime tries to find an assembly with **probing**. The .NET runtime tries to find an assembly with either a .dll or a .exe file extension in the application directory, or in a subdirectory thereof, that has the same name as the assembly searched for. If the assembly is not found here, the search continues. You can configure search directories with the `<probing>` element in the `<runtime>` section of application configuration files. This XML configuration can also be done easily by selecting the properties of the application with the .NET Framework Configuration tool. We can configure the directories where the probing should occur by using the search path:

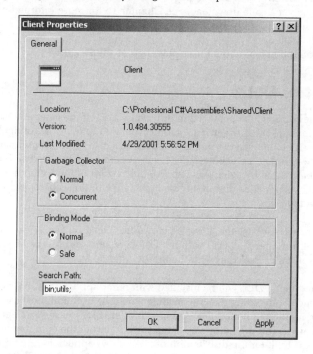

The XML file produced has these entries:

```xml
<?xml version="1.0"?>
<configuration>
    <runtime>
        <gcConcurrent enabled="enabled" />
        <assemblyBinding xmlns="urn:schemas-microsoft-com:asm.v1">
            <probing privatePath="bin;utils;" xmlns="" />
        </assemblyBinding>
    </runtime>
</configuration>
```

The `<probing>` element has just a single required attribute: `privatePath`. This application configuration file tells the runtime that assemblies should be searched for in the base directory of the application, followed by the `bin` and the `util` directory. Both directories are subdirectories of the application base directory. It's not possible to reference a private assembly outside the application base directory or a subdirectory thereof. An assembly outside of the application base directory must have a shared name and can be referenced using the `<codeBase>` element as we've done before.

Deployment

How the assemblies should be packaged and distributed depends on the application type. Windows Forms applications should be packaged in a Windows Installer Package and distributed using the Windows Installer. Controls inside web pages should be packaged in a `.cab` file or just the DLL. Distribution can be via a code download. See Chapter 16 for more information about controls. ASP.NET applications should be distributed using `xcopy` or `ftp`.

Now we will talk a little more about the deployment of simple DLLs.

Deployment of DLLs

The packaging of DLLs can be achieved in different ways – if the assembly exists as just a single DLL, this is sufficient for packaging. By using a cabinet file, multiple DLLs, configuration files, and other dependent files can be put into the single, compressed `.cab` file. This also benefits downloading speeds, but you have to watch that the cabinet file doesn't get too large because of too many assemblies. A cabinet file can be created by using the Cab Project Wizard of the Setup and Deployment Projects with Visual Studio .NET. Files that should be included with this cabinet can be easily included with the menu Project | Add | File.

Another useful format for packaging is a Windows Installer Package. Visual Studio .NET supports creating Microsoft Installer Packages with the Setup Wizard and Merge Modules that can be used within Windows Installer Packages with the Merge Module Project.

It can be expected that a DLL will be installed with other applications that need this DLL, but not as a standalone product. So building a **merge module** would be useful in most cases. A merge module allows the creation of reusable setup modules. A merge module file (`.msm`) is a single package that contains DLLs, registry entries, resource files, and setup logic to install the component. When a Windows Installer Package is built for the distribution of a Windows application, the merge module can be easily included with this installer package. The complete .NET runtime is available as a merge module and so can be included with installation programs.

Creating a Merge Module

A merge module can be easily created within Visual Studio .NET. Of course, InstallShield or Wise for Windows do have a lot more features than the Merge Module Project in Visual Studio, but the Merge Module Project is included within Visual Studio .NET and will solve a lot of installation issues where the "bigger brothers" are not needed.

When selecting Build | Deploy Solution with the opened class library project, a message box appears saying that a deployment project must be created. Merge Module Project should be selected. A File System View is opened in Visual Studio .NET; the left pane shows directories where the files can be configured for installation. Three folders are created automatically:

- ❏ The **common files folder** is used for common files that are shared between applications. With default installations, it points to C:\Program Files\Common Files. This folder can be used for shared assemblies that are not installed in the global assembly cache. For such assemblies the <codeBase> configuration is needed as we have seen earlier.

- ❏ Assemblies put into the **global assembly cache folder** will be installed in the global assembly cache during installation.

- ❏ The **module retargetable folder** is mostly used for merge modules. The merge module will be used from an MSI Package. The MSI package can then define in which directories the files of the retargetable folder should be installed.

We can also add special folders like the Program Files folder, the user's desktop folder, etc.

Selecting the Module Retargetable Folder using the context menu Add | Project Output we see this dialog:

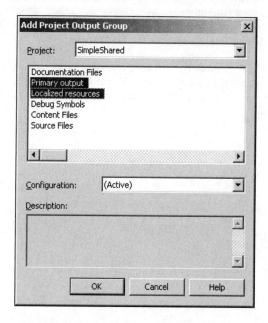

Now it's just necessary to select the Primary output, which includes DLL and EXE files, and (if available) Localized resources that include the satellite assemblies. All the referenced assemblies are automatically included in the merge module. This merge module can now be used within Windows Installer packages for other applications.

Summary

Assemblies are the new installation unit for the .NET platform. Microsoft learned from problems with previous architectures and did a complete redesign to avoid the old problems. In this chapter, we discussed the features of assemblies: they are self-describing and no type library and registry information is needed. Version dependencies are exactly recorded so that with assemblies, the DLL Hell we had with old DLLs is no more. Because of these features, not only development but also deployment and administration become a lot easier.

We discussed cross-language support and created a C# class that derives from a VB.NET class that makes use of a managed C++ class, and looked at the differences in the generated MSIL code.

We explored the use of resources and how this helps with localization of applications. We created satellite assemblies manually and with the built-in help of Visual Studio .NET. Besides using resources for localization we also looked at how to implement date and number formatting that is dependent on the language of the user.

We discussed the differences between private and shared assemblies, and how shared assemblies can be created. With private assemblies we don't have to pay attention to uniqueness and versioning issues as these assemblies are copied and only used by a single application. Sharing assemblies has the requirement to use a key for uniquness, and to define the version. We looked at the global assembly cache that can be used as an intelligent store for shared assemblies.

We looked at overriding versioning issues to use a version of an assembly different from the one that was used during development; this is done through publisher policies and application configuration files. We also discussed how probing works with private assemblies, and finally, we considered the deployment of assemblies.

9

Data Access with .NET

In this chapter, we'll be discussing how to get at data from your C# programs using ADO.NET. Over the course of this chapter, we'll be covering the following areas:

❑ Connecting to the database – how to utilize the new `SqlConnection` and `OleDbConnection` classes to connect to and disconnect from the database. Connections utilize the same form of connection strings as did OLEDB providers (and therefore ADO), and these are briefly discussed. We then go through a set of best practices for utilizing database connections, and show how to ensure that a connection is closed after use, which is one of the sources of poor application performance.

❑ Executing Commands – ADO.NET has the concept of a command object, which may execute SQL directly, or may issue a stored procedure with return values. The various options on command objects are discussed in depth, with examples to show how commands can be used for each of the options presented by the `Sql` and `OleDB` classes.

❑ Stored Procedures – How to call stored procedures using command objects, and how the results of those stored procedures may be integrated back into the data cached on the client.

❑ The ADO.NET object model – this is significantly different from the objects available with ADO, and the `DataSet`, `DataTable`, `DataRow`, and `DataColumn` classes are all discussed. A `DataSet` can also include relationships between tables, and also constraints. These issues are also discussed.

❑ Using XML and XML Schemas – ADO.NET is built upon an XML framework, so we'll examine how some of the support for XML has been added to the data classes.

We'll also present a guide to the naming conventions that preside in the world of ADO.NET and explain some of the reasoning behind them. First, though, let's take a brief tour of ADO.NET and see what's on offer.

ADO.NET Overview

Like most of the .NET Framework, ADO.NET is more than just a thin veneer over some existing API. The similarity to ADO is in name only – the classes and method of accessing data are completely different.

ADO (Microsoft's ActiveX Data Objects) was a library of COM components that has had many incarnations over the last few years. Currently at version 2.7, ADO consists primarily of the `Connection`, `Command`, `Recordset`, and `Field` objects. A connection would be opened to the database, some data selected into a recordset, consisting of fields, that data would then be manipulated, updated on the server, and the connection would be closed. ADO also introduced the concept of a disconnected recordset, which was used where keeping the connection open for long periods of time was not desirable.

There were several problems that ADO did not address satisfactorily, most notably the unwieldiness (in physical size) of a disconnected recordset. This support was more necessary than ever with the evolution of "web-centric" computing, so a fresh approach was taken. There are a number of similarities between ADO.NET programming and ADO (not only the name), so upgrading from ADO shouldn't be too difficult. What's more, if you're using SQL Server, there's a fantastic new set of managed classes that are very highly tuned to squeeze maximum performance out of the database. This alone should be reason enough to move.

ADO.NET ships with two database client namespaces – one for SQL Server, the other for databases exposed through an OLE DB interface. If your database of choice has an OLE DB driver, you will be able to easily connect to it from .NET – just use the OLE DB classes and connect through your current database driver.

Namespaces

All of the examples in this chapter access data in one way or another. The following namespaces expose the classes and interfaces used in .NET data access:

- ❑ `System.Data` – All generic data access classes
- ❑ `System.Data.Common` – Classes shared (or overridden) by individual data providers
- ❑ `System.Data.OleDb` – OLE DB provider classes
- ❑ `System.Data.SqlClient` – SQL Server provider classes
- ❑ `System.Data.SqlTypes` – SQL Server data types

The main classes in ADO.NET are listed below:

Shared Classes

ADO.NET contains a number of classes that are used regardless of whether you are using the SQL Server classes or the OLE DB classes.

The following are contained in the `System.Data` namespace:

❑ `DataSet` – This object may contain a set of `DataTables`, can include relationships between these tables, and is designed for disconnected use.

❑ `DataTable` – A container of data. A `DataTable` consists of one or more `DataColumns`, and when populated will have one or more `DataRows` containing data.

❑ `DataRow` – A number of values, akin to a row from a database table, or a row from a spreadsheet.

❑ `DataColumn` – Contains the definition of a column, such as the name and data type.

❑ `DataRelation` – A link between two `DataTables` within a `DataSet`. Used for foreign key and master/detail relationships.

❑ `Constraint` – Defines a rule for a `DataColumn` (or set of data columns), such as unique values.

These next two classes are to be found in the `System.Data.Common` namespace:

❑ `DataColumnMapping` – Maps the name of a column from the database with the name of a column within a `DataTable`.

❑ `DataTableMapping` – Maps a table name from the database to a `DataTable` within a `DataSet`.

Database Specific Classes

In addition to the shared classes above, ADO.NET contains a number of database-specific classes shown below. These classes implement a set of standard interfaces defined within the `System.Data` namespace, allowing the classes to be used if required in a generic manner. For example, both the `SqlConnection` and `OleDbConnection` classes implement the `IDbConnection` interface.

❑ `SqlCommand, OleDbCommand` – A wrapper for SQL statements or stored procedure calls.

❑ `SqlCommandBuilder, OleDbCommandBuilder` – A class used to generate SQL commands (such as `INSERT`, `UPDATE`, and `DELETE` statements) from a `SELECT` statement.

❑ `SqlConnection, OleDbConnection` – The connection to the database. Similar to an ADO `Connection`.

❑ `SqlDataAdapter, OleDbDataAdapter` – A class used to hold select, insert, update, and delete commands, which are then used to populate a `DataSet` and update the `Database`.

❑ `SqlDataReader, OleDbDataReader` – A forward only, connected data reader.

❑ `SqlParameter, OleDbParameter` – Defines a parameter to a stored procedure.

❑ `SqlTransaction, OleDbTransaction` – A database transaction, wrapped in an object.

The most important new feature of the ADO.NET classes is that they are designed to work in a disconnected manner, which is important in today's highly web-centric world. It is now common practice to architect a service (such as an online bookshop) to connect to a server, retrieve some data, and then work on that data on the client PC before reconnecting and passing the data back for processing. The disconnected nature of ADO.NET enables this type of behavior.

ADO 2.1 introduced the disconnected recordset, which would permit data to be retrieved from a database, passed to the client for processing, and then reattached to the server. This was often cumbersome to use, as disconnected behavior hadn't been designed in from the start. The ADO.NET classes are different – in all but one case (the Sql/OleDb DataReader) they are designed for use offline from the database.

The classes and interfaces used for data access in the .NET Framework will be introduced as the chapter continues. I will mainly concentrate on the Sql classes when connecting to the database, because the Framework SDK samples install an MSDE database (SQL Server). In most cases the OleDb classes mimic exactly the Sql code.

Using Database Connections

In order to access the database, you need to provide connection parameters, such as the machine that the database is running on, and possibly your login credentials. Anyone who has worked with ADO will be immediately familiar with the .NET connection classes, OleDbConnection and SqlConnection:

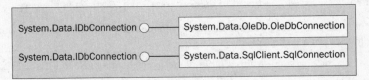

The following code snippet illustrates how to create, open, and close a connection to the Northwind database. In the examples within this chapter I use the Northwind database, which is installed with the .NET Framework SDK samples:

```
using System.Data.SqlClient;

string source = "server=(local)\\NetSDK;" +
                "uid=QSUser;pwd=QSPassword;" +
                "database=Northwind";
SqlConnection conn = new SqlConnection(source);
conn.Open();

// Do something useful

conn.Close();
```

The connection string should be very familiar to you if you've ever used ADO or OLE DB before – indeed, you should be able to cut and paste from your old code if you use the OleDb provider. In the example connection string, the parameters used are as follows. The parameters are delimited by a semicolon in the connection string.

❏ `server=(local)\\NetSDK` – This denotes the database server to connect to. SQL Server permits a number of separate database server processes to be running on the same machine, so here we're connecting to the `NetSDK` processes on the local machine.

❏ `uid=QSUser` – This parameter describes the database user. You can also use `User ID`.

❏ `pwd=QSPassword` – And this is the password for that user. The .NET SDK comes with a set of sample databases, and this user/password combination is added during the installation of the .NET samples. You can also use `Password`.

❏ `database=Northwind` – This describes the database instance to connect to – each SQL Server process can expose several database instances.

The example opens a database connection using the defined connection string, and then closes that connection. Once the connection has been opened, you can issue commands against the data source, and when you're finished, the connection can be closed.

SQL Server has another mode of authentication – it can use Windows integrated security, so that the credentials supplied at logon are passed through to SQL Server. This is catered for by removing the `uid` and `pwd` portions of the connection string , and adding in `Integrated Security=SSPI`.

In the download code available for this chapter, you will find a file `Login.cs` that simplifies the examples in this chapter. It is linked to all the example code, and includes database connection information used for the examples; you can alter this to supply your own server name, user, and password as appropriate. This by default uses Windows integrated security; however, you can change the username and password as appropriate.

Now that we know how to open connections, before we move on we should consider some good practices concerning the handling of connections.

Using Connections Efficiently

In general, when using "scarce" resources in .NET, such as database connections, windows, or graphics objects, it is good practice to ensure that each resource is closed after use. Although the designers of .NET have implemented automatic garbage collection, which will tidy up eventually, it is necessary to actively release resources as early as possible.

This is all too apparent when writing code that accesses a database, as keeping a connection open for slightly longer than necessary can affect other sessions. In extreme circumstances, not closing a connection can lock other users out of an entire set of tables, considerably hurting application performance. Closing database connections should be considered mandatory, so this section shows how to structure your code so as to minimize the risk of leaving a resource open.

There are two main ways to ensure that database connections and the like are released after use.

Option One – try/catch/finally

The first option to ensure that resources are cleaned up is to utilize `try...catch...finally` blocks, and ensure that you close any open connections within the finally block. Here's a short example:

```
try
{
    // Open the connection
    conn.Open();
    // Do something useful
}
catch ( Exception ex )
{
    // Do something about the exception
}
finally
{
    // Ensure that the connection is freed
    conn.Close ( ) ;
}
```

Within the `finally` block you can release any resources you have used. The only trouble with this method is that you have to ensure that you close the connection – it is all too easy to forget to add in the `finally` clause, so something less prone to vagaries in coding style might be worthwhile.

Also, you may find that you open a number of resources (say two database connections and a file) within a given method, so the cascading of `try...catch...finally` blocks can sometimes become less easy to read. There is however another way to guarantee resource cleanup – the `using` statement.

Option Two – The using Block Statement

During development of C#, .NET's method of clearing up objects after they are no longer referenced using nondeterministic destruction became a topic of very heated discussion. In C++, as soon as an object went out of scope, its destructor would be automatically called. This was great news for designers of resource-based classes, as the destructor was the ideal place to close the resource if the user had forgotten to do so. A C++ destructor is called in any and every situation when an object goes out of scope – so for instance if an exception was raised and not caught, all objects with destructors would have them called.

With C# and the other managed languages, there is no concept of automatic, deterministic destruction – instead there is the garbage collector, which will dispose of resources at some point in the future. What makes this nondeterministic is that you have little say over when this process actually happens. Forgetting to close a database connection could cause all sorts of problems for a .NET executable. Luckily, help is at hand. The following code demonstrates how to use the `using` clause to ensure that objects that implement the `IDisposable` interface (discussed in Chapter 2) are cleared up immediately the block exits.

```
string source = "server=(local)\\NetSDK;" +
                "uid=QSUser;pwd=QSPassword;" +
                "database=Northwind";

using ( SqlConnection conn = new SqlConnection ( source ) )
```

```
{
    // Open the connection
    conn.Open ( ) ;

    // Do something useful
}
```

The using clause was introduced in Chapter 2. The object within the using clause must implement the IDisposable interface, or a compilation error will be flagged if the object does not support this interface. The Dispose() method will automatically be called on exiting the using block.

Looking at the IL code for the Dispose() method of SqlConnection (and OleDbConnection), both of these check the current state of the connection object, and if open will call the Close() method.

When programming, you should use at least one of these methods, and probably both. Wherever you acquire resources it is good practice to utilize the using () statement, as even though we all mean to write the Close() statement, sometimes we forget, and in the face of exceptions the using clause does the right thing. There is no substitute for good exception handling either, so in most instances I would suggest you use both methods together as in the following example:

```
try
{
    using (SqlConnection conn = new SqlConnection ( source ))
    {
        // Open the connection
        conn.Open ( ) ;

        // Do something useful

        // Close it myself
        conn.Close ( ) ;
    }
}
catch (Exception e)
{
    // Do something with the exception here...
}
```

Here I have explicitly called Close() which isn't strictly necessary as the using clause will ensure that this is done anyway; however, you should ensure that any resources such as this are released as soon as possible – you may have more code in the rest of the block and there's no point locking a resource unnecessarily.

In addition, if an exception is raised within the using block, the IDisposable.Dispose method will be called on the resource guarded by the using clause, which in this case will ensure that the database connection is always closed. This produces easier to read code than having to ensure you close a connection within an exception clause.

One last word – if you are writing a class that wraps a resource, whatever that resource may be, always implement the IDisposable interface to close the resource. That way anyone coding with your class can utilize the using() statement and guarantee that the resource will be cleared up.

Transactions

Often when there is more than one update to be made to the database, these updates must be performed within the scope of a transaction. A transaction in ADO.NET is begun by calling one of the BeginTransaction() methods on the database connection object. These methods return an object that implements the IDbTransaction interface, defined within System.Data.

The following sequence of code initiates a transaction on a SQL Server connection:

```
string source = "server=(local)\\NetSDK;" +
                "uid=QSUser;pwd=QSPassword;" +
                "database=Northwind";
SqlConnection conn = new SqlConnection(source);
conn.Open();
SqlTransaction tx = conn.BeginTransaction();

// Execute some commands, then commit the transaction

tx.Commit();
conn.Close();
```

When you begin a transaction, you can choose the isolation level for commands executed within that transaction. The level determines how isolated your transaction is from others occurring on the database server. Certain database engines may support fewer than the four presented here. The options are as follows:

Isolation Level	Description
ReadCommitted	The default for SQL Server. This level ensures that data written by one transaction will only be accessible in a second transaction after the first commits.
ReadUncommitted	This permits your transaction to read data within the database, even data that has not yet been committed by another transaction. As an example, if two users were accessing the same database, and the first inserted some data without concluding their transaction (by means of a Commit or Rollback), then the second user with their isolation level set to ReadUncommitted could read the data.
RepeatableRead	This level, which extends the ReadCommitted level, ensures that if the same statement is issued within the transaction, regardless of other potential updates made to the database, the same data will always be returned. This level does require extra locks to be held on the data, which could adversely affect performance.
	This level guarantees that, for each row in the initial query, no changes can be made to that data. It does however permit "phantom" rows to show up – these are completely new rows that another transaction may have inserted while your transaction is running.

Isolation Level	Description
Serializable	This is the most "exclusive" transaction level, which in effect serializes access to data within the database. With this isolation level, phantom rows can never show up, so a SQL statement issued within a serializable transaction will always retrieve the same data.

The negative performance impact of a Serializable transaction should not be underestimated – if you don't absolutely need to use this level of isolation, it is advisable to stay away from it. |

The SQL Server default isolation level, ReadCommitted, is a good compromise between data coherence and data availability, as fewer locks are required on data than in RepeatableRead or Serializable modes. However, there are situations where the isolation level should be increased, and so within .NET you can simply begin a transaction with a different level from the default. There are no hard and fast rules as to which levels to pick – that comes with experience.

One last word on transactions – if you are currently using a database that does not support transactions, it is well worth changing to a database that does!

Commands

I briefly touched on the idea of issuing commands against a database in the *Using Database Connections* section. A command is, in its simplest form, a string of text containing SQL statements that is to be issued to the database. A command could also be a stored procedure, or the name of a table that will return all columns and all rows from that table (in other words, a SELECT *-style clause).

A command can be constructed by passing the SQL clause as a parameter to the constructor of the SqlCommand class, as shown below:

```
string source = "server=(local)\\NetSDK;" +
                "uid=QSUser;pwd=QSPassword;" +
                "database=Northwind";
string select = "SELECT ContactName,CompanyName FROM Customers";
SqlConnection conn = new SqlConnection(source);
conn.Open();
SqlCommand cmd = new SqlCommand(select, conn);
```

The SqlCommand and OleDbCommand classes have a property called CommandType, which is used to define whether the command is a SQL clause, a call to a stored procedure, or a full table statement (which simply selects all columns and rows from a given table). The following table summarizes the CommandType enumeration:

CommandType	Example

Text
(default)
	`String select = "SELECT ContactName FROM Customers";`
	
	`SqlCommand cmd = new SqlCommand(select , conn);`

StoredProcedure	`SqlCommand cmd = new SqlCommand("CustOrderHist", conn);`
	
	`cmd.CommandType = CommandType.StoredProcedure;`
	
	`cmd.Parameters.Add("@CustomerID", "QUICK");`

TableDirect	`OleDbCommand cmd = new OleDbCommand("Categories", conn);`
	
	`cmd.CommandType = CommandType.TableDirect;`

When executing a stored procedure, it may be necessary to pass parameters to that procedure. The example above sets the @CustomerID parameter directly, although there are other ways of setting the parameter value, which we will look at later in the chapter.

> Note: The `TableDirect` command type is only valid for the `OleDb` provider – an exception is thrown by the `Sql` provider if you attempt to use this command type with it.

Executing Commands

Once you have the command defined, you need to execute it. There are a number of ways to issue the statement, depending on what you expect to be returned (if anything) from that command. The `SqlCommand` and `OleDbCommand` classes provide the following execute methods:

❑ `ExecuteNonQuery()` – Execute the command but do not return any output

❑ `ExecuteReader()` – Execute the command and return a typed `IDataReader`

❑ `ExecuteScalar()` – Execute the command and return a single value

In addition to the above methods, the `SqlCommand` class also exposes the following method

❑ `ExecuteXmlReader()` – Execute the command, and return an `XmlReader` object, which can be used to traverse the XML fragment returned from the database.

The example code in this section can be found in the `Chapter 09\01_ExecutingCommands` subdirectory of the code download.

ExecuteNonQuery()

This method is commonly used for UPDATE, INSERT, or DELETE statements, where the only returned value is the number of records affected. This method can, however, return results if you call a stored procedure that has output parameters.

```
using System;
using System.Data.SqlClient;
public class ExecuteNonQueryExample
{
    public static void Main(string[] args)
    {
        string source = "server=(local)\\NetSDK;" +
                        "uid=QSUser;pwd=QSPassword;" +
                        "database=Northwind";
        string select = "UPDATE Customers " +
                        "SET ContactName = 'Bob' " +
                        "WHERE ContactName = 'Bill'";
        SqlConnection  conn = new SqlConnection(source);
        conn.Open();
        SqlCommand cmd = new SqlCommand(select, conn);
        int rowsReturned = cmd.ExecuteNonQuery();
        Console.WriteLine("{0} rows returned.", rowsReturned);
        conn.Close();
    }
}
```

ExecuteNonQuery() returns the number of rows affected by the command as an int.

ExecuteReader()

This method executes the command and returns a SqlDataReader or OleDbDataReader object, depending on the provider in use. The object returned can be used to iterate through the record(s) returned, as shown in the following code:

```
using System;
using System.Data.SqlClient;
public class ExecuteReaderExample
{
    public static void Main(string[] args)
    {
        string source = "server=(local)\\NetSDK;" +
                        "uid=QSUser;pwd=QSPassword;" +
                        "database=Northwind";
        string select = "SELECT ContactName,CompanyName FROM Customers";
        SqlConnection conn = new SqlConnection(source);
        conn.Open();
        SqlCommand cmd = new SqlCommand(select, conn);
        SqlDataReader reader = cmd.ExecuteReader();
        while(reader.Read())
        {
            Console.WriteLine("Contact : {0,-20} Company : {1}" ,
                            reader[0] , reader[1]);
        }
    }
}
```

The `SqlDataReader` and `OleDbDataReader` objects will be discussed later in this chapter.

ExecuteScalar()

On many occasions it is necessary to return a single result from a SQL statement, such as the count of records in a given table, or the current date/time on the server. The `ExecuteScalar` method can be used in such situations:

```
using System;
using System.Data.SqlClient;
public class ExecuteScalarExample
{
    public static void Main(string[] args)
    {
        string source = "server=(local)\\NetSDK;" +
                        "uid=QSUser;pwd=QSPassword;" +
                        "database=Northwind";
        string select = "SELECT COUNT(*) FROM Customers";
        SqlConnection conn = new SqlConnection(source);
        conn.Open();
        SqlCommand cmd = new SqlCommand(select, conn);
        object o = cmd.ExecuteScalar();
        Console.WriteLine ( o ) ;
    }
}
```

The method returns an object, which you can cast into the appropriate type if required.

ExecuteXmlReader() (SqlClient Provider Only)

As its name implies, this method will execute the command and return an `XmlReader` object to the caller. SQL Server permits a SQL `SELECT` statement to be extended with a `FOR XML` clause. This clause can take one of three options:

❑   `FOR XML AUTO` – builds a tree based on the tables in the `FROM` clause

❑   `FOR XML RAW` – result set rows are mapped to elements, with columns mapped to attributes

❑   `FOR XML EXPLICIT` –you must specify the shape of the XML tree to be returned

Professional SQL Server 2000 XML (Wrox Press, ISBN 1-861005-46-6) includes a complete description of these options. For this example I shall use AUTO:

```
using System;
using System.Data.SqlClient;
using System.Xml;
public class ExecuteXmlReaderExample
{
    public static void Main(string[] args)
    {

        string source = "server=(local)\\NetSDK;" +
                        "uid=QSUser;pwd=QSPassword;" +
                        "database=Northwind";
        string select = "SELECT ContactName,CompanyName " +
                        "FROM Customers FOR XML AUTO";
        SqlConnection conn = new SqlConnection(source);
        conn.Open();
        SqlCommand cmd = new SqlCommand(select, conn);

        XmlReader xr = cmd.ExecuteXmlReader();
        xr.Read();
        string s;
        do
        {
            s = xr.ReadOuterXml();
            if (s!="")
                Console.WriteLine(s);
        } while (s!= "");
        conn.Close();
    }
}
```

Note that we have to import the System.Xml namespace in order to output the returned XML. This namespace and further XML capabilities of the .NET Framework are explored in more detail in Chapter 11.

Here we include the FOR XML AUTO clause in the SQL statement, then call the ExecuteXmlReader() method. A screenshot of the possible output from this code is shown below:

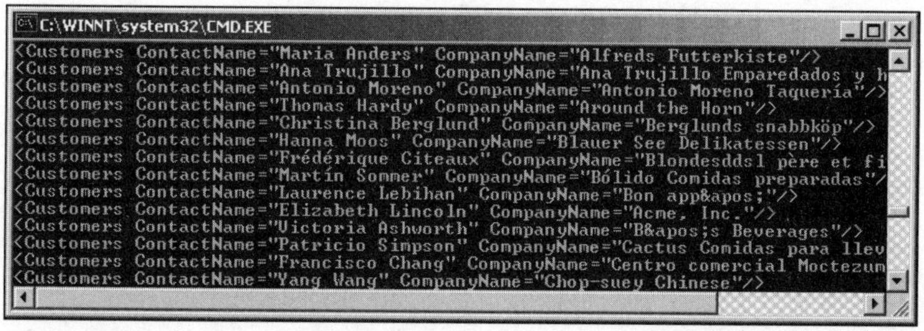

In the SQL clause, we specified FROM Customers, so an element of type Customers is shown in the output. To this are added attributes, one for each column selected from the database. This builds up an XML fragment for each row selected from the database.

Calling Stored Procedures

Calling a stored procedure with a command object is just a matter of defining the name of the stored procedure, adding a parameter's definition for each parameter of the procedure, then executing the command with one of the methods presented in the previous section.

In order to make the examples in this section more useful, I have defined a set of stored procedures that can be used to insert, update, and delete records from the Region table in the Northwind example database. I have chosen this table despite its small size, as it can be used to define examples for each of the types of stored procedures you will commonly write.

Calling a Stored Procedure that Returns Nothing

The simplest example of calling a stored procedure is one that returns nothing to the caller. There are two such procedures defined below, one for updating a pre-existing Region record, and the other for deleting a given Region record.

Record Update

Updating a Region record is fairly trivial, as there is only one column that can be modified (assuming primary keys cannot be updated). You can type these examples directly into the SQL Server Query Analyzer, or run the StoredProcs.sql file in the Chapter 09\02_StoredProcs subdirectory, which will install each of the stored procedures in this section:

```
CREATE PROCEDURE RegionUpdate (@RegionID INTEGER,
                               @RegionDescription NCHAR(50)) AS
    SET NOCOUNT OFF
    UPDATE Region
        SET RegionDescription = @RegionDescription
        WHERE RegionID = @RegionID
GO
```

An update command on a more real-world table might need to re-select and return the updated record in its entirety. This stored procedure takes two input parameters (@RegionID and @RegionDescription), and issues an UPDATE statement against the database.

To run this stored procedure from within .NET code, you need to define a SQL command and execute it:

```
SqlCommand aCommand = new SqlCommand("RegionUpdate", conn);

aCommand.CommandType = CommandType.StoredProcedure;
aCommand.Parameters.Add(new SqlParameter ("@RegionID",
                                          SqlDbType.Int,
                                          0,
                                          "RegionID"));
```

```
aCommand.Parameters.Add(new SqlParameter("@RegionDescription",
                                          SqlDbType.NChar,
                                          50,
                                          "RegionDescription"));
aCommand.UpdatedRowSource = UpdateRowSource.None;
```

This code creates a new SqlCommand object named aCommand, and defines it as a stored procedure. We then add each parameter in turn, and finally set the expected output from the stored procedure to one of the values in the UpdateRowSource enumeration, which is discussed later in this chapter.

The stored procedure takes two parameters: the unique primary key of the Region record being updated, and the new description to be given to this record.

Once the command has been created, it can be executed by issuing the following commands:

```
aCommand.Parameters[0].Value = 999;
aCommand.Parameters[1].Value = "South Western England";
aCommand.ExecuteNonQuery();
```

Here we are setting the value of the parameters, then executing the stored procedure. As the procedure returns nothing, ExecuteNonQuery() will suffice.

Command parameters may be set by ordinal as shown above, or set by name.

Record Deletion

The next stored procedure required is one that can be used to delete a Region record from the database:

```
CREATE PROCEDURE RegionDelete (@RegionID INTEGER) AS
    SET NOCOUNT OFF
    DELETE FROM Region
    WHERE         RegionID = @RegionID
GO
```

This procedure only requires the primary key value of the record. The code uses a SqlCommand object to call this stored procedure as follows:

```
SqlCommand aCommand = new SqlCommand("RegionDelete" , conn);
aCommand.CommandType = CommandType.StoredProcedure;
aCommand.Parameters.Add(new SqlParameter("@RegionID" , SqlDbType.Int , 0 ,
                                          "RegionID"));
aCommand.UpdatedRowSource = UpdateRowSource.None;
```

This command only accepts a single parameter as shown in the following code, which will execute the RegionDelete stored procedure; here we see an example of setting the parameter by name:

```
aCommand.Parameters["@RegionID"].Value= 999;
aCommand.ExecuteNonQuery();
```

Calling a Stored Procedure that Returns Output Parameters

Both of the previous examples execute stored procedures that return nothing. If a stored procedure includes output parameters, then these need to be defined within the .NET client so that they can be filled when the procedure returns.

The following example shows how to insert a record into the database, and return the primary key of that record to the caller.

Record Insertion

The Region table only consists of a primary key (RegionID) and description field (RegionDescription). To insert a record, this numeric primary key needs to be generated, then a new row inserted into the database. I have chosen to simplify the primary key generation in this example by creating one within the stored procedure. The method used is exceedingly crude, which is why I have devoted a section to key generation later in the chapter. For now this primitive example will suffice:

```
CREATE PROCEDURE RegionInsert(@RegionDescription NCHAR(50),
                              @RegionID INTEGER OUTPUT)AS
    SET NOCOUNT OFF
    SELECT @RegionID = MAX(RegionID)+ 1
    FROM Region
    INSERT INTO Region(RegionID, RegionDescription)
    VALUES(@RegionID, @RegionDescription)
GO
```

The insert procedure creates a new Region record. As the primary key value is generated by the database itself, this value is returned as an output parameter from the procedure (**@RegionID**). This is sufficient for this simple example, but for a more complex table (especially one with default values), it is more common not to utilize output parameters, and instead select the entire inserted row and return this to the caller. The .NET classes can cope with either scenario.

```
SqlCommand  aCommand = new SqlCommand("RegionInsert" , conn);
aCommand.CommandType = CommandType.StoredProcedure;
aCommand.Parameters.Add(new SqlParameter("@RegionDescription" ,
                                         SqlDbType.NChar ,
                                         50 ,
                                         "RegionDescription"));
aCommand.Parameters.Add(new SqlParameter("@RegionID" ,
                                         SqlDbType.Int,
                                         0 ,
                                         ParameterDirection.Output ,
                                         false ,
                                         0 ,
                                         0 ,
                                         "RegionID" ,
                                         DataRowVersion.Default ,
                                         null));
aCommand.UpdatedRowSource = UpdateRowSource.OutputParameters;
```

Here, the definition of the parameters is much more complex. The second parameter, @RegionID, is defined to include its parameter direction, which in this example is Output. In addition to this flag, on the last line of the code, we utilize the UpdateRowSource enumeration to indicate that we expect to return data from this stored procedure via output parameters. This flag is mainly used when issuing stored procedure calls from a DataTable (covered later in the chapter).

Calling this stored procedure is similar to the previous examples, except in this instance we need to read the output parameter after executing the procedure:

```
aCommand.Parameters["@RegionDescription"].Value = "South West";
aCommand.ExecuteNonQuery();
int newRegionID = (int) aCommand.Parameters["@RegionID"].Value;
```

After executing the command, we read the value of the @RegionID parameter and cast this to an integer.

You may be wondering what to do if the stored procedure you call returns output parameters and a set of rows. In this instance, define the parameters as appropriate, and rather than calling ExecuteNonQuery(), call one of the other methods (such as ExecuteReader()) that will permit you to traverse any record(s) returned.

Quick Data Access: The Data Reader

A data reader is the simplest and fastest way of selecting some data from a data source, but also the least capable. You cannot directly instantiate a data reader object – an instance is returned from a SqlCommand or OleDbCommand object having called the ExecuteReader() method – from a SqlCommand object, a SqlDataReader object is returned, and from the OleDbCommand object, a OleDbDataReader object is returned.

The following code demonstrates how to select data from the Customers table in the Northwind database. The example connects to the database, selects a number of records, loops through these selected records and outputs them to the console.

This example utilizes the OLE DB provider as a brief respite from the SQL provider. In most cases the classes have a one-to-one correspondence with their SqlClient cousins, so for instance there is the OleDbConnection object, which is similar to the SqlConnection object used in the previous examples.

To execute commands against an OLE DB data source, the OleDbCommand class is used. The following code shows an example of executing a simple SQL statement and reading the records by returning an OleDbDataReader object.

The code for this example can be found in the Chapter 09\03_DataReader directory.

Note the second using directive below that makes available the OleDb classes:

```
using System;
using System.Data.OleDb;
```

All the data providers currently available are shipped within the same DLL, so it is only necessary to reference the System.Data.dll assembly to import all classes used in this section:

```
public class DataReaderExample
{
    public static void Main(string[] args)
    {
        string source = "Provider=SQLOLEDB;" +
                        "server=(local)\\NetSDK;" +
                        "uid=QSUser;pwd=QSPassword;" +
                        "database=northwind";
        string select = "SELECT ContactName,CompanyName FROM Customers";
        OleDbConnection conn = new OleDbConnection(source);
        conn.Open();
        OleDbCommand cmd = new OleDbCommand(select , conn);
        OleDbDataReader aReader = cmd.ExecuteReader();
        while(aReader.Read())
           Console.WriteLine("'{0}' from {1}" ,
                             aReader.GetString(0) , aReader.GetString(1));
        aReader.Close();
        conn.Close();
    }
}
```

The preceding code includes many familiar aspects of C# covered in other chapters. To compile the example, issue the following command:

```
csc /t:exe /debug+ DataReaderExample.cs /r:System.Data.dll
```

The following code from the example above creates a new OLE DB .NET database connection, based on the source connection string:

```
OleDbConnection conn = new OleDbConnection(source);
conn.Open();
OleDbCommand cmd = new OleDbCommand(select, conn);
```

The third line creates a new OleDbCommand object, based on a particular SELECT statement, and the database connection to be used when the command is executed. When you have a valid command, you then need to execute it, which returns an initialized OleDbDataReader:

```
OleDbDataReader aReader = cmd.ExecuteReader();
```

An OleDbDataReader is a forward-only "connected" cursor. In other words, you can only traverse through the records returned in one direction, and the database connection used is kept open until the data reader has been closed.

An **OleDbDataReader** keeps the database connection open until explicitly closed.

The `OleDbDataReader` class cannot be directly instantiated – it is always returned by a call to the `ExecuteReader()` method of the `OleDbCommand` class. Once you have an open data reader, there are various ways to access the data contained within the reader.

When the `OleDbDataReader` object is closed (via an explicit call to `Close()`, or the object being garbage collected), the underlying connection may also be closed, depending on which of the `ExecuteReader()` methods is called. If you call `ExecuteReader()` and pass `CommandBehavior.CloseConnection`, you can force the connection to be closed when the reader is closed.

The `OleDbDataReader` class has an indexer that permits access (although not type-safe access) to any field using the familiar array style syntax:

```
object o = aReader[0];
object o = aReader["CategoryID"];
```

Assuming that the `CategoryID` field was the first in the `SELECT` statement used to populate the reader, these two lines are functionally equivalent, although the second is slower than the first – I wrote a simple test application that performed a million iterations of accessing the same column from an open data reader, just to get some numbers that were big enough to read. I know – you probably don't read the same column a million times in a tight loop, but every (micro) second counts, and you might as well write code that is as close to optimal as possible.

Just for interest, the numeric indexer took on average 0.09 seconds for the million accesses, and the textual one 0.63 seconds. The reason for this difference is that the textual method looks up the column number internally from the schema and then accesses it using its ordinal. If you know this information beforehand you can do a better job of accessing the data.

So should you use the numeric indexer? Maybe, but there is a better way.

In addition to the indexers presented above, the `OleDbDataReader` has a set of type-safe methods that can be used to read columns. These are fairly self-explanatory, and all begin with `Get`. There are methods to read most types of data, such as `GetInt32`, `GetFloat`, `GetGuid`, and so on.

My million iterations using `GetInt32` took 0.06 seconds. The overhead in the numeric indexer is incurred while getting the data type, calling the same code as `GetInt32`, then boxing (and in this instance unboxing) an integer. So, if you know the schema beforehand, are willing to use cryptic numbers instead of column names, and you can be bothered to use a type-safe function for each and every column access, you stand to gain somewhere in the region of a ten fold speed increase over using a textual column name (when selecting those million copies of the same column).

Needless to say, there is a tradeoff between maintainability and speed. If you must use numeric indexers, define constants within class scope for each of the columns that you will be accessing.

The code above can be used to select data from any OLE DB database; however, there are a number of SQL Server-specific classes that can be used with the obvious portability tradeoff.

The following example is the same as the above, except in this instance I have replaced the OLE DB provider and all references to OLE DB classes with their SQL counterparts. The changes in the code from the previous example have been highlighted. The example is in the `04_DataReaderSql` directory:

```
using System;
using System.Data.SqlClient;
public class DataReaderSql
{
    public static int Main(string[] args)
    {
        string source = "server=(local)\\NetSDK;" +
                        "uid=QSUser;pwd=QSPassword;" +
                        "database=northwind";
        string select = "SELECT ContactName,CompanyName FROM Customers";
        SqlConnection conn = new SqlConnection(source);
        conn.Open();
        SqlCommand cmd = new SqlCommand(select , conn);
        SqlDataReader aReader = cmd.ExecuteReader();
        while(aReader.Read())
            Console.WriteLine("'{0}' from {1}" , aReader.GetString(0) ,
                              aReader.GetString(1));
        aReader.Close();
        conn.Close();
        return 0;
    }
}
```

Notice the difference? If you're typing this in then do a global replace on OleDb with Sql, change the data source string and recompile. It's that easy!

I ran the same performance tests on the indexers for the SQL provider, and this time the numeric indexers were both exactly the same at 0.13 seconds for the million accesses, and the string-based indexer ran at about 0.65 seconds. You would expect the native SQL Server provider to be faster than going through OleDb, which up until I tested this section under the release version of .NET it was. I'm reasonably sure that this is an anomaly due to the simplistic test approach I am using (selecting the same value 1,000,000 times), and would expect a real-world test to show better performance from the managed SQL provider.

If you are interested in running the code on your own computer to see what performance is like, see the 05_IndexerTestingOleDb and 06_IndexerTestingSql examples included in the code download.

Managing Data and Relationships: The DataSet

The DataSet class has been designed as an offline container of data. It has no notion of database connections. In fact, the data held within a DataSet doesn't necessarily need to have come from a database – it could just as easily be records from a CSV file, or points read from a measuring device.

A DataSet consists of a set of data tables, each of which will have a set of data columns and data rows. In addition to defining the data, you can also define *links* between tables within the DataSet. One common scenario would be when defining a parent-child relationship (commonly known as master/detail). One record in a table (say Order) links to many records in another table (say Order_Details). This relationship can be defined and navigated within the DataSet.

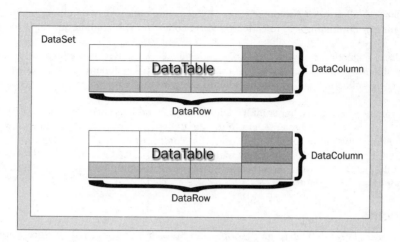

The following sections describe the classes that are used with a `DataSet`.

Data Tables

A data table is very similar to a physical database table – it consists of a set of columns with particular properties, and may contain zero or more rows of data. A data table may also define a primary key, which can be one or more columns, and may also contain constraints on columns. The generic term for this information used throughout the rest of the chapter is **schema**.

There are several ways to define the schema for a particular data table (and indeed the `DataSet` as a whole). These are discussed after we introduce data columns and data rows.

The following diagram shows some of the objects that are accessible through the data table:

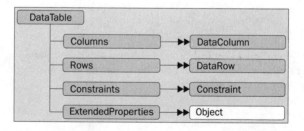

A `DataTable` object (and also a `DataColumn`) can have an arbitrary number of extended properties associated with it. This collection can be populated with any user-defined information pertaining to the object. For example, a given column might have an input mask used to validate the contents of that column – the typical example would be the US social security number. Extended properties are especially useful when the data is constructed within a middle tier and returned to the client for some processing. You could, for example, store validation criteria (such as `min` and `max`) for numeric columns.

When a data table has been populated, either by selecting data from a database, reading data from a file, or manually populating within code, the Rows collection will contain this retrieved data.

The Columns collection contains DataColumn instances that have been added to this table. These define the schema of the data, such as the data type, nullability, default values, and so on. The Constraints collection can be populated with either unique or primary key constraints.

One example of where the schema information for a data table is used is when displaying that data in a DataGrid (which we'll discuss at length in the next chapter). The DataGrid control uses properties such as the data type of the column to decide what control to use for that column. A bit field within the database will be displayed as a checkbox within the DataGrid. If a column is defined within the database schema as NOT NULL, then this fact will be stored within the DataColumn so that it can be tested when the user attempts to move off a row.

Data Columns

A DataColumn object defines properties of a column within the DataTable, such as the data type of that column, whether the column is read only, and various other facts. A column can be created in code, or can be automatically generated by the runtime.

When creating a column, it is also useful to give it a name; otherwise the runtime will generate a name for you in the form Column$n$ where n is an incrementing number.

The data type of the column can be set either by supplying it in the constructor, or by setting the DataType property. Once you have loaded data into a data table you cannot alter the type of a column – you'll just receive an ArgumentException.

Data columns can be created to hold the following .NET Framework data types:

Boolean	Decimal	Int64	TimeSpan
Byte	Double	Sbyte	UInt16
Char	Int16	Single	UInt32
DateTime	Int32	String	UInt64

Once created, the next thing to do with a DataColumn object is to set up other properties, such as the nullability of the column or the default value. The following code fragment shows a few of the more common options to set on a DataColumn:

```
DataColumn customerID = new DataColumn("CustomerID" , typeof(int));
customerID.AllowDBNull = false;
customerID.ReadOnly = false;
customerID.AutoIncrement = true;
customerID.AutoIncrementSeed = 1000;
DataColumn name = new DataColumn("Name" , typeof(string));
name.AllowDBNull = false;
name.Unique = true;
```

The following properties can be set on a `DataColumn`:

Property	Description
AllowDBNull	If `true`, permits the column to be set to `DBNull`.
AutoIncrement	Defines that this column value is automatically generated as an incrementing number.
AutoIncrementSeed	The initial seed value for an `AutoIncrement` column.
AutoIncrementStep	Defines the step between automatically generated column values, with a default of one.
Caption	Can be used for displaying the name of the column on screen.
ColumnMapping	Defines how a column is mapped into XML when a `DataSet` is saved by calling `DataSet.WriteXml`.
ColumnName	The name of the column. This is auto-generated by the runtime if not set in the constructor.
DataType	The `System.Type` value of the column.
DefaultValue	Can define a default value for a column.
Expression	This property defines the expression to be used in a computed column.

Data Rows

This class makes up the other part of the `DataTable` class. The columns within a data table are defined in terms of the `DataColumn` class. The actual data within the table is accessed using the `DataRow` object. The following example shows how to access rows within a data table. The code for this example is available in the `07_SimpleDatasetSql` directory. First, the connection details:

```
string source = "server=(local)\\NetSDK;" +
                "uid=QSUser;pwd=QSPassword;" +
                "database=northwind";
string select = "SELECT ContactName,CompanyName FROM Customers";
SqlConnection  conn = new SqlConnection(source);
```

The following code introduces the `SqlDataAdapter` class, which is used to place data into a `DataSet`. The `SqlDataAdapter` will issue the SQL clause, and fill a table in the `DataSet` called `Customers` with the output of this following query. We'll be discussing the data adapter class further in the *Populating a DataSet* section.

```
SqlDataAdapter da = new SqlDataAdapter(select, conn);
DataSet ds = new DataSet();
da.Fill(ds , "Customers");
```

In the code below, you may notice the use of the `DataRow` indexer to access values from within that row. The value for a given column can be retrieved using one of the several overloaded indexers. These permit you to retrieve a value knowing the column number, name, or `DataColumn`:

```
foreach(DataRow row in ds.Tables["Customers"].Rows)
    Console.WriteLine("'{0}' from {1}" , row[0] ,row[1]);
```

One of the most appealing aspects of a `DataRow` is that it is versioned. This permits you to receive various values for a given column in a particular row. The versions are described in the following table:

`DataRowVersion` Value	Description
Current	The value existing at present within the column. If no edit has occurred, this will be the same as the original value. If an edit (or edits) have occurred, the value will be the last valid value entered.
Default	The default value (in other words, any default set up for the column).
Original	The value of the column when originally selected from the database. If the `DataRow`'s `AcceptChanges` method is called, then this value will update to be the `Current` value.
Proposed	When changes are in progress for a row, it is possible to retrieve this modified value. If you call `BeginEdit()` on the row and make changes, each column will have a proposed value until either `EndEdit()` or `CancelEdit()` is called.

The version of a given column could be used in many ways. One example is when updating rows within the database, in which instance it is common to issue an SQL statement such as the following:

```
UPDATE Products
SET    Name = Column.Current
WHERE  ProductID = xxx
AND    Name = Column.Original;
```

Obviously this code would never compile, but it shows one use for original and current values of a column within a row.

To retrieve a versioned value from the `DataRow`, use one of the indexer methods that accept a `DataRowVersion` value as a parameter. The following code snippet shows how to obtain all values of each column in a `DataTable`:

```
foreach (DataRow row in ds.Tables["Customers"].Rows )
{
   foreach ( DataColumn dc in ds.Tables["Customers"].Columns )
   {
     Console.WriteLine ("{0} Current  = {1}" , dc.ColumnName ,
                                          row[dc,DataRowVersion.Current]);
     Console.WriteLine ("      Default  = {0}" , row[dc,DataRowVersion.Default]);
     Console.WriteLine ("      Original = {0}" , row[dc,DataRowVersion.Original]);
   }
}
```

The whole row has a state flag called RowState, which can be used to determine what operation is needed on the row when it is persisted back to the database. The RowState property is set to keep track of all the changes made to the DataTable, such as adding new rows, deleting existing rows, and changing columns within the table. When the data is reconciled with the database, the row state flag is used to determine what SQL operations should occur. These flags are defined by the DataRowState enumeration:

DataRowState Value	Description
Added	The row has been newly added to a DataTable's Rows collection. All rows created on the client are set to this value, and will ultimately issue SQL INSERT statements when reconciled with the database.
Deleted	This indicates that the row has been marked as deleted from the DataTable by means of the DataRow.Delete() method. The row still exists within the DataTable, but will not normally be viewable on screen (unless a DataView has been explicitly set up). DataViews will be discussed in the next chapter. Rows marked as deleted in the DataTable will be deleted from the database when reconciled.
Detached	A row is in this state immediately after it is created, and can also be returned to this state by calling DataRow.Remove(). A detached row is not considered to be part of any data table, and as such no SQL for rows in this state will be issued.
Modified	A row will be Modified if the value in any column has been changed.
Unchanged	The row has not been changed since the last call to AcceptChanges().

The state of the row depends also on what methods have been called on the row. The AcceptChanges() method is generally called after successfully updating the data source (that is, after persisting changes to the database).

The most common way to alter data in a DataRow is to use the indexer; however, if you have a number of changes to make you also need to consider the BeginEdit() and EndEdit() methods.

When an alteration is made to a column within a DataRow, the ColumnChanging event is raised on the row's DataTable. This permits you to override the ProposedValue property of the DataColumnChangeEventArgs class classes, and change it as required. This is one way of performing some data validation on column values. If you call BeginEdit() before making changes, the ColumnChanging event will not be raised. This permits you to make multiple changes and then call EndEdit() to persist these changes. If you wish to revert to the original values, call CancelEdit().

A DataRow can be linked in some way to other rows of data. This permits the creation of navigable links between rows, which is common in master/detail scenarios. The DataRow contains a GetChildRows() method that will return an array of associated rows from another table in the same DataSet as the current row. These are discussed in the *Data Relationships* section later in this chapter.

Schema Generation

There are three ways to create the schema for a DataTable. These are:

- Let the runtime do it for you
- Write code to create the table(s)
- Use the XML schema generator

Runtime Schema Generation

The DataRow example shown earlier presented the following code for selecting data from a database and populating a DataSet:

```
SqlDataAdapter da = new SqlDataAdapter(select , conn);
DataSet ds = new DataSet();
da.Fill(ds , "Customers");
```

This is obviously easy to use, but it has a few drawbacks too. One example is that you have to make do with the column names selected from the database, which may be fine, but in certain instances you might want to rename a physical database column (say PKID) to something more user-friendly.

You could naturally rename columns within your SQL clause, as in SELECT PID AS PersonID FROM PersonTable; I would always recommend not renaming columns within SQL, as the only place a column really needs to have a "pretty" name is on screen.

Another potential problem with automated DataTable/DataColumn generation is that you have no control over the column types that the runtime chooses for your data. It does a fairly good job of deciding the correct data type for you, but as usual there are instances where you need more control. You might for example have defined an enumerated type for a given column, so as to simplify user code written against your class. If you accept the default column types that the runtime generates, the column will likely be an integer with a 32-bit range, as opposed to an enum with five options.

Lastly, and probably most problematic, is that when using automated table generation, you have no type-safe access to the data within the DataTable – you are at the mercy of indexers, which return instances of object rather than derived data types. If you like sprinkling your code with typecast expressions then skip the following sections.

Hand-Coded Schema

Generating the code to create a DataTable, replete with associated DataColumns is fairly easy. The examples within this section will access the Products table from the Northwind database shown below. The code for this section is available in the 08_ManufacturedDataSet example.

Products			
Column Name	Data Type	Length	Allow Nulls
🔑 ProductID	int	4	
ProductName	nvarchar	40	
SupplierID	int	4	✓
CategoryID	int	4	✓
QuantityPerUnit	nvarchar	20	✓
UnitPrice	money	8	✓
UnitsInStock	smallint	2	✓
UnitsOnOrder	smallint	2	✓
ReorderLevel	smallint	2	✓
Discontinued	bit	1	

The following code manufactures a `DataTable`, which corresponds to the above schema.

```
public static void ManufactureProductDataTable(DataSet ds)
{
    DataTable   products = new DataTable("Products");
    products.Columns.Add(new DataColumn("ProductID", typeof(int)));
    products.Columns.Add(new DataColumn("ProductName", typeof(string)));
    products.Columns.Add(new DataColumn("SupplierID", typeof(int)));
    products.Columns.Add(new DataColumn("CategoryID", typeof(int)));
    products.Columns.Add(new DataColumn("QuantityPerUnit", typeof(string)));
    products.Columns.Add(new DataColumn("UnitPrice", typeof(decimal)));
    products.Columns.Add(new DataColumn("UnitsInStock", typeof(short)));
    products.Columns.Add(new DataColumn("UnitsOnOrder", typeof(short)));
    products.Columns.Add(new DataColumn("ReorderLevel", typeof(short)));
    products.Columns.Add(new DataColumn("Discontinued", typeof(bool)));
    ds.Tables.Add(products);
}
```

You can alter the code in the `DataRow` example to utilize this newly generated table definition as follows:

```
string source = "server=localhost;" +
                "integrated security=sspi;" +
                "database=Northwind";
string select = "SELECT * FROM Products";
SqlConnection conn = new SqlConnection(source);
SqlDataAdapter cmd = new SqlDataAdapter(select, conn);
DataSet ds = new DataSet();
ManufactureProductDataTable(ds);
cmd.Fill(ds, "Products");
foreach(DataRow row in ds.Tables["Products"].Rows)
    Console.WriteLine("'{0}' from {1}", row[0], row[1]);
```

The `ManufactureProductDataTable()` method creates a new `DataTable`, adds each column in turn, and finally appends this to the list of tables within the `DataSet`. The `DataSet` has an indexer that takes the name of the table and returns that `DataTable` to the caller.

The above example is still not really type-safe, as I'm using indexers on columns to retrieve the data. What would be better is a class (or set of classes) derived from `DataSet`, `DataTable`, and `DataRow`, that define type-safe accessors for tables, rows, and columns. You can generate this code yourself – it's not particularly tedious and you end up with truly type-safe data access classes.

If you don't like the sound of generating these type-safe classes yourself then help is at hand. The .NET Framework includes support for using XML schemas to define a `DataSet`, `DataTable`, and the other classes that we have touched on in this section. The *XML Schemas* section later in the chapter details this method; but first, we will look at relationships and constraints within a `DataSet`.

Data Relationships

When writing an application, it is often necessary to obtain and cache various tables of information. The `DataSet` class is the container for this information. With regular OLE DB it was necessary to provide a strange SQL dialect to enforce hierarchical data relationships, and the provider itself was not without its own subtle quirks.

The `DataSet` class on the other hand has been designed from the start to establish relationships between data tables with ease. For the code in this section I decided to hand-generate and populate two tables with data. So, if you haven't got SQL Server or the `NorthWind` database to hand, you can run this example anyway. The code is available in the `09_DataRelationships` directory:

```
DataSet ds = new DataSet("Relationships");
ds.Tables.Add(CreateBuildingTable());
ds.Tables.Add(CreateRoomTable());
ds.Relations.Add("Rooms",
                 ds.Tables["Building"].Columns["BuildingID"],
                 ds.Tables["Room"].Columns["BuildingID"]);
```

The tables simply contain a primary key and name field, with the `Room` table having `BuildingID` as a foreign key.

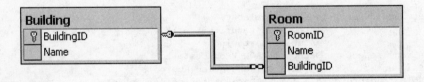

These tables were kept deliberately simple, as my fingers were wearing out at this point so I didn't want to add too many columns to either one.

I then added some default data to each table. Once that was done, I could then iterate through the buildings and rooms using the code below.

```
foreach(DataRow theBuilding in ds.Tables["Building"].Rows)
{
   DataRow[] children = theBuilding.GetChildRows("Rooms");
   int roomCount = children.Length;
   Console.WriteLine("Building {0} contains {1} room{2}",
                     theBuilding["Name"],
                     roomCount,
                     roomCount > 1 ? "s" : "");
   // Loop through the rooms
   foreach(DataRow theRoom in children)
      Console.WriteLine("Room: {0}", theRoom["Name"]);
}
```

The big difference between the DataSet and the old-style hierarchical Recordset object is in the way the relationship is presented. In a hierarchical Recordset, the relationship was presented as a pseudo-column within the row. This column itself was a Recordset that could be iterated through. Under ADO.NET, however, a relationship is traversed simply by calling the GetChildRows() method:

```
DataRow[] children = theBuilding.GetChildRows("Rooms");
```

This method has a number of forms, but the simple example shown above just uses the name of the relationship to traverse between parent and child rows. It returns an array of rows that can be updated as appropriate by using the indexers as shown in earlier examples.

What's more interesting with data relationships is that they can be traversed both ways. Not only can you go from a parent to the child rows, but you can also find a parent row (or rows) from a child record simply by using the ParentRelations property on the DataTable class. This property returns a DataRelationCollection, which can be indexed using the [] array syntax (for example, ParentRelations["Rooms"]), or as an alternative the GetParentRows() method can be called as shown below:

```
foreach(DataRow theRoom in ds.Tables["Room"].Rows)
{
   DataRow[] parents = theRoom.GetParentRows("Rooms");
   foreach(DataRow theBuilding in parents)
      Console.WriteLine("Room {0} is contained in building {1}",
                        theRoom["Name"],
                        theBuilding["Name"]);
}
```

There are two methods with various overrides available for retrieving the parent row(s) – GetParentRows() (which returns an array of zero or more rows), or GetParentRow() (which retrieves a single parent row given a relationship).

Data Constraints

Changing the data type of columns created on the client is not the only thing a DataTable is good for. ADO.NET permits you to create a set of constraints on a column (or columns), which are then used to enforce rules within the data.

The runtime currently supports the following constraint types, embodied as classes in the System.Data namespace.

Constraint	Description
ForeignKeyConstraint	Enforce a link between two DataTables within a DataSet
UniqueConstraint	Ensure that entries in a given column are unique

Setting a Primary Key

As is common for a table in a relational database, you can supply a primary key, which can be based on one or more columns from the DataTable.

The code below creates a primary key for the Products table, whose schema we constructed by hand earlier, and can be found in the 08_ManufactureDataSet folder.

Note that a primary key on a table is just one form of constraint. When a primary key is added to a DataTable, the runtime also generates a unique constraint over the key column(s). This is because there isn't actually a constraint type of PrimaryKey – a primary key is simply a unique constraint over one or more columns.

```
public static void ManufacturePrimaryKey(DataTable dt)
{
    DataColumn[] pk = new DataColumn[1];
    pk[0] = dt.Columns["ProductID"];
    dt.PrimaryKey = pk;
}
```

As a primary key may contain several columns, it is typed as an array of DataColumns. A table's primary key can be set to those columns simply by assigning an array of columns to the property.

To check the constraints for a table, you can iterate through the ConstraintCollection. For the auto-generated constraint produced by the above code, the name of the constraint is Constraint1. That's not a very useful name, so to avoid this problem it is always best to create the constraint in code first, then define which column(s) make up the primary key, as we shall do now.

As a long time database programmer, I find named constraints much simpler to understand, as most databases produce cryptic names for constraints, rather than something simple and legible. The code below names the constraint before creating the primary key:

```
DataColumn[] pk = new DataColumn[1];
pk[0] = dt.Columns["ProductID"];
dt.Constraints.Add(new UniqueConstraint("PK_Products", pk[0]));
dt.PrimaryKey = pk;
```

Unique constraints can be applied to as many columns as you wish.

Setting a Foreign Key

In addition to unique constraints, a `DataTable` may also contain foreign key constraints. These are primarily used to enforce master/detail relationships, but can also be used to replicate columns between tables if you set the constraint up correctly. A master/detail relationship is one where there is commonly one parent record (say an order) and many child records (order lines), linked by the primary key of the parent record.

A foreign key constraint can only operate over tables within the same `DataSet`, so the following example utilizes the `Categories` table from the `Northwind` database, and assigns a constraint between it and the `Products` table.

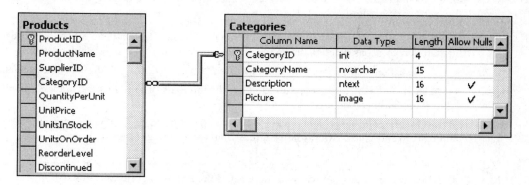

The first step is to generate a new data table for the `Categories` table. The `08_ManufactureDataSet` example includes this code:

```
DataTable categories = new DataTable("Categories");
categories.Columns.Add(new DataColumn("CategoryID", typeof(int)));
categories.Columns.Add(new DataColumn("CategoryName", typeof(string)));
categories.Columns.Add(new DataColumn("Description", typeof(string)));
categories.Constraints.Add(new UniqueConstraint("PK_Categories",
                            categories.Columns["CategoryID"]));
categories.PrimaryKey = new DataColumn[1]
                          {categories.Columns["CategoryID"]};
```

The last line of the above code creates the primary key for the `Categories` table. The primary key in this instance is a single column; however, it is possible to generate a key over multiple columns using the array syntax shown.

Then I need to create the constraint between the two tables:

```
DataColumn parent = ds.Tables["Categories"].Columns["CategoryID"];
DataColumn child = ds.Tables["Products"].Columns["CategoryID"];
ForeignKeyConstraint fk =
    new ForeignKeyConstraint("FK_Product_CategoryID", parent, child);
fk.UpdateRule = Rule.Cascade;
fk.DeleteRule = Rule.SetNull;
ds.Tables["Products"].Constraints.Add(fk);
```

This constraint applies to the link between `Categories.CategoryID` and `Products.CategoryID`. There are four different constructors for `ForeignKeyConstraint`, but again I would suggest using those that permit you to name the constraint.

Setting Update and Delete Constraints

In addition to defining the fact that there is some type of constraint between parent and child tables, you can define what should happen when a column in the constraint is updated.

The above example sets the update rule and the delete rule. These rules are used when an action occurs to a column (or row) within the parent table, and the rule is used to decide what should happen to row(s) within the child table that could be affected. There are four different rules that can be applied through the `Rule` enumeration:

❑   `Cascade` – If the parent key was updated then copy the new key value to all child records. If the parent record was deleted, delete the child records also. This is the default option.

❑   `None` – No action whatsoever. This option will leave orphaned rows within the child data table.

❑   `SetDefault` – Each child record affected has the foreign key column(s) set to their default value, if one has been defined.

❑   `SetNull` – All child rows have the key column(s) set to `DBNull`. (Following on from the naming convention that Microsoft uses, this should really be `SetDBNull`).

> **Constraints are only enforced within a `DataSet` if the `EnforceConstraints`**
> **property of the `DataSet` is `true`.**

I have covered the main classes that make up the constituent parts of the `DataSet`, and shown how to manually generate each of these classes in code. There is another way to define a `DataTable`, `DataRow`, `DataColumn`, `DataRelation`, and `Constraint` – by using the XML schema file(s) and the XSD tool that ships with .NET. The following section describes how to set up a simple schema and generate type-safe classes to access your data.

XML Schemas

XML is firmly entrenched into ADO.NET – indeed, the remoting format for passing data between objects is now XML. With the .NET runtime, it is now possible to describe a `DataTable` within an XML schema definition file (XSD). What's more, you can define an entire `DataSet`, with a number of `DataTables`, a set of relationships between these tables, and include various other details to fully describe the data.

When you have defined an XSD file, there is a new tool in the runtime that will convert this schema to the corresponding data access class(es), such as the type-safe product `DataTable` class shown above. In this section we'll start with a simple XSD file that describes the same information as the `Products` sample previously shown, and then extend this to include some extra functionality. This file is `Products.xsd`, found in the `10_XSD_DataSet` folder:

```
<?xml version="1.0" encoding="utf-8" ?>
<xs:schema
    id="Products"
    targetNamespace="http://tempuri.org/XMLSchema1.xsd"
    elementFormDefault="qualified"
    xmlns="http://tempuri.org/XMLSchema1.xsd"
    xmlns:mstns="http://tempuri.org/XMLSchema1.xsd"
    xmlns:xsd="http://www.w3.org/2001/XMLSchema"
    xmlns:msdata="urn:schemas-microsoft-com:xml-msdata">
  <xs:element name="Product">
    <xs:complexType>
      <xs:sequence>
        <xs:element name="ProductID" type="xs:int" />
        <xs:element name="ProductName" type="xs:string" />
        <xs:element name="SupplierID" type="xs:int" minOccurs="0" />
        <xs:element name="CategoryID" type="xs:int" minOccurs="0" />
        <xs:element name="QuantityPerUnit" type="xs:string" minOccurs="0" />
        <xs:element name="UnitPrice" type="xs:decimal" minOccurs="0" />
        <xs:element name="UnitsInStock" type="xs:short" minOccurs="0" />
        <xs:element name="UnitsOnOrder" type="xs:short" minOccurs="0" />
        <xs:element name="ReorderLevel" type="xs:short" minOccurs="0" />
        <xs:element name="Discontinued" type="xs:boolean" />
      </xs:sequence>
    </xs:complexType>
  </xs:element>
</xs:schema>
```

We'll take a closer look at some of the options within this file in Chapter 11; for now, this file basically defines a schema with the `id` attribute set to `Products`. A complex type called `Product` is defined, which contains a number of elements, one for each of the fields within the `Products` table.

These items map onto data classes as follows. The `Products` schema maps to a class derived from `DataSet`. The `Product` complex type maps to a class derived from `DataTable`. Each sub-element maps to a class derived from `DataColumn`. The collection of all columns maps onto a class derived from `DataRow`.

Thankfully there is a tool within the .NET Framework that will produce all of the code for these classes given only the input XSD file. Because its sole job in life is to perform various functions on XSD files, the tool itself is called `XSD.EXE`.

Generating Code with XSD

Assuming you save the above file as `Product.xsd`, you would convert the file into code by issuing the following command in a command prompt:

```
xsd Product.xsd /d
```

This creates the file `Product.cs`.

There are various switches that can be used with XSD to alter the output generated. Some of the more commonly used are shown in the table below.

Switch	Description
/dataset (/d)	Generate classes derived from DataSet, DataTable, and DataRow.
/language:<language>	Permits you to choose which language the output file will be written in. C# is the default, but you can choose VB for a Visual Basic .NET file.
/namespace:<namespace>	Define the namespace that the generated code should reside within. The default is no namespace.

An abridged version of the output from XSD for the Products schema is shown below. I've removed some of the less necessary code to concentrate on the most important aspects, and done some reformatting so that it will fit within the confines of a couple of pages. To see the complete output, run XSD.EXE on the Products schema (or one of your own making) and take a look at the .cs file generated. The example includes the entire sourcecode plus the Product.xsd file, and can be found in the 10_XSD_DataSet directory:

```
//------------------------------------------------------------------------
// <autogenerated>
//      This code was generated by a tool.
//      Runtime Version: 1.0.3512.0
//
//      Changes to this file may cause incorrect behavior and will be lost if
//      the code is regenerated.
// </autogenerated>
//------------------------------------------------------------------------

//
// This source code was auto-generated by xsd, Version=1.0.3512.0.
//
using System;
using System.Data;
using System.Xml;
using System.Runtime.Serialization;

[Serializable()]
[System.ComponentModel.DesignerCategoryAttribute("code")]
[System.Diagnostics.DebuggerStepThrough()]
[System.ComponentModel.ToolboxItem(true)]
public class Products : DataSet
{
    private ProductDataTable tableProduct;
    public Products()
    public ProductDataTable Product
    public override DataSet Clone()
    public delegate void ProductRowChangeEventHandler ( object sender,
                                            ProductRowChangeEvent e);

    [System.Diagnostics.DebuggerStepThrough()]
    public class ProductDataTable : DataTable, System.Collections.IEnumerable

    [System.Diagnostics.DebuggerStepThrough()]
    public class ProductRow : DataRow
}
```

I have taken some liberties with this sourcecode, as I have split it into three sections and removed any protected and private members so that we can concentrate on the public interface. The emboldened `ProductDataTable` and `ProductRow` definitions show the positions of two nested classes, which we're going to implement next. We'll look at the code for these after a brief explanation of the `DataSet` derived class.

The `Products()` constructor calls a private method, `InitClass()`, which constructs an instance of the `DataTable` class derived class `ProductDataTable`, and adds the table to the `Tables` collection of the `DataSet`. The `Products` data table can be accessed by the following code:

```
DataSet ds = new Products();
DataTable products = ds.Tables["Products"];
```

Or, more simply by using the property `Product`, available on the derived `DataSet` object:

```
DataTable products = ds.Product;
```

As the `Product` property is strongly typed, you could naturally use `ProductDataTable` rather than the `DataTable` reference I showed above.

The `ProductDataTable` class includes far more code:

```
[System.Diagnostics.DebuggerStepThrough()]
public class ProductDataTable : DataTable, System.Collections.IEnumerable
{
    private DataColumn columnProductID;
    private DataColumn columnProductName;
    private DataColumn columnSupplierID;
    private DataColumn columnCategoryID;
    private DataColumn columnQuantityPerUnit;
    private DataColumn columnUnitPrice;
    private DataColumn columnUnitsInStock;
    private DataColumn columnUnitsOnOrder;
    private DataColumn columnReorderLevel;
    private DataColumn columnDiscontinued;

    internal ProductDataTable() : base("Product")
    {
        this.InitClass();
    }
```

The `ProductDataTable` class, derived from `DataTable` and implementing the `IEnumerable` interface, defines a private `DataColumn` instance for each of the columns within the table. These are initialized again from the constructor by calling the private `InitClass()` member. Each column is given an internal accessor, which the `DataRow` class described later uses.

```
[System.ComponentModel.Browsable(false)]
public int Count
{
    get { return this.Rows.Count; }
}
internal DataColumn ProductIDColumn
{
    get { return this.columnProductID; }
}
// Other row accessors removed for clarity - there is one for each of the columns
```

Adding rows to the table is taken care of by the two overloaded (and significantly different, except unfortunately by name) AddProductRow() methods. The first takes an already constructed DataRow and returns a void. The latter takes a set of values, one for each of the columns in the DataTable, constructs a new row, sets the values within this new row, adds the row to the DataTable and returns the row to the caller. Such widely different functions shouldn't really have the same name, in my opinion.

```
public void AddProductRow(ProductRow row)
{
   this.Rows.Add(row);
}

public ProductRow AddProductRow ( string ProductName , int SupplierID ,
                                  int CategoryID , string QuantityPerUnit ,
                                  System.Decimal UnitPrice , short UnitsInStock ,
                                  short UnitsOnOrder , short ReorderLevel ,
                                  bool Discontinued )
{
   ProductRow rowProductRow = ((ProductRow)(this.NewRow()));
   rowProductRow.ItemArray = new object[]
   {
      null,
      ProductName,
      SupplierID,
      CategoryID,
      QuantityPerUnit,
      UnitPrice,
      UnitsInStock,
      UnitsOnOrder,
      ReorderLevel,
      Discontinued
   };
   this.Rows.Add(rowProductRow);
   return rowProductRow;
}
```

Just like the InitClass() member in the DataSet derived class, which added the table into the DataSet, the InitClass() member in ProductDataTable adds in columns to the DataTable. Each column's properties are set as appropriate, and the column is then appended to the columns collection.

```
private void InitClass()
{
   this.columnProductID = new DataColumn ( "ProductID",
                                           typeof(int),
                                           null,
                                           System.Data.MappingType.Element);
   this.Columns.Add(this.columnProductID);
   // Other columns removed for clarity

   this.columnProductID.AutoIncrement = true;
   this.columnProductID.AllowDBNull = false;
   this.columnProductID.ReadOnly = true;
   this.columnProductName.AllowDBNull = false;
   this.columnDiscontinued.AllowDBNull = false;
}

public ProductRow NewProductRow()
{
    return ((ProductRow)(this.NewRow()));
}
```

The last method I want to discuss, `NewRowFromBuilder()`, is called internally from the `DataTable`'s `NewRow()` method. Here it creates a new strongly typed row. The `DataRowBuilder` instance is created by the `DataTable`, and its members are only accessible within the `System.Data` assembly.

```
protected override DataRow NewRowFromBuilder(DataRowBuilder builder)
{
    return new ProductRow(builder);
}
```

The last class to discuss is the `ProductRow` class, derived from `DataRow`. This class is used to provide type-safe access to all fields in the data table. It wraps the storage for a particular row, and provides members to read (and write) each of the fields in the table.

In addition, for each nullable field, there are functions to set the field to null, and check if the field is null. The example below shows the functions for the `SupplierID` column:

```
[System.Diagnostics.DebuggerStepThrough()]
public class ProductRow : DataRow
{
    private ProductDataTable tableProduct;

    internal ProductRow(DataRowBuilder rb) : base(rb)
    {
        this.tableProduct = ((ProductDataTable)(this.Table));
    }

    public int ProductID
    {
        get { return ((int)(this[this.tableProduct.ProductIDColumn])); }
        set { this[this.tableProduct.ProductIDColumn] = value; }
    }
   // Other column accessors/mutators removed for clarity

    public bool IsSupplierIDNull()
    {
        return this.IsNull(this.tableProduct.SupplierIDColumn);
    }

    public void SetSupplierIDNull()
    {
        this[this.tableProduct.SupplierIDColumn] = System.Convert.DBNull;
    }
}
```

Now that the sourcecode for these data access classes has been generated by XSD.EXE, we can incorporate the classes into code. The following code utilizes these classes to retrieve data from the `Products` table and display that data to the console:

```
using System;
using System.Data;
using System.Data.SqlClient;

public class XSD_DataSet
{
    public static void Main()
```

```
    {
        string source = "server=(local)\\NetSDK;" +
                        "uid=QSUser;pwd=QSPassword;" +
                        "database=northwind";
        string select = "SELECT * FROM Products";
        SqlConnection conn = new SqlConnection(source);
        SqlDataAdapter da = new SqlDataAdapter(select , conn);
        Products ds = new Products();
        da.Fill(ds , "Product");
        foreach(Products.ProductRow row in ds.Product )
        Console.WriteLine("'{0}' from {1}" ,
                            row.ProductID ,
                            row.ProductName);
    }
}
```

The main areas of interest are highlighted. The output of the XSD file contains a class derived from `DataSet`, `Products`, which is created and then filled by the use of the data adapter. The `foreach` statement utilizes the strongly-typed `ProductRow` and also the `Product` property, which returns the `Product` data table.

To compile this example, issue the following commands:

xsd product.xsd /d

and

csc /recurse:*.cs

The first generates the `Products.cs` file from the `Products.XSD` schema, and then the `csc` command utilizes the `/recurse:*.cs` parameter to go through all files with the extension `.cs` and add these to the resulting assembly.

Populating a DataSet

Once you have fully defined the schema of your data set, replete with `DataTables`, `DataColumns`, `Constraints`, and whatever else was necessary, you need to be able to populate the `DataSet` with some information. There are two main ways to read data from an external source and insert it into the `DataSet`:

❑ Use a data adapter

❑ Read XML into the `DataSet`

Populating a DataSet Using a DataAdapter

The section on data rows briefly introduced the `SqlDataAdapter` class, as shown in the following code:

```
    string select = "SELECT ContactName,CompanyName FROM Customers";
    SqlConnection conn = new SqlConnection(source);
    SqlDataAdapter da = new SqlDataAdapter(select , conn);
    DataSet ds = new DataSet();
    da.Fill(ds , "Customers");
```

The two highlighted lines show the `SqlDataAdapter` in use – the `OleDbDataAdapter` is again virtually identical in functionality to the `Sql` equivalent.

The `SqlDataAdapter` and `OleDbDataAdapter` are two of the classes that are derived from a common base class rather than a set of interfaces, as are most of the other `SqlClient-` or `OleDb-` specific classes. The inheritance hierarchy is shown below:

```
System.Data.Common.DataAdapter
    System.Data.Common.DbDataAdapter
        System.Data.OleDb.OleDbDataAdapter
        System.Data.SqlClient.SqlDataAdapter
```

In order to retrieve data into a `DataSet`, it is necessary to have some form of command that is executed to select that data. The command in question could be a SQL `SELECT` statement, a call to a stored procedure, or for the OLE DB provider, a `TableDirect` command. The example above utilizes one of the constructors available on `SqlDataAdapter` that converts the passed SQL `SELECT` statement into a `SqlCommand`, and issues this when the `Fill()` method is called on the adapter.

Going back to the example on stored procedures earlier in the chapter, I defined stored procedures to `INSERT`, `UPDATE`, and `DELETE`, but didn't present a procedure to `SELECT` data. We'll fill that gap in this next section, and show how you can call a stored procedure from an `SqlDataAdapter` to populate data in a `DataSet`.

Using a Stored Procedure in a DataAdapter

First off we need to define a stored procedure and install it into the database. The code for this example is available in the `11_DataAdapter` directory. The stored procedure to `SELECT` data is as follows:

```
CREATE PROCEDURE RegionSelect AS
    SET NOCOUNT OFF
    SELECT * FROM Region
GO
```

Again this example is fairly trivial, and not really worthy of a stored procedure, as a direct SQL statement would normally suffice. This stored procedure can be typed directly into the SQL Server Query Analyzer, or you can run the `StoredProc.sql` file that is provided for use by this example.

Next, we need to define a `SqlCommand` that will execute this stored procedure. Again the code is very simple, and most of it was already presented in the earlier section on issuing commands:

```
private static SqlCommand GenerateSelectCommand(SqlConnection conn )
{
    SqlCommand  aCommand = new SqlCommand("RegionSelect" , conn);
    aCommand.CommandType = CommandType.StoredProcedure;
    aCommand.UpdatedRowSource = UpdateRowSource.None;
    return aCommand;
}
```

This method generates the `SqlCommand` that will call the `RegionSelect` procedure when executed. All that remains is to hook this command up to a `SqlDataAdapter`, and call the `Fill()` method:

```
DataSet ds = new DataSet();
// Create a data adapter to fill the DataSet
SqlDataAdapter da = new SqlDataAdapter();
// Set the data adapter's select command
da.SelectCommand = GenerateSelectCommand (conn);
da.Fill(ds , "Region");
```

Here I create a new `SqlDataAdapter`, assign the generated `SqlCommand` to the `SelectCommand` property of the data adapter, and then call `Fill()`, which will execute the stored procedure and insert all rows returned into the `Region` `DataTable` (which in this instance is generated by the runtime).

There's more to a data adapter than just selecting data by issuing a command. In the *Persisting DataSet Changes* section I will explore the rest of the facilities of the data adapter.

Populating a DataSet from XML

In addition to generating the schema for a given `DataSet` and associated tables and so on, a `DataSet` can read and write data in native XML, such as a file on disk, a stream, or a text reader.

To load XML into a `DataSet`, simply call one of the `ReadXML()` methods, such as that shown below, which will read data from a disk file:

```
DataSet ds = new DataSet();
ds.ReadXml(".\\MyData.xml");
```

The `ReadXml()` method attempts to load any inline schema information from the input XML, and if found, uses this schema in the validation of any data loaded from that file. If no inline schema is found then the `DataSet` will extend its internal structure as data is loaded. This is similar to the behavior of `Fill()` in the previous example, which retrieves the data and constructs a `DataTable` based on the data selected.

Persisting DataSet Changes

After editing data within a `DataSet`, it is probably necessary to persist these changes. The most common example would be selecting data from a database, displaying it to the user, and returning those updates back to the database.

In a less "connected" application, changes might be persisted to an XML file, transported to a middle-tier application server, and then processed to update several data sources.

A `DataSet` can be used for either of these examples, and what's more it's really easy to do.

Updating with Data Adapters

In addition to the `SelectCommand` that an `SqlDataAdapter` most likely includes, you can also define an `InsertCommand`, `UpdateCommand`, and `DeleteCommand`. As these names imply, these objects are instances of `SqlCommand` (or `OleDbCommand` for the `OleDbDataAdapter`), so any of these commands could be straight SQL or a stored procedure.

With this level of flexibility, you are free to tune the application by judicious use of stored procedures for frequently used commands (say `SELECT` and `INSERT`), and use straight SQL for less commonly used commands such as `DELETE`.

For the example in this section I have resurrected the stored procedure code from the *Calling Stored Procedures* section for inserting, updating, and deleting `Region` records, coupled these with the `RegionSelect` procedure written above, and produced an example utilizes each of these commands to retrieve and update data in a `DataSet`. The main body of code is shown below; the full sourcecode is available in the `12_DataAdapter2` directory.

Inserting a New Row

There are two ways to add a new row to a `DataTable`. The first way is to call the `NewRow()` method, which returns a blank row that you then populate and add to the `Rows` collection, as follows:

```
DataRow r = ds.Tables["Region"].NewRow();
r["RegionID"]=999;
r["RegionDescription"]="North West";
ds.Tables["Region"].Rows.Add(r);
```

The second way to add a new row would be to pass an array of data to the `Rows.Add()` method as shown in the following code:

```
DataRow r = ds.Tables["Region"].Rows.Add
            (new object [] { 999 , "North West" });
```

Each new row within the `DataTable` will have its `RowState` set to `Added`. The example dumps out the records before each change is made to the database, so after adding the following row (either way) to the `DataTable`, the rows will look something like the following. Note that the right-hand column shows the row state.

```
New row pending inserting into database
    1    Eastern                                    Unchanged
    2    Western                                    Unchanged
    3    Northern                                   Unchanged
    4    Southern                                   Unchanged
  999 North West                                    Added
```

To update the database from the `DataAdapter`, call one of the `Update()` methods as shown below:

```
da.Update(ds , "Region");
```

For the new row within the `DataTable`, this will execute the stored procedure (in this instance `RegionInsert`), and subsequently I dump the records in the `DataTable` again.

```
New row updated and new RegionID assigned by database
   1    Eastern                                      Unchanged
   2    Western                                      Unchanged
   3    Northern                                     Unchanged
   4    Southern                                     Unchanged
   5    North West                                   Unchanged
```

Look at the last row in the `DataTable`. I had set the `RegionID` in code to 999, but after executing the `RegionInsert` stored procedure the value has been changed to 5. This is intentional – the database will often generate primary keys for you, and the updated data in the `DataTable` is due to the fact that the `SqlCommand` definition within our sourcecode has the `UpdatedRowSource` property set to `UpdateRowSource.OutputParameters`:

```
SqlCommand aCommand = new SqlCommand("RegionInsert" , conn);

aCommand.CommandType = CommandType.StoredProcedure;
aCommand.Parameters.Add(new SqlParameter("@RegionDescription" ,
                        SqlDbType.NChar ,
                        50 ,
                        "RegionDescription"));
aCommand.Parameters.Add(new SqlParameter("@RegionID" ,
                        SqlDbType.Int,
                        0 ,
                        ParameterDirection.Output ,
                        false ,
                        0 ,
                        0 ,
                        "RegionID" ,    // Defines the SOURCE column
                        DataRowVersion.Default ,
                        null));
aCommand.UpdatedRowSource = UpdateRowSource.OutputParameters;
```

What this means is that whenever a data adapter issues this command, the output parameters should be mapped back to the source of the row, which in this instance was a row in a `DataTable`. The flag states what data should be updated – the stored procedure has an output parameter that is mapped back into the `DataRow`. The column it applies to is `RegionID`, as this is defined within the command definition.

The values for `UpdateRowSource` are as follows:

UpdateRowSource Value	Description
Both	A stored procedure may return output parameters and also a complete database record. Both of these data sources are used to update the source row.
FirstReturnedRecord	This infers that the command returns a single record, and that the contents of that record should be merged into the original source `DataRow`. This is useful where a given table has a number of default (or computed) columns, as after an `INSERT` statement these need to be synchronized with the `DataRow` on the client. An example might be 'INSERT (columns) INTO (table) WITH (primarykey)', then 'SELECT (columns) FROM (table) WHERE (primarykey)'. The returned record would then be merged into the original row.

UpdateRowSource Value	Description
None	All data returned from the command is discarded.
OutputParameters	Any output parameters from the command are mapped onto the appropriate column(s) in the DataRow.

Updating an Existing Row

Updating a row that already exists within the DataTable is just a case of utilizing the DataRow class's indexer with either a column name or column number, as shown in the following code:

```
r["RegionDescription"]="North West England";
r[1] = "North East England";
```

Both of these statements are equivalent (in this example):

```
Changed RegionID 5 description
    1    Eastern                              Unchanged
    2    Western                              Unchanged
    3    Northern                             Unchanged
    4    Southern                             Unchanged
    5    North West England                   Modified
```

Prior to updating the database, the row updated has its state set to Modified as shown above.

Deleting a Row

Deleting a row is a matter of calling the Delete() method:

```
r.Delete();
```

A deleted row has its row state set to Deleted, but you cannot read columns from the deleted DataRow as these are no longer valid. When the adaptor's Update() method is called, all deleted rows will utilize the DeleteCommand, which in this instance executes the RegionDelete stored procedure.

Writing XML Output

As you have seen already, the DataSet has great support for defining its schema in XML, and as you can read data from an XML document, you can also write data to an XML document.

The DataSet.WriteXml() method permits you to output various parts of the data stored within the DataSet. You can elect to output just the data, or the data and the schema. The following code shows an example of both for the Region example shown above:

```
ds.WriteXml(".\\WithoutSchema.xml");
ds.WriteXml(".\\WithSchema.xml" , XmlWriteMode.WriteSchema);
```

The first file, `WithoutSchema.xml` is shown below:

```
<?xml version="1.0" standalone="yes"?>
<NewDataSet>
    <Region>
        <RegionID>1</RegionID>
        <RegionDescription>Eastern                    </RegionDescription>
    </Region>
    <Region>
        <RegionID>2</RegionID>
        <RegionDescription>Western                    </RegionDescription>
    </Region>
    <Region>
        <RegionID>3</RegionID>
        <RegionDescription>Northern                   </RegionDescription>
    </Region>
    <Region>
        <RegionID>4</RegionID>
        <RegionDescription>Southern                   </RegionDescription>
    </Region>
</NewDataSet>
```

The closing tag on `RegionDescription` is over to the right of the page as the database column is defined as `NCHAR(50)`, which is a 50 character string padded with spaces.

The output produced in the `WithSchema.xml` file includes, not surprisingly, the XML schema for the `DataSet` as well as the data itself:

```
<?xml version="1.0" standalone="yes"?>
<NewDataSet>
    <xs:schema id="NewDataSet" xmlns=""
            xmlns:xs="http://www.w3.org/2001/XMLSchema"
            xmlns:msdata="urn:schemas-microsoft-com:xml-msdata">
        <xs:element name="NewDataSet" msdata:IsDataSet="true">
            <xs:complexType>
                <xs:choice maxOccurs="unbounded">
                    <xs:element name="Region">
                        <xs:complexType>
                            <xs:sequence>
                                <xs:element name="RegionID"
                                            msdata:AutoIncrement="true"
                                            msdata:AutoIncrementSeed="1"
                                            type="xs:int" />
                                <xs:element name="RegionDescription"
                                            type="xs:string" />
                            </xs:sequence>
                        </xs:complexType>
                    </xs:element>
                </xs:choice>
            </xs:complexType>
        </xs:element>
    </xs:schema>
    <Region>
        <RegionID>1</RegionID>
        <RegionDescription>Eastern                    </RegionDescription>
```

```
        </Region>
        <Region>
           <RegionID>2</RegionID>
           <RegionDescription>Western                    </RegionDescription>
        </Region>
        <Region>
           <RegionID>3</RegionID>
           <RegionDescription>Northern                   </RegionDescription>
        </Region>
        <Region>
           <RegionID>4</RegionID>
           <RegionDescription>Southern                   </RegionDescription>
        </Region>
     </NewDataSet>
```

Note the use in this file of the `msdata` schema, which defines extra attributes for columns within a `DataSet`, such as `AutoIncrement` and `AutoIncrementSeed` – these attributes correspond directly with the properties definable on a `DataColumn`.

Working with ADO.NET

This last section will attempt to address some common scenarios when developing data access applications with ADO.NET.

Tiered Development

Producing an application that interacts with data is often done by splitting the application up into tiers. A common model is to have an application tier (the front end), a data services tier, and the database itself.

One of the difficulties with this model is deciding what data to transport between tiers, and the format that it should be transported in. With ADO.NET you'll be pleased to hear that these wrinkles have been ironed out, and support for this style of architecture has been designed in from the start.

Copying and Merging Data

Ever tried copying an entire OLE DB recordset? In .NET it's easy to copy a `DataSet`:

```
DataSet source = {some dataset};
DataSet dest = source.Copy();
```

This will create an exact copy of the source `DataSet` – each `DataTable`, `DataColumn`, `DataRow`, and `Relation` will be copied across verbatim, and all data will be in exactly the same state as it was in the source. If all you want to copy is the schema of the `DataSet`, you can try the following:

```
DataSet source = {some dataset};
DataSet dest = source.Clone();
```

This will again copy all tables, relations, and so on. However, each copied `DataTable` will be empty. It really couldn't be more straightforward.

A common requirement when writing a tiered system, whether based on Win32 or the web, is to be able to ship as little data as possible between tiers. This reduces the amount of resources consumed.

To cope with this requirement, the `DataSet` has the `GetChanges()` method. This simple method performs a huge amount of work, and returns a `DataSet` with only the changed rows from the source dataset. This is ideal for passing between tiers, as only a minimal set of data has to be passed across the wire.

The following example shows how to generate a "changes" `DataSet`:

```
DataSet source = {some dataset};
DataSet dest = source.GetChanges();
```

Again, this is trivial. Under the covers things are a little more interesting. There are two overloads of the `GetChanges()` method. One overload takes a value of the `DataRowState` enumeration, and returns only rows that correspond to that state (or states). `GetChanges()` simply calls `GetChanges(Deleted | Modified | Added)`, and first checks to ensure that there are some changes by calling `HasChanges()`. If no changes have been made, then a `null` is returned to the caller immediately.

The next operation is to clone the current `DataSet`. Once done, the new `DataSet` is set up to ignore constraint violations (`EnforceConstraints = false`), and then each changed row for every table is copied into the new `DataSet`.

Once you have a `DataSet` that just contains changes, you can then move these off to the data services tier for processing. Once the data is updated in the database, the "changes" `DataSet` can be returned to the caller (as there may, for example, be some output parameters from the stored procedures that have updated values in the columns). These changes can then be merged into the original `DataSet` using the `Merge()` method. This sequence of operations is depicted below:

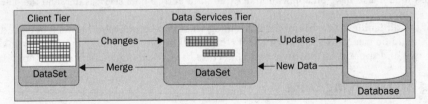

Key Generation with SQL Server

The `RegionInsert` stored procedure presented earlier in the chapter was one example of generating a primary key value on insertion into the database. The method for generating the key was fairly crude and wouldn't scale well, so for a real application you should look at utilizing some other strategy for generating keys.

Your first instinct might be simply to define an identity column, and return the `@@IDENTITY` value from the stored procedure. The following stored procedure shows how this might be defined for the `Categories` table in the `Northwind` example database. Type this stored procedure into SQL Query Analyzer, or run the `StoredProcs.sql` file in the `13_SQLServerKeys` directory:

```
CREATE PROCEDURE CategoryInsert(@CategoryName NVARCHAR(15),
                               @Description NTEXT,
                               @CategoryID INTEGER OUTPUT) AS
    SET NOCOUNT OFF
    INSERT INTO Categories (CategoryName, Description)
       VALUES(@CategoryName, @Description)
    SELECT @CategoryID = @@IDENTITY
GO
```

This inserts a new row into the `Category` table, and returns the generated primary key to the caller. You can test the procedure by typing in the following SQL in Query Analyzer:

```
DECLARE @CatID int;
EXECUTE CategoryInsert 'Pasties' , 'Heaven Sent Food' , @CatID OUTPUT;
PRINT @CatID;
```

When executed as a batch of commands, this will insert a new row into the `Categories` table, and return the identity of the new record, which is then displayed to the user.

Let's say that some months down the line, someone decides to add in a simple audit trail, which will record all insertions and modifications made to the category name. You define a table such as that shown below, which will record the old and new value of the category:

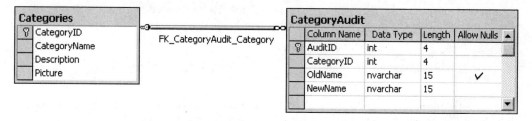

The creation script for this table is included in the `StoredProcs.sql` file. The `AuditID` column is defined as an `IDENTITY` column. You then construct a couple of database triggers that will record changes to the `CategoryName` field:

```
CREATE TRIGGER CategoryInsertTrigger
    ON Categories
    AFTER UPDATE
AS
    INSERT INTO CategoryAudit(CategoryID , OldName , NewName )
        SELECT old.CategoryID, old.CategoryName, new.CategoryName
        FROM Deleted AS old,
             Categories AS new
        WHERE old.CategoryID = new.CategoryID;
GO
```

For those of you used to Oracle stored procedures, SQL Server doesn't exactly have the concept of OLD and NEW rows, instead for an insert trigger there is an in memory table called `Inserted`, and for deletes and updates the old rows are available within the `Deleted` table.

This trigger retrieves the `CategoryID` of the record(s) affected, and stores this together with the old and new value of the `CategoryName` column.

Now, when you call your original stored procedure to insert a new `CategoryID`, you receive an identity value; however, this is no longer the identity value from the row inserted into the `Categories` table, it is now the new value generated for the row in the `CategoryAudit` table. Ouch!

To view the problem first hand, open up a copy of SQL Server Enterprise manager, and view the contents of the `Categories` table.

	CategoryID	CategoryName	Description
	1	Beverages	Soft drinks, coffees, teas, beers, and ales
	2	Condiments	Sweet and savory sauces, relishes, spreads, and seasonings
	3	Confections	Desserts, candies, and sweet breads
	4	Dairy Products	Cheeses
	5	Grains/Cereals	Breads, crackers, pasta, and cereal
	6	Meat/Poultry	Prepared meats
	7	Produce	Dried fruit and bean curd
	8	Seafood	Seaweed and fish
▶	20	Pasties	Heaven Sent Grub
✱			

This lists all the categories I have in my instance of the database.

The next identity value for the `Categories` table should be `21`, so we'll insert a new row by executing the code shown below, and see what `ID` is returned as follows:

```
DECLARE @CatID int;
EXECUTE CategoryInsert 'Pasties' , 'Heaven Sent Food' , @CatID OUTPUT;
PRINT @CatID;
```

The output value of this on my PC was 17. If I look into the `CategoryAudit` table, I find that this is the identity of the newly inserted audit record, not that of the category record created.

	AuditID	CategoryID	OldName	NewName
▶	17	30	<NULL>	Vegetables
✱				

The problem lies in the way that `@@IDENTITY` actually works. It returns the LAST identity value created by your session, so as shown above it isn't completely reliable.

There are two other identity functions that you can utilize instead of `@@IDENTITY`, but neither are free from possible problems. The first, `SCOPE_IDENTITY()`, will return the last identity value created within the current "scope". SQL Server defines scope as a stored procedure, trigger, or function. This may work most of the time, but if for some reason someone adds another `INSERT` statement into the stored procedure, then you will receive this value rather than the one you expected.

The other, `IDENT_CURRENT()` will return the last identity value generated for a given table in any scope, so for instance, if two users were accessing SQL Server at exactly the same time, it might be possible to receive the other user's generated identity value.

As you might imagine, tracking down a problem of this nature isn't easy. The moral of the story is to beware when utilizing `IDENTITY` columns in SQL Server.

Naming Conventions

Having worked with database applications all my working life, I've picked up a few recommendations for naming entities, which are worth sharing. I know, this isn't really .NET related, but the conventions are useful especially when naming constraints as above. Feel free to skip this section if you already have your own views on the subject.

Database Tables

❑ Always use singular names – `Product` rather than `Products`. This one is largely due to having to explain to customers a database schema – it's much better grammatically to say "The `Product` table contains products" than "The `Products` table contains products". Have a look at the `Northwind` database as an example of how not to do this.

❑ Adopt some form of naming convention for the fields that go into a table – ours is `<Table>_ID` for the primary key of a table (assuming that the primary key is a single column), `Name` for the field considered to be the user-friendly name of the record, and `Description` for any textual information about the record itself. Having a good table convention means you can look at virtually any table in the database and instinctively know what the fields are used for.

Database Columns

❑ Use singular rather than plural names again.

❑ Any columns that link to another table should be named the same as the primary key of that table. So, a link to the `Product` table would be `Product_ID`, and to the `Sample` table `Sample_ID`. This isn't always possible, especially if one table has multiple references to another. In that case use your own judgment.

❑ Date fields should have a suffix of `_On`, as in `Modified_On`, `Created_On`. Then it's easy to read some SQL output and infer what a column means just by its name.

❑ Fields that record the user should be suffixed with `_By`, as in `Modified_By` and `Created_By`. Again, this aids legibility.

Constraints

❑ If possible, include in the name of the constraint the table and column name, as in `CK_<Table>_<Field>`. Examples would be `CK_PERSON_SEX` for a check constraint on the `SEX` column of the `PERSON` table. A foreign key example would be `FK_Product_Supplier_ID`, for the foreign key relationship between product and supplier.

❑ Show the type of constraint with a prefix, such as `CK` for a check constraint and `FK` for a foreign key constraint. Feel free to be more specific, as in `CK_PERSON_AGE_GT0` for a constraint on the age column indicating that the age should be greater than zero.

❑ If you have to trim the length of the constraint, do it on the table name part rather than the column name. When you get a constraint violation, it's usually easy to infer which table was in error, but sometimes not so easy to check which column caused the problem. Oracle has a 30-character limit on names, which you can easily hit.

Stored Procedures

Just like the obsession many have fallen into over the past few years of putting a 'C' in front of each and every class they have declared (you know you have!), many SQL Server developers feel compelled to prefix every stored procedure with 'sp_' or something similar. It's not a good idea.

SQL Server uses the 'sp_' prefix for all (well, most) system stored procedures. So, on the one hand, you risk confusing your users into thinking that 'sp_widget' is something that comes as standard with SQL Server. In addition, when looking for a stored procedure, SQL Server will treat procedures with the 'sp_' prefix differently from those without.

If you use this prefix, and do not qualify the database/owner of the stored procedure, then SQL Server will look in the current scope, then jump into the master database and look up the stored procedure there. Without the 'sp_' prefix your users would get an error a little earlier. What's worse, and also possible to do, is to create a local stored procedure (one within your database) that has the same name and parameters as an system stored procedure. I'd avoid this at all costs – if in doubt, don't prefix.

Above all, when naming entities, whether within the database or within code, *be consistent*.

Performance

The current set of managed providers available for .NET are somewhat limited – you can choose OleDb or SqlClient; OleDb permits connection to any data source exposed with an OLE DB driver (such as Oracle), and the SqlClient provider is tailored for SqlServer.

The SqlClient provider has been written completely in managed code, and uses as few layers as possible to connect to the database. This provider writes **TDS** (**Tabular Data Stream**) packets direct to SQL Server, which should be substantially faster than the OleDb provider, which naturally has to go through a number of layers before actually hitting the database.

To test the theory, the following code was run against the same database on the same machine, the only difference being the use of the SqlClient managed provider over the ADO provider:

```
SqlConnection conn = new SqlConnection(Login.Connection);
conn.Open();
SqlCommand cmd = new SqlCommand ( "update tempdata set AValue=1 Where ID=1" ,
                                  conn);

DateTime    initial, elapsed ;
initial = DateTime.Now ;
for(int i = 0; i < iterations; i++)
    cmd.ExecuteNonQuery();
elapsed = DateTime.Now ;

conn.Close();
```

Naturally the OLE DB version utilizes `OleDbCommand` rather than `SqlCommand`. I created a simple database table with two columns as shown below, and manually added a single row:

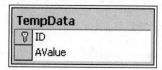

The SQL clause used was a simple `UPDATE` command:

```
UPDATE TempData SET AValue = 1 WHERE ID = 1.
```

The SQL was kept deliberately simple to attempt to highlight the differences in the providers. The results (in seconds) achieved for various combinations of iterations were as follows :

Provider	100	1000	10000	50000
OleDb	0.109	0.798	7.95	39.11
Sql	0.078	0.626	6.23	29.27

If you are only targeting SQL Server then the obvious choice is the `Sql` provider. Back in the real world, if you target anything other than SQL Server you naturally have to use the `OleDb` provider. Or do you?

As Microsoft has done an excellent job of making database access generic with the `System.Data.Common` classes, it would be better to write code against those classes, and use the appropriate managed provider at run time. It's fairly simple to swap between `OleDb` and `Sql` now, and if other database vendors write managed providers for their products, you will be able to swap out ADO for a native provider with little (or no) code changes. For an example of the versatility of .NET data access, The "Scientific Data Center" case study in "*Data-Centric .NET Programming with C#*" (Wrox Press, ISBN 1-861005-92-x) details using C# to query a MySQL database.

Summary

The subject of data access is a large one, especially in .NET as there is an abundance of new material to cover. This chapter has provided an outline of the main classes in the ADO.NET namespaces, and shown how to use the classes when manipulating data from a data source.

Firstly, we explored the use of the `Connection` object, through the use of both the `SqlConnection` (SQL Server specific) and `OleDbConnection` (for any OLE DB data sources). The programming model for these two classes is so similar that one can normally be substituted for the other and the code will continue to run.

After illustrating how to connect to and disconnect from the data source, we then discussed how to do it properly, so that scarce resources, such as database connections, could be closed as early as possible. Both of the connection classes implement the `IDisposable` interface, called when the object is placed within a `using` clause. If there's one thing I'd like you to take away from this chapter is the importance of closing database connections as early as possible.

We then discussed database commands, through examples that executed with no returned data, to calling stored procedures with input and output parameters. Various execute methods were described, including the `ExecuteXmlReader` method available only on the SQL Server provider. This vastly simplifies the selection and manipulation of XML-based data.

The generic classes within the `System.Data` namespace were all described in detail, from the `DataSet` class through `DataTable`, `DataColumn`, `DataRow` and on to relationships and constraints. The `DataSet` class is an excellent container of data, and various methods make it ideal for cross tier data flow. The data within a `DataSet` can be represented in XML for transport, and in addition, methods are available that will pass a minimal amount of data between tiers. The ability of having many tables of data within a single `DataSet` can greatly increase its usability; being able to maintain relationships automatically between master/details rows will be expanded upon in the next chapter.

Having the schema stored within a `DataSet` is one thing, but .NET also includes the data adapter that along with various `Command` objects can be used to select data into a `DataSet` and subsequently update data in the data store. One of the beneficial aspects of a data adapter is that a distinct command can be defined for each of the four actions – `SELECT`, `INSERT`, `UPDATE` and `DELETE`. The system can create a default set of commands based on database schema information and a `SELECT` statement, but for the best performance, a set of stored procedures can be used, with the `DataAdapter`'s commands defined appropriately to pass only the necessary information to these stored procedures.

As XML and XSD schemas have become feverishly popular over the past couple of years, we discussed how to convert an XSD schema into a set of database classes using the XSD tool `XSD.EXE` that ships with .NET. The classes produced are ready to be used within an application, and their automatic generation can save many hours of laborious typing.

During the last few pages of the chapter we've gone through some best practices and naming conventions for database development. Although not strictly .NET-related, these were thought to be a worthwhile inclusion. A set of conventions should always be adhered to when programming, whether in C# against a SQL Server database or in Perl scripts on Linux.

Armed with this knowledge, we're now in a good position to move on to the next chapter, where we'll explore the use of Visual Studio and .NET's Windows Forms data controls.

10

Viewing .NET Data

The last chapter was devoted to various ways of selecting and changing data. This chapter will carry on from where that one left off, and will demonstrate how you can display data to the user by binding to various Windows controls.

The data binding capabilities of .NET are similar to ADO and the Visual Basic controls. All .NET languages are now capable of using the same controls and methods, which can make life a good deal easier. The most revolutionary aspect of the .NET data access model is the new `DataGrid` control. We'll spend the first part of this chapter describing its features.

One of the best features of the new `DataGrid` control is its flexibility – the data source can be an `Array`, `DataTable`, `DataView`, `DataSet`, or a component that implements either the `IListSource` or `IList` interface. With the large number of options available we'll spend some time early on in the chapter showing how each of these sources of data can be used and viewed within the `DataGrid`.

Data binding is a common requirement, and although VB 6 (and to a certain extent MFC) had data binding capabilities, under .NET, all managed languages gain the ability to link to data. What's more, once bound to a column of data, a control will be updated automatically when the current "row" of data changes. In this chapter we will explore some of the capabilities of data binding, and show how to connect data to Windows Forms controls. We'll also see some of the inner workings of data binding to get a better understanding of how it works.

Data sources have become much more integrated into Visual Studio .NET, and in this chapter we'll show how to use the Server Explorer to create a connection and generate a `DataSet`, all without writing a line of code. We'll also cover the use of the XSD schema editor within Visual Studio .NET, giving an example of the code generated by the editor.

The chapter concludes with an example of how to utilize hit testing and reflection on rows in the `DataGrid`. This example brings together some aspects discussed elsewhere in the book, such as responding to events, reflection, custom attributes, and there's some data access thrown in too!

The DataGrid Control

The `DataGrid` is a completely new control, written specifically for .NET, and it permits various views of data to be displayed. In its simplest guise, you can display data (as in a `DataSet`) by calling the `SetDataBinding()` method. More complex capabilities are also built into the control, which we'll come to throughout the course of this chapter.

Displaying Tabular Data

The last chapter showed numerous ways of selecting data and getting it into a data table, although the data was displayed in a very basic fashion; we simply used `Console.WriteLine()`.

The first example here will show how to retrieve some data and display it in a `DataGrid` control. The following is a screenshot from the application we're about to build. The sourcecode for this application is available in the `\01_DisplayTabularData` directory:

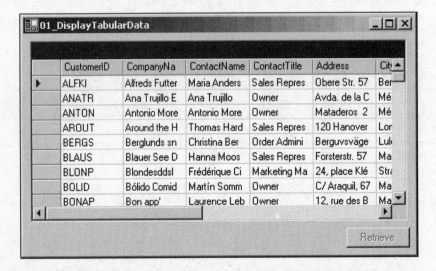

The application (simple as it is), selects every record from the customer table within the `Northwind` database, and displays these records to the user in the `DataGrid`. The code is fairly short and we will step through it in its entirety here:

```
using System;
using System.Windows.Forms;
using System.Data;
using System.Data.SqlClient;

public class DisplayTabularData : System.Windows.Forms.Form
```

```
{
    private System.Windows.Forms.Button retrieveButton;
    private System.Windows.Forms.DataGrid dataGrid;
    public DisplayTabularData()
    {
        this.AutoScaleBaseSize = new System.Drawing.Size(5, 13);
        this.ClientSize = new System.Drawing.Size(464, 253);
        this.Text = "01_DisplayTabularData";
```

Next we create the grid control, and set up its properties. The second line: `dataGrid.BeginInit();` disables firing of events on the grid, which is useful when making many modifications to the control. If events are not inhibited, each change to the grid could force a redraw on screen. We then set the location and size of the control, define the tab index, and anchor the control to both the top left and bottom right corners of the window, so that its proportions will track those of the main application window.

```
this.dataGrid = new System.Windows.Forms.DataGrid();
dataGrid.BeginInit();
dataGrid.Location = new System.Drawing.Point(8, 8);
dataGrid.Size = new System.Drawing.Size(448, 208);
dataGrid.TabIndex = 0;
dataGrid.Anchor = AnchorStyles.Bottom | AnchorStyles.Top |
                  AnchorStyles.Left | AnchorStyles.Right;
this.Controls.Add(this.dataGrid);
dataGrid.EndInit();
```

Now we create the button. The same basic steps are followed in initializing the button:

```
this.retrieveButton = new System.Windows.Forms.Button();
retrieveButton.Location = new System.Drawing.Point(384, 224);
retrieveButton.Size = new System.Drawing.Size(75, 23);
retrieveButton.TabIndex = 1;
retrieveButton.Anchor = AnchorStyles.Bottom | AnchorStyles.Right;
retrieveButton.Text = "Retrieve";
retrieveButton.Click += new System.EventHandler
                            (this.retrieveButton_Click);
this.Controls.Add(this.retrieveButton);
}
```

We also have a `Click` event, which calls the `retrieveButton_Click` event handler:

```
protected void retrieveButton_Click(object sender, System.EventArgs e)
{
    retrieveButton.Enabled = false;
    string source = "server=(local)\\NetSDK;" +
                    "uid=QSUser;pwd=QSPassword;" +
                    "database=Northwind";
```

After selecting the data from the `Customers` table and filling the data set, I call `SetDataBinding` to bind the data set to the grid. To this method I pass the data set and the name of the table within the `DataSet` that I wish to display. A grid can only display the data from one `DataTable` at a time, even if the `DataSet` contains multiple tables. Further on in the chapter, I will show an example of displaying data from a `DataSet` with multiple `DataTables`. Of course, the data within the `DataSet` could naturally come from many actual database tables (or a view over many tables):

```
        string select = "SELECT * FROM Customers" ;
        SqlConnection conn = new SqlConnection(source);
        SqlDataAdapter da = new SqlDataAdapter( select , conn);
        DataSet ds = new DataSet();
        da.Fill(ds , "Customers");
        dataGrid.SetDataBinding(ds , "Customers");
    }
    static void Main()
    {
        Application.Run(new DisplayTabularData());
    }
}
```

To compile this example, type the following at a command prompt:

csc /t:winexe /debug+ /r:System.dll /r:System.Data.dll /r:system.windows.forms.dll /recurse:*.cs

The /recurse:*.cs parameter will compile all .cs files in your current directory and all subdirectories – I use it as shorthand, so I don't have to remember all the files in the application, but you do have to ensure that you've only got the expected files in the directory.

Data Sources

The DataGrid is a very flexible way to display data; in addition to calling SetDataBinding() with a DataSet and the name of the table to display, this method can be called with any of the following data sources:

❑   An array – The grid can bind to any one dimensional array

❑   DataTable

❑   DataView

❑   DataSet or DataViewManager

❑   Components that implement the IListSource interface

❑   Components that implement the IList interface

The following sections will give an example of each of these data sources.

Displaying Data from a Array

At first glance this seems to be easy. Create an array, fill it with some data, and call SetDataBinding (array, null) on the DataGrid. Here's some example code:

```
string[] stuff = new string[] {"One", "Two", "Three"};
dataGrid.SetDataBinding(stuff, null);
```

As you may have noticed, SetDataBinding accepts two parameters. The first is the data source, which is the array in this instance. The second parameter should be null unless the data source is a DataSet or DataViewManager, in which case it should be the name of the table that you wish to display.

You could replace the code in the previous example's `retrieveButton_Click` event handler with the array code above. The problem with this code is the resulting display:

As you can see, rather than displaying the strings defined within the array, the grid is actually displaying the length of those strings. The reason for this is that when using an array as the source of data for a `DataGrid`, the grid looks for the first public property of the object within the array, and displays this value rather than the string you were expecting. The first (and only) public property of a string is its length, so that is what is displayed.

One way to rectify this is to create a wrapper class for strings, such as that shown below:

```
protected class Item
{
    public Item(string text)
    {
        m_text = text;
    }
    public string Text
    {
        get{return m_text;}
    }
    private string m_text;
}
```

When adding an array of this `Item` class (which could as well be a `struct` for all the processing that it does), you will receive the expected output. The sourcecode for this example is available in the `02_DataSourceArray` directory:

DataTable

There are two main ways to display a DataTable within a DataGrid:

❑ If your DataTable is standalone, call SetDataBinding(DataTable, null)

❑ If your DataTable is contained within a DataSet, call SetDataBinding(DataSet, "<Table Name>")

The example screenshot, taken from the code available in \03_DatasourceDataTable, shows some of the columns:

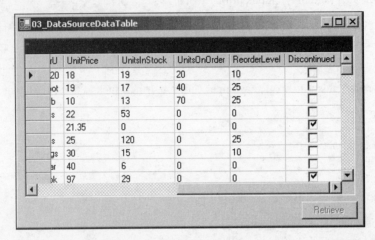

Note the display of the last column; it shows a checkbox instead of the more common edit control. The DataGrid, in the absence of any other information, will read the schema from the data source (which in this case is the Products table), and infer from the column types what control is to be displayed.

The data in the database does not change when you alter fields in the data grid, as the data is only stored locally on your computer – there is no active connection to the database. We'll come on to updating the original data source later, in the *Updating the Data Source* section.

Don't get too excited, though – the only two types that are currently supported are textboxes and checkboxes – any other sort of mapping has to be done manually.

Displaying Data from a DataView

A DataView provides a means to filter and sort data within a DataTable. When you have selected data from the database, it is common to permit the user to sort that data, such as by clicking on column headings. In addition, you may want to filter the data to show only certain rows, such as all those that have been changed by the user. A DataView allows you to limit the rows shown to the user; however, it does not limit the columns from the DataTable.

> A **DataView** does not allow you to change which columns are displayed, just which rows.

An example of how to limit the columns shown is provided later in the chapter, in the *DataGridTableStyle and DataGridColumnStyle* section.

The code to create a `DataView` based on an existing `DataTable` is shown below. The example code for this section is available in the `\04_DataSourceDataView` directory.

```
DataView dv = new DataView(dataTable);
```

Once created, you can then alter settings on the `DataView`, which affect the data and operations permitted on that data when the view is displayed within the data grid. Some examples are:

❑ Setting `AllowEdit = false` disables all column edit functionality for rows

❑ Setting `AllowNew = false` will disable the new row functionality

❑ Setting `AllowDelete = false` will disable the delete row capability

❑ Setting the `RowStateFilter` to display only rows of a given state

❑ Setting the `RowFilter` to filter rows

❑ Sorting the rows by certain columns

We'll see examples of using the `RowStateFilter` in the next section – the other options are fairly self-explanatory.

Filtering Rows by Data

Once you have created a `DataView`, you can alter the data displayed by that view by setting the `RowFilter` property. This property, typed as a string, is used as a means of filtering based on certain criteria – the value of the string is used as the filter criteria. Its syntax is similar to a `WHERE` clause in regular SQL, but it is issued against data already selected from the database.

Some examples of filter clauses are shown in the following table:

Clause	Description
`UnitsInStock > 50`	Show only those rows where the `UnitsInStock` column is greater than 50.
`Client = 'Smith'`	Return only those records for a given client.
`County LIKE 'C*'`	Return all records where the `County` field begins with a C – so for example this would return rows for Cornwall, Cumbria, Cheshire, and Cambridgeshire. You can use "%" as a single character wildcard, whereas the "*" denotes a general wildcard that will match zero or more characters.

The runtime will do its best to coerce the data types used within the filter expression into the appropriate types for the source columns. As an example, it is perfectly legal to write `"UnitsInStock > '50'"` in the earlier example, even though the column is an integer. If you do, however, provide a filter string that is invalid, then an `EvaluateException` will be thrown.

Filtering Rows on State

Each row within a `DataView` has a defined row state, which will be one of the following values. This state can also be used to filter the rows viewed by the user.

`DataViewRowState`	Description
Added	All rows that have been newly created.
CurrentRows	All rows except those that have been deleted.
Deleted	All rows that were originally selected and have been deleted – does not show newly created rows that have been deleted.
ModifiedCurrent	Lists all rows that have been modified, and shows the current value of each column.
ModifiedOriginal	Lists all rows that have been modified, but shows the original value of the column and not the current value.
OriginalRows	All rows which were originally selected from a data source. Does not include new rows. Shows the original values of the columns (that is, not the current values if changes have been made).
Unchanged	All rows that have not changed in any way.

To view the effect of these states on a grid, I've written an example that displays two grids – one being data selected from the database that you can interact with, the other showing rows in one of the above states:

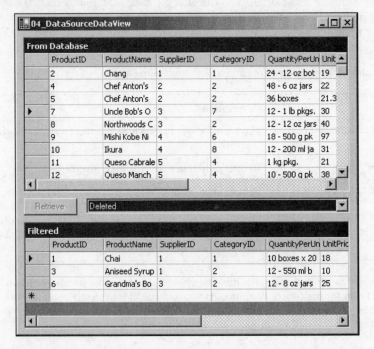

The filter not only applies to the rows that are visible, but also to the state of the columns within those rows. This is evident when choosing the `ModifiedOriginal` or `ModifiedCurrent` selections. These states were described in the previous chapter, and are based on the `DataRowVersion` enumeration. If, for example, you have updated a row in some form, then the row will show up when you choose either `ModifiedOriginal` or `ModifiedCurrent`; however, the actual value will either be the `Original` value selected from the database (if you choose `ModifiedOriginal`), or the current value in the `DataColumn` if you choose `ModifiedCurrent`.

Sorting Rows

As well as filtering data, it is sometimes necessary to sort the data within a `DataView`. You can click on a column header within the `DataGrid` control, and this will sort a column in either ascending or descending order. The only trouble is that the control can only sort by one column, whereas the underlying `DataView` can sort by many columns:

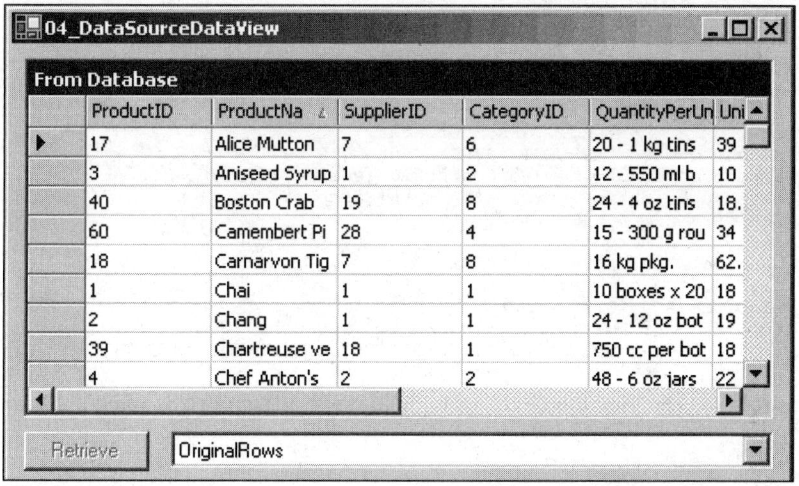

When a column is sorted, either by clicking on the header (as shown on the `ProductName` column) or within code, the `DataGrid` displays an arrow bitmap to indicate which column the sort has been applied to.

To programmatically set the sort order on a column, use the `Sort` property of the `DataView`:

```
dataView.Sort = "ProductName";
dataView.Sort = "ProductName ASC, ProductID DESC";
```

The first line above will sort the data based on the `ProductName` column, as shown in the previous image. The second line will sort in the data in ascending order, based on the `ProductName` column, then in descending order of `ProductID`.

The `DataView` supports both ascending and descending sort orders on columns – the default being ascending. If you do choose to sort on more than one column within the `DataView`, the `DataGrid` will cease to display any sort arrows.

If you have done any Win32 programming with ListView controls, you'll appreciate the work that the .NET team have done for sorting within the grid. As each column within the grid can be strongly typed, its sort order is not based upon the string representation of the column. Instead, it is based on the actual data.

The upshot is that if you have a date column within the DataGrid, and you try to sort it, the grid will do date comparisons to sort rather than string comparisons.

Displaying Data from a DataSet

The DataGrid comes in to its own when displaying data from a DataSet. As with the preceding examples, the DataGrid can only display a single DataTable at a time. However, as you'll see in this example, it is possible to navigate relationships within the DataSet on screen. The following code can be used to generate such a DataSet based on the Customers and Orders tables within the Northwind database. The code is available in the \05_DataSourceDataSet directory. The example adds in these two DataTables, and then creates a relationship between these tables called CustomerOrders:

```
string source = "server=(local)\\NetSDK;" +
                "uid=QSUser;pwd=QSPassword;" +
                "database=northwind";
string orders = "SELECT * FROM Orders";
string customers = "SELECT * FROM Customers";
SqlConnection conn = new SqlConnection(source);
SqlDataAdapter da = new SqlDataAdapter(orders, conn);
DataSet ds = new DataSet();
da.Fill(ds, "Orders");
da = new SqlDataAdapter(customers , conn);
da.Fill(ds, "Customers");
ds.Relations.Add("CustomerOrders",
                 ds.Tables["Customers"].Columns["CustomerID"],
                 ds.Tables["Orders"].Columns["CustomerID"]);
```

Once created, you can bind the DataSet to the DataGrid simply by calling SetDataBinding():

```
dataGrid1.SetDataBinding(ds, "Customers");
```

This will produce a display something like the following screenshot:

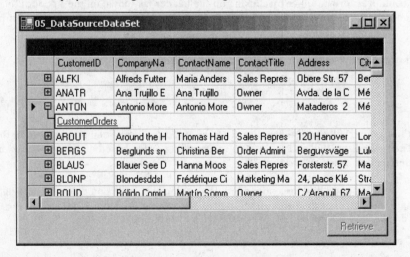

You may immediately notice that unlike the other `DataGrids` that we have seen in this chapter, there is a + to the left of each record. This reflects the fact that we created a `DataSet` with a navigable relationship, between customers and orders. You can have a number of such relationships defined in code.

When you click on the + sign, the list of relationships is shown (or hidden if already visible). Clicking on the name of the relationship will navigate the grid to the linked records, in this case listing all orders placed by the selected customer:

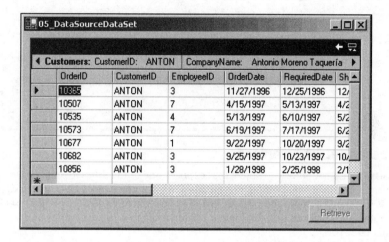

The `DataGrid` control also includes a couple of new icons in the top right corner. The arrow permits you to navigate back to the parent row, and will change the display to that on the previous page. The header row showing details of the parent record can be shown or hidden by clicking on the other button.

Displaying Data in a DataViewManager

The display of data in a `DataViewManager` is the same as that for the `DataSet` just shown. However, when a `DataViewManager` is created for a `DataSet`, an individual `DataView` is created for each `DataTable`, which then permits you to alter the displayed rows, based on a filter or the row state as shown in the `DataView` example. Even if you don't expect the need to filter data, I would suggest always wrapping a `DataSet` in a `DataViewManager` for display, as it gives you more options when revising your code.

The following code creates a `DataViewManager` based on the `DataSet` from the previous example, and then alters the `DataView` for the `Customers` table to show only customers from the UK:

```
DataViewManager dvm = new DataViewManager(ds);
dvm.DataViewSettings["Customers"].RowFilter = "Country='UK'";
dataGrid.SetDataBinding(dvm, "Customers");
```

The output of this code is shown below. The example can be found in the
\06_DataSourceDataViewManager directory.

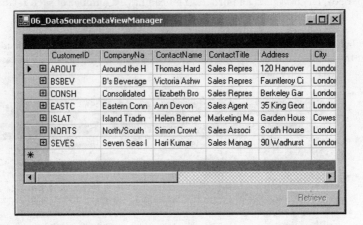

IListSource and IList Interfaces

The `DataGrid` also supports any object that exposes one of the interfaces `IListSource` or `IList`.
`IListSource` only has one method, `GetList()`, which returns an `IList` interface. `IList` on the
other hand is somewhat more interesting, and is implemented by a large number of classes in the
runtime. Some of the classes that implement this interface are `Array`, `ArrayList`, and
`StringCollection`.

When using `IList`, the same caveat for the object within the collection holds true as for the `Array`
implementation shown earlier – if you use a `StringCollection` as the data source for the `DataGrid`,
the length of the strings is displayed within the grid, not the text of the item as you would hope.

DataGrid Class Hierarchy

The class hierarchy for the main parts of the `DataGrid` is shown below:

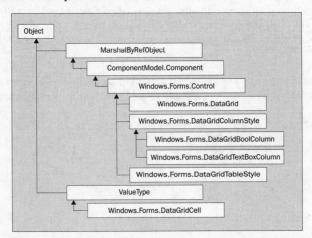

The DataGrid consists of zero or more DataGridTableStyles. These styles consist of zero or more DataGridColumnStyles. A given cell in the grid can be accessed by means of the DataGridCell struct.

However, there's more to DataGridTableStyle and DataGridColumnStyle than simply letting the runtime create them for you. The following sections will describe these and the other main classes shown in the above figure. The following sections will discuss these in detail, and show how you can alter many facets of the on-screen display of data using these classes.

DataGridTableStyle and DataGridColumnStyle

A DataGridTableStyle contains the visual representation of a DataTable. The DataGrid contains a collection of these styles, accessible by the TableStyles property. When a DataTable is displayed, a check is made through all DataGridTableStyle objects to find one with its MappingName property equal to the TableName property of the DataTable. On finding a match, that style will be used in the display of the table.

The DataGridTableStyle permits you to define visual parameters for the DataGrid, such as the background and foreground color, the font used in the column header, and various other properties. The DataGridColumnStyle allows you to refine the display options on a column-by-column basis, such as setting the alignment for the data in the column, the text that is displayed for a null value, and the width of the column on screen.

When the DataGrid displays a DataTable with a defined DataGridTableStyle, you can define which columns of data are actually displayed by adding (or not adding) a DataGridColumnStyle. Only columns that have a defined style will be displayed, which can be useful for "hiding" columns such as primary key values that are not normally displayed. You may also define a column style as ReadOnly.

The code below shows an example of creating a DataGridTableStyle. The code creates a DataGridTableStyle object, adds in two DataGridColumnStyle objects, and then displays all of the data within the Customers table. We'll show the code in its entirety, as this will be the basis for several examples in this section. The first part of the code should be familiar from our earlier example:

```
using System;
using System.Windows.Forms;
using System.Data;
using System.Data.SqlClient;
public class CustomDataGridTableStyle : System.Windows.Forms.Form
{
    private System.Windows.Forms.Button retrieveButton;
    private System.Windows.Forms.DataGrid dataGrid;
    public CustomDataGridTableStyle()
    {
        this.AutoScaleBaseSize = new System.Drawing.Size(5, 13);
        this.ClientSize = new System.Drawing.Size(464, 253);
        this.Text = "07_CustomDataGridTableStyle";
        this.dataGrid = new System.Windows.Forms.DataGrid();
        dataGrid.BeginInit();
        dataGrid.Location = new System.Drawing.Point(8, 8);
        dataGrid.Size = new System.Drawing.Size(448, 208);
```

```
      dataGrid.TabIndex = 0;
      dataGrid.Anchor = AnchorStyles.Bottom | AnchorStyles.Top |
                        AnchorStyles.Left | AnchorStyles.Right;
      this.Controls.Add(this.dataGrid);
      dataGrid.EndInit();
      this.retrieveButton = new System.Windows.Forms.Button();
      retrieveButton.Location = new System.Drawing.Point(384, 224);
      retrieveButton.Size = new System.Drawing.Size(75, 23);
      retrieveButton.TabIndex = 1;
      retrieveButton.Anchor = AnchorStyles.Bottom | AnchorStyles.Right;
      retrieveButton.Text = "Retrieve";
      retrieveButton.Click += new
                        System.EventHandler(this.retrieveButton_Click);
      this.Controls.Add(this.retrieveButton);
}
protected void retrieveButton_Click(object sender, System.EventArgs e)
{
      retrieveButton.Enabled = false;
```

These generate the `DataSet` that will be used, then create the `DataGridTableStyles` for use in the
example, and finally bind the `DataGrid` to the `DataSet`. The `CreateDataSet` method is nothing
particularly new as we will see later; it simply retrieves all rows from the `Customers` table:

```
      DataSet ds = CreateDataSet();
      CreateStyles(dataGrid);
      dataGrid.SetDataBinding(ds, "Customers");
}
```

The `CreateStyles()` method is, however, more interesting. The first few lines create the new
`DataGridTableStyle` object, and set its `MappingName` property. This property is used when the
`DataGrid` displays a given `DataTable`. The `DataGrid` can display rows in alternating colors. The
code here also defines the color for every second row, and the output is displayed in the screenshot later
in this section:

```
      private void CreateStyles(DataGrid dg)
      {
          DataGridTableStyle style = new DataGridTableStyle();
          style.MappingName = "Customers";
          style.AlternatingBackColor = System.Drawing.Color.Bisque;
          DataGridTextBoxColumn customerID = new DataGridTextBoxColumn();
          customerID.HeaderText = "Customer ID";
          customerID.MappingName = "CustomerID";
          customerID.Width = 200;
          DataGridTextBoxColumn name = new DataGridTextBoxColumn();
          name.HeaderText = "Name";
          name.MappingName = "CompanyName";
          name.Width = 300;
```

When the columns have been defined, they are added to the `GridColumnStyles` collection of the `DataGridTableStyle` object, which itself is then added to the `TableStyles` property of the `DataGrid`:

```
        style.GridColumnStyles.AddRange
                    (new DataGridColumnStyle[]{customerID , name});
        dg.TableStyles.Add(style);
    }
    private DataSet CreateDataSet()
    {
        string source = "server=(local)\\NetSDK;" +
                        "uid=QSUser;pwd=QSPassword;" +
                        "database=northwind";
        string customers = "SELECT * FROM Customers";
        SqlConnection con = new SqlConnection(source);
        SqlDataAdapter da = new SqlDataAdapter(customers , con);
        DataSet ds = new DataSet();
        da.Fill(ds, "Customers");
        return ds;
    }
    static void Main()
    {
        Application.Run(new CustomDataGridTableStyle());
    }
}
```

After creating the `DataGridTableStyle` object, we created two objects derived from `DataGridColumnStyle` – in this instance they are textboxes. Each column has a number of properties defined. The following table lists some of the key properties:

Property	Description
Alignment	One of the `HorizontalAlignment` enumerated values – `Left`, `Center`, or `Right`. This indicates how data in the column is justified.
FontHeight	The size of the font in pixels. This will default to that of the `DataGrid` if no value is set. This property is `protected`, so can only be modified if you create your own subclass.
HeaderText	The text displayed in the column heading.
MappingName	The column in the `DataTable` represented by the displayed column.
NullText	The text displayed within the column if the underlying data value is `DBNull`.
PropertyDescriptor	This will be discussed later in the chapter.
ReadOnly	A flag indicating whether the column is read-write or read-only.
Width	The width of the column in pixels.

The display resulting from this code is shown below. The example is available in the \07_CustomDataGridTableStyle directory:

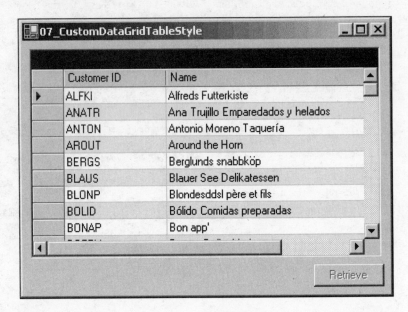

Data Binding

The previous examples have all used the DataGrid control, which is only one of the controls within the .NET runtime that can be used to display data. The process of linking a control to a data source is called **data binding**.

If you have any experience with programming Windows applications in MFC, at one time or another, you'll probably have utilized the **Dialog Data Exchange** (**DDX**) capabilities, to hook member variables of one class to a Win32 control. You'll probably be pleased to know that you can close the door on DDX, as it's considerably easier to hook data to controls in .NET. You can bind data not only to Windows controls, but also to web pages using ASP.NET. Binding controls to web pages will be covered in Chapter 14.

Simple Binding

A control that supports single binding typically displays only a single value at once, such as a textbox or radio button. The following example shows how to bind a column from a DataTable to a TextBox:

```
DataSet ds = CreateDataSet();
textBox1.DataBindings.Add("Text", ds , "Products.ProductName");
```

After retrieving some data from the `Products` table and storing this in the returned `DataSet` with the `CreateDataSet()` method as above, the second line then binds the `Text` property of the control (textBox1) to the `Products.ProductName` column. If you were to write this code and retrieve data from the `Northwind` database, you would see something like the following on screen:

The textbox is indeed displaying something from the database. To check that it is the right column and value, you could use the SQL Server Query Analyzer tool to verify the contents of the `Products` table:

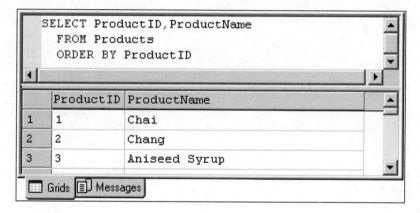

Having a single text box on screen with no way to scroll to the next or the previous record and no way to update the database is not very useful, so the next section will show a more realistic example, and introduce the other objects that are necessary in order for data binding to work. I'll begin with an overview of some of the classes used.

Data Binding Objects

The diagram overleaf shows a class hierarchy for the objects that are used in data binding. In this section we'll discuss the `BindingContext`, `CurrencyManager`, and `PropertyManager` classes of the `System.Windows.Forms` namespace, and show how they interact when data is bound to one or more controls on a form. The shaded objects are those that are utilized in binding.

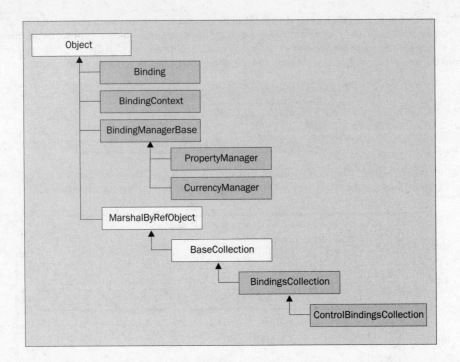

In the previous example, we used the `DataBindings` property of the `TextBox` control to bind a column from a `DataSet` to the `Text` property of the control. The `DataBindings` property is an instance of the `ControlBindingsCollection` shown above:

```
textBox1.DataBindings.Add("Text", ds, "Products.ProductName");
```

This line added a `Binding` object to the `ControlBindingsCollection`.

Binding Context

Each Windows form has a `BindingContext` property. Incidentally, `Form` is derived from `Control`, which is where this property is actually defined, so most controls have this property. A `BindingContext` object has a collection of `BindingManagerBase` instances. These instances are created and added to the binding manager object when a control is data bound:

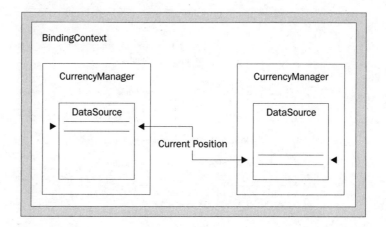

The `BindingContext` may contain several data sources, wrapped in either a `CurrencyManager` or a `PropertyManager`. The decision on which class is used is based on the data source itself.

If the data source contains a list of items, such as a `DataTable`, `DataView`, or any object that implements the `IList` interface, then a `CurrencyManager` will be used, as this can maintain the current position within that data source. If the data source returns only a single value then a `PropertyManager` will be stored within the `BindingContext`.

A `CurrencyManager` or `PropertyManager` is only created once for a given data source. If you bind two textboxes to a row from a `DataTable`, only one `CurrencyManager` will be created within the binding context.

Each control added to a form is linked to the form's binding manager, so all controls share the same instance. When a control is initially created, its `BindingContext` property is null. When the control is added to the `Controls` collection of the form, this sets the `BindingContext` to that of the form.

To bind a control to a form, you need to add an entry to its `DataBindings` property, which is an instance of `ControlBindingsCollection`. The code shown below creates a new binding:

```
textBox1.DataBindings.Add("Text", ds, "Products.ProductName");
```

Internally, the `Add()` method of `ControlBindingsCollection` creates a new instance of a `Binding` object from the parameters passed to this method, and adds this to the bindings collection:

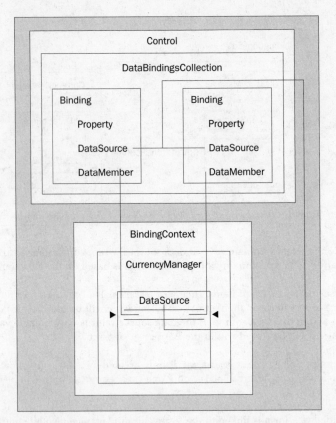

The image above shows roughly what is going on when you add a `Binding` to a `Control`. The binding links the control to a data source, which is maintained within the `BindingContext` of the `Form` (or control itself). Changes within the data source are reflected into the control, as are changes in the control.

Binding

This class links a property of the control to a member of the data source. When that member changes, the control's property is updated to reflect this change. The opposite is also true – if the text within the textbox is updated, this change is reflected in the data source.

Bindings can be set up from any column to any property of the control, so, for instance, you would bind a column to a textbox and could also bind another column to the textbox color (or length).

You could bind properties of a control to completely different data sources – maybe the color of the cell is defined in a colors table, and the actual data is defined within another table.

CurrencyManager and PropertyManager

When a `Binding` object is created, a corresponding `CurrencyManager` or `PropertyManager` object will also be created if this is the first time that data from the given source has been bound. The purpose of this class is to define the position of the "current" record within the data source, and to coordinate all list bindings when this current record is changed.

The following example displays two fields from the `Products` table, and includes a way to move between records by means of a `TrackBar` control:

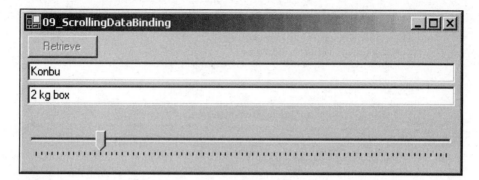

The example code for this application is shown in its entirety. The code is available in the `\09_ScrollingDataBinding` directory:

```
using System;
using System.Windows.Forms;
using System.Data;
using System.Data.SqlClient;

public class ScrollingDataBinding : System.Windows.Forms.Form
{
    private Button retrieveButton;
    private TextBox textName;
    private TextBox textQuan;
    private TrackBar trackBar;
    private DataSet ds;
```

The application creates the window, and all controls for that window, within the `ScrollingDataBinding` constructor:

```
public ScrollingDataBinding()
{
    this.AutoScaleBaseSize = new System.Drawing.Size(5, 13);
    this.ClientSize = new System.Drawing.Size(464, 253);
    this.Text = "09_ScrollingDataBinding";
    this.retrieveButton = new Button();
    retrieveButton.Location = new System.Drawing.Point(4, 4);
    retrieveButton.Size = new System.Drawing.Size(75, 23);
    retrieveButton.TabIndex = 1;
    retrieveButton.Anchor = AnchorStyles.Top | AnchorStyles.Left;
    retrieveButton.Text = "Retrieve";
    retrieveButton.Click += new System.EventHandler
                                (this.retrieveButton_Click);
    this.Controls.Add(this.retrieveButton);
    this.textName = new TextBox();
    textName.Location = new System.Drawing.Point(4, 31);
    textName.Text = "Please click retrieve...";
```

```
            textName.TabIndex = 2;
            textName.Anchor = AnchorStyles.Top | AnchorStyles.Left |
                          AnchorStyles.Right ;
            textName.Size = new System.Drawing.Size(456, 20);
            textName.Enabled = false;
            this.Controls.Add(this.textName);
            this.textQuan = new TextBox();
            textQuan.Location = new System.Drawing.Point(4, 55);
            textQuan.Text = "";
            textQuan.TabIndex = 3;
            textQuan.Anchor = AnchorStyles.Top | AnchorStyles.Left |
                          AnchorStyles.Top;
            textQuan.Size = new System.Drawing.Size(456, 20);
            textQuan.Enabled = false;
            this.Controls.Add(this.textQuan);
            this.trackBar = new TrackBar();
            trackBar.BeginInit();
            trackBar.Dock = DockStyle.Bottom ;
            trackBar.Location = new System.Drawing.Point(0, 275);
            trackBar.TabIndex = 4;
            trackBar.Size = new System.Drawing.Size(504, 42);
            trackBar.Scroll += new System.EventHandler(this.trackBar_Scroll);
            trackBar.Enabled = false;
            this.Controls.Add(this.trackBar);
        }
```

When the **Retrieve** button is clicked, the event handler selects all records from the `Products` table, and stores this data within the private dataset `ds`:

```
        protected void retrieveButton_Click(object sender, System.EventArgs e)
        {
            retrieveButton.Enabled = false ;
            ds = CreateDataSet();
```

Next, the two text controls are bound:

```
            textName.DataBindings.Add("Text" , ds ,
                              "Products.ProductName");
            textQuan.DataBindings.Add("Text" , ds ,
                              "Products.QuantityPerUnit");
            trackBar.Minimum - 0 ;
            trackBar.Maximum = this.BindingContext[ds,"Products"].Count - 1;
            textName.Enabled = true;
            textQuan.Enabled = true;
            trackBar.Enabled = true;
        }
```

Here we have a trivial record scrolling mechanism, which responds to movements of the `TrackBar` thumb:

```
        protected void trackBar_Scroll(object sender , System.EventArgs e)
        {
            this.BindingContext[ds,"Products"].Position = trackBar.Value;
        }
        private DataSet CreateDataSet()
        {
```

```
        string source = "server=(local)\\NetSDK;" +
                        "uid=QSUser;pwd=QSPassword;" +
                        "database=northwind";
        string customers = "SELECT * FROM Products";
        SqlConnection con = new SqlConnection(source);
        SqlDataAdapter da = new SqlDataAdapter(customers , con);
        DataSet ds = new DataSet();
        da.Fill(ds , "Products");
        return ds;
    }
    static void Main()
    {
        Application.Run(new ScrollingDataBinding());
    }
}
```

When the data is originally retrieved, the maximum position on the track bar is set to be the number of records. Then, in the scroll method above, we set the position of the `BindingContext` for the products `DataTable` to the position of the scroll bar thumb. This effectively changes the current record from the `DataTable`, so all controls bound to the current row (in this example the two textboxes) are updated.

In this section we've covered binding to various data sources, such as arrays, data tables, data views, and various other containers of data, how to sort and filter that data, and how the underlying binding mechanism in .NET works. In the next section we'll discuss how Visual Studio has been extended to permit data access to be better integrated with the application.

Visual Studio and Data Access

With the new version of Visual Studio come some new ways to bolt data access into your applications. This section will discuss some of the ways that Visual Studio .NET allows data to be integrated into the GUI, so that you can interact with data just as you would with regular controls.

The tools available allow you to create a database connection, using either the `OleDbConnection` or `SqlConnection` classes. The class you will use depends on which database you wish to connect to. Once you have defined a connection, you can then create a `DataSet` and populate it from within Visual Studio .NET. This generates an XSD file for the `DataSet`, just as we did manually in the previous chapter, and automatically generates the `.cs` code for you. This results in the creation of a type-safe `DataSet`.

In this section I'll show you how to create a connection, select some data, generate a `DataSet`, and use all of the generated objects to produce a simple application.

Creating a Connection

To begin this section, create a new Windows application. Once created, you'll most probably see a blank form. The first task is to create a new database connection. Bring up the **Server Explorer** – either type *Ctrl + Alt + S*, or select **Server Explorer** item from the **View** menu. This will display a window similar to that shown overleaf:

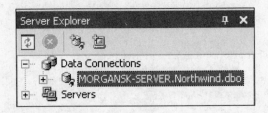

Within this window you can manage various aspects of data access. For this example, you need to create a connection to the Northwind database. Selecting the **Add Connection...** option from the context menu available on the **Data Connections** item will bring up a wizard where you can select which OLE DB provider to use – choose **Microsoft OLE DB Provider for SQL Server** as you will be connecting to the Northwind database installed as part of the Framework SDK samples. The second page of the **Data Link** dialog is shown here:

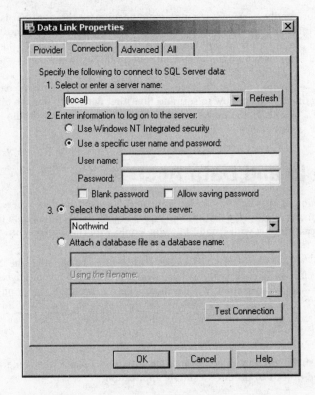

Depending on how you have installed your Framework samples databases, you may have an instance of the Northwind database residing in SQL Server, one in a local MSDE (Microsoft Data Engine) database, or possibly both.

To connect to the MSDE database (if you have one), type (local)\NETSDK for the name of the server. To connect to a regular SQL Server instance, type (local) as shown above for the current machine, or the name of the desired server on the network.

Next you need to choose the login information – you can either use integrated NT security, or specify a username and password. The choice you make again depends on how your database has been set up. For the local MSDE database, you can use a specific username and password, which are **QSUser** and **QSPassword** respectively.

Select the **Northwind** database from the drop-down list of databases, and to ensure you have everything set up correctly, click on the **Test Connection** button. This will attempt to connect to the database and should display a message box when complete. Of course, you'll have to set the server up appropriately for your machine's configuration, so the user name, password, and the server name may all be different.

To create a connection object, click and drag the newly added server onto the main application window. This will create a member variable of type `System.Data.SqlClient.SqlConnection`, or `System.Data.OleDb.OleDbConnection` if you chose a different provider, and add the following code into the `InitializeComponent` method of the main form:

```
this.sqlConnection1 = new System.Data.SqlClient.SqlConnection();

//
// sqlConnection1
//

this.sqlConnection1.ConnectionString = "data source=skinnerm\\NETSDK;" +
                                        "initial catalog=Northwind;" +
                                        "user id=QSUser;password=QSPassword;" +
                                        "persist security info=True;" +
                                        "workstation id=SKINNERM;" +
                                        "packet size=4096";
```

As you can see, the connection string information is persisted directly in code.

When you have added this object to the project, you will notice that the `sqlConnection1` object appears in the tray area at the bottom of the Visual Studio window:

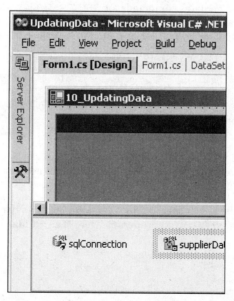

You can alter properties of this object by selecting it and showing the **Properties** dialog (*F4*).

Selecting Data

When you have defined a data connection, you can then select a table (or view) from the available list, and drag that table into an active form from your project:

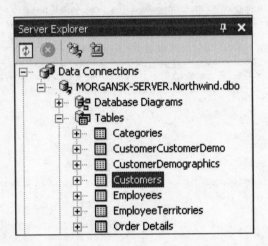

For this example, I have chosen the **Customers** table. When you drag this object into your project (you can drop this on the form or the server controls palette), it will add an object to your form derived from `SqlDataAdapter`, or `OleDbDataAdapter` if you're not using SQL Server.

The data adapter generated contains commands for SELECT, INSERT, UPDATE, and DELETE. Needless to say, these may (and probably should), be tailored to call stored procedures rather than using straight SQL. The wizard-generated code will do for now, however. Visual Studio .NET adds the following code to your `.cs` file:

```
private System.Data.SqlClient.SqlCommand sqlSelectCommand1;
private System.Data.SqlClient.SqlCommand sqlInsertCommand1;
private System.Data.SqlClient.SqlCommand sqlUpdateCommand1;
private System.Data.SqlClient.SqlCommand sqlDeleteCommand1;
private System.Data.SqlClient.SqlDataAdapter sqlDataAdapter1;
```

There is an object defined for each of the SQL commands, and a `SqlDataAdapter`. Further down the file, in the `InitializeComponent()` method, the wizard has generated code to create each one of these commands and the data adapter too. The code is fairly verbose, so I have only included excerpts here.

There are two aspects of the code generated by Visual Studio .NET that are worth looking at – the `UpdateCommand` and `InsertCommand` properties. Here is an abridged version showing the pertinent information:

```
//
// sqlInsertCommand1
//
```

```
    this.sqlInsertCommand1.CommandText = @"INSERT INTO dbo.Customers
                              (CustomerID, CompanyName, ContactName,
                              ContactTitle, Address, City, Region,
                              PostalCode, Country, Phone, Fax)
        VALUES(@CustomerID, @CompanyName, @ContactName, @ContactTitle,
               @Address, @City, @Region, @PostalCode, @Country, @Phone, @Fax);
        SELECT CustomerID, CompanyName, ContactName, ContactTitle, Address,
               City, Region, PostalCode, Country, Phone, Fax
        FROM dbo.Customers WHERE (CustomerID = @Select2_CustomerID)";
    this.sqlInsertCommand1.Connection = this.sqlConnection1;

    //
    // sqlUpdateCommand1
    //

    this.sqlUpdateCommand1.CommandText = @"UPDATE dbo.Customers
            SET CustomerID = @CustomerID, CompanyName = @CompanyName,
                ContactName = @ContactName, ContactTitle = @ContactTitle,
                Address = @Address, City = @City, Region = @Region,
                PostalCode = @PostalCode, Country = @Country,
                Phone = @Phone, Fax = @Fax
            WHERE (CustomerID = @Original_CustomerID)
            AND (Address = @Original_Address) AND (City = @Original_City)
            AND (CompanyName = @Original_CompanyName)
            AND (ContactName = @Original_ContactName)
            AND (ContactTitle = @Original_ContactTitle)
            AND (Country = @Original_Country)
            AND (Fax = @Original_Fax)
            AND (Phone = @Original_Phone)
            AND (PostalCode = @Original_PostalCode)
            AND (Region = @Original_Region);
            SELECT CustomerID, CompanyName, ContactName, ContactTitle,
                   Address, City, Region, PostalCode, Country, Phone, Fax
            FROM dbo.Customers
            WHERE (CustomerID = @Select2_CustomerID)";
    this.sqlUpdateCommand1.Connection = this.sqlConnection1;
```

The main area of interest in these commands is the SQL that has been generated. For both the INSERT and UPDATE commands there are actually two SQL statements: one to do the INSERT or UPDATE, and the other to reselect the row from the database.

These seemingly redundant clauses are used as a way to re-synchronize the data on the client machine with that on the server. There may be defaults applied to columns when inserted, or database triggers that fire to update some of the columns in the inserted/updated record, so re-syncing the data has some benefit. The @Select2_CustomerID parameter used to reselect the data is the same value passed into the INSERT/UPDATE statement for the primary key; the name is just something auto-generated by the wizard.

For tables that include an IDENTITY column, the SQL generated utilizes the @@IDENTITY value after the INSERT statement. As described in the previous chapter, relying on @@IDENTITY to produce primary keys can lead to some interesting bugs, so that's one area of the SQL you may want to change. Similarly, if you have no calculated columns it seems a little wasteful to re-select all columns from the original table just in case something has been updated.

The wizard-generated code works, but is less than optimal. For a production system, you would probably want to replace some, if not all of these SQL clauses with calls to stored procedures. If your `INSERT` or `UPDATE` clauses didn't need to re-synchronize the data then the removal of the redundant SQL clause could speed up the application a little.

Generating a DataSet

Now you have defined the data adapter, you can use it to create a `DataSet`. To generate the `DataSet`, click on the data adapter and display the properties for the object (*F4*). Towards the bottom of the property sheet you'll notice the following three options:

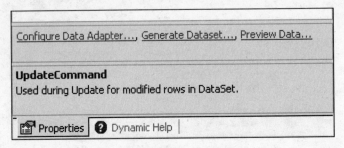

Clicking on **Generate DataSet...** will permit you to choose a name for the new `DataSet` object, and to choose which tables to add into that `DataSet`. If you have dragged several tables from the Server Explorer onto the form, you can link them together from within the dialog box, into a single `DataSet`.

What is actually created is an XSD schema, defining the `DataSet` and each table that you have included within the `DataSet`. This is similar to the hand-crafted example in the previous chapter, but in this instance the XSD file has been created for you:

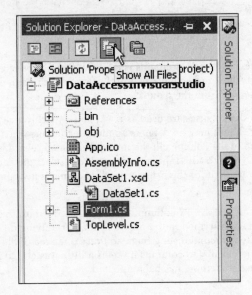

In addition to the XSD file there is a (hidden) `.cs` file that defines a number of type safe classes. To view this generated file, click on the **Show All Files** toolbar button as shown above, and then expand the XSD file. You'll notice a `.cs` file with the same name as the XSD file. The classes defined are as follows:

❑ A class derived from `DataSet`

❑ A class derived from `DataTable` for the data adapter you chose

❑ A class derived from `DataRow`, defining the columns accessible within the `DataTable`

❑ A class derived from `EventArgs`, used when a row changes

You may have guessed what tool is used to generate this file and these classes – it's `XSD.EXE`, discussed in the last chapter.

You can naturally choose to update the XSD file once the wizards have done their thing, but don't be tempted to edit the `.cs` file to tweak it in some way, as it will be regenerated when you recompile the project, and all those changes will be lost.

Updating the Data Source

Now that we have created an application that can select data from the database, I'll show you how trivial it is to persist the changes back to the database. If you have followed along with the last few steps, you should have an application that contains connection, data adapter and `DataSet` objects. All that is left to do is hook the `DataSet` up to a `DataGrid`, add on some logic to retrieve data from the database and display it, then simply persist any changes back to the database.

We'll set up a form as shown below, and then I'll go through the code behind the scenes, which is available in the `\10_UpdatingData` subdirectory.

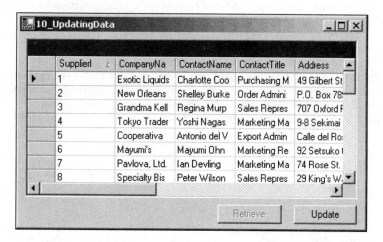

The form consists of a `DataGrid` control and two buttons. When the user clicks the **Retrieve** button, the following code is executed.

```
private void retrieveButton_Click(object sender, System.EventArgs e)
{
    sqlDataAdapter1.Fill (customerDataSet , "Customer") ;
    dataGrid1.SetDataBinding (customerDataSet , "Customer") ;
}
```

This code utilizes the data adapter created earlier (by dragging a database table from the Server Explorer) to fill a `DataSet`. We fill the `Customer` data table with all records from the database. The call to `SetDataBinding()` will then display these records on screen.

After navigating through the data and making some changes, you can then click on the **Update** button. The code behind this is shown next.

```
private void updateButton_Click(object sender, System.EventArgs e)
{
    sqlDataAdapter1.Update(customerDataSet , "Customer" ) ;
}
```

Again this code is trivially simple, as the data adapter is doing most of the work. The `Update()` method loops through the data in the selected table of the `DataSet`, and for each change made will execute the appropriate SQL statement against the database. Note that this method returns an `int`, which is the number of rows modified by the update.

The use of the data adapter was discussed in detail in the previous chapter, but to recap, it represents SQL statements for `SELECT`, `INSERT`, `UPDATE`, and `DELETE` operations. When the `Update()` method is called, this executes the appropriate statement for each modified row. This will cause all modified rows to execute an `UPDATE` statement, all deleted rows to issue a `DELETE` statement, and so on. If you have hand crafted a set of SQL commands, you have the option of defining calls to stored procedures instead of simply issuing many different SQL statements, as in general, the use of stored procedures produces much better performing code.

If you want all the benefits of using stored procedures, but don't have the time or knowledge to write your own, there's an easy way to do it in Visual Studio .NET. Display the context menu for the data adapter and choose the **Configure Data Adapter** menu option. This will display a wizard where it is possible to choose the source of data for the adapter:

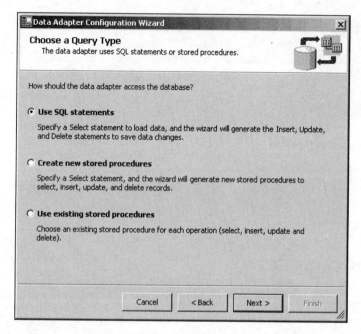

After selecting **Create new stored procedures,** clicking **Next** will walk through the process of automatically generating new stored procedures for SELECT, INSERT, UPDATE, and DELETE statements, and ultimately modifies the code generated within the project to add calls to these stored procedures instead of the calls to straight SQL statements.

In addition to generating new stored procedures, you can also select existing stored procedures to populate the four SQL commands on the adapter. This would be useful when hand-crafted stored procedures are already available, or when some other function is performed by a procedure such as auditing changes or updating linked records.

Building a Schema

I spent a few pages in the previous chapter defining an XSD schema by hand, which isn't the only way to do it. Visual Studio includes an editor for creating XSD schemas – from the **Project** menu, choose **Add New Item,** then select the **XML Schema** item from the **Data** category, and call it TestSchema.xsd:

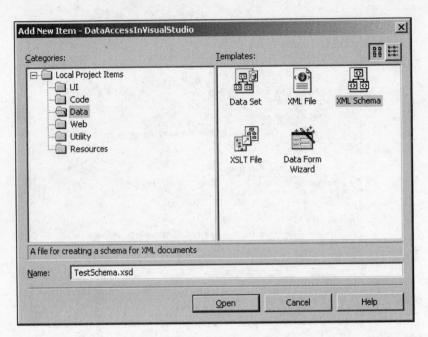

This will add two new files to your project – the .xsd file and a corresponding .xsx file (which is just used by the designer to store layout information for the schema elements that are designed). To create a corresponding set of code for the schema, choose the **Generate Dataset** option from the **Schema** menu as shown below.

Choosing this option will add an extra C# file to the project, which again will show up beneath the XSD file in the Solution Explorer. This file is automatically generated whenever changes are made to the XSD Schema, and so should not be edited manually; it is generated, as in the last chapter, with the XSD.EXE tool.

If you click from **Schema** view to **XML** view, you will see the raw schema template:

```
<?xml version="1.0" encoding="utf-8" ?>
<xs:schema id="TestSchema"
        targetNamespace="http://tempuri.org/TestSchema.xsd"
        elementFormDefault="qualified"
        xmlns="http://tempuri.org/TestSchema.xsd"
        xmlns:mstns="http://tempuri.org/TestSchema.xsd"
        xmlns:xs="http://www.w3.org/2001/XMLSchema">
</xs:schema>
```

This XSD script generates the following C# in the file `TestSchema.cs`. In the following code I have omitted the bodies of the methods and formatted for easier reading – you can inspect the code generated when you work through the example yourself:

```
using System;
using System.Data;
using System.Xml;
using System.Runtime.Serialization;

[Serializable()]
[System.ComponentModel.DesignerCategoryAttribute("code")]
[System.Diagnostics.DebuggerStepThrough()]
[System.ComponentModel.ToolboxItem(true)]
public class TestSchema : DataSet
{
    public TestSchema() { ... }

    protected TestSchema(SerializationInfo info, StreamingContext context)
    { ... }
    public override DataSet Clone() { ... }
    protected override bool ShouldSerializeTables() { ... }
    protected override bool ShouldSerializeRelations() { ... }
    protected override void ReadXmlSerializable(XmlReader reader) { ... }
    protected override System.Xml.Schema.XmlSchema GetSchemaSerializable()
    { ... }
    internal void InitVars() { ... }
    private void InitClass() { ... }
    private void SchemaChanged(object sender,
                System.ComponentModel.CollectionChangeEventArgs e)
    { ... }
}
```

I'll use this as the starting point for this section, so that you can see what code changes are made as items are added into the XSD schema. The two main things to note are that an XSD schema is mapped to a `DataSet`, and that this `DataSet` is serializable – note the protected constructor that can be used by an `ISerializable` implementation. We'll see more about serialization in Chapter 11.

Adding an Element

The first thing to do is add a new top-level element. Right-click on the workspace and choose **Add | New Element**:

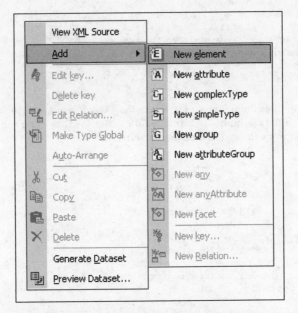

This will create a new, unnamed element on screen. You should type in a name for the element; in this example we'll use **Product**. I've also added some attributes to the element:

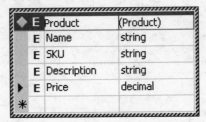

When you save the XSD file, the C# file will be modified and a number of new classes generated. We'll discuss the most pertinent aspects of the code generated in this file, `TestSchema.cs`:

```
public class TestSchema : DataSet
{
    private ProductDataTable tableProduct;
    [System.ComponentModel.DesignerSerializationVisibilityAttribute
            (System.ComponentModel.DesignerSerializationVisibility.Content)]
    public ProductDataTable Product
    {
        get
        {
            return this.tableProduct;
        }
    }
}
```

A new member variable of the class `ProductDataTable` (described in a moment) is created. This object is returned by the `Product` property, and is constructed within the updated `InitClass()` method. From this small section of code, it's evident that the user of these classes can now construct a `DataSet` from the class in this file, and use `DataSet.Products` to return the products `DataTable`.

Generated DataTable

The code below is generated for the `DataTable` (Product) that was added to the schema template:

```
public delegate void ProductRowChangeEventHandler
                    (object sender, ProductRowChangeEvent e);
public class ProductDataTable : DataTable, System.Collections.IEnumerable
{
    internal ProductDataTable() : base("Product")
    {
        this.InitClass();
    }
    [System.ComponentModel.Browsable(false)]
    public int Count
    {
        get { return this.Rows.Count;}
    }
    public ProductRow this[int index]
    {
        get { return ((ProductRow)(this.Rows[index]));}
    }
    public event ProductRowChangeEventHandler ProductRowChanged;
    public event ProductRowChangeEventHandler ProductRowChanging;
    public event ProductRowChangeEventHandler ProductRowDeleted;
    public event ProductRowChangeEventHandler ProductRowDeleting;
```

The generated `ProductDataTable` class is derived from `DataTable`, and includes an implementation of the `IEnumerable` interface. Four events are defined that use the delegate defined above the class when raised. This delegate is passed an instance of the `ProductRowChangeEvent` class, again defined by Visual Studio .NET.

The generated code includes a class derived from `DataRow`, which permits type-safe access to columns within the table. You can create a new row in one of two ways:

- ❑ Call the `NewRow()` (or generated `NewProductRow()`) method to return a new instance of the row class. Pass this new row to the `Rows.Add ()` method (or the type-safe `AddProductRow()`).

- ❑ Call the `Rows.Add()` (or generated `AddProductRow()`) method, and pass an array of objects, one for each column in the table.

The `AddProductRow()` methods are shown below:

```
public void AddProductRow(ProductRow row)
{
    this.Rows.Add(row);
}
public ProductRow AddProductRow ( ... )
```

```
{
    ProductRow rowProductRow = ((ProductRow)(this.NewRow()));
    rowProductRow.ItemArray = new Object[0];
    this.Rows.Add(rowProductRow);
    return rowProductRow;
}
```

As can be seen from the code, the second method not only creates a new row, it then inserts that row into the Rows collection of the DataTable, and then returns this object to the caller. The bulk of the other methods on the DataTable are for raising events, which I won't discuss here.

Generated DataRow

The ProductRow class generated is shown below:

```
public class ProductRow : DataRow
{
    private ProductDataTable tableProduct;
    internal ProductRow(DataRowBuilder rb) : base(rb)
    {
        this.tableProduct = ((ProductDataTable)(this.Table));
    }
    public string Name { ... }
    public bool IsNameNull { ... }
    public void SetNameNull { ... }
    // Other accessors/mutators omitted for clarity
}
```

When attributes are added to an element, a property is added to the generated DataRow class as shown above. The property has the same name as the attribute, so in the example above for the Product row, there would be properties for Name, SKU, Description, and Price.

For each attribute added, several changes are made to the .cs file. In the following example, suppose we have added an attribute called ProductId, of type int.

At first the ProductDataTable class (derived from DataTable) has a private member added, which is the new DataColumn:

```
private DataColumn columnProductId;
```

This is joined by a property named ProductIDColumn as shown below. This property is defined as internal:

```
internal DataColumn ProductIdColumn
{
    get { return this.columnProductId; }
}
```

The `AddProductRow()` method shown above is also modified; it now takes an integer `ProductID`, and stores the value entered in the newly created column:

```
public ProductRow AddProductRow ( ... , int ProductId)
{
    ProductRow rowProductRow = ((ProductRow)(this.NewRow()));
    rowProductRow.ItemArray = new Object[] { ... , ProductId};
    this.Rows.Add(rowProductRow);
    return rowProductRow;
}
```

Finally, in the `ProductDataTable`, there is a modification to the `InitClass()` method:

```
private void InitClass()
{
    ...
    this.columnProductID = new DataColumn("ProductID", typeof(int), null,
                                System.Data.MappingType.Attribute);
    this.Columns.Add(this.columnProductID);
    this.columnProductID.Namespace = "";
}
```

This creates the new `DataColumn` and adds it to the `Columns` collection of the `DataTable`. The final parameter to the `DataColumn` constructor defines how this column is mapped back into XML; this is of use when the `DataSet` is saved to an XML file, for example.

The `ProductRow` class is updated to add an accessor for this column:

```
public int ProductId
{
    get { return ((int)(this[this.tableProduct.ProductIdColumn])); }
    set { this[this.tableProduct.ProductIdColumn] = value; }
}
```

Generated EventArgs

The final class added into the sourcecode is a derivation of `EventArgs`, which provides methods for directly accessing the row that has changed (or is changing), and the action being applied to that row. This code has been omitted for brevity.

Other Common Requirements

A common requirement when displaying data is to provide a pop-up menu for a given row. There are numerous ways of doing this, but I'll concentrate on one that can simplify the code required, especially if the display context is a `DataGrid`, where a `DataSet` with some relations is displayed. The problem here is that the context menu depends on the row being selected, and that row could come from any source `DataTable` within the `DataSet`.

As the context menu functionality is likely to be fairly general purpose, the implementation here utilizes a base class (`ContextDataRow`) which supports the menu building code, and each data row class wishing to support a pop-up menu derives from this base class.

When the user right-clicks on any part of a row in the `DataGrid`, we'll look up the row and check if it derives from `ContextDataRow`, and if so, `PopupMenu()` can be called. You could implement this by using an interface; however, in this instance a base class is probably simpler.

This example will show how to generate `DataRow` and `DataTable` classes, which can be used to provide type-safe access to data, in much the same way as the previous XSD sample. However, this time the code will be hand crafted, and it also shows one use for custom attributes and reflection.

The following illustration shows the class hierarchy for this example:

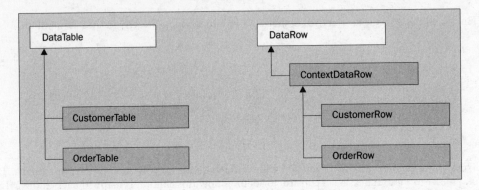

The full code for this example is available in the `\11_Miscellaneous` directory:

```
using System;
using System.Windows.Forms;
using System.Data;
using System.Data.SqlClient;
using System.Reflection;

public class ContextDataRow : DataRow
{
    public ContextDataRow(DataRowBuilder builder) : base(builder)
    {
    }
    public void PopupMenu(System.Windows.Forms.Control parent, int x, int y)
    {

        // Use reflection to get the list of popup menu commands
        MemberInfo[] members = this.GetType().FindMembers (MemberTypes.Method,
                        BindingFlags.Public | BindingFlags.Instance ,
                        new System.Reflection.MemberFilter(Filter),
                        null);
        if (members.Length > 0)
        {

        // Create a context menu

        ContextMenu menu = new ContextMenu();

        // Now loop through those members and generate the popup menu
        // Note the cast to MethodInfo in the foreach
```

```
        foreach (MethodInfo meth in members)
        {

            // Get the caption for the operation from the
            // ContextMenuAttribute

            ContextMenuAttribute[] ctx = (ContextMenuAttribute[])
                meth.GetCustomAttributes(typeof(ContextMenuAttribute), true);
            MenuCommand callback = new MenuCommand(this, meth);
            MenuItem item = new MenuItem(ctx[0].Caption, new
                             EventHandler(callback.Execute));
            item.DefaultItem = ctx[0].Default;
            menu.MenuItems.Add(item);
        }
        System.Drawing.Point pt = new System.Drawing.Point(x,y);
        menu.Show(parent, pt);
    }
}

private bool Filter(MemberInfo member, object criteria)
{
    bool bInclude = false;

    // Cast MemberInfo to MethodInfo

    MethodInfo meth = member as MethodInfo;
    if (meth != null)
        if (meth.ReturnType == typeof(void))
        {
            ParameterInfo[] parms = meth.GetParameters();
            if (parms.Length == 0)
            {

                // Lastly check if there is a ContextMenuAttribute on the
                // method...

                object[] atts = meth.GetCustomAttributes
                        (typeof(ContextMenuAttribute), true);
                bInclude = (atts.Length == 1);
            }
        }
    return bInclude;
}
}
```

The context data row class is derived from `DataRow`, and contains just two member functions. The first, `PopupMenu`, uses reflection to look for methods that correspond to a particular signature, and it displays a pop-up menu of these options to the user. `Filter()` is used as a delegate by `PopupMenu` when enumerating methods. It simply returns `true` if the member function does correspond to the appropriate calling convention:

```
MemberInfo[] members = this.GetType().FindMembers(MemberTypes.Method,
            BindingFlags.Public | BindingFlags.Instance,
            new System.Reflection.MemberFilter(Filter),
            null);
```

This single statement is used to filter all methods on the current object, and return only those that match the following criteria:

- ❑ The member must be a method
- ❑ The member must be a public instance method
- ❑ The member must return `void`
- ❑ The member must accept zero parameters
- ❑ The member must include the `ContextMenuAttribute`

The last of these is a custom attribute, written specifically for this example. I'll discuss this after completing the dissection of the `PopupMenu` method:

```
ContextMenu menu = new ContextMenu();
foreach (MethodInfo meth in members)
{
    // ... Add the menu item
}
System.Drawing.Point pt = new System.Drawing.Point(x,y);
menu.Show(parent, pt);
```

A context menu instance is created, and we loop through each method that matches the above criteria, and add the item to the menu. The menu is subsequently displayed as shown in the following screenshot:

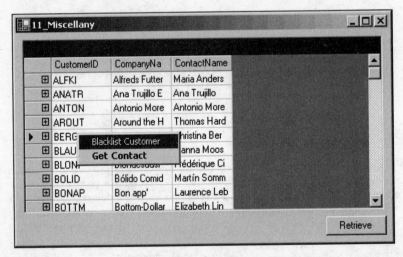

The main area of difficulty within this example is the following section of code, repeated once for each member function that is to be displayed on the pop-up menu:

```
System.Type ctxtype = typeof(ContextMenuAttribute);
ContextMenuAttribute[] ctx = (ContextMenuAttribute[])
                        meth.GetCustomAttributes(ctxtype);
MenuCommand callback = new MenuCommand(this, meth);
```

```
MenuItem item = new MenuItem(ctx[0].Caption,
                new EventHandler(callback.Execute));
item.DefaultItem = ctx[0].Default;
menu.MenuItems.Add(item);
```

Each method that should show up on the context menu is attributed with the `ContextMenuAttribute`. This defines a user-friendly name for the menu option, as a C# method name cannot include spaces, and it's wise to use real English on pop-up menus rather than some internal code. The attribute is retrieved from the method, and a new menu item created and added to the menu items collection of the pop-up menu.

This example code also shows the use of a simplified Command class (a common design pattern). The `MenuCommand` class used in this instance is triggered from the user choosing an item on the context menu, and it forwards the call to the receiver of the method – in this case the object and method that was attributed. This also helps keep the code in the receiver object more isolated from the user interface code. This code is explained in the following sections.

Manufactured Tables and Rows

The XSD example earlier in the chapter showed the code produced when the Visual Studio editor was used to generate a set of data access classes, and you may be wondering what the minimal set of code for these classes looks like. The following class shows the required methods for a `DataTable`, which are fairly minimal:

```
public class CustomerTable : DataTable
{
    public CustomerTable() : base("Customers")
    {
        this.Columns.Add("CustomerID", typeof(string));
        this.Columns.Add("CompanyName", typeof(string));
        this.Columns.Add("ContactName", typeof(string));
    }
    protected override System.Type GetRowType()
    {
        return typeof(CustomerRow);
    }
    protected override DataRow NewRowFromBuilder(DataRowBuilder builder)
    {
        return(DataRow) new CustomerRow(builder);
    }
}
```

The first prerequisite of a `DataTable` is that you override the `GetRowType()` method. This is used by the .NET internals when generating new rows for the table. You should return the type of the class used to represent each row.

The next prerequisite is that you implement `NewRowFromBuilder()`, again called by the runtime when creating new rows for the table. That's enough for a minimal implementation. Our implementation includes adding columns to the `DataTable`. Since we know beforehand what the columns are in this example, we can add them accordingly. The corresponding `CustomerRow` class is fairly simple. It implements properties for each of the columns within the row, and then implements the methods that ultimately are displayed on the context menu:

```
public class CustomerRow : ContextDataRow
{
    public CustomerRow(DataRowBuilder builder) : base(builder)
    {
    }
    public string CustomerID
    {
        get { return (string)this["CustomerID"];}
        set { this["CustomerID"] = value;}
    }

    // Other properties omitted for clarity

    [ContextMenu("Blacklist Customer")]
    public void Blacklist()
    {
        // Do something
    }
    [ContextMenu("Get Contact",Default=true)]
    public void GetContact()
    {
        // Do something else
    }
}
```

The class simply derives from `ContextDataRow`, including the appropriate getter/setter methods on properties named the same as each field, and then a set of methods may be added that are used when reflecting on the class:

```
[ContextMenu("Blacklist Customer")]
public void Blacklist()
{

    // Do something
}
```

Each method that you wish to have displayed on the context menu has the same signature, and includes the custom `ContextMenu` attribute.

Using an Attribute

The idea behind writing the `ContextMenu` attribute was to be able to supply a free text name for a given menu option. I have also implemented a `Default` flag, which is used to indicate the default menu choice. The entire attribute class is presented here:

```
[AttributeUsage(AttributeTargets.Method,AllowMultiple=false,Inherited=true)]
public class ContextMenuAttribute : System.Attribute
{
    public ContextMenuAttribute(string caption)
    {
        Caption = caption;
        Default = false;
```

```
  }
  public readonly string Caption;
  public bool Default;
}
```

Here, the `AttributeUsage` attribute on the class marks the `ContextMenuAttribute` as only being usable on a method, and it also defines that there may be only one instance of this object on any given method. The `Inherited=true` clause defines whether the attribute can be placed on a superclass method, and still reflected upon by a subclass.

You can probably think of a number of other members to add to this attribute. Some examples are:

- ❑ A hotkey for the menu option
- ❑ An image to be displayed
- ❑ Some text to be displayed in the toolbar as the mouse pointer rolls over the menu option
- ❑ A help context ID

Dispatching Methods

When a menu is displayed within .NET, each menu option is linked to the processing code for that option by means of a delegate. In implementing the mechanism for hooking menu choices to code, you basically have two choices:

- ❑ Implement a method with the same signature as the `System.EventHandler`. This is defined as shown below:

```
public delegate void EventHandler(object sender, EventArgs e);
```

- ❑ Define a proxy class, which implements the above delegate, and forwards calls to the received class. This is known as the Command pattern, and is what I have chosen for this example.

The Command pattern separates the sender and the receiver of the call by means of a simple intermediate class. You may think this is overkill for such an example, but it makes the methods on each `DataRow` simpler (as they don't need the parameters passed to the delegate), and it is more extensible:

```
public class MenuCommand
{
  public MenuCommand(object receiver, MethodInfo method)
  {
    Receiver = receiver;
    Method = method;
  }
  public void Execute(object sender, EventArgs e)
  {
    Method.Invoke(Receiver, new object[] {} );
  }
  public readonly object Receiver;
  public readonly MethodInfo Method;
}
```

The class simply provides an `EventHandler` delegate (the `Execute` method), which invokes the desired method on the receiver object. Our example handles two different types of row: rows from the `Customers` table, and rows from the `Orders` table. Naturally, the processing options for each of these types of data are likely to differ. The previous image showed the operations available for a `Customer` row. The image below shows the options for an `Order` row:

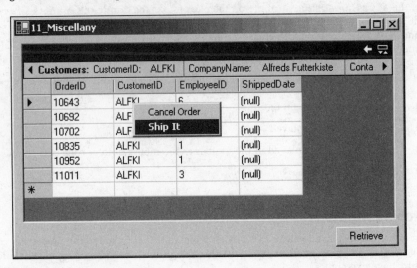

Getting the Selected Row

The last piece of the puzzle for this example is how to work out which row within the `DataSet` the user has clicked upon. Your first thought might be "it must be a property on the `DataGrid`", but try as you like you won't find it there. You might look at the hit test information that you can obtain from within the `MouseUp()` event handler, but that only helps if you are displaying data from a single `DataTable`.

Going back to how the grid is filled for a moment, the line of code is:

```
dataGrid.SetDataBinding(ds,"Customers");
```

Remember the section on `DataBinding`? This method adds a new `CurrencyManager` into the `BindingContext`, which represents the current `DataTable` and the `DataSet`. Now, the `DataGrid` has two properties, `DataSource` and `DataMember`, which are set when you call `SetDataBinding()`. `DataSource` in this instance will be a `DataSet`, and `DataMember` will be `Customers`.

We have a data source, a data member, and know that this information is stored within the `BindingContext` of the form. All we need to do is look up the information:

```
protected void dataGrid_MouseUp(object sender, MouseEventArgs e)
{
    // Perform a hit test
    if(e.Button == MouseButtons.Right)
    {
        // Find which row the user clicked on, if any
        DataGrid.HitTestInfo hti = dataGrid.HitTest(e.X, e.Y);

        // Check if the user hit a cell
```

```
if(hti.Type == DataGrid.HitTestType.Cell)
{
    // Find the DataRow that corresponds to the cell
    //the user has clicked upon
```

After calling `dataGrid.HitTest()` to calculate where the user has clicked the mouse, we then retrieve the `BindingManagerBase` instance for the data grid:

```
BindingManagerBase bmb = this.BindingContext[ dataGrid.DataSource,
                                              dataGrid.DataMember];
```

This uses the `DataGrid`'s `DataSource` and `DataMember` to name the object we want to be returned. All we want to do now is find the row the user clicked on, and display the context menu. With a right mouse click on a row, the current row indicator doesn't normally move, but that's not good enough for us. We want to move the row indicator and then pop up the menu. From the `HitTestInfo` object we have the row number, so all I need to do is move the `BindingManagerBase` object's current position:

```
bmb.Position = hti.Row;
```

This changes the cell indicator, and at the same time means that when I call into the class to get the Row, I end up with the current row and not the last one selected:

```
DataRowView drv = bmb.Current as DataRowView;
if(drv != null)
{
    ContextDataRow ctx = drv.Row as ContextDataRow;
    if(ctx != null) ctx.PopupMenu(dataGrid,e.X,e.Y);
}
        }
    }
}
```

As the `DataGrid` is displaying items from a `DataSet`, the `Current` object within the `BindingManagerBase` collection is a `DataRowView`, which is tested by an explicit cast in the code above. If this succeeds, I can then retrieve the actual row that the `DataRowView` wraps by performing another cast to check if it is indeed a `ContextDataRow`, and finally pop up a menu.

In the example, you'll notice that I have created two data tables, `Customers` and `Orders`, and defined a relationship between these tables, so that when you click on `CustomerOrders` you see a filtered list of orders. When you do this, the `DataGrid` changes the `DataMember` from `Customers` to `Customers.CustomerOrders`, which just so happens to be the correct thing that the `BindingContext` indexer uses to retrieve the data being shown.

Summary

This chapter has introduced some of the methods of displaying data under .NET. There are a large number of classes to be explored in `System.Windows.Forms`, and we've shown how to use the `DataGrid` to display data from many different data sources, such as an `Array`, `DataTable`, or `DataSet`.

The DataGrid control has many innovative capabilities – not least the ability to navigate parent-child relationships defined within a DataSet. This, together with the ability to use other customization capabilities of the control, makes it well worth using when displaying data. We also took a quick look at how easy it is to actually update the original data source with any new data.

Displaying data in a grid is not always appropriate, so we've discussed simple data binding in the chapter also, whereby a column of data is linked to a single control in the user interface. The binding capabilities of .NET make this type of user interface very easy to support, as it's generally just a case of binding a control to a column and letting .NET get on with the rest.

We explored the integration of Visual Studio .NET and XML schemas, with a section on XSD and automatic code generation, and a hand-crafted example to show a minimal implementation. Using an XSD schema to generate DataSet code can save a great deal of typing, as the tool takes care of all of the underlying code.

Hopefully, these last two chapters have given you an appetite for the other XML facilities of .NET, which are tackled further in the next chapter.

11

Manipulating XML

XML plays a significant role in the .NET Framework. Not only does the Framework allow you to make use of XML in your application; the Framework itself uses XML for configuration files and sourcecode documentation, as well as SOAP, Web Services, and ADO.NET just to name a few.

To accommodate this extensive use of XML, the .NET Framework includes the `System.Xml` namespace. This namespace is loaded with classes that we can use for the processing of XML, and we will be discussing many of these classes in this chapter.

We will look at how to use the `XmlDocument` class, which is the implementation of the DOM, as well as what .NET offers as a replacement for SAX (the `XmlReader` and `XmlWriter` classes). We will also discuss the class implementations of XPath and XSLT. We'll see how XML and ADO.NET work together and how easy it is to transform one to the other. We will also discuss how you can serialize your objects to XML and create an object from (deserialize) an XML document using classes in the `System.Xml.Serialization` namespace. More to the point, we will look at how you can incorporate XML into your C# applications.

You should note that the XML namespace allows you to get similiar results in a number of different ways. It is not possible to include all the variations in one chapter, so we will examine one possible way of doing something, and we will try and mention the other ways that the same task could be accomplished.

Since we don't have the space to teach you XML from scratch, we are assuming that you are already somewhat familiar with XML technology for this chapter. Therefore, you should know what elements, attributes, and nodes are, and you should also know what is meant by a well-formed document. You should also be familiar with SAX and DOM. If you to find out more about XML, Wrox's *Beginning XML* (ISBN 1-861003-41-2), and *Professional XML* (ISBN 1-861003-11-0) are great places to head for information.

Let's begin this chapter by taking a look at the current status of XML standards.

XML Standards Support in .NET

The World Wide Web Consortium (W3C) has developed a set of standards that give XML its power and potential. Without these standards, XML would not have the impact on the development world that it does. The W3C website (http://www.w3.org/) is a valuable source of all things XML.

As of February 2002, the .NET Framework supports the following W3C standards:

❑ XML 1.0 (http://www.w3.org/TR/1998/REC-xml-19980210), including DTD support

❑ XML Namespaces (http://www.w3.org/TR/REC-xml-names), both stream-level and DOM

❑ XML Schemas (http://www.w3.org/2001/XMLSchema)

❑ XPath expressions (http://www.w3.org/TR/xpath)

❑ XSLT transformations (http://www.w3.org/TR/xslt)

❑ DOM Level 1 Core (http://www.w3.org/TR/REC-DOM-Level-1/)

❑ DOM Level 2 Core (http://www.w3.org/TR/DOM-Level-2-Core/)

❑ SOAP 1.1 (http://www.w3.org/TR/SOAP)

The level of standards support will be changing both as the Framework matures, and as the W3C updates the recommended standards. Because of this, you will always need to make sure you stay up-to-date with the standards and the level of support provided by Microsoft.

Introducing the System.Xml Namespace

Support for processing XML is provided by the classes in the System.Xml namespace in .NET. Let's take a look (in no particular order) at some of the more important classes that the System.Xml namespace has for us to use. Here are the main XML reader and writer classes that we will be discussing:

Class Name	Description
XmlReader	An abstract reader class that provides fast, non-cached XML data. XmlReader is forward only, like the SAX parser.
XmlWriter	An abstract writer class that provides fast, non-cached XML data in stream or file format.

Class Name	Description
XmlTextReader	Extends XmlReader. Provides fast forward-only stream access to XML data.
XmlTextWriter	Extends XmlWriter. Fast forward-only generation of XML streams.

Some other useful classes for handling XML include the following:

Class Name	Description
XmlNode	An abstract class that represents a single node in an XML document. Base class for several classes in the XML namespace.
XmlDocument	Extends XmlNode. This is the W3C Document Object Model (DOM) implementation. It provides a tree representation in memory of an XML document, enabling navigation and editing.
XmlDataDocument	Extends XmlDocument. This is a document that can be loaded from XML data or from relational data in an ADO.NET DataSet. Allows the mixing of XML and relational data in the same view.
XmlResolver	An abstract class that resolves external XML-based resources such as DTD and schema references. Also used to process <xsl:include> and <xsl:import> elements.
XmlUrlResolver	Extends XmlResolver. Resolves external resources named by a URI (Uniform Resource Identifier).

Many of the classes in the System.Xml namespace provide a means to manage XML documents and streams, while others (for example the XmlDataDocument class) provide a bridge between XML data stores and the relational data stored in DataSets.

> It is worth noting that the XML namespace is available to any language that is part of the .NET family. This means that all of the examples in this chapter could also be written in VB.NET, Managed C++, and so on.

Using MSXML in .NET

What if you have a ton of code developed using Microsoft's latest parser (currently MSXML 4.0)? Do you have to toss it away and start over if you want to use it with .NET? On the other hand, what if you are comfortable using the MSXML 4.0 DOM? Do you have to switch to .NET right away?

The answer is "no". XML 4.0, 3.0 or 2.0 can be used directly in your applications. Once you add a reference to the MSXML4 DLL to your solution, you can start writing some code.

The next few examples will use books.xml as the source of data. This file can be downloaded from the Wrox web site (http://www.wrox.com/), but it is also included in several examples in the .NET SDK. The books.xml file is a book catalog for an imaginary bookstore. It includes book information such as genre, author name, price, and ISBN number. All of the code examples in this chapter are also available on the Wrox web site. In order to run the examples, the XML data files will need to be in a path structure that looks something like this:

```
/XMLChapter/Sample1
/XMLChapter/Sample2
/XMLChapter/Sample3
...
```

Actually, you can call the directories anything you wish, but the relative position is important. You can also modify the examples to point to anywhere you wish. The example code will be commented to show which line(s) to change if you wish to do this.

This is what the books.xml file looks like:

```xml
<?xml version='1.0'?>
<!-- This file represents a fragment of a book store inventory database -->
<bookstore>
    <book genre="autobiography" publicationdate="1981" ISBN="1-861003-11-0">
        <title>The Autobiography of Benjamin Franklin</title>
        <author>
            <first-name>Benjamin</first-name>
            <last-name>Franklin</last-name>
        </author>
        <price>8.99</price>
    </book>
    <book genre="novel" publicationdate="1967" ISBN="0-201-63361-2">
        <title>The Confidence Man</title>
        <author>
            <first-name>Herman</first-name>
            <last-name>Melville</last-name>
        </author>
        <price>11.99</price>
    </book>
    <book genre="philosophy" publicationdate="1991" ISBN="1-861001-57-6">
        <title>The Gorgias</title>
        <author>
            <name>Plato</name>
        </author>
        <price>9.99</price>
    </book>
</bookstore>
```

Let's look at some code that uses MSXML 4.0 to load a listbox with the ISBNs from books.xml. You'll find the full code in the MSXML_Sample folder of the download. You can copy this into the Visual Studio IDE or create a new Windows Form from scratch. This form contains a listbox and a button, as you can see opposite. Both use the default names of listBox1 and button1, with the Text property of button1 set to Load XML.

One thing that should be pointed out is that since MSXML 4 is a COM-based component, we will need to create the interop assembly. The easiest way is to select **Add Reference** from the **Project** menu in the Visual Studio IDE. Go to the **COM** tab and select **Microsoft XML, v4.0** (or **v3.0, v2.6**). You will see **MSXML2** as the added namespace **Solution Explorer**. Why is it **MSXML2**? When you import a COM component the namespace is given to the new assembly is the typelib name for the COM component. In this case it is **MSXML2**. If you use `TLBIMP` you can change the namespace to something else if you wish to.

Let's now have a look at the most important lines from the `MSXML_sample` example code.

Since we now have the reference, we add the line:

```
using MSXML2;
```

We also need a class-level variable.

```
private DOMDocument40 doc;
```

Now we are ready to use MSXML in our application.

We want to take the ISBN from the listbox, and, using a simple XPath search, find the book node that it matches and display the node text (the book title and book price) in a `MessageBox`. XML Path Language (XPath) is an XML notation that can be used for querying and filtering text in an XML document. We will look more closely at how to use XPath in .NET later in the chapter.

Here is the event handler code for selecting an entry in the listbox:

```
protected void listBox1_SelectedIndexChanged (
                        object sender, System.EventArgs e)
{
    string srch=listBox1.SelectedItem.ToString();
    IXMLDOMNode nd=doc.selectSingleNode(
                        "bookstore/book[@ISBN='" + srch + "']");
    MessageBox.Show(nd.text);
}
```

Now we'll look at the event handler for clicking the button. First, we load the `books.xml` file – note that if you're running the executable from somewhere that isn't the `bin/debug` or `bin/release` folder, you'll need to adjust the path appropriately:

```
protected void button1_Click (object sender, System.EventArgs e)
{
    doc=new DOMDocument40 ();
    doc.load("..\\..\\..\\books.xml");
```

The next lines declare that `nodes` is a `NodeList` of book nodes. In this case there are three `book` nodes:

```
IXMLDOMNodeList nodes;
nodes = doc.selectNodes("bookstore/book");
IXMLDOMNode node=nodes.nextNode();
```

Then we loop through the nodes, and add the text value of the `ISBN` attribute to `listBox1`:

```
while(node!=null)
{
    listBox1.Items.Add(node.attributes.getNamedItem("ISBN").text);
        node=nodes.nextNode ();
}
}
```

The left-hand screenshot below shows the sample executing. After clicking the button, the listbox is loaded with the book ISBNs. The output after selecting an ISBN is shown in the right-hand screenshot below.

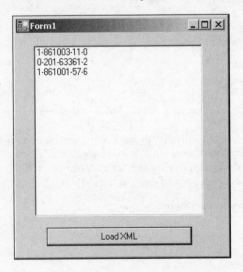
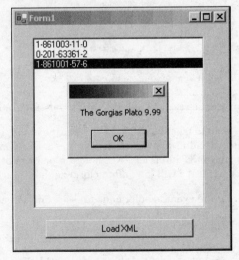

Using System.Xml Classes

If you have done any work with MSXML 3.0 or 4.0, the code above will look pretty familiar. So why would you want to do this if the .NET Framework is supposed to have all of these wonderful XML classes to use?

While the System.Xml namespace is powerful and relatively easy to use, it is different from the MSXML 3.0 model. If you are comfortable using MSXML 3.0, then use it until you become familiar with the System.Xml namespace.

However, System.Xml classes have several advantages over MSXML classes. First, System.Xml is managed code, so by using it you will gain all of the code security and type safety of using managed code. Also, using COM interop incurs some overhead. Most importantly, however, the System.Xml namespace is easy to use and offers a great deal of flexibility. By the end of this chapter this will have become very evident to you.

You should note that we will be using the books.xml file for several examples in the chapter, and the code sample we just looked at will be the basis for many examples too.

Reading and Writing Streamed XML

Now that we have seen how things can be done today, let's take a look at what .NET will allow us to do. We start by looking at how to read and write XML.

The XmlReader and XmlWriter classes will feel familiar to anyone who has ever used SAX. XmlReader-based classes provide a very fast, forward-only, read-only cursor that streams the XML data for processing. Since it is a streaming model, the memory requirements are not very demanding. However, you don't have the navigation flexibility and the read/write capabilities that would be available from a DOM-based model. XmlWriter-based classes will produce an XML document that conforms to the W3C's XML 1.0 Namespace Recommendations.

XmlReader and XmlWriter are both abstract classes. The graphic below shows what classes are derived from XmlReader and XmlWriter:

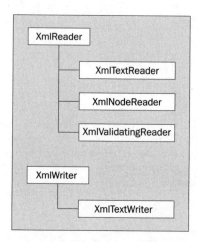

XmlTextReader and XmlTextWriter work with either a stream-based object or TextReader/TextWriter objects from the System.IO namespace. XmlNodeReader uses an XmlNode as its source instead of a stream. The XmlValidatingReader adds DTD and schema validation and therefore offers data validation. We'll look at these in a little more detail later in the chapter.

Using the XmlTextReader Class

Again, XmlTextReader is a lot like SAX. One of the biggest differences, however, is that while SAX is a **push** type of model (that is, it pushes data out to the application, and the developer has to be ready to accept it), the XmlTextReader has a **pull** model, where data is pulled in to the application requesting it. This gives an easier and more intuitive programming model. Another advantage to this is that a pull model can be selective about the data that is sent to the application: if you don't want all of the data, then you don't need to process it. In a push model, all of the XML data has to be processed by the application whether it is needed or not.

Let's take a look at a very simple example of reading XML data, and then we can take a closer look at the XmlTextReader class. You'll find the code in the XmlReaderSample1 folder. Instead of using the namespace MSXML2 as in the previous example, we will now be using the following:

```
using System.Xml;
```

We also remove need to remove the following line from the module level code:

```
private DOMDocument40 doc;
```

This is what our button click event handler looks like now:

```
protected void button1_Click (object sender, System.EventArgs e)
{
    //Modify this path to find books.xml
    string fileName = "..\\..\\..\\books.xml";
    //Create the new TextReader Object
    XmlTextReader tr = new XmlTextReader(fileName);
    //Read in a node at a time
    while(tr.Read())
    {
      if(tr.NodeType == XmlNodeType.Text)
      listBox1.Items.Add(tr.Value);
    }
}
```

This is XmlTextReader at its simplest. First we create a string object with the name of the XML file. We then create a new XmlTextReader passing in the fileName string. XmlTextReader has thirteen different constructor overloads. We can pass in various combinations of strings (filenames and URLs), streams and NameTables (when an element or attribute name occurs several times, it can be stored in a NameTable, which allows for faster comparisons).

Just after an `XmlTextReader` object has been initialized, no node is selected. This is the only time that a node isn't current. When we go into the `tr.Read()` loop, the first `Read()` will move us to the first node in the document. This would typically be the XML declaration node. In this sample, as we move to each node we compare `tr.NodeType` against the `XmlNodeType` enumeration, and when we find a text node, we add the text value to the listbox. Here is a screenshot after the listbox is loaded:

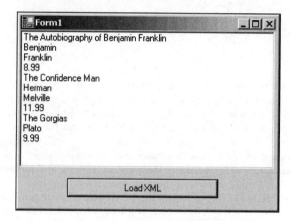

Read Methods

There are several ways to move through the document. As we just saw, `Read()` takes us to the next node. We can then check to see if the node has a value (`HasValue()`) or, as you will see shortly, if the node has any attributes (`HasAttributes()`). We can also use the `ReadStartElement()` method, which will check to see if the current node is the start element, and then position you on to the next node. If you are not on the start element, an `XmlException` is raised. Calling this method is the same as calling the `IsStartElement()` method, followed by a `Read()`.

The `ReadString()` and `ReadChars()` methods both read in the text data from an element. `ReadString()` returns a string object containing the data, while `ReadChars()` reads the data into an array of chars.

`ReadElementString()` is similar to `ReadString()`, except that you can optionally pass in the name of an element. If the next content node is not a start tag, or if the `Name` parameter does not match the current node `Name`, then an exception is raised.

Here is an example of how `ReadElementString()` can be used (you'll find the code in the `XmlReaderSample2` folder). Notice that this example uses `FileStreams`, so you will need to make sure that you include the `System.IO` namespace via a `using` statement.

```
protected void button1_Click (object sender, System.EventArgs e)
{
    //use a filestream to get the data
    FileStream fs = new FileStream("..\\..\\..\\books.xml",FileMode.Open);
    XmlTextReader tr = new XmlTextReader(fs);
    while(!tr.EOF)
    {
        //if we hit an element type, try and load it in the listbox
        if(tr.MoveToContent() == XmlNodeType.Element && tr.Name=="title")
```

```
        {
            listBox1.Items.Add(tr.ReadElementString());
        }
        else
        {
            //otherwise move on
            tr.Read();
        }
    }
}
```

In the `while` loop we use `MoveToContent()` to find each node of type `XmlNodeType.Element` with the name `title`. We use the `EOF` property of the `XmlTextReader` as the loop condition. If the node is not of type `Element` or not named `title`, the `else` clause will issue a `Read()` method to move to the next node. When we find a node that matches the criteria, we add the result of a `ReadElementString()` to the `listbox`. This should leave us with just the book titles in the listbox. Notice that we don't have to issue a `Read()` call after a successful `ReadElementString()`. This is because `ReadElementString()` consumes the entire `Element`, and positions you on the next node.

If you remove `&& tr.Name=="title"` from the `if` clause, you will now have to catch the `XmlException` exception when it is thrown. If you look at the data file, you will see that the first element that `MoveToContent()` will find is the `<bookstore>` element. Since it is an element, it will pass the check in the `if` statement. However, since it does not contain a simple text type, it will cause `ReadElementString()` to raise an `XmlException`. One way to work around this is to put the `ReadElementString()` call in a function of its own. Then, if the call to `ReadElementString()` fails inside this function, we can deal with the error and return back to the calling function.

Let's do this; we'll call this new method `LoadList()`, and pass in the `XmlTextReader` as a parameter. This is what the sample code looks like with these changes (you'll find the code in the `XmlReaderSample3` folder):

```
protected void button1_Click (object sender, System.EventArgs e)
{
    //use a filestream to get the data
    FileStream fs = new FileStream("..\\..\\..\\books.xml",FileMode.Open);
    XmlTextReader tr = new XmlTextReader(fs);
    while(!tr.EOF)
    {
        //if we hit an element type, try and load it in the listbox
        if(tr.MoveToContent() == XmlNodeType.Element)
        {
            LoadList(tr);
        }
        else
        {
            //otherwise move on
            tr.Read();
        }
    }
}
private void LoadList(XmlReader reader)
```

```
{
    try
    {
        listBox1.Items.Add(reader.ReadElementString());
    }
    // if an XmlException is raised, ignore it.
    catch(XmlException er){}
}
```

This is what you should see when you run this code:

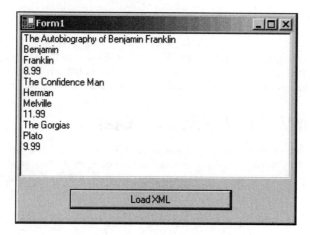

Looks familiar? It's the same result that we had before. What we are seeing is that there is more then one way to accomplish the same goal. This is where the flexibility of the classes in the `System.Xml` namespace starts to become apparent.

Retrieving Attribute Data

As you play with the sample code, you may notice that when the nodes are read in, you don't see any attributes. This is because attributes are not considered part of a document's structure. When you are on an element node, you can check for the existence of attributes, and optionally retreive the attribute values.

For example, the `HasAttributes` property will return `true` if there are any attributes, otherwise `false` is returned. The `AttributeCount` property will tell you how many attributes there are, and the `GetAttribute()` method will get an attribute by name or by index. If you want to iterate through the attributes one at a time, there are also `MoveToFirstAttribute()` and `MoveToNextAttribute()` methods.

Here is an example of iterating through the attributes from `XmlReaderSample4`:

```
protected void button1_Click (object sender, System.EventArgs e)
{
    //set this path to match your data path structure
    string fileName = "..\\..\\..\\books.xml";
    //Create the new TextReader Object
    XmlTextReader tr = new XmlTextReader(fileName);
```

```
    //Read in node at a time
  while(tr.Read())
  {
     //check to see if it's a NodeType element
     if(tr.NodeType == XmlNodeType.Element)
     {
        //if it's an element, then let's look at the attributes.
        for(int i = 0; i < tr.AttributeCount; i++) {
           listBox1.Items.Add(tr.GetAttribute(i));
        }
     }
  }
}
```

This time we are looking for element nodes. When we find one, we loop through all of the attributes, and using the `GetAttribute()` method, we load the value of the attribute into the listbox. In this example those attributes would be `genre`, `publicationdate`, and `ISBN`.

Using the XmlValidatingReader Class

If you want to validate an XML document, you'll need to use the `XmlValidatingReader` class. It contains the same functionality as `XmlTextReader` (both classes extend `XmlReader`) but `XmlValidatingReader` adds a `ValidationType` property, a `Schemas` property and a `SchemaType` property.

You set the `ValidationType` property to the type of validation that you want to do. The valid values for this property are:

Property Value	Description
Auto	If a DTD is declared in a `<!DOCTYPE...>` declaration, that DTD will be loaded and processed. Default attributes and general entities defined in the DTD will be made available.
	If an XSD `schemalocation` attribute is found, the XSD is loaded and processed, and will return any default attributes defined in the schema.
	If a namespace with the MSXML `x-schema:` prefix is found, it will load and process the XDR schema and return any default attributes defined.
DTD	Validate according to DTD rules.
Schema	Validate according to XSD schema.
XDR	Validate according to XDR schema.
None	No validation is performed.

Once this property is set, a `ValidationEventHandler` will need to be assigned. This is an event that gets raised when a validation error occurs. You can then react to the error in any way you see fit.

Let's look at an example of how this works. First we will add an XDR (XM- Data Reduced) schema namespace to our `books.xml` file, and rename this file `booksVal.xml`. It now looks like this:

```
<?xml version='1.0'?>
<!-- This file represents a fragment of a book store inventory database -->
<bookstore xmlns="x-schema:books.xdr">
    <book genre="autobiography" publicationdate="1981" ISBN="1-861003-11-0">
        <title>The Autobiography of Benjamin Franklin</title>

        <author>
            <first-name>Benjamin</first-name>
            <list-name>Franklin</list-name>
        </author>
        <price>8.99</price>
    </book>
    ...
</bookstore>
```

Notice that the bookstore element now has the attribute `xmlns="x-schema:books.xdr"`. This will point to the following XDR schema, called `books.xdr`:

```
<?xml version="1.0"?>
<Schema xmlns="urn:schemas-microsoft-com:xml-data"
        xmlns:dt="urn:schemas-microsoft-com:datatypes">
    <ElementType name="first-name" content="textOnly"/>
    <ElementType name="last-name" content="textOnly"/>
    <ElementType name="name" content="textOnly"/>
    <ElementType name="price" content="textOnly" dt:type="fixed.14.4"/>
    <ElementType name="author" content="eltOnly" order="one">
        <group order="seq">
            <element type="name"/>
        </group>
        <group order="seq">
            <element type="first-name"/>
            <element type="last-name"/>
        </group>
    </ElementType>
    <ElementType name="title" content="textOnly"/>
    <AttributeType name="genre" dt:type="string"/>
    <ElementType name="book" content="eltOnly">
        <attribute type="genre" required="yes"/>
        <element type="title"/>
        <element type="author"/>
        <element type="price"/>
    </ElementType>
    <ElementType name="bookstore" content="eltOnly">
        <element type="book"/>
    </ElementType>
</Schema>
```

Now everything looks good except for the fact that we have a couple of attributes in the XML file that are not defined in the schema (publicationdate and ISBN from the book element). We have added these in order to show that validation is really taking place by raising a validation error. We can use the following code (from XmlReaderSample5) to verify this.

First, you will also need to add:

```
using System.Xml.Schema;
```

to your class. Then add the following to the button event handler:

```
protected void button1_Click (object sender, System.EventArgs e)
{
    //change this to match your path structure.
    string fileName = "..\\..\\..\\booksVal.xml";
    XmlTextReader tr=new XmlTextReader(fileName);
    XmlValidatingReader trv = new XmlValidatingReader(tr);

    //Set validation type

    trv.ValidationType=ValidationType.XDR;

    //Add in the Validation eventhandler

    trv.ValidationEventHandler +=
                    new ValidationEventHandler(this.ValidationEvent);

    //Read in node at a time

    while(trv.Read())
    {
        if(trv.NodeType == XmlNodeType.Text)
        listBox1.Items.Add(trv.Value);
    }
}

public void ValidationEvent (object sender, ValidationEventArgs args)
{
    MessageBox.Show(args.Message);
}
```

Here we create an XmlTextReader to pass to the XmlValidatingReader. Once the XmlValidatingReader (trv) is created, we can use it in much the same way that we used XmlTextReader in the previous examples. The differences are that we specify the ValidationType, and add a ValidationEventHandler. You can handle the validation error any way that you see fit; in this example we are showing a MessageBox with the error. This is what the MessageBox looks like when the ValidationEvent is raised:

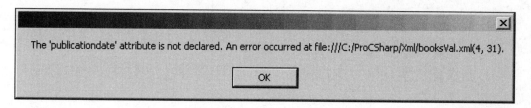

Unlike some parsers, once a validation error occurs, `XmlValidatingReader` will keep on reading. It's up to you to stop the reading and deal with the errors accordingly if you believe that the error is serious enough.

Using the Schemas Property

The `Schemas` property of `XmlValidatingReader` holds an `XmlSchemaCollection`, which is found in the `System.Xml.Schema` namespace. This collection holds pre-loaded XSD and XDR schemas. This allows for very fast validation, especially if you need to validate several documents, since the schema will not have to be reloaded on each validation. In order to utilize this performance gain, you create an `XmlSchemaCollection` object. The `Add()` method, used to populate an `XmlSchemaCollection`, has four overloads. You can pass in an `XmlSchema`-based object, an `XmlSchemaCollection`-based object, a `string` with the `namespace` along with a `string` with the URI of the schema file, and finally a `string` with the `namespace` and an `XmlReader`-based object that contains the schema.

Using the XmlTextWriter Class

The `XmlTextWriter` class allows you write out XML to a stream, a file, or a `TextWriter` object. Like `XmlTextReader`, it does so in a forward-only, non-cached manner. `XmlTextWriter` is highly configurable, allowing you to specify such things as whether or not to indent, the amount to indent, what quote character to use in attribute values, and whether namespaces are supported.

Let's look at a simple example to see how the `XmlTextWriter` class can be used. This can be found in the `XmlWriterSample1` folder:

```
private void button1_Click(object sender, System.EventArgs e)
{
    // change to match your path structure
    string fileName="..\\..\\..\\booknew.xml";
    // create the XmlTextWriter
    XmlTextWriter tw=new XmlTextWriter(fileName,null);
    // set the formatting to indented
    tw.Formatting=Formatting.Indented;
    tw.WriteStartDocument();
    // Start creating elements and attributes
    tw.WriteStartElement("book");
    tw.WriteAttributeString("genre","Mystery");
    tw.WriteAttributeString("publicationdate","2001");
    tw.WriteAttributeString("ISBN","123456789");
    tw.WriteElementString("title","The Case of the Missing Cookie");
    tw.WriteStartElement("author");
    tw.WriteElementString("name","Cookie Monster");
```

```
        tw.WriteEndElement();
        tw.WriteElementString("price","9.99");
        tw.WriteEndElement();
        tw.WriteEndDocument();
        //clean up
        tw.Flush();
        tw.Close();
    }
```

Here we are writing to a new XML file called `booknew.xml`, and adding the data for a new book. Note that `XmlTextWriter` will overwrite an existing file with a new one. We will look at inserting a new element or node into an existing document later in the chapter. We are instantiating the `XmlTextWriter` object using a `FileStream` object as a parameter. We could also pass in a string with a filename and path, or a `TextWriter`-based object. The next thing that we do is set the `Indenting` property. Once this is set, child nodes are automatically indented from the parent. `WriteStartDocument()` will add the document declaration. Now we start writing data. First comes the `book` element, and then we add the `genre`, `publicationdate`, and `ISBN` attributes. Now we write the `title`, `author`, and `price` elements. Notice that the `author` element has a child element name.

When we click on the button, we'll produce the `booknew.xml` file, which looks like this:

```xml
<?xml version="1.0"?>
<book genre="Mystery" publicationdate="2001" ISBN="123456789">
  <title>The Case of the Missing Cookie</title>
  <author>
    <name>Cookie Monster</name>
  </author>
  <price>9.99</price>
</book>
```

The nesting of elements is controlled by paying attention to when you start and finish writing elements and attributes. You can see this when we add the `name` child element to the `authors` element. Note how the `WriteStartElement()` and `WriteEndElement()` method calls are arranged, and how that arrangement produces the nested elements in the output file.

To go along with the `WriteElementString()` and `WriteAttributeString()` methods, there are several other specialized write methods. `WriteCData()` will output a CData section (`<!CDATA[...]]>`), writing out the text it takes as a parameter. `WriteComment()` writes out a comment in proper XML format. `WriteChars()` writes out the contents of a char buffer. This works in similar way to the `ReadChars()` method that we looked at earlier; they both use the same type of parameters. `WriteChars()` needs a buffer (an array of characters), the starting position for writing (an integer) and the number of characters to write (an integer).

Reading and writing XML using the `XmlReader` and `XmlWriter`-based classes is surprisingly flexible and simple to use. Next, we will look at how the DOM is implemented in the `System.Xml` namespace, through the `XmlDocument` and `XmlNode` classes.

Using the DOM in .NET

The Document Object Model (DOM) implementation in .NET supports the W3C DOM Level 1 and Core DOM Level 2 specifications. The DOM is implemented through the XmlNode class, which is an abstract class that represents a node of an XML document.

There is also an XmlNodeList class, which is an ordered list of nodes. This is a live list of nodes, and any changes to any node are immediately reflected in the list. XmlNodeList supports indexed access or iterative access. There is another abstract class, XmlCharacterData, that extends XmlLinkedNode, and provides text manipulation methods for other classes.

The XmlNode and XmlNodeList classes make up the core of the DOM implementation in the .NET Framework. Here is a list of some of the classes that are based on XmlNode:

Class Name	Description
XmlLinkedNode	Returns the node immediately before or after the current node. Adds NextSibling and PreviousSibling properties to XmlNode.
XmlDocument	Represents the entire document. Implements the DOM Level 1 and Level 2 specifications.
XmlDocumentFragment	Represents a fragment of the document tree.
XmlAttribute	An attribute object of an XmlElement object.
XmlEntity	A parsed or unparsed entity node.
XmlNotation	Contains a notation declared in a DTD or schema.

The following classes extend XmlCharacterData:

Class Name	Description
XmlCDataSection	An object that represents a CData section of a document.
XmlComment	Represents an XML comment object.
XmlSignificantWhitespace	Represents a node with whitespace. Nodes created only if the PreserveWhiteSpace flag is true.
XmlWhitespace	Represents whitespace in element content. Nodes are created only if the PreserveWhiteSpace flag is true.
XmlText	The textual content of an element or attribute.

Finally, the next collection of classes extend the `XmlLinkedNode` class:

Class Name	Description
`XmlDeclaration`	Represents the declaration node (`<?xml version='1.0'...>`)
`XmlDocumentType`	Data relating to the document type declaration
`XmlElement`	An XML element object
`XmlEntityReferenceNode`	Represents an entity reference node
`XmlProcessingInstruction`	Contains an XML processing instruction

As you can see, .NET makes available a class to fit just about any XML type that you may encounter. Because of this, you end up with a very flexible and powerful toolset. We won't look at every class in detail, but we will use several examples to give you an idea of what you can accomplish. This is what the inheritance diagram looks like:

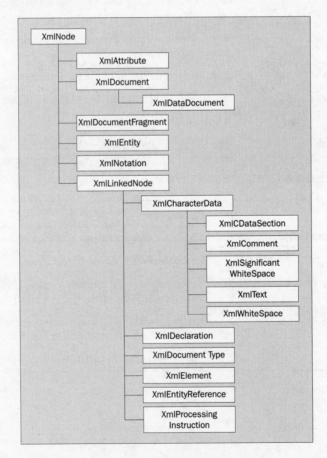

Using the XmlDocument Class

XmlDocument and its derived class XmlDataDocument (we look at this later in the chapter) are the classes that you will be using to represent the DOM in .NET. Unlike XmlReader and XmlWriter, XmlDocument gives you read and write capabilities as well as random access to the DOM tree. XmlDocument resembles the DOM implementation in MSXML. If you have programmed with MSXML then you will feel comfortable using XmlDocument.

Let's introduce an example that creates an XmlDocument object, loads a document from disk, and loads a listbox with data from the title elements. This is similar to one of the examples that we constructed in the XmlReader section. This difference here is that we will be selecting the nodes we want to work with instead of going through the entire document as the XmlReader-based example did.

Here is our code. Look at how simple it looks in comparison to the XmlReader example (the file can be found in the DOMSample1 folder of the download):

```
private void button1_Click(object sender, System.EventArgs e)
{
    // doc is declared at the module level
    // change path to match your path structure
    doc.Load("..\\..\\..\\books.xml");
    // get only the nodes that we want
    XmlNodeList nodeLst=doc.GetElementsByTagName("title");
    // iterate through the XmlNodeList

    foreach(XmlNode node in nodeLst) listBox1.Items.Add(node.InnerText);
}
```

Note that we also add the following declaration at the module level for the examples in this section:

```
private XmlDocument doc=new XmlDocument();
```

If this is all that we wanted to do, using the XmlReader would have been a much more efficient way to load the listbox, because we just go through the document once, and then we are finished with it. This is exactly the type of work that XmlReader was designed for. If, however, we wanted to revisit a node, then using XmlDocument is a better way. Let's extend the previous example by adding another event handler (this is DOMSample2):

```
private void listBox1_SelectedIndexChanged(object sender, System.EventArgs e)
{
    //create XPath search string
    string srch="bookstore/book[title='" + listBox1.SelectedItem.ToString()
                                    + "']";
    //look for the extra data
    XmlNode foundNode = doc.SelectSingleNode(srch);
    if(foundNode != null)
        MessageBox.Show(foundNode.InnerText);
    else
        MessageBox.Show("Not found");
}
```

In this example, we load the listbox with the titles from the `books.xml` document, as in the previous example. When we click on the listbox, it causes the `SelectedIndexChanged()` event handler to fire. In this case, we take the text of the selected item in the listbox (the book title) create an XPath statement and pass it to the `SelectSingleNode()` method of the `doc` object. This returns the `book` element that the `title` is part of (`foundNode`). Then we display the `InnerText` of the node in a message box. We can keep clicking on items in the listbox as many times as we want, since the document is loaded and stays loaded until we release it.

A quick comment regarding the `SelectSingleNode()` method. This is an XPath implementation in the `XmlDocument` class. There are the methods `SelectSingleNode()` and `SelectNodes()`. Both of these methods are defined in `XmlNode`, which `XmlDocument` in based on. `SelectSingleNode()` returns an `XmlNode` and `SelectNodes()` returns an `XmlNodeList`. However, the `System.Xml.XPath` namespace contains a richer XPath implementation, and we will be looking at that in a later section.

Inserting Nodes

Earlier we looked at an example using `XmlTextWriter` that created a new document. The limitation was that it would not insert a node into a current document. With the `XmlDocument` class we can do just that. Change the `button1_Click()` event handler from the last example to the following (`DOMSample3` in the download code):

```
private void button1_Click(object sender, System.EventArgs e)
{
    //change path to match your structure
    doc.Load("..\\..\\..\\books.xml");
    //create a new 'book' element
    XmlElement newBook=doc.CreateElement("book");
    //set some attributes
    newBook.SetAttribute("genre","Mystery");
    newBook.SetAttribute("publicationdate","2001");
    newBook.SetAttribute("ISBN","123456789");
    //create a new 'title' element
    XmlElement newTitle=doc.CreateElement("title");
    newTitle.InnerText="The Case of the Missing Cookie";
    newBook.AppendChild(newTitle);
    //create new author element
    XmlElement newAuthor=doc.CreateElement("author");
    newBook.AppendChild(newAuthor);
    //create new name element
    XmlElement newName=doc.CreateElement("name");
    newName.InnerText="C. Monster";
    newAuthor.AppendChild(newName);
    //create new price element
    XmlElement newPrice=doc.CreateElement("price");
    newPrice.InnerText="9.95";
    newBook.AppendChild(newPrice);
    //add to the current document
    doc.DocumentElement.AppendChild(newBook);
    //write out the doc to disk
    XmlTextWriter tr=new XmlTextWriter("..\\..\\..\\booksEdit.xml",null);
```

```
      tr.Formatting=Formatting.Indented;
      doc.WriteContentTo(tr);
      tr.Close();
      //load listBox1 with all of the titles, including new one
      XmlNodeList nodeLst=doc.GetElementsByTagName("title");
      foreach(XmlNode node in nodeLst)
        listBox1.Items.Add(node.InnerText);
    }
```

After executing this code, you end up with the same functionality as the previous example, but there is one additional book in the listbox, *The Case of the Missing Cookie* (a soon-to-be classic). Clicking on the cookie caper title will show all of the same info as the other titles. Breaking the code down a little, we can see that this is actually a fairly simple process. The first thing that we do is create a new book element:

```
XmlElement newBook = doc.CreateElement("book");
```

CreateElement() has three overloads that allow you to specify:

❑   The element name

❑   The name and namespace URI

❑   The prefix, localname, and namespace

Once the element is created we need to add attributes:

```
newBook.SetAttribute("genre","Mystery");
newBook.SetAttribute("publicationdate","2001");
newBook.SetAttribute("ISBN","123456789");
```

Now that we have the attributes created, we need to add the other elements of a book:

```
XmlElement newTitle = doc.CreateElement("title");
newTitle.InnerText = "The Case of the Missing Cookie";
newBook.AppendChild(newTitle);
```

Once again we create a new XmlElement-based object (newTitle). Then we set the InnerText property to the title of our new classic, and append the element as a child to the book element. We repeat this for the rest of the elements in this book element. Note that we add the name element as a child to the author element. This will give us the proper nesting relationship as in the other book elements.

Finally, we append the newBook element to the doc.DocumentElement node. This is the same level as all of the other book elements. We have now updated an existing document with a new element.

The last thing to do is to write out the new XML document to disk. In this example we create a new XmlTextWriter, and pass it to the WriteContentTo() method. WriteContentTo() and WriteTo() both take an XmlTextWriter as a parameter. WriteContentTo() saves the current node and all of its children to the XmlTextWriter, whereas WriteTo() just saves the current node. Because doc is an XmlDocument-based object, it represents the entire document and so that is what is saved. We could also use the Save() method. It will always save the entire document. Save() has four overloads. You can specify a string with the file name and path, a Stream-based object, a TextWriter-based object, or an XmlWriter-based object.

We also call the Close() method on XmlTextWriter to flush the internal buffers and close the file.

This is what we get when we run this example. Notice the new entry at the bottom of the list:

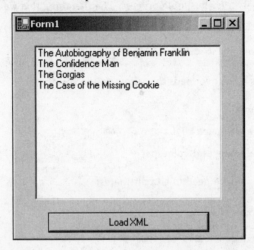

If we wanted to create a document from scratch, we could use the XmlTextWriter, which we saw in action earlier in the chapter. We can also use XmlDocument. Why would you use one in preference to the other? If the data that you want streamed to XML is available and ready to write, then the XmlTextWriter class would be the best choice. However, if you need to build the XML document a little at a time, inserting nodes into various places, then creating the document with XmlDocument may be the better choice. We can accomplish this by changing the following line:

```
doc.Load("..\\..\\..\\books.xml");
```

to (this code is in example DOMSample4):

```
//create the declaration section
XmlDeclaration newDec = doc.CreateXmlDeclaration("1.0",null,null);
doc.AppendChild(newDec);
//create the new root element
XmlElement newRoot = doc.CreateElement("newBookstore");
doc.AppendChild(newRoot);
```

First, we create a new `XmlDeclaration`. The parameters are the version (always 1.0 for now), the encoding, and the standalone flag. The encoding parameter should be set to a string that is part of the `System.Text.Encoding` class if null isn't used. `null` defaults to UTF-8. The standalone flag can be either yes, no, or `null`. If it is `null` then the attribute is not used and will not be included in the document.

The next element that is created will become the `DocumentElement`. In this case, we called it `newBookstore` so that you can see the difference. The rest of the code is the same as the previous example, and works in the same way. This is `booksEdit.xml`, which is generated from the code:

```
<?xml version="1.0"?>
<newBookstore>
    <book genre="Mystery" publicationdate="2001" ISBN="123456789">
        <title>The Case of the Missing Cookie</title>
        <author>
            <name>C. Monster</name>
        </author>
        <price>9.95</price>
    </book>
</newBookstore>
```

We have not looked at every nook and cranny of the `XmlDocument` class, or of the other classes that help to create the DOM model in .NET. However, we have seen the power and flexibility that the DOM implementation in .NET offers. You will want to use the `XmlDocument` class when you want to have random access to the document, or the `XmlReader` based classes when you want a streaming type model instead. Remember that there is a cost for the flexibility of the `XmlNode`-based `XmlDocument`. Memory requirements are higher and the performance of reading the document is not as good as using `XmlReader`. So think carefully about which method is best for the situation.

Using XPath and XSLT in .NET

In this section, we are going to look at support for XPath and XSL Transforms (XSLT) in the .NET Framework. XPath support is through the `System.Xml.XPath` namespace, and XSLT through the `System.Xml.Xsl` namespace. The reason that we are looking at them together is that the `XPathNavigator` class of the `System.XPath` namespace provides a very performance-oriented way of performing XSL Transforms in .NET.

XPath is the query language for XML. You would use XPath to select a subset of elements based on element text values or perhaps based on attribute values. XSLT is used to transform a base document into another document of different structure or type.

We will first look at `System.XPath` and then discuss how it is used to feed the `System.Xml.Xsl` classes.

The System.XPath Namespace

The System.XPath namespace is built for speed. It provides a read-only view of your XML documents, so there are no editing capabilities here. Classes in this namespace are built to do fast iteration and selections on the XML document in a cursor fashion.

Here is a table that lists the key classes in System.XPath, and gives a short description of the purpose of each class:

Class Name	Description
XPathDocument	A view of the entire XML document. Read-only.
XPathNavigator	Provides the navigation capabilities to an XPathDocument.
XPathNodeIterator	Provides iteration capabilities to a node set. XPath equivalent to a nodeset in Xpath.
XPathExpression	A compiled XPath expression. Used by SelectNodes, SelectSingleNodes, Evaluate, and Matches.
XPathException	XPath exception class.

XPathDocument

XPathDocument doesn't offer any of the functionality of the XmlDocument class. If you need editing capabilities, then XmlDocument is the choice to go for; if you're utilizing ADO.NET, then XmlDataDocument (we will see this later in the chapter) is what you'll use. However, if speed is of concern, then use XPathDocument as your store. It has four overloads allowing you to open an XML document from a file and path string, a TextReader object, an XmlReader object, or a Stream-based object.

XPathNavigator

XPathNavigator contains all of the methods for moving and selecting elements that you need. Some of the "move" methods defined in this class are:

Method Name	Description
MoveTo()	Takes an XPathNavigator as a parameter. Move the current position to be the same as that passed in to XPathNavigator.
MoveToAttribute()	Move to the named attribute. Takes the attribute name and namespace as parameters.
MoveToFirstAttribute()	Move to the first attribute in the current element. Returns true if successful.
MoveToNextAttribute()	Move to the next attribute in the current element. Returns true if successful.

Method Name	Description
MoveToFirst()	Move to the first sibling in the current node. Returns `true` if successful, otherwise returns `false`.
MoveToLast()	Move to the last sibling in the current node. Returns `true` if successful.
MoveToNext()	Move to the next sibling in the current node. Returns `true` if successful.
MoveToPrevious()	Move to the previous sibling in the current node. Returns `true` if successful.
MoveToFirstChild()	Move to the first child of the current element. Returns `true` if successful.
MoveToId()	Move to the element with the ID supplied as a parameter. There needs to be a schema for the document, and the data type for the element must be of type `ID`.
MoveToParent()	Move to the parent of the current node. Returns `true` if successful.
MoveToRoot()	Move to the root node of the document.

There several `Select()` methods for selecting a subset of nodes to work with. All of these `Select()` methods return an `XPathNodeIterator` object.

There are also `SelectAncestors()` and `SelectChildren()` methods that can be used. Both return an `XPathNodeIterator`. While `Select()` takes an XPath expression as a parameter, the other select methods take an `XPathNodeType` as a parameter.

You can extend `XPathNavigator` to use such things as the file system or Registry as the store instead of an `XPathDocument`.

XPathNodeIterator

`XPathNodeIterator` can be thought of as the equivalent of a `NodeList` or a `NodeSet` in XPath. This object has three properties and two methods:

❑ `Clone` – Creates a new copy of itself

❑ `Count` – Number of nodes in the `XPathNodeIterator` object

❑ `Current` – Returns an `XPathNavigator` pointing to the current node

❑ `CurrentPosition()` – Returns an integer with the current position

❑ `MoveNext()` – Moves to the next node that matches the XPath expression that created the `XpathNodeIterator`

Using Classes from the XPath Namespace

The best way to see how these classes are used is to look at some code. Let's load up the books.xml document and move around in it so that you can see how the navigation works. In order to use the examples, we first add a reference to the System.Xml.Xsl and System.Xml.XPath namespaces:

```
using System.Xml.XPath;
using System.Xml.Xsl;
```

For this example we are using the file booksxpath.xml. It is similar to the books.xml that we have been using previously, except there are a couple of extra books added. Here's the form code, which can be found in the XPathXSLSample1 folder:

```
private void button1_Click(object sender, System.EventArgs e)
{

    //modify to match your path structure
    XPathDocument doc=new XPathDocument("..\\..\\..\\booksxpath.xml");
    //create the XPath navigator
    XPathNavigator nav=doc.CreateNavigator();
    //create the XPathNodeIterator of book nodes
    // that have genre attribute value of novel
    XPathNodeIterator iter=nav.Select("/bookstore/book[@genre='novel']");

    while(iter.MoveNext())
    {
        LoadBook(iter.Current);
    }
}

private void LoadBook(XPathNavigator lstNav)
{
    //We are passed an XPathNavigator of a particular book node
    //we will select all of the descendents and
    //load the list box with the names and values

    XPathNodeIterator iterBook=lstNav.SelectDescendants
                            (XPathNodeType.Element,false);
    while(iterBook.MoveNext())
        listBox1.Items.Add(iterBook.Current.Name + ": "
                                        + iterBook.Current.Value);

}
```

The first thing we do in the button1_Click() method is to create the XPathDocument (called doc), passing in the file and path string of the document we want opened. The next line is where the XPathNavigator is created:

```
XPathNavigator nav = doc.CreateNavigator();
```

In the example you can see that we use the `Select()` method to retrieve a set of nodes that all have `novel` as the value of the `genre` attribute. We then use the `MoveNext()` method to iterate through all of the novels in the book list.

To load the data into the listbox, we use the `XPathNodeIterator.Current` property. This will create a new `XPathNavigator` object based on just the node that the `XPathNodeIterator` is pointing at. In this case, we are creating an `XPathNavigator` for one `book` node in the document.

The `LoadBook()` method takes this `XPathNavigator` and creates another `XPathNodeIterator` by issuing another type of select method, the `SelectDescendants()` method. This will give us an `XPathNodeIterator` of all of the child nodes and children of the child nodes of the `book` node that we passed to the `LoadBook()` method.

Then we do another `MoveNext()` loop on the `XPathNodeIterator` and load the listbox with the element names and element values.

This is what the screen looks like after running the code. Notice that novels are the only books listed now:

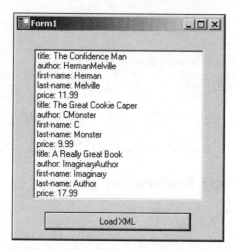

What if we wanted to add up the cost of these books? `XPathNavigator` includes the `Evaluate()` method for just this reason. `Evaluate()` has three overloads. The first one contains a string that is the XPath function call. The second overload uses the `XPathExpression` object as a parameter, and the third uses `XPathExpression` and an `XPathNodeIterator` as parameters. The changes are highlighted below (this version of the code can be found in `XPathXSLSample2`):

```
private void button1_Click(object sender, System.EventArgs e)
{
    //modify to match your path structure
    XPathDocument doc = new XPathDocument("..\\..\\..\\booksxpath.XML");
    //create the XPath navigator
    XPathNavigator nav = doc.CreateNavigator();
    //create the XPathNodeIterator of book nodes
    // that have genre attribute value of novel
    XPathNodeIterator iter = nav.Select("/bookstore/book[@genre='novel']");
    while(iter.MoveNext())
```

```
    {
        LoadBook(iter.Current.Clone());
    }

        //add a break line and calculate the sum
        listBox1.Items.Add("========================");
        listBox1.Items.Add("Total Cost = "
                    + nav.Evaluate("sum(/bookstore/book[@genre='novel']/price)"));
    }
```

This time, we see the total cost of the books evaluated in the listbox:

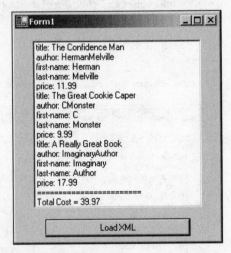

The System.Xml.Xsl Namespace

The System.Xml.Xsl namespace contains the classes that the .NET Framework uses to support XSL Transforms. The contents of this namespace are available to any store whose classes implement the IXPathNavigable interface. In the .NET Framework, that would currently include XmlDocument, XmlDataDocument, and XPathDocument. Again, just as with XPath, use the store that makes the most sense. If you plan to create a custom store, such as one using the file system, and you want to be able to do transforms, be sure to implement the IXPathNavigable interface in your class.

XSLT is based on a streaming pull model. Because of this, you can chain several transforms together. You could even apply a custom reader between transforms if needed. This allows a great deal of flexibility in design.

Transforming XML

The first example we will look at takes the books.xml document and transforms it into a simple HTML document for display using the XSLT file books.xsl. (This code can be found in the XPathXSLSample3 folder.) We will need to add the following using statements:

```
    using System.IO;
    using System.Xml.Xsl;
    using System.Xml.XPath;
```

Here is the code to perform the transform:

```
private void button1_Click(object sender, System.EventArgs e)
{
    //create the new XPathDocument
    XPathDocument doc = new XPathDocument("..\\..\\..\\booksxpath.xml");
    //create a new XslTransform
    XslTransform transForm = new XslTransform();
    transForm.Load("..\\..\\..\\books.xsl");
    //this FileStream will be our output
    FileStream fs=new FileStream("..\\..\\..\\booklist.html",
                                FileMode.Create);
    //Create the navigator
    XPathNavigator nav = doc.CreateNavigator();
    //Do the transform. The output file is created here
    transForm.Transform(nav, null, fs);
}
```

This is about as simple a transform as can be. We create an `XPathDocument`-based object and an `XslTransform`-based object. We load the `booksxpath.xml` file into the `XPathDocument`, and `books.xsl` file into the `XslTransform`.

In this example, we also create a `FileStream` object to write the new HTML document to disk. If this were an ASP.NET application, we would have used a `TextWriter` object and passed it into the `HttpResponse` object instead. If we were transforming to another XML document we would have used an `XmlWriter` based object.

After the `XPathDocument` and `XslTransform` objects are ready, we create the `XPathNavigator` on the `XPathDocument`, and pass the `XPathNavigator` and the `FileStream` into the `Transform()` method of the `XslTransform` object. `Transform()` has several overloads, passing in combinations of navigators, `XsltArgumentList` (more on this later), and `IO` streams. The navigator parameter can be `XPathNavigator`, or anything that implements the `IXPathNavigable` interface. The `IO` streams can be a `TextWriter`, `Stream`, or `XmlWriter`-based object.

The `books.xsl` document is a fairly straightforward stylesheet. The document looks like this:

```
<xsl:stylesheet version="1.0"
                    xmlns:xsl="http://www.w3.org/1999/XSL/Transform">

<xsl:template match="/">
    <html>
        <head>
            <title>Price List</title>
        </head>
        <body>
            <table>
                <xsl:apply-templates/>
            </table>
        </body>
    </html>
```

```
        </xsl:template>

    <xsl:template match="bookstore">
        <xsl:apply-templates select="book"/>
    </xsl:template>

    <xsl:template match="book">
        <tr><td>
            <xsl:value-of select="title"/>
        </td><td>
            <xsl:value-of select="price"/>
        </td></tr>
    </xsl:template>

</xsl:stylesheet>
```

Using XsltArgumentList

Earlier we mentioned `XsltArgumentList`. This is a way that you can bind an object with methods to a namespace. Once this is done, you can invoke the methods during the transform. Let's look at an example to see how this works (found in `XPathXSLSample4`). Add the highlighted code to your sample code:

```
private void button1_Click(object sender, System.EventArgs e)
{
    //new XPathDocument
    XPathDocument doc=new XPathDocument("..\\..\\..\\booksxpath.xml");
    //new XslTransform
    XslTransform transForm=new XslTransform();
    transForm.Load("..\\..\\..\\booksarg.xsl");
    //new XmlTextWriter since we are creating a new XML document
    XmlWriter xw=new XmlTextWriter("..\\..\\argSample.xml",null);
    //create the XsltArgumentList and new BookUtils object
    XsltArgumentList argBook=new XsltArgumentList();
    BookUtils bu=new BookUtils();
    //this tells the argumentlist about BookUtils
    argBook.AddExtensionObject("urn:ProCSharp",bu);
    //new XPathNavigator
    XPathNavigator nav=doc.CreateNavigator();
    //do the transform
    transForm.Transform(nav,argBook,xw);
    xw.Close();
}

//simple test class

public class BookUtils
{
    public BookUtils(){}

    public string ShowText()
    {
        return "This came from the ShowText method!";
    }
}
```

This is what the output of the transform looks like (`argSample.xml`):

```xml
<?xml version="1.0"?>
<books>
   <discbook>
      <booktitle>The Autobiography of Benjamin Franklin</booktitle>
      <showtext>This came from the ShowText method!</showtext>
   </discbook>
   <discbook>
      <booktitle>The Confidence Man</booktitle>
      <showtext>This came from the ShowText method!</showtext>
   </discbook>
   <discbook>
      <booktitle>The Gorgias</booktitle>
      <showtext>This came from the ShowText method!</showtext>
   </discbook>
   <discbook>
      <booktitle>The Great Cookie Caper</booktitle>
      <showtext>This came from the ShowText method!</showtext>
   </discbook>
   <discbook>
      <booktitle>A Really Great Book</booktitle>
      <showtext>This came from the ShowText method!</showtext>
   </discbook>
</books>
```

In this example, we define a new class, `BookUtils`. In this class we have one rather useless method that returns the string `"This came from the ShowText method!"`. In the `button1_Click()` event, we create the `XPathDocument` and `XslTransform` just as we did before, with a couple of exceptions. This time we are going to create an XML document, so we use the `XmlWriter` instead of the `FileStream` that we used before. The next change is here:

```
XsltArgumentList argBook=new XsltArgumentList();
BookUtils bu=new BookUtils();
argBook.AddExtensionObject("urn:ProCSharp",bu);
```

This is where we create the `XsltArgumentList`. We create an instance of our `BookUtils` object, and when we call the `AddExtensionObject()` method, we pass in a namespace for our extension, and the object that we want to be able to call methods from. When we make the `Transform()` call, we pass in the `XsltArgumentList` (`argBook`) along with the `XPathNavigator` and the `XmlWriter` object we made.

Here is the `booksarg.xsl` document (based upon `books.xsl`):

```xml
<xsl:stylesheet version="1.0" xmlns:xsl="http://www.w3.org/1999/XSL/Transform"
                        xmlns:bookUtil="urn:ProCSharp">
   <xsl:output method="xml" indent="yes"/>

   <xsl:template match="/">
      <xsl:element name="books">
         <xsl:apply-templates/>
```

```
        </xsl:element>
    </xsl:template>

    <xsl:template match="bookstore">
        <xsl:apply-templates select="book"/>
    </xsl:template>

    <xsl:template match="book">
        <xsl:element name="discbook">
            <xsl:element name="booktitle">
                <xsl:value-of select="title"/>
            </xsl:element>
            <xsl:element name="showtext">
                <xsl:value-of select="bookUtil:ShowText()"/>
            </xsl:element>
        </xsl:element>
    </xsl:template>

</xsl:stylesheet>
```

The two important new lines are highlighted. First we add the namespace that we created when we added the object to the `XsltArgumentList`. Then when we want to make the method call, we use standard XSLT namespace prefixing syntax and make the method call.

Another way we could have accomplished this is with XSLT scripting. You can include C#, VB, and JavaScript code in the stylesheet. The great thing about this is that unlike current non-.NET implementations the script is compiled at the `XslTransform.Load()` call; this way you are executing already compiled scripts, much the same way that ASP.NET works.

Let's modify the previous XSLT file in this way. First we add the script to the stylesheet. You can see these changes below in `booksscript.xsl`:

```
<xsl:stylesheet version="1.0" xmlns:xsl="http://www.w3.org/1999/XSL/Transform"
                             xmlns:msxsl="urn:schemas-microsoft-com:xslt"
                             xmlns:user="http://wrox.com">

    <msxsl:script language="C#" implements-prefix="user">

        string ShowText()
            {
                return "This came from the ShowText method!";

            }
    </msxsl:script>

    <xsl:output method="xml" indent="yes"/>
        <xsl:template match="/">
    <xsl:element name="books">
        <xsl:apply-templates/>
    </xsl:element>
        </xsl:template>
    <xsl:template match="bookstore">
```

```
        <xsl:apply-templates select="book"/>
    </xsl:template>
        <xsl:template match="book">
        <xsl:element name="discbook">
        <xsl:element name="booktitle">
            <xsl:value-of select="title"/>
        </xsl:element>
        <xsl:element name="showtext">
            <xsl:value-of select="user:ShowText()"/>
        </xsl:element>
      </xsl:element>
    </xsl:template>

    </xsl:stylesheet>
```

Once again the changes are highlighted. We set the scripting namespace, add the code (which was copied and pasted in from the Visual Studio .NET IDE), and make the call in the stylesheet. The output looks the same as that of the previous example.

To summarize, the key thing to keep in mind when performing transforms is to remember to use the proper XML data store. Use `XPathDocument` if you don't need edit capabilities, `XmlDataDocument` if you're getting your data from ADO.NET, and `XmlDocument` if you need to be able to edit the data. The process is the same regardless.

XML and ADO.NET

XML is the glue that binds ADO.NET to the rest of the world. ADO.NET was designed from the ground up to work within the XML environment. XML is used to transfer the data to and from the data store and the application or web page. Since ADO.NET uses XML as the transport in remoting scenarios, data can be exchanged with applications and systems that are not even aware of ADO.NET. Because of the importance of XML in ADO.NET, there are some powerful features in ADO.NET that allow the reading and writing of XML documents. The `System.Xml` namespace also contains classes that can consume or utilize ADO.NET relational data.

Converting ADO.NET Data to XML

The first example that we are going to look at uses ADO.NET, streams, and XML to pull some data from the `Northwind` database into a `DataSet`, load an `XmlDocument` object with the XML from the `DataSet`, and load the XML into a listbox. In order to run the next few examples, you need to add the following `using` statements:

```
using System.Data;
using System.Xml;
using System.Data.SqlClient;
using System.IO;
```

Since we will be using XmlDocument, we also need to add the following at the module level:

```
private XmlDocument doc = new XmlDocument();
```

Also, for the ADO.NET samples we have added a DataGrid to the forms. This will allow us to see the data in the ADO.NET DataSet since it is bound to the grid, as well as the data from the generated XML documents that we load in the listbox. Here is the code for the first example, which can be found in the ADOSample1 folder:

```
private void button1_Click(object sender, System.EventArgs e)
{
    //create a dataset
    DataSet ds = new DataSet("XMLProducts");
    //connect to the northwind database and
    //select all of the rows from products table
    //make sure your login matches your version of SqlServer
    SqlConnection conn = new SqlConnection
                (@"server=GLYNNJ_CS\NetSDK;uid=sa;pwd=;database=northwind");
    SqlDataAdapter da = new SqlDataAdapter("SELECT * FROM Products",conn);
```

After we create the SqlDataAdapter, da, and the DataSet, ds, we instantiate a MemoryStream object, a StreamReader object, and a StreamWriter object. The StreamReader and StreamWriter objects will use the MemoryStream to move the XML around:

```
    MemoryStream memStrm=new MemoryStream();
    StreamReader strmRead=new StreamReader(memStrm);
    StreamWriter strmWrite=new StreamWriter(memStrm);
```

We will use a MemoryStream so that we don't have to write anything to disk, however, we could have used any object that was based on the Stream class such as FileStream. Next, we fill the DataSet and bind it to the DataGrid. The data in the DataSet will now be displayed in the DataGrid:

```
    da.Fill(ds,"products");
    //load data into DataGrid
    dataGrid1.DataSource=ds;
    dataGrid1.DataMember="products";
```

This next step is where the XML is generated. We call the WriteXml() method from the DataSet class. This method generates an XML document. There are two overloads to WriteXml(): one takes a string with the file path and name, and the other adds a mode parameter. This mode is an XmlWriteMode enumeration, with possible values:

❑ IgnoreSchema

❑ WriteSchema

❑ DiffGram

`IgnoreSchema` is used if you don't want `WriteXml()` to write an inline schema at the start of your XML file; use the `WriteSchema` parameter if you do want one. We will look at `DiffGrams` later in the section.

```
    ds.WriteXml(strmWrite,XmlWriteMode.IgnoreSchema);
    memStrm.Seek(0,SeekOrigin.Begin);
    //read from the memory stream to an XmlDocument object
    doc.Load(strmRead);
    //get all of the products elements
    XmlNodeList nodeLst=doc.GetElementsByTagName("ProductName");
    //load them into the list box
    foreach(XmlNode nd in nodeLst)
      listBox1.Items.Add(nd.InnerText);
}
private void listBox1_SelectedIndexChanged(object sender,
                                      System.EventArgs e)
{
    //when you click on the listbox,
    //a message box appears with the unit price
    string srch="XMLProducts/products[ProductName=" +
                    '"'+ listBox1.SelectedItem.ToString() + '"' + "]";
    XmlNode foundNode=doc.SelectSingleNode(srch);
    if(foundNode!=null)
      MessageBox.Show(foundNode.SelectSingleNode("UnitPrice").InnerText);
    else
      MessageBox.Show("Not found");
}
```

Here is a screenshot, so you can see the data in the list as well as the bound `DataGrid`:

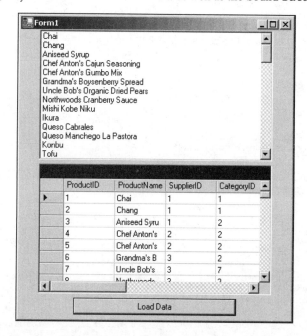

If we had only wanted the schema, we could have called WriteXmlSchema() instead of WriteXml(). This method has four overloads. One takes a string, which is the path and file name of where to write the XML document. The second overload uses an object that is based on the XmlWriter class. The third overload uses an object that is based on the TextWriter class. The fourth overload is the one that we used in the example and is derived from the Stream class.

Also, if we wanted to persist the XML document to disk, we would have used something like this:

```
string file = "c:\\test\\product.xml";
ds.WriteXml(file);
```

This would give us a well-formed XML document on disk that could be read in by another stream, or by DataSet, or used by another application or web site. Since no XmlMode parameter is specified, this XmlDocument would have the schema included. In our example, we use the stream as a parameter to the XmlDocument.Load() method.

Once the XmlDocument is prepared, we load the listbox using the same XPath statement that we used before. If you look closely, you'll see that we changed the listBox1_SelectedIndexChanged() event slightly. Instead of showing the InnerText of the element, we do another XPath search using SelectSingleNode() to get the UnitPrice element. So now every time you click on a product in the listbox, a MessageBox appears with the UnitPrice. We now have two views of the data, but more importantly, we can manipulate the data using two different models. We can use the System.Data namespace to use the data or we can use the System.Xml namespace on the data. This can lead to some very flexible designs in your applications, because now you are not tied to just one object model to program with. This is the real power to the ADO.NET and System.Xml combination. You have multiple views of the same data, and multiple ways to access the data.

In the next example we will simplify the process by eliminating the three streams and by using some of the ADO capabilities built into the System.Xml namespace. We will need to change the module-level line of code:

```
private XmlDocument doc = new XmlDocument();
```

to:

```
private XmlDataDocument doc;
```

We need this because we are now going to be using the XmlDataDocument. Here is the code, which can be found in the ADOSample2 folder:

```
private void button1_Click(object sender, System.EventArgs e)
{
    //create a dataset
    DataSet ds=new DataSet("XMLProducts");
    //connect to the northwind database and
    //select all of the rows from products table
    //make changes to connect string to match your login and server name
    SqlConnection conn=new SqlConnection
            (@"server=GLYNNJ_CS\NetSDK;uid=sa;pwd=;database=northwind");
```

```
SqlDataAdapter da=new SqlDataAdapter("SELECT * FROM products",conn);
//fill the dataset
da.Fill(ds,"products");
//load data into grid
dataGrid1.DataSource=ds;
dataGrid1.DataMember="products";
doc=new XmlDataDocument(ds);

//get all of the products elements

XmlNodeList nodeLst=doc.GetElementsByTagName("ProductName");

//load them into the list box
//we'll use a for loop this time

for(int ctr=0;ctr<nodeLst.Count;ctr++)
   listBox1.Items.Add(nodeLst[ctr].InnerText);
}
```

As you can see, the code to load the `DataSet` into the XML document has been simplified. Instead of using the `XmlDocument` class, we are using the `XmlDataDocument` class. This class was built specifically for using data with a `DataSet` object.

The `XmlDataDocument` is based on the `XmlDocument` class, so it has all of the functionality that the `XmlDocument` class has. One of the main differences is the overloaded constructor that the `XmlDataDocument` has. Note the line of code that instantiates the `XmlDataDocument` (doc):

```
doc = new XmlDataDocument(ds);
```

It passes in the `DataSet` that we created, ds, as a parameter. This creates the XML document from the `DataSet`, and we don't have to use the `Load()` method. In fact, if you instantiate a new `XmlDataDocument` object without passing in a `DataSet` as the parameter, it will contain a `DataSet` with the name `NewDataSet` that has no `DataTables` in the `tables` collection. There is also a `DataSet` property that you can set after an `XmlDataDocument` based object is created.

Say the following line of code is added after the `DataSet.Fill()` call:

```
ds.WriteXml("c:\\test\\sample.xml", XmlWriteMode.WriteSchema);
```

In this case, the following XML file, `sample.xml`, is produced in the folder `c:\test`:

```
<?xml version="1.0" standalone="yes"?>
<XMLProducts>
   <xs:schema id="XMLProducts" xmlns=""
            xmlns:xs="http://www.w3.org/2001/XMLSchema"
            xmlns:msdata="urn:schemas-microsoft-com:xml-msdata">
      <xs:element name="XMLProducts" msdata:IsDataSet="true">
         <xs:complexType>
            <xs:choice maxOccurs="unbounded">
               <xs:element name="products">
                  <xs:complexType>
```

651

```
                <xs:sequence>
                    <xs:element name="ProductID" type="xs:int"
                                minOccurs="0" />
                    <xs:element name="ProductName" type="xs:string"
                                minOccurs="0" />
                    <xs:element name="SupplierID" type="xs:int"
                                minOccurs="0" />
                    <xs:element name="CategoryID" type="xs:int"
                                minOccurs="0" />
                    <xs:element name="QuantityPerUnit" type="xs:string"
                                minOccurs="0" />
                    <xs:element name="UnitPrice" type="xs:decimal"
                                minOccurs="0" />
                    <xs:element name="UnitsInStock" type="xs:short"
                                minOccurs="0" />
                    <xs:element name="UnitsOnOrder" type="xs:short"
                                minOccurs="0" />
                    <xs:element name="ReorderLevel" type="xs:short"
                                minOccurs="0" />
                    <xs:element name="Discontinued" type="xs:boolean"
                                minOccurs="0" />
                </xs:sequence>
            </xs:complexType>
        </xs:element>
      </xs:choice>
    </xs:complexType>
  </xs:element>
</xs:schema>
<products>
    <ProductID>1</ProductID>
    <ProductName>Chai</ProductName>
    <SupplierID>1</SupplierID>
     <CategoryID>1</CategoryID>
    <QuantityPerUnit>10 boxes x 20 bags</QuantityPerUnit>
    <UnitPrice>18</UnitPrice>
    <UnitsInStock>39</UnitsInStock>
    <UnitsOnOrder>0</UnitsOnOrder>
    <ReorderLevel>10</ReorderLevel>
    <Discontinued>false</Discontinued>
</products>
</XMLProducts>
```

Only the first `products` element is shown. The actual XML file would contain all of the products in the `Products` table of `Northwind` database.

Converting Relational Data

This looks simple enough for a single table, but what about relational data, such as multiple `DataTables` and `Relations` in the `DataSet`? It all still works the same way. Let's make the following changes to the code that we've been using (this version can be found in `ADOSample3`):

```
private void button1_Click(object sender, System.EventArgs e)
{
    //create a dataset
    DataSet ds=new DataSet("XMLProducts");
    //connect to the northwind database and
    //select all of the rows from products table and from suppliers table
    //make sure your connect string matches your server configuration
    SqlConnection conn=new SqlConnection
            (@"server=GLYNNJ_CS\NetSDK;uid=sa;pwd=;database=northwind");
```

```
SqlDataAdapter daProd=new SqlDataAdapter("SELECT * FROM products",conn);
SqlDataAdapter daSup=new SqlDataAdapter("SELECT * FROM suppliers",conn);
//Fill DataSet from both SqlAdapters
daProd.Fill(ds,"products");
daSup.Fill(ds,"suppliers");
//Add the relation
ds.Relations.Add(ds.Tables["suppliers"].Columns["SupplierId"],
                 ds.Tables["products"].Columns["SupplierId"]);
//Write the XML to a file so we can look at it later
ds.WriteXml("..\\..\\..\\SuppProd.xml",XmlWriteMode.WriteSchema);
//load data into grid
dataGrid1.DataSource=ds;
dataGrid1.DataMember="suppliers";
//create the XmlDataDocument
doc=new XmlDataDocument(ds);
//Select the productname elements and load them in the grid
XmlNodeList nodeLst=doc.SelectNodes("//ProductName");
foreach(XmlNode nd in nodeLst)
    listBox1.Items.Add(nd.InnerXml);
}
```

In this sample we are creating two `DataTables` in the `XMLProducts DataSet`: `Products` and `Suppliers`. The relation is that `Suppliers` supply `Products`. We create a new relation on the column `SupplierId` in both tables. This is what the `DataSet` looks like:

Products				Suppliers	
PK	**ProductID**			**PK**	**SupplierID**
FK1	**ProductName** SupplierID CategoryID QuantityPerUnit UnitPrice UnitsinStock UnitsOnOrder ReorderLevel Discontinued	SupplierID →			**CompanyName** ContactName ContactTitle Address City Region PostalCode Country Phone Fax HomePage

By making the same `WriteXml()` method call that we did in the previous example, we will get the following XML file (`SuppProd.xml`):

```xml
<?xml version="1.0" standalone="yes"?>
<XMLProducts>
    <xs:schema id="XMLProducts" xmlns=""
            xmlns:xs="http://www.w3.org/2001/XMLSchema"
            xmlns:msdata="urn:schemas-microsoft-com:xml-msdata">
        <xs:element name="XMLProducts" msdata:IsDataSet="true">
            <xs:complexType>
```

```
<xs:choice maxOccurs="unbounded">
    <xs:element name="products">
        <xs:complexType>
            <xs:sequence>
                <xs:element name="ProductID" type="xs:int"
                        minOccurs="0" />
                <xs:element name="ProductName" type="xs:string"
                        minOccurs="0" />
                <xs:element name="SupplierID" type="xs:int"
                        minOccurs="0" />
                <xs:element name="CategoryID" type="xs:int"
                        minOccurs="0" />
                <xs:element name="QuantityPerUnit" type="xs:string"
                        minOccurs="0" />
                <xs:element name="UnitPrice" type="xs:decimal"
                        minOccurs="0" />
                <xs:element name="UnitsInStock" type="xs:short"
                        minOccurs="0" />
                <xs:element name="UnitsOnOrder" type="xs:short"
                        minOccurs="0" />
                <xs:element name="ReorderLevel" type="xs:short"
                        minOccurs="0" />
                <xs:element name="Discontinued" type="xs:boolean"
                        minOccurs="0" />
            </xs:sequence>
        </xs:complexType>
    </xs:element>
    <xs:element name="suppliers">
        <xs:complexType>
            <xs:sequence>
                <xs:element name="SupplierID" type="xs:int"
                        minOccurs="0" />
                <xs:element name="CompanyName" type="xs:string"
                        minOccurs="0" />
                <xs:element name="ContactName" type="xs:string"
                        minOccurs="0" />
                <xs:element name="ContactTitle" type="xs:string"
                        minOccurs="0" />
                <xs:element name="Address" type="xs:string"
                        minOccurs="0" />
                <xs:element name="City" type="xs:string"
                        minOccurs="0" />
                <xs:element name="Region" type="xs:string"
                        minOccurs="0" />
                <xs:element name="PostalCode" type="xs:string"
                        minOccurs="0" />
                <xs:element name="Country" type="xs:string"
                        minOccurs="0" />
                <xs:element name="Phone" type="xs:string"
                        minOccurs="0" />
                <xs:element name="Fax" type="xs:string"
                        minOccurs="0" />
                <xs:element name="HomePage" type="xs:string"
```

```
                              minOccurs="0" />
                    </xs:sequence>
                 </xs:complexType>
               </xs:element>
            </xs:choice>
         </xs:complexType>
         <xs:unique name="Constraint1">
            <xs:selector xpath=".//suppliers" />
            <xs:field xpath="SupplierID" />
         </xs:unique>
         <xs:keyref name="Relation1" refer="Constraint1">
            <xs:selector xpath=".//products" />
            <xs:field xpath="SupplierID" />
         </xs:keyref>
      </xs:element>
   </xs:schema>
   <products>
      <ProductID>1</ProductID>
      <ProductName>Chai</ProductName>
      <SupplierID>1</SupplierID>
      <CategoryID>1</CategoryID>
      <QuantityPerUnit>10 boxes x 20 bags</QuantityPerUnit>
      <UnitPrice>18</UnitPrice>
      <UnitsInStock>39</UnitsInStock>
      <UnitsOnOrder>0</UnitsOnOrder>
      <ReorderLevel>10</ReorderLevel>
      <Discontinued>false</Discontinued>
   </products>
<suppliers>
      <SupplierID>1</SupplierID>
      <CompanyName>Exotic Liquids</CompanyName>
      <ContactName>Charlotte Cooper</ContactName>
      <ContactTitle>Purchasing Manager</ContactTitle>
      <Address>49 Gilbert St.</Address>
      <City>London</City>
      <PostalCode>EC1 4SD</PostalCode>
      <Country>UK</Country>
      <Phone>(171) 555-2222</Phone>
   </suppliers>
</XMLProducts>
```

The schema includes both `DataTables` that were in the `DataSet`. In addition, the data includes all of the data from both tables. For the sake of brevity, we only show the first `suppliers` and `products` records here. As before we could have saved just the schema or just the data by passing in the correct `XmlWriteMode` parameter.

Converting XML to ADO.NET Data

Let's say that you have an XML document that you would like to get into an ADO.NET `DataSet`. You would want to do this so you could load the XML into a database, or perhaps bind the data to a .NET data control such as `DataGrid`. This way you could actually use the XML document as your data store, and could eliminate the overhead of the database altogether. If your data is reasonably small in size, then this is an attractive possibility. Here is some code to get you started (`ADOSample4`):

```
private void button1_Click(object sender, System.EventArgs e)
{

    //create a new DataSet
    DataSet ds=new DataSet("XMLProducts");
    //read in the XML document to the Dataset
    ds.ReadXml("..\\..\\..\\prod.xml");
    //load data into grid
    dataGrid1.DataSource=ds;
    dataGrid1.DataMember="products";
    //create the new XmlDataDocument
    doc=new XmlDataDocument(ds);
    //load the product names into the listbox
    XmlNodeList nodeLst=doc.SelectNodes("//ProductName");

    foreach(XmlNode nd in nodeLst)
        listBox1.Items.Add(nd.InnerXml);
}
```

It is that easy. We instantiate a new `DataSet` object. Then we call the `ReadXml()` method, and you now have XML in a `DataTable` in your `DataSet`. As with the `WriteXml()` methods, `ReadXml()` has an `XmlReadMode` parameter. `ReadXml()` has a couple more options in the `XmlReadMode` too. This table describes them:

Value	Description
Auto	Sets the `XmlReadMode` to the most appropriate setting.
	If data is in `DiffGram` format, `DiffGram` is selected.
	If a schema has already been read, or an inline schema is detected, then `ReadSchema` is selected.
	If no schema has been assigned to the `DataSet`, and none is detected inline, then `IgnoreSchema` is selected.
DiffGram	Reads in the `DiffGram` and applies the changes to the `DataSet`. `DiffGrams` are described later in the chapter.
Fragment	Reads documents that contain XDR schema fragments, such as the type created by SQL Server.
IgnoreSchema	Ignores any inline schema that may be found. Reads data into the current `DataSet` schema. If data does not match `DataSet` schema it is discarded.
InferSchema	Ignores any inline schema. Creates the schema based on data in the XML document. If a schema exists in the `DataSet`, that schema is used, and extended with additional columns and tables if needed. An exception is thrown if a column exists, but is of a different data type.
ReadSchema	Reads the inline schema and loads the data. Will not overwrite a schema in the `DataSet`, but will throw an exception if a table in the inline schema already exists in the `DataSet`.

There is also the `ReadXmlSchema()` method. This will read in a standalone schema and create the tables, columns, and relations accordingly. You would use this if your schema is not inline with your data. `ReadXmlSchema()` has the same four overloads: string with file and path name, `Stream`-based object, `TextReader`-based object and an `XmlReader`-based object.

To show that the data tables are getting created properly, let's load the XML document that contains the `Products` and `Suppliers` tables that we used in an earlier example. This time however, let's load the listbox with the `DataTable` names and the `DataColumn` names and data types. We can look at this and compare it back to the original `Northwind` database to see that all is well. Here is the code that we will use, which can be found in `ADOSample5`:

```
private void button1_Click(object sender, System.EventArgs e)
{
    //create the DataSet
    DataSet ds=new DataSet("XMLProducts");
    //read in the XML document
    ds.ReadXml("..\\..\\..\\SuppProd.xml");
    //load data into grid
    dataGrid1.DataSource=ds;
    dataGrid1.DataMember="products";
    //load the listbox with table, column and datatype info
    foreach(DataTable dt in ds.Tables)
    {
        listBox1.Items.Add(dt.TableName);
        foreach(DataColumn col in dt.Columns)
        {
            listBox1.Items.Add(
                    '\t' + col.ColumnName + " - " + col.DataType.FullName);
        }
    }
}
```

Note the addition of the two `foreach` loops. The first loop is getting the table name from each table in the `Tables` collection of the `DataSet`. Inside the inner `foreach` loop we get the name and data type of each column in the `DataTable`. We load this data into the listbox, allowing us to display it. Here is a screenshot of the output:

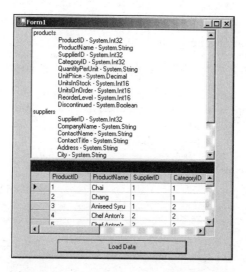

Looking at the listbox you can check that the `DataTables` were created with the columns all having the correct names and data types.

Something else you may want to note is that since the last two examples didn't transfer any data to or from a database, no `SqlDataAdapter` or `SqlConnection` was defined. This shows the real flexibility of both the `System.Xml` namespace and ADO.NET: you can look at the same data in multiple formats. If you need to do a transform and show the data in HTML format, or if you need to bind to a grid, you can take the same data, and with just a method call, have it in the required format.

Reading and Writing a DiffGram

A DiffGram is an XML document that contains the before and after data of an edit session. This can include any combination of data changes, additions, and deletions. A `DiffGram` can be used as an audit trail or for a commit/rollback process. Most DBMS systems today have this built in, but if you happen to be working with a DBMS that does not have these features or if XML is your data store and you do not have a DBMS, you can implement commit/rollback features yourself.

Let's see some code that shows how a `DiffGram` is created and how a `DataSet` can be created from a `DiffGram` (this code can be found in the `ADOSample6` folder).

The beginning part of this code should look familiar. We define and set up a new `DataSet`, ds, a new `SqlConnection`, conn, and a new `SqlDataAdapter`, da. We connect to the database, select all of the rows from the `Products` table, create a new `DataTable` named products, and load the data from the database into the `DataSet`:

```
private void button1_Click(object sender, System.EventArgs e)
{
    //new DataSet
    DataSet ds=new DataSet("XMLProducts");
    //Make connection and load products rows
    SqlConnection conn=new SqlConnection
                (@"server=GLYNNJ_CS\NetSDK;uid=sa;pwd=;database=northwind");
    SqlDataAdapter da=new SqlDataAdapter("SELECT * FROM products",conn);
    //fill the DataSet
    da.Fill(ds,"products");
    //edit first row
    ds.Tables["products"].Rows[0]["ProductName"]="NewProdName";
```

In this next code block we do two things. First, we modify the `ProductName` column in the first row to `NewProdName`. Second, we create a new row in the `DataTable`, set the column values, and finally add the new data row to the `DataTable`.

```
    //add new row
    DataRow dr=ds.Tables["products"].NewRow();;
    dr["ProductId"]=100;
    dr["CategoryId"]=2;
    dr["Discontinued"]=false;
    dr["ProductName"]="This is the new product";
    dr["QuantityPerUnit"]=12;
    dr["ReorderLevel"]=1;
    dr["SupplierId"]=12;
```

```
dr["UnitPrice"]=23;
dr["UnitsInStock"]=5;
dr["UnitsOnOrder"]=0;
ds.Tables["products"].Rows.Add(dr);
```

The next block is the interesting part of the code. First, we write out the schema with
`WriteXmlSchema()`. This is important because you cannot read back in a `DiffGram` without the
schema. `WriteXml()` with the `XmlWriteMode.DiffGram` parameter passed to it actually creates the
`DiffGram`. The next line accepts the changes that we made. It is important that the `DiffGram` is
created before calling `AcceptChanges()`, otherwise there would not appear to be any modifications to
the data.

```
//Write the Schema
ds.WriteXmlSchema("..\\..\\..\\diffgram.xsd");
//generate the DiffGram
ds.WriteXml("..\\..\\..\\diffgram.xml",XmlWriteMode.DiffGram);
ds.AcceptChanges();
//load data into grid

dataGrid1.DataSource=ds;
dataGrid1.DataMember="products";

//new XmlDataDocument
doc=new XmlDataDocument(ds);
//load the productnames in the list
XmlNodeList nodeLst=doc.SelectNodes("//ProductName");
foreach(XmlNode nd in nodeLst)
    listBox1.Items.Add(nd.InnerXml);
}
```

In order to get the data back into a `DataSet`, we can do the following:

```
DataSet dsNew=new DataSet();
dsNew.ReadXmlSchema("..\\..\\..\\diffgram.xsd");
dsNew.XmlRead("..\\..\\..\\diffgram.xml",XmlReadMode.DiffGram);
```

Here we are creating a new `DataSet`, dsNew. The call to the `ReadXmlSchema()` method creates a new
`DataTable` based on the schema information. In this case it would be a clone of the `products`
`DataTable`. Now we can read in the `DiffGram`. The `DiffGram` does not contain schema information,
so it is important that the `DataTable` be created and ready before you call the `ReadXml()` method.

Here is a sample of what the `DiffGram` (`diffgram.xml`) looks like:

```
<?xml version="1.0" standalone="yes"?>
<diffgr:diffgram xmlns:msdata="urn:schemas-microsoft-com:xml-msdata"
                 xmlns:diffgr="urn:schemas-microsoft-com:xml-diffgram-v1">
  <XMLProducts>
    <products diffgr:id="products1" msdata:rowOrder="0"
            diffgr:hasChanges="modified">
      <ProductID>1</ProductID>
      <ProductName>NewProdName</ProductName>
```

```
        <SupplierID>1</SupplierID>
        <CategoryID>1</CategoryID>
        <QuantityPerUnit>10 boxes x 20 bags</QuantityPerUnit>
        <UnitPrice>18</UnitPrice>
        <UnitsInStock>39</UnitsInStock>
        <UnitsOnOrder>0</UnitsOnOrder>
        <ReorderLevel>10</ReorderLevel>
        <Discontinued>false</Discontinued>
      </products>
      ...
      <products diffgr:id="products78" msdata:rowOrder="77"
               diffgr:hasChanges="inserted">
        <ProductID>100</ProductID>
        <ProductName>This is the new product</ProductName>
        <SupplierID>12</SupplierID>
        <CategoryID>2</CategoryID>
        <QuantityPerUnit>12</QuantityPerUnit>
        <UnitPrice>23</UnitPrice>
        <UnitsInStock>5</UnitsInStock>
        <UnitsOnOrder>0</UnitsOnOrder>
        <ReorderLevel>1</ReorderLevel>
        <Discontinued>false</Discontinued>
      </products>
    </XMLProducts>
    <diffgr:before>
      <products diffgr:id="products1" msdata:rowOrder="0">
        <ProductID>1</ProductID>
        <ProductName>Chai</ProductName>
        <SupplierID>1</SupplierID>
        <CategoryID>1</CategoryID>
        <QuantityPerUnit>10 boxes x 20 bags</QuantityPerUnit>
        <UnitPrice>18</UnitPrice>
        <UnitsInStock>39</UnitsInStock>
        <UnitsOnOrder>0</UnitsOnOrder>
        <ReorderLevel>10</ReorderLevel>
        <Discontinued>false</Discontinued>
      </products>
    </diffgr:before>
  </diffgr:diffgram>
```

Notice how each DataTable row is repeated, and that there is a diffgr:id attribute for each <products> element (we've only shown the first and last of the <products> elements in order to save space). diffgr is the namespace prefix for urn:schemas-microsoft-com:xml-diffgram-v1. For rows that were modified or inserted, ADO.NET adds a diffgr:hasChanges attribute. There's also a <diffgr:before> element after the <XMLProducts> element, which contains a <products> element indicating the previous contents of any modified rows. Obviously the inserted row didn't have any previous contents, so this doesn't have an element in <diffgr:before>.

After the DiffGram has been read into the DataTable, it is in the state that it would be in after changes were made to the data but before AcceptChanges() is called. At this point you can actually roll back changes by calling the RejectChanges() method. By looking at the DataRow.Item property and passing in either DataRowVersion.Original or DataRowVersion.Current, we can see the before and after values in the DataTable.

If you keep a series of `DiffGrams` it is important that you are able to reapply them in the proper order. You probably would not want to try to roll back changes for more then a couple of iterations. You could, however use the `DiffGrams` as a form of logging or for auditing purposes if the DBMS that is being used does not offer these facilities.

Serializing Objects in XML

Serializing is the process of persisting an object to disk. Another part of your application, or even a separate application, can deserialize the object and it will be in the same state it was in prior to serialization. The .NET Framework includes a couple of ways to do this.

In this section, we are going to take a look at the `System.Xml.Serialization` namespace, which contains classes used to serialize objects into XML documents or streams. This means that an object's public properties and public fields are converted into XML elements and/or attributes.

The most important class in the `System.Xml.Serialization` namespace is `XmlSerializer`. To serialize an object, we first need to instantiate an `XmlSerializer` object, specifying the type of the object to serialize. Then we need to instantiate a stream/writer object to write the file to a stream/document. The final step is to call the `Serialize()` method on the `XMLSerializer`, passing it the stream/writer object, and the object to serialize.

Data that can be serialized can be primitive types, fields, arrays, and embedded XML in the form of `XmlElement` and `XmlAttribute` objects.

To deserialize an object from an XML document, we go through the reverse process to that above. We create a stream/reader and an `XmlSerializer` object, and then pass the stream/reader to the `Deserialize()` method. This method returns the deserialized object, although it needs to be cast to the correct type.

> **The XML serializer cannot convert private data, only public data, and it cannot serialize object graphs.**

However, these should not be serious limitations; by carefully designing your classes, they should be easily avoided. If you do need to be able to serialize public and private data as well as an object graph containing many nested objects, then you will want to use the `System.Runtime.Serialization.Formatters.Binary` namespace.

Some of the other things that you can do with `System.Xml.Serialization` classes are:

- ❑ Determine if the data should be an attribute or element
- ❑ Specify the namespace
- ❑ Change the attribute or element name

The links between your object and the XML document are the custom C# attributes that annotate your classes. These attributes are what are used to inform the serializer how to write out the data. There is a tool that is included with the .NET Framework that can help you create these attributes for you if you wish; xsd.exe can do the following:

- Generate an XML schema from an XDR schema file
- Generate an XML schema from an XML file
- Generate DataSet classes from an XSD schema file
- Generate run-time classes that have the custom attributes for XmlSerialization
- Generate an XSD file from classes that you have already developed
- Limit which elements are created in code
- Determine which programming language the generated code should be in (C#, VB.NET, or JScript.NET)
- Create schemas from types in compiled assemblies

You should refer to the Framework documentation for details of command-line options for xsd.exe.

Despite these capabilities, you don't *have* to use xsd.exe to create the classes for serialization. The process is quite simple. Let's take a look at a simple application that serializes a class that reads in the Products data we saved earlier in the chapter. This can be found in the SerialSample1 folder. At the beginning of the example we have very simple code that creates a new Product object, pd, and fills it with some data:

```
private void button1_Click(object sender, System.EventArgs e)
{
    //new products object
    Products pd=new Products();
    //set some properties
    pd.ProductID=200;
    pd.CategoryID=100;
    pd.Discontinued=false;
    pd.ProductName="Serialize Objects";
    pd.QuantityPerUnit="6";
    pd.ReorderLevel=1;
    pd.SupplierID=1;
    pd.UnitPrice=1000;
    pd.UnitsInStock=10;
    pd.UnitsOnOrder=0;
```

The Serialize() method of the XmlSerializer class actually performs the serialization, and it has six overloads. One of the parameters required is a stream to write the data out to. It can be a Stream, TextWriter, or an XmlWriter. In our example we create a TextWriter-based object, tr. The next thing to do is to create the XmlSerializer-based object sr. The XmlSerializer needs to know type information for the object that it is serializing, so we use the typeof keyword with the type that is to be serialized. After the sr object is created, we call the Serialize() method, passing in the tr (Stream-based object), and the object that you want serialized, in this case pd. Be sure to close the stream when you are finished with it.

```
        //new TextWriter and XmlSerializer
        TextWriter tr=new StreamWriter("..\\..\\..\\serialprod.xml");
        XmlSerializer sr=new XmlSerializer(typeof(Products));
        //serialize object
        sr.Serialize(tr,pd);
        tr.Close();
    }
```

Now let's examine the `Products` class, the class that is to be serialized. The only differences between this and any other class that you may write are the C# attributes that have been added. The `XmlRootAttribute` and `XmlElementAttribute` classes in the attributes inherit from the `System.Attribute` class. Don't confuse these attributes with the attributes in an XML document. A C# attribute is simply some declarative information that can be retrieved at runtime by the CLR (see Chapter 6 for more details). In this case, the attributes describe how the object should be serialized:

```
//class that will be serialized.
//attributes determine how object is serialized

[System.Xml.Serialization.XmlRootAttribute(Namespace="", IsNullable=false)]
public class Products
{
    [System.Xml.Serialization.XmlElementAttribute(IsNullable=false)]
    public int ProductID;
    [System.Xml.Serialization.XmlElementAttribute(IsNullable=false)]
    public string ProductName;
    [System.Xml.Serialization.XmlElementAttribute()]
    public int SupplierID;
    [System.Xml.Serialization.XmlElementAttribute()]
    public int CategoryID;
    [System.Xml.Serialization.XmlElementAttribute()]
    public string QuantityPerUnit;
    [System.Xml.Serialization.XmlElementAttribute()]
    public System.Decimal UnitPrice;
    [System.Xml.Serialization.XmlElementAttribute()]
    public short UnitsInStock;
    [System.Xml.Serialization.XmlElementAttribute()]
    public short UnitsOnOrder;
    [System.Xml.Serialization.XmlElementAttribute()]
    public short ReorderLevel;
    [System.Xml.Serialization.XmlElementAttribute()]
    public bool Discontinued;
}
```

The `XmlRootAttribute()` invocation in the attribute above the `Products` class definition identifies this class as a root element (in the XML file produced upon serialization). The attribute containing `XmlElementAttribute()` identifies that the member below the attribute represents an XML element.

If we take a look at the XML document that is created during serialization, you will see that it looks like any other XML document that we may have created, which is the point of the exercise. Let's take a look at the document:

```
<?xml version="1.0" encoding="utf-8"?>
<Products xmlns:xsd="http://www.w3.org/2001/XMLSchema"
          xmlns:xsi="http://www.w3.org/2001/XMLSchema-instance">
   <ProductID>200</ProductID>
   <ProductName>Serialize Objects</ProductName>
   <SupplierID>1</SupplierID>
   <CategoryID>100</CategoryID>
   <QuantityPerUnit>6</QuantityPerUnit>
   <UnitPrice>1000</UnitPrice>
   <UnitsInStock>10</UnitsInStock>
   <UnitsOnOrder>0</UnitsOnOrder>
   <ReorderLevel>1</ReorderLevel>
   <Discontinued>false</Discontinued>
</Products>
```

There is nothing out of the ordinary here. We could use this any way that you would use an XML document. We could do a transform on it and display it as HTML, load into a `DataSet` using ADO.NET, load an `XmlDocument` with it, or, as you can see in the example, deserialize it and create an object in the same state that pd was in prior to serializing it (which is exactly what we're doing with our second button).

Next we will add another button event handler to deserialize a new `Products`-based object newPd. This time we will be using a `FileStream` object to read in the XML:

```
private void button2_Click(object sender, System.EventArgs e)
{
    //create a reference to products type
    Products newPd;
    //new filestream to open serialized object
    FileStream f=new FileStream("..\\..\\..\\serialprod.xml",FileMode.Open);
```

Once again, we create a new `XmlSerializer`, passing in the type information of `Product`. We can then make the call to the `Deserialize()` method. Note that we still need to do an explicit cast when we create the newPd object. At this point newPd is in exactly the same state as pd was:

```
    //new serializer
    XmlSerializer newSr=new XmlSerializer(typeof(Products));
    //deserialize the object
    newPd=(Products)newSr.Deserialize(f);
    //load it in the list box.
    listBox1.Items.Add(newPd.ProductName);
    f.Close();
}
```

The example that we just looked at is very simple – let's look at a more complex example using the `XmlSerializer` class. We'll make each field `private`, accessible only via `get` and `set` properties in the `Products` class. We will also add a `Discount` attribute to the XML file, to demonstrate that attributes can be serialized too.

This example can be found in the `SerialSample2` folder; here's what our new `Products` class looks like:

```
[System.Xml.Serialization.XmlRootAttribute()]
public class Products
{
    private int prodId;
    private string prodName;
    private int suppId;
    private int catId;
    private string qtyPerUnit;
    private Decimal unitPrice;
    private short unitsInStock;
    private short unitsOnOrder;
    private short reorderLvl;
    private bool discont;
    private int disc;

    //add the Discount attribute
    [XmlAttributeAttribute(AttributeName="Discount")]
    public int Discount
    {
        get {return disc;}
        set {disc=value;}
    }

    [XmlElementAttribute()]
    public int ProductID
    {
        get {return prodId;}
        set {prodId=value;}
    }

    ...
    // properties for most of the fields are not shown for sake of brevity
    ...

    [XmlElementAttribute()]
    public bool Discontinued
    {
        get {return discont;}
        set {discont=value;}
    }
}
```

You will also need to make the following modifications to the button click event handlers:

```
private void button1_Click(object sender, System.EventArgs e)
{
    //new products object
    Products pd=new Products();
    //set some properties
    pd.ProductID=200;
```

```
        pd.CategoryID=100;
        pd.Discontinued=false;
        pd.ProductName="Serialize Objects";
        pd.QuantityPerUnit="6";
        pd.ReorderLevel=1;
        pd.SupplierID=1;
        pd.UnitPrice=1000;
        pd.UnitsInStock=10;
        pd.UnitsOnOrder=0;
        pd.Discount=2;
        //new TextWriter and XmlSerializer
        TextWriter tr=new StreamWriter("..\\..\\..\\serialprod1.xml");
        XmlSerializer sr=new XmlSerializer(typeof(Products));

        //serialize object
        sr.Serialize(tr,pd);
        tr.Close();
    }
    private void button2_Click(object sender, System.EventArgs e)
    {
        //create a reference to products type
        Products newPd;
        //new filestream to open serialized object
        FileStream f=new FileStream("..\\..\\..\\serialprod1.xml",FileMode.Open);
        //new serializer
        XmlSerializer newSr=new XmlSerializer(typeof(Products));
        //deserialize the object
        newPd=(Products)newSr.Deserialize(f);
        //load it in the list box.
        listBox1.Items.Add(newPd.ProductName);
        f.Close();
    }
```

Running this code will give the same results as the earlier example, but with one difference. The output for this (serialprod1.xml) looks like this:

```xml
<?xml version="1.0" encoding="utf-8"?>
<Products xmlns:xsd="http://www.w3.org/2001/XMLSchema"
          xmlns:xsi="http://www.w3.org/2001/XMLSchema-instance"
          Discount="2">
    <ProductID>200</ProductID>
    <ProductName>Serialize Objects</ProductName>
    <SupplierID>1</SupplierID>
    <CategoryID>100</CategoryID>
    <QuantityPerUnit>6</QuantityPerUnit>
    <UnitPrice>1000</UnitPrice>
    <UnitsInStock>10</UnitsInStock>
    <UnitsOnOrder>0</UnitsOnOrder>
    <ReorderLevel>1</ReorderLevel>
    <Discontinued>false</Discontinued>
</Products>
```

Notice the `Discount` attribute on the `Products` element. So, now that you have property accessors defined, you can add more complex validation code in the properties.

What about situations where we have derived classes, and possibly properties that return an array? `XmlSerializer` has that covered as well. Let's look at a slightly more complex example that deals with these issues.

First we define three new classes, `Product`, `BookProduct` (derived from `Product`), and `Inventory` (which contains both of the other classes):

```
public class Product
{
   private int prodId;
   private string prodName;
   private int suppId;
   public Product() {}
   public int  ProductID
   {
      get {return prodId;}
      set {prodId=value;}
   }
   public string ProductName
   {
      get {return prodName;}
      set {prodName=value;}
   }
   public int SupplierID
   {
      get {return suppId;}
      set {suppId=value;}
   }
}

public class BookProduct : Product
{
   private string isbnNum;
   public BookProduct() {}
   public string ISBN
   {
      get {return isbnNum;}
      set {isbnNum=value;}
   }
}

public class Inventory
{
   private Product[] stuff;
   public Inventory() {}
   //need to have an attribute entry for each data type
   [XmlArrayItem("Prod",typeof(Product)),
   XmlArrayItem("Book",typeof(BookProduct))]
   public Product[] InventoryItems
   {
      get {return stuff;}
      set {stuff=value;}
   }
}
```

The `Inventory` class is the one of real interest to us here. If we are to serialize this class, we need to insert an attribute containing `XmlArrayItem` constructors for each type that can be added to the array. You should note that `XmlArrayItem` is the name of the .NET attribute represented by the `XmlArrayItemAttribute` class.

The first parameter supplied to these constructors is what we would like the element name to be in the XML document that is created during serialization. If we leave off the `ElementName` parameter, the elements will be given the same name as the object type (`Product` and `BookProduct` in this case). The second parameter that must be specified is the type of the object.

There is also an `XmlArrayAttribute` class that you would use if the property were returning an array of objects or primitive type. Since we are returning different types in the array, we use `XmlArrayItemAttribute`, which allows the higher level of control.

In the `button1_Click()` event handler, we create a new `Product` object and a new `BookProduct` object (`newProd` and `newBook`). We add data to the various properties of each object, and add the objects to a `Product` array. We then create a new `Inventory` object and pass in the array as a parameter. We can then serialize the `Inventory` object to recreate it at a later time:

```
private void button1_Click(object sender, System.EventArgs e)
{
    //create new book and bookproducts objects
    Product newProd=new Product();
    BookProduct newBook=new BookProduct();
    //set some properties
    newProd.ProductID=100;
    newProd.ProductName="Product Thing";
    newProd.SupplierID=10;
    newBook.ProductID=101;
    newBook.ProductName="How to Use Your New Product Thing";
    newBook.SupplierID=10;
    newBook.ISBN="123456789";
    //add the items to an array
    Product[] addProd={newProd,newBook};
    //new inventory object using the addProd array
    Inventory inv=new Inventory();
    inv.InventoryItems=addProd;
    //serialize the Inventory object
    TextWriter tr=new StreamWriter("..\\..\\..\\order.xml");
    XmlSerializer sr=new XmlSerializer(typeof(Inventory));
    sr.Serialize(tr,inv);
    tr.Close();
}
```

This is what the XML document looks like:

```
<?xml version="1.0" encoding="utf-8"?>
<Inventory xmlns:xsd="http://www.w3.org/2001/XMLSchema">
        xmlns:xsi="http://www.w3.org/2001/XMLSchema-instance">
    <InventoryItems>
      <Prod>
        <ProductID>100</ProductID>
        <ProductName>Product Thing</ProductName>
        <SupplierID>10</SupplierID>
      </Prod>
      <Book>
        <ProductID>101</ProductID>
        <ProductName>How to Use Your New Product Thing</ProductName>
        <SupplierID>10</SupplierID>
        <ISBN>123456789</ISBN>
      </Book>
    </InventoryItems>
</Inventory>
```

The `button2_Click()` event handler implements deserialization of the `Inventory` object. Notice that we iterate through the array in the newly-created `newInv` object to show that it is the same data:

```
private void button2_Click(object sender, System.EventArgs e)
{
    Inventory newInv;
    FileStream f=new FileStream("..\\..\\..\\order.xml",FileMode.Open);
    XmlSerializer newSr=new XmlSerializer(typeof(Inventory));
    newInv=(Inventory)newSr.Deserialize(f);
    foreach(Product prod in newInv.InventoryItems)
        listBox1.Items.Add(prod.ProductName);
    f.Close();
}
```

Serialization Without Sourcecode Access

Well this all works great, but what if you don't have access to the sourcecode for the types that are being serialized? You can't add the attribute if you don't have the source. There is another way. You can use the `XmlAttributes` class and the `XmlAttributeOverrides` class. Together these classes will allow you to accomplish exactly what we have just done, but without adding the attributes. Let's look at an example of how this works, taken from the `SerialSample4` folder.

For this example, imagine that the `Inventory`, `Product`, and the derived `BookProduct` classes are in a separate DLL, and that we don't have the source. The `Product` and `BookProduct` classes are the same as in the previous example, but you should note that there are now no attributes added to the `Inventory` class:

```
public class Inventory
{
    private Product[] stuff;
    public Inventory() {}
    public Product[] InventoryItems
    {
        get {return stuff;}
        set {stuff=value;}
    }
}
```

Let's now deal with the serialization in the `button1_Click()` event handler:

```
private void button1_Click(object sender, System.EventArgs e)
{
```

The first step in the serialization process is to create an `XmlAttributes` object, and an `XmlElementAttribute` object for each data type that you will be overriding:

```
XmlAttributes attrs=new XmlAttributes();
attrs.XmlElements.Add(new XmlElementAttribute("Book",typeof(BookProduct)));
attrs.XmlElements.Add(new XmlElementAttribute("Product",typeof(Product)));
```

Here you can see that we are adding new `XmlElementAttribute` objects to the `XmlElements` collection of the `XmlAttributes` class. The `XmlAttributes` class has properties that correspond to the attributes that can be applied; `XmlArray` and `XmlArrayItems`, which we looked at in the previous example, are just a few of these. We now have an `XmlAttributes` object with two `XmlElementAttribute`-based objects added to the `XmlElements` collection.

The next thing we have to do is create an `XmlAttributeOverrides` object:

```
XmlAttributeOverrides attrOver=new XmlAttributeOverrides();
attrOver.Add(typeof(Inventory),"InventoryItems",attrs);
```

The `Add()` method of this class has two overloads. The first one takes the type information of the object to override and the `XmlAttributes` object that we created earlier. The other overload, which is the one we are using, also takes a string value that is the member in the overridden object. In our case we want to override the `InventoryItems` member in the `Inventory` class.

When we create the `XmlSerializer` object, we add the `XmlAttributeOverrides` object as a parameter. Now the `XmlSerializer` knows which types we want to override and what we need to return for those types.

```
//create the Product and Book objects
Product newProd=new Product();
BookProduct newBook=new BookProduct();
newProd.ProductID=100;
newProd.ProductName="Product Thing";
newProd.SupplierID=10;
newBook.ProductID=101;
newBook.ProductName="How to Use Your New Product Thing";
newBook.SupplierID=10;
newBook.ISBN="123456789";
Product[] addProd={newProd,newBook};

Inventory inv=new Inventory();
inv.InventoryItems=addProd;
TextWriter tr=new StreamWriter("..\\..\\..\\inventory.xml");
XmlSerializer sr=new XmlSerializer(typeof(Inventory),attrOver);
sr.Serialize(tr,inv);
tr.Close();
}
```

If we execute the `Serialize()` method we will end up with this XML output:

```
<?xml version="1.0" encoding="utf-8"?>
<Inventory xmlns:xsd="http://www.w3.org/2001/XMLSchema">
        xmlns:xsi="http://www.w3.org/2001/XMLSchema-instance">
    <Product>
        <ProductID>100</ProductID>
        <ProductName>Product Thing</ProductName>
        <SupplierID>10</SupplierID>
    </Product>
    <Book>
        <ProductID>101</ProductID>
        <ProductName>How to Use Your New Product Thing</ProductName>
        <SupplierID>10</SupplierID>
        <ISBN>123456789</ISBN>
    </Book>
</Inventory>
```

As you can see, we get the same XML as we did with the earlier example. In order to deserialize this object and recreate the `Inventory`-based object that we started out with, we need to create all of the same `XmlAttributes`, `XmlElementAttribute`, and `XmlAttributeOverrides` objects that we created when we serialized the object. Once we do that we can read in the XML and recreate the `Inventory` object just as we did before. Here is the code to deserialize the `Inventory` object:

```
private void button2_Click(object sender, System.EventArgs e)
{
    //create the new XmlAttributes collection
    XmlAttributes attrs=new XmlAttributes();
    //add the type information to the elements collection
    attrs.XmlElements.Add(new XmlElementAttribute("Book",typeof(BookProduct)));
    attrs.XmlElements.Add(new XmlElementAttribute("Product",typeof(Product)));
    XmlAttributeOverrides attrOver=new XmlAttributeOverrides();
    //add to the Attributes collection

    attrOver.Add(typeof(Inventory),"InventoryItems",attrs);
    //need a new Inventory object to deserialize to
    Inventory newInv;
    //deserialize and load data into the listbox from deserialized object
    FileStream f=new FileStream("..\\..\\..\\inventory.xml",FileMode.Open);
    XmlSerializer newSr=new XmlSerializer(typeof(Inventory),attrOver);
    newInv=(Inventory)newSr.Deserialize(f);
    if(newInv!=null)
    {
        foreach(Product prod in newInv.InventoryItems)
            listBox1.Items.Add(prod.ProductName);
    }
    f.Close();
}
```

Notice that the first few lines of code are identical to the code we used to serialize the object.

The `System.Xml.XmlSerialization` namespace provides a very powerful toolset for serializing objects to XML. By serializing and de-serializing objects to XML instead of to binary format, you are given the option of doing something else with this XML, greatly adding to the flexibility of your designs.

Summary

In this chapter we explored many of the corners of the `System.Xml` namespace of the .NET Framework. We looked at how to read and write XML documents using the very fast `XmlReader` and `XmlWriter`-based classes. We looked at how the DOM is implemented in .NET, and how to use the power of DOM. We saw that XML and ADO.NET are indeed very closely related. A `DataSet` and an XML document are just two different views of the same underlying architecture. And, of course, we visited XPath and XSL Transforms.

Finally, we serialized objects out to XML, and were able to bring them back to life with just a couple of method calls.

XML is going to be, if it isn't already, an important part of your application development over the next several years. The .NET Framework has made available a very rich and powerful toolset for working with XML. For a further exploration of XML and C#, with emphasis on XPath and XSLT, see "*Data-Centric .NET Programming with C#*" (Wrox Press, ISBN 1-861005-92-x).

In the next chapter we will be looking at how to handle files and the Registry using C# classes.

12

File and Registry Operations

In this chapter, we will examine how to perform tasks involving reading from and writing to files and the system registry in C#. In particular, we are going to cover:

❑ Exploring the directory structure, finding out what files and folders are present and checking their properties

❑ Moving, copying, and deleting files and folders

❑ Reading and writing text in files

❑ Reading and writing keys in the Registry

Microsoft has provided very intuitive object models covering these areas, and during this chapter we will show you how to use .NET base classes to perform the tasks mentioned above. For the case of file system operations, the relevant classes are almost all found in the `System.IO` namespace, while registry operations are dealt with by a couple of classes in the `Microsoft.Win32` namespace.

> *The .NET base classes also include a number of classes and interfaces in the*
> `System.Runtime.Serialization` *namespace that are concerned with serialization – that is the process of converting some data (for example, the contents of a document) into a stream of bytes for storage somewhere. We won't be focusing on these classes in this chapter; we will be focusing on the classes that are available to give you direct access to files.*

Note that although security affects all areas, security is particularly important when modifying files or registry entries. The whole area of security is covered separately in Chapter 23. In this chapter, however, we will simply assume that you have sufficient access rights to run all the examples that modify files or registry entries, which should be the case if you are running from an account with administrator privileges.

Managing the File System

The classes that are used to browse around the file system and perform operations, such as moving, copying, and deleting files, are shown in the following diagram. The namespace of each class is shown in brackets beneath the class name in the diagram:

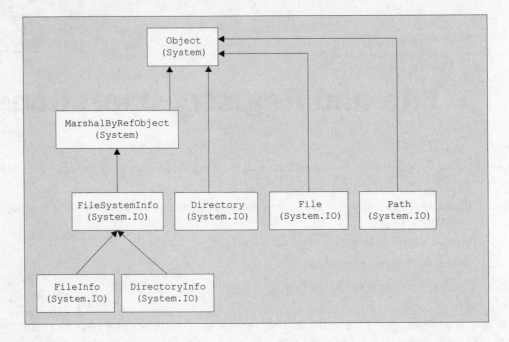

The purposes of these classes are:

❑ `System.MarshalByRefObject` – Base object class for .NET classes that are remotable; permits marshaling of data between application domains

❑ `FileSystemInfo` – Base class that represents any file system object

❑ `FileInfo` and `File` – These classes represent a file on the file system

❑ `DirectoryInfo` and `Directory` – These classes represent a folder on the file system

❑ `Path` – This class contains static members that you can use to manipulate pathnames

On Windows, the objects that contain files and are used to organize the file system are termed **folders**. *For example, in the path* C:\My Documents\ReadMe.txt, ReadMe.txt *is a file and* My Documents *is a folder. Folder is a very Windows-specific term: On virtually every other operating system the term* **directory** *is used in place of folder, and in accordance with the Microsoft's desire for .NET to ultimately be platform-independent, the corresponding .NET base classes are called* Directory *and* DirectoryInfo. *However, due to the potential for confusion with LDAP directories (as discussed in Chapter 13), and because this is a Windows book, we'll stick to the term* **folder** *in this discussion.*

.NET Classes that Represent Files and Folders

You will notice from the above list that there are two classes used to represent a folder and two classes for a file. Which one of these classes you use will depend largely on how many times you need to access that folder or file:

❏ `Directory` and `File` contain only static methods and are never instantiated. You use these classes by supplying the path to the appropriate file system object whenever you call a member method. If you only want to do one operation on a folder or file then using these classes is more efficient, because it saves the overhead of instantiating a .NET class.

❏ `DirectoryInfo` and `FileInfo` implement roughly the same public methods as `Directory` and `File`, as well as some public properties and constructors, but they are stateful and the members of these classes are not static. You need to actually instantiate these classes and then each instance is associated with a particular folder or file. This means that these classes are more efficient if you're performing multiple operations using the same object, because they will read in the authentication and other information for the appropriate file system object on construction, and then will not need to read that information again, no matter how many methods and so on you call against each object (class instance). In comparison, the corresponding stateless classes will need to check the details of the file or folder again with every method you call.

In this section, we will be mostly using the `FileInfo` and `DirectoryInfo` classes, but it happens that many (though not all) of the methods we call are also implemented by `File` and `Directory` (although in those cases these methods require an extra parameter – the pathname of the file system object, and a couple of the methods have slightly different names). For example:

```
FileInfo myFile = new FileInfo(@"C:\Program Files\My Program\ReadMe.txt");
myFile.CopyTo(@"D:\Copies\ReadMe.txt");
```

Has the same effect as:

```
File.Copy(@"C:\Program Files\My Program\ReadMe.txt", @"D:\Copies\ReadMe.txt");
```

The first code snippet above will take slightly longer to execute, because of the need to instantiate a `FileInfo` object, `myFile`, but it leaves `myFile` ready for you to perform further actions on the same file.

You instantiate a `FileInfo` or `DirectoryInfo` class by passing to the constructor a string containing the path to the corresponding file system. We've just illustrated the process for a file. For a folder the code looks similar:

```
DirectoryInfo myFolder = new DirectoryInfo(@"C:\Program Files");
```

If the path represents an object that does not exist, then an exception will not be thrown at construction, but will instead be thrown the first time that you call a method that actually requires the corresponding file system object to be there. You can find out whether the object exists and is of the appropriate type by checking the `Exists` property, which is implemented by both of these classes:

```
FileInfo test = new FileInfo(@"C:\Windows");
Console.WriteLine(test.Exists.ToString());
```

Note that for this property to return true, the corresponding file system object must be of the appropriate type. In other words, if you instantiate a FileInfo object supplying the path of a folder, or you instantiate a DirectoryInfo object, giving it the path of a file, Exists will have the value false. On the other hand, most of the properties and methods of these objects will return a value if at all possible – they won't necessarily throw an exception just because the wrong type of object has been called, unless they are asked to do something that really is impossible. For example, the above code snippet will first display false (because C:\Windows is a folder – at least on my computer!), but will still then correctly display the time the folder was created – because a folder still has that information. On the other hand, if we then tried to open the folder as if it was a file, using the FileInfo.Open() method, we'd then get an exception.

After you have established whether the corresponding file system object exists, you can (if you are using the FileInfo or DirectoryInfo class) find out information about it using a number of properties, including:

Name	Description
CreationTime	Time file or folder was created
DirectoryName (FileInfo), Parent (DirectoryInfo)	Full pathname of the containing folder
Exists	Whether file or folder exists
Extension	Extension of the file; returns blank for folders
FullName	Full pathname of the file or folder
LastAccessTime	Time file or folder was last accessed
LastWriteTime	Time file or folder was last modified
Name	Name of the file or folder
Root	The root portion of the path (DirectoryInfo only)
Length	The size of the file in bytes (FileInfo only)

You can also perform actions on the file system object using these methods:

Name	Purpose
Create()	Creates a folder or empty file of the given name. For a FileInfo this also returns a stream object to let you write to the file. *We cover streams later in the chapter.*
Delete()	Deletes the file or folder. For folders there is an option for the Delete to be recursive.

Name	Purpose
MoveTo()	Moves and/or renames the file or folder.
CopyTo()	(FileInfo only) Copies the file. Note that there is no copy method for folders. If copying complete directory trees you'll need to individually copy each file and create new folders corresponding to the old folders.
GetDirectories()	(DirectoryInfo only) Returns an array of DirectoryInfo objects representing all folders contained in this folder.
GetFiles()	(DirectoryInfo only) Returns an array of FileInfo objects representing all files contained in this folder.
GetFileSystemObjects()	(DirectoryInfo only) Returns FileInfo and DirectoryInfo objects representing all objects contained in this folder, as an array of FileSystemInfo references.

Note that the above tables give the main properties and methods, and are not intended to be exhaustive.

> *In the above tables we've not listed most of the properties or methods that allow you to write to or read the data in files. This is actually done using stream objects, which we'll cover later in the chapter. FileInfo also implements a number of methods Open(), OpenRead(), OpenText(), OpenWrite(), Create(), and CreateText() that return stream objects for this purpose.*

Interestingly, the creation time, last access time, and last write time are all writable:

```
// displays the creation time of a file, then changes it and displays it
// again
 FileInfo test = new FileInfo(@"C:\My Documents\MyFile.txt");
Console.WriteLine(test.Exists.ToString());
Console.WriteLine(test.CreationTime.ToString());
test.CreationTime = new DateTime(2001, 1, 1, 7, 30, 0);
Console.WriteLine(test.CreationTime.ToString());
```

Being able to manually modify these properties might seem strange, but it can be quite useful. For example, if you have a program that effectively modifies a file by simply reading it in, then deleting it and creating new file with the new contents, then you'd probably want to modify the creation date to match the original creation date of the old file.

The Path Class

The Path class is not a class that you would instantiate. Rather, it exposes some static methods that make operations on pathnames easier. For example, suppose you want to display the full pathname for a file, ReadMe.txt in the folder C:\My Documents. You could find the path to the file with the following:

```
Console.WriteLine(Path.Combine(@"C:\My Documents", "ReadMe.txt"));
```

Using the `Path` class is a lot easier than trying to fiddle about with separation symbols manually, especially because the `Path` class is aware of different formats for pathnames on different operating systems. At the time of writing, Windows is the only operating system supported by .NET, but if, for example, .NET was later ported to Unix, `Path` would be able to cope with Unix paths, in which /, rather than \, is used as a separator in pathnames. `Path.Combine()` is the method of this class that you are likely to use most often, but `Path` also implements other methods that supply information about the path or the required format for it.

In the following section we present an example that illustrates how to browse directories and view the properties of files.

Example: A File Browser

In this section we'll present a sample C# application called `FileProperties`, which presents a simple user interface that allows you to browse around the file system, and view the creation time, last access time, last write time, and size of files.

The `FileProperties` application looks like this. You type in the name of a folder or file in the main textbox at the top of the window and click the **Display** button. If you type in the path to a folder, its contents are listed in the listboxes. If you type in the path to a file, its details are displayed in the textboxes at the bottom of the form and the contents of its parent folder are displayed in the listboxes. The screenshot shows `FileProperties` being used to examine a folder:

The user can very easily navigate around the file system by clicking on any of the folders in the right-hand listbox to move down to that folder, or by clicking the Up button to move up to the parent folder. In the above screenshot I typed in C:\7043 into the main textbox to get the contents of that folder then used the listbox to navigate down. The user can also select a file by clicking on its name in the listbox – in which case its properties are displayed in the textboxes. The next screenshot shows this:

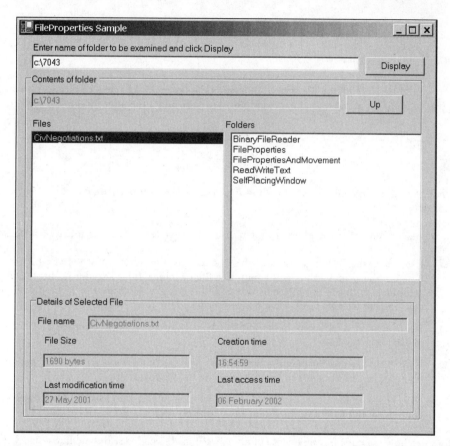

Note that if we'd wanted, we could also display the creation time, last access time, and last modification time for folders too – DirectoryInfo does implement the appropriate properties. We are going to display these properties only for a selected file to keep things simple.

We create the project as a standard C# Windows application in Visual Studio.NET, and add the various textboxes and the listbox from the Windows Forms area of the toolbox. We've also renamed the controls with the more intuitive names of textBoxInput, textBoxFolder, buttonDisplay, buttonUp, listBoxFiles, listBoxFolders, textBoxFileName, txtBoxCreationTime, textBoxLastAccessTime, textBoxLastWriteTime, and txtBoxFileSize.

Then we need to add some code. Firstly, we need to indicate that we will be using the `System.IO` namespace:

```
using System;
using System.Drawing;
using System.Collections;
using System.ComponentModel;
using System.Windows.Forms;
using System.Data;
using System.IO;
```

We need to do this for all the file system-related examples in this chapter, but we won't explicitly show this part of the code in the remaining examples. We then add a member field to the main form:

```
public class Form1 : System.Windows.Forms.Form
{
    private string currentFolderPath;
```

`currentFolderPath` will store the path of the folder whose contents are currently being shown in the listboxes.

Now we need to add event handlers for the user-generated events. The possible user inputs are:

❑ User clicks the **Display** button: In this case we need to figure out whether what the user has typed in the main textbox is the path to a file or folder. If it's a folder we list the files and subfolders of this folder in the listboxes. If it is a file, we still do this for the folder containing that file, but we also display the file properties in the lower textboxes.

❑ User clicks on a file name in the **Files** listbox: In this case we display the properties of this file in the lower textboxes.

❑ User clicks on a folder name in the **Folders** listbox: In this case we clear all the controls and then display the contents of this subfolder in the listboxes.

❑ User clicks on the **Up** button: In this case we clear all the controls and then display the contents of the parent of the folder being displayed in the listboxes.

Before we show the code for the event handlers, we'll list the code for the methods that will actually do all the work. First, we need to clear the contents of all the controls. This method is fairly self-explanatory:

```
protected void ClearAllFields()
{
    listBoxFolders.Items.Clear();
    listBoxFiles.Items.Clear();
    textBoxFolder.Text = "";
    textBoxFileName.Text = "";
    textBoxCreationTime.Text = "";
    textBoxLastAccessTime.Text = "";
    textBoxLastWriteTime.Text = "";
    textBoxFileSize.Text = "";
}
```

Secondly, we define a method, `DisplayFileInfo()`, which handles the process of displaying the information for a given file in the textboxes. This method takes one parameter, the full pathname of the file, and it works by creating a `FileInfo` object based on this path:

```
protected void DisplayFileInfo(string fileFullName)
{
   FileInfo theFile = new FileInfo(fileFullName);
   if (!theFile.Exists)
      throw new FileNotFoundException("File not found: " + fileFullName);
   textBoxFileName.Text = theFile.Name;
   textBoxCreationTime.Text = theFile.CreationTime.ToLongTimeString();
   textBoxLastAccessTime.Text = theFile.LastAccessTime.ToLongDateString();
   textBoxLastWriteTime.Text = theFile.LastWriteTime.ToLongDateString();
   textBoxFileSize.Text = theFile.Length.ToString() + " bytes";
}
```

Note that we take the precaution of throwing an exception if there are any problems locating a file here. The exception will be handled in the calling routine (one of the event handlers). Finally, we define a method, `DisplayFolderList()`, which displays the contents of a given folder in the two listboxes. The full pathname of the folder is passed in as a parameter to this method:

```
protected void DisplayFolderList(string folderFullName)
{
   DirectoryInfo theFolder = new DirectoryInfo(folderFullName);
   if (!theFolder.Exists)
      throw new DirectoryNotFoundException("Folder not found: "
                                    + folderFullName);
   ClearAllFields();
   textBoxFolder.Text = theFolder.FullName;
   currentFolderPath = theFolder.FullName;

   // list all subfolders in folder
   foreach(DirectoryInfo nextFolder in theFolder.GetDirectories())
      listBoxFolders.Items.Add(nextFolder.Name);

   // list all files in folder
   foreach(FileInfo nextFile in theFolder.GetFiles())
      listBoxFiles.Items.Add(nextFile.Name);
}
```

Now we will examine the event handlers. The handler for the event of the user clicking the **Display** button is the most complex, since it needs to handle three different possibilities for the text the user typed in; it could be the pathname of a folder, the pathname of a file, or neither:

```
protected void OnDisplayButtonClick(object sender, EventArgs e)
{
   try
   {
      string folderPath = textBoxInput.Text;
      DirectoryInfo theFolder = new DirectoryInfo(folderPath);
      if (theFolder.Exists)
      {
```

```
            DisplayFolderList(theFolder.FullName);
            return;
        }
        FileInfo theFile = new FileInfo(folderPath);
        if (theFile.Exists)
        {
            DisplayFolderList(theFile.Directory.FullName);
            int index = listBoxFiles.Items.IndexOf(theFile.Name);
            listBoxFiles.SetSelected(index, true);
            return;
        }
        throw new FileNotFoundException("There is no file or folder with "
                                    + "this name: " + textBoxInput.Text);

    }
    catch(Exception ex)
    {
        MessageBox.Show(ex.Message);
    }
}
```

In the above code, we establish if the supplied text represents a folder or file by in turn instantiating `DirectoryInfo` and `FileInfo` instances and examining the `Exists` property of each object. If neither exists, then we throw an exception. If it's a folder, we call `DisplayFolderList()` to populate the listboxes. If it's a file, we need to populate the listboxes and sort out the textboxes that display the file properties. We handle this case by first populating the listboxes. We then programmatically select the appropriate file name in the **Files** listbox. This has exactly the same effect as if the user had selected that item – it will raise the item-selected event. We can then simply exit the current event handler, knowing that the selected item event handler will immediately be called to display the file properties.

The following code is the event handler that gets called when an item in the files listbox is selected, either by the user or, as indicated above, programmatically. It simply constructs the full pathname of the selected file, and passes this to the `DisplayFileInfo()` method that we presented earlier:

```
protected void OnListBoxFilesSelected(object sender, EventArgs e)
{
    try
    {
        string selectedString = listBoxFiles.SelectedItem.ToString();
        string fullFileName = Path.Combine(currentFolderPath, selectedString);
        DisplayFileInfo(fullFileName);
    }
    catch(Exception ex)
    {
        MessageBox.Show(ex.Message);
    }
}
```

The event handler for the selection of a folder in the **Folders** listbox is implemented in a very similar way, except that in this case we call `DisplayFolderList()` to update the contents of the listboxes:

```
protected void OnListBoxFoldersSelected(object sender, EventArgs e)
{
   try
   {
      string selectedString = listBoxFolders.SelectedItem.ToString();
      string fullPathName = Path.Combine(currentFolderPath, selectedString);
      DisplayFolderList(fullPathName);
   }
   catch(Exception ex)
   {
      MessageBox.Show(ex.Message);
   }
}
```

Finally, when the **Up** button is clicked, `DisplayFolderList()` must also be called, except that this time we need to obtain the path of the parent of the folder currently being displayed. This is obtained through the `FileInfo.DirectoryName` property, which returns the parent folder path:

```
protected void OnUpButtonClick(object sender, EventArgs e)
{
   try
   {
      string folderPath = new FileInfo(currentFolderPath).DirectoryName;
      DisplayFolderList(folderPath);
   }
   catch(Exception ex)
   {
      MessageBox.Show(ex.Message);
   }
}
```

Note that for this project, we have not displayed the code that adds the event handlers to the relevant events for the controls. We do not need to add this code manually, since, as noted in Chapter 7, we can use the **Properties** window in Visual Studio to associate each event handler with the event.

Moving, Copying, and Deleting Files

We have already mentioned that moving and deleting files or folders is done by the `MoveTo()` and `Delete()` methods of the `FileInfo` and `DirectoryInfo` classes. The equivalent methods on the `File` and `Directory` classes are `Move()` and `Delete()`. The `FileInfo` and `File` classes also respectively implement methods, `CopyTo()` and `Copy()`. No methods exist to copy complete folders, however – you need to do that by copying each file in the folder.

Use of all these methods is quite intuitive – and you can find full details in MSDN. In this section we are going to illustrate their use for the particular cases of calling the static `Move()`, `Copy()`, and `Delete()` methods on the `File` class. To do this we will develop our previous `FileProperties` example into a new example, `FilePropertiesAndMovement`. This example will have the extra feature that whenever the properties of a file are displayed, the application gives us the option of deleting that file, or moving or copying it to another location.

Example: FilePropertiesAndMovement

The new example looks like this:

From this screenshot, we can see that it is very similar in appearance to the `FileProperties` example, except that there is an additional group of three buttons and a textbox at the bottom of the window. These controls are only enabled when the example is actually displaying the properties of a file – at other times, they are disabled. We've also squashed the existing controls up a bit to stop the main form from getting too big. When the properties of a file are displayed, `FilePropertiesAndMovement` automatically places the full pathname of that file in the bottom textbox for the user to edit. The user can then click on any of the buttons to perform the appropriate operation. When they do, an appropriate message box is displayed that confirms the action. In the above case, if the user clicks on Copy To we will see this message:

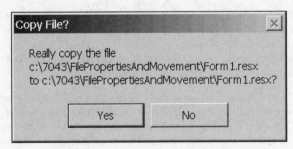

Assuming the user confirms the action, it will go ahead. In the case of moving or deleting a file, we obviously can't carry on displaying the contents of that file in the same location. As well as this, if we copy a file to another filename in the same folder, our display will also be out of date. In all of these cases, the example resets its controls to display only the containing folder after the file operation.

To code this up, we need to add the relevant controls, as well as their event handlers to the code for the `FileProperties` example. We have given the new controls the names `buttonDelete`, `buttonCopyTo`, `buttonMoveTo`, and `textBoxNewPath`.

We'll look first at the event handler that gets called when the user hits the **Delete** button;

```
protected void OnDeleteButtonClick(object sender, EventArgs e)
{
   try
   {
      string filePath = Path.Combine(currentFolderPath,
                                 textBoxFileName.Text);
      string query = "Really delete the file\n" + filePath + "?";
      if (MessageBox.Show(query,
         "Delete File?", MessageBoxButtons.YesNo) == DialogResult.Yes)
      {
         File.Delete(filePath);
         DisplayFolderList(currentFolderPath);
      }
   }
   catch(Exception ex)
   {
      MessageBox.Show("Unable to delete file. The following exception"
                     + " occurred:\n" + ex.Message, "Failed");
   }
}
```

The code for this method is contained in a `try` block because of the obvious risk of an exception being thrown if, for example, we don't have permission to delete the file, or the file got moved by another process in the time between our example displaying it, and the user hitting the **Delete** button. We construct the path of the file to be deleted from the `CurrentParentPath` field, which will contain the path of the parent folder, and the text in the `textBoxFileName` textbox, which will contain the name of the file.

The methods to move and copy the file are structured in a very similar manner:

```
protected void OnMoveButtonClick(object sender, EventArgs e)
{
   try
   {
      string filePath = Path.Combine(currentFolderPath,
                                 textBoxFileName.Text);
      string query = "Really move the file\n" + filePath + "\nto "
                     + textBoxNewPath.Text + "?";
      if (MessageBox.Show(query,
         "Move File?", MessageBoxButtons.YesNo) == DialogResult.Yes)
      {
```

```
            File.Move(filePath, textBoxNewPath.Text);
            DisplayFolderList(currentFolderPath);
        }
    }
    catch(Exception ex)
    {
        MessageBox.Show("Unable to move file. The following exception"
                    + " occurred:\n" + ex.Message, "Failed");
    }
}

protected void OnCopyButtonClick(object sender, EventArgs e)
{
    try
    {
        string filePath = Path.Combine(currentFolderPath,
                                    textBoxFileName.Text);
        string query = "Really copy the file\n" + filePath + "\nto "
                    + textBoxNewPath.Text + "?";
        if (MessageBox.Show(query,
            "Copy File?", MessageBoxButtons.YesNo) == DialogResult.Yes)
        {
            File.Copy(filePath, textBoxNewPath.Text);
            DisplayFolderList(currentFolderPath);
        }
    }
    catch(Exception ex)
    {
        MessageBox.Show("Unable to copy file. The following exception"
                    + " occurred:\n" + ex.Message, "Failed");
    }
}
```

We're not quite done yet. We also need to make sure the new buttons and textbox are enabled and disabled at the appropriate times. To enable them when we are displaying the contents of a file, we add the following code to `DisplayFileInfo()`:

```
protected void DisplayFileInfo(string fileFullName)
{
    FileInfo theFile = new FileInfo(fileFullName);
    if (!theFile.Exists)
        throw new FileNotFoundException("File not found: " + fileFullName);

    textBoxFileName.Text = theFile.Name;
    textBoxCreationTime.Text = theFile.CreationTime.ToLongTimeString();
    textBoxLastAccessTime.Text = theFile.LastAccessTime.ToLongDateString();
    textBoxLastWriteTime.Text = theFile.LastWriteTime.ToLongDateString();
    textBoxFileSize.Text = theFile.Length.ToString() + " bytes";

    // enable move, copy, delete buttons
    textBoxNewPath.Text = theFile.FullName;
    textBoxNewPath.Enabled = true;
    buttonCopyTo.Enabled = true;
```

```
        buttonDelete.Enabled = true;
        buttonMoveTo.Enabled = true;
    }
```

We also need to make one change to `DisplayFolderList`:

```
    protected void DisplayFolderList(string folderFullName)
    {
        DirectoryInfo theFolder = new DirectoryInfo(folderFullName);
        if (!theFolder.Exists)
            throw new DirectoryNotFoundException("Folder not found: " + folderFullName);

        ClearAllFields();
        DisableMoveFeatures();
        textBoxFolder.Text = theFolder.FullName;
        currentFolderPath = theFolder.FullName;

        // list all subfolders in folder
        foreach(DirectoryInfo nextFolder in theFolder.GetDirectories())
            listBoxFolders.Items.Add(NextFolder.Name);

        // list all files in folder
        foreach(FileInfo nextFile in theFolder.GetFiles())
            listBoxFiles.Items.Add(NextFile.Name);
    }
```

`DisableMoveFeatures` is a small utility function that disables the new controls:

```
        void DisableMoveFeatures()
        {
            textBoxNewPath.Text = "";
            textBoxNewPath.Enabled = false;
            buttonCopyTo.Enabled = false;
            buttonDelete.Enabled = false;
            buttonMoveTo.Enabled = false;
        }
```

We also need to add extra code to `ClearAllFields()` to clear the extra textbox:

```
        protected void ClearAllFields()
        {
            listBoxFolders.Items.Clear();
            listBoxFiles.Items.Clear();
            textBoxFolder.Text = "";
            textBoxFileName.Text = "";
            textBoxCreationTime.Text = "";
            textBoxLastAccessTime.Text = "";
            textBoxLastWriteTime.Text = "";
            textBoxFileSize.Text = "";
            textBoxNewPath.Text = "";
        }
```

With that, the code is complete.

Reading and Writing to Files

Reading and writing to files is in principle very simple; however, it is not done through the `DirectoryInfo` or `FileInfo` objects that we've just been examining. Instead, it is done through a number of classes that represent a generic concept called a **stream**, which we will examine next.

Streams

The idea of a stream has been around for a very long time. A stream is an object used to transfer data. The data can be transferred in one of two directions:

❑ If the data is being transferred from some outside source into your program then we talk about **reading** from the stream

❑ If the data is being transferred from your program to some outside source then we talk about **writing** to the stream

Very often, the outside source will be a file, but that is not necessarily the case. Other possibilities include:

❑ Reading or writing data on the network using some network protocol, where the intention is for this data to be picked up by or sent from another computer

❑ Reading or writing to a named pipe

❑ Reading or writing to an area of memory

Of these examples, Microsoft has supplied a .NET base class for writing to or reading from memory, `System.IO.MemoryStream`, while `System.Net.Sockets.NetworkStream` handles network data. There are no base stream classes for writing to or reading from pipes, but there is a generic stream class, `System.IO.Stream`, from which you would inherit if you wished to write such a class. `Stream` does not make any assumptions about the nature of the external data source.

The outside source might even be a variable within your own code. This might sound paradoxical, but the technique of using streams to transmit data between variables can be a useful trick for converting data between data types. The C language used something like this to convert between integer data types and strings or to format strings using a function, `sprintf`.

The advantage of having a separate object for the transfer of data, rather than using the `FileInfo` or `DirectoryInfo` classes to do this, is that by separating the concept of transferring data from the particular data source, it makes it easier to swap data sources. Stream objects themselves contain a lot of generic code that concerns the movement of data between outside sources and variables in your code, and by keeping this code separate from any concept of a particular data source, we make it easier for this code to be reused (through inheritance) in different circumstances. As an example of this, the `StringReader` and `StringWriter` classes mentioned above are part of the same inheritance tree as two classes that we will be using later on to read and write text files, `StreamReader` and `StreamWriter`. The classes will almost certainly share a substantial amount of code behind the scenes.

The actual hierarchy of stream-related classes in the `System.IO` namespace looks like this:

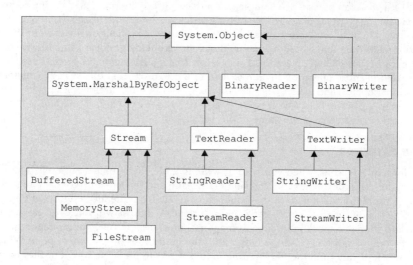

As far as reading and writing files is concerned, the classes that we are going to be most concerned with are:

❑   `FileStream`. This class is intended for reading and writing binary data in a binary file – though if you wish you can use it to read from or write to any file.

❑   `StreamReader` and `StreamWriter`. These classes are designed specifically for reading from and writing to text files.

Although we won't be using them in our examples, we'll also mention a couple of other classes that you may find useful, `BinaryReader` and `BinaryWriter`. If you wish to use these classes, you should refer to the MSDN documentation for details of their operation.

These classes do not actually implement streams themselves, but they are able to provide wrappers around other stream objects. `BinaryReader` and `BinaryWriter` provide extra formatting of binary data, which allows you to directly read or write the contents of C# variables to the relevant stream. The easiest way to think about it is that the `BinaryReader` and `BinaryWriter` sit between the stream and your code, providing extra formatting:

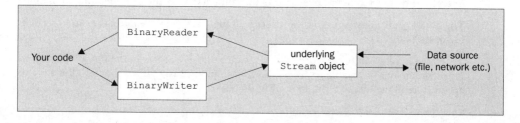

The difference between using these classes and directly using the underlying stream objects is that a basic stream works in bytes. For example, suppose as part of the process of saving some document you want to write the contents of a variable of type `long` to a binary file. Each `long` occupies 8 bytes, and if you used a plain ordinary binary stream you would have to explicitly write each of those 8 bytes of memory. In C# code that would mean you'd have to explicitly perform some bitwise operations to extract each of those 8 bytes from the `long` value. Using a `BinaryWriter` instance, you can encapsulate the entire operation in an overload of the `BinaryWriter.Write()` method that takes a `long` as a parameter, and which will place those 8 bytes into the stream (and hence if the stream is directed to a file, in the file). A corresponding `BinaryReader.Read()` method will extract 8 bytes from the stream and recover the value of the `long`.

Buffered Streams

For performance reasons, when you read or write to a file, the output is buffered. This means that if your program asks for the next 2 bytes of a file stream, and the stream passes the request on to Windows, Windows will not go to the trouble of connecting to the file system and then locating and reading the file off the disk, just to get 2 bytes. Instead, Windows will retrieve a large block of the file in one go, and store this block in an area of memory known as a **buffer**. Subsequent requests for data from the stream will be satisfied from the buffer until the buffer runs out, at which point Windows will grab another block of data from the file. Writing to files works in the same way. For files this is done automatically by the operating system, but it may be the case that you need to write a stream class to read from some other device that isn't buffered. If so, you can derive your class from `BufferedStream`, which implements a buffer itself. (`BufferedStream` is not, however, designed for the situation in which an application frequently alternates between reading and writing data.)

Reading and Writing to Binary Files

Reading and writing to binary files is usually done using the `FileStream` class.

The FileStream Class

A `FileStream` instance is used to read or write data to or from a file. In order to construct a `FileStream`, you need four pieces of information:

- ❑ The **file** you want to access.

- ❑ The **mode**, which indicates how you want to open the file. For example, are you intending to create a new file or open an existing file, and if opening an existing file should any write operations be interpreted as overwriting the contents of the file or appending to the file?

- ❑ The **access**, indicating how you want access to file – are you intending to read or write to the file or do both?

- ❑ The **share** access – in other words do you want exclusive access to the file, or are you willing for other streams to be able to access this file simultaneously? If so, should other streams have access to read the file, to write to it, or to do both?

The first of these pieces of information is usually represented by a string that contains the full pathname of the file, and in this chapter we will only consider those constructors that require a string here. Besides those constructors, however, there are some additional ones that take an old Windows-API style Windows handle to a file instead. The remaining three pieces of information are represented by three .NET enumerations respectively called `FileMode`, `FileAccess`, and `FileShare`. The values of these enumerations should be self-explanatory, and they are:

Enumeration	Values
FileMode	Append, Create, CreateNew, Open, OpenOrCreate, or Truncate
FileAccess	Read, ReadWrite, or Write
FileShare	Inheritable, None, Read, ReadWrite, or Write

Note that in the case of `FileMode`, exceptions can be thrown if you request a mode that is inconsistent with the existing status of the file. `Append`, `Open`, and `Truncate` will throw an exception if the file does not already exist, and `CreateNew` will throw an exception if it does. `Create` and `OpenOrCreate` will cope with either scenario, but `Create` will delete any existing file to replace it with a new, initially empty, one. The `FileAccess` and `FileShare` enumerations are bitwise flags – so values can be combined with the C# bitwise `OR` operator, `|`.

There are a large number of constructors for the `FileStream`. The three simplest ones work as follows:

```
// creates file with read-write access and allows other streams read access
FileStream fs = new FileStream(@"C:\C# Projects\Project.doc",
                FileMode.Create);
```

```
// as above, but we only get write access to the file
FileStream fs2 = new FileStream(@"C:\C# Projects\Project2.doc",
                FileMode.Create, FileAccess.Write);
```

```
// as above but other streams don't get any access to the file while
// fs3 is open
FileStream fs3 = new FileStream(@"C:\C# Projects\Project3.doc",
                FileMode.Create, FileAccess.Write, FileShare.None);
```

From this code we can see that these overloads of the constructors have the effect of providing default values of `FileAccess.ReadWrite` and `FileShare.Read` to the third and fourth parameters. It is also possible to create a file stream from a `FileInfo` instance in various ways:

```
FileInfo myFile4 = new FileInfo(@"C:\C# Projects\Project4.doc");
FileStream fs4 = myFile4.OpenRead();
```

```
FileInfo myFile5= new FileInfo(@"C:\C# Projects\Project5doc");
FileStream fs5 = myFile5.OpenWrite();
```

```
FileInfo myFile6= new FileInfo(@"C:\C# Projects\Project6doc");
FileStream fs6 = myFile6.Open(FileMode.Append, FileAccess.Write,
                    FileShare.None);
```

```
FileInfo myFile7 = new FileInfo(@"C:\C# Projects\Project7.doc");
FileStream fs7 = myFile7.Create();
```

`FileInfo.OpenRead()` supplies a stream that gives you read-only access to an existing file, while `FileInfo.OpenWrite()` gives you read-write access. `FileInfo.Open()` allows you to specify the mode, access, and file share parameters explicitly.

You won't be surprised to learn that once you've finished with a stream, you should close it:

```
fs.Close();
```

Closing the stream frees up the resources associated with it, and allows other applications to set up streams to the same file. In between opening and closing the stream, you'll want to read data from it and/or write data to it. `FileStream` implements a number of methods to do this.

`ReadByte()` is the simplest way of reading data. It grabs one byte from the stream, and casts the result to an `int` having a value between 0 and 255. If we have reached the end of the stream, it returns -1:

```
int NextByte = fs.ReadByte();
```

If you prefer to read a number of bytes at a time, you can call the `Read()` method, which reads a specified number of bytes into an array. `Read()` returns the number of bytes actually read – if this value is zero then you know you're at the end of the stream. Here's an example where we read into a `Byte` array `ByteArray`:

```
int nBytesRead = fs.Read(ByteArray, 0, nBytes);
```

The second parameter to `Read()` is an offset, which you can use to request that the `Read` operation starts populating the array at some element other than the first, and the third parameter is the number of bytes to read into the array.

If you wish to write data to a file, then there are two parallel methods available, `WriteByte()` and `Write()`. `WriteByte()` writes a single byte to the stream:

```
byte NextByte = 100;
fs.WriteByte(NextByte);
```

`Write()`, on the other hand, writes out an array of bytes. For instance, if we initialized the `ByteArray` we mentioned before with some values, we could use the following code to write out the first nBytes of the array:

```
fs.Write(ByteArray, 0, nBytes);
```

As with Read(), the second parameter allows you to start writing from some point other than the beginning of the array. Both WriteByte() and Write() return void.

Besides these methods, FileStream implements various other methods and properties to do with bookkeeping tasks like determining how many bytes are in the stream, locking the stream, or flushing the buffer. These other methods aren't usually required for basic reading and writing, and if you need them, full details are in the MSDN documentation.

Example: BinaryFileReader

We'll illustrate the use of the FileStream class by writing an example, BinaryFileReader, which reads in and displays any file. The example is as usual created in Visual Studio .NET as a Windows application. We've added one menu item, which brings up a standard OpenFileDialog asking what file to read in, then displays the file. As we are reading in binary files, we need to be able to display non-printable characters. The way we will do this is by displaying each byte of the file individually, showing 16 bytes on each line of a multiline textbox. If the byte represents a printable ASCII character we'll display that character, otherwise we'll display the value of the byte in hexadecimal format. In either case, we pad out the displayed text with spaces so that each 'byte' displayed occupies four columns so the bytes line up nicely under each other.

This is what the BinaryFileReader looks like when viewing a text file, (since the BinaryFileReader can view any file, it's quite possible to use it on text files as well as binary ones). In this case, the example has read in a file that contains some negotiations that went on in a recent game of *Civilization* (Sid Meier's well-known computer game):

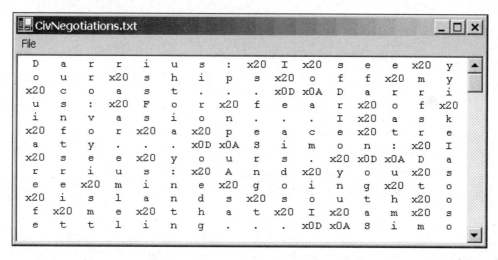

Clearly this format is more suited to looking at the values of individual bytes rather than to displaying text! Later in the chapter, we'll develop an example that is specifically designed to read text files – then we will be able to see what this file really says. On the other hand, the advantage of this example is that we can look at the contents of any file.

For this example, we won't demonstrate writing to files. That's because we don't want to get bogged down in the complexities of trying to translate the contents of a textbox like the one above into a binary stream! We will demonstrate writing to files later on when we develop an example that can read or write, but only to text files.

Let's look at the code used to get these results. First, we need an extra `using` statement, since besides `System.IO`, this example is going to use the `StringBuilder` class from the `System.Text` namespace to construct the strings in the textbox:

```
using System.IO;
using System.Text;
```

Next, we add a couple of fields to the main form class – one representing the file dialog, and a string that gives the path of the file currently being viewed:

```
public class Form1 : System.Windows.Forms.Form
{
    private OpenFileDialog chooseOpenFileDialog = new OpenFileDialog();
    private string chosenFile;
```

We also need to add some standard Windows Forms code to deal with the handlers for the menu and the file dialog:

```
public Form1()
{
    InitializeComponent();
    menuFileOpen.Click += new EventHandler(OnFileOpen);
    chooseOpenFileDialog.FileOk += new
        CancelEventHandler(OnOpenFileDialogOK);
}
void OnFileOpen(object Sender, EventArgs e)
{
    chooseOpenFileDialog.ShowDialog();
}
void OnOpenFileDialogOK(object Sender, CancelEventArgs e)
{
    chosenFile = chooseOpenFileDialog.FileName;
    this.Text = Path.GetFileName(chosenFile);
    DisplayFile();
}
```

From this we see that once the user clicks **OK** to select a file in the file dialog, we call a method, `DisplayFile()`, which actually does the work of reading in the file:

```
void DisplayFile()
{
    int nCols = 16;
    FileStream inStream = new FileStream(chosenFile, FileMode.Open,
                                                FileAccess.Read);

    long nBytesToRead = inStream.Length;
    if (nBytesToRead > 65536/4)
```

```
        nBytesToRead = 65536/4;
    int nLines = (int)(nBytesToRead/nCols) + 1;
    string [] lines = new string[nLines];
    int nBytesRead = 0;
    for (int i=0 ; i<nLines ; i++)
    {
        StringBuilder nextLine = new StringBuilder();
        nextLine.Capacity = 4*nCols;
        for (int j = 0 ; j<nCols ; j++)
        {
            int nextByte = inStream.ReadByte();
            nBytesRead++;
            if (nextByte < 0 || nBytesRead > 65536)
                break;
            char nextChar = (char)nextByte;
            if (nextChar < 16)
                nextLine.Append(" x0" + string.Format("{0,1:X}",
                                                (int)nextChar));
            else if
                (char.IsLetterOrDigit(nextChar) ||
                                char.IsPunctuation(nextChar))
                nextLine.Append("   " + nextChar + " ");
            else
                nextLine.Append(" x" + string.Format("{0,2:X}",
                                            (int)nextChar));
        }
        lines[i] = nextLine.ToString();
    }
    inStream.Close();
    this.textBoxContents.Lines = lines;
}
```

There's quite a lot going on in this method, so we'll break it down. We instantiate a `FileStream` object for the selected file specifying that we wish to open an existing file for reading. We then work out how many bytes there are to read in and how many lines should be displayed. The number of bytes will normally be the number of bytes in the file. Textboxes can only display a maximum of 65,536 characters, however, and with our chosen format, we are displaying 4 characters for every byte in the file, so we will need to cap the number of bytes shown if the file is longer than $65,536/4 = 16,384$.

> *If you want to display longer files in this sort of environment, you might want to look up the*
> `RichTextBox` *class in the* `System.Windows.Forms` *namespace.* `RichTextBox` *is similar*
> *to a textbox, but has many more advanced formatting facilities and does not have a limit on how*
> *much text it can display. We are using* `TextBox` *here to keep the example simple and focused on*
> *the process of reading in files.*

The bulk of the method is given over to two nested `for` loops that construct each line of text to be displayed. We use a `StringBuilder` class to construct each line for performance reasons: We will be appending suitable text for each byte to the string that represents each line 16 times. If on each occasion we allocate a new string and take a copy of the half-constructed line, we are not only going to be spending a lot of time allocating strings, but will be wasting a lot of memory on the heap. Notice that our definition of "printable" characters is anything that is a letter, digit, or punctuation, as indicated by the relevant static `System.Char` methods. We've excluded any character with a value less than 16 from the printable list, however, which means we'll trap the carriage return (13) and line feed (10) as binary characters (a multiline textbox isn't able to display these characters properly if they occur individually within a line).

A couple of other points; Using the Properties Window, we changed the Font for the text box to a fixed width font – we chose Courier New 9pt regular, and also set the textbox to have vertical and horizontal scroll bars.

Finally, we close the stream and set the contents of the textbox to the array of strings that we've built up.

Reading and Writing to Text Files

Theoretically, it's perfectly possible to use the `FileStream` class to read in and display text files. We have, after all, just demonstrated doing that. The format in which we displayed the `CivNegotiations.txt` file above wasn't particularly user-friendly, but that wasn't due to any intrinsic problem with the `FileStream` class – that was just because of the way we had chosen to display the results in the textbox.

Having said that, if you know that a particular file contains text, you will usually find it more convenient to read and write it using the `StreamReader` and `StreamWriter` classes. That's because these classes work at a slightly higher level, and are specifically geared to reading and writing text. The methods that they implement are able to automatically detect where convenient points to stop reading text are, based upon the contents of the stream. In particular:

❑   These classes implement methods to read or write one line of text at a time, `StreamReader.ReadLine()` and `StreamWriter.WriteLine()`. In the case of reading, this means that is the stream will automatically figure out for you where the next carriage return is, and stop reading at that point. In the case of writing, it means that the stream will automatically append the carriage return-line feed combination to the text that it writes out.

❑   By using the `StreamReader` and `StreamWriter` classes you don't need to worry about the encoding (the text format) used in the file. Possible encodings include ASCII (1 byte for each character), or any or the Unicode-based formats, UNICODE, UTF7, and UTF8. Text files on Windows 9x systems are always in ASCII, because Windows 9x doesn't support Unicode, but Windows NT, 2000, and XP all do support Unicode, and so text files might theoretically contain Unicode, UTF7, or UTF8 data instead of ASCII data. The convention is that if the file is in ASCII format, it will simply contain the text. If is in any Unicode format, this will be indicated by the first two or three bytes of the file, which are set to particular combinations of values to indicate the format.

These bytes are known as the **byte code markers**. When you open a file using any of the standard Windows applications, such as Notepad or WordPad, you don't need to worry about this because these applications are aware of the different encoding methods and will automatically read the file correctly. This is also the case for the `StreamReader` class, which will correctly read in a file in any of these formats, while the `StreamWriter` class is capable of formatting the text it writes out using whatever encoding technique you request. On the other hand, if you wanted to read in and display a text file using the `FileStream` class, you would have to handle all this yourself.

The StreamReader Class

`StreamReader` is used to read text files. Constructing a `StreamReader` is in some ways simpler than constructing a `FileStream` instance, because some of the `FileStream` options are not required. In particular, the mode and access types are not relevant, because the only thing you can do with a `StreamReader` is read! As well as this, there is no direct option to specify the sharing permissions. However, there are a couple of new options:

❑   We need to specify what to do about the different encoding methods. We can instruct the `StreamReader` to examine the byte code markers in the file to determine the encoding method, or we can simply tell the `StreamReader` to assume that the file uses a specified encoding method.

❑   Instead of supplying a file name to be read from, we can supply a reference to another stream.

This last option deserves a bit more discussion, because it illustrates another advantage of basing our model for reading and writing data around the concept of streams. Because the `StreamReader` works at a relatively high level, you might find it useful if you are in the situation in which you have another stream that is there to read data from some other source, but you would like to use the facilities provided by `StreamReader` to process that other stream as if it contained text. You can do so by simply passing the output from this stream to a `StreamReader`. In this way, `StreamReader` can be used to read and process data from any data source – not only files. This is essentially the situation we discussed earlier with regard to the `BinaryReader` class. However, in this book we will only use `StreamReader` to connect directly to files.

The result of these possibilities is that `StreamReader` has a large number of constructors. Not only that, but there are a couple of `FileInfo` methods that return `StreamReader` references too: `OpenText()` and `CreateText()`. Here we will just illustrate some of the constructors.

The simplest constructor takes just a file name. This `StreamReader` will examine the byte order marks to determine the encoding:

```
StreamReader sr = new StreamReader(@"C:\My Documents\ReadMe.txt");
```

Alternatively, if you prefer to specify that UTF8 encoding should be assumed:

```
StreamReader sr = new StreamReader(@"C:\My Documents\ReadMe.txt",
                        Encoding.UTF8);
```

We specify the encoding by using one of several properties on a class, `System.Text.Encoding`. This class is an abstract base class, from which a number of classes are defined, which implement methods that actually perform the text encoding. Each property returns an instance of the appropriate class, and the possible properties we can use here are:

❑   `ASCII`

❑   `Unicode`

❑   `UTF7`

❑   `UTF8`

❑   `BigEndianUnicode`

The following example demonstrates hooking a `StreamReader` up to a `FileStream`. The advantage of this is that we can explicitly specify whether to create the file and the share permissions, which we cannot do if we directly attach a `StreamReader` to the file:

```
FileStream fs = new FileStream(@"C:\My Documents\ReadMe.txt",
                    FileMode.Open, FileAccess.Read, FileShare.None);
StreamReader sr = new StreamReader(fs);
```

For this example, we specify that the `StreamReader` will look for byte code markers to determine the encoding method used, as it will do in the following examples, in which the `StreamReader` is obtained from a `FileInfo` instance:

```
FileInfo myFile = new FileInfo(@"C:\My Documents\ReadMe.txt");
StreamReader sr = myFile.OpenText();
```

Just as with a `FileStream`, you should always close a `StreamReader` after use. Failure to do so will result in the file remaining locked to other processes (unless you used a `FileStream` to construct the `StreamReader` and specified `FileShare.ShareReadWrite`):

```
sr.Close();
```

Now we've gone to the trouble of instantiating a `StreamReader`, we can do something with it. As with the `FileStream`, we'll simply point out the various ways there are to read data, and leave the other, less commonly used, `StreamReader` methods to the MSDN documentation.

Possibly the easiest method to use is `ReadLine()`, which keeps reading until it gets to the end of a line. It does not include the carriage return-line feed combination that marks the end of the line in the returned string:

```
string nextLine = sr.ReadLine();
```

Alternatively, you can grab the entire remainder of the file (or strictly, the remainder of the stream) in one string:

```
string restOfStream = sr.ReadToEnd();
```

You can read a single character:

```
int nextChar = sr.Read();
```

This overload of `Read()` casts the returned character to an `int`. This is so that it has the option of returning a value of -1 if the end of the stream has been reached.

Finally, you can read a given number of characters into an array, with an offset:

```
// to read 100 characters in.

int nChars = 100;
char [] charArray = new char[nChars];
int nCharsRead = sr.Read(charArray, 0, nChars);
```

`nCharsRead` will be less than `nChars` if we have requested to read more characters than are left in the file.

The StreamWriter Class

This works in basically the same way as the `StreamReader`, except that you can only use `StreamWriter` to write to a file (or to another stream). Possibilities for constructing a `StreamWriter` include:

```
StreamWriter sw = new StreamWriter(@"C:\My Documents\ReadMe.txt");
```

The above code will use UTF8 Encoding, which is regarded by .NET as the default encoding method. If you want to you can specify an alternative encoding:

```
StreamWriter sw = new StreamWriter(@"C:\My Documents\ReadMe.txt", true,
    Encoding.ASCII);
```

In this constructor, the second parameter is a `Boolean` that indicates whether the file should be opened for appending. There is, oddly, no constructor that takes only a file name and an encoding class.

Of course, you may want to hook a `StreamWriter` up to a file stream to give you more control over the options for opening the file:

```
FileStream fs = new FileStream(@"C:\My Documents\ReadMe.txt",
    FileMode.CreateNew, FileAccess.Write, FileShare.Read);
StreamWriter sw = new StreamWriter(fs);
```

`FileInfo` does not implement any methods that return a `StreamWriter`.

Alternatively, if you want to create a new file and start writing data to it, you'll find this sequence useful:

```
FileInfo myFile = new FileInfo(@"C:\My Documents\NewFile.txt");
StreamWriter sw = myFile.CreateText();
```

Just as with all other stream classes it is important to close a `StreamWriter` when you have finished with it:

```
sw.Close();
```

Writing to the stream is done using any of four overloads of `StreamWriter.Write()`. The simplest writes out a string, and appends it with a carriage return-line feed combination:

```
string nextLine = "Groovy Line";
sw.Write(nextLine);
```

It is also possible to write out a single character:

```
char nextChar = 'a';
sw.Write(nextChar);
```

An array of characters is also possible:

```
char [] charArray = new char[100];

// initialize these characters

sw.Write(charArray);
```

It is even possible to write out a portion of an array of characters:

```
int nCharsToWrite = 50;
int startAtLocation = 25;
char [] charArray = new char[100];

// initialize these characters

sw.Write(charArray, startAtLocation, nCharsToWrite);
```

Example: ReadWriteText

The ReadWriteText example displays the use of the StreamReader and StreamWriter classes. It is similar to the earlier ReadBinaryFile example, but it assumes the file to be read in is a text file and displays it as such. It is also capable of saving the file (with any modifications you've made to the text in the textbox). It will save any file in Unicode format.

The screenshot shows ReadWriteText being used to display the same CivNegotiations file that we saw earlier. This time, however, we are able to read the contents a bit more easily!

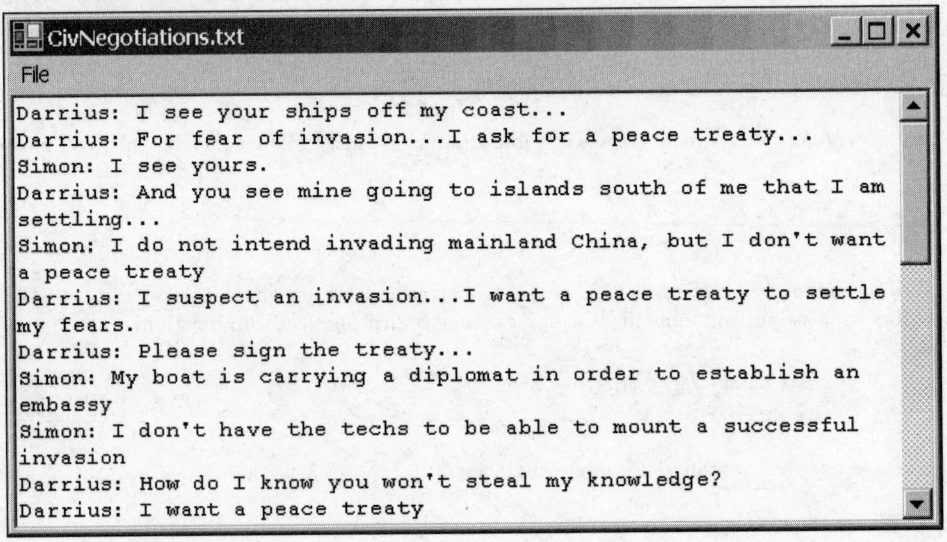

We won't go over the details of adding the event handlers for the open file dialog, because they are basically the same as with the `BinaryFileReader` example. As with that example, opening a new file causes the `DisplayFile()` method to be called. The only real differences between this example and the previous one are the implementation of `DisplayFile`, and also that we now have the option to save a file. This is represented by another menu option, **Save**. The handler for this option calls another method we've added to the code, `SaveFile()`. (Note that the new file always overwrites the original file – this example does not have an option to write to a different file.)

We'll look at `SaveFile()` first, since that is the simplest function. We simply write each line of the textbox, in turn, to a `StreamWriter` stream, relying on the `StreamReader.WriteLine()` method to append the trailing carriage return and line feed at the end of each line:

```
void SaveFile()
{
    StreamWriter sw = new StreamWriter(chosenFile, false,
                             Encoding.Unicode);
    foreach (string line in textBoxContents.Lines)
        sw.WriteLine(line);
    sw.Close();
}
```

`ChosenFile` is a string field of the main form, which contains the name of the file we have read in (just as for the previous example). Notice that we specify Unicode encoding when we open the stream. If we'd wanted to write files in some other format then we'd simply need to change the value of this parameter. The second parameter to this constructor would be set to `true` if we wanted to append to a file, but we don't in this case. The encoding must be set at construction time for a `StreamWriter`. It is subsequently available as a read-only property, `Encoding`.

Now we'll examine how files are read in. The process of reading in is complicated by the fact that we don't know until we've read in the file how many lines it is going to contain (in other words, how many `(char)13(char)10` sequences are in the file – since `char(13)char(10)` is the carriage return-line feed combination that occurs at the end of a line). We solve this problem by initially reading the file into an instance of the `StringCollection` class, which is in the `System.Collections.Specialized` namespace. This class is designed to hold a set of strings that can be dynamically expanded. It implements two methods that we will be interested in: `Add()`, which adds a string to the collection, and `CopyTo()`, which copies the string collection into a normal array (a `System.Array` instance). Each element of the `StringCollection` object will hold one line of the file.

The `DisplayFile()` method calls another method, `ReadFileIntoStringCollection()`, which actually reads in the file. After doing this, we now know how many lines there are, so we are in a position to copy the `StringCollection` into a normal, fixed size array and feed this array into the textbox. Since when we make the copy it is only the references to the strings that get copied, not the strings themselves, the process is reasonably efficient:

```
void DisplayFile()
{
    StringCollection linesCollection = ReadFileIntoStringCollection();
    string [] linesArray = new string[linesCollection.Count];
    linesCollection.CopyTo(linesArray, 0);
    this.textBoxContents.Lines = linesArray;
}
```

The second parameter of `StringCollection.CopyTo()` indicates the index within the destination array of where we want the collection to start.

Now we will examine the `ReadFileIntoStringCollection()` method. We use a `StreamReader` to read in each line. The main complication here is the need to count the characters read in to make sure we don't exceed the capacity of the textbox:

```
StringCollection ReadFileIntoStringCollection()
{
    const int MaxBytes = 65536;
    StreamReader sr = new StreamReader(chosenFile);
    StringCollection result = new StringCollection();
    int nBytesRead = 0;
    string nextLine;
    while ( (nextLine = sr.ReadLine()) != null)
    {
        nBytesRead += nextLine.Length;
        if (nBytesRead > MaxBytes)
            break;
        result.Add(nextLine);
    }
    sr.Close();
    return result;
}
```

That completes the code for the example.

If we run `ReadWriteText`, read in the `CivNegotiations` file, and then save it, the file will be in Unicode format. We wouldn't be able to tell this from any of the usual Windows applications: Notepad, WordPad, and even our own `ReadWriteText` example, will still read the file in and display it correctly under Windows NT/2000/XP, although because Windows 9x doesn't support Unicode, applications like Notepad won't be able to understand the Unicode file on those platforms. (If you download the example from the Wrox Press web site, you can try this!) However, if we try to display the file again using our earlier `BinaryFileReader` example, we can see the difference immediately, as shown in the following screenshot. The two initial bytes that indicate the file is in Unicode format are visible, and thereafter we see that every character is represented by two bytes. This last fact is very obvious, because the high-order byte of every character in this particular file is zero, so every second byte in this file now displays x00:

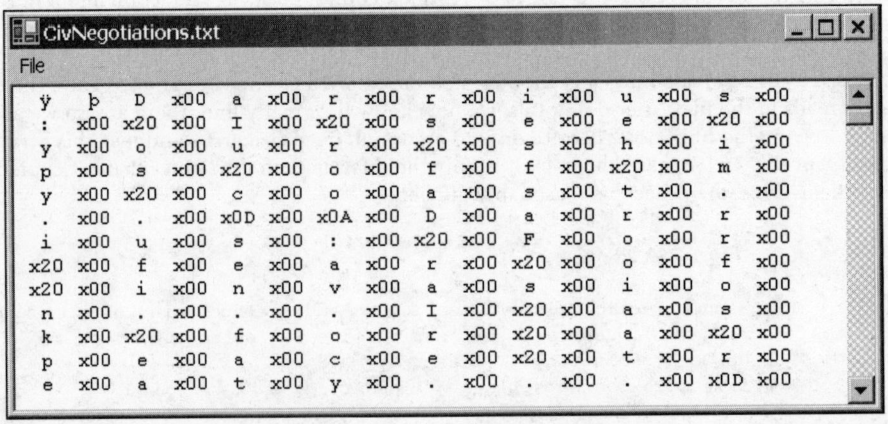

Reading and Writing to the Registry

In all versions of Windows since Windows 95, the Registry has been the central repository for all configuration information relating to Windows setup, user preferences, and installed software and devices. Almost all commercial software these days uses the Registry to store information about itself, and COM components must place information about themselves in the Registry in order to be called by clients. The .NET Framework and its accompanying concept of zero-impact installation has slightly reduced the significance of the Registry for applications in the sense that assemblies are entirely self-contained, so no information about particular assemblies needs to be placed in the Registry – even for shared assemblies. In addition, the .NET Framework has brought the concept of isolated storage, by which applications can store information that is particular to each user in files, with the .NET Framework taking care of making sure that data is stored separately for each user registered on a machine. (Isolated storage is beyond the scope of this book, but if you are interested, you can find the relevant .NET base classes in the `System.IO.IsolatedStorage` namespace.)

The fact that applications can now be installed using the Windows Installer also frees developers from some of the direct manipulation of the Registry that used to be involved in installing applications. However, despite this, the possibility exists that if you distribute any complete application, your application will use the Registry to store information about its configuration. If you want your application to show up in the **Add/Remove Programs** dialog under the control panel, then this will involve appropriate registry entries being made. You may also need to use the Registry for backwards compatibility with legacy code.

As you'd expect from a library as comprehensive as the .NET library, it includes classes that give you access to the Registry. There are two classes concerned with the Registry, and both are in the `Microsoft.Win32` namespace. The classes are `Registry` and `RegistryKey`. Before we examine these classes, we will briefly review the structure of the Registry itself.

The Registry

The Registry has a hierarchical structure much like that of the file system. The usual way to view or modify the contents of the Registry is with one of two utilities – `regedit` or `regedt32`. Of these, `regedit` comes with all versions of Windows, since Windows 95 as standard. `regedt32` comes with Windows NT and Windows 2000 – it is less user-friendly than `regedit`, but allows access to security information that `regedit` is unable to view. For our discussion here, we'll use `regedit`, which you can launch by typing in `regedit` at the **Run...** dialog or command prompt.

When you first launch `regedit` up you'll see something like this:

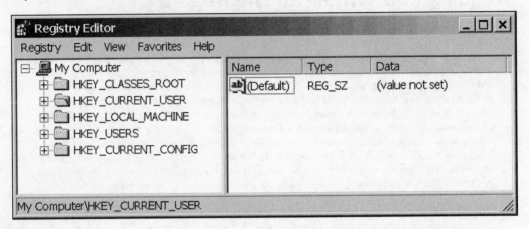

`regedit` has a similar treeview/listview style user interface to Windows Explorer, which matches the hierarchical structure of the Registry itself. As we'll soon see, however, there are some differences.

In a file system, the topmost level nodes can be thought of as being the partitions on your disks, `C:\`, `D:\`, and so on. In the Registry, the equivalent to a partition is the **registry hive**. It is not possible to change which hives are there – they are fixed, and there are seven of them, although only five are actually visible through `regedit`:

❑ HKEY_CLASSES_ROOT (HKCR) contains details of types of files on the system (`.txt`, `.doc`, and so on), and which applications are able to open files of each type. It also contains registration information for all COM components (this latter area is usually the largest single area of the Registry, since Windows these days comes with a huge number of COM components).

❑ HKEY_CURRENT_USER (HKCU) contains details of user preferences for the user currently logged on to the machine.

❑ HKEY_LOCAL_MACHINE (HKLM) is a huge hive that contains details of all software and hardware installed on the machine. It also includes the HKCR hive: HKCR is actually not really an independent hive in its own right, but is simply a convenient mapping onto the registry key HKLM/SOFTWARE/Classes.

❑ HKEY_USERS (HKUSR) contains details of user preferences for all users. As you might guess, it also contains the HKCU hive, which is simply a mapping onto one of the keys in HKEY_USERS.

❑ HKEY_CURRENT_CONFIG (HKCF) contains details of hardware on the machine.

The remaining two keys contain information that is of a temporary nature, and which changes frequently:

❑ HKEY_DYN_DATA is a general container for any volatile data that needs to be stored somewhere in the Registry

❑ HKEY_PERFORMANCE_DATA contains information concerning the performance of running applications

Within the hives is a tree structure of registry **keys**. Each key is in many ways analogous to a folder or file on the file system. However, there is one very important difference. The file system distinguishes between files (which are there to contain data), and folders (which are primarily there to contain other files or folders), but in the Registry there are only keys. A key may contain both data and other keys.

If a key contains data, then this will be present as a series of values. Each value will have an associated name, data type, and data. In addition, a key may have a default value, which is unnamed.

We can see this structure by using `regedit` to examine registry keys. The screenshot shows the contents of the key `HKCU\Control Panel\Appearance`, which contains the details of the chosen color scheme of the currently logged in user. `regedit` shows which key is being examined by displaying it with an open folder icon in the tree view:

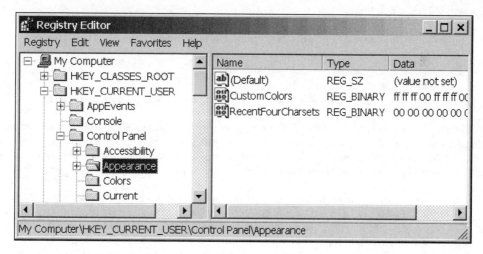

The `HKCU\Control Panel\Appearance` key has three named values set, although the default value does not contain any data. The column in the screenshot marked **Type** details the data type of each value. Registry entries may be formatted as one of three data types. The types are:

- ❑ REG_SZ (which roughly corresponds to a .NET string instance – the matching is not exact because the registry data types are not .NET data types)
- ❑ REG_DWORD (corresponds roughly to `uint`)
- ❑ REG_BINARY (array of bytes)

An application that wishes to store data in the Registry will do so by creating a number of registry keys, usually under the key `HKLM\Software\<CompanyName>`. Note that it is not necessary for these keys to contain any data. Sometimes the very fact of whether a key exists provides the data that an application needs.

The .NET Registry Classes

Access to the Registry is via two classes in the `Microsoft.Win32` namespace, `Registry` and `RegistryKey`. A `RegistryKey` instance represents a registry key. This class implements methods to browse down into child keys, to create new keys or to read or modify the values in the key. In other words, to do everything you would normally wish to do with a registry key (except set security levels for the key). `RegistryKey` will be the class you use for almost all your work with the Registry. `Registry`, by contrast, is a class that you will never instantiate. Its role is simply to provide you with `RegistryKey` instances that represent the top-level keys – the different hives – in order to start you off navigating through the Registry. `Registry` provides these instances through static properties, and there are seven of them, called respectively `ClassesRoot`, `CurrentConfig`, `CurrentUser`, `DynData`, `LocalMachine`, `PerformanceData`, and `Users`. I bet you can't guess which of these properties corresponds to which hive!

So, for example, to obtain a `RegistryKey` instance that represents the HKLM key, you would write:

```
RegistryKey hklm = Registry.LocalMachine;
```

The process of obtaining a reference to a `RegistryKey` object is known as opening the key.

Although you might expect that the methods exposed by `RegistryKey` would be similar to those implemented by `DirectoryInfo`, given that the Registry has a similar hierarchical structure to the file system, this actually isn't the case. Often, the way that you access the Registry is different from the way that you would use files and folders, and `RegistryKey` implements methods that reflect this.

The most obvious difference is in how you open a registry key at a given location in the Registry. The `Registry` class does not have any public constructor that you can use, nor does it have any methods that let you go directly to a key, given its name. Instead, you are expected to browse down to that key from the top of the relevant hive. If you want to instantiate a `RegistryKey` object, the only way is to start off with the appropriate static property of `Registry`, and work down from there. So, for example, if you want to read some data in the HKLM/`Software`/`Microsoft` key, you'd get a reference to it like this:

```
RegistryKey hklm = Registry.LocalMachine;
RegistryKey hkSoftware = hklm.OpenSubKey("Software");
RegistryKey hkMicrosoft = hkSoftware.OpenSubKey("Microsoft");
```

A registry key accessed in this way will give you read-only access. If you want to be able to write to the key (that includes writing to its values or creating or deleting direct children of it), you need to use another override to `OpenSubKey`, which takes a second parameter, of type `bool`, that indicates whether you want read-write access to the key. So for example, if you want to be able to modify the `Microsoft` key (and assuming you are a systems administrator with permission to do this) you would write this:

```
RegistryKey hklm = Registry.LocalMachine;
RegistryKey hkSoftware = hklm.OpenSubKey("Software");
RegistryKey hkMicrosoft = hkSoftware.OpenSubKey("Microsoft", true);
```

Incidentally, since this key contains information used by Microsoft's applications, in most cases you probably shouldn't be modifying this particular key.

The `OpenSubKey()` method is the one you will call if you are expecting the key to already be present. If the key isn't there, it will return a `null` reference. If you wish to create a key, then you should use the `CreateSubKey()` method (which automatically gives you read-write access to the key through the reference returned):

```
RegistryKey hklm = Registry.LocalMachine;
RegistryKey hkSoftware = hklm.OpenSubKey("Software");
RegistryKey hkMine = hkSoftware.CreateSubKey("MyOwnSoftware");
```

The way that `CreateSubKey()` works is quite interesting. It will create the key if it doesn't already exist, but if it does already exist, then it will quietly return a `RegistryKey` instance that represents the existing key. The reason for the method behaving in this manner is to do with how you will normally use the Registry. The Registry, on the whole, contains long-term data such as configuration information for Windows and for various applications. It's not very common, therefore, that you find yourself in a situation where you need to explicitly create a key.

What is much more common is that your application needs to make sure that some data is present in the Registry – in other words create the relevant keys if they don't already exist, but do nothing if they do. `CreateSubKey()` fills that need perfectly. Unlike the situation with `FileInfo.Open()`, for example, there is no chance with `CreateSubKey()` of accidentally removing any data. If deleting registry keys is your intention, then you'll need to explicitly call the `RegistryKey.DeleteSubKey()` method. This makes sense given the importance of the Registry to Windows. The last thing you want is to accidentally completely break Windows by deleting a couple of important keys while you're debugging your C# registry calls!

Once you've located the registry key you want to read or modify, you can use the `SetValue()` or `GetValue()` methods to set or get at the data in it. Both of these methods take a string giving the name of the value as a parameter, and `SetValue()` requires an additional object reference containing details of the value. Since the parameter is defined as an object reference, it can actually be a reference to any class you want. `SetValue()` will decide from the type of class actually supplied whether to set the value as a `REG_SZ`, `REG_DWORD`, or `REG_BINARY` value. For example:

```
RegistryKey hkMine = HkSoftware.CreateSubKey("MyOwnSoftware");
hkMine.SetValue("MyStringValue", "Hello World");
hkMine.SetValue("MyIntValue", 20);
```

This code will set the key to have two values: `MyStringValue` will be of type `REG_SZ`, while `MyIntValue` will be of type `REG_DWORD`. These are the only two types we will consider here, and use in the example that we present later.

`RegistryKey.GetValue()` works in much the same way. It is defined to return an object reference, which means it is free to actually return a `string` reference if it detects the value is of type `REG_SZ`, and an `int` if that value is of type `REG_DWORD`:

```
string stringValue = (string)hkMine.GetValue("MyStringValue");
int intValue = (int)hkMine.GetValue("MyIntValue");
```

Finally, once you've finished reading or modifying the data, you should close the key:

```
hkMine.Close();
```

`RegistryKey` implements a large number of methods and properties. The tables give a selection of the most useful ones:

Properties

Property Name	Description
Name	Name of the key (read-only)
SubKeyCount	The number of children of this key
ValueCount	How many values the key contains

Methods

Method Name	Purpose
Close()	Closes the key
CreateSubKey()	Creates a subkey of a given name (or opens it if it already exists)
DeleteSubKey()	Deletes a given subkey
DeleteSubKeyTree()	Recursively deletes a subkey and all its children
DeleteValue()	Removes a named value from a key
GetSubKeyNames()	Returns an array of strings containing the names of the subkeys
GetValue()	Returns a named value
GetValueNames()	Returns an array of strings containing the names of all the values of the key
OpenSubKey()	Returns a reference to a `RegistryKey` instance that represents a given subkey
SetValue()	Sets a named value

Example: SelfPlacingWindow

We will illustrate the use of the registry classes with an application, which we will call the `SelfPlacingWindow`. This example is a simple C# Windows application, which actually has almost no features. The only thing you can do with it is click on a button, which brings up a standard Windows color dialog box (represented by the `System.Windows.Forms.ColorDialog` class), to let you choose a color, which will become the background color of the form.

Despite this lack of features, the self-placing window scores over just about every other application that we have developed in this book in one important and very user-friendly way. If you drag the window around the screen, change its size, or maximize or minimize it before you exit the application, it will remember the new position, as well as the background color, so that the next time it is launched it can automatically resume the way you chose last time. It remembers this information, because it writes it to the Registry whenever it shuts down. In this way, we get to demonstrate not only the .NET registry classes themselves, but also a very typical use for them, which you'll almost certainly want to replicate in any serious commercial Windows Forms application you write.

The location that `SelfPlacingWindow` stores its information in the Registry is a key, `HKLM\Software\WroxPress\SelfPlacingWindow`. `HKLM` is the usual place for application configuration information, but note that it is not user-specific. If you wanted to be more sophisticated in a real application, you'd probably want to replicate the information inside the `HK_Users` hive as well, so that each user can have their own profile.

It's also worth noting that, if you are implementing this in a real .NET application, you may want to consider using isolated storage instead of the Registry to store this information. On the other hand, since isolated storage is only available in .NET, you'll need to use the Registry if you need any interoperability with non-.NET apps.

The very first time that you run the example, it will look for this key and not find it, obviously! Therefore it is forced to use a default size, color, and position that we set in the developer environment. The example also features a listbox in which it displays any information read in from the Registry. On its first run, it will look like this:

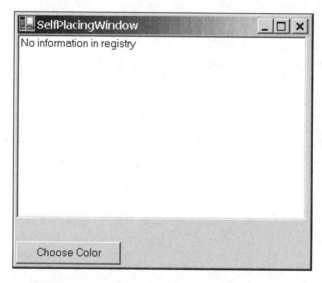

If we now modify the background color and resize the `SelfPlacingWindow` or move it around on the screen a bit before exiting, it will, just before it exits, create the `HKLM\Software\WroxPress\SelfPlacingWindow` key and write its new configuration information into it. We can examine the information using `regedit`:

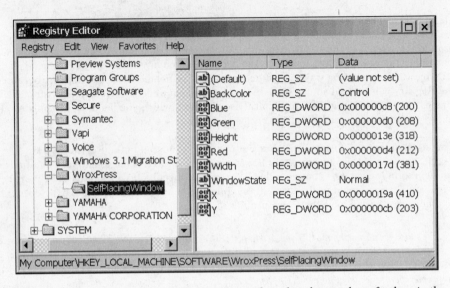

We can see from this screenshot that `SelfPlacingWindow` has placed a number of values in the registry key.

The values `Red`, `Green`, and `Blue` give the color components that make up the selected background color. If you're not familiar with color components, don't worry, as these will be explained later in Chapter 19, *Graphics with GDI+*. For now, just take it that any color display on the system can be completely described by these three components, which are each represented by a number between 0 and 255 (or `0x00` and `0xff` in hexadecimal). The values given here make up a bright green color. There are also four more `REG_DWORD` values, which represent the position and size of the window: `X` and `Y` are the coordinates of top left of the window on the desktop – that is to say the numbers of pixels across from the top left of the screen and the numbers of pixels down. `Width` and `Height` give the size of the window. `WindowsState` is the only value for which we have used a string data type (`REG_SZ`), and it can contain one of the strings `Normal`, `Maximised`, or `Minimised`, depending on the final state of the window when we exited the application.

If we now launch SelfPlacingWindow again it will read this registry key, and automatically position itself accordingly (I know it's a black and white book, but I can promise you that background color really is bright green!):

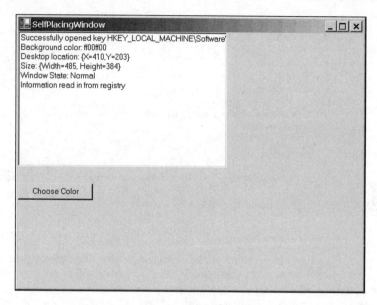

This time when we exit SelfPlacingWindow, it will overwrite the previous registry settings with whatever new values are relevant at the time that we exit it. To code up the example, we create the usual Windows Forms project in Visual Studio.NET, and add the listbox and button, using the developer environment's toolbox. We will change the names of these controls respectively to listBoxMessages and buttonChooseColor. We also need to ensure that we use the Microsoft.Win32 namespace:

```
using System;
using System.Drawing;
using System.Collections;
using System.ComponentModel;
using System.Windows.Forms;
using System.Data;
using Microsoft.Win32;
```

We need to add one field (chooseColorDialog) to the main Form1 class, which will represent the color dialog box:

```
public class Form1 : System.Windows.Forms.Form
{
    private System.Windows.Forms.ListBox listBoxMessages;
    private System.Windows.Forms.Button buttonChooseColor;
    private ColorDialog chooseColorDialog = new ColorDialog();
```

Quite a lot of action takes place in the `Form1` constructor:

```
public Form1()
{
    InitializeComponent();
    buttonChooseColor.Click += new EventHandler(OnClickChooseColor);
    try
    {
        if (ReadSettings() == false)
            listBoxMessages.Items.Add("No information in registry");
        else
            listBoxMessages.Items.Add("Information read in from registry");
            StartPosition = FormStartPosition.Manual;
    }
    catch (Exception e)
    {
        listBoxMessages.Items.Add("A problem occurred reading in data
                                   from registry:");
        listBoxMessages.Items.Add(e.Message);
    }
}
```

In this constructor, we start off by setting up the event handler for when the user clicks on the button. The handler is a method called `OnClickChooseColor`, which we will cover soon. Reading in the configuration information is done using another method that we will write called `ReadSettings()`. `ReadSettings()` returns `true` if it finds the information in the Registry, and `false` if it doesn't (which it should be since this is the first time we have run the application). We place this part of the constructor in a `try` block, just in case any exceptions are generated while reading in the registry values (this might happen if some user has come in and played around with the Registry using `regedit`).

The `StartPosition = FormStartPosition.Manual;` statement tells the form to take its initial starting position from the `DeskTopLocation` property instead of using the Windows default location (the default behavior). Possible values are taken from the `FormStartPosition` enumeration.

`SelfPlacingWindow` is also one of the few applications in this book in which we have a serious use for adding code to the `Dispose()` method. Remember that `Dispose()` is called whenever the application terminates normally, so this is the ideal place from which to save the configuration information to the Registry. This is done using another method that we will write, `SaveSettings()`:

```
protected override void Dispose( bool disposing )
{
    if( disposing )
    {
        if (components != null)
        {
            components.Dispose();
        }
    }
    SaveSettings();
    base.Dispose( disposing );
}
```

The `SaveSettings()` and `ReadSettings()` methods are the ones that contain the registry code we are interested in, but before we examine them we have one more piece of housekeeping: to handle the event of the user clicking that button. This involves displaying the color dialog and setting the background color to whatever color the user chose:

```
void OnClickChooseColor(object Sender, EventArgs e)
{
    if(chooseColorDialog.ShowDialog() == DialogResult.OK)
        BackColor = chooseColorDialog.Color;
}
```

Now let's look at how we save the settings:

```
void SaveSettings()
{
    RegistryKey softwareKey =
                Registry.LocalMachine.OpenSubKey("Software", true);
    RegistryKey wroxKey = softwareKey.CreateSubKey("WroxPress");
    RegistryKey selfPlacingWindowKey =
                wroxKey.CreateSubKey("SelfPlacingWindow");
    selfPlacingWindowKey.SetValue("BackColor",
                (object)BackColor.ToKnownColor());
    selfPlacingWindowKey.SetValue("Red", (object)(int)BackColor.R);
    selfPlacingWindowKey.SetValue("Green", (object)(int)BackColor.G);
    selfPlacingWindowKey.SetValue("Blue", (object)(int)BackColor.B);
    selfPlacingWindowKey.SetValue("Width", (object)Width);
    selfPlacingWindowKey.SetValue("Height", (object)Height);
    selfPlacingWindowKey.SetValue("X", (object)DesktopLocation.X);
    selfPlacingWindowKey.SetValue("Y", (object)DesktopLocation.Y);
    selfPlacingWindowKey.SetValue("WindowState",
                (object)WindowState.ToString());
}
```

There's quite a lot going on here. We start off by navigating through the Registry to get to the `HKLM\Software\WroxPress\SelfPlacingWindow` registry key using the technique we demonstrated earlier, starting with the `Registry.LocalMachine` static property that represents the `HKLM` hive.

Then we use the `RegistryKey.OpenSubKey()` method, rather than `RegistryKey.CreateSubKey()` to get to the `HKLM/Software` key. That's because we can be very confident this key already exists – if it doesn't then there's something very seriously wrong with our computer, as this key contains settings for a lot of system software! We also indicate that we need write access to this key. That's because if the `WroxPress` key doesn't already exist we will need to create it – which involves writing to the parent key.

The next key to navigate to is `HKLM\Software\WroxPress` – and here we are not certain whether the key already exists, so we use `CreateSubKey()` to automatically create it if it doesn't. Note that `CreateSubKey()` automatically gives us write access to the key in question. Once we have reached `HKLM\Software\WroxPress\SelfPlacingWindow`, it is simply a matter of calling the `RegistryKey.SetValue()` method a number of times to either create or set the appropriate values. There are, however, a couple of complications.

Firstly, you might notice that we are using a couple of classes that we've not encountered before. The `DeskTopLocation` property of the `Form` class indicates the position of the top left corner of the screen, and is of type `Point`. We'll cover the `Point` structure in Chapter 19. What we need to know here is that it contains two `int` values, `X` and `Y`, which represent the horizontal and vertical position on the screen. We also look up three member properties of the `Form.BackColor` property, which is an instance of the `Color` class: R, G, and B: `Color` you'll guess represents a color, and these properties on it give the red, green, and blue components that make up the color and are all of type `byte`. We also use the `Form.WindowState` property – this contains an enumeration that gives the current state of the window – `Minimized`, `Maximized`, or `Normal`.

The other complication here is that we need to be a little careful about our casts: `SetValue()` takes two parameters – a `string` that gives the name of the key, and a `System.Object` instance, which contains the value. `SetValue()` has a choice of format for storing the value – it can store it as `REG_SZ`, `REG_BINARY`, or `REG_DWORD` – and it is actually pretty intelligent about making a sensible choice depending on the data type that has been given. Hence for the `WindowState`, we pass it a `string`, and `SetValue()` sensibly determines that this should be translated to `REG_SZ`. Similarly, for the various positions and dimensions we supply `int`s, which will be converted into `REG_DWORD`. However, the color components are more complicated as we want these to be stored as `REG_DWORD` too because they are numeric types. However, if `SetValue()` sees that the data is of type `byte`, it will store it as a string – as `REG_SZ` in the Registry. In order to prevent this, we cast the color components to `int`s.

We've also explicitly cast all the values to the type `object`. We don't really need to do this as the cast from any other data type to `object` is implicit, but we are doing so in order to make it clear what's going on and remind ourselves that `SetValue()` is defined to take just an object reference as its second parameter.

The `ReadSettings()` method is a little longer because for each value read in, we also need to interpret it, display the value in the listbox, and make the appropriate adjustments to the relevant property of the main form. `ReadSettings()` looks like this:

```
bool ReadSettings()
{
    RegistryKey softwareKey =
                Registry.LocalMachine.OpenSubKey("Software");
    RegistryKey wroxKey = softwareKey.OpenSubKey("WroxPress");
    if (wroxKey == null)
        return false;
    RegistryKey selfPlacingWindowKey =
                wroxKey.OpenSubKey("SelfPlacingWindow");
    if (selfPlacingWindowKey == null)
        return false;
    else
        listBoxMessages.Items.Add("Successfully opened key " +
                selfPlacingWindowKey.ToString());
    int redComponent = (int)selfPlacingWindowKey.GetValue("Red");
    int greenComponent = (int)selfPlacingWindowKey.GetValue("Green");
    int blueComponent = (int)selfPlacingWindowKey.GetValue("Blue");
    this.BackColor = Color.FromArgb(redComponent, greenComponent,
                blueComponent);
    listBoxMessages.Items.Add("Background color: " + BackColor.Name);
    int X = (int)selfPlacingWindowKey.GetValue("X");
```

```
            int Y = (int)selfPlacingWindowKey.GetValue("Y");
            this.DesktopLocation = new Point(X, Y);
            listBoxMessages.Items.Add("Desktop location: " +
                    DesktopLocation.ToString());
            this.Height = (int)selfPlacingWindowKey.GetValue("Height");
            this.Width = (int)selfPlacingWindowKey.GetValue("Width");
            listBoxMessages.Items.Add("Size: " + new
                    Size(Width,Height).ToString());
            string initialWindowState =
                    (string)selfPlacingWindowKey.GetValue("WindowState");
            listBoxMessages.Items.Add("Window State: " + initialWindowState);
            this.WindowState = (FormWindowState)FormWindowState.Parse
                    (WindowState.GetType(), initialWindowState);
            return true;
        }
```

In `ReadSettings()` we first have to navigate to the `HKLM/Software/WroxPress/SelfPlacingWindow` registry key. In this case, however, we are hoping to find the key there so that we can read it. If it's not there, then it's probably the first time we have run the example. In this case, we just want to abort reading the keys, and we certainly don't want to create any keys. Now we use the `RegistryKey.OpenSubKey()` method all the way down. If at any stage `OpenSubkey()` returns a `null` reference then we know that the registry key isn't there and we can simply return the value `false` back to the calling code.

When it comes to actually reading the keys, we use the `RegistryKey.GetValue()` method, which is defined as returning an object reference – which means this method can actually return an instance of literally any class it chooses. Like `SetValue()`, it will return a class of object appropriate to the type of data it found in the key – so we can usually assume that the REG_SZ keys will give us a string and the other keys will give us an `int`. We also cast the return reference from `SetValue()` accordingly. If there is an exception, say someone has fiddled with the Registry and mangled the value types, then our cast will cause an exception to be thrown – which will be caught by the handler in the `Form1` constructor.

The rest of this code uses one more data type that you might not be familiar with – again because we don't cover it until the graphics chapter – the `Size` structure. This is similar to a `Point` structure, but is used to represent sizes rather than coordinates. It has two member properties, `Width` and `Height`, and we use the `Size` structure here simply as a convenient way of packaging up the size of the form for displaying in the listbox.

Summary

In this chapter, we have examined how to use the .NET base classes to access the Registry and the file system from your C# code. We've seen that in both cases the base classes expose simple, but powerful, object models that make it very simple to perform almost any kind of action in these areas. In the case of the Registry, these are creating, modifying, or reading keys, and in the case of the file system, copying files, moving, creating, and deleting files and folders, and reading and writing both binary and text files.

In this chapter we have assumed that you are running your code from an account that has sufficient access rights to do whatever the code needs to do. Obviously, the question of security is an important one where file access is concerned, and we will examine that area in Chapter 23, *.NET Security*.

13

Working with the Active Directory

A major (maybe the most important) feature that was introduced with Windows 2000 is the **Active Directory**. The Active Directory is a **directory service,** which provides a central, hierarchical store for user information, network resources, services, etc. It is also possible to extend the information in this directory service to store custom data that is of interest for the enterprise.

For example, Microsoft's Exchange Server 2000 uses the Active Directory intensively to store public folders and other items.

Before the Active Directory was available, the Exchange Server used its own private store for its objects. It was necessary for a system administrator to configure two user IDs for a single person: a user account in the Windows NT domain so that a logon was possible, and a user in the Exchange Directory. This was necessary because additional information for users was needed (such as e-mail addresses, phone numbers, and so on), and the user information for the NT domain was not extensible to let us put the required information in there. Now the system administrator only needs to configure a single user for a person in the Active Directory; the information for a user object can be extended so that it fits the requirements of the Exchange Server. We can also extend this information.

User information is stored in the Active Directory. Suppose we extend this information with a skills list. This way, it would easily be possible to track down a C# developer by searching for the required C# skill .

In this chapter, we will look at how we can use the .NET Framework to access and manipulate the data in a directory service using classes from the System.DirectoryServices namespace.

> *To use the examples in this chapter you need a Windows 2000 Server with the Active Directory installed and configured. The classes of the System.DirectoryServices namespace can also be used for Novell Directory Services and Windows NT 4, with small modifications to the code presented here.*

In this chapter we will cover:

❑ The architecture of the Active Directory – features and basic concepts

❑ Some of the tools available for administration of the Active Directory, and their benefit to programming

❑ How to read and modify data in the Active Directory

❑ Searching for objects in the Active Directory

❑ After discussing the architecture and how to program the Active Directory we are going to create a Windows application where we can specify properties and a filter to search for user objects

Architecture of the Active Directory

Before we start programming we have to know how the Active Directory works, what it is used for, and what data we can store there.

Features

The features of the Active Directory can be grouped into the following list:

❑ The data in the Active Directory is grouped **hierarchically**. Objects can be stored inside other container objects. Instead of having a single, large list of users, the users can be grouped inside organizational units. An organizational unit can contain other organizational units, so we can build a tree.

❑ The Active Directory uses a **multi-master replication**. In Windows NT 4 domains the **primary domain controller**, **PDC**, was the master. In Windows 2000 with the Active Directory every **domain controller**, **DC**, is a master. If the PDC in a Windows NT 4 domain is down, no user can change their password; the system administrator can only update users when the PDC is up and running. With the Active Directory, updates can be applied to any DC. This model is much more scalable, as updates can happen to different servers concurrently. The disadvantage of this model is that replication is more complex. We will talk about the replication issues later in this chapter.

❑ The **replication topology** is flexible, to support replications across slow links in WANs. How often data should be replicated is configurable by the domain administrators.

❑ The Active Directory supports **open standards**. **LDAP**, the **Lightweight Directory Access Protocol**, is one of the standards that can be used to access the data in the Active Directory. LDAP is an Internet standard that can be used to access a lot of different directory services. With LDAP a programming interface, LDAP API, is also defined. The LDAP API can be used to access the Active Directory with the C language. Microsoft's preferred programming interface to directory services is **ADSI**, the **Active Directory Service Interface**. This, of course, is not an open standard. In contrast to the LDAP API, ADSI makes it possible to access all features of the Active Directory. Another standard that's used within the Active Directory is **Kerberos**, which is used for authentication. The Windows 2000 Kerberos service can also be used to authenticate UNIX clients.

❑ With the Active Directory we have a **fine-grained security**. Every object stored in the Active Directory can have an associated access-control list that defines who can do what with that object.

The objects in the directory are **strongly typed,** which means that the type of an object is exactly defined; no attributes that are not specified may be added to an object. In the **Schema,** the object types as well as the parts of an object (attributes) are defined. Attributes can be mandatory or optional.

For more information about ADSI you can read Simon Robinson's *Professional ADSI Programming,* Wrox Press, ISBN 1-861002-26-2.

Active Directory Concepts

Before programming the Active Directory, we need to begin with some basic terms and definitions.

Objects

We store objects in the Active Directory. An object refers to something concrete such as a user, a printer, or a network share. Objects have mandatory and optional attributes that describe them. Some examples of the attributes of a user object are the first name, last name, e-mail address, phone number, and so on.

The following figure shows a container object called Wrox Press that contains some other objects; two user objects, a contact object, a printer object, and a user group object:

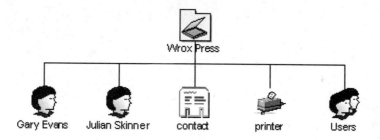

Schema

Every object is an instance of a class that is defined in the **schema.** The schema **defines the types,** and is itself stored within objects in the Active Directory. We have to differentiate between classSchema and attributeSchema. The types of objects are defined in the classSchema, as well as detailing what mandatory and optional attributes an object has. The attributeSchema defines what an attribute looks like, and what the allowed syntax for a specific attribute is.

We can define custom types and attributes, and add these to the schema. Be aware, however, that a new schema type can never be removed from the Active Directory. It's possible to mark it as inactive so that new objects cannot be created any more, but there can be existing objects of that type, so it's not possible to remove classes or attributes that are defined in the schema. The Windows 2000 Administrator doesn't have enough rights to create new schema entries; the Windows 2000 Domain Enterprise Administrator is needed here.

Configuration

Besides objects and class definitions that are stored as objects, the configuration of the Active Directory itself is stored within the Active Directory. The configuration of the Active Directory stores the information about all sites, such as the replication intervals, that is set up by the system administrator. The configuration itself is stored in the Active Directory, so we can access the configuration information like all other objects in the Active Directory.

Active Directory Domain

A domain is a security boundary of a Windows network. In the Active Directory domain, the objects are stored in a hierarchical order. The Active Directory itself is made up of one or more domains. The hierarchical order of objects within a domain is presented in the figure below, in which we see a domain represented by a triangle. Container objects such as `Users`, `Computers`, and `Books` can store other objects. Each oval in the picture represents an object, with the lines between the objects representing parent-child relationships. For instance, `Books` is the parent of `.NET` and `Java`, and `Pro C#`, `Beg C#`, and `ASP.NET` are child objects of the `.NET` object.

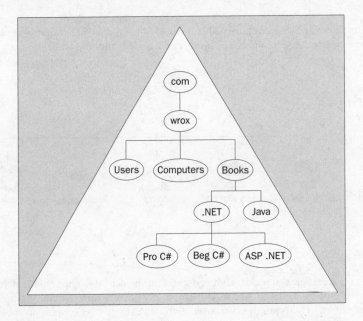

Domain Controller

A single domain can have multiple domain controllers, each of which stores all of the objects within the domain. There is no master server, and all DCs are treated equally; we have a multi-master model. The objects are replicated across the servers inside the domain.

Site

A **site** is a location in the network holding at least one DC. If we have multiple locations in the enterprise, which are connected with slow network links, we can use multiple sites for a single domain. For backup or scalability reasons, each site can have one or more DCs running. Replication between servers in a site can happen at shorter intervals due to the faster network connection. Replication is configured to occur at larger time intervals between servers across sites, depending on the speed of the network. Of course, the domain administrator can configure this.

Domain Tree

Multiple domains can be connected by trust relationships. These domains share a **common schema**, a **common configuration**, and a **global catalog** (we will talk about global catalogs soon). A common schema and a common configuration mean that this data is replicated across domains. Domain trees share the same class and attribute schema. The objects themselves are not replicated across domains.

Domains connected in such a way form a Domain Tree. Domains in a domain tree have a **contiguous, hierarchical namespace**. This means that the domain name of the child domain is the name of that child domain appended to the name of the parent domain. Between domains, trusts that use the Kerberos protocol are established.

For example, we have the root domain `wrox.com`, which is the **parent domain** of the **child domains** `india.wrox.com` and `uk.wrox.com`. A trust is set up between the parent and the child domains, so that accounts from one domain can be authenticated by another domain.

Forest

Multiple domain trees connected using a common schema, a common configuration, and a global catalog without a contiguous namespace, are called a forest. A forest is a set of domain trees. A forest can be used if the company has a sub-company where a different domain name should be used. Let's say that `asptoday.com` should be relatively independent of the domain `wrox.com`, but it should be possible to have a common management, and be possible for users from `asptoday.com` to access resources from the `wrox.com` domain, and the other way around. With a forest we can have trusts between multiple domain trees.

Global Catalog

A search for an object can span multiple domains. If we look for a specific `user` object with some attributes we have to search every domain. Starting with `wrox.com`, the search continues to `uk.wrox.com` and `india.wrox.com`; across slow links such a search could take a while.

To make searches faster, all objects are copied to the **global catalog, GC**. The GC is replicated in every domain of a forest. There's at least one server in every domain holding a GC. For performance and scalability reasons, we can have more than one GC server in a domain. Using a GC, a search through all the objects can happen on a single server.

The GC is a **read-only cache** of all the objects, which can only be used for searches; the domain controllers must be used to do updates.

Not all attributes of an object are stored in the GC. We can define whether or not an attribute should be stored with an object. The decision whether to store an attribute in the GC depends on the frequency of its use in searches. A picture of a user isn't useful in the GC, because you would never search for a picture. Conversely, the phone number would be a useful addition to the store. You can also define that an attribute should be indexed so that a query for it is faster.

Replication

As programmers we are unlikely to ever configure replication, but because it affects the data we store in the Active Directory, we have to know how it works. The Active Directory uses a **multi-master** server architecture. Updates can and will happen to every domain controller in the domain. The **replication latency** defines how long it takes until an update happens.

❑ The configurable **change notification** happens, by default, every 5 minutes inside a site if some attributes change. The DC where a change occurred informs one server after the other with 30-second intervals, so the fourth DC can get the change notification after 7 minutes. The default change notification across sites is set to 180 minutes. Intra- and inter-site replication can each be configured to other values.

❑ If no changes occurred, the **scheduled replication** occurs every 60 minutes inside a site. This is to ensure that a change notification wasn't missed.

❑ For security-sensitive information such as account lockout **immediate notification** can occur.

With a replication, only the changes are copied to the DCs. With every change of an attribute a version number (USN, update sequence number) and a time stamp are recorded. These are used to help resolve conflicts if updates happened to the same attribute on different servers.

Let's look at one example. The mobile phone attribute of the user John Doe has the USN number 47. This value is already replicated to all DCs. One system administrator changes the phone number. The change occurs on the server DC1; the new USN of this attribute on the server DC1 is now 48, whereas the other DCs still have the USN 47. For someone still reading the attribute, the old value can be read until the replication to all domain controllers has occurred.

Now the rare case can happen that another administrator changes the phone number attribute, and here a different DC was selected because this administrator received a faster response from the server DC2. The USN of this attribute on the server DC2 is also changed to 48.

At the notification intervals, notification happens because the USN for the attribute changed, and the last time replication occurred was with a USN value 47. With the replication mechanism it is now detected that the servers DC1 and DC2 both have a USN of 48 for the phone number attribute. What server is the winner is not really important, but one server must win. To resolve this conflict the time stamp of the change is used. Because the change happened later on DC2 the value stored in the DC2 domain controller gets replicated.

> When reading objects, we have to be aware that the data is not necessarily current. The currency of the data depends on replication latencies. When updating objects, another user can still read some old values after the update. It's also possible that different updates can happen at the same time.

Characteristics of Active Directory Data

The Active Directory doesn't replace a relational database or the Registry – but what kind of data would we store in it?

❑   We have **hierarchical data** within the Active Directory. We can have containers that store further containers, and also objects. Containers themselves are objects, too.

❑   The data should be used for **read-mostly**. Because of replication occurring at certain time-intervals, we cannot be sure that we will read up-to-date data. In applications we must be aware that the information we read is possibly not the current up-to-date information.

❑   Data should be of global interest to the enterprise; this is because adding a new data type to theschema replicates to it all the servers in the enterprise. For data types that are only of interest to a small number of users, the Domain Enterprise Administrator wouldn't normally install new schema types.

❑   The data stored should be of **reasonable size** because of replication issues. If the data size is 100K, it is fine to store this data in the directory if the data changes only once per week. However, if the data changes once per hour, then data of this size is too large. Always think about replicating the data to different servers: where the data gets transferred to, and at what intervals. If you have larger data it's possible to put a link into the Active Directory, and store the data itself in a different place.

To summarize, the data we store in the Active Directory should be hierarchically organized, of reasonable size, and important for the enterprise.

Schema

Active Directory objects are strongly typed. The schema defines the types of the objects, mandatory and optional attributes, and the syntaxes and constraints of these attributes. In the schema we can differentiate between class-schema and attribute-schema objects. A class is a collection of attributes. With the classes, single inheritance is supported. As can be seen in the following class diagram, the user class derives from the organizationalPerson class, organizationalPerson is a subclass of person, and the base class is top. The classSchema that defines a class describes the attributes with the systemMayContain attribute.

The diagram to the right shows only a few of all the `systemMayContain` values. Using the ADSI Edit tool, you can easily see all the values; we will look at this in the next section.

In the root class `top` we can see that every object can have common name (`cn`), `displayName`, `objectGUID`, `whenChanged`, and `whenCreated` attributes. The `person` class derives from `top`. A `person` object also has a `userPassword` and a `telephoneNumber`. `OrganizationalPerson` derives from `person`. In addition to the attributes of `person` it has a `manager`, `department`, and `company`; and a `user` has extra attributes needed to log on to a system:

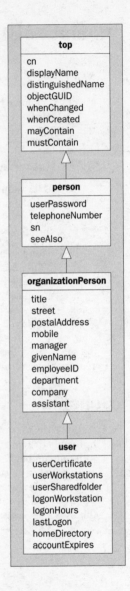

Administration Tools for the Active Directory

We will not really talk about the administration of the Active Directory. Administration is the responsibility of the Windows 2000 system administrators, and we want to talk about programming the Active Directory. However, looking into some of the administration tools can help to give us an idea of the Active Directory, what data is in there, and what can be done programmatically.

The system administrator has a lot of tools to enter new data, update data, and configure the Active Directory:

❑ The **Active Directory Users and Computers** MMC snap-in is used to enter new users and update user data

❑ The **Active Directory Sites and Services** MMC snap-in is used to configure sites in a domain and replication between these sites

❑ The **Active Directory Domains and Trusts** MMC snap-in can be used to build up a trust relationship between domains in a tree

❑ **ADSI Edit** is the editor of the Active Directory, where every object can be viewed and edited

In addition to the tools for the system administrator, we get a tool with the Microsoft Platform SDK: **ADSI Viewer**.

Active Directory Users and Computers

The Active Directory Users and Computers snap-in is the tool that's mainly used by System Administrators to manage users. Select Start | Programs | Administrative Tools | Active Directory Users and Computers:

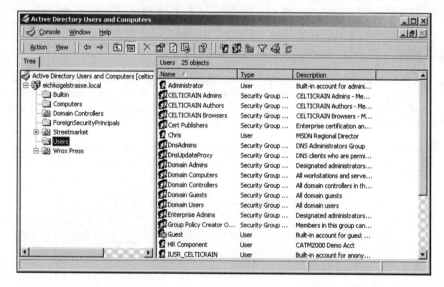

With this tool we can add new users, groups, contacts, organizational units, printers, shared folders, or computers, and modify existing ones. In the next screenshot you can see the attributes that can be entered for a user object: office, phone numbers, e-mail addresses, web pages, organization information, addresses, groups, and so on. This is much more information than was ever possible in an NT 4 domain:

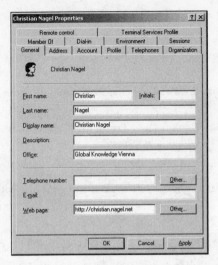

Active Directory Users and Computers can also be used in big enterprises with maybe millions of objects. It's not necessary to look through a list with a thousand objects, because we can select a custom filter so that only some of the objects are displayed. We can also do an LDAP query to search for the objects in the enterprise. We shall explore these possibilities later in the chapter.

ADSI Edit

ADSI Edit is the editor of the Active Directory. This tool is not installed automatically; on the Windows 2000 Server CD you can find a directory named Supporting Tools. When the supporting tools are installed you'll find ADSI Edit from the start menu: Start | Programs | Windows 2000 Support Tools | Tools | ADSI Edit.

ADSI Edit offers greater control than the Active Directory Users and Computers tool; with ADSI Edit everything can be configured, and we can also look at the schema and the configuration. This tool is not that easy to use, however, and it is very easy to enter wrong data:

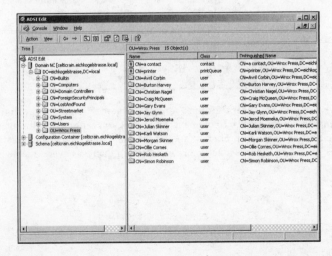

By opening the Properties window of an object, we can view and change every attribute of an object in the Active Directory. We see mandatory and optional attributes, with their types and values:

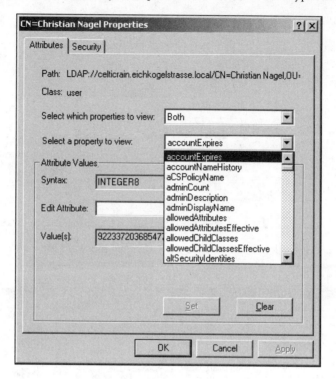

ADSI Viewer

You should also install the Active Directory Browser that's part of the Microsoft Platform SDK. The Microsoft Platform SDK is not part of the Visual Studio .NET distribution. You get a CD with the MSDN subscription, or you can download it from the MSDN Web. After installing the Platform SDK you can start the tool by selecting Start | Programs | Microsoft Platform SDK | Tools | ADSI Viewer.

The ADSI Viewer has two modes. With File | New we can start a query or use the Object Viewer to display and modify attributes of objects. After starting the Object Viewer we can specify an LDAP path, as well as username and password to open the object. In the next section, we will start doing this programmatically, and you will be able to see what form the LDAP path can take. Here I'm specifying LDAP://OU=Wrox Press, DC=eichkogelstrasse, DC=local to access a organizational unit object:

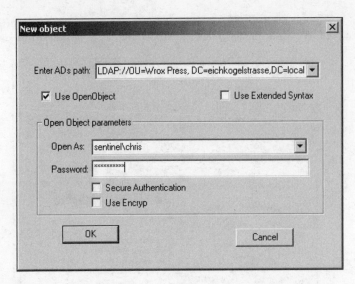

If the object we specify with the path and the username and password are valid, we get the Object Viewer screen, where we can view and modify the properties of the object and its child objects:

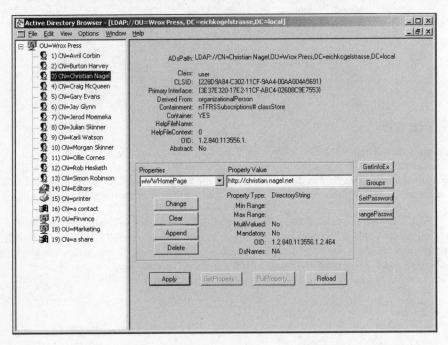

Active Directory Service Interfaces (ADSI)

The **Active Directory Service Interfaces** (**ADSI**) is a programmatic interface to directory services. ADSI defines some COM interfaces that are implemented by ADSI providers. This means that the client can use different directory services with the same programmatic interfaces. The .NET Framework classes in the System.DirectoryServices namespace make use of the ADSI interfaces.

In the following picture we can see some ADSI Providers (LDAP, WinNT, and NDS) that implement COM interfaces like IADs and IUnknown. The assembly System.DirectoryServices makes use of the ADSI providers:

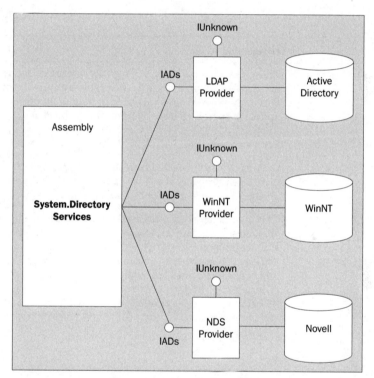

Programming the Active Directory

To develop programs for the Active Directory, we use classes from the System.DirectoryServices namespace and have to reference the System.DirectoryServices assembly. With these classes we can query objects, view and update properties, search for objects, and move objects to other container objects. In the following code segments we use a simple C# console application to demonstrate how the classes in the System.DirectoryServices namespace can be used.

In this section, we'll cover:

❑ Classes in the `System.DirectoryServices` namespace

❑ The process of connecting to the Active Directory – binding

❑ Getting directory entries, and creating new objects and updating existing entries

❑ Searching the Active Directory

Classes in System.DirectoryServices

The following table shows the major classes in the `System.DirectoryServices` namespace:

Class	Description
DirectoryEntry	This class is the main class of the `System.DirectoryServices` namespace. An object of this class represents an object in the Active Directory store. We use this class to bind to an object, and to view and update properties. The properties of the object are represented in a `PropertyCollection`. Every item in the `PropertyCollection` has a `PropertyValueCollection`.
DirectoryEntries	`DirectoryEntries` is a collection of `DirectoryEntry` objects. The `Children` property of a `DirectoryEntry` object returns a list of objects in a `DirectoryEntries` collection.
DirectorySearcher	This class is the main class used for searching for objects with specific attributes. To define the search the `SortOption` class and the enumerations `SearchScope`, `SortDirection`, and `ReferalChasingOption` can be used. The search results in a `SearchResult` or a `SearchResultCollection`. We also get `ResultPropertyCollection` and `ResultPropertyValueCollection` objects.

Binding

To get the values of an object in the Active Directory, we have to connect to the Active Directory. The connecting process is called **binding**. The binding path can look like this:

```
LDAP://dc01.globalknowledge.net/OU=Marketing, DC=GlobalKnowledge, DC=Com
```

With the binding process we can specify these items:

❑ The **Protocol** specifies the provider to be used

❑ The **Server Name** of the domain controller

❑ The **Port Number** of the server process

❑   The **Distinguished Name** of the object; this identifies the object we want to access

❑   The **Username** and **Password** if a user that's different to the account running the current process is needed for accessing the Active Directory

❑   An **Authentication** type can also be specified if encryption is needed

Let's have a more detailed look into these options:

Protocol

The first part of a binding path specifies the ADSI provider. The provider is implemented as a COM server; for identification a `progID` can be found in the Registry directly under `HKEY_CLASSES_ROOT`. The providers we get with Windows 2000 are listed in this table:

Provider	Description
LDAP	LDAP Server, such as the Exchange directory and the Windows 2000 Active Directory Server.
GC	GC is used to access the global catalog in the Active Directory. It can be used for fast queries.
IIS	With the ADSI provider for IIS it's possible to create new web sites and administer it in the IIS catalog.
WinNT	To access the user database of old Windows NT 4 domains we can use the ADSI provider for WinNT. The fact that NT 4 users only have a few attributes remains unchanged. It is also possible to use this protocol to bind to a Windows 2000 domain, but here you are also restricted to the attributes that are available with NT 4.
NDS	This `progID` is used to communicate with Novell Directory Services.
NWCOMPAT	With NWCOMPAT we can access old Novell directories, such as Novell Netware 3.x.

Server Name

The **server name** follows the protocol in the binding path. The server name is optional if you are logged on to an Active Directory domain. Without a server name **serverless binding** occurs; this means that Windows 2000 tries to get the "best" domain controller in the domain that's associated with the user doing the bind. If there's no server inside a site, the first domain controller that can be found will be used.

A serverless binding can look like `LDAP://OU=Sales, DC=GlobalKnowledge, DC=Com`.

Port Number

After the server name we can specify the **port number** of the server process, by using the syntax `:xxx`. The default port number for the LDAP server is port 389: `LDAP://dc01.globalknowledge.net:389`. The Exchange server uses the same port number as the LDAP server. If the Exchange server is installed on the same system – for example, as a domain controller of the Active Directory – a different port can be configured.

731

Distinguished Name

The fourth part that we can specify in the path is the **distinguished name (DN).** The distinguished name is a guaranteed unique name that identifies the object we want to access. With the Active Directory we can use LDAP syntax that is based on X.500 to specify the name of the object.

For example, we could have this distinguished name:

```
CN=Christian Nagel, OU=Trainer, DC=GlobalKnowledge, DC=com
```

This distinguished name specifies a Common Name (CN) of `Christian Nagel` in the Organizational Unit (OU) called `Trainer` in the Domain Component (DC) called `GlobalKnowledge` of the domain `GlobalKnowledge.com`. The part that is specified rightmost is the root object of the domain. The name has to follow the hierarchy in the object tree.

The LDAP specification for the string representation of distinguished names can be found in RFC 2253: http://www.ietf.org/rfc/rfc2253.txt.

Relative Distinguished Name

A **relative distinguished name (RDN)** is used to reference objects within a container object. With an RDN the specification of OU and DC is not needed, as a common name is enough. `CN=Christian Nagel` is the relative distinguished name inside the organizational unit. A relative distinguished name can be used if we already have a reference to a container object and we want to access child objects.

Default Naming Context

If a distinguished name is not specified in the path, the binding process will be made to the default naming context. We can read the default naming context with the help of `rootDSE`. LDAP 3.0 defines `rootDSE` as the root of a directory tree on a directory server. For example:

```
LDAP://rootDSE
```

or:

```
LDAP://servername/rootDSE
```

By enumerating all properties of the `rootDSE` we can get the information about the `defaultNamingContext` that will be used when no name is specified. `schemaNamingContext` and `configurationNamingContext` specify the required names to be used to access the schema and the configuration in the Active Directory store.

The following code is used to get all properties of the `rootDSE`:

```
using (DirectoryEntry de = new DirectoryEntry())
{
    de.Path = "LDAP://celticrain/rootDSE";
    de.Username = @"sentinel\chris";
    de.Password = "someSecret";

    PropertyCollection props = de.Properties;
```

```
    foreach (string prop in props.PropertyNames)
    {
       PropertyValueCollection values = props[prop];
       foreach (string val in values)
       {
          Console.Write(prop + ": ");
          Console.WriteLine(val);
       }
    }
 }
```

Besides outputting other properties, this program shows the defaultNamingContext
DC=eichkogelstrasse, DC=local, the context that can be used to access the schema: CN=Schema,
CN=Configuration, DC=eichkogelstrasse, DC=local, and the naming context of the
configuration: CN=Configuration, DC=eichkogelstrasse, DC=local:

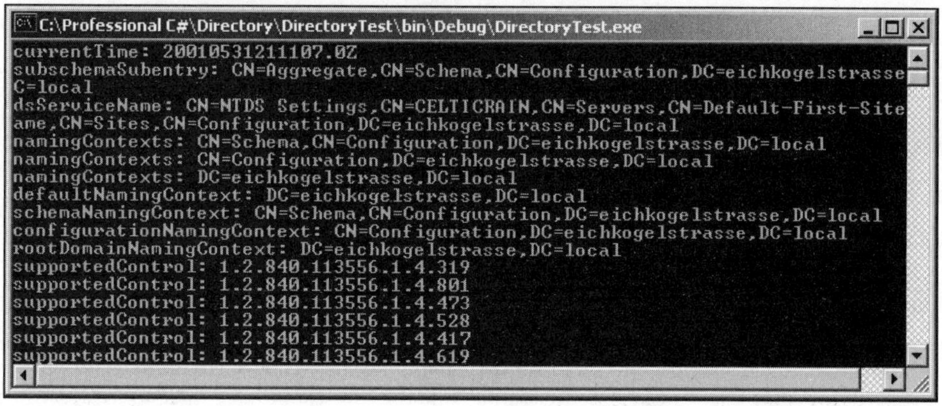

Object Identifier

Every object has a unique identifier, a GUID. A GUID is a unique 128-bit number as you may already/
know from COM development. We can bind to an object using the GUID. This way we always get to
the same object no matter if the object was moved to a different container. The GUID is generated at
object creation and always remains the same.

We can get to a GUID string representation with DirectoryEntry.NativeGuid. This string
representation can then be used to bind to the object.

This example shows the path name for a serverless binding to bind to a specific object represented by a GUID:

```
LDAP://<GUID=14abbd652aae1a47abc60782dcfc78ea>
```

Object Names in Windows NT Domains

The WinNT provider doesn't allow LDAP syntax in the name part of the binding string. With this
provider the object is specified using ObjectName, ClassName. Valid binding strings for a Windows
NT domain are:

```
WinNT:
WinNT://DomainName
WinNT://DomainName/UserName, user
WinNT://DomainName/ServerName/MyGroup, group
```

The user and group postfixes specify that we access objects of type user or group.

Username

If a user other than the user of the current process must be used for accessing the directory (maybe this user doesn't have the required permissions to access the Active Directory), explicit **user credentials** must be specified for the binding process. With Active Directory we have a number of ways to set the username.

Downlevel Logon

With a downlevel logon the username can be specified with the pre-Windows 2000 domain name:

```
domain\username
```

Distinguished Name

The user can also be specified by a distinguished name of a user object, for example:

```
CN=Administrator, CN=Users, DC=eichkogelstrasse, DC=local
```

User Principal Name (UPN)

The **user principal name** (**UPN**) of an object is defined with the userPrincipalName attribute. The system administrator specifies this with the logon information in the Account tab of the User properties with the Active Directory Users and Computers tool. Note that this is not the e-mail address of the user.

This information also uniquely identifies a user, and can be used for a logon:

```
Nagel@eichkogelstrasse.local
```

Authentication

For secure encrypted authentication the **authentication** type can also be specified. The authentication can be set with the AuthenticationType property of the DirectoryEntry class. The value that can be assigned is one of the AuthenticationTypes enumeration values. Because the enumeration is marked with the [Flags] attribute, multiple values can be specified. Some of the possible values are where the data sent is encrypted, ReadonlyServer, where we specify that we need only read access, and Secure for secure authentication.

Binding with the DirectoryEntry Class

The System.DirectoryServices.DirectoryEntry class can be used to specify all the binding information. We can use the default constructor and define the binding information with the properties Path, Username, Password, and AuthenticationType, or pass all the information in the constructor:

```
DirectoryEntry de = new DirectoryEntry();
de.Path = "LDAP://celticrain/DC=eichkogelstrasse, DC=local";
de.Username = "nagel@eichkogelstrasse.local";
de.Password = "someSecret";

// use the current user credentials
DirectoryEntry de2 = new DirectoryEntry(
                      "LDAP://DC=eichkogelstrasse, DC=local");
```

Even if constructing the `DirectoryEntry` object is successful, this doesn't mean that the binding was a success. Binding will happen the first time a property is read to avoid unnecessary network traffic. At the first access of the object, it can be seen if the object exists, and if the specified user credentials are correct.

Getting Directory Entries

Now that we know how to specify the binding attributes to an object in the Active Directory, let's read the attributes of an object.

Properties of User Objects

The `DirectoryEntry` class has some properties to get information about the object: the `Name`, `Guid`, and `SchemaClassName` properties. The first time we access a property of the `DirectoryEntry` object, the binding occurs and the cache of the underlying ADSI object is filled. We will discuss this, more detail later. When we access the other properties, we're reading them just from the cache, and communication with the server isn't necessary for data from the same object.

In this example we are accessing a `user` object with the common name `Christian Nagel` in the organization unit `Wrox Press`:

```
using (DirectoryEntry de = new DirectoryEntry())
{
    de.Path = "LDAP://celticrain/CN=Christian Nagel, " +
              "OU=Wrox Press, DC=eichkogelstrasse, DC=local";

    Console.WriteLine("Name: " + de.Name);
    Console.WriteLine("GUID: " + de.Guid);
    Console.WriteLine("Type: " + de.SchemaClassName);
    Console.WriteLine();

    //...
}
```

An Active Directory object holds much more information, with the information available depending on the type of the object; the `Properties` property returns a `PropertyCollection`. Each property is itself a collection, because a single property can have multiple values, for example, the `user` object can have multiple phone numbers. In our example, we go through the values with an inner `foreach` loop. The collection that is returned from `properties[name]` is an `object` array. The attribute values can be strings, numbers, or other types. We will just use the `ToString()` method to display the values.

```
    Console.WriteLine("Properties: ");
    PropertyCollection properties = de.Properties;
    foreach (string name in properties.PropertyNames)
    {
        foreach (object o in properties[name])
        {
            Console.WriteLine(name + ": " + o.ToString());
        }
    }
```

In the resulting output we see all attributes of the user object Christian Nagel. We can see that otherTelephone is a multivalue property that has many phone numbers. Some of the property values just display the type of the object, System.__ComObject, for example lastLogoff, lastLogon, and nTSecurityDescriptor. To get the values of these attributes we have to use the ADSI COM interfaces directly from the classes in the System.DirectoryServices namespace.

In Chapter 17 you can read about how to work with COM objects and interfaces.

```
C:\Professional C#\Directory\DirectoryTest\bin\Debug\DirectoryTest.exe
Name: CN=Christian Nagel
GUID: 14abbd65-2aae-1a47-abc6-0782dcfc78ea
Type: user

Properties:
accountExpires: System.__ComObject
badPasswordTime: System.__ComObject
badPwdCount: 0
codePage: 0
cn: Christian Nagel
company: Global Knowledge
countryCode: 0
description: Author
displayName: Christian Nagel
givenName: Christian
instanceType: 4
lastLogoff: System.__ComObject
lastLogon: System.__ComObject
logonCount: 0
nTSecurityDescriptor: System.__ComObject
distinguishedName: CN=Christian Nagel,OU=Wrox Press,DC=eichkogelstrasse,DC=loca
l
objectCategory: CN=Person,CN=Schema,CN=Configuration,DC=eichkogelstrasse,DC=loc
al
objectClass: top
objectClass: person
objectClass: organizationalPerson
objectClass: user
objectGUID: System.Byte[]
objectSid: System.Byte[]
homePhone: +43(1)112233
mobile: +43(664)32344344
otherTelephone: +43(1)3333333333
otherTelephone: +43(1)2222222222
otherTelephone: +43(1)1111111111
primaryGroupID: 513
pwdLastSet: System.__ComObject
name: Christian Nagel
sAMAccountName: Nagel
sAMAccountType: 805306368
sn: Nagel
userAccountControl: 512
userPrincipalName: Nagel@eichkogelstrasse.local
uSNChanged: System.__ComObject
uSNCreated: System.__ComObject
whenChanged: 15.05.2001 15:30:35
whenCreated: 03.05.2001 20:10:44
wWWHomePage: http://christian.nagel.net
Press any key to continue_
```

Access a Property Directly by its Name

With `DirectoryEntry.Properties` we can access all properties. If a property name is known we can access the values directly:

```csharp
foreach (string homePage in de.Properties["wWWHomePage"])
   Console.WriteLine("Home page: " + homePage);
```

Object Collections

Objects are stored hierarchically in the Active Directory. Container objects contain children. We can enumerate these child objects with the `Children` property of the class `DirectoryEntry`. In the other direction, we can get the container of an object with the `Parent` property.

A `user` object doesn't have children, so now I'm using an organizational unit instead. Non-container objects return an empty collection with the `Children` property. Let's get all `user` objects from the organizational unit `Wrox Press` in the domain `eichkogelstrasse.local`. The `Children` property returns a `DirectoryEntries` collection that collects `DirectoryEntry` objects. We iterate through all `DirectoryEntry` objects to display the name of the child objects:

```csharp
using (DirectoryEntry de = new DirectoryEntry())
{
   de.Path = "LDAP://celticrain/OU=Wrox Press, " +
             "DC=eichkogelstrasse, DC=local";

   Console.WriteLine("Children of " + de.Name);
   foreach (DirectoryEntry obj in de.Children)
   {
      Console.WriteLine(obj.Name);
   }
}
```

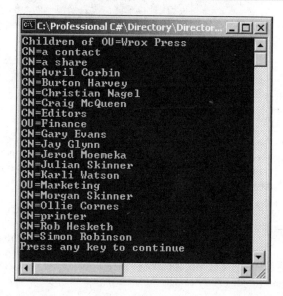

In this example we've seen all the objects in the organizational unit: `users`, `contacts`, `printers`, `shares`, and others. If we want to see only some object types we can use the `SchemaFilter` property of the `DirectoryEntries` class. The `SchemaFilter` property returns a `SchemaNameCollection`. With this `SchemaNameCollection` we can use the `Add()` method to define the object types we want to see. In our case we are just interested in seeing the `user` objects, so `user` is added to this collection:

```
using (DirectoryEntry de = new DirectoryEntry())
{
    de.Path = "LDAP://celticrain/OU=Wrox Press, " +
              "DC=eichkogelstrasse, DC=local";

    Console.WriteLine("Children of " + de.Name);
    de.Children.SchemaFilter.Add("user");
    foreach (DirectoryEntry obj in de.Children)
    {
        Console.WriteLine(obj.Name);
    }
}
```

As a result we only see the `user` objects in the organizational unit:

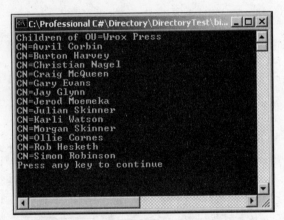

Cache

To reduce the network transfers, ADSI uses a cache for the object properties. As we mentioned earlier, the server isn't accessed when we create a `DirectoryEntry` object; instead when we first read a value from the directory store all the properties are written into the cache, so that a round trip to the server isn't necessary when we read the next property.

Writing any changes to objects will only change the cached object; setting properties doesn't generate network traffic. To transfer any changed data to the server, `DirectoryEntry.CommitChanges()` will flush the cache and take care of this. To get the newly written data from the directory store, we can use `DirectoryEntry.RefreshCache()` to read the properties. Of course if you change some properties without calling `CommitChanges()` and do a `RefreshCache()`, all your changes will be lost because we read the values from the directory service again using `RefreshCache()`.

It is possible to turn off this property cache by setting the `DirectoryEntry.UsePropertyCache` property to `false`. However, unless debugging, it's better not to turn off the cache because of the extra round trips to the server that will be generated.

Creating New Objects

When we want to create new Active Directory objects such as users, computers, printers, contacts, and so on, we can do this programmatically with the `DirectoryEntries` class.

To add new objects to the directory we first have to bind to a container object, such as an organizational unit, where new objects can be inserted – objects that can't contain other objects can't be used. Here I'm using the container object with the distinguished name `CN=Users, DC=eichkogelstrasse, DC=local`:

```
DirectoryEntry de = new DirectoryEntry();
de.Path = "LDAP://celticrain/CN=Users, DC=eichkogelstrasse, DC=local";
```

We can get to the `DirectoryEntries` object with the `Children` property of a `DirectoryEntry`:

```
DirectoryEntries users = de.Children;
```

With `DirectoryEntries` we have methods to add, remove, and find objects in the collection. Here I'm creating a new `user` object. With the `Add()` method, we need the name of the object and a type name. We can get to the type names directly using ADSI Edit.

```
DirectoryEntry user = users.Add("CN=John Doe", "user");
```

The object now has the default property values. To assign specific property values we can add properties with the `Add()` method of the `Properties` property. Of course, all of the properties must exist in the schema for the `user` object. If a specified property doesn't exist you'll get a `COMException` "The specified directory service attribute or value doesn't exist":

```
user.Properties["company"].Add("Some Company");
user.Properties["department"].Add("Sales");
user.Properties["employeeID"].Add("4711");
user.Properties["samAccountName"].Add("JDoe");
user.Properties["userPrincipalName"].Add("JDoe@eichkogelstrasse.local");
user.Properties["givenName"].Add("John");
user.Properties["sn"].Add("Doe");
user.Properties["userPassword"].Add("someSecret");
```

Finally, to write the data to the Active Directory, we have to flush the cache:

```
user.CommitChanges();
```

Updating Directory Entries

Objects in the Active Directory can be updated as easily as they can be read. After reading the object, we are able to change the values. To remove all values of a single property the method `PropertyValueCollection.Clear()` can be called. With `Add()` new values can be added to a property. `Remove()` and `RemoveAt()` remove specific values from a property collection.

We can change a value simply by setting it to the specified value. With the following code example the mobile phone number is set to a new value by using an indexer for the `PropertyValueCollection`. With the indexer a value can only be changed if it exists. Therefore, we should always check with `DirectoryEntry.Properties.Contains()` if the attribute is available:

```
using (DirectoryEntry de = new DirectoryEntry())
{
    de.Path = "LDAP://celticrain/CN=Christian Nagel, " +
              "OU=Wrox Press, DC=eichkogelstrasse, DC=local";

    if (de.Properties.Contains("mobile"))
    {
        de.Properties["mobile"][0] = "+43(664)3434343434";
    }
    else
    {
        de.Properties["mobile"].Add("+43(664)3434343434");
    }

    de.CommitChanges();
}
```

With the `else` part in our example we add a new property for the mobile phone number if it doesn't already exist with the method `PropertyValueCollection.Add()`. If we would use the `Add()` method with already existing properties the resulting effect depends on the type of the property – a single-value or a multi-value property. Using the `Add()` method with a single value property that already exists we get a COMException: A constraint violation occurred. Using `Add()` with a multi value property, however, succeeds, and an additional value is added to the property.

The property mobile for a `user` object is defined as a single-value property, so additional mobile phone numbers cannot be added. However a user can have more than one mobile phone number. For multiple mobile phone numbers we have the property `otherMobile`. `otherMobile` is a multi-value property that allows setting multiple phone numbers, and so calling `Add()` multiple times. There is one important check for multi-value properties: they are checked for uniqueness. If case the second phone number is added to the same `user` object again we get a COMException: The specified directory service attribute or value already exists.

> Remember to call `DirectoryEntry.CommitChanges()` after creating or updating new directory objects. Otherwise only the cache gets updated, and the changes are not sent to the directory service.

Accessing Native ADSI Objects

Often it is a lot easier to call methods of predefined ADSI interfaces instead of searching for the names of object properties. Some ADSI objects also support methods that can't be directly used from the DirectoryEntry class. One example of a practical use is the IADsServiceOperations interface that has methods to start and stop Windows services. Windows Services will be discussed in Chapter 22.

The classes of the System.DirectoryServices namespace use the underlying ADSI COM objects as we discussed before in this chapter. The DirectoryEntry class supports calling methods of the underlying objects directly by using the Invoke() method.

The first parameter of Invoke() requires the method name that should be called in the ADSI object; the params keyword of the second parameter allows a flexible number of additional arguments that can be passed to the ADSI method:

```
public object Invoke(string methodName, params object[] args);
```

You can find the methods that can be called with the Invoke() method in the ADSI documentation. Every object in the domain supports the methods of the IADs interface. The user object that we created previously also supports the methods of the IADsUser interface.

In the following code example, we use the method IADsUser.SetPassword() to change the password of the previously created user object:

```
using (DirectoryEntry de = new DirectoryEntry())
{
   de.Path = "LDAP://celticrain/CN=John Doe, " +
             "CN=Users, DC=eichkogelstrasse, DC=local";

   de.Invoke("SetPassword", "anotherSecret");
   de.CommitChanges();
}
```

Instead of using Invoke() it is also possible to use the underlying ADSI object directly. To use these objects we have to add a reference to the Active DS Type Library using **Project | Add Reference**. This creates a wrapper class where we can access these objects in the namespace ActiveDs.

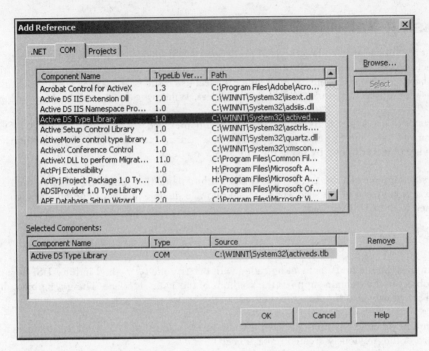

The native object can be accessed with the `NativeObject` property of the `DirectoryEntry` class. In our example, the object `de` is a `user` object, so we can cast it to `ActiveDs.IADsUser`. `SetPassword()` is a method that is documented in the `IADsUser` interface, so we can call it directly instead of using the `Invoke()` method. By setting the `AccountDisabled` property of `IADsUser` to `false`, we can enable the account. As in our previous examples the changes are written to the directory service by calling `CommitChanges()` with the `DirectoryEntry` object:

```
ActiveDs.IADsUser user = (ActiveDs.IADsUser)de.NativeObject;
user.SetPassword("someSecret");
user.AccountDisabled = false;
de.CommitChanges();
```

Searching in the Active Directory

Since the Active Directory is a data store that's optimized for **read-mostly** access, we will generally be searching it for values. To search in the Active Directory, the .NET Framework has the `DirectorySearcher` class.

We can only use `DirectorySearcher` with the LDAP provider; it doesn't work with the other providers such as NDS or IIS.

In the constructor of the `DirectorySearcher` class we can define four important parts for the search. We can also use a default constructor and define the search options with properties.

SearchRoot

The search root specifies where the search should start. The default of the `SearchRoot` is the root of the domain you're currently using. The `SearchRoot` is specified with the `Path` of a `DirectoryEntry` object.

Filter

The filter defines the values where we want to get hits. The filter is a string that must be enclosed in parentheses.

Relational operators such as `<=`, `=`, and `>=` are allowed in expressions. `(objectClass=contact)` will search all objects of type `contact`; `(lastName>=Nagel)` searches all objects where the `lastName` property is equal to or larger than `Nagel`, which means that it follows in the alphabet.

Expressions can be combined with the `&` and `|` prefix operators. For instance, `(&(objectClass=user)(description=Auth*))` searches all objects of type user where the property description starts with the string `Auth`. Because the `&` and `|` operators are at the beginning of the expressions it's possible to combine more than two expressions with a single prefix operator.

The default filter is `(objectClass=*)` so all objects are valid.

The filter syntax is defined in RFC 2254, "*The String Representation of LDAP Search Filters*". This RFC can be found at http://www.ietf.org/rfc/rfc2254.txt.

PropertiesToLoad

With `PropertiesToLoad` we define a `StringCollection` of all the properties that we are interested in. Objects can have a lot of properties, most of which will not be important for our search request. We define the properties that should be loaded into the cache. The default properties we get if nothing is specified are the `Path` and the `Name` of the object.

SearchScope

`SearchScope` is an enumeration that defines how deep the search should extend:

- ❏ `SearchScope.Base` only searches the attributes in the object where the search started, so we get at most one object.

- ❏ With `SearchScope.OneLevel` the search continues in the child collection of the base object. The base object itself is not searched for a hit.

- ❏ `SearchScope.Subtree` defines that the search should go down the complete tree.

The default `SearchScope` is `Subtree`.

Search Limits

A search for specific objects in a directory service can span multiple domains. To limit the search to the number of objects or the time taken we have some additional properties to define, as shown in the following table:

Property	Description
ClientTimeout	The maximum time the client waits for the server to return a result. If the server does not respond no records are returned.
PageSize	With a **paged search** the server returns a number of objects defined with the PageSize instead of the complete result. This reduces the time for the client to get a first answer and the memory needed. The server sends a cookie to the client, which is sent back to the server with the next search request, so that the search can continue at the point where it finished.
ServerPageTimeLimit	For paged searches this value defines the time a search should continue to return a number of objects that's defined with the PageSize value. If the time is reached before the PageSize value, the objects that were found up to that point are returned to the client. The default value is −1, which means infinite.
ServerTimeLimit	Defines the maximum time the server will search for objects. When this time is reached all objects that are found up to this point are returned to the client. The default is 120 seconds, and you cannot set the search to a higher value.
ReferalChasing	A search can cross multiple domains. If the root that's specified with SearchRoot is a parent domain or no root was specified, the search can continue to child domains. With this property we can specify if the search should continue on different servers.
	ReferalChasingOption.None means that the search does not continue onto other servers.
	With the value ReferalChasingOption.Subordinate it's specified that the search should go on to child domains. When the search starts at DC=Wrox, DC=COM the server can return a result set and the referral to DC=France, DC=Wrox, DC=COM. The client can continue the search in the subdomain.
	ReferalChasingOption.External means that the server can refer the client to an independent server that is not in the subdomain. This is the default option.
	With ReferalChasingOption.All both external and subordinate referrals are returned.

In our search example we want to search for all user objects in the organizational unit Wrox Press, where the property description has a value of Author.

First, we bind to the organizational unit Wrox Press. This is where the search should start. We are creating a DirectorySearcher object where the SearchRoot is set. The filter is defined as (&(objectClass=user)(description=Auth*)), so that we find all objects of type user with a description of Auth following by something else. The scope of the search should be a sub-tree, so that child organizational units within Wrox Press are searched, too:

```
using (DirectoryEntry de =
    new DirectoryEntry("LDAP://OU=Wrox Press, DC=eichkogelstrasse, DC=local"))
using (DirectorySearcher searcher = new DirectorySearcher())
{
    searcher.SearchRoot = de;
    searcher.Filter = "(&(objectClass=user)(description=Auth*))";
    searcher.SearchScope = SearchScope.Subtree;
```

The properties we want to have in the result of the search are name, description, givenName, and wWWHomePage:

```
    searcher.PropertiesToLoad.Add("name");
    searcher.PropertiesToLoad.Add("description");
    searcher.PropertiesToLoad.Add("givenName");
    searcher.PropertiesToLoad.Add("wWWHomePage");
```

We are ready to do the search. However, the result should also be sorted. DirectorySearcher has a property Sort, where we can set a SortOption. The first argument in the constructor of the SortOption class defines the property that we use to sort by; the second argument defines the direction of the sort. The SortDirection enumeration has values Ascending and Descending.

To start the search we can use the method FindOne() to find the first object, or FindAll(). FindOne() returns a simple SearchResult, whereas FindAll() returns a SearchResultCollection. We want to get all the authors, so FindAll() is used here:

```
    searcher.Sort = new SortOption("givenName", SortDirection.Ascending);

    SearchResultCollection results = searcher.FindAll();
```

With a foreach loop we are accessing every SearchResult in the SearchResultCollection. A SearchResult represents a single object in the search cache. The Properties property returns a ResultPropertyCollection, where we access all properties and values with the property name and the indexer:

```
    SearchResultCollection results = searcher.FindAll();

    foreach (SearchResult result in results)
    {
        ResultPropertyCollection props = result.Properties;
        foreach (string propName in props.PropertyNames)
        {
            Console.Write(propName + ": ");
            Console.WriteLine(props[propName][0]);
        }
        Console.WriteLine();
    }
}
```

If you would like to get to the complete object after a search that's also possible: `SearchResult` has a method `GetDirectoryEntry()` that returns the corresponding `DirectoryEntry` of the found object.

The resulting output shows the beginning of the list of all authors of Professional C# with the properties we've chosen:

```
C:\Professional C#\Directory\GetUser\bin\Debug\GetUser.exe            _ □ ×
givenname: Burton
description : Author
name: Burton Harvey
adspath: LDAP://celticrain/CN=Burton Harvey,OU=Wrox Press,DC=eichkogelstrasse,DC
=local

givenname: Christian
description : Author
adspath: LDAP://celticrain/CN=Christian Nagel,OU=Wrox Press,DC=eichkogelstrasse,
DC=local
name: Christian Nagel
wwwhomepage: http://christian.nagel.net
```

Searching for User Objects

In the final section of this chapter we will build a Windows Forms application called `UserSearch`. This application is flexible in that a specific domain controller, username, and password to access the Active Directory can be entered, or the user of the running process is used. In this application we will access the schema of the Active Directory to get the properties of a `user` object. The user can enter a filter string to search all `user` objects of a domain. It's also possible to set the properties of the `user` objects that should be displayed.

User Interface

The user interface shows numbered steps to indicate how to use the application:

1. In the first step **Username**, **Password**, and the **Domain Controller** can be entered. All this information is optional. If no domain controller is entered the connection works with serverless binding. If the username is missing the security context of the current user is taken.

2. A button allows all the property names of the `user` object to be loaded dynamically in the `listBoxProperties` listbox.

3. After the property names are loaded, the properties that should be displayed can be selected. The `SelectionMode` of the listbox is set to `MultiSimple`.

4. The filter to limit the search can be entered. The default value that's set in this dialog box searches for all `user` objects: `(objectClass=user)`.

5. Now the search can start:

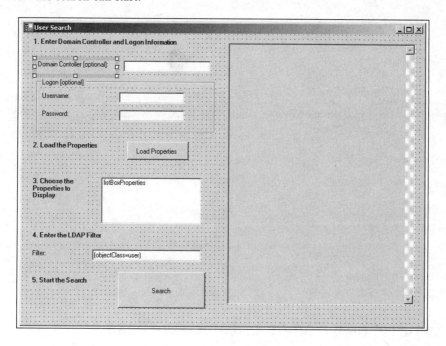

Get the Schema Naming Context

This application just has two handler methods: the first handler method for the button to load the properties, and the second to start the search in the domain. In the first part we read the properties of the `user` class dynamically from the schema to display it in the user interface.

In the handler `buttonLoadProperties_Click()` method, `SetLogonInformation()` reads the username, password, and hostname from the dialog and stores them in members of the class. Next the method `SetNamingContext()` sets the LDAP name of the schema and the LDAP name of the default context. This schema LDAP name is used in the call to set the properties in the listbox: `SetUserProperties()`:

```
private void buttonLoadProperties_Click(object sender, System.EventArgs e)
{
    try
    {
        SetLogonInformation();
        SetNamingContext();

        SetUserProperties(schemaNamingContext);
    }
```

```
    catch (Exception ex)
    {
        MessageBox.Show("Check your inputs! " + ex.Message);
    }
}
protected void SetLogonInformation()
{
    username = (textBoxUsername.Text == "" ? null : textBoxUsername.Text);
    password = (textBoxPassword.Text == "" ? null : textBoxPassword.Text);
    hostname = textBoxHostname.Text;
    if (hostname != "") hostname += "/";
}
```

In the helper method SetNamingContext(), we are using the root of the directory tree to get the properties of the server. We are just interested in the value of two properties: schemaNamingContext and defaultNamingContext:

```
protected string SetNamingContext()
{
    using (DirectoryEntry de = new DirectoryEntry())
    {
        string path = "LDAP://" + hostname + "rootDSE";
        de.Username = username;
        de.Password = password;
        de.Path = path;
        schemaNamingContext = de.Properties["schemaNamingContext"][0].ToString();
        defaultNamingContext =
                    de.Properties["defaultNamingContext"][0].ToString();
    }
}
```

Get the Property Names of the User Class

We have the LDAP name to access the schema. We can use this to access the directory and read the properties. We are not only interested in the properties of the user class, but also of the base classes of user: Organizational-Person, Person, and Top. In this program, the names of the base classes are hard-coded. It would be also possible to read the base class dynamically with the subClassOf attribute. GetSchemaProperties() returns a string array with all property names of the specific object type. All the property names are collected in the StringCollection properties:

```
protected void SetUserProperties(string schemaNamingContext)
{
    StringCollection properties = new StringCollection();
    string[] data = GetSchemaProperties(schemaNamingContext, "User");
    properties.AddRange(GetSchemaProperties(schemaNamingContext,
                    "Organizational-Person"));
    properties.AddRange(GetSchemaProperties(schemaNamingContext, "Person"));
    properties.AddRange(GetSchemaProperties(schemaNamingContext, "Top"));
    listBoxProperties.Items.Clear();
    foreach (string s in properties)
    {
        listBoxProperties.Items.Add(s);
    }
}
```

In GetSchemaProperties() we are accessing the Active Directory again. This time rootDSE is not used, rather the LDAP name to the schema that we discovered earlier. The property systemMayContain holds a collection of all attributes that are allowed in the class objectType:

```
protected string[] GetSchemaProperties(string schemaNamingContext,
                                       string objectType)
{
    string[] data;
    using (DirectoryEntry de = new DirectoryEntry())
    {
        de.Username = username;
        de.Password = password;

        de.Path = "LDAP://" + hostname + "CN=" + objectType + "," +
                  schemaNamingContext;

        DS.PropertyCollection properties = de.Properties;
        DS.PropertyValueCollection values = properties["systemMayContain"];

        data = new String[values.Count];
        values.CopyTo(data, 0);
    }
    return data;
}
```

Note the presence of `DS.PropertyCollection` in the above code – this is because in a Windows Forms application, the `PropertyCollection` class of the `System.DirectoryServices` namespace has a naming conflict with `System.Data.PropertyCollection`, and to avoid long names like `System.DirectoryServices.PropertyCollection`, I shortened the namespace name using the following:

```
using DS = System.DirectoryServices;
```

Step 2 in the application is completed. The `listbox` has all the property names of the `user` objects.

Search For User Objects

The handler for the search button just calls the helper method `FillResult()`:

```
private void buttonSearch_Click(object sender, System.EventArgs e)
{
    try
    {
        FillResult();
    }
    catch (Exception ex)
    {
        MessageBox.Show("Check your input: " + ex.Message);
    }
}
```

In `FillResult()` we are doing a normal search in the complete Active Directory Domain as we've seen earlier. `SearchScope` is set to `Subtree`, the `Filter` to the string we get from a `TextBox`, and the properties that should be loaded into the cache are set by the values the user selected in the listbox:

```
protected void FillResult()
{
    using (DirectoryEntry root = new DirectoryEntry())
    {
        root.Username = username;
        root.Password = password;
        root.Path = "LDAP://" + hostname + defaultNamingContext;

        using (DirectorySearcher searcher = new DirectorySearcher())
        {
            searcher.SearchRoot = root;
            searcher.SearchScope = SearchScope.Subtree;
            searcher.Filter = textBoxFilter.Text;
            searcher.PropertiesToLoad.AddRange(GetProperties());

            SearchResultCollection results = searcher.FindAll();
            StringBuilder summary = new StringBuilder();
            foreach (SearchResult result in results)
            {
                foreach (string propName in
                result.Properties.PropertyNames)
                {
                    foreach (string s in result.Properties[propName])
                    {
                        summary.Append(" " + propName + ": " + s + "\r\n");
                    }
                }
                summary.Append("\r\n");
            }
            textBoxResults.Text = summary.ToString();
        }
    }
}
```

Starting the application we get a list of all objects where the filter is valid:

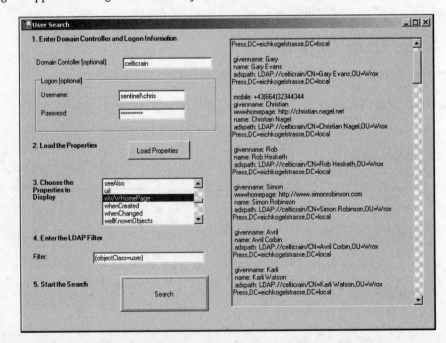

Summary

In this chapter we've seen the architecture of the Active Directory: the important concepts of domains, trees, and forests. We can access information in the complete enterprise. Writing applications that access the Active Directory we have to be aware that the data we read may not be up-to-date because of the replication latency.

The classes in the `System.DirectoryServices` namespaces give us easy ways to access the Active Directory by wrapping to the ADSI providers. The `DirectoryEntry` class makes it possible to read and write objects directly in the data store.

With the `DirectorySearcher` class we can do complex searches and define filters, timeouts, properties to load, and a scope. Using the Global Catalog we can speed up the search for objects in the complete enterprise, because it stores a read-only version of all objects in the forest.

ASP.NET Pages

If you are new to the world of C# and .NET in general you may wonder why a chapter on ASP.NET has been included in this book. It's a whole new language, right? Well, not really. In fact, as we will see, it is possible to use C# to create ASP.NET pages. But we're getting ahead of ourselves here – first off we should discuss exactly what ASP.NET is.

ASP.NET, or Active Server Pages .NET, ships as part of the .NET Framework and is a technology that allows for the dynamic creation of documents on a web server when they are requested via HTTP. This mostly means HTML documents, although it is equally possible to create, say, WML documents for consumption on WAP browsers, or indeed anything else with a MIME type.

In some ways ASP.NET is similar to many other technologies, such as PHP, ASP, ColdFusion, and so on – but there is one important difference. ASP.NET, as its name suggests, has been designed to be fully integrated with the .NET Framework, part of which includes support for C#.

It is quite possible that you have had experience of the last Microsoft technology for achieving dynamic content generation – ASP. If this is the case then you will probably know that programming in this technology used scripting languages such as VBScript or JScript. This worked, but it did mean that some things were awkward for those of us used to 'proper', compiled programming languages, and it certainly resulted in a loss of performance.

One major difference, related to the use of more advanced programming languages, is the provision of a complete server-side object model for use at runtime. ASP.NET gives access to all of the controls on a page as objects, in a rich environment. On the server side we also have access to any other .NET classes we may require, allowing for the integration of many useful services. Controls used on a page expose a lot of functionality; in fact we can do almost as much as with Windows Forms classes, which gives plenty of flexibility. For this reason, ASP.NET pages generating HTML content are often called **Web Forms**.

In this chapter we will take a more detailed look at ASP.NET, including how it works, what we can do with it, and where C# fits in.

ASP.NET Introduction

ASP.NET works with Internet Information Server (IIS) to deliver content in response to HTTP requests. ASP.NET pages are found in .aspx files, and the basic architecture looks like this:

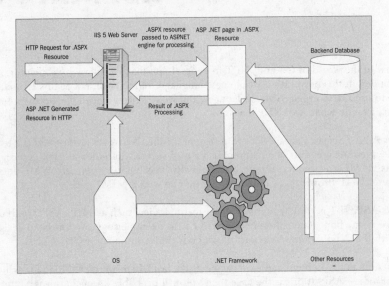

During ASP.NET processing we have access to all .NET classes, custom components created in C# or other languages, databases, and so on. In fact, we have as much power as we would have running a C# application – using C# in ASP.NET is in effect running a C# application.

An ASP.NET file may contain any of the following:

❑   Processing instructions for the server

❑   Code in C#, VB.NET, JScript.NET, or any other language that the .NET Framework supports now or might support in the future

❑   Content in whatever form is appropriate for the generated resource, such as HTML

❑   Embedded ASP.NET server controls

So, in fact we could have an ASP.NET file as simple as:

```
Hello!
```

with no additional code or instructions at all. This would simply result in an HTML page being returned (as HTML is the default output of ASP.NET pages) containing just this text.

As we will see later in this chapter, it is also possible to split certain portions of the code into other files, which can provide a more logical structure.

State Management in ASP.NET

One of the key properties of ASP.NET pages is that they are effectively stateless. By default, no information is stored on the server between user requests (although there are methods for doing this should you wish, as we'll see later). At first glance this seems a little strange, as state management is something that seems essential for user-friendly interactive sessions. However, ASP.NET provides a rather nice way around this problem, in such a way as to make session management almost completely transparent. It just happens.

Basically, information about, for example, the state of controls on a Web Form (such as data entered in textboxes, or selections from drop-down lists) is stored in a hidden **viewstate** field that is part of the page generated by the server and passed to the user. Subsequent actions, such as triggering events that require server-side processing like submitting form data, result in this information being sent back to the server, known as **postback**. On the server this information is used to repopulate the page object model allowing us to operate on it as if the changes had been made locally.

We'll see this in action shortly and point out the details.

ASP.NET Web Forms

As mentioned earlier, much of the functionality in ASP.NET is achieved using Web Forms. Before long we'll dive in and create a simple Web Form to give us a starting point to explore this technology. First, though, we should look at a couple of quick points pertinent to Web Form design. It should be noted that many ASP.NET developers simply use a text editor such as Notepad to create files. This is made easier by the fact that it is possible, as noted earlier, to combine all code in one file. We achieve this by enclosing code in <script> tags, using two attributes on the opening <script> tag as follows:

```
<script language="c#" runat="server">

    // Server-side code goes here.

</script>
```

The runat="server" attribute here is crucial (and we'll see it time and again in this chapter), as it instructs the ASP.NET engine to execute this code on the server rather than sending it to the client, thus giving us access to the rich environment discussed earlier. We can place our functions, event handlers, and so on, in server-side script blocks.

If we omit the `runat="server"` attribute we are effectively providing client-side code, which will fail if it uses any of the server-side style coding we will see in this chapter. However, there might be times when we want to provide client-side code (indeed, ASP.NET generates some itself sometimes, depending on browser capabilities and what Web Form code is used). Unfortunately we can't use C# here, as to do this would require the .NET Framework on the client, which might not always be the case. Hence JScript is probably the next best option as it is supported on the widest variety of client browsers. To change the language we simply change the value of the `language` attribute as follows:

```
<script language="jscript">

    // Client-side code goes here; we can also use "vbscript".

</script>
```

It is equally possible to create ASP.NET files in Visual Studio .NET, which is great for us as we are already familiar with this environment for C# programming. However, the default project setup for web applications in this environment has a slightly more complex structure than a single `.aspx` file. This isn't a problem for us though, and does make things a bit more logical (read: more programmer-like and less web developer-like). Based on this we'll use Visual Studio .NET throughout this chapter for our ASP.NET programming.

`.aspx` files may also include code in blocks enclosed by `<%` and `%>` tags. However, function definitions and variable declarations cannot go here. Instead we can insert code that is executed as soon as the block is reached, which is useful when outputting simple HTML content. This behavior is similar to that of old-style ASP pages, with one important difference: the code is compiled, not interpreted. This results in far better performance.

Now it's time for an example. Create a new project of type **ASP.NET Web Application** called **PCSWebApp1** as shown below:

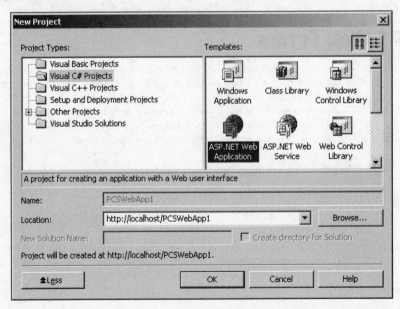

By default, VS.NET will use FrontPage extensions to set up a web application at the required location, which may be remote if your web server is on a different machine. However, it also provides an alternative (and slightly faster) method for doing this, using the file system over a LAN (which is of course impossible if your remote web server isn't on the same LAN as your development server). If the first method fails then VS.NET will try the second.

Regardless of which method is used, VS.NET keeps a local cache of all project files, and keeps these in sync with the files on the web server.

After a few moments Visual Studio .NET should have set up the following:

❑ A new solution, `PCSWebApp1`, containing the C# Web Application `PCSWebApp1`

❑ `AssemblyInfo.cs` – the standard VS.NET file describing the assembly

❑ `Global.asax` – application global information and events (see later in this chapter)

❑ `PCSWebApp1.vsdisco` – a file describing any Web Services in the project, enabling dynamic discovery (see next chapter for details)

❑ `Web.config` – configuration information for the application (see later in this chapter)

❑ `WebForm1.aspx` – the first ASP.NET page in the web application

We'll cover all of the generated files over the course of this and the next two chapters; for now we should concentrate on the meat of the application, which is the `.aspx` file that VS.NET has generated for us.

We can view `.aspx` files in two ways – in design or code view (well actually it's three, if you count the HTML view in the designer). This is the same as for Windows Forms, as we saw earlier in the book. The initial view in VS.NET is the design view:

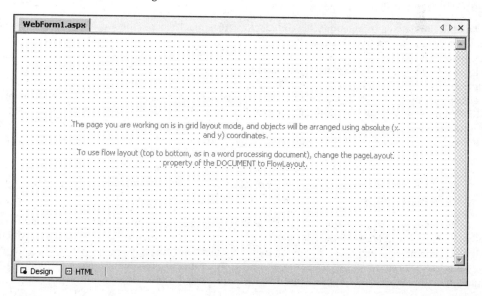

The text shown in this view by default isn't text that we'll see in our application, it's just a note from VS.NET to say what layout mode is in use. Here we are using *GridLayout* mode, which allows extra flexibility in control positioning, but we can change this to *FlowLayout* if we require a more traditional HTML-type positioning scheme. We'll look at this a little later.

If we select the HTML view from the buttons below the layout display we'll see the code generated inside the .aspx file:

```
<%@ Page language="c#" Codebehind="WebForm1.aspx.cs" AutoEventWireup="false"
        Inherits="PCSWebApp1.WebForm1" %>
<!DOCTYPE HTML PUBLIC "-//W3C//DTD HTML 4.0 Transitional//EN" >
<html>
    <head>
        <title>WebForm1</title>
        <meta name="GENERATOR" Content="Microsoft Visual Studio 7.0">
        <meta name="CODE_LANGUAGE" Content="C#">
        <meta name="vs_defaultClientScript" content="JavaScript">
        <meta name="vs_targetSchema"
            content="http://schemas.microsoft.com/intellisense/ie5">
    </head>
    <body MS_POSITIONING="GridLayout">
        <form id="Form1" method="post" Runat="server">
        </form>
    </body>
</html>
```

The <html> element here has been populated with a little metadata that doesn't really concern us, and a <form> element to contain ASP.NET code. The most important thing about this element is the runat attribute. Just as with the server-side code blocks we saw at the start of this section this is set to server, meaning that the processing of the form will take place on the server. If we don't include this then no server-side processing will be performed and the form won't do anything. There can only be one server-side <form> element in an ASP.NET page.

The other interesting thing about this code is the <%@ Page %> tag at the top. This tag defines page characteristics that are important to us as C# web application developers. Firstly there is a language attribute that specifies that we will use C# throughout our page, as we saw earlier with <script> blocks (the default for web applications is VB.NET, although this can be changed using the Web.config configuration file). The next three attributes are necessary, as the code driving the page has been set up by VS.NET to reside in a separate file, WebForm1.aspx.cs. This file, which we'll look at in a moment, contains a class definition that is used as the base class for the Web Forms page. Now we start to see how ASP.NET ties in with a rich object model! This base class will be used in conjunction with code in this file to generate the HTML that reaches the user.

> Note that not all .aspx files require this multi-layer model; it is possible just to use the base .NET Web Form class as the base class for the page, which is the default. In this case the .aspx file would include all of our C# code in <script> blocks as mentioned earlier.

Since we are providing a customized base class for the page we might also have customized events. To ensure that the ASP.NET engine is aware of this we use the AutoEventWireup attribute, which signifies whether the Page_Load() event handler (called, surprisingly enough, on loading the page) is automatically wired up to the OnPageLoad event. By setting this attribute to false we must provide our own code to do this if required, but this does allow us a bit more freedom in what we do.

Next we'll look at the "code-behind" code generated for this file. To do this, right-click on **WebForm1.aspx** in the Solution Explorer and select **View Code**. This should load the code in `WebForm1.aspx.cs` into the text editor. First off, we see the default set of namespace references required for basic usage:

```
using System;
using System.Collections;
using System.ComponentModel;
using System.Data;
using System.Drawing;
using System.Web;
using System.Web.SessionState;
using System.Web.UI;
using System.Web.UI.WebControls;
using System.Web.UI.HtmlControls;
```

Moving on we see a namespace declaration for our web application followed by the definition of `WebForm1`, the base class used for the `.aspx` page. This class inherits from `System.Web.UI.Page`, the base class for Web Forms:

```
namespace PCSWebApp1
{
    /// <summary>
    /// Summary description for WebForm1.
    /// </summary>
    public class WebForm1 : System.Web.UI.Page
    {
```

The rest of the code in this form performs various initialization tasks, and includes the code required to design Web Forms in VS.NET. No constructor is included (the .NET default one is used), but there is an event handler called `Page_Load()` that we can use to add any code we require when the page is loaded:

```
        private void Page_Load(object sender, System.EventArgs e)
        {
            // Put user code to initialize the page here
        }
```

The rest of the code is enclosed in a `#region` block, so to view it we need to expand it:

```
        #region Web Form Designer generated code
        override protected void OnInit(EventArgs e)
        {
            //
            // CODEGEN: This call is required by the ASP.NET Web Form Designer.
            //
            InitializeComponent();
            base.OnInit(e);
        }

        /// <summary>
        /// Required method for Designer support - do not modify
        /// the contents of this method with the code editor.
```

```
/// </summary>
private void InitializeComponent()
{
    this.Load += new System.EventHandler(this.Page_Load);
}
#endregion
```

Here the OnInit() event handler inherited from System.Web.UI.Control is overridden. This event handler is executed when the page initializes, and results in InitializeComponent() being called before the base implementation of OnInit() is processed. InitializeComponent() simply wires up the Page_Load() event handler to the Load event of the page, necessary as AutoEventWireup was set to false.

Strictly speaking, this is more code than is required for a simple ASP.NET Web Form page, which can be as simple as we saw right at the start of the chapter (albeit as a trivial example). However, the structure created does lend itself to reusability and expansion using C# techniques, without causing a noticeable amount of overhead, so we'll run with it.

ASP.NET Server Controls

Our generated code doesn't do very much as yet, so next we need to add some content. We can do this in VS.NET using the Web Form designer, which supports drag-and-drop and adding via code in just the same way as the Windows Forms designer.

There are four types of control that we can add to our ASP.NET pages:

❑ **HTML server controls** – controls that mimic HTML elements, which will be familiar to HTML developers.

❑ **Web server controls** – a new set of controls, some of which have the same functionality as HTML controls but with a common naming scheme for properties etc. to ease development, and provide consistency with analogous Windows Forms controls. There are also some completely new and very powerful controls as we will see later.

❑ **Validation controls** – a set of controls capable of performing validation of user input in a simple way.

❑ **Custom and user controls** – controls defined by the developer, which can be defined in a number of ways as we will see in Chapter 16.

We'll see a complete list of web server and validation controls in the next section, along with usage notes. HTML controls will not be covered in this chapter. These controls don't do anything more than the web server controls, and the web server controls provide a richer environment for those more used to programming than HTML design (which I'm assuming applies to the majority of the audience of this book). Learning how to use the web server controls will provide enough knowledge to use HTML server controls without much difficulty, should you be interested. You could also look at Professional ASP.NET 1.0 ISBN 1-861007-03-5 *or* ASP.NET Programmer's Reference ISBN 1-861005-30-X, *both published by Wrox Press.*

Let's add a couple of web server controls to our project. All web server and validation controls are used in the following XML element-type form:

```
<asp:X runat="server" attribute="value">Contents</asp:X>
```

Where *X* is the name of the ASP.NET server control, `attribute="value"` is one or more attribute specifications, and `Contents` specifies the control content, if any. Some controls allow properties to be set using attributes and control-element content, such as `Label` (used for simple text display) where `Text` can be specified in either way. Other controls may use an element containment scheme to define their hierarchy, for example `Table` (which, spookily enough, defines a table), which can contain `TableRow` elements in order to specify table rows declaratively.

Note that, as the syntax for controls is based on XML (although they may be used embedded in non-XML code such as HTML), it is an error to omit the closing tags, omit the `/>` for empty elements, or overlap controls.

Finally, we once again see the `runat="server"` attribute on web server controls. It is just as essential here as it is elsewhere, and it is a common mistake to miss this attribute off (trust me, you'll do it occasionally), resulting in dead Web Forms.

We'll keep things simple for this first example. Change the HTML design view for `WebForm1.aspx` as follows:

```
<%@ Page language="c#" Codebehind="WebForm1.aspx.cs" AutoEventWireup="false"
        Inherits="PCSWebApp1.WebForm1" %>
<!DOCTYPE HTML PUBLIC "-//W3C//DTD HTML 4.0 Transitional//EN" >
<html>
    <head>
        <title>WebForm1</title>
        <meta name="GENERATOR" Content="Microsoft Visual Studio 7.0">
        <meta name="CODE_LANGUAGE" Content="C#">
        <meta name="vs_defaultClientScript" content="JavaScript">
        <meta name="vs_targetSchema"
            content="http://schemas.microsoft.com/intellisense/ie5">
    </head>
    <body MS_POSITIONING="GridLayout">
        <form id="Form1" method="post" Runat="server">
            <asp:Label Runat="server" ID="resultLabel"/><br>
            <asp:Button Runat="server" ID="triggerButton" Text="Click Me"/>
        </form>
    </body>
</html>
```

Here we have added two web-form controls, a label and a button.

Note that as you do this, VS.NET IntelliSense predicts your code entry just like in C# design.

Going back to the design screen we can see that our controls have been added, and named using their ID attributes. As with Windows Forms we have full access to properties, events, and so on through the **Properties** window, and can see instant feedback in code or design whenever we make changes.

Next, have another look at `WebForm1.aspx.cs`. The following two members have been added to our `WebForm1` class:

```
protected System.Web.UI.WebControls.Button triggerButton;
protected System.Web.UI.WebControls.Label resultLabel;
```

Any server controls we add will automatically become part of the object model for our form that we are building in this code-behind file. This is an instant bonus for Windows Forms developers – the similarities are beginning to make themselves known!

To make this application actually do something, let's add an event handler for clicking on the button. Here we can either enter a method name in the **Properties** window for the button or just double-click on the button to get the default event handler. If we double-click on the button we'll automatically add an event handling method as follows:

```
private void triggerButton_Click(object sender, System.EventArgs e)
{
}
```

This is hooked up to the button by some code added to `InitializeComponent()`:

```
private void InitializeComponent()
{
    this.triggerButton.Click +=
                        new System.EventHandler(this.triggerButton_Click);
    this.Load += new System.EventHandler(this.Page_Load);
}
```

Modify the code in `triggerButton_Click()` as follows:

```
protected void triggerButton_Click(object sender, System.EventArgs e)
{
    resultLabel.Text = "Button clicked!";
}
```

Now we're ready to make it go. Build the application from VS.NET in the normal way and all the files will be compiled and/or placed on the web server ready for use. To test the web application out we can either run the application (which will give us full use of VS.NET debugging facilities), or just point a browser at http://localhost/PCSWebApp1/WebForm1.aspx. Either way you should see the **Click Me** button on a web page. Before pressing the button, take a quick look at the code received by the browser using **View | Source** (in IE). The `<form>` section should look something like the following:

```
<form name="Form1" method="post" action="WebForm1.aspx" id="Form1">
    <input type="hidden" name="__VIEWSTATE" value="dDwtOTk1MjE0NDA4Ozs+" />
    <span id="resultLabel"></span><br>
    <input type="submit" name="triggerButton" value="Click Me"
        id="triggerButton" />
</form>
```

The web server controls have generated straight HTML, <span> and <input> for <asp:Label> and <asp:Button>, respectively. There is also a <input type="hidden"> field with the name __VIEWSTATE. This encapsulates the state of the form as mentioned earlier. This information is used when the form is posted back to the server to recreate the UI, keeping track of changes etc. Note that the <form> element has been configured for this; it will post data back to WebForm1.aspx (specified in action) via an HTTP POST operation (specified in method). It has also been assigned the name Form1.

After clicking the button and seeing the text appear, check out the source HTML again (spacing added for clarity below):

```
<form name="Form1" method="post" action="WebForm1.aspx" id="Form1">
    <input type="hidden" name="__VIEWSTATE"
           value="dDwtOTk1MjE0NDA4O3O2w8aTwxPjs+O2w8dDw7bDxpPDE+Oz47bD
                  x0PHA8cDxsPFR1eHQ7PjtsPEJ1dHRvbiBjbGlja2VkITs+Pjs+Ozs+
                  Oz4+Oz4+Oz4=" />
    <span id="resultLabel">Button clicked!</span><br>
    <input type="submit" name="triggerButton" value="Click Me"
           id="triggerButton" />
</form>
```

This time the value of the viewstate contains more information, as the HTML result relies on more than the default output from the ASP.NET page. In complex forms this may be a very long string indeed, but we shouldn't complain, as so much is done for us behind the scenes. We can almost forget about state management, keeping field values between posts, and so on.

The Control Palette

In this section we'll take a quick look at the available controls before we put more of them together into a full, and more interesting, application. We'll divide this section up into web server controls and validation controls. Note that we refer to 'properties' in the control descriptions – in all cases the corresponding attribute for use in ASP.NET code is identically named. We haven't attempted to provide a complete reference here, so we've missed out many properties and only included the most frequently used ones. A complete reference can be found in *ASP.NET Programmer's Reference* ISBN 1-861005-30-X.

Web Server Controls

Almost all the web server controls inherit from System.Web.UI.WebControls.WebControl, which in turn inherits from System.Web.UI.Control. Those that don't use this inheritance instead derive either directly from Control or from a more specialized base class that derives (eventually) from Control. As such the web server controls have many common properties and events that we can use if required. There are quite a lot of these, so we won't attempt to cover them all here, just as with the properties and events of the web server controls themselves.

Many of the frequently used inherited properties are those that deal with display style. This can be controlled simply, using properties such as ForeColor, BackColor, Font, and so on, but can also be controlled using CSS (Cascading Style Sheet) classes. This is achieved by setting the string property CssClass to the name of a CSS class in a separate file. Other notable properties include Width and Height to size a control, AccessKey and TabIndex to ease user interaction, and Enabled to set whether the control's functionality is activated in the Web Form.

Of the events, we are likely to use the inherited `Load` event most often, to perform initialization on a control, and `PreRender`, to perform last-minute modifications before HTML is output by the control.

There are plenty more events and properties for us to make use of, and we'll see many of these in more detail in our later chapter concerning *Custom Controls* (Chapter 16).

The list of web server controls is as follows:

Control	Description
PlaceHolder	This control doesn't render any output, but can be handy for grouping other controls together, or for adding controls programmatically to a given location. Contained controls can be accessed using the `Controls` property.
Label	Simple text display; use the `Text` property to set and programmatically modify displayed text.
Literal	Performs the same function as `Label`, but has no styling properties, just a `Text` one.
Xml	A more complicated text display control, used for displaying XML content, which may be transformed using an XSLT stylesheet. The XML content is set using one of the `Document`, `DocumentContent`, or `DocumentSource` properties (depending on what format the original XML is in), and the XSLT stylesheet (optional) using either `Transform` or `TransformSource`.
TextBox	Provides a textbox that users can edit. Use the `Text` property to access the entered data, and the `TextChanged` event to act on selection changes on postback. If automatic postback is required (as opposed to using a button, say) set the `AutoPostBack` property to `true`.
DropDownList	Allows the user to select one of a list of choices, either by choosing it directly from a list or typing the first letter or two. Use the `Items` property to set the item list (this is a `ListItemCollection` class containing `ListItem` objects) and the `SelectedItem` and `SelectedIndex` properties to determine what is selected. The `SelectedIndexChanged` event can be used to determine whether the selection has changed, and this control also has an `AutoPostBack` property so that this selection change will trigger a postback operation.
ListBox	Allows the user to make one or more selections from a list. Set `SelectionMode` to `Multiple` or `Single` to set how many items may be selected at once and `Rows` to determine how many items to display. Other properties and events as for `DropDownList`.
Image	Displays an image. Use `ImageUrl` for the image reference, and `AlternateText` to provide text if the image fails to load.

Control	Description
AdRotator	Displays several images in succession, with a different one displayed after each server round trip. Use the AdvertisementFile property to specify the XML file describing the possible images and the AdCreated event to perform processing before each image is sent back. Can also use the Target property to name a window to open when an image is clicked.
CheckBox	Displays a box that can be checked or unchecked. The state is stored in the Boolean property Checked, and the text associated with the checkbox in Text. The AutoPostBack property can be used to initiate automatic postback and the CheckedChanged event to act on changes.
CheckBoxList	Creates a group of checkboxes. Properties and events are identical to other list controls, such as DropDownList.
RadioButton	Displays a button that can be turned on or off. Generally these are grouped such that only one in the group can be active. Use the GroupName property to link RadioButton controls into a group. Other properties and events are as per CheckBox.
RadioButtonList	Creates a group of radio buttons where only one button in the group can be selected at a time. Properties and events are as per other list controls.
Calendar	Allows the user to select a date from a graphical calendar display. This control has many style-related properties, but essential functionality can be achieved using the SelectedDate and VisibleDate properties (of type System.DateTime) to get access to the date selected by the user and the month to display (which will always contain VisibleDate). The key event to hook up to is SelectionChanged. Postback from this control is automatic.
Button	A standard button for the user to click. Use the Text property for text on the button, and the Click event to respond to clicks (server postback is automatic). Can also use the Command event to respond to clicks, which gives access to additional CommandName and CommandArgument properties on receipt.
LinkButton	Identical to Button, but displays button as a hyperlink.
ImageButton	Displays an image that doubles as a clickable button. Properties and events are inherited from Button and Image.
HyperLink	HTML hyperlink. Set the destination with NavigateUrl and the text to display with Text. You can also use ImageUrl to specify an image to display for the link and Target to specify the browser window to use. This control has no non-standard events, so use a LinkButton instead if additional processing is required when the link is followed.

Table continued on following page

Control	Description
Table	Specifies a table. Use this in conjunction with `TableRow` and `TableCell` at design time or programmatically assign rows using the `Rows` property, of type `TableRowCollection`. You can also use this property for run-time modifications. This control has several styling properties unique to tables, as do `TableRow` and `TableCell`.
TableRow	Specifies a row within a `Table`. The key property is `Cells`, which is a `TableCellCollection` class containing `TableCell` objects.
TableCell	Specifies an individual cell within a `TableRow`. Use `Text` to set the text to display, `Wrap` to determine whether to wrap text, and `RowSpan` and `ColumnSpan` to set how much of the table is covered by the cell.
Panel	A container for other controls. You can use `HorizontalAlign` and `Wrap` to specify how the contents are arranged.
Repeater	Used to output data from a data query, allowing great flexibility using templates. We'll look at this control in detail later in the chapter.
DataList	Similar to the `Repeater` control, but has more flexibility when it comes to arranging data and formatting. Can automatically render a table, which may be editable, for example. Again, this is a subject for later in the chapter.
DataGrid	Similar to `Repeater` and `DataList` with a few extra facilities, such as sorting. See later.

Validation Controls

Validation controls provide a method of validating user input without (in most cases) writing any code at all. Whenever postback is initiated each validation control checks the control it is validating and changes its `IsValid` property accordingly. If this property is `false` then the user input for the validated control has failed validation. The page containing all the controls also has an `IsValid` property – if any of the validation controls has its version of this property set to `false` then this will be `false` also. We can check this property from our server-side code and act on it.

However, validation controls have a second function. Not only do they validate controls at run time, they can also output helpful hints to the user automatically. Simply setting the `ErrorMessage` property to the text you want means the user will see it when they attempt to post back invalid data.

The text stored in `ErrorMessage` may be output at the point where the validation control is located, or at a separate point, along with the messages from all other validation controls on a page. This latter behavior is achieved using the `ValidationSummary` control, which displays all error messages along with additional text as required.

On browsers that support it, these controls even generate client-side JavaScript functions to streamline their validation behavior. This means that in some cases postback won't even occur – as the validation controls can prevent this in certain circumstances and output error messages without needing to involve the server.

All validation controls inherit from `BaseValidator`, and so share several important properties. Perhaps the most important is the `ErrorMessage` property discussed above, in which case the `ControlToValidate` property must come a close second. This property specifies the programmatic ID of the control that is being validated. Another important property is `Display`, which determines whether to place text at the validation summary position (if set to none), or at the validator position. We also have the choice to make space for the error message even when it's not being displayed (set `Display` to `Static`) or to dynamically allocate space when required, which might shift page contents around slightly (set `Display` to `Dynamic`).

We'll look at an example shortly; first let's briefly describe the various validation controls.

Control	Description
RequiredFieldValidator	Used to check if the user has entered data in a control such as a `TextBox`.
CompareValidator	Used to check that data entered fulfils simple requirements, by use of an operator set using the `Operator` property and a `ValueToCompare` property to validate against. `Operator` may be one of `Equal`, `GreaterThan`, `GreaterThanEqual`, `LessThan`, `LessThanEqual`, `NotEqual`, and `DataTypeCheck`. The last of these simply compares the data type of `ValueToCompare` with the data in the control to be validated. `ValueToCompare` is a string property, but is interpreted as different data types based on its contents.
RangeValidator	Validates that data in the control to validate falls between `MaximumValue` and `MinimumValue` property values.
RegularExpressionValidator	Validates the contents of a field based on a regular expression stored in `ValidationExpression`. This can be useful for known sequences such as zip codes, phone numbers, IP numbers, and so on.
CustomValidator	Used to validate data in a control using a custom function. `ClientValidationFunction` is used to specify a *client-side* function used to validate a control (which means, unfortunately, that we can't use C#). This function should return a Boolean value indicating whether validation was successful. Alternatively, we can use the `ServerValidate` event to specify a server-side function to use for validation. This function is a `bool` type event handler that receives a string containing the data to validate instead of an `EventArgs` parameter. We return `true` if validation succeeds, otherwise `false`.

Table continued on following page

Control	Description
ValidationSummary	Displays validation errors for all validation controls that have an `ErrorMessage` set. The display can be formatted by setting the `DisplayMode` (`BulletList`, `List`, or `SingleParagraph`) and `HeaderText` properties. The display can be disabled by setting `ShowSummary` to `false`, and displayed in a pop-up message box by setting `ShowMessageBox` to `true`.

Server Control Example

Now we've seen what's available to us, and played with a simple example, it's time to look at a more involved scenario. Here we will create the framework for a web application, a meeting room booking tool. For now this will just include the front end and simple event processing; later we will extend this with ADO.NET and data binding to include server-side business logic.

The Web Form we are going to create will contain fields for user name, event name, meeting room, and attendees, along with a calendar to select a date (we're assuming for the purposes of this example that the events last for entire days). We will include validation controls for all fields except the calendar, which we will validate on the server side, and provide a default date in case none has been entered.

For UI testing we will also have a `Label` control on the form that we can use to display submission results.

To kick things off, create a new web application project in Visual Studio .NET, named **PCSWebApp2**. Next we design the form, which is generated using the following code in `WebForm1.aspx` (with auto-generated code not highlighted):

```
<%@ Page language="c#" Codebehind="WebForm1.aspx.cs" AutoEventWireup="false"
    Inherits="PCSWebApp2.WebForm1" %>
<!DOCTYPE HTML PUBLIC "-//W3C//DTD HTML 4.0 Transitional//EN" >
<html>
  <head>
    <title>WebForm1</title>
    <meta name="GENERATOR" Content="Microsoft Visual Studio 7.0">
    <meta name="CODE_LANGUAGE" Content="C#">
    <meta name="vs_defaultClientScript" content="JavaScript">
    <meta name="vs_targetSchema"
        content="http://schemas.microsoft.com/intellisense/ie5">
  </head>
  <body MS_POSITIONING="GridLayout">
    <form id="Form1" method="post" Runat="server">
      <h1 align="center">
        Enter details and set a day to initiate an event.
      </h1>
      <br>
```

After the title of the page, which is written out enclosed in HTML `<h1>` tags to get large, title-style text, the main body of the form is enclosed in an HTML `<table>`. We could use a web server control table, but this introduces unnecessary complexity as we are using a table purely for formatting the display, not to be a dynamic UI element (an important point to bear in mind when designing Web Forms – don't add web server controls unnecessarily). The table is divided up into three columns, the first holding simple text labels, the second holding UI fields corresponding to the text labels (along with validation controls for these), and the third containing a calendar control for date selection, which spans four rows. The fifth row contains a submission button spanning all columns, and the sixth row contains a `ValidationSummary` control to display error messages when required (all the other validation controls have `Display="None"` as they will use this summary for display). Beneath the table is a simple label that we can use to display results for now, before we add database access later.

```
<table bordercolor="#000000" cellspacing="0" cellpadding="8"
       rules="none" align="center" bgcolor="#fff99e" border="2"
       width="540">
  <tr>
    <td valign="top">Your Name:</td>
    <td valign="top">
      <asp:TextBox ID="nameBox" Runat="server" Width="160px"/>
      <asp:RequiredFieldValidator ID="validateName"
                           Runat="server"
                           ErrorMessage="You must enter a name."
                           ControlToValidate="nameBox"
                           Display="None"/>
    </td>
    <td valign="center" rowspan="4">
      <asp:Calendar ID="calendar" Runat="server"
               BackColor="White"/>
    </td>
  </tr>
  <tr>
    <td valign="top">Event Name:</td>
    <td valign="top">
      <asp:TextBox ID="eventBox" Runat="server" Width="160px"/>
      <asp:RequiredFieldValidator ID="validateEvent"
                           Runat="server"
                           ErrorMessage="You must enter an event name."
                           ControlToValidate="eventBox"
                           Display="None"/>
    </td>
  </tr>
  <tr>
```

Most of the ASP.NET code in this file is remarkably simple, and much can be learned simply by reading through it. Of particular note in the code is the way in which list items are attached to the controls for selecting a meeting room and multiple attendees for the event:

```
    <td valign="top">Meeting Room:</td>
    <td valign="top">
      <asp:DropDownList ID="roomList" Runat="server" Width="160px">
        <asp:ListItem Value="1">The Happy Room</asp:ListItem>
        <asp:ListItem Value="2">The Angry Room</asp:ListItem>
```

```
                                    <asp:ListItem Value="3">The Depressing Room</asp:ListItem>
                                    <asp:ListItem Value="4">The Funked Out Room</asp:ListItem>
                            </asp:DropDownList>
                            <asp:RequiredFieldValidator ID="validateRoom" Runat="server"
                                        ErrorMessage="You must select a room."
                                        ControlToValidate="roomList" Display="None"/>
                    </td>
            </tr>
            <tr>
                    <td valign="top">Attendees:</td>
                    <td valign="top">
                        <asp:ListBox ID="attendeeList" Runat="server"
                                    Width="160px"
                                    SelectionMode="Multiple" Rows="6">
                            <asp:ListItem Value="1">Bill Gates</asp:ListItem>
                            <asp:ListItem Value="2">Monica Lewinsky</asp:ListItem>

                            <asp:ListItem Value="3">Vincent Price</asp:ListItem>
                            <asp:ListItem Value="4">Vlad the Impaler</asp:ListItem>
                            <asp:ListItem Value="5">Iggy Pop</asp:ListItem>
                            <asp:ListItem Value="6">William
                                            Shakespeare</asp:ListItem>
                        </asp:ListBox>
```

Here we are associating `ListItem` objects with the two web server controls. These objects are not web server controls in their own right (they simply inherit from `System.Object`), which is why we don't need to use `Runat="server"` on them. When the page is processed the `<asp:ListItem>` entries are used to create `ListItem` objects, which are added to the `Items` collection of their parent list control. This makes it easier for us to initialize lists than having to write code for this ourselves (we'd have to create a `ListItemCollection` object, add `ListItem` objects, and then pass the collection to the list control). Of course, we can still do all of this programmatically if preferred.

```
                        <asp:RequiredFieldValidator ID="validateAttendees"
                                    Runat="server"
                                    ErrorMessage="You must have at least one attendee."
                                    ControlToValidate="attendeeList" Display="None"/>
                    </td>
            </tr>
            <tr>
                    <td align="center" colspan="3">
                        <asp:Button ID="submitButton" Runat="server" Width="100%"
                                    Text="Submit meeting room request"/>
                    </td>
            </tr>
            <tr>
                    <td align="center" colspan="3">
                        <asp:ValidationSummary ID="validationSummary"
                                    Runat="server"
                                    HeaderText="Before submitting your request:"/>
                    </td>
            </tr>
        </table>
        <br>
        Results:
        <asp:Label Runat="server" ID="resultLabel" Text="None."/>
    </form>
  </body>
</html>
```

In design view the form we have created looks like this:

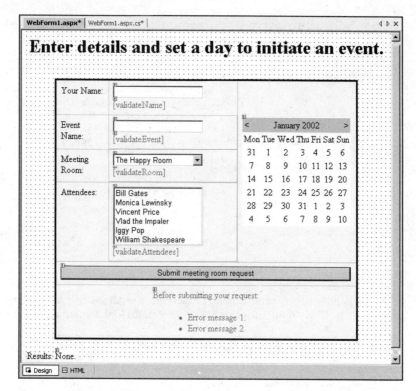

This is a fully functioning UI, which maintains its own state between server requests, and validates user input. Considering the brevity of the above code this is quite something. In fact, it leaves us very little to do, at least for this example; we just have to wire up the button click event for the submission button.

Actually, that's not quite true. So far we have no validation for the calendar control. Still, this is simple as it is impossible to clear the selection in this control, so all we have to do is give it an initial value. We can do this in the Page_Load() event handler for our page in the code-behind file:

```
private void Page_Load(object sender, System.EventArgs e)
{
    if (!this.IsPostBack)
    {
        calendar.SelectedDate = System.DateTime.Now;
    }
}
```

Here we just select today's date as a starting point. Note that we first check to see if Page_Load() is being called as the result of a postback operation by checking the IsPostBack property of the page. If a postback is in progress this property will be true and we leave the selected date alone (we don't want to lose the user's selection, after all).

To add the button click handler simply double-click on the button and add the following code:

```
private void submitButton_Click(object sender, System.EventArgs e)
{
    if (this.IsValid)
    {
        resultLabel.Text = roomList.SelectedItem.Text +
                            " has been booked on " +
                            calendar.SelectedDate.ToLongDateString() +
                            " by " + nameBox.Text + " for " +
                            eventBox.Text + " event. ";
        foreach (ListItem attendee in attendeeList.Items)
        {
            if (attendee.Selected)
            {
                resultLabel.Text += attendee.Text + ", ";
            }
        }
        resultLabel.Text += " and " + nameBox.Text +
                            " will be attending.";
    }
}
```

Here we just set the `resultLabel` control `Text` property to a result string, which will then appear below the main table. In IE the result of such a submission might look something like the following:

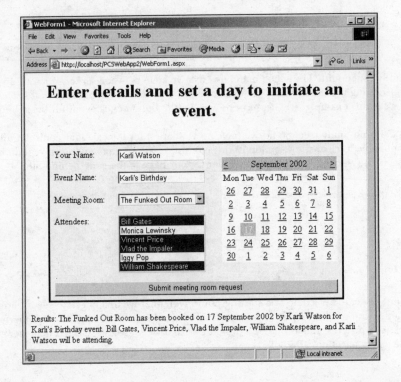

unless there are errors, in which case the ValidationSummary will activate instead:

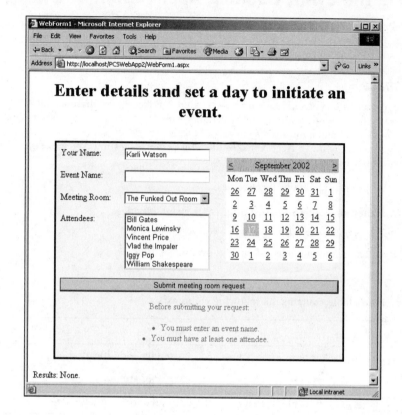

ADO.NET and Data Binding

The Web Form application we created in the last section is perfectly functional, but only contains static data. In addition, the event booking process does not include persisting event data. In order to solve both of these problems we can make use of ADO.NET to access data stored in a database, such that we can store and retrieve event data along with the lists of rooms and attendees.

Data binding makes the process of retrieving data even easier. Controls such as listboxes (and some of the more specialized controls we'll look at a bit later) come enabled for this technique. They can be bound to any object that exposes an IEnumerable, ICollection, or IListSource interface, which includes DataTable objects.

In this section we will start by updating our event booking application to be data-aware, and then move on to take a look at some of the other things we can do with data binding, using some of the other data-aware web controls.

Updating the Event Booking Application

To keep things separate from the last example, create a new web application project called PCSWebApp3 and copy the code across from the PCSWebApp2 application created earlier. Before we start on our new code, let's look at the database we will be accessing.

The Database

For the purposes of this example we will use a Microsoft Access database called PCSWebApp3.mdb, which may be found along with the downloadable code for this book. For an enterprise-scale application it would make more sense to use a SQL Server database, but the techniques involved are practically identical and MS Access makes life a bit easier for testing. We will point out the differences in code as they occur.

The database provided contains three tables:

❑ Attendees, containing a list of possible event attendees

❑ Rooms, containing a list of possible rooms for events

❑ Events, containing a list of booked events

Attendees

The Attendees table contains the following columns:

Column	Type	Notes
ID	AutoNumber, primary key	Attendee identification number
Name	Text, required, 50 chars	Name of attendee
Email	Text, optional, 50 chars	E-mail address of attendee

The supplied database includes entries for 20 attendees, all of who have (made up) e-mail addresses. It is envisioned that in a more developed application e-mails could automatically be sent to attendees when a booking is made, but this is left to the reader as an optional exercise using techniques found elsewhere in this book.

Rooms

The Rooms table contains the following columns:

Column	Type	Notes
ID	AutoNumber, primary key	Room identification number
Room	Text, required, 50 chars	Name of room

20 records are supplied in the database.

Events

The Events table contains the following columns:

Column	Type	Notes
ID	AutoNumber, primary key	Event identification number
Name	Text, required, 255 chars	Name of event
Room	Number, required	ID of room for event
AttendeeList	Memo, required	List of attendee names
EventDate	Date/Time, required	Date of event

A few events are supplied in the downloadable database.

Binding to the Database

The two controls we'd like to bind to data are attendeeList and roomList. To do this we have to set the DataSource properties of these controls to tables containing our data. Our code must load data into these tables and perform this binding at run time. Both of these controls also have DataTextField and DataValueField properties that specify what columns to use for displaying list items and setting value properties, respectively. In both cases we can set these properties at design time and they will be used as soon as the DataSource property is set to populate the list items in the control.

Remove the existing entries from the ASP.NET code for these controls such that the declarations read as follows:

```
...
<asp:DropDownList ID="roomList" Runat="server" Width="160px"
                  DataTextField="Room" DataValueField="ID" >
</asp:DropDownList>
...
<asp:ListBox ID="attendeeList" Runat="server" Width="160px"
             SelectionMode="Multiple" Rows="6"
             DataTextField="Name"
             DataValueField="ID" />
</asp:ListBox>
...
```

The next task is to create a connection to the database. There are several ways to do this, as we saw in Chapter 9 earlier. We'll hand-code it to keep things simple. As we are using an Access database the provider type for this connection is the Microsoft Jet 4.0 OLE DB Provider, so we need to add a System.Data.OleDb.OleDbConnection object to our form called oleDbConnection1:

```
public class WebForm1 : System.Web.UI.Page
{
    ...
    protected System.Data.OleDb.OleDbConnection oleDbConnection1;
```

For a SQL Server connection the object added would be a `SqlClient.SqlConnection` object.

We then need to add some code to `InitializeComponent()` to set the `ConnectionString` property of `oleDbConnection1` so it is all ready for us to use:

```
private void InitializeComponent()
{
    this.oleDbConnection1 = new System.Data.OleDb.OleDbConnection();
    ...
    this.oleDbConnection1.ConnectionString =
        @"Provider=Microsoft.Jet.OLEDB.4.0;Password="""";User ID=Admin;Data " +
                    "Source=C:\\Inetpub\\wwwroot\\PCSWebApp3\\PCSWebApp3.mdb";
```

We want to perform our data binding in the `Page_Load()` event handler, such that the controls are fully populated when we want to use them in other parts of our code. We will read data from the database regardless of whether a postback operation is in progress (even though the list controls will persist their contents via the viewstate) to ensure that we have access to all the data we might need, although we don't need to perform the data binding itself in a postback. This might seem slightly wasteful, but I will again leave it as an exercise to the reader to add additional logic to the code to optimize this behavior. Here we are concentrating on how to get things working, without going into too much detail.

All of our code will be placed in-between calling the `Open()` and `Close()` methods of our connection object:

```
private void Page_Load(object sender, System.EventArgs e)
{
    oleDbConnection1.Open();
    if (!this.IsPostBack)
    {
        calendar.SelectedDate = System.DateTime.Now;
    }
    oleDbConnection1.Close();
}
```

We'll see why the calendar date setting is left inside this postback-checking code shortly.

For our data exchange we need to use several objects to store our data in. We can declare these at the class level such that we have access to them from other functions. We need a `DataSet` object to store the database information, three `OleDb.OleDbDataAdapter` objects to execute queries on the dataset, and a `DataTable` object to store our events for later access. Declare these as follows:

```
public class WebForm1 : System.Web.UI.Page
{
    ...
    protected System.Data.DataSet ds;
    protected System.Data.DataTable eventTable;
    protected System.Data.OleDb.OleDbDataAdapter daAttendees;
    protected System.Data.OleDb.OleDbDataAdapter daRooms;
    protected System.Data.OleDb.OleDbDataAdapter daEvents;
```

SQL Server versions of all the OLE DB objects exist, and their usage is identical.

Page_Load() now needs to create the DataSet object:

```
private void Page_Load(object sender, System.EventArgs e)
{
    ...
    oleDbConnection1.Open();
    ds = new DataSet();
```

Then we must assign the OleDbDataAdapter objects with queries and a link to the connection object:

```
ds = new DataSet();
daAttendees = new System.Data.OleDb.OleDbDataAdapter(
            "SELECT * FROM Attendees", oleDbConnection1);
daRooms = new System.Data.OleDb.OleDbDataAdapter(
            "SELECT * FROM Rooms", oleDbConnection1);
daEvents = new System.Data.OleDb.OleDbDataAdapter(
            "SELECT * FROM Events", oleDbConnection1);
```

Next we execute the queries using calls to Fill():

```
daEvents = new System.Data.OleDb.OleDbDataAdapter(
            "SELECT * FROM Events", oleDbConnection1);
daAttendees.Fill(ds, "Attendees");
daRooms.Fill(ds, "Rooms");
daEvents.Fill(ds, "Events");
```

Now we come to the data binding itself. As mentioned earlier, this simply involves setting the DataSource property on our bound controls to the tables we want to bind to:

```
daEvents.Fill(ds, "Events");
attendeeList.DataSource = ds.Tables["Attendees"];
roomList.DataSource = ds.Tables["Rooms"];
```

This sets the properties, but data binding itself won't occur until we call the DataBind() method of the form, which we'll do in a moment. Before we do this we'll populate the DataTable object with the event table data:

```
roomList.DataSource = ds.Tables["Rooms"];
eventTable = ds.Tables["Events"];
```

We will only data bind if a postback is not in progress; otherwise, we will simply be refreshing data (which we're assuming is static in the database for the duration of an event booking request). Data binding in a postback would also wipe the selections in the roomList and attendeeList controls. We could make a note of these before binding and then renew them, but it is simpler to call DataBind() in our existing if statement (this is the reason that this statement was kept in the region of code where the data connection was open):

```
        eventTable = ds.Tables["Events"];
        if (!this.IsPostBack)
        {
            calendar.SelectedDate = System.DateTime.Now;
            this.DataBind();
        }
        oleDbConnection1.Close();
    }
```

Running the application now will result in the full attendee and room data being available from our data bound controls.

> **Please note that in order for the code to run you may have to explicitly close any open connections to the database, either in Access or in Server Explorer. To do this simply right-click on the data source in Server Explorer and choose Close.**

Customizing the Calendar Control

Before we discuss adding events to the database let's make a modification to our calendar display. It would be nice to display any day where a booking has previously been made in a different color, and prevent such days from being selectable. This requires modifications to the way we set dates in the calendar, and the way day cells are displayed.

We'll start with date selection. There are three places where we need to check for dates where events are booked and modify the selection accordingly: when we set the initial date in Page_Load(), when the user attempts to select a date from the calendar, and when an event is booked and we wish to set a new date to prevent the user booking two events on the same day before selecting a new date. As this is going to be a common feature we may as well create a private method to perform this calculation. This method should accept a trial date as a parameter and return the date to use, which will either be the same date as the trial date, or the next available day after the trial date.

Add this method, getFreeDate(), to the code-behind file:

```
private System.DateTime getFreeDate(System.DateTime trialDate)
{
    if (eventTable.Rows.Count > 0)
    {
        System.DateTime testDate;
        bool trialDateOK = false;
        while (!trialDateOK)
        {
            trialDateOK = true;
            foreach (System.Data.DataRow testRow in eventTable.Rows)
            {
                testDate = (System.DateTime)testRow["EventDate"];
                if (testDate.Date == trialDate.Date)
                {
                    trialDateOK = false;
                    trialDate = trialDate.AddDays(1);
                }
            }
        }
    }
    return trialDate;
}
```

This simple code uses the `eventTable` object that we populated in `Page_Load()` to extract event data. First we check for the trivial case where no events have been booked, in which case we can just confirm the trial date by returning it. Next we iterate through the dates in the `Event` table comparing them with the trial date. If we find a match we add one day to the trial date and perform another search.

Extracting the date from the `DataTable` is remarkably simple:

```
testDate = (System.DateTime)testRow["EventDate"];
```

Casting the column data into `System.DateTime` works fine.

The first place we will use `getFreeDate()`, then, is back in `Page_Load()`. This simply means making a minor modification to the code that sets the calendar `SelectedDate` property:

```
if (!this.IsPostBack)
{
    System.DateTime trialDate = System.DateTime.Now;
    calendar.SelectedDate = getFreeDate(trialDate);
    this.DataBind();
}
```

Next we need to respond to date selection on the calendar. To do this we simply need to add an event handler for the `SelectionChanged` event of the calendar, and force the date to be checked against existing events. Double-click on the calendar in the Designer and add this code:

```
private void calendar_SelectionChanged(object sender,
                                       System.EventArgs e)
{
    System.DateTime trialDate = calendar.SelectedDate;
    calendar.SelectedDate = getFreeDate(trialDate);
}
```

The code here is identical to that in `Page_Load()`.

The third place that we must perform this check is in response to the booking button being pressed. We'll come back to this in a little while, as we have many changes to make here.

Next we want to color the day cells of the calendar to signify existing events. To do this we need to add an event handler for the `DayRender` event of the calendar object. This event is raised each time an individual day is rendered, and gives us access to the cell object being displayed and the date of this cell through the `Cell` and `Date` properties of the `DayRenderEventArgs` parameter we receive in the handler function. We simply need to compare the date of the cell being rendered to the dates in our `eventTable` object, and color the cell using the `Cell.BackColor` property if there is a match:

```
protected void calendar_DayRender(object sender,
              System.Web.UI.WebControls.DayRenderEventArgs e)
{
    if (eventTable.Rows.Count > 0)
    {
        System.DateTime testDate;
```

```
           foreach (System.Data.DataRow testRow in eventTable.Rows)
           {
               testDate = (System.DateTime)testRow["EventDate"];
               if (testDate.Date == e.Day.Date)
               {
                   e.Cell.BackColor = Color.Red;
               }
           }
       }
   }
```

Here we are using red, which will give us a display along the lines of:

Here the 15th, 27th, 28th, 29th, and 30th of March all contain events, and the user has selected the 17th. With the addition of the date-selection logic it is now impossible to select a day that is shown in red; if an attempt is made then a later date is selected instead. For example, clicking on the 28th of March on the calendar shown above will result in the 31st being selected.

Adding Events to the Database

The submitButton_Click() event handler currently assembles a string from the event characteristics and displays it in the resultLabel control. To add an event to the database we simply need to reformat the string created into a SQL INSERT query and execute it.

Much of the following code will therefore look familiar:

```
protected void submitButton_Click(object sender, System.EventArgs e)
{
    if (this.IsValid)
    {
        String attendees = "";
        foreach (ListItem attendee in attendeeList.Items)
        {
            if (attendee.Selected)
            {
                attendees += attendee.Text + " (" + attendee.Value + "), ";
```

```
            }
        }
        attendees += " and " + nameBox.Text;
        String dateString =
                   calendar.SelectedDate.Date.Date.ToShortDateString();
        String oleDbCommand = "INSERT INTO Events (Name, Room, " +
                             "AttendeeList, EventDate) VALUES ('" +
                             eventBox.Text + "', '" +
                             roomList.SelectedItem.Value + "', '" +
                             attendees + "', '" + dateString + "')";
```

Once we have created our SQL query string we can use it to build an `OleDb.OleDbCommand` object:

```
        System.Data.OleDb.OleDbCommand insertCommand =
                    new System.Data.OleDb.OleDbCommand(oleDbCommand,
                                                       oleDbConnection1);
```

Next we reopen the connection that was closed in `Page_Load()` (again, this is perhaps not the most efficient way of doing things, but it works fine for demonstration purposes), and execute the query:

```
        oleDbConnection1.Open();
        int queryResult = insertCommand.ExecuteNonQuery();
```

`ExecuteNonQuery()` returns an integer representing how many table rows were affected by the query. If this is equal to 1 then we know that our insertion was successful. If so then we put a success message in `resultLabel`, execute a new query to repopulate `eventTable` and our dataset with our new list of events (we clear the dataset first, otherwise events will be duplicated), and change the calendar selection to a new, free, date:

```
        if (queryResult == 1)
        {
            resultLabel.Text = "Event Added.";
            daEvents = new System.Data.OleDb.OleDbDataAdapter(
                        "SELECT * FROM Events", oleDbConnection1);
            ds.Clear();
            daEvents.Fill(ds, "Events");
            eventTable = ds.Tables["Events"];
            calendar.SelectedDate =
                        getFreeDate(calendar.SelectedDate.AddDays(1));
        }
```

If `ExecuteNonQuery()` returns a number other than 1 we know that there has been a problem. For this example we won't worry too much about this, and simply display a failure notification in `resultLabel`:

```
        else
        {
            resultLabel.Text = "Event not added due to DB access "
                               + "problem.";
        }
```

Finally, we close the connection again:

```
            oleDbConnection1.Close();
        }
    }
```

and our data-aware version of the event booking application is complete.

Note that due to the syntax of the SQL INSERT query we must avoid using certain characters in the event name, such as apostrophes " ' ", as they will cause an error. It would be relatively easy to enforce a custom validation rule that prevented the user from using such characters, or to perform some type of character escaping before inserting data and after reading data, but the code for this will not be covered here.

More on Data Binding

When we looked at the available Server Controls earlier in this chapter we saw three that dealt with data display: DataGrid, Repeater, and DataList. These are all extremely useful when it comes to outputting data to a web page, as they perform many tasks automatically that would otherwise require a fair amount of coding.

To start with, let's look at the simplest of these to use, DataGrid. As a simple example of this control let's add an event-detail display to the bottom of the display of PCSWebApp3. This enables us to ignore database connections for now, as we have already configured our application for this access.

Add the following to the bottom of WebForm1.aspx in the PCSWebApp3 project:

```
        <br>Results:
        <asp:Label ID=resultLabel Runat="server"
                   Text="None."></asp:label>
        <br>
        <br>
        <asp:DataGrid Runat="server" ID="eventDetails1" />
        </form>
    </body>
</HTML>
```

Also, add the following to Page_Load() in WebForm1.aspx.cs:

```
        attendeeList.DataSource = ds.Tables["Attendees"];
        roomList.DataSource = ds.Tables["Rooms"];
        eventTable = ds.Tables["Events"];
        eventDetails1.DataSource = eventTable;
        if (!this.IsPostBack)
        {
            System.DateTime trialDate = System.DateTime.Now;
            calendar.SelectedDate = getFreeDate(trialDate);
            this.DataBind();
        }
        else
        {
            eventDetails1.DataBind();
        }
        oleDbConnection1.Close();
    }
```

Note that the event list may have changed between requests if another user has added an event, so we need to call `DataBind()` on the `DataGrid` to reflect these changes. Remember that calling `DataBind()` on the whole form will result in room and attendee selections being lost, so this is a fair compromise.

If you load the application in your web browser again you should see a list underneath the booking details section containing the full list of events:

ID	Name	Room	AttendeeList	EventDate
1	My Birthday	4	Iggy Pop (5), Sean Connery (7), Albert Einstein (10), George Clooney (14), Jules Verne (18), Robin Hood (20), and Karli Watson	17.09.2001 00:00:00
2	Dinner	1	Bill Gates (1), Monika Lewinsky (2), and Bruce Lee	05.08.2001 00:00:00
5	Discussion of darkness	6	Vlad the Impaler (4), Darth Vader and Beelzebub	29.10.2001 00:00:00
6	Christmas with Pals	9	Dr Frank N Furter (11), Bobby Davro (15), John F Kennedy (16), Stephen King (19), and Karli Watson	25.12.2001 00:00:00
7	Escape	17	Monika Lewinsky (2), Stephen King (19), and Spartacus	10.05.2001 00:00:00
8	Planetary Conquest	14	Bill Gates (1), Albert Einstein (10), Dr Frank N Furter (11), Bobby Davro (15), and Darth Vader	15.06.2001 00:00:00
9	Homecoming Celebration	7	William Shakespeare (6), Christopher Columbus (12), Robin Hood (20), and Ulysses	22.06.2001 00:00:00
10	Dalek Reunion Ball	12	Roger Moore (8), George Clooney (14), Bobby Davro (15), and Davros	12.06.2001 00:00:00
11	Romantic meal for two	13	George Clooney (14), and Donna Watson	29.03.2001 00:00:00

We can also make one further modification in `submitButton_Click()` to ensure that this data is updated when new records are added:

```
if (queryResult == 1)
{
    resultLabel.Text = "Event Added.";
    daEvents = new System.Data.OleDb.OleDbDataAdapter(
                "SELECT * FROM Events", oleDbConnection1);
    ds.Clear();
    daEvents.Fill(ds, "Events");
    eventTable = ds.Tables["Events"];
    calendar.SelectedDate =
                getFreeDate(calendar.SelectedDate.AddDays(1));
    eventDetails1.DataBind();
}
```

Note that we call `DataBind()` on the `DataGrid`, not on `this`. This prevents all data bound controls from being refreshed, which would be unnecessary. All data-bindable controls support this method, which is normally called by the form if we call the top-level (`this`) `DataBind()` method.

As you might expect, the `DataGrid` control contains many properties that we can use to format the displayed data in a more user-friendly way, but I'll leave these for you to discover.

Data Display with Templates

The other two data displaying controls, `Repeater` and `DataList`, require you to use templates to format data for display. Templates, in an ASP.NET sense, are parameterized sections of HTML that are used as elements of output in certain controls. They enable us to customize exactly how data is output to the browser, and can result in professional-looking displays without too much effort.

There are several templates available to customize various aspects of list behavior, but the one template that is essential for both `Repeater` and `DataList` is `<ItemTemplate>`, which is used in the display of each data item. We declare this template (and all the others) inside the control declaration, for example:

```
<asp:DataList Runat="server" ... >
   <ItemTemplate>
      ...
   </ItemTemplate>
</asp:DataList>
```

Within template declarations we will normally want to output sections of HTML along with parameters from the data that is bound to the control. There is a special syntax that we can use to output such parameters:

```
<%# expression %>
```

expression might be simply an expression binding the parameter to a page or control property, but is more likely to consist of a `DataBinder.Eval()` expression. This useful function can be used to output data from a table bound to a control simply by specifying the column, using the following syntax:

```
<%# DataBinder.Eval(Container.DataItem, "ColumnName") %>
```

There is also an optional third parameter that allows us to format the data returned, which has identical syntax to string formatting expressions used elsewhere.

The full list of available templates and when they are used is shown below:

Template	Description
`<ItemTemplate>`	Template to use for list items
`<HeaderTemplate>`	Template to use for output before the list
`<FooterTemplate>`	Template to use for output after the list

Table continued on following page

Template	Description
`<SeparatorTemplate>`	Template for use between items in list
`<AlternatingItemTemplate>`	Template for alternate items; can aid visibility
`<SelectedItemTemplate>`	(`DataList` only) Template to use for selected items in the list
`<EditItemTemplate>`	(`DataList` only) Template to use for items in a list that are being edited

Again, the easiest way to look at this is with an example, and we can use our existing data query in PCSWebApp3 to achieve this.

Using Templates Example

We'll extend the table at the top of the page to contain a `DataList` displaying each of the events stored in the database. We'll make these events selectable such that details of any event can be displayed by clicking on its name.

The changes to the code in `WebForm1.aspx` in the `PCSWebApp3` project are shown below:

```
<tr>
    <td align=middle colSpan=3>
        <asp:ValidationSummary ID=validationSummary Runat="server"
                HeaderText="Before submitting your request:"/>
    </td>
</tr>
<tr>
    <td align="left" colSpan="3" width="100%">
        <table cellspacing="4">
            <tr>
                <td width="40%" bgcolor="#ccffcc" >
                    <asp:DataList Runat="server" ID="eventDetails2"
                            OnSelectedIndexChanged=
                            "eventDetails2_SelectedIndexChanged">
                    <ItemTemplate>
                        <asp:LinkButton Runat="server"
                                    CommandName="Select"
                                    ForeColor="#0000ff"
                                    ID="Linkbutton1"
                                    CausesValidation="false">
                        <%# DataBinder.Eval(Container.DataItem,
                                    "Name")%>
                        </asp:LinkButton>

                        <br>
                    </ItemTemplate>
                    <SelectedItemTemplate>
                        <b><%# DataBinder.Eval(Container.DataItem,
                                    "Name") %></b>
                        <br>
```

```
                        </SelectedItemTemplate>
                    </asp:DataList>
                </td>
                <td valign="top">
                    <asp:Label Runat="server" ID="edName"
                                Font-Name="Arial" Font-Bold="True"
                                Font-Italic="True" Font-Size="14">
                        Select an event to view details.
                    </asp:Label>
                    <br>
                    <asp:Label Runat="server" ID="edDate"/>
                    <br>
                    <asp:Label Runat="server" ID="edRoom"/>
                    <br>
                    <asp:Label Runat="server" ID="edAttendees"/>
                </td>
            </tr>
        </table>
    </td>
  </tr>
</table>
```

Here we have added a new table row containing a table with a `DataList` in one column and a detail view in the other. The detail view is simply four labels for event properties, one of which contains the text "**Select an event to view details.**" when no event is selected (the situation when the form is first loaded).

The `DataList` uses `<ItemTemplate>` and `<SelectedItemTemplate>` to display event details. To facilitate selection we raise a `Select` command from the event name link rendered in `<ItemTemplate>`, which automatically changes the selection. We also use the `OnSelectedIndexChanged` event, triggered when the `Select` command changes the selection, to populate the event detail labels. The event handler we get if we double-click on `eventDetails2` in the Designer is shown below. You'll need to change the protection level of the method from `protected` to `private`. (Note that we need to `DataBind()` first to update the selection.)

```
private void eventDetails2_SelectedIndexChanged(object sender,
                                                System.EventArgs e)
{
    eventDetails2.DataBind();
    DataRow selectedEventRow =
                        eventTable.Rows[eventDetails2.SelectedIndex];
    edName.Text = (string)selectedEventRow["Name"];
    edDate.Text = "<b>Date:</b> " +
            ((DateTime)selectedEventRow["EventDate"]).ToLongDateString();
    edAttendees.Text = "<b>Attendees:</b> " +
                            (string)selectedEventRow["AttendeeList"];
    DataRow selectedEventRoomRow =
            ds.Tables["Rooms"].Rows[(int)selectedEventRow["Room"] - 1];
    edRoom.Text = "<b>Room:</b> " + selectedEventRoomRow["Room"];
}
```

This uses data in `ds` and `eventTable` to populate the details.

As with the `DataGrid` we used earlier, we need to set the data for `eventDetails2` and bind in `Page_Load()`:

```
eventDetails1.DataSource = eventTable;
eventDetails2.DataSource = eventTable;
...
    eventDetails1.DataBind();
    eventDetails2.DataBind();
```

and re-bind in `submitButton_Click()`:

```
eventDetails1.DataBind();
eventDetails2.DataBind();
```

Now event details are available in the table:

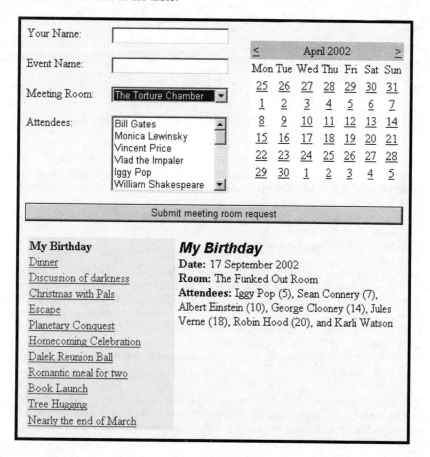

There is *much* more that we can do with templates and data bound controls in general, enough in fact to fill a whole book. However, this should be enough to get you started with your experimentation.

Application Configuration

One thing that has been alluded to throughout this chapter, but without any details being supplied, is the existence of a conceptual application containing web pages and configuration settings. This is an important concept to grasp, especially when configuring your web sites for multiple concurrent users.

A few notes on terminology and application lifetime are necessary here. An **application** is defined as all files in your project, and is configured by the `Web.config` file. An `Application` object is created when an application is started for the first time, which will be when the first HTTP request arrives. Also at this time the `Application_Start` event is triggered and a pool of `HttpApplication` instances is created. Each incoming request receives one of these instances, which performs request processing. Note that this means `HttpApplication` objects do not need to cope with concurrent access, unlike the global `Application` object. When all `HttpApplication` instances finish their work the `Application_End` event fires and the application terminates, destroying the `Application` object.

The event handlers for the events mentioned above (along with handlers for all other events discussed here) must be defined in the `Global.asax` file, which contains blanks for you to fill in, for example:

```
protected void Application_Start(Object sender, EventArgs e)
{

}
```

When an individual user uses the web application a **session** is started. Similar to the application, this involves the creation of a user-specific `Session` object, along with the triggering of a `Session_Start` event. Within a session individual **requests** trigger `Application_BeginRequest` and `Application_EndRequest` events. These may occur several times over the scope of a session as different resources within the application are accessed. Individual sessions may be terminated manually, or will time out if no further requests are received. Session termination triggers a `Session_End` event and the destruction of the `Session` object.

With this process in mind, then, how does this help us? Well, there are several things we can do to streamline our application. Consider the example application we have been developing in this chapter. Every time our `.aspx` page is accessed a recordset is populated with the contents of `PCSWebApp3.mdb`. This recordset is only ever used for reading data, as the method of inserting events into the database is different. In cases like this we could populate the recordset in the `Application_Start` event handler and make it available to all users. The only time we would need to refresh the recordset would be if an event were added. This will drastically improve performance with multiple users, as in most requests no DB access will be required.

Another technique we can use is to store session-level information for use by individual users across requests. This might include user-specific information extracted from a data store when the user first connects, and available until the user ceases to submit requests, or explicitly logs out.

We won't detail these techniques here, as this is something better dealt with in specialized ASP.NET books, such as *Professional ASP.NET 1.0* (ISBN 1-861007-03-5) but it helps to have a broad understanding of the processes nevertheless. In the next chapter, dealing with Web Services, we will see some of these techniques in action.

Summary

This chapter has provided an overview of web application creation with ASP.NET. We have seen how we can use every bit as much C# as we have looked at in this book, combined with web server controls to provide a truly rich development environment. We have developed a meeting room booking application to illustrate many of the techniques available, such as the variety of server controls that exist, and data binding with ADO.NET.

In the next two chapters we will see two more important web subjects: Web Services and Custom Controls. We will continue to develop the example from this chapter in these chapters, taking it in radically different directions to illustrate the tools at our disposal.

In conclusion, ASP.NET is a powerful new weapon in the web developer's arsenal. The server-side processing is second to none, and being able to use the full power of C# and the .NET Framework is an attractive proposition.

15

Web Services

Web Services are a new way of performing remote method calls over HTTP that can make use of the **SOAP** (**Simple Object Access Protocol**). In the past this issue has been fraught with difficulty, as anyone who has any DCOM (Distributed COM) experience will bear witness to. The act of instantiating an object on a remote server, calling a method, and obtaining the result was far from simple – and the necessary configuration was even trickier.

SOAP simplifies matters immensely. This technology is an XML-based standard that details how method calls may be made over HTTP in a reproducible manner. A remote SOAP server is capable of understanding these calls and performing all the hard work for us, such as instantiating the required object, making the call, and returning a SOAP-formatted response to the client.

The .NET Framework makes it very easy for us to make use of all this. As with ASP.NET, we are able to use the full array of C# and .NET techniques on the server, but (perhaps more importantly) the simple consumption of Web Services can be achieved from any platform with HTTP access to the server. In other words, it is conceivable that Linux code could, for example, use .NET Web Services, or even Internet-enabled fridges.

In addition, Web Services may be completely described using **WSDL** (**Web Service Description Language**), allowing dynamic discovery of Web Services at run time. WSDL provides descriptions of all methods (along with the types required to call them) using XML with XML schemas. There are a wide variety of types available to Web Services, which range from simple primitive types to full `DataSet` objects, such that full in-memory databases can be marshaled to a client, which can result in a dramatic reduction in load on a database server.

In this chapter we will:

❑ Look at the syntax of SOAP and WSDL, then move on to see how they are used by Web Services

❑ We will discuss how to expose and consume Web Services

❑ Work through a complete example building on the meeting room booker from the last chapter to illustrate their use

❑ See how to exchange data using SOAP Headers

SOAP

As mentioned above, one method used to exchange data with Web Services is SOAP. This technology has had a lot of press, especially since Microsoft decided to adopt it for use in the .NET Framework. Now, though, the excitement seems to be dying down a bit as the SOAP specification is finalized. When you think about it, finding out exactly how SOAP works is a bit like finding out about how HTTP works – interesting, but not essential. Most of the time we never have to worry about the format of the exchanges made with Web Services, they just happen, we get the results we want, and everyone is happy.

For this reason we won't go into a huge amount of depth in this section, but we will see some simple SOAP requests and responses so you can get a feel for what is going on under the hood should you so desire.

Let's imagine that we want to call a method in a Web Service with the following signature:

```
int DoSomething(string stringParam, int intParam)
```

The SOAP headers and body required for this are shown below, with the address of the Web Service (more on this later) at the top:

```
POST /SomeLocation/myWebService.asmx HTTP/1.1
Host: karlivaio
Content-Type: text/xml; charset=utf-8
Content-Length: length
SOAPAction: "http://tempuri.org/DoSomething"

<?xml version="1.0" encoding="utf-8"?>
<soap:Envelope xmlns:xsi="http://www.w3.org/2001/XMLSchema-instance"
               xmlns:xsd="http://www.w3.org/2001/XMLSchema"
               xmlns:soap="http://schemas.xmlsoap.org/soap/envelope/">
    <soap:Body>
       <DoSomething xmlns="http://tempuri.org/">
           <stringParam>string</stringParam>
           <intParam>int</intParam>
       </DoSomething>
    </soap:Body>
</soap:Envelope>
```

The *length* parameter here specifies the total byte size of the content, and will vary depending on the values sent in the *string* and *int* parameters.

The `soap` namespace referenced here defines various elements that we use to build up our message. When we send this over HTTP the actual data sent will be slightly different (but related). For example, we could call the above method using the simple GET method:

```
GET /PCSWebSrv1/Service1.asmx/DoSomething?stringParam=string&intParam=int HTTP/1.1
Host: hostname
```

The SOAP response of this method will be as follows:

```
HTTP/1.1 200 OK
Content-Type: text/xml; charset=utf-8
Content-Length: length

<?xml version="1.0" encoding="utf-8"?>
<soap:Envelope xmlns:xsi="http://www.w3.org/2001/XMLSchema-instance"
               xmlns:xsd="http://www.w3.org/2001/XMLSchema"
               xmlns:soap="http://schemas.xmlsoap.org/soap/envelope/">
   <soap:Body>
      <DoSomethingResponse xmlns="http://tempuri.org/">
         <DoSomethingResult>int</DoSomethingResult>
      </DoSomethingResponse>
   </soap:Body>
</soap:Envelope>
```

where `length` is again varied according to the contents, in this case `int`.

Again, the actual response over HTTP may be far simpler, for example:

```
HTTP/1.1 200 OK
Content-Type: text/xml; charset=utf-8
Content-Length: length

<?xml version="1.0"?>
<int xmlns="http://tempuri.org/">int</int>
```

This is a far simpler XML format.

As discussed at the start of this section, the beauty of all this is that we can ignore it completely. It is only if we want to do something really odd that the exact syntax becomes important.

WSDL

WSDL completely describes Web Services, the methods available, and the various ways of calling these methods. Again, the exact details of this won't really benefit us that much, but a general understanding is useful.

WSDL is another fully XML-compliant syntax, and specifies Web Services by the methods available, the types used by these methods, the formats of request and response messages sent to and from methods via various protocols (pure SOAP, HTTP GET, etc.), and various bindings between the above.

Perhaps the most important part of a WSDL file is the type-definition section. This uses XML schemas to describe the format for data exchange via the XML elements that may be used, and their relationships.

For example, the Web Service method used as an example in the last section:

```
int DoSomething(string stringParam, int intParam)
```

would have types declared for the request as follows:

```
<?xml version="1.0" ?>
<definitions xmlns:http="http://schemas.xmlsoap.org/wsdl/http/"
             xmlns:soap="http://schemas.xmlsoap.org/wsdl/soap/"
             xmlns:s="http://www.w3.org/2001/XMLSchema"
             ...other namespaces...>
    <types>
        <s:schema elementFormDefault="qualified"
                  targetNamespace="http://tempuri.org/">
            <s:element name="DoSomething">
                <s:complexType>
                    <s:sequence>
                        <s:element minOccurs="0" maxOccurs="1" name="stringParam"
                                   type="s:string" />
                        <s:element minOccurs="1" maxOccurs="1" name="intParam"
                                   type="s:int" />
                    </s:sequence>
                </s:complexType>
            </s:element>
            <s:element name="DoSomethingResponse">
                <s:complexType>
                    <s:sequence>
                        <s:element minOccurs="1" maxOccurs="1" name="DoSomethingResult"
                                   type="s:int" />
                    </s:sequence>
                </s:complexType>
            </s:element>
            <s:element name="int" type="s:int" />
        </s:schema>
    </types>
    ...other definitions...
</definitions>
```

These types are all that are required for the SOAP and HTTP requests and responses we saw earlier, and are bound to these operations later in the file. All the types are specified using standard XML schema syntax, for example:

```
<s:element name="DoSomethingResponse">
    <s:complexType>
        <s:sequence>
            <s:element minOccurs="1" maxOccurs="1" name="DoSomethingResult"
                       type="s:int" />
        </s:sequence>
    </s:complexType>
</s:element>
```

This specifies that an element called `DoSomethingResponse` has a child element called `DoSomethingResult` that contains an integer. This integer must occur 0 or 1 times, meaning that it may be omitted.

If we have access to the WSDL for a Web Service then we can use it. As we will see shortly, this isn't that difficult to do.

Now we've had a brief look at SOAP and WSDL it's time to move on to look at how we create and consume Web Services.

Web Services

The discussion of Web Services falls into two categories:

❑   Exposing Web Services, which concerns writing Web Services and placing them on web servers

❑   Consuming Web Services, which concerns using the services you design on a client

We will look at these subjects in the two sections that follow.

Exposing Web Services

Web Services are exposed by placing code either directly into `.asmx` files or by referencing Web Service classes from these files. As with ASP.NET pages, creating a Web Service in VS .NET uses the latter method, and we will too for demonstration purposes.

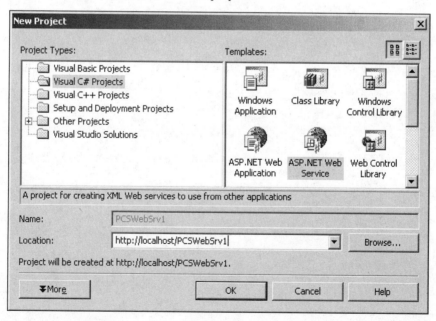

Creating a Web Service project called **PCSWebSrv1** as shown above results in a similar set of files being generated to those for a web application project. In fact, the only difference is that instead of a file called WebForm1.aspx being generated, a file called Service1.asmx is created. The .vsdisco file generated is responsible for identifying the Web Service such that Visual Studio .NET can add a web reference to it, as we will see shortly.

The code in Service1.asmx isn't directly accessible through VS .NET, but inspection with Notepad reveals the following single line of code:

```
<%@ WebService Language="c#" Codebehind="Service1.asmx.cs"
   Class="PCSWebSrv1.Service1" %>
```

This references the code file that we can see in VS .NET, Service1.asmx.cs, accessible by right-clicking on Service1.asmx in the Solution Explorer and selecting **View Code**. The generated code, with comments removed for brevity, is shown below:

```csharp
using System;
using System.Collections;
using System.ComponentModel;
using System.Data;
using System.Diagnostics;
using System.Web;
using System.Web.Services;

namespace PCSWebSrv1
{

    public class Service1 : System.Web.Services.WebService
    {
        public Service1()
        {
            InitializeComponent();
        }

        #region Component Designer generated code

        private IContainer components = null;

        private void InitializeComponent()
        {
        }

        protected override void Dispose( bool disposing )
        {
            if(disposing && components != null)
            {
                components.Dispose();
            }
            base.Dispose(disposing);
        }

        #endregion
    }
}
```

This code contains several standard namespace references, and defines the `PCSWebSrv1` namespace. The namespace contains the definition of the Web Service class `Service1` (which we saw referenced above in `Service1.asmx`), descended from `System.Web.Services.WebService`. It also contains similar code to that found in the ASP.NET page code-behind file, which we saw in the last chapter. This code is required in order to design Web Services in VS .NET, part of which is a private member to contain any components that can be added to the Web Service. In order for the Web Service class to free resources properly there is also a `Dispose()` method, which will clean up any components in this collection. It is now up to us to provide additional methods on this Web Service class.

Adding a method accessible through the Web Service simply requires defining the method as `public` and giving it the `WebMethod` attribute. This attribute simply labels the methods we want to be accessible. We'll look at the types we can use for the return type and parameters shortly, but for now add the following method:

```
[WebMethod]
public String CanWeFixIt()
{
    return "Yes we can!";
}
```

Now compile the project.

We can check things are working by pointing our web browser at `Service1.asmx`:

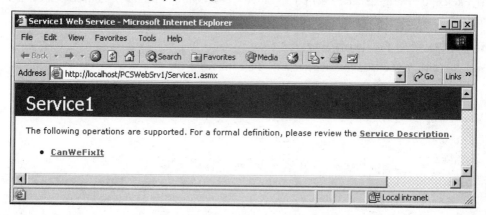

Clicking on the method name gives us information about the SOAP request and response, as well as examples of how the request and response will look via HTTP GET and HTTP POST methods. We can also test the method by clicking on the Invoke button provided. If the method requires simple parameters we can enter these on this form as well. If we do this we will see the XML returned by the method call:

```
<?xml version="1.0" encoding="utf-8"?>
<string xmlns="http://tempuri.org/">Yes we can!</string>
```

This demonstrates that our method is working perfectly.

Following the **Service Description** link from the browser screen shown above allows us to view the WSDL description of the Web Service. The most important part as far as we are concerned is the description of the element types for requests and responses:

```
<types>
    <s:schema elementFormDefault="qualified"
              targetNamespace="http://tempuri.org/">
        <s:element name="CanWeFixIt">
            <s:complexType />
        </s:element>
        <s:element name="CanWeFixItResponse">
            <s:complexType>
                <s:sequence>
                    <s:element minOccurs="0" maxOccurs="1" name="CanWeFixItResult"
                               type="s:string" />
                </s:sequence>
            </s:complexType>
        </s:element>
        <s:element name="string" nillable="true" type="s:string" />
    </s:schema>
</types>
```

The description also contains descriptions of the types required for requests and responses, as well as various bindings for the service, making it quite a long file.

Types Available for Web Services

Web Services can be used to exchange any of the following types:

String	Char	Byte
Boolean	Int16	Int32
Int64	UInt16	UInt32
UInt64	Single	Double
Guid	Decimal	DateTime
XmlQualifiedName	Class	struct
XmlNode	DataSet	enum

Arrays of all the above types are also allowed. Note also that only public properties and fields of `Class` and `struct` types are marshaled.

Consuming Web Services

Now we know how to create Web Services it's time to look at how we use them. To do this we need to generate a proxy class in our code that knows how to communicate with a given Web Service. Any calls from our code to the Web Service will go through this proxy, which looks identical to the Web Service, giving our code the illusion that we have a local copy of it. In actual fact there is a lot of HTTP communication going on, but we are shielded from the details. There are two ways of doing this. We can either use the `WSDL.exe` command-line tool or the **Add Web Reference** menu option in VS .NET.

Using WSDL.exe from the command line generates a .cs file containing a proxy class, based on the WSDL description of the Web Service. We specify this using the URL of the Web Service, for example:

```
WSDL http://localhost/PCSWebSrv1/Service1.asmx?WSDL
```

This will generate a proxy class for the example from the last section in a file called Service1.cs. The class will be named after the Web Service, in this case Service1, and contain methods that call identically named methods of the service. To use this class we simply add the .cs file generated to a project and use code along the lines of:

```
Service1 myService = new Service1();
String result = myService.CanWeFixIt();
```

By default the class generated will be placed in the root namespace, so no using statement is necessary, but we can specify a different namespace to use with the **/n: <namespace>** WSDL.exe command-line option.

This technique works fine but can be a pain to continually redo if the service is being developed and changing continuously. Of course, it could be executed in the build options for a project in order to automatically update the generated proxy before each compile, but there is a better way.

We'll illustrate this better way by creating a client for the example in the last section, in a new web application called **PCSWebClient1**. Create this project now and replace the existing form declaration in the .aspx page generated with the following code:

```
<form method="post" runat="server">
   <asp:Label Runat="server" ID="resultLabel"/><br>
   <asp:Button Runat="server" ID="triggerButton"
               Text="Invoke CanWeFixIt()"/>
</form>
```

In a moment we'll bind the button-click event handler to the Web Service. First we need to add a reference to the Web Service to our project. To do this, right-click on the new client project in the Solution Explorer and select the **Add Web Reference...** option. In the window that appears type in the URL of the Web Service Service1.asmx file:

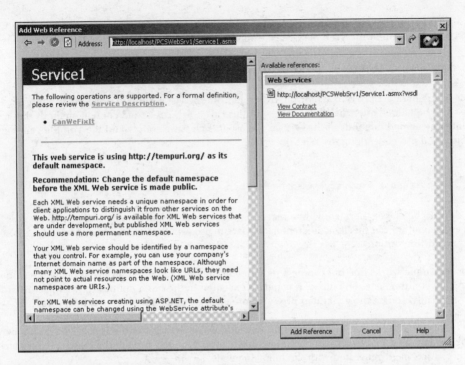

From here we can add a reference with the **Add Reference** button. Pressing this button now will result in three files being added to the **Web References** section of the project in Solution Explorer, `Reference.map`, `Service1.disco`, and `Service1.wsdl`:

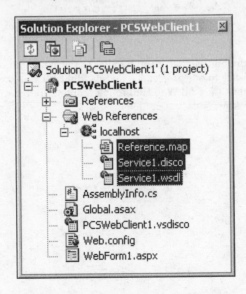

The folder containing our web reference is named after the server where the service is located, which is localhost here. This is also the namespace we need to reference to use the proxy class, so it makes sense to rename this, which we can do by right-clicking on it. Let's rename this folder as myWebService and add the using statement to our code:

```
using PCSWebClient1.myWebService;
```

Now we can use the service in our class without fully qualifying its name.

Add an event handler to the button on the form (double-click on the button) with the following code:

```
private void triggerButton_Click(object sender, System.EventArgs e)
{
    Service1 myService = new Service1();
    resultLabel.Text = myService.CanWeFixIt();
}
```

Running the application and clicking the button will now result in the result of CanWeFixIt() being displayed in the browser window.

This Web Service might change later, but with this method we can simply right-click on the web reference folder in the Server Explorer and select **Update Web Reference**. This will generate a new proxy class for us to use.

Extending the Meeting Room Booker Example

Now we know the basics of creating and consuming Web Services, let's apply our knowledge to extending the meeting room booker application from the last chapter. Specifically, we will extract the database access aspects from the application and place them into a Web Service. This Web Service will have two methods:

❑ GetData(), which will return a DataSet containing all three tables in the PCSWebApp3. mdb database

❑ AddEvent(), which will add an event and return an updated version of the DataSet that includes the change

In addition, we'll design the Web Service with some of the load-reducing techniques from the last chapter in mind. Specifically, we will store the DataSet at the application level in the Web Service application. This means that multiple requests for the data won't require additional database requests to work. The data in this application-level DataSet will only be refreshed when new data is added to the database. This means that changes made to the database by other means, such as manual editing, will *not* be reflected in this DataSet. Still, as long as we know that our Web Service is the only thing with direct access to the data we have nothing to worry about.

The Meeting Room Booking Web Service

Create a new Web Service project in VS .NET called PCSWebSrv2. The first thing we'll add to this project is some code in the Application_Start() handler in Global.asax.cs. We want to load all the data in PCSWebApp3.mdb into a dataset and store it. This will mostly involve code that we've already seen, as getting the database into a DataSet is something we've already done. In fact, we can copy all the code we need from WebForm1.aspx.cs in PCSWebApp3 from the last chapter – including the database connection string in InitializeComponent() (which we won't show here because yours is likely to be different) – with only a few modifications:

```
protected void Application_Start(Object sender, EventArgs e)
{
    System.Data.DataSet ds;
    System.Data.OleDb.OleDbConnection oleDbConnection1;
    System.Data.OleDb.OleDbDataAdapter daAttendees;
    System.Data.OleDb.OleDbDataAdapter daRooms;
    System.Data.OleDb.OleDbDataAdapter daEvents;

    oleDbConnection1 = new System.Data.OleDb.OleDbConnection();
    oleDbConnection1.ConnectionString = @" ... ";
    oleDbConnection1.Open();
    ds = new DataSet();
    daAttendees = new System.Data.OleDb.OleDbDataAdapter(
                    "SELECT * FROM Attendees", oleDbConnection1);
    daRooms = new System.Data.OleDb.OleDbDataAdapter(
                    "SELECT * FROM Rooms", oleDbConnection1);
    daEvents = new System.Data.OleDb.OleDbDataAdapter(
                    "SELECT * FROM Events", oleDbConnection1);
    daAttendees.Fill(ds, "Attendees");
    daRooms.Fill(ds, "Rooms");
    daEvents.Fill(ds, "Events");
    oleDbConnection1.Close();

    Application["ds"] = ds;
}
```

The important code to note here is in the last line. Application (and Session) objects have a collection of name-value pairs that we can use to store data in. Here we are creating a name in the Application store called ds, which takes the serialized value of the ds DataSet containing the Attendees, Rooms, and Events tables from our database. This value will be accessible to all instances of the Web Service at any time.

In order for the above code to work we also need to add a reference to the System.Data namespace to Global.asax.cs:

```
...
using System.Data;
```

This technique is very useful for read-only data as multiple threads will be able to access it, reducing the load on our database. Note, though, that the Events table is likely to change, and we'll have to update the application-level DataSet when this happens. We'll look at this shortly.

Next we need to add the `GetData()` method to our service in `Service1.asmx.cs`:

```
[WebMethod]
public DataSet GetData()
{
    return (DataSet)Application["ds"];
}
```

This uses the same syntax as `Application_Load()` to access the `DataSet`, which we simply cast to the correct type and return.

The `AddEvent()` method is slightly more complicated. Conceptually, we need to do the following:

❑ Accept event data from the client

❑ Create a SQL `INSERT` statement using this data

❑ Connect to the database and execute the SQL statement

❑ If the addition is successful then refresh the data in `Application["ds"]`

❑ Return a success or failure notification to the client (we'll leave it up to the client to refresh their `DataSet` if required)

Starting from the top, we'll accept all fields as strings:

```
[WebMethod]
public int AddEvent(String eventName, String eventRoom,
                    String eventAttendees, String eventDate)
{
}
```

Next we declare the objects we'll need for database access, connect to the database, and execute our query, all using similar code to that in `PCSWebApp3` (again, we need the connection string here, but we won't show it):

```
[WebMethod]
public int AddEvent(String eventName, String eventRoom,
                    String eventAttendees, String eventDate)
{
    System.Data.OleDb.OleDbConnection oleDbConnection1;
    System.Data.OleDb.OleDbDataAdapter daEvents;
    DataSet ds;

    oleDbConnection1 = new System.Data.OleDb.OleDbConnection();
    oleDbConnection1.ConnectionString = @" ... ";
    String oleDbCommand = "INSERT INTO Events (Name, Room, AttendeeList," +
                    " EventDate) VALUES ('" + eventName + "', '" +
                    eventRoom + "', '" + eventAttendees + "', '" +
                    eventDate + "')";
    System.Data.OleDb.OleDbCommand insertCommand =
        new System.Data.OleDb.OleDbCommand(oleDbCommand,
                                           oleDbConnection1);
    oleDbConnection1.Open();

    int queryResult = insertCommand.ExecuteNonQuery();
}
```

We use `queryResult` to store the number of rows affected by the query as before. We can check this to see if it is 1 to gauge our success. If we are successful then we execute a new query on the database to refresh the `Events` table in our `DataSet`. It is vital to lock the application data while we perform our updates, to ensure that no other threads can access `Application["ds"]` while we update it. We can do this using the `Lock()` and `UnLock()` methods of the `Application` object:

```
[WebMethod]
public int AddEvent(String eventName, String eventRoom,
                    String eventAttendees, String eventDate)
{
    ...
    int queryResult = insertCommand.ExecuteNonQuery();
    if (queryResult == 1)
    {
        daEvents = new System.Data.OleDb.OleDbDataAdapter(
                       "SELECT * FROM Events", oleDbConnection1);
        ds = (DataSet)Application["ds"];
        ds.Tables["Events"].Clear();
        daEvents.Fill(ds, "Events");
        Application.Lock();
        Application["ds"] = ds;
        Application.UnLock();
        oleDbConnection1.Close();
    }
}
```

Finally, we return `queryResult`, allowing the client to know if the query was successful:

```
[WebMethod]
public int AddEvent(String eventName, String eventRoom,
                    String eventAttendees, String eventDate)
{
    ...
    return queryResult;
}
```

And with that, we have completed our Web Service. As before, we can test this service out simply by pointing a web browser at the `.asmx` file, so we can add records and look at the XML representation of the `DataSet` returned by `GetData()` without writing any client code.

The Meeting Room Booker Client

The client we'll use will be a development of the `PCSWebApp3` web application from the last chapter. We'll call this application, unsurprisingly enough, `PCSWebApp4`, and use the code from `PCSWebApp3` as a starting point.

We'll make two major modifications to the project. Firstly, we'll remove all direct database access from this application and use the Web Service instead. Secondly, we'll introduce an application-level store of the `DataSet` returned from the Web Service that is only updated when necessary, meaning that even less of a load is placed on the database.

The first thing to do to our new web application is to add a web reference to the `PCSWebSrv2/Service1.asmx` service. We can do this in the same way we saw earlier in the chapter through right-clicking on the project in Server Explorer, locating the `.asmx` file, selecting **Add Reference**, and calling the folder `eventDataService`.

The first thing we'll do, then, is to add code to `Global.asax.cs` in much the same way as we did for our Web Service. This code, though, is a lot simpler. First we reference the Web Service and the `System.Data` namespace:

```
...
using System.Data;
using PCSWebApp4.eventDataService;
```

Next we fill a `DataSet` and place it into an application-level data store called `ds`:

```
protected void Application_Start(Object sender, EventArgs e)
{
    Service1 dataService = new Service1();
    DataSet ds = dataService.GetData();
    Application["ds"] = ds;
}
```

This `DataSet` is now available to all instances of `PCSWebApp4`, meaning that multiple users can read data without any calls to the Web Service, or indeed to the database.

Now we have this `DataSet` we need to modify `WebForm1.aspx.cs` to use it. The first thing that we can do is remove the declarations of `oleDbConnection1`, `daAttendees`, `daRooms`, and `daEvents`, as we won't be performing any database access. We can also remove the initialization code for `oleDbConnection1`, found in `InitializeComponent()`. Next we need to add a `using` statement for `PCSWebApp4.eventDataService`, as we did for `Global.asax.cs`, and change `Page_Load()` as follows:

```
private void Page_Load(object sender, System.EventArgs e)
{
    ds = (DataSet)Application["ds"];
    attendeeList.DataSource = ds.Tables["Attendees"];
    roomList.DataSource = ds.Tables["Rooms"];
    eventTable = ds.Tables["Events"];
    eventDetails1.DataSource = eventTable;
    eventDetails2.DataSource = eventTable;
    if (!this.IsPostBack)
    {
        System.DateTime trialDate = System.DateTime.Now;
        calendar.SelectedDate = getFreeDate(trialDate);
        this.DataBind();
    }
    else
    {
        eventDetails1.DataBind();
        eventDetails2.DataBind();
    }
}
```

Most of the code remains the same, all we need to do is to use `Application["ds"]` instead of getting the `DataSet` ourselves.

We also need to change `submitButton_Click()` to use the Web Service `AddData()` method. Again, much of the code remains unchanged:

```
private void submitButton_Click(object sender, System.EventArgs e)
{
    if (this.IsValid)
    {
        String attendees = "";
        foreach (ListItem attendee in attendeeList.Items)
        {
            if (attendee.Selected)
            {
                attendees += attendee.Text + " (" + attendee.Value + "), ";
            }
        }
        attendees += " and " + nameBox.Text;
        String dateString =
                    calendar.SelectedDate.Date.Date.ToShortDateString();
        Service1 dataService = new Service1();
        int queryResult = dataService.AddEvent(eventBox.Text,
                                        roomList.SelectedItem.Value,
                                        attendees,
                                        dateString);

        if (queryResult == 1)
        {
            resultLabel.Text = "Event Added.";
            ds = dataService.GetData();
            Application.Lock();
            Application["ds"] = ds;
            Application.UnLock();

            eventTable = ds.Tables["Events"];
            calendar.SelectedDate =
                        getFreeDate(calendar.SelectedDate.AddDays(1));
            eventDetails1.DataSource = eventTable;
            eventDetails1.DataBind();
            eventDetails2.DataSource = eventTable;
            eventDetails2.DataBind();
        }
        else
        {
            resultLabel.Text = "Event not added due to DB access problem.";
        }
    }
}
```

In fact, all we've really done is simplify things a great deal. This is often the case when using well-designed Web Services – we can forget about much of the workings and instead concentrate on the user experience.

There isn't a huge amount to comment on in this code. Continuing to make use of `queryResult` is a bonus, and locking the application is essential as already noted.

The PCSWebApp4 web application should look and function exactly like PCSWebApp3, but perform substantially better. We can also use the same Web Service for other applications very easily – simply displaying events on a page, for example, or even editing events, attendee names, and rooms if we add some more methods. Doing this won't break PCSWebApp4 as it will simply ignore any new methods created.

Exchanging Data using SOAP Headers

One final topic to look at in this chapter is using SOAP headers to exchange information, rather than including information in method parameters. The reason for covering it is that it is a very nice system to use for maintaining a user login. We won't go into detail about setting up your server for SSL connections, or the various methods of authentication that can be configured using IIS, as these do not affect the Web Service code we need to get this behavior.

The situation is as follows. Let's say we have a service that contains a simple authentication method with a signature as follows:

```
AuthenticationToken AuthenticateUser(string userName, string password);
```

Where AuthenticationToken is a type we define that can be used by the user in later method calls, for example:

```
void DoSomething(AuthenticationToken token, OtherParamType param);
```

Once a user has 'logged on' they then have access to other methods using the token they receive from AuthenticateUser(). This technique is typical of secure web systems, although it may be implemented in a far more complex way.

We can simplify this further by using a SOAP header to exchange tokens (or any other data). We can restrict methods such that they may only be called if a specified SOAP header is included in the method call, thus simplifying their structure to something along the lines of:

```
void DoSomething(OtherParamType param);
```

The advantage here is that, once we have set the header on the client, it persists, so after an initial bit of setting up we can ignore authentication tokens in all further web method calls.

To see this in action create a new Web Service project called PCSWebSrv3, and add a new class called AuthenticationToken.cs as follows:

```
using System;
using System.Web.Services.Protocols;

namespace PCSWebSrv3
{
    public class AuthenticationToken : SoapHeader
    {
        public Guid InnerToken;
    }
}
```

We'll use a GUID to identify the token, a common procedure, as we can be sure that it is unique.

To declare that the Web Service can have a custom SOAP header we simply add a public member to the service class, of our new type:

```
public class Service1 : System.Web.Services.WebService
{
     public AuthenticationToken AuthenticationTokenHeader;
```

We also need a using statement for System.Web.Services.Protocols in the Service1.asmx.cs file. This namespace contains an attribute called SoapHeaderAttribute which we can use to mark those web methods that require the extra SOAP header in order to work.

Before we add such a method though, let's add a very simple Login() method that clients can use to obtain an authentication token:

```
[WebMethod]
public Guid Login(string userName, string password)
{
   if ((userName == "Karli") && (password == "Cheese"))
   {
      Guid currentUser = Guid.NewGuid();
      Application["currentUser"] = currentUser;
      return currentUser;
   }
   else
   {
      Application["currentUser"] = Guid.Empty;
      return Guid.Empty;
   }
}
```

If the correct username and password are used then a new Guid is generated, stored in an Application-level variable, and returned to the user. If authentication fails then an empty Guid is returned and stored at the Application level.

Next we have a method that requires the header, as specified by the SoapHeaderAttribute attribute:

```
[WebMethod]
[SoapHeaderAttribute("AuthenticationTokenHeader",
                 Direction = SoapHeaderDirection.In,
                 Required = true)]
public string DoSomething()
{
   if ((AuthenticationTokenHeader.InnerToken
                          == (Guid)Application["currentUser"]) &&
                 (AuthenticationTokenHeader.InnerToken != Guid.Empty))
   {
      return "Authentication OK.";
   }
   else
   {
      return "Authentication failed.";
   }
}
```

This returns one of two strings, depending on whether the required header isn't an empty `Guid` and matches the one stored in `Application["currentUser"]`.

Next we need to create a quick client to test this service. Create a new web application called **PCSWebClient3**, with the following simple code for the user interface:

```
<form id="Form1" method="post" runat="server">
   User Name:
   <asp:TextBox Runat="server" ID="userNameBox" /><br>
   Password:
   <asp:TextBox Runat="server" ID="passwordBox" /><br>
   <asp:Button Runat="server" ID="loginButton" Text="Log in" /><br>
   <asp:Label Runat="server" ID="tokenLabel" /><br>
   <asp:Button Runat="server" ID="invokeButton" Text="Invoke DoSomething()" /><br>
   <asp:Label Runat="server" ID="resultLabel" /><br>
</form>
```

Add the `PCSWebSrv3` service as a web reference with the folder name `authenticateService`, and add the following `using` statement to `WebForm1.aspx.cs`:

```
using PCSWebClient3.authenticateService;
```

We will use a protected member to store the web reference proxy, and another to store a Boolean value indicating whether the user is authenticated or not:

```
public class WebForm1 : System.Web.UI.Page
{
    protected System.Web.UI.WebControls.TextBox userNameBox;
    protected System.Web.UI.WebControls.TextBox passwordBox;
    protected System.Web.UI.WebControls.Button loginButton;
    protected System.Web.UI.WebControls.Label tokenLabel;
    protected System.Web.UI.WebControls.Button invokeButton;
    protected System.Web.UI.WebControls.Label resultLabel;
    protected Service1 myService;
    protected bool authenticated;
```

We will initialize this member in `Page_Load()`. Once we have a header to use with this Web Service we'll store it in the `ViewState` collection of the form (a useful way to persist information between postbacks, which works in a similar way to storing information at the Application or Session level). `Page_Load()` looks to see if there is a stored header and assigns the header to the proxy accordingly (assigning the header in this way is the only step we need to take for the data to be sent as a SOAP header). This way any event handlers that are being called (such as the one for the web method invoking button) won't need to worry about assigning a header – that step has already been taken:

```
    private void Page_Load(object sender, System.EventArgs e)
    {
        myService = new Service1();
        AuthenticationToken header = new AuthenticationToken();
        if (ViewState["AuthenticationTokenHeader"] != null)
        {
            header.InnerToken = (Guid)ViewState["AuthenticationTokenHeader"];
```

```
        }
        else
        {
            header.InnerToken = Guid.Empty;
        }
        myService.AuthenticationTokenValue = header;
    }
```

Next we add an event handler for the Log in button by double-clicking on it in the Designer:

```
        private void loginButton_Click(object sender, System.EventArgs e)
        {
            Guid authenticationTokenHeader = myService.Login(userNameBox.Text,
                                                             passwordBox.Text);
            tokenLabel.Text = authenticationTokenHeader.ToString();
            ViewState.Add("AuthenticationTokenHeader", authenticationTokenHeader);
        }
```

This handler uses any data entered in the two text boxes to call Login(), displays the Guid returned, and stores the Guid in the ViewState collection.

Finally, we have to add a handler in the same way for the Invoke DoSomething() button:

```
        private void invokeButton_Click(object sender, System.EventArgs e)
        {
            resultLabel.Text = myService.DoSomething();
        }
```

This handler simply outputs the text returned by DoSomething().

When we run this application we can press the Invoke DoSomething() button straight away, as Page_Load() has assigned the correct header (if we haven't assigned a header then an exception will be thrown, as we have specified that the header is required for this method). This will result in a failure message, returned from DoSomething():

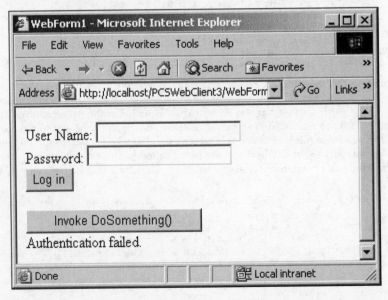

If we try to log in with any user name and password except "Karli" and "Cheese" we will get the same result. If, on the other hand, we log in using these credentials and then call DoSomething() we get the success message:

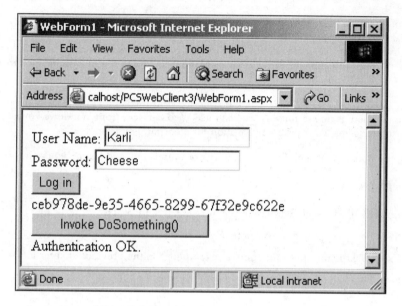

We can also see the Guid used for validation.

Of course, applications that use this technique of exchanging data via SOAP headers are likely to be far more complicated. They will need to store login tokens in a more sensible way than just one Application-level variable, perhaps in a database. For completeness we can also expire these tokens when a certain amount of time has passed, and provide the facility for users to log out if they wish, which would simply mean removing the token. We could even validate the token against the IP address used by the user for further security. The key points here though are that the username and password of the user are only sent once, and that using a SOAP header simplifies later method calls.

Summary

In this chapter we have seen how to create and consume Web Services using C# and the VS .NET development platform. Doing this is perhaps surprisingly simple, but is instantly recognizable as something that could prove to be incredibly useful. Already we are seeing many announcements about new Web Services, and I suspect that they will be everywhere before long.

It has also been pointed out, and I'll reiterate it here to push the point home, that Web Services may be accessed from any platform. This is due to the SOAP protocol, which doesn't limit us to .NET.

The main example developed in this chapter illustrates how we can create .NET distributed applications with ease. We have assumed here that you are using a single server to test things out, but there is no reason why the Web Service shouldn't be completely separate from the client. It may even be on a separate server to the database if an additional data tier is required.

The use of data caching throughout is another important technique to master for use in large-scale applications, which may have thousands of users connecting simultaneously. Of course, in such a situation using Microsoft Access as a data source might not necessarily be the best idea!

Exchanging data via SOAP headers, introduced in the last example, is another useful technique that can be worked into your applications. The example used the exchange of a login token, but there is no reason why more complex data shouldn't be exchanged in this way. Perhaps this could be used for simple 'password protection' of Web Services, without having to resort to imposing more complex security.

Finally, it is worth bearing in mind that Web Service consumers don't necessarily have to be web applications. There is no reason why we can't use Web Services from Windows Form applications – which certainly seems like an attractive option for a corporate intranet.

All in all, the potential of Web Services certainly astounds me, and I hope you're impressed too!

In this chapter we have:

- ❑ Looked at how Web Services implement SOAP and WSDL
- ❑ Seen how to expose and consume Web Services
- ❑ Extended the meeting room booker example from the previous chapter to use Web Services
- ❑ Seen how to exchange data using SOAP Headers

16

User Controls and Custom Controls

It has often been the case with web development that the tools available, however powerful, don't quite match up with your requirements for a specific project. Perhaps a given control doesn't quite work as you'd like it to, or perhaps one section of code, intended for reuse on several pages, would be unworkably complex in the hands of multiple developers. In cases such as these there is a strong argument for building your own controls. Such controls can, at their simplest, wrap multiple existing controls together, perhaps with additional properties specifying layout. They can also be completely unlike any existing control. Using a control you have built yourself can be as simple as using any other control in ASP.NET (if you have written them well), which can certainly ease web site coding.

In the past it has been tricky to implement such custom-built controls, especially on large-scale systems where complex registration procedures may be required in order to use them. Even on simple systems, the coding required to create a custom control could become a very involved process. The scripting capabilities of older web languages also suffered by not giving the perfect access to your cunningly crafted object models, and resulted in poor performance all round.

The .NET Framework provides an ideal setting for the creation of custom controls, using simple programming techniques. Every aspect of ASP.NET server controls is exposed for you to customize should you wish, including such capabilities as templating, client-side scripting, and so on. However, there is no need to write code for all of these eventualities if you don't want or need to; simpler controls can be a lot easier to create.

In addition, the dynamic discovery of assemblies that is inherent in a .NET system makes installation of web applications on a new web server as simple as copying the directory structure containing your code. To make use of the controls you have created you simply copy the assemblies containing those controls along with the rest of the code. You can even place frequently used controls in an assembly located in the global assembly cache (GAC) on the web server, such that all web applications on the server have access to them.

In this chapter we will look at two different kinds of controls:

❑ User controls – converting existing ASP.NET pages into controls

❑ Custom controls – grouping the functionality of several controls, extending existing controls, and creating new controls from scratch

We'll illustrate user controls by creating a simple control that displays a card suit (club, diamond, heart, or spade), so that we can embed it in other ASP.NET pages with ease. In the case of custom controls, we'll create a straw poll control allowing the user to vote for a candidate in a list and see how the vote is progressing.

As is implied by the above discussion, custom control building is a large and at times complicated topic. For a more complete treatment please refer to Professional ASP.NET Server Controls (ISBN: 1-861005-64-4), also published by Wrox Press.

User Controls

User controls are controls that you create using ASP.NET code, just as you would in standard ASP.NET web pages. The difference is that once you have created a user control you can reuse it in multiple ASP.NET pages with a minimum of difficulty.

For example, let's say that you have created a page that displays some information from a database, perhaps information about an order. Instead of creating a fixed page that does this, it is possible to place the relevant code into a user control, and then insert that control into as many different web pages as you wish.

In addition, it is possible to define properties and methods for user controls. For instance, you could specify a property for the background color for displaying your database table in a web page, or a method to re-run a database query to check for changes.

Let's dive in and create a simple user control, discussing the relevant points as they come up, then build on it to see how we can add methods and properties.

A Simple User Control

In VS .NET, create a new web application called **PCSUserCWebApp1**. Once the standard files have been generated, select the **Project | Add New Item...** menu option, and add a **Web User Control** called `PCSUserC1.ascx` as shown:

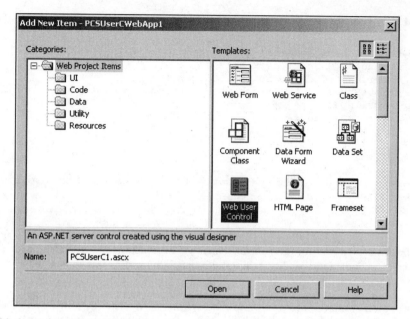

The files added to our project, with the extensions `.ascx` and `.ascx.cs`, work in a very similar way to the `.aspx` files we've seen already. The `.ascx` file will contain our ASP.NET code and look very similar to a normal `.aspx` file. The `.ascx.cs` file is our code-behind file, which defines the user control, much in the same way that forms are defined in `.aspx.cs` files.

`.ascx` files can be viewed in designer or HTML view just like `.aspx` files. Looking at the file in HTML view reveals an important difference: there is no HTML code-present, and in particular no `<form>` element. This is because user controls will be inserted inside ASP.NET forms in other files, and so don't need a `<form>` tag of their own. The generated code is as follows:

```
<%@ Control Language="c#" AutoEventWireup="false"
Codebehind="PCSUserC1.ascx.cs"
    Inherits="PCSUserCWebApp1.PCSUserC1"
    TargetSchema="http://schemas.microsoft.com/intellisense/ie5"%>
```

This is very similar to the `<%@ Page %>` directive generated in `.aspx` files, except that `Control` is specified rather than `Page`, and a `TargetSchema` attribute is included. This attribute specifies what browser the control is being designed for, in this case Internet Explorer 5, which affects what items are available to add from the VS .NET toolbox.

Looking at the generated code in the `.ascx.cs` file reveals another important difference from ASP.NET pages: the class generated inherits from `System.Web.UI.UserControl`. Again, this is because the control will be used inside a form, it isn't a form itself.

Our simple control will be one that displays a graphic corresponding to one of the four standard suits in cards (club, diamond, heart, spade). The graphics required for this are shipped as part of VS .NET; you can find them in: `C:\Program Files\Microsoft Visual Studio.NET\Common7\Graphics\bitmaps\assorted`, with the filenames `CLUB.BMP`, `DIAMOND.BMP`, `HEART.BMP`, and `SPADE.BMP`. Copy these into your project's directory so that we can use them in a moment.

Let's add some code to our new control. In the HTML view of `PCSUserC1.ascx` add the following:

```
<%@ Control Language="c#" AutoEventWireup="false"
Codebehind="PCSUserC1.ascx.cs"
    Inherits="PCSUserCWebApp1.PCSUserC1"
    TargetSchema="http://schemas.microsoft.com/intellisense/ie5"%>
<table cellspacing=4>
    <tr valign="middle">
      <td>
         <asp:Image Runat="server" ID="suitPic" ImageURL="club.bmp"/>
      </td>
      <td>
         <asp:Label Runat="server" ID="suitLabel">Club</asp:Label>
      </td>
    </tr>
</table>
```

This defines a default state for our control, which will be a picture of a club along with a label. Before we add any additional functionality we'll test this default by adding this control to our project web page `WebForm1.aspx`.

In order to use a custom control in a `.aspx` file, we first need to specify how we will refer to it, that is, the name of the tag that will represent the control in our HTML. To do this we use the `<%@ Register %>` directive at the top of the code as follows:

```
<%@ Register TagPrefix="PCS" TagName="UserC1" Src="PCSUserC1.ascx" %>
```

The `TagPrefix` and `TagName` attributes specify the tag name to use (in the form `TagPrefix:"TagName"`), and we use the `Src` attribute to point to the file containing our user control. Now we can use our control by adding the following element:

```
<form id="Form1" method="post" runat="server">
    <PCS:UserC1 Runat="server" ID="myUserControl"/>
</form>
```

User controls aren't declared by default in the code behind our form, so we also need to add the following declaration to `WebForm1.aspx.cs`:

```
public class WebForm1 : System.Web.UI.Page
{
    protected PCSUserC1 myUserControl;
    ...
```

This is all we need to do to test our user control, and running the project results in the following:

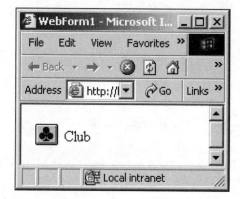

As it stands this control groups two existing controls together, an image and a label in a table layout. As such it falls into the category of a **composite** control.

To gain control over the suit being displayed, we can use an attribute on the `<PCS:UserC1>` element. Attributes on user control elements are automatically mapped to properties on user controls, so all we have to do to make this work is add a property to the code behind our control, `PCSUserC1.ascx.cs`. We'll call this property `Suit`, and let it take any suit value. To make it easier for us to represent the state of the control, we'll define an enumeration to hold the four suit names, inside the `PCSUserCWebApp1` namespace in the `PCSUserC1.ascx.cs` file:

```
namespace PCSUserCWebApp1
{
    ...
    public enum suit
    {
        club, diamond, heart, spade
    }
    ...
}
```

The `PCSUserC1` class needs a member variable to hold the suit type, `currentSuit`:

```
public class PCSUserC1 : System.Web.UI.UserControl
{
    protected System.Web.UI.WebControls.Image suitPic;
    protected System.Web.UI.WebControls.Label suitLabel;
    protected suit currentSuit;
```

And a property to access this member variable, `Suit`:

```
public suit Suit
{
    get
    {
```

```
            return currentSuit;
        }
        set
        {
            currentSuit = value;
            suitPic.ImageUrl = currentSuit.ToString() + ".bmp";
            suitLabel.Text = currentSuit.ToString();
        }
    }
}
```

The set accessor here sets the URL of the image to one of the files we copied earlier, and the text displayed to the suit name.

Now the control is finished we need to add code to WebForm1.aspx to access this new property. We could simply specify the suit using the property we have just added:

```
<PCS:UserC1 Runat="server" id="myUserControl" Suit="diamond"/>
```

The ASP.NET processor is intelligent enough to get the correct enumeration item from the string provided. To make things a bit more interesting and interactive, though, we'll use a radio button list to select a suit:

```
<form id="Form1" method="post" runat="server">
    <PCS:UserC1 Runat="server" ID="myUserControl"/>
    <asp:RadioButtonList Runat="server" ID="suitList"
                            AutoPostBack="True">
        <asp:ListItem Value="club"
Selected="True">Club</asp:ListItem>
        <asp:ListItem Value="diamond">Diamond</asp:ListItem>
        <asp:ListItem Value="heart">Heart</asp:ListItem>
        <asp:ListItem Value="spade">Spade</asp:ListItem>
    </asp:RadioButtonList>
</form>
```

We also need to add an event handler for the SelectedIndexChanged event of the list, which we can do simply by double-clicking on the radio button list control in design view.

> Note that we have set the AutoPostBack property of this list to True, as the
> suitList_SelectedIndexChanged() event handler won't be executed on the server unless a
> postback is in operation, and this control doesn't trigger a post back by default.

The suitList_SelectedIndexChanged() method needs the following code in WebForm1.aspx.cs:

```
protected void suitList_SelectedIndexChanged(object sender,
                                              System.EventArgs e)
{
    myUserControl.Suit = (suit)Enum.Parse(typeof(suit),

suitList.SelectedItem.Value);
}
```

We know that the `Value` attributes on the `<ListItem>` elements represent valid values for the `suit` enumeration we defined earlier, so we simply parse these as enumeration types and use them as values of the `Suit` property of our user control. We cast the returned `object` type to `suit` using simple casing syntax, as this can't be achieved implicitly.

Now we can change the suit when we run our web application:

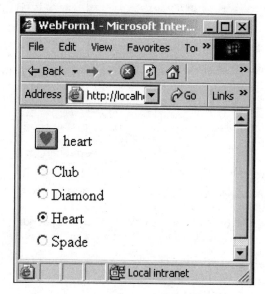

Next we'll give our control some methods. Again, this is very simple; we just need to add methods to our `PCSUserC1` class:

```
public void Club()
{
    Suit = suit.club;
}

public void Diamond()
{
    Suit = suit.diamond;
}

public void Heart()
{
    Suit = suit.heart;
}

public void Spade()
{
    Suit = suit.spade;
}
```

These four methods, `Club()`, `Diamond()`, `Heart()`, and `Spade()`, change the suit displayed on the screen to the respective suit clicked.

We'll call these functions from four `ImageButton` controls in our `.aspx` page:

```
      </asp:RadioButtonList>
      <asp:ImageButton Runat="server" ID="clubButton"
                       ImageUrl="CLUB.BMP"
                       OnClick="clubButton_Click"/>
      <asp:ImageButton Runat="server" ID="diamondButton"
                       ImageUrl="DIAMOND.BMP"
                       OnClick="diamondButton_Click"/>
      <asp:ImageButton Runat="server" ID="heartButton"
                       ImageUrl="HEART.BMP"
                       OnClick="heartButton_Click"/>
      <asp:ImageButton Runat="server" ID="spadeButton"
                       ImageUrl="SPADE.BMP"
                       OnClick="spadeButton_Click"/>
</form>
```

With the following event handlers:

```
      protected void clubButton_Click(object sender,
                            System.Web.UI.ImageClickEventArgs e)
      {
         myUserControl.Club();
         suitList.SelectedIndex = 0;
      }

      protected void diamondButton_Click(object sender,
                               System.Web.UI.ImageClickEventArgs e)
      {
         myUserControl.Diamond();
         suitList.SelectedIndex = 1;
      }

      protected void heartButton_Click(object sender,
                            System.Web.UI.ImageClickEventArgs e)
      {
         myUserControl.Heart();
         suitList.SelectedIndex = 2;
      }

      protected void spadeButton_Click(object sender,
                            System.Web.UI.ImageClickEventArgs e)
      {
         myUserControl.Spade();
         suitList.SelectedIndex = 3;
      }
```

Now we have four new buttons we can use to change the suit:

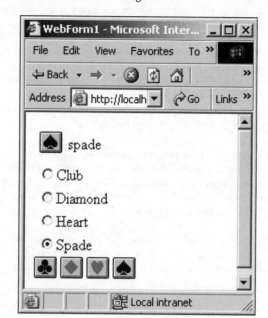

Now we've created our user control we can use it in any other web page simply by using the `<%@ Register %>` directive and the two source code files (`PCSUserC1.ascx` and `PCSUserC1.ascx.cs`) we have created for the control.

Custom Controls

Custom controls go a step beyond user controls in that they are entirely self-contained in C# assemblies, requiring no separate ASP.NET code. This means that we don't need to go through the process of assembling a UI in an `.ascx` file. Instead, we have complete control over what is written to the output stream, that is, the exact HTML generated by our control.

In general, it will take longer to develop custom controls than user controls, because the syntax is more complex and we often have to write significantly more code to get results. A user control may be as simple as a few other controls grouped together as we've seen, whereas a custom control can do just about anything short of making you a cup of coffee.

To get the most customizable behavior for our custom controls we can derive a class from `System.Web.UI.WebControls.WebControl`. If we do this then we are creating a **full** custom control. Alternatively, we can extend the functionality of an existing control, creating a **derived** custom control. Finally, we can group existing controls together, much like we did in the last section but with a more logical structure, to create a **composite** custom control.

Whatever we create can be used in ASP.NET pages in pretty much the same way. All we need to do is to place the generated assembly somewhere where the web application that will use it can find it, and register the element names to use with the `<%@ Register %>` directive. I say 'somewhere' because there are two options: we can either put the assembly in the `bin` directory of the web application, or place it in the GAC if we want all web applications on the server to have access to it.

The `<%@ Register %>` directive takes a slightly different syntax for custom controls:

```
<%@ Register TagPrefix="PCS" Namespace="PCSCustomWebControls"
             Assembly="PCSCustomWebControls"%>
```

We use the `TagPrefix` option in the same way as before, but we don't use the `TagName` or `Src` attributes. This is because the custom control assembly we use may contain several custom controls, and each of these will be named by its class, so `TagName` is redundant. In addition, since we can use the dynamic discovery capabilities of the .NET Framework to find our assembly we simply have to name it and the namespace in it that contains our controls.

In the example line of code above, we are saying that we want to use an assembly called `PCSCustomWebControls.dll` with controls in the `PCSCustomWebControls` namespace, and use the tag prefix `PCS`. If we have a control called `Control1` in this namespace we could use it with the ASP.NET code:

```
<PCS:Control1 Runat="server" ID="MyControl1"/>
```

With custom controls it is also possible to reproduce some of the control nesting behavior such as we see in list controls:

```
<asp:DropDownList ID="roomList" Runat="server" Width="160px">
    <asp:ListItem Value="1">The Happy Room</asp:ListItem>
    <asp:ListItem Value="2">The Angry Room</asp:ListItem>
    <asp:ListItem Value="3">The Depressing Room</asp:ListItem>
    <asp:ListItem Value="4">The Funked Out Room</asp:ListItem>
</asp:DropDownList>
```

We can create controls that should be interpreted as being children of other controls in a very similar way to this. We'll see how to do this later in this section.

Custom Control Project Configuration

Let's start putting some of this theory into practice. We'll use a single assembly to hold all of the example custom controls in this chapter for simplicity, which we can create in Visual Studio .NET by choosing a new project of type **Web Control Library**. We'll call our library **PCSCustomWebControls**:

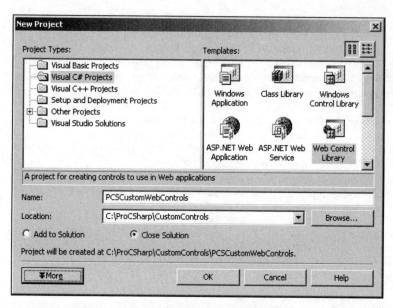

Here I have created the project in C:\ProCSharp\CustomControls. There is no need for the project to be created on the web server as with web applications, since it doesn't need to be externally accessible in the same way. Of course, we can create web control libraries anywhere, as long as we remember to copy the generated assembly somewhere where the web application that uses it can find it!

One technique we can use to facilitate testing is to add a web application project to the same solution. We'll call this application **PCSCustomWebControlsTestApp**. For now, this is the only application that will use our custom control library, so to speed things up a little we can make the output assembly for our library be created in the correct bin directory (this means that we don't have to copy the file across every time we recompile). We can do this through the property pages for the **PCSCustomWebControls** project:

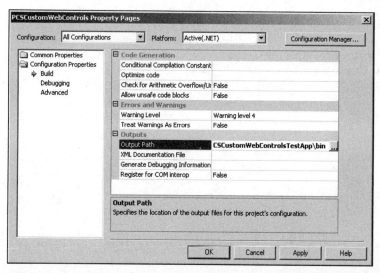

Note that we have changed the Configuration dropdown to All Configurations, so debug and release build will be placed in the same place. The Output Path has been changed to C:\Inetpub\wwwroot\PCSCustomWebControlsTestApp\bin. To make debugging easier we can also change the Start URL option on the Debugging property page to http://localhost/PCSCustomWebControlsTestApp/WebForm1.aspx and the Debug Mode to URL, so we can just execute our project in debug mode to see our results.

We can make sure that this is all working by testing out the control that is supplied by default in the .cs file for our custom control library, WebCustomControl1. We just need to make the following changes to the code in WebForm1.aspx, which simply reference the newly-created control library and embed the default control in this library into the page body:

```
<%@ Page language="c#" Codebehind="WebForm1.aspx.cs"
AutoEventWireup="false"
        Inherits="PCSCustomWebControlsTestApp.WebForm1" %>
<%@ Register TagPrefix="PCS" Namespace="PCSCustomWebControls"
        Assembly="PCSCustomWebControls"%>
<!DOCTYPE HTML PUBLIC "-//W3C//DTD HTML 4.0 Transitional//EN" >
<HTML>
    <HEAD>
        <title>WebForm1</title>
        <meta name="GENERATOR"content="Microsoft Visual Studio 7.0" >
        <meta name="CODE_LANGUAGE"content="C#" >
        <meta name="vs_defaultClientScript"content="JavaScript" >
        <meta name="vs_targetSchema"
            content="http://schemas.microsoft.com/intellisense/ie5" >
    </HEAD>
    <body MS_POSITIONING="GridLayout">
        <form id="Form1" method="post" runat="server">
            <PCS:WebCustomControl1 ID="testControl" Runat="server"
                            Text="Testing again..."/>
        </form>
    </body>
</html>
```

In fact, there is an even better way of doing this once the control library project is compiled. Add a new tab to the Toolbox called Custom Controls, right-click it and choose the Customize Toolbox... menu option. Next choose the .NET Framework Components tab and browse to the PCSCustomWebControls assembly. Once this is loaded you can choose controls from it in the list:

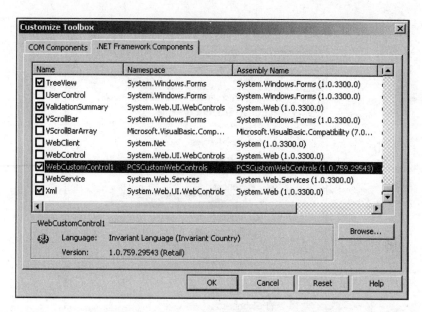

Select WebCustomControl1 as shown above and the new control will appear in the toolbox ready for adding to our form:

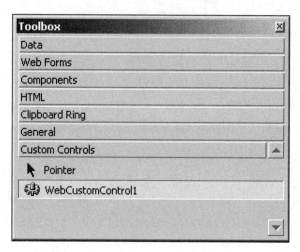

Also, add a project reference to `PCSCustomWebControls` in the test app:

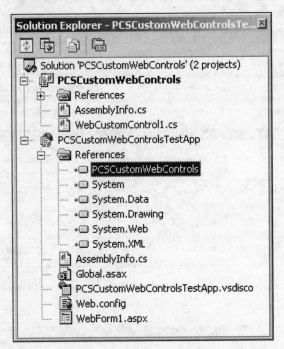

Now add a `using` statement to our `PCSCustomWebControlsTestApp` namespace in `WebForm1.aspx.cs`:

```
using PCSCustomWebControls;
```

This will enable us to use our custom controls from the code behind the form without full name qualification.

The nice thing about this is that if we add the control from the toolbox the `<%@ Register %>` directive is added automatically – although the tag prefix is assigned automatically. I got `cc1` for mine when I tried it, which is fine although doing this ourselves gives us greater flexibility that could improve code readability.

Now, as long as we have the PCSCustomWebControls library configured as our startup application we can hit the **Debug** button to see our results:

Basic Custom Controls

As can be inferred from the results in the last section, the sample control generated by default is simply a version of the standard <asp:Label> control. The code generated in the .cs file for the project, WebCustomControl1.cs, is as follows (omitting the standard and XML documentation comments):

```
using System;
using System.Web.UI;
using System.Web.UI.WebControls;
using System.ComponentModel;
using PCSCustomWebControls;

namespace PCSCustomWebControls
{
    [DefaultProperty("Text"),
     ToolboxData("<{0}:WebCustomControl1 runat=server>
                 </{0}:WebCustomControl1>")]
    public class WebCustomControl1 : System.Web.UI.WebControls.WebControl
    {
        private string text;

        [Bindable(true), Category("Appearance"), DefaultValue("")]
        public string Text
        {
            get
            {
                return text;
            }

            set
            {
                text = value;
            }
        }

        protected override void Render(HtmlTextWriter output)
        {
            output.Write(Text);
        }
    }
}
```

The single class defined here is the `WebCustomControl1` class (note how the class name mapped straight onto an ASP.NET element in the simple example we saw before), which is derived from the `WebControl` class as discussed earlier. Two attributes are provided for this class: `DefaultProperty` and `ToolboxData`. The `DefaultProperty` attribute specifies what the default property for the control will be if used in languages that support this functionality. The `ToolboxData` attribute specifies exactly what HTML will be added to an `.aspx` page if this control is added using the Visual Studio toolbox (as we saw above, once the project is compiled we can add the control to the toolbox by configuring the toolbox to use the assembly created). Note that a `{0}` placeholder is used to specify where the tag prefix will be placed.

The class contains one property: `Text`. This is a very simple text property much like those we've seen before. The only point to note here is the three attributes:

❑   `Bindable` – whether the property can be bound to data

❑   `Category` – where the property will be displayed in the property pages

❑   `DefaultValue` – the default value for the property

Exposing properties in this way works in exactly the same way as it did for custom controls, and is definitely preferable to exposing public fields.

The remainder of the class consists of the `Render()` method. This is the single most important method to implement when designing custom controls, as it is where we have access to the output stream to display our control content. There are only two cases where we don't need to implement this method:

❑   Where we are designing a control that has no visual representation (usually known as a component)

❑   Where we are deriving from an existing control and don't need to change its display characteristics

Custom controls may also expose custom methods, raise custom events, and respond to child controls (if any exist). We'll look at all of this in the remainder of this chapter, where we'll see how to:

❑   Create a derived control

❑   Create a composite control

❑   Create a more advanced control

The final example will be a straw poll control, capable of allowing the user to vote for one of several candidates, and displaying voting progress graphically. Options will be defined using nested child controls, in the manner described earlier.

We'll start simply, though, and create a simple derived control.

The RainbowLabel Derived Control

For this first example we'll derive a control from a `Label` control and override its `Render()` method to output multicolored text. To keep the code for example controls in this chapter separate we'll create new source files as necessary, so for this control add a new `.cs` code file called `RainbowLabel.cs` to the `PCSCustomWebControls` project and add the following code:

```csharp
using System;
using System.Web.UI;
using System.Web.UI.WebControls;
using System.ComponentModel;
using System.Drawing;

namespace PCSCustomWebControls
{
    public class RainbowLabel : System.Web.UI.WebControls.Label
    {
        private Color[] colors = new Color[] {Color.Red, Color.Orange,
                                              Color.Yellow,
                                              Color.GreenYellow,
                                              Color.Blue, Color.Indigo,
                                              Color.Violet};

        protected override void Render(HtmlTextWriter output)
        {
            string text = Text;

            for (int pos=0; pos < text.Length; pos++)
            {
                int rgb = colors[pos % colors.Length].ToArgb() & 0xFFFFFF;
                output.Write("<font color='#" + rgb.ToString("X6") + "'>"
                            + text[pos] + "</font>");
            }
        }
    }
}
```

This class derives from the existing Label control (System.Web.UI.WebControls.Label) and doesn't require any additional properties as the inherited Text one will do fine. We have added a new private field, colors[], which contains an array of colors that we'll cycle through when we output text.

The main functionality of the control is in Render(), which we have overridden as we want to change the HTML output. Here we get the string to display from the Text property and display each character in a color from the colors[] array.

To test this control we need to add it to the form in PCSCustomWebControlsTestApp:

```
<form method="post" runat="server" ID="Form1">
    <PCS:RainbowLabel Runat="server" Text="Multicolored label!"
                    ID="rainbowLabel1"/>
</form>
```

This gives us:

Maintaining State in Custom Controls

Each time a control is created on the server in response to a server request it is created from scratch. This means that any simple field of the control will be reinitialized. In order for controls to maintain state between requests they must use the ViewState maintained on the client, which means we need to write controls with this in mind.

To illustrate this, we'll add an additional capability to the RainbowLabel control. We'll add a method called Cycle() that cycles through the colors available, which will make use of a stored offset field to determine which color should be used for the first letter in the string displayed. This field will need to make use of the ViewState of the control in order to be persisted between requests.

We'll show the code for both with and without ViewState storage cases to illustrate the trap that is all too easy to fall into. First we'll look at code that fails to make use of the ViewState:

```
public class RainbowLabel : System.Web.UI.WebControls.Label
{
    private Color[] colors = new Color[] {Color.Red, Color.Orange,
                                          Color.Yellow,
                                          Color.GreenYellow,
                                          Color.Blue, Color.Indigo,
                                          Color.Violet};

    private int offset = 0;

    protected override void Render(HtmlTextWriter output)
    {
        string text = Text;
        for (int pos=0; pos < text.Length; pos++)
        {
            int rgb = colors[(pos + offset) % colors.Length].ToArgb()
                                                  & 0xFFFFFF;
            output.Write("<font color='#" + rgb.ToString("X6") + "'>"
                        + text[pos] + "</font>");
        }
    }
}
```

```
    public void Cycle()
    {
        offset = ++offset;
    }
}
```

Here we initialize the offset field to zero, then allow the Cycle() method to increment it, using the %
operator to ensure that it wraps round to 0 if it reaches 7 (the number of colors in the colors array).

To test this we need a way of calling cycle(), and the simplest way to do that is to add a button to
our form:

```
<form method="post" runat="server" ID="Form1">
    <PCS:RainbowLabel Runat="server" Text="Multicolored label!"
                      ID="rainbowLabel1"/>
    <asp:Button Runat="server" ID="cycleButton"
                            Text="Cycle colors"/>
</form>
```

Add an event handler by double-clicking on the button in design view and add the following code
(you'll need to change the protection level to protected):

```
protected void cycleButton_Click(object sender, System.EventArgs e)
{
    this.rainbowLabel1.Cycle();
}
```

If you run this code you'll find that the colors change the first time you click the button, but further
clicks will leave the colors as they are.

If this control persisted itself on the server between requests then it would work adequately, as the
offset field would maintain its state without us having to worry about it. However, this technique
wouldn't make sense for a web application, with thousands of users potentially using it at the same time.
Creating a separate instance for each user would be counterproductive.

In any case, the solution is quite simple. We have to use the ViewState property bag of our control to
store and retrieve data. We don't have to worry about how this is serialized, recreated, or anything else,
we just put things in and take things out, safe in the knowledge that state will be maintained between
requests in the standard ASP.NET way.

To place the offset field into the ViewState we simply use:

```
ViewState["_offset"] = offset;
```

ViewState consists of name-value pairs, and here we are using one called _offset. We don't have to
declare this anywhere, it will be created the first time this code is used.

Similarly, to retrieve state we use:

```
offset = (int)ViewState["_offset"];
```

If we do this when nothing is stored in the ViewState under that name we will get a null value. Casting a null value in code such as the above will throw an exception, so we can either test for this or check whether the object type retrieved from ViewState is null before we cast it, which is what we'll do in our code.

In fact, we can update our code in a very simple way – simply by replacing the existing offset member with a private offset property that makes use of viewstate, with code as follows:

```
public class RainbowLabel : System.Web.UI.WebControls.Label
{
    ...
    private int offset
    {
        get
        {
            object rawOffset = ViewState["_offset"];
            if (rawOffset != null)
            {
                return (int)rawOffset;
            }
            else
            {
                ViewState["_offset"] = 0;
                return 0;
            }
        }
        set
        {
            ViewState["_offset"] = value;
        }
    }
    ...
}
```

This time, the control allows the Cycle() method to work each time.

In general, we might see ViewState being used for simple public properties, for example:

```
public string Name
{
    get
    {
        return (string)ViewState["_name"];
    }
    set
    {
        ViewState["_name"] = value;
    }
}
```

One further point about using the `ViewState` concerns child controls. If our control has children and is used more than once on a page, then we have the problem that the children will share their `ViewState` by default. In almost every case this isn't the behavior we'd like to see, and luckily we have a simple solution. By implementing `INamingContainer` on the parent control we force child controls to use qualified storage in the `ViewState`, such that child controls will not share their `ViewState` with similar child controls with a different parent.

Using this interface doesn't require any property or method implementation, we just need to say that we are using it, as if it were simply a marker for interpretation by the ASP.NET server. We'll need to do this in the next section.

Creating a Composite Custom Control

As a simple example of a composite custom control, we can combine the control from the last section with the cycle button we had in the test form.

We'll call this composite control `RainbowLabel2`, and place it in a new file, `RainbowLabel2.cs`. This control needs to:

❏   Inherit from WebControl (not Label this time)

❏   Support INamingContainer

❏   Possess two fields to hold its child controls

The code for these three things requires the following modifications to the code obtained by generating a new class file:

```
using System;
using System.Web.UI;
using System.Web.UI.WebControls;
using System.ComponentModel;

namespace PCSCustomWebControls
{
    public class RainbowLabel2 : System.Web.UI.WebControls.WebControl,
                                 INamingContainer
    {
        private RainbowLabel rainbowLabel = new RainbowLabel();
        private Button cycleButton = new Button();
    ...
```

In order to configure a composite control we need to ensure that any child controls are added to the `Controls` collection and properly initialized. We do this by overriding the `CreateChildControls()` method and placing the required code there (here we should call the base `CreateChildControls()` implementation, which won't affect our class but may prevent unexpected surprises):

```
        protected override void CreateChildControls()
        {
            cycleButton.Text = "Cycle colors.";
            cycleButton.Click += new System.EventHandler(cycleButton_Click);
```

```
        Controls.Add(cycleButton);
        Controls.Add(rainbowLabel);
        base.CreateChildControls();
    }
```

Here we just use the Add() method of Controls to get things set up correctly. We've also added an event handler for the button so that we can make it cycle colors, which is achieved in exactly the same way as for other events. The handler is the now familiar:

```
    protected void cycleButton_Click(object sender, System.EventArgs e)
    {
        rainbowLabel.Cycle();
    }
```

This call simply makes the label colors cycle.

To give users of our composite control access to the text in the rainbowLabel child we can add a property that maps to the Text property of the child:

```
    public string Text
    {
        get
        {
            return rainbowLabel.Text;
        }
        set
        {
            rainbowLabel.Text = value;
        }
    }
```

The last thing to do is to implement Render(). The base implementation of this method takes each control in the Controls collection of the class and tells it to render itself. Since Render() is a protected method it doesn't call Render() for each of these controls; instead it calls the public method RenderControl(). This has the same effect, because RenderControl() calls Render(), so we don't have to change any more code in the RainbowLabel class. To get more control over this rendering (for example in composite controls that output HTML around that generated by child controls) we can call this method ourselves:

```
    protected override void Render(HtmlTextWriter output)
    {
        rainbowLabel.RenderControl(output);
        cycleButton.RenderControl(output);
    }
```

We just pass the HtmlTextWriter instance we receive to the RenderControl() method for a child, and the HTML normally generated by that child will be rendered.

We can use this control in much the same way as `RainbowLabel`:

```
<form method="post" runat="server" ID="Form1">
    <PCS:RainbowLabel2 Runat="server"
                       Text="Multicolored label composite"
                       ID="rainbowLabel2"/>
</form>
```

This time a button to cycle the colors is included.

A Straw Poll Control

Next we'll use and build on the techniques we've covered so far to make a more involved custom control. The end result of this will enable the following ASP.NET code:

```
<form method="post" runat="server" ID="Form1">
    <PCS:StrawPoll Runat="server" ID="strawPoll1"
                   PollStyle="voteonly"
                   Title="Who is your favorite James Bond?">
        <PCS:Candidate Name="Sean Connery" Votes="101"/>
        <PCS:Candidate Name="Roger Moore" Votes="83"/>
        <PCS:Candidate Name="George Lazenby" Votes="32"/>
        <PCS:Candidate Name="Timothy Dalton" Votes="28"/>
        <PCS:Candidate Name="Pierce Brosnan" Votes="95"/>
    </PCS:StrawPoll>
</form>
```

to give us:

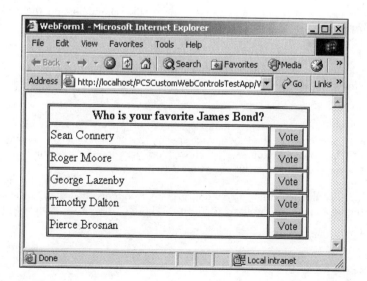

And when we click on a vote button the display will change to a straw poll control:

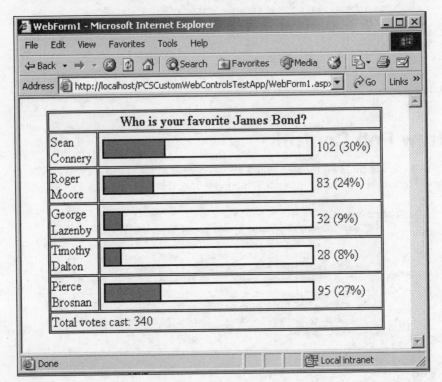

Alternatively, we can view results and voting buttons at the same time, and allow multiple votes, mainly for testing purposes.

The ASP.NET code explicitly sets the Name and Votes property for each Candidate. This is fine for this example, although it is foreseeable that a more advanced version of this control might be data-bound to get these results. However, we won't cover this in this chapter, because that could get quite involved.

When the ASP.NET code is parsed, structures such as this one are interpreted in a consistent way: each child element is interpreted in the way that we specify in a **control builder** class associated with the parent control. This control builder, for which we'll see the code shortly, handles anything nested inside the control it is associated with, including literal text.

The two controls we need to create are Candidate to hold individual candidates, and StrawPoll, which will contain and render the straw poll control. Both of these will be placed in a new source file: StrawPoll.cs.

The Candidate Controls

To start with, we'll create our `Candidate` controls, each of which will store a name and the number of votes cast for that candidate. In addition, these controls will maintain a voting button, and handle any clicks of this button.

So, we need:

- ❑ Code for the Name and Votes properties (stored in the ViewState)
- ❑ Initialization code in CreateChildControls()
- ❑ Code for our button click handler

We'll also include a utility method, `Increment()`, which will add a vote to the current vote count for the `Candidate` instance. This utility method will be called by the button click handler.

We'll also need to support `INamingContainer`, as we'll have multiple instances of these controls with their own children.

The code for the `Candidate` class will go in `Candidate.cs`, which we should add to our project along with the standard `namespace` and `using` statements as per the `RainbowLabel` controls we saw earlier. The code is as follows:

```
public class Candidate : System.Web.UI.WebControls.WebControl,
                         INamingContainer
{
    public string Name
    {
        get
        {
            object rawName = ViewState["_name"];
            if (rawName != null)
            {
                return (string)rawName;
            }
            else
            {
                ViewState["_name"] = "Candidate";
                return "Candidate";
            }
        }
        set
        {
            ViewState["_name"] = value;
        }
    }

    public long Votes
    {
        get
        {
            object rawVotes = ViewState["_votes"];
            if (rawVotes != null)
```

```
                    {
                        return (long)rawVotes;
                    }
                    else
                    {
                        ViewState["_votes"] = (long)0;
                        return 0;
                    }
                }
                set
                {
                    ViewState["_votes"] = value;
                }
            }

            public void Increment()
            {
                Votes += 1;
            }

            public void Reset()
            {
                Votes = 0;
            }

            protected override void CreateChildControls()
            {
                Button btnVote = new Button();
                btnVote.Text = "Vote";
                btnVote.Click += new System.EventHandler(btnVote_Click);
                Controls.Add(btnVote);
                base.CreateChildControls();
            }

            protected void btnVote_Click(object sender, System.EventArgs e)
            {
                Increment();
            }
        }
```

Note that Render() hasn't been overridden here. This is because this control has a single child, the voting button, and no other information to display. So, we can just go with the default, which will simply be a rendering of the button.

The StrawPoll Control Builder

Next we'll look at how we can translate the ASP.NET code for each option into a control that is a child of our StrawPoll control. To do this we need to associate a control builder with the StrawPoll class (defined in StrawPoll.cs), using the ControlBuilderAttribute attribute. We also need to specify that child controls should not be parsed as properties of the StrawPoll class by setting the ParseChildren attribute to false:

```
[ ControlBuilderAttribute(typeof(StrawPollControlBuilder)) ]
[ ParseChildren(false) ]
public class StrawPoll : System.Web.UI.WebControls.WebControl,
                         INamingContainer
{
}
```

Here we are using a class called `StrawPollControlBuilder`, defined in `StrawPollControlBuilder.cs`, as follows:

```
internal class StrawPollControlBuilder : ControlBuilder
{
    public override Type GetChildControlType(string tagName,
                                             IDictionary attribs)
    {
        if (tagName.ToLower().EndsWith("candidate"))
            return typeof(Candidate);

        return null;
    }

    public override void AppendLiteralString(string s)
    {
        // Do nothing, to avoid embedded text being added to control
    }
}
```

Here we override the `GetChildControlType()` method of the base `ControlBuilder` class to return the type of our `Candidate` class in response to a tag named `<Candidate>`. In fact, to make sure things work smoothly in as many situations as possible, we just look for any tag name that ends with the string "candidate", with letters in upper or lower case.

We also override the `AppendLiteralString()` method so that any intervening text, including white space, is ignored and won't cause us any problems.

Once this is set up, and assuming we don't place any other controls in `StrawPoll`, we will have all of our `Candidate` controls contained in the `Controls` collection of `StrawPoll`. This collection won't contain any other controls.

Note that the control builder makes use of a collection of attributes. In order to support this we need to add the following using statement to our namespace:

```
using System.Collections;
```

841

Straw Poll Style

Before we look at the `StrawPoll` class itself, there is one more design consideration. The straw poll should be able to display itself in three forms:

- Voting buttons only
- Results only
- Voting buttons and results

We can define an enumeration for this that we can use as a property of our `StrawPoll` control (putting this in `StrawPoll.cs` is fine):

```
public enum pollStyle
{
    voteonly,
    valuesonly,
    voteandvalues
}
```

As we saw earlier, properties that are enumerations are easy to use – we can simply use the text names as attribute values in ASP.NET.

The Straw Poll Control

Now we can start putting things together. To start with we'll define two properties, `Title` for the title to display for the control, and `PollStyle` to hold the enumerated display type. Both of these will use the `ViewState` for persistence:

```
[ ControlBuilderAttribute(typeof(StrawPollControlBuilder)) ]
[ ParseChildren(false) ]
public class StrawPoll : System.Web.UI.WebControls.WebControl,
                         INamingContainer
{
    public string Title
    {
        get
        {
            object rawTitle = ViewState["_title"];
            if (rawTitle != null)
            {
                return (string)rawTitle;
            }
            else
            {
                ViewState["_title"] = "Straw Poll";
                return "Straw Poll";
            }
        }
        set
        {
```

```
            ViewState["_title"] = value;
        }
    }

    public pollStyle PollStyle
    {
        get
        {
            object rawPollStyle = ViewState["_pollStyle"];
            if (rawPollStyle != null)
            {
                return (pollStyle)rawPollStyle;
            }
            else
            {
                ViewState["_pollStyle"] = pollStyle.voteandvalues;
                return pollStyle.voteandvalues;
            }
        }
        set
        {
            ViewState["_pollStyle"] = value;
        }
    }
}
```

The remainder of this class is taken up with the Render() method. This will display the whole straw poll control along with any options, taking into account the poll style to use. We'll display voting buttons simply by calling the RenderControl() method of child Candidate controls, and display the votes cast graphically and numerically using the Votes properties of child Candidate controls to generate simple HTML.

The code is as follows, commented for clarity:

```
    protected override void Render(HtmlTextWriter output)
    {
        Candidate currentCandidate;
        long iTotalVotes = 0;
        long iPercentage = 0;
        int iColumns = 2;

        // Start table, display title
        if (PollStyle == pollStyle.voteandvalues)
        {
            iColumns = 3;
        }
        output.Write("<TABLE border='1' bordercolor='black'
                    + " bgcolor='#DDDDBB'"
                    + " width='90%' cellpadding='1' cellspacing='1'"
                    + " align='center'>");
        output.Write("<TR><TD colspan='" + iColumns
                                    + "' align='center'"
```

```
                        + " bgcolor='#FFFFDD'>");
        output.Write("<B>" + Title + "</B></TD></TR>");

        if (Controls.Count == 0)
        {
            // Default text when no options contained
            output.Write("<TR><TD bgcolor='#FFFFDD'>No options to"
                        + " display.</TR></TD>");
        }
        else
        {
            // Get total votes
            for (int iLoop = 0; iLoop < Controls.Count; iLoop++)
            {
                // Get option
                currentCandidate = (Candidate)Controls[iLoop];
                // Sum votes cast
                iTotalVotes += currentCandidate.Votes;
            }

            // Render each option
            for (int iLoop = 0; iLoop < Controls.Count; iLoop++)
            {
                // Get option
                currentCandidate = (Candidate)Controls[iLoop];
                // Place option name in first column
                output.Write("<TR><TD bgcolor='#FFFFDD' width='15%'> "
                            + currentCandidate.Name + " </TD>");
                // Add voting option to second column if required
                if (PollStyle != pollStyle.valuesonly)
                {
                    output.Write("<TD width='1%' bgcolor='#FFFFDD'>"
                                + "<FONT color='#FFFFDD'>.</FONT>");
                    currentCandidate.RenderControl(output);
                    output.Write("<FONT color='#FFFFDD'>.</FONT></TD>");
                }

                // Place graph, value, and percentage in third
                // column if required
                if (PollStyle != pollStyle.voteonly)
                {
                    if (iTotalVotes > 0)
                    {
                        iPercentage = (currentCandidate.Votes * 100) /
                                        iTotalVotes;
                    }
                    else
                    {
                        iPercentage = 0;
                    }
                    output.Write("<TD bgcolor='#FFFFDD'>"
                        + "<TABLE width='100%'>"
                        + "<TR><TD><TABLE border='1' bordercolor='black'"
```

```
                              + " width='100%' cellpadding='0'"
                              + " cellspacing='0'>");
                output.Write("<TR><TD bgcolor='red' width='"
                              + iPercentage
                              + "%'><FONT color='red'>.</FONT></TD>");
                output.Write("<TD bgcolor='white' width='"
                              + (100-iPercentage)
                              + "%'><FONT color='white'>."
                              + "</FONT></TD></TR></TABLE></TD>");
                output.Write("<TD width='75'>"
                              + currentCandidate.Votes + " ("
                              + iPercentage
                              + "%)</TD></TR></TABLE></TD>");
            }
            // End row
            output.Write("</TR>");
        }
        // Show total votes cast if values displayed
        if (PollStyle != pollStyle.voteonly)
        {
            output.Write("<TR><TD bgcolor='#FFFFDD' colspan='"
                          + iColumns
                          + "'>Total votes cast: " + iTotalVotes
                          + "</TD></TR>");
        }
    }
    // Finish table
    output.Write("</TABLE>");
}
```

There is one more thing to do. If the straw poll is being displayed in voteonly mode then voting should trigger a change of display to valuesonly mode. To do this we need a minor modification in the voting button handler in our Candidate class:

```
protected void btnVote_Click(object sender, System.EventArgs e)
{
    Increment();
    StrawPoll parent = (StrawPoll)Parent;
    if (parent.PollStyle == pollStyle.voteonly)
    {
        parent.PollStyle = pollStyle.valuesonly;
    }
}
```

Now you are free to vote for you favorite James Bond to your heart's content!

Adding an Event Handler

It is often the case with custom controls that you want to raise custom events, and allow users of the control to act on them. This can be used to excellent effect, as is immediately apparent if you look at the existing server controls that ASP.NET supplies. For example, the `Calendar` control is nothing more than a well-formatted selection of hyperlinks. We could build something like that ourselves using the techniques built up above. However, it has the useful function that when you click on a date other than the selected one it raises a `SelectionChanged` event. We can act on this event, either ignoring it if the selection is OK to change, or performing some processing, which we did in the last chapter when we checked to see if the selected date was already booked. In a similar vein, it would be nice if our straw poll control had a `Voted` event, which will notify the form that a vote has been made, and supply it with all the information needed to act on this.

To register a custom event we have to add code such as the following to a control:

```
public event EventHandler Voted;

protected void OnVoted(EventArgs e)
{
    Voted(this, e);
}
```

Then, whenever we want to raise the event, we simply call `OnVoted()`, passing the event arguments.

Whenever we call `OnVoted()` an event is raised that the user of the control can act on. To do this the user needs to register an event handler for this event:

```
strawPoll1.Voted += new EventHandler(this.strawPoll1_Voted);
```

The user will also need to provide the handler code, `strawPoll1_Voted()`.

We'll extend this slightly by having custom arguments for our event, in order to make the `Candidate` that triggers the event available. We'll call our custom argument object `CandidateEventArgs`, defined in a new class, `CandidateEventArgs.cs`, as follows:

```
public class CandidateEventArgs : EventArgs
{
    public Candidate OriginatingCandidate;

    public CandidateEventArgs(Candidate originator)
    {
        OriginatingCandidate = originator;
    }
}
```

We've simply added an additional public field to the existing `EventArgs` class. As we've changed the arguments we're using, we also need a specialized version of the `EventHandler` delegate that can be declared in the `PCSCustomWebControls` namespace as follows:

```
public delegate void CandidateEventHandler(object sender,
                                           CandidateEventArgs e);
```

We can use these examples in `StrawPoll` as follows:

```
public class StrawPoll : System.Web.UI.WebControls.WebControl,
                         INamingContainer
{
    public event CandidateEventHandler Voted;

    protected void OnVoted(CandidateEventArgs e)
    {
        Voted(this, e);
    }
    ...
```

We'll also have a method to raise the event, called from child `Candidate` controls when voting buttons are clicked:

```
    internal void ChildVote(CandidateEventArgs e)
    {
        OnVoted(e);
    }
```

We also need to make a further modification to the button click handler in `Candidate` to call this method, supplying it with the correct parameters:

```
    protected void btnVote_Click(object sender, System.EventArgs e)
    {
        Increment();
        StrawPoll parent = (StrawPoll)Parent;
        if (parent.PollStyle == pollStyle.voteonly)
        {
            parent.PollStyle = pollStyle.valuesonly;
        }
        CandidateEventArgs eCandidate = new CandidateEventArgs(this);
        parent.ChildVote(eCandidate);
    }
```

Now we're ready to implement the handler on the page using the control. We simply have to specify it in our ASP.NET page, adding a label to use in the handler:

```
<form id=Form1 method=post runat="server">
  <PCS:StrawPoll Runat="server" ID=strawPoll1 PollStyle="voteonly"
              Title="Who is your favorite James Bond?"
              Voted="strawPoll1_Voted">
```

```
            <PCS:Option Name="Sean Connery" Votes="101"/>
            <PCS:Option Name="Roger Moore" Votes="83"/>
            <PCS:Option Name="George Lazenby" Votes="32"/>
            <PCS:Option Name="Timothy Dalton" Votes="28"/>
            <PCS:Option Name="Pierce Brosnan" Votes="95"/>
        </PCS:StrawPoll>
        <br>
        <br>
        <asp:Label Runat="server" ID="resultLabel" Text="No vote cast."/>
    </form>
```

Then we add the event handler itself:

```
        protected void strawPoll1_Voted(object sender, CandidateEventArgs
e)
        {
            resultLabel.Text = "You voted for "
                        + e.OriginatingCandidate.Name + ".";
        }
```

We also need to register this event handler in `InitializeComponent()` (we'll need a `using` statement for `PCSCustomWebControls` to do this):

```
        this.strawPoll1.Voted +=
        new
PCSCustomWebControls.CandidateEventHandler(this.strawPoll1_Voted);
```

Now when we vote we will get feedback on our vote:

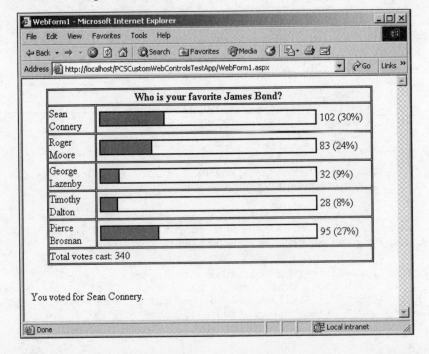

Summary

In this chapter we have looked at the various ways we can create reusable ASP.NET server controls using C#. We have seen how to create simple user controls from existing ASP.NET pages, and also how to create custom controls from scratch.

There is a lot we can do with custom controls, and unfortunately it would have been impossible to cover all of it in a single chapter. However, hopefully there is enough information here to get you started. In particular it would have been interesting to have looked at data-binding, and how we can create our controls with this in mind, and a more in-depth look at many areas (particularly an extended coverage of properties and control builders) would also have been fruitful. Unfortunately, topics such as these are really better suited to more specialized books. You can find lots of great information in *Professional ASP.NET Server Controls* ISBN 1-861005-64-4, also published by Wrox Press.

In this chapter we have covered the following:

- ❑ Building and consuming simple User Controls
- ❑ Building and consuming Custom Controls
- ❑ Maintaining State in Custom Controls
- ❑ Creating a Composite Custom Control
- ❑ Adding Custom Event Handlers

17

COM Interoperability

In this chapter we will look at COM interoperability with .NET. COM components and .NET components are not innately compatible because they rely on different internal architectures. Since many organizations rely extensively on COM components for their middle-tier services, it will be important for many .NET solutions to exploit these legacy components. The .NET Framework does indeed provide facilities for manipulating COM components from managed, .NET code, and also consuming .NET components from unmanaged code: code that is not managed by the .NET runtime.

At the heart of COM interoperability is the idea of wrapper classes that translate specific calls from a managed client into COM-specific invocation requests on the unmanaged COM component. Thus a .NET application can be fooled into thinking it is dealing with another .NET component, and a COM component can believe it is dealing with a standard COM-aware client. Conversely, another type of wrapper allows .NET components to be consumed from unmanaged code.

In this chapter, we'll show you how to achieve interoperability between COM and .NET.

We'll start with a brief review of COM, followed by a look at using COM components from .NET, in which we will cover:

❑   Early and late binding to COM components and Runtime Callable Wrappers

❑   Generating managed metadata wrappers using `TlbImp.exe` and Visual Studio .NET

❑   Examples of early binding and late binding to COM components, and using an ADODB `Recordset` in .NET

❑   Releasing COM objects

❑   Using ActiveX controls in .NET

Then, we'll look at using .NET components from COM clients, and cover:

❑ COM-Callable Wrappers, and requirements of .NET classes so they can be used from unmanaged COM clients

❑ Binding to a .NET component

❑ Exporting type libraries, with RegAsm.exe and TlbExp.exe

Finally, we'll take a look at platform invocation services, and how .NET can interoperate with unmanaged code in any DLL, such as the Win32 API.

A Quick Tour of COM

COM stands for Component Object Model. For newcomers to the Windows platform, understanding how COM works can be somewhat inscrutable, even if you're a devotee of CORBA. The advent of .NET and .NET components may allow you to avoid the intricacies of COM programming.

COM provides a modular, object-oriented approach to code reuse. It defines standard ways of locating and identifying the functionality of other components, and the components can be written in and used from a variety of languages.

However, COM components are not particularly easy to code, with the functionality offered by the component dependent on the language used to code it. Another particular problem with COM components is that they can be difficult to deploy. Developers of COM server components are supposed to ensure that new versions of their components are compatible with older versions, but they sometimes fail at this, and the installation of a new application that references a new version of a COM component can suddenly cause existing applications to fail. Problems of this variety are known as DLL Hell, and are the cause of a lot of head-scratching and wasted time. As we discussed in Chapter 8, .NET assemblies are a solution to this problem, making componentized architecture more accessible to everyday programmers.

How COM Works

To understand why COM components and .NET components aren't innately compatible, it helps to have a general understanding of how COM works. A grossly simplified explanation follows. For more detailed information of how COM works, see *Professional ATL COM Programming* from Wrox Press (ISBN 1-861001-40-1).

COM imposes a standard for the interfaces through which client code talks to component classes. Because client code communicates with component classes only through these standardized interfaces, it can remain blissfully ignorant of the language-specific details of how those component classes are implemented.

The component's IUnknown interface helps maintain a reference count of the number of clients using the component. When this reference count drops down to zero, the component can unload itself. All COM objects must implement the IUnknown interface. Reference counting is handled by the AddRef() and Release() methods of IUnknown, and interface discovery is handled by its QueryInterface() method. Furthermore, by implementing interfaces recognized by COM+ Services, a COM class can make use of prewritten functionality for security, object pooling, and resource conservation.

A component's class and its interfaces can be uniquely identified by a GUID. When a component is registered, these GUID values are written to the Registry and contain mappings to corresponding information on the location of the component and other attributes such as its threading model, for example. When a client creates a component, COM uses these GUIDs in the Registry to locate and bind to the components.

Using COM Components in .NET

Most organizations might not be willing to throw out legacy COM components. Consequently, you can expect to reference legacy COM components from new .NET code, at least in your first .NET enterprise projects. Specifically, if you're building a new .NET application on top of an existing database, you will probably be using existing COM data access objects as your project's data access layer. While accessing data through the legacy components, your .NET components will enforce business rules and deliver data to an ASP.NET or Windows Forms user interface.

Binding to COM Components

Before a client can invoke a COM component object's methods and properties, it needs information about these methods and properties; there are two different techniques that client programs can use to determine this information.

Early binding allows clients to obtain compile-time type information from the component's type library. This allows for stronger type checking during compile time. It is also much faster than the late binding approach that we'll see next. The COM interoperability techniques that we'll look at first rely on early binding.

On the other hand, late-bound clients bind to components at run time. They do not have rich type information available at compile time. Late-bound code typically refers to client objects through generic data types, such as `object`, and relies on the runtime to dynamically ascertain the method addresses.

COM interoperability uses "wrapper" classes and "proxy" components, conventions common in the programming world in general. A wrapper class surrounds a class that adheres to another architecture, providing a familiar interface to it for clients that would not recognize the wrappered class's native interface. Similarly, a client can use a proxy component to access a component that adheres to a different architecture or is geographically remote.

Runtime Callable Wrappers

A .NET application does not communicate directly with a COM component. Instead, it works through a managed wrapper of the component. This wrapper, known as a Runtime-Callable Wrapper (RCW), acts like a managed proxy to the unmanaged COM component. It is able to handle the calling of methods on the component, and pass back any return values in a form suitable for the CLR.

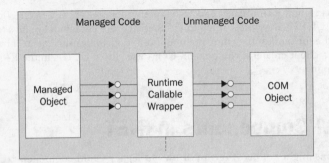

Once a metadata wrapper assembly is generated, either by the Type Library Importer (TlbImp.exe) or from within Visual Studio .NET, methods can be called on the COM component by calling corresponding methods in the managed metadata wrappers, giving the appearance that method calls are being made to a managed object.

Thus the target of any method calls to the COM component is *not* the component itself, but the RCW. The RCW also controls the lifetime of the COM component, which we shall discuss more in the *Releasing COM Objects* section.

The metadata wrapper generated from the type library contains wrapper classes that the C# client can reference and then use it to create the component and invoke its methods. An RCW is created on the fly whenever the component is created, and it acts like a managed proxy to the unmanaged COM component. The RCW handles the marshaling of managed types to COM-specific data types, and also unmarshals return types from COM back into managed data types.

First, we shall look at the two ways two to generate managed metadata wrappers:

❑   Using the TlbImp.exe utility

❑   From within Visual Studio .NET

Creating a Wrapper with TlbImp.exe

TlbImp.exe is invoked from the command-line, and converts the COM-specific type definitions in a COM type library into equivalent definitions for a .NET wrapper assembly. By default TlbImp.exe will name the resulting wrapper with the same name as the COM component DLL. You can provide TlbImp.exe with an out command-line argument so that the resulting wrapper assembly will have a different name from the COM DLL:

```
Visual Studio .NET Command Prompt                                    _ □ ×
C:\ProCSharp\ComInterop>TlbImp DataAccess.dll /out:DataAccessRCW.dll /verbose
Microsoft (R) .NET Framework Type Library to Assembly Converter 1.0.3328.4
Copyright (C) Microsoft Corporation 1998-2001.  All rights reserved.

Resolving reference to type library 'ADODB'.
Assembly 'C:\ProCSharp\ComInterop\ADODB.dll' loaded.
Type _CustomerTable imported.
Type CustomerTable imported.
Type _ItemTable imported.
Type ItemTable imported.
Type _OrderDetailTable imported.
Type OrderDetailTable imported.
Type _OrderTable imported.
Type OrderTable imported.
Type library imported to C:\ProCSharp\ComInterop\DataAccessRCW.dll

C:\ProCSharp\ComInterop>
```

TlbImp is shorthand for **Type Library Importer**. When you execute this program against a COM DLL, it interrogates the COM DLL's type library and translates the information therein into a .NET format, converting COM standard data types into those recognized by .NET. Once you've run TlbImp.exe against a COM DLL, the output DLL can be referenced in the usual way like any other assembly by using the /r: compiler option.

Don't forget to provide an out argument if you use TlbImp.exe to generate a wrapper from a DLL that is in the current directory! If you do not to provide one, the TlbImp.exe program will complain that it cannot overwrite the original file:

```
C:\WINNT2\system32\cmd.exe                                           _ □ ×
C:\ProCSharp\ComInterop>TlbImp DataAccess.dll
Microsoft (R) .NET Framework Type Library to Assembly Converter 1.0.3328.4
Copyright (C) Microsoft Corporation 1998-2001.  All rights reserved.

TlbImp error: Output file would overwrite input file

C:\ProCSharp\ComInterop>
```

Creating a Wrapper from Visual Studio .NET

To generate a managed metadata wrapper from Visual Studio .NET, you need to use the References dialog, which is available from the Add Reference... option on the Project menu. The COM tab displays a list of the components that are registered as COM components on the local machine, and allows us to import COM components to use in our .NET project. The Browse button allows you to search the file system for the COM DLL that your .NET project needs.

When you locate your chosen DLL, selecting it adds it to the list of components on the **COM** tab of the form:

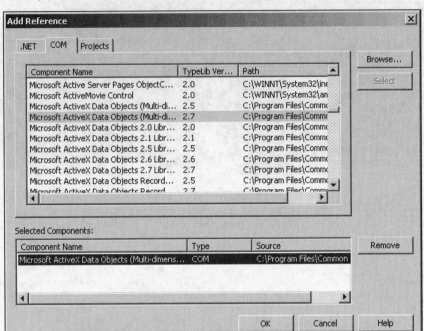

Once you've used the References dialog to locate a COM DLL and add it to the list of COM references, you can use that COM component in your .NET code. Visual Studio .NET generates a metadata wrapper assembly, putting the classes provided by that component into a namespace with the same name as the original COM component. You create a reference, instantiate, and invoke COM object wrappers with the same syntax with which you reference, instantiate, and invoke objects native to C#.

The Visual Studio .NET IDE will even use IntelliSense to help you remember the component's class members. The screenshot below shows the IntelliSense dropdown that lists the classes in the `DataAccess` namespace. The original `DataAccess` DLL contained classes such as `Customer`, `Order`, `OrderItem,` and `Product`:

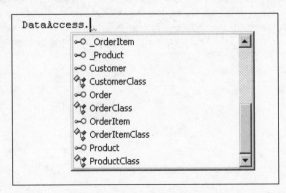

The screenshot shows something interesting – in the original DLL, we had a class named `Customer`, but the screenshot shows that in the wrapper, we have a **Customer** interface, and a class called **CustomerClass**. To create an instance of the `Customer` class in the original DLL, we have to use the name `CustomerClass`.

This is because for each class actually imported into the wrapper assembly, two wrapper classes are generated. One is an interface associated with the same GUID as the original COM class's default interface, and with the same name as this COM class. The other class is a *concrete* class, and to use the COM component, we need to create instances of this class. The concrete class has the word `Class` appended to the original COM class name. The concrete class implements all the interfaces that are supported by the original COM class.

Using a C++ COM Component

For our example, we will use a simple C++ COM component, created in Visual C++ 6 with the ATL COM Wizard. We will not cover the creation of an ATL COM component here, and as most of the code is automatically generated by Visual C++ 6, we show only the code directly relevant to our example here.

For those familiar with the process of creating COM components in Visual Studio 6, this is perhaps a good opportunity to reflect on the progress Microsoft has made with the various automatic code generation facilities in Visual Studio .NET!

A new ATL COM AppWizard project is started from Visual C++ 6, with a project name of RCWTEST. A single class is added, `Factorial`, with a single method, `GetFactorial()` in the class's default interface `IFactorial`. The parameters for the method are shown in the screenshot below. Note we will be using an `unsigned int` to return the value of the factorial.

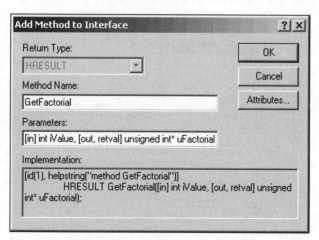

The code for the GetFactorial() method is below; this goes in the Factorial.cpp file.

```
STDMETHODIMP CFactorial::GetFactorial(int iValue, unsigned int* uFactorial)
{
    unsigned int uSubTotal = iValue;
    for (int i = 1; i < iValue; i++)
        uSubTotal *= i;

    *uFactorial = uSubTotal;
    return S_OK;
}
```

The GetFactorial() method simply takes an int, iValue, and returns an unsigned int uFactorial, which is the factorial value of iValue. We now build the project.

We use TlbImp.exe on the created type library, as seen in the screenshot below.

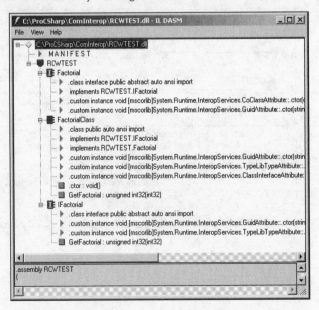

The above command generates a wrapper assembly called RCWTEST.dll from the component's type library, RCWTEST.tlb. We use the VERBOSE option to specify that full output will be displayed.

We'll have a look at how the COM-specific information in the RCWTEST component has been transformed into .NET information by viewing RCWTEST.dll from ildasm:

Looking at the screenshot, we can see a couple of things:

The type library importer has placed all generated types in the RCWTEST namespace. By default, the namespace name is based on the name of the wrapper assembly. However, you can generate a namespace of your choice by using the /namespace command-line option with TlbImp.

As with the IntelliSense screenshot earlier, we can see the two generated managed wrapper classes – Factorial, and FactorialClass.

The type library importer converts the COM-specific parameter types used by the GetFactorial() method to the managed equivalents. GetFactorial() expects an int data type to be passed; this has been transformed into an int32 managed type. You'll also notice that the unsigned int uFactorial parameter in GetFactorial() has been transformed into the method's return value, an unsigned int32 managed type.

As we have discussed earlier, the wrapper automatically performs data type mapping as we cross from managed to unmanaged code. For example, certain VB-specific data types used in an unmanaged VB 6 COM component are mapped into the following C# types: an Integer becomes a short, a Long integer becomes a C# int, a Variant goes to an object, and a Double becomes a double. There is a more detailed table of data types conversions in the .NET Framework documentation.

We test the COM component from a straightforward C# Windows Application. We have a form, with two TextBoxes, textInput and textOutput, and a button. To make use of the COM component, we add a reference to the RCWTEST DLL from the COM tab of the References dialog, and a metadata wrapper assembly is generated. The code for the button's click handler is simple:

```
private void button1_Click(object sender, System.EventArgs e)
{
    int number = int.Parse(this.textInput.Text);
    RCWTEST.FactorialClass factorial = new RCWTEST.FactorialClass();
    int result = factorial.GetFactorial(number);
    this.textOutput.Text = result.ToString();
}
```

The screenshot below shows the output:

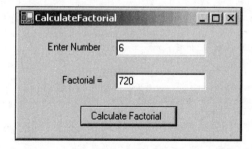

The important lines in the example concern the creation of the `Factorial` class, and the calling of the method to return the factorial of the input number:

```
RCWTESTLib.FactorialClass factorial = new RCWTESTLib.FactorialClass();
int result = factorial.GetFactorial(number);
```

We're simply creating an instance of the .NET wrapper, and allowing it to delegate its work to the real COM object behind the scenes.

Of course, this isn't an enterprise-level application, unless your enterprise involves calculating the factorial of small numbers, so let's look at another, more interesting scenario.

Filling a DataSet with a Recordset

Consider the scenario of a COM data access object in the business object layer of an n-tier data-centric application. The question is, how can we handle the ADO `Recordset` object in .NET? For example, can we fill a `DataSet` from this `Recordset`?

The role of the particular component we will be looking at is simply to retrieve all products from the `Products` table in the `Northwind` database with a `UnitPrice` more than a value that we supply to the component. Of course, in an enterprise-level application, there would be error-handling, and stored procedures would be used for the bulk of the database access, and you'd also be unlikely to query the `Northwind` database for your information.

We have the following snippet of a VB 6-based component, part of a `Products` class in a `DataAccess` DLL

```
Public Function Select_(ByVal Price As Integer) As ADODB.Recordset
    Dim ConnectionString As String
    ConnectionString = "Provider=SQLOLEDB.1;uid=sa;password=;" & _
                       "database=Northwind;Data Source=(local)"
    Dim strQuery As String
    strQuery = "SELECT * FROM Products WHERE UnitPrice > " & Price
    Set Select_ = ExecuteQuery_(ConnectionString, strQuery)
End Function

Public Function ExecuteQuery_(ByVal strConnection As String, _
                             ByVal SQLQuery As String) As ADODB.Recordset
    Dim objConnection As ADODB.Connection
    Dim objRecordset As ADODB.Recordset
    Set objConnection = New ADODB.Connection
    Call objConnection.Open(strConnection)
    Set objRecordset = New ADODB.Recordset
    objRecordset.CursorLocation = adUseClient
    objRecordset.Open SQLQuery, objConnection, adOpenStatic, _
                      adLockBatchOptimistic
    Set objRecordset.ActiveConnection = Nothing
    objConnection.Close
    Set ExecuteQuery_ = objRecordset
End Function
```

Select_ returns a Recordset, consisting of all products with UnitPrice greater than our supplied Price.

To handle the Recordset in .NET, we will be using an overload of the Fill() method of the OleDbDataAdapter class; we saw this class in Chapter 9. The overload we will use accepts a DataSet, a Recordset or Record object, and a string for the name of a source table.

We create a Windows Form application, with a TextBox, a button, and a DataGrid control that we will bind our DataSet to, displaying all the products with UnitPrice greater than the value entered into the TextBox. First, we add a reference to the DataAccess.dll, which we saw the code for above. Note that this will also automatically add a reference to ADODB, since we referenced ADO 2.6 in the original DataAccess project.

The code for the button's click handler consists of the following:

```
private void button1_Click(object sender, System.EventArgs e)
{
    short number = short.Parse(this.textBox1.Text);

    DataSet ds = new DataSet("FromRecordset");
    OleDbDataAdapter da = new OleDbDataAdapter();
```

We now create an instance of the Products class, and create an ADODB Recordset. We will use Recordset rather than RecordsetClass, and we will see why in a moment.

```
    DataAccess.ProductsClass prod = new DataAccess.ProductsClass();
    Recordset rs = new ADODB.Recordset();
```

Next, we use Select_ to populate our Recordset rs. If we have created rs as RecordsetClass, then the compiler would report that we are unable to implicitly convert Recordset to RecordsetClass.

```
    rs = prod.Select_(number);
```

Finally, we use the overload of the Fill() method we mentioned earlier to fill the DataSet, and then bind this to the DataGrid, and the data is displayed!

```
    da.Fill(ds, rs, "Products");
    dataGrid1.SetDataBinding(ds,"Products");
}
```

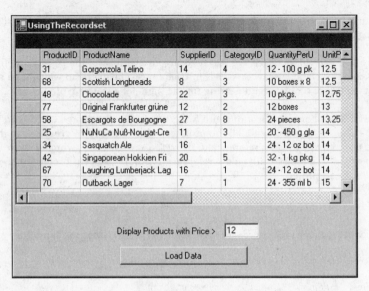

In the screenshot above, the rows are sorted by unit price with a simple click on the **UnitPrice** column – it would have been much more difficult to achieve this with the `Recordset` itself.

Late Binding to COM Components

So far, we have looked at early binding, so now we will look at how we can late-bind to a COM component using reflection in C#.

We shall late-bind to our `RCWTEST` component here. We will use the same form as before, and add a reference to the `System.Reflection` namespace. The code that follows will replace the code in the button's click handler.

When you late bind to a COM object in a C# program, you call the `GetTypeFromProgID()` static method of the `Type` class to instantiate an object representing the COM object's type. The `Type` class is a member of the `System` namespace, and in the code below, we configure a `Type` object for the `RCWTEST` component.

```
int number = int.Parse(this.textInput.Text);

Type factorialType;
factorialType = Type.GetTypeFromProgID("RCWTEST.Factorial");
```

Once you have a `Type` object encapsulating the COM object's type information, you use it to create an instance of the COM object itself. This is accomplished by passing the `Type` object to the `CreateInstance()` static method of the `Activator` class. `CreateInstance()` instantiates the COM object and returns a late-bound instance to it, which you can store in an `object` reference.

```
object objFactorial;
objFactorial = Activator.CreateInstance(factorialType);
```

At this point, your C# code has a late-bound reference to a full-fledged instance of the COM class.

Unfortunately, you can't invoke methods directly on the `object` reference. Instead, to talk to the COM object, you have to rely on the `InvokeMember()` method of the `Type` object that you first created. When you call `InvokeMember()`, you pass it a reference to the COM object, along with the name of the COM method that you are invoking and an `object` array of any input arguments to that method.

For our factorial example, we only need the one input parameter.

```
object[] aryInputArgs = new object[] {number};

object objResult = factorialType.InvokeMember("GetFactorial",
                                     BindingFlags.InvokeMethod,
                                     null,
                                     objFactorial,
                                     aryInputArgs);
```

Finally, we cast the object containing our return value into a `uint`, and display the output in the textbox.

```
uint result = (uint)objResult;
this.textOutput.Text = result.ToString();
```

Although C#'s late binding facilities allow you to avoid the hassle of wrapper assemblies, you need to be aware of some of its associated drawbacks:

- ❑ Late binding can be dangerous. When you use early binding, the compiler is able to consult the COM component's type library to make sure that all of the methods that you call on the COM object actually exist. In late binding, however, a typo in an `InvokeMember()` call can generate a run-time error.

- ❑ Late binding can be slow. Each time you use `InvokeMember()` on an `object` reference, the runtime has to look up the desired member in the COM class's function library before invoking it. This exacts an additional performance overhead on your program.

Releasing COM Objects

The lifetime of the RCW is controlled by the CLR, since the RCW is a managed creation. The COM component is freed from memory when the garbage collector calls the `Finalize()` method of the RCW. At this point, the RCW calls `IUnknown::Release()` on the COM component, and the COM component is released from memory. However, if you wish to explicitly remove the COM component from memory, for example if the component is holding on to valuable resources such as database connections, you can call the `ReleaseComObject()` static method of the `Marshal` class, in the `System.Runtime.InteropServices` namespace.

```
Marshal.ReleaseComObject(factorial);
```

This would remove our `factorial` COM component from memory, by forcing the RCW to release any references to the component. In general, `ReleaseComObject()` decreases the reference count on the object.

Using ActiveX Controls in .NET

ActiveX controls support interfaces that interact with ActiveX containers that host these controls. Generally, ActiveX controls represent reusable graphical controls that can be hosted in ActiveX control containers. It's also possible to have windowless ActiveX controls.

Just as you can import standard COM components for use in .NET projects, you can import ActiveX controls, too. AxImp.exe is the utility program that allows you to do this.

AxImp.exe

To import an ActiveX component into .NET with AxImp.exe, you invoke AxImp.exe from the command line, and specify the name of the ActiveX (*.ocx) file that you wish to import.

For an example, in the screenshot below we're importing the Windows Media Player ActiveX control (msdxm.ocx):

```
C:\WINNT\system32>AxImp msdxm.ocx
Generated Assembly: C:\WINNT\system32\MediaPlayer.dll
Generated Assembly: C:\WINNT\system32\AxMediaPlayer.dll

C:\WINNT\system32>
```

As you can see, the AxImp.exe program outputs two files. Here's why:

❑   The first output file, MediaPlayer.dll, is the assembly proxy. It contains metadata type information that allows C# clients to create and invoke the methods and properties of the ActiveX control as if it were a managed component.

❑   The second file, AxMediaPlayer.dll, is the Windows control. It allows you to use the graphical aspect of the imported ActiveX control as a Windows control in .NET Windows Forms projects, as the classes in AxMediaPlayer.dll present the ActiveX control as a managed Windows Form control.

To use the assembly proxy generated from an ActiveX component in Visual Studio by AxImp.exe, you just add a reference to the assembly proxy with Visual Studio .NET's References dialog, which we saw earlier in the chapter. We intend to use our Windows Media Player control on a Windows Form, so we will need to add references to both MediaPlayer.dll and AxMediaPlayer.dll.

Once you've referenced the proxy assembly (and the Windows control wrapper), you're ready to use the ActiveX component in your code.

Hosting an ActiveX Control on a Windows Form

It's straightforward to host an ActiveX control on a Windows Form from within Visual Studio .NET. To do so, right-click on the Toolbox and select Customize Toolbox. From the COM Components tab, select the control you wish to import; we will be using the Windows Media Player control.

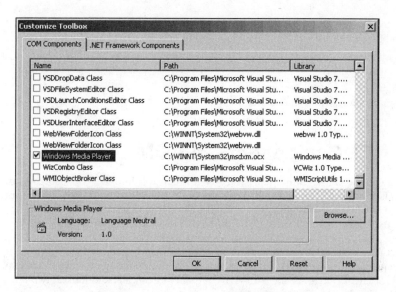

Once you've selected your control, you can drag it from the Toolbox onto your form, and you're ready to use the ActiveX component in your code. At this point the references are added to your project. We have two references added when we import our example control – one is called MediaPlayer, the other is AxMediaPlayer. This is because classes in the AxMediaPlayer wrapper assembly use classes in the MediaPlayer wrapper assembly internally. Thus both assemblies are needed and added. stdole is also added, since this holds managed metadata type information for some standard OLE interfaces and data types, and is therefore required when importing ActiveX controls.

The instance of the control on the form is named `axMediaPlayer1`. From the Properties dialog, you can access the properties of the ActiveX control as a standard control on the form, and right-clicking on the control itself and selecting Properties allows you to access the custom property page of the ActiveX control:

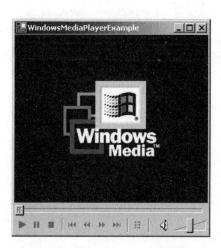

The imported ActiveX control can be coded against like any other Windows Form control. For example, if we add the following code to the form's constructor after the `InitializeComponent()` call:

```
this.axMediaPlayer1.FileName = "c:\\ProCSharp\\WroxTrailer.mpeg";
```

then our application will display a video clip.

Using .NET Components in COM

Just as you can use COM components and ActiveX controls in .NET code, so you can use .NET components in standard, unmanaged code, too. Only a few features of .NET assemblies are not accessible via COM, including parameterized constructors, static methods, and constant fields. Additionally, accessing overloaded .NET methods from COM requires a little work.

In this section, we shall look at how .NET components can be exposed to COM clients through a wrapper, analogous to the RCW, and discuss some of the requirements for classes that can be consumed from a COM client. Then, we have a .NET component example, and look at two utilities that facilitate COM clients binding to .NET components:

- ❑ `RegAsm.exe`, used to register a .NET component with the COM runtime
- ❑ `TlbExp.exe`, used to export type libraries for early-binding to .NET components

COM-Callable Wrappers

As we have the RCW for using COM components with .NET clients, so we have the corresponding notion of a COM Callable Wrapper, through which an unmanaged COM client can consume a .NET component. After all, a .NET object has no knowledge of COM, nor any real interest in COM-specific type information.

In order for a COM client to reference a .NET component, a **COM-Callable Wrapper** (CCW) needs to be generated for the component. This wrapper is used by COM clients as a proxy for the .NET component. When a COM client calls a .NET object, both the .NET object and a CCW are created. Note that only one CCW is created for each managed object, regardless of the number of COM clients that might be calling the object.

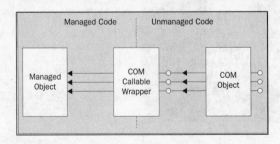

A type library containing COM-specific information for the .NET component is generated by the `TlbExp.exe` tool (or `RegAsm.exe` with a `/tlb:` option), which we shall look at later, and this library can be used by unmanaged clients to bind to the components.

COM clients maintain reference counts on the CCW proxy, rather than on the actual .NET component. The CCW lives only as along as any COM clients have references on the object. The CCW dies when the COM client releases the last reference to it. When this happens, the CCW marks the managed .NET component for garbage collection. Analogous to the RCW, the CCW is responsible for marshaling the method call parameters that move back and forward between the COM client and the .NET component.

Requirements of .NET Components

To ensure that a COM client can use your .NET component, there are some requirements on your .NET classes:

- ❏ Classes must be public, with a default public constructor

- ❏ Since only public types are exported to the type library, consequently, only methods, properties, and so on, that are public will be visible to COM

Without a default public constructor, it may still be possible for a COM client to create the object by some other means. Furthermore, your classes should not be abstract and they should explicitly implement any interfaces.

The C# Factorial Component

As an example, consider the following code in a C# Class Library called `CSharpFactorial`. It simply accepts a number as an input argument and returns the factorial of that number, as our earlier C++ example did. We will make use of this component from a simple VBScript client later:

```
using System;
namespace CSharpFactorial
{
    public class Factorial
    {

        //THIS METHOD COMPUTES THE
        //FACTORIAL FOR A NUMBER.
        public int ComputeFactorial(int n)
        {
            int intFactorial=n;
            for (int i=1;i<n;i++)
            {
                intFactorial*=i;
            }
            return intFactorial;
        }
        // A private method that will not be available to COM
        private int DoubleNumber (int n)
        {
            return n*2;
        }
    }
}
```

Note the private method `DoubleNumber()`.

Before we can use our component with a VBScript client, we have to install the assembly `CSharpFactorial.dll` into the global assembly cache. This is familiar to us from Chapter 8, so we will not spend time on it here.

Now we need to register the component with the `RegAsm.exe` tool:

RegAsm.exe

RegAsm (Register Assembly) is in charge of entering a .NET component's type information into the system Registry so that the COM runtime can access it. Once you've registered a .NET component with RegAsm, standard COM clients can bind to the component. The process of registering the component only has to be done one time. After it is registered, all COM clients can access it.

To finish off the task of registering our example `CSharpFactorial` DLL, we simply use `RegAsm.exe` thus:

```
regasm CSharpFactorial.dll
```

The VBScript COM Client

Now that the assembly has been registered with COM via RegAsm, we're free to bind to the .NET assembly through COM. For demonstration purposes, we'll be using VBScript. Simply type the following code into any text editor and save it as `Factorial.vbs`. Assuming that you have Windows Script Host installed, the file will run as a script when invoked. Note that VBScript employs late binding for COM components.

```
Option Explicit

Dim objFactorial
Dim lngResult
Dim lngInputValue

Set objFactorial=CreateObject("CSharpFactorial.Factorial")
lngInputValue=InputBox("Number?")
lngResult=objFactorial.ComputeFactorial(CLng(lngInputValue))
Call MsgBox(lngResult)
```

When you execute the VB script, it uses COM to instantiate the .NET object, calls a method on that object, and displays the value returned from the .NET object in a message box:

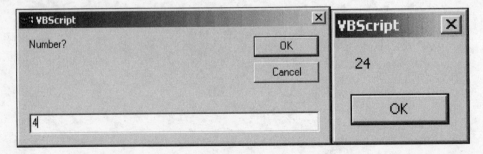

As you probably know, VBScript uses late binding – that's why it was able to create our .NET object in the example here. Unfortunately, this approach does not solve any of the aforementioned dangers associated with late binding.

Early Binding to .NET Components

If a COM client wants to early-bind to a .NET component, we have two options. Firstly, we can tell RegAsm that we want to generate a type library using the /tlb switch:

```
RegAsm CSharpFactorial.dll /tlb:CSharpFactorial.tlb
```

```
Command Prompt                                                    _ | □ | ×
C:\ProCSharp\ComInterop>RegAsm CSharpFactorial.dll /tlb:CSharpFactorial.tlb
Microsoft (R) .NET Framework Assembly Registration Utility 1.0.3512.0
Copyright (C) Microsoft Corporation 1998-2001.  All rights reserved.

Types registered successfully
Assembly exported to 'C:\ProCSharp\ComInterop\CSharpFactorial.tlb', and the type
 library was registered successfully

C:\ProCSharp\ComInterop>
```

Alternatively, we can use the Type Library Exporter program, TlbExp.exe.

TlbExp.exe

The Type Library Exporter, TlbExp.exe, inspects an assembly and exports all its public types into a corresponding type library containing COM-specific type information; a .tlb file that can be made available to unmanaged COM clients.

Once TlbExp (or RegAsm with the /tlb: option) has created a type library file for a .NET component, non-.NET development languages such as VB 6 can reference it, using it to effectively achieve early binding to the .NET components:

```
Command Prompt                                                    _ | □ | ×
C:\ProCSharp\ComInterop>TlbExp CSharpFactorial.dll
Microsoft (R) .NET Framework Assembly to Type Library Converter 1.0.3705.0
Copyright (C) Microsoft Corporation 1998-2001.  All rights reserved.

Assembly exported to C:\ProCSharp\ComInterop\CSharpFactorial.tlb

C:\ProCSharp\ComInterop>
```

Let's use `TlbExp` on our `CSharpFactorial` example, and have a look at the resulting type library with the `OleView` utility:

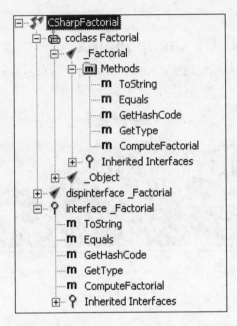

We can see our `ComputeFactorial` method, but no `DoubleNumber` method; this is expected, since `DoubleNumber` was private.

Platform Invocation Services

We've talked about interoperability between COM components and .NET. While we're on the subject of interoperability, let's talk about another kind: that which is between .NET code and functions available from unmanaged Win32 DLLs. The technology for achieving this is called Platform Invocation Services, or **PInvoke** for short.

As we mentioned at the start of the chapter, unmanaged code is not managed by the .NET runtime. When a .NET application's thread-of-execution enters a segment of unmanaged code, the .NET runtime no longer has control over what that code does, and is unable to enforce garbage collection or security rules on it. For this reason, applications that use unmanaged code must be endowed with a trust by the system administrator.

Platform Invocation Services allow .NET code to interoperate with code that is not only unsafe, but also authentically unmanaged.

Accessing Unmanaged Code

To use Platform Invocation Services to call an unmanaged, external function, we must declare the target function at the top of a C# file. Providing no implementation, this declaration gives the target function's name, lists its input arguments, and associates the function with the name of the DLL from which the function is available. This is done through the DllImport attribute of the System.Runtime.InteropServices namespace.

The following simple console application example uses the Windows API to create a message box:

```
using System;
using System.Runtime.InteropServices;

namespace Wrox.ProCSharp.ComInterop.UnmanagedExample
{
   class PInvokeExample
   {
//Declare the external, unmanaged function.
      [DllImport ("user32.dll")]
      public static extern int MessageBoxA (int Modal,
                                       string Message,
                                       string Caption,
                                       int Options);

      //Program starts here.
      public static void Main (string[] args)
      {
         //Invoke the unmanaged function using PInvoke.
         MessageBoxA(0,"PInvoke worked!","PInvoke Example",0);
      }
   }
}
```

When the code calls the unmanaged function, PInvoke loads the function's DLL into memory, locates the address of the function, and marshals the C# input arguments to types that the DLL function will understand. Then PInvoke activates the function, moving the application's thread-of-execution into the unmanaged DLL. As the example above shows, a call to an unmanaged function looks just like the call to an ordinary, managed one.

An important thing to note about the above code is the use of the extern keyword in the unmanaged function's declaration. This indicates that the function is defined externally, so we don't have to supply a definition within our code itself. Now, client .NET code can invoke the exported function by calling the managed declaration that we tagged with the [DllImport] attribute.

Although we chose to give the wrapper function the same name as the Windows API call to which it maps, we could give it a different name as well, as we do in the example below. Here, we change the name MessageBoxA to one that more accurately specifies how the API call will be used. We do this by using the EntryPoint parameter with the DllImport attribute to specify an alias name for the external function:

```
[DllImport("user32.dll",EntryPoint="MessageBoxA")]
public static extern int ErrorMessage(int Modal,
                                      string Message,
                                      string Caption,
                                      int Options);
```

With an alias defined for the managed declaration, C# clients can invoke the exported function using this alias name, as shown below

```
ErrorMessage(0, "PInvoke worked with alias name!", "PInvoke Example",0);
```

The Drawback to Pinvoke

As you've seen, it's pretty easy to reference and invoke an unmanaged function from .NET code. Unfortunately, there is a potential drawback to using unmanaged code in this fashion.

Although Microsoft has consistently sidestepped the issue of platform interoperability, many people suspect that it is on the horizon for .NET. With platform interoperability in place, you could run a .NET program on any platform from Macintosh to Unix, provided that the platform was equipped with a .NET runtime. However, when you use PInvoke, you couple your .NET code to the Windows operating system.

When you consider using PInvoke, first check to see that the functionality you need isn't exposed somewhere by the .NET base classes; the most useful stuff is in there. If the .NET runtime were ever ported to a different platform, the .NET base classes would be ported, too, and your code would have a good chance of running correctly on the new platform with few (if any) changes.

Summary

In this chapter, we've looked at interoperability between COM and .NET. We looked at early and late binding to COM components, and generating managed metadata wrappers using TlbImp.exe and Visual Studio .NET.

After some examples of consuming COM components from .NET code, we saw how to release COM objects and use ActiveX controls as we would any other Windows control.

In our exploration of using .NET components from COM clients, we looked at binding to a .NET component, and exporting type libraries with RegAsm.exe and TlbExp.exe. We finished the chapter with a look at platform invocation services, and how .NET can interoperate with unmanaged code in any DLL, such as the Win32 API.

As this chapter has demonstrated, COM and .NET are distinct technologies that can work together if you apply the proper techniques. Using interoperability tools such as TlbImp.exe, RegAsm.exe, and TlbExp.exe, developers can use legacy COM components as building blocks for new .NET applications, and also use .NET components from unmanaged COM clients.

Compared to COM components, assemblies are easier to build, deploy, and maintain. Developers of web applications and programs to be used by organizations internally will find .NET assemblies to be a welcome respite from DLL Hell, and that the simplicity and elegance of the .NET deployment model could be a good enough reason for companies to migrate their existing COM components to .NET.

18
COM+ Services

In this chapter, we will look at COM+ Services; what they are, how they have developed, and how they work; and how COM+ Services can be used from .NET.

We'll tackle the first subject in the first part of this chapter. Even if you're an old hand with COM+ Service's forerunner, MTS, you'll benefit from the coverage of new services like message queuing and events. As you'll see, COM+ Services provide much more than transaction support; they are a wealth of prefabricated functionality from which every professional C# programmer can benefit.

The last part of the chapter will address the second subject: how COM+ Services can be used in .NET. There, we'll take a look at the classes, interfaces, and attributes that are in the `System.EnterpriseServices` namespace. We'll also take a look at the `RegSvcs.exe` tool. It's at this point that we'll drill down into code samples.

Let's begin by taking a look at how COM+ Services came about.

COM+ Services in Perspective

In the bad old days of programming, the application developer had to build everything from scratch. If the developer wanted database functionality, for example, then they would have to implement it, devising a mechanism for maintaining indexes and searching for records through flat files. In those freewheeling frontier days of software engineering, people wasted a lot of time re-inventing the wheel.

As the programming techniques evolved, vendors packed useful functionality into reusable server components. As time went on, more and more useful functionality was pressed downward out of application programs and into the level of server programs, and even the operating system.

COM+ Services make life easier for enterprise developers by providing valuable functionality that their components can easily employ. When a component needs a capability such as transaction enforcement, the developer can rely on COM+ Services to provide a robust solution.

Firstly, let's take a quick look at the COM+ programmer's best friend: the Component Services "snap-in".

The Component Services Snap-In

Seasoned developers may recall that the MTS administrator was accessed from the Windows NT Option Pack option on the Start menu. In keeping with its new status as an integral part of the operating system, COM+ Services is listed more prominently on the Administrative Tools menu in Windows 2000, under the title Component Services.

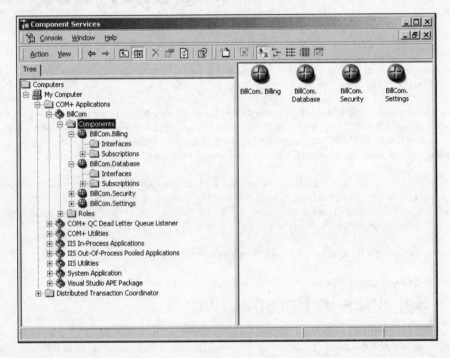

The left pane of the Component Services window contains a hierarchical tree with computer, COM+ application, and component nodes. (In the parlance of Component Services, an application is a group of COM+ components that are administered as a whole; this was called a package in MTS.) Each component class in an application is represented by a golden sphere with a plus sign in the middle; the sphere spins when the component is being accessed.

Features of COM+ Services

COM+ Services began life as a Windows NT add-on called Microsoft Transaction Server, MTS. Subsequently, Windows 2000 subsumed MTS as an integral part of the operating system, renaming it in the process. In addition to all of the original features of MTS, COM+ Services boast exciting new ones that further reduce the amount of code that the component developer has to write. The features of COM+ Services include:

- Automatic transaction handling

- Just-In-Time (JIT) object activation

- Security

- Event support

- Object pooling

- Component message queuing

- Component load balancing

A **configured** class has a set of COM+ -specific declarative attributes, which specify the required COM+ services. At run time, COM+ ensures that it provides the required services to the COM+ objects. COM+ provides its services through **contexts**, which are implemented as objects called the **object context**. All COM+ classes are instantiated in a context, and each object lives in precisely one context. Classes that are not configured ignore their associated contexts.

We should first be aware that there are two different types of COM+ applications:

- A **library application** is a collection of component classes, that when instantiated, are created within the calling client's process

- A server application is a collection of component classes, that, when instantiated, are created in a dedicated surrogate process that is separate from the calling client's process

Most ASP-based applications typically used components stored in server applications. Because Server Application components are hosted in a dedicated, surrogate process, the failure of a server component doesn't crash the web server. For standard (non-.NET COM applications), you set the Activation type property on the Activation tab of the application's Properties window:

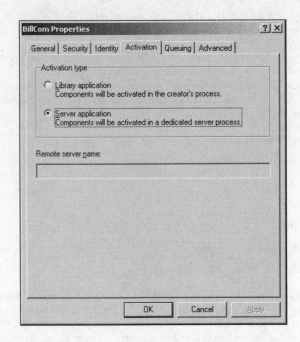

As you'll see later, there's a different procedure for specifying a .NET assembly's activation type. You'll learn how to do it programmatically, with attributes.

Transactions

A transaction is a set of operations that succeed or fail as a unit, that is, if one operation in the set fails, all the other previously completed operations in the transaction must be rolled back to the original state before the transaction was started.

Consider a web site that features credit card processing for orders. If a user orders a product from the site, it is essential that not only is the user's account charged, but that an order record is placed in the order database as well. If there's a problem entering an order record into the database, the charging of the credit card must be undone, and the order also needs to be canceled, otherwise a user will be charged for an item that they will never receive.

In the old days, developers had to cook up their own transaction enforcement schemes in order to get the sort of functionality mentioned above. These schemes usually involved lots of Boolean variables and elaborate error-handling strategies, and were bug-prone. More recently, the ADODB.Connection object offered support for transactions in a form that was quite elegant. Now, by means of the ContextUtil object that we'll look at shortly, COM+ Services presents developers with a transaction mechanism that is robust, ready-made, and even easier to use than the ADODB.Connection approach.

How Transactions Work

The Distributed Transaction Coordinator (DTC), a component of the Windows operating system, is in charge of administering transactions. Components that can enlist and participate in transactions must match an interface that the DTC understands, and must provide a resource manager that is capable of rolling back or committing units of work when told to do so by the DTC. This high degree of abstraction allows components as diverse as database engines and credit card processors to work together.

The DTC enforces transactions through a process called the two-phase commit. When enforcing a transaction, the DTC first asks every resource manager participating in the transaction whether it will be able to complete its work; this is the first phase. If and only if the DTC receives an OK from every participant, it tells each participant to go ahead and commit the changes; this is the second phase. If one of the participants experiences problems in the first phase, the DTC will tell every participant to undo its work.

Every transaction operation – such as a credit card charge and the subsequent insertion of an order record – has a context with which it is associated. To say that an operation occurs in the context of a transaction is to say that the operation is a part of the transaction, and can suggest to the DTC that the transaction be rolled back or committed. Such an operation effectively has the power to "veto" the committal of all the operations in its context.

COM+ provides its services through **contexts**, which are implemented as objects called the **object context**. All COM+ classes, configured and non-configured, are instantiated in a context. Each object lives in precisely one context.

COM+ provides services to configured classes at run time, when required, through contexts. Non-configured classes, on the other hand, ignore their associated contexts as they are not aware of such object contexts.

Transactions in n-Tier Architectures

Architecturally, the typical client-server application that makes use of COM+ transactions consists of a layer of data access objects that perform the grunt work of adding, deleting, retrieving, and updating records in the database, wrapped with a layer of business objects that enforce the business rules, topped by a Windows Form-based or browser-based user interface.

It's common for a single business object method to call several different methods on several different data access objects. If one of the data access methods fails to execute properly, the business object method can use the COM+ transaction mechanism to ask the DTC to roll the operation back, ensuring that the data is left in a consistent state.

Just-In-Time Activation (JIT)

Because object instantiation consumes server resources, developers have traditionally had to be careful about when in the program it was performed. Specifically, they had to be sure that heavily used, multi-user programs with a lot of traffic only created objects when required, and deallocated them immediately when they were no longer needed. Fortunately for us, COM+ Services provides another approach that frees the developer from this concern.

With Just-In-Time activation, a developer can instantiate objects once at the beginning of the program, and then use them whenever needed, without worrying about the resources that they consume while they are dormant. Invisibly, COM+ Services deallocates the space occupied by the objects when they're unused, and resurrects them at the moment that the client code invokes their methods. Thus, the client code can hold references to many objects for as long as it wants, confident that COM+ Services will provide the objects as necessary, and deallocate their memory whenever possible.

JIT-activated classes must manage state wisely. If COM+ Services deallocates the space occupied by your object between subsequent calls to it, there's no guarantee that the same property values will persist between the first and second call. In other words, classes designed to be used with COM+ services should be stateless.

We've all used server objects that require some initialization before their methods can be invoked. The `ADODB.Connection` object is one example; you need to initialize its `ConnectionString` property before you can tell it to `Execute()` a SQL query. Because a JIT object can't persist state between calls, you can't initialize it and invoke its methods in separate steps. Instead, a call to a JIT object must pass to that object all the values that it needs to perform its work.

Security

There are two aspects to the security model that COM+ Services provide.

The first aspect is authentication. Briefly, COM+ Services allow you to place restrictions on who has access to serviced components and the methods that they provide. Using the Component Services snap-in, you can set an application's authentication level to determine when authentication is performed: upon the client's connection to the server object, or with each network packet of communication to the object, or as each method is invoked, etc.

The second aspect to the COM+ Services security model is a component's impersonation level. Since a server object performs work on behalf of a client, it can sometimes be useful for a server object to assume the access privileges and identity of the client that it serves. The impersonation level allows you to determine this.

Role-based security is the convention typically associated with client-server applications that utilize COM+ Services. In this approach, a server object first checks that its client belongs to a certain Windows security role before performing work on its behalf.

Events

The architecture of the COM+ event mechanism differs from the traditional mechanism of using connection points.

This event service has often been termed the "publisher-subscriber" model. In this approach, you develop an event interface and register it with COM+ Services. Next, you register classes that want to be able to raise events defined in the interface as publishers. Last, you register classes that want to be able to handle events defined in the event interface as subscribers. When a publisher/server object raises an event, COM+ Services is in charge of notifying all of the subscribers. Because the subscriber classes are not directly coupled to the publisher classes, but instead rely on COM+ Services to serve as an intermediary, this architecture is often described as "loosely-coupled" events.

To implement this scheme, you must follow these steps:

- ❏ Create an event class DLL that implements the event interface
- ❏ Register the event class DLL with COM+ Services
- ❏ Create a server component that internally instantiates the event class and invokes methods on the instance in order to raise events
- ❏ Register the server component as a publisher with COM+ Services
- ❏ Create client components that implement the event interface in order to catch events
- ❏ Register the client components as subscribers with COM+ Services

When these steps are completed, a publisher class can raise an event simply by creating an instance of the event class and invoking one of its methods. As noted above, COM+ services will tell each subscriber class that the event has been raised. However, despite the robustness of this approach, there are at least two drawbacks to the way that COM+ Services implements this event model.

- ❏ Because subscriber objects are notified of raised events one at a time, each subscriber object has the potential to make the others wait if its event handler is slow
- ❏ At least at the time of writing, COM+ Services does not have the ability to raise events from publisher objects to subscriber objects on different machines

Again, the principal advantage of the publisher-subscriber event architecture is that the publisher and subscriber classes remain loosely coupled, able to communicate without maintaining direct references to each other.

Object Pooling

In terms of processor cycles and bytes, it's expensive to instantiate and initialize certain objects. This expense is compounded for a web server that must serve tens of thousands of users simultaneously. So that users don't experience delays while the web server struggles to create component objects, COM+ Services provides object pooling.

As you might infer, this COM+ service allows the maintenance of a pool of objects that are created and waiting for use even before they are needed. When a server session needs a particular component object, it just requests one from the pool of available ones, getting one immediately if one is ready, or waiting in a queue until a new one becomes available. When the object is released by the client, COM+ Services does not destroy it, but instead allows it to persist in the pool, ready in the event that another client needs it. Because you can determine the minimum and maximum number of objects in the pool, you can discretely control how much of the server's resources are dedicated to the component class.

Object pooling is useful when the components being pooled have expensive initialization requirements. For example, a web site might have many option lists that are generated from tables in a database. Rather than building the option list on the fly every time a page is viewed, the lists can be generated by the pooled component when it is instantiated. Since pooled components maintain state, the options lists that it maintains can then be retrieved by any web page that needs to display a list. The expensive initialization, in this case querying the database and building option lists, only happens once per object, when it is instantiated by COM+.

Note that even though pooled components maintain their state, you cannot simply import all of your legacy COM components into COM+ as pooled components and expect them to work properly. During multiple method invocations there is no guarantee that you will receive a reference to the same object during each call.

Message Queuing

Special conditions may arise during the course of a program's execution. The database server may crash, or the user may attempt, purposefully or accidentally, to submit work from a disconnected terminal. Traditionally, developers have had to make special provisions in their application code to deal with these anomalies.

Now, the COM+ message queuing service will allow developers to avoid coding for disconnected situations. Briefly, the queuing service will record method calls from a client object to a server object that is unavailable, so that they can be played back to the server object when it once again comes online. The client code remains unaware that anything out of the ordinary has happened, and that COM+ Services is acting as an intermediary.

As you might imagine, message queuing comes in handy when you're designing applications that must run from both disconnected and connected machines. Also, message queuing is an integral part of Microsoft's new BizTalk Server, a new server program that can orchestrate how data moves through and between organizations. When you install Windows 2000 Server, message queuing is an option that you can install or leave out.

Component Load Balancing

Even with the benefits that object pooling and Just-In-Time activation provide for maximizing server resources, there may be times when one server machine just isn't strong enough to serve all of an application's clients. In such situations, developers can make use of COM+'s Component Load Balancing Service. This service distributes application objects out across a farm of co-operating web servers, so that no one server is overwhelmed by object requests and so that end users continue to enjoy smooth, consistent performance.

The crux of the Component Load Balancing strategy is the Component Load Balancing server, or the CLB. The CLB is a Windows Advanced Server or Windows Data Server machine that serves as a manager to the other servers in the farm. The CLB is in charge of distributing the object requests between the available servers.

The algorithm that the CLB server uses for picking object hosts is a sophisticated one. It proceeds in order down a list of available servers, handing creation requests to the first server that is available. Because this list is sorted from most robust to least robust server, stronger servers are more likely to host requests.

Once a connection is established between the client application and the server machine that the CLB has assigned to the client, communication proceeds between them without subsequent intervention by the CLB. Because there's no guarantee that the client's server object will continue to be hosted on the same server machine, components must be stateless, and object pooling is not available.

Using COM+ Services with .NET Assemblies

Now that we understand what the various COM+ Services are, let's look at how the services can be used with .NET. The .NET Framework still relies on COM+ to provide run time services to .NET components, and provides this integration with a collection of classes in the System.EnterpriseServices namespace. An **Enterprise Service** is a COM+ service provided through the System.EnterpriseServices namespace. A **serviced component** is a .NET class designed to use Enterprise Services, and a **serviced assembly** is a .NET assembly that contains at least one serviced component.

To create a class as a serviced component, the class must inherit from the ServicedComponent class of the System.EnterpriseServices namespace, or from other classes that derive from this class, and must also define a public default constructor.

```
public class ComPlusExample : ServicedComponent
{
   public ComPlusExample()
   {
   }
}
```

> Note that to use the **System.EnterpriseServices** namespace, you need to manually add a reference to the **System.EnterpriseServices.dll**, either with **Project | Add Reference** from Visual Studio .NET, or by adding **/r:System.EnterpriseServices.dll** if compiling from the command line.

By prefixing class definitions with attributes defined in the System.EnterpriseServices namespace, you're able to specify how COM+ Services treat those classes. The C# compiler knows how to translate the attributes into the necessary code "hooks" that COM+ Services expect from components.

The attributes defined in the System.EnterpriseServices namespace include:

- ❑ Transaction
- ❑ ObjectPooling
- ❑ JustInTimeActivation
- ❑ EventClass
- ❑ ApplicationActivation

In addition to these attributes, the System.EnterpriseServices namespace defines various classes and enumerations as well, several of which we'll examine in detail shortly.

The following sections explain how we can use .NET Enterprise Service classes in our applications.

Configuring Assemblies

First, we need to add a set of assembly attributes to the assembly in `AssemblyInfo.cs` of any Enterprise Services application that we wish to use:

```
[assembly:ApplicationActivation(ActivationOption.Server)]
[assembly:ApplicationID("448934a3-324f-34d3-2343-129ab3c43b2c")]
[assembly:ApplicationName("EnterpriseServiceApplication")]
[assembly:Description("Description of your assembly here.")]
```

Let's examine each of these attributes in turn.

Remember earlier when we mentioned that there are two kinds of COM+ applications, server applications and library applications? The first attribute in the code sample, the `ApplicationActivation` attribute, allows you to specify which of these two kinds of applications a particular assembly is. The acceptable values for this attribute are defined in the `ActivationOption` enumeration. By specifying the application's type programmatically with this attribute, there is no need to open up the Component Services manager and do so manually. This enumeration has two values, `ActivationOption.Library` and `ActivationOption.Server`.

The second attribute, `ApplicationID`, is the GUID of the application. The `ApplicationName` attribute allows you to specify the name of the COM+ Services application that will be created to host the .NET assembly when the assembly is imported into COM+ Services. In our example, we've used the value `EnterpriseServiceName`. The `Description` attribute allows you to associate a description with the assembly.

Deploying an Assembly for COM+ Services

Deploying an assembly that is to be used with COM+ Services is only a little more involved than deploying any other .NET assembly.

The simplest way is to copy the assembly to the COM+ application's directory, known as **dynamic registration**. Doing this means that the assembly is not placed in the global assembly cache. However, there is a catch – only a user who is a member of the `Administrators` group can register a serviced component. This means that with dynamic registration, the user of your application must be a member of the `Administrators` group.

The other way to register a serviced component is by **manual registration** – administrator privileges are still required. Firstly, you have to provide the assembly with a strong name, and then register the assembly in the global assembly cache. We can use the `gacutil` utility to do this:

```
gacutil -i AssemblyName.dll
```

Registering of assemblies, the global assembly cache, and the use of strong names were discussed at length in Chapter 8.

The next step is to explicitly register the assembly with COM+ Services yourself, prior to any client program's execution. The program for doing this registration, `RegSvcs.exe`, is provided by Microsoft as part of the .NET SDK. When you run `RegSvcs` against a .NET component, it will create a COM+ application with the name specified by the `ApplicationName` attribute in the assembly and import the assembly into it.

```
Command Prompt                                                    _ □ ×
C:\ProCSharp\ComPlus>RegSvcs TransactionTest.dll TransactionTest
Microsoft (R) .NET Framework Services Installation Utility Version 1.0.3512.0
Copyright (C) Microsoft Corporation 1998-2001.  All rights reserved.

Installed Assembly:
        Assembly: C:\ProCSharp\ComPlus\TransactionTest.dll
        Application: TransactionTest
        TypeLib: c:\procsharp\complus\TransactionTest.tlb

C:\ProCSharp\ComPlus>
```

The typical syntax for RegSvcs is as follows:

RegSvcs ComponentName [COM+AppName] [Typelibrary.tlb]

With the second argument (COM+AppName), you can specify a different name for the COM+ application that will be created, and you can determine the name of the type library file that will be generated by providing a third argument (TypeLibrary.tlb)

You may be wondering why RegSvcs.exe is necessary; as you may recall from the previous chapter on COM interoperability, .NET assemblies adhere to a different architecture from COM components. It's the job of RegSvcs.exe to resolve these discrepancies, so that .NET assemblies meet the interface expected by COM+ Services. To fulfill its job, RegSvcs.exe does four things:

❑   It loads and registers the .NET assembly

❑   It creates a type library for the .NET assembly

❑   It imports the type library into a COM+ Services application

❑   It uses metadata inside the DLL to properly configure the type library inside the COM+ Services application

Using Transactions with .NET Assemblies

There are two things that you have to do in order to equip a .NET class for transactions. Firstly, you have to modify the class with an attribute to indicate its level of transactional support. Secondly, you have to add code to the class to control its behavior when it participates in transactions. There is a way to tell COM+ how to automatically control its transactional behavior by using the [AutoComplete] attribute, covered a little later on.

Specifying Transactional Support

If you've used transactions from COM+ Services before, you may have seen the Transaction support setting on a class's Property window in the Component Services snap-in. This setting allows you to set the level of transactional support that COM+ Services will grant to a standard COM component.

In .NET, you can determine an assembly's level of transactional support differently, not by means of a graphical window in the Component Services snap-in, but programmatically, by means of the Transaction attribute defined in the System.EnterpriseServices namespace. For example, in the example below, we've specified that the following class should support transactions. Given this attribute value, our component will be configured to support transactions when it is imported into COM+ Services by RegSvcs.exe.

```
[Transaction(TransactionOption.Supported)]
public class TxExample : ServicedComponent
{
}
```

Supported is only one of five values that you can assign to a component's Transaction attribute, and they are listed in the TransactionOption enumeration, which is part of the System.EnterpriseServices namespace.

Attribute	Description
Supported	Objects of the class *can* enlist in the transactional context of its calling clients, *if those calling clients did indeed begin a transaction*. Such an object cannot instigate a transaction by itself.
Required	COM+ Services knows that objects of the class can only execute within the context of a transaction. If such an object is invoked by a client that has a transaction context, the object inherits the client's transaction context. If, however, the object is invoked by a client that does *not* have a transaction context, COM+ Services creates a context for the object.
RequiresNew	COM+ Services creates a brand new transaction for the class every time that it is invoked. Even if the object's client already has a transaction, COM+ Services creates a new one for the server object. As you might infer, classes configured in this way can only roll back their own transactions, and not the work of their clients.
Disabled	COM+ Services provides no transactional support for the class, even if such support is specified elsewhere in code. (In other words, calls that the class makes to ContextUtil to commit or roll back transactions are ignored. We'll see more about ContextUtil in the next section.)
NotSupported	The class does not enlist in transactions started by its clients; in other words, it's not placed in their context. When so configured, the objects of that class do not vote on whether the calling transaction is committed or rolled back.

In practice, most developers only use one or two of these settings. The Supported value is great for a class that will need to serve both transactional and non-transactional classes. For most other transactional classes in most situations, you can usually get away with designating the Required value. However, this is not to say that you will sometimes encounter situations in which one of the more complex values is needed; for further information, consult *Professional Windows DNA* , (Wrox Press, ISBN 1-861004-45-1).

Coding Transactions with ContextUtil

Modifying a class with the Transaction attribute is only part of what you have to do in order to enable it for transactions. You also have to specify how each *method* in that class will behave when invoked as part of a transaction. This is accomplished by means of the ContextUtil class of the System.EnterpriseServices namespace.

To put it simply, the ContextUtil class exposes a transaction's context. Once you have a reference to the transaction's context, you can explicitly cause that context to be committed or rolled back. The methods that you need to call for committing and rolling back transactions are exposed as *static* methods on the ContextUtil class, so you don't have to create an instance of the ContextUtil class in order to invoke them.

We will now move on to an example that makes use of ContextUtil, to demonstrate the use of COM+ transactions.

The example will simply attempt to update the UnitsOnOrder and UnitsInStock columns of Products table in the Northwind database – however, the UnitsInStock column has a constraint that will prevent the value falling below 0, so any attempt to obtain non-existent stock would fail. Accordingly, the corresponding order placed will have to be withdrawn, achieved by rolling back the transaction.

First, we create a new Class Library called TransactionTest, add a reference to System.EnterpriseServices, and begin with the usual namespaces:

```
using System;
using System.Data;
using System.Data.SqlClient;
using System.EnterpriseServices;

namespace Wrox.ProCSharp.ComPlus.TransactionTest
{
```

And now we mark our class, TxTest, with the Required option of the Transaction attribute, enabling the class to use COM+ transactions.

```
[Transaction(TransactionOption.Required)]
public class TxTest : ServicedComponent
{
    public TxTest()
    {
    }
```

The OrderProduct() method begins by defining a connection to the Northwind database.

```
public bool OrderProduct(int ProductID, int Units)
{
    SqlConnection conn = new SqlConnection("Data Source=(local);" +
                    "Initial Catalog=Northwind;User ID=sa;Password=");
    try
    {
```

Next, we use the `IsInTransaction` property of `ContextUtil` to determine if we are currently participating in a transaction – if we're not, then an exception is thrown.

```
if (!ContextUtil.IsInTransaction)
    throw new Exception("Not in transaction");
```

The next few lines open the connection to the database, and attempt to update the relevant columns for the relevant products, throwing an exception if an insufficient number of rows is returned. Attempting to decrease the `UnitsInStock` column below 0 will result in an exception, due to the `CK_UnitsInStock` constraint on the `Products` table. Note that the `UnitsOnOrder` column is updated first; thus, if there is an error updating the `UnitsInStock` column, we definitely need to roll back any changes made.

```
conn.Open();
SqlCommand cmd = new SqlCommand("UPDATE Products SET UnitsOnOrder = "+
                                "UnitsOnOrder + " + Units +
                                " WHERE ProductID = " + ProductID, conn);

int rowsAffected = cmd.ExecuteNonQuery();
if (rowsAffected != 1)
    throw new Exception("Invalid number of rows affected");

cmd = new SqlCommand("UPDATE Products SET UnitsInStock = " +
                     "UnitsInStock - " + Units +
                     " WHERE ProductID = " + ProductID, conn);

rowsAffected = cmd.ExecuteNonQuery();
if (rowsAffected != 1)
    throw new Exception("Invalid number of rows affected");
```

At this point, there must be enough available stock since we have successfully updated both columns, and so we call `ContextUtil`'s `SetComplete()` method, effectively telling the DTC through the resource manager that, as far as it's concerned, the transaction needs to be committed.

```
ContextUtil.SetComplete();
return true;
}
```

In the `catch` block, we advise that there was an error, and invoke `ContextUtil`'s `SetAbort()` method. This method casts its vote for the cancellation of the transaction in which it is involved, and the DTC, after receiving this vote from the resource manager, will instruct each participant in the transaction to roll back any work attempted. We also return a value of `false` to indicate `OrderProduct()`'s failure.

```
catch (Exception e)
{
    Console.WriteLine("Transaction aborted with error: {0}", e.Message);
    ContextUtil.SetAbort();
    return false;
}
```

Finally, we close any open connections in the `finally` block.

```
        finally
        {
            if (conn.State == ConnectionState.Open)
            conn.Close();
        }
    }
}
```

Remember, you don't have to create an instance of the `ContextUtil` object in order to invoke its `SetComplete()` and `SetAbort()` methods, since they are static methods.

After building the project, we install the assembly into the global assembly cache, and then register the assembly with COM+ Services by using `regsvcs`. A look in the Component Services window shows us that our service is indeed registered.

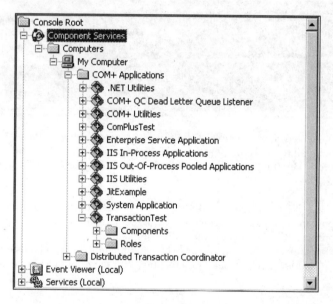

We test the code with a simple Console Application client. Remember to add a reference to `System.EnterpriseServices` and the `TransactionTest.dll`

```
using System;
using Wrox.ProCSharp.ComPlus.TransactionTest;

namespace Wrox.ProCSharp.ComPlus.TransactionTestClient
{
    class Class1
    {

        [STAThread]
```

```
        static void Main(string[] args)
        {
            TxTest txObj = new TxTest();
            bool result = txObj.OrderProduct(1,20);
            Console.WriteLine("OrderProduct returned {0} for 20 orders.", result);
            result = txObj.OrderProduct(1,20);
            Console.WriteLine("OrderProduct returned {0} for a further 20 "+
                                                      "orders.", result);

            Console.ReadLine();
        }
    }
}
```

The product in the `Products` table with a `ProductId` of 1 is `Chai`, and there are 39 units in stock. Thus we would expect the first call, `OrderProduct(1,20)`, to be successful, and the second attempt to fail.

Most transaction-enabled code resembles the above example. It calls `SetComplete()` just before its exit point to commit all the work that has successfully been performed, or it calls `SetAbort()` in its error handler to roll everything back because of the error. Pretty easy, eh? There's another way that's even easier.

Microsoft provides a .NET attribute called `AutoComplete`. Methods modified with this attribute automatically apply the approach described above. Even though such methods never explicitly reference the `ContextUtil` class, they implicitly complete their transactions if they exit normally, or roll back all work if they exit due to an error (when an unhandled exception is thrown). Our `OrderProduct()` method above would look like this with the `AutoComplete` attribute applied:

```
        [AutoComplete]
        public bool OrderProduct(int ProductID, int Units)
        {
            ...
```

Since the `AutoComplete` attribute is specified, this method call, when invoked, automatically votes in favor of the transaction committing if the method completes, or votes to abort the transaction if an unhandled exception is thrown. In our example above, we would need to call `SetAbort()` because our exceptions are handled.

Other Useful ContextUtil Methods and Properties

While we're on the subject of the `ContextUtil` class, let's look at a couple of other properties and methods that may prove useful to you in C# programming.

First, the `IsCallerInRole()` method provides for role-based security. As an input variable, this method accepts a string variable containing the name of a particular Windows 2000 security role. It returns a Boolean value indicating whether or not the user who is currently invoking the object is a member of the specified role.

In the code sample below, we've added a check to make sure that the user attempting to invoke `OrderProduct()` is an authorized member of `Administrators` role. If the user isn't in the role, `OrderProduct()` throws an exception.

```
[Transaction(TransactionOption.Required)]
public class TxTest : ServicedComponent
    ...
    public bool OrderProduct(int ProductID, int Units)
    {
        if (!ContextUtil.IsCallerInRole("Administrators"))
        {
            throw new Exception ("You are not authorized to place orders.");
        }

    // Continue Transaction Code here...
    }
```

A useful `ContextUtil` property that we've already seen is the `IsInTransaction`. `IsInTransaction` holds a Boolean value indicating whether the object is currently involved in a transaction.

As a professional C# programmer, you'll probably develop transactional components for use on a remote machine at remote installation that you do not control. To make sure that assemblies requiring transactional support are properly configured for it, you can make use of the `IsInTransaction` property of `ContextUtil`, and throw an error if this property is set to `false`. In our above example, you can test out this property by setting the `TxTest` class's attribute to `TransactionOption.Disabled`.

This completes our discussion of COM+ transactions and the `ContextUtil` class. Let's move on to object pooling.

Using Object Pooling with .NET Assemblies

It's not difficult to configure a .NET component for object pooling. Doing so entails modifying the class with an attribute.

The ObjectPooling Attribute

The attribute with which you should modify the class is `ObjectPooling`. This attribute receives four arguments:

❑ The `Enabled` argument is first. It should be assigned a value of `true`

❑ The `MinPoolSize` argument specifies the minimum number of object instances that COM+ Services should maintain in the class's object pool

❑ The `MaxPoolSize` argument specifies the maximum number of object instances that COM+ Services should maintain in the class's object pool

❑ The `CreationTimeOut` argument specifies the length of time (in milliseconds) that COM+ Services should attempt to get an object from the pool before returning a failure

Here's an example of an `ObjectPooling` attribute with all four arguments applied to a class. We'll combine this snippet into a larger code sample near the end of this section.

```
[ObjectPooling (Enabled=True, MinPoolSize=1, MaxPoolSize=100, CreationTimeout=30)]
public class CreditCard:ServicedComponent
{
```

All serviced components must inherit from the `ServicedComponent` class. To use object pooling, there are three protected methods you have to override.

❑ The `CanBePooled()` method is used by COM+ Services to ascertain whether the class can be pooled. This method should return a value of `true` to indicate that the class can be pooled. If the object cannot be pooled for any reason in its lifetime, such as an error situation from which it cannot gracefully recover, it should return `false`. This tells COM+ to discard the object, and create a new object to take its place.

❑ The `Activate()` method is invoked by COM+ Services on a pooled object just before that object is handed to a new client. Endow this method with code for any initialization that the object should do between uses.

❑ The `Deactivate()` method, `Activate()`'s counterpart, is fired by COM+ Services when the object is released by a client to return to the available pool.

The following code snippet shows a sample class configured for object pooling.

```
[ObjectPooling (Enabled=true,
                MinPoolSize=1,
                MaxPoolSize=100,
                CreationTimeout=30)]
public class ObjPoolTest : ServicedComponent
{
    public ObjPoolTest()
    {
        // EXPENSIVE INTIALIZATION DONE HERE IF REQUIRED
        // SINCE THE OBJECT IS POOLED, THIS WILL ONLY HAPPEN
        // THE FIRST TIME THIS OBJECT IS CREATED
    }
    // THIS METHOD WOULD BE INVOKED
    // BY COM SERVICES TO DETERMINE IF THE
    // OBJECT IS POOLED.
    protected override bool CanBePooled()
    {
        // YOU SHOULD RETURN true
        // UNLESS THE OBJECT SHOULD NOT BE REUSED
        return true;
    }
    // THIS METHOD WOULD BE INVOKED
    // BY COM SERVICES WHEN THE OBJECT
    // IS BEING GIVEN TO A CLIENT.
    protected override void Activate()
    {
        //INITIALIZATION CODE WOULD GO HERE.
```

```
        }

        // THIS METHOD WOULD BE INVOKED
        // BY COM SERVICES WHEN THE OBJECT IS
        // BEING RETURNED TO THE POOL.
        protected override void Deactivate()
        {
            // TERMINATION CODE WOULD GO HERE.
        }

        //THIS METHOD WOULD BE INVOKED BY THE CLIENT.
        public bool OrderProduct(int ProductID, int Units)
        {
            // CODE FOR ORDERING A PRODUCT
        }
    }
```

Using JIT Activation with .NET Assemblies

To configure a .NET class for JIT activation, you merely modify the class with the
JustInTimeActivation attribute, providing a value of true. Here, we present a simple example that
demonstrates the activation and de-activation of an object.

We simply override the Activate() and Deactivate() methods to indicate when our object is
activated and deactivated.

```
[JustInTimeActivation(true)]
    public class JitTest : ServicedComponent
    {
        public JitTest()
        {
        }

        protected override void Activate()
        {
            Console.WriteLine("Activated!!!");
        }

        protected override void Deactivate()
        {
            Console.WriteLine("De-Activated!!!");
        }
```

We have a very simple method, DoSomething(). The only thing of note here is the
DeactivateOnReturn property of ContextUtil. By setting this to true, we are setting the **done** bit
of the COM+ context ; this bit is inspected by COM+ when a method call finishes, and the object will
be deactivated if this bit is set.

```
        public int number = 0 ;

        public void DoSomething()
        {
                Console.WriteLine("This is our JIT object in action - " +
                                                "Attempt {0}.",number);

                number++;
                ContextUtil.DeactivateOnReturn = true;
        }
}
```

The attempt to increase number here also demonstrates the importance of using stateless objects with Just-In-Time activation. The object is deactivated at the end of the DoSomething() method, and any state the object has is removed from memory. The next method call to our object will activate it, but all its properties will have been re-initialized. You can witness this all with a simple test client like the following:

```
Console.WriteLine("There is no JIT object yet....");
JitTest jitObj = new JitTest();
Console.WriteLine("Now we call a method on our JIT object.");
jitObj.DoSomething();
Console.WriteLine("We have returned from the method....");
jitObj.DoSomething();
```

Note how the count is not incremented between method invocations:

```
Command Prompt

There is no JIT object yet....
Now we call a method on our JIT object.
This is our JIT object in action - Attempt 0.
We have returned from the method....
This is our JIT object in action - Attempt 0.
```

Delving deeper into COM+ Services becomes more involved than we have room for here – we have only been able to scratch the surface with our transaction example, and discussion of object pooling and Just-In-Time activation.

To further explore these COM+ Services, and the use of Messaging Services and Queued Components in .NET, we refer the reader to *Data-Centric .NET Programming with C#* (Wrox Press, ISBN 1-861005-92-x).

Summary

As we've just seen, COM+ Services offers a rich set of functionality that can be leveraged when building distributed enterprise applications. Before you embark on your next enterprise development project, take some time to become more familiar with the functionality of COM+ Services. The *Professional Windows DNA* book from Wrox Press, mentioned earlier, is a good start.

In this chapter we've looked briefly at some of the available COM+ Services, and how to register your serviced components, and seen some examples of using the automatic transaction handling and Just-In-Time activation.

COM+ Services offer a wealth of functionality that would take a long time to replicate, and even longer to completely debug. What's more, the approaches that COM+ Services take to transaction support, resource conservation, and inter-process communication are quite generic: once you've learned them, you can apply them to a wide variety of problem domains.

19

Graphics with GDI+

This is the second of the two chapters in this book that cover the elements of interacting directly with the user; displaying information on the screen and accepting user input. In Chapter 7 we focused on Windows Forms, where we learned how to display a dialog box or SDI or MDI window, and how to place various controls on it such as buttons, textboxes, and listboxes. We used these familiar, predefined controls at a high level and relied on the fact that they are able to take full responsibility for getting themselves drawn on the display device.

Although these standard controls are powerful, and are by themselves quite adequate for the complete user interface for many applications, there are situations in which you need more flexibility in your user interface. For example, you may want to draw text in a given font in a precise position in a window, display images without using a picture box control, or draw simple shapes or other graphics. None of this can be done with the controls from Chapter 7. To display that kind of output, the application must take direct responsibility for telling the operating system precisely what needs to be displayed where in its window.

Therefore, in this chapter we're going to show you how to draw a variety of items including:

- ❑   Lines and simple shapes
- ❑   Images from bitmap and other image files
- ❑   Text

In the process, we'll also need to use a variety of helper objects including pens (to define the characteristics of lines), brushes (to define how areas are filled in), and fonts (to define the shape of the characters of text). We'll also go into some detail on how devices interpret and display different colors.

We'll start, however, by discussing a technology called **GDI+**. GDI+ consists of the set of .NET base classes that are available to carry out custom drawing on the screen. These classes arrange for the appropriate instructions to be sent to graphics device drivers to ensure the correct output is placed on the monitor screen (or printed to a hard copy).

Understanding Drawing Principles

In this section, we'll examine the basic principles that we need to understand in order to start drawing to the screen. We'll start by giving an overview of GDI, the underlying technology on which GDI+ is based, and see how it and GDI+ are related. Then we'll move on to a couple of simple examples.

GDI and GDI+

In general, one of the strengths of Windows – and indeed of modern operating systems in general – lies in their ability to abstract the details of particular devices away from the developer. For example, you don't need to understand anything about your hard drive device driver in order to programmatically read and write files to disk; you simply call the appropriate methods in the relevant .NET classes (or in pre-.NET days, the equivalent Windows API functions). This principle is also very true when it comes to drawing. When the computer draws anything to the screen, it does so by sending instructions to the video card. However, there are many hundreds of different video cards on the market, most of which have different instruction sets and capabilities. If you had to take that into account, and write specific code for each video driver, writing any such application would be an almost impossible task. This is why the Windows **Graphical Device Interface** (**GDI**) has always been around since the earliest versions of Windows.

GDI provides a layer of abstraction, hiding the differences between the different video cards. You simply call the Windows API function to do the specific task, and internally the GDI figures out how to get your particular video card to do whatever it is you want. Not only this, but if you have several display devices – monitors and printers, say – GDI achieves the remarkable feat of making your printer look the same as your screen as far as your application is concerned. If you want to print something instead of displaying it, you simply inform the system that the output device is the printer and then call the same API functions in exactly the same way.

As you can see, the DC is a very powerful object and you won't be surprised to learn that under GDI *all* drawing had to be done through a device context. The DC was even used for operations that don't involve drawing to the screen or to any hardware device, such as modifying images in memory.

Although GDI exposes a relatively high-level API to developers, it is still an API that is based on the old Windows API, with C-style functions. **GDI+** to a large extent sits as a layer between GDI and your application, providing a more intuitive, inheritance-based object model. Although GDI+ is basically a wrapper around GDI, Microsoft has been able through GDI+ to provide new features and claims to have made some performance improvements.

The GDI+ part of the .NET base class library is huge, and we will scarcely scratch the surface of its features in this chapter. That's a deliberate decision, because trying to cover more than a tiny fraction of the library would have effectively turned this chapter into a huge reference guide that simply listed classes and methods. It's more important to understand the fundamental principles involved in drawing, so that you will be in a good position to explore the classes available yourself. Full lists of all the classes and methods available in GDI+ are of course available in the MSDN documentation.

Developers coming from a VB background, in particular, are likely to find the concepts involved in drawing quite unfamiliar, since VB's focus lies so strongly in controls that handle their own painting. Those coming from a C++/MFC background are likely to be in more comfortable territory since MFC does require developers to take control of more of the drawing process, using GDI. However, even if you have a good background in GDI, you'll find a lot of the material is new.

GDI+ Namespaces

Here's an overview of the main namespaces you'll need to look in to find the GDI+ base classes:

Namespace	Contains
System.Drawing	Most of the classes, structs, enums, and delegates concerned with the basic functionality of drawing
System.Drawing.Drawing2D	Provides most of the support for advanced 2D and vector drawing, including antialiasing, geometric transformations, and graphics paths
System.Drawing.Imaging	Various classes that assist in the manipulation of images (bitmaps, GIF files, and so on)
System.Drawing.Printing	Classes to assist when specifically targeting a printer or print preview window as the "output device"
System.Drawing.Design	Some predefined dialog boxes, property sheets, and other user interface elements concerned with extending the design-time user interface
System.Drawing.Text	Classes to perform more advanced manipulation of fonts and font families

You should note that almost all of the classes and structs that we use in this chapter will be taken from the System.Drawing namespace.

Device Contexts and the Graphics Object

In GDI, the way that you identify which device you want your output to go to is through an object known as the **device context (DC).** The DC stores information about a particular device and is able to translate calls to the GDI API functions into whatever instructions need to be sent to that device. You can also query the device context to find out what the capabilities of the corresponding device are (for example, whether a printer prints in color or only black and white), so you can adjust your output accordingly. If you ask the device to do something it's not capable of, the DC will normally detect this, and take appropriate action (which depending on the situation might mean throwing an error or modifying the request to get the closest match that the device is actually capable of).

However, the DC doesn't only deal with the hardware device. It acts as a bridge to Windows and is able to take account of any requirements or restrictions placed on the drawing by Windows. For example, if Windows knows that only a portion of your application's window needs to be redrawn, the DC can trap and nullify attempts to draw outside that area. Due to the DC's relationship with Windows, working through the device context can simplify your code in other ways.

For example, hardware devices need to be told where to draw objects, and they usually want coordinates relative to the top left corner of the screen (or output device). Usually, however, your application will be thinking of drawing something at a certain position within the client area (the area reserved for drawing) of its own window, possibly using its own coordinate system. Since the window might be positioned anywhere on the screen, and a user might move it at any time, translating between the two coordinate systems is potentially a difficult task. However, the DC always knows where your window is and is able to perform this translation automatically.

With GDI+, the device context is wrapped up in the .NET base class `System.Drawing.Graphics`. Most drawing is done by calling methods on an instance of `Graphics`. In fact, since the `Graphics` class is the class that is responsible for actually handling most drawing operations, very little gets done in GDI+ that doesn't involve a `Graphics` instance somewhere, so understanding how to manipulate this object is the key to understanding how to draw to display devices with GDI+.

Drawing Shapes

We're going to start off with a short example, `DisplayAtStartup`, to illustrate drawing to an application's main window. The examples in this chapter are all created in Visual Studio.NET as C# Windows applications. Recall that for this type of project the code wizard gives us a class called `Form1`, derived from `System.Windows.Form`, which represents the application's main window. Unless otherwise stated, in all code samples, new or modified code means code that we've added to the wizard-generated code.

> *In .NET usage, when we are talking about applications that display various controls, the terminology* form *has largely replaced* window *to represent the rectangular object that occupies an area of the screen on behalf of an application. In this chapter, we've tended to stick to the term* window, *since in the context of manually drawing items it's rather more meaningful. We'll also talk about the Form when we're referring to the .NET class used to instantiate the form/window. Finally, we'll use the terms drawing and painting interchangeably to describe the process of displaying some item on the screen or other display device.*

The first example will simply create a form and draw to it in the constructor, when the form starts up. I should say at the start that this is not actually the best or the correct way to draw to the screen – we'll quickly find that this example has a problem in that it is unable to redraw anything when it needs to after starting up. However the sample will illustrate quite a few points about drawing without our having to do very much work.

For this sample, we start Visual Studio .NET and create a Windows application. We first set the background color of the form to white. We've put this line in the `InitializeComponent()` method so that Visual Studio .NET recognizes the line and is able to alter the design view appearance of the form. We could have used the design view to set the background color, but this would have resulted in pretty much the same line being added automatically:

```
private void InitializeComponent()
{
    this.components = new System.ComponentModel.Container();
    this.Size = new System.Drawing.Size(300,300);
    this.Text = "Display At Startup";

    this.BackColor = Color.White;
```

Then we add code to the Form1 constructor. We create a Graphics object using the Form's CreateGraphics() method. This Graphics object contains the Windows DC we need to draw with. The device context created is associated with the display device, and also with this window:

```
public Form1()
{
    InitializeComponent();

    Graphics dc = this.CreateGraphics();
    this.Show();
    Pen bluePen = new Pen(Color.Blue, 3);
    dc.DrawRectangle(bluePen, 0,0,50,50);
    Pen redPen = new Pen(Color.Red, 2);
    dc.DrawEllipse(redPen, 0, 50, 80, 60);
}
```

As you can see, we then call the Show() method to display the window. This is really a fudge to force the window to display immediately, because we can't actually do any drawing until the window has been displayed – there's nothing to draw onto.

Finally, we display a rectangle, at coordinates (0,0), and with width and height 50, and an ellipse with coordinates (0,50) and with width 80 and height 50. Note that coordinates (x,y) means x pixels to the right and y pixels down from the top left corner of the client area of the window – and these are the coordinates of the top left corner of the shape being displayed:

The overloads that we are using of the DrawRectangle() and DrawEllipse() methods each take five parameters. The first parameter of each is an instance of the class System.Drawing.Pen. A Pen is one of a number of supporting objects to help with drawing – it contains information about how lines are to be drawn. Our first pen says that lines should be blue and with a width of 3 pixels, the second says that lines should be red and have a width of 2 pixels. The final four parameters are coordinates and size. For the rectangle, they represent the (x,y) coordinates of the top left hand corner of the rectangle, and its width and height. For the ellipse these numbers represent the same thing, except that we are talking about a hypothetical rectangle that the ellipse just fits into, rather than the ellipse itself.

Running this code gives this result:

I know – the book's printed in grayscale. As with all the screenshots in this chapter, you'll just have to take my word for it that the colors are correct. Or you can always try running the examples yourself!

This screenshot demonstrates a couple of points. First, you can see clearly what the client area of the window means. It's the white area – the area that has been affected by our setting the BackColor property. And notice that the rectangle nestles up in the corner of this area, as you'd expect when we specified coordinates of (0,0) for it. Second, notice how the top of the ellipse overlaps the rectangle slightly, which you wouldn't expect from the coordinates we gave in the code. That results from where Windows places the lines that border the rectangle and ellipse. By default, Windows will try to center the line on where the border of the shape is – that's not always possible to do exactly, because the line has to be drawn on pixels (obviously), but normally the border of each shape theoretically lies between two pixels. The result is that lines that are 1 pixel thick will get drawn just *inside* the top and left sides of a shape, but just *outside* the bottom and right sides – which means that shapes that strictly speaking are next to each other will have their borders overlap by one pixel. We've specified wider lines; therefore the overlap is greater. It is possible to change the default behavior by setting the Pen.Alignment property, as detailed in the MSDN documentation, but for our purposes the default behavior is adequate.

Unfortunately, if you actually run the sample you'll notice the form behaves a bit strangely. It's fine if you just leave it there, and it's fine if you drag it around the screen with the mouse. Try minimizing it then restoring it, however, and our carefully drawn shapes just vanish! The same thing happens if you drag another window across the sample. If you drag another window across it so that it only obscures a portion of our shapes, then drag the other window away again, you'll find the temporarily obscured portion has disappeared and you're left with half an ellipse or half a rectangle!

So what's going on? The problem arises when part of a window gets hidden, because Windows usually immediately discards all the information concerning exactly what was being displayed there. It has to – otherwise the memory usage for storing screen data would be astronomical. A typical computer might be running with the video card set to display 1024 x 768 pixels, perhaps with 24-bit color mode. We'll cover what 24-bit color means later in the chapter, but for now I'll say that implies that each pixel on the screen occupies 3 bytes. That means 2.25MB to display the screen. However, it's not uncommon for a user to sit there working, with 10 or 20 minimized windows in the taskbar. Let's do a worst-case scenario: 20 windows, each of which would occupy the whole screen if it wasn't minimized. If Windows actually stored the visual information those windows contained, ready for when the user restored them, you'd be talking about 45MB! These days, a good graphics card might have 64MB of memory and be able to cope with that, but it's only a couple of years ago that 4MB was considered generous in a graphics card – and the excess would need to be stored in the computer's main memory. A lot of people still have old machines – for example, my backup computer that has a 4 MB graphics card. Clearly it wouldn't be practical for Windows to manage its user interface like that.

The moment any part of a window gets hidden, the 'hidden' pixels get lost, because Windows frees the memory that was holding those pixels. It does, however, note that a portion of the window is hidden, and when it detects that it is no longer hidden, it asks the application that owns the window to redraw its contents. There are a couple of exceptions to this rule – generally for cases in which a small portion of a window is hidden very temporarily (a good example is when you select an item from the main menu and that menu item drops down, temporarily obscuring part of the window below). In general, however, you can expect that if part of your window gets hidden, your application will need to redraw it later.

That's the source of the problem for our sample application. We placed our drawing code in the Form1 constructor, which is called just once when the application starts up, and you can't call the constructor again to redraw the shapes when required later on.

In Chapter 7, when we covered controls, we didn't need to know about any of that. This is because the standard controls are pretty sophisticated and they are able to redraw themselves correctly whenever Windows asks them to. That's one reason why when programming controls you don't need to worry about the actual drawing process at all. If we are taking responsibility for drawing to the screen in our application then we also need to make sure our application will respond correctly whenever Windows asks it to redraw all or part of its window. In the next section, we will modify our sample to do just that.

Painting Shapes Using OnPaint()

If the above explanation has made you worried that drawing your own user interface is going to be terribly complicated, don't worry. Getting your application to redraw itself when necessary is actually quite easy.

Windows notifies an application that some repainting needs to be done by raising a Paint event. Interestingly, the Form class has already implemented a handler for this event so you don't need to add one yourself. The Form1 handler for the Paint event will at some point in its processing call up a virtual method, OnPaint(), passing to it a single PaintEventArgs parameter. This means that all we need to do is override OnPaint() to perform our painting.

Although we've chosen to work by overriding OnPaint(), it's equally possible to achieve the same results by simply adding our own event handler for the Paint event (a Form1_Paint() method, say) – in much the same way as you would for any other Windows Forms event. This other approach is arguably more convenient, since you can add a new event handler through the VS .NET properties window, saving yourself from typing some code. However, our approach, of overriding OnPaint(), is slightly more flexible in terms of letting us control when the call to the base class window processing occurs, and is the approach recommended in the documentation. We suggest you use this approach for consistency.

We'll create a new Windows Application called DrawShapes to do this. As before, we set the background color to white using the Properties Window. We'll also change the Form's text to 'DrawShapes sample'. Then we add the following code to the generated code for the Form1 class:

```
protected override void OnPaint( PaintEventArgs e )
{
    base.OnPaint(e);
    Graphics dc = e.Graphics;
    Pen bluePen = new Pen(Color.Blue, 3);
    dc.DrawRectangle(bluePen, 0,0,50,50);
    Pen redPen = new Pen(Color.Red, 2);
    dc.DrawEllipse(redPen, 0, 50, 80, 60);
}
```

Notice that OnPaint() is declared as protected, because it is normally used internally within the class, so there's no reason for any other code outside the class to know about its existence.

PaintEventArgs is a class that is derived from the EventArgs class normally used to pass in information about events. PaintEventArgs has two additional properties, of which the more important is a Graphics instance, already primed and optimized to paint the required portion of the window. This means that you don't have to call CreateGraphics() to get a DC in the OnPaint() method – you've already been provided with one. We'll look at the other additional property soon – it contains more detailed information about which area of the window actually needs repainting.

In our implementation of OnPaint(), we first get a reference to the Graphics object from PaintEventArgs, then we draw our shapes exactly as we did before. At the end we call the base class's OnPaint() method. This step is important. We've overridden OnPaint() to do our own painting, but it's possible that Windows may have some additional work of its own to do in the painting process – any such work will be dealt with in an OnPaint() method in one of the .NET base classes.

> *For this example, you'll find that removing the call to base.OnPaint() doesn't seem to have any effect, but don't ever be tempted to leave this call out. You might be stopping Windows from doing its work properly and the results could be unpredictable.*

OnPaint() will also be called when the application first starts up and our window is displayed for the first time, so there is no need to duplicate the drawing code in the constructor.

Running this code gives the same results initially as for our previous example – except that now our application behaves itself properly when you minimize it or hide parts of the window.

Using the Clipping Region

Our DrawShapes sample from the last section illustrates the main principles involved with drawing to a window, although it's not very efficient. The reason is that it attempts to draw everything in the window, irrespective of how much needs to be drawn. Consider the situation shown in this screenshot. I ran the DrawShapes example, but while it was on the screen I opened another window and moved it over the DrawShapes form, so it hid part of it.

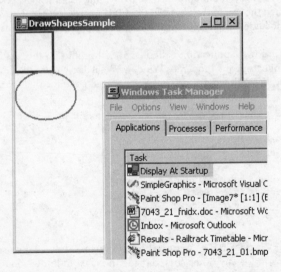

So far, so good. However, when I move the overlapping window so that the DrawShapes window is fully visible again, Windows will as usual send a Paint event to the form, asking it to repaint itself. The rectangle and ellipse both lie in the top left corner of the client area, and so were visible all the time; therefore, there's actually nothing that needs to be done in this case apart from repaint the white background area. However, Windows doesn't know that, so it thinks it should raise the Paint event, resulting in our OnPaint() implementation being called. OnPaint() will then unnecessarily attempt to redraw the rectangle and ellipse.

Actually, in this case, the shapes will not get repainted. The reason is to do with the device context. Windows has pre-initialized the device context with information concerning what area actually needed repainting. In the days of GDI, the region that is marked for repainting used to be known as the **invalidated region**, but with GDI+ the terminology has largely changed to **clipping region**. The device context knows what this region is; therefore, it will intercept any attempts to draw outside this region, and not pass the relevant drawing commands on to the graphics card. That sounds good, but there's still a potential performance hit here. We don't know how much processing the device context had to do before it figured out that the drawing was outside the invalidated region. In some cases it might be quite a lot, since calculating which pixels need to be changed to what color can be very processor-intensive (although a good graphics card will provide hardware acceleration to help with some of this).

The bottom line to this is that asking the Graphics instance to do some drawing outside the invalidated region is almost certainly wasting processor time and slowing your application down. In a well designed application, your code will actively help the device context out by carrying out a few simple checks, to see if the proposed drawing work is likely to be actually needed, before it calls the relevant Graphics instance methods. In this section we're going to code up a new example – DrawShapesWithClipping – by modifying the DisplayShapes example to do just that. In our OnPaint() code, we'll do a simple test to see whether the invalidated region intersects the area we need to draw in, and only call the drawing methods if it does.

First, we need to obtain the details of the clipping region. This is where an extra property, ClipRectangle, on the PaintEventArgs comes in. ClipRectangle contains the coordinates of the region to be repainted, wrapped up in an instance of a struct, System.Drawing.Rectangle. Rectangle is quite a simple struct – it contains four properties of interest: Top, Bottom, Left, and Right. These respectively contain the vertical coordinates of the top and bottom of the rectangle, and the horizontal coordinates of the left and right edges.

Next, we need to decide what test we'll use to determine whether drawing should take place. We'll go for a simple test here. Notice, that in our drawing, the rectangle and ellipse are both entirely contained within the rectangle that stretches from point (0,0) to point (80,130) of the client area; actually, point (82,132) to be on the safe side, since we know that the lines may stray a pixel or so outside this area. So we'll check whether the top left corner of the clipping region is inside this rectangle. If it is, we'll go ahead and redraw. If it isn't, we won't bother.

Here is the code to do this:

```
protected override void OnPaint( PaintEventArgs e )
{
    base.OnPaint(e);
    Graphics dc = e.Graphics;

    if (e.ClipRectangle.Top < 132 && e.ClipRectangle.Left < 82)
    {
        Pen bluePen = new Pen(Color.Blue, 3);
        dc.DrawRectangle(bluePen, 0,0,50,50);
        Pen redPen = new Pen(Color.Red, 2);
        dc.DrawEllipse(redPen, 0, 50, 80, 60);
    }
}
```

Note that what gets displayed is exactly the same as before – but performance is improved now by the early detection of some cases in which nothing needs to be drawn. Notice, also that we've chosen a fairly crude test of whether to proceed with the drawing. A more refined test might be to check separately, whether the rectangle needs to be drawn, or whether the ellipse needs to be redrawn, or both. However, there's a balance here. You can make your tests in OnPaint() more sophisticated, improving performance, but you'll also make your own OnPaint() code more complex. It's almost always worth putting some test in, because you've written the code so you understand far more about what is being drawn than the Graphics instance, which just blindly follows drawing commands.

Measuring Coordinates and Areas

In our last example, we encountered the base struct, Rectangle, which is used to represent the coordinates of a rectangle. GDI+ actually uses several similar structures to represent coordinates or areas, and we're at a convenient point in the chapter to go over the main ones. We'll look at the following structs, which are all defined in the System.Drawing namespace:

Struct	Main Public Properties
struct Point struct PointF	X, Y
struct Size struct SizeF	Width, Height
struct Rectangle struct RectangleF	Left, Right, Top, Bottom, Width, Height, X, Y, Location, Size

Note that many of these objects have a number of other properties, methods, or operator overloads not listed here. In this section we'll just discuss the most important ones.

Point and PointF

We'll look at Point first. Point is conceptually the simplest of these structs. Mathematically, it's completely equivalent to a 2D vector. It contains two public integer properties, which represent how far you move horizontally and vertically from a particular location (perhaps on the screen). In other words, look at this diagram:

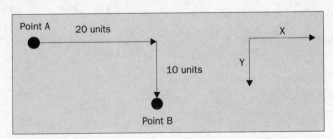

In order to get from point A to point B, you move 20 units across and 10 units down, marked as x and y on the diagram as this is how they are commonly referred to. We could create a `Point` struct that represents that as follows:

```
Point ab = new Point(20, 10);
Console.WriteLine("Moved {0} across, {1} down", ab.X, ab.Y);
```

X and Y are read-write properties, which means you can also set the values in a `Point` like this:

```
Point ab = new Point();
ab.X = 20;
ab.Y = 10;
Console.WriteLine("Moved {0} across, {1} down", ab.X, ab.Y);
```

Note that although conventionally horizontal and vertical coordinates are referred to as x and y coordinates (lowercase), the corresponding `Point` properties are X and Y (uppercase) because the usual convention in C# is for public properties to have names that start with an uppercase letter.

`PointF` is essentially identical to `Point`, except that X and Y are of type `float` instead of `int`. `PointF` is used when the coordinates are not necessarily integer values. A cast has been defined so that you can implicitly convert from `Point` to `PointF`. (Note that because `Point` and `PointF` are structs, this cast involves actually making a copy of the data). There is no corresponding reverse case – to convert from `PointF` to `Point` you have to explicitly copy the values across, or use one of three conversion methods, `Round()`, `Truncate()`, and `Ceiling()`:

```
PointF abFloat = new PointF(20.5F, 10.9F);
// converting to Point
Point ab = new Point();
ab.X = (int)abFloat.X;
ab.Y = (int)abFloat.Y;
Point ab1 = Point.Round(abFloat);
Point ab2 = Point.Truncate(abFloat);
Point ab3 = Point.Ceiling(abFloat);

// but conversion back to PointF is implicit
PointF abFloat2 = ab;
```

You may be wondering what a "unit" is measured in. By default, GDI+ will interpret units as pixels along the screen (or printer, whatever the graphics device is) – so that's how the `Graphics` object methods will view any coordinates that they get passed as parameters. For example, the point new `Point(20,10)` represents 20 pixels across the screen and 10 pixels down. Usually these pixels will be measured from the top left corner of the client area of the window, as has been the case in our examples up to now. However, that won't always be the case – for example, on some occasions you may wish to draw relative to the top left corner of the whole window (including its border), or even to the top left corner of the screen. In most cases, however, unless the documentation tells you otherwise, you can assume you're talking pixels relative to the top left corner of the client area.

We'll have more to say on this subject later on, after we've examined scrolling, when we mention the three different coordinate systems in use, world, page, and device coordinates.

Size and SizeF

Like `Point` and `PointF`, sizes come in two varieties. The `Size` struct is for when you are using `int`s; `SizeF` is available if you need to use `float`s. Otherwise `Size` and `SizeF` are identical. We'll focus on the `Size` struct here.

In many ways the `Size` struct is identical to the `Point` struct. It has two integer properties that represent a distance horizontally and a distance vertically – the main difference is that instead of `X` and `Y`, these properties are named `Width` and `Height`. We can represent our earlier diagram by:

```
Size ab = new Size(20,10);
Console.WriteLine("Moved {0} across, {1} down", ab.Width, ab.Height);
```

Although strictly speaking, a `Size` mathematically represents exactly the same thing as a `Point`; conceptually it is intended to be used in a slightly different way. A `Point` is used when we are talking about where something is, and a `Size` is used when we are talking about how big it is. However, because `Size` and `Point` are so closely related, there are even supported explicit conversions between these two:

```
Point point = new Point(20, 10);
Size size = (Size) point;
Point anotherPoint = (Point) size;
```

As an example, think about the rectangle we drew earlier, with top left coordinate (0,0) and size (50,50). The size of this rectangle is (50,50) and might be represented by a `Size` instance. The bottom right corner is also at (50,50), but that would be represented by a `Point` instance. To see the difference, suppose we drew the rectangle in a different location, so it's top left coordinate was at (10,10):

```
dc.DrawRectangle(bluePen, 10,10,50,50);
```

Now the bottom right corner is at coordinate (60,60), but the size is unchanged – that's still (50,50).

The addition operator has been overloaded for `Point`s and `Size`s, so that it is possible to add a `Size` to a `Point` giving another `Point`:

```
static void Main(string[] args)
{
    Point topLeft = new Point(10,10);
    Size rectangleSize = new Size(50,50);
    Point bottomRight = topLeft + rectangleSize;
    Console.WriteLine("topLeft = " + topLeft);
    Console.WriteLine("bottomRight = " + bottomRight);
    Console.WriteLine("Size = " + rectangleSize);
}
```

This code, running as a simple console application, called `PointsAndSizes`, produces this output:

```
Command Prompt                                                    _ □ X
C:\ProCSharp\GdiPlus>PointsAndSizes
topLeft = {X=10,Y=10}
bottomRight = {X=60,Y=60}
Size = {Width=50, Height=50}


C:\ProCSharp\GdiPlus>_
```

Notice that this output also shows how the ToString() method has been overridden in both Point and Size to display the value in {X, Y} format.

It is also possible to subtract a Size from a Point to give a Point, and you can add two Sizes together, giving another Size. It is not possible, however, to add a Point to another Point. Microsoft decided that adding Points doesn't conceptually make sense, and so chose not to supply any overload to the + operator that would have allowed that.

You can also explicitly cast a Point to a Size and vice versa:

```
Point topLeft = new Point(10,10);
Size s1 = (Size)topLeft;
Point p1 = (Point)s1;
```

With this cast s1.Width is assigned the value of topLeft.X, and s1.Height is assigned the value of topLeft.Y. Hence, s1 contains (10,10). p1 will end up storing the same values as topLeft.

Rectangle and RectangleF

These structures represent a rectangular region (usually of the screen). Just as with Point and Size, we'll only consider the Rectangle struct here. RectangleF is basically identical except that those of its properties that represent dimensions all use float, whereas those of Rectangle use int.

A Rectangle can be thought of as composed of a point, representing the top left corner of the rectangle, and a Size, which represents how large it is. One of its constructors actually takes a Point and a Size as its parameters. We can see this by rewriting our earlier code from the DrawShapes sample that draws a rectangle:

```
Graphics dc = e.Graphics;
Pen bluePen = new Pen(Color.Blue, 3);
Point topLeft = new Point(0,0);
Size howBig = new Size(50,50);
Rectangle rectangleArea = new Rectangle(topLeft, howBig);
dc.DrawRectangle(bluePen, rectangleArea);
```

This code also uses an alternative override of Graphics.DrawRectangle(), which takes a Pen and a Rectangle struct as its parameters.

You can also construct a Rectangle by supplying the top left horizontal coordinate, top left vertical coordinate, width, and height separately, and in that order, as individual numbers:

```
Rectangle rectangleArea = new Rectangle(0, 0, 50, 50)
```

`Rectangle` makes quite a few read-write properties available to set or extract its dimensions in different combinations:

Property	Description
int Left	x-coordinate of left-hand edge
int Right	x-coordinate of right-hand edge
int Top	y-coordinate of top
int Bottom	y-coordinate of bottom
int X	same as Left
int Y	same as Top
int Width	width of rectangle
int Height	height of rectangle
Point Location	top left corner
Size Size	size of rectangle

Note that these properties are not all independent – for example setting `Width` will also affect the value of `Right`.

Region

We'll mention the existence of the `System.Drawing.Region` class here, though we don't have space to go details in this book. `Region` represents an area of the screen that has some complex shape. For example the shaded area in the diagram could be represented by `Region`:

As you can imagine, the process of initializing a `Region` instance is itself quite complex. Broadly speaking, you can do it by indicating either what component simple shapes make up the region or what path you take as you trace round the edge of the region. If you do need to start working with areas like this, then it's worth looking up the `Region` class.

A Note about Debugging

We're just about ready to do some more advanced drawing now. First,however, I just want to say a few things about debugging. If you have a go at setting break points in the examples in this chapter you will quickly notice that debugging drawing routines isn't quite as simple as debugging other parts of your program. This is because entering and leaving the debugger often causes Paint messages to be sent to your application. The result can be that setting a breakpoint in your OnPaint() override simply causes your application to keep painting itself over and over again, so it's unable to do anything else.

A typical scenario is as follows. You want to find out why your application is displaying something incorrectly, so you set a break point in OnPaint(). As expected, the application hits the break point and the debugger comes in, at which point your developer environment MDI window comes to the foreground. If you're anything like me, you probably have the developer environments set to full screen display so you can more easily view all the debugging information, which means it always completely hides the application you are debugging.

Moving on, you examine the values of some variables and hopefully find out something useful. Then you hit *F5* to tell the application to continue, so that you can go on to see what happens when the application displays something else, after it's done some processing. Unfortunately, the first thing that happens is that the application comes to the foreground and Windows efficiently detects that the form is visible again and promptly sends it a Paint event. This means, of course, that your break point gets hit again straight away. If that's what you want fine, but more commonly what you really want is to hit the breakpoint *later,* when the application is drawing something more interesting, perhaps after you've selected some menu option to read in a file or in some other way changed what gets displayed. It looks like you're stuck. Either you don't have a break point in OnPaint() at all, or your application can never get beyond the point where it's displaying its initial startup window.

There are a couple of ways around this problem.

If you have a big screen the easiest way is simply to keep your developer environment window tiled rather than maximized and keep it well away from your application window – so your application never gets hidden in the first place. Unfortunately, in most cases that is not a practical solution, because that would make your developer environment window too small. An alternative that uses the same principle is to have your application declare itself as the topmost application while you are debugging. You do this by setting a property in the Form class, TopMost, which you can easily do in the InitializeComponent() method:

```
private void InitializeComponent()
{
    this.TopMost = true;
```

You can also set this property through the Properties Window in Visual Studio .NET.

Being a TopMost window means your application can never be hidden by other windows (except other topmost windows). It always remains above other windows even when another application has the focus. This is how the Task Manager behaves.

Even with this technique you have to be careful, because you can never quite be certain when Windows might decide for some reason to raise a `Paint` event. If you really want to trap some problem that occurs in `OnPaint()` for some specific circumstance (for example, the application draws something after you select a certain menu option, and something goes wrong at that point), then the best way to do this is to place some dummy code in `OnPaint()` that tests some condition, which will only be `true` in the specified circumstances – and then place the break point inside the `if` block, like this:

```
protected override void OnPaint( PaintEventArgs e )
{
    // Condition() evaluates to true when we want to break
    if ( Condition() == true)
    {
        int ii = 0;   // <-- SET BREAKPOINT HERE!!!
    }
}
```

This is effectively a quick-and-easy way of putting in a conditional break point.

Drawing Scrollable Windows

Our earlier `DrawShapes` sample worked very well, because everything we needed to draw fitted into the initial window size. In this section we're going to look at what we need to do if that's not the case.

We shall expand our `DrawShapes` sample to demonstrate scrolling. To make things a bit more realistic, we'll start by creating an example, `BigShapes`, in which we will make the rectangle and ellipse a bit bigger. Also, while we're at it we'll demonstrate how to use the `Point`, `Size`, and `Rectangle` structs by using them to assist in defining the drawing areas. With these changes, the relevant part of the `Form1` class looks like this:

```
// member fields
private Point rectangleTopLeft = new Point(0, 0);
private Size rectangleSize = new Size(200,200);
private Point ellipseTopLeft = new Point(50, 200);
private Size ellipseSize = new Size(200, 150);
private Pen bluePen = new Pen(Color.Blue, 3);
private Pen redPen = new Pen(Color.Red, 2);

protected override void OnPaint( PaintEventArgs e )
{
    base.OnPaint(e);
    Graphics dc = e.Graphics;

    if (e.ClipRectangle.Top < 350 || e.ClipRectangle.Left < 250)
    {
        Rectangle rectangleArea =
            new Rectangle (rectangleTopLeft, rectangleSize);
        Rectangle ellipseArea =
            new Rectangle (ellipseTopLeft, ellipseSize);
        dc.DrawRectangle(bluePen, rectangleArea);
        dc.DrawEllipse(redPen, ellipseArea);
    }
}
```

Notice, that we've also turned the `Pen`, `Size`, and `Point` objects into member fields – this is more efficient than creating a new `Pen` every time we need to draw anything, as we have been doing up to now.

The result of running this example looks like this:

We can see a problem instantly. The shapes don't fit in our 300x300 pixel drawing area.

Normally, if a document is too large to display, an application will add scrollbars to let you scroll the window and look at a chosen part of it. This is another area in which, with the kind of user interface that we were dealing with in Chapter 7, we'd let the .NET runtime and the base classes handle everything. If your form has various controls attached to it then the `Form` instance will normally know where these controls are and it will therefore know if its window becomes so small that scrollbars become necessary. The `Form` instance will also automatically add the scrollbars for you, and not only that, but it's also able to correctly draw whichever portion of the screen you've scrolled to. In that case there is nothing you need to explicitly do in your code. In this chapter, however, we're taking responsibility for drawing to the screen; therefore, we're going to have to help the `Form` instance out when it comes to scrolling.

> *In the last paragraph we said "if a document is too large to display". This probably made you think in terms of something like a Word or Excel document. With drawing applications, however, it's better to think of the document as whatever data the application is manipulating that it needs to draw. For our current example, the rectangle and ellipse between them constitute the document.*

Getting the scrollbars added is actually very easy. The `Form` can still handle all that for us – the reason it hasn't in the above `ScrollShapes` sample is that Windows doesn't know they are needed – because it doesn't know how big an area we will want to draw in. How big an area is that? More accurately, what we need to figure out is the size of a rectangle that stretches from the top left corner of the document (or equivalently, the top left corner of the client area before we've done any scrolling), and which is just big enough to contain the entire document. In this chapter, we'll refer to this area as the document area. Looking at the diagram of the 'document' we can see that for this example the document area is (250, 350) pixels.

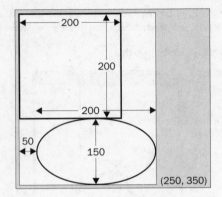

It is easy to tell the form how big the document is. We use the relevant property, `Form.AutoScrollMinSize`. Therefore we can add this code to either the `InitializeComponent()` method or the `Form1` constructor:

```
private void InitializeComponent()
{
    this.components = new System.ComponentModel.Container();
    this.Size = new System.Drawing.Size(300,300);
    this.Text = "Scroll Shapes";
    this.BackColor = Color.White;
    this.AutoScrollMinSize = new Size(250, 350);
}
```

Alternatively the `AutoScrollMinSize` property can be set through the Visual Studio .NET properties window.

Setting the minimum size at application startup and leaving it thereafter is fine in this particular application, because we know that is how big the screen area will always be. Our "document" never changes size while this particular application is running. Bear in mind, however, that if your application does things like display contents of files or something else for which the area of the screen might change, you will need to set this property at other times (and in that case you'll have to sort out the code manually – the Visual Studio .NET Properties window can only help you with the initial value that a property has when the form is constructed).

Setting `AutoScrollMinSize` is a start, but it's not yet quite enough. To see that, let's look at what our sample – which in this version is downloadable as the `ScrollShapes` sample – looks like now. Initially we get the screen that correctly displays the shapes:

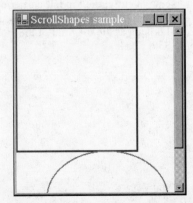

Notice that, not only has the form correctly set the scrollbars, but it's even correctly sized them to indicate what proportion of the document is currently displayed. You can try resizing the window while the sample is running – you'll find the scrollbars respond correctly, and even disappear if we make the window big enough that they are no longer needed.

However, now look at what happens if we actually use one of the scrollbars and scroll down a bit:

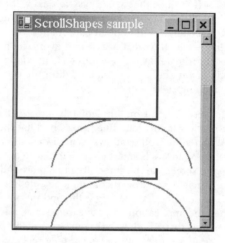

Clearly something has gone wrong!

In fact, what's gone wrong is that we haven't taken into account the position of the scrollbars in the code in our OnPaint() override. We can see this very clearly if we force the window to completely repaint itself by minimizing and restoring it. The result looks like this:

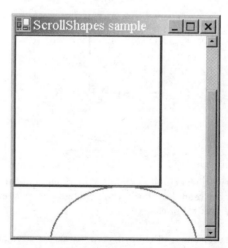

The shapes have been painted, just as before, with the top left corner of the rectangle nestled into the top left corner of the client area – just as if we hadn't moved the scrollbars at all.

Before we go over how to correct this problem, we'll take a closer look at precisely what is happening in these screenshots. Doing so is quite instructive, both because it'll help us to understand exactly how the drawing is done in the presence of scrollbars and because it'll be quite good practice. If you start using GDI+, I promise you that sooner or later, you'll find yourself presented with a strange drawing like one of those above, and having to try to figure out what has gone wrong.

We'll look at the last screenshot first since that one is easy to deal with. The ScrollShapes sample has just been restored so the entire window has just been repainted. Looking back at our code it instructs the graphics instance to draw a rectangle with top left coordinates (0,0) – relative to the top left corner of the client area of the window – which is what has been drawn. The problem is, that the graphics instance by default interprets coordinates as relative to the client window – it doesn't know anything about the scrollbars. Our code as yet does not attempt to adjust the coordinates for the scrollbar positions. The same goes for the ellipse.

Now, we can tackle the earlier screenshot, from immediately after we'd scrolled down. We notice that here the top two-thirds or so of the window look fine. That's because these were drawn when the application first started up. When you scroll windows, Windows doesn't ask the application to redraw what was already on the screen. Windows is smart enough to figure out for itself which bits of what's currently being displayed on the screen can be smoothly moved around to match where the scrollbars now are. That's a much more efficient process, since it may be able to use some hardware acceleration to do that too. The bit in this screenshot that's wrong is the bottom third of the window. This part of the window didn't get drawn when the application first appeared, since before we started scrolling it was outside the client area. This means that Windows asks our ScrollShapes application to draw this area. It'll raise a Paint event passing in just this area as the clipping rectangle. And that's exactly what our OnPaint() override has done.

One way of looking at the problem is that we are at the moment expressing our coordinates relative to the top left corner of the start of the 'document' – we need to convert them to express them relative to the top left corner of the client area instead. The following diagram should make this clear:

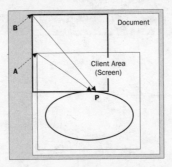

To make the diagram clearer we've actually extended the document further downwards and to the right, beyond the boundaries of the screen, but this doesn't change our reasoning. We've also assumed a small horizontal scroll as well as a vertical one.

In the diagram the thin rectangles mark the borders of the screen area and of the entire document. The thick lines mark the rectangle and ellipse that we are trying to draw. P marks some arbitrary point that we are drawing, which we're going to take as an example. When calling the drawing methods we've supplied the graphics instance with the vector from point B to (say) point P, expressed as a Point instance. We actually need to give it the vector from point A to point P.

The problem is that we don't know what the vector from A to P is. We know what B to P is – that's just the coordinates of P relative to the top left corner of the document – the position where we want to draw point P in the document. We also know what the vector from B to A is – that's just the amount we've scrolled by; this is stored in a property of the Form class called AutoScrollPosition. However, we don't know the vector from A to P.

Now, if you were good at math at school, you might remember what the solution to this is – you just have to subtract vectors. Say, for example, to get from B to P you move 150 pixels across and 200 pixels down, while to get from B to A you have to move 10 pixels across and 57 pixels down. That means to get from A to P you have to move 140 (=150 minus 10) pixels across and 143 (=200 minus 57) pixels down. The Graphics class actually implements a method that will do these calculations for us. It's called TranslateTransform(). You pass it the horizontal and vertical coordinates that say where the top left of the client area is relative to the top left corner of the document, (our AutoScrollPosition property, that is the vector from B to A in the diagram). Then the Graphics device will from then on work out all its coordinates taking into account where the client area is relative to the document.

After all that explanation, all we need to do is add this line to our drawing code:

```
dc.TranslateTransform(this.AutoScrollPosition.X, this.AutoScrollPosition.Y);
```

In fact in our example, it's a little more complicated because we are also separately testing whether we need to do any drawing by looking at the clipping region. We need to adjust this test to take the scroll position into account too. When we've done that, the full drawing code for the sample (downloadable from the Wrox Press web site as ScrollShapes) looks like this:

```
protected override void OnPaint( PaintEventArgs e )
{
   base.OnPaint(e);
  Graphics dc = e.Graphics;
   Size scrollOffset = new Size(this.AutoScrollPosition);
   if (e.ClipRectangle.Top+scrollOffset.Width < 350 ||
      e.ClipRectangle.Left+scrollOffset.Height < 250)
   {
      Rectangle rectangleArea = new Rectangle
         (rectangleTopLeft+scrollOffset, rectangleSize);
      Rectangle ellipseArea = new Rectangle
         (ellipseTopLeft+scrollOffset, ellipseSize);
      dc.DrawRectangle(bluePen, rectangleArea);
      dc.DrawEllipse(redPen, ellipseArea);
   }
}
```

Now we have our scroll code working perfectly, we can at last obtain a correctly scrolled screenshot!

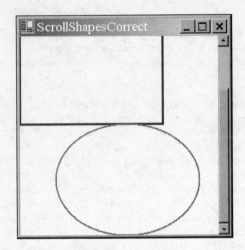

World, Page, and Device Coordinates

The distinction between measuring position relative to the top left corner of the document and measuring it relative to the top left corner of the screen (desktop), is so important that GDI+ has special names for these coordinate systems:

- ❑ **World coordinates** are the position of a point measured in pixels from the top left corner of the document

- ❑ **Page coordinates** are the position of a point measured in pixels from the top left corner of the client area

Developers familiar with GDI will note that world coordinates correspond to what in GDI were known as logical coordinates. Page coordinates correspond to what used to be known as device coordinates. Those developers should also note that the way you code up conversion between logical and device coordinates has changed in GDI+. In GDI, conversions took place via the device context, using the LPtoDP() and DPtoLP() Windows API functions. In GDI+, it's the Control class, from which both Form and all the various Windows Forms controls derive, that maintains the information needed to carry out the conversion.

GDI+ also distinguishes a third coordinate system, which is now known as **device coordinates**. Device coordinates are similar to page coordinates, except that we do not use pixels as the unit of measurement – instead we use some other unit that can be specified by the user by calling the `Graphics.PageUnit` property. Possible units, besides the default of pixels, include inches and millimeters. Although we won't use the `PageUnit` property in this chapter, it can be useful as a way of getting around the different pixel densities of devices. For example, 100 pixels on most monitors will occupy something like an inch. However, laser printers can have anything up to thousands of dpi (dots per inch) – which means that a shape specified to be 100 pixels wide will look a lot smaller when printed on it. By setting the units to, say, inches – and specifying that the shape should be 1 inch wide, you can ensure that the shape will look the same size on the different devices.

Colors

In this section, we're going to look at the ways that you can specify what color you want something to be drawn in.

Colors in GDI+ are represented by instances of the System.Drawing.Color struct. Generally, once you've instantiated this struct, you won't do much with the corresponding Color instance – just pass it to whatever other method you are calling that requires a Color. We've encountered this struct before – when we set the background color of the client area of the window in each of our samples, as well as when we set the colors of the various shapes we were displaying. The Form.BackColor property actually returns a Color instance. In this section, we'll look at this struct in more detail. In particular, we'll examine several different ways that you can construct a Color.

Red-Green-Blue (RGB) Values

The total number of colors that can be displayed by a monitor is huge – over 16 million. To be exact the number is 2 to the power 24, which works out at 16,777,216. Obviously we need some way of indexing those colors so we can indicate which of these is the color we want to display at a given pixel.

The most common way of indexing colors is by dividing them into the red, green, and blue components. This idea is based on the principle that any color that the human eye can distinguish can be constructed from a certain amount of red light, a certain amount of the green light, and a certain amount of blue light. These colors are known as **components**. In practice, it's found that if we divide the amount of each component light into 256 possible intensities, then that gives a sufficiently fine gradation to be able to display images that are perceived by the human eye to be of photographic quality. We therefore specify colors by giving the amounts of these components on a scale of 0 to 255 where 0 means that the component is not present and 255 means that it is at its maximum intensity.

We can now see where are quoted figure of 16,777,216 colors comes from, since that number is just 256 cubed.

This gives us our first way of telling GDI+ about a color. You can indicate a color's red, green, and blue values by calling the static function Color.FromArgb(). Microsoft has chosen not to supply a constructor to do this task. The reason is that there are other ways, besides the usual RGB components, to indicate a color. Because of this, Microsoft felt that the meaning of parameters passed to any constructor they defined would be open to misinterpretation:

```
Color redColor = Color.FromArgb(255,0,0);
Color funnyOrangyBrownColor = Color.FromArgb(255,155,100);
Color blackColor = Color.FromArgb(0,0,0);
Color whiteColor = Color.FromArgb(255,255,255);
```

The three parameters are respectively the quantities of red, green, and blue. There are a number of other overloads to this function, some of which also allow you to specify something called an alpha-blend (that's the A in the name of the method, FromArgb()). Alpha blending is beyond the scope of this chapter, but it allows you to paint a color semi-transparently by combining it with whatever color was already on the screen. This can give some beautiful effects and is often used in games.

The Named Colors

Constructing a `Color` using `FromArgb()` is the most flexible technique, since it literally means you can specify any color that the human eye can see. However, if you want a simple, standard, well-known color such as red or blue, it's a lot easier to just be able to name the color you want. Hence Microsoft has also provided a large number of static properties in `Color`, each of which returns a named color. It is one of these properties that we used when we set the background color of our windows to white in our samples:

```
this.BackColor = Color.White;

// has the same effect as:
// this.BackColor = Color.FromArgb(255, 255 , 255);
```

There are several hundred such colors. The full list is given in the MSDN documentation. They include all the simple colors: `Red`, `White`, `Blue`, `Green`, `Black`, and so on, as well as such delights as `MediumAquamarine`, `LightCoral`, and `DarkOrchid`. There is also a `KnownColor` enumeration, which lists the named colors.

Incidentally, although it might look that way, these named colors have not been chosen at random. Each one represents a precise set of RGB values, and they were originally chosen many years ago for use on the Internet. The idea was to provide a useful set of colors right across the spectrum whose names would be recognized by web browsers – thus saving you from having to write explicit RGB values in your HTML code. A few years ago these colors were also important because early browsers couldn't necessarily display very many colors accurately, and the named colors were supposed to provide a set of colors that would be displayed correctly by most browsers. These days that aspect is less important since modern web browsers are quite capable of displaying any RGB value correctly.

Graphics Display Modes and the Safety Palette

Although we've said that in principle monitors can display any of the over 16 million RGB colors, in practice this depends on how you've set the display properties on your computer. In Windows, there are traditionally three main color options (although some machines may provide other options depending on the hardware): true color (24-bit), high color (16-bit), and 256 colors. (On some graphics cards these days, true color is actually marked as 32-bit for reasons to do with optimizing the hardware, though in that case only 24 bits of the 32 bits are used for the color itself.)

Only true-color mode allows you to display all of the RGB colors simultaneously. This sounds the best option, but it comes at a cost: 3 bytes are needed to hold a full RGB value which means 3 bytes of graphics card memory are needed to hold each pixel that is displayed. If graphics card memory is at a premium (a restriction that's less common now than it used to be) you may choose one of the other modes. High color mode gives you 2 bytes per pixel. That's enough to give 5 bits for each RGB component. So instead of 256 gradations of red intensity you just get 32 gradations; the same for blue and green, which gives a total of 65,536 colors. That is just about enough to give apparent photographic quality on a casual inspection, though areas of subtle shading tend to be broken up a bit.

256-color mode gives you even fewer colors. However, in this mode, you get to choose which colors. What happens is that the system sets up something known as a **palette**. This is a list of 256 colors chosen from the 16 million RGB colors. Once you've specified the colors in the palette, the graphics device will be able to display just those colors. The palette can be changed at any time – but the graphics device can still only display 256 different colors on the screen at any one time. 256-color mode is only really used when high performance and video memory is at a premium. Most games will use this mode – and they can still achieve decent-looking graphics because of a very careful choice of palette.

In general, if a display device is in high-color or 256-color mode and it is asked to display a particular RGB color, it will pick the nearest mathematical match from the pool of colors that it is able to display. It's for this reason that it's important to be aware of the color modes. If you are drawing something that involves subtle shading or photographic quality images, and the user does not have 24-bit color mode selected, they may not see the image the same way you intended it. So if you're doing that kind of work with GDI+, you should test your application in different color modes. (It is also possible for your application to programmatically set a given color mode, though we won't go into that in this chapter.)

The Safety Palette

For reference, we'll quickly mention the safety palette, which is a very commonly-used default palette. The way it works is that we set six equally spaced possible values for each color component. Namely, the values 0, 51, 102, 153, 204, and 255. In other words, the red component can have any of these values. So can the green component. So can the blue component. So possible colors from the safety palette include: (0,0,0), black; (153,0,0), a fairly dark shade of red; (0, 255,102), green with a smattering of blue added; and so on. This gives us a total of 6 cubed = 216 colors. The idea is that this gives us an easy way of having a palette that contains colors from right across the spectrum and of all degrees of brightness, although in practice this doesn't actually work that well because equal mathematical spacing of color components doesn't mean equal perception of color differences by the human eye. Because the safety palette used to be widely used, however, you'll still find a fair number of applications and images exclusively use colors from the safety palette.

If you set Windows to 256-color mode, you'll find the default palette you get is the safety palette, with 20 Windows standard colors added to it, and 20 spare colors.

Pens and Brushes

In this section, we'll review two helper classes that are needed in order to draw shapes. We've already encountered the Pen class, used to tell the graphics instance how to draw lines. A related class is System.Drawing.Brush, which tells it how to fill regions. For example, the Pen is needed to draw the outlines of the rectangle and ellipse in our previous samples. If we'd needed to draw these shapes as solid, it would have been a brush that would have been used to specify how to fill them in. One aspect of both of these classes is that you will hardly ever call any methods on them. You simply construct a Pen or Brush instance with the required color and other properties, and then pass it to drawing methods that require a Pen or Brush.

We will look at brushes first, then pens.

> *Incidentally, if you've programmed using GDI before you have noticed from the first couple of examples that pens are used in a different way in GDI+. In GDI the normal practice was to call a Windows API function, SelectObject(), which actually associated a pen with the device context. That pen was then used in all drawing operations that required a pen until you informed the device context otherwise, by calling SelectObject() again. The same principle held for brushes and other objects such as fonts or bitmaps. With GDI+, as mentioned earlier, Microsoft has instead gone for a stateless model in which there is no default pen or other helper object. Rather, you simply specify with each method call the appropriate helper object to be used for that particular method.*

Brushes

GDI+ has several different kinds of brush – more than we have space to go into in this chapter, so we'll just explain the simpler ones to give you an idea of the principles. Each type of brush is represented by an instance of a class derived from the abstract class `System.Drawing.Brush`. The simplest brush, `System.Drawing.SolidBrush`, simply indicates that a region is to be filled with solid color:

```
Brush solidBeigeBrush = new SolidBrush(Color.Beige);
Brush solidFunnyOrangyBrownBrush =
                       new SolidBrush(Color.FromArgb(255,155,100));
```

Alternatively, if the brush is one of the Internet named colors you can construct the brush more simply using another class, `System.Drawing.Brushes`. `Brushes` is one of those classes that you never actually instantiate (it's got a private constructor to stop you doing that). It simply has a large number of static properties, each of which returns a brush of a specified color. You'd use `Brushes` like this:

```
Brush solidAzureBrush = Brushes.Azure;
Brush solidChocolateBrush = Brushes.Chocolate;
```

The next level of complexity is a hatch brush, which fills a region by drawing a pattern. This type of brush is considered more advanced so it's in the `Drawing2D` namespace, represented by the class `System.Drawing.Drawing2D.HatchBrush`. The `Brushes` class can't help you with hatch brushes – you'll need to construct one explicitly, by supplying the hatch style and two colors – the foreground color followed by the background color (you can omit the background color, in which case it defaults to black). The hatch style comes from an enumeration, `System.Drawing.Drawing2D.HatchStyle`. There are a large number of `HatchStyle` values available, so it's easiest to refer to the MSDN documentation for the full list. To give you an idea, typical styles include `ForwardDiagonal`, `Cross`, `DiagonalCross`, `SmallConfetti`, and `ZigZag`. Examples of constructing a hatch brush include:

```
Brush crossBrush = new HatchBrush(HatchStyle.Cross, Color.Azure);

// background color of CrossBrush is black

Brush brickBrush = new HatchBrush(HatchStyle.DiagonalBrick,
                            Color.DarkGoldenrod, Color.Cyan);
```

Solid and hatch brushes are the only brushes available under GDI. GDI+ has added a couple of new styles of brush:

❑ `System.Drawing.Drawing2D.LinearGradientBrush` fills in an area with a color that varies across the screen

❑ `System.Drawing.Drawing2D.PathGradientBrush` is similar, but in this case the color varies along a path around the region to be filled

We won't go into these brushes in this chapter. We'll note though that both can give some spectacular effects if used carefully.

Pens

Unlike brushes, pens are represented by just one class – `System.Drawing.Pen`. The pen is, however, actually slightly more complex than the brush, because it needs to indicate how thick lines should be (how many pixels wide) and, for a wide line, how to fill the area inside the line. Pens can also specify a number of other properties, which are beyond the scope of this chapter, but which include the `Alignment` property that we mentioned earlier, which indicates where in relation to the border of a shape a line should be drawn, as well as what shape to draw at the end of a line (whether to round off the shape).

The area inside a thick line can be filled with solid color, or it can be filled using a brush. Hence, a `Pen` instance may contain a reference to a `Brush` instance. This is quite powerful, as it means you can draw lines that are colored in by using – say – hatching or linear shading. There are four different ways that you can construct a `Pen` instance that you have designed yourself. You can do it by passing a color, or you can do it by passing in a brush. Both of these constructors will produce a pen with a width of one pixel. Alternatively, you can pass in a color or a brush, and additionally a `float`, which represents the width of the pen. (It needs to be a `float` in case we are using non-default units such as millimeters or inches for the `Graphics` object that will do the drawing – so we can for example specify fractions of an inch.) So for example, you can construct pens like this:

```
Brush brickBrush = new HatchBrush(HatchStyle.DiagonalBrick,
                                  Color.DarkGoldenrod, Color.Cyan);
```

```
Pen solidBluePen = new Pen(Color.FromArgb(0,0,255));
Pen solidWideBluePen = new Pen(Color.Blue, 4);
Pen brickPen = new Pen(brickBrush);
Pen brickWidePen = new Pen(brickBrush, 10);
```

Additionally, for the quick construction of pens, you can use the class `System.Drawing.Pens` which, like the `Brushes` class, simply contains a number of stock pens. These pens all have width one pixel and come in the usual sets of Internet named colors. This allows you to construct pens in this way:

```
Pen solidYellowPen = Pens.Yellow;
```

Drawing Shapes and Lines

We've almost finished the first part of the chapter, in which we've covered all the basic classes and objects required in order to draw specified shapes and so on to the screen. We'll round off by reviewing some of the drawing methods the `Graphics` class makes available, and presenting a short example that illustrates the use of several brushes and pens.

`System.Drawing.Graphics` has a large number of methods that allow you to draw various lines, outline shapes, and solid shapes. Once again there are too many to provide a comprehensive list here, but the following table gives the main ones and should give you some idea of the variety of shapes you can draw.

Method	Typical parameters	What it draws
DrawLine	Pen, start and end points	A single straight line
DrawRectangle	Pen, position, and size	Outline of a rectangle
DrawEllipse	Pen, position, and size	Outline of an ellipse
FillRectangle	Brush, position, and size	Solid rectangle
FillEllipse	Brush, position, and size	Solid ellipse
DrawLines	Pen, array of points	Series of lines, connecting each point to the next one in the array
DrawBezier	Pen, 4 points	A smooth curve through the two end points, with the remaining two points used to control the shape of the curve
DrawCurve	Pen, array of points	A smooth curve through the points
DrawArc	Pen, rectangle, two angles	Portion of circle within the rectangle defined by the angles
DrawClosedCurve	Pen, array of points	Like DrawCurve but also draws a straight line to close the curve
DrawPie	Pen, rectangle, two angles	Wedge-shaped outline within the rectangle
FillPie	Brush, rectangle, two angles	Solid wedge-shaped area within the rectangle
DrawPolygon	Pen, array of points	Like DrawLines but also connects first and last points to close the figure drawn

Before we leave the subject of drawing simple objects, we'll round off with a simple example that demonstrates the kinds of visual effect you can achieve by use of brushes. The example is called ScrollMoreShapes, and it's essentially a revision of ScrollShapes. Besides the rectangle and ellipse, we'll add a thick line and fill the shapes in with various custom brushes. We've already explained the principles of drawing so we'll present the code without too many comments. First, because of our new brushes, we need to indicate we are using the System.Drawing.Drawing2D namespace:

```
using System;
using System.Drawing;
using System.Drawing.Drawing2D;
using System.Collections;
using System.ComponentModel;
using System.Windows.Forms;
using System.Data;
```

Next some extra fields in our Form1 class, which contain details of the locations where the shapes are to be drawn, as well as various pens and brushes we will use:

```
private Rectangle rectangleBounds = new Rectangle(new Point(0,0),
                                                    new Size(200,200));
private Rectangle ellipseBounds = new Rectangle(new Point(50,200),
                                                    new Size(200,150));
private Pen bluePen = new Pen(Color.Blue, 3);
private Pen redPen = new Pen(Color.Red, 2);
private Brush solidAzureBrush = Brushes.Azure;
private Brush solidYellowBrush = new SolidBrush(Color.Yellow);
static private Brush brickBrush = new HatchBrush(HatchStyle.DiagonalBrick,
                                                    Color.DarkGoldenrod, Color.Cyan);
private Pen brickWidePen = new Pen(brickBrush, 10);
```

The brickBrush field has been declared as static, so that we can use its value to initialize the brickWidePen field. C# won't let us use one instance field to initialize another instance field, because it's not defined which one will be initialized first, but declaring the field as static solves the problem. Since only one instance of the Form1 class will be instantiated, it is immaterial whether the fields are static or instance fields.

Here is the OnPaint() override:

```
protected override void OnPaint( PaintEventArgs e )
{
   base.OnPaint(e);
   Graphics dc = e.Graphics;
   Point scrollOffset = this.AutoScrollPosition;
   dc.TranslateTransform(scrollOffset.X, scrollOffset.Y);
   if (e.ClipRectangle.Top+scrollOffset.X < 350 ||
       e.ClipRectangle.Left+scrollOffset.Y < 250)
   {
      dc.DrawRectangle(bluePen, rectangleBounds);
      dc.FillRectangle(solidYellowBrush, rectangleBounds);
      dc.DrawEllipse(redPen, ellipseBounds);
      dc.FillEllipse(solidAzureBrush, ellipseBounds);
      dc.DrawLine(brickWidePen, rectangleBounds.Location,
                           ellipseBounds.Location+ellipseBounds.Size);
   }
}
```

As before we also set the AutoScrollMinSize to (250,350). Now the results:

Notice that the thick diagonal line has been drawn on top of the rectangle and ellipse, because it was the last item to be painted.

Displaying Images

One of the most common things you may want to do with GDI+ is display an image that already exists in a file. This is actually a lot simpler than drawing your own user interface, because the image is already pre-drawn. Effectively, all you have to do is load the file and instruct GDI+ to display it. The image can be a simple line drawing, an icon, or a complex image such as a photograph. It's also possible to perform some manipulations on the image, such as stretching it or rotating it, and you can choose to display only a portion of it.

In this section, just for a change, we'll present the sample first. Then we'll discuss some of the issues you need to be aware of when displaying images. We can do this, because the code needed to display an image really is so simple.

The class we need is the .NET base class, `System.Drawing.Image`. An instance of `Image` represents one image – if you like, one picture. Reading in an image takes one line of code:

```
Image myImage = Image.FromFile("FileName");
```

`FromFile()` is a static member of `Image` and is the usual way of instantiating an image. The file can be any of the commonly-supported graphics file formats, including `.bmp`, `.jpg`, `.gif`, and `.png`.

Displaying an image is also very simple, assuming you have a suitable `Graphics` instance to hand – a simple call to either `Graphics.DrawImageUnscaled()` or `Graphics.DrawImage()` will suffice. There are quite a few overloads of these methods, allowing you a lot of flexibility in the information you supply in terms of where the image is located and how big it is to be drawn. But we will use `DrawImage()`, like this:

```
dc.DrawImage(myImage, points);
```

In this line of code, `dc` is assumed to be a `Graphics` instance, while `myImage` is the `Image` to be displayed. `points` is an array of `Point` structs, where `points[0]`, `points[1]`, and `points[2]` are the coordinates of top left, top right, and bottom left corner of the image.

> *Images are probably the area in which developers familiar with GDI will notice the biggest difference with GDI+. In GDI, displaying an image involved several nontrivial steps. If the image was a bitmap, loading it was reasonably simple, but if it was any other file type, loading it would involve a sequence of calls to OLE objects. Actually getting a loaded image onto the screen involved getting a handle to it, selecting it into a memory device context, then performing a block transfer between device contexts. Although the device contexts and handles are still there behind the scenes, and will be needed if you want to start doing sophisticated editing of the images from your code, simple tasks have now been extremely well wrapped up in the GDI+ object model.*

We'll illustrate the process of displaying an image with an example called `DisplayImage`. The example simply displays a `.bmp` file in the application's main window. To keep things simple, the path of the `.bmp` file is hard coded into the application (so if you run the example you'll need to change it to reflect the location of the file in your system). The `.bmp` file we'll display is a group photograph of attendees from a recent COMFest event.

COMFest (www.comfest.co.uk) is an informal group of developers in the UK who meet to discuss the latest technologies and swap ideas. The picture includes all the attendees at COMFest 4, except for the author of this chapter who was (conveniently) taking the picture!

As usual for this chapter, the `DisplayImage` project is a standard C# Visual Studio .NET-generated Windows application. We add the following fields to our `Form1` class:

```
Image piccy;
private Point [] piccyBounds;
```

We then load the file in the `Form1()` constructor:

```
public Form1()
{
    InitializeComponent();

    piccy =
        Image.FromFile(@"C:\ProCSharp\GdiPlus\Images\CF4Group.bmp");
    this.AutoScrollMinSize = piccy.Size;
    piccyBounds = new Point[3];
    piccyBounds[0] = new Point(0,0);            // top left
    piccyBounds[1] = new Point(piccy.Width,0);   // top right
    piccyBounds[2] = new Point(0,piccy.Height);   // bottom left
}
```

Note that the size in pixels of the image is obtained as its `Size` property, which we use to set the document area. We also set up the `piccyBounds` array, which is used to identify the position of the image on the screen. We have chosen the coordinates of the three corners to draw the image in its actual size and shape here, but if we'd wanted the image to be resized, stretched, or even sheared into a non-rectangular parallelogram, we could do so simply by changing the values of the `Points` in the `piccyBounds` array.

The image is displayed in the `OnPaint()` override:

```
protected override void OnPaint(PaintEventArgs e)
{
    base.OnPaint(e);
    Graphics dc = e.Graphics;
    dc.ScaleTransform(1.0f, 1.0f);
    dc.TranslateTransform(this.AutoScrollPosition.X, this.AutoScrollPosition.Y);
    dc.DrawImage(piccy, piccyBounds);
}
```

Finally, we'll take particular note of the modification made to the code wizard-generated `Form1.Dispose()` method:

```
protected override void Dispose(bool disposing)
{
    piccy.Dispose();
```

```
if( disposing )
{
    if (components != null)
    {
        components.Dispose();
    }
}
base.Dispose( disposing );
}
```

Disposing of the image as soon as possible when it's no longer needed is important, because images generally eat a lot of memory while in use. After `Image.Dispose()` has been called the `Image` instance no longer refers to any actual image, and so can no longer be displayed (unless you load a new image).

Running this code produces these results:

Issues When Manipulating Images

Although displaying images is very simple, it still pays to have some understanding what's going on behind the scenes.

The most important point to understand about images is that they are always rectangular. That's not just a convenience, but because of the underlying technology. It's because all modern graphics cards have hardware built-in that can very efficiently copy blocks of pixels from one area of memory to another area of memory, provided that the block of pixels represents a rectangular region. This hardware-accelerated operation can occur virtually as one single operation, and as such is extremely fast. Indeed, it is the key to modern high-performance graphics. This operation is known as a **bitmap block transfer** (or **BitBlt**). `Graphics.DrawImageUnscaled()` internally uses a `BitBlt`, which is why you can see a huge image, perhaps containing as many as a million pixels, appearing almost instantly. If the computer had to copy the image to the screen individually pixel by pixel, you'd see the image gradually being drawn over a period of up to several seconds.

`BitBlts` are very efficient; therefore almost all drawing and manipulation of images is carried out using them. Even some editing of images will be done by `BitBlt`ing portions of images between DCs that represent areas of memory. In the days of GDI, the Windows 32 API function `BitBlt()` was arguably the most important and widely used function for image manipulation, though with GDI+ the `BitBlt` operations are largely hidden by the GDI+ object model.

It's not possible to BitBlt areas of images that are not rectangular, although similar effects can be easily simulated. One way is to mark a certain color as transparent for the purposes of a BitBlt, so that areas of that color in the source image will not overwrite the existing color of the corresponding pixel in the destination device. It is also possible to specify that in the process of a BitBlt, each pixel of the resultant image will be formed by some logical operation (such as a bitwise AND) on the colors of that pixel in the source image and in the destination device before the BitBlt. Such operations are supported by hardware acceleration, and can be used to give a variety of subtle effects. We're not going to go into details of this here. We'll remark however, that the Graphics object implements another method, DrawImage(). This is similar to DrawImageUnscaled(), but comes in a large number of overloads that allow you to specify more complex forms of BitBlt to be used in the drawing process. DrawImage() also allows you to draw (BitBlt) only a specified part of the image, or to perform certain other operations on it such as scaling it (expanding or reducing it in size) as it is drawn.

Drawing Text

We've left the very important topic of displaying text until this late in the chapter because drawing text to the screen is (in general) more complex than drawing simple graphics. Although displaying a line or two of text when you're not that bothered about the appearance is extremely easy – it takes one single call to the Graphics.DrawString() method, if you are trying to display a document that has a fair amount of text in it, you rapidly find that things become a lot more complex. This is for two reasons:

❑ If you're concerned about getting the appearance just right, you need to understand fonts. Where shape drawing requires brushes and pens as helper objects, the process of drawing text correspondingly requires fonts as helper objects. And understanding fonts is not trivial task.

❑ Text needs to be very carefully laid out in the window. Users generally expect words to follow naturally from one another – to be lined up with clear spaces in between. Doing that is harder than you'd think. For a start, unlike the case for shapes, you don't usually know in advance how much space on the screen a word is going to take up. That has to be calculated (using the Graphics.MeasureString() method). Also, how much space on the screen a word occupies will affect whereabouts on the screen every subsequent word in the document gets placed. If your application does line wrapping then it'll need to carefully assess word sizes before deciding where to place the break. The next time you run Word for Windows, look carefully at the way Word is continually repositioning text as you do your work: there's a lot of complex processing going on there. The chances are that any GDI+ application you work on won't be anything like as complex as Word, but if you need to display any text then many of the same considerations still apply.

So, good quality text processing is tricky to get right, but putting a line of text on the screen, assuming you know the font and where you want it to go, is actually very simple. Therefore, the next thing we'll do is present a quick example that shows how to display a couple of pieces of text. After that, the plan for the rest of the chapter is to review some of the principles of fonts and font families before moving on to our more realistic text-processing example, the CapsEditor sample, which will demonstrate some of the issues involved when you're trying to control text layout on-screen, and will also show how to handle user input.

Simple Text Example

This example, `DisplayText`, is our usual Windows Forms effort. This time we've overridden `OnPaint()` and added member fields as follows:

```
private System.ComponentModel.Container components = null;
private Brush blackBrush = Brushes.Black;
private Brush blueBrush = Brushes.Blue;
private Font haettenschweilerFont = new Font("Haettenschweiler", 12);
private Font boldTimesFont = new Font("Times New Roman", 10, FontStyle.Bold);
private Font italicCourierFont = new Font("Courier", 11, FontStyle.Italic |
    FontStyle.Underline);

protected override void OnPaint(PaintEventArgs e)
{
    base.OnPaint(e);
    Graphics dc = e.Graphics;
    dc.DrawString("This is a groovy string", haettenschweilerFont, blackBrush,
                10, 10);
    dc.DrawString("This is a groovy string " +
                "with some very long text that will never fit in the box",
                boldTimesFont, blueBrush,
                new Rectangle(new Point(10, 40), new Size(100, 40)));
    dc.DrawString("This is a groovy string", italicCourierFont, blackBrush,
                new Point(10, 100));
}
```

Running this example produces this:

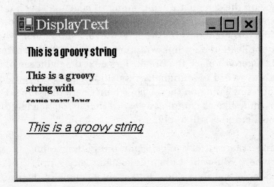

The example demonstrates the use of the `Graphics.DrawString()` method to draw items of text. `DrawString()` comes in a number of overloads, of which we demonstrate three. The different overloads all, however, require parameters that indicate the text to be displayed, the font that the string should be drawn in, and the brush that should be used to construct the various lines and curves that make up each character of text. There are a couple of alternatives for the remaining parameters. In general, however, it is possible to specify either a `Point` (or equivalently, two numbers), or a `Rectangle`.

If you specify a `Point`, the text will start with its top left corner at that `Point` and simply stretch out to the right. If you specify a `Rectangle`, then the `Graphics` instance will lay the string out inside that rectangle. If the text doesn't fit into the bounds of the rectangle, then it'll be cut off, as you see from the screenshot. Passing a rectangle to `DrawString()` means that the drawing process will take longer, as `DrawString()` will need to figure out where to put line breaks, but the result may look nicer, provided the string fits in the rectangle!

This example also shows a couple of ways of constructing fonts. You always need the name of the font, and its size (height). You can also optionally pass in various styles that modify how the text is to be drawn (bold, underline, and so on).

Fonts and Font Families

We all think intuitively that we have a fairly good understanding of fonts; after all we look at them almost all the time. A font describes exactly how each letter should be displayed. Selection of the appropriate font and providing a reasonable variety of fonts within a document are important factors in improving readability.

Oddly, our intuitive understanding usually isn't quite correct. Most people, if asked to name a font, will say things like 'Arial' or 'Times New Roman' or 'Courier'. In fact, these are not fonts at all – they are **font families**. The font family tells you in generic terms the visual style of the text, and is a key factor in the overall appearance of your application. Most of us will have become used to recognizing the styles of the most common font families, even if we're not consciously aware of this.

An actual **font** would be something like Arial 9-point italic. In other words, the size and other modifications to the text are specified as well as the font family. These modifications might include whether it is **bold,** *italic,* underlined, or displayed in SMALL CAPS or as a $_{subscript}$; this is technically referred to the **style**, though in some ways the term is misleading since the visual appearance is determined as much by the font family.

The way the size of the text is measured is by specifying its height. The height is measured in **points** – a traditional unit, which represents 1/72 of an inch (0.351 mm). So letters in a 10-point font are roughly 1/7" or 3.5 mm high. However, you won't get seven lines of 10 point text into one inch of vertical screen or paper space, because you need to allow for the spacing between the lines as well.

> *Strictly speaking, measuring the height isn't quite as simple as that, since there are several different heights that you need to consider. For example, there is the height of tall letters like the A or F (this is the measurement that we really mean when we talk about the height), the additional height occupied by any accents on letters like Å or Ñ (the **internal leading**), and the extra height below the base line needed for the tails of letters like y and g (the **descent**). However, for this chapter we won't worry about that. Once you specify the font family and the main height, these subsidiary heights are determined automatically – you can't independently choose their values.*

When you're dealing with fonts you may also encounter some other terms that are commonly used to describe certain font families.

- ❑ A **serif** font family is one that has little tick marks at the ends of many of the lines that make up the characters (These ticks are known as serifs). Times New Roman is a classic example of this.

❏ **Sans serif** font families, by contrast, don't have these ticks. Good examples of sans serif fonts are Arial, and Verdana. The lack of tick marks often gives text a blunt, in-your-face appearance, so sans serif fonts are often used for important text.

❏ A **True Type** font family is one that is defined by expressing the shapes of the curves that make up the characters in a precise mathematical manner. This means that that the same definition can be used to calculate how to draw fonts of any size within the family. These days, virtually all the fonts you will use are true type fonts. Some older font families from the days of Windows 3.1 were defined by individually specifying the bitmap for each character separately for each font size, but the use of these fonts is now discouraged.

Microsoft has provided two main classes that we need to deal with when selecting or manipulating fonts. These are:

❏ System.Drawing.Font

❏ System.Drawing.FontFamily

We have already seen the main use of the Font class. When we wish to draw text we instantiate an instance of Font and pass it to the DrawString() method to indicate how the text should be drawn. A FontFamily instance is used (surprisingly enough) to represent a family of fonts.

One use of the FontFamily class is if you know you want a font of a particular type (Serif, Sans Serif or Monospace), but don't mind which font. The static properties GenericSerif, GenericSansSerif, and GenericMonospace return default fonts that satisfy these criteria:

```
FontFamily sansSerifFont = FontFamily.GenericSansSerif;
```

Generally speaking, however, if you're writing a professional application, you will want to choose your font in a more sophisticated way than this. Most likely, you will implement your drawing code so that it checks the font families available, and selects the appropriate one, perhaps by taking the first available one on a list of preferred fonts. And if you want your application to be very user-friendly, the first choice on the list will probably be the one that the user selected last time they ran your software. Usually, if you're dealing with the most popular font families, such as Arial and Times New Roman, you'll be safe. However, if you do try to display text using a font that doesn't exist the results aren't always predictable and you're quite likely to find that Windows just substitutes the standard system font, which is very easy for the system to draw but it doesn't look very pleasant – and if it does appear in your document it's likely to give the impression of very poor-quality software.

You can find out what fonts are available on your system using a class called InstalledFontCollection, which is in the System.Drawing.Text namespace. This class implements a property, Families, which is an array of all the fonts that are available to use on your system:

```
InstalledFontCollection insFont = new InstalledFontCollection();
FontFamily [] families = insFont.Families;
foreach (FontFamily family in families)
{

    // do processing with this font family

}
```

Example: Enumerating Font Families

In this section, we will work through a quick example, EnumFontFamilies, which lists all the font families available on the system and illustrates them by displaying the name of each family using an appropriate font (the 10-point regular version of that font family). When the sample is run it will look something like this:

Of course, the results that you get will depend on what fonts you have installed on your computer.

For this sample we have as usual created a standard C# Windows Application – this time named EnumFontFamilies. We start off by adding an extra namespace to be searched. We will be using the InstalledFontCollection class, which is defined in System.Drawing.Text.

```
using System;
using System.Drawing;
using System.Drawing.Text;
```

We then add the following constant to the Form1 class:

```
private const int margin = 10;
```

margin will be the size of the left and top margin between the text and the edge of the document – it stops the text from appearing right at the edge of the client area.

This is designed as a quick-and-easy way of showing off font families; therefore the code is crude and in many cases doesn't do things the way you ought to in a real application. For example, I've just hard-coded in a guessed value for the document size of (200,1500) and set the AutoScrollMinSize property to this value using the Visual Studio .NET Properties window. Normally you would have to examine the text to be displayed to work out the document size. We will do that in the next section.

Here is the OnPaint() method:

```
protected override void OnPaint(PaintEventArgs e)
{
    base.OnPaint(e);
    int verticalCoordinate = margin;
    Point topLeftCorner;
    InstalledFontCollection insFont = new InstalledFontCollection();
    FontFamily [] families = insFont.Families;
    e.Graphics.TranslateTransform(AutoScrollPosition.X,
                                  AutoScrollPosition.Y);
    foreach (FontFamily family in families)
    {
        if (family.IsStyleAvailable(FontStyle.Regular))
        {
            Font f = new Font(family.Name, 10);
            topLeftCorner = new Point(margin, verticalCoordinate);
            verticalCoordinate += f.Height;
            e.Graphics.DrawString (family.Name, f,
                                   Brushes.Black,topLeftCorner);
            f.Dispose();
        }
    }
}
```

In this code we start off by using an `InstalledFontCollection` object to obtain an array that contains details of all the available font families. For each family, we instantiate a 10 point Font. We use a simple constructor for Font – there are many more that allow additional options to be specified. The constructor we've picked takes two parameters, the name of the family and the size of the font:

```
Font f = new Font(family.Name, 10);
```

This constructor constructs a font that has the regular style. To be on the safe side, however, we first check that this style is available for each font family before attempting to display anything using that font. This is done using the `FontFamily.IsStyleAvailable()` method, and this check is important, because not all fonts are available in all styles:

```
if (family.IsStyleAvailable(FontStyle.Regular))
```

`FontFamily.IsStyleAvailable()` takes one parameter, a `FontStyle` enumeration. This enumeration contains a number of flags that may be combined with the bitwise OR operator. The possible flags are Bold, Italic, Regular, Strikeout, and Underline.

Finally, note that we use a property of the Font class, Height, which returns the height needed to display text of that font, in order to work out the line spacing:

```
Font f = new Font(family.Name, 10);
topLeftCorner = new Point(margin, verticalCoordinate);
verticalCoordinate += f.Height;
```

Again, to keep things simple, our version of `OnPaint()` reveals some bad programming practices. For a start, we haven't bothered to check what area of the document actually needs drawing – we just try to display everything. Also, instantiating a `Font` is, as remarked earlier, a computationally intensive process, so we really ought to save the fonts rather than instantiating new copies every time `OnPaint()` is called. As a result of the way the code has been designed, you may notice that this example actually takes a noticeable time to paint itself. In order to try to conserve memory and help the garbage collector out we do, however, call `Dispose()` on each font instance after we have finished with it. If we didn't, then after 10 or 20 paint operations, there'd be a lot of wasted memory storing fonts that are no longer needed.

Editing a Text Document: The CapsEditor Sample

We now come to the extended example in this chapter. The `CapsEditor` example is designed to illustrate how the principles of drawing that we've learned up till now need to be applied in a more realistic example. The example won't require any new material, apart from responding to user input via the mouse, but it will show how to manage the drawing of text so that the application maintains performance while ensuring that the contents of the client area of the main window are always kept up to date.

The `CapsEditor` program is functionally quite simple. It allows the user to read in a text file, which is then displayed line by line in the client area. If the user double-clicks on any line, that line will be changed to all uppercase. That's literally all the sample does. Even with this limited set of features, we'll find that the work involved in making sure everything gets displayed in the right place while considering performance issues is quite complex. In particular, we have a new element here, that the contents of the document can change – either when the user selects the menu option to read a new file, or when they double-click to capitalize a line. In the first case we need to update the document size so the scrollbars still work correctly, and we have to redisplay everything. In the second case, we need to check carefully whether the document size is changed, and what text needs to be redisplayed.

We'll start by reviewing the appearance of `CapsEditor`. When the application is first run, it has no document loaded, and displays this:

The File menu has two options: **Open** and **Exit**. **Exit** exits the application, while **Open** brings up the standard `OpenFileDialog` and reads in whatever file the user selects. The next screenshot shows `CapsEditor` being used to view its own source file, `Form1.cs`. I've also randomly double-clicked on a couple of lines to convert them to uppercase:

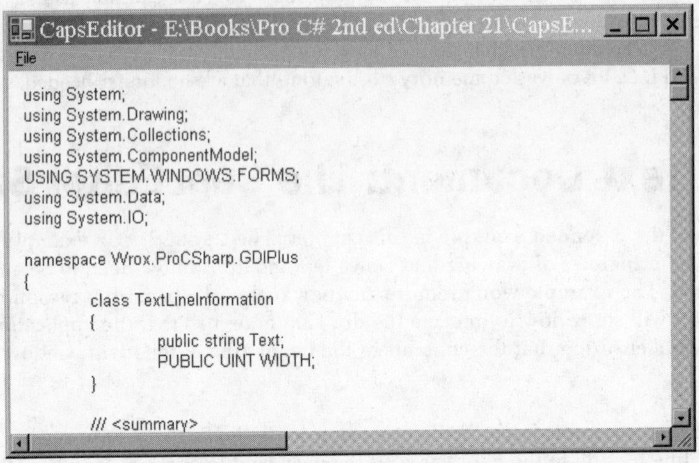

```
CapsEditor - E:\Books\Pro C# 2nd ed\Chapter 21\CapsE...
File

using System;
using System.Drawing;
using System.Collections;
using System.ComponentModel;
USING SYSTEM.WINDOWS.FORMS;
using System.Data;
using System.IO;

namespace Wrox.ProCSharp.GDIPlus
{
        class TextLineInformation
        {
                public string Text;
                PUBLIC UINT WIDTH;
        }

        /// <summary>
```

The sizes of the horizontal and vertical scrollbars are, by the way, correct. The client area will scroll just enough to view the entire document. `CapsEditor` doesn't try to wrap lines of text – the example is already complicated enough without doing that. It just displays each line of the file exactly as it is read in. There are no limits to the size of the file, but we are assuming it is a text file and doesn't contain any non-printable characters.

We'll start off by adding a `using` command:

```
using System;
using System.Drawing;
using System.Collections;
using System.ComponentModel;
using System.Windows.Forms;
using System.Data;
using System.IO;
```

This is because we'll be using the `StreamReader` class which is in `System.IO`. Next we'll add in some fields to the `Form1` class:

```
#region Constant fields
private const string standardTitle = "CapsEditor";
                                            // default text in titlebar
private const uint margin = 10;
                    // horizontal and vertical margin in client area
#endregion

#region Member fields
private ArrayList documentLines = new ArrayList();   // the 'document'
```

```
        private uint lineHeight;        // height in pixels of one line
        private Size documentSize;      // how big a client area is needed to
                                        // display document
        private uint nLines;            // number of lines in document
        private Font mainFont;          // font used to display all lines
        private Font emptyDocumentFont; // font used to display empty message
        private Brush mainBrush = Brushes.Blue;
                                        // brush used to display document text
        private Brush emptyDocumentBrush = Brushes.Red;
                            // brush used to display empty document message
        private Point mouseDoubleClickPosition;
            // location mouse is pointing to when double-clicked
        private OpenFileDialog fileOpenDialog = new OpenFileDialog();
            // standard open file dialog
        private bool documentHasData = false;
            // set to true if document has some data in it
        #endregion
```

Most of these fields should be self-explanatory. The documentLines field is an ArrayList that contains the actual text of the file that has been read in. In a real sense, this is the field that contains the data in the "document". Each element of documentLines contains information for one line of text that has been read in. Since it's an ArrayList, rather than a plain array, we can dynamically add elements to it as we read in a file. You'll notice I've also liberally used #region preprocessor directives to block up bits of the program to make it easier to edit.

I said each documentLines element contains information about a line of text. This information is actually an instance of another class I've defined, TextLineInformation:

```
    class TextLineInformation
    {
        public string Text;
        public uint Width;
    }
```

TextLineInformation looks like a classic case where you'd normally use a struct rather than a class since it's just there to group together a couple of fields. However, its instances are always accessed as elements of an ArrayList, which expects its elements to be stored as reference types, so declaring TextLineInformation as a class makes things more efficient by saving a lot of boxing and unboxing operations.

Each TextLineInformation instance stores a line of text – and that can be thought of as the smallest item that is displayed as a single item. In general, for each similar item in a GDI+ application, you'd probably want to store the text of the item, as well as the world coordinates of where it should be displayed and its size (the page coordinates will change frequently, whenever the user scrolls, whereas world coordinates will normally only change when other parts of the document are modified in some way). In this case we've only stored the Width of the item. The reason is because the height in this case is just the height of whatever our selected font is. It's the same for all lines of text so there's no point storing it separately for each one; we store it once, in the Form1.lineHeight field. As for the position – well in this case the x coordinate is just equal to the margin, and the y coordinate is easily calculated as:

```
margin + lineHeight*(however many lines are above this one)
```

If we'd been trying to display and manipulate, say, individual words instead of complete lines, then the x position of each word would have to be calculated using the widths of all the previous words on that line of text, but I wanted to keep it simple here, which is why we're treating each line of text as one single item.

Let's deal with the main menu now. This part of the application is more the realm of Windows Forms – the subject of Chapter 7, than of GDI+. I added the menu options using the design view in Visual Studio .NET, but renamed them as `menuFile`, `menuFileOpen`, and `menuFileExit`. I then added event handlers for the **File Open** and **File Exit** menu options using the Visual Studio .NET Properties window. The event handlers have their VS .NET-generated names of `menuFileOpen_Click()` and `menuFileExit_Click()`.

We need some extra initialization code in the `Form1()` constructor:

```
public Form1()
{
    InitializeComponent();

    CreateFonts();
    fileOpenDialog.FileOk += new
        System.ComponentModel.CancelEventHandler(
        this.OpenFileDialog_FileOk);
    fileOpenDialog.Filter =
        "Text files (*.txt)|*.txt|C# source files (*.cs)|*.cs";

}
```

The event handler added here is for when the user clicks **OK** on the **File Open** dialog. We have also set the filter for the open file dialog so that we can only load up text files – we've opted for `.txt` files as well as C# source files, so we can use the application to examine the sourcecode for our samples.

`CreateFonts()` is a helper method that sorts out the fonts we intend to use:

```
private void CreateFonts()
{
    mainFont = new Font("Arial", 10);
    lineHeight = (uint)mainFont.Height;
    emptyDocumentFont = new Font("Verdana", 13, FontStyle.Bold);
}
```

The actual definitions of the handlers are pretty standard stuff:

```
protected void OpenFileDialog_FileOk(object Sender, CancelEventArgs e)
{
    this.LoadFile(fileOpenDialog.FileName);
}

protected void menuFileOpen_Click(object sender, EventArgs e)
{
    fileOpenDialog.ShowDialog();
}


protected void menuFileExit_Click(object sender, EventArgs e)
{
    this.Close();
}
```

We'll examine the `LoadFile()` method now. It's the method that handles the opening and reading in of a file (as well as ensuring a `Paint` event gets raised to force a repaint with the new file):

```
private void LoadFile(string FileName)
{
    StreamReader sr = new StreamReader(FileName);
    string nextLine;
    documentLines.Clear();
    nLines = 0;
    TextLineInformation nextLineInfo;
    while ( (nextLine = sr.ReadLine()) != null)
    {
        nextLineInfo = new TextLineInformation();
        nextLineInfo.Text = nextLine;
        documentLines.Add(nextLineInfo);
        ++nLines;
    }
    sr.Close();
    documentHasData = (nLines>0) ? true : false;

    CalculateLineWidths();
    CalculateDocumentSize();

    this.Text = standardTitle + " - " + FileName;
    this.Invalidate();
}
```

Most of this function is just standard file-reading stuff, as covered in Chapter 12. Notice how as the file is read in, we progressively add lines to the `documentLines` ArrayList, so this array ends up containing information for each of the lines in order. After we've read in the file, we set the `documentHasData` flag, which indicates whether there is actually anything to display. Our next task is to work out where everything is to be displayed, and, having done that, how much client area we need to display the file – the document size that will be used to set the scrollbars. Finally, we set the title bar text and call `Invalidate()`. `Invalidate()` is an important method supplied by Microsoft, so we'll break for a couple of pages to explain its use, before we examine the code for the `CalculateLineWidths()` and `CalculateDocumentSize()` methods.

The Invalidate() Method

`Invalidate()` is a member of `System.Windows.Forms.Form` that we've not met before. It marks an area of the client window as invalid and, therefore, in need of repainting, and then makes sure a `Paint` event is raised. There are a couple of overrides to `Invalidate()`: you can pass it a rectangle that specifies (in page coordinates) precisely which area of the window needs repainting, or if you don't pass any parameters it'll just mark the entire client area as invalid.

You may wonder why we are doing it this way. If we know that something needs painting, why don't we just call `OnPaint()` or some other method to do the painting directly? The answer is that in general, calling painting routines directly is regarded as bad programming practice – if your code decides it wants some painting done, in general you should call `Invalidate()`. Here's why:

❑ Drawing is almost always the most processor-intensive task a GDI+ application will carry out, so doing it in the middle of other work holds up the other work. With our example, if we'd directly called a method to do the drawing from the `LoadFile()` method, then the `LoadFile()` method wouldn't return until that drawing task was complete. During that time, our application can't respond to any other events. On the other hand, by calling `Invalidate()` we are simply getting Windows to raise a `Paint` event before immediately returning from `LoadFile()`. Windows is then free to examine the events that are waiting to be handled. How this works internally is that the events sit as what are known as **messages** in a **message queue**. Windows periodically examines the queue and if there are events in it, it picks one and calls the corresponding event handler. Although the `Paint` event may be the only one sitting in the queue (so `OnPaint()` gets called immediately anyway), in a more complex application there may be other events that ought to get priority over our `Paint` event. In particular, if the user has decided to quit the application, this will be marked by a message known as `WM_QUIT`.

❑ Related to the first reason, if you have a more complicated, multithreaded, application, you'll probably want just one thread to handle all the drawing. Using `Invalidate()` to route all drawing through the message queue provides a good way of ensuring that the same thread (whatever thread is responsible for the message queue – this will be the thread that called `Application.Run()`) does all the drawing, no matter what other thread requested the drawing operation.

❑ There's an additional performance-related reason. Suppose at about the same time a couple of different requests to draw part of the screen come in. Maybe your code has just modified the document and wants to ensure the updated document is displayed, while at the same time the user has just moved another window that was covering part of the client area out of the way. By calling `Invalidate()`, you are giving windows a chance to notice that this has occurred. Windows can then merge the `Paint` events if appropriate, combining the invalidated areas, so that the painting is only done once.

❑ Finally, the code to do the painting is probably going to be one of the most complex parts of the code in your application, especially if you have a very sophisticated user interface. The guys who have to maintain your code in a couple of years time will thank you for having kept your painting code all in one place and as simple as you reasonably can – something that's easier to do if you don't have too many pathways into it from other parts of the program.

The bottom line from all this is that it is good practice to keep all your painting in the `OnPaint()` routine, or in other methods called from that method. However, you have to strike a balance; if you want to replace just one character on the screen and you know perfectly well that it won't affect anything else that you've drawn, then you may decide that it's not worth the overhead of going through `Invalidate()`, and just write a separate drawing routine.

> *In a very complicated application, you may even write a full class that takes responsibility for drawing to the screen. A few years ago when MFC was the standard technology for GDI-intensive applications, MFC followed this model, with a C++ class, C<ApplicationName>View that was responsible for painting. However, even in this case, this class had one member function, OnDraw(), which was designed to be the entry point for most drawing requests.*

Calculating Item Sizes and Document Size

We'll return to the `CapsEditor` example now and examine the `CalculateLineWidths()` and `CalculateDocumentSize()` methods that are called from `LoadFile()`:

```
private void CalculateLineWidths()
{
    Graphics dc = this.CreateGraphics();
    foreach (TextLineInformation nextLine in documentLines)
    {
        nextLine.Width = (uint)dc.MeasureString(nextLine.Text,
                                                mainFont).Width;
    }
}
```

This method simply runs through each line that has been read in and uses the `Graphics.MeasureString()` method to work out and store how much horizontal screen space the string requires. We store the value, because `MeasureString()` is computationally intensive. If we hadn't made the `CapsEditor` sample so simple that we can easily work out the height and location of each item, this method would almost certainly have needed to be implemented in such a way as to compute all those quantities too.

Now we know how big each item on the screen is, and we can calculate where each item goes, we are in a position to work out the actual document size. The height is basically the number of lines multiplied by the height of each line. The width will need to be worked out by iterating through the lines to find the longest. For both height and width, we will also want to make an allowance for a small margin around the displayed document, to make the application look more attractive.

Here's the method that calculates the document size:

```
private void CalculateDocumentSize()
{
    if (!documentHasData)
    {
        documentSize = new Size(100, 200);
    }
    else
    {
        documentSize.Height = (int)(nLines*lineHeight) + 2*(int)margin;
        uint maxLineLength = 0;
        foreach (TextLineInformation nextWord in documentLines)
        {
            uint tempLineLength = nextWord.Width + 2*margin;
            if (tempLineLength > maxLineLength)
                maxLineLength = tempLineLength;
        }
        documentSize.Width = (int)maxLineLength;
    }
    this.AutoScrollMinSize = documentSize;
}
```

This method first checks whether there is any data to be displayed. If there isn't we cheat a bit and use a hard-coded document size, which I happen to know is big enough to display the big red <Empty Document> warning. If we'd wanted to really do it properly, we'd have used `MeasureString()` to check how big that warning actually is.

Once we've worked out the document size, we tell the `Form` instance what the size is by setting the `Form.AutoScrollMinSize` property. When we do this, something interesting happens behind the scenes. In the process of setting this property, the client area is invalidated and a `Paint` event is raised, for the very sensible reason that changing the size of the document means scrollbars will need to be added or modified and the entire client area will almost certainly be repainted. Why do I say that's interesting? It illustrates perfectly what I was saying earlier about using the `Form.Invalidate()` method. You see, if you look back at the code for `LoadFile()` you'll realize that our call to `Invalidate()` in that method is actually redundant. The client area will be invalidated anyway when we set the document size. I left the explicit call to `Invalidate()` in the `LoadFile()` implementation to illustrate how in general you should normally do things. In fact in this case, all calling `Invalidate()` again will do is needlessly request a duplicate `Paint` event. However, this in turn illustrates what I was saying about how `Invalidate()` gives Windows the chance to optimize performance. The second `Paint` event won't in fact get raised: Windows will see that there's a `Paint` event already sitting in the queue and will compare the requested invalidated regions to see if it needs to do anything to merge them. In this case both `Paint` events will specify the entire client area, so nothing needs to be done, and Windows will quietly drop the second `Paint` request. Of course, going through that process will take up a little bit of processor time, but it'll be an negligible amount of time compared to how long it takes to actually do some painting.

OnPaint()

Now we've seen how `CapsEditor` loads the file, it's time to look at how the painting is done:

```
protected override void OnPaint(PaintEventArgs e)
{
    base.OnPaint(e);
    Graphics dc = e.Graphics;
    int scrollPositionX = this.AutoScrollPosition.X;
    int scrollPositionY = this.AutoScrollPosition.Y;
    dc.TranslateTransform(scrollPositionX, scrollPositionY);

    if (!documentHasData)
    {
        dc.DrawString("<Empty document>", emptyDocumentFont,
            emptyDocumentBrush, new Point(20,20));
        base.OnPaint(e);
        return;
    }

    // work out which lines are in clipping rectangle
    int minLineInClipRegion =
                WorldYCoordinateToLineIndex(e.ClipRectangle.Top -
                                                scrollPositionY);
    if (minLineInClipRegion == -1)
        minLineInClipRegion = 0;
    int maxLineInClipRegion =
                WorldYCoordinateToLineIndex(e.ClipRectangle.Bottom -
                                                scrollPositionY);
    if (maxLineInClipRegion >= this.documentLines.Count ||
        maxLineInClipRegion == -1)
    maxLineInClipRegion = this.documentLines.Count-1;

    TextLineInformation nextLine;
    for (int i=minLineInClipRegion; i<=maxLineInClipRegion ; i++)
    {
```

```
            nextLine = (TextLineInformation)documentLines[i];
            dc.DrawString(nextLine.Text, mainFont, mainBrush,
                        this.LineIndexToWorldCoordinates(i));
        }
    }
```

At the heart of this `OnPaint()` override is a loop that goes through each line of the document, calling `Graphics.DrawString()` to paint each one. The rest of this code is mostly to do with optimizing the painting – the usual stuff about figuring out what exactly needs painting instead of rushing in and telling the graphics instance to redraw everything.

We start off by checking if there is any data in the document. If there isn't, we draw a quick message saying so, call the base class's `OnPaint()` implementation, and exit. If there is data, then we start looking at the clipping rectangle. The way we do this is by calling another method that we've written, `WorldYCoordinateToLineIndex()`. We'll examine this method next, but essentially it takes a given y position relative to the top of the document, and works out what line of the document is being displayed at that point.

The first time we call the `WorldYCoordinateToLineIndex()` method, we pass it the coordinate value `e.ClipRectangle.Top - scrollPositionY`. This is just the top of the clipping region, converted to world coordinates. If the return value is -1, we'll play safe and assume we need to start at the beginning of the document (this is the case if the top of the clipping region is in the top margin).

Once we've done all that, we essentially repeat the same process for the bottom of the clipping rectangle, in order to find the last line of the document that is inside the clipping region. The indices of the first and last lines are respectively stored in `minLineInClipRegion` and `maxLineInClipRegion`, so then we can just run a `for` loop between these values to do our painting. Inside the painting loop, we actually need to do roughly the reverse transformation to the one performed by `WorldYCoordinateToLineIndex()`. We are given the index of a line of text, and we need to check where it should be drawn. This calculation is actually quite simple, but we've wrapped it up in another method, `LineIndexToWorldCoordinates()`, which returns the required coordinates of the top left corner of the item. The returned coordinates are world coordinates, but that's fine, because we have already called `TranslateTransform()` on the `Graphics` object so that we need to pass it world, rather than page, coordinates when asking it to display items.

Coordinate Transforms

In this section, we'll examine the implementation of the helper methods that we've written in the `CapsEditor` sample to help us with coordinate transforms. These are the `WorldYCoordinateToLineIndex()` and `LineIndexToWorldCoordinates()` methods that we referred to in the last section, as well as a couple of other methods.

First, `LineIndexToWorldCoordinates()` takes a given line index, and works out the world coordinates of the top left corner of that line, using the known margin and line height:

```
    private Point LineIndexToWorldCoordinates(int index)
    {
        Point TopLeftCorner = new Point(
            (int)margin, (int)(lineHeight*index + margin));
        return TopLeftCorner;
    }
```

We also used a method that roughly does the reverse transform in `OnPaint()`. `WorldYCoordinateToLineIndex()` works out the line index, but it only takes into account a vertical world coordinate. This is because it is used to work out the line index corresponding to the top and bottom of the clip region.

```
private int WorldYCoordinateToLineIndex(int y)
{
    if (y < margin)
        return -1;
    return (int)((y-margin)/lineHeight);
}
```

There are three more methods, which will be called from the handler routine that responds to the user double-clicking the mouse. First, we have a method that works out the index of the line being displayed at given world coordinates. Unlike `WorldYCoordinateToLineIndex()`, this method takes into account the x and y positions of the coordinates. It returns −1 if there is no line of text covering the coordinates passed in:

```
private int WorldCoordinatesToLineIndex(Point position)
{
    if (!documentHasData)
        return -1;
    if (position.Y < margin || position.X < margin)
        return -1;
    int index = (int)(position.Y-margin)/(int)this.lineHeight;
    // check position isn't below document
    if (index >= documentLines.Count)
        return -1;
    // now check that horizontal position is within this line
    TextLineInformation theLine =
                        (TextLineInformation)documentLines[index];
    if (position.X > margin + theLine.Width)
        return -1;

    // all is OK. We can return answer
    return index;
}
```

Finally, on occasions we also need to convert between line index and page, rather than world, coordinates. The following methods achieve this:

```
private Point LineIndexToPageCoordinates(int index)
{
    return LineIndexToWorldCoordinates(index) +
                                new Size(AutoScrollPosition);
}

private int PageCoordinatesToLineIndex(Point position)
{
    return WorldCoordinatesToLineIndex(position - new
                        Size(AutoScrollPosition));
}
```

Note that when converting *to* page coordinates, we add the `AutoScrollPosition`, which is negative.

Although these methods by themselves don't look particularly interesting, they do illustrate a general technique that you'll probably often need to use. With GDI+, we'll often find ourselves in a situation where we have been given some coordinates (for example the coordinates of where the user has clicked the mouse) and we'll need to figure out what item is being displayed at that point. Or it could happen the other way round – given a particular display item, whereabouts should it be displayed? Hence, if you are writing a GDI+ application, you'll probably find it useful to write methods that do the equivalent of the coordinate transformation methods illustrated here.

Responding to User Input

So far, with the exception of the File menu in the `CapsEditor` sample, everything we've done in this chapter has been one way: the application has talked to the user, by displaying information on the screen. Almost all software of course works both ways: the user can talk to the software as well. We're now going to add that facility to `CapsEditor`.

Getting a GDI+ application to respond to user input is actually a lot simpler than writing the code to draw to the screen, and indeed we've already covered how handle user input in Chapter 7. Essentially, you override methods from the `Form` class that get called from the relevant event handler – in much the same way that `OnPaint()` is called when a `Paint` event is raised.

For the case of detecting when the user clicks or moves the mouse the methods you may wish to override include:

Method	Called when:
`OnClick(EventArgs e)`	mouse is clicked
`OnDoubleClick(EventArgs e)`	mouse is double-clicked
`OnMouseDown(MouseEventArgs e)`	left mouse button pressed
`OnMouseHover(MouseEventArgs e)`	mouse stays still somewhere after moving
`OnMouseMove(MouseEventArgs e)`	mouse is moved
`OnMouseUp(MouseEventArgs e)`	left mouse button is released

If you want to detect when the user types in any text, then you'll probably want to override these methods:

Method	Called when:
`OnKeyDown(KeyEventArgs e)`	a key is depressed
`OnKeyPress(KeyPressEventArgs e)`	a key is pressed and released
`OnKeyUp(KeyEventArgs e)`	a pressed key is released

Notice that some of these events overlap. For example, if the user presses a mouse button this will raise the `MouseDown` event. If the button is immediately released again, this will raise the `MouseUp` event and the `Click` event. Also, some of these methods take an argument that is derived from `EventArgs` rather than an instance of `EventArgs` itself. These instances of derived classes can be used to give more information about a particular event. `MouseEventArgs` has two properties X and Y, which give the device coordinates of the mouse at the time it was pressed. Both `KeyEventArgs` and `KeyPressEventArgs` have properties that indicate which key or keys the event concerns.

That's all there is to it. It's then up to you to think about the logic of precisely what you want to do. The only point to note is that you'll probably find yourself doing a bit more logic work with a GDI+ application than you would have with a `Windows.Forms` application. That's because in a `Windows.Forms` application you are typically responding to quite high-level events (`TextChanged` for a textbox, for example). By contrast with GDI+, the events tend to be more basic – user clicks the mouse, or hits the key *h*. The action your application takes is likely to depend on a sequence of events rather than a single event. For example, say your application works like Word for Windows, where in order to select some text the user clicks the left mouse button, then moves the mouse, then releases the left mouse button. Your application will receive the `MouseDown` event, but there's not much you can do with this event except record that the mouse was clicked with the cursor in a certain position. Then, when the `MouseMove` event is received, you'll want to check from the record whether the left button is currently down, and if so highlight text as the user selects it. When the user releases the left mouse button, your corresponding action (in the `OnMouseUp()` method) will need to check whether any dragging took place while the mouse button was down, and act accordingly. Only at this point is the sequence complete.

Another point to consider is that, because certain events overlap, you will often have a choice of which event you want your code to respond to.

The golden rule really is to think carefully about the logic of every combination of mouse movement or click and keyboard event that the user might initiate, and ensure that your application responds in a way that is intuitive and in accordance with the expected behavior of applications in *every* case. Most of your work here will be in thinking rather than in coding, though the coding you do will be quite fiddly, as you may need to take into account a lot of combinations of user input. For example, what should your application do if the user starts typing in text while one of the mouse buttons is held down? It might sound like an improbable combination, but sooner or later some user is going to try it!

For the `CapsEditor` example, we are keeping things very simple, so we don't really have any combinations to think about. The only thing we are going to respond to is when the user double-clicks – in which case we capitalize whatever line of text the mouse pointer is hovering over.

This should be a fairly simple task, but there is one snag. We need to trap the `DoubleClick` event, but the table above shows that this event takes an `EventArgs` parameter, not a `MouseEventArgs` parameter. The trouble is that we'll need to know where the mouse is when the user double-clicks, if we are to correctly identify the line of text to be capitalized – and you need a `MouseEventArgs` parameter to do that. There are two workarounds. One is to use a static method that is implemented by the `Form1` object, `Control.MousePosition`, to find out the mouse position, like so:

```
protected override void OnDoubleClick(EventArgs e)
{
    Point MouseLocation = Control.MousePosition;
    // handle double click
```

In most cases this will work. However, there could be a problem if your application (or even some other application with a high priority) is doing some computationally intensive work at the moment the user double-clicks. It just might happen in that case that the `OnDoubleClick()` event handler doesn't get called until perhaps half a second or so *after* the user has double-clicked. You don't really want delays like that, because they usually annoy users intensely, but even so, occasionally it does happen, and sometimes for reasons beyond the control of your app (a slow computer for instance). Trouble is, half a second is easily enough time for the mouse to get moved halfway across the screen – in which case your call to `Control.MousePosition` will return completely the wrong location!

A better way here is to rely on one of the many overlaps between mouse-event meanings. The first part of double-clicking a mouse involves pressing the left button down. This means that if OnDoubleClick() is called then we know that OnMouseDown() has also just been called, with the mouse at the same location. We can use the OnMouseDown() override to record the position of the mouse, ready for OnDoubleClick(). This is the approach we take in CapsEditor:

```
protected override void OnMouseDown(MouseEventArgs e)
{
    base.OnMouseDown(e);
    this.mouseDoubleClickPosition = new Point(e.X, e.Y);
}
```

Now let's look at our OnDoubleClick() override. There's quite a bit more work to do here:

```
protected override void OnDoubleClick(EventArgs e)
{
    int i = PageCoordinatesToLineIndex(this.mouseDoubleClickPosition);
    if (i >= 0)
    {
        TextLineInformation lineToBeChanged =
                        (TextLineInformation)documentLines[i];
        lineToBeChanged.Text = lineToBeChanged.Text.ToUpper();
        Graphics dc = this.CreateGraphics();
        uint newWidth =(uint)dc.MeasureString(lineToBeChanged.Text,
                                        mainFont).Width;
        if (newWidth > lineToBeChanged.Width)
            lineToBeChanged.Width = newWidth;
        if (newWidth+2*margin > this.documentSize.Width)
        {
            this.documentSize.Width = (int)newWidth;
            this.AutoScrollMinSize = this.documentSize;
        }
        Rectangle changedRectangle = new Rectangle(
                                LineIndexToPageCoordinates(i),
                                new Size((int)newWidth,
                                (int)this.lineHeight));
        this.Invalidate(changedRectangle);
    }
    base.OnDoubleClick(e);
}
```

We start off by calling PageCoordinatesToLineIndex() to work out which line of text the mouse pointer was hovering over when the user double-clicked. If this call returns −1 then we weren't over any text, so there's nothing to do; except, of course, call the base class version of OnDoubleClick() to let Windows do any default processing.

Assuming we've identified a line of text, we can use the string.ToUpper() method to convert it to uppercase. That was the easy part. The hard part is figuring out what needs to be redrawn where. Fortunately, because we kept the sample so simplistic, there aren't too many combinations. We can assume for a start, that converting to uppercase will always either leave the width of the line on the screen unchanged, or increase it. Capital letters are bigger than lowercase letters; therefore, the width will never go down. We also know that since we are not wrapping lines, our line of text won't overflow to the next line and push out other text below. Our action of converting the line to uppercase won't, therefore, actually change the locations of any of the other items being displayed. That's a big simplification!

The next thing the code does is use `Graphics.MeasureString()` to work out the new width of the text. There are now just two possibilities:

❏ The new width might make our line the longest line, and cause the width of the entire document to increase. If that's the case then we'll need to set `AutoScrollMinSize` to the new size so that the scrollbars are correctly placed.

❏ The size of the document might be unchanged.

In either case, we need to get the screen redrawn, by calling `Invalidate()`. Only one line has changed; therefore, we don't want to have the entire document repainted. Rather, we need to work out the bounds of a rectangle that contains just the modified line, so that we can pass this rectangle to `Invalidate()`, ensuring that just that line of text will be repainted. That's precisely what the above code does. Our call to `Invalidate()` will result in `OnPaint()` being called, when the mouse event handler finally returns. Bearing in mind our comments earlier in the chapter about the difficulty in setting a break point in `OnPaint()`, if you run the sample and set a break point in `OnPaint()` to trap the resultant painting action, you'll find that the `PaintEventArgs` parameter to `OnPaint()` does indeed contain a clipping region that matches the specified rectangle. And since we've overloaded `OnPaint()` to take careful account of the clipping region, only the one required line of text will be repainted.

Printing

In this chapter we've focused so far entirely on drawing to the screen. However, at some point you will probably also want to be able to produce a hard copy of the data too. That's the topic of this section. We're going to extend the `CapsEditor` sample so that it is able to print preview and print the document that is being edited.

Unfortunately, we don't have enough space to go into too much detail about printing here, so the printing functionality we will implement will be very basic. Usually, if you are implementing the ability for an application to print data, you will add three items to the application's main **File** menu:

❏ **Page Setup** – allows the user to choose options such as which pages to print, which printer to use, etc.

❏ **Print Preview** – opens a new Form that displays a mock-up of what the printed copy should look

❏ **Print** – actually prints the document

In our case, to keep things simple, we won't implement a **Page Setup** menu option. Printing will only be possible using default settings. We will note, however, that, if you do want to implement **Page Setup**, then Microsoft has already written a page setup dialog class for you to use. It is the class `System.Windows.Forms.PrintDialog`. You will normally want to write an event handler that displays this form, and saves the settings chosen by the user.

In many ways printing is just the same as displaying to a screen. You will be supplied with a device context (`Graphics` instance) and call all the usual display commands against that instance. Microsoft has written a number of classes to assist you in doing this; the two main ones that we need to use are `System.Drawing.Printing.PrintDocument` and `System.Drawing.Printing.PrintPreviewDialog`. These two classes handle the process of making sure that drawing instructions passed to a device context get appropriately handled for printing, leaving you to think about the logic of what to print where.

There are some important differences between printing/print previewing on the one hand, and displaying to the screen on the other hand. Printers cannot scroll – instead they have pages. So you'll need to make sure you find a sensible way of dividing your document into pages, and draw each page as requested. Among other things that means calculating how much of your document will fit onto a single page, and therefore how many pages you'll need, and which page each part of the document needs to be written to.

Despite the above complications, the process of printing is quite simple. Programmatically, the steps you need to go through look roughly like this:

❑ **Printing**
You instantiate a PrintDocument object, and call its Print() method. This method will internally cause an event, PrintPage, to be raised to signal the printing of the first page. PrintPage takes a PrintPageEventArgs parameter, which supplies information concerning paper size and setup, as well as a Graphics object used for the drawing commands. You should therefore have written an event handler for this event, and have implemented this handler to print a page. This event handler should also set a Boolean property of the PrintPageEventArgs, HasMorePages, to either true or false to indicate whether there are more pages to be printed. The PrintDocument.Print() method will repeatedly raise the PrintPage event until it sees that HasMorePages has been set to false.

❑ **Print Previewing**
In this case, you instantiate both a PrintDocument object and a PrintPreviewDialog object. You attach the PrintDocument to the PrintPreviewDialog (using the property PrintPreviewDialog.Document) and then call the dialog's ShowDialog() method. This method will modally display the dialog – which turns out to be a standard Windows print preview form, and which displays pages of the document. Internally, the pages are displayed once again by repeatedly raising the PrintPage event until the HasMorePages property is false. There's no need to write a separate event handler for this; you can use the same event handler as used for printing each page since the drawing code ought to be identical in both cases (after all, whatever is print previewed ought to look identical to the printed version!).

Implementing Print and Print Preview

Now we've gone over the broad steps to be taken, let's see how this works in code terms. The code is downloadable as the PrintingCapsEdit project, and consists of the CapsEditor project, with the changes highlighted below made.

We start off by using the VS .NET design view to add two new items to the File menu: **Print** and **Print Preview**. We also use the properties window to name these items menuFilePrint and menuFilePrintPreview, and to set them to be disabled when the application starts up (we can't print anything until a document has been opened!). We arrange for these menu items to be enabled by adding the following code to the main form's LoadFile() method, which we recall is responsible for loading a file into the CapsEditor application:

```
private void LoadFile(string FileName)
{
    StreamReader sr = new StreamReader(FileName);
    string nextLine;
    documentLines.Clear();
    nLines = 0;
    TextLineInformation nextLineInfo;
    while ( (nextLine = sr.ReadLine()) != null)
```

```
    {
        nextLineInfo = new TextLineInformation();
        nextLineInfo.Text = nextLine;
        documentLines.Add(nextLineInfo);
        ++nLines;
    }
    sr.Close();
    if (nLines > 0)
    {
        documentHasData = true;
        menuFilePrint.Enabled = true;
        menuFilePrintPreview.Enabled = true;
    }
    else
    {
        documentHasData = false;
        menuFilePrint.Enabled = false;
        menuFilePrintPreview.Enabled = false;
    }

    CalculateLineWidths();
    CalculateDocumentSize();

    this.Text = standardTitle + " - " + FileName;
    this.Invalidate();
}
```

The highlighted code above is the new code we have added to this method. Next we add a member field to the Form1 class:

```
public class Form1 : System.Windows.Forms.Form
{
    private int pagesPrinted = 0;
```

This field will be used to indicate which page we are currently printing. We are making it a member field, since we will need to remember this information between calls to the PrintPage event handler.

Next, the event handlers for when the user selects the Print or Print Preview menu options:

```
private void menuFilePrintPreview_Click(object sender, System.EventArgs e)
{
    this.pagesPrinted = 0;
    PrintPreviewDialog ppd = new PrintPreviewDialog();
    PrintDocument pd = new PrintDocument();
    pd.PrintPage += new PrintPageEventHandler
        (this.pd_PrintPage);
    ppd.Document = pd;
    ppd.ShowDialog();
}

private void menuFilePrint_Click(object sender, System.EventArgs e)
{
    this.pagesPrinted = 0;
    PrintDocument pd = new PrintDocument();
    pd.PrintPage += new PrintPageEventHandler
        (this.pd_PrintPage);
    pd.Print();
}
```

We've already explained the broad procedure involved in printing, and we can see that these event handlers are simply implementing that procedure. In both cases we are instantiating a `PrintDocument` object and attaching an event handler to its `PrintPage` event. For the case of printing, we call `PrintDocument.Print()`, while for print previewing, we attach the `PrintDocument` object to a `PrintPreviewDialog`, and call the preview dialog object's `ShowDialog()` method. The real work is going to be done in that event handler to the `PrintPage` event – and this is what that handler looks like:

```
private void pd_PrintPage(object sender, PrintPageEventArgs e)
{
   float yPos = 0;
   float leftMargin = e.MarginBounds.Left;
   float topMargin = e.MarginBounds.Top;
   string line = null;

   // Calculate the number of lines per page.
   int linesPerPage = (int)(e.MarginBounds.Height /
      mainFont.GetHeight(e.Graphics));
   int lineNo = this.pagesPrinted * linesPerPage;

   // Print each line of the file.
   int count = 0;
   while(count < linesPerPage && lineNo < this.nLines)
   {
      line = ((TextLineInformation)this.documentLines[lineNo]).Text;
      yPos = topMargin + (count * mainFont.GetHeight(e.Graphics));
      e.Graphics.DrawString(line, mainFont, Brushes.Blue,
         leftMargin, yPos, new StringFormat());
      lineNo++;
      count++;
   }

   // If more lines exist, print another page.
   if(this.nLines > lineNo)
      e.HasMorePages = true;
   else
      e.HasMorePages = false;
   pagesPrinted++;
}
```

After declaring a couple of local variables, the first thing we do is work out how many lines of text can be displayed on one page – which will be the height of a page divided by the height of a line and rounded down. The height of the page can be obtained from the `PrintPageEventArgs.MarginBounds` property. This property is a `RectangleF` struct that has been initialized to give the bounds of the page. The height of a line is obtained from the `Form1.mainFont` field, which we recall from the `CapsEditor` sample is the font used for displaying the text. There is no reason here for not using the same font for printing too. Note that for the `PrintingCapsEditor` sample, the number of lines per page is always the same, so we arguably could have cached the value the first time we calculated it. However, the calculation isn't too hard, and in a more sophisticated application the value might change, so it's not bad practice to recalculate it every time we print a page.

We also initialize a variable called `lineNo`. This gives the zero-based index of the line of the document that will be the first line of this page. This information is important because in principle, the `pd_PrintPage()` method could have been called to print any page, not just the first page. `lineNo` is computed as the number of lines per page times the number of pages that have so far been printed.

Next we run through a loop, printing each line. This loop will terminate either when we find that we have printed all the lines of text in the document, or when we find that we have printed all the lines that will fit on this page – whichever condition occurs first. Finally, we check whether there is any more of the document to be printed, and set the `HasMorePages` property of our `PrintPageEventArgs` accordingly, and also increment the `pagesPrinted` field, so that we know to print the correct page the next time the `PrintPage` event handler is invoked.

One point to note about this event handler is that we do not worry about where the drawing commands are being sent. We simply use the `Graphics` object that was supplied with the `PrintPageEventArgs`. The `PrintDocument` class that Microsoft has written will internally take care of making sure that, if we are printing, the `Graphics` object will have been hooked up to the printer, while if we are print previewing then the `Graphics` object will have been hooked up to the print preview form on the screen.

Finally, we need to ensure the `System.Drawing.Printing` namespace is searched for type definitions:

```
using System;
using System.Drawing;
using System.Drawing.Printing;
using System.Collections;
using System.ComponentModel;
using System.Windows.Forms;
using System.Data;
using System.IO;
```

All that remains is to compile the project and check that the code works. We can't really show screenshots of a printed document(!) but this is what happens if you run `CapsEdit`, load a text document (as before, we've picked the C# source file for the project), and select **Print Preview**:

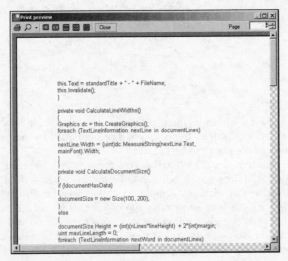

In the screenshot, we have scrolled through to page 5 of the document, and set the preview to display normal size. The `PrintPreviewDialog` has supplied quite a lot of features for us, as can be seen from the toolbar at the top of the form. The options available include actually printing the document, zooming in or out, and displaying two, three, four or six pages together. These options are all fully functional, without our needing to do any work. For example, if we change the zoom to auto and click to display four pages (third toolbar button from the right), we get this.

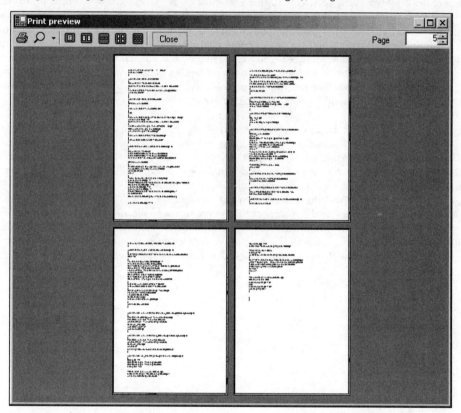

Summary

In this chapter, we've covered the area of drawing to a display device, where the drawing is done by your code rather than by some predefined control or dialog – the realm of GDI+. GDI+ is a powerful tool, and there are many .NET base classes available to help you draw to a device. We've seen that the process of drawing is actually relatively simple – in most cases you can draw text or sophisticated figures or display images with just a couple of C# statements. However, managing your drawing – the behind-the-scenes work involving working out what to draw, where to draw it, and what does or doesn't need repainting in any given situation – is far more complex and requires careful algorithm design. For this reason, it is also important to have a good understanding of how GDI+ works, and what actions Windows takes in order to get something drawn. In particular, because of the architecture of Windows, it is important that where possible drawing should be done by invalidating areas of the window and relying on Windows to respond by issuing a Paint event.

There are many more .NET classes concerned with drawing than we've had space to cover in this chapter, but if you've worked through it and understood the principles involved in drawing, you'll be in an excellent position to explore them, by looking at their lists of methods in the documentation and instantiating instances of them to see what they do. In the end, drawing, like almost any other aspect of programming, requires logic, careful thought, and clear algorithms. Apply that and you'll be able to write sophisticated user interfaces that don't depend on the standard controls. Your software will benefit hugely in both user-friendliness and visual appearance: There are many applications out there that rely entirely on controls for their user interface. While this can be effective, such applications very quickly end up looking just like each other. By adding some GDI+ code to do some custom drawing you can mark out your software as distinct and make it appear more original – which can only help your sales!

20

Accessing the Internet

In Chapters 14-16, we saw how you can use C# to write powerful, efficient, and dynamic web pages using ASP.NET, as well as web services. For the most part, the clients accessing ASP.NET pages will be users running Internet Explorer or other web browsers. However, you might want to add web-browsing features to your own application, or need your applications to programmatically obtain information from a web site. In this latter case, it is usually better for the site to implement a web service – but if you are accessing outside sites you may not have any control over how the site is implemented.

In this chapter, we will cover facilities provided through the .NET base classes for using various network protocols, particularly HTTP and TCP, to access networks and the Internet as a client. In particular, we will cover:

❑ Downloading files from the World Wide Web

❑ Using Internet Explorer as an ActiveX control

❑ Manipulating IP addresses and performing DNS lookups

❑ Socket programming with TCP, UDP, and socket classes

The two namespaces we are most interested in for networking are the System.Net and the System.Net.Sockets namespaces. The System.Net namespace is generally concerned with higher-level operations, for example, downloading and uploading files, and making web requests using HTTP and other protocols, while System.Net.Sockets contains classes to perform lower-level operations. You will find these classes more useful when you want to work directly with sockets or protocols such as TCP/IP. The methods in these classes closely mimic the Windows socket (Winsock) API functions derived from the Berkeley sockets interface.

We are going to take a fairly practical approach in this chapter, mixing examples with a discussion of the relevant theory and networking concepts as appropriate. This chapter is not a guide to computer networking, but an introduction to using the .NET Framework for network communication.

We will start with the simplest case of sending a request to a server and storing the information sent back.

The WebClient Class

If you only want to request a file from a particular URI, then you will find that the easiest .NET class to use is `System.Net.WebClient`. This class is an extremely high-level class designed to perform basic operations with only one or two commands. The .NET Framework currently supports URIs beginning with `http:`, `https:`, and `file:` identifiers.

> *It is worth noting that the term URL (Uniform Resource Locator) is no longer in use in new technical specifications, and URI (**Uniform Resource Identifier**) is now preferred. URI has roughly the same meaning as URL, but is a bit more general since URI does not imply we are using one of the familiar protocols, such as HTTP or FTP.*

Downloading Files

There are two methods available for downloading a file using `WebClient`. The method we choose depends on how we want to process the file contents. If we simply want to save the file to disk we use the `DownloadFile()` method. This method takes two parameters: the URI of the file, and a location (path and filename) to save the requested data.

```
WebClient Client = new WebClient();
Client.DownloadFile("http://www.Wrox.com/index.asp", "index.htm");
```

More commonly, your application will want to process the data retrieved from the web site. In order to do this you use the `OpenRead()` method. `OpenRead()` returns a `Stream` reference you can then use to retrieve the data into memory.

```
WebClient Client = new WebClient();
Stream strm = Client.OpenRead("http://www.Wrox.com/default.asp");
```

Basic Web Client Example

Our first example will demonstrate the `WebClient.OpenRead()` method. We will display the contents of the downloaded page in a `ListBox` control. We create the project as a standard C# Windows application, add a `ListBox` called `listBox1` with the docking property set to `DockStyle.Fill`. At the beginning of the file, we will need to add the `System.Net` and `System.IO` namespaces to our list of `using` directives. We then make the following changes to the constructor of the main form

```
public Form1()
{
    InitializeComponent();
```

```
    System.Net.WebClient Client = new WebClient();
    Stream strm = Client.OpenRead("http://www.wrox.com");
    StreamReader sr = new StreamReader(strm);
    string line;
    while ( (line=sr.ReadLine()) != null )
    {
       listBox1.Items.Add(line);
    }

    strm.Close();
}
```

In this example, we connect a `StreamReader` from the `System.IO` namespace to the network stream. This allows us to obtain data from the stream as text through the use of higher-level methods, such as `ReadLine()`. This is an excellent example of the point made in Chapter 12 about the benefits of abstracting data movement into the concept of a stream.

Running this sample produces the following results:

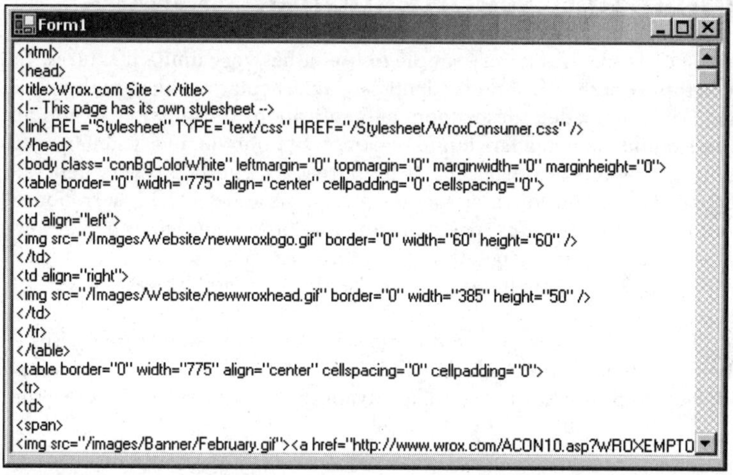

There is also an `OpenWrite()` method in the `WebClient` class. This method returns a writeable stream for you to send data to a URI. You can also specify the method used to send the data to the host; the default method is POST. The following code snippet assumes a writeable directory named `accept` on the local machine. The code will create a file in the directory with the name `newfile.txt` and the contents "**Hello World**".

```
WebClient webClient = new WebClient();

Stream stream = webClient.OpenWrite("http://localhost/accept/newfile.txt",
                                    "PUT");

StreamWriter streamWriter = new StreamWriter(stream);
streamWriter.WriteLine("Hello World");
streamWriter.Close();
```

Uploading Files

The `WebClient` class also features `UploadFile()` and `UploadData()` methods. `UploadFile()` uploads a file to a specified location given the local filename, while `UploadData()` uploads binary data supplied as an array of bytes to the specified URI (there is also a `DownloadData()` method for retrieving an array of bytes from a URI).

```
WebClient client = new WebClient();
client.UploadFile("http://www.ourwebsite.com/NewFile.htm",
                  "C:\\WebSiteFiles\\NewFile.htm");
byte [] image;
// code to initialise image so it contains all the binary data for
// some jpg file
client.UploadData("http://www.ourwebsite.com/NewFile.jpg", image);
```

WebRequest and WebResponse Classes

Although the `WebClient` class is very simple to use, it has very limited features. In particular, you cannot use it to supply authentication credentials – a particular problem with uploading data is that not many sites will accept uploaded files without authentication! It is possible to add header information to requests and to examine any headers in the response, but only in a very generic sense – there is no specific support for any one protocol. This is because `WebClient` is a very general-purpose class designed to work with any protocol for sending a requests and receiving a response (such as HTTP, or FTP). It cannot handle any features specific to any one protocol, such as cookies, which are specific to HTTP. If you want to take advantage of these features you need to use a family of classes based on two other classes in the `System.Net` namespace: `WebRequest` and `WebResponse`.

We will start off by showing you how to download a web page using these classes – this is the same example as before, but using `WebRequest` and `WebResponse`. In the process we will uncover the class hierarchy involved, and then see how to take advantage of extra HTTP features supported by this hierarchy.

The following code shows the modifications we need to make the `BasicWebClient` sample use the `WebRequest` and `WebResponse` classes.

```
public Form1()
{
    InitializeComponent();

    WebRequest wrq = WebRequest.Create("http://www.wrox.com");
    WebResponse wrs = wrq.GetResponse();
    Stream strm = wrs.GetResponseStream();
    StreamReader sr = new StreamReader(strm);
    string line;
    while ( (line = sr.ReadLine()) != null)
    {
        listBox1.Items.Add(line);
    }
    strm.Close();
}
```

In the code we start by instantiating an object representing a web request. We don't do this using a constructor, but instead call the static method `WebRequest.Create()`. As we will explain in more detail later, the `WebRequest` class is part of a hierarchy of classes supporting different network protocols. In order to receive a reference to the correct object for the request type, a factory mechanism is in place. The `WebRequest.Create()` method will create the appropriate object for the given protocol.

The `WebRequest` class represents the request for information to send to a particular URI. The URI is passed as a parameter to the `Create()` method. A `WebResponse` represents the data we retrieve from the server. By calling the `WebRequest.GetResponse()` method, we actually send the request to the web server and create a `WebResponse` object to examine the return data. As with the `WebClient` object, we can obtain a stream to represent the data, but, in this case we use the `WebResponse.GetResponseStream()` method.

Other WebRequest and WebResponse Features

We will quickly mention a couple of the other areas supported by `WebRequest`, `WebResponse`, and other related classes.

HTTP Header Information

An important part of the HTTP protocol is the ability to send extensive header information with both request and response streams. This information can include cookies, and the details of the particular browser sending the request (the user agent). As you would expect, the .NET Framework provides full support for accessing the most significant data. The `WebRequest` and `WebResponse` classes provide some support for reading the header,information. However, two derived classes provide additional HTTP-specific information: `HttpWebRequest` and `HttpWebResponse`. As we will explain in more detail later, creating a `WebRequest` with an HTTP URI results in an `HttpWebRequest` object instance. Since `HttpWebRequest` is derived from `WebRequest`, you can use the new instance anywhere a `WebRequest` is required. In addition, you can cast the instance to an `HttpWebRequest` reference and access properties specific to the HTTP protocol. Likewise, the `GetResponse()` method call will actually return an `HttpWebResponse` instance as a `WebResponse` reference when dealing with HTTP. Again, you can perform a simple cast to access the HTTP-specific features.

We can examine a couple of the header properties by adding the following code before the `GetResponse()` method call.

```
WebRequest wrq = WebRequest.Create("http://www.wrox.com");
HttpWebRequest hwrq = (HttpWebRequest)wrq;

listBox1.Items.Add("Request Timeout (ms) = " + wrq.Timeout);
listBox1.Items.Add("Request Keep Alive = " + hwrq.KeepAlive);
listBox1.Items.Add("Request AllowAutoRedirect = " + hwrq.AllowAutoRedirect);
```

The `Timeout` property is specified in milliseconds, and the default value is 100,000. You can set the timeout property to control how long the `WebRequest` object will wait on the response before throwing a `WebException`. You can check the `WebException.Status` property to see the reason for an exception. This enumeration includes status codes for timeouts, connection failures, protocol errors, and more.

The `KeepAlive` property is a specific extension to the HTTP protocol, so we access this property through an `HttpWebRequest` reference. `KeepAlive` allows multiple requests to use the same connection, saving time in closing and reopening connections on subsequent requests. The default value for this property is `true`.

961

The `AllowAutoRedirect` property is also specific to the `HttpWebRequest` class. Use this property to control if the web request should automatically follow redirection responses from the web server. Again, the default value is `true`. If you want to allow only a limited number of redirections, set the `MaximumAutomaticRedirections` property of the `HttpWebRequest` to the desired number.

While the request and response classes expose most of the important headers as properties, you can also use the `Headers` property itself to view the entire collection of headers. Add the following code after the `GetResponse()` method call to place all of the headers in the listbox control:

```
WebRequest wrq = WebRequest.Create("http://www.wrox.com");
WebResponse wrs = wrq.GetResponse();
WebHeaderCollection whc = wrs.Headers;
for(int i = 0; i < whc.Count; i++)
{
    listBox1.Items.Add("Header " + whc.GetKey(i) + " : " + whc[i]);
}
```

This example code produces the following list of headers:

Authentication

A further property in the `WebRequest` class is the `Credentials` property. If we needed authentication credentials to accompany our request, we could create an instance of the `NetworkCredential` class (also from the `System.Net` namespace) with a username and password. You could place the following code **before** the call to `GetResponse()`.

```
NetworkCredential myCred = new NetworkCredential("myusername", "mypassword");
wrq.Credentials = myCred;
```

Asynchronous Page Requests

An additional feature of the `WebRequest` class is the ability to request pages asynchronously. This feature is significant since there can be quite a long delay between sending a request off to a host and receiving the response. Methods such as `WebClient.DownloadData()` and `WebRequest.GetResponse()` will not return until the response from the server is complete. You might not want your application frozen due to a long period of inactivity, and in such scenarios it is better to use the `BeginGetResponse()` and `EndGetResponse()` methods. `BeginGetResponse()` works asynchronously and returns almost immediately. Under the covers, the runtime will asynchronously manage a background thread to retrieve the response from the server. Instead of returning a `WebResponse` object, `BeginGetResponse()` returns an object implementing the `IAsyncResult` interface. With this interface you can poll or wait for the response to become available, and then invoke `EndGetResponse()` to gather the results.

You can also pass a callback delegate into the `BeginGetResponse()` method. The target of a callback delegate is a method returning `void` and accepting an `IAsyncResult` reference as a parameter. When the worker thread is finished gathering the response, the runtime invokes the callback delegate to inform you of the completed work. As shown in the following code, calling `EndGetResponse()` in the callback method allows you to retrieve the `WebResponse` object.

```
public Form1()
{
    InitializeComponent();

    WebRequest wrq = WebRequest.Create("http://www.wrox.com");
    wrq.BeginGetResponse(new AsyncCallback(OnResponse), wrq);
}

protected void OnResponse(IAsyncResult ar)
{
    WebRequest wrq = (WebRequest)ar.AsyncState;
    WebResponse wrs = wrq.EndGetResponse(ar);

    // read the response ...
}
```

Notice how you can retrieve the original `WebRequest` object by passing the object as the third parameter to `BeginGetResponse()`. The third parameter is an object reference known as the state parameter. During the callback method you can retrieve the same state object using the `AsyncState` property of `IAsyncResult`.

Displaying Output as an HTML Page

Our examples show how the .NET base classes make it very easy to download and process data from the Internet. However, so far we have only displayed files as plain text. Quite often you will want to view an HTML file in an Internet Explorer style interface where the rendered HTML allows you to see what the web document actually looks like. Unfortunately, the .NET base classes don't include any intrinsic support for a control with an Internet Explorer-style interface. You will need to either programmatically call up Internet Explorer, or host the web browser as an ActiveX control.

You can programmatically start an Internet Explorer process and navigate to a web page using the `Process` class in the `System.Diagnostics` namespace.

```
Process myProcess = new Process();
myProcess.StartInfo.FileName = "iexplore.exe";
myProcess.StartInfo.Arguments = "http://www.wrox.com";
myProcess.Start();
```

However, the above code launches Internet Explorer as a separate window. Your application has no connection to the new window and therefore cannot control the browser.

On the other hand, using the browser as an ActiveX control allows you to display and control the browser as an integrated part of your application. The web browser control is quite sophisticated, featuring a large number of methods, properties, and events.

The easiest way to incorporate this control, using Visual Studio .NET, is to add the control to the toolbox. To do this, right-click on the toolbox in Visual Studio .NET and select Customize Toolbox from the context menu to bring up the following dialog. You should select the COM Components tab, and check Microsoft Web Browser.

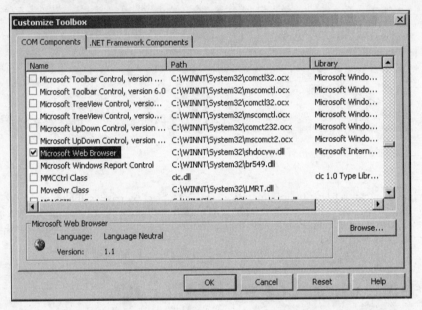

The Web Browser control now appears in the toolbox. You can click and drop the control onto your forms in the same manner as would you drop native .NET controls from the toolbox. Visual Studio .NET will automatically generate all the COM interoperability code required to host the web browser control in your application's form. We will demonstrate this technique with another example, DisplayWebPage, which will display a web page retrieved from the Internet in a typical Windows form.

We create DisplayWebPage as a standard C# Windows application, and drop the Web Browser ActiveX control onto the form. By default, Visual Studio .NET names the control axWebBrowser1. We then add the following code to the Form1 constructor:

```
public Form1()
{
    // Required for Windows Form Designer support
    InitializeComponent();
    int zero = 0;
    object oZero = zero;
    string emptyString = "";
    object oEmptyString = emptyString;
    axWebBrowser1.Navigate("http://www.wrox.com",
                           ref oZero,
                           ref oEmptyString,
                           ref oEmptyString,
                           ref oEmptyString);
}
```

In this code we use the `Navigate()` method of the `WebBrowser` control, which actually sends an HTTP request and displays the output from a given URI. The first parameter to this method is a string containing the URI to navigate to. The second parameter accepts a number of flags to modify the navigation behavior, for example, if the browser adds the new URI to the history list or not. The third parameter contains the name of the target frame (if any) used to display the resource. The fourth parameter contains POST data to send with the request, and the final parameter allows you to pass additional HTTP header information. For our purposes, we can pass the default values for zero and the empty string into the last four parameters. These parameters are defined as optional parameters, but C# does not support optional parameters so we supply them explicitly. We also explicitly declare object references for these variables to pass them by reference.

Calling `Navigate()` with the parameters shown above is the same as typing the URL into the Internet Explorer address bar. This code is the only code we need to add to the `DisplayWebPage` project. If we run the example we get the results shown below (we have also used Visual Studio .NET to change the title text of the main form).

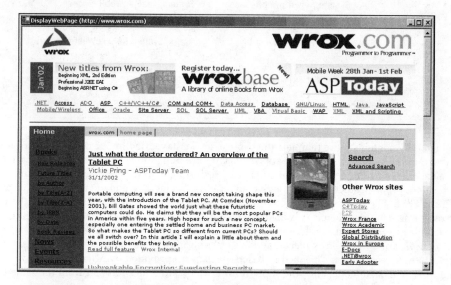

The Web Request and Web Response Hierarchy

In this section we will take a closer look at the architecture underlying the `WebRequest` and `WebResponse` classes.

The inheritance hierarchy of the classes involved is shown in the following diagram.

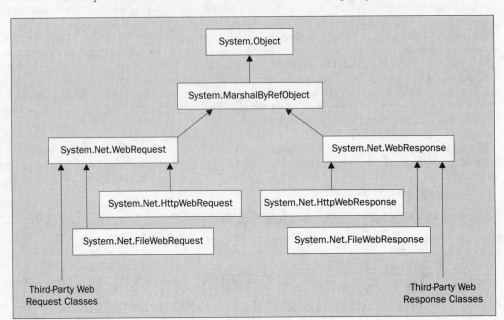

The hierarchy contains more than just the two classes we have used in our code. We also should point out that the WebRequest and WebResponse classes are both abstract, and cannot be instantiated. These base classes provide general functionality for dealing with web requests and responses independent of the protocol used for a given operation. Requests are made using a particular protocol (HTTP, FTP, SMTP, etc.) and a derived class written for the given protocol will handle the request. Microsoft refers to this scheme as "pluggable protocols". Remember in the code we examined earlier, our variables were defined as references to the base classes; however, WebRequest.Create() actually gave us an HttpWebRequest object, and the GetResponse() method actually returned an HttpWebResponse object. This factory-based mechanism provided by Microsoft hides many of the details from the client code, allowing support for a wide variety of protocols from the same code base.

The fact that we needed an object specifically capable of dealing with the HTTP protocol is clear from the URI that we supplied to WebRequest.Create(). WebRequest.Create() examines the protocol specifier in the URI to instantiate and return an object of the appropriate class. This keeps your code free from having to know anything about the derived classes or specific protocol used. When you need to access specific features of a protocol, you might need the properties and methods of the derived class, in which case you can cast your WebRequest or WebResponse reference to the derived class.

With this architecture we should be able to send requests using any of the common protocols. However, Microsoft currently only provides derived classes to cover the HTTP, HTTPS, and FILE protocols. If you want to utilize other protocols, for example, FTP or SMTP, then you will need to either fall back on the Windows API, write your own classes, or wait for an independent software vendor to write some the suitable .NET classes.

Utility Classes

In this section we will cover a couple of utility classes to make web programming easier when dealing with URIs and IP addresses.

URIs

`Uri` and `UriBuilder` are two classes in the `System` (note: not `System.Net`) namespace, and they are both intended to represent a URI. `UriBuilder` allows you to build a URI given the strings for the component parts, while the `Uri` class allows you to parse, combine, and compare URIs.

For the `Uri` class, the constructor requires a completed URI string.

```
Uri MSPage = new
        Uri("http://www.Microsoft.com/SomeFolder/SomeFile.htm?Order=true");
```

The class exposes a large number of read-only properties. A `Uri` object is not intended to be modified once it has been constructed.

```
string Query = MSPage.Query;                    // Order=true;
string AbsolutePath = MSPage.AbsolutePath;      // SomeFolder/SomeFile.htm
string Scheme = MSPage.Scheme;                  // http
int Port = MSPage.Port;                         // 80 (the default for http)
string Host = MSPage.Host;                      // www.Microsoft.com
bool IsDefaultPort = MSPage.IsDefaultPort;      // true since 80 is default
```

`URIBuilder`, on the other hand, implements fewer properties: just enough to allow you to build up a complete URI. These properties are read-write.

You can supply the components to build up a URI to the constructor:

```
Uri MSPage = new
    UriBuilder("http", "www.Microsoft.com", 80, "SomeFolder/SomeFile.htm")
```

Or you can build the components up by assigning values to the properties:

```
UriBuilder MSPage = new UriBuilder();
MSPage.Scheme ="http";
MSPage.Host = "www.Microsoft.com";
MSPage.Port = 80;
MSPage.Path = "SomeFolder/SomeFile.htm";
```

Once you have completed initializing the `UriBuilder`, you can obtain the corresponding `Uri` object with the `Uri` property:

```
Uri CompletedUri = MSPage.Uri;
```

The Display Page Example

We will illustrate the use of `UriBuilder` along with creating an Internet Explorer process with an example: `DisplayPage`. This example allows the user to type in the component parts of a URL. Note that we mean URL, not URI, since this is an HTTP request. The user can then click a button marked View Page and the application will display the completed URL in a textbox, and display the page using the web browser ActiveX control.

The example is a standard C# Windows application and looks as follows:

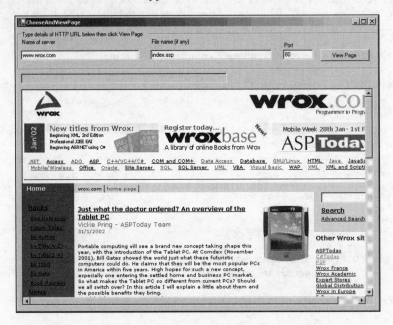

The textbox names are `txtBoxServer`, `txtBoxPath`, `txtBoxPort`, and `txtBoxURI` respectively. The code to add to the example is entirely in the `ViewPage` button event handler:

```
private void ViewPage_Click (object sender, System.EventArgs e)
{
    UriBuilder Address = new UriBuilder();
    Address.Host = txtBoxServer.Text;
    Address.Port = int.Parse(txtBoxPort.Text);
    Address.Scheme = Uri.UriSchemeHttp;
    Address.Path = txtBoxPath.Text;

    Uri AddressUri = Address.Uri;

    Process myProcess = new Process();
    myProcess.StartInfo.FileName = "iexplore.exe";
    txtBoxURI.Text = AddressUri.ToString();
    myProcess.StartInfo.Arguments = AddressUri.ToString();
    myProcess.Start();
}
```

IP Addresses and DNS Names

On the Internet we identify servers as well as clients by IP address or hostname (also referred to as a DNS name). Generally speaking, the hostname is the human-friendly name that you type in a web browser window, such as www.wrox.com or www.microsoft.com. An IP address, on the other hand, is the identifier computers use to identify each other. IP addresses are the identifiers used to ensure web requests and responses reach the appropriate machines. It is even possible for a computer to have more than one IP address.

Most human beings prefer the friendly host names like http://www.wrox.com over the direct use of IP addresses. For these names to work we must first send a network request to translate the hostname into an IP address, a task carried out by one or more DNS servers.

A DNS server stores a table mapping hostnames to IP addresses for all the computers it knows about, as well as the IP addresses of other DNS servers to look up the hostnames it does not know about. Your local computer should always know about at least one DNS server. Network administrators configure this information when a computer is set up.

Before sending out a request, your computer will first ask the DNS server to tell it the IP address corresponding to the host name you have typed in. Once armed with the correct IP address, the computer can address the request and send it over the network. All of this work normally happens behind the scenes to the user simply browsing the web.

.NET Classes for IP Addresses

The .NET Framework supplies a number of classes that are able to assist with the process of looking up IP addresses and finding out information about host computers.

IPAddress

IPAddress represents an IP address. The address itself is available as the Address property, and may be converted to dotted decimal format with the ToString() method. IPAddress also implements a static Parse() method, which effectively performs the reverse conversion of ToString() – converting from a dotted decimal string to an IPAddress.

```
IPAddress ipAddress = IPAddress.Parse("234.56.78.9");
long address = ipAddress.Address;
string ipString = ipAddress.ToString();
```

In the above example, the long integer address will be assigned 156121322, and the string ipString will be assigned the text "234.56.78.9".

IPAddress also provides a number of constant static fields to return special addresses. For example, the Loopback address allows a machine to send messages to itself, while the Broadcast address allows multicasting to the local network.

```
// The following line will set loopback to "127.0.0.1".
// the loopback address indicates the local host.
string loopback = IPAddress.Loopback.ToString();
```

```
// The following line will set broadcast address to "255.255.255.255".
// the broadcast address is used to send a message to all machines on
// the local network.
string broadcast = IPAddress.Broadcast.ToString();
```

IPHostEntry

The `IPHostEntry` class encapsulates information relating to a particular host computer. This class makes the hostname available via the `HostName` property (which returns a string), and the `AddressList` property returns an array of `IPAddress` objects. We are going to use the `IPHostEntry` class in the in next example: `DNSLookupResolver`.

Dns

The `Dns` class is able to communicate with your default DNS server in order to retrieve IP addresses. The two important (static) methods are `Resolve()`, which uses the DNS server to obtain the details of a host with a given host name, and `GetHostByAddress()`, which also returns details of the host, but this time using the IP address. Both methods return an `IPHostEntry` object.

```
IPHostEntry wroxHost = Dns.Resolve("www.wrox.com");
IPHostEntry wroxHostCopy = Dns.GetHostByAddress("204.148.170.161");
```

In this code both `IPHostEntry` objects will contain details of the Wrox.com servers.

The `Dns` class differs from the `IPAddress` and `IPHostEntry` classes since it has the ability to actually communicate with servers to obtain information. In contrast, `IPAddress` and `IPHostEntry` are more along the lines of simple data structures with convenient properties to allow access to the underlying data.

DnsLookup Example

We will illustrate the DNS and IP-related classes with an example that looks up DNS names. This screenshot shows the `DnsLookup` example in action:

The sample application simply invites the user to type in a DNS name using the main textbox. When the user clicks the Resolve button, the sample uses the `Dns.Resolve()` method to retrieve an `IPHostEntry` reference and display the hostname and IP addresses. Note how the hostname displayed may be different from the name typed in. This can occur if one DNS name (www.microsoft.com) simply acts as a proxy for another DNS name (www.microsoft.akadns.net).

The `DnsLookup` application is a standard C# Windows application, with the controls added as shown in the screenshot, giving them the names `txtBoxInput`, `btnResolve`, `txtBoxHostName`, and `listBoxIPs` respectively. Then we simply add the following method to the `Form1` class as the event handler for the `buttonResolve` click event.

```
void btnResolve_Click (object sender, EventArgs e)
{
    try
    {
        IPHostEntry iphost = Dns.Resolve(txtBoxInput.Text);
        foreach (IPAddress ip in iphost.AddressList)
        {
            long ipaddress = ip.Address;
            listBoxIPs.Items.Add(ipaddress);
            listBoxIPs.Items.Add("    " + ip.ToString());
        }
        txtBoxHostName.Text = iphost.HostName;
    }
    catch(Exception ex)
    {
        MessageBox.Show("Unable to process the request because " +
            "the following problem occurred:\n" +
             ex.Message, "Exception occurred");
    }
}
```

Notice how in this code we are careful to trap any exceptions. An exception may occur if the user types in an invalid DNS name, or if the network is down.

After retrieving the `IPHostEntry` instance, we use the `AddressList` property to obtain an array containing the IP addresses, which we then iterate through with a `foreach` loop. For each entry we display the IP address as an integer and as a string, using the `IPAddress.ToString()` method.

Lower-Level Protocols

In this section we will briefly mention some of the .NET classes used to communicate at a lower level.

Network communications work on several different levels. The classes we have covered in this chapter so far work at the highest level: the level at which specific commands are processed. It is probably easiest to understand this concept if we think of file transfer using FTP. Although today's GUI applications hide many of the FTP details, it was not so long ago when we executed FTP from a command-line prompt. In this environment we explicitly typed commands to send to the server for downloading, uploading, and listing files.

FTP is not the only high-level protocol relying on textual commands. HTTP, SMTP, POP, and other protocols are based on a similar type of behavior. Again, many of the modern graphical tools hide the transmission of commands from the user, so you are generally not aware of them. For example, when you type a URL into a web browser, and the web request goes off to a server, the browser is actually sending a (plain text) GET command to the server, which serves a similar purpose to the FTP get command. It may also send a POST command, which indicates that the browser has attached other data to the request.

However, these protocols are not sufficient by themselves to achieve communication between computers. Even if both the client and the server understand, for example, the HTTP protocol, it will still not be possible for them to understand each other unless there is also agreement on exactly how to transmit the characters: what binary format will be used, and getting down to the lowest level, what voltages will be used to represent 0s and 1s in the binary data? Since there are so many items to configure and agree upon, developers and hardware engineers in the networking field often refer to a protocol stack. When you list all of the various protocols and mechanisms required for communication between two hosts, you create a protocol stack with high-level protocols on the top and low-level protocols on the bottom. This approach results in a modular and layered approach to achieving efficient communication.

Luckily, for most development work, we don't need to go far down the stack or work with voltage levels, but if you are writing code that requires efficient communication between computers, it's not unusual to write code that works directly at the level of sending binary data packets between computers. This is the realm of protocols such as TCP, and Microsoft has supplied a number of classes that allow you to conveniently work with binary data at this level.

Lower-Level Classes

The System.Net.Sockets namespace contains the relevant classes. These classes, for example, allow you, to directly send out TCP network requests or to listen to TCP network requests on a particular port. The main classes are:

Class	Purpose
Socket	Low-level class that deals with actually managing connections. Classes such as WebRequest, TcpClient, and UdpClient use this class internally.
NetworkStream	Derived from Stream. Represents a stream of data from the network.
TcpClient	Lets you create and use TCP connections.
TcpListener	Lets you listen for incoming TCP connection requests.
UdpClient	Lets you create connections for UDP clients. (UDP is an alternative protocol to TCP, but is much less widely used – mostly on local networks.)

Using the TCP Classes

The transmission control protocol (TCP) classes offer simple methods for connecting and sending data between two endpoints. An endpoint is the combination of an IP address and a port number. Existing protocols have well defined port numbers, for example, HTTP uses port 80, while SMTP uses port 25. The Internet Assigned Number Authority, IANA, (http://www.iana.org/) assigns port numbers to these well-known services. Unless you are implementing a well-known service, you will want to select a port number above 1,024.

TCP traffic makes up the majority of traffic on the Internet today. TCP is often the protocol of choice because it offers guaranteed delivery, error correction, and buffering. The `TcpClient` class encapsulates a TCP connection and provides a number of properties to regulate the connection, including buffering, buffer size, and timeouts. Reading and writing is accomplished by requesting a `NetworkStream` object via the `GetStream()` method.

The `TcpListener` class listens for incoming TCP connections with the `Start()` method. When a connection request arrives you can use the `AcceptSocket()` method to return a socket for communication with the remote machine, or use the `AcceptTcpClient()` method to use a higher-level `TcpClient` object for communication. The easiest way to demonstrate the `TcpListener` and `TcpClient` classes working together is to present an example.

TcpSend and TcpReceive Example

To demonstrate these classes we need to build two applications. The first application, the **TcpSend** client application, is shown below. This application opens a TCP connection to a server and sends the C# sourcecode for itself.

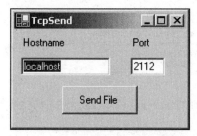

Once again we create a C# Windows Application. The form consists of two textboxes (`txtHost` and `txtPort`) for the host name and port respectively, as well as a button (`btnSend`) to click and start a connection. First, we ensure that we include the relevant namespaces:

```
using System.Net;
using System.Net.Sockets;
using System.IO;
```

The event handler for the button's click event is listed below.

```
private void btnSend_Click(object sender, System.EventArgs e)
{
    TcpClient tcpClient = new TcpClient(txtHost.Text, Int32.Parse(txtPort.Text));
```

```
    NetworkStream ns = tcpClient.GetStream();
    FileStream fs = File.Open("..\\..\\form1.cs", FileMode.Open);

    int data = fs.ReadByte();
    while(data != -1)
    {
       ns.WriteByte((byte)data);
       data = fs.ReadByte();
    }

    fs.Close();
    ns.Close();
    tcpClient.Close();
}
```

This example creates the `TcpClient` using a host name and a port number. Alternatively, if you have an instance of the `IPEndPoint` class, you can pass the instance to the `TcpClient` constructor. After retrieving an instance of the `NetworkStream` class we open the sourcecode file and begin to read bytes. Like many of the binary streams, we need to check for the end of stream by comparing the return value of the `ReadByte()` method to `-1`. Once our loop has read all of the bytes and sent them along to the network stream, we make sure to close all of the open files, connections, and streams.

On the other side of the connection, the `TcpReceive` application displays the received file after the transmission is finished. This application is shown below.

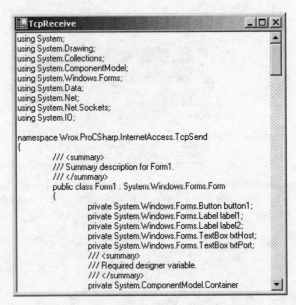

The form consists of a single RichTextBox control, named `txtDisplay`. The `TcpReceive` application uses a `TcpListener` to wait for the incoming connection. In order to avoid freezing the application interface, we use a background thread to wait for and then read from the connection. Thus we need to include the `System.Threading` namespace as well:

```
using System.Net;
using System.Net.Sockets;
using System.IO;
using System.Threading;
```

Inside the form's constructor we spin up a background thread:

```
public Form1()
{
    InitializeComponent();

    Thread thread = new Thread(new ThreadStart(Listen));
    thread.Start();
}
```

The remaining important code is below:

```
public void Listen()
{
    TcpListener tcpListener = new TcpListener(2112);
    tcpListener.Start();

    TcpClient tcpClient = tcpListener.AcceptTcpClient();

    NetworkStream ns = tcpClient.GetStream();
    StreamReader sr = new StreamReader(ns);
    string result = sr.ReadToEnd();
    Invoke(new UpdateDisplayDelegate(UpdateDisplay),
            new object[] {result} );

    tcpClient.Close();
    tcpListener.Stop();
}

public void UpdateDisplay(string text)
{
    txtDisplay.Text= text;
}

protected delegate void UpdateDisplayDelegate(string text);
```

The thread begins execution in the `Listen()` method and allows us to make the blocking call to `AcceptTcpClient()` without halting the interface. Notice how we have hard-coded port number 2112 into the application, so you will need to enter the same port number from the client application.

We use the `TcpClient` object returned by `AccepTcpClient()` to open a new stream for reading. Similar to the example earlier in the chapter, we create a `StreamReader` to easily convert the incoming network data into a string. Before we close the client and stop the listener, we update the form's textbox. We do not want to directly access the textbox from our background thread, so we use the form's `Invoke()` method with a delegate, and pass the result string as the first element in an array of `object` parameters. `Invoke()` ensures our call is correctly marshaled into the thread owning the control handles in the user interface.

975

TCP versus UDP

The other protocol to cover in this section is UDP (User Datagram Protocol). UDP is a simple protocol with few features but also little overhead. Developers often use UDP in applications where the speed and performance requirements outweigh the reliability needs, for example, video streaming. In contrast, TCP offers a number of features to confirm the delivery of data. TCP provides error correction and re-transmission in the case of lost or corrupted packets. Finally, TCP buffers incoming and outgoing data and also guarantees a sequence of packets scrambled in transmission are reassembled before delivery to the application. Even with the extra overhead, TCP is the most widely used protocol across the Internet because of the higher reliability.

UDP Class

As you might expect, the `UdpClient` class features a smaller and simpler interface compared to `TcpClient`. This reflects the relatively simpler nature of the protocol in comparison to TCP. While both TCP and UDP classes use a socket underneath the covers, the `UdpClient` client does not contain a method to return a network stream for reading and writing. Instead, the member function `Send()` accepts an array of bytes as a parameter, while the `Receive()` function returns an array of bytes. Also, since UDP is a connectionless protocol, you can wait to specify the endpoint for the communication as a parameter to the `Send()` and `Receive()` methods, instead of earlier in a constructor or `Connect()` method. You can also change the endpoint on each subsequent send or receive.

The following code fragment uses the `UdpClient` class to send a message to an echo service. A server with an echo service running accepts TCP or UDP connections on port 7. The echo service simply echoes any data sent to the server back to the client. This service is useful for diagnostics and testing, although many system administrators disable echo services for security reasons.

```csharp
using System;
using System.Text;
using System.Net;
using System.Net.Sockets;


namespace Wrox.ProCSharp.InternetAccess.UdpExample
{

    class Class1
    {
        [STAThread]
        static void Main(string[] args)
        {
            UdpClient udpClient = new UdpClicnt();

            string sendMsg = "Hello Echo Server";
            byte [] sendBytes = Encoding.ASCII.GetBytes(sendMsg);

            udpClient.Send(sendBytes, sendBytes.Length, "SomeEchoServer.net", 7);

            IPEndPoint endPoint = new IPEndPoint(0,0);
            byte [] rcvBytes = udpClient.Receive(ref endPoint);
            string rcvMessage = Encoding.ASCII.GetString(rcvBytes,
                                                         0,
                                                         rcvBytes.Length);

            // should print out "Hello Echo Server"
            Console.WriteLine(rcvMessage);
        }
    }
}
```

We make heavy use of the `Encoding.ASCII` class to translate strings into arrays of `byte` and vice versa. Also notice we pass an `IPEndPoint` by reference into the `Receive()` method. Since UDP is not a connection oriented protocol, each call to `Receive()` may pick up data from a different end point, so `Receive()` populates this parameter with the IP address and port of the sending host.

Both `UdpClient` and `TcpClient` offer a layer of abstraction over the lowest of the low level classes: the `Socket`.

Socket Class

The `Socket` class offers the highest level of control in network programming. One of the easiest ways to demonstrate the class is to rewrite the `TcpReceive` application with the `Socket` class. The updated `Listen()` method is listed below.

```
public void Listen()
{
    Socket listener = new Socket(AddressFamily.InterNetwork,
                                 SocketType.Stream,
                                 ProtocolType.Tcp);
    listener.Bind(new IPEndPoint(IPAddress.Any, 2112));
    listener.Listen(0);

    Socket socket = listener.Accept();
    Stream netStream = new NetworkStream(socket);
    StreamReader reader = new StreamReader(netStream);

    string result = reader.ReadToEnd();

    Invoke(new UpdateDisplayDelegate(UpdateDisplay),
           new object[] {result} );
    socket.Close();
    listener.Close();
}
```

The `Socket` class requires a few more lines of code to complete the same task. For starters, the constructor arguments need to specify an IP addressing scheme for a streaming socket with the TCP protocol. These arguments are just one of the many combinations available to the `Socket` class, and the `TcpClient` class configured these settings for you. We then bind the listener socket to a port and begin to listen for incoming connections. When an incoming request arrives we can use the `Accept()` method to create a new socket for handling the connection. We ultimately attach a `StreamReader` instance to the socket to read the incoming data, in much the same fashion as before.

The `Socket` class also contains a number of methods for asynchronously accepting, connecting, sending, and receiving. You can use these methods with callback delegates in the same way we used the asynchronous page requests with the `WebRequest` class. If you really need to dig into the internals of the socket, the `GetSocketOption()` and `SetSocketOption()` methods are available. These methods allow you to see and configure options including timeout, time-to-live, and other low-level options.

Summary

In this chapter we have reviewed the .NET Framework classes available in the `System.Net` namespace for communication across networks. We have seen some of the .NET base classes that deal with opening client connections on the network and Internet, and how to send requests to, and receive responses from servers; the most obvious use of this being to receive HTML pages. By taking advantage of COM interoperability in .NET, you can easily make use of Internet Explorer from your desktop applications.

As a rule of thumb, when programming with classes in the `System.Net` namespace, you should always try to use the most generic class possible. For instance, using the `TCPClient` class instead of the `Socket` class isolates your code from many of the lower-level socket details. Moving one step higher, the `WebRequest` class allows you to take advantage of the pluggable protocol architecture of the .NET Framework. Your code will be ready to take advantage of new application-level protocols as Microsoft and other third parties introduce new functionality.

Finally, we saw the use of the asynchronous capabilities in the networking classes, which give a Windows Forms application the professional touch of a responsive user interface.

21

Distributed Applications with .NET Remoting

In this chapter we will explore .NET Remoting. .NET Remoting can be used for accessing objects in another application domain, for example on another server. In Chapter 15, we discussed ASP.NET web services; these allow us to call objects on a remote server. .NET Remoting also offers programming web services, but it is more complex than ASP.NET, and also much more flexible. With .NET Remoting, we can offer web services from any application type, such as a Windows service or a Windows application. .NET Remoting offers great flexibility for the use of different network protocols and control of the formatting of any data that is sent across application domains.

In this chapter we will develop .NET Remoting objects, clients, and servers using the HTTP and TCP channel with the SOAP and binary formatter. First we will define the channel and formatter programmatically before we change the application to use configuration files instead, where only a few .NET Remoting methods are required. We will also write small programs to use .NET Remoting asynchronously, and calling event handlers in the client application.

The .NET Remoting classes can be found in the namespace System.Runtime.Remoting and sub-namespaces thereof. Many of these classes can be found in the core assembly mscorlib, and some that are needed only for cross-network communication are available in the assembly System.Runtime.Remoting.

The .NET Remoting topics we look at in this chapter, are as follows:

- ❑ An overview of .NET Remoting
- ❑ Contexts, which are used to group objects with similar execution requirements
- ❑ Implementing a simple remote object, client, and server

❑   The .NET Remoting architecture

   ❑ Channels, messages, and sinks

   ❑ SOAP and binary formatters

   ❑ Activating well-known objects and client-activated objects

   ❑ Passing objects across the network

   ❑ Lifetime Management of stateful client-activated objects

❑   .NET Remoting Configuration files

❑   Hosting .NET Remoting objects in ASP.NET

❑   Using Soapsuds to access the metadata of remote objects

❑   Calling .NET Remoting methods asynchronously

❑   Calling methods in the client with the help of events

❑   Using the CallContext to automatically pass data to the server

.NET Remoting is a massive subject, but this chapter will provide you with the information and relevant examples you need to get started, and to gain a practical handle on the topic. For a deeper examination of .NET Remoting, see Professional C# Web Services: Building .NET Web Services with ASP.NET and .NET Remoting *(Wrox Press, 1-861004-39-7).*

Let's begin by finding out what .NET Remoting is.

What is .NET Remoting?

In Chapter 15, we talked about the SOAP protocol that is used with ASP.NET Web services, which allow us to call objects on a remote server. The use of a web server and the SOAP protocol is not always efficient enough for intranet applications. The SOAP protocol causes a lot of overhead when transferring a lot of data. For a fast intranet solution, we could use simple sockets as we've done in the last chapter. In the "old world" however, you may have already written programs using DCOM. With DCOM, we are used to calling methods on objects running on a server. The programming model is the same whether objects are used on the server or on the client.

Without DCOM, we have to deal with ports and sockets, pay attention to the target platforms because of possibly different data representations, and build a custom protocol, where messages are sent to the socket so that we finally call some methods. DCOM handles all these issues for us.

The replacement for DCOM is **.NET Remoting**. In contrast to DCOM, .NET Remoting can also be used in Internet solutions. DCOM is not flexible and efficient enough for use in Internet solutions. It's possible to adapt and extend every part of the architecture with .NET Remoting, so it fits for nearly all remoting scenarios.

Two expressions can describe .NET Remoting: **Web Services Anywhere** and **CLR Object Remoting**. Let's have a closer look at what these two phrases mean.

Web Services Anywhere

The expression **Web Services Anywhere** is used with .NET Remoting. It means that with .NET Remoting, web services can be used in *any application* over *any transport,* using *any payload encoding.* .NET Remoting is an extremely flexible architecture.

Using SOAP and HTTP together is just one way to call remote objects. The transport channel is pluggable, and can be replaced. We get HTTP and TCP channels represented by the classes `HttpChannel` and `TcpChannel`. We can build transport channels to use UDP, IPX, SMTP, a shared memory mechanism, or message queuing – the choice is yours entirely.

> *The term **pluggable** is often used with .NET Remoting. Pluggable means that a specific part is designed so that it can be replaced by a custom implementation.*

The payload is used to transport the parameters of a method call. This payload encoding can also be replaced. Microsoft delivers SOAP and binary encoding mechanisms. We can use the SOAP formatter using the HTTP channel, but it's also possible to use HTTP using the binary formatter. Of course, both of these formatters can also be used with the TCP channel.

.NET Remoting not only makes it possible to use web services in every .NET application, but also allows us to *offer* web services in *every* application. It doesn't matter if we build a console or a Windows application, a Windows Service, or a COM+ component – web services can be used anywhere!

CLR Object Remoting

CLR Object Remoting sits on top of web services anywhere. CLR Object Remoting makes it easy to use web services. All of the language constructs, such as constructors, delegates, interfaces, methods, properties, and fields, can be used with remote objects. Calling a remote object can be as easy as calling a local object. CLR Object Remoting deals with activation, distributed identities, lifetimes, and call contexts.

.NET Remoting Overview

.NET Remoting can be used for accessing objects in another application domain. .NET Remoting can always be used whether the two objects live inside a single process, in separate processes, or on separate systems.

Remote assemblies can be configured to work locally in the application domain or as a part of a remote application. If the assembly is part of the remote application then the client receives a proxy to talk to instead of the real object. The proxy is a representative of the remote object in the client process, used by the client application to call methods. When the client calls a method in the proxy, the proxy sends a message into the channel that is passed on to the remote object.

.NET applications work within an application domain. An application domain can be seen as a sub-process within a process. Traditionally, processes were used as an isolation boundary. An application running in one process cannot access and destroy memory in another process. For applications to communicate with each other, cross-process communication is needed. With .NET, the application domain is the new safety boundary inside a process, because the MSIL code is type-safe and verifiable. As we discussed in Chapter 8, different applications can run inside the same process but within different application domains. Objects inside the same application domain can interact directly; a proxy is needed in order to access objects in a different application domain.

Before we look into the internal functionality of .NET Remoting, let's have a look at the major elements of the architecture:

❑ A **remote object** is an object that's running on the server. The client doesn't call methods on this object directly, but uses a proxy instead. With .NET it's easy to differentiate remote objects from local objects: every class that's derived from MarshalByRefObject never leaves its application domain. The client can call methods of the remote object via a proxy.

❑ A **channel** is used for communication between the client and the server. There are client and server parts of the channel. With the .NET Framework, we get two channel types that communicate via TCP or HTTP. We can also create a custom channel that communicates using a different protocol.

❑ **Messages** are sent into the channel. Messages are created for communication between the client and the server. These messages hold the information about the remote object, the method name called, and all of the arguments.

❑ The **formatter** defines how messages are transferred into the channel. With the .NET Framework, we have SOAP and binary formatters. The SOAP formatter can be used to communicate with web services that are not based on the .NET Framework. Binary formatters are much faster and can be used efficiently in an intranet environment. Of course, you also have the possibility to create a custom formatter.

❑ A **formatter provider** is used to associate a formatter with a channel. By creating a channel, we can specify what formatter provider to use, and this in turn defines the formatter that will be used to transfer the data into the channel.

❑ The client calls methods on a **proxy** instead of the remote object. There are two types of proxies: the **transparent proxy** and the **real proxy**. To the client, the transparent proxy looks like the remote object. On the transparent proxy, the client can call the methods implemented by the remote objects. In turn, the transparent proxy calls the Invoke() method on the real proxy. The Invoke() method uses the message sink to pass the message to the channel.

❑ A **message sink,** or just a **sink,** is an interceptor object. We have such interceptors on both the client and on the server. A sink is associated with the channel. The real proxy uses the message sink to pass the message into the channel, so the sink can do some interception before the message goes into the channel. Depending on where the sink it used, it is known as an envoy sink, a server context sink, an object context sink, and so on.

❑ The client can use an **activator** to create a remote object on the server or to get a proxy of a server-activated object.

❑ RemotingConfiguration is a utility class to configure remote servers and clients. This class can be used either to read configuration files, or to configure remote objects dynamically.

`ChannelServices` is a utility class to register channels and then to dispatch messages to them.

To get a better insight into the functionality, let's look at a conceptual picture of how these pieces fit together:

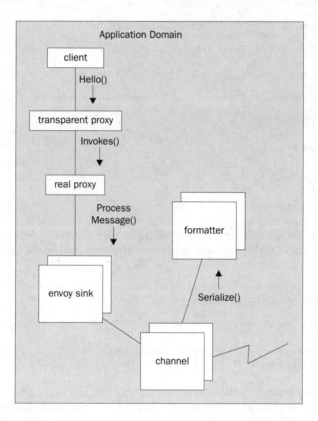

When the client calls methods on a remote object, it actually calls methods on a transparent proxy instead. The transparent proxy looks like the real object – it implements the public methods of the real object. The transparent proxy knows about the public methods of the real object by using the reflection mechanism to read the metadata from the assembly.

In turn, the transparent proxy calls the real proxy. The real proxy is responsible for sending the message to the channel. The real proxy is pluggable; we can replace it with a custom implementation. A custom implementation can be used to write a log, or to use another way to find a channel, and so on. The default implementation of the real proxy locates the collection (or chain) of envoy sinks and passes the message to the first envoy sink. An envoy sink can intercept and change the message. Examples of such sinks are debugging sinks, security sinks, and synchronization sinks.

The last envoy sink sends the message into the channel. How the messages are sent over the wire depends on the formatter. As previously stated, we have SOAP and binary formatters. The formatter however, is also pluggable. The channel is responsible for either connecting to a listening socket on the server or sending the formatted data. With a custom channel you can do something different; we just have to implement the code to do what's necessary to transfer the data to the other side:

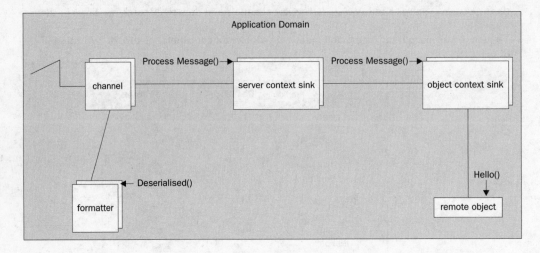

Let's continue with the server side.

❑ The channel receives the formatted messages from the client and uses the formatter to unmarshal the SOAP or binary data into messages. Then the channel calls server-context sinks.

❑ The server-context sinks are a chain of sinks, where the last sink in the chain continues the call to the chain of object-context sinks.

❑ The last object-context sink then calls the method in the remote object.

Note that the object-context sinks are confined to the object context, and the server-context sinks are confined to the server context. A single server-context sink can be used to access a number of object sinks.

> *.NET Remoting is extremely customizable: we can replace the real proxy, add sink objects, or replace the formatter and channel. Of course, we can also use all what's already provided.*

If you're wondering about the overhead when going through these layers, there's not much overhead if nothing is happening in there. If you add your own functionality, the overhead will depend on that.

Contexts

Before we look at using .NET Remoting to build servers and clients that communicate across a network, let's look at the cases where a channel is needed inside an application domain: calling objects across contexts.

If you've written COM+ components, you already know about COM+ contexts. Contexts in .NET are very similar. A context is a boundary containing a collection of objects. Likewise, with a COM+ context, the objects in such a collection require the same usage rules that are defined by the context attributes.

As you already know, a single process can have multiple application domains. An application domain is something like a sub-process with security boundaries. We discussed application domains in Chapter 8.

An application domain can have different contexts. A context is used to group objects with similar execution requirements. Contexts are composed from a set of properties and are used for interception: when a **context-bound object** is accessed from a different context, an **interceptor** can do some work before the call reaches the object. Examples where this can be used are for thread synchronization, transactions, and security management.

A class that is derived from `MarshalByRefObject` is bound to the application domain. Outside the application domain a proxy is needed to access the object. A class derived from `ContextBoundObject` that itself derives from `MarshalByRefObject` is bound to a context. Outside the context, a proxy is needed to access the object.

Context-bound objects can have **context attributes**. A context-bound object without context attributes is created in the context of the creator. A context-bound object with context attributes is created in a new context, or in the creator's context if the attributes are compatible.

To further understand contexts we have to know some terms:

❑ Creating an application domain creates the **default context** in this application domain. If a new object is instantiated that needs different context properties a new context is created.

❑ **Context attributes** can be assigned to classes derived from `ContextBoundObject`. We can create a custom attribute class by implementing the interface `IContextAttribute`. The .NET Framework has one context attribute class in the namespace `System.Runtime.Remoting.Contexts: SynchronizationAttribute`.

❑ Context attributes define **context properties** that are needed for an object. A context property class implements the interface `IContextProperty`. Active properties contribute message sinks to the call chain. The class `ContextAttribute` implements both `IContextProperty` and `IContextAttribute`, and can be used as a base class for custom attributes.

❑ A **message sink** is an interceptor for a method call. With a message sink we can intercept method calls. Properties can contribute to message sinks.

Activation

A new context is created if an instance of a class that's created needs a context different from the calling context. The attribute classes that are associated with the target class are asked if all the properties of the current context are acceptable. If any of these properties are unacceptable, the runtime asks for all property classes associated with the attribute class and creates a new context. The runtime then asks the property classes for the sinks they want to install. A property class can implement one of the `IContributeXXXSink` interfaces to contribute sink objects. There are several of these interfaces to go with the variety of sinks.

Attributes and Properties

With context attributes we define the properties of a context. A context attribute class primarily is an attribute. You can read more about attributes in Chapter 4. Context attribute classes must implement the interface IContextAttribute. A custom context attribute class can derive from the class ContextAttribute, because this class already has a default implementation of this interface.

With the .NET Framework we have one context attribute class: System.Runtime.Remoting.Contexts.SynchronizationAttribute. The Synchronization attribute defines synchronization requirements – it specifies the synchronization property that is needed by the object. We can specify that multiple threads cannot access the object concurrently, but the thread accessing the object can change.

With the constructor of this attribute we can set four values:

❑ NOT_SUPPORTED defines that the class should not be instantiated in a context where the synchronization is set

❑ REQUIRED specifies that we need a context with synchronization

❑ With REQUIRES_NEW we always get a new context

❑ SUPPORTED means that it doesn't matter what context we get, the object can live in it

Communication between Contexts

So, how does the communication between contexts happen? The client uses a proxy instead of the real object. The proxy creates a message that is transferred to a channel, and sinks can do interception. Does this sound familiar? It ought to. The same mechanism is used for communication across different application domains or different systems. A TCP or HTTP channel is not required for the communication across contexts, but a channel is used here too. CrossContextChannel can use the same virtual memory in both the client and server sides of the channel, and formatters are not required for crossing contexts.

Remote Objects, Clients, and Servers

Before we step into the details of the .NET Remoting architecture, let's look briefly at a remote object and a very small, simple client-server application that uses this remote object. After that, we will look in more detail at all the required steps and options.

The remote object we implement is called `Hello`. `HelloServer` is the main class of the application on the server, and `HelloClient` is for the client:

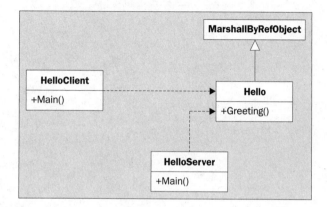

Remote Objects

Remote objects are needed for distributed computing. An object that should be called remotely from a different system must be derived from `System.MarshalByRefObject`. `MarshalByRefObject` objects are **confined to the application domain** in which they were created. This means that they are never passed across application domains; instead a proxy object is used to access the remote object from another application domain. The other application domain can live inside the same process, in another process, or on another system.

A remote object has **distributed identity**. Because of this, a reference to the object can be passed to other clients, and they will still access the same object. The proxy knows about the identity of the remote object.

The `MarshalByRefObject` class has, in addition to the inherited methods from the `Object` class, methods to initialize and get the lifetime services. The lifetime services define how long the remote object lives. Lifetime services and the leasing features will be dealt with later in this chapter.

To see .NET Remoting in action, we will begin with a simple Class Library to create a remote object. The class `Hello` derives from `System.MarshalByRefObject`. In the constructor and destructor, a message is written to the console so that we know about the object's lifetime. In addition, we have just a single method, `Greeting()`, that will be called from the client.

In order to easily distinguish between the assembly and the class in the following sections, we have given them different names in the arguments of the method calls used. The name of the assembly is `RemoteHello`, and the class is named `Hello`.

```
using System;

namespace Wrox.ProCSharp.Remoting
{

    public class Hello : System.MarshalByRefObject
```

```
    {
        public Hello()
        {
            Console.WriteLine("Constructor called");
        }
        ~Hello()
        {
            Console.WriteLine("Destructor called");
        }

        public string Greeting(string name)
        {
            Console.WriteLine("Greeting called");
            return "Hello, " + name;
        }
    }
}
```

A Simple Server

For the server we create a new C# console application `HelloServer`. To use the `TcpServerChannel` class, we have to reference the `System.Runtime.Remoting` assembly. It's also required that we reference the `RemoteHello` assembly that we created earlier.

In the `Main()` method a `System.Runtime.Remoting.Channels.Tcp.TcpServerChannel` is created with the port number 8086. This channel is registered with the `System.Runtime.Remoting.Channels.ChannelServices` class to make it available for remote objects. The remote object type is registered using `System.Runtime.Remoting.RemotingConfiguration.RegisterWellKnownServiceType`. Here we specify the type of the class in the remote object, the URI that is used by the client, and a mode. The mode `WellKnownObject.SingleCall` means that a new instance is created for every method call; we do not hold state in the remote object.

> *.NET Remoting allows creating **stateless** and **stateful** remote objects. In our first example we use **well-known single-call** objects that don't hold state. The other object type is called **client-activated**. Client-activated objects hold state. Later in this chapter we look at the object activation sequence, and go into more detail about these differences, and how these object types can be used.*

After registration of the remote object, we keep the server running until a key is pressed:

```
using System;
using System.Runtime.Remoting;
using System.Runtime.Remoting.Channels;
using System.Runtime.Remoting.Channels.Tcp;

namespace Wrox.ProCSharp.Remoting
{

    public class HelloServer
    {
        [STAThread]
```

```
    public static void Main(string[] args)
    {
        TcpServerChannel channel = new TcpServerChannel(8086);
        ChannelServices.RegisterChannel(channel);
        RemotingConfiguration.RegisterWellKnownServiceType(
                                    typeof(Hello), "Hi",
                                    WellKnownObjectMode.SingleCall);
        System.Console.WriteLine("hit to exit");
        System.Console.ReadLine();
    }
  }
}
```

A Simple Client

The client is again a C# console application: HelloClient. Here the System.Runtime.Remoting assembly is also referenced so that we can use the TcpClientChannel class. In addition, we also have to reference our RemoteHello assembly. Although we will create the object on the remote server, we need the assembly on the client for the proxy to read the metadata during run time.

In the client program we're creating a TcpClientChannel object that's registered in ChannelServices. For the TcpChannel we are using the default constructor, so a free port is selected. Next the Activator class is used to return a proxy to the remote object. The proxy is of type System.Runtime.Remoting.Proxies.__TransparentProxy. This object looks like the real object. This is all achieved by reflection, where the metadata of the real object is read. The transparent proxy uses the real proxy to send messages to the channel:

```
using System;
using System.Runtime.Remoting.Channels;
using System.Runtime.Remoting.Channels.Tcp;

namespace Wrox.ProCSharp.Remoting
{

    public class HelloClient
    {
        [STAThread]
        public static void Main(string[] args)
        {
            ChannelServices.RegisterChannel(new TcpClientChannel());
            Hello obj = (Hello)Activator.GetObject(
                                    typeof(Hello), "tcp://localhost:8086/Hi");
            if (obj == null)
            {
                Console.WriteLine("could not locate server");
                return;
            }
            for (int i=0; i< 5; i++)
            {
                Console.WriteLine(obj.Greeting("Christian"));
            }
        }
    }
}
```

When we start the server and the client program Hello, Christian appears five times in the client console. In the console window of the server application we see a similar output to this window:

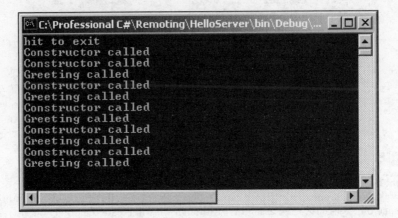

The first constructor is called the first time a method of the object is called remotely. Then for every method call a new instance gets created because we selected the WellKnownObjectMode.SingleCall activation mode. Depending on timing and resources needed, you may also see some destructor calls. If you start the client a few times you are sure to see some destructor calls.

.NET Remoting Architecture

After we've seen a simple client and server in action, we need an overview of the .NET architecture before we can go into the details. Based on the previously created program we will look at the details of the architecture and will see mechanisms for extensibility.

In this section, we shall explore all the topics in this list:

❑ The functionality of a channel and how a channel can be configured

❑ Formatters and how they are used

❑ The utility classes ChannelServices and RemotingConfiguration

❑ Different ways to activate remote objects, and how stateless and stateful objects can be used with .NET Remoting

❑ Functionality of Message Sinks

❑ How to pass objects by value and by reference

❑ Lifetime Management of stateful objects with .NET Remoting leasing mechanisms

Channels

A channel is used to communicate between a .NET client and a server. The .NET Framework ships with channel classes that communicate using TCP or HTTP. We can create custom channels for other protocols.

The **HTTP channel** is used by most web services. It uses the HTTP protocol for communication. Because firewalls usually have port 80 opened so that the clients can access web servers, our .NET Remoting web services can listen to port 80 so that they can be used by these clients easily.

It's also possible to use the **TCP channel** on the Internet, but here the firewalls must be configured so that clients can access a specified port that's used by the TCP channel. The TCP channel can be used to communicate more efficiently in an intranet compared to the HTTP channel.

When performing a method call on the remote object, the client channel object sends a message to the remote channel object.

Both the server and the client application must create a channel. This code shows how a `TcpServerChannel` can be created on the server side:

```
using System.Runtime.Remoting.Channels.Tcp;
   ...
TcpServerChannel channel = new TcpServerChannel(8086);
```

The port on which the TCP socket is listening is specified in the constructor argument. The server channel must specify a well-known port, and the client must use this port when accessing the server. For creating a `TcpClientChannel` on the client, however, it isn't necessary to specify a well-known port. The default constructor of `TcpClientChannel` chooses an available port, which is passed to the server at connection-time so that the server can send data back to the client.

Creating a new channel instance immediately switches the socket to the listening state, which can be verified by typing `netstat -a` at the command line.

The HTTP channels can be used similarly to the TCP channels. We can specify the port where the server can create the listening socket.

A server can listen to multiple channels. Here we are creating both an HTTP and a TCP channel in the file `HelloServer.cs`:

```
using System;
using System.Runtime.Remoting;
using System.Runtime.Remoting.Channels;
using System.Runtime.Remoting.Channels.Tcp;
using System.Runtime.Remoting.Channels.Http;

namespace Wrox.ProCSharp.Remoting
{

    public class HelloServer
    {
        [STAThread]
        public static void Main(string[] args)
        {
            TcpServerChannel tcpChannel = new TcpServerChannel(8086);
```

```
        HttpServerChannel httpChannel = new HttpServerChannel(8085);

        //...
        // register the channel and remote object as we have done previously
    }
```

A channel class must implement the `IChannel` interface. The `IChannel` interface has these two properties:

- `ChannelName` is a read-only property that returns the name of the channel. The name of the channel depends on the type – for example the HTTP channel is named `HTTP`.

- `ChannelPriority` is a read-only property. More than one channel can be used for communication between a client and a server. The priority defines the order of the channel. On the client, the channel with the higher priority is chosen first to connect to the server. The bigger the priority value, the higher the priority. The default value is 1, but negative values are allowed to create lower priorities.

Additional interfaces are implemented depending on whether the channel is a client-channel or a server-channel. The server versions of the channels implement the `IChannelReceiver` interface, the client versions implement the `IChannelSender` interface.

The `HttpChannel` and `TcpChannel` classes can be used for both the client and the server. They implement `IChannelSender` and `IChannelReceiver`. These interfaces derive from `IChannel`.

The client-side `IChannelSender` has, in addition to `IChannel`, a single method called `CreateMessageSink()`, which returns an object that implements `IMessageSink`. The `IMessageSink` interface can be used for putting synchronous as well as asynchronous messages into the channel. With the server-side interface `IChannelReceiver`, the channel can be put into listening mode using `StartListening()`, and stopped again with `StopListening()`. We also have a `ChannelData` property to access the received data.

We can get information about the configuration of the channels using properties of the channel classes. For both channels, we have a `ChannelName`, a `ChannelPriority`, and a `ChannelData` property. The `ChannelData` property can be used to get information about the URIs that are stored in the `ChannelDataStore` class. With the `HttpChannel` there's also a `Scheme` property. The code below shows a helper method, `ShowChannelProperties()`, in our file `HelloServer.cs` that displays this information:

```
protected static void ShowChannelProperties(IChannelReceiver channel)
{
    Console.WriteLine("Name: " + channel.ChannelName);
    Console.WriteLine("Priority: " + channel.ChannelPriority);
    if (channel is HttpChannel)
    {
        HttpChannel httpChannel = channel as HttpChannel;
        Console.WriteLine("Scheme: " + httpChannel.ChannelScheme);
    }
    ChannelDataStore data = (ChannelDataStore)channel.ChannelData;
    foreach (string uri in data.ChannelUris)
    {
        Console.WriteLine("URI: " + uri);
    }
    Console.WriteLine();
}
```

The method `ShowChannelProperties()` is called after creating the channels in our `Main()` method:

```
TcpServerChannel tcpChannel = new TcpServerChannel(8086);
ShowChannelProperties(tcpChannel);
HttpServerChannel httpChannel = new HttpServerChannel(8085);
ShowChannelProperties(httpChannel);
```

With our TCP and HTTP channels, we get this information:

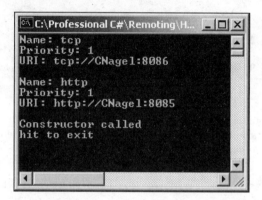

As we can see here, the default name for the `TcpServerChannel` is `tcp`, and the HTTP channel is called `http`. Both channels have a default priority of 1 and I've set the ports 8085 and 8086 in the constructors. The URI of the channels shows the protocol, hostname (in my case `CNagel`), and port number.

Setting Channel Properties

We can set all the properties of a channel in a list using the constructor `TcpServerChannel(IDictionary, IServerChannelSinkProvider)`. The `Hashtable` class implements `IDictionary`, so I'm setting the `Name`, `Priority`, and `Port` property with help of this class.

In order to use the `Hashtable` class we have to declare the use of the `System.Collections` namespace. In addition to the `IDictionary` parameter we can pass an `IServerChannelSinkProvider` parameter. I pass a `SoapServerFormatterSinkProvider` instead of the `BinaryServerFormatterSinkProvider`, which is the default of the `TcpServerChannel`. The default implementation of the `SoapServerFormatterSinkProvider` class associates a `SoapServerFormatterSink` class with the channel that uses a `SoapFormatter` to convert the data for the transfer:

```
IDictionary properties = new Hashtable();
properties["name"] = "TCP Channel with a SOAP Formatter";
properties["priority"] = "20";
properties["port"] = "8086";
SoapServerFormatterSinkProvider sinkProvider =
                    new SoapServerFormatterSinkProvider();
TcpServerChannel tcpChannel =
                    new TcpServerChannel(properties, sinkProvider);
ShowChannelProperties(tcpChannel);
```

The new output we get from our server startup code shows the new properties of the TCP channel:

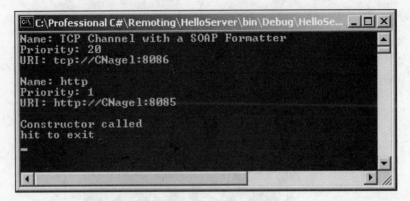

Depending on the channel types, different properties can be specified. Both the TCP and the HTTP channel support the name and `priority` channel property that we used in our example. These channels also support other properties such as `bindTo`, which specifies an IP address for binding that can be used if the computer has multiple IP addresses configured. `rejectRemoteRequests` is supported by the TCP server channel to allow client connections only from the local computer.

Pluggability of a Channel

A custom channel can be created to send the messages using a transport protocol other than HTTP or TCP, or you can extend the existing channels:

❑ The sending part must implement the `IchannelSender` interface. The most important part is the `CreateMessageSink()` method, which the client sends a URL, and with this a connection to the server can be instantiated. Here a message sink must be created, which is then used by the proxy to send messages to the channel.

❑ The receiving part must implement the `IchannelReceiver` interface. We have to start the listening in the `ChannelData get` property. Then we can wait in a separate thread to receive data from the client. After unmarshaling the message, we can use `ChannelServices.SyncDispatchMessage()` to dispatch the message to the object.

Formatters

The .NET Framework delivers two formatter classes:

❑ `System.Runtime.Serialization.Formatters.Binary.BinaryFormatter`

❑ `System.Runtime.Serialization.Formatters.Soap.SoapFormatter`

Formatters are associated with channels through formatter sink objects and formatter sink providers.

Both of these formatter classes implement the interface `System.Runtime.Remoting.Messaging.IRemotingFormatter`, which defines the methods `Serialize()` and `Deserialize()` to transfer the data to and from the channel.

The formatter is also pluggable. When you're writing a custom formatter class, an instance must be associated with the channel you want to use. This is done using a formatter sink and a formatter sink provider. The formatter sink provider, for example, `SoapServerFormatterSinkProvider`, can be passed as an argument when creating a channel as we saw earlier. A formatter sink provider implements the interface `IServerChannelSinkProvider` for the server, and `IClientChannelSinkProvider` for the client. Both of these interfaces define a `CreateSink()` method where a formatter sink must be returned. The `SoapServerFormatterSinkProvider` returns an instance of the class `SoapServerFormatterSink`. On the client side, we have the `SoapClientFormatterSink` class that uses the `SyncProcessMessage()` and `AsyncProcessMessage()` methods of the `SoapFormatter` class to serialize the message. The `SoapServerFormatterSink` deserializes the message, again using the `SoapFormatter`.

All these sink and provider classes can be extended and replaced with custom implementations.

ChannelServices and RemotingConfiguration

The `ChannelServices` utility class is used to register channels into the .NET Remoting runtime. With this class we can also access all registered channels. This is extremely useful if configuration files are used to configure the channel, because here the channel is created implicitly, as we will see later.

A channel is registered using the static method `ChannelServices.RegisterChannel()`.

You can see here the server code to register our HTTP and TCP channels:

```
TcpChannel tcpChannel = new TcpChannel(8086);
HttpChannel httpChannel = new HttpChannel(8085);
ChannelServices.RegisterChannel(tcpChannel);
ChannelServices.RegisterChannel(httpChannel);
```

The `ChannelServices` utility class can now be used to dispatch synchronous and asynchronous messages, and to unregister specific channels. The `RegisteredChannels` property returns an `IChannel` array of all the channels we registered. We can also use the `GetChannel()` method to get to a specific channel by its name. With the help of `ChannelServices` we could write a custom administration utility that manages our channels. Here is a small example that shows how the server channel can be stopped from listening for incoming requests:

```
HttpServerChannel channel =(HttpServerChannel)ChannelServices.GetChannel("http");
channel.StopListening(null);
```

The `RemotingConfiguration` class is another .NET Remoting utility class. On the server side it's used to register remote object types for server-activated objects, and to marshal remote objects to a marshaled object reference class `ObjRef`. `ObjRef` is a serializable representation of an object that's sent over the wire. On the client side, `RemotingServices` is used to unmarshal a remote object in order to create a proxy from the object reference.

Here is the server-side code to register a well-known remote object type to the `RemotingServices`:

```
RemotingConfiguration.RegisterWellKnownServiceType(
                        typeof(Hello),                    // Type
                        "Hi",                             // URI
                        WellKnownObjectMode.SingleCall);  // Mode
```

The first argument of RegisterWellKnownServiceType(), Hello specifies the type of the remote object. The second argument, "Hi", is the uniform resource identifier of the remote object that will be used from the client to access the remote object. The last argument is the mode of the remote object. The mode can be a value of the WellKnownObjectMode enumeration: SingleCall or Singleton.

❑ **SingleCall** means that the object holds no state. With every call to the remote object a new instance is created. A SingleCall object is created from the server with the RemotingConfiguration.RegisterWellKnownServiceType() method, and a WellKnownObjectMode.SingleCall argument. This is very efficient on the server because it means that we don't need to hold any resources for maybe thousands of clients.

❑ With a **Singleton** the object is shared for all clients of the server; typically, such object types can be used if you want to share some data between all clients. This shouldn't be a problem for read-only data, but with read-write data you have to be aware of locking issues and scalability. A Singleton object is created by the server with the RemotingConfiguration.RegisterWellKnownServiceType() method and a WellKnownObjectMode.Singleton argument. We have to pay attention to locking of resources held by the Singleton object; we have to make sure that data can't be corrupted when clients are accessing the Singleton concurrently, but we also have to check that the locking is done efficiently enough so that the required scalability is reached.

Server for Client Activated Objects

If a remote object should hold state for a specific client, we can use client-activated objects. In the next section we will look at how to call server-activated or client-activated objects on the client side. On the server side client-activated objects must be registered in a different way from server-activated objects.

Instead of calling RemotingConfiguration.RegisterWellKnownType(), we have to call RemotingConfiguration.RegisterActivatedServiceType(). With this method, only the type is specified, and not the URI. The reason for this is that for client-activated objects, the clients can instantiate different object types with the same URI. The URI for all client-activated objects must be defined using RemotingConfiguration.ApplicationName:

```
RemotingConfiguration.ApplicationName = "HelloServer";
RemotingConfiguration.RegisterActivatedServiceType(typeof(Hello));
```

Object Activation

Clients can use and create remote objects using the Activator class. We can get a proxy to a server-activated or well-known remote object using the GetObject() method. The CreateInstance() method returns a proxy to a client-activated remote object.

Instead of using the Activator class, the new operator can also be used to activate remote objects. To make this possible, the remote object must also be configured within the client using the RemotingConfiguration class.

Application URL

In all activation scenarios, we have to specify a URL to the remote object. This URL is the same one you'd use when browsing with a web browser. The first part specifies the protocol followed by the server name or IP address, the port number, and a URI that was specified when registering the remote object on the server in this form:

```
protocol://server:port/URI
```

We are continually using two URL examples in our code. We specify the protocols http and tcp, the server name is localhost, the port numbers are 8085 and 8086, and the URI is Hi, as follows:

```
http://localhost:8085/Hi
tcp://localhost:8086/Hi
```

Activating Well-Known Objects

In our previous, simple client example we activated well-known objects. Now let us take a more detailed look at the activation sequence.

```
using System;
using System.Runtime.Remoting;
using System.Runtime.Remoting.Channels;
using System.Runtime.Remoting.Channels.Tcp;

// ...

TcpClientChannel channel = new TcpClientChannel();
ChannelServices.RegisterChannel(channel);
```

```
Hello obj = (Hello)Activator.GetObject(typeof(Hello),
                            "tcp://localhost:8086/Hi");
```

GetObject() is a static method of System.Activator that calls RemotingServices.Connect() to return a proxy object to the remote object. The first argument specifies the type of the remote object. The proxy implements all public and protected methods and properties, so that the client can call these methods as it would on the real object. The second argument is the URL to the remote object. We are using the string tcp://localhost:8086/Hi. tcp is the protocol, localhost:8086 is the hostname and the port number, and finally Hi is the URI of the object that was specified using RemotingConfiguration.RegisterWellKnownServiceType().

Instead of using Activator.GetObject(), we could also use RemotingServices.Connect() directly:

```
Hello obj = (Hello)RemotingServices.Connect(typeof(Hello),
                            "tcp://localhost:8086/Hi");
```

If you prefer to do a simple new to activate well-known remote objects, the remote object can be registered on the client using RemotingConfiguration.RegisterWellKnownClientType(). The arguments needed here are similar: the type of the remote object and the URI. new doesn't really create a new remote object, instead it returns a proxy similar to Activator.GetObject(). If the remote object is registered with a flag WellKnownObjectMode.SingleCall, the rule always stays the same – the remote object is created with every method call:

```
RemotingConfiguration.RegisterWellKnownClientType(typeof(Hello),
                                        "tcp://localhost:8086/Hi");

Hello obj = new Hello();
```

Activating Client-Activated Objects

Remote objects can hold state for a client. Activator.CreateInstance() creates a client-activated remote object. Using the Activator.GetObject() method, the remote object is created on a method call, and is destroyed when the method is finished. The object doesn't hold state on the server. The situation is different with Activator.CreateInstance(). With the static CreateInstance() method an activation sequence is started to create the remote object. This object lives until the lease time is expired and a garbage collection occurs. We will talk about the leasing mechanism later in this chapter.

Some of the overloaded Activator.CreateInstance() methods can only be used to create local objects. To create remote objects a method is needed where it's possible to pass activation attributes. One of these overloaded methods is used in our example. This method accepts two string parameters, the first is the name of the assembly and the second is the type, and a third parameter, an array of objects. The channel and the object name are specified in the object array with the help of a UrlAttribute. To use the UrlAttribute class the namespace System.Runtime.Remoting.Activation must be specified:

```
object[] attrs = {new UrlAttribute("tcp://localhost:8086/Hello") };
ObjectHandle handle = Activator.CreateInstance(
            "RemoteHello", "Wrox.ProCSharp.Remoting.Hello", attrs);
if (handle == null)
{
    Console.WriteLine("could not locate server");
     return 0;
}
Hello obj = (Hello)handle.Unwrap();
Console.WriteLine(obj.Greeting("Christian"));
```

Of course, for client-activated objects it's again possible to use the new operator instead of the Activator class. This way we have to register the client-activated object using RemotingConfiguration.RegisterActivatedClientType(). In the architecture of client-activated objects the new operator not only returns a proxy but also creates the remote object:

```
RemotingConfiguration.RegisterActivatedClientType(typeof(Hello),
                                "tcp://localhost:8086/HelloServer");

Hello obj = new Hello();
```

Proxy Objects

The `Activator.GetObject()` and `Activator.CreateInstance()` methods return a proxy to the client. We actually get two proxies, a transparent proxy and a real proxy. The transparent proxy looks like the remote object – it implements all public methods of the remote object. These methods just call the `Invoke()` method of the `RealProxy`, where a message containing the method to call is passed. The real proxy sends the message to the channel with the help of message sinks.

With `RemotingServices.IsTransparentProxy()`, we can check if our object is really a transparent proxy. We can also get to the real proxy using `RemotingServices.GetRealProxy()`. Using the Visual Studio .NET debugger, it's now easy to get all the properties of the real proxy:

```
ChannelServices.RegisterChannel(new TCPChannel());
Hello obj = (Hello)Activator.GetObject(typeof(Hello),
                                "tcp://localhost:8086/Hi");
if (obj == null)
{
    Console.WriteLine("could not locate server");
    return 0;
}
if (RemotingServices.IsTransparentProxy(obj))
{
    Console.WriteLine("Using a transparent proxy");
    RealProxy proxy = RemotingServices.GetRealProxy(obj);

    // proxy.Invoke(message);

}
```

Pluggability of a Proxy

The real proxy can be replaced with a custom proxy. A custom proxy can extend the base class `System.Runtime.Remoting.RealProxy`. We receive the type of the remote object in the constructor of the custom proxy. Calling the constructor of the `RealProxy` creates a transparent proxy in addition to the real proxy. In the constructor, the registered channels can be accessed with the help of the `ChannelServices` class to create a message sink `IChannelSender.CreateMessageSink()`. Besides implementing the constructor, a custom channel has to override the `Invoke()` method. In `Invoke()` a message is received that can be analyzed and sent to the message sink.

Messages

The proxy sends a message into the channel. On the server side, a method call can be made after analyzing the message – so let's look at messages.

We have some message classes for method calls, responses, return messages, and so on. What all the message classes have in common is that they implement the `IMessage` interface. This interface has a single property: `Properties`. This property represents a dictionary with the `IDictionary` interface where the URI to the object, the called `MethodName`, `MethodSignature`, `TypeName`, `Args`, and the `CallContext` are packaged.

Below is the hierarchy of the message classes and interfaces:

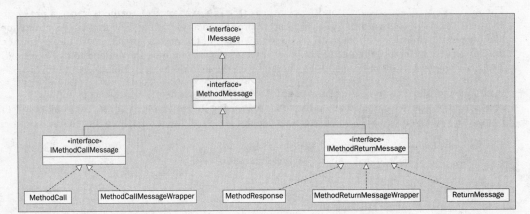

The message that is sent to the real proxy is a `MethodCall`. With the interfaces `IMethodCallMessage` and `IMethodMessage` we have easier access to the properties of the message than through the `IMessage` interface. Instead of having to use the `IDictionary` interface, we have direct access to the method name, the URI, the arguments, and so on. The real proxy returns a `ReturnMessage` to the transparent proxy.

Message Sinks

The `Activator.GetObject()` method calls `RemotingServices.Connect()` to connect to a well-known object. In the `Connect()` method, an `Unmarshal()` happens where not only the proxy, but also envoy sinks, are created. The proxy uses a chain of envoy sinks to pass the message to the channel. All the sinks are interceptors that can change the messages and perform some additional actions such as creating a lock, writing an event, performing security checking, and so on.

All message sinks implement the interface `IMessageSink`. This interface defines one property and two methods:

- ❑ The property `NextSink` is used by a sink to get to the next sink and pass the message along.

- ❑ For synchronous messages, `SyncProcessMessage()` is invoked by a previous sink or by the remoting infrastructure. It has an `IMessage` parameter to send a message and to return a message.

- ❑ For asynchronous messages, `AsyncProcessMessage()` is invoked by a previous sink in the chain, or by the remoting infrastructure. `AsyncProcessMessage()` has two parameters: a message and a message sink that receives the reply.

Let's take a look at the three different message sinks available for use.

Envoy Sink

We can get to the chain of envoy sinks by the `IEnvoyInfo` interface. The marshaled object reference `ObjRef` has a `EnvoyInfo` property that returns the `IEnvoyInfo` interface. The envoy list is created from the server context, so the server can inject functionality into the client. Envoys can collect identity information about the client and pass that information to the server.

Server-Context Sink

When the message is received on the serverside of the channel, it is passed to the server-context sinks. The last of the server-context sinks routes the message to the object-sink chain.

Object Sink

The object sink is associated with a particular object. If the object class defines particular context attributes, context sinks are created for the object.

Passing Objects in Remote Methods

The parameter types of remote method calls aren't just limited to basic data types, but can also be classes that we define ourselves. For remoting we have to differentiate between three types of classes:

❑ **Marshal-by-value** classes are serialized through the channel. Classes that should be marshaled must implement either the `ISerializable` interface, or must be marked using the `[Serializable]` attribute. Objects of these classes don't have a remote identity, because the complete object is marshaled through the channel, and the object that is serialized to the client is independent of the server object (or the other way around). Marshal-by-value classes are also called **unbound classes** because they don't have data that depends on the application domain.

❑ **Marshal-by-reference** classes do have a remote identity. The objects are not passed across the wire, but instead a proxy is returned. A class that is marshaled by reference must derive from `MarshalByRefObject`. `MarshalByRefObjects` are known as **application domain bound objects**. A specialized version of `MarshalByRefObject` is `ContextBoundObject`: the abstract class `ContextBoundObject` is derived from `MarshalByRefObject`. If a class is derived from `ContextBoundObject`, a proxy is needed even in the same application domain when context boundaries are crossed. Such objects are called **context-bound objects**, and they are only valid in the creation context.

❑ Classes that are not serializable and don't derive from `MarshalByRefObject` are **not remotable**. Classes of these types cannot be used as parameters in a remote object's public methods. These classes are bound to the application domain where they are created. Non-remotable classes should be used if the class has a data member that is only valid in the application domain, such as a Win32 file handle.

To see marshaling in action, we will change the remote object to send two objects to the client: the class MySerialized will be sent marshal-by-value, the class MyRemote marshal-by-reference. In the methods a message is written to the console so that we can verify if the call was made on the client or on the server. In addition, the Hello class is changed to return a MySerialized and a MyRemote instance:

```
using System;

namespace Wrox.ProCSharp.Remoting
{
    [Serializable]
    public class MySerialized
    {
        public MySerialized(int val)
        {
            a = val;
        }
        public void Foo()
        {
            Console.WriteLine("MySerialized.Foo called");
        }
        public int A
        {
            get
            {
                Console.WriteLine("MySerialized.A called");
                return a;
            }
            set
            {
                a = value;
            }
        }
        protected int a;
    }
    public class MyRemote : System.MarshalByRefObject
    {
        public MyRemote(int val)
        {
            a = val;
        }
        public void Foo()
        {
            Console.WriteLine("MyRemote.Foo called");
        }
        public int A
        {
            get
            {
                Console.WriteLine("MyRemote.A called");
                return a;
            }
        }
```

```
            set
            {
                a = value;
            }
        }
        protected int a;
    }

    public class Hello : System.MarshalByRefObject
    {
        public Hello()
        {
            Console.WriteLine("Constructor called");
        }
        ~Hello()
        {
            Console.WriteLine("Destructor called");
        }
        public string Greeting(string name)
        {
            Console.WriteLine("Greeting called");
            return "Hello, " + name;
        }
        public MySerialized GetMySerialized()
        {
            return new MySerialized(4711);
        }
        public MyRemote GetMyRemote()
        {
            return new MyRemote(4712);
        }
    }
}
```

The client application also needs to be changed to see the effects when using marshaled-by-value and marshaled-by-reference objects. We are calling the methods GetMySerialized() and GetMyRemote() to retrieve the new objects. We're also checking if the transparent proxy is used in the Main() method of the file HelloClient.cs:

```
ChannelServices.RegisterChannel(new TcpChannel());
Hello obj = (Hello)Activator.GetObject(typeof(Hello),
                                "tcp://localhost:8086/Hi");
if (obj == null)
{
    Console.WriteLine("could not locate server");
    return;
}
MySerialized ser = obj.GetMySerialized();
if (!RemotingServices.IsTransparentProxy(ser))
{
    Console.WriteLine("ser is not a transparent proxy");
}
ser.Foo();
```

```
        MyRemote rem = obj.GetMyRemote();
        if (RemotingServices.IsTransparentProxy(rem))
        {
            Console.WriteLine("rem is a transparent proxy");
        }
        rem.Foo();
```

In the client console window, we can see that the ser object is called on the client. This object is not a transparent proxy because it's serialized to the client. In contrast, the rem object on the client *is* a transparent proxy. Methods called on this object are transferred to the server:

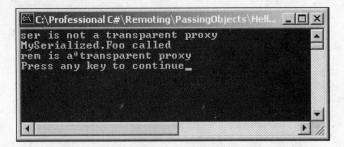

In the server output we see that the Foo() method is called with the remote object MyRemote:

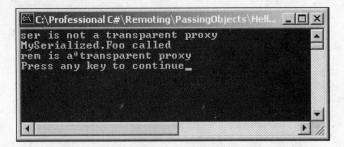

Directional Attributes

Remote objects are never transferred over the wire, whereas value types and serializable classes are transferred. Sometimes we want to send the data only in one direction. This can be especially important when the data is transferred over the network. For example, if you want to send data in a collection to the server for the server to perform some calculation on this data and return a simple value to the client, it would not be very efficient to send the collection back to the client. With COM it was possible to declare directional attributes [in], [out], and [in, out] to the arguments if the data should be sent to the server, to the client, or in both directions.

With C# we have similar attributes as part of the language: `ref` and `out` method parameters. The `ref` and `out` method parameters can be used for value types and for reference types that are serializable. Using the `ref` parameter, the argument is marshaled in both directions, `out` goes from the server to the client, and using no parameter sends the data to the server.

You can read more about the `out` *and* `ref` *keywords in Chapter 2.*

Lifetime Management

How do a client and a server detect if the other side is not available anymore, and what are the problems we get into?

For a client, the answer can be simple. As soon as the client does a call to a method on the remote object we get an exception of type `System.Runtime.Remoting.RemotingException`. We just have to handle this exception and do what's necessary, for example perform a retry, write to a log, inform the user, and so on.

What about the server? When does the server detect if the client is not around anymore, meaning that the server can go ahead and clean up any resources it's holding for the client? We could wait until the next method call from the client – but maybe it will never arrive. In the COM realm, the DCOM protocol used a ping mechanism. The client sent a ping to the server with the information about the object referenced. A client can have hundreds of objects referenced on the server, and so the information in the ping can be very large. To make this mechanism more efficient it wasn't the information about all objects that was sent, but just the difference from the last ping.

This ping mechanism was efficient on a LAN, but is not suitable for Internet solutions – imagine thousands or millions of clients sending ping information to the server! .NET Remoting has a much more scalable solution for lifetime management: the **Leasing Distributed Garbage Collector (LDGC)**.

This lifetime management is *only active for client-activated objects.* `SingleCall` objects can be destroyed after every method call because they don't hold state. Client-activated objects do have state and we should be aware of the resources used. For client-activated objects that are referenced outside the application domain a lease is created. A lease has a lease time. When the lease time reaches zero the lease expires and the remote object is disconnected and, finally, is garbage-collected.

Lease Renewals

If the client calls a method on the object when the lease has expired, we get an exception. If we have a client where the remote object could be needed for more than 300 seconds (the default value for lease-times), we have three ways to renew a lease:

❑ An **implicit renewal** of the lease is automatically done when the client calls a method on the remote object. If the current lease time is less than the `RenewOnCallTime` value, the lease is set to `RenewOnCallTime`.

❑ With an **explicit renewal** the client can specify the new lease time. This is done with the `Renew()` method of the `ILease` interface. We can get to the `ILease` interface by calling the `GetLifetimeService()` method of the transparent proxy.

❑ **Sponsoring** is the third possibility to renew leases. The client can create a sponsor that implements the ISponsor interface and registers the sponsor in the leasing services using the Register() method of the ILease interface. The sponsor defines the lease extension time. When a lease expires the sponsor is asked for an extension of the lease. The sponsoring mechanism can be used if you want long-lived remote objects on the server.

Leasing Configuration Values

Let's look at the values that can be configured:

❑ LeaseTime defines the time until a lease expires.

❑ RenewOnCallTime is the time the lease is set on a method call if the current lease time has a lower value.

❑ If a sponsor is not available within the SponsorshipTimeout, the remoting infrastructure looks for the next sponsor. If there are no more sponsors, the lease expires.

❑ The LeaseManagerPollTime defines the time interval at which the lease manager checks for expired objects.

The default values are listed in this table:

Lease Configuration	Default Value (seconds)
LeaseTime	300
RenewOnCallTime	120
SponsorshipTimeout	120
LeaseManagerPollTime	10

Classes Used for Lifetime Management

The ClientSponsor is one sponsor that implements the ISponsor interface. It can be used on the client side for lease-extension. With the ILease interface we can get all information about the lease, all the lease properties and the current lease time and state. The state is specified with the LeaseState enumeration. With the LifetimeServices utility class we can get and set the properties for the lease of all remote objects in the application domain.

Getting Lease Information Example

In this small code example we are accessing the lease information by calling the GetLifetimeService() method of the transparent proxy. For the ILease interface we have to use the namespace System.Runtime.Remoting.Lifetime:

> Remember, you can use this only for client-activated objects. **SingleCall** objects are instantiated with every method call anyway, so the leasing mechanism doesn't apply.

```
        ILease lease = (ILease)obj.GetLifetimeService();
        if (lease != null)
        {
            Console.WriteLine("Lease Configuration:");
            Console.WriteLine("InitialLeaseTime: " +
                              lease.InitialLeaseTime);
            Console.WriteLine("RenewOnCallTime: " +
                              lease.RenewOnCallTime);
            Console.WriteLine("SponsorshipTimeout: " +
                              lease.SponsorshipTimeout);
            Console.WriteLine(lease.CurrentLeaseTime);
        }
```

This is the output we see in the client console window:

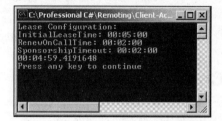

Changing Default Lease Configurations

The server itself can change the default lease configuration *for all remote objects* using the
`System.Runtime.Remoting.Lifetime.LifetimeServices` utility class:

```
        LifetimeServices.LeaseTime = TimeSpan.FromMinutes(10);
        LifetimeServices.RenewOnCallTime = TimeSpan.FromMinutes(2);
```

If you want different default lifetimes depending on the type of the remote object, you can change the
lease configuration of the remote object by overriding the `InitializeLifetimeService()` method
of the base class `MarshalByRefObject`:

```
    public class Hello : System.MarshalByRefObject
    {
        public Hello()
        {
            Console.WriteLine("Constructor called");
        }
        ~Hello()
        {
            Console.WriteLine("Destructor called");
        }
        public override Object InitializeLifetimeService()
        {
            ILease lease = (ILease)base.InitializeLifetimeService();
            lease.InitialLeaseTime = TimeSpan.FromMinutes(10);
            lease.RenewOnCallTime = TimeSpan.FromSeconds(40);
            return lease;
        }
    }
```

The lifetime services configuration can also be done using a configuration file as we see next.

Miscellaneous .NET Remoting Features

In the final section of this chapter we shall explore the following .NET Remoting features such as

❑   How application configuration files can be used to define remoting channels

❑   Hosting .NET Remoting Servers in a IIS Server by using the ASP.NET runtime

❑   Different ways to get the type information of the server for building the client with the utility SOAPSuds

❑   How tracking services can help with debugging

❑   Calling .NET Remoting methods asynchronously

❑   Implementing events to callback methods in the client

❑   Using call contexts to pass some data to the server behind the scenes automatically

Configuration Files

Instead of writing the channel and object configuration in the sourcecode, configuration files can be used. This way the channel can be reconfigured, additional channels can be added, and so on, without changing the sourcecode. Like all the other configuration files on the .NET platform, XML is used. The same application and configuration files that you read about in Chapter 8 are used here, too. We will add security configurations into the same files in Chapter 23. For .NET Remoting, we have some XML elements and attributes to configure the channel and the remote objects. The file should have the same name as the executable followed by .config. For the server HelloServer.exe the configuration file is HelloServer.exe.config.

In the code download, you'll find the following example configuration files in the root directory of the client and server examples, under the names clientactivated.config and wellknown.config. With the client example you will also find the file wellknownhttp.config that specifies an HTTP channel to a well-known remote object. To use these configurations, the files must be renamed as above and placed in the directory containing the executable file.

Here is just one example of how such a configuration file could look. We will walk through all the different configuration options:

```
<configuration>
    <system.runtime.remoting>
        <application name="Hello">
            <service>
                <wellknown mode="SingleCall"
                    type="Wrox.ProCSharp.Remoting.Hello, RemoteHello"
                            objectUri="Hi" />
            </service>
            <channels>
                <channel ref="tcp" port="6791" />
                <channel ref="http" port="6792" />
            </channels>
        </application>
    </system.runtime.remoting>
</configuration>
```

<configuration> is the XML root element for all .NET configuration files. All the remoting configurations can be found in the sub-element <system.runtime.remoting>. <application> is a subelement of <system.runtime.remoting>.

Let's look at the main elements and attributes of the parts within <system.runtime.remoting>:

❑ With the <application> element we can specify the name of the application using the attribute name. On the server side, this is the name of the server, and on the client side it's the name of the client application. As an example for a server configuration, <application name="Hello"> defines the remote application name Hello, which is used as part of the URL by the client to access the remote object.

❑ On the server, the element <service> is used to specify a collection of remote objects. It can have <wellknown> and <activated> subelements to specify the type of the remote object as *well-known* or *client-activated.*

❑ The client part of the <service> element is <client>. Like the <service> element, it can have <wellknown> and <activated> subelements to specify the type of the remote object. Unlike the <service> counterpart, <client> has a url attribute to specify the URL to the remote object.

❑ <wellknown> is a element that's used on the server and the client to specify well-known remote objects. The server part could look like this:

```
<wellknown mode="SingleCall"
    type="Wrox.ProCSharp.Remoting.Hello, RemoteHello"
        objectURI="Hi" />
```

While the mode attribute SingleCall or Singleton can be specified, the type is the type of the remote class including the namespace Wrox.ProCSharp.Remoting.Hello, followed by the assembly name RemoteHello. objectURI is the name of the remote object that's registered in the channel.

On the client, the type attribute is the same as for the server version. mode and objectURI are not needed, but instead the url attribute is used to define the path to the remote object: protocol, hostname, port-number, application-name, and the object URI:

```
<wellknown type="Wrox.ProCSharp.Remoting.Hello, RemoteHello"
              url="tcp://localhost:6791/Hello/Hi" />
```

❑ The <activated> element is used for client-activated objects. With the type attribute the type and assembly must be defined both for the client and the server application:

```
<activated type="Wrox.ProCSharp.Remoting.Hello, RemoteHello" />
```

❑ To specify the channel, the <channel> element is used. It's a subelement of <channels> so that a collection of channels can be configured for a single application. Its use is similar for clients and servers. With the XML attribute ref we reference a channel name that is configured in the configuration file machine.config. We will look into this file next. For the server channel we have to set the port number with the XML attribute port. The XML attribute displayName is used to specify a name for the channel that is used from the .NET Framework Configuration tool, as we will see later.

```
<channels>
   <channel ref="tcp" port="6791" displayName="TCP Channel" />
   <channel ref="http" port="6792" displayName="HTTP Channel" />
</channels>
```

Predefined Channels in machine.config

In the machine.config configuration file that you can find in the directory
<windir>\Microsoft.NET\Framework\<version>\CONFIG, predefined channels can be found.
These predefined channels can be used in your application, or you can specify your own channel class.

In the XML file below you can see an extract of the machine.config file showing the predefined
channels. The <channel> element is used as a subelement of <channels> to define channels. Here
the attribute id specifies a name of a channel that can be referenced with the ref attribute. With the
type attribute the class of the channel is specified followed by the assembly; for example, the channel
class System.Runtime.Remoting.Channels.Http.HttpChannel can be found in the assembly
System.Runtime.Remoting. Because the System.Runtime.Remoting assembly is shared, the
strong name of the assembly must be specified with Version, Culture, and PublicKeyToken.

```xml
<system.runtime.remoting>
  <!-- ... -->
    <channels>
      <channel id="http" type="System.Runtime.Remoting.Channels.Http.HttpChannel,
         System.Runtime.Remoting, Version=1.0.3300.0, Culture=neutral,
         PublicKeyToken=b77a5c561934e089"/>
      <channel id="http client"
         type="System.Runtime.Remoting.Channels.Http.HttpClientChannel,
         System.Runtime.Remoting, Version=1.0.3300.0, Culture=neutral,
         PublicKeyToken=b77a5c561934e089"/>
      <channel id="http server"
         type="System.Runtime.Remoting.Channels.Http.HttpServerChannel,
         System.Runtime.Remoting, Version=1.0.3300.0, Culture=neutral,
         PublicKeyToken=b77a5c561934e089"/>
      <channel id="tcp" type="System.Runtime.Remoting.Channels.Tcp.TcpChannel,
         System.Runtime.Remoting, Version=1.0.3300.0, Culture=neutral,
         PublicKeyToken=b77a5c561934e089"/>
      <channel id="tcp client"
         type="System.Runtime.Remoting.Channels.Tcp.TcpClientChannel,
         System.Runtime.Remoting, Version=1.0.3300.0, Culture=neutral,
         PublicKeyToken=b77a5c561934e089"/>
      <channel id="tcp server"
         type="System.Runtime.Remoting.Channels.Tcp.TcpServerChannel,
         System.Runtime.Remoting, Version=1.0.3300.0, Culture=neutral,
         PublicKeyToken=b77a5c561934e089"/>
    </channels>
  <!-- ... -->
<system.runtime.remoting>
```

Server Configuration for Well-Known Objects

This example file, wellknown.config, has the value Hello for the name property. We are using the
TCP channel to listen on port 6791, and the HTTP channel to listen on port 6792. The remote object
class is Wrox.ProCSharp.Remoting.Hello in the assembly RemoteHello, the object is called Hi in
the channel, and we are using the mode SingleCall:

```
<configuration>
   <system.runtime.remoting>
      <application name="Hello">
         <service>
            <wellknown mode="SingleCall"
                       type="Wrox.ProCSharp.Remoting.Hello, RemoteHello"
                       objectUri="Hi" />
         </service>
         <channels>
            <channel ref="tcp" port="6791"
               displayName="TCP Channel (HelloServer)" />
            <channel ref="http" port="6792"
               displayName="HTTP Channel (HelloServer)" />
         </channels>
      </application>
   </system.runtime.remoting>
</configuration>
```

Client Configuration for Well-Known Objects

For well-known objects, we have to specify the assembly and the channel in the client configuration file `wellknown.config`. The types for the remote object can be found in the `RemoteHello` assembly, `Hi` is the name of the object in the channel, and the URI for the remote type `Wrox.ProCSharp.Remoting.Hello` is `tcp://localhost:6791/Hi`. In the client we are also using a TCP channel, but in the client no port is specified, so a free port is selected:

```
<configuration>
   <system.runtime.remoting>
      <application name="Client">
         <client url="tcp:/localhost:6791/Hello"
                 displayName="Hello client for well-known objects">
            <wellknown type = "Wrox.ProCSharp.Remoting.Hello, RemoteHello"
                            url="tcp://localhost:6791/Hello/Hi" />
         </client>
         <channels>
            <channel ref="tcp" displayName="TCP Channel (HelloClient)" />
         </channels>
      </application>
   </system.runtime.remoting>
</configuration>
```

A small change in the configuration file, and we're using the HTTP channel (as can be seen in `wellknownhttp.config`):

```
            <client url="http:/localhost:6792/Hello">
               <wellknown type="Wrox.ProCSharp.Remoting.Hello, RemoteHello"
                               url="http://localhost:6792/Hello/Hi" />
            </client>
            <channels>
               <channel ref="http" displayName="HTTP Channel (HelloClient)" />
            </channels>
```

Server Configuration for Client-Activated Objects

By changing only the configuration file (which can be found in `clientactivated.config`), we can change the server configuration from server-activated to client-activated objects. Here the `<activated>` subelement of the `<service>` element is specified. With the `<activated>` element for the server configuration, just the `type` attribute must be specified. The `name` attribute of the `application` element defines the URI:

```
<configuration>
    <system.runtime.remoting>
        <application name="HelloServer">
            <service>
                <activated type="Wrox.ProCSharp.Remoting.Hello, RemoteHello" />
            </service>
            <channels>
                <channel ref="http" port="6788"
                        displayName="HTTP Channel (HelloServer)" />

                <channel ref="tcp" port="6789"
                    displayName="TCP Channel (HelloServer)" />
            </channels>
        </application>
    </system.runtime.remoting>
</configuration>
```

Client Configuration for Client-Activated Objects

The `clientactivated.config` file defines the client-activated remote object using the `url` attribute of the `<client>` element and the `type` attribute of the `<activated>` element:

```
<configuration>
    <system.runtime.remoting>
        <application>
            <client url="http://localhost:6788/HelloServer"
                    displayName="Hello client for client-activated objects">
                <activated type="Wrox.ProCSharp.Remoting.Hello, RemoteHello" />
            </client>
            <channels>
                <channel ref="http" displayName="HTTP Channel (HelloClient)" />
                <channel ref="tcp" displayName="TCP Channel (HelloClient)" />
            </channels>
        </application>
    </system.runtime.remoting>
</configuration>
```

Server Code Using Configuration Files

In the server code we have to configure remoting using the static method `Configure()` from the `RemotingConfiguration` class. Here all the channels that are defined are built up and instantiated. Maybe we also want to know about the channel configurations from the server application – that's why I've created the static methods `ShowActivatedServiceTypes()` and `ShowWellKnownServiceTypes()`; they are called after loading and starting the remoting configuration:

```
public static void Main(string[] args)
{
    RemotingConfiguration.Configure("HelloServer.exe.config");
    Console.WriteLine("Application: " + RemotingConfiguration.ApplicationName);
    ShowActivatedServiceTypes();
    ShowWellKnownServiceTypes();
    System.Console.WriteLine("hit to exit");
    System.Console.ReadLine();
    return;
}
```

These two functions show configuration information of well-known and client-activated types:

```
public static void ShowWellKnownServiceTypes()
{
    WellKnownServiceTypeEntry[] entries =
    RemotingConfiguration.GetRegisteredWellKnownServiceTypes();
    foreach (WellKnownServiceTypeEntry entry in entries)
    {
        Console.WriteLine("Assembly: " + entry.AssemblyName);
        Console.WriteLine("Mode: " + entry.Mode);
        Console.WriteLine("URI: " + entry.ObjectUri);
        Console.WriteLine("Type: " + entry.TypeName);
    }
}
public static void ShowActivatedServiceTypes()
{
    ActivatedServiceTypeEntry[] entries =
    RemotingConfiguration.GetRegisteredActivatedServiceTypes();
    foreach (ActivatedServiceTypeEntry entry in entries)
    {
        Console.WriteLine("Assembly: " + entry.AssemblyName);
        Console.WriteLine("Type: " + entry.TypeName);
    }
}
```

Client Code Using Configuration Files

In the client code, we only have to configure the remoting services using the configuration file client.exe.config. After that, we can use the new operator to create new instances of the Remote class, no matter whether we work with server-activated or client-activated remote objects. Be aware, however – there's a small difference! With client-activated objects it's now possible to use **non-default constructors** with the new operator. This isn't possible for server-activated objects, and it doesn't make sense there: SingleCall objects can have no state because they are destroyed with every call; Singleton objects are created just once. Calling non-default constructors is only useful for client-activated objects because it is only for this kind of objects that the new operator really calls the constructor in the remote object.

In the Main() method of the file HelloClient.cs we can now change the remoting code to use the configuration file with RemotingConfiguration.Configure(), and we create the remote object with the new operator:

```
RemotingConfiguration.Configure("HelloClient.exe.config");
Hello obj = new Hello();
if (obj == null)
{
   Console.WriteLine("could not locate server");
   return 0;
}
for (int i=0; i < 5; i++)
{
   Console.WriteLine(obj.Greeting("Christian"));
}
```

Delayed Loading of Client Channels

With the configuration file machine.config, two channels are configured that can be used automatically if the client doesn't configure a channel.

```
<system.runtime.remoting>
   <application>
      <channels>
         <channel ref="http client" displayName="http client (delay loaded)"
                  delayLoadAsClientChannel="true"/>
         <channel ref="tcp client" displayName="tcp client (delay loaded)"
                  delayLoadAsClientChannel="true"/>
      </channels>
   </application>
</system.runtime.remoting>
```

The XML attribute delayLoadAsClientChannel with a value true defines that the channel should be used from a client that doesn't configure a channel. The runtime tries to connect to the server using the delay loaded channels. So it is not necessary to configure a channel in the client configuration file, and a client configuration file for the well-known object we have used earlier can look as simple as this:

```
<configuration>
   <system.runtime.remoting>
      <application name="Client">
         <client url="tcp:/localhost:6791/Hello">
            <wellknown type = "Wrox.ProCSharp.Remoting.Hello, RemoteHello"
                       url="tcp://localhost:6791/Hello/Hi" />
         </client>
      </application>
   </system.runtime.remoting>
</configuration>
```

Lifetime Services in Configuration Files

Leasing configuration for remote servers can also be done with the application configuration files. The <lifetime> element has the attributes leaseTime, sponsorshipTimeOut, renewOnCallTime, and pollTime as you see here:

```
<configuration>
   <system.runtime.remoting>
      <application>
         <lifetime leaseTime = "15M" sponsorshipTimeOut = "4M"
                   renewOnCallTime = "3M" pollTime = "30s"/>
      </application>
   </system.runtime.remoting>
</configuration>
```

Using configuration files, it is possible to change the remoting configuration by editing files instead of working with sourcecode. We can easily change the channel to use HTTP instead of TCP, change a port, the name of the channel, and so on. With the addition of a single line the server can listen to two channels instead of one.

.NET Framework Configuration Tool

The System Administrator can use the .NET Framework Configuration Tool to reconfigure existing configuration files. You can find this tool with the Administrative Tools in the Control Panel.

Adding the application `HelloClient.exe` where we used the client configuration file to the configured applications in this tool, we can configure the URL of the remote object by selecting the hyperlink View Remoting Services Properties:

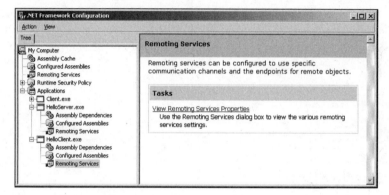

For the client application we can see the value of the `displayName` attribute in the combo box to select the remote application, and we can change the URL of the remote object:

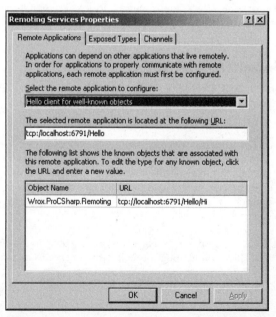

Adding the server application to this tool we can change the configuration of the remote object and the channels as the two pictures below demonstrate:

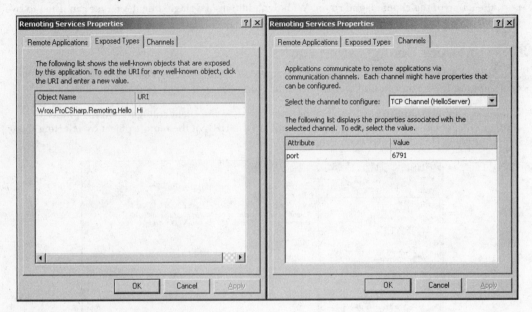

Hosting Applications

Up to this point all our sample servers were running in self-hosted .NET servers. A self-hosted server must be launched manually. A .NET remoting server can also be started in a lot of other application types. In a **Windows Service** the server can be automatically started at boot-time, and in addition the process can run with the credentials of the system account. We'll see more about Windows Services in Chapter 22.

Hosting Remote Servers in ASP.NET

There's special support for .NET Remoting servers for ASP.NET. ASP.NET can be used for the automatic startup of remote servers. Contrary to EXE-hosted applications, ASP.NET Remoting uses a different file for configuration.

To use the infrastructure from the Internet Information Server and ASP.NET, we just have to create a class that derives from `System.MarshalByRefObject` and has a default constructor. The code used earlier for our server to create and register the channel is no longer necessary; that's done by the ASP.NET runtime. We just have to create a virtual directory on the web server that maps a directory to where we put the configuration file `web.config`. The assembly of the remote class must reside in the `bin` subdirectory.

To configure a virtual directory on the web server we can use the Internet Information Services MMC. Selecting the Default Web Site and opening the Action menu creates a new Virtual Directory.

The configuration file web.config on the web server must be put in the home directory of the virtual web site. With the default IIS configuration, the channel that will be used listens to port 80:

```
<configuration>
   <system.runtime.remoting>
      <application>
         <service>
            <wellknown mode="SingleCall"
                type="Wrox.ProCSharp.Remoting.Hello, RemoteHello"
                objectUri="HelloService.soap" />
         </service>
      </application>
   </system.runtime.remoting>
</configuration>
```

The client can now connect to the remote object using the following configuration file. The URL that must be specified for the remote object here is the web server localhost, followed by the web application name RemoteHello (specified when creating the virtual web site), and the URI of the remote object HelloService.soap that we defined in the file web.config. It's not necessary to specify the port number 80, because that's the default port for the HTTP protocol. Not specifying a <channels> section means that we use the delay loaded HTTP channel from the configuration file machine.config:

```
<configuration>
   <system.runtime.remoting>
      <application>
         <client url="http:/localhost/RemoteHello">
            <wellknown type="Wrox.ProCSharp.Remoting.Hello, RemoteHello"
                       url="http://localhost/RemoteHello/HelloService.soap" />
         </client>
      </application>
   </system.runtime.remoting>
</configuration>
```

> **Hosting remote objects in ASP.NET only supports well-known objects.**

Classes, Interfaces, and SoapSuds

In the client-server examples we've done up until now, we have always copied the assembly of the remote object not only to the server, but also to the client application. This way we have the MSIL code of the remote object in both the client and the server applications, although in the client application only the metadata is needed. However, copying the remoting object assembly means that it's not possible for the client and server to be programmed independently. A much better way to use just the metadata is to use interfaces or the SoapSuds.exe utility instead.

Interfaces

We have a cleaner separation of the client and server code using interfaces. An interface simply defines the methods without implementation. We separate the contract between the client and the server from the implementation. Here are the necessary steps to use an interface:

1. Define an interface that will be placed in a separate assembly.

2. Implement the interface in the remote object class. To do this, the assembly of the interface must be referenced.

3. On the server side no more changes are required. The server can be programmed and configured in the usual ways.

4. On the client side, reference the assembly of the interface instead of the assembly of the remote class.

5. The client can now use the interface of the remote object rather than the remote object class. The object can be created using the `Activator` class as we've done earlier. You can't use the `new` operator in this way, because the interface itself cannot be instantiated.

The interface defines the contract between the client and server. The two applications can now be developed independently of each other. If you also stick to the old COM rules about interfaces (that interfaces should never be changed) you will not have any versioning problems.

Soapsuds

We can also use the `Soapsuds` utility to get the metadata from an assembly if an HTTP channel and the SOAP formatter are used. `Soapsuds` can convert assemblies to XML Schemas, XML Schemas to wrapper classes, and also works in the other directions.

The following command converts the type `Hello` from the assembly `RemoteHello` to the assembly `HelloWrapper` where a transparent proxy is generated that calls the remote object:

```
soapsuds -types:Wrox.ProCSharp.Remoting.Hello,RemoteHello
         -oa:HelloWrapper.dll
```

With `Soapsuds` we can also get the type information directly from a running server if the IITTP channel and the SOAP formatter are used:

```
soapsuds -url:http://localhost:6792/hello/hi?wsdl -oa:HelloWrapper.dll
```

In the client we can now reference the `Soapsuds`-generated assembly instead of the original one. Some of the options are listed in this table:

Option	Description
-url	Retrieve schema from the specified URL
-proxyurl	If a proxy server is required to access the server, specify the proxy with this option
-types	Specify a type and assembly to read the schema information from it
-is	Input schema file
-ia	Input assembly file
-os	Output schema file
-oa	Output assembly file

Generating a WSDL Document with .NET Remoting

In Chapter 15 we discussed the WSDL protocol used by ASP.NET Web Services. WSDL is also supported by .NET Remoting when an HTTP channel and the SOAP formatter are used. This can be tested easily by using a browser to access a remote object. Adding ?wsdl to the URI of the remote object returns a WSDL document, as you can see in the screenshot below, which shows the output from accessing our remote server we created earlier.

.NET Remoting uses the RPC style of WSDL documents, unlike ASP.NET Web Services, which uses the Document style by default.

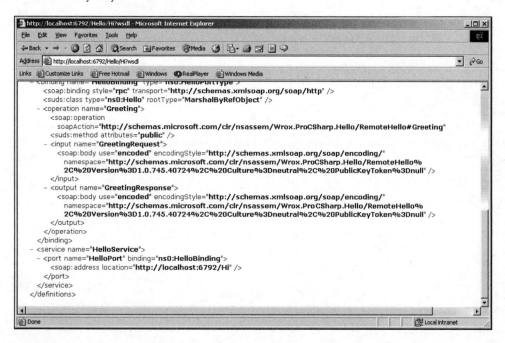

We can access the WSDL document across the network only if we use a well-known remote object type. For client-activated objects the URI is created dynamically. With client activated objects we can use the assembly with the -ia option of soapsuds to get the metadata.

Tracking Services

For debugging and troubleshooting applications using .NET, remoting tracking services can be used. The System.Runtime.Remoting.Services.TrackingService class provides a tracking service to get information about when marshaling and unmarshaling occur, when remote objects are called and disconnected, and so on:

❑ With the TrackingServices utility class we can register and unregister a handler that implements ITrackingHandler.

❑ The ITrackingHandler interface is called when an event happens on a remote object, or a proxy. We can implement three methods in the handler: MarshaledObject(), UnmarshaledObject(), and DisconnectedObject().

To see tracking services in action in both the client and the server, we create a new class library, TrackingHandler. The TrackingHandler class implements the ITrackingHandler interface. In the methods we receive two arguments: the object itself and an ObjRef. With the ObjRef we can get information about the URI, the channel, and the envoy sinks. We can also attach new sinks to add a contributor to all the called methods. In our example we're writing the URI and information about the channel to the console:

```
using System;
using System.Runtime.Remoting;
using System.Runtime.Remoting.Services;

namespace Wrox.ProCSharp.Remoting
{
    public class TrackingHandler : ITrackingHandler
    {
        public TrackingHandler()
        {
        }
        public void MarshaledObject(object obj, ObjRef or)
        {
            Console.WriteLine("--- Marshaled Object " +
                              obj.GetType() + " ---");
            Console.WriteLine("Object URI: " + or.URI);
            object[] channelData = or.ChannelInfo.ChannelData;
            foreach (object data in channelData)
            {
                ChannelDataStore dataStore = data as ChannelDataStore;
                if (dataStore != null)
                {
                    foreach (string uri in dataStore.ChannelUris)
                    {
                        Console.WriteLine("Channel URI: " + uri);
                    }
                }
            }
            Console.WriteLine("---------");
            Console.WriteLine();
```

```
    }
    public void UnmarshaledObject(object obj, ObjRef or)
    {
        Console.WriteLine("Unmarshal");
    }
    public void DisconnectedObject(object obj)
    {
        Console.WriteLine("Disconnect");
    }
    }
  }
}
```

The server program is changed to register the `TrackingHandler`. Just two lines need to be added to register the handler:

```
using System.Runtime.Remoting.Services;

//...

    public static void Main(string[] args)
    {
        TrackingServices.RegisterTrackingHandler(new TrackingHandler());
        TcpChannel channel = new TcpChannel(8086);

        //...
```

When starting the server, a first instance is created during registration of the well-known type and we get the following output. `MarshaledObject()` gets called and displays the type of the object to marshal – `Wrox.ProCSharp.Remoting.Hello`. With the object URI we see a GUID that's used internally in the remoting runtime to distinguish different instances and the URI we specified. With the channel URI the configuration of the channel can be verified. In this case the hostname is `CNagel`:

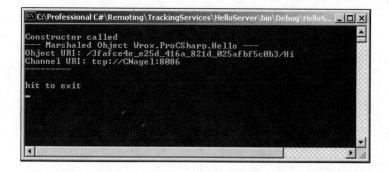

Asynchronous Remoting

If server methods take a while to complete and the client needs to do some different work at the same time, it isn't necessary to start a separate thread to do the remote call. By doing an asynchronous call, the method starts but returns immediately to the client. Asynchronous calls can be made on a remote object as they are made on a local object with the help of a delegate.

To make an asynchronous method, we create a delegate, `GreetingDelegate`, with the same argument and return value as the `Greeting()` method of the remote object. With the `delegate` keyword a new class `GreetingDelegate` that derives from `MulticastDelegate` is created. You can verify this by using `ildasm` and checking the assembly. The argument of the constructor of this delegate class is a reference to the `Greeting()` method. We start the `Greeting()` call using the `BeginInvoke()` method of the delegate class. The second argument of `BeginInvoke()` is an `AsyncCallback` instance that defines the method `HelloClient.Callback()`, which is called when the remote method is finished. In the `Callback()` method the remote call is finished using `EndInvoke()`:

```
using System;
using System.Runtime.Remoting;
namespace Wrox.ProCSharp.Remoting
{
    public class HelloClient
    {
        private delegate String GreetingDelegate(String name);
        private static string greeting;
        [STAThread]
        public static void Main(string[] args)
        {
            RemotingConfiguration.Configure("HelloClient.exe.config");
            Hello obj = new Hello();
            if (obj == null)
            {
                Console.WriteLine("could not locate server");
                return 0;
            }
            // synchronous version
            // string greeting = obj.Greeting("Christian");
            // asynchronous version

            GreetingDelegate d = new GreetingDelegate(obj.Greeting);
            IAsyncResult ar = d.BeginInvoke("Christian", null, null);

            // do some work and then wait
            ar.AsyncWaitHandle.WaitOne();
            if (ar.IsCompleted)
            {
                greeting = d.EndInvoke(ar);
            }

            Console.WriteLine(greeting);
        }
    }
}
```

You can read more about delegates and events in Chapter 4.

OneWay Attribute

A method that has a void return and only input parameters can be marked with the OneWay attribute. The OneWay attribute makes a method automatically asynchronous, not matter how the client calls it. Adding the method TakeAWhile() to our remote object class RemoteHello creates a **fire-and-forget** method. If the client calls it by the proxy, the proxy immediately returns to the client. On the server, the method finishes some time later:

```
[OneWay]
public void TakeAWhile(int ms)
{
    Console.WriteLine("TakeAWhile started");
    System.Threading.Thread.Sleep(ms);
    Console.WriteLine("TakeAWhile finished");
}
```

Remoting and Events

With .NET Remoting not only can the client call methods on the remote object across the network, but the server can also call methods in the client. For this, a mechanism that we already know from the basic language features is used: **delegates and events**.

In principle, the architecture is simple. The server has a remotable object that the client can call, and the client has a remotable object that the server can call:

❑   The remote object in the server must declare an external function (a delegate) with the signature of the method that the client will implement in a handler

❑   The arguments that are passed with the handler function to the client must be marshalable, so all the data sent to the client must be serializable

❑   The remote object must also declare an instance of the delegate function modified with the event keyword; the client will use this to register a handler

❑   The client must create a sink object with a handler method that has the same signature as the delegate defined, and it has to register the sink object with the event in the remote object

To help explain this, let's take a look at an example. To see all the parts of event handling with .NET Remoting we will create five classes; Server, Client, RemoteObject, EventSink, and StatusEventArgs.

The Server class is a remoting server such as the one we already know. The Server class will create a channel based on information from a configuration file and register the remote object that's implemented in the RemoteObject class in the remoting runtime. The remote object declares the arguments of a delegate and fires events in the registered handler functions. The argument that's passed to the handler function is of type StatusEventArgs. The class StatusEventArgs must be serializable so it can be marshaled to the client.

The Client class represents the client application. This class creates an instance of the EventSink class and registers the StatusHandler() method of this class as a handler for the delegate in the remote object. EventSink must be remotable like the RemoteObject class, because this class will also be called across the network:

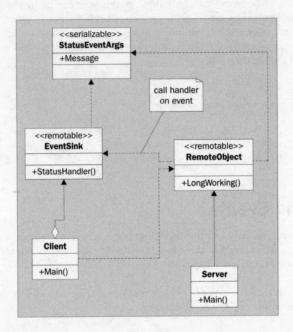

Remote Object

The remote object class is implemented in the file RemoteObject.cs. The remote object class must be derived from MarshalByRefObject, as we already know from our previous examples. To make it possible that the client can register an event handler that can be called from within the remote object, we have to declare an external function with the delegate keyword. We declare the delegate StatusEvent() with two arguments: the sender (so the client knows about the object that fired the event) and a variable of type StatusEventArgs. Into the argument class we can put all the additional information we want to send to the client.

The method that will be implemented in the client has some strict requirements. It may have only input parameters; return types, ref, and out parameters are not allowed; and the argument types must be either [Serializable], or remotable (derived from MarshalByRefObject). These requirements are fulfilled by the parameters we define with our StatusEvent delegate:

```
public delegate void StatusEvent(object sender, StatusEventArgs e);

public class RemoteObject : MarshalByRefObject
{
```

Within the `RemoteObject` class we declare an instance of the delegate function, `Status`, modified with the `event` keyword. The client must add an event handler to the `Status` event to receive status information from the remote object:

```
public class RemoteObject : MarshalByRefObject
{
    public RemoteObject()
    {
        Console.WriteLine("RemoteObject constructor called");
    }
    public event StatusEvent Status;
```

In the `LongWorking()` method we're checking if a event handler is registered before the event is fired with `Status(this, e)`. To verify that the event is fired asynchronously, we fire an event at the start of the method before doing the `Thread.Sleep()`, and after the sleep:

```
public void LongWorking(int ms)
{
    Console.WriteLine("RemoteObject: LongWorking() Started");
    StatusEventArgs e = new StatusEventArgs(
                        "Message for Client: LongWorking() Started");
    // fire event
    if (Status != null)
    {
        Console.WriteLine("RemoteObject: Firing Starting Event");
        Status(this, e);
    }
    System.Threading.Thread.Sleep(ms);
    e.Message = "Message for Client: LongWorking() Ending";
    // fire ending event
    if (Status != null)
    {
        Console.WriteLine("RemoteObject: Firing Ending Event");
        Status(this, e);
    }
    Console.WriteLine("RemoteObject: LongWorking() Ending");
}
```

Event Arguments

As you've seen in the `RemoteObject` class, the class `StatusEventArgs` is used as argument for the delegate. With the `[Serializable]` attribute an instance of this class can be transferred from the server to the client. We are using a simple property of type `string` to send a message to the client:

```
[Serializable]
public class StatusEventArgs
{
    public StatusEventArgs(string m)
    {
        message = m;
    }
    public string Message
    {
        get
        {
            return message;
```

```
      }
      set
      {
         message = value;
      }
   }
   private string message;
}
```

Server

The server is implemented within a console application. We are only waiting for a user to end the server after reading the configuration file, and setting up the channel and the remote object:

```csharp
using System;
using System.Runtime.Remoting;
namespace Wrox.ProCSharp.Remoting
{
   class Server
   {
      [STAThread]
      static void Main(string[] args)
      {
         RemotingConfiguration.Configure("Server.exe.config");
         Console.WriteLine("Hit a key to exit");
         Console.ReadLine();
      }
   }
}
```

Server Configuration File

The server configuration file, Server.exe.config, is also created as we've already discussed. There is just one important point: because the client first registers the event handler and then calls the remote method, the remote object must keep state for the client. It isn't possible to use SingleCall objects with events, so the RemoteObject class is configured as a client-activated type:

```xml
<configuration>
   <system.runtime.remoting>
      <application name="CallbackSample">
         <service>
            <activated type="Wrox.ProCSharp.Remoting.RemoteObject,
                           RemoteObject" />
         </service>
         <channels>
            <channel ref="http" port="6791" />
         </channels>
      </application>
   </system.runtime.remoting>
</configuration>
```

Event Sink

The event sink implements the handler StatusHandler() that's defined with the delegate. As previously noted when we declared the delegate, the method can have only input parameters, and only a void return. These are exactly the requirements for [OneWay] methods as we've seen earlier with Asynchronous Remoting. StatusHandler() will be called asynchronously. The EventSink class must also inherit from the class MarshalByRefObject to make it remotable because it will be called remotely, from the server:

```
using System;
using System.Runtime.Remoting.Messaging;
namespace Wrox.ProCSharp.Remoting
{
   public class EventSink : MarshalByRefObject
   {
      public EventSink()
      {
      }
      [OneWay]
      public void StatusHandler(object sender, StatusEventArgs e)
      {
         Console.WriteLine("EventSink: Event occurred: " + e.Message);
      }
   }
}
```

Client

The client reads the client configuration file with the RemotingConfiguration class: this is no different from the clients we've seen so far. The client creates an instance of the remotable sink class EventSink locally. The method that should be called from the remote object on the server is passed to the remote object:

```
using System;
using System.Runtime.Remoting;
namespace Wrox.ProCSharp.Remoting
{
   class Client
   {
      static void Main(string[] args)
      {
         RemotingConfiguration.Configure("Client.exe.config");
```

The differences start here. We have to create an instance of the remotable sink class EventSink locally. Since this class will not be configured with the <client> element, it's instantiated locally. Next, the remote object class RemoteObject is instantiated. This class is configured in the <client> element, so it's instantiated on the remote server:

```
         EventSink sink = new EventSink();
         RemoteObject obj = new RemoteObject();
```

Now can we register the handler method of the `EventSink` object in the remote object. `StatusEvent` is the name of the delegate that was defined in the server. The `StatusHandler()` method has the same arguments as are defined in the `StatusEvent`.

By calling the `LongWorking()` method, the server will call back into the method `StatusHandler()` at the beginning and end of the method:

```
// register client sink in server - subscribe to event

obj.Status += new StatusEvent(sink.StatusHandler);
obj.LongWorking(5000);
```

Now we are no longer interested in receiving events from the server and unsubscribe from the event. The next time we call `LongWorking()` no events will be received:

```
// unsubscribe from event

obj.Status -= new StatusEvent(sink.StatusHandler);
obj.LongWorking(5000);
Console.WriteLine("Hit to exit");
Console.ReadLine();
          }
       }
   }
```

Client Configuration File

The configuration file for the client, `client.exe.config`, is nearly the same configuration file for client-activated objects that we've already seen. The difference can be found in defining a port number for the channel. Since the server must reach the client with a known port, we have to define the port number for the channel as an attribute of the `<channel>` element. It isn't necessary to define a `<service>` section for our `EventSink` class, because this class will be instantiated from the client with the `new` operator locally. The server does not access this object by its name; instead it will receive a marshaled reference to the instance:

```
<configuration>
   <system.runtime.remoting>
      <application name="Client">
         <client url="http://localhost:6791/CallbackSample">
            <activated type="Wrox.ProCSharp.Remoting.RemoteObject,
                           RemoteObject" />
         </client>
         <channels>
            <channel ref="http" port="777" />
         </channels>
      </application>
   </system.runtime.remoting>
</configuration>
```

Running Programs

We see the resulting output on the server. The constructor of the remote object is called once because we have a client-activated object. Next, we see the call to `LongWorking()` has started and we are firing the events to the client. The next start of the `LongWorking()` method doesn't fire events, because the client has already unregistered its interest in the event:

```
C:\Professional C#\Remoting\Callback\Server\bi...
Hit to exit
RemoteObject constructor called
RemoteObject: LongWorking() Started
RemoteObject: Firing Starting Event
RemoteObject: Firing Ending Event
RemoteObject: LongWorking() Ending
RemoteObject: LongWorking() Started
RemoteObject: LongWorking() Ending
```

In the client output we can see that the events made it across the network:

```
C:\Professional C#\Remoting\Callback\Client\bin\Debug\Client.exe
EventSink: Event occurred: Message for Client: LongWorking() Started
EventSink: Event occurred: Message for Client: LongWorking() Ending
Hit to exit
```

Call Contexts

Client-activated objects can hold state for a specific client. With client-activated objects, we need resources on the server. With server-activated `SingleCall` objects, a new instance is created for every instance call, and no resources are held on the server; these objects can't hold state for a client. For state management we can keep state on the client side; details of the state of that object are sent with every method call to the server. We don't have to change all method signatures to include an additional parameter that passes the state to the server, because we can use **call contexts**.

A call context flows with a logical thread and is passed with every method call. A **logical thread** is started from the calling thread and flows through all method calls that are started from the calling thread, passing through different contexts, different application domains, and different processes.

We can assign data to the call context using `CallContext.SetData()`. The class of the object that's used as data for the `SetData()` method must implement the interface `ILogicalThreadAffinative`. We can get this data again in the same logical thread (but possibly a different physical thread) using `CallContext.GetData()`.

For the data of the call context I'm creating a new C# Class Library with the newly created class `CallContextData`. This class will be used to pass some data from the client to the server with every method call. The class that's passed with the call context must implement the `System.Runtime.Remoting.Messaging.ILogicalThreadAffinative` interface. This interface doesn't have a method; it's just a markup for the runtime to define that instances of this class should flow with a logical thread. The `CallContextData` class must also be marked with the `Serializable` attribute so it can be transferred through the channel:

```
using System;
using System.Runtime.Remoting.Messaging;
namespace Wrox.ProCSharp.Remoting
{
    [Serializable]
    public class CallContextData : ILogicalThreadAffinative
    {
        public CallContextData()
        {
        }
        public string Data
        {
            get
            {
                return data;
            }
            set
            {
                data = value;
            }
        }
        protected string data;
    }
}
```

In our `Hello` class, the `Greeting()` method is changed so that we access the call context. For the use of the `CallContextData` class we have to reference the previously created assembly `CallContextData` in the file `CallContextData.dll`. To work with the `CallContext` class, the namespace `System.Runtime.Remoting.Messaging` must be opened. Because the context works similar to a browser-based cookie, where the client automatically sends data to the web server, I'm giving the name `cookie` to the variable that holds the data that is sent from the client to the server:

```
public string Greeting(string name)
{
    Console.WriteLine("Greeting started");
    CallContextData cookie =
        (CallContextData)CallContext.GetData("mycookie");
    if (cookie != null)
    {
        Console.WriteLine("Cookie: " + cookie.Data);
    }
    Console.WriteLine("Greeting finished");
    return "Hello, " + name;
}
```

In the client code we pass the call context information by creating an instance of `CallContextData`, and declare that the values referenced by the cookie variable should be sent to the server by calling `CallContext.SetData()`. Now every time we call the `Greeting()` method in the `for` loop, the context data is automatically passed to the server.

```
CallContextData cookie = new CallContextData();
cookie.Data = "information for the server";
CallContext.SetData("mycookie", cookie);
for (int i=0; i < 5; i++)
{
    Console.WriteLine(obj.Greeting("Christian"));
}
```

Such a call context can be used to send information about the user, the name of the client system, or simply a unique identifier that's used on the server side to get some state information from a database.

Summary

In this chapter we've seen that .NET Remoting can make the task of invoking methods across the network straightforward. A remote object just has to inherit form `MarshalByRefObject`. In the server application only a single method is needed to load the configuration file so that the channels and remote objects are both set up and running. Within the client, we load the configuration file and can use the new operator to instantiate the remote object.

We also used .NET Remoting without the help of configuration files. On the server, we simply created a channel and registered a remote object. On the client, we created a channel and used the remote object.

We have seen in this chapter that although .NET Remoting can be that straightforward, the architecture is also flexible and can be extended. All parts of this technology such as channels, proxies, formatters, message sinks, and so on, are pluggable and can be replaced with custom implementations.

We used HTTP and TCP channels for the communication across the network, and SOAP and binary formatters to format the parameters before sending.

We discussed the use of stateless and stateful object types that are used by well-known and client-activated objects. With client-activated objects we have seen how the leasing mechanism is used to specify the lifetime of remote objects.

We have also seen that .NET Remoting is very well integrated in other parts of the .NET Framework, such as calling asynchronous methods, performing callbacks using the delegate and event keywords, among others.

Now, let's build on this experience by exploring Windows Services in our next chapter.

22

Windows Services

In Chapter 20 we had a look at networking and Chapter 21 covered servers using .NET Remoting. The server processes that we've looked at so far must be started manually. In this chapter, we will look at Windows Services, programs that can be started automatically at boottime without needing someone to log on to the machine.

In this chapter we will explore:

❑ The architecture of Windows Services; the functionality of a service program, service control program, and service configuration program.

❑ How to implement a Windows Service with the classes found in the `System.ServiceProcess` namespace.

❑ Installation programs to configure the Windows Service in the Registry.

❑ Writing a program to control the Windows Service using the `ServiceController` class.

❑ How to implement event handling. Because Windows Services usually run without any users interactively logged in, and typically don't have a user interface, errors can't be displayed in a message box. Event handling is a good way to report errors.

❑ Adding event logging to other application types.

❑ Implementing performance monitoring for a Windows Service. Performance monitoring can be used to get information about a normal running service.

First, we'll begin with a look at what a Windows Service actually is.

What is a Windows Service?

Windows Services are applications that can be automatically started when the operating system boots. They can run without having an interactive user logged on to the system. We can configure a Windows Service to be run from a specially configured user account; or from the system user account – a user account that has even more privileges than that of the System Administrator.

> Windows Services don't run on Windows 95, 98, or ME; the NT kernel is a requirement. Windows Services do run on Windows NT 4, Windows 2000, and Windows XP.

From now on, unless any confusion should arise, we shall refer to a Windows Service simply as a service.

Here are few examples of services:

❏ Simple TCP/IP Services is a service program that hosts some small TCP/IP servers: echo, daytime, quote, and others

❏ World Wide Publishing Service is the service of the Internet Information Server

❏ Event Log is a service to log messages to the event log system

❏ Microsoft Search is a service that creates indexes of data on the disk

We can use the Component Services administrative tool to see all of the services on a system. On a Windows 2000 Server this program can be accessed from Start | Programs | Administrative Tools | Services; on Windows 2000 Professional the program is accessible from Settings | Control Panel | Administrative Tools | Services:

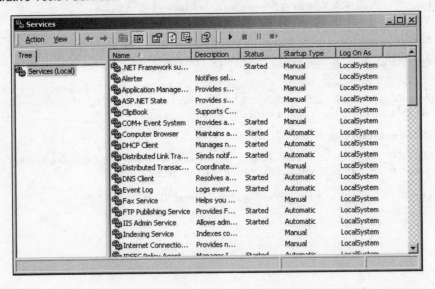

Windows Services Architecture

Three program types are necessary to operate a Windows Service.

❑ A service program

❑ A service control program

❑ A service configuration program

The **service program** itself provides the actual functionality we are looking for. With a **service control** program, it's possible to send control requests to a service, such as start, stop, pause, and continue. Finally, we need a **service configuration** program. With a service configuration program, a service can be installed; it's copied to the file system, written into the Registry, and configured as a service. While .NET components can be installed simply with an xcopy because they don't need the use of the Registry, installation for services does require Registry configuration. A service configuration program can also be used to change the configuration of that service at a later point.

We shall now look at these three ingredients of a Windows Service.

Service Program

Before looking at the .NET implementation of a service, let's look at it from an independent viewpoint and discover what the Windows architecture of services looks like, and what the inner functionality of a service is.

The service program implements the functionality of the service. It needs three parts:

❑ A main function

❑ A service-main function

❑ A handler

Before we discuss these parts, we first need to introduce the **Service Control Manager** (**SCM**). The SCM plays a very important role for services, sending requests to our service to start and stop it.

Service Control Manager (SCM)

The Service Control Manager is the part of the operating system that communicates with the service. Let's have a look at how this communication works with a UML sequence diagram:

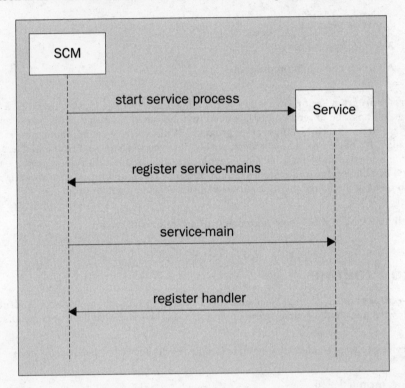

> At boot time, each process for which a service is set to automatically start is started, and so the main function of this process gets called. The service has the responsibility to register the service-main function for each of its services. The main function is the entry point of the service program, and in here, the entry points for the service-main functions must be registered with the SCM.

A main function may register more than one service-main function. It must register a service-main function for each service it provides. A service program can provide a lot of services in a single program; for example, <windows>\system32\services.exe is the service program that includes Alerter, Application Management, Computer Browser, and DHCP Client, among others.

The SCM now calls the service-main function for each service that should be started. The **service-main** function contains the actual functionality of the service. One important task of the service-main function is to register a handler with the SCM.

The **handler** function is the third part of the service program. The handler must respond to events from the SCM. Services can be stopped, suspended, and resumed, and the handler must react to these events.

Once a handler has been registered with the SCM, the service control program can post requests to the SCM to stop, suspend, and resume the service. The service control program is independent of the SCM and the service itself. We get many service control programs with the operating system; one is the MMC Services snap-in that we've seen earlier. We can also write our own service control program; a good example of this is the SQL Server Service Manager:

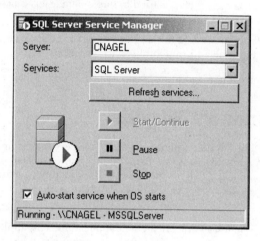

Service Control Program

As the name suggests, with a service control program we can control the service. For stopping, suspending, and resuming the service, we can send control codes to the service, and the handler should react to these events. It's also possible to ask the service about the actual status, and to implement a custom handler that responds to custom control codes.

Service Configuration Program

We can't use xcopy installation with services, since services must be configured in the Registry. We can set the startup type to automatic, manual, or disabled. We have to configure the user of the service program, and dependencies of the service – for example, the services that must be started before this one can start. All these configurations are made within a service configuration program. The installation program can use the service configuration program to configure the service, but this program can also be used at a later time to change service configuration parameters.

System.ServiceProcess Namespace

In the .NET Framework, we can find service classes in the System.ServiceProcess namespace that implement the three parts of a service:

- ❑ We inherit from the ServiceBase class to implement a service. The ServiceBase class is used to register the service and answer start and stop requests.

- ❑ The ServiceController class is used to implement a service control program. With this class we can send requests to services.

- ❑ The ServiceProcessInstaller and ServiceInstaller classes are, as the names suggest, classes to install and configure service programs.

Now we are ready to create a new service.

Creating a Windows Service

The service we are creating will host a quote server. With every request made from a client the quote server returns a random quote from a quote file. The first part of the solution will be done with three assemblies, one for the client and two for the server. The assembly QuoteServer holds the actual functionality. We will read the quote file in a memory cache, and answer requests for quotes with the help of a socket server.

The QuoteClient is a Windows Forms rich-client application. This application creates a client socket to communicate with the QuoteServer. The third assembly we will build is the actual service. The QuoteService starts and stops the QuoteServer; the service will control the server:

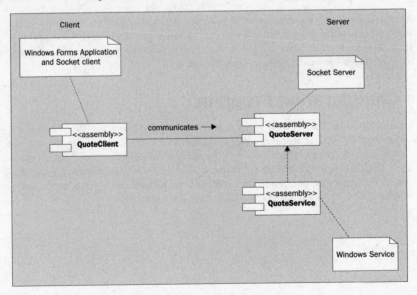

Before creating the service part of our program, we build a simple socket server in an extra C# class library that will be used from our service process.

A Class Library Using Sockets

We could build any functionality in the service such as scanning for files to do a backup or a virus check, or starting a .NET Remoting server, for example. But with any program we can offer as a service there are some similarities. The program must be possible to start (and return to the caller), and possibly to stop and suspend. We will look at such an implementation with a socket server.

With Windows 2000 or Windows XP, the Simple TCP/IP Services can be installed as part of the Windows components. Part of the Simple TCP/IP Services is a "quote of the day" TCP/IP server, short name "qotd". This simple service listens to port 17 and answers every request with a random message from the file `<windir>\system32\drivers\etc\quotes`. We will build a similar server here. Our server returns a Unicode string, in contrast to the good old "qotd" server that returns an ASCII string.

First we create a Class Library called `QuoteServer`. Let's step through the sourcecode of our `QuoteServer` class in the file `QuoteServer.cs`:

```
using System;
using System.IO;
using System.Threading;
using System.Net.Sockets;
using System.Text;
using System.Collections.Specialized;

namespace Wrox.ProCSharp.WinServices
{

    /// <summary>
    ///     Socket server example.
    /// </summary>

    public class QuoteServer
    {
        private TcpListener listener;
        private int port;
        private string filename;
        private StringCollection quotes;
        private Random random;
        private Thread listenerThread;
```

The constructor `QuoteServer()` is overloaded, so that a filename and a port can be passed to the call. The constructor where just the filename is passed uses the default port 7890 for the server. The default constructor defines the default filename for the quotes as `quotes.txt`:

```
        public QuoteServer() : this ("quotes.txt")
        {
        }
        public QuoteServer(string filename) : this(filename, 7890)
```

```
    {
    }
    public QuoteServer(string filename, int port)
    {
        this.filename = filename;
        this.port = port;
    }
```

ReadQuotes() is a helper method that reads all the quotes from a file that was specified in the constructor. All the quotes are added to the StringCollection quotes. In addition, we are creating an instance of the Random class that will be used to return random quotes:

```
    protected void ReadQuotes()
    {
        quotes = new StringCollection();
        Stream stream = File.OpenRead(filename);
        StreamReader streamReader = new StreamReader(stream);
        string quote;
        while ((quote = streamReader.ReadLine()) != null)
        {
            quotes.Add(quote);
        }
        streamReader.Close();
        stream.Close();
        random = new Random();
    }
```

Another helper method is GetRandomQuoteOfTheDay(). This method returns a random quote from the StringCollection quotes:

```
    protected string GetRandomQuoteOfTheDay()
    {
        int index = random.Next(0, quotes.Count);
        return quotes[index];
    }
```

In the Start() method, the complete file containing the quotes is read in the StringCollection quotes by using the helper method ReadQuotes(). After this, a new thread is started, which immediately calls the Listener() method – this may be familiar to you from our TcpReceive example in Chapter 20.

We are using a thread because the Start() method may not block and wait for a client; it must return immediately to the caller (SCM). The SCM would assume the start failed if the method didn't return to the caller in a timely fashion (30 seconds):

```
    public void Start()
    {
        ReadQuotes();
        listenerThread = new Thread(
            new ThreadStart(this.Listener));
        listenerThread.Start();
    }
```

The thread function `Listener()` creates a `TcpListener` instance. In the `AcceptSocket()` method, we are waiting for a client to connect. As soon as a client connects, `AcceptSocket()` returns with a socket associated with the client. We're calling `GetRandomQuoteOfTheDay()` to send the returned random quote to the client using `socket.Send()`:

```
protected void Listener()
{
    try
    {
        listener = new TcpListener(port);
        listener.Start();
        while (true)
        {
            Socket socket = listener.AcceptSocket();
            string message = GetRandomQuoteOfTheDay();
            UnicodeEncoding encoder = new UnicodeEncoding();
            byte[] buffer = encoder.GetBytes(message);
            socket.Send(buffer, buffer.Length, 0);
            socket.Close();
        }
    }
    catch (SocketException e)
    {
        Console.WriteLine(e.Message);
    }
}
```

As well as the `Start()` method, we have some methods to control the service: `Stop()`, `Suspend()`, and `Resume()`:

```
public void Stop()
{
    listener.Stop();
}
public void Suspend()
{
    listenerThread.Suspend();
}
public void Resume()
{
    listenerThread.Resume();
}
```

Another method that will be publicly available is `RefreshQuotes()`. If the file containing the quotes changes, then we start a re-read of the file with this method:

```
public void RefreshQuotes()
{
    ReadQuotes();
}
    }
}
```

Before building a service around our server, it's useful to build a test program that just creates an instance of the QuoteServer *and calls* Start(). *This way, we can test the functionality without the need to handle service-specific issues. This test server must be started manually, and we can easily walk through the code with a debugger.*

The test program is a C# console application, TestQuoteServer. We have to reference the assembly of the QuoteServer class. The file containing the quotes must be copied to the directory c:\ProCSharp\WinServices (or you have to change the argument in the constructor to specify where you have copied the file). After calling the constructor, the Start() method of the QuoteServer instance is called. Start() returns immediately after creating a thread, so we keep the console application running until Return is pressed:

```
static void Main(string[] args)
{
    QuoteServer qs = new QuoteServer(@"c:\ProCSharp\WinServices\quotes.txt",
                                     4567);
    qs.Start();
    Console.WriteLine("Hit return to exit");
    Console.ReadLine();
    qs.Stop();
}
```

Note that the QuoteServer will be running on port 4567 on localhost using this program – you will need to use these settings in the client later.

TcpClient Example

The client is a simple Windows application where we can enter the host name and the port number of the server. This application uses the TcpClient class to connect to the running server, and receives the returned message, displaying it in a RichTextBox. There's also a status bar at the bottom of the form. The entire form looks like this:

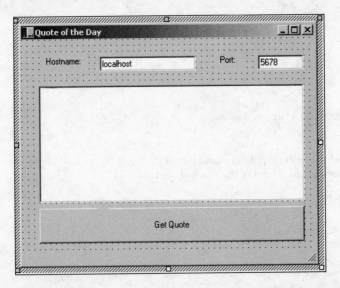

We have to make the following `using` directives in our code:

```
using System;
using System.Drawing;
using System.Collections;
using System.ComponentModel;
using System.Windows.Forms;
using System.Data;
using System.Net;
using System.Net.Sockets;
using System.Text;
```

The remainder of the code is automatically generated by the IDE, so we won't go into it in detail here. The major functionality of the client lies in the handler for the click event of the **Get Quote** button:

```
protected void buttonQuote_Click (object sender, System.EventArgs e)
{
    statusBar.Text = "";
    string server = textBoxHostname.Text;
    try
    {
        int port = Convert.ToInt32(textBoxPortNumber.Text);
    }
    catch (FormatException ex)
    {
        statusBar.Text = ex.Message;
        return;
    }
    TcpClient client = new TcpClient();
    try
    {
        client.Connect(textBoxHostname.Text,
                    Convert.ToInt32(textBoxPortNumber.Text));
        NetworkStream stream = client.GetStream();
        byte[] buffer = new Byte[1024];
        int received = stream.Read(buffer, 0, 1024);
        if (received <= 0)
        {
            statusBar.Text = "Read failed";
            return;
        }
        textBoxQuote.Text = Encoding.Unicode.GetString(buffer);
    }
    catch (SocketException ex)
    {
        statusBar.Text = ex.Message;
    }
    finally
    {
        client.Close();
    }
}
```

After starting the test server and this Windows application client, we can test the functionality. A successful run can have this output using the settings in the following screenshot:

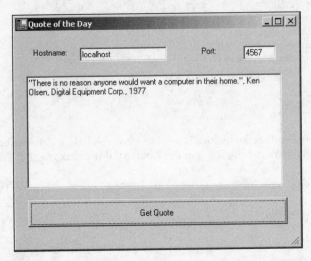

Let's now go on and implement what we are here for in this chapter – the service functionality in the server. The program is already running, so what more do we need? Well, the server program should be automatically started at boottime without anyone logged on to the system, and we want to control it using service control programs.

Windows Service Project

Using the new project wizard for C# Windows Services, we can now start to create a Windows Service. I'm naming the project QuoteService. Pay attention not to select a Web Service project!

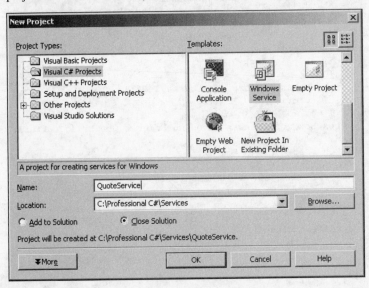

After pressing **OK** to create the Windows Service application, the Designer surface appears as in Windows Forms applications, but you can't insert any Windows Forms components because the application cannot directly display anything on the screen. We will use the Designer surface later in the chapter to add other components, such as performance counters and event logging.

Selecting the properties of this service opens up this Properties editor window:

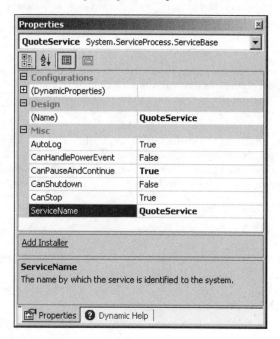

Here, properties of the service can be configured:

❑ AutoLog means that events are automatically written to the event log for starting and stopping the service.

❑ CanPauseAndContinue, CanShutdown, and CanStop means that the service can handle the specific pause, continue, shutdown, and stop requests.

❑ ServiceName is the name of the service that's written to the Registry and is used to control the service.

❑ CanHandlePowerEvent is a valid option for services running on a Windows 2000 system. We will talk about the power options in the *Windows 2000 Service Features* section later in the chapter.

> The default service name is `WinService1` – no matter what the project is named. You can install only a single `WinService1` service. If you get installation errors during your testing process, this may be the reason. Make sure, therefore, that you change the name of the service with the **Properties** editor to a more suitable name at the beginning of the service development.

Changing these properties with the **Properties** editor sets the values of our `ServiceBase`-derived class in the `InitalizeComponent()` method. You already know this method from Windows Forms applications. With services it's used in a similar way.

A wizard will generate the code, but we will change the file name to `QuoteService.cs`, the name of the namespace to `Wrox.ProCSharp.WinServices`, and the class name to `QuoteService`. We'll take a detailed look at this code later, but for now, we'll have a look at the `ServiceBase` class.

ServiceBase Class

The `ServiceBase` class is the base class for all .NET services. Our class `QuoteService` derives from `ServiceBase`; this class communicates with the service control manager using an undocumented helper class, `System.ServiceProcess.NativeMethods`, which is just a wrapper class to the Win32 API calls. The class is private, so we can't use it in our code.

The following sequence diagram shows the interaction of the SCM, our class `QuoteService`, and the classes from the `System.ServiceProcess` namespace. In the sequence diagram below, we can see the lifelines of objects vertically and communication going on in the horizontal direction. The communication is time-ordered from top to bottom:

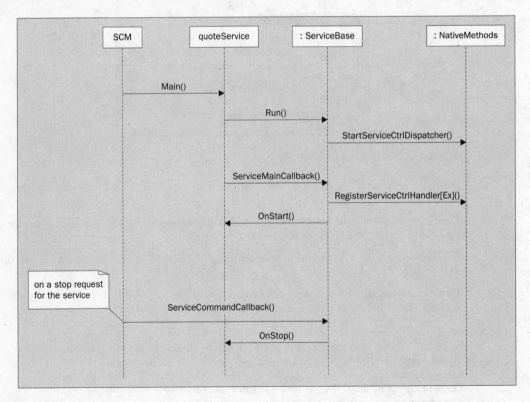

The SCM starts the process of a service that should be started. At startup, the `Main()` method is called. In the `Main()` method of our service we call the `Run()` method of the base class `ServiceBase`. `Run()` registers the method `ServiceMainCallback()` using `NativeMethods.StartServiceCtrlDispatcher()` in the SCM and writes an entry to the event log.

The next step is that the SCM calls the registered method `ServiceMainCallback()` in our service program. `ServiceMainCallback()` itself registers the handler in the SCM using `NativeMethods.RegisterServiceCtrlHandler[Ex]()` and sets the status of the service in the SCM. Next, the `OnStart()` method gets called. In `OnStart()` we have to implement the startup code. If `OnStart()` is successful, the string **"Service started successfully"** is written to the event log.

The handler is implemented in the `ServiceCommandCallback()` method. The SCM calls this method when changes are requested from the service. The `ServiceCommandCallback()` method routes the requests further to `OnPause()`, `OnContinue()`, `OnStop()`, `OnCustomCommand()`, and `OnPowerEvent()`.

Main Function

Let's look into the application-wizard - generated main function of the service process. In the main function, an array of `ServiceBase` classes, `ServicesToRun` is declared. One instance of the `QuoteService` class is created and passed as the first element to the `ServicesToRun` array. If more than one service should run inside this service process, it's necessary to add more instances of the specific service classes to the array. This array is then passed to the static `Run()` method of the `ServiceBase` class. With the `Run()` method of `ServiceBase`, we are giving the SCM references to the entry points of our services. The main thread of our service process is now blocked and waits for the service to terminate.

Here's the automatically generated code:

```
// The main entry point for the process
static void Main()
{
    System.ServiceProcess.ServiceBase[] ServicesToRun;

    // More than one user Service may run within the same process. To
    // add another service to this process, change the following line
    // to create a second service object. For example,
    //
    //    ServicesToRun = New System.ServiceProcess.ServiceBase[]
    //    {
    //        new WinService1(), new MySecondUserService()
    //    };
    //

    ServicesToRun = new System.ServiceProcess.ServiceBase[]
    {
        new QuoteService()
    };
    System.ServiceProcess.ServiceBase.Run(ServicesToRun);
}
```

If there's only a single service in the process the array can be removed – the `Run()` method accepts a single object derived from the class `ServiceBase`, so the `Main()` method could be reduced to this:

```
System.ServiceProcess.ServiceBase.Run(new QuoteService());
```

If there is more than one service, like the Windows program `Services.exe` that includes multiple services, and we need some shared initialization for the services, then this shared initialization must be done before the `Run()` method, because the main thread is blocked until the service process is stopped, and any following instructions would not be reached before the end of the service.

The initialization should not take too long: it shouldn't take longer than 30 seconds. If the initialization code were to take longer than this, then the service control manager assume that the service startup failed. We have to take into account the slowest machines where this service should run when considering this 30 second limit. If the initialization takes longer, we could start the initialization in a different thread so that the main thread calls `Run()` in time. An event object can then be used to signal that the thread completed its work.

Service-Start

At service start the `OnStart()` method is called - in here we can start our socket server. The `QuoteServer.dll` assembly must be referenced for the use of the `QuoteServer`. The thread calling `OnStart()` may not be blocked; this method must return to the caller, which is the `ServiceMainCallback()` method of the `ServiceBase` class. The `ServiceBase` class registers the handler and informs the SCM that the service started successfully after calling `OnStart()`:

```
protected override void OnStart(string[] args)
{
    quoteServer = new QuoteServer(@"c:\ProCSharp\WinServices\quotes.txt",
                                  5678);
    quoteServer.Start();
}
```

The `quoteServer` variable is declared as a private member in the class:

```
namespace Wrox.ProCSharp.WinServices
{
    public class QuoteService : System.ServiceProcess.ServiceBase
    {

        /// <summary>
        /// Required designer variable.
        /// </summary>

        private System.ComponentModel.Container components = null;
        private QuoteServer quoteServer;
```

Handler Methods

When the service is stopped, the `OnStop()` method gets called. We should stop the service functionality in this method:

```
protected override void OnStop()
{
    quoteServer.Stop();
}
```

In addition to OnStart() and OnStop(), we can override the following handlers in our class:

❑ OnPause() gets called when the service should be paused.

❑ OnContinue() gets called when the service should return to normal operation after being paused. To make it possible for the overridden methods OnPause() and OnContinue() to be called, the CanPauseAndContinue property must be set to true.

❑ OnShutdown() is called when Windows is undergoing system shutdown. Normally, the behavior of this method should be similar to the OnStop() implementation; if more time would be needed for a shutdown additional time can be requested. Similar to OnPause() and OnContinue(), a property must be set to enable this behavior: CanShutdown must be set to true.

❑ OnCustomCommand() is a handler that can serve custom commands that are sent by a service control program. The method signature of OnCustomCommand() has an int argument where we get the custom command number. The value can be in the range 128 to 256; values below 128 are system-reserved values. In our service we are re-reading the quotes file with the custom command 128:

```
protected override void OnPause()
{
    quoteServer.Suspend();
}
protected override void OnContinue()
{
    quoteServer.Resume();
}
protected override void OnShutdown()
{
    OnStop();
}
public const int commandRefresh = 128;
protected override void OnCustomCommand(int command)
{
    switch (command)
    {
        case commandRefresh:
            quoteServer.RefreshQuotes();
            break;
        default:
            break;
    }
}
```

Don't forget to add in a reference to our QuoteServer.dll file.

Threading and Services

With services, we have to deal with threads. As stated earlier, the SCM will assume that the service failed if the initialization takes too long. To deal with this, we have to create a thread.

The `OnStart()` method in our service class must return in time. If we call a blocking method like `AcceptSocket()` from the `TcpListener` class, we have to start a thread to do this. With a networking server that deals with multiple clients, a thread pool is also very useful. `AcceptSocket()` should receive the call and hand the processing off to another thread from the pool. This way, no one waits for the execution of code and the system seems responsive.

Service Installation

A service must be configured in the Registry. All services can be found in `HKEY_LOCAL_MACHINE\System\CurrentControlSet\Services`. You can view the Registry entries using `regedit`. The type of the service, display name, path to the executable, startup configuration, and so on, are all found here:

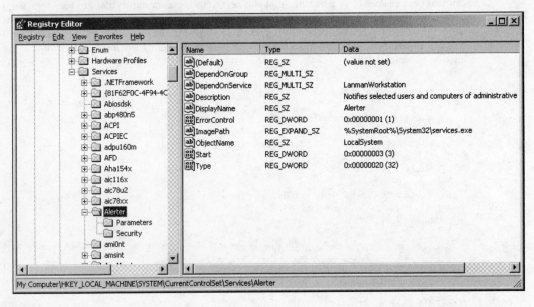

This configuration can be done using the installer classes from the `System.ServiceProcess` namespace. We shall look at these now.

Installation Program

We can add an installation program to the service by switching to the Design View with Visual Studio .NET and then selecting the **Add Installer** option from the context menu. With this option a new `ProjectInstaller` class is created, and a `ServiceInstaller` and a `ServiceProcessInstaller` instance are created.

The class diagram of the installer classes for services should help understanding of the generated code from the wizard:

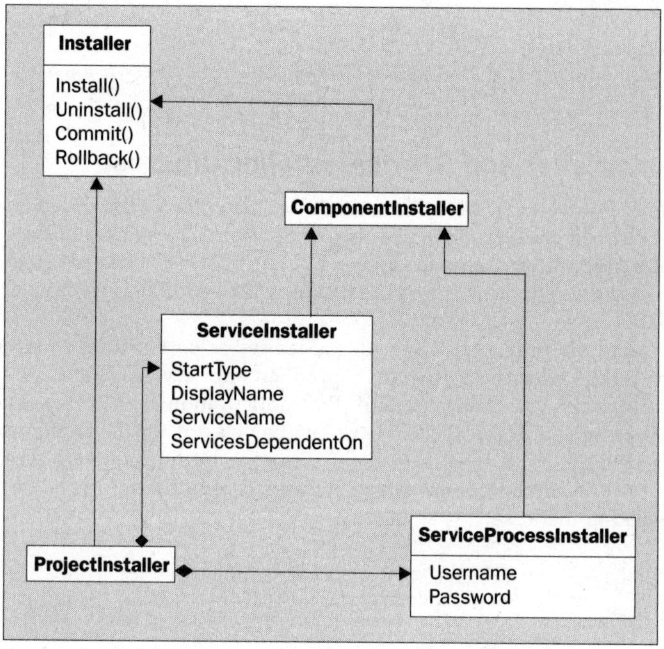

With this diagram in mind, let's go through the sourcecode in the file `ProjectInstaller.cs` that was created with the **Add Installer** option.

Installer Class

The class `ProjectInstaller` is derived from `System.Configuration.Install.Installer`. This is the base class for all custom installers. With the `Installer` class, it's possible to build transaction-based installations. With a transaction-based installation, it's possible to roll back to the previous state if the installation fails, and any changes made by this installation so far will be undone. As you can see in the figure above, the `Installer` class has `Install()`, `Commit()`, `Rollback()`, and `Uninstall()` methods, and they are called from installation programs.

The attribute `RunInstaller(true)` means that the class `ProjectInstaller` should be invoked when installing an assembly. Custom action installers as well as `installutil.exe` (which we will use later) check for this attribute:

```
using System;
using System.Collections;
using System.ComponentModel;
using System.Configuration.Install;

namespace Wrox.ProCSharp.WinServices
{
```

```
/// <summary>
///      Summary description for ProjectInstaller.
/// </summary>

[RunInstaller(true)]
public class ProjectInstaller : System.Configuration.Install.Installer
{
```

ServiceProcessInstaller and ServiceInstaller Classes

Similar to Windows Forms applications, InitializeComponent() is called inside the constructor of the ProjectInstaller class. In InitializeComponent(), instances of the ServiceProcessInstaller class and the ServiceInstaller class are created. Both of these classes derive from the ComponentInstaller class, which itself derives from Installer.

Classes derived from ComponentInstaller can be used as parts within an installation process. Remember that a service process can include more than one service. The ServiceProcessInstaller class is used for the configuration of the process that defines values for all services in this process, and the ServiceInstaller class is for the configuration of the service, so one instance of ServiceInstaller is needed for each service. If there are three services inside the process, then we have to add additional ServiceInstaller objects – three ServiceInstaller instances are needed in that case:

```
private System.ServiceProcess.ServiceProcessInstaller
              serviceProcessInstaller1;
private System.ServiceProcess.ServiceInstaller serviceInstaller1;

/// <summary>
///      Required designer variable.
/// </summary>

private System.ComponentModel.Container components = null;
public ProjectInstaller()
{
   // This call is required by the Designer.
   InitializeComponent();

   // TODO: Add any initialization after the InitComponent call
}
/// <summary>
///      Required method for Designer support - do not modify
///      the contents of this method with the code editor.
/// </summary>
private void InitializeComponent()
{
   this.serviceProcessInstaller1 =
              new System.ServiceProcess.ServiceProcessInstaller();
   this.serviceInstaller1 =
              new System.ServiceProcess.ServiceInstaller();
   //
   // serviceProcessInstaller1
   //
   this.serviceProcessInstaller1.Password = null;
   this.serviceProcessInstaller1.Username = null;
```

```
        //
        // serviceInstaller1
        //
        this.serviceInstaller1.ServiceName = "QuoteService";

        //
        // ProjectInstaller
        //
        this.Installers.AddRange(
            new System.Configuration.Install.Installer[]
                {this.serviceProcessInstaller1,
                 this.serviceInstaller1});
        }
    }
}
```

`ServiceProcessInstaller` installs an executable that implements the class `ServiceBase`. `ServiceProcessInstaller` has properties for the complete process. Properties shared by all the services inside the process include:

Property	Description
Username, Password	Indicates the user account under which the service runs if the `Account` property is set to `ServiceAccount.User`
Account	With this property we can specify the account type of the service. We will discuss the possible values next
HelpText	`HelpText` is a read-only property that returns the help text for setting the user name and password

The process that is used to run the service can be specified with the `Account` property of the `ServiceProcessInstaller` class using this enumeration:

Value	Meaning
LocalSystem	Setting this value specifies that the service uses a highly privileged user account on the local system, but this account presents an anonymous user to the network. Thus it doesn't have rights on the network.
LocalService	This account type presents the computer's credentials to any remote server.
NetworkService	Similar to `LocalService`, this value specifies that the computer's credentials are passed to remote servers, but unlike `LocalService` such a service acts as a non-privileged user on the local system. As the name says, this account should be used only for services that need resources from the network.
User	Setting the `Account` property to `ServiceAccount.User` means that we can define the account that should be used from the service.

ServiceInstaller is the class needed for every service; it has properties for each service inside a process: StartType, DisplayName, ServiceName, and ServicesDependedOn:

Property	Description
StartType	The StartType property indicates if the service is manually or automatically started. Possible values: ServiceStartMode.Automatic, ServiceStartMode.Manual, ServiceStartMode.Disabled. With ServiceStartMode.Disabled the service cannot be started. This option is useful for services that shouldn't be started on a system. You may wish to set the option to Disabled if a required hardware controller is not available, for example.
DisplayName	DisplayName is the friendly name of the service that is displayed to the user. This name is also used by management tools that control and monitor the service.
ServiceName	ServiceName is the name of the service. This value must be identical to the ServiceName property of the ServiceBase class in the service program. This name associates the configuration of the ServiceInstaller to the required service program.
ServicesDependentOn	Specifies an array of services that must be started before this service can be started. When the service is started, all these dependent services are started automatically, and then our service will start.

> **If you change the name of the service in the ServiceBase-derived class be sure to also change the ServiceName property in the ServiceInstaller object!**

In the testing phases set the StartType to Manual. This is advised because if you can't stop the service because of a bug in your program, then you still have the possibility to reboot the system. But if you have the StartType set to Automatic, the service would be started automatically with the reboot! You can change this configuration at a later time when you're sure it works.

ServiceInstallerDialog Class

Another installer class in the System.ServiceProcess.Design namespace is the ServiceInstallerDialog. This class can be used if we want the System Administrator to enter the username and password during the installation.

If we set the `Account` property of the class `ServiceProcessInstaller` to `ServiceAccount.User`, and the `Username` and `Password` properties to `null`, then the dialog shown below will automatically be displayed at installation time. It's also possible to cancel the installation here:

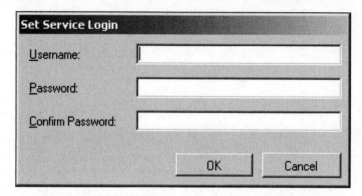

installutil

After adding the installer classes to the project we can now use the `installutil.exe` utility to install and uninstall the service. This utility can be used to install any assembly that has an `Installer` class. `installutil.exe` calls the method `Install()` of the class that derives from the `Installer` class for installation, and `Uninstall()` for the uninstallation.

The command-line inputs for the installation and uninstallation of our service are, respectively:

```
installutil quoteservice.exe
installutil /u quoteservice.exe
```

> If the installation fails be sure to check the installation log files
> `InstallUtil.InstallLog` and `<servicename>.InstallLog`. Often you can find
> very useful information such as "**The specified service already exists**".

Client

After the service has been successfully installed, we can start the service manually from the Services MMC (see next section for further details), and we can start our client; the following screenshot of the service inaction shows the settings:

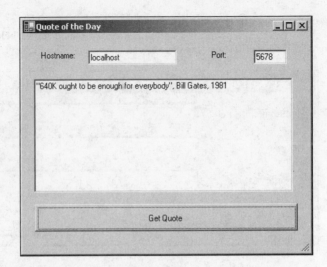

Monitoring and Controlling the Service

To monitor and control services we have some utilities. There's a Services MMC snap-in that's part of the Computer Management administration tool. With every Windows system we also get a command-line utility, `net.exe`, which allows us to control services. `sc.exe` is an additional command-line utility that has much more functionality than the `net.exe` command that's part of the Platform SDK. We will also create a small Windows application that makes use of the `System.ServiceProcess.ServiceController` class to monitor and control services.

MMC Computer Management

Using the Services snap-in to the Microsoft Management Console (MMC) we can view the status of all services. It's also possible to send control requests to services to stop, enable, and disable them, as well as change their configuration. The Services snap-in is a service control program as well as a service configuration program:

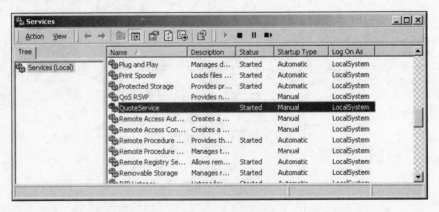

Double-clicking on our QuoteService opens up this dialog:

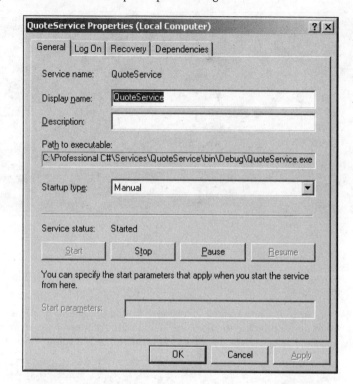

We see the service name, description, and the path to the executable, the startup type, and the status. The service is currently started. The account for the service process can be changed with the Log On tab in this dialog.

net.exe

The Services snap-in is easy to use, but the System Administrator cannot automate it, because it's not usable within an administrative script. For this task there is a command-line utility: net.exe. This tool can be used to control services. net start shows all running services, net start *servicename* starts a service, net stop *servicename* sends a stop request to the service. It's also possible to pause and continue a service with net pause and net continue (only if the service allows it, of course).

This console window shows the result of net start:

```
C:\WINNT\System32\cmd.exe                                    _ □ ×

C:\>net start
These Windows 2000 services are started:

   COM+ Event System
   Computer Browser
   DHCP Client
   Distributed Link Tracking Client
   DNS Client
   Event Log
   FTP Publishing Service
   IIS Admin Service
   IPSEC Policy Agent
   Logical Disk Manager
   Machine Debug Manager
   Messenger
   Network Connections
   Plug and Play
   Print Spooler
   Protected Storage
   QuoteService
   Remote Procedure Call (RPC)
   Remote Registry Service
   Removable Storage
   RIP Listener
```

sc.exe

There's a little known utility that's delivered with Visual Studio .NET, but starting with Windows XP is also part of the operating system: sc.exe.

sc.exe is a great tool to play with services. A lot more can be done with sc.exe compared to the net.exe utility. With sc it's possible to check the actual status of a service, or configure, remove, and add services. This tool also assists with the de-installation of the service if it fails to function correctly any more:

```
C:\WINNT2\System32\cmd.exe - sc                                        _ □ ×

C:\Program Files\Microsoft Platform SDK\Bin\WinNT>sc
DESCRIPTION:
        SC is a command line program used for communicating with the
        NT Service Controller and services.
USAGE:
        sc <server> [command] [service name] <option1> <option2>...

        The option <server> has the form "\\ServerName"
        Further help on commands can be obtained by typing: "sc [command]"
        Commands:
          query-----------Queries the status for a service, or
                          enumerates the status for types of services.
          queryex---------Queries the extended status for a service, or
                          enumerates the status for types of services.
          start-----------Starts a service.
          pause-----------Sends a PAUSE control request to a service.
          interrogate-----Sends an INTERROGATE control request to a service.
          continue--------Sends a CONTINUE control request to a service.
          stop------------Sends a STOP request to a service.
          config----------Changes the configuration of a service (persistant).
          description-----Changes the description of a service
          failure---------Changes the actions taken by a service upon failure.
          qc--------------Queries the configuration information for a service.
          qdescription----Queries the description for a service.
          qfailure--------Queries the actions taken by a service upon failure.
          delete----------Deletes a service (from the registry).
          create----------Creates a service. (adds it to the registry).
          control---------Sends a control to a service.
          sdshow----------Displays a service's security descriptor.
          sdset-----------Sets a service's security descriptor.
          GetDisplayName--Gets the DisplayName for a service.
          GetKeyName------Gets the ServiceKeyName for a service.
          EnumDepend------Enumerates Service Dependencies.

        The following commands don't require a service name:
        sc <server> <command> <option>
          boot------------(ok | bad) Indicates whether the last boot should
                          be saved as the last-known-good boot configuration
          Lock------------Locks the Service Database
          QueryLock-------Queries the LockStatus for the SCManager Database
EXAMPLE:
        sc start MyService

Would you like to see help for the QUERY and QUERYEX commands? [ y | n ]:
```

Visual Studio .NET Server Explorer

It's also possible to control services using the Server Explorer within Visual Studio .NET; **Services** is underneath **Servers** and the name of your computer. By selecting a service and opening the context menu a service can be started and stopped. This context menu can also be used to add a `ServiceController` class to the project. If you want to control a specific service in your application, drag and drop a service from the Server Explorer to the Designer: a `ServiceController` instance is added to the application. The properties of this object are automatically set to access the selected service, and the `System.ServiceProcess.dll` is referenced. You can use this instance to control a service in the same way that we can with the application we will develop in the next section.

ServiceController Class

We will create a small Windows application using the `ServiceController` class to monitor and control Windows Services.

The user interface to this application has a list box to show all services, four textboxes to display the display name, status, type, and name of the service, and four buttons to send control events.

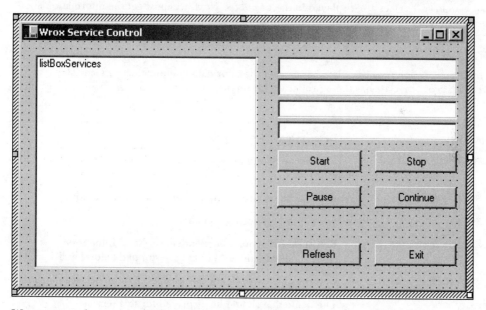

We are using the `System.ServiceProcess.ServiceController` class, so the file `System.ServiceProcess.dll` must be referenced.

We are implementing the `RefreshServiceList()` method that is called within the constructor of the `ServiceControlForm` class. This method fills a `ListBox` with the display names of all services. `GetServices()` is a static method of the `ServiceController` class, and it returns a `ServiceController` array representing all Windows Services. The `ServiceController` class also has a static method, `GetDevices()`, that returns a `ServiceController` array representing all device drivers.

The ListBox is filled by simply binding ServiceController.GetServices() to the ListBox:

```
        private System.ServiceProcess.ServiceController[] services;

        public ServiceControlForm()
        {

            //
            // Required for Windows Form Designer support
            //

            InitializeComponent();
            RefreshServiceList();
        }
        protected void RefreshServiceList()
        {
            services = ServiceController.GetServices();
            listBoxServices.DisplayMember = "DisplayName";
            listBoxServices.DataSource = services;
        }
```

Now, all Windows Services are displayed in the ListBox. Next, we must get the information about a service to display it in the textboxes.

Monitoring the Service

Using the ServiceController class, we can get the information about each service. The ServiceController class has these properties for service information, some of which we've met before:

Property	Description
CanPauseAndContinue	If pause and continue requests can be sent to the service, true is returned.
CanShutdown	true if the service has a handler for a system shutdown.
CanStop	true if the service is stoppable.
DependentServices	Returns a collection of dependent services. If the service is stopped all dependent services are stopped beforehand.
ServicesDependentOn	Returns of a collection of the services that this service depends on.
DisplayName	The name that should be displayed for this service.
MachineName	The name of the machine that the service runs on.
ServiceName	Name of the service.

Property	Description
ServiceType	The service can be run inside a shared process where more than one service uses the same process (Win32ShareProcess), or run so there's just one service in a process (Win32OwnProcess). If the service can interact with the desktop the type is InteractiveProcess.
Status	Status of the service. The status can be running, stopped, paused, or in some intermediate mode like start pending, stop pending, and so on. The status values are defined in the enumeration ServiceControllerStatus.

In our application, we are using the properties DisplayName, ServiceName, ServiceType, and Status to display the service information. Also, CanPauseAndContinue and CanStop are used to enable or disable the **Pause**, **Continue**, and **Stop** buttons.

OnSelectedIndexChanged() is a handler for the ListBox; it's called when the user selects a service in the ListBox. In OnSelectedIndexChanged() we set the display and service name directly with properties of the ServiceController class. The status and type cannot be set that easily, because a string should be displayed instead of a number, which is what the ServiceController class returns. SetServiceStatus() is a helper function that walks through the enumeration of the Status property to display a string for the status, and also to enable or disable the buttons. GetServiceTypeName() builds up the name of the service type.

The ServiceType we get from ServiceController.ServiceType represents a set of flags that can be combined using the bitwise OR operator. The InteractiveProcess bit can be set together with Win32OwnProcess and Win32ShareProcess. First, we check to see that the InteractiveProcess bit is set before we go on to check for the other values:

```
protected string GetServiceTypeName(ServiceType type)
{
   string serviceType = "";
   if ((type & ServiceType.InteractiveProcess) != 0)
   {
      serviceType = "Interactive ";
      type -= ServiceType.InteractiveProcess;
   }
   switch (type)
   {
      case ServiceType.Adapter:
         serviceType += "Adapter";
         break;
      case ServiceType.FileSystemDriver:
      case ServiceType.KernelDriver:
      case ServiceType.RecognizerDriver:
         serviceType += "Driver";
         break;
      case ServiceType.Win32OwnProcess:
         serviceType += "Win32 Service Process";
```

```
            break;
        case ServiceType.Win32ShareProcess:
            serviceType += "Win32 Shared Process";
            break;
        default:
            serviceType += "unknown type " + type.ToString();
            break;
    }
    return serviceType;
}
protected void SetServiceStatus(ServiceController controller)
{
    buttonStart.Enabled = true;
    buttonStop.Enabled = true;
    buttonPause.Enabled = true;
    buttonContinue.Enabled = true;
    if (!controller.CanPauseAndContinue)
    {
        buttonPause.Enabled = false;
        buttonContinue.Enabled = false;
    }
    if (!controller.CanStop)
    {
        buttonStop.Enabled = false;
    }
    ServiceControllerStatus status = controller.Status;
    switch (status)
    {
        case ServiceControllerStatus.ContinuePending:
            textBoxServiceStatus.Text = "Continue Pending";
            buttonContinue.Enabled = false;
            break;
        case ServiceControllerStatus.Paused:
            textBoxServiceStatus.Text = "Paused";
            buttonPause.Enabled = false;
            buttonStart.Enabled = false;
            break;
        case ServiceControllerStatus.PausePending:
            textBoxServiceStatus.Text = "Pause Pending";
            buttonPause.Enabled = false;
            buttonStart.Enabled = false;
            break;
        case ServiceControllerStatus.StartPending:
            textBoxServiceStatus.Text = "Start Pending";
            buttonStart.Enabled = false;
            break;
        case ServiceControllerStatus.Running:
            textBoxServiceStatus.Text = "Running";
            buttonStart.Enabled = false;
            buttonContinue.Enabled = false;
            break;
        case ServiceControllerStatus.Stopped:
            textBoxServiceStatus.Text = "Stopped";
```

```
                        buttonStop.Enabled = false;
                        break;
                case ServiceControllerStatus.StopPending:
                        textBoxServiceStatus.Text = "Stop Pending";
                        buttonStop.Enabled = false;
                        break;
                default:
                        textBoxServiceStatus.Text = "Unknown status";
                        break;

        }
        protected void OnSelectedIndexChanged (object sender,
                        System.EventArgs e)
        {
            ServiceController controller =
                        (ServiceController)listBoxServices.SelectedItem;
            textBoxDisplayName.Text = controller.DisplayName;
            textBoxServiceType.Text =
                        GetServiceTypeName(controller.ServiceType);
            textBoxServiceName.Text = controller.ServiceName;
            SetServiceStatus(controller);
        }
```

Controlling the Service

With the ServiceController class we can also send control requests to the service:

Method	Description
Start()	Start() tells the SCM that the service should be started. In our service program OnStart() is called.
Stop()	Stop() calls OnStop() in our service program with the help of the SCM if the property CanStop is true in the service class.
Pause()	Pause() calls OnPause() if the property CanPauseAndContinue is true.
Continue()	Continue calls OnContinue() if the property CanPauseAndContinue is true.
ExecuteCommand()	With ExecuteCommand() it's possible to send a custom command to the service.

The code to control the services follows here. Because the code for starting, stopping, suspending, and pausing is similar, only one handler is used for the four buttons:

```
        protected void buttonCommand_Click(object sender, System.EventArgs e)
        {
            Cursor.Current = Cursors.WaitCursor;
            ServiceController controller =
```

```
                      (ServiceController)listBoxServices.SelectedItem;
        if (sender == this.buttonStart)
        {
            controller.Start();
            controller.WaitForStatus(ServiceControllerStatus.Running);
        }
        else if (sender == this.buttonStop)
        {
            controller.Stop();
            controller.WaitForStatus(ServiceControllerStatus.Stopped);
        }
        else if (sender == this.buttonPause)
        {
            controller.Pause();
            controller.WaitForStatus(ServiceControllerStatus.Paused);
        }
        else if (sender == this.buttonContinue)
        {
            controller.Continue();
            controller.WaitForStatus(ServiceControllerStatus.Running);
        }
        int index =listBoxServices.SelectedIndex;
        RefreshServiceList();
        listBoxServices.SelectedIndex = index;
        Cursor.Current = Cursors.Default;
    }

protected void buttonExit_Click(object sender, System.EventArgs e)
{
    Application.Exit();
}
protected void buttonRefresh_Click(object sender, System.EventArgs e)
{
    RefreshServiceList();
}
```

As the action of controlling the services can take some time, the cursor is switched to the wait cursor in the first statement. Then, a ServiceController method is called depending on the pressed button. With the WaitForStatus() method, we are waiting to check that the service changes the status to the requested value, but we only wait a maximum of 10 seconds. After this time, the information in the ListBox is refreshed; and the same service as before is selected, and the new status of this service is displayed.

The completed application looks like this:

Troubleshooting

Troubleshooting services is different from troubleshooting normal applications.

In this section, we will look at the following troubleshooting topics:

- ❑ The problems of interactive services
- ❑ Event logging
- ❑ Performance monitoring

The best way to begin building a service is to create an assembly with the desired functionality and a test client, before the service is actually created. Here you can do normal debugging and error handling. As soon as the application is running you can build a service using this assembly. Of course, there still can be problems with the service:

- ❑ Don't display errors in a message box from the service (except for interactive services that are running on the client system). Instead, use the event logging service to write errors to the event log. Of course, you can display a message box to inform the user about errors in the client application that uses the service.

- ❑ The service can't be started from within a debugger, but a debugger can be attached to the running service process. Open the solution with the sourcecode of the service and set breakpoints. From the Visual Studio .NET Debug menu select Processes and attach the running process of the service.

- ❑ The Windows 2000 Performance Monitor can be used to monitor the activity of services. We can add our own performance objects to the service. This can add some useful information for debugging. For example, with our service, we could set up an object to give the total number of quotes returned, the time it takes to initialize, and so on.

Interactive Services

If an interactive service runs with a logged-on user it can be helpful to display message boxes to the user. If the service should run on a server that would be locked inside a computer room, the service should never display a message box. When you open a message box, to wait for some user input, the user input probably won't happen for some days as nobody is looking at the server in the computer room; but it can get even worse than that – if the service isn't configured as an interactive service, the message box opens up on a different, hidden, window station. In this case, no one can answer that message box because it is hidden, and the service is blocked.

> **Never open dialogs for services running on a server system. Nobody will answer this dialog.**

In those cases where you really want to interact with the user, an interactive service can be configured. Some examples of such interactive services are the Print Spooler that displays paper-out messages to the user, and the NetMeeting Remote Desktop Sharing service.

To configure an interactive service, the option **Allow service to interact with desktop** in the **Services** configuration tool must be set. This changes the type of the service by adding the `SERVICE_INTERACTIVE_PROCESS` flag to the type:

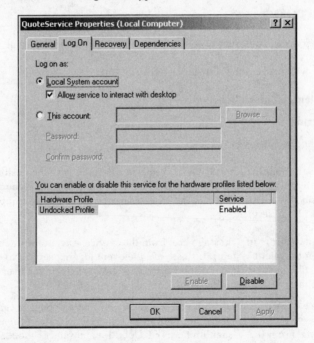

Event Logging

Services can report errors and other information by adding events to the event log. A service class derived from `ServiceBase` automatically logs events when the `AutoLog` property is set to `true`. The `ServiceBase` class checks this property and writes a log entry at start, stop, pause, and continue requests.

In this section, we will explore:

- ❑ Error-logging architecture
- ❑ Classes for event logging from the `System.Diagnostics` namespace
- ❑ Adding event logging, to services and to other application types
- ❑ Creating an event-log listener with the `EnableRaisingEvents` property of the `EventLog` class

First, here's an example of a log entry from a service:

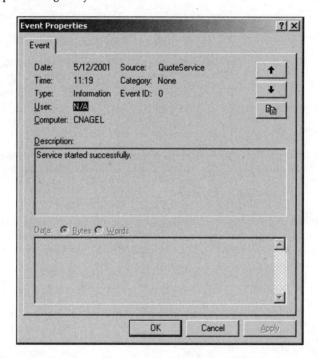

For custom event logging, we can use classes from the `System.Diagnostics` namespace.

Event Logging Architecture

By default, the Event Log is stored in three log files: Application, Security, and System. Looking at the Registry configuration of the event log service the three entries can be seen at `HKEY_LOCAL_MACHINE\System\CurrentControlSet\Services\Eventlog` with configurations pointing to the specific files. The System log file is used from the system and device drivers. Applications and services write to the Application log. The Security log is a read-only log for applications. The auditing feature of the operating system uses the Security log.

We can read these events using the administrative tool Event Viewer. The Event Viewer can be started directly from the Server Explorer of Visual Studio .NET by right-clicking on the Event Logs item, and selecting the Launch Event Viewer entry from the context menu:

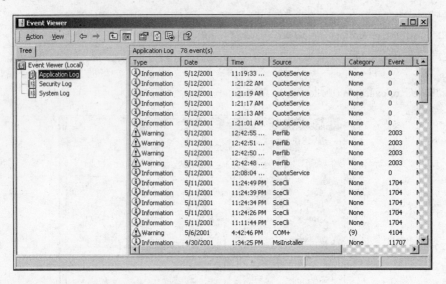

In the Event log we can see this information:

❑ The type can be Information, Warning, or Error. Information is an infrequent successful operation, Warning a problem that's not immediately significant, and Error a major problem. Additional types are FailureAudit and SuccessAudit, but these types are only used for the Security log.

❑ Date and Time show the time when the event occurred.

❑ The Source is the name of the software that logs the event. The source for the Application log is configured in:

```
HKEY_LOCAL_MACHINE\
    System\CurrentControlSet\Services\
        Eventlog\Application\[ApplicationName]
```

Below this key the value EventMessageFile is configured to point to a resource DLL that holds error messages.

❑ A Category can be defined so that event logs can be filtered when using the Event Viewer. Categories can be defined by an event source.

❑ The Event identifier specifies a particular event message.

Event Logging Classes

The System.Diagnostics namespace has some classes for event logging:

❑ With the EventLog class we can read and write entries in the event log, and establish applications as event sources.

❑ The EventLogEntry class represents a single entry in the event log. With the EventLogEntryCollection we can iterate through EventLogEntry items.

❑ The EventLogInstaller class is the installer for an EventLog component. EventLogInstaller calls EventLog.CreateEventSource() to create an event source.

❑ With the help of the EventLogTraceListener traces can be written to the event log. This class implements the abstract class TraceListener.

Adding Event Logging

If the AutoLog property of the ServiceBase class is set to true, event logging is automatically turned on. The ServiceBase class logs an informational event at startup, stop, pause, and continue requests of the service. In the ServiceInstaller class an EventLogInstaller instance is created so that an event log source is configured. This event log source has the same name as the service. If we want to write events we can use the static WriteEntry() method of the EventLog class. The Source property was already set in the ServiceBase class:

```
EventLog.WriteEntry ("event log message");
```

This method logs an informational event. If warning or error events should be created an overloaded method of WriteEvent() can be used to specify the type:

```
EventLog.WriteEntry("event log message", EventLogEntryType.Warning);
EventLog.WriteEntry("event log message", EventLogEntryType.Error);
```

Adding Event Logging to Other Application Types

With services the ServiceBase class automatically adds event-logging features. If you would like to use event logging within other application types, this can easily be done using Visual Studio .NET.

❑ Use the Toolbox to add an EventLog component to the designer.

❑ Set the Log property of the EventLog component to Application and the Source property to a name you choose. This name is typically the name of the application that shows up in the Event Viewer.

❑ Logs can now be written with the WriteEntry() method of the EventLog instance.

❑ An installer can be added from the Add Installer context menu item of the EventLog component. This creates the ProjectInstaller class that configures the event source in the Registry.

❑ The application can now be registered with the installutil command. installutil calls the ProjectInstaller class and registers the event source.

In the sense of xcopy-installation the last two steps are not really necessary. If the Source property of the EventLog instance is set, this source is automatically registered when an event log is written the first time. That's really easy to do, but for a real application I would prefer adding the installer: with installutil /u the event log configuration gets unregistered. If the application is just deleted, this Registry key remains unless EventLog.DeleteEventSource() is called.

Trace

It's also possible that all your trace messages are redirected to the event log. You shouldn't really do this, because on a normal running system the event log gets overblown with trace messages, and the System Administrator could miss the really important logs if this happens. Turning on trace messages to the event log can be a useful testing feature for problematic services. Tracing is possible with debug as well as with release code.

To send trace messages to the event log an EventLogTraceListener object must be created and added to the listener's list of the Trace class:

```
EventLogTraceListener listener = new EventLogTraceListener(eventLog1);
Trace.Listeners.Add(listener);
```

Now, all trace messages are sent to the event log:

```
Trace.WriteLine("trace message");
```

Creating an Event Log Listener

Now it would be useful if we could write an application that receives an event when a service encounters a problem. We will create a simple Windows application that monitors the events of our Quote service.

This Windows application has just a ListBox and an Exit button:

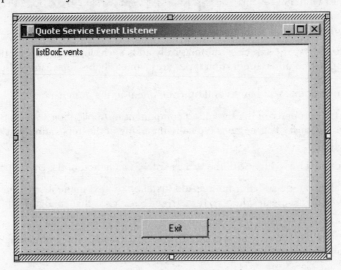

An `EventLog` component is added to this project by dragging and dropping it from the **Toolbox**. We set the `Log` property to `Application`, and the `Source` to the source of our service, `QuoteService`. The `EventLog` class also has a property, `EnableRaisingEvents`. Until now, we haven't talked about this property. The default value is `false`; setting it to `true` means that an event is generated each time this event occurs, and we can write an event handler for the `EntryWritten` Windows event.

In the file `EventListener.cs` of our project, the properties are set in `InitializeComponent()`:

```
private void InitializeComponent()
{
    this.eventLogQuote = new System.Diagnostics.EventLog();
    this.buttonExit = new System.Windows.Forms.Button();
    this.listBoxEvents = new System.Windows.Forms.ListBox();
    ((System.ComponentModel.ISupportInitialize)
                    (this.eventLogQuote)).BeginInit();
    this.SuspendLayout();

    //
    // eventLogQuote
    //

    this.eventLogQuote.EnableRaisingEvents = true;
    this.eventLogQuote.Log = "Application";
    this.eventLogQuote.Source = "QuoteService";
    this.eventLogQuote.SynchronizingObject = this;
    this.eventLogQuote.EntryWritten +=
            new System.Diagnostics.EntryWrittenEventHandler
                                (this.OnEntryWritten);
```

The `OnEntryWritten()` handler receives an `EntryWrittenEventArgs` object as argument, from which we can get the complete information about an event. With the `Entry` property we get an `EventLogEntry` object with information about the time, event source, type, category, and so on:

```
protected void OnEntryWritten (object sender,
    System.Diagnostics.EntryWrittenEventArgs e)
{
    DateTime time = e.Entry.TimeGenerated;
    string message = e.Entry.Message;
    listBoxEvents.Items.Add(time + " " + message);
}
```

The running application displays all events for the `QuoteService`:

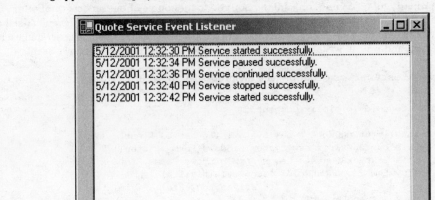

Performance Monitoring

Performance monitoring can be used to get information about the normal running of the service. Performance monitoring is a great tool that helps us to understand the workload of the system, and to observe changes and trends.

Windows 2000 has a lot of performance objects, such as `System`, `Memory`, `Objects`, `Process`, `Processor`, `Thread`, `Cache`, and so on. Each of these objects has many counts to monitor. For example, with the `Process` object the user time, handle count, page faults, thread count, and so on, can be monitored for all processes, or for specific process instances. Some applications, such as SQL Server, also add application-specific objects.

For our quote service, we could be interested in getting the information about the number of client requests, how big the data is that is sent over the wire, and so on.

Performance Monitoring Classes

The `System.Diagnostics` namespace has these classes for performance monitoring:

❑ `PerformanceCounter` can be used both to monitor counts and to write counts. New performance categories can also be created with this class.

❑ With the `PerformanceCounterCategory` we can walk through all existing categories as well as create new ones. We can programmatically get all the counters of a category.

❑ The `PerformanceCounterInstaller` class is used for the installation of performance counters. The use is similar to the `EventLogInstaller` we discussed previously.

Performance Counter Builder

We can create a new performance counter category by selecting the performance counters in the Server Explorer and selecting the menu entry **Create New Category...** in the context menu. This starts the Performance Counter Builder:

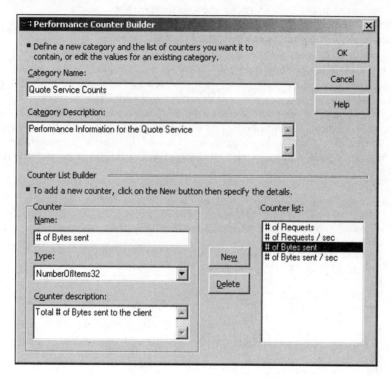

I'm setting the name of the category to be `Quote Service`. Here is a table showing all performance counters of our service:

Name	Description	Type
# of Bytes sent	Total # of bytes sent to the client	`NumberOfItems32`
# of Bytes sent / sec	# of bytes sent to the client in one second	`RateOfCountsPerSecond32`
# of Requests	Total # of requests	`NumberOfItems32`
# of Requests / sec	# of requests in one second	`RateOfCountsPerSecond32`

The Performance Counter Builder writes the configuration to the performance database. This can also be done dynamically using the `Create()` method of the `PerformanceCounterCategory` class in the `System.Diagnostics` namespace. An installer for other systems can easily be added later using Visual Studio .NET.

Adding Performance Counts

Next, we want to add the performance counts to the quote server. The `QuoteService` class has no knowledge about the information needed for the performance counts. We want to collect the number of requests, but after the start of the service `QuoteService` receives no requests. The information is completely contained in the `QuoteServer` class we built earlier.

Add Visual Studio .NET Designer Support to the Class Library

We could add instances of the `PerformanceCounter` class manually in the code, or we can use the Visual Studio .NET designer. With the Designer we can drag and drop `PerformanceCounter` components from the Toolbox. Designer support can be easily added to a component library by deriving the class from `System.ComponentModel.Component`. The method `InitializeComponent()` that will be used from the Designer to set the properties of the components will be added automatically as soon as the first component is dropped onto the Designer surface, but we do have to add a call to `InitializeComponent()` in the constructor. To remember the number of bytes sent and the request number we also add two private variables: `requestPerSec` and `bytesPerSec`.

```
public class QuoteServer : System.ComponentModel.Component
{
    private TcpListener listener;
    private int port;
    private string filename;
    private StringCollection quotes;
    private Random random;
    private Thread listenerThread;
    private System.Diagnostics.EventLog eventLog;

    private int requestsPerSec;
    private int bytesPerSec;

    public QuoteServer(): this("quotes.txt")
    {
    }
    public QuoteServer(string filename) : this(filename, 7890)
    {
    }
    public QuoteServer(string filename, int port)
    {
        this.filename = filename;
        this.port = port;

        InitializeComponent();
    }
}
```

Add PerformanceCounter Components

Now it's possible to add PerformanceCounter components from the Toolbox. For our service, we add four instances where the `CategoryName` property is set to "Quote Service Count" for all objects, and the `CounterName` property is set to one of the values available in the selected category. The `ReadOnly` property must be set to false.

The following code is generated into `InitalizeComponent()` by adding the **PerformanceCounter** components to the Designer and setting the properties as above:

```
private void InitializeComponent()
{
    //...
    //
    // performanceCounterRequestsPerSec
    //
    this.performanceCounterRequestsPerSec.CategoryName =
                        "Quote Service Counts";
    this.performanceCounterRequestsPerSec.CounterName =
                        "# of Requests / sec";
    this.performanceCounterRequestsPerSec.ReadOnly = false;
    //
    // performanceCounterBytesSentTotal
    //
    this.performanceCounterBytesSentTotal.CategoryName =
                        "Quote Service Counts";
    this.performanceCounterBytesSentTotal.CounterName =
                        "# of Bytes sent";
    this.performanceCounterBytesSentTotal.ReadOnly = false;
    //
    // performanceCounterBytesSentPerSec
    //
    this.performanceCounterBytesSentPerSec.CategoryName =
                        "Quote Service Counts";
    this.performanceCounterBytesSentPerSec.CounterName =
                        "# of Bytes sent / sec";
    this.performanceCounterBytesSentPerSec.ReadOnly = false;
    //
    // performanceCounterRequestsTotal
    //
    this.performanceCounterRequestsTotal.CategoryName =
                        "Quote Service Counts";
    this.performanceCounterRequestsTotal.CounterName =
                        "# of Requests";
    this.performanceCounterRequestsTotal.ReadOnly = false;

    //...
```

The performance counts that show the total values are incremented directly in the `Listener()` method (shown below) of the `QuoteServer` class. We use `PerformanceCounter.Increment()` to count the number of total requests, and `IncrementBy()` to count the number of bytes sent.

For the performance counts that show the value by seconds, just two variables, `requestsPerSec` and `bytesPerSec`, are updated in the `Listener()` method:

```
protected void Listener()
{
    try
    {
        listener = new TCPListener(port);
```

```
listener.Start();
while (true)
{
    Socket socket = listener.Accept();

    string message = GetRandomQuoteOfTheDay();
    UnicodeEncoding encoder = new UnicodeEncoding();
    byte[] buffer = encoder.GetBytes(message);
    socket.Send(buffer, buffer.Length, 0);
    socket.Close();

    performanceCounterRequestsTotal.Increment();
    performanceCounterBytesSentTotal.IncrementBy(buffer.Length);

    requestsPerSec++;
    bytesPerSec += buffer.Length;
}
}
catch (Exception e)
{
    string message = "Quote Server failed in Listener: "
                     + e.Message;
    eventLog.WriteEntry(message, EventLogEntryType.Error);
}
}
```

To show updated values every second, we use a **Timer** component. The `OnTimer()` method gets called once per second and sets the performance counts using the `RawValue` property of the `PerformanceCounter` class:

```
protected void OnTimer (object sender, System.EventArgs e)
{
    performanceCounterBytesSentPerSec.RawValue = bytesPerSec;
    performanceCounterRequestsPerSec.RawValue = requestsPerSec;
    bytesPerSec = 0;
    requestsPerSec = 0;
}
```

perfmon.exe

Now we can monitor our service. The **Performance** tool can be started from **Administrative Tools |
Performance**. Pressing the + button in the toolbar, we can add performance counts. The Quote Service
shows up as a performance object. All the counters we configured show up in the counter list:

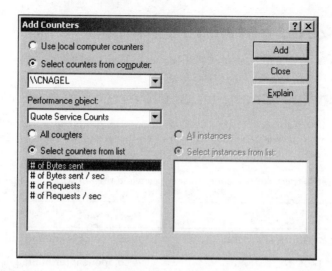

After the counts are added we can see the counts of our service over time. Using this performance tool, we can also create log files to analyze the performance at a later time:

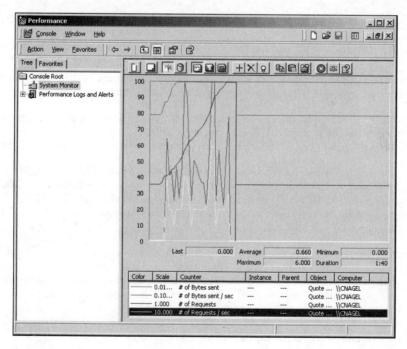

Windows 2000 Service Features

Let's take a look at the features of Windows Services in Windows 2000.

Network Binding Changes and Power Events

With Windows 2000, it's not necessary to reboot the system as often as it was with Windows NT; for example, it's not necessary to reboot the system when the IP address changes. To make this possible, a service receives events when the address changes and can act accordingly.

Windows 2000 sends these control codes to services when the network binding changes:

Control code	Description
SERVICE_CONTROL_NETBINDADD	A new component for binding is available.
SERVICE_CONTROL_NETBINDREMOVE	A component for binding has been removed. It's necessary to re-read the binding information and unbind from the removed component.
SERVICE_CONTROL_NETBINDENABLE	A previously disabled binding is now enabled.
SERVICE_CONTROL_NETBINDDISABLE	A previously enabled binding is now disabled.

If the service is using a binding, it's necessary to re-read the binding information and remove the bindings that are no longer available. Thus the service can react to networking changes so a reboot is not necessary.

Windows 2000 also adds a lot of power management support. There's support to hibernate the system – the memory gets written to disk, so a faster boot is possible. It's also possible to suspend the system in order to reduce the power consumption, but it can automatically be awakened when needed.

For all power events, the service can receive the control code SERVICE_CONTROL_POWEREVENT with additional parameters. The reason for the event is passed through these parameters. The reason could be low battery power, or that the system is going to a suspended state, or a power status change. Depending on the reason code the service should slow down, suspend background threads, close network connections, close files, and so on.

The classes in the System.ServiceProcess namespace have support for these Windows 2000 features, too. In the same way as we can configure a service so that it reacts to pause and continue events with the CanPauseAndContinue property, we can also set a property for power management: CanHandlePowerEvent. Windows 2000 services that handle power events are registered in the SCM with the Win32 API method RegisterServiceCtrlHandlerEx().

With a CanHandlePowerEvent value of true the method:

```
protected virtual bool OnPowerEvent(PowerBroadcastStatus powerStatus);
```

will be called as soon as the power status changes. Some of the values we get from the `PowerBroadcastStatus` enumeration are listed in this table:

Value	Description
BatteryLow	The battery power is low. We should reduce the functionality of the service to a minimum.
PowerStatusChange	A switch from battery power to A/C happened, or the battery power slips below a threshold, and so on.
QuerySuspend	The system requests permissions to go into a suspended mode. We could deny the permissions, or prepare to go into the suspended mode by closing files, disconnecting network connections, and so on.
QuerySuspendFailed	Change into the suspended mode was denied for the system. We can go on with the functionality as before.
Suspend	Nobody denied the request to go into the suspended mode. The system will be suspended soon.

Recovery

Automatic recovery is a feature that's just a configuration issue and can be used for all services running on Windows 2000. If a service process crashes then the service can be automatically restarted, or a special file can be configured to run, or the complete system can be automatically rebooted. There's usually a reason why a service crashes and therefore we don't want to automatically reboot the system continuously; we can differentiate responses to first, second, and subsequent failures.

We can configure the recovery options using the properties in the Computer Management MMC Administrator tool:

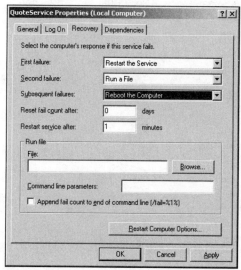

COM+ Applications as Services

Starting with Windows XP it's possible that a COM+ application (as long as it is configured as a server application) can run as a service. What's the advantage of this? With Windows XP a service can have direct access to COM+ services such as transactions, object pooling, and so on. If we want to use COM+ Services with Windows 2000 in a Windows Service we have to build two separate applications: one application deals with the service functionality, the second with the COM+ services. Let's look at the advantages this brings us:

❑ It's easier to create a service application. We no longer have to deal with the service-specific installation as this can be done directly from the COM+ configuration.

❑ A COM+ application can act like a service. It can be automatically started at boot time, it can have the rights of the system account, and it can react to service control codes we are sending from a service control program.

❑ The service application that's created as a COM+ application can have direct access to the COM+ services such as transaction management, object pooling, and so on.

Summary

In this chapter, we've seen what Windows Services are and how they can be created using the .NET Framework. Applications can start automatically at boot time with Windows Services, and we can use a privileged system account as the user of the service.

The .NET Framework has great support for Windows Services. All the plumbing code that's necessary for building, controlling, and installing services is built into the classes of the .NET Framework in the `System.ServiceProcess` namespace. Also, all the support technologies needed for Windows Services, such as event logging, and performance monitoring, can easily be accessed using `System.Diagnostics` classes.

23

.NET Security

You're sitting at your machine and you click a button on an application you're using. Behind the scenes, your application responds to the fact that you are attempting to use a feature for which it does not have the relevant module. It connects to the Internet, downloads the module into the Global Assembly Cache, and begins executing, and all without you being prompted.

This kind of behind-the-scenes upgrade functionality will become the norm in the not-too-distant future, but clearly there is a concern here over the security implications relating to what we call **mobile code**. In clear terms, what evidence do we actually have that the code your computer is downloading can be trusted? How do we know that the module we requested is, in fact, the one that we are receiving? What does the CLR do behind the scenes to ensure, for example, a control on a web site is not reading our private e-mails?

.NET enforces a security policy around assemblies. It uses the evidence it has about assemblies, for example where they are from or who publishes them, to split the assemblies into groups with similar characteristics. For example, the runtime places all code from the local intranet into a specific group. It then uses the security policy (normally defined by a system administrator using the Code Access Security Policy Tool (caspol.exe) command-line utility, or the Microsoft Management Console) to decide what permissions the code should be granted at a very granular level. What do you need to do to enable security on a machine or for a specific application? Nothing – all code automatically runs within the security context of the CLR, although you can turn security off if for some reason you need to.

In addition to high levels of confidence that the code we are executing can be trusted, it is also important to be sure we are permitting the user of our application access to the features they need, but no more. Effective management of users and roles is something else .NET can help us with by virtue of its role-based security.

In this chapter we will look through the features available in .NET to help us manage security, including how .NET protects us from malicious code, how we administer security policies, and how we access the security sub-system programmatically. We will also take a look at deploying .NET applications securely and see a number of short example applications to solidify the concepts in this chapter for you.

Code Access Security

Code access security is a feature of .NET that manages code dependent on our level trust of it. If the CLR trusts the code enough to allow it to run, it will begin executing the code. Depending on the permissions provided to the assembly, however, it may run within a restricted environment. If the code is not trusted enough to run, or if it runs but then attempts to perform an action for which it does not have the relevant permissions, a security exception (of type SecurityException, or a subclass of it) is thrown. The code access security system means we can stop malicious code running, but we can also allow code to run within a protected environment where we are confident it cannot do any damage.

For example, if a user attempted to run an application that attempted to execute code downloaded from the Internet, the default security policy would raise an exception and the application would fail to start. In a similar way, if the user ran an application from a network drive it would begin executing, but if the application then attempted to access a file on the local drive, the runtime would raise an exception and, depending on the error handling in the application, would either gracefully degrade or exit.

For most applications, .NET's code access security is a significant benefit but one that sits at the back of the room quietly helping us out. It provides high levels of protection from malicious code, but generally, we do not need to get involved. However, one area we will be involved in is the management of security policy, and this is especially true when configuring desktops to trust code from the locations of software suppliers who are delivering applications to us.

Another area where code access security is more important is where we are building an application that includes an element whose security we want to closely control. For example, if there is a database within your organization containing extremely sensitive data, you would use code access security to state what code is allowed to access that database, and what code must not access it.

It is important to realize how code access security is about protecting resources (local drive, network, user interface) from malicious code; it is not primarily a tool for protecting software from users. For security in relation to users, you will generally use Windows 2000's built-in user security subsystem, or make use of .NET's role-based security, which we will look at later in the chapter.

Code access security is based upon two high-level concepts; **Code Groups**, and **Permissions**. Let's look at these before we start as they form the foundations of what follows:

- ❑ **Code Groups** bring together code with similar characteristics, although the most important property is usually where the code came from. For example, code groups include "Internet" (code sourced from the Internet) and "Intranet" (code sourced from the LAN). The information used to place assemblies into code groups is called **evidence**. Other evidence is collected by the CLR, including the publisher of the code, the strong name, and (where applicable) the URI from which it was downloaded. Code groups are arranged in a hierarchy, and assemblies are nearly always matched to several code groups. The code group at the root of the hierarchy is called "All Code" and contains all other code groups. The hierarchy is used in deciding which code groups an assembly belongs to; if an assembly does not provide evidence that matches it to a group in the tree, no attempt is made to match it to code groups below.

❑ **Permissions** are the actions we allow each code group to perform. For example, permissions include "able to access the user interface" and "able to access local storage". The system administrator usually manages the permissions at the Enterprise level, the Machine level, and the User level.

The Virtual Execution System within the CLR loads and runs programs. It provides the functionality needed to execute managed code and uses assembly metadata to connect modules together at run time. When the VES loads an assembly, the VES matches the assembly to one or more of a number of code groups. Each code group is assigned one or more permissions that specify what actions assemblies in that code group can do. For example, if the `MyComputer` code group is assigned the permission `FileIOPermission`, this means that assemblies from the local machine can read and write to the local file system.

Code Groups

Code groups have an entry requirement called a **Membership Condition**. For an assembly to be filed into a code group, it must match the group's membership condition. Membership conditions are things like "the assembly is from the site http://www.microsoft.com" or "the Publisher of this software is Microsoft Corporation".

Each code group has one, and only one, membership condition. Here are the types of code group membership conditions available in .NET:

❑ **Zone** –the region from which the code originated.

❑ **Site** – the web site from which the code originated.

❑ **Strong name** – a unique, verifiable name for the code, often called a 'shared name'.

❑ **Publisher** – the publisher of the code.

❑ **URL** – the specific location from which the code originated.

❑ **Hash value** – the hash value for the assembly.

❑ **Skip verification** – code requests it bypasses code verification checks. Code verification ensures the code accesses types in a well-defined and acceptable way. The runtime cannot enforce security on code that is not type safe.

❑ **Application directory** – the location of the assembly within the application.

❑ **All code** – all code fulfills this condition.

❑ **Custom** – a user-specified condition.

The first type of membership condition in the list is the **Zone** condition, which is one of the most commonly used. A zone is the region of origin of a piece of code and is one of the following: **MyComputer, Internet, Intranet, Trusted**, or **Untrusted**. These zones are managed using the Security Options in Internet Explorer, and we'll see more about these later in the chapter when we look at how to manage security policy. Although the settings are managed within Internet Explorer, they apply to the entire machine. Clearly, these configuration options are not available in non-Microsoft browsers and, in fact, in-page controls written using the .NET Framework will not work in browsers other than Internet Explorer.

Code groups are arranged in a hierarchy, with the **All Code** membership condition at the root:

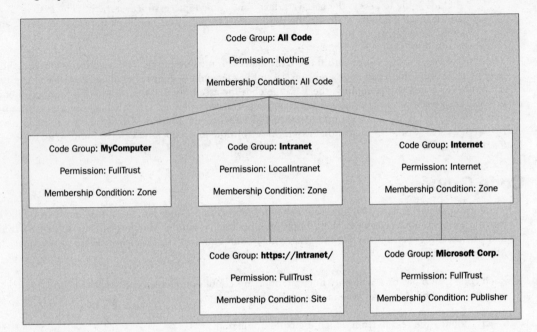

You can see that each code group has a single membership condition and specifies the permissions that the code group has been granted. We'll see more about permissions later. Note that if an assembly does not match the membership condition in a code group, the CLR does not attempt to match code groups below it.

Caspol.exe – Code Access Security Policy Tool

The command-line Code Access Security Policy tool is the one we'll spend the most time looking at in this chapter. It lets us view and manage security policy. To get a list of options for the tool, just type the following at the command prompt:

```
>caspol.exe -?
```

Alternatively, to send the output to a text file use:

```
>caspol.exe > caspol.txt
```

.NET also includes a snap-in for the Microsoft Management Console to manage code access security; however, we will restrict ourselves to the command-line utility as the examples are easier to follow, and you'll also be in a position to create scripts to alter security policy, which is very useful when applying policies to large numbers of machines.

Let's have a look at the code groups on a machine using `caspol.exe`. The output of the command lists the hierarchical structure of the code groups on the machine, and next to each it gives a description of the code group. Type this command:

```
>caspol.exe -listdescription
```

Alternatively, the `-listdescription` parameter has a shortcut: `-ld`. You will see something like this:

```
Microsoft (R) .NET Framework CasPol 1.0.3705.0
Copyright (C) Microsoft Corporation 1998-2001. All rights reserved.

Security is ON
Execution checking is ON
Policy change prompt is ON

Level = Machine

Full Trust Assemblies:

1. All_Code: Code group grants no permissions and forms the root of the code gro
up tree.
   1.1. My_Computer_Zone: Code group grants full trust to all code originating o
n the local computer
      1.1.1. Microsoft_Strong_Name: Code group grants full trust to code signed
with the Microsoft strong name.
      1.1.2. ECMA_Strong_Name: Code group grants full trust to code signed with
the ECMA strong name.
   1.2. LocalIntranet_Zone: Code group grants the intranet permission set to cod
e from the intranet zone. This permission set grants intranet code the right to
use isolated storage, full UI access, some capability to do reflection, and limi
ted access to environment variables.
      1.2.1. Intranet_Same_Site_Access: All intranet code gets the right to conn
ect back to the site of its origin.
      1.2.2. Intranet_Same_Directory_Access: All intranet code gets the right to
 read from its install directory.
   1.3. Internet_Zone: Code group grants code from the Internet zone the Interne
t permission set. This permission set grants Internet code the right to use isol
ated storage and limited UI access.
      1.3.1. Internet_Same_Site_Access: All Internet code gets the right to conn
ect back to the site of its origin.
   1.4. Restricted_Zone: Code coming from a restricted zone does not receive any
 permissions.
   1.5. Trusted_Zone: Code from a trusted zone is granted the Internet permissio
n set. This permission set grants the right to use isolated storage and limited
UI access.
      1.5.1. Trusted_Same_Site_Access: All Trusted Code gets the right to connec
t back to the site of its origin.
Success
```

The .NET security subsystem ensures that code from each code group is allowed to do only certain things. For example, code from the Internet zone will, by default, have much stricter limits than code from the local drive. For example, code from the local drive is normally granted access to data stored on the local drive, but assemblies from the Internet are not granted this permission by default.

Using `caspol`, and its equivalent in the Microsoft Management Console, we can specify what level of trust we have for each code access group, as well as managing code groups and permissions in a more granular fashion.

Let's take another look at the code access groups, but this time in a slightly more compact view. Make sure you're logged in as a local Administrator, open up a command prompt, and type this command:

```
>caspol.exe -listgroups
```

You will see something like this:

```
Microsoft (R) .NET Framework CasPol 1.0.3705.0
Copyright (C) Microsoft Corporation 1998-2001. All rights reserved.

Security is ON
Execution checking is ON
Policy change prompt is ON

Level = Machine

Code Groups:

1.  All code: Nothing
    1.1.  Zone - MyComputer: FullTrust
        1.1.1.  StrongName - 002400000480000094000000060200000024000052534131000040
0000100010007D1FA57C4AED9F0A32E84AA0FAEFD0DE9E8FD6AEC8F87FB03766C834C99921EB23BE
79AD9D5DCC1DD9AD236132102900B723CF980957FC4E177108FC607774F29E8320E92EA05ECE4E82
1C0A5EFE8F1645C4C0C93C1AB99285D622CAA652C1DFAD63D745D6F2DE5F17E5EAF0FC4963D261C8
A12436518206DC093344D5AD293: FullTrust
        1.1.2.  StrongName - 00000000000000000400000000000000: FullTrust
    1.2.  Zone - Intranet: LocalIntranet
        1.2.1.  All code: Same site Web.
        1.2.2.  All code: Same directory FileIO - Read, PathDiscovery
    1.3.  Zone - Internet: Internet
        1.3.1.  All code: Same site Web.
    1.4.  Zone - Untrusted: Nothing
    1.5.  Zone - Trusted: Internet
        1.5.1.  All code: Same site Web.
Success
```

You'll notice that near the start of the output it says, `Security is ON`. Later in the chapter, we see that it can be turned off and then back on.

The `Execution Checking` setting is on by default, which means all assemblies must be granted the permission to execute before they can run. If execution checking is turned off using `caspol` (`caspol.exe -execution on|off`), assemblies that do not have the permission to run can execute, although they may well cause security exceptions if they attempt to act contrary to the security policy later in their execution.

The `Policy change prompt` option specifies whether we see an `"Are you sure"` warning message when we attempt to alter the security policy.

As code is broken down into these groups, we can manage security at a more granular level, and apply full trust to a much smaller percentage of code. Note that each group has a label (such as 1.2). These labels are auto-generated by .NET, and can differ between machines. We do not generally manage security for each assembly; we do it using a code group.

You may be curious how `caspol.exe` operates when a machine has several side-by-side installations of .NET. Under these circumstances, the copy of `caspol.exe` that you run will only alter the security policy for its associated installation of .NET. To keep security policy management simpler, you may well want to remove previous copies of .NET as you install successive versions.

Viewing an Assembly's Code Groups

Assemblies are matched to code groups dependent upon the membership conditions they match. If we go back to our example code groups and load an assembly from the https://intranet/ web site, it would match code groups like this:

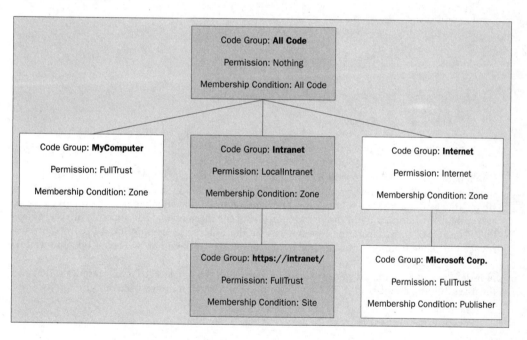

The assembly, as with all others, is a member of the root code group (All Code); as it came from the local network it is also a member of the Intranet code group; but as it was loaded from the specific site https://intranet it is also granted `FullTrust`, which means it can run unrestricted.

We can easily view the code groups that an assembly is a member of using a command like this:

```
>caspol.exe -resolvegroup assembly.dll
```

Running this command on an assembly on the local drive produces output like this:

```
Microsoft (R) .NET Framework CasPol 1.0.3705.0
Copyright (C) Microsoft Corporation 1998-2001. All rights reserved.


Level = Enterprise

Code Groups:

1.  All code: FullTrust


Level = Machine

Code Groups:

1.  All code: Nothing
     1.1.  Zone - MyComputer: FullTrust


Level = User

Code Groups:

1.  All code: FullTrust

Success
```

You'll notice that code groups are listed on three levels – **Enterprise**, **Machine**, and **User**. For now, just stay focused on the Machine level. We'll look at the other two in much more detail later in the chapter. If you are curious about the relationship between the three, the effective permission given to an assembly is the intersection of the permissions from the three levels. For example, if you remove the FullTrust permission from the Internet zone at the Enterprise-level policy, all permissions are revoked for code from the Internet zone, and the settings of the other two levels become irrelevant.

Now let's use this command against the same assembly, but across HTTP to a remote server, we'll see the assembly is a member of different groups that have much more restrictive permissions:

```
>caspol.exe -resolvegroup http://server/assembly.dll


Microsoft (R) .NET Framework CasPol 1.0.3705.0
Copyright (C) Microsoft Corporation 1998-2001. All rights reserved.


Level = Enterprise

Code Groups:

1.  All code: FullTrust
```

```
Level = Machine

Code Groups:

1.  All code: Nothing
    1.1.   Zone - Internet: Internet
        1.1.1.  All code: Same site Web.


Level = User

Code Groups:

1.  All code: FullTrust

Success
```

The assembly grants the `Internet` permissions and the `Same Site Web` permissions. The intersection of the permissions will allow the code limited UI access, and will allow it to make connections back to the site it originated from.

Let's take a closer look at permissions – the freedom we allow assemblies matched to each code group.

Code Access Permissions and Permissions Sets

Imagine yourself administering security policy on a network of desktop machines in a large enterprise scenario. In this environment it's clearly immensely useful for the CLR to collect evidence on code before it executes it, but equally, you as the administrator must have the opportunity to strictly control what code is allowed to do on the several hundred machines you manage once the CLR knows where it came from. This is where permissions come into the equation.

Once an assembly has been matched to code groups, the CLR looks at the security policy to calculate the permissions it grants to an assembly. When managing permissions in Windows 2000 we generally don't apply permissions to users, we apply permissions to groups. The same is true with assemblies; we apply permissions to code groups rather than individual assemblies, which makes the management of security policy in .NET a much easier task.

The security policy specifies what actions assemblies in a code group are permitted to perform. Let's look at the code access permissions provided by the CLR. As you can see from the following list, there are many of them, giving us a high degree of control over what code is allowed to do or not allowed to do:

❑ **DirectoryServicesPermission** – the ability to access Active Directory through the `System.DirectoryServices` classes.

❑ **DnsPermission** – the ability to use the TCP/IP Domain Name System (DNS).

❑ **EnvironmentPermission** – the ability to read and write environment variables.

❑ **EventLogPermission** – the ability to read and write to the event log.

- ❑ **FileDialogPermission** – the ability to access files that have been selected by the user in the **Open** dialog box. Typically used when `FileIOPermission` is not granted to allow limited access to files.

- ❑ **FileIOPermission** – the ability to work with files (reading, writing, and appending to file, as well as creating and altering folders and accessing.

- ❑ **IsolatedStorageFilePermission** – the ability to access private virtual file systems.

- ❑ **IsolatedStoragePermission** – the ability to access isolated storage; storage that is associated with an individual user and with some aspect of the code's identity, such as its web site, signature, or publisher.

- ❑ **MessageQueuePermission** – the ability to use message queues through the Microsoft Message Queue.

- ❑ **OleDbPermission** – the ability to access databases with OLE DB.

- ❑ **PerformanceCounterPermission** – the ability to make use of performance counters.

- ❑ **PrintingPermission** – the ability to print.

- ❑ **ReflectionPermission** – the ability to discover information about a type at run time using `System.Reflection`.

- ❑ **RegistryPermission** – the ability to read, write, create, or delete registry keys and values.

- ❑ **SecurityPermission** – the ability to execute, assert permissions, call into unmanaged code, skip verification, and other rights.

- ❑ **ServiceControllerPermission** – the ability to access (running or stopped) Windows Services.

- ❑ **SocketPermission** – the ability to make or accept TCP/IP connections on a transport address.

- ❑ **SQLClientPermission** – the ability to access SQL databases.

- ❑ **UIPermission** – the ability to access the user interface.

- ❑ **WebPermission** – the ability to make or accept connections to/from the web.

With each of these permission classes, we can often specify an even deeper level of granularity. For example, later in the chapter you'll see an example of requesting not just file access, but a specific level of file access.

In terms of best practice, you are well advised to ensure any attempts to make use of the resources relating to the permissions in this list are enclosed within `try…catch` error handling blocks, so that your application degrades gracefully should it be running under restricted permissions. The design of your application should specify how your application should act under these circumstances; you should not assume that it will be running under the same security policy under which you develop it. For example, if your application cannot access the local drive, should it exit, or operate in an alternative fashion?

An assembly will be associated with several code groups; the effective permission of an assembly within the security policy is the union of all permissions from all the code groups to which it belongs. That is, each code group that an assembly matches will extend what it is allowed to do. Do note that code groups down the tree will often be assigned more relaxed permissions than those above.

There is another set of permissions that are assigned by the CLR on the basis of the identity of the code, which cannot be explicitly granted. These permissions relate directly to the evidence the CLR has collated about the assembly, and are called **Identity Permissions**. Here are the names of the classes for the identity permissions:

❏ **PublisherIdentityPermission** – the software publisher's digital signature

❏ **SiteIdentityPermission** – the location of the web site from which the code originated

❏ **StrongNameIdentityPermission** – the assembly's strong name

❏ **URLIdentityPermission** – the URL from which the code came (including the protocol, for example, `https://`)

❏ **ZoneIdentityPermission** – the zone from which the assembly originates

Usually, we'll apply permissions in blocks, which is why .NET also gives us **Permission Sets**. These are lists of code access permissions grouped into a named set. Here are the named permission sets we get straight out of the box:

❏ **FullTrust** – no permission restrictions.

❏ **Execution** – the ability to run, but not to access any protected resources.

❏ **Nothing** – no permissions and unable to execute.

❏ **LocalIntranet** – the default policy for the local intranet, a subset of the full set of permissions. For example, file IO is restricted to read access on the share where the assembly originates.

❏ **Internet** – the default policy for code of unknown origin. This is the most restrictive policy listed. For example, code executing in this permission set has no file IO capability, cannot read or write event logs, and cannot read or write environment variables.

❏ **Everything** – all the permissions are listed under this set, except the permission to skip code verification. The administrator can alter any of the permissions in this permission set. This is useful where the default policy needs to be tighter.

> *Do note that of these you can only change the definitions of the Everything permission set – the first five are fixed and cannot be changed.*

Identity permissions cannot be included in permission sets because the CLR is the only body able to grant identity permissions to code. For example, if a piece of code is from a specific publisher, it would make little sense for the administrator to give it the identity permissions associated with another publisher. The CLR grants identity permissions where necessary, and we can then make use of them if we wish.

Viewing an Assembly's Permissions

Imagine you're using an application written by Microsoft, and you attempt to use a feature that you have not used before. The application does not have a copy of the code stored locally, so it requests it and the code is then downloaded into the Global Assembly Cache. Under a scenario like this, with code from the Internet published by a named organization that has signed the assembly with a certificate, we'll find the assembly's code group membership looks something like this:

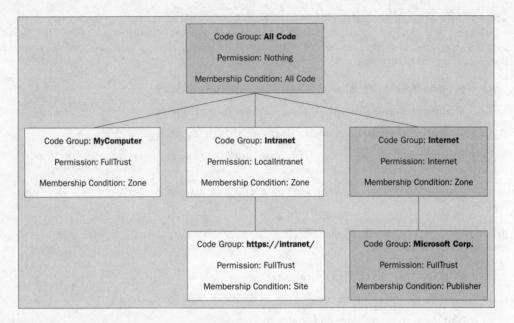

According to our policy in this example, although the `All Code` and `Internet` code groups bring only limited permissions, membership of the code group in the bottom right-hand corner grants the assembly the `FullTrust` permission. The overall effective permission is the **union** of permissions across the matching code groups. When the permissions are merged in this way, the effective permission is that of the highest permissions granted. That is, each code group an assembly belongs to brings additional permissions.

Just as we can look at the code groups an assembly belongs to, we can also look at the permissions assigned to the code groups to which it belongs. When we do this we'll see not only the code access permissions (what the code is allowed to do), but also the code identity permissions that will give us access to the evidence the code presented to the runtime. To see the permissions for an assembly's code groups, we use a command like this:

```
>caspol.exe -resolveperm assembly.dll
```

Let's try this on an assembly, and look at the code access and identity permissions it is granted when we access it over a local intranet. If we type the following command we see the code access permissions and then the three identity permissions at the end:

```
>caspol.exe -resolveperm http://intranet/assembly.dll
```

```
Microsoft (R) .NET Framework CasPol 1.0.3705.0
Copyright (C) Microsoft Corporation 1998-2001. All rights reserved.

Resolving permissions for level = Enterprise
Resolving permissions for level = Machine
Resolving permissions for level = User
```

```
Grant =
<PermissionSet class="System.Security.PermissionSet"
               version="1">
   <IPermission class="System.Security.Permissions.FileDialogPermission,
                       mscorlib, Version=1.0.3300.0, Culture=neutral,
                       PublicKeyToken=b77a5c561934e089"
                version="1"
                Access="Open"/>
   <IPermission class="System.Security.Permissions.IsolatedStorageFilePermission,
                       mscorlib, Version=1.0.3300.0, Culture=neutral,
                       PublicKeyToken=b77a5c561934e089"
                version="1"
                Allowed="DomainIsolationByUser"
                UserQuota="10240"/>
   <IPermission class="System.Security.Permissions.SecurityPermission,
                       mscorlib, Version=1.0.3300.0, Culture=neutral,
                       PublicKeyToken=b77a5c561934e089"
                version="1"
                Flags="Execution"/>
   <IPermission class="System.Security.Permissions.UIPermission,
                       mscorlib, Version=1.0.3300.0, Culture=neutral,
                       PublicKeyToken=b77a5c561934e089"
                version="1"
                Window="SafeTopLevelWindows"
                Clipboard="OwnClipboard"/>
   <IPermission class="System.Net.WebPermission,
                       System, Version=1.0.3300.0, Culture=neutral,
                       PublicKeyToken=b77a5c561934e089"
                version="1">
      <ConnectAccess>
         <URI uri="(https|http)://some\.host\.com/.*"/>
      </ConnectAccess>
   </IPermission>
   <IPermission class="System.Drawing.Printing.PrintingPermission,
                       System.Drawing, Version=1.0.3300.0, Culture=neutral,
                       PublicKeyToken=b03f5f7f11d50a3a"
                version="1"
                Level="SafePrinting"/>
   <IPermission class="System.Security.Permissions.SiteIdentityPermission,
                       mscorlib, Version=1.0.3300.0, Culture=neutral,
                       PublicKeyToken=b77a5c561934e089"
                version="1"
                Site="some.host.com"/>
   <IPermission class="System.Security.Permissions.UrlIdentityPermission,
                       mscorlib, Version=1.0.3300.0, Culture=neutral,
                       PublicKeyToken=b77a5c561934e089"
                version="1"
                Url="http://some.host.com/dev/testdll.dll"/>
   <IPermission class="System.Security.Permissions.ZoneIdentityPermission,
                       mscorlib, Version=1.0.3300.0, Culture=neutral,
                       PublicKeyToken=b77a5c561934e089"
                version="1"
                Zone="Internet"/>
</PermissionSet>

Success
```

The output shows each of the permissions in XML, including the class defining the permission, the assembly containing the class, the permission version, and an encryption token. The output suggests it is possible for us to create our own permissions, and you'll see more about that later. We can also see that each of the identity permissions includes more detailed information on, for example, the UrlIdentityPermission class, which provides access to the URL from which the code originated.

Note how at the start of the output `caspol.exe` resolved the permissions at the `Enterprise`, `Machine`, and `User` levels and then listed the effective granted permissions. Let's look at these now.

Policy Levels: Machine, User, and Enterprise

Up to now we have looked at security in the context of a single machine. It's often necessary to specify security policies for specific users or for an entire organization, and that is why .NET provides not one, but three levels of code groups:

- ❑ Machine
- ❑ Enterprise
- ❑ User

The code group levels are independently managed and exist in parallel:

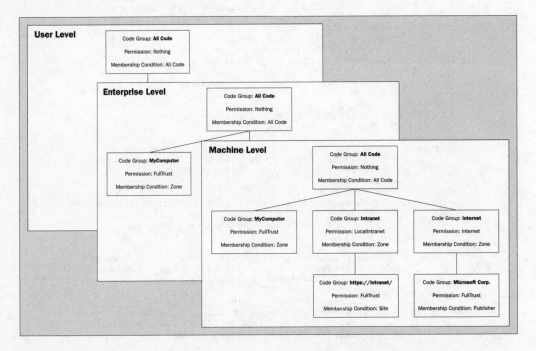

If there are three security policies, how do we know which applies? The effective permission is the **intersection** of the permissions from the three levels. Each of the three levels has the ability to veto the permissions allowed by another – this is clearly good news for administrators as their settings will override user settings.

To work with code groups and permissions on the user or enterprise levels using `caspol.exe`, add either the `-enterprise` or `-user` argument to change the command's mode. `caspol.exe` works at the `Machine` level by default and that's how we've been using it up to now. Let's see the code groups listing at the `User` level:

```
>caspol.exe -user -listgroups
```

The output of the command on a default installation looks like this:

```
Security is ON
Execution checking is ON
Policy change prompt is ON

Level = User

Code Groups:

1.  All code: FullTrust
Success
```

Now let's run the same command, but this time to see the code groups at the `Enterprise` level:

```
>caspol.exe -enterprise -listgroups
```

The output of the command looks like this:

```
Security is ON
Execution checking is ON
Policy change prompt is ON

Level = Enterprise

Code Groups:

1.  All code: FullTrust
Success
```

As you can see, by default, both the `User` level and the `Enterprise` level are configured to allow `FullTrust` for the single code group `All Code`. The result of this is that the default setting for .NET security places no restrictions at the Enterprise or User level, and the enforced policy is dictated solely by the machine-level policy. For example, if we were to assign a more restrictive permission or permission set to either the enterprise or user levels than `FullTrust`, those restrictions would restrict the overall permissions, and probably override permissions at the Machine level. The effective permissions are intersected, so, for example, if we want to apply `FullTrust` to a code group, that permission must be assigned to the code group on each of the three policy levels.

When we run `caspol.exe` as an administrator, it defaults to the Machine level, but if we log out and log back in as a user who is not in the Administrator user group, `caspol.exe` will instead default to the User level. In addition, `caspol.exe` will not allow us to alter the security policy in a way that renders the `caspol.exe` utility itself inoperable.

Now we've had a high-level look at the security architecture in .NET, let's look at how we can access its features programmatically.

Support for Security in the Framework

For .NET security to work, we must, as programmers, trust the CLR to enforce the security policy. How does it do this? When a call is made to a method that demands specific permissions (for example, accessing a file on the local drive), the CLR will walk up the stack to ensure that every caller in the call chain has the permissions being demanded.

The word "performance" is probably ringing in your mind at this point, and clearly that is a concern, but to gain the benefits of a managed environment like .NET this is the price we pay. The alternative is that assemblies that are not fully trusted could make calls to trusted assemblies and our system is open to attack.

For reference, the parts of the .NET Framework library namespace most applicable to this chapter are:

- ❑ System.Security.Permissions
- ❑ System.Security.Policy
- ❑ System.Security.Principal

Note that evidence-based code access security works in tandem with Windows logon security. If you attempt to run a .NET desktop application, it must be granted the relevant .NET code access security permissions, but you as the logged-in user must also be running under a Windows account that has the relevant permissions to execute the code. With desktop applications, this means the current user must have been granted the relevant rights to access the relevant assembly files on the drive. For Internet applications, the account under which Internet Information Server is running must have access to the assembly files.

Demanding Permissions

Let's create a Windows Forms application that contains a button that, when clicked, will perform an action that accesses the drive. Let's say, for example, that if the application does not have the relevant permission to access the local drive (`FileIOPermission`), we will mark the button as unavailable (grayed).

In the code that follows, look at the constructor for the form that creates a `FileIOPermission` object, calls its `Demand()` method, and then acts on the result:

```
using System;
using System.Drawing;
using System.Collections;
using System.ComponentModel;
using System.Windows.Forms;
using System.Data;
using System.Security;
using System.Security.Permissions;

namespace SecurityApp1
{
    public class Form1 : System.Windows.Forms.Form
    {
        private System.Windows.Forms.Button button1;
```

```
private System.ComponentModel.Container components;

public Form1()
{
    InitializeComponent();

    try
    {
        FileIOPermission fileioperm = new
            FileIOPermission(FileIOPermissionAccess.AllAccess,@"c:\");
        fileioperm.Demand();
    }
    catch
    {
        button1.Enabled = false;
    }
}

protected override void Dispose(bool disposing)
{
    if( disposing )
    {
        if (components != null)
        {
            components.Dispose();
        }
    }
    base.Dispose( disposing );
}

#region Windows Form Designer generated code
/// <summary>
/// Required method for Designer support - do not modify
/// the contents of this method with the code editor.
/// </summary>
private void InitializeComponent()
{
    this.button1 = new System.Windows.Forms.Button();
    this.SuspendLayout();
    //
    // button1
    //
    this.button1.Location = new System.Drawing.Point(48, 8);
    this.button1.Name = "button1";
    this.button1.Size = new System.Drawing.Size(192, 23);
    this.button1.TabIndex = 0;
    this.button1.Text = "Button Requires FileIOPermission";
    //
    // Form1
    //
    this.AutoScaleBaseSize = new System.Drawing.Size(5, 13);
    this.ClientSize = new System.Drawing.Size(292, 37);
    this.Controls.AddRange(new System.Windows.Forms.Control[]
                        {this.button1});
```

```
        this.Name = "Form1";
        this.Text = "Form1";
        this.ResumeLayout(false);

    }
    #endregion

    /// <summary>
    /// The main entry point for the application.
    /// </summary>
    [STAThread]
    static void Main()
    {
        Application.Run(new Form1());
    }
  }
}
```

You'll notice that `FileIOPermission` is contained within the `System.Security.Permissions` namespace, which is home to the full set of permissions, and also provides classes for declarative permission attributes and enumerations for the parameters used to create permissions objects (for example, when creating a `FileIOPermission` specifying whether we need full access, or read-only).

If we run the application from the local drive where the default security policy allows access to local storage, the application will appear like this:

However, if we copy the executable to a network share and run it again, we're operating within the `LocalIntranet` permission sets, which blocks access to local storage, and the button will be grayed:

If we implemented the functionality to make the button access the disk when we click it, we would not have to write any security code, as the relevant class in the .NET Framework will demand the file permissions, and the CLR will ensure each caller up the stack has those permissions before proceeding. If we were to run our application from the intranet, and it attempted to open a file on the local disk, we would see an exception unless the security policy had been altered to grant access to the local drive.

If you want to catch exceptions thrown by the CLR when code attempts to act contrary to its granted permissions, you can catch the exception of the type `SecurityException`, which provides access to a number of useful pieces of information including a human-readable stack trace (`SecurityException.StackTrace`) and a reference to the method that threw the exception (`SecurityException.TargetSite`). `SecurityException` even provides us with the `SecurityException.PermissionType` property that returns the type of `Permission` object that caused the security exception to occur. If you're having problems diagnosing security exceptions, this should be one of your first ports of call. Simply remove the `try` and `catch` blocks from the above example code to see the exception in the following screenshot:

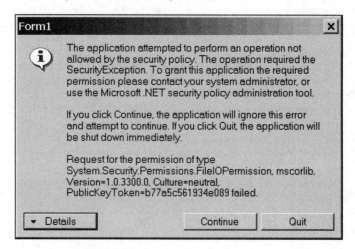

Requesting Permissions

As you saw above, demanding permissions is where you state quite clearly what you need at run time; however, you can configure an assembly so it makes a softer request for permissions right at the start of execution where it states what it needs before it begins executing.

You can request permissions in three ways:

❑ **Minimum** Permissions – the permissions your code must have to run

❑ **Optional** Permissions – the permissions your code can use but is able to run effectively without

❑ **Refused** Permissions – the permissions that you want to ensure are not granted to your code

Why would you want to request permissions when your assembly starts? There are several reasons:

❑ If your assembly needs certain permissions to run, it makes sense to state this at the start of execution rather than during execution to ensure the user does not experience a road block after beginning work in your program.

❑ You will only be granted the permissions you request and no more. Without explicitly requesting permissions your assembly may be granted more permissions then it needs to execute. This increases the risk of your assembly being used for malicious purposes by other code.

❑ If you only request a minimum set of permissions, you are increasing the likelihood that your assembly will run since you cannot predict the security policies in effect at an end user's location.

Requesting permissions is likely to be most useful if you're doing more complex deployment, and there is a higher risk that your application will be installed on a machine that does not grant the requisite permissions. It's usually preferable for the application to know right at the start of execution if it will not be granted permissions, rather than partway through execution.

To successfully request the permissions your assembly needs, you must keep track of exactly what permissions your assembly is using. In particular, you must be aware of the permission requirements of the calls your assembly is making into other class libraries, including the .NET Framework.

Let's look at three examples from an `AssemblyInfo.cs` file, demonstrating using attributes to request permissions. If you are following this with the code download, these examples can be found in the `SecurityApp2` project. The first attribute requests that the assembly have `UIPermission` granted, which will allow the application access to the user interface. The request is for the minimum permissions, so if this permission is not granted the assembly will fail to start:

```
using System.Security.Permissions;
[assembly:UIPermissionAttribute(SecurityAction.RequestMinimum, Unrestricted=true)]
```

Next, we have a request that the assembly be refused access to the C:\ drive. This attribute's setting means the entire assembly will be blocked from accessing this drive:

```
[assembly:FileIOPermissionAttribute(SecurityAction.RequestRefuse, Read="C:\\")]
```

Finally, here's an attribute that requests our assembly be optionally granted the permission to access unmanaged code:

```
[assembly:SecurityPermissionAttribute(SecurityAction.RequestOptional,
                    Flags = SecurityPermissionFlag.UnmanagedCode)]
```

In this scenario we would add this attribute to an application that accesses unmanaged code in at least one place. In this case, we have specified that this permission is optional, the suggestion being that the application can run without the permission to access unmanaged code. If the assembly is not granted permission to access unmanaged code, and attempts to do so, a `SecurityException` will be raised, which the application should expect and handle accordingly. The full list of available `SecurityAction` enumeration values is shown below, and some of these values are covered in more detail later.

Security Action	Description
Assert	Allows code to access resources not available to the caller
Demand	Requires all callers in the call stack to have the specified permission
Deny	Denies a permission by forcing any subsequent demand for the permission to fail

Security Action	Description
InheritanceDemand	Requires derived classes to have the specified permission granted
LinkDemand	Requires the immediate caller to have the specified permission
PermitOnly	Similar to deny, subsequent demands for resources not explicitly listed by PermitOnly are refused.
RequestMinimum	Applied at assembly scope, this contains a permission required for an assembly to operate correctly
RequestOptional	Applied at assembly scope, this asks for permissions the assembly can use, if available, to provide additional features and functionality
RequestRefuse	Applied at assembly scope when there is a permission you do not want your assembly to have

When we are considering the permission requirements of our application, we usually have to decide between one of two options:

❑ Request all the permissions we need at the start of execution, and degrade gracefully or exit if those permissions are not granted

❑ Avoid requesting permissions at the start of execution, but be prepared to handle security exceptions throughout our application

Once an assembly has been configured using permission attributes in this way, we can use the permview.exe utility to view the permissions by aiming it at the assembly file containing the assembly manifest:

```
>permview.exe <path>\SecurityApp2\bin\Debug\SecurityApp2.exe
```

The output for an application using the three attributes we have been through looks like this:

```
Microsoft (R) .NET Framework Permission Request Viewer.  Version 1.0.3705.0
Copyright (C) Microsoft Corporation 1998-2001. All rights reserved.

minimal permission set:
<PermissionSet class="System.Security.PermissionSet"
                    version="1">
   <IPermission class="System.Security.Permissions.UIPermission, mscorlib,
                  Version=1.0.3300.0, Culture=neutral,
                  PublicKeyToken=b77a5c561934e089"
                  version="1"
```

```
                            Unrestricted="true"/>
    </PermissionSet>

    optional permission set:
    <PermissionSet class="System.Security.PermissionSet" version="1">
        <IPermission class="System.Security.Permissions.SecurityPermission, mscorlib,
                        Version=1.0.3300.0, Culture=neutral,
                        PublicKeyToken=b77a5c561934e089"
                        version="1"
                        Flags="UnmanagedCode"/>
    </PermissionSet>

    refused permission set:
    <PermissionSet class="System.Security.PermissionSet"
                        version="1">
        <IPermission class="System.Security.Permissions.FileIOPermission, mscorlib,
                        Version=1.0.3300.0, Culture=neutral,
                        PublicKeyToken=b77a5c561934e089"
                        version="1"
                Read="c:\"/>
    </PermissionSet>
```

In addition to requesting permissions, we can also request permissions sets, the advantage being that we can request a whole set of permissions all at once. As the Everything permission set can be altered through the security policy while an assembly is running, it cannot be requested. For example, if an assembly requested at run time that it must be granted all permissions in the Everything permission set to execute, and the administrator then tightened the Everything permission set while the application is running, they might be unaware that it is still operating with a wider set of permissions than the policy dictates.

Here's an example, of how to request a built-in permission set:

```
[assembly:PermissionSetAttribute(SecurityAction.RequestMinimum,
                        Name = "FullTrust")]
```

In this example the assembly requests that as a minimum it be granted the FullTrust built-in permission set. If it is not granted this set of permissions, the assembly will throw a security exception at run time.

Implicit Permission

When permissions are granted, there is often an implicit statement that we are also granted other permissions. For example, if we are assigned the FileIOPermission for C:\ there is an implicit assumption that we also have access to its subdirectories (Windows account security allowing).

If you want to check whether a granted permission implicitly brings us another permission as a subset, you can do this:

```
// Example from SecurityApp3

   class Class1
   {
      static void Main(string[] args)
      {
         CodeAccessPermission permissionA =
            new FileIOPermission(FileIOPermissionAccess.AllAccess, @"C:\");
         CodeAccessPermission permissionB =
            new FileIOPermission(FileIOPermissionAccess.Read, @"C:\temp");
         if (permissionB.IsSubsetOf(permissionA))
         {
            Console.WriteLine("PermissionB is a subset of PermissionA");
         }
         else
         {
            Console.WriteLine("PermissionB is NOT a subset of PermissionA");
         }
      }
   }
```

The output looks like this:

```
PermissionB is a subset of PermissionA
```

Denying Permissions

There will be circumstances under which we want to perform an action and be absolutely sure that the method we call is acting within a protected environment where it cannot do anything untoward. For example, let's say we want to make a call to a third-party class in a way that we are confident it will not access the local disk.

To do that, we create an instance of the permission we want to ensure the method is not granted, and then call its Deny() method before making the call to the class:

```
using System;
using System.IO;
using System.Security;
using System.Security.Permissions;
namespace SecurityApp4
{
   class Class1
   {
      static void Main(string[] args)
      {
         CodeAccessPermission permission =
            new FileIOPermission(FileIOPermissionAccess.AllAccess,@"C:\");
```

```
            permission.Deny();
            UntrustworthyClass.Method();
            CodeAccessPermission.RevertDeny();
        }
    }
    class UntrustworthyClass
    {
        public static void Method()
        {
            try
            {
                StreamReader din = File.OpenText(@"C:\textfile.txt");
            }
            catch
            {
                Console.WriteLine("Failed to open file");
            }
        }
    }
}
```

If you build this code the output will state `Failed to open file`, as the untrustworthy class does not have access to the local disk.

Note that the `Deny()` call is made on an instance of the `permission` object, whereas the `RevertDeny()` call is made statically. The reason for this is that the `RevertDeny()` call reverts all deny requests within the current stack frame; this means if you have made several calls to `Deny()` you only need make one follow-up call to `RevertDeny()`.

Asserting Permissions

Imagine that we have an assembly that has been installed with full trust on a user's system. Within that assembly is a method that saves auditing information to a text file on the local disk. If we later install an application that wants to make use of the auditing feature, it will be necessary for the application to have the relevant `FileIOPermission` permissions to save the data to disk.

This seems excessive, however, as really all we want to do is perform a highly restricted action on the local disk. At times like these, it would be useful if assemblies with limiting permissions could make calls to more trusted assemblies, which can temporarily increase the scope of the permissions on the stack, and perform operations on behalf of the caller that it does not have the permissions to do itself.

To achieve this, assemblies with high enough levels of trust can assert permissions that they require. If the assembly has the permissions it needs to assert additional permissions, it removes the need for callers up the stack to have such wide-ranging permissions.

The code opposite contains a class called `AuditClass` that implements a method called `Save()`, which takes a string and saves audit data to `C:\audit.txt`. The `AuditClass` method asserts the permissions it needs to add the audit lines to the file. To test it out, the `Main()` method for the application explicitly denies the file permission that the `Audit` method needs:

```
using System;
using System.IO;
using System.Security;
using System.Security.Permissions;
namespace SecurityApp5
{
    class Class1
    {
        static void Main(string[] args)
        {
            CodeAccessPermission permission =
                new FileIOPermission(FileIOPermissionAccess.Append,
                                @"C:\audit.txt");
            permission.Deny();
            AuditClass.Save("some data to audit");
            CodeAccessPermission.RevertDeny();
        }
    }
    class AuditClass
    {
        public static void Save(string value)
        {
            try
            {
                FileIOPermission permission =
                    new FileIOPermission(FileIOPermissionAccess.Append,
                                @"C:\audit.txt");
                permission.Assert();
                FileStream stream = new FileStream(@"C:\audit.txt",
                    FileMode.Append, FileAccess.Write);

                // code to write to audit file here...
                CodeAccessPermission.RevertAssert();
                Console.WriteLine("Data written to audit file");
            }
            catch
            {
                Console.WriteLine("Failed to write data to audit file");
            }
        }
    }
}
```

When this code is executed, you'll find the call to the AuditClass method does not cause a security exception, even though when it was called it did not have the required permissions to carry out the disk access.

As with RevertDeny(), RevertAssert() is a static method, and it reverts all assertions within the current frame.

It's important to be very careful when using assertions. We are explicitly assigning permissions to a method that has been called by code that may well not have those permissions, and this could open a security hole. For example, in the auditing example, even if the security policy dictated that an installed application can not write to the local disk, our assembly would be able to write to the disk when the auditing assembly asserts `FileIOPermissions` for writing. To perform the assertion the auditing assembly must have been installed with permission for `FileIOAccess` and `SecurityPermission`. The `SecurityPermission` allows an assembly to perform an assert, and the assembly will need both the `SecurityPermission` and the permission being asserted to complete successfully.

Creating Code Access Permissions

The .NET Framework implements code access security permissions that provide protection for the resources that it exposes. There may be occasions when you want to create your own permissions, however, and in that event you can do so by subclassing `CodeAccessPermission`. Deriving from this class gives you the benefits of the .NET code access security system, including stack walking and policy management.

Here are two examples of cases where you might want to roll your own code access permissions:

❑ **Protecting a resource not already protected by the Framework**. For example, you have developed a .NET application for home automation that is implemented using an onboard hardware device. By creating your own code access permissions, you have a highly granular level of control over the access given to the home automation hardware.

❑ **Providing a finer degree of management than existing permissions**. For example, although the .NET Framework provides permissions that allow granular control over access to the local file system, you may have an application where you want to control access to a specific file or folder much more tightly. In this scenario, you may find it useful to create a code access permission that relates specifically to that file or folder, and without that permission no managed code can access that area of the disk.

Declarative Security

You can deny, demand, and assert permissions by calling classes in the .NET Framework, but you can also use attributes and specify permission requirements declaratively.

The main benefit of using declarative security is that the settings are accessible via reflection. (It's also easier on the fingers as there's less to type!) Being able to access this information through reflection can be of enormous benefit to system administrators, who will often want to view the security requirements of applications.

For example, we can specify that a method must have permission to read from C:\ to execute:

```
using System;
using System.Security.Permissions;
namespace SecurityApp6
{
    class Class1
    {
        static void Main(string[] args)
```

```
        {
            MyClass.Method();
        }
    }

    [FileIOPermission(SecurityAction.Assert, Read="C:\\")]
    class MyClass
    {
        public static void Method()
        {

            // implementation goes here

        }
    }
}
```

Be aware that if you use attributes to assert or demand permissions, you cannot catch any exceptions that are raised if the action fails, as there is no imperative code around in which you can place a `try-catch-finally` clause.

Role-Based Security

As we have seen, code access security gives the CLR the ability to make intelligent decisions behind the scenes as to whether code should run or not and with what permissions based on the evidence it presents. In addition to this, .NET provides role-based security that specifies whether code can perform actions on the basis of evidence about the user and their role, rather than just the code. You'll probably be glad to hear that it does this without walking the stack!

Role-based security is especially useful in situations where access to resources is an issue, a primary example being the finance industry, where employees' roles define what information they can access and what actions they can perform.

Role-based security is also ideal for use in conjunction with Windows 2000 accounts, Microsoft Passport, or a custom user directory to manage access to web-based resources. For example, a web site could restrict access to its content until a user registers their details with the site, and then additionally provide access to special content only if the user is a paying subscriber. In many ways, ASP.NET makes role-based security easier because much of the code is based on the server.

For example, if we want to implement a web service that requires authentication, we could use Windows 2000's accounts subsystem and write the web method in such a way that it ensures the user is a member of a specific Windows 2000 user group before allowing access to the method's functionality.

The Principal

.NET gives the current thread easy access to the application user, which it refers to as a `Principal`. The principal is at the core of the role-based security that .NET provides, and through it, we can access the user's `Identity`, which will usually map to a user account of one of these types:

❑ Windows account

❑ Passport account

❑ ASP.NET cookie-authenticated user

As an added bonus, the role-based security in .NET has been designed so that you can create your own principals by implementing the `IPrincipal` interface. If you are not relying on Windows authentication, Passport, or simple cookie authentication, you should look at creating your own using a custom `principal` class.

With access to the principal we can make security decisions based on the principal's identity and roles. A role is a collection of users who have the same security permissions, and is the unit of administration for users. For example, if we're using Windows authentication to authenticate our users, we will use the `WindowsIdentity` type as our choice of `Identity`. We can use that type to find out whether the user is a member of a specific Windows user account group, and we can then use that information to decide whether to grant or deny access to code and resources.

You'll generally find that it's much easier to manage security if you allow access to resources and functionality on the basis of roles rather than individual users. Imagine a scenario where you have three methods that each provides access to a feature over which you need tight control to ensure only authorized personnel can access it. If the application had, say, four users, we could quite easily specify within each method which users can and which users cannot access the method. However, imagine a time in the future where the number of features has extended to nine; to allow access to an additional user potentially requires changing every one of the nine methods even though this is an administrative task! Even worse, as users move between roles in the company we would need to change the code each time that happens too. If we had instead implemented the system using roles, we could then simply add users to and remove users from roles, rather than adding and removing individual users to and from the application. This simplifies the application, as for each method we simply request that the user be a member of a specific role. It also simplifies the management of roles, as the administrator can do it rather than the application developer. Put simply, the developer should be concerned with ensuring that, for example, managers but not secretaries can access a method; that Julie and Bob can, but not Conrad.

.NET's role-based security builds on that provided in MTS and COM+ 1.0, and provides a flexible framework that can be used to build fences around sections of the application that need to be protected. If COM+ 1.0 is installed on a machine, its role-based security will interoperate with .NET; however, COM is not required for .NET's role-based security to function.

Windows Principal

Let's create a console application that gives us access to our principal in an application, where we want access to the underlying Windows account. We'll need to reference the System.Security.Principal and System.Threading namespaces. First of all, we must specify that we want .NET to automatically hook up our principal with the underlying Windows account, as .NET does not automatically populate the thread's CurrentPrincipal property for security reasons. We do that like this:

```
using System;
using System.Security.Principal;
using System.Security.Permissions;
using System.Threading;

namespace SecurityApp7
{
    class Class1
    {
        static void Main(string[] args)
        {
            AppDomain.CurrentDomain.SetPrincipalPolicy(
                PrincipalPolicy.WindowsPrincipal);
```

It's possible to use WindowsIdentity.GetCurrent() to access the Windows account details; however, that method is best used when you're only going to look at the principal once. If you want to access the principal a number of times it is more efficient to set the policy so the current thread provides access to the principal for you. When we use the SetPrincipalPolicy method we are specifying that the principal in the current thread should hold a WindowsIdentity object for us. All identity classes like WindowsIdentity implement the IIdentity interface. The interface contains three properties (AuthenticationType, IsAuthenticated, and Name) for all derived identity classes to implement.

Let's add some code to access the principal's properties from the Thread object:

```
            WindowsPrincipal principal =
                (WindowsPrincipal)Thread.CurrentPrincipal;
            WindowsIdentity identity = (WindowsIdentity)principal.Identity;
            Console.WriteLine("IdentityType:" + identity.ToString());
            Console.WriteLine("Name:" + identity.Name);
            Console.WriteLine("'Users'?:" + principal.IsInRole("BUILTIN\\Users"));
            Console.WriteLine("'Administrators'?:" +
                principal.IsInRole(WindowsBuiltInRole.Administrator));
            Console.WriteLine("Authenticated:" + identity.IsAuthenticated);
            Console.WriteLine("AuthType:" + identity.AuthenticationType);
            Console.WriteLine("Anonymous?:" + identity.IsAnonymous);
            Console.WriteLine("Token:" + identity.Token);
        }
    }
}
```

The output from this console application will look something like this depending on your machine configuration and the roles associated with the account under which you're signed in:

```
IdentityType:System.Security.Principal.WindowsIdentity
Name:MACHINE\alaric
'Users'?:True
'Administrators'?:True
Authenticated:True
AuthType:NTLM
Anonymous?:False
Token:256
```

Clearly, it is enormously beneficial to be able to access details about the current user and their roles so easily, and using this information we can make decisions about what actions to permit and to deny. The ability to make use of roles and Windows user groups provides the added benefit that administration can be done using standard user administration tools, and we can usually avoid altering the code when user roles change. Let's look at roles in more detail.

Roles

Imagine a scenario where we have an intranet application relying on Windows accounts. The system has a group called `Manager` and one called `Assistant`; users are assigned to these groups dependent upon their role within the organization. Let's say our application contains a feature that displays information about employees that we only want those in the `Managers` group to access. We can easily use code that checks whether the current user is a member of the `Managers` group and permit or deny access based on this.

However, if we later decide to rearrange our account groups and introduce a group called `Personnel` that also has access to employee details, we have a problem. We have to go through all the code and update it to include rules for this new group.

A better solution would be to create a permission called something like `ReadEmployeeDetails` and assign it to groups where necessary. If our code applies a check for the `ReadEmployeeDetails` permission, to update the application to allow those in the `Personnel` group access to employee details is simply a matter of creating the group, placing the users in it, and assigning the `ReadEmployeeDetails` permission.

Declarative Role-Based Security

Just as with code access security, we can implement role-based security requests ("the user must be in the Administrators group") using imperative requests (as you saw in the preceding section), or using attributes. We can state permission requirements declaratively at the class level like this:

```
using System;
using System.Security;
using System.Security.Principal;
using System.Security.Permissions;

namespace SecurityApp8
{
```

```
class Class1
{
    static void Main(string[] args)
    {
        AppDomain.CurrentDomain.SetPrincipalPolicy(
            PrincipalPolicy.WindowsPrincipal);
        try
        {
            ShowMessage();
        }
        catch (SecurityException exception)
        {
            Console.WriteLine("Security exception caught (" +
                            exception.Message + ")");
            Console.WriteLine("The current principal must be in the local"
                            + "Users group");
        }
    }

    [PrincipalPermissionAttribute(SecurityAction.Demand,
                                Role = "BUILTIN\\Users")]
    static void ShowMessage()
    {
        Console.WriteLine("The current principal is logged in locally ");
        Console.WriteLine("(they are a member of the local Users group)");
    }
}
```

The ShowMessage() method will throw an exception unless we execute the application in the context of a user in the Windows 2000 local Users group. For a web application, the account under which the ASP.NET code is running must be in the group, although in a real-world example you would certainly avoid adding this account to the administrators group!

If you run the code above using an account in the local Users group, the output will look like this:

```
The current principal is logged in locally
(they are a member of the local Users group)
```

For more information on role-based security in .NET, your first stop should be the MSDN documentation for the System.Security.Principal namespace.

Managing Security Policy

Although .NET's security features are wide ranging and far in advance of anything seen before on Windows, there are some limitations that we should be aware of:

❑ .NET security policy does not enforce security on unmanaged code (although it provides some protection against calls to unmanaged code).

❑ If a user copies an assembly to their local machine, the assembly has FullTrust and security policy is effectively bypassed. To work around this, we can limit the permissions granted to local code.

❑ .NET security policy provides very little help in dealing with script-based viruses and malicious Win32 .EXE files, which Microsoft is dealing with in different ways. For example, recent versions of Outlook do not allow you to run executable files from e-mails – the user is warned they may contain a virus and forced to save them to disk where there are opportunities for administrative restraints to be installed, including blocking access to the local drive and providing an opportunity for anti-virus software to act.

However, .NET helps enormously in assisting the operating system in making intelligent decisions about how much trust to give to code, whether it is from an intranet application, a control on a web page, or a Windows Forms application downloaded from a software supplier on the Internet.

The Security Configuration File

As we've seen already, the glue that connects together code groups, permissions, and permission sets is our three levels of security policy (Enterprise, Machine, and User). Security configuration information in .NET is stored in XML configuration files that are protected by Windows security. For example, the Machine-level security policy is only writable to users in the Administrator, Power User, and SYSTEM Windows 2000 groups.

On Windows 2000, the files that store the security policy are located in the following places:

❑ Enterprise policy Configuration:
C:\WinNT\Microsoft.NET\Framework\v1.0.xxxx\Config\enterprise.config

❑ Machine policy configuration:
C:\WinNT\Microsoft.NET\Framework\v1.0.xxxx\Config\security.config

❑ User policy configuration: %USERPROFILE%\application data\Microsoft\CLR
security config\vxx.xx\security.config

The version number marked with several x's will vary depending on the version of the .NET Framework you have on your machine. If necessary, it's possible to manually edit these configuration files, for example, if an administrator needs to configure policy for a user without logging into their account. However, in general it's recommended to use caspol.exe or the Runtime Security Policy node in the .NET Framework Configuration MMC snap-in to manage security policy.

A Simple Example

Given everything you've read so far, let's create a simple application that accesses the local drive, the kind of behavior we're likely to want to manage carefully. The application is a C# Windows Forms application with a listbox and a button. If you click the button, the listbox is populated from a file called animals.txt in the root of the C:\ drive:

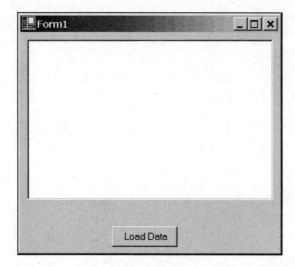

The application was created using Visual Studio.NET and the only changes were to add the listbox and **Load Data** button to the form and to add an event to the button that looks like this:

```
// Example from SecurityApp9

private void button1_Click(object sender, System.EventArgs e)
{
    StreamReader stream = File.OpenText(@"C:\animals.txt");
    String str;
    while ((str=stream.ReadLine()) != null)
    {
        listBox1.Items.Add(str);
    }
}
```

It opens a simple text file from the root of the C:\ drive, which contains a list of animals on separate lines, and loads each line into a string, which it then uses to create each item in the listbox.

If we run the application from our local machine and click the button, we'll see the data loaded from the root of the C:\ drive and displayed in the listbox as we'd expect. Behind the scenes the runtime has granted our assembly the permission it needs to execute, access the user interface, and read data from the local disk:

You may remember that the permissions on the intranet zone code group are more restrictive than on the local machine, in particular, they do not allow access to the local disk (except in the folder from which the application runs). If we run the application again, but this time from a network share, it will run just as before as it is granted the permissions to execute and access the user interface, however, if we now click the Load Data button on the form, a security exception is thrown:

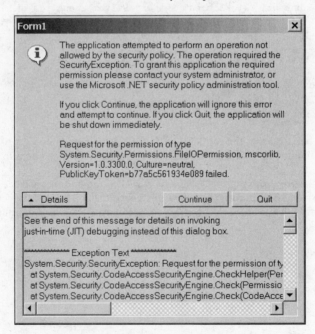

You'll see in the exception message text that it mentions the
`System.Security.Permissions.FileIOPermission` object; this is the permission that our
application was not granted that was demanded by the class in the Framework that we are using to load
the data from the file on the local disk.

By default, the Intranet code group is granted the `LocalIntranet` permission set; let's change the
permission set to `FullTrust` so any code from the intranet zone can run completely unrestricted.

First, we need to get the numeric label of the `LocalIntranet` code group. We can do this with the
following command.

```
>caspol.exe -listgroups
```

This will output something like this:

```
Code Groups:

1.  All code: Nothing
    1.1.  Zone - MyComputer: FullTrust
        1.1.1.  StrongName -
00240000004800000940000000602000000240000525341310004000001000010007D1FA57C4AED9F0A3
2E84AA0FAEFD0DE9E8FD6AEC8F87FB03766C834C99921EB23BE79AD9D5DCC1DD9AD236132102900B72
3CF980957FC4E177108FC607774F29E8320E92EA05ECE4E821C0A5EFE8F1645C4C0C93C1AB99285D62
2CAA652C1DFAD63D745D6F2DE5F17E5EAF0FC4963D261C8A12436518206DC093344D5AD293:
FullTrust
        1.1.2.  StrongName - 0000000000000000400000000000000: FullTrust
    1.2.  Zone - Intranet: LocalIntranet
        1.2.1.  All code: Same site Web.
        1.2.2.  All code: Same directory FileIO - Read, PathDiscovery
    1.3.  Zone - Internet: Internet
        1.3.1.  All code: Same site Web.
    1.4.  Zone - Untrusted: Nothing
    1.5.  Zone - Trusted: Internet
        1.5.1.  All code: Same site Web.
```

Notice the `LocalIntranet` group is listed as 1.2. We now use the following command to apply full
trust.

```
>caspol.exe -chggroup 1.2 FullTrust
```

If we now run the application from the network share again and click the button, we'll see that the
listbox is populated from the file in the root of the `C:\` drive and no exception occurs.

In scenarios like these where we're making use of resources that are governed by permissions, it is
advisable to extend the code so security exceptions are caught, so that the application can degrade
gracefully. For example, in our application we can add a `try-catch` block around the file access code
and if a `SecurityException` is thrown we display a line in the listbox saying, **Permission denied
accessing file:**

```
// Code from SecurityApp9

private void button1_Click(object sender, System.EventArgs e)
{
    try
    {
        StreamReader din = File.OpenText(@"C:\animals.txt");
        String str;
        while ((str=din.ReadLine()) != null)
        {
            listBox1.Items.Add(str);
        }
    }
    catch (SecurityException exception)
    {
        listBox1.Items.Add("Permission denied accessing file");
    }
}
```

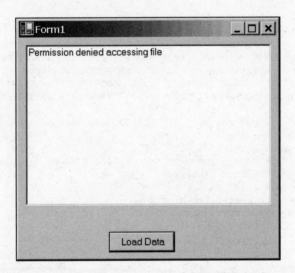

In reality, if we wanted to run a specific application from a network share, we'd most likely opt for a solution that didn't open up our client machine to all code on the intranet. Instead, we would use code groups and membership conditions to tightly control the requirements of the application – perhaps using its location on the intranet, a strong name, or a certificate proving the identity of the publisher.

Managing Code Groups and Permissions

In managing security on .NET, we find that if an assembly is failing with a security exception we usually have three choices:

❑   Ease the policy permissions

❑   Move the assembly

❑   Apply a strong name to the assembly

When making these kinds of decisions you must ensure that you to take into account your level of trust of the assembly.

Turning Security On and Off

By default .NET security is enabled. If, for any reason, you need to turn it off, you can do it like this:

```
>caspol.exe -security off
```

To turn security back on, use this:

```
>caspol.exe -security on
```

Generally, the security risks inherent in opening a machine up by turning off security mean that it's only necessary to turn off security for testing and debugging.

> **Something you should be aware of is that the command above does not need administrative privileges; this means any user (or a virus) could turn off .NET security. You are well advised to alter the Windows file security on the `caspol` utility to guard against malicious or misinformed usage.**

Resetting Security Policy

If you need to return the security configuration to its original state, you can type this command:

```
>caspol.exe -reset
```

This command resets the security policy to the installation default.

Creating a Code Group

We can create our own code groups and then apply specific permissions to them. For example, we could specify that we want to trust all code from the web site www.wrox.com and give it full access to our system (without trusting code from any other web site).

Earlier we ran caspol to list the available group and number assignments. We saw then the fact that Zone: Internet is labeled 1.3, so we now type this command:

```
>caspol.exe -addgroup 1.3 -site www.wrox.com FullTrust
```

Note that this command will ask for confirmation as we are attempting to explicitly alter the security policy on the machine. If we now run the caspol.exe -listgroups command again, we'll see the new code group has been added and assigned FullTrust:

```
...
1.2.   Zone - Intranet: LocalIntranet
   1.2.1.   All code: Same site Web.
   1.2.2.   All code: Same directory FileIO - Read, PathDiscovery
1.3.   Zone - Internet: Internet
   1.3.1.   All code: Same site Web.
   1.3.2.   Site - www.wrox.com: FullTrust
1.4.   Zone - Untrusted: Nothing
1.5.   Zone - Trusted: Internet
   1.5.1.   All code: Same site Web.
```

Let's look at another example. Let's say we want to create a code group under the `Intranet` code group (`1.2`) that grants `FullTrust` to all applications running from a specific network share:

```
>caspol.exe -addgroup 1.2 -url file:///\\intranetserver/sharename/* FullTrust
```

Deleting a Code Group

To remove a code group we have created, we can type a command like this:

```
>caspol.exe -remgroup 1.3.2
```

It will ask for confirmation that you want to alter the security policy, and if you give positive confirmation it will state that the group has been removed.

> Be aware that although you cannot delete the code group **All Code**, it is possible to delete code groups at the level below, including the groups for **Internet**, **MyComputer**, and **LocalIntranet**.

Changing a Code Group's Permissions

To ease or restrict the permissions assigned to a code group, we can use `caspol.exe` again. Let's say we want to apply `FullTrust` to the `Intranet` zone, first we need to get the label that represents the `Intranet` code group:

```
>caspol.exe -listgroups
```

The output shows the `Intranet` code group:

```
Code Groups:

1.  All code: Nothing
   1.1.   Zone - MyComputer: FullTrust
      1.1.1.   StrongName -
00240000048000000940000000602000000240000525341310004000001000010007D1FA57C4AED9F0A3
2E84AA0FAEFD0DE9E8FD6AEC8F87FB03766C834C99921EB23BE79AD9D5DCC1DD9AD236132102900B72
```

```
3CF980957FC4E177108FC607774F29E8320E92EA05ECE4E821C0A5EFE8F1645C4C0C93C1AB99285D62
2CAA652C1DFAD63D745D6F2DE5F17E5EAF0FC4963D261C8A12436518206DC093344D5AD293:
FullTrust
     1.1.2.   StrongName - 00000000000000000400000000000000: FullTrust
  1.2.   Zone - Intranet: LocalIntranet
     1.2.1.   All code: Same site Web.
     1.2.2.   All code: Same directory FileIO - Read, PathDiscovery
  1.3.   Zone - Internet: Internet
     1.3.1.   All code: Same site Web.
  1.4.   Zone - Untrusted: Nothing
  1.5.   Zone - Trusted: Internet
     1.5.1.   All code: Same site Web.
```

Once we have the `Intranet` code group's label, `1.2`, we enter a second command to alter the code group's permissions:

```
>caspol.exe -chggroup 1.2 FullTrust
```

The command will ask us to confirm the change to the security policy, and if we now run the `caspol.exe -listgroups` command again, we can see the permission on the end of the `Intranet` line has changed to `FullTrust`:

```
Code Groups:

1.   All code: Nothing
   1.1.   Zone - MyComputer: FullTrust
      1.1.1.   StrongName -
00240000004800000940000000602000000240000525341310004000001000100007D1FA57C4AED9F0A3
2E84AA0FAEFD0DE9E8FD6AEC8F87FB03766C834C99921EB23BE79AD9D5DCC1DD9AD236132102900B72
3CF980957FC4E177108FC607774F29E8320E92EA05ECE4E821C0A5EFE8F1645C4C0C93C1AB99285D62
2CAA652C1DFAD63D745D6F2DE5F17E5EAF0FC4963D261C8A12436518206DC093344D5AD293:
FullTrust
      1.1.2.   StrongName - 00000000000000000400000000000000: FullTrust
   1.2.   Zone - Intranet: FullTrust
      1.2.1.   All code: Same site Web.
      1.2.2.   All code: Same directory FileIO - Read, PathDiscovery
   1.3.   Zone - Internet: Internet
      1.3.1.   All code: Same site Web.
   1.4.   Zone - Untrusted: Nothing
   1.5.   Zone - Trusted: Internet
      1.5.1.   All code: Same site Web.
```

Creating and Applying Permissions Sets

We can create new permission sets using a command like this:

```
>caspol.exe -addpset MyCustomPermissionSet permissionset.xml
```

This command specifies that we are creating a new permissions set called `MyCustomPermissionSet`, and basing it on the contents of the specified XML file. The XML file must contain a standard format specifying a `PermissionSet`. For reference, here's the permission set file for the `Everything` permission set, which you can trim down to the permission set you want to create:

```
<PermissionSet class="System.Security.NamedPermissionSet"
               version="1"
          Name="Everything" Description="Allows unrestricted access to
          all resources covered by built-in permissions">
    <IPermission class="System.Security.Permissions.EnvironmentPermission,
              mscorlib, Version=1.0.3300.0, Culture=neutral,
                        PublicKeyToken=b77a5c561934e089"
              version="1"
              Unrestricted="true"/>
    <IPermission class="System.Security.Permissions.FileDialogPermission,
              mscorlib, Version=1.0.3300.0, Culture=neutral,
                             PublicKeyToken=b77a5c561934e089"
              version="1"
              Unrestricted="true"/>
    <IPermission class="System.Security.Permissions.FileIOPermission,
              mscorlib, Version=1.0.3300.0, Culture=neutral,
                        PublicKeyToken=b77a5c561934e089"
              version="1"
              Unrestricted="true"/>
    <IPermission class="System.Security.Permissions.IsolatedStorageFilePermission,
              mscorlib, Version=1.0.3300.0, Culture=neutral,
                        PublicKeyToken=b77a5c561934e089"
              version="1"
              Unrestricted="true"/>
    <IPermission class="System.Security.Permissions.ReflectionPermission,
           mscorlib, Version=1.0.3300.0, Culture=neutral,
                        PublicKeyToken=b77a5c561934e089"
              version="1"
              Unrestricted="true"/>
    <IPermission class="System.Security.Permissions.RegistryPermission,
           mscorlib, Version=1.0.3300.0, Culture=neutral,
                        PublicKeyToken=b77a5c561934e089"
              version="1"
              Unrestricted="true"/>
    <IPermission class="System.Security.Permissions.SecurityPermission,
           mscorlib, Version=1.0.3300.0, Culture=neutral,
                        PublicKeyToken=b77a5c561934e089"
              version="1"
              Flags="Assertion, UnmanagedCode, Execution, ControlThread,
              ControlEvidence, ControlPolicy,
              SerializationFormatter, ControlDomainPolicy,
              ControlPrincipal, ControlAppDomain, RemotingConfiguration,
              Infrastructure"/>
    <IPermission class="System.Security.Permissions.UIPermission,
           mscorlib, Version=1.0.3300.0, Culture=neutral,
                        PublicKeyToken=b77a5c561934e089"
              version="1"
              Unrestricted="true"/>
    <IPermission class="System.Net.DnsPermission, System, Version=1.0.3300.0,
```

```
            Culture=neutral, PublicKeyToken=b77a5c561934e089"
                version="1"
                Unrestricted="true"/>
<IPermission class="System.Drawing.Printing.PrintingPermission,
        System.Drawing, Version=1.0.3300.0, Culture=neutral,
                        PublicKeyToken=b03f5f7f11d50a3a"
                version="1"
                Unrestricted="true"/>
<IPermission class="System.Diagnostics.EventLogPermission, System,
            Version=1.0.3300.0, Culture=neutral,
                        PublicKeyToken=b77a5c561934e089"
                version="1"
                Unrestricted="true"/>
<IPermission class="System.Net.SocketPermission, System, Version=1.0.3300.0,
            Culture=neutral, PublicKeyToken=b77a5c561934e089"
                version="1"
                Unrestricted="true"/>
<IPermission class="System.Net.WebPermission, System, Version=1.0.3300.0,
            Culture=neutral, PublicKeyToken=b77a5c561934e089"
                version="1"
                Unrestricted="true"/>
<IPermission class="System.Diagnostics.PerformanceCounterPermission, System,
            Version=1.0.3300.0, Culture=neutral,
                        PublicKeyToken=b77a5c561934e089"
                version="1"
                Unrestricted="true"/>
<IPermission class="System.DirectoryServices.DirectoryServicesPermission,
        System.DirectoryServices, Version=1.0.3300.0,
            Culture=neutral, PublicKeyToken=b03f5f7f11d50a3a"
                version="1"
                Unrestricted="true"/>
<IPermission class="System.Messaging.MessageQueuePermission, System.Messaging,
            Version=1.0.3300.0, Culture=neutral,
                    PublicKeyToken=b03f5f7f11d50a3a"
                version="1"
                Unrestricted="true"/>
<IPermission class="System.ServiceProcess.ServiceControllerPermission,
        System.ServiceProcess, Version=1.0.3300.0, Culture=neutral,
        PublicKeyToken=b03f5f7f11d50a3a"
                version="1"
                Unrestricted="true"/>
<IPermission class="System.Data.OleDb.OleDbPermission, System.Data,
            Version=1.0.3300.0, Culture=neutral,
                        PublicKeyToken=b77a5c561934e089"
                version="1"
                AllowBlankPassword="False"
                Unrestricted="true"/>
<IPermission class="System.Data.SqlClient.SqlClientPermission, System.Data,
            Version=1.0.3300.0, Culture=neutral,
                        PublicKeyToken=b77a5c561934e089"
                version="1"
                AllowBlankPassword="False"
                Unrestricted="true"/>
```

```
</PermissionSet>
```

To view all permission sets in XML format, you can use this command:

```
>caspol.exe -listpset
```

If you want to give a new definition to an existing permission set by applying an XML `PermissionSet` configuration file, you can use this command:

```
>caspol.exe -chgpset permissionset.xml MyCustomPermissionSet
```

Distributing Code Using a Strong Name

.NET provides the ability for us to match an assembly to a code group when the assembly's identity and integrity have been confirmed using a strong name. This scenario is very common when assemblies are being deployed across networks, for example, distributing software over the Internet.

If you are a software company, and you want to provide code to your customers via the Internet, you build an assembly and give it a strong name. The strong name ensures that the assembly can be uniquely identified, and also provides protection against tampering. Your customers can incorporate this strong name into their code access security policy; an assembly that matches this unique strong name can then be assigned permissions explicitly. As you saw in the chapter on assemblies, the strong name includes checksums for hashes of all the files within an assembly, so we have strong evidence that the assembly has not been altered since the publisher created the strong name.

Note that, if your application uses an installer, the installer will install assemblies that have already been given a strong name. The strong name is generated once for each distribution before being sent to customers; the installer does not run these commands. The reason for this is that the strong name provides an assurance that the assembly has not been modified since it left your company; a common way to achieve this is to give your customer not only the application code, but also, separately, a copy of the strong name for the assembly. You may find it beneficial to pass the strong name to your customer using a secure form (perhaps fax or encrypted e-mail) to guard against the assembly being tampered with enroute.

Let's look at an example where we want to create an assembly with a strong name that we can distribute in such a way that the recipient of the assembly can use the strong name to grant the `FullTrust` permission to the assembly.

First, we need to create a key pair, as strong names make use of public key encryption. The public and private keys are stored in the file we specify, and are used to sign the strong name. To create a key pair, we use the Strong Name Tool (`sn.exe`), which in addition to helping us create key pairs can also be used to manage keys and strong names. Let's create a key; do this by typing the following command:

```
>sn.exe -k key.snk
```

We then place the keyfile (`key.snk` in our case) in the folder where Visual Studio builds our output file (normally the **Debug** folder) and add the key to our code using an assembly attribute. Once we have added this attribute to `AssemblyInfo.cs`, we just rebuild the assembly. The recompilation ensures the hash is recalculated and the assembly is protected against malicious modifications:

```
[assembly: AssemblyKeyFileAttribute("key.snk")]
```

Our assembly has now been compiled and signed; it has a unique identifying strong name. We can now create a new code group on the machine where we want the assembly to execute, which has a membership condition that requires a match for the strong name of our assembly.

The following command states that we want to create a new code group using the strong name from the specified assembly manifest file, that we do not mind which version of the assembly is used, and that we want the code group to be granted the FullTrust permissions:

```
>caspol.exe -addgroup 1 -strong -file \bin\debug\SecurityApp10.exe
          -noname -noversion FullTrust
```

The application in this example will now run from any zone, even the Internet zone, because the strong name provides powerful evidence that the assembly can be trusted. If we look at our code groups using caspol.exe -listgroups, we'll see the new code group (1.6 and its associated public key in hexadecimal):

```
Code Groups:

1.  All code: Nothing
    1.1.  Zone - MyComputer: FullTrust
        1.1.1.  StrongName -
00240000048000009400000060200000024000052534131000400000100010007D1FA57C4AED9F0A3
2E84AA0FAEFD0DE9E8FD6AEC8F87FB03766C834C99921EB23BE79AD9D5DCC1DD9AD236132102900B72
3CF980957FC4E177108FC607774F29E8320E92EA05ECE4E821C0A5EFE8F1645C4C0C93C1AB99285D62
2CAA652C1DFAD63D745D6F2DE5F17E5EAF0FC4963D261C8A12436518206DC093344D5AD293:
FullTrust
        1.1.2.  StrongName - 00000000000000000400000000000000: FullTrust
    1.2.  Zone - Intranet: LocalIntranet
        1.2.1.  All code: Same site Web.
        1.2.2.  All code: Same directory FileIO - Read, PathDiscovery
    1.3.  Zone - Internet: Internet
        1.3.1.  All code: Same site Web.
    1.4.  Zone - Untrusted: Nothing
    1.5.  Zone - Trusted: Internet
        1.5.1.  All code: Same site Web.
    1.6.  StrongName -
00240000048000009400000060200000024000052534131000400000100010000D51335D1B5B64BE976
AD8B08030F8E36A0DBBC3EEB5F8A18D0E30E8951DA059B440281997D760FFF61A6252A284061C1D714
EFEE5B329F410983A01DB324FA85BCE6C4E6384A2F3BC1FFA01E2586816B23888CFADD38D5AA5DF041
ACE2F81D9E8B591556852E83C473017A1785203B12F56B6D9DC23A8C9F691A0BC525D7B7EA:
FullTrust
Success
```

If you want to access the strong name in an assembly you can use the secutil.exe tool against the assembly manifest file. Let's use secutil.exe to view the strong name information for our assembly. We'll add the -hex option, so the public key is shown in hexadecimal (like caspol.exe), and then also the argument -strongname that specifies that we want to view the strong name. Type this command, and you'll see a listing containing the strong name public key, the assembly name, and the assembly version:

```
>secutil.exe -hex -strongname securityapp10.exe

Microsoft (R) .NET Framework SecUtil 1.0.3705.0
Copyright (C) Microsoft Corporation 1998-2001. All rights reserved.

Public Key =
0x00240000048000009400000006020000002400005253413130004000001000100D51335D1B5B64BE9
76AD8B08030F8E36A0DBBC3EEB5F8A18D0E30E8951DA059B440281997D760FFF61A6252A284061C1D7
14EFEE5B329F410983A01DB324FA85BCE6C4E6384A2F3BC1FFA01E2586816B23888CFADD38D5AA5DF0
41ACE2F81D9E8B591556852E83C473017A1785203B12F56B6D9DC23A8C9F691A0BC525D7B7EA
Name =
SecurityApp10
Version =
1.0.756.38019
Success
```

The curious among you may be wondering what the two strong name code groups installed by default refer to. One is a strong name key for Microsoft code, and the other strong name key is for the parts of .NET that have been submitted to the ECMA for standardization, which Microsoft will have much less control over.

Distributing Code Using Certificates

In the last section, we looked at how we can apply a unique strong name to an assembly so system administrators can explicitly grant permissions to assemblies that match that strong name using a code access group. Although this method of security policy management can be very effective, it's sometimes necessary to work at a higher level, where the administrator of the security policy grants permissions on the basis of the publisher of the software, rather than each individual software component. You'll probably have seen a similar method used before when you have downloaded executables from the Internet that have been Authenticode signed.

To provide information about the software publisher, we make use of digital certificates, and sign assemblies so that consumers of the software can verify the identity of the software publisher. In a commercial environment we would obtain a certificate from a company such as Verisign or Thawte.

The benefit of purchasing a certificate from a supplier such as this, rather than creating your own, is that it provides high levels of trust in its authenticity; the supplier acts as a trusted third-party. For test purposes however .NET includes a command-line utility we can use to create a test certificate. The process of creating certificates and using them to publish software is complex, but to give you a picture of what's involved we'll walk through an example without going into too much detail; if we did this chapter would be twice as long!

Let's imagine we're a company called ABC Corporation, and let's create a certificate for our software product "ABC Suite". First off, we need to create a test certificate; type the following command:

```
>makecert -sk ABC -n "CN=ABC Corporation" abccorptest.cer
```

The command creates a test certificate under the name "ABC Corporation" and saves it to a file called abccorptest.cer. The -sk ABC argument creates a key container location, which is used by the public key cryptography.

To sign our assembly with the certificate, we use the signcode.exe utility on the assembly file containing the assembly manifest. Often the easiest way to sign an assembly is to use the signcode.exe in its wizard mode; to start the wizard, just type signcode.exe with no parameters:

If we click Next, we're asked to specify where the file is that we wish to sign. For an assembly, we sign the file containing the manifest:

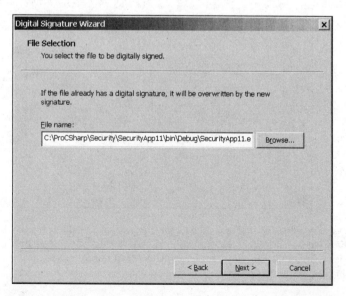

If we click **Next** the next screen is the Signing Options page:

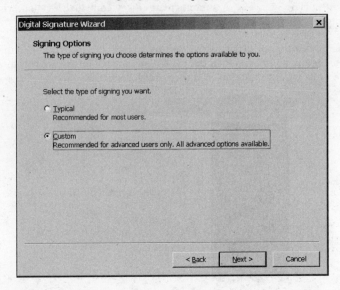

Select **Custom** and then **Next**. We're then asked to specify the certificate we want to use to sign the assembly. If we click **Select from File** and browse to the `abccorptest.cer` file, we'll see this confirmation screen:

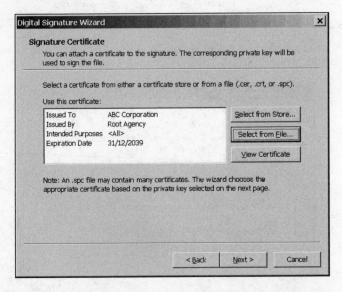

The following screen then appears that asks us for our private key file. This key file was created by the `makecert` utility, so we can select the options as shown in the next screenshot. The cryptographic service provider is an application that implements the cryptographic standards. Public key cryptography was covered in Chapter 8, *Assemblies*:

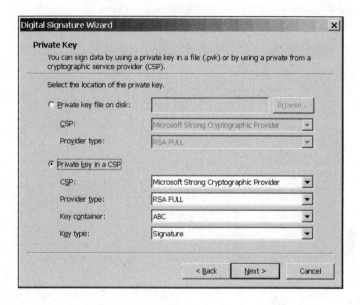

We're then asked a series of question about the way the signing is performed, including this screen, which asks us to specify the encryption algorithm:

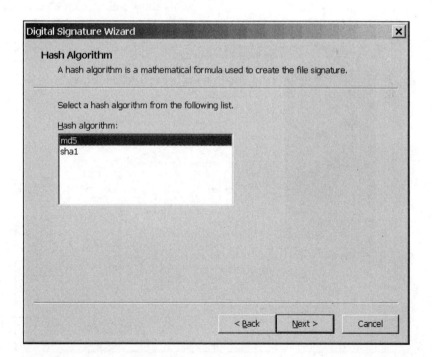

Next, we specify the name of our application and the URL for a web page that gives more information about it:

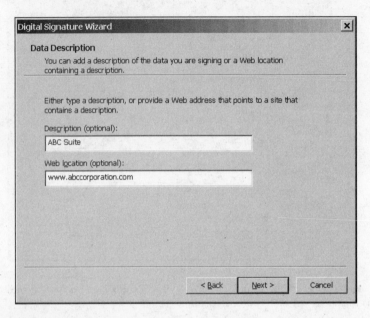

That's pretty much the end of the process; the last screen confirms the details of the certificate and the fact that the assembly has been successfully signed:

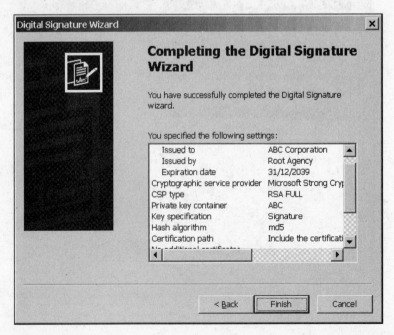

As our executable is now signed with the certificate, a recipient of the assembly has access to strong evidence as to who published the software; the runtime can examine the certificate and match the publisher of the assembly to a code group with high levels of confidence as to the identity of the code, because the trusted thirdparty certifies the publisher's identity.

Let's look at the signed assembly in a bit more detail. Although we're using a test certificate, we can temporarily configure .NET to treat test certificates more like trusted certificates issued by a trusted thirdparty using `setreg.exe`, which lets us configure public key and certificate settings in the Registry. If we enter the following command, our machine will be configured to trust the test root certificate, which gives us a more meaningful test environment:

```
>setreg.exe 1 true
```

When you are ready to reset the value, pass `false` as the last parameter. Let's check out our assembly and verify its trust level using the `chktrust.exe` utility:

```
>chktrust.exe securityapp11.exe
```

This command will pop up a window like this:

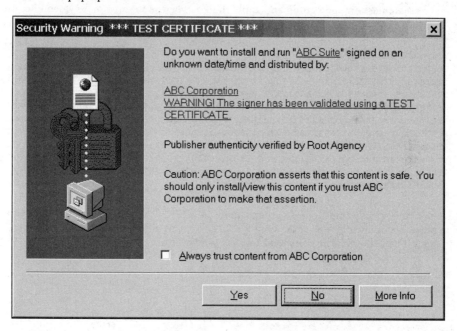

Note that `chktrust.exe` has successfully confirmed the publisher of the software using the certificate, but also reminded us that, although the certificate has been verified, it is still a test certificate.

Let's now turn our attention to a machine that we want to configure to trust software from the ABC Corporation. To do this we can create a new code access group that matches this software from ABC Corporation. To do that we grab a hexadecimal representation of the certificate from the assembly using the `secutil.exe` tool:

```
>secutil.exe -hex -x securityapp11.exe
```

The command will output something like this:

```
Microsoft (R) .NET Framework SecUtil 1.0.3705.0
Copyright (c) Microsoft Corp 1999-2001. All rights reserved.

X.509 Certificate =
0x3082017B30820125A0030201020210D69BE8D88D8FF9B54A9C689A71BB7E33300D06092A864886F7
0D0101040500301631143012060355040313B526F6F74204167656E6379301E170D30313035323831
38333133305A170D3339313233313233353935395A301A3118301606035504031430F41424320436F72
706F726174696F6E305C300D06092A864886F70D0101010500034B003048024100ECBEFB348C1364B0
A3AE14FA9805F893AD180C7B2E57ADABBBE7EF94694A1E92BC5B4B59EF76FBDAC8D04D3DF2140B7616
550FE2D5AE5F15E03CBB54932F5CBB0203010001A34B304930470603551D010440303E801012E4092D
061D1D4F008D6121DC166463A118301631143012060355040313B526F6F74204167656E6379821006
376C00AA00648A11CFB8D4AA5C35F4300D06092A864886F70D010104050004341001D1B5F6FBB0C4C0E
85A9BB5FDA5FEC1B8D9C229BB0FB8A7CBE3340A527A5B25EAA2A70205DD71571607291272D5A81981C
73028AB849FF273465FAEF2F4C7174
Success
```

Let's now create the new code group and apply the `FullTrust` permission to assemblies published by
the ABC Corporation using this (rather long) command:

```
>caspol -addgroup 1 -pub -hex
3082017B30820125A0030201020210D69BE8D88D8FF9B54A9C689A71BB7E33300D06092A864886F70D
01010405003016311430120603550403130B526F6F74204167656E6379301E170D3031303532383138
333133305A170D3339313233313233353935395A301A3118301606035504031430F41424320436F7270
6F726174696F6E305C300D06092A864886F70D0101010500034B003048024100ECBEFB348C1364B0A3
AE14FA9805F893AD180C7B2E57ADABBBE7EF94694A1E92BC5B4B59EF76FBDAC8D04D3DF2140B761655
0FE2D5AE5F15E03CBB54932F5CBB0203010001A34B304930470603551D010440303E801012E4092D06
1D1D4F008D6121DC166463A118301631143012060355040313B526F6F74204167656E637982100637
6C00AA00648A11CFB8D4AA5C35F4300D06092A864886F70D010104050004341001D1B5F6FBB0C4C0E85
A9BB5FDA5FEC1B8D9C229BB0FB8A7CBE3340A527A5B25EAA2A70205DD71571607291272D5A81981C73
028AB849FF273465FAEF2F4C7174 FullTrust
```

The parameters specify that the code group should be added at the top level (`1.`), and that the code
group membership condition is of the type `Publisher`, and the last parameter specifies the permission
set to grant (`FullTrust`). The command will ask for confirmation:

```
Microsoft (R) .NET Framework CasPol 1.0.3705.0
Copyright (C) Microsoft Corporation 1998-2001. All rights reserved.

The operation you are performing will alter security policy.
Are you sure you want to perform this operation? (yes/no)
y
Added union code group with "-pub" membership condition to the Machine level.
Success
```

Our machine is now configured to trust fully all assemblies that have been signed with the certificate
from ABC Corporation. To confirm that, we can run a `caspol.exe -lg` command, which lists the new
code access group (1.7):

```
Security is ON
Execution checking is ON
Policy change prompt is ON

Level = Machine

Code Groups:

1.  All code: Nothing
    1.1.   Zone - MyComputer: FullTrust
        1.1.1.   StrongName -
002400000480000009400000006020000002400005253413100040000010001007D1FA57C4AED9F0A3
2E84AA0FAEFD0DE9E8FD6AEC8F87FB03766C834C99921EB23BE79AD9D5DCC1DD9AD236132102900B72
3CF980957FC4E177108FC607774F29E8320E92EA05ECE4E821C0A5EFE8F1645C4C0C93C1AB99285D62
2CAA652C1DFAD63D745D6F2DE5F17E5EAF0FC4963D261C8A12436518206DC093344D5AD293:
FullTrust
        1.1.2.   StrongName - 0000000000000000004000000000000000: FullTrust
    1.2.   Zone - Intranet: LocalIntranet
        1.2.1.   All code: Same site Web.
        1.2.2.   All code: Same directory FileIO - Read, PathDiscovery
    1.3.   Zone - Internet: Internet
        1.3.1.   All code: Same site Web.
    1.4.   Zone - Untrusted: Nothing
    1.5.   Zone - Trusted: Internet
        1.5.1.   All code: Same site Web.
    1.6.   StrongName -
002400000480000009400000006020000002400005253413100040000010001000D51335D1B5B64BE976
AD8B08030F8E36A0DBBC3EEB5F8A18D0E30E8951DA059B440281997D760FFF61A6252A284061C1D714
EFEE5B329F410983A01DB324FA85BCE6C4E6384A2F3BC1FFA01E2586816B23888CFADD38D5AA5DF041
ACE2F81D9E8B591556852E83C473017A1785203B12F56B6D9DC23A8C9F691A0BC525D7B7EA:
FullTrust
    1.7.   Publisher -
3048024100E85C3867F321729F1097C86F6B6696ED9DA7D6C6038A6A64354D185890841E3C5D5BADDB
FA42BF3EE25A5552EACDE8F0395F60B7241E026D35B9EE25655F6F230203010001: FullTrust
Success
```

As another check, let's ask `caspol.exe` to tell us what code groups our assembly matches:

```
>caspol.exe -resolvegroup securityapp11.exe

Level = Enterprise

Code Groups:

1.  All code: FullTrust


Level = Machine

Code Groups:
```

```
1.  All code: Nothing
    1.1.  Zone - MyComputer: FullTrust
    1.2.  Publisher -
3048024100E85C3867F321729F1097C86F6B6696ED9DA7D6C6038A6A64354D185890841E3C5D5BADDB
FA42BF3EE25A5552EACDE8F0395F60B7241E026D35B9EE25655F6F230203010001: FullTrust


Level = User

Code Groups:

1.  All code: FullTrust

Success
```

In the center of the results we can see that the assembly has been successfully matched to our new code group and granted the `FullTrust` permission set.

Managing Zones

Earlier we talked about the zones that Windows provides and that we manage using Internet Explorer's security tools. The four zones we manage in this way are:

- ❏   `Internet` – all web sites you haven't placed in other zones

- ❏   `Intranet` – all web sites that are on your organization's intranet

- ❏   `Trusted Sites` – web sites that you trust not to damage your data

- ❏   `Restricted Sites` – web sites that could potentially damage your computer

These settings are managed from within Internet Explorer because they apply to sites visited using the browser that access .NET code (whether downloaded, or in page controls). If you are using a non-Microsoft browser, it will most likely not support .NET code, and so there will be no options to manage the associated zones.

Any user on a machine can alter the zone settings; however, the security settings for the zones that they specify only apply to their account. That is, it is not possible for one user to alter another user's zone settings. That said, there is a risk here as a user might alter the zone settings without understanding what they are doing and inadvertently open their machine up to attack.

To alter the settings associated with each zone, open Internet Explorer and open the Internet Options dialogue box from the Tools menu. In the Options box, move to the Security tab:

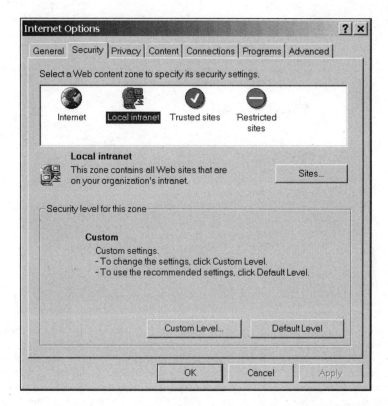

At the top you can see the four zones, and having selected one of the zones by clicking on its icon, you can use the Sites... button to specify sites that you want included in that zone. For example, if you want to configure the Local intranet zone, you will use this dialogue box:

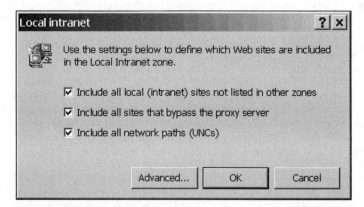

The options here give us enough scope to accurately define what constitutes the intranet in our organization. In addition, the Advanced... button gives us access to a dialogue box where we can specify URI's for particular sites we want included in the Local intranet zone:

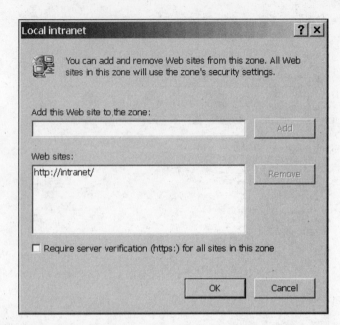

Note the option at the bottom of this dialogue box, which is provided for each of the zones except the Internet zone. It allows you to specify that you only trust sites in this zone when they are accessed over secure HTTP using Secure Sockets Layer (SSL) encryption. If you trust a site that is accessed over an unencrypted connection, you are potentially risking an attack as your traffic may be intercepted. If you want to verify that a site is held within a specific zone, visit the site and look at the bottom right hand corner of the Internet Explorer window, which will display the name of the zone for the web address you are currently viewing.

As well as being able to specify the scope of the zone by detailing sites you trust or do not trust, you can also specify what actions are permitted within each zone using the security-level settings. These specify things like whether a prompt should be given for ActiveX controls, and whether cookies are accepted.

Summary

In this chapter, we've covered how assemblies are matched to code groups, and how those code groups are assigned permissions by the security policy at the user, enterprise, and machine level, and we've seen how we can use tools to manage this policy. We've also seen how, for an assembly to execute, it must have the relevant permissions at the three policy levels, as well as the correct role-based permissions and the relevant Windows account permissions. We've also looked at the options available to us in distributing code using strong names and digital certificates.

Clearly, there are more security checks in place with .NET than we have seen before on Windows, and much of the security comes "for free" as we do not need to do much to make use of it at the basic level. However, when we do want to extend it we are provided with the classes and frameworks to do that.

Security is an ongoing challenge, and although Microsoft has not solved all the problems, the managed security environment provided by .NET is a significant step forwards as it provides a framework within which code is challenged before it executes. It's no coincidence that these developments are occurring at a time when Microsoft is moving towards distributing its products over the web, as a secure distribution method for that is essential.

Principles of Object-Oriented Programming

In general, when learning a new language, a fair part of your effort is spent in learning the syntax of that language: how to declare variables, how to control the flow of execution, and so on. However, in order to write quality code in a language, you also need to understand the principles and methodologies behind the language. C# is a fully object-oriented language, so in order to create well-designed C# code you need to get to grips with its object-oriented features, and that means learning about **Object-Oriented Programming** (**OOP**).

In OOP, we aim to write easily maintainable and reusable pieces of code that can collectively perform very complex tasks. However, the whole structure of an object-oriented program is very different from the structure of an equivalent program written in procedural language. In this appendix, we are going to introduce the principles of object-oriented programming. Although we will have to learn some C# syntax (since we'll be presenting the examples in C#) the emphasis is on learning those principles which apply to OOP in general, no matter which language you are using.

OOP is an extremely powerful methodology. Once you've become used to writing your code using it, you will probably wonder how you ever got by without it. You'll find that it gives your code an intuitive, "natural" structure that is not possible with procedural languages, and is not really possible even in VB 6, which does implement a few object-oriented features.

We'll start by looking in some detail at the nature of an object before moving on to examine the concept of **inheritance**. Inheritance allows the code for classes to be reused in a very convenient manner, and is at the heart of object-oriented programming. We'll look both at how to code up inheritance in C# and at how you would normally use inheritance in your programs in more conceptual terms.

A Note for VB 6 Programmers

If you are a skilled Visual Basic 6 developer, but do not have C++ or Java experience, then you will find many of the concepts in this chapter completely new. Visual Basic does allow you to code something that is often referred to as an object: the VB class module. Some texts even refer to this as involving object-oriented programming, although this actually bears little resemblance to the original concepts of OOP. It is more accurate to say that VB implements a few of the more basic features of OOP. A VB class module is essentially a COM component, but wrapped up in a way that hides much of what it does. In particular it does not support inheritance of its methods in the same way that inheritance is used in C# and conventional OOP.

When you start reading this Appendix you'll probably think at first that we're just describing what you're used to in the class modules. However, because of its support for a different kind of inheritance (implementation inheritance), C# classes are much more powerful than VB class modules, and are often used very differently. If you want to write good C# .NET applications and assemblies, you will need to read this chapter. Objects and inheritance are not just new language features. In a well-designed object-oriented program, the whole architecture of the program is often arranged around inheritance, so you'll find once you're comfortable with the concept, you'll be structuring your programs in a completely different way to how you would have done in VB, and your programs will be easier for others to maintain as a result. If, however, you do already feel very comfortable with manipulating objects in VB, but have not yet used inheritance, you may want to skip straight to the section on inheritance.

> *Note that whenever we refer to "VB" or "Visual Basic" in this Appendix, we are more specifically referring to VB 6.*

What is an Object?

In everyday life, an object is anything that is identifiably a single material item. It could be a car, a house, a book, a document, or a pay check. For our purposes, we're going to extend that a bit and think of an object as anything whatsoever that is a single item that you might want to represent in a program. We'll therefore also include living "objects", such as a person, an employee, or a customer, as well as more abstract "objects", such as a company, a database, or a country.

The reason for thinking about objects in this way is partly so that we'll be able to write code that models the real world, to the extent that it contains objects, and partly to provide a way of breaking up a large program into smaller, more manageable, units. The idea really comes from the concept of a **black box** that you may have encountered in school science.

The idea of a black box is that there are a lot of objects in life that you are able to use but of which you don't understand the mechanism. Look at your car radio, for example. Most people don't know exactly how a car radio works, but know what it does and are still able to use it. Not only that, but you can take out your radio, plug in a different one and it'll do basically the same thing, even though the internal workings of it might be completely different. Black boxes formalize this idea that there's a difference between what something does, which you usually know, and how it works (which you usually don't need to know) and that two objects can do the same thing, but work differently inside.

Replacing one object with another does have some subtle effects. Car radios might have different knobs and switches, but the basic function is unchanged. Another important point is that the basic user interface is unchanged; I plug one car stereo into the slot in much the same way as I would another.

If you understand all that, then you basically understand object-oriented programming, because OOP is about applying these same concepts to computer programming. If, in other areas of our lives, we use things that have a well-designed interface, whose function we know, and we know how to use them, but don't care how they work, why not do the same thing in your programs? In other words, break each program into lots of units, each designed to perform a clearly specified role within the program. That's basically what an object is.

If you start thinking about your programs this way, you gain quite a few advantages. You'll find it becomes easier to design the programs. The architecture of the programs becomes more intuitive and easier to understand, because it more closely reflects whatever it is that the program is abstracting from real life. It becomes easier for multiple developers to work together, since they can work on different objects in the code; they only need to know what each other's objects do, and how to interface with them. They don't have to worry about the details of how each other's code works.

Objects in Programming

We've now established what an object is in general terms and seen a couple of examples from everyday life. We now need to see more specifically how to apply the concepts to programming.

If you've programmed on Windows before then you've almost certainly already been using objects extensively in your programs. For example, think about the various controls that you can place in windows – textboxes, listboxes, buttons, and so on. Microsoft has written these controls for you, so that you don't need to know, for example, how a textbox works internally. You just know that it does certain things. For example, you can set its `Text` property and the new text will appear on the screen, or you can set its `Width` property, and the textbox will immediately resize itself for you.

In programming, we need to distinguish between a **class** and an **object**. A class is the generic definition of what an object is – the template. For example, a class could be "car radio" – the abstract idea of a car radio. The class specifies what properties an object should have to be a car radio.

Class Members

So far, we've emphasized that there are two sides to an object – what it does, which is usually publicly known, and how it works, which is usually hidden. In programming, the "what it does" is normally represented in the first instance by **methods**, which are blocks of functionality that you can use. A method is just C# parlance for a function. The "how it works" is represented both by methods, and by any data (variables) that the object stores. In Java and C++, this data is described as member variables, while in VB this data would be represented by any module-level variables in the class module. In C# the terminology is **fields**. In general, a class is defined by its fields and methods.

We'll also use the term **member** by itself to denote anything that is part of a class, be it a field, method, or any of the other items just mentioned that can be defined within a class.

Defining a Class

The easiest way to understand how to code up a class is by looking at an example. Therefore, over the next few sections of this Appendix, we're going to develop a simple class called `Authenticator`. We'll assume we're in the process of writing a large application, which at some point requires users to log in, supplying a password. `Authenticator` is the name of the class that will handle this aspect of the program. We won't worry about the rest of the application – we'll just concentrate on writing this class, but we will also write a small piece of test harness code to check that `Authenticator` works as intended.

`Authenticator` allows us to do two things: set a new password, and check whether a password is valid. The C# code we need to define the class looks like this:

```csharp
public class Authenticator
{
    private string password = "";

    public bool IsPasswordCorrect(string tryPassword)
    {
        return (tryPassword == password) ? true : false;
    }

    public bool ChangePassword(string oldPassword, string newPassword)
    {
        if (oldPassword == password)
        {
            password = newPassword;
            return true;
        }
        else
            return false;
    }
}
```

The keyword `class` in C# indicates that we are going to define a new class (type of object). The word immediately following `class` is the name we're going to use for this class. Then the actual definition of the object follows in braces – the definition consisting of variables (fields) and methods – in our case one field, `password`, and two methods, `IsPasswordCorrect()` and `ChangePassword()`.

Access Modifiers

The only field in `Authenticator`, `password`, stores the current password (initially an empty string when an `Authenticator` object is created), and is marked by the keyword `private`. This means that it is not visible outside the class, only to code that is part of the `Authenticator` class itself. Marking a field or method as `private` effectively ensures that that field or method will be part of the internal working of the class, as opposed to the external interface. The advantage of this is that if you decide to change the internal working (perhaps you later decide not to store `password` as a string but to use some other more specialized data type), you can just make the change, and you know it won't break or affect any other code outside the `Authenticator` class definition. This is because any other code couldn't possibly have been accessing this field anyway.

Any code that uses the Authenticator class can only access the methods that have been marked with the keyword public – in this case the IsPasswordCorrect() and ChangePassword() methods. Both of these methods have been implemented in such a way that nothing will be done (other than returning true or false) unless the calling code supplies the current correct password, as you'd expect for software that implements security. The implementations of these functions both access the password field, but that's fine because this code forms part of the Authenticator class itself. Notice that these public functions simultaneously give us the interface to the external world (in other words, any other code that uses the Authenticator class), and define what the Authenticator class does, as viewed by the rest of the world.

> *private and public are not the only access modifiers available to define what code is allowed to know about the existence of a member. Later in this Appendix we'll encounter protected, which makes the member available to this class and certain related classes. C# also allows members to be declared as internal and protected internal, which restrict access to other code within the same assembly.*

Instantiating and Using Objects

Now we've defined the Authenticator class, how do we use it in our code? The easiest way to understand that is to think of the class as a new type of variable. You're used to the predefined variable types – in C# these are things like int, float, double, and so on. Well, by defining the Authenticator class, we've effectively told the compiler that there's a new type of variable called an Authenticator. The class definition contains everything the compiler needs to know to be able to process this variable type. Therefore, just as the compiler knows that a double contains a floating-point number stored in a certain format, and you can do things with doubles such as adding them together, we've told the compiler that a variable of type Authenticator contains a string and allows you to call the IsPasswordCorrect() and ChangePassword() methods.

> *Although we've described a class as a new type of variable, the more common terminology is **data type**, or simply **type**.*

Creating a user-defined variable (an object) is known as **instantiation**, because we create an **instance** of the object. An instance is simply any particular occurrence of the object. So, if our Authenticator object is simply another kind of variable, we should be able to use it just like any other variable. We can, and in the next example we demonstrate this.

Create the MainEntryPoint class, as shown below, and place it in the Wrox.ProCSharp.OOProg namespace along with the Authenticator class we created earlier:

```
using System;

namespace Wrox.ProCSharp.OOProg
{
    class MainEntryPoint
    {
        static void Main()
        {
            Authenticator simon = new Authenticator();
```

```
        bool done;
        done = simon.ChangePassword("", "MyNewPassword");
        if (done == true)
            Console.WriteLine("Password for Simon changed");
        else
            Console.WriteLine("Failed to change password for Simon");

        done = simon.ChangePassword("", "AnotherPassword");
        if (done == true)
            Console.WriteLine("Password for Simon changed");
        else
            Console.WriteLine("Failed to change password for Simon");

        if (simon.IsPasswordCorrect("WhatPassword"))
            Console.WriteLine("Verified Simon\'s password");
        else
            Console.WriteLine("Failed to verify Simon\'s password");
    }
}

public class Authenticator
{
    // implementation as shown earlier
}
}
```

The `MainEntryPoint` class is a full-blown class like `Authenticator` – it can have its own members (that is, its own fields, methods and so on). However, we've chosen to use this class solely as a container for the program entry point – the `Main()` method. Doing it this way means that the `Authenticator` class can sit as a class in its own right, able to be used in other programs if we wish (either by cutting and pasting the code or by compiling it separately into an assembly). `MainEntryPoint` only really exists as a class because of the syntactical requirement of C# that even the program's main entry point has to be defined within a class, rather than sitting as an independent function.

Since all the action is happening in the `Main()` method, let's take a closer look at it. The first line of interest is:

```
Authenticator simon = new Authenticator();
```

Here we are declaring and instantiating a new `Authenticator` object instance. Don't worry too much about the `= new Authenticator()` bit. It's part of C# syntax, and is there because in C#, classes are always accessed by reference. We could actually use the following line if we just wanted to declare a new `Authenticator` object called `simon`:

```
Authenticator simon;
```

This can hold a reference to an `Authenticator` object, without actually creating any object (in much the same way that the line `Dim obj As Object` in VB doesn't actually create any object). The `new` operator in C# is what actually instantiates an `Authenticator` object.

Calling class methods is done using the period symbol (.) appended to the name of the variable:

```
done = simon.ChangePassword("", "MyNewPassword");
```

Here we have called the `ChangePassword()` method on the `simon` instance, and fed the return value into the `done` Boolean variable. We can retrieve class fields in a similar way. Note, however, that we could not do this:

```
string SimonsPassword = simon.password;
```

This code will actually cause a compilation error, because the `password` field was explicitly marked as `private`, so other code outside the `Authenticator` class cannot explicitly access it. If we changed the `password` field to be `public`, then the line above would compile, and would feed the value of `password` into the string variable.

You should note that if you are accessing member methods or fields from inside the same class, you can simply give the name of the member directly.

Now that you understand how to instantiate objects, call class methods, and retrieve public fields, the logic in the `Main()` method should be pretty clear. If we save this code as `Authenticator.cs`, then compile and run it, this is what we see:

```
Authenticator
Password for Simon changed
Failed to change password for Simon
Failed to verify Simon's password
```

There are a couple of points to note from the code. Firstly, you'll notice that so far we're not actually doing anything new compared to – say – how you'd code up a VB class module, or to the basic C# syntax that we covered in Chapter 2. The reason for going over this code here was to make sure we are clear about the concepts behind classes.

Second, the above example uses the `Authenticator` class directly in other code within the same source file. You'll often want to write classes that are used by other projects that you or others work on. In order to do this, you write the class in exactly the same way, but compile the code for the class into a library. How to do this is covered in Chapter 8.

Using Static Members

You may have noticed in our example that the `Main()` method was declared as `static`. In this section we are going to discuss what effect this `static` keyword has.

Creating Static Fields

It's important to understand that each instance of a class (each object) has its own set of all the fields you've defined in the class by default. For example, if you write:

```
Authenticator julian = new Authenticator();
Authenticator karli = new Authenticator();
karli.ChangePassword("OldKarliPassword", "NewKarliPassword")
julian.ChangePassword("OldJulianPassword", "NewJulianPassword")
```

The instances `karli` and `julian` each contain their own string called `password`. Changing the password in `karli` has no effect on the password in `julian`, and vice versa (unless the two references happen to be pointing to the same address in memory, which is something we'll come to later). The situation is a bit like this:

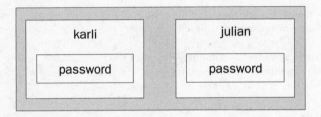

There are some cases in which this might not be the behavior you want. For example, suppose in our `Authenticator` class we wished to define a minimum length for all `passwords` (and therefore for all of the `password` fields in all instances). We do not want each password to have its own minimum length. Therefore, we really want the minimum length to be stored only once in memory, no matter how many instances of `Authenticator` we create.

To indicate that a field should only be stored once, no matter how many instances of the class we create, we place the keyword `static` in front of the field declaration in our code:

```
public class Authenticator
{
    private static uint minPasswordLength = 6;
    private string password = "";
```

Storing a copy of `minPasswordLength` with each `Authenticator` instance would not only have wasted memory, but also caused problems if we wanted to be able to change its value! By declaring the field as `static`, we ensure that it will only be stored once, and this field is shared among all instances of the class. Note that in this code snippet we also set an initial value. Fields declared with the `static` keyword are referred to as **static fields** or **static data**, while fields that are not declared as static are referred to as **instance fields** or **instance data**. Another way of looking at it is that an instance field belongs to an object, while a static field belongs to the class.

> **VB developers shouldn't confuse this with static variables in VB, which are variables whose values remain between invocations of a method.**

If a field has been declared as `static`, then it exists when your program is running from the moment that the particular module or assembly containing the definition of the class is loaded. This will be as soon as your code tries to use something from that assembly, so you can always guarantee a static variable is there when you want to refer to it. This is independent of whether you actually create any instances of that class. By contrast, instance fields only exist when there are variables of that class currently in scope – one set of instance fields for each variable.

> *In some ways static fields perform the same functions as global variables performed for older languages such as C and FORTRAN.*

You should note that the `static` keyword is independent of the accessibility of the member to which it applies. A class member can be `public static` or `private static`.

Creating Static Methods

As we saw in the example earlier, by default a method such as `ChangePassword()` is called against a particular instance, as indicated by the name of the variable in front of the `"."` operator. That method then implicitly has access to all the members (fields, methods, and so on) of that particular instance.

However, just as with fields, it is possible to declare methods as `static`, provided that they do not attempt to access any instance data or other instance methods. For example, we might wish to provide a method to allow users to view the minimum password length:

```
public class Authenticator
{
    private static uint minPasswordLength = 6;
    public static uint GetMinPasswordLength()
    {
        return minPasswordLength;
    }
    ...
```

The code for `Authenticator` with this modification is available on the Wrox Press web site as the `Authenticator2` sample.

In our earlier `Authenticator` example, the `Main()` method of the `MainEntryPoint` class was declared as `static`. This allows it to be invoked as the entry point to the program, despite the fact that no instance of the `MainEntryPoint` class was ever created.

Accessing Static Members

The fact that static methods and fields are associated with a class rather than an object is reflected in how you access them. Instead of specifying the name of a variable before the `"."` operator, you specify the name of the class, like this:

```
Console.WriteLine(Authenticator.GetMinPasswordLength());
```

Also notice that in the above code, we access the `Console.WriteLine()` method by specifying the name of the class, `Console`. That is because `WriteLine()` is a static method too – we don't need to instantiate a `Console` object to use `WriteLine()`.

How Instance and Static Methods are Implemented in Memory

We said earlier that each object stores its own copy of that class's instance fields. This is, however, not the case for methods. If each object had its own copy of the code for a method it would be incredibly wasteful of memory, since the code for the methods remains the same across all object instances. Therefore, instance methods, just like static methods, are stored only once, and associated with the class as a whole. Later on, we'll learn about other types of class member (constructors, properties, and so on) that contain code rather than data, and the same applies to these.

The full picture looks something like this:

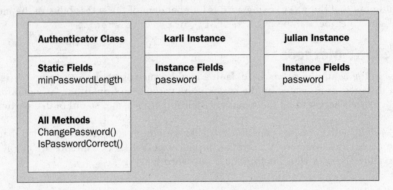

If instance methods are only stored once, how is a method able to access the correct copy of each field? In other words, when you write:

```
karli.ChangePassword("OldKarliPassword", "NewKarliPassword")
julian.ChangePassword("OldJulianPassword", "NewJulianPassword")
```

How is the compiler able to generate code that accesses Karli's password with the first method call and Julian's with the second? The answer is that instance methods actually take an extra implicit parameter, which is a reference to where in memory the relevant class instance is stored. You can almost think of it as that the above code is the user-friendly version that you have to write, because it's how C# syntax works, but what's actually happening in your compiled code is:

```
ChangePassword(karli, "OldKarliPassword", "NewKarliPassword")
ChangePassword(julian "OldJulianPassword", "NewJulianPassword")
```

Declaring a method as static makes calling it slightly more efficient, because it will not be passed this extra parameter. On the other hand, if a method is declared as static, but attempts to access any instance data, the compiler will raise an error for the obvious reason that you can't access instance data unless you have the address of a class instance!

This means that in our Authenticator sample we could not declare either ChangePassword() or IsPasswordCorrect() as static, because both of these methods access the password field, which is not static.

Interestingly, although the hidden parameter that comes with instance methods is never declared explicitly, you do actually have access to it in your code. You can get to it using the keyword `this`. As another example, we could rewrite the code for the `ChangePassword()` method as follows:

```
public bool ChangePassword(string oldPassword, string newPassword)
{
    if (oldPassword == this.password)
    {
        this.password = newPassword;
        return true;
    }
    else
        return false;
}
```

Generally, you wouldn't write your code like this unless you need to distinguish variable names – all we've achieved here is to make the method longer and slightly harder to read.

A Note About Reference Types

Before we leave the discussion of classes, we ought to point out one potential gotcha that can occur in C# because C# regards all classes as reference types. This can have some unexpected effects when it comes to comparing instances of classes for equality, and setting instances of classes equal to each other. For example, look at this:

```
Authenticator User1;
Authenticator User2 = new Authenticator();
Authenticator User3 = new Authenticator();
User1 = User2;
User2.ChangePassword ("", "Tardis")  // This sets password for User1 as well!
User3.ChangePassword ("", "Tardis")
if (User2 == User3)
{
    // contents of this if block will NOT be executed even though
    // objects referred to by User2 and User3 are contain identical values,
    // because the variables refer to different objects
}
if (User2 == User1)
{
    // any code here will be executed because User1 and User2 refer
    // to the same memory
}
```

In this code we declare three variables of type `Authenticator`: `User1`, `User2`, and `User3`. However, we only actually instantiate two objects of the `Authenticator` class, because we only use the `new` operator twice. Then we set the variable `User1` equal to `User2`. Unlike with a value type, this does *not* copy any of the contents of `User2`. Rather, it means that `User1` is set to refer to the same memory as `User2` is referring to. What that means is that any changes we make to `User2` also affect `User1`, because they are not separate objects; both variables refer to the same data. We can also say that they **point to** the same data, and the actual data referred to is sometimes described as the **referent**. So when we set the password of `User2` to `Tardis`, we are implicitly also setting the password of `User1` to `Tardis`. This is very different from how value types would behave.

The situation gets even less intuitive when we try to compare User2 and User3 in the next statement:

```
if (User2 == User3)
```

You might expect that this condition would return true, since User2 and User3 have both been set to the same password, so both instances contain identical data. The comparison operator for reference types, however, doesn't compare the contents of the data by default – it simply tests to see whether the two references are referring to the same address in memory. Because they are not, this test will return false, which means anything inside this if block will not be executed. By contrast, comparing User2 with User1 will return true because these variables do point to the same address in memory.

Note that this behavior does not apply to strings, because the == operator has been overloaded for strings. Comparing two strings with "==" will always compare string content (any other behavior for strings would be extremely confusing!).

Overloading Methods

To **overload** a method is to create several methods each with the same name, but each with a different signature. The reason why you might want to use overloading is best seen with an example. Consider how in C# we write data to the command line, using the Console.WriteLine() method. For example, if we want to display the value of an integer, we can write this:

```
int x = 10;
Console.WriteLine(x);
```

While to display a string we can write:

```
string message = "Hello";
Console.WriteLine(message);
```

Even though we are passing different data types to the same method, both of these examples compile. This is because there are actually lots of Console.WriteLine() methods, but each has a different signature – one of them takes an int as a parameter, while another one takes a string, and so on. There is even a two parameter overload of the method that allows for formatted output, and lets you write code like this:

```
string Message = "Hello";
Console.WriteLine("The message is {0}", Message);
```

Obviously, Microsoft provides all of these `Console.WriteLine()` methods because it realizes that there are many different data types that you might want to display the value of.

Method overloading is very useful, but there are some pitfalls to be aware of when using it. Suppose we write:

```
short y = 10;
Console.WriteLine(y);
```

A quick look at the documentation will reveal that no overload of `WriteLine()` takes a short. So what will the compiler do? Well in principle, it could generate code that converts the short to an int, and call the int version of `Console.WriteLine()`. Or it could convert the short to a long and call `Console.WriteLine(long)`. Or it could even convert the short to a string.

In this situation, each language will have a set of rules for what conversion will be the one that is actually performed (for C#, the conversion to an int is the preferred one). However you can see the potential for confusion. For this reason, if you define method overloads, you need to take care to do so in a way that won't cause any unpredictable results. This issue is discussed in more detail for C# in Chapter 6.

When to Use Overloading

Generally, you should consider overloading a method when you need a number of methods that take different parameters, but conceptually do the same thing, as with `Console.WriteLine()` above. The main situations in which you will normally use overloading are as follows.

Optional Parameters

One common use of method overloads is to allow certain parameters to a method to be optional and to have default values if the client code chooses not to specify their values explicitly. For example, consider this code:

```
public void DoSomething(int x, int y)
{
    // do whatever
}

public void DoSomething(int x)
{
    DoSomething(x, 10);
}
```

These overloads allow client code to call `DoSomething()`, supplying one required parameter and one optional parameter. If the optional parameter isn't supplied, we effectively assume the second int is 10. Most modern compilers will also inline method calls in this situation so there is no performance loss. This is certainly true of the .NET JIT compiler.

Some languages, including VB and C++, allow default parameters to be specified explicitly in function declarations, with a syntax that looks like `public void DoSomething(int X, int Y=10)`*. C# does not allow this, so in C# you need to simulate default parameters by providing multiple overloads of methods as shown in the above example.*

Different Input Types

We have already seen an example (`Console.WriteLine()`) of this very common reason for defining overloads.

Different Output Types

This situation is far less common, but you may occasionally have a method that calculates or obtains some quantity, and depending on the circumstances, you might wish this to be returned in more than one different way. For example, in an airline company, you might have a class that represents aircraft timetables, and you might wish to define a method that tells you where an aircraft should be at a particular time. Depending on the situation, you might want the method to return either a string description of the position ("over Atlantic Ocean en route to London") or the latitude and longitude of the position.

We cannot distinguish overloads using the return type of a method. However, you can do so using out parameters. So you could define these:

```
void GetAircraftLocation(DateTime Time, out string Location)
{
...
}

void GetAircraftLocation(DateTime Time, out float Latitude, out float Longitude)
{
...
}
```

Note, however, that in most cases, using overloads to obtain different out parameters does not lead to an architecturally neat design. In the above example, a better design would perhaps involve defining a `Location` struct that contains the location string as well as the latitude and longitude, and returning this from the method call, hence avoiding the need for overloads.

Properties

Earlier we said that, in general, a class is defined by its fields and methods. However, there are some other types of class members – constructors, indexers, properties, delegates, and events. For the most part these other items are used only in more advanced situations, and are not essential to understanding the principles of object-oriented design. For that reason, we are not going to discuss most of them in this appendix. They are introduced as required in Chapters 5-7. Properties are in extremely common use, however, and can significantly simplify the external user interface exposed by classes. For this reason, we'll discuss them here.

VB programmers will find that C# properties correspond almost exactly to properties in VB class modules and are used in just the same way.

Properties exist for the situation in which you wish to make a method call look like a field. We can see what a property is by looking again at the `minPasswordLength` field in our `Authenticator` class. Let's extend the class so that users can read and modify this field without having to use a `GetMinPasswordLength()` method like the one we introduced earlier. We can do this using properties.

A property is a method or pair of methods that are exposed to the outside world as if they are fields. To create a property for the minimum password length we modify the code for the `Authenticator` class as follows:

```
public static uint MinPasswordLength
{
    get
    {
        return minPasswordLength;
    }
    set
    {
        minPasswordLength = value;
    }
}
```

As we can see from this, we define a property in much the same way as a field, except that after the name of the property, we have a code block enclosed by curly braces. In the code block there may be two methods called `get` and `set`. These are known as the **get accessor** and the **set accessor**. Note that although no parameter is explicitly mentioned in the definition of the `set` accessor, there is an implicit parameter passed in, and referred to by the name `value`. Also, the `get` accessor always returns the same data type as the property was declared as (in this case a `uint`).

Now, to retrieve the value of `minPasswordLength` using this property, we use this syntax:

```
uint i = Authenticator.MinPasswordLength;
```

What will actually happen here is that `MinPasswordLength` property's `get` accessor is called. In this case, this method is implemented to simply return the value of the `minPasswordLength` field.

To set the `MinPasswordLength` field using the property, we would use the following code:

```
Authenticator.MinPasswordLength = 7;
```

This code will cause the `MinPasswordLength`'s `set` accessor to be called, which is implemented to assign the required value (seven here) to the `minPasswordLength` field. We said earlier that the `set` accessor has an implicit parameter, called `value`.

Note that in this particular example, the property in question happens to be static. In general that is not necessary. Just as for methods, you will normally declare properties as static only if they only refer to static data.

Data Encapsulation

You may wonder what the point of all the above code is. Wouldn't it have been simpler to simply make the minPasswordLength field public, so that we could access it directly and not have to bother about any properties? The answer is that fields represent the internal data of an object, so they are anintegral part of the functionality of an object. Now, in object-oriented programming, we aim to make it so that users of objects only need to know what an object does, not how it does it. So making fields directly accessible to users defeats the ideology behind object-oriented programming.

Ideology is all very well, but there must be practical reasons behind it. One reason is this: if we make fields directly visible to external users, we lose control over what they do to the fields. They might modify the fields in such a way as to break the intended functionality of the object (give the fields inappropriate values, say). However, if we use properties to control access to a field, this is not a problem because we can add functionality to the property that checks for inappropriate values. Related to this, we can also provide read-only properties by omitting the set accessor completely. The principle of hiding fields from client code in this way is known as **data encapsulation**.

You should only use properties to do something that appears only to set or retrieve a value – otherwise you should use methods. That means that the set accessor must only take one parameter and return a void, while the get accessor cannot take any parameters. For example, it would not be possible to rewrite the IsPasswordValid() method in the Authenticator class as a property. The parameter types and return value for this method are not of the correct type.

Introducing Inheritance

One characteristic of objects in everyday life is that they tend to come in families of related things that share aspects of their design. My sofa is just like my armchairs, except that it can seat more than one person. A CD does the same sort of thing as a cassette tape, but with extra direct-access facilities.

Another example focuses upon cars. My car at the moment is a 13-year-old Ford Escort. Back in the 1980s, Ford had three big-selling cars out that all had a very similar design – the Escort, the Orion, and the Fiesta. The reason I'm thinking about these cars in particular is that they shared a lot more than just being Ford cars. They had different-shaped body shells, and the Fiesta was smaller, but internally their engines and other components were built in much the same way, often using the same components.

This is an example of **implementation inheritance**, and the equivalent in object-oriented programming would be some classes (EscortCar, OrionCar, and FiestaCar, perhaps?), which not only expose methods with the same names, but actually the same methods, in the sense that when you call the methods you are running the same code.

Let's now extend this example. Say that I swapped my Escort for another Escort that has a diesel engine. Both cars have exactly the same body shell (the user interface is the same) but under the hood, the engines are different. That's an example of **interface inheritance**, and the equivalent in computer programming would be two classes, EscortCar and EscortDieselCar, which happen to expose methods that have the same names, purposes, and signatures, but different implementations.

Developers experienced in Java or in C++ and COM will recognize that implementation inheritance is the kind of inheritance that is supported by Java/C++ and other traditional object-oriented languages, while the more restricted interface inheritance was the only form of inheritance that was supported by COM and COM objects. VB supports only interface inheritance, through the Implements *keyword. The great thing about C# is it supports both types of inheritance.*

As far as C# programming is concerned, we're looking at the issue of how to define a new class, while reusing features from an existing class. The benefits are twofold – first, inheritance provides a convenient way to reuse existing, fully tested code in different contexts, thereby saving a lot of coding time, and second, inheritance can provide even more structure to your programs by giving a finer degree of granularity to your classes.

At this point we're going to move on to a new coding example, based on a cell phone company, which will demonstrate how implementation inheritance works in a C# program. Inheritance of classes in C# is always implementation inheritance. We'll leave interface inheritance for a while.

Using Inheritance in C#

The example we'll use to demonstrate inheritance is going to be of a fictitious cell phone company, which we'll call Mortimer Phones. We're going to develop a class that represents a customer account and is responsible for calculating that customer's phone bill. It's going to develop into a much longer, more complex sample than the Authenticator class, and as it develops we'll quickly find that one simple class is not adequate; rather, we are going to need a number of related classes, and in the next section inheritance will magically enter as the solution.

We're going to write a class that works out the monthly bill for each customer of Mortimer Phones. The class is called Customer, and each instance of this class represents one customer's account. In terms of public interface, the class will contain two properties:

❑   Name representing the customer's name (read-write)

❑   Balance, representing the amount owed (read-only)

There will also be two methods:

❑   RecordPayment(), which is called to indicate that the customer has paid a certain amount of their bill.

❑   RecordCall(), which is called when the customer has made a phone call. It works out the cost of the call and adds it to that customer's balance.

The RecordCall() method is potentially quite a complex function, since in the real world it would involve figuring out what the type of call was from the number called, then applying the appropriate tariff, and keeping a history of the calls. To keep things simple here, we'll assume there are just two types of calls: calls to landlines, and calls to other cell phones, and that each of these are charged at a flat rate of 2 cents a minute for landlines and 30 cents a minute for other cell phones. Our RecordCall method will simply be passed the type of call as a parameter, and we won't worry about keeping a call history.

With this simplification, we can look at the code for the project. The project was as usual created as a console application, and the first thing in it is an enumeration for the types of call:

```
namespace Wrox.ProCSharp.OOProg
{
    using System;
    public enum TypeOfCall
    {
        CallToCellPhone, CallToLandline
    }
```

Now, let's look at the definition of the Customer class:

```
    public class Customer
    {
        private string name;
        private decimal balance;

        public string Name
        {
            get
            {
                return name;
            }
            set
            {
                name = value;
            }
        }

        public decimal Balance
        {
            get
            {
                return balance;
            }
        }

        public void RecordPayment(decimal amountPaid)
        {
            balance -= amountPaid;
        }

        public void RecordCall(TypeOfCall callType, uint nMinutes)
        {
            switch (callType)
            {
                case TypeOfCall.CallToLandline:
                    balance += (0.02M * nMinutes);
                    break;
                case TypeOfCall.CallToCellPhone:
                    balance += (0.30M * nMinutes);
                    break;
                default:
                    break;
            }
        }
    }
}
```

This code should be reasonably self-explanatory. Note that we've hard-code the call charges of 2 cents/minute (land line) and 30 cents/minute (pay-as-you-go charges for a cell phone) into the program. In real life, they'd more likely be read in from a relational database, or some file that allows the values to be changed easily.

Now let's add some code in the program's `Main()` method that displays the amounts of bills currently owing:

```
public class MainEntryPoint
{
    public static void Main()
    {
        Customer arabel = new Customer();
        arabel.Name = "Arabel Jones";
        Customer mrJones = new Customer();
        mrJones.Name = "Ben Jones";
        arabel.RecordCall(TypeOfCall.CallToLandline, 20);
        arabel.RecordCall(TypeOfCall.CallToCellPhone, 5);
        mrJones.RecordCall(TypeOfCall.CallToLandline, 10);
        Console.WriteLine("{0,-20} owes ${1:F2}", arabel.Name, arabel.Balance);
        Console.WriteLine("{0,-20} owes ${1:F2}", mrJones.Name, mrJones.Balance);
    }
}
```

Running this code gives the following results:

```
MortimerPhones
Arabel Jones          owes $1.90
Ben Jones             owes $0.20
```

Adding Inheritance

Currently, the Mortimer Phones example is heavily simplified. In particular, it only has one tariff for all customers, which is not remotely realistic. I'm registered under a tariff in which I pay a fixed rate each month, but there are loads of other schemes.

The way we're working at the moment, if we try to take all of the different tariffs into account, our `RecordCall()` method is going to end up containing various nested `switch` statements and looking something like this (assuming the `Tariff` field is an enumeration):

```
public void RecordCall(TypeOfCall callType, uint nMinutes)
{
    switch (tariff)
    case Tariff.Tariff1:
    {
        switch (callType)
        {
        case TypeOfCall.CallToLandline:
```

```
        // work out amount

    case TypeOfCall.CallToCellPhone:

        // work out amount
        // other cases
   // etc.


    }
    case Tariff.Tariff2:
    {
        switch (callType)
        {

// etc.


    }
```

That is not a satisfactory solution. Small `switch` statements are nice, but huge `switch` statements with large numbers of options – and in particular embedded `switch` statements – make for code that is difficult to follow. It also means that whenever a new tariff is introduced the code for the method will need to be changed. This could accidentally introduce new bugs into the parts of the code responsible for processing existing tariffs.

The problem is really to do with the way the code for the different tariffs is mixed up in a `switch` statement. If we could cleanly separate the code for the different tariffs the problem would be solved. This is one of the issues that inheritance addresses.

We want to separate out the code for different types of customers. We'll start by defining a new class, specifically represents customers on a new tariff, which we'll call the Nevermore60 tariff. Nevermore60 is designed for customers who use their cell phones a lot. Customers on this tariff pay a higher rate of 50 cents a minute for the first 60 minutes of calls to other cell phones, then a reduced rate of 20 cents a minute for all additional calls, so if they make a large enough number of calls they save money compared to the previous tariff.

We'll save actually implementing the new payment calculations for a little while longer, and we'll initially define `Nevermore60Customer` like this:

```
public class Nevermore60Customer : Customer
{

}
```

In other words, the class has no methods, no properties, nothing of its own. On the other hand, it's defined in a slightly different way from how we've defined any classes before. After the class name is a colon, followed by the name of our earlier class, `Customer`. This tells the compiler that `Nevermore60Customer` is **derived** from `Customer`. That means that every member in `Customer` also exists in `Nevermore60Customer`. Alternatively, to use the correct terminology, each member of `Customer` is **inherited** in `Nevermore60Customer`. Also, `Nevermore60Customer` is said to be a **derived class**, while `Customer` is said to be the **base class**. You'll also sometimes encounter derived classes referred to as subclasses, and base classes as superclasses or parent classes.

Since we've not yet put anything else in the `Nevermore60Customer` class, it is effectively an exact copy of the definition of the `Customer` class. We can create instances of and call methods against the `Nevermore60Customer` class, just as we could with `Customer`. To see this, we'll modify one of the customers, `Arabel`, to be a `Nevermore60Customer`:

```
public static void Main()
{
    Nevermore60Customer arabel = new Nevermore60Customer();
    ...
}
```

In this code, we've changed just one line, the declaration of `Arabel`, to make this customer a `Nevermore60Customer` instance. All the method calls remain the same, and this code will produce exactly the same results as our earlier code. If you want to try this out, it's the `MortimerPhones2` code sample.

By itself, having a copy of the definition of the `Customer` class might not look very useful. The power of this comes from the fact we can now make some modifications or additions to `Nevermore60Customer`. We can effectively say to the compiler, "`Nevermore60Customer` is almost the same as `Customer`, but with these differences." In particular, we're going to modify the way that `Nevermore60Customer` works out the charge for each phone call according to the new tariff.

The differences we can specify in principle are:

❑   We can add new members (of any type: fields, methods, properties, and so on) to the derived class, where these members are not defined in the base class

❑   We can replace the implementation of existing members, such as methods or properties, that are already present in the base class

For our example, we will replace, or **override**, the `RecordCall()` method in `Customer` with a new implementation of the `RecordCall()` method in `Nevermore60Customer`. Not only that, but whenever we need to add a new tariff, we can simply create another new class derived from `Customer`, with a new override of `RecordCall()`. In this way we can add code to cope with many different tariffs, while keeping the new code separate from all the existing code that is responsible for calculations using existing tariffs.

> *Don't confuse method overriding with method overloading – the similarity in these names is unfortunate as they are completely different, unrelated, concepts. Method overloading has nothing to do with inheritance or virtual methods.*

So let's modify the code for the `Nevermore60Customer` class, so that it implements the new tariff. To do this we need not only to override the `RecordCall()` method, but also to add a new field that indicates the number of high cost minutes that have been used:

```
public class Nevermore60Customer : Customer
{
    private uint highCostMinutesUsed;
    public override void RecordCall(TypeOfCall callType, uint nMinutes)
```

```
    {
        switch (callType)
        {
            case TypeOfCall.CallToLandline:
                balance += (0.02M * nMinutes);
                break;
            case TypeOfCall.CallToCellPhone:
        uint highCostMinutes, lowCostMinutes;
        uint highCostMinutesToGo =
            (highCostMinutesUsed < 60) ? 60 - highCostMinutesUsed : 0;
        if (nMinutes > highCostMinutesToGo)
        {
            highCostMinutes = highCostMinutesToGo;
            lowCostMinutes = nMinutes - highCostMinutes;
        }
        else
        {
            highCostMinutes = nMinutes;
            lowCostMinutes = 0;
        }
        highCostMinutesUsed += highCostMinutes;
        balance += (0.50M * highCostMinutes + 0.20M *
            lowCostMinutes);
        break;
            default:
                break;
        }
    }
}
```

You should note that the new field we've added, highCostMinutesUsed, is only stored in instances of Nevermore60Customer. It is not stored in instances of the base class, Customer. The base class itself is never implicitly modified in any way by the existence of the derived class. This must always be the case, because when you code up the base class, you don't necessarily know what other derived classes might be added in the future – and you wouldn't want your code to be broken when someone adds a derived class!

As you can see, the algorithm to compute the call cost in this case is rather more complex, though if you follow through the logic you will see it does meet our definition for the Nevermore60 tariff. Notice that the extra keyword override has been added to the definition of the RecordCall() method. This informs the compiler that this method is actually an override of a method that is already present in the base class, and we must include this keyword.

Before this code will compile, we need to make a couple of modifications to the base class, Customer, too:

```
public class Customer
{
    private string name;
    protected decimal balance;

// etc.

    public virtual void RecordCall(TypeOfCall callType, uint nMinutes)
    {
        switch (callType)
```

The first change we've made is to the `balance` field. Previously it was defined with the `private` keyword, meaning that no code outside the `Customer` class could access it directly. Unfortunately this means that, even though `Nevermore60Customer` is derived from `Customer`, the code in the `Nevermore60Customer` class cannot directly access this field (even though a `balance` field is still present inside every `Nevermore60Customer` object). That would prevent `Nevermore60Customer` from being able to modify the balance when it records calls made, and so prevent the code we presented for the `Nevermore60Customer.RecordCall()` method from compiling.

The access modifier keyword `protected` solves this problem. It indicates that any class that is derived from `Customer`, as well as `Customer` itself, should be allowed access to this member. The member is still invisible, however, to code in any other class that is not derived from `Customer`. Essentially, we're assuming that, because of the close relationship between a class and its derived class, it's fine for the derived class to know a bit about the internal workings of the base class, at least as far as protected members are concerned.

> *There is actually a controversial point here about good programming style. Many developers would regard it as better practice to keep all fields private, and write a protected accessor method to allow derived classes to modify the balance. In this case, allowing the* `balance` *field to be* `protected` *rather than* `private` *prevents our example from becoming more complex than it already is.*

The second change we've made is to the declaration of the `RecordCall()` method in the base class. We've added the keyword `virtual`. This changes the manner in which the method is called when the program is run, in a way that facilitates overriding it. C# will not allow derived classes to override a method unless that method has been declared as `virtual` in the base class. We will be looking at virtual methods and overriding later in this appendix.

Class Hierarchies and Class Design

In a procedural language, and even to some extent in a language like VB, the emphasis is very much on breaking the program down into functions. Object orientation shifts the emphasis of program design away from thinking about what functionality the program has to considering what objects the program consists of.

Inheritance is also an extremely important feature of object-oriented programming, and a crucial stage in the design of your program is deciding on **class hierarchies** – the relationships between your classes. In general, as with our Mortimer Phones example, you will find that you have a number of specialized objects that are all particular types of more generic objects.

When you're designing classes it's normally easiest to use a diagram known as a **class hierarchy diagram**, which illustrates the relationships between the various base and derived classes in your program. Traditionally, class hierarchy diagrams are drawn with the base class at the top and arrows pointing from derived classes to their immediate base classes. For example, the hierarchy of our Mortimer Phones examples from `MortimerPhones3` onwards look like this:

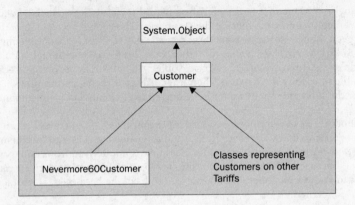

The above class hierarchy diagram emphasizes that inheritance can be direct or indirect. In our example, `Nevermore60Customer` is directly derived from `Customer`, but indirectly derived from `Object`. Although the examples in our discussion are tending to focus on direct derivation, all the principles apply equally when a class indirectly derives from another class.

Another example is one of the hierarchies from the .NET base classes. In Chapter 7, we see how to use the base classes that encapsulate windows (or to give them their more modern .NET terminology, forms). You may not have realized just how rich a hierarchy could be behind some of the controls that you can place on windows:

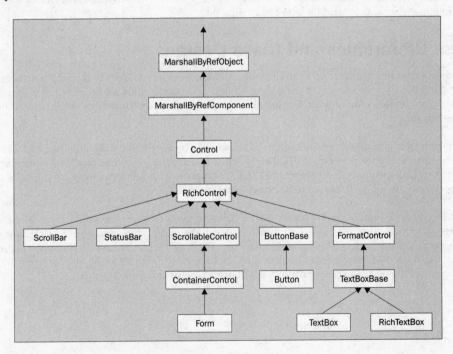

The `Form` class represents the generic window, while `ScrollBar`, `StatusBar`, `Button`, `TextBox`, and `RichTextBox` represent the familiar corresponding controls. The rich hierarchy behind these classes allows a very finetuning of what implementations of which methods can be made common to a number of different classes. Many of these classes will also implement certain interfaces, by which they can make their nature as windows known to client code.

It's also important to realize that class hierarchies are, like any other aspect of programming, an area in which there may be many possible solutions, each of which having its own advantages and disadvantages. For our Mortimer Phones example, there may be other ways to design classes. One argument against our chosen hierarchy is that customers often change their tariffs – and do we really want to have to destroy a customer object and instantiate a new one of a different class whenever that happens?. Perhaps it would be better to have just one customer class, which contains a reference to a tariff object, and have a class hierarchy of tariffs?

A large application will not have just one hierarchy, but will typically implement a large number possibly stretching into hundreds of classes. That may sound daunting, but the alternative, before object-oriented programming came into being, was to have literally thousands of functions making up your program, with no way to group them into manageable units. Classes provide a very effective way of breaking your program into smaller sections. This not only helps maintenance, but also makes your program easier to understand because the classes represent the actual objects that your program is representing in a very intuitive way.

It's also important with your classes to think carefully about the separation between the public interface that is presented to client code, and the private internal implementation. In general the more of a class you are able to keep private, the more modular your program will become, in the sense that you can make modifications or improvements to the internal implementation of one class and be certain that it will not break or even have any effect on any other part of the program. That's the reason that we've emphasized that member fields in particular will almost invariably be private, unless they are either constant or they form part of a struct whose main purpose is to group together a small number of fields. We haven't always kept to that rule rigidly in this appendix, but that's largely so we can keep the samples as simple as possible.

The Object Class

One point that you might not realize from the code is that in our Mortimer Phones examples, `Customer` is itself derived from another class, the class `System.Object`. This is a rule that is enforced by .NET and C#: There is a base class called `Object`, which all other .NET classes must ultimately derive from. In C# code, if you write a class and do not specify a base class, the compiler will supply `System.Object` as the base class by default. This means that *all* objects in the .NET Framework have certain methods inherited from the `Object` class, including the `ToString()` and `GetType()` methods that are discussed in Chapter 2. We look at the `Object` class in more detail in Chapters 5.

Single and Multiple Inheritance

In C#, each derived class can only inherit from one base class (although we can create as many different classes that are derived from the same base class as we want). The terminology to describe this is **single inheritance**. Some other languages, including C++, allow you to write classes that have more than one base class, which is known as **multiple inheritance**.

Polymorphism and Virtual Members

Let's go back to our Mortimer Phones example. Earlier, we encountered this line of code:

```
Nevermore60Customer Arabel = new Nevermore60Customer();
```

In fact, we could have instantiated the `Nevermore60Customer` object like this too:

```
Customer Arabel = new Nevermore60Customer();
```

Because `Nevermore60Customer` is derived from `Customer`, it's actually perfectly legitimate for a reference to a `Customer` to be set up to point to either a `Customer` or a `Nevermore60Customer`, or to an instance of any other class that is derived directly or indirectly from `Customer`. Notice that all we've changed here is the declaration of the reference variable. The actual object that gets instantiated with new is still a `Nevermore60Customer` object. If for example, you try to call `GetType()` against it, it'll tell you it's a `Nevermore60Customer`.

Being able to point to derived classes with a base reference may look like just a syntactical convenience, but it's actually essential if we want to be able use derived classes easily – and it's an essential feature of any language that aims to allow object-oriented programming. We can understand why if we think about how a real cell phone company will want to store the various `Customer`-derived classes. You see in our example we only had two customers, so it was easy to define separate variables, but more realistically we'd have hundreds of thousands of customers and we might want to do something like read them from a database into an array, then process them using the array, perhaps with code that looks like this:

```
Customer[] customers = new Customer[NCustomers];

    // do something to initialize customers

foreach (Customer nextCustomer in customers)
{
    Console.WriteLine("{0,-20} owes ${1:F2}", nextCustomer.Name,
                                               nextCustomer.Balance);
}
```

If we use an array of `Customer` references, each element can point to any type of customer, no matter what `Customer`-derived class is used to represent that customer. However, if variables could not store references to derived types we'd have to have lots of arrays – an array of `Customers`, an array of `Nevermore60Customers`, and another array for each type of class.

Now that we've ensured that we can mix different types of class in one array, but this will give the compiler a new problem. Suppose we have a snippet of code like this:

```
Customer aCustomer;

// Initialize aCustomer to a particular tariff

aCustomer.RecordCall(TypeOfCall.CallToLandline, 20);
```

What the compiler can see is a `Customer` reference, and we are to call the `RecordCall()` method on it. The trouble is that `aCustomer` might refer to a `Customer` instance or it might refer to a `Nevermore60Customer` instance or it might refer to an instance of some other class derived from `Customer`. Each of these classes might have its own implementation of `RecordCall()`. How will the compiler determine which method should be called? There are two answers to this, depending on whether the method in the base class is declared as `virtual` and the derived class method as an `override`:

❏   If the methods are not declared as virtual and override respectively then the compiler will simply use the type that the reference was declared to be. In this case, since `aCustomer` is of type `Customer`, it will arrange for the `Customer.RecordCall()` method to be called, no matter what `aCustomer` is actually referring to.

❏   If the methods are declared as virtual and override respectively then the compiler will generate code that checks what the `aCustomer` reference is actually pointing to at run time. It then identifies which class this instance belongs to, and calls the appropriate `RecordCall()` override. This determination of which overload should be called will need to be made separately each time the statement is executed. For example, if the `virtual` method call occurs inside a `foreach` loop which executes 100 times, then on each iteration through the loop the reference might be pointing to a different instance and therefore to a different class of object.

In most cases, the second behavior is the one we want. If we have a reference, for example, to a `Nevermore60Customer`, then it's highly unlikely that we'd want to call any override of any method other than the one that applies to `Nevermore60Customer` instances. In fact, you might wonder why you'd ever want the compiler to use the first, non-virtual, approach, since it looks like that means in many cases the "wrong" override will be called up. Why we don't just make `virtual` methods the normal behavior, and say that every method is automatically `virtual`? This is, incidentally, the approach taken by Java, which automatically makes all methods `virtual`. There are three good reasons, however, for not doing this in C#:

❏   **Performance**.
When a virtual method is called, a run-time determination needs to be made to identify which override needs to be called. For a non-virtual function, this information is available at compile-time. (The compiler can identify the relevant override from the type that the reference is declared as!) This means that for a non-virtual function, the compiler can perform optimizations such as inlining code to improve performance. Inlining virtual methods is not possible, which will hurt performance. Another, more minor, factor, is that the determination of the method itself gives a very small performance penalty. This penalty amounts to no more than an extra address lookup in a table of virtual function addresses (called a vtable), and so is insignificant in most cases, but may be important in very tight and frequently executed loops.

❏   **Design**
It may be the case that when you design a class there are some methods that should not be overridden. This actually happens a lot, especially with methods that should only be used internally within the class by other methods, or whose implementations reflect the internal class design. When you design a class, you choose which features of its implementation you make public, protected, or private. It's unlikely that you'll want methods that are primarily concerned with the internal operation of the class to be overrideable, so you typically won't declare these methods as virtual.

❑ **Versioning**
Virtual methods can cause a particular problem connected with releasing new versions of base classes. We examine these problems and the solutions in Chapter 3, when we discuss versioning.

The ability of a variable to be used to reference objects of different types, and to automatically call the appropriate version of the method of the object it references, is more formally known as **polymorphism**. However, you should note that in order to make use of polymorphism, the method you are calling must exist on the base class as well as the derived class. For example, suppose we add some other method, such as a property called HighCostMinutesLeft, to Nevermore60Customer in order to allow users to find out this piece of information. Then the following would be legal code:

```
Nevermore60Customer mrLeggit = new Nevermore60Customer();

    // processing

int minutesLeft = mrLeggit.HighCostMinutesLeft;
```

The following, however, would not be legal code, because the HighCostMinutesLeft property doesn't exist in the Customer base class:

```
Customer mrLeggit = new Nevermore60Customer();

    // processing

int minutesLeft = mrLeggit.HighCostMinutesLeft;
```

We also ought to mention some other points about virtual members:

❑ It is not only methods that can be overridden or hidden. You can do the same thing with any other class member that has an implementation, including properties.

❑ Fields cannot be declared as virtual or overridden. However, it is possible to hide a base version of a field by declaring another field of the same name in a derived class. In that case, if you wanted to access the base version from the derived class, you'd need to use the syntax base.<field_name>. Actually, you probably wouldn't do that anyway, because you'd have all your fields declared as private.

❑ Static methods and so on cannot be declared as virtual, but they can be hidden in the same way that instance methods etc. can be. It wouldn't make sense to declare a static member as virtual; virtual means that the compiler looks up the instance of a class when it calls that member, but static members are not associated with any class instance.

❑ Just because a method has been declared as virtual, that doesn't mean that it has to be overridden. In general, if the compiler encounters a call to a virtual method, it will look for the definition of the method first in the class concerned. If the method isn't defined or overridden in that class, it will call the base class version of the method. If the method isn't derived there, it'll look in the next base class, and so on, so that the method executed will be the one closest in the class hierarchy to the class concerned. (Note that this process occurs at compile time, when the compiler is constructing the vtable for each class. There is no impact at runtime.)

Method Hiding

Even if a method has not been declared as `virtual` in a base class, then it is still possible to provide another method with the same signature in a derived class. The **signature** of a method is the set of all information needed to describe how to call that method: its name, number of parameters, and parameter types. The new method will not, however, override the method in the base class. Rather, it is said to **hide** the base class method. As we've implied earlier, what this means is that the compiler will always examine the data type that the variable used to reference the instance is declared as when deciding which method to call. If a method hides a method in a base class, then you should normally add the keyword `new` to its definition. Not doing so does not constitute an error, but it will cause the compiler to give you a warning.

Realistically, method hiding is not something you'll often deliberately want to do, but we'll demonstrate how it would work by adding a new method called `GetFunnyString()` to our `Customer` class, and hiding it in `Nevermore60Customer()`. `GetFunnyString()` just displays some information about the class, and is defined like this:

```
public class Customer
{
    public string GetFunnyString()
    {
        return "Plain ordinary customer. Kaark!";
    }
```

...

```
public class Nevermore60Customer : Customer
{
    public new string GetFunnyString()
    {
        return "Nevermore60. Nevermore!";
    }
```

...

`Nevermore60Customer`'s version of this function will be the one called up, but only if called using a variable that is declared as a reference to `Nevermore60Customer` (or some other class derived from `Nevermore60Customer`). We can demonstrate this with this client code:

```
public static void Main()
{
    Customer cust1;
    Nevermore60Customer cust2;
    cust1 = new Customer();
    Console.WriteLine("Customer referencing Customer: "
        + cust1.GetFunnyString());
    cust1 = new Nevermore60Customer();
    Console.WriteLine("Customer referencing Nevermore60Customer: "
        + cust1.GetFunnyString());
    cust2 = new Nevermore60Customer();
    Console.WriteLine("Nevermore60Customer referencing: "
        + cust2.GetFunnyString());
}
```

This code is downloadable as the `MortimerPhones3Funny` sample. Running the sample gives this result:

```
MortimerPhones3Funny
Customer referencing Customer: Plain ordinary customer. Kaark!
Customer referencing Nevermore60Customer: Plain ordinary customer. Kaark!
Nevermore60Customer referencing: Nevermore60. Nevermore!
```

Abstract Functions and Base Classes

So far, every time we've defined a class we've actually created instances of that class, but that's not always the case. In many situations, you'll define a very generic class that you intend to derive other more specialized classes from, but don't ever intend to actually use. C# provides the keyword `abstract` for this purpose. If a class is declared as `abstract` it is not possible to instantiate it.

For example, suppose we have an abstract class `MyBaseClass`, declared like this:

```
abstract class MyBaseClass
{
...
```

In this case the following statement will not compile:

```
MyBaseClass MyBaseRef = new MyBaseClass();
```

However, it's perfectly legitimate to have `MyBaseClass` references, so long as they only point to derived classes. For example, you can derive a new class from `MyBaseClass`:

```
class MyDerivedClass : MyBaseClass
{
...
```

In this case, the following is all perfectly valid code:

```
MyBaseClass myBaseRef;
myBaseRef = new MyDerivedClass();
```

It's also possible to define a method as `abstract`. This means that the method is treated as a `virtual` method, and that you are not actually implementing the method in that class, on the assumption that it will be overridden in all derived classes. If you declare a method as `abstract` you do not need to supply a method body:

```
abstract class MyBaseClass
{
    public abstract int MyAbstractMethod();    // look no body!
    ...
```

If any method in a class is `abstract`, then that implies the class itself should be `abstract`, and the compiler will raise an error if the class is not so declared. Also, any non-abstract class that is derived from this class *must* override the `abstract` method. These rules prevent you from ever actually instantiating a class that doesn't have implementations of all its methods.

At this stage, you're probably wondering what the use of abstract methods and classes is. They are actually extremely useful for two reasons. One is that they often allow a better design of class hierarchy, in which the hierarchy more closely reflects the situation you are trying to model. The other is that the use of abstract classes can shift certain potential bugs from hard-to-locate run-time errors into easy-to-locate compile-time errors. It's a bit hard to see how that works in practice without looking at an example, so let's improve the program architecture of `MortimerPhones` by rearranging the class hierarchy.

Defining an Abstract Class

Before we start, let me say that we're not redesigning the Mortimer Phones sample just for the fun of it. There's actually a bit of a design flaw in the class hierarchy at the moment. Our class `Customer` represents pay-as-you-go customers as the base class for all the other customer types. We're treating that kind of tariff as if it's a special tariff from which all the others are derived. That's not really an accurate representation of the situation. In reality, the pay-as-you-go tariff is just one of a range of tariffs – there's nothing special about it – and a more carefully designed class hierarchy would reflect that. Therefore, in this section, we're going to rework the `MortimerPhones` sample to give it the class hierarchy shown in the diagram:

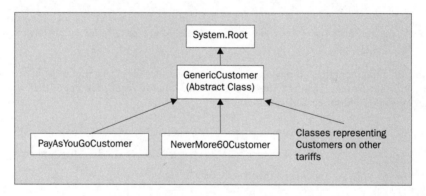

Our old `Customer` class is gone. In its place is a new abstract base class, `GenericCustomer`. `GenericCustomer` implements all the stuff that is common to all types of customers, such as methods and properties that have the same implementation for all customers and so are not virtual. This will include such things as retrieving the balance or the customer's name or recording a payment.

`GenericCustomer` will not, however, provide any implementation of the `RecordCall()` method, which works out the cost of a given call and adds it to the customer's account. The implementation of this method is different for each tariff, so we require that every derived class supplies its own. Instead, `GenericCustomer`'s `RecordCall()` method will be declared as `abstract`.

Having done that, we need to add a class that represents the pay-as-you-go customers. The `PayAsYouGoCustomer` class does this job, supplying the override to `RecordCall()` that with our previous hierarchy was defined in the base `Customer` class.

You may wonder whether it is really worth the effort in redesigning the class hierarchy for the sample in this way. After all, the old hierarchy worked perfectly well didn't it? There is actually a practical reason for regarding the new hierarchy as a better designed architecture, in that it removes a possible subtle source of bugs.

In a real application, RecordCall() probably wouldn't be the only virtual method that needed to be implemented separately for each tariff. What happens if later on someone adds a new derived class, representing a new tariff, but forgets to add the overrides of some of these methods? Well, with the old class hierarchy, the compiler would have automatically substituted the corresponding method in the base class. With that hierarchy, the base class represented pay-as-you-go customers, so we would have ended up with subtle run-time bugs involving the wrong versions of methods being called. With our new hierarchy, however, that won't happen. Instead, we'll get a compile-time error, with the compiler complaining that the relevant abstract methods haven't been overridden in the new class.

Anyway, on to the new code, and as you may by now have guessed, this is the MortimerPhones4 sample. With the new hierarchy, the code for GenericCustomer looks like this. Most of the code is the same as for our old Customer class – in the following code we've highlighted the few lines that are different. Note the abstract declaration for the RecordCall() method:

```
public abstract class GenericCustomer
{
    ...
    public void RecordPayment(decimal amountPaid)
    {
        balance -= amountPaid;
    }
    public abstract void RecordCall(TypeOfCall callType, uint nMinutes);
}
```

Now for the implementation of pay-as-you-go customers. Again, notice that most of the code is taken directly from the former, obsolete, Customer, class. The only real difference is that RecordCall() is now an override rather than a virtual method:

```
public class PayAsYouGoCustomer : GenericCustomer
{
    public override void RecordCall(TypeOfCall callType, uint nMinutes)
    {
        // same implementation as for Customer
    }
}
```

We won't display the full code for Nevermore60Customer here as the RecordCall() override in this class is long and completely unchanged from the earlier version of the example. The only change we need to make to this class is to derive it from GenericCustomer instead of from the Customer class, which no longer exists:

```
public class Nevermore60Customer : GenericCustomer
{
    private uint highCostMinutesUsed;
    public override void RecordCall(TypeOfCall callType, uint nMinutes)
    {
        // same implementation as for old Nevermore60Customer
    }
    ...
```

To finish off, we'll add some new client code to demonstrate the operation of the new class hierarchy. This time we've actually used an array to store the various customers, so this code shows how an array of references to the abstract base class can be used to reference instances of the various derived class, with the appropriate overrides of the methods being called:

```
public static void Main()
{
    GenericCustomer arabel = new Nevermore60Customer();
    arabel.Name = "Arabel Jones";
    GenericCustomer mrJones = new PayAsYouGoCustomer();
    mrJones.Name = "Ben Jones";
    GenericCustomer [] customers = new GenericCustomer[2];
    customers[0] = arabel;
    customers[0].RecordCall(TypeOfCall.CallToLandline, 20);
    customers[0].RecordCall(TypeOfCall.CallToCellPhone, 5);
    customers[1] = mrJones;
    customers[1].RecordCall(TypeOfCall.CallToLandline, 10);
    foreach (GenericCustomer nextCustomer in customers)
    {
        Console.WriteLine("{0,-20} owes ${1:F2}", nextCustomer.Name,
                                                  nextCustomer.Balance);
    }
}
```

Running this code, once again, produces the correct results for the amounts owed:

```
MortimerPhones4
Arabel Jones           owes $2.90
Ben Jones          owes $0.20
```

Sealed Classes and Methods

In many ways you can think of a sealed class or method as the opposite of an abstract class or method. Whereas declaring something as abstract means that it must be overridden or inherited from, declaring it as sealed means that it cannot be. Not all object-oriented languages support this concept, but it can be useful. In C# the syntax looks like this.

```
sealed class FinalClass
{
...
```

C# also supports declaring an individual override method as sealed, preventing any further overrides of it.

The most likely situation when you'll mark a class or method as `sealed` will be if it is very much internal to the operation of the library, class, or other classes that you are writing, so you are fairly sure that any attempt to override some of its functionality will cause problems. You might also mark a class or method as `sealed` for commercial reasons, in order to prevent a third party from extending your classes in a manner that is contrary to the licensing agreements. In general, however, you should be careful about marking a class or member as `sealed`, since by doing so you are severely restricting how it can be used. Even if you don't think it would be useful to inherit from a class or override a particular member of it, it's still possible that at some point in the future someone will encounter a situation you hadn't anticipated in which it is useful to do so.

Interfaces

Earlier in this appendix, we indicated that there were two types of inheritance: implementation inheritance and interface inheritance. So far we've said a lot about implementation inheritance; in this section we are going to look more closely at interface inheritance.

In general, an interface is a contract that says that a class must implement certain features (usually methods and properties), but which doesn't specify any implementations of those methods and properties. Therefore you don't instantiate an interface; instead a class can declare that it **implements** one or more interfaces. In C#, as in most languages that support interfaces, this essentially means that the class inherits from the interface.

To get an idea of how an interface looks in programming terms, we'll show the syntax for the definition of an interface that is defined in the .NET base classes, `IEnumerator`, from the `System.Collections` namespace. `IEnumerator` looks like this:

```
interface IEnumerator
{
   // Properties
   object Current {get; }

   // Methods
   bool MoveNext();
   void Reset();
}
```

As you can see, the `IEnumerator` interface has two methods and one property. This interface is important in implementing collections, and is designed to encapsulate the functionality of moving through the items in a collection. `MoveNext()` moves to the next item, `Reset()` returns to the first item, while `Current` retrieves a reference to the current item.

Beyond the lack of method implementations, the main point to note is the lack of any modifiers on the members. Interface members are always public, and cannot be declared as virtual or static.

So why have interfaces? Up to now we've treated classes as having certain members, and not concerned ourselves about grouping any members together – our classes have simply contained a list of various miscellaneous methods, fields, properties, and so on. There are often situations in which in order to be able to use a class in a certain way, we need to know that the class implements certain features. An example is provided by the `foreach` loop in C#. In principle, it is possible to use `foreach` to iterate through a class instance, provided that that class is able to act as if it is a collection. How can the .NET runtime tell whether a class instance represents a collection? It queries the instance to find out whether it implements the `System.Collections.IEnumerable` interface. If it does, then the runtime uses the methods on this interface to iterate through the members of the collection. If it doesn't, then `foreach` will raise an exception.

You might wonder why in this case we don't just see if the class implements the required methods and properties. The answer is that that wouldn't be a very reliable way of checking. For example, you can probably think of all sorts of different reasons why a class might happen to implement a method called `MoveNext()`, or one called `Reset()`, which don't have anything to do with collections. If the class declares that it implements the interfaces needed for collections, then you know that it really is a collection.

A second reason for using interfaces is for interoperability with COM. Before .NET came on the scene, COM, and its later versions DCOM and COM+, provided the main way that applications could communicate with each other on the Windows platform, and the particular object model that COM used was heavily dependent on interfaces. Indeed, it was through COM that the concept of an interface first became commonly known. We should stress, however, that C# interfaces are not the same as COM interfaces. COM interfaces have very strict requirements, such as that they must use GUIDs as identifiers, which are not necessarily present in C# interfaces. However, using attributes (a C# feature that we cover in the Chapter 4), it is possible to dress up a C# interface so it acts like a COM interface, and hence provide compatibility with COM. We discuss COM interoperability in Chapter 17.

We won't go into any more depth about interfaces here, but we do look more closely at the subject in Chapter 3.

Construction and Disposal

For this final section of the appendix, we are going to leave inheritance behind, and look at another topic that is important in OOP programming: creation and disposal of objects – or to use the usual terminology – construction and destruction of objects. Say you have this code:

```
{
    int x;
    // more code
}
```

You will be aware that when x is created (comes into scope), memory gets allocated for it, and that when it goes out of scope, that memory is reclaimed by the system. If you are familiar with C#, you'll also be aware that x gets initialized with the value zero when the variable comes into scope. For integers, the language defines what initializations happen automatically when an `int` gets created. But wouldn't it be nice if we could do the same for our own classes? Well, most modern OOP languages will support the ability to do this – and C# is no exception. This support happens through something called a **constructor**. A constructor is a special method called automatically whenever an object of a given class gets created. You don't have to write a constructor for a class, but if you want some custom initialization to take place automatically, you should place the relevant code in the constructor.

Similarly, OOP languages, including C#, support something called a **destructor**. A destructor is a method called automatically whenever an object is destroyed (the variable goes out of scope). Reclaiming memory aside, destructors are particularly useful for classes that represent a connection to a database, or an open file, or those that have methods to read from and write to the database/file. In that case, the destructor can be used to make sure that you don't leave any database connections or file handles hanging open when the object goes out of scope.

Having said all that, the facilities offered by the .NET Framework and the garbage collector mean that destructors are not only used a lot less often in C# than they are in pre-.NET languages, but also that the syntax for defining them is more complex (indeed, destructors are almost the only thing that is more complex to code up in C# than in C++!). For that reason we won't look any more closely at destructors in this appendix. How to write destructors in C# is covered in Chapter 3. Here, we will concentrate on constructors, to give you an idea of how the concept works.

VB developers will note that there are some similarities between constructors and the `Initialize()` *and* `Form_Load()` *methods of VB class modules. Constructors, however, are far more flexible and powerful.*

Creating Constructors

When you see a constructor definition in C#, it looks much like a method definition, but the difference is that you don't usually call a constructor explicitly. It's like a method that is always called on your behalf whenever an instance of a class is created. In addition, because you never call the method explicitly, there is no way you can get access to any return value, which means that constructors never return anything. You can identify a constructor in a class definition because it always has the same name as the class itself. For example, if we have a class named `MyClass`, a skeleton constructor would be defined as follows:

```
public class MyClass
{
    public MyClass()
    {
    }
    ...
```

This constructor so far does nothing – we haven't added any code to it. Let's add an integer field `MyField` to the class and initialize it to 10:

```
public class MyClass
{
    public MyClass()
    {
        myField = 10;
    }
    private int myField;
    ...
```

It's as simple as that. Notice that no return type is specified, not even `void`. The compiler recognizes the constructor from the fact that it has the same name as the containing class. You should note that one implication of this is that it is not possible to write a method that has the same name as the class it belongs to, because if you do the compiler will interpret it as a constructor.

From the above code, you may wonder if we've actually achieved anything new. After all, in terms of C# syntax, we could equally have written

```
public class MyClass
    private int myField = 10;
```

which achieves the same effect – specifying how to initialize each object without explicitly indicating a constructor. Indeed, we have already done something like this in all our `Authenticator` samples, in which we specified that the password field should automatically be initialized to an empty string. The answer is really that here we are trying to introduce the concept of a constructor. The above code is really just C# shorthand for specifying construction code implicitly – and is a shorthand that is specific to C#. Behind the shorthand there is still a constructor at work. Besides, by writing a constructor explicitly, it means we can write code to compute initial values at runtime – the shorthand requires values to be known at compile-time, as constants.

It's not necessary to provide a constructor for your class – we haven't supplied one for any of our examples so far. In general, if you don't explicitly supply any constructor, the compiler will just make a default one up for you behind the scenes. It'll be a very basic constructor that just initializes all the member fields to their normal default values (empty string for strings, zero for numeric data types, and `false` for `bool`s).

Initializing to default values is something that happens in C# because C# initializes all members of a class. If you are coding in a different language, this behavior may be different. For example, by default C++ never initializes anything unless you explicitly indicate that's what you want. So in C++, if you don't supply a constructor to a class, then its members won't get initialized to anything (unless they have constructors instead).

Passing Parameters to Constructors

Let's go back to our `Authenticator` class. Say we wanted to modify the class so that we can specify the initial password when we first instantiate the class. It is possible to do this by supplying a constructor that takes parameters. In this regard, a constructor behaves like a method in that we can define whatever parameters we want for it, and this is where constructors really score over VB's `Initialize` or `Form_Load`.

For the `Authenticator`, we'd probably add a constructor that takes an initial password as a parameter:

```
public class Authenticator
{
    public Authenticator(string initialPassword)
    {
        password = initialPassword;
    }
    private string password = "";
    private static uint minPasswordLength = 6;
    ...
```

The advantage of using such a constructor is that it means an `Authenticator` object is guaranteed to be initialized the instant it is created. It is, therefore, not possible for other code to access the object before it has been initialized, as would be possible if we initialized it by calling a method after instantiating an object.

Now, to instantiate the object we would use a line of code similar to the following:

```
Authenticator NewUser = new Authenticator("MyPassword45");
```

Here we have created an instance with the password MyPassword45. You should note that the following line will not compile any more:

```
Authenticator NewUser2 = new Authenticator();
```

This is because we do not supply any parameters to the constructor, and constructor requires one parameter. However, if we wanted to, we could simply create an overload for the constructor that didn't take any parameter arguments, and simply set a default password in this constructor overload (this would not be a very secure approach though!).

More Uses of Constructors

Although the only thing we've done with constructors is to initialize the values of fields, a constructor does act as a normal method so you can place any instructions you wish in it – for example, you might perform some calculations to work out the initial values of the fields. If your class encapsulates access to a file or database, the constructor might attempt to open the file. The only thing that you cannot do in a constructor is return any value (such as indicating status) to the calling code.

Another novel use is to use a constructor to count how many instances of a class have been created while the program is running. If we wanted to do that for the Authenticator class, we could create a static field, nInstancesCreated, and amend the code for the constructor as follows:

```
public class Authenticator
{
    private static uint nInstancesCreated = 0;

    public Authenticator(string initialPassword)
    {
        ++nInstancesCreated;
        Password = initialPassword;
    }

    private string password = 10;
    private static uint minPasswordLength = 6;
    ...
```

This example is here more to demonstrate the kind of flexibility that being able to specify your own constructors gives you than because it's likely to have much practical benefit. Counting instances is, it should be said, something you're unlikely to want to do in release builds of code, but it's something that you might want to do for debugging purposes.

Summary

The aim of this appendix has been to introduce you to the basic concepts of object-oriented (OO) design in C#:

❑   classes, objects, and instances

❑   fields, methods, and properties

❑   overloading

❑   inheritance and class hierarchies

❑   polymorphism

❑   interfaces

OO programming methodology is strongly reflected in the design of the C# language, and of Intermediate Language too – we will see this as we begin to use the .NET base classes. Microsoft has done this because with our current understanding of programming techniques, it simply is the most appropriate way of coding up any large library or application.

B

C# Compilation Options

This appendix lists the various C# compiler options that you may use if you have to compile your C# projects without the benefit of Visual Studio .NET, or if you want to carry out compiler operations not supported by Visual Studio .NET. They have been arranged as a series of tables according to category. First, however, we will give a brief overview of how to use the C# compiler.

Using the C# Compiler

Freely distributed with the .NET Framework SDK, the C# compiler, csc.exe, can be invoked from a DOS command line or from the VS.NET IDE that most readers will probably end up using. In order to use the C# compiler you need to set up certain environment variables. Let's look at the steps to do this now.

Open up the System Properties window, Start | Settings | Control Panel | System, and switch to the Advanced tab:

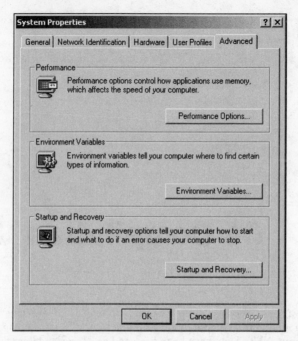

Now click on the Environment Variables button. In the System variables window double-click on the Path variable so that we can edit it, and add in the path to the version of the Framework that you have installed on your computer (on my computer this is C:\WINNT\Microsoft.NET\Framework\v1.0.3705):

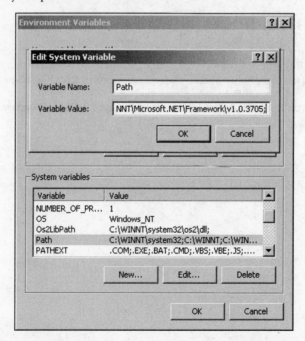

Note that you will need to use a semicolon to separate this path variable from those that are already in there.

The compiler's behavior is controlled by command-line arguments. When you tell an IDE like VS.NET to compile a C# program, the IDE consults its settings to dynamically build the command string with the command-line arguments and uses this string to shell out to a `csc.exe` process. Although using an IDE like VS.NET certainly saves you a lot of time and keystrokes, it's good to know the command-line options for controlling the C# compiler in case you want to automate your organization's build process through scripts, batch files, and so on.

Input and Output Files

When invoking the C# compiler from the command line, you indicate your source file simply by listing its filename after the name of the compiler, `csc`. You indicate the name for the target file by using the output argument:

```
csc SourceFile.cs /out:TargetFile.exe
```

Compiling Different Project Types

C# can be used to create different kinds of projects, such as console applications, Windows Form applications, components, and more. You use the `/target` command-line option to tell the C# compiler what kind of project it needs to build:

❑ The `/target:exe` argument tells the C# compiler to produce a console application.

❑ The `/target:winexe` argument tells the C# compiler to produce a Windows Form application.

❑ The `/target:library` argument tells the C# compiler to produce a standalone assembly containing a manifest.

❑ The `/target:module` arguments also tells the C# compiler to produce an assembly file, but without a manifest. Manifest-less assemblies produced with the `/target:module` argument can be subsumed into other assembly components that do contain manifests.

Response Files

To make automating builds easier, the C# compiler supports **response files**. A response file contains a listing of command-line options and can be linked in by a reference to the file when the compiler is invoked. You denote a response file on the command line by prefixing it with the "@" symbol:

```
csc /out:TargetFile.exe  @<responsefilename> SourceFile.cs
```

Compiler Options

The first table shows the various file formats that can be output by the compiler:

Option	Purpose
`/doc:<filename>`	Processes XML documentation comments (marked with three slashes, `///`) and outputs to the specified XML file.
`/nooutput`	Compiles code but does not create an output file; useful for debugging purposes as the console will show warnings and errors.
`/out:<filename>`	Specifies the name of the output file. If this is not specified the compiler generates a standard `.exe` file with the same name as the source file (minus the extension).
`/target:<option>` `/t:<option>`	Specifies the format of the output file. The four options are: `exe`: produces a standard executable (the default setting). `library`: produces a code library (DLL). `module`: produces a code module (assembly with no manifest), which is later added to an assembly (using `/addmodule`). `winexe`: creates a Windows executable.

Unless the `/target:module` option is specified the compiler will add a manifest to the EXE that is created (or the first DLL if no EXE is created). Note that `/target` can be abbreviated to `/t`.

The next table explains the command-line option for determining compiler optimizations.

Option	Purpose
`/optimize<+	->` `/o<+	->`	Enables or disables optimizations carried out by the compiler to produce smaller, faster, and more efficient output. This is disabled by default. To enable, use the syntax: `/optimize` or `/optimize+` To disable, use this syntax: `/optimize-`

The following table describes options that are used when creating and referring to .NET assemblies:

Option	Purpose
`/addmodule:<module>`	Specifies one or more modules to be included in the specified assembly. If more than one module is specified, they are separated by semicolons. This option is not available in Visual Studio .NET.

`/nostdlib<+ | ->`	Specifies whether or not to import the standard library (`mscorlib.dll`), which is imported by default.
	
	If you want to implement your own System namespace and classes, you may want the compiler *not* to load the standard library. The syntax for doing this is:
	
	`/nostdlib` or `/nostdlib+`
	
	The syntax for importing it is:
	
	`/nostdlib-`

`/reference:<assembly>` `/r:<assembly>`	Imports metadata from an assembly file. You can specify the full path to the assembly, or anywhere specified by the PATH environment variable, or a relative path starting at the current project. If more than one file is specified, they are separated by semicolons.

The following table explains the options that apply to debugging and error checking:

Option	Purpose
`/bugreport:<filename>`	Creates the specified file that contains any bug information produced by the compiler. The contents of the file include: ❑ A copy of all sourcecode ❑ A listing of compiler options ❑ Information on the compiler version, operating system etc. ❑ Any compiler output ❑ Description of problem and possible solution (optional) This option is not available in Visual Studio .NET

Table continued on following page

Option	Purpose
`/checked<+ | ->`	Specifies whether integer overflows raise a run-time error. This applies only to code outside of the scope of `checked` and `unchecked` blocks. This is disabled by default. The syntax for overflow checking is: `/checked` or `/checked+` To disable overflow checking use this syntax: `/checked-`
`/debug<+ | ->` `/debug:<option>`	Generates debugging information. To enable this use the syntax: `/debug` or `/debug+` To disable use this: `/debug-` Debugging is disabled by default. If you specify that debugging information should be output, then you have two options regarding the type of debugging information that is produced: `/debug:full`: enables the attaching of a debugger to the operating program. `/debug:pdbonly`: allows sourcecode debugging when the program is started in the debugger but will only display assembler when the running program is attached to the debugger.
`/fullpaths`	Specifies the full path to the file containing the error. This option is not available in Visual Studio .NET.
`/nowarn:<number>`	Suppresses the compiler's ability to generate specified warnings. The `<number>` option specifies which warning number to suppress. If more than one is specified, they are separated by commas. This option is not available in Visual Studio .NET.
`/warn:<option>` `/w:<option>`	Sets the minimum warning level that you want to display. The options are: 0: suppresses all warnings 1: displays only severe warnings 2: displays severe warnings plus warnings of medium severity 3: displays severe warnings plus warnings of medium and low severity 4: displays all warnings including informational warnings

Option	Purpose
/warnaserror<+ | ->	Treats all warnings as errors. To enable, this use this syntax: /warnaserror or /warnaserror+ To disable use this syntax: /warnaserror- This is disabled by default.

This table show how to set preprocessor directives:

Option	Purpose
/define:<name> /d:<name>	Defines preprocessor symbol specified by <name>

This table explains the options associated with including external resources:

Option	Purpose
/linkresource:<filename> /linkres:<filename>	Creates a link to the specified .NET resource. Two optional additional parameters (delimited by commas) are: identifier: the logical name for the resource; the name used to load the resource (the default is the filename) mimetype: a string representing the media type for the resource (the default is none) This option is not available in Visual Studio .NET.
/resource:<filename> /res:<filename>	Embeds a .NET-specified resource into the output file. Two optional additional parameters (delimited by commas) are: identifier: the logical name for the resource; the name used to load the resource (the default is the filename). mimetype: a string representing the media type for the resource (the default is none).
/win32icon:<filename>	Inserts the specified Win32 icon (.ico) file into the output file.
/win32res:<filename>	Inserts the specified Win32 resource (.res) file into the output file. This option is not available in Visual Studio .NET.

The final table lists various miscellaneous compiler options:

Option	Purpose
@<filename>	Specifies a file that contains all the compiler options and source files that will be processed by the compiler as if they had been entered at the command line.
/baseaddress:<address>	Specifies the preferred base address at which to load a DLL. The value of <address> can be decimal, hexadecimal, or octal.
/codepage:<id>	Specifies the code page (value passed as the <id> option) to use for all sourcecode files in the compilation. Use this option if you use a character set in the C# files which isn't the default for your system. This option is not available in Visual Studio .NET.
/help /?	Lists compiler options to standard output. This option is not available in Visual Studio .NET.
/incremental<+ | -> /incr<+ | ->	Allows incremental compilation of sourcecode files, that is, it compiles only those functions that have been altered since the previous compilation. Information about the state of the previous compilation is stored in two files, a .dbg file (or .pdb if /debug has been specified) to hold debug information and a .incr file to hold state information. To enable this use either syntax: /incremental or /incremental+ To disable use this syntax: /incremental- This is disabled by default.
/main:<class>	Specifies the location of the Main() method, if more than one exists in the sourcecode.
/nologo	Suppresses the output of the compiler banner information. This option is not available in Visual Studio .NET.
/recurse:<dir\file>	Searches subdirectories for source files to compile. There are two options: dir (optional): the directory or subdirectory to start the search from. If not specified, it is the directory of the current project. file: the file or files to search for. You can use wildcards.
/unsafe	Allows the compilation of code that uses the unsafe keyword.

Index

B